Edited by Joseph B. Roberts, Jr.
and Harris J. Andrews

STOEGER PUBLISHING COMPANY, ACCOKEEK, MARYLAND

STOEGER PUBLISHING COMPANY
is a division of Benelli USA

Benelli USA
Vice President and General Manager:
Stephen Otway
Vice President of Marketing and Communications:
Stephen McKelvain

Stoeger Publishing Company
President: Jeffrey Reh
Publisher: Jennifer Thomas
Managing Editor: Harris J. Andrews
Creative Director: Cynthia T. Richardson
Graphic Designer: William Graves
Special Accounts Manager: Julie Brownlee
Publishing Assistant: Stacy Logue
Contributing Editor: Stanton Wormley
Proofreaders: Stacy Logue & Amy Jones
Illustrator for revisions: William Graves

Published November 2007 by:
Stoeger Publishing Company
17603 Indian Head Highway, Suite 200
Accokeek, Maryland 20607

BK0614
ISBN-13: 978-0-88317-335-0
ISBN-10: 0-88317-335-2
Library of Congress Control Number: 2007936925

Manufactured in Canada.

Distributed to the book trade and
to the sporting goods trade by:
Stoeger Industries
17603 Indian Head Highway, Suite 200
Accokeek, Maryland 20607
301 283-6300 Fax: 301 283-6986
www.stoegerbooks.com

For information, contact the National Rifle Association
11250 Waples Mill Road, Fairfax, Virginia 22030-9400

FOREWORD

A modern firearm, or an antique one for that matter, tends to be among the most complex and advanced artifacts produced by any industrialized society. With their multitude of finely machined, interconnected parts and the stresses to which they are subjected by the nature of their function and operation — intense internal pressures, mechanical wear, recoil stress, moisture, oxidation and abuse by careless or inattentive owners — all firearms need regular servicing and, sooner or later, repairs. Many gunsmiths make a good part of their living by servicing and repairing guns brought into their shops by frustrated owners. With this compilation of articles we are not trying to put a dent in any gunsmith's livelihood. As a matter of fact, every worthwhile gunsmith I know has greasy, shopworn copies of previous editions of the NRA Firearms Assembly Guides ready at hand. But we do hope to help gun owners better understand their guns, and how to take them apart for maintenance and simple repair.

Cartridge and rifle innovator Charles Newton is credited with the first illustrated view of his High Power Rifle in the 15th edition of the Newton Arms Co. catalog, likely from 1915, with clear concise instructions on disassembly. He is, according to former American Rifleman Technical editor Pete Dickey, "the father of the Exploded View."

American Rifleman printed its first "Exploded View" in 1952. Written and illustrated by the late E.J. Hoffschmidt, it gave a brief history of the Browning Hi Power, with an "Exploded View" parts drawing that showed all the parts and their relationship to each other, along with detailed and illustrated disassembly instructions. Back then, this was a pretty revolutionary concept. Most makers would merely have a photograph or a line drawing of the parts, and a list with prices so you could order replacements. Some credit Rifleman's "Exploded Views" with the clear, concise disassembly instructions found in most owner's manuals today.

Over the years, hundreds of "Exploded Views" of rifle, shotgun, pistols and revolvers have appeared in the pages of American Rifleman, written by dozens of writers and illustrators—myself included--and the vast majority of them are included here. To this day, they are the most commonly requested articles of the tens of thousands Rifleman has published over the years. You get most everything you need; the gun's background, when it was made, how to take it apart and a complete listing of all the parts. And in this book, they are all together.

One of the best features of this book is the appendix at the end giving brand names and model numbers that generally follow the guns included in the book. Those listed are mechanically and operationally similar to those covered here, but might be different enough to require gunsmith attention if you are not careful. When in doubt—or if you are taking apart a gun for the first time—take digital photos or make simple hand sketches of the parts in relation to each other as you remove each one. It's a good idea, even if you have the "Exploded View." Also, there are a number of guns here that only give fieldstripping directions. That's for good reason, as anyone who has unwittingly fully disassembled a Browning Auto-5 can attest. I've done it, and don't recommend it to even those I dislike. Some guns have tricks, some require special jigs and tools, and some are just a bear even if you know what you are doing.

For many men, reading the instructions is the last resort. As one who has taken guns apart weekly for more than 15 years, I can assure you that, unless you want to bring a bag of jumbled parts to a smirking gunsmith, the directions are, indeed, the place to start.

Mark A. Keefe, IV
Editor-In-Chief
American Rifleman
Fairfax, Virginia

CONTENTS

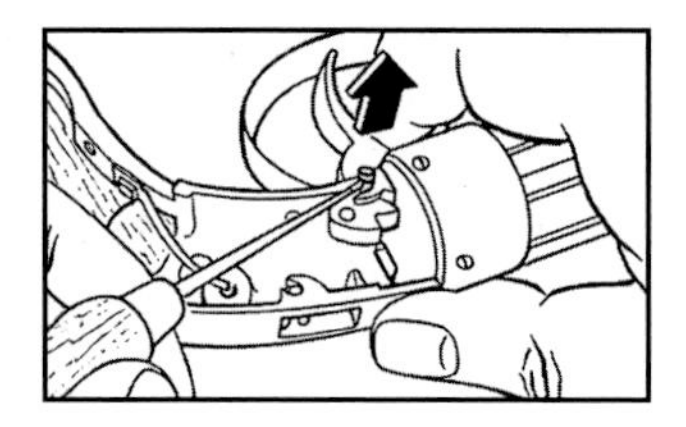

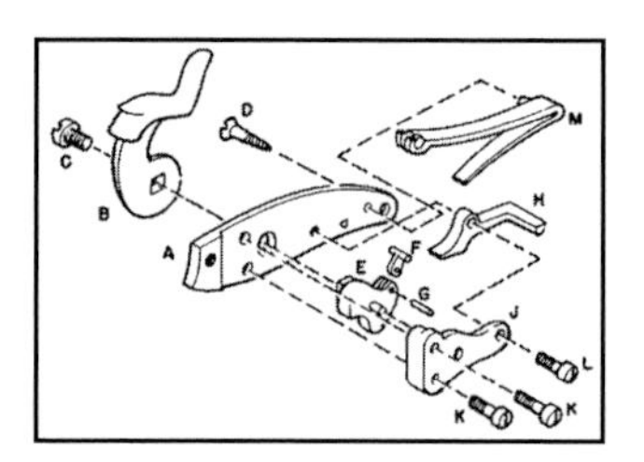

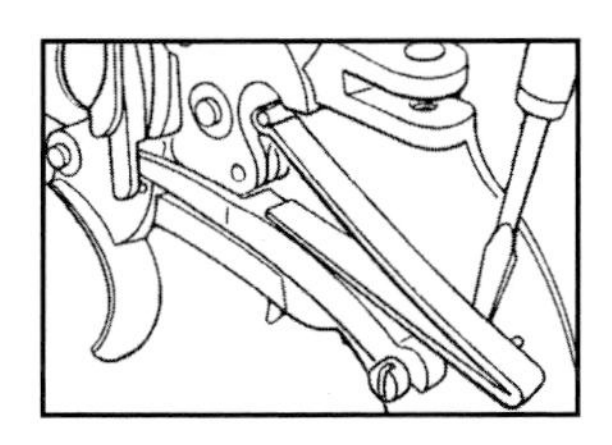

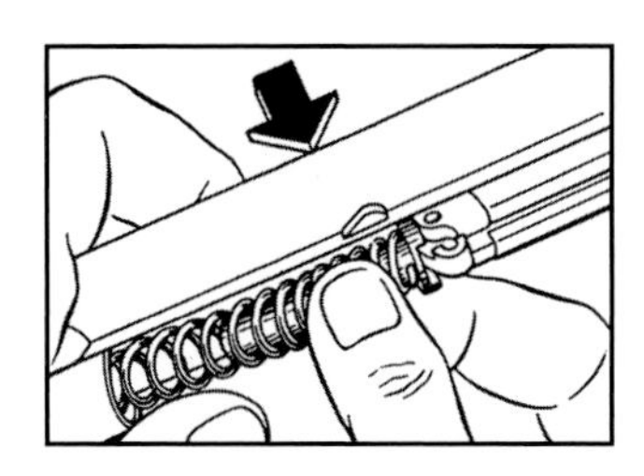

WHAT THE NRA IS & WHAT IT DOES

The National Rifle Association was organized as a non-profit, membership corporation in the State of New York in November 1871, by a small group of National Guard officers. The object for which it was formed was the ...improvement of its members in marksmanship, and to promote the introduction of the system of aiming drill and rifle practice as a part of the military drill of the National Guard....

In 1877, its name was changed to the National Rifle Association of America (NRA). During its years of existence, NRA Headquarters has been located in New York, New Jersey and, since 1908, in Washington, D.C.

The NRA represents and promotes the best interests of gun owners and shooter-sportsmen and supports their belief in the ideals of the United States of America and its way of life. It is dedicated to firearms safety education as a public service, marksmanship training as a contribution to individual preparedness for personal and national defense, and the sports of shooting and hunting as wholesome forms of recreation. It stands squarely behind the premise that ownership of firearms must not be denied to law-abiding Americans.

The purposes and objectives of the National Rifle Association of America are:

- To protect and defend the Constitution of the United States, especially with reference to the inalienable right of the individual American citizen guaranteed by such Constitution to acquire, possess, transport, carry, transfer ownership of, and enjoy the right to use arms, in order that the people may always be in a position to exercise their legitimate individual rights of self-preservation and defense of family, person, and property, as well as to serve effectively in the appropriate militia for the common defense of the Republic and the individual liberty of its citizens;
- To promote public safety, law and order, and the national defense;
- To train members of law enforcement agencies, the armed forces, the militia, and people of good repute in marksmanship and in the safe handling and efficient use of small arms;
- To foster and promote the shooting sports, including the advancement of amateur competitions in marksmanship at the local, state, regional, national and international levels;
- To promote hunter safety, and to promote and defend hunting as a shooting sport and as a viable and necessary method of fostering the propagation, growth, conservation and wise use of our renewable wildlife resources.

INTRODUCTION

Disassembling a handgun seems easy enough. The carefully designed and finely machined parts should go together in a logical order and it should simply be a matter of unscrewing the right screws, driving out a pin or so, and pulling the thing apart. Unfortunately it isn't always that easy! That unexpected heavy spring under brutal tension; a cluster (assembly in firearms trade parlance) of minute, interlocked parts and springs; a pin precisely milled to only drive in one direction; can all contrive to make even field stripping some handguns an exercise in frustration and occasionally a small scale disaster.

A clear understanding of the interior design of a firearm and how its multitude of parts interact is vital for anyone trying to disassemble and then successfully reassemble it. Having access to a clear, well-labeled "exploded view" diagram is the next best thing to having an experienced gunsmith sitting at one's elbow. The logical, perspective-view schematic diagrams contained in this book clearly show the construction and relationship of components of hundreds of antique and modern firearms.

Most of the exploded views included in The NRA Official Guide were laboriously drawn by hand by highly experienced professional draftsmen using traditional drafting and inking tools. Modern engineers, however, use sophisticated computer drafting programs or "CAD" (Computer Assisted Drawing) systems to produce mechanical drawings. Whether drawn by hand or by machine, the scaled, detailed views are key to understanding the "guts" of any pistol or revolver.

In addition, the *Official Guide* contains illustrated, step-by-step disassembly instructions and brief historical and technical descriptions of each firearm. The instruction sections include photographs of the primary models of the handgun in question and a selection of color photographs of various models included in the book.

Drawn from the files of the National Rifle Association's American Rifleman magazine, this collection was originally published as *Firearms Assembly: the NRA Guide to Pistols and Revolvers* in 1980. These articles were the product of the knowledge and skills of the magazine's contributors — gunsmiths, firearms aficionados, collectors and hunters — and they provide valuable information on many of the important, popular and innovative handguns of the last two centuries. The book has been revised and expanded before, and the latest revision by Stoeger Publishing simply adds to the scope and usefulness of a well-respected guidebook and shop companion.

Stoeger Publishing's new edition, *The NRA Official Guide to Firearms Assembly: Pistols & Revolvers,* has been upgraded with new information and additional new entries covering current popular and interesting pistols and revolvers. Each handgun features an exploded-view diagram and supporting, step-by-step instructions detailing the process for field stripping and disassembly. In many cases articles provide useful re-assembly tips and cautions concerning the mechanical "quirks" of various guns.

ACKNOWLEDGEMENTS

The following authors and editors, along with the NRA Technical Staff, wrote and illustrated the articles printed in American Rifleman magazine that formed the text contained in the original editions of: *Firearms Assembly: The NRA Guide to Pistols and Revolvers.*

Pete Dickey
John F. Finnegan
Charlie Gara
Inigo Diaz-Guardamino
Augustin Guisasola
Robert W. Hunnicutt
Edward J. Hoffschmidt
John Karns
Mark A. Keefe, IV
Charles Lanham
George Lees
James S. McLellan
Ludwig Olsen
Dennis Riordan
James M. Triggs
Stephen K. Vogel
M. D. Waite
Doug Wicklund
Thomas E. Wessel

GALLERY OF PISTOLS & REVOLVERS

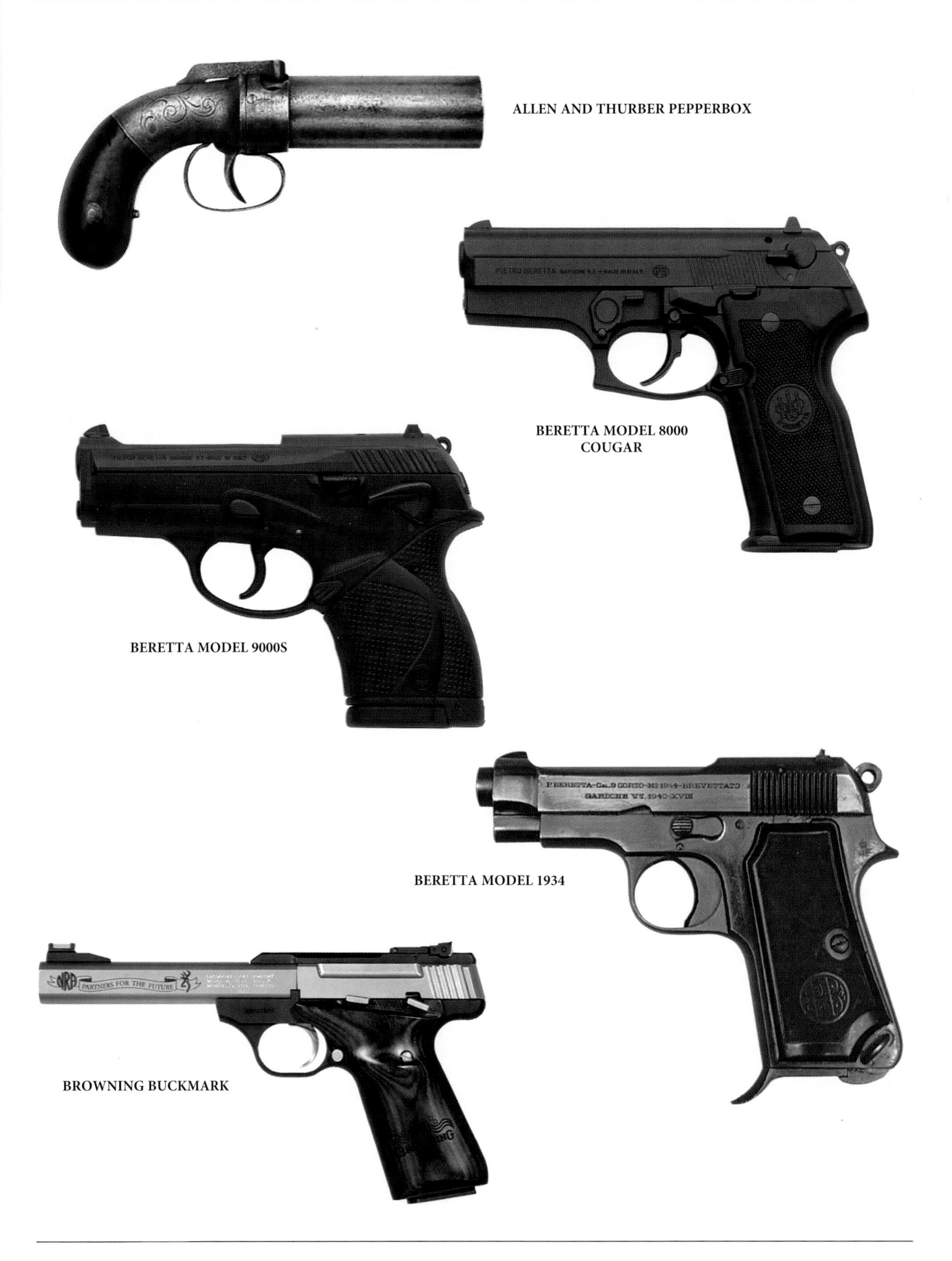

ALLEN AND THURBER PEPPERBOX

BERETTA MODEL 8000
COUGAR

BERETTA MODEL 9000S

BERETTA MODEL 1934

BROWNING BUCKMARK

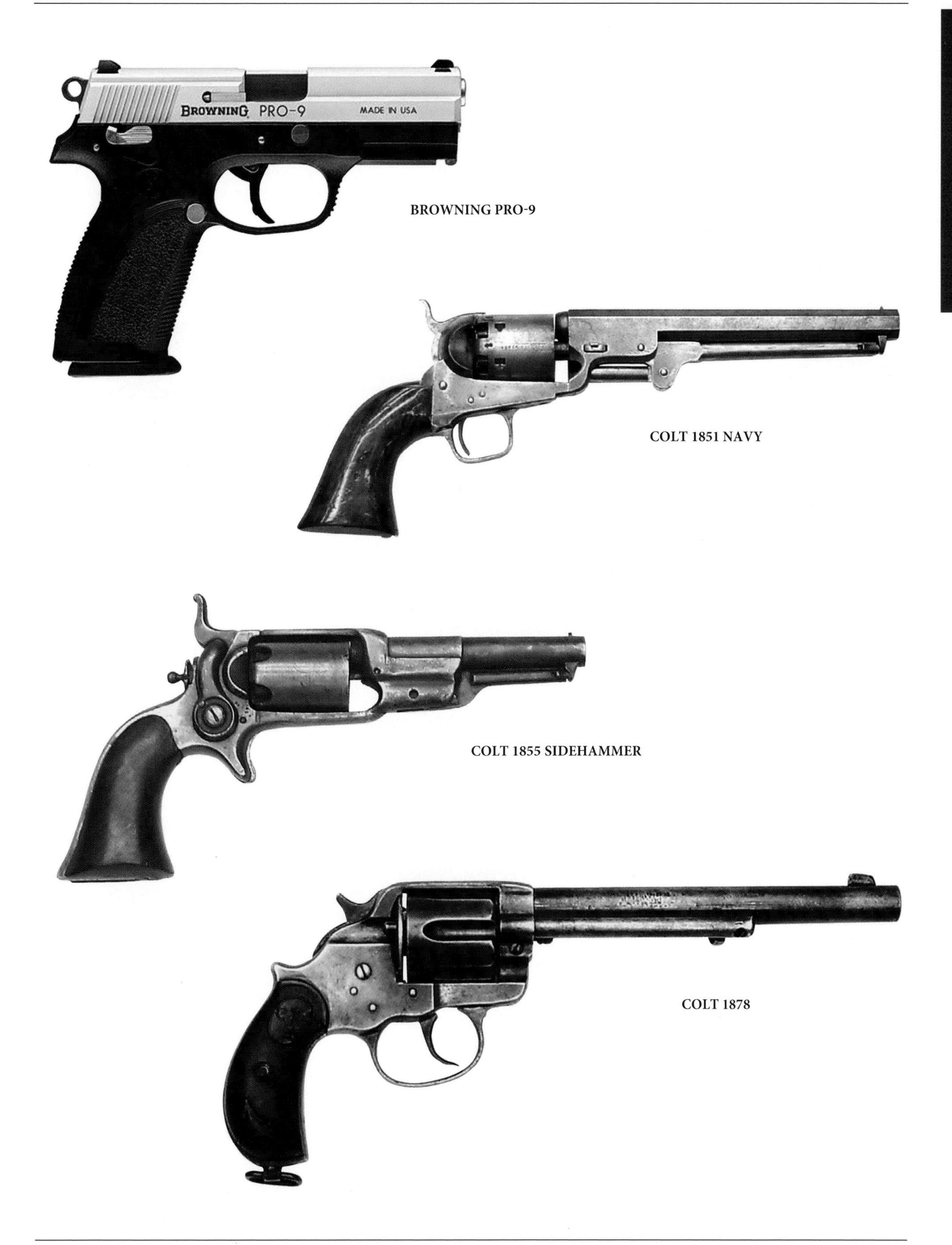

BROWNING PRO-9

COLT 1851 NAVY

COLT 1855 SIDEHAMMER

COLT 1878

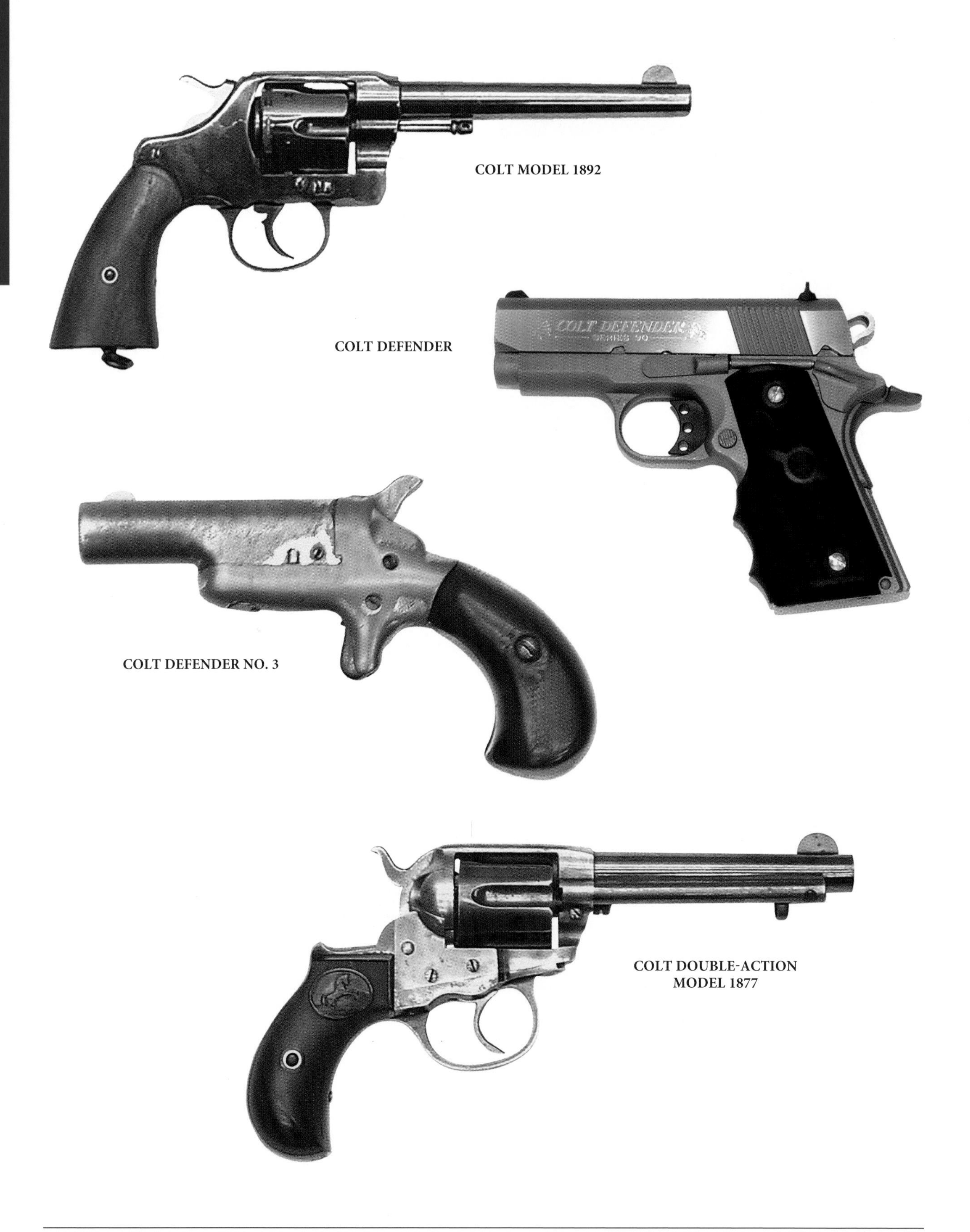

COLT MODEL 1892

COLT DEFENDER

COLT DEFENDER NO. 3

COLT DOUBLE-ACTION MODEL 1877

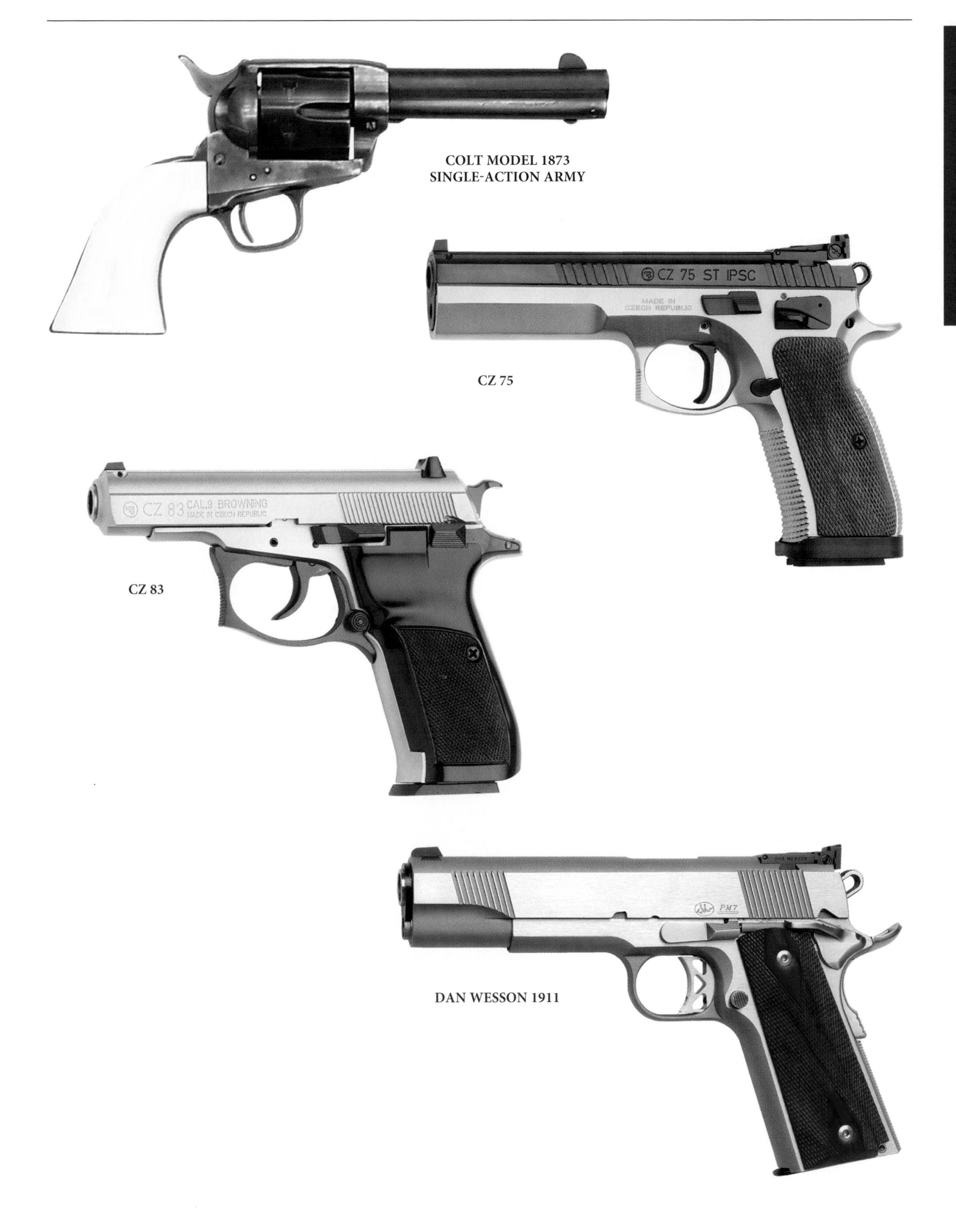

COLT MODEL 1873
SINGLE-ACTION ARMY

CZ 75

CZ 83

DAN WESSON 1911

GLOCK G17

H&K USP 40

KAHR P9

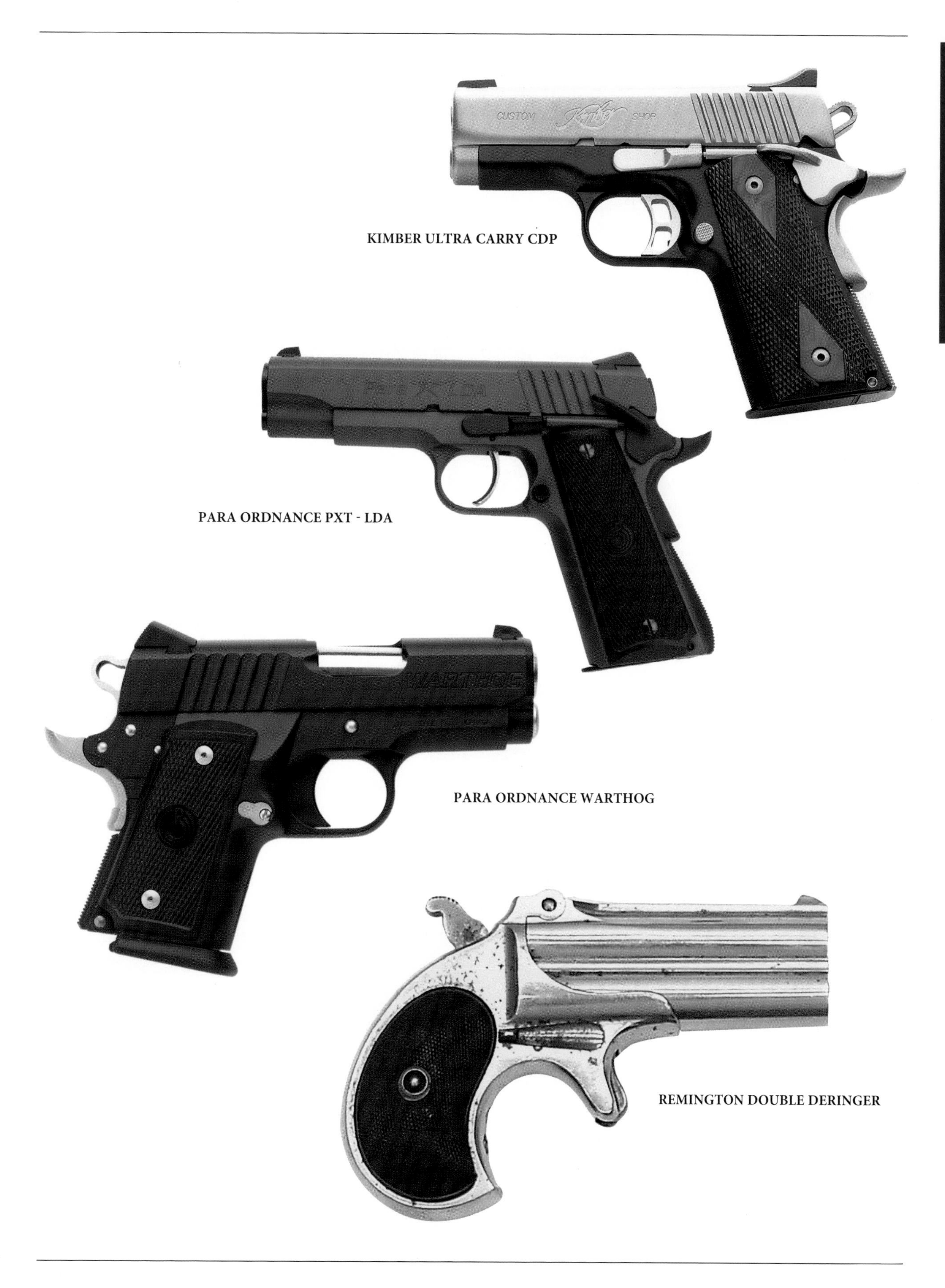

KIMBER ULTRA CARRY CDP

PARA ORDNANCE PXT - LDA

PARA ORDNANCE WARTHOG

REMINGTON DOUBLE DERINGER

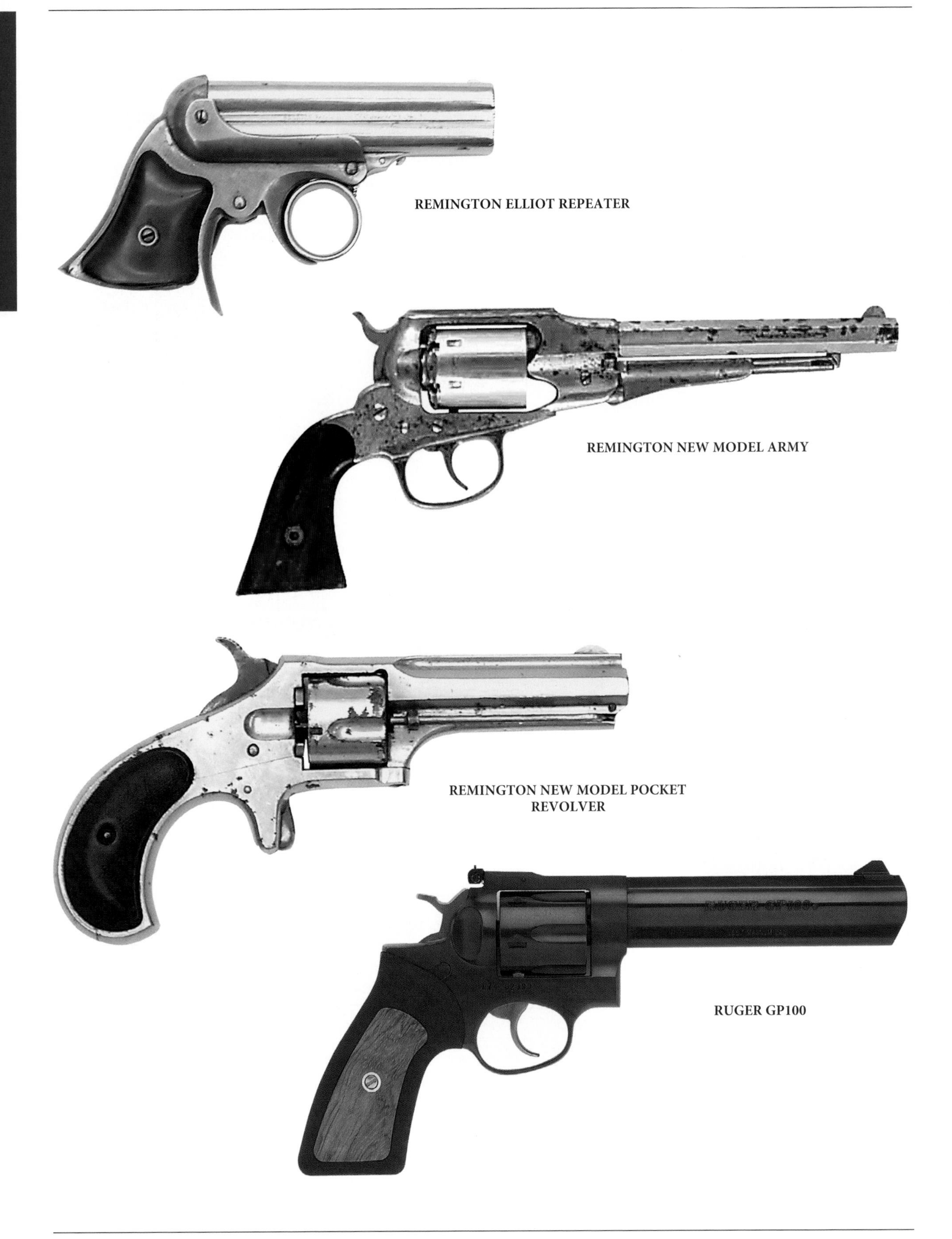
REMINGTON ELLIOT REPEATER

REMINGTON NEW MODEL ARMY

REMINGTON NEW MODEL POCKET REVOLVER

RUGER GP100

RUGER NEW VAQUERO

RUGER P95

SIG ARMS P226

SMITH & WESSON SIGMA

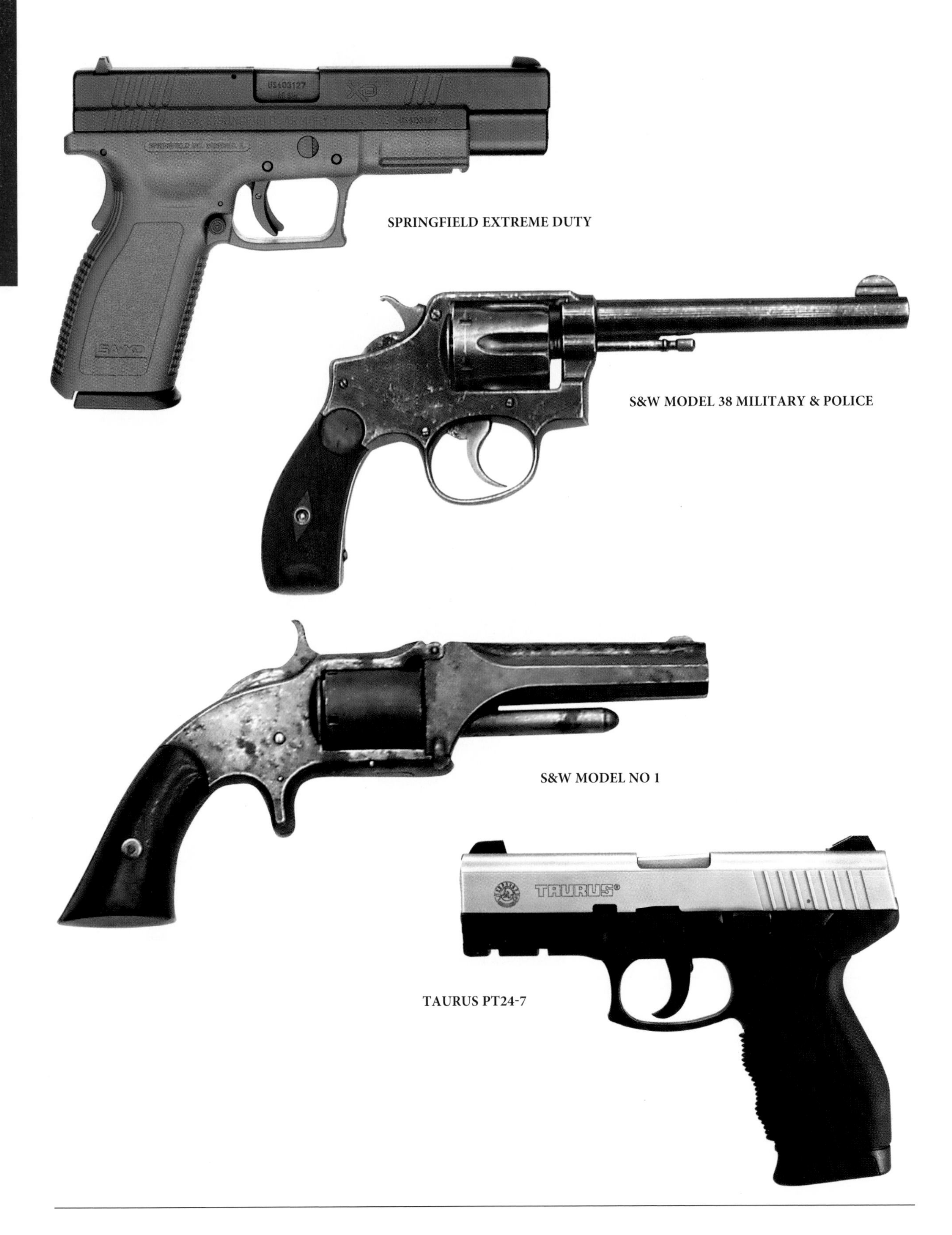

SPRINGFIELD EXTREME DUTY

S&W MODEL 38 MILITARY & POLICE

S&W MODEL NO 1

TAURUS PT24-7

FIREARMS DISASSEMBLY INSTRUCTIONS WITH EXPLODED VIEWS

WARNING: **Before attempting to field strip or disassemble ANY firearm, always keep your finger off the trigger and hold the weapon with the muzzle pointed in a safe direction.**

ALWAYS assume that a firearm is loaded and capable of being discharged until you have personally verified that it is not loaded.

ALWAYS open and inspect any loading port, remove any magazine, open the action and inspect the chamber and loading areas before beginning to disassemble any firearm.

ALLEN AND THURBER PEPPERBOX

PARTS LEGEND

1. Barrel retaining screw
2. Barrel group
3. Hammer
4. Sear
5. Sear screw
6. Mainspring link
7. Mainspring
8. Right grip
9. Frame
10. Left grip
11. Grip screw
12. Side-plate screw
13. Side-plate
14. Trigger
15. Hand operating pin
16. Barrel latch screw
17. Barrel latch
18. Detent pin
19. Detent retaining pin
20. Detent spring
21. Nipple shield
22. Shield screws
23. Trigger pin
24. Hand
25. Hand retaining screw
26. Hand spring
27. Spring retaining screw
28. Mainspring tension screw
29. Trigger guard
30. Hammer pin

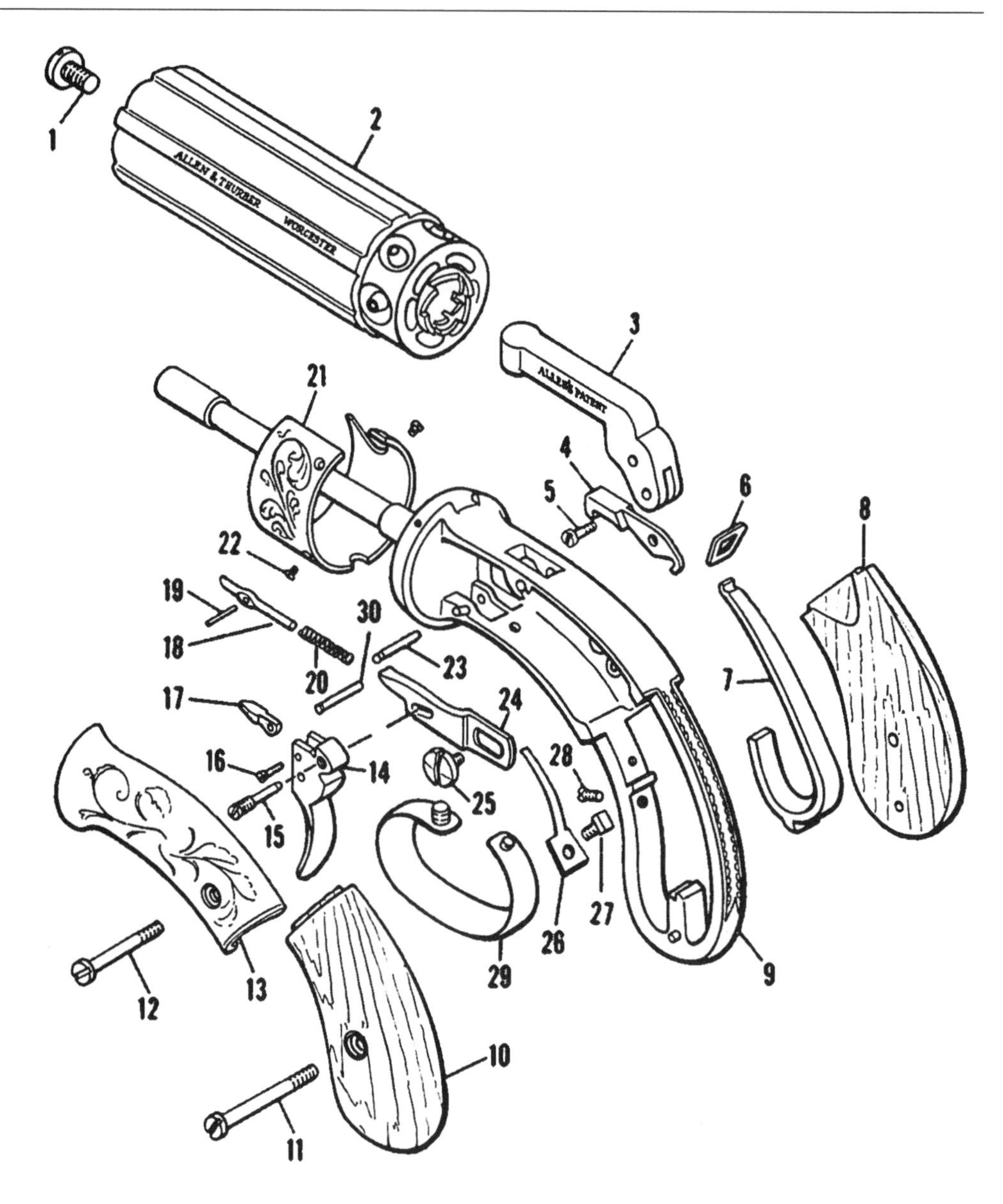

The pepperbox pistol holds a unique position in American firearms history. It bridged the gap between the single-shot pistol and the revolver with stationary barrel. Pepperbox guns were handy, fairly reliable, and supplied a series of quick shots. They proved popular throughout the United States and were carried West in great numbers during the gold rush era.

While there were flintlock pepperboxes, they were clumsy and expensive. The common pepperbox, as we know it today, came about after development of the percussion cap.

Ethan Allen saw the possibilities of a percussion pepperbox and in 1834 patented his self-cocking gun. A few years later, with the aid of his brother-in-law, he founded the Allen and Thurber Gun Co. They made guns from 1837 to 1842 in Grafton, Massachusetts. In 1842 they moved to Norwich, Connecticut and, in 1855, they moved back to Massachusetts and settled in Worcester. Despite all these moves, a steady flow of pepperboxes were turned out. A wide variety of models was offered. The revolving barrels ranged from 2 to 5 inches in length and in calibers from .28 up to .36.

Allen and Thurber guns were well-made. The barrels were bored from a block of cast steel. The frame was also cast steel. Operating parts were machined from bar stock and hardened where necessary. Walnut was used for the grips in most cases and the frames were generally scroll engraved.

The self-cocking lock mechanism was unique for its time. It is fairly simple and contains a minimum number of parts. Lack of shielding between the caps in some of the earlier pepperboxes resulted in occasional multiple discharges. Allen overcame this by putting a snug-fitting shield around the nipple area which kept the caps in place and also helped keep the sparks from igniting the other loaded barrels.

The revolver, with its fixed rifled barrel and compact design, to say nothing of its reduced weight, soon overshadowed the pepperbox design. The invention of the metallic cartridge gave the pepperbox its final kiss of death, since it was impractical to try to convert a pepperbox to fire fixed ammunition.

DISASSEMBLY

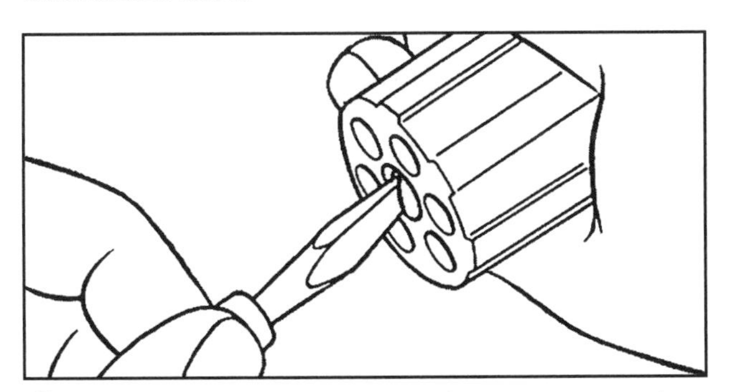

1 The Allen and Thurber pepperbox barrel group rotates around a central pin fixed to the frame. To remove the barrel group, remove the barrel retaining screw (1) and pull the trigger until the hammer just clears the nipple. Then pull barrel group forward off pin. Use a good grade of penetrating oil on all the screw heads and threads.

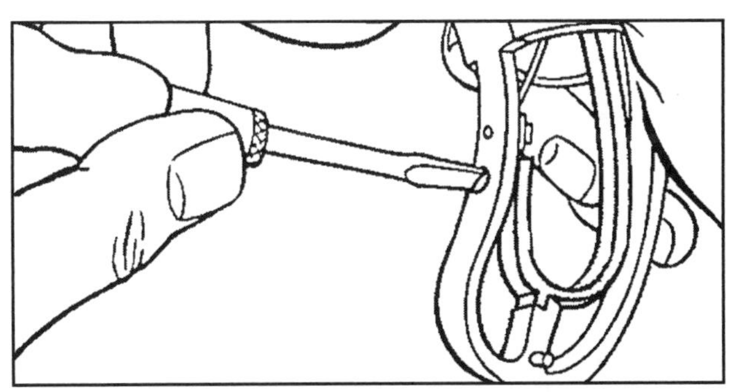

2 The trigger pull can be adjusted to a certain extent by loosening or tightening the mainspring tension screw (28) . When this screw is removed, the mainspring (7) can be pushed out of its seat in the frame and lifted free.

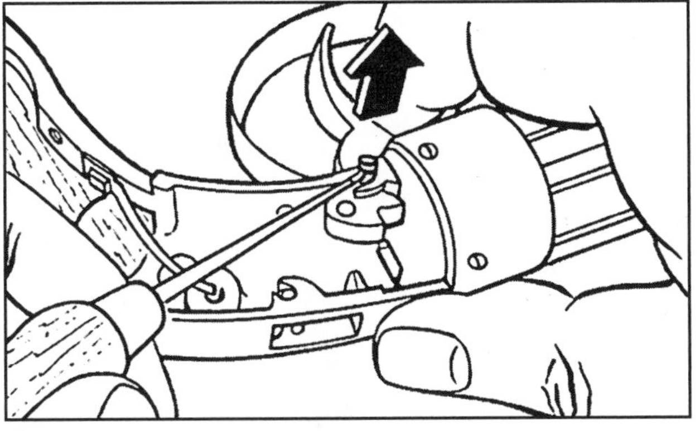

3 There are only 2 hinge pins (23 and 30) in the entire gun, one retaining the trigger, the other retaining the hammer. Since both of these pins are blind pins and do not extend through the frame, a notch was cut in the frame and an undercut was machined into the pins. If a thin screwdriver or pick is inserted as shown, the pins can be easily pried out.

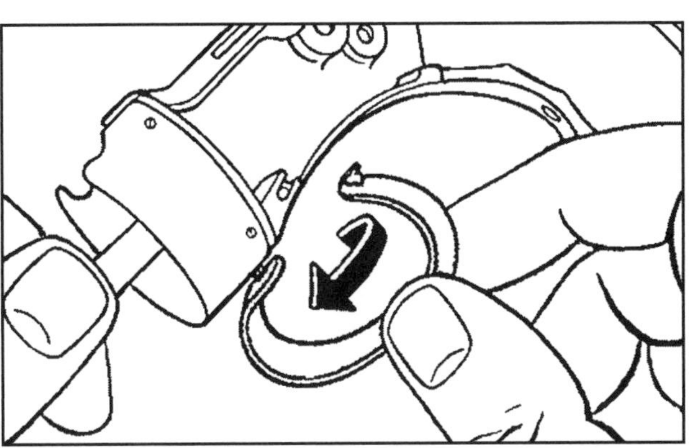

4 Once the side-plate has been removed, internal parts can be easily unscrewed and removed. To remove the trigger guard (29), push rear of the guard forward and pull down on it slightly. When it comes free of the frame, unscrew as shown.

ASTRA 357 DA REVOLVER

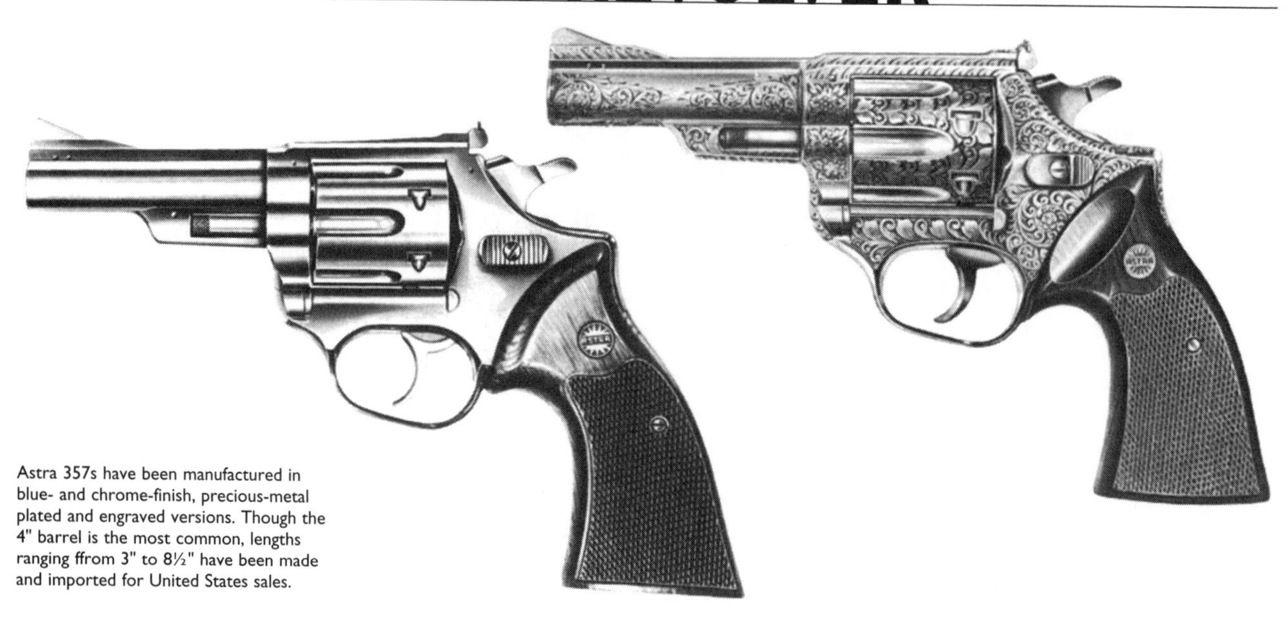

Astra 357s have been manufactured in blue- and chrome-finish, precious-metal plated and engraved versions. Though the 4" barrel is the most common, lengths ranging ffrom 3" to 8½" have been made and imported for United States sales.

PARTS LEGEND

1. Frame
2. Crane
3. Cylinder with extractor and pins
4. Barrel
5. Hammer
6. Trigger
7. Bolt
8. Thumbpiece
9. Cylinder stop
10. Rebound slide
11. Sear
12. Sideplate
13. Front sight
14. Trigger lever
15. Hand
16. Rear sight leaf
17. Sight slide
18. Rear sight elevator
19. Locking bolt
20. Firing pin
21. Firing pin retaining pin
22. Front sight pin (2)
23. Locking bolt pin
24. Barrel pin
25. Bolt plunger
26. Sight leaf screw
27. Cylinder pin
28. Extractor rod collar
29. Windage screw
30. Elevator screw
31. Thumbpiece screw
32. Flat head sideplate screw
33. Front & lower side-plate screw (2)
34. Top sideplate screw
35. Hammer strut
36. Extractor rod
37. Bolt spring
38. Sear spring
39. Locking bolt spring
40. Firing pin spring
41. Sight slide spring
42. Cylinder stop spring
43. Extractor spring
44. Center pin spring
45. Hand torsion spring
46. Rebound slide spring
47. Hammer spring
48. Right grip
49. Regulating ring
50. Grip screw
51. Left grip
52. Grip pin
53. Safety pin
54. Safety
55. Cylinder stop plunger
56. Cylinder stop screw
57. Sear plunger
58. Hand plunger

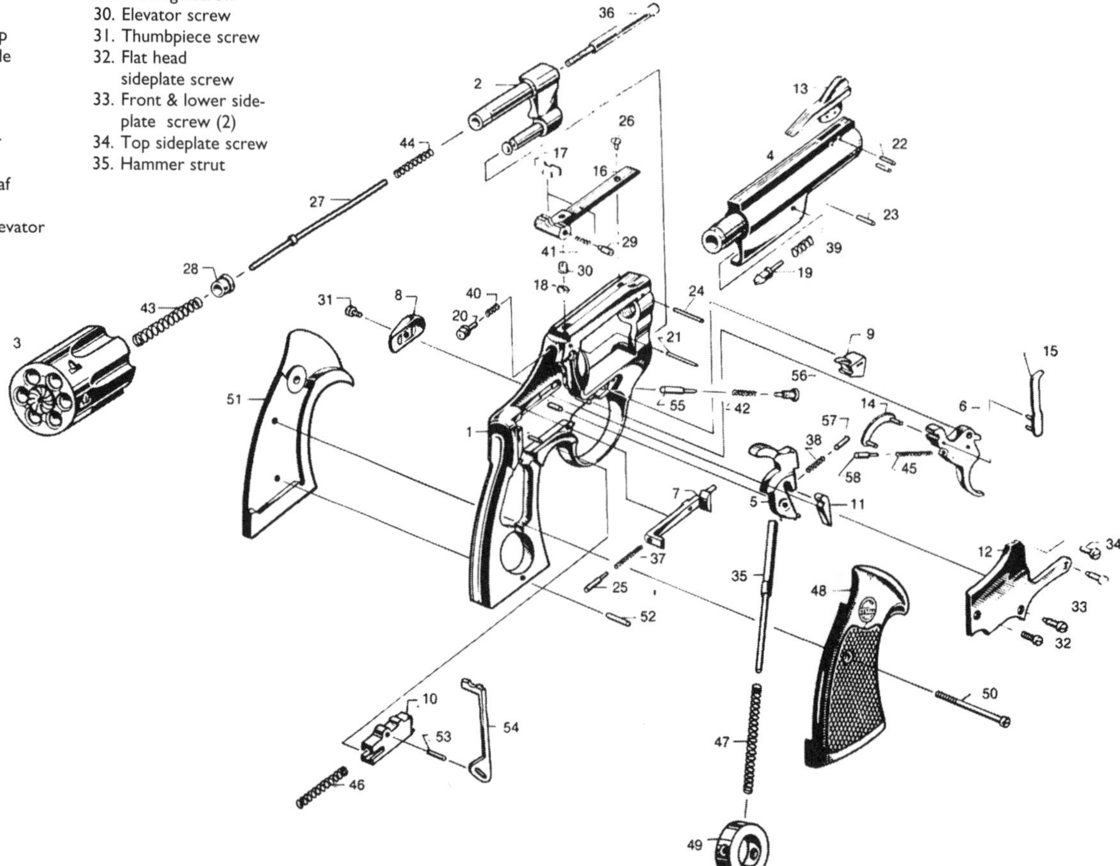

The name Astra was registered in 1914 by Esperanza y Unceta, some six years after the founding of the firm at Eibar, Spain. The present plant was built in 1913 in Guernica, Spain, where it remains. The firm name was changed in 1926 to Unceta y Cia., and changed again in 1953 to Astra-Unceta y Cia., S.A.

Up until 1960, Astra, as it has come to be known, had manufactured many semi-automatic pistols, but no revolvers. In that year, they introduced the Cadix revolver in .22, .32 and .38 Spl. calibers. The Cadix line proved profitable to Astra, and in 1969 the company began the development of a revolver similar to the Cadix but built on a medium-sized frame to handle the .357 Mag. cartridge. Initial deliveries were made in September of 1971. Like the Cadix, the Astra 357 was similar in its internal construction to contemporary Smith & Wesson revolvers. Internally, the most significant difference is the coiled, music-wire mainspring which, around its strut, impinges on an internal ring in the butt of the revolver. This ring (also found on the earlier Cadix) has four annular holes which are counterbored to varying depths. The ring can be turned manually after the removal of the grips and mainspring assembly, so that different trigger pull weights can be achieved.

In 1971, the .357 was available with 3-, 4- or 6-inch barrel lengths, and in 1976 an 8½-inch version was introduced.

By mid-1979, approximately 55,000 .357s had been made and sold in blue, chrome, and engraved versions. A 4-inch barrel version was introduced in stainless steel and was discontinued in 1987. In addition to the 55,000 unit quantity, over 16,000 similar guns in .38 Special caliber were produced, but these are seldom encountered in the United States.

The standard .38 Special gun is designated the Model 960, and a single-action version with screw-adjustable trigger, designed for competition shooting, is termed the Match Model. The Astra .357 was imported into the United States from 1972 to 1988.

DISASSEMBLY

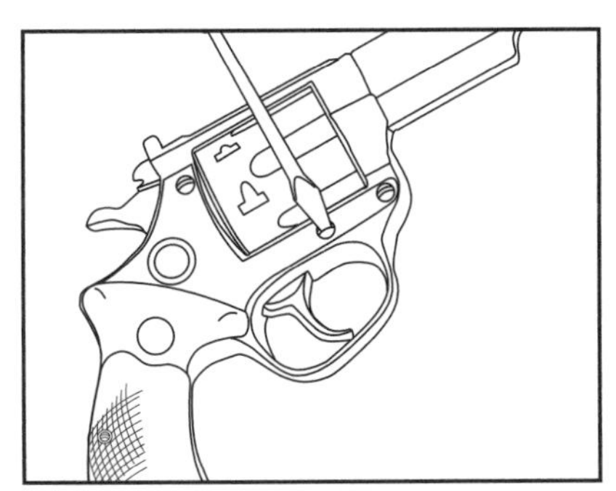

1 To remove the cylinder assembly, back off the front sideplate screw (33). Then, moving the thumbpiece (8) forward, swing out the cylinder assembly and push it and its crane (2) free of the frame.

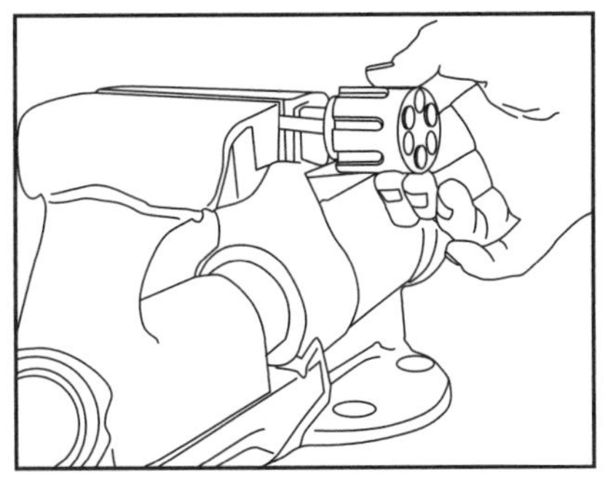

2 Clamp the extractor (36) in a padded vise and, with two or three empty cartridge cases in the chambers to prevent damage to the extractor and its guide pins, turn the cylinder clockwise to free it from the extractor rod.

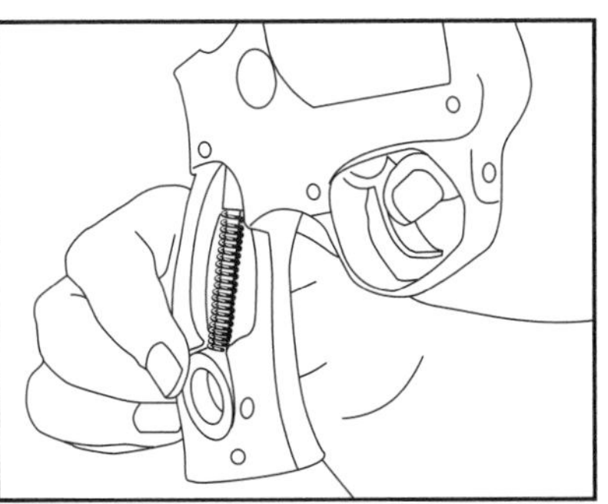

3 Once the grips are removed, and before taking off the sideplate, grasp the regulating ring (49) and move it sideways from the frame, taking care to restrain the strut (35) and hammer spring (47).

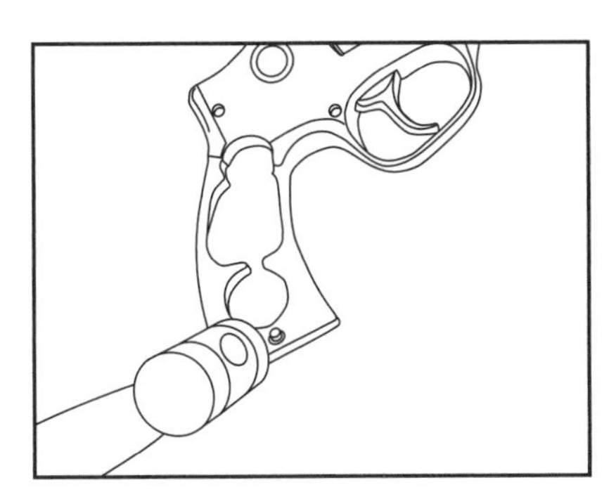

4 Remove the sideplate screws (32, 33, 34) and tap the frame lightly with a wooden or plastic mallet at the right of the grip to loosen the sideplate (12). Do not pry the sideplate from its seat.

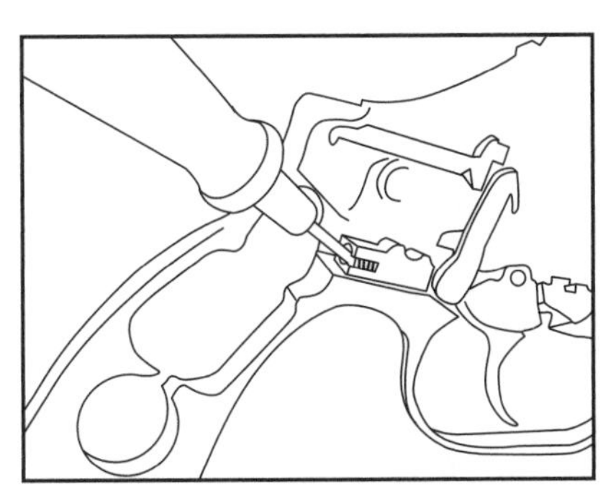

5 Remove the rebound slide (10) and its spring (46) by compressing the spring with a screwdriver while lifting up on the rebound slide and pulling it off the fixed frame pin. Take care that the rebound slide spring is not lost, by keeping a cloth overthe gun to trap the spring and prevent injury.

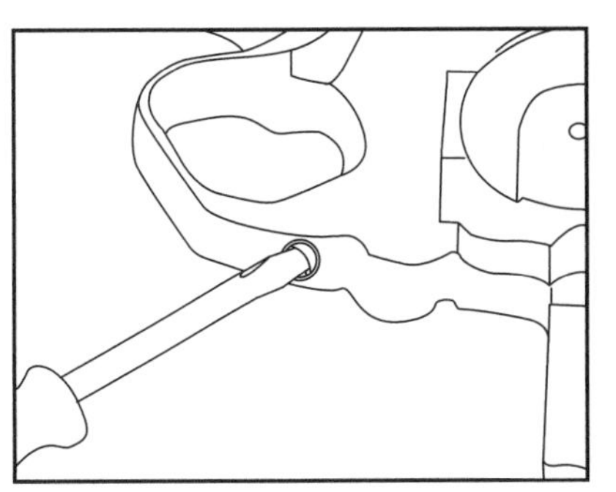

6 To remove the cylinder stop (9), back out its screw (56) located at the front of the frame and remove the cylinder stop spring (42) and the cylinder stop plunger (55). With a screwdriver, push the narrow side of the cylinder stop to force it out of the frame. Reassemble in reverse order.

ASTRA MODEL 400 & 600 PISTOLS

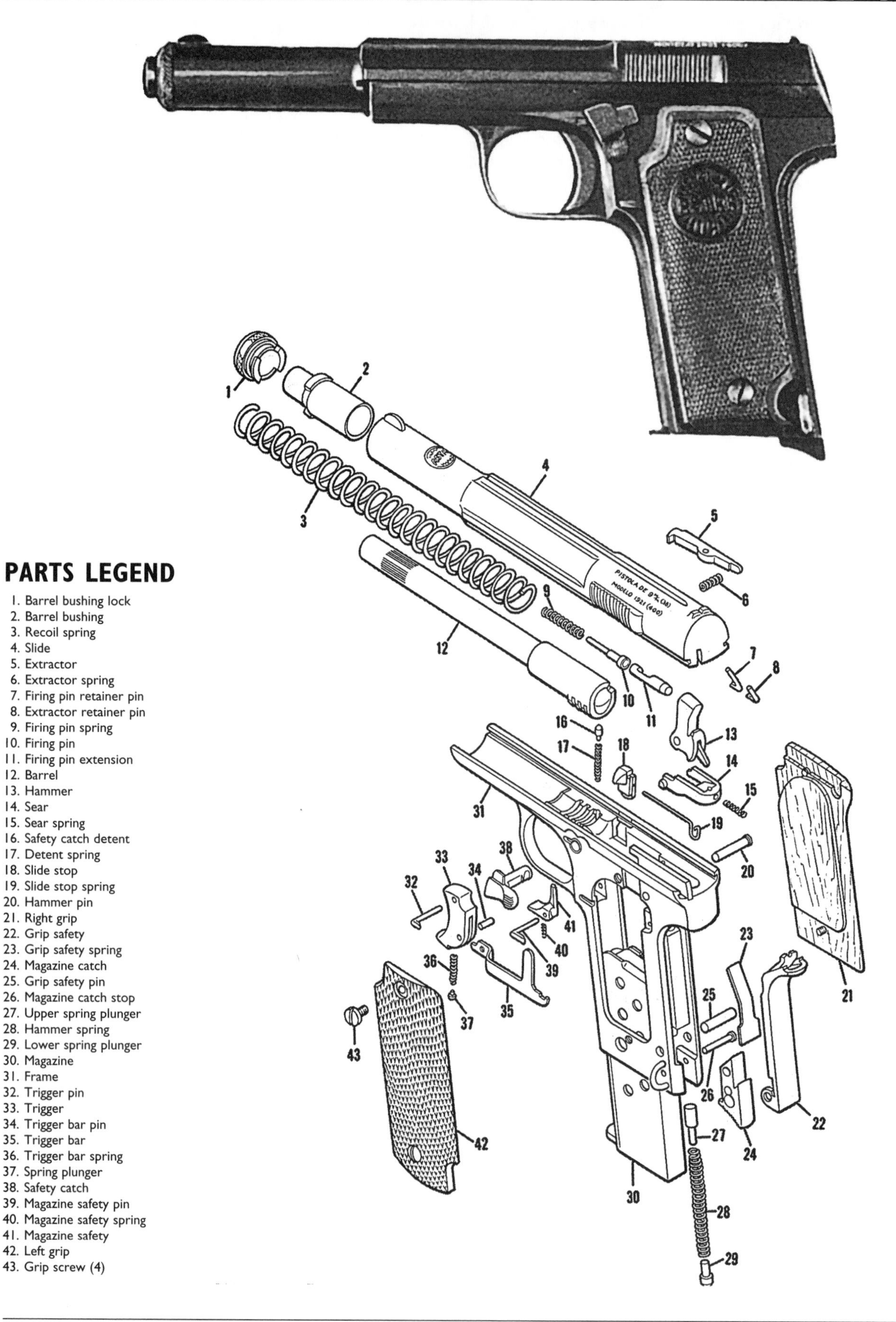

PARTS LEGEND

1. Barrel bushing lock
2. Barrel bushing
3. Recoil spring
4. Slide
5. Extractor
6. Extractor spring
7. Firing pin retainer pin
8. Extractor retainer pin
9. Firing pin spring
10. Firing pin
11. Firing pin extension
12. Barrel
13. Hammer
14. Sear
15. Sear spring
16. Safety catch detent
17. Detent spring
18. Slide stop
19. Slide stop spring
20. Hammer pin
21. Right grip
22. Grip safety
23. Grip safety spring
24. Magazine catch
25. Grip safety pin
26. Magazine catch stop
27. Upper spring plunger
28. Hammer spring
29. Lower spring plunger
30. Magazine
31. Frame
32. Trigger pin
33. Trigger
34. Trigger bar pin
35. Trigger bar
36. Trigger bar spring
37. Spring plunger
38. Safety catch
39. Magazine safety pin
40. Magazine safety spring
41. Magazine safety
42. Left grip
43. Grip screw (4)

The Spanish-made Astra Model 400 (Model 1921) semi-automatic pistol was a blowback-operated arm capable of firing either the 9 mm Largo (9 mm Bergmann) cartridge or the .38 Automatic Colt Pistol cartridge. Being blowback-operated, the gun's breech was not locked in firing. A locked breech is usually considered necessary to handle the more powerful 9 mm loads, but in the Model 400 pistol the opening of the breech was delayed through the use of a heavy slide and a powerful recoil spring. The Model 400 was produced from 1921 through 1945.

During World War II, the German Army obtained the Astra pistol in cal. 9 mm Parabellum (9 mm. Luger). This gun was known as the Model 600 and has the inscription "PIST. PATR. 08" stamped on the barrel opposite the ejection port in the slide. Model 600 pistols used by the German Army have the German Ordnance acceptance mark on the right side of the grip overhang. After World War II, 14,000 Model 600 pistols were sold to West Germany for police use. It was also offered commercially.

The Models 400 and 600 pistols featured a thumb safety locking the trigger and slide, a grip safety locking the sear, and a magazine safety that blocked the trigger when the magazine is removed.

The disassembly procedures for the Models 400 and 600 pistols are essentially identical.

DISASSEMBLY

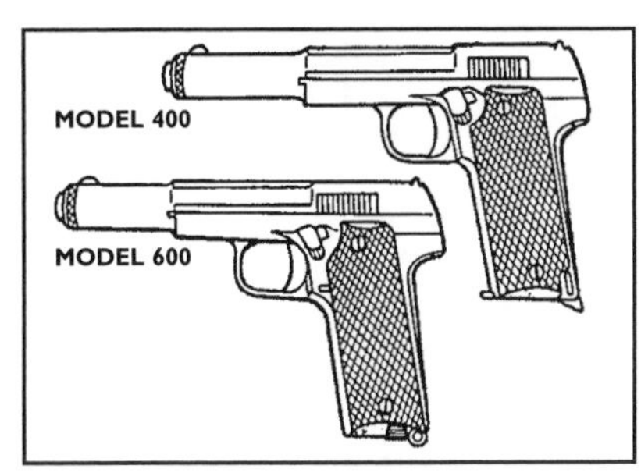

1 Mechanically, the Models 400 and 600 are similar. The Model 600 is ¾" shorter. The front-to-back grip depth is less in the Model 600 because of the shorter cartridge it fires. Most parts are not interchangeable but the take-down sequence is similar.

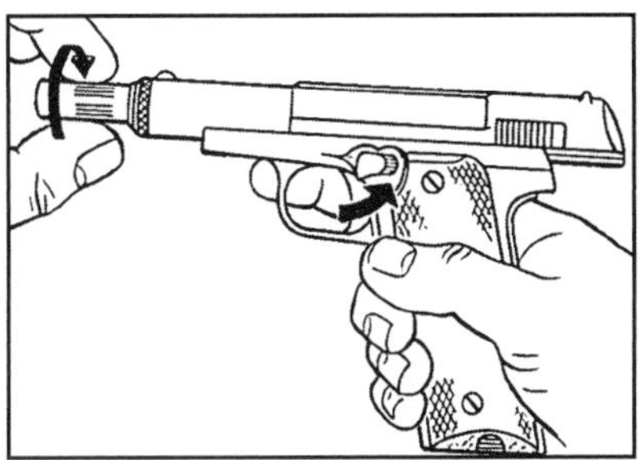

2 To field strip for general cleaning, first clear chamber and remove magazine (30). Pull slide (4) to rear, then rotate safety catch (38) up as slide is moved forward until catch engages slide. Rotate barrel (12) as shown, until it is released from frame (31) and engaged with slide. Release safety catch and move barrel and slide forward off frame.

3 To disassemble, first clear chamber and remove magazine. Place pistol, muzzle up, on table. Depress barrel bushing (2) with magazine floorplate or screwdriver. Turn barrel bushing lock (1) either way until it holds barrel bushing. Grip barrel bushing and lock firmly with both hands and turn lock about ¼-turn, releasing recoil spring (3). Remove recoil spring, bushing, and lock. Barrel and slide are removed from frame as in fieldstripping.

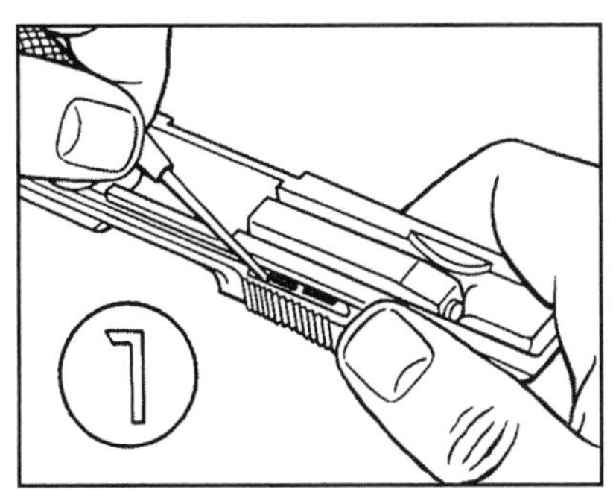

4 L-shaped retainer pins (7 & 8) retain the extractor (5) and the firing pin extension (11). Remove pins by prying up with a small screwdriver or punch. When reassembling firing pin spring (9), firing pin (10), and firing pin extension (11), align cut-out on the firing pin extension before inserting the retainer pin (7).

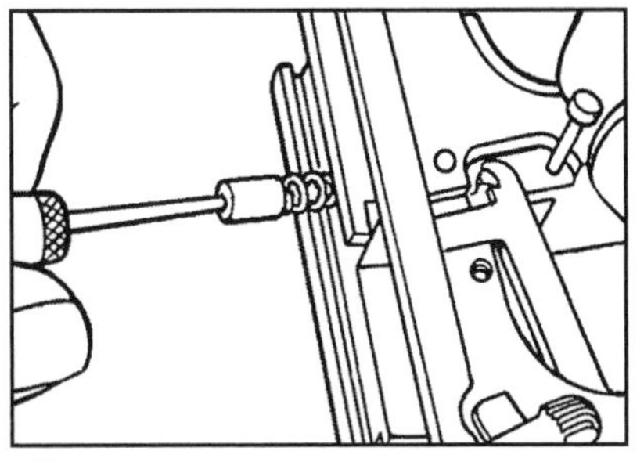

5 Remove the four grip screws (43) and the grips (21 & 42). Replace magazine (30) in frame. Insert punch through hole in frame below trigger bar (35). Hold hammer (13) with thumb and pull trigger, allowing hammer to fall until upper plunger (27) stops against punch. Remove magazine. Drift out hammer pin (20) from left side and remove hammer. Hold upper plunger with drift and remove punch. Remove upper and lower plungers (27 & 29) and hammer spring (28). Note that the Model 600 has no lower plunger.

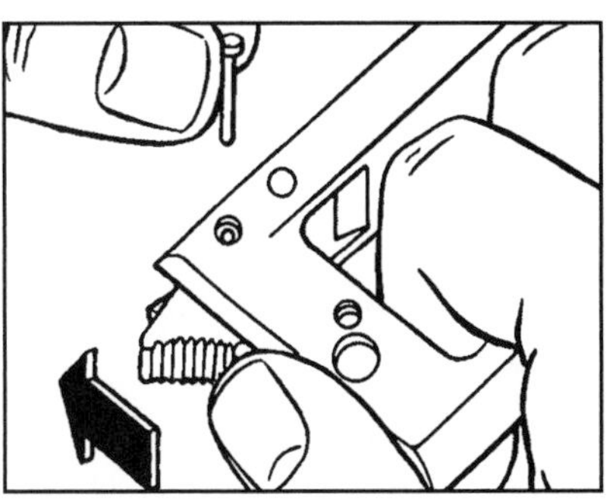

6 Most Model 400 pistols have magazine catch as shown here. Remove magazine catch stop (26). Drift out grip safety pin (25), remove grip safety (22), and push out magazine catch (24) in direction indicated. It is unnecessary to remove side magazine catch on late Models 400 and 600 pistols.

ASTRA CADIX DA REVOLVER

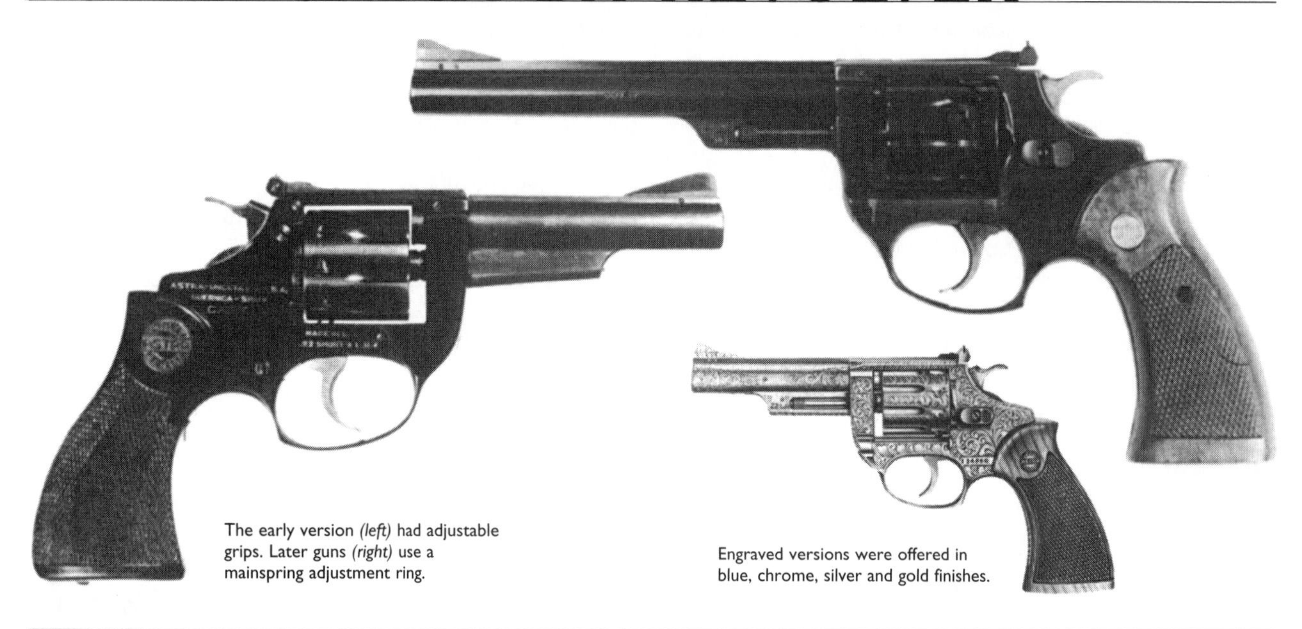

The early version *(left)* had adjustable grips. Later guns *(right)* use a mainspring adjustment ring.

Engraved versions were offered in blue, chrome, silver and gold finishes.

PARTS LEGEND

1. Frame
2. Crane
3. Cylinder
4. Extractor
5. Barrel
6. Hammer
7. Trigger
8. Grip adjusting block
9. Bolt
10. Thumbpiece
11. Cylinder stop
12. Rebound slide
13. Sear
14. Sideplate
15. Front sight
16. Trigger lever
17. Grip
18. Hand
19. Rear sight leaf
20. Sight slide
21. Elevating stud
22. Locking bolt
23. Firing pin
24. Firing pin bushing
25. Firing pin retaining pin
26. Lever spring pin
27. Lever spring collar pin
28. Front sight pin
29. Locking bolt pin
30. Mainspring
31. Rebound slide spring
32. Barrel pin
33. Sear pin
34. Hand spring pin
35. Bushing retaining pin
36. Cylinder lever pin
37. Bolt plunger
38. Sight leaf screw
39. Center pin
40. Hand spring
41. Extractor rod collar
42. Center pin spring
43. Windage screw
44. Elevation screw
45. Thumbpiece screw
46. Flat head sideplate screw
47. Rear sideplate screw
48. Front sideplate screw
49. Top sideplate screw
50. Extractor pin
51. Cylinder stop spring
52. Sight slide spring
53. Firing pin spring
54. Hammer strut
55. Extractor rod
56. Mainspring seat
57. Grip adjusting screw
58. Bolt spring
59. Sear spring
60. Locking bolt spring

DETAIL

A. Left grip
B. Frame
C. Adjustment ring
D. Right grip
E. Grip screw

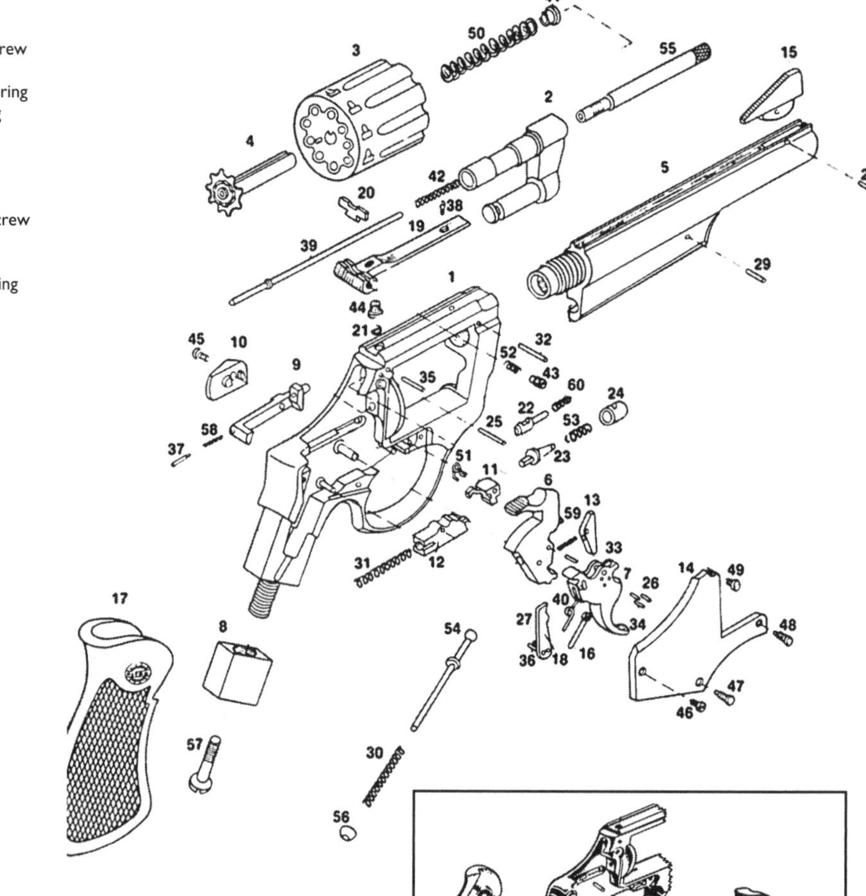

The Spanish gunmaking firm of Esperanza y Unceta was founded in Eibar in 1908. A new factory was built in Guernica in 1913 and a year later the brand name Astra was registered. In 1926, the firm name was changed to Unceta y Cia., and changed again in 1953 to Astra-Unceta y Cia. Here and in Europe it is known simply as Astra.

Semi-automatic pistols formed the bulk of Astra's production for half a century, and it supplied guns ranging from the Campo Giro to the Junior Colt.

Although well-made S&W-type revolvers were cataloged and sold by Unceta y Cia. in the 1920s and '30s, these were not made in Guernica but in Eibar by a contracting firm. Revolvers did not become a part of Astra's production until 1958. In January of that year, the first true Astra revolver prototypes were produced and given the name Cadix — the archaic spelling of the Spanish port Cadiz.

The early revolvers were essentially S&W derivations in .22 cal. with shrouded extractor rods, but included some interesting innovations. The swing-out cylinder held not six but nine .22 Long Rifle (or Short or Long) cartridges; the frame profiling was distinctly different from that of the S&W wheelguns; and the one-piece plastic grip was affixed to a spacer block on the frame tang, permitting the grip to be adjusted vertically to suit differing hand sizes. Versions with 2-, 4- and 6-inch barrels were produced.

Despite its large cylinder capacity, the Cadix was small in size and inevitably (1962) a five-shot .38 Spl. version came along, followed by a six-shot .32 and nine-shot .22 Mag. in 1969. The 2-inch-barreled .38 proved a most popular addition to the line of the U.S. importers of the time, Firearms International Corp., and many Cadix revolvers were sold here. The small .38 dispensed with the adjustable-grip feature, substituting a conventional grip frame and two-piece walnut grip panels. By 1968, adjustable grips had disappeared from all models in favor of a conventional grip and a mainspring adjustment ring as shown in the photographs and accompanying exploded drawing.

More than 300,000 Cadix revolvers were made before Astra went out of business in 1997. The Cadix was imported into the United States from about 1960 through 1968.

DISASSEMBLY

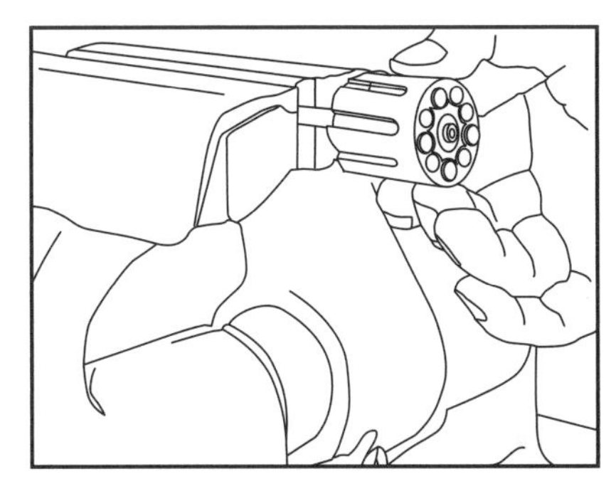

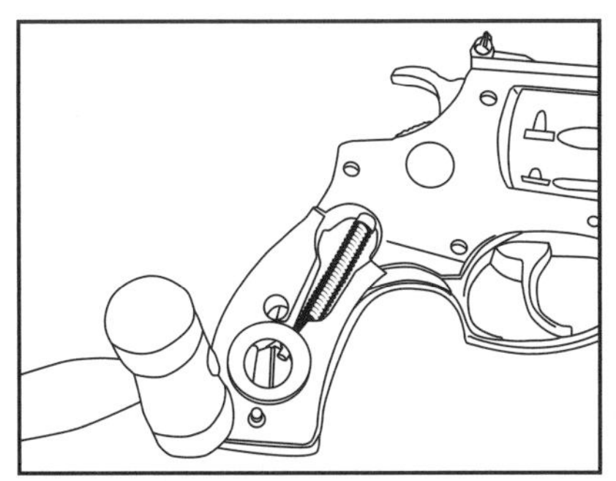

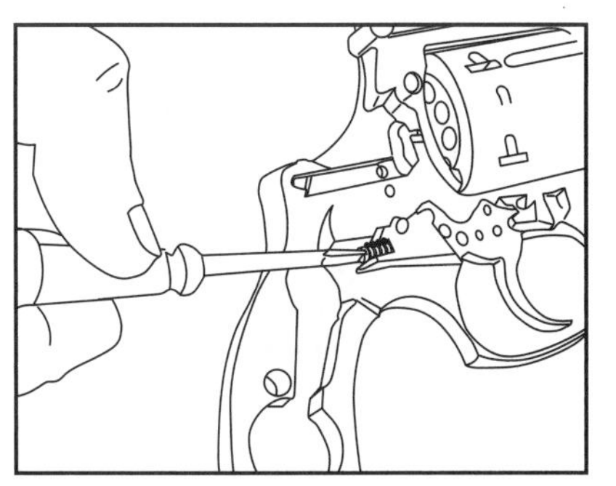

1 Disassembly Instructions—All Types First check that the revolver is unloaded by moving the thumbpiece (10) forward and swinging the cylinder (3) out to the left. The grip (17) or grip plates (A, D) (depending on model), are taken off by removing screws (57) or (E).

Remove the cylinder, its crane (2) and attendant parts by loosening the front sideplate screw (48) and sliding the opened cylinder assembly forward off the frame (1). Disassembly of the cylinder is accomplished by clamping the extractor rod (55) in a padded vise with two or three empty cartridges chambered to prevent damage to the extractor guide pins. The cylinder is then turned clockwise to free it from the extractor rod.

2 The sideplate (14) can now be taken off to expose the internal parts by first removing its screws (46, 47, 48, 49) and then tapping the right side of the frame with a plastic or wooden mallet to loosen the plate which can then be removed with the fingers. Do not pry with metal tools which can damage the finish or internal parts.

3 With the sideplate removed, the internal parts and their function are apparent. No further disassembly should be required for maintenance.

If it is required that the rebound slide (12) be removed, caution is necessary as it is powered by a heavy spring that could cause injury if released unexpectedly. Eye protection is mandatory.

Compress the rebound slide spring (31) with a screwdriver and lift it over the frame pin which restrains it.

ASTRA CONSTABLE PISTOL

PARTS LEGEND

1. Slide
2. Barrel
3. Barrel pin
4. Recoil spring
5. Firing pin spring
6. Firing pin retainer
7. Safety plunger
8. Extractor spring
9. Extractor retainer
10. Extractor
11. Sear spring and take-down yoke spring
12. Takedown yoke
13. Takedown plunger spring
14. Takedown plunger
15. Takedown plunger pin
16 Trigger spring
17. Trigger
18. Trigger pin
19. Hammer
20. Hammer pin
21. Mainspring
22. Sear plunger
23. Sear
24. Sear pin
25. Sear bar
26. Disconnector
27. Magazine catch
28. Magazine catch spring
29. Magazine button plunger
30. Magazine catch button
31. Grip screws
32. Magazine complete
33. Frame
34. Firing pin
35. Slide retainer
36. Disconnector spring
37. Right grip
38. Left grip
39. Rear sight
40. Thumb safety
41. Hammer strut
42. Sight slide
43. Sight slide spring
44. Windage screw

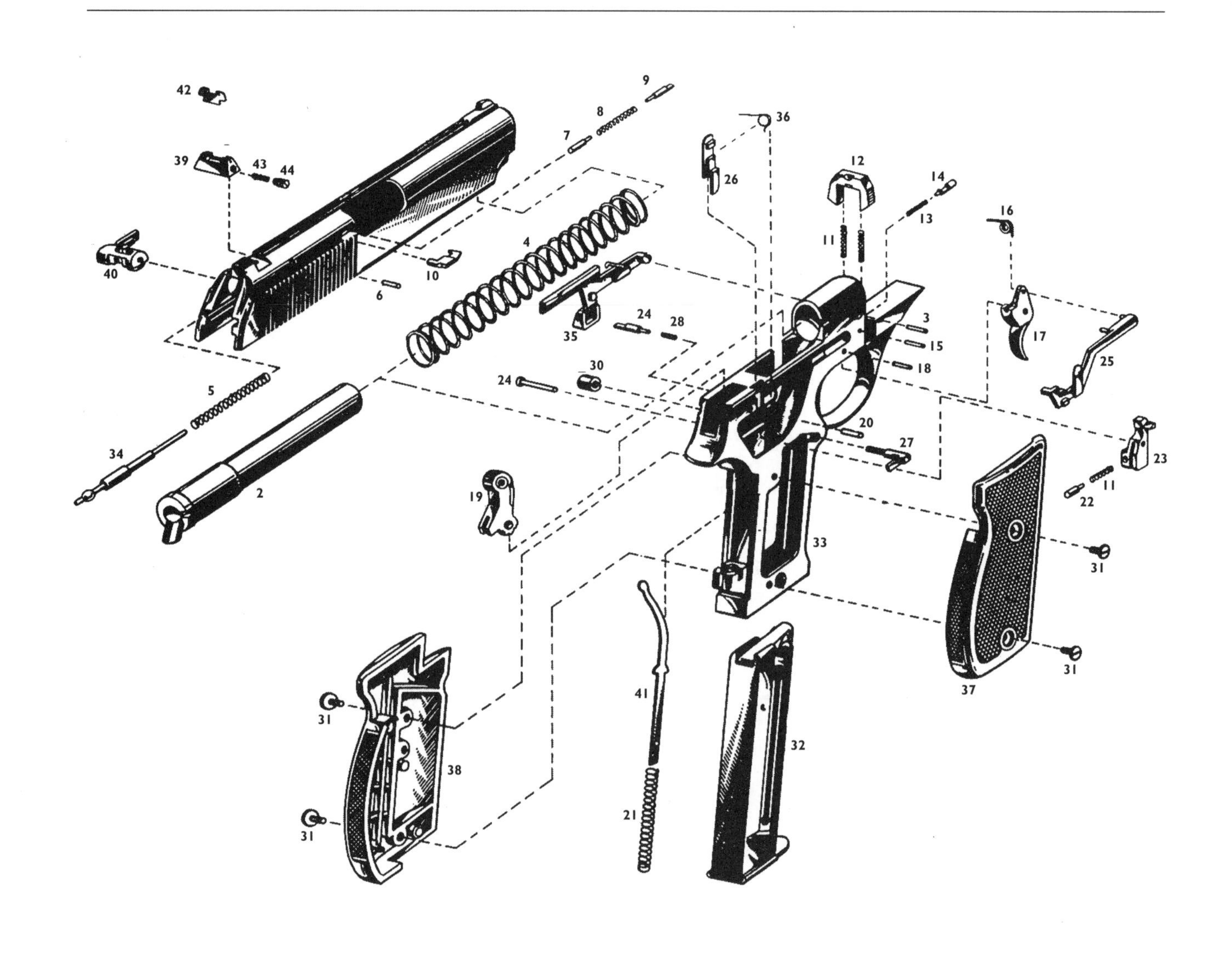

In the mid-1960s, Astra began the development of their first double-action semi-automatic pistol, the Constable. It was not until 1970, however, that the first production models were offered for sale in the United States.

These original pistols in calibers .32, .380 and .22 Long Rifle were all equipped with plastic grips affixed with a single screw on each side and an integral thumb shelf on the left side. Early guns had fixed rear sights and positive firing pins. The positive firing pin meant that if the pistol, with chamber loaded, were to be carried with the chamber loaded, the hammer fully down and the safety off, the firing pin would impinge on the cartridge primer. Safe carrying the pistol, then, required either that the pistol be carried with the chamber empty, or with the chamber loaded, the hammer down and the safety engaged.

Later pistols were equipped with flat plastic grips lacking the thumbrest, affixed with two screws on each side, and a rear sight adjustable for windage. Still later, positive firing pins were changed to firing pins of the inertia type making it safer to carry the gun. This change in the firing pin was accompanied by minor changes to the safety, the disconnector and the slide retainer. The firing pin change took place in the .380 A.C.P. and .32 calibers at Serial No. 1091101, and in the .22 caliber pistols at Serial No. 1140551.

A 13-shot version of the .380 Constable, designated the Constable A-60, was also produced, and brought into the United States between 1986 and 1991.

Constables were imported by Interarms, of Alexandria, Virginia. By 1988, Interarms had dropped both the .32 and the .22 Long Rifle guns from their catalogs. Importation of all Constable models ceased after 1991.

Astra Constables were, like other Astra products, of good quality and well-finished throughout. At various times they were offered in blue, chrome and chrome-engraved finishes. The Constable Sport Model, in .22 Long Rifle only, was fitted with a six-inch barrel, a windage- and elevation-adjustable rear sight, and a barrel counterweight.

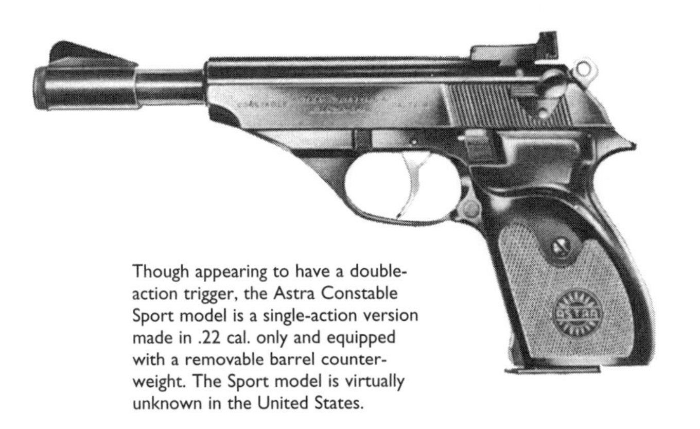

Though appearing to have a double-action trigger, the Astra Constable Sport model is a single-action version made in .22 cal. only and equipped with a removable barrel counter-weight. The Sport model is virtually unknown in the United States.

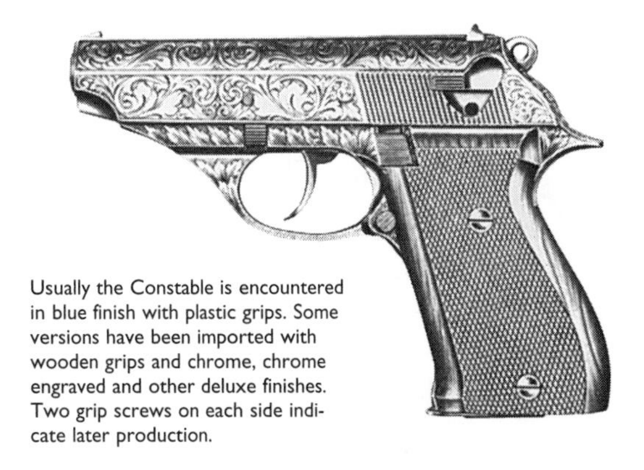

Usually the Constable is encountered in blue finish with plastic grips. Some versions have been imported with wooden grips and chrome, chrome engraved and other deluxe finishes. Two grip screws on each side indicate later production.

DISASSEMBLY

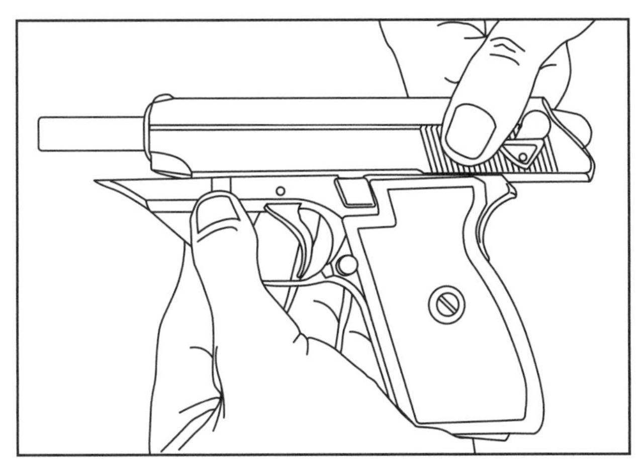

1 Depress the magazine catch button (30) and remove the magazine (32) from the pistol. Retract the slide (1) and release it after checking that the chamber is empty. Leave the hammer (19) at the full cock position. With the thumb and index finger of the left hand, pull down the takedown latch (12) located in front of the trigger and with the right hand pull the slide fully to the rear.

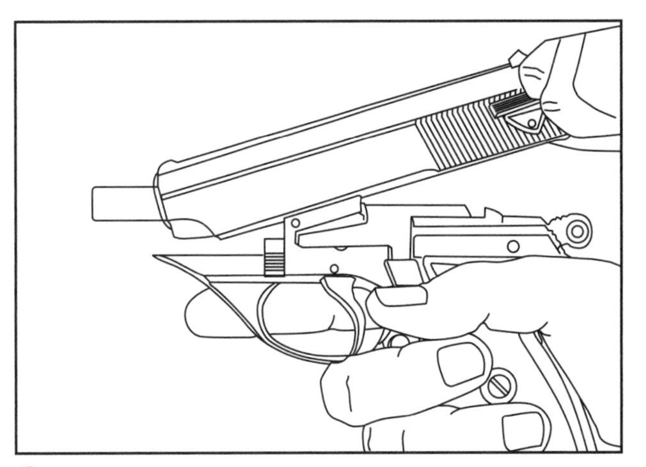

2 The slide may then be lifted clear of the frame (33) and removed by sliding it forward off the barrel. This is all that is necessary to clean and lubricate the pistol. Further disassembly is not recommended.

BALLESTER-MOLINA PISTOL

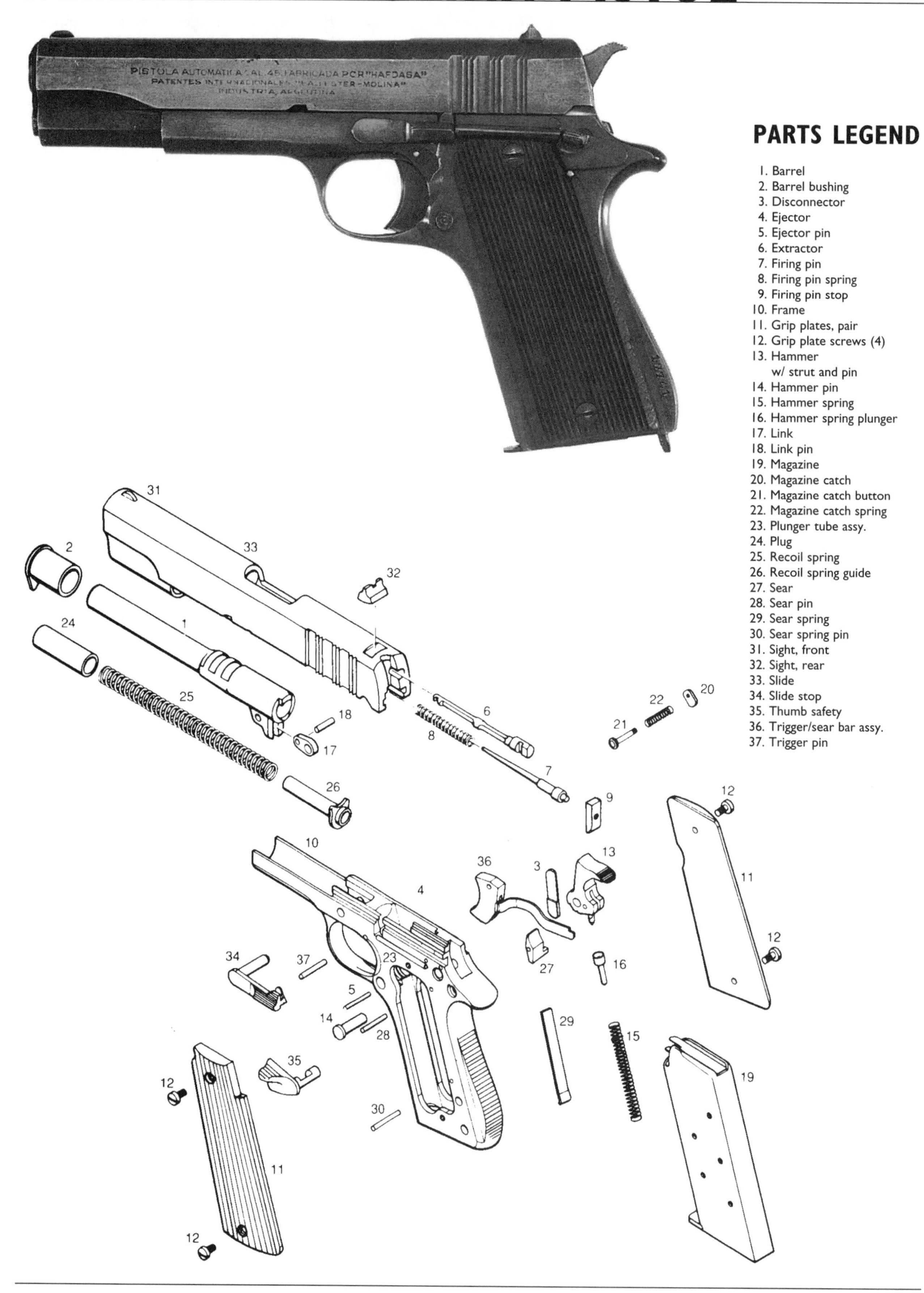

PARTS LEGEND

1. Barrel
2. Barrel bushing
3. Disconnector
4. Ejector
5. Ejector pin
6. Extractor
7. Firing pin
8. Firing pin spring
9. Firing pin stop
10. Frame
11. Grip plates, pair
12. Grip plate screws (4)
13. Hammer
    w/ strut and pin
14. Hammer pin
15. Hammer spring
16. Hammer spring plunger
17. Link
18. Link pin
19. Magazine
20. Magazine catch
21. Magazine catch button
22. Magazine catch spring
23. Plunger tube assy.
24. Plug
25. Recoil spring
26. Recoil spring guide
27. Sear
28. Sear pin
29. Sear spring
30. Sear spring pin
31. Sight, front
32. Sight, rear
33. Slide
34. Slide stop
35. Thumb safety
36. Trigger/sear bar assy.
37. Trigger pin

In 1929 Dr. Arturo Ballester Janer and Ing. Eugenio Molina formed Hispano Argentina Fabrica de Au-tomoviles S.A. (HAFDASA) in Buenos Aires for the manufacture of automo-biles, trucks, buses and diesel engines for the Argentine market. The firm also went on to make small arms of several types, but none became as well-known as its .45 cal. pistol, made from 1937-1953.

For the first three years the pistol was marked Ballester-Rigaud (lng. Rorice Rigaud being the engineer behind the project), but thereafter the more familiar Ballester-Molina marking was standard.

The pistols were issued to Argentine military and police forces, sold commercially throughout Latin America, and reportedly were sold to the British in World War II for use by the Eighth Army in North Africa as well as for clandestine forces. Surplus Ballester-Molinas were imported into the U.S. In the 1960s, and were well-received by collectors and shooters. A .22 cal. "trainer" version made for commercial and military sales from 1940 to 1953 is rarely encountered in the U.S.

In 1981 the "Ballester--Molina" name was registered by the U.S. Patent and Trade-mark Office by Carlos Jose Luis Ballester Molina of Buenos Aires, a de-scendent of the origi-nal founders of the firm seeking to reintroduce the pistol.

The Ballester-Molina was a somewhat modified version of the M1911A1 Government Model pistol, and utilizes the same swinging link to effect lockup. Its slide differs from the original M1911 design mainly in the serrations and the lack of a second (disassembly) notch. The frame assembly of the Ballester-Molina diverges from the Government Model design in its hammer-blocking safety, sear, sear spring, disconnector, pivoting trigger, grips and magazine release, as well as in lacking a separate mainsping housing. In many ways, the Ballester-Molina is a near-clone of the Star Modelo P of the 1930s.

DISASSEMBLY

Press the magazine catch button (21), remove the magazine (19), retract the slide (33) to assure an empty chamber and release the slide. Push in the plug (24) and maintain con-trol of it while turning the barrel bushing (2) 90 degrees clockwise. Slowly release the plug and remove it, the recoil spring (25) and the barrel bushing.

Retract the slide and push the shaft of the slide stop (34) that protrudes from the right side of the frame (10). Remove the slide stop to free the slide that can now be moved for-ward off the frame to free the recoil spring guide (26) and barrel (1) with its link and pin (17 & 18). Push the firing pin (7) in with a punch and pry the firing pin stop down to free the pin and its spring (8). The extractor (6) can be pried out of its recess in the slide.

Remove the four grip plate screws (12) and grip plates (11).

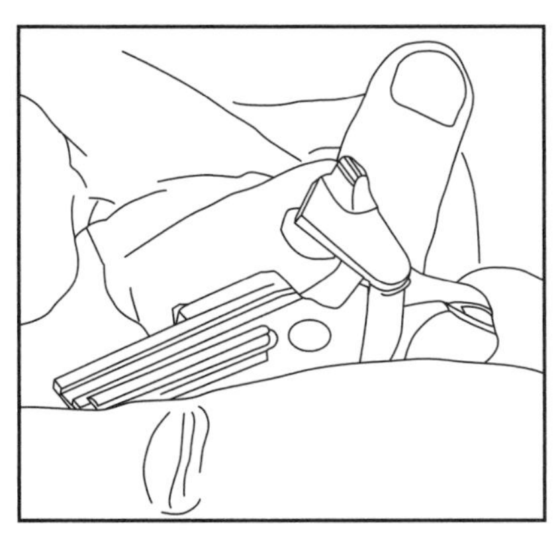

1 Pull the hammer (13) back past the fully cocked position, turn the thumb safety (35) 180 degrees and withdraw it (Fig. A). Grasp the hammer and control its full descent while pulling the trigger. Drift out the large hammer pin (14) from the right side and remove the hammer with its strut and pin, and the hammer spring and plunger (15 & 16).

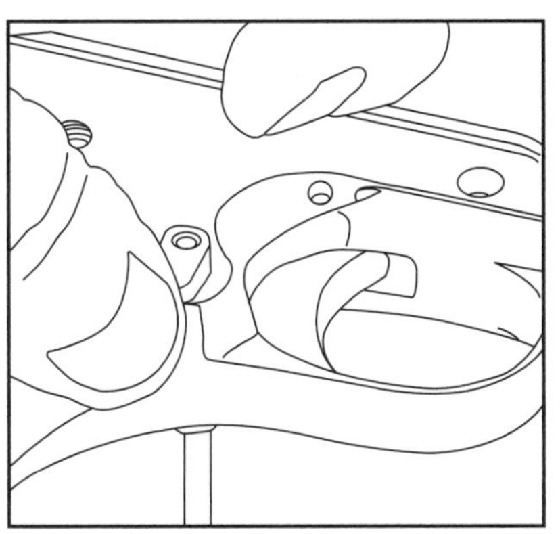

2 Push the magazine catch button (21) in as far as it will go with a punch and turn the now fully exposed magazine catch (20) off the threaded stem of the button (Fig. B). If the assembly is so tightly joined that this cannot be done, do not depress the button but, with padded pliers turn the magazine catch button (21) counterclockwise to free it from the catch and spring (20 & 22).

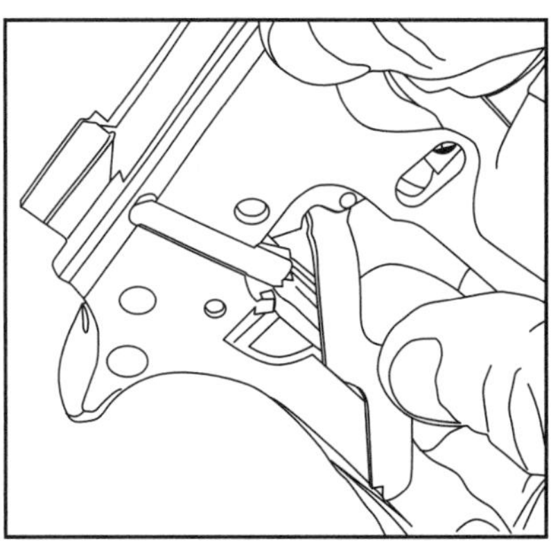

3 Drifting out the trigger pin (37) permits removal of the trigger/sear bar assembly (36) through the magazine well, thus allowing the disconnector (3) to be slid down and out of its dovetail in the frame (Fig. C).

Drift the combination safety stop/sear pin (28) to the left and remove the sear and sear spring (27 & 29). The ejector pin (5), though tightly fitted, may be removed to free the ejector (4) if required, but the plunger tube assembly (23), containing a spring and detent plungers for the safety and slide stop, is staked in place and should not be removed. Reverse the above procedures for reassembly.

BERETTA MODEL 90 PISTOL

PARTS LEGEND

1. Extractor
2. Extractor plunger
3. Extractor spring
4. Slide
5. Rear sight
6. Firing pin retainer
7. Firing pin spring
8. Firing pin
9. Right grip
10. Grip screw (2)
11. Magazine bottom
12. Magazine follower
13. Magazine body
14. Recoil spring
15. Slide catch plunger
16. Slide catch spring
17. Slide catch
18. Slide catch pin
19. Frame
20. Barrel nut
21. Barrel
22. Trigger bar
23. Trigger bar spring
24. Safety spring
25. Safety plunger
26. Ejector spring
27. Ejector-empty magazine indicator
28. Trigger spring
29. Trigger
30. Trigger pin
31. Trigger sleeve
32. Magazine catch
33. Magazine catch screw
34. Magazine catch spring
35. Hammer stop pin
36. Hammer pin
37. Sear pin
38. Safety
39. Left grip
40. Sear
41. Sear spring
42. Hammer
43. Hammer strut
44. Hammer spring
45. Magazine spring
46. Magazine bottom plate

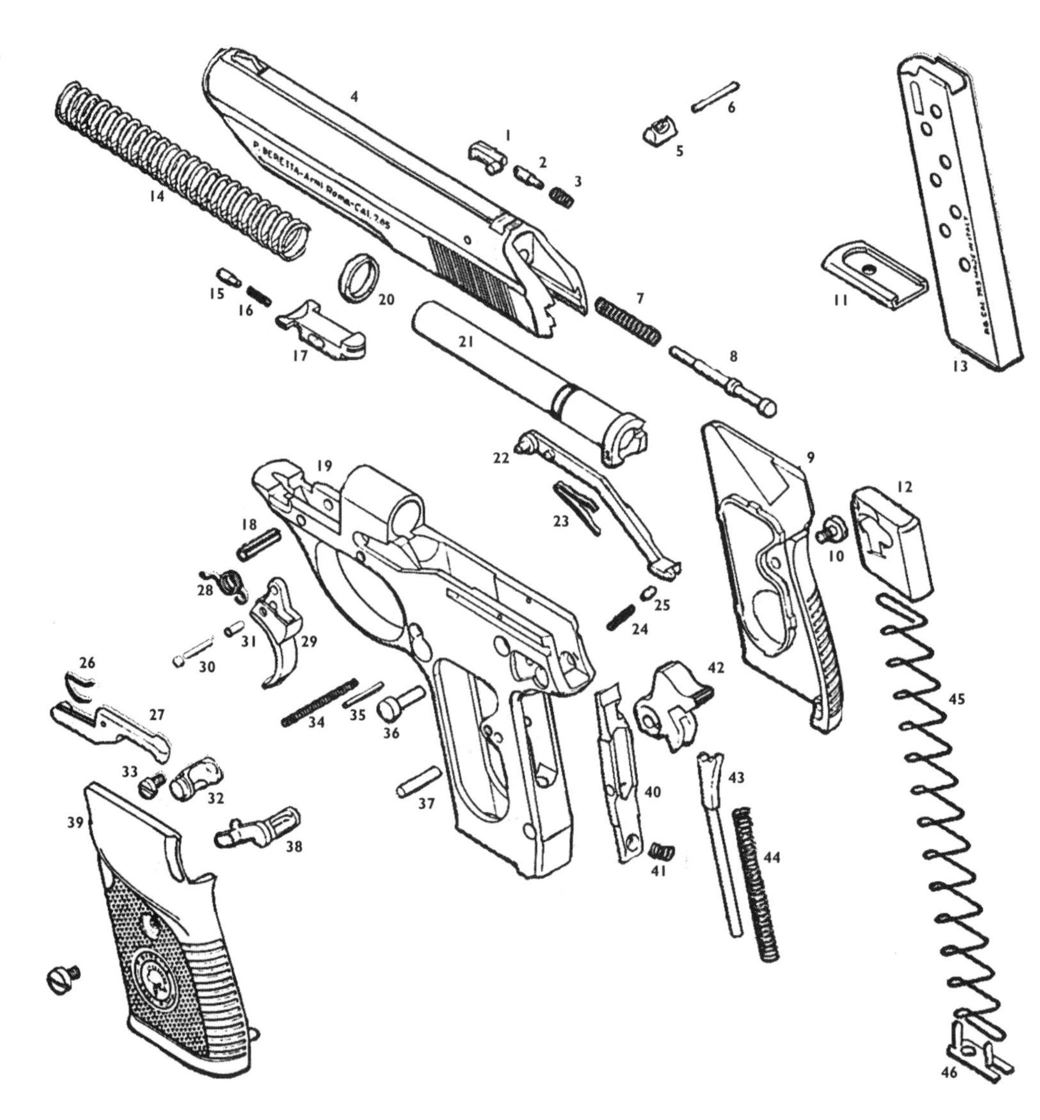

The Beretta Model 90, produced in Italy by the firm of P. Beretta, was a blowback-operated arm firing the 7.65mm (.32 ACP) cartridge. The Model 90 featured an eight-shot magazine, black ergonomic Tenite grips, a double-action lock mechanism with rebounding hammer, a lightweight alloy frame, an exposed hammer and a manually-operated safety on the upper left of the frame. Barrel length was 3⅝ inches; over-all length was 6⅝ inches, and its weight was 19½ ounces.

Due to its double-action lock mechanism and rebounding hammer, the Model 90 can be safely carried with the chamber loaded, the hammer down and the safety disengaged. Engaging the safety allows the pistol to be carried with the hammer cocked and chamber loaded. An additional safety feature is found in the extractor, which protrudes from the slide when a cartridge is in the chamber, and thus serves as a loaded chamber indicator. The slide locks open after the last shot.

Aiming is by way of a fixed, square-notch rear sight and square-blade front sight, and is aided by a flat rib integral with the slide top. Fine serrations on the rib give a dull non-reflective surface. The Model 90 was produced from 1969 to 1983.

DISASSEMBLY

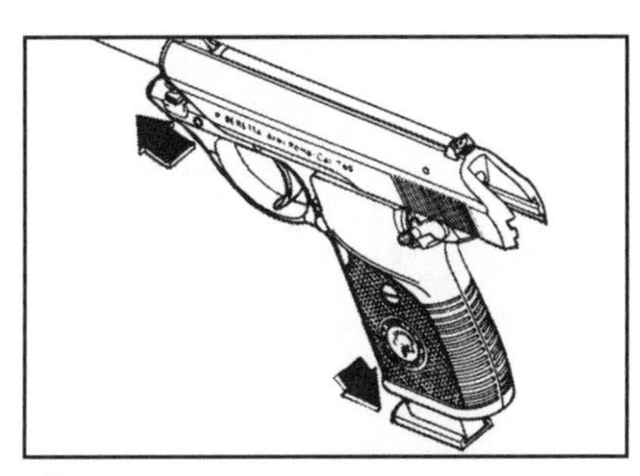

1 To field-strip the Model 90, depress magazine catch (32), and withdraw and unload magazine. Disengage safety (38), and pull slide (4) fully to the rear to clear chamber. Replace magazine and draw slide rearward until it locks open. Grasp serrated finger-pieces of slide catch (17), and pull catch forward and up. Remove magazine.

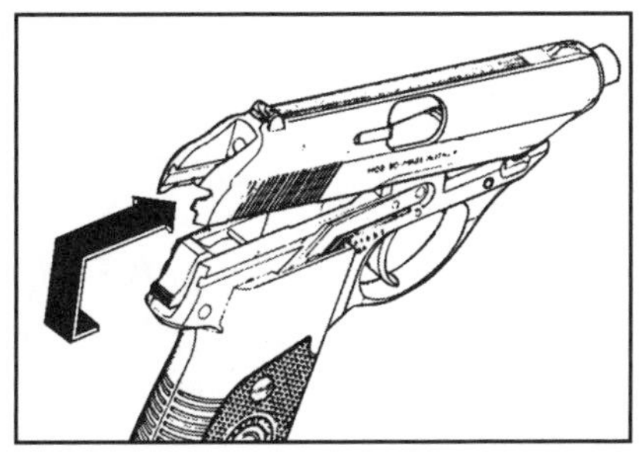

2 Grasp slide firmly, pull fully rear-ward and lift rear end out of frame (19). Ease slide forward off barrel (21), and remove recoil spring (14). This is sufficient takedown for normal cleaning. Position tightest coil of recoil spring to rear during reassembly. Slide catch closes automatically as the slide moves over it.

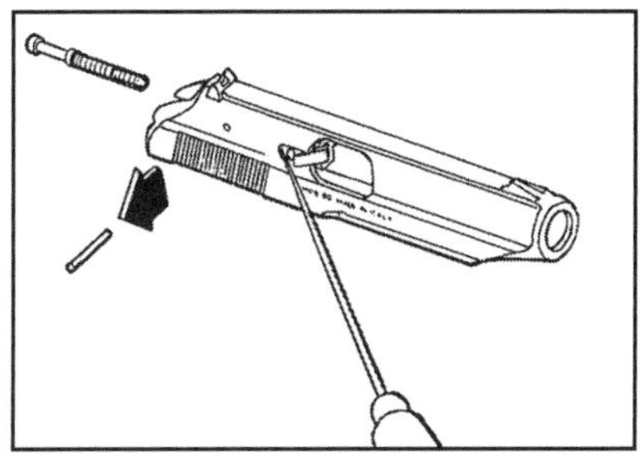

3 For further disassembly, drive out firing pin retainer (6) to free firing pin (8) and spring (7). Depress extractor plunger (2) well into slide with ice pick or awl, pivot extractor (1) toward breech face and remove. Ease out plunger and spring (3).

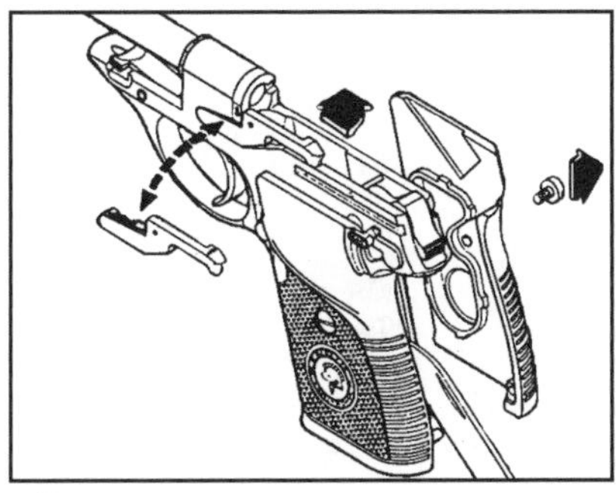

4 Place left thumb against forward portion of ejector (27) so that its spring (26) cannot fly loose. Push rear of ejector to the right, levering forward end out of frame. On replacement, small hooked end of spring must seat into frame notch just forward of barrel flange (arrow). Remove barrel nut (20) with 15mm wrench to release barrel. Nylon inserts in barrel nut face toward frame in assembly. Remove right grip screw (10) and insert knife blade between the grips. Pry right grip (9) outward off positioning pin fixed to bottom of left grip (39). Engage safety, and remove left grip.

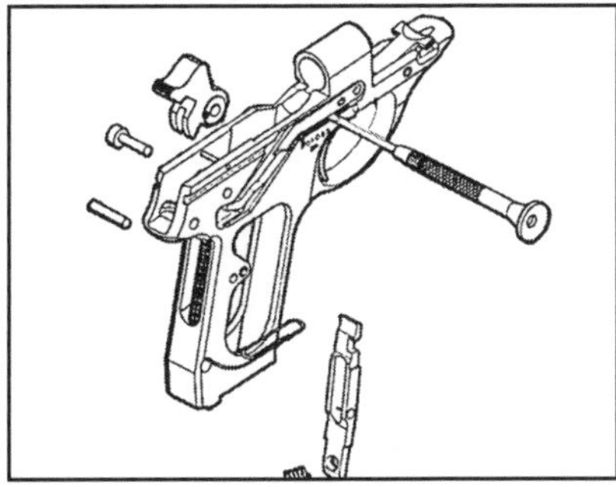

5 Insert a straightened paper clip through small hole in the hammer strut (43), working through the frame tunnel provided. Release safety, pull trigger (29), and lower hammer (42) with thumb. Push out hammer pin (36) and lift out hammer. Push out sear pin (37) to release sear (40) and spring (41). Hold trigger depressed and insert small screwdriver between trigger bar (22) and spring (23). Lever the spring downward free of trigger bar, then pry the bar outward and off.

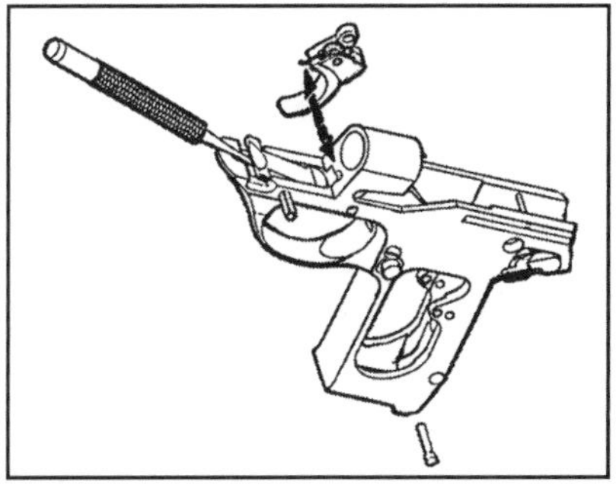

6 Push out trigger pin (30). Pivot trigger assembly forward, and remove from below. On replacement, small hooked end of trigger spring (28) must seat into frame tunnel (arrow). Drift out slide catch pin (18) to remove slide catch, spring (16), and plunger (15). To reassemble slide catch parts, start pin through frame and partially into catch. Position catch in take-down attitude, and install spring and plunger through hole in its forward end. Depress plunger with a thin punch inserted through the frame channel provided, and tap pin to fully seat it.

BERETTA MODEL 92F (M9) PISTOL

Adopted by the United States military in 1984 as the M9 pistol, the Beretta 92F 9 mm also has been chosen by many police agencies.

PARTS LEGEND

1. Barrel
2. Locking block
3. Locking block plunger
4. Locking block plunger retaining pin
5. Slide
6. Extractor
7. Extractor pin
8. Extractor spring
9. Rear sight
10. Trigger bar release plunger
11. Trigger bar release plunger spring
12. Firing pin
13. Firing pin spring
14. Left safety lever
15. Firing pin plunger
16. Recoil spring
17. Recoil spring guide
18. Frame
19. Disassembly latch
20. Slide catch spring
21. Slide catch
22. Trigger
23. Trigger pin
24. Trigger spring
25. Trigger bar
26. Trigger bar spring
27. Disassembly latch release button
28. Disassembly latch release button spring
29. Hammer release lever
30. Ejector
31. Hammer release lever pin
32. Ejector spring pin
33. Hammer
34. Hammer pin
35. Hammer strut
36. Hammer spring
37. Hammer spring cap
38. Sear
39. Sear spring
40. Sear pin
41. Magazine release button
42. Magazine release button spring
43. Hammer spring cap spring pin
44. Grip (LH/RH)
45. Grip screws (4)
46. Grip screw bushings (4)
47. Magazine tube
48. Magazine follower
49. Magazine spring
50. Magazine lock plate
51. Magazine base
52. Firing pin block spring
53. Firing pin block
54. Firing pin retaining spring
55. Safety plunger spring
56. Safety plunger
57. Right safety lever
58. Right safety lever spring pin (2)
59. Firing pin block lever
60. Magazine catch spring bush (short)
61. Magazine catch spring bush (long)
62. Grip spring washers (4)

The Beretta Model 92F pistol was adopted in 1984 as a U.S. government military standard pistol. Its official military designation is the M9 pistol or PDW (Personal Defense Weapon). More recent import variants of this Beretta 9mm are marked as Model 92FS, and incorporate a slide-mounted ambidextruous safety/decocking lever and other design changes. The Model 92 has been made in a number of variants differing in size, features, operation and safety modes, and finish.

Tracing its ancestry back to the earlier, single-action Beretta Models 1934 .380 and 1951 "Brigadier" 9mm pistols, the double-action 92F's disassembly instructions may be applied in part to other Model 92 variants as well as to the Brazilian-made Taurus 92, although the latter features a frame-mounted sear-blocking safety. In contrast, the 92F's slide-mounted safety, when engaged, blocks the hammer from contacting the firing pin and disconnects the trigger and sear. The 92F's firing pin is also prevented from moving forward to strike a primer unless the trigger is pulled, preventing discharge if the gun is dropped muzzle-first.

DISASSEMBLY

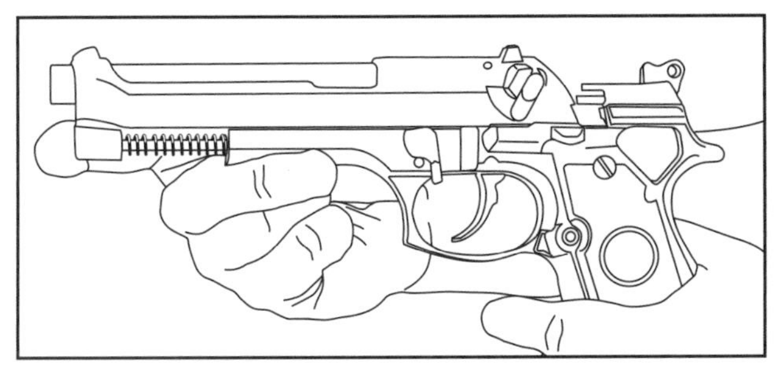

1 Clear the pistol by removing the magazine, retracting the slide, and checking the chamber and magazine well.

With the slide forward and the hammer down, press the disassembly latch release button (27) and swing the disassembly latch (19) down and forward. Move the slide assembly forward off the frame (18).

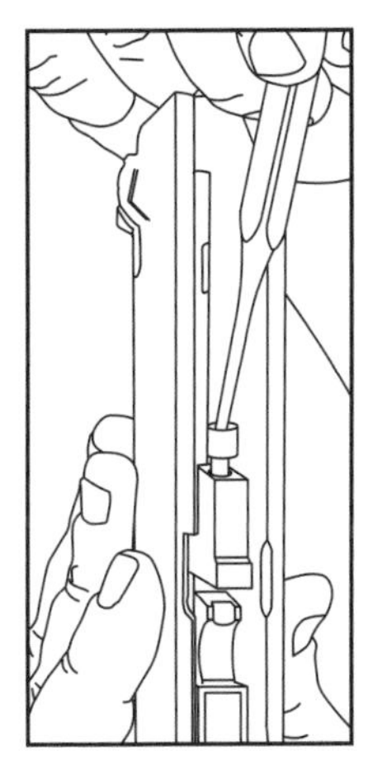

2 With the slide assembly resting upside down on a firm surface, lift the recoil spring guide (17) from its step on the locking block (2) and, restraining the guide, remove the spring (16) and guide to the rear. Push the plunger (3) at the rear of the barrel underlug (1) to detach the locking block from the slide lugs.

3 Move the barrel forward to clear the extractor (6) and remove from the slide.

This completes basic field-stripping of the Beretta 92F. NOTE: Further disassembly is not recommended by the manufacturer unless performed by a competent gunsmith. Should further disassembly be necessary, full disassembly instructions follow. Remove the grips (44), taking care not to lose the grip screw washers (62). Press the back of the magazine release button (41) down and away for removal. Reinstalling the magazine release can be done with the button oriented to the left or right.

Depress the upper arm of the trigger bar spring (26) from its groove in the underside of the trigger bar (25) and slowly release the spring out and away to the right. Remove the trigger bar. Pull the slide catch (21) out to remove the catch and its spring (20). The trigger pin (23) can be drifted out to the left, freeing the trigger (22) and its spring (24).

Drift out the hammer spring cap spring pin (43) to free the cap (37) and slowly release tension on the hammer spring (36) to remove. Tapping out the hammer pin (34) will allow the removal of the hammer (33) and strut (35). Drift out the sear pin (40) to release the sear (38) and its spring (39) into the magazine well. Tap out the hammer release lever pin (31) and the ejector spring pin (32) to free the ejector (30) and the hammer release lever (29) for removal upwards from the frame.

Remove the firing pin block lever (59) by lifting up and out.

With the slide-mounted safety in "safe" position, drift out the two right safety lever spring pins (58). Pull the right safety lever (57) to the right for removal. Tap out the firing pin retaining spring pin (54) to remove the firing pin block (53) and its spring (52). With a punch, dislodge the firing pin plunger (15), depress the rear face of the firing pin (12), and pull the left safety lever (14) up and to the left for removal, taking care not to lose the safety plunger (56) and its spring (55), the trigger bar release plunger (10) and its spring (11). Slowly release pressure on the firing pin to remove it and its spring (13). Drift out the extractor pin (7) and pry out the extractor (6) and extractor spring (8).

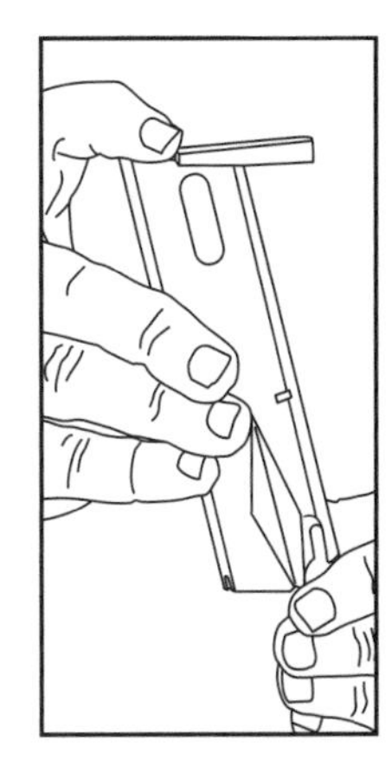

To disassemble the magazine, use a punch to depress the stud on the lock plate (50). Release the magazine base (51) by sliding it forward, taking care to restrain the magazine spring (49) and lock plate as tension is released.

BERETTA MODEL 950B JETFIRE

PARTS LEGEND

1. Slide
2. Firing pin spring
3. Firing pin
4. Firing pin retaining pin
5. Right grip
6. Right grip screw
7. Recoil and barrel latch spring
8. Sear
9. Trigger bar
10. Trigger spring plunger
11. Trigger spring
12. Trigger
13. Trigger bar pin
14. Barrel
15. Hinge pin
16. Trigger guard and barrel spring
17. Trigger pin
18. Barrel latch
19. Latch stop screw
20. Recoil and barrel latch spring pin
21. Hammer pin
22. Frame
23. Left grip screw
24. Left grip
25. Magazine catch button
26. Magazine catch spring
27. Magazine
28. Sear pin
29. Sear spring
30. Hammer
31. Hammer strut
32. Hammer spring
33. Hammer spring retainer
34. Magazine catch

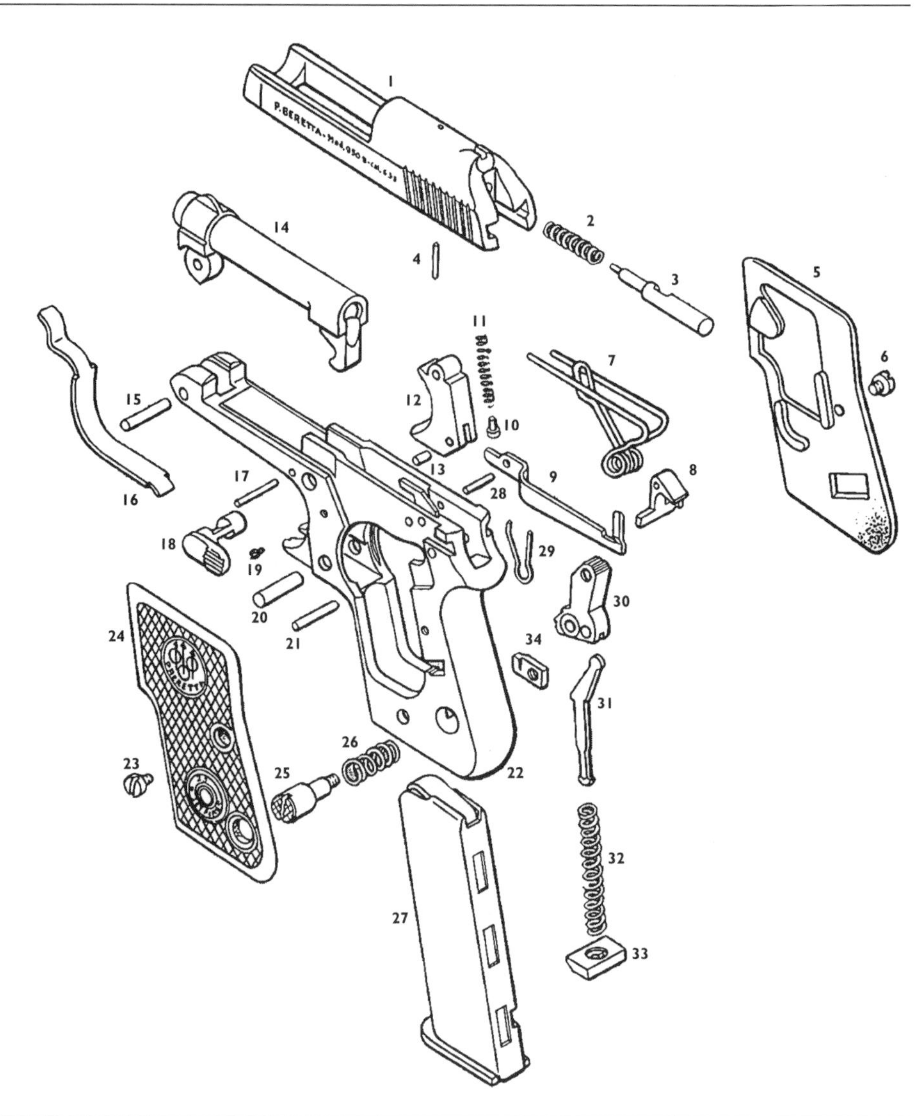

Made by the Italian arms firm of Pietro Beretta, the Model 950B Jetfire .25 ACP semi-automatic pistol, first sold in the U.S. around 1953, is a slightly modified version of the Beretta Model 950 pistol introduced not long after World War II.

The barrel of the Model 950B pistol is hinged at the muzzle end can be tipped up for cleaning, loading and unloading, making it unnecessary to retract the slide manually to load or unload the gun. The Jetfire lacks an extractor; upon firing, the fired case acts as a piston and blows back the slide until the ejector kicks the case clear of the pistol.

Rather than a surrounding or under the barrel recoil spring, the 950B features a frame-mounted combination recoil and barrel latch spring, whose upper ends engage recesses in the slide. Two such recoil springs were utilized in the older Model 950. The Model 950 and Model 950B pistols lack mechanical safeties, but their exposed hammers can be placed in half-cock position.

Disassembly instructions for the Jetfire can also be used for the Beretta Minx, a pistol also chambered for the .22 Short.

DISASSEMBLY

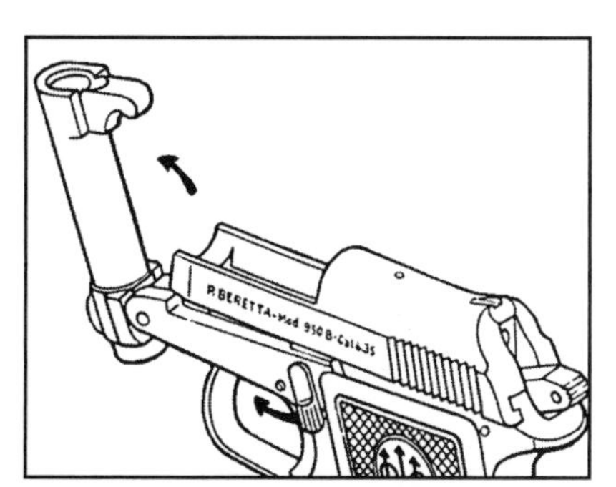

1 The takedown procedure for the Beretta Model 950B Jetfire pistol is simple and easy. First remove the magazine (27), then press forward on the barrel latch (18) to tip up the barrel (14). Now, clear the chamber and then swing the barrel up to vertical position. Cock the hammer (30) and lift the front of the slide (1) slightly, until it is free of the frame (22). Pull the slide forward approximately ⅛" and lift the slide free of the frame.

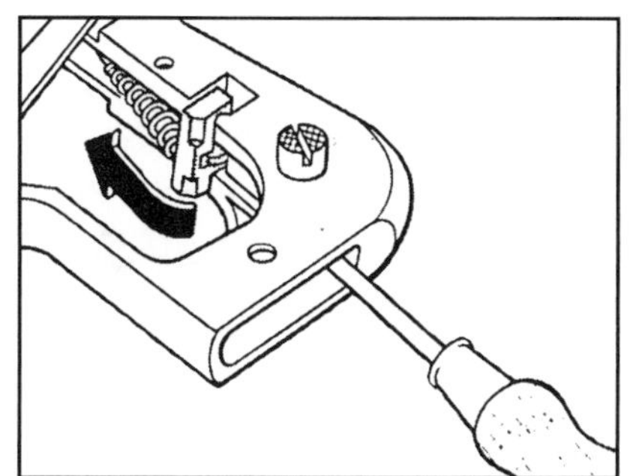

2 Before driving steel pins in or out of an aluminum alloy frame, it is sound practice to relieve the spring tension on the part retained by the pin. Lower the hammer and remove the hammer spring assembly before removing the hammer pin (21). Insert a narrow screwdriver into the magazine well as shown. Push up and outward on the hammer spring retainer (33) until it is free of its recess in the frame. This will relieve the tension on the hammer pin and hammer.

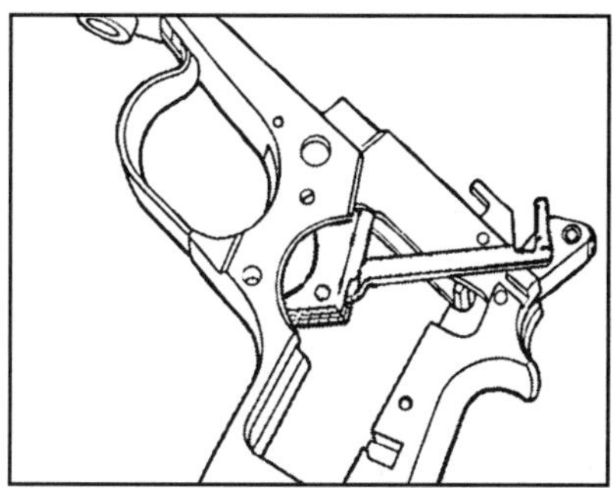

3 After the trigger pin (17) has been removed, the trigger will snap back under the influence of the trigger spring (11). To remove the trigger, lift the tail of the trigger bar (9) up over the sear and pull the trigger assembly out through the cutout in the left side of the frame. Reverse the procedure for reassembly. When the trigger bar is back in its proper place below the sear, rotate the upper portion of the trigger until it lines up with the hole in the frame. Insert trigger pin.

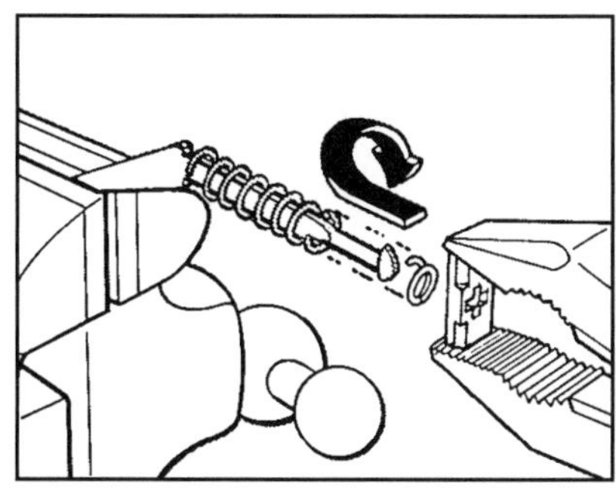

4 The hammer spring (32) and hammer strut (31) are assembled as a unit for easy handling. To disassemble this unit, hold the hammer strut in a padded vise as shown. Grasp the hammer spring retainer (33) with pliers and push toward the spring until the tail of the strut is clear of its seat in the retainer. Rotate the retainer 90° and ease the retainer off the tail of the strut. Be sure to use care in removing the retainer because it is under spring tension.

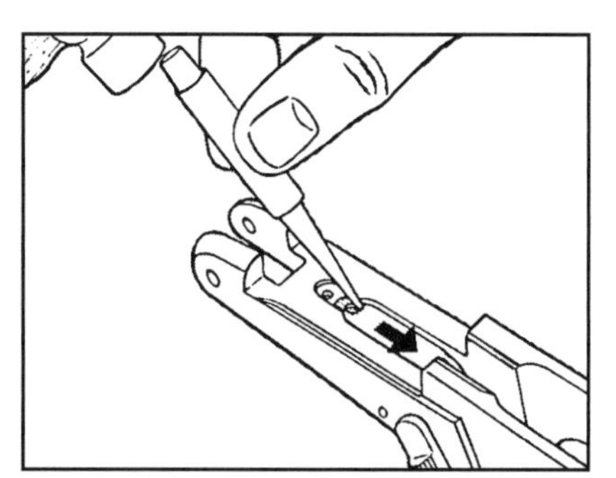

5 In taking down the Beretta Model 950 Jetfire pistol, after the barrel hinge pin (15) and barrel (14) have been removed, the trigger guard can be pulled free of the frame. The barrel latch (18) must be removed in order to further disassemble the gun. To remove the barrel latch, first remove the tiny latch spring screw, and then gently drive the spring rearward out of its recess in the frame. The barrel latch can now be pulled from the frame of the pistol.

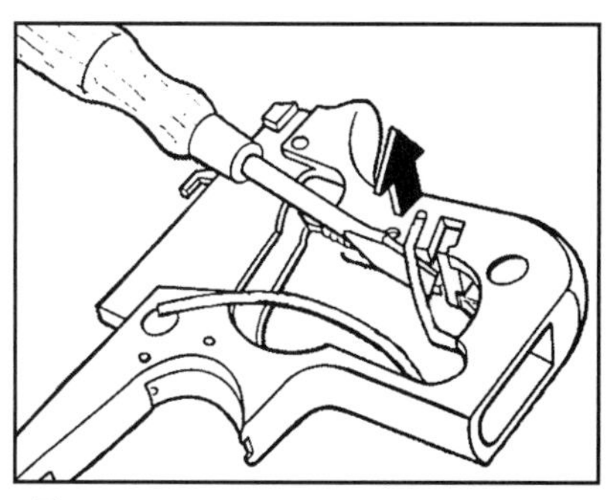

6 In further disassembly of the Model 950, remove both grips to expose the separate recoil springs which must be removed one at a time. Lift the long leg of the recoil spring out of its recess in the frame. Next pry the short leg gently out of its recess as shown. Gently wiggle the spring out of its seat in the curved recess in the frame. The long legs of the springs are ground thinner on one side. This ground side must face toward the frame in reassembly.

BERETTA MODEL 1934 PISTOL

PARTS LEGEND

1. Slide
2. Extractor
3. Extractor spring
4. Extractor pin
5. Rear sight
6. Firing pin spring
7. Firing pin
8. Right-hand grip
9. Grip screw (see 31)
10. Hammer
11. Hammer strut
12. Sear lever
13. Hammer spring
14. Hammer strut nut
15. Magazine catch spring
16. Spring follower
17. Magazine catch
18. Magazine
19. Magazine catch pin
20. Magazine catch hinge pin
21. Sear lever pin
22. Sear plate
23. Sear plate screw
24. Trigger bar
25. Trigger spring plunger
26. Trigger spring
27. Trigger
28. Trigger bar pin
29. Trigger pin
30. Safety catch
31. Grip screw (see 9)
32. Left-hand grip
33. Receiver
34. Recoil spring guide
35. Recoil spring
36. Barrel
37. Ejector
38. Ejector pin
39. Hammer pin

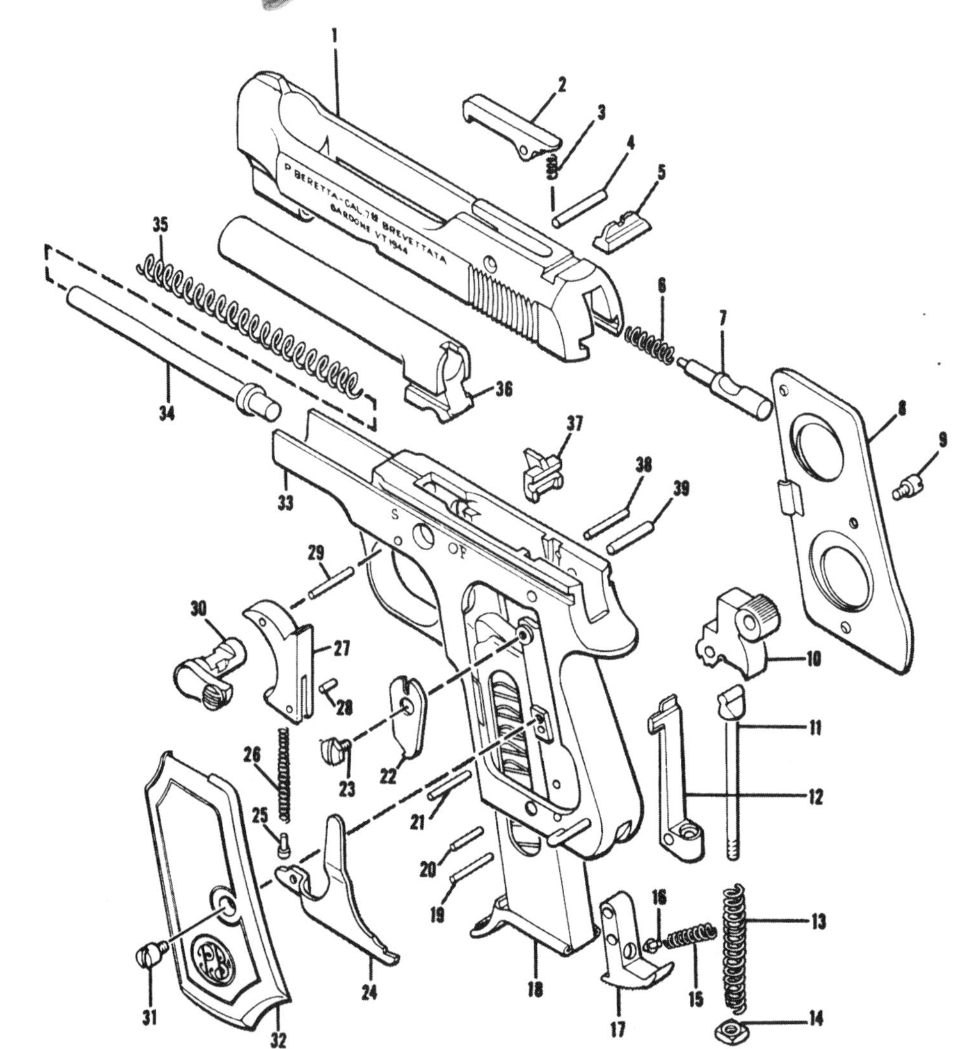

One of the best-known products of the Italian firm of Pietro Beretta was the Model 1934, a single-action, exposed-hammer pistol chambered for the .380 ACP (9mm *Kurz*) cartridge. The official Italian Army sidearm during World War II, it was also widely used by Italian police.

Composed of a relatively small number of simple working parts, the pistol was easy to mass-produce. Not as sophisticated as some contemporary German pocket pistols, the Model 1934 was nevertheless a handy, rugged and reliable little gun. A version of the Model 1934 in .32 ACP (7.65mm), known as the Model 1935, was also produced. Similar to the earlier Model 1923 in 9mm Glisenti, and the .32 ACP Model 31, the Model 1934 had a total run of more than 1,000,000 guns from 1934-1980.

The simplicity of the design is exemplified by its disconnector mechanism. An arm on the trigger bar extends up into a recess in the slide. Unless the slide is fully forward, this arm will not allow the trigger bar to engage the sear plate. Upon firing, slide recoil causes the trigger bar to be cammed downward out of contact with the sear plate, allowing the sear to be reset. The trigger bar re-engages the sear again only when the slide has returned fully forward.

Although reliable, the gun has drawbacks. When the last shot is fired, the slide is held open by the magazine follower. Allowing the slide to go forward requires the removal of the magazine, a clumsy, two-handed operation. This problem was eliminated by grinding the back edge of the magazine follower as shown in illustration 4. This prevents the slide locking back after the last shot, allowing easy magazine removal.

Another awkward feature is the position and function of the safety catch. Since the safety locks only the trigger; it is theoretically possible for the gun to fire if dropped on the hammer.

DISASSEMBLY

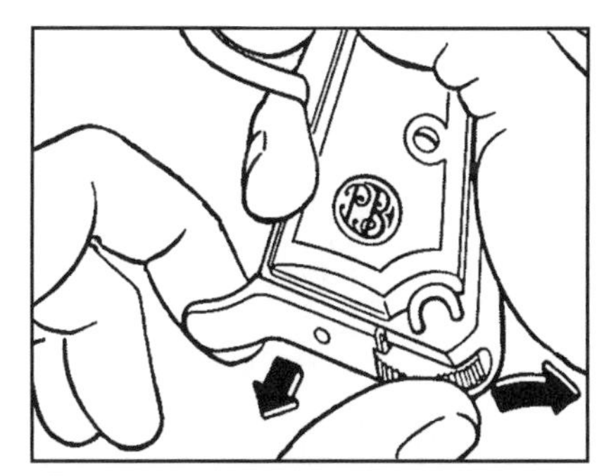

1 Before attempting to field-strip the gun, remove magazine (18) and retract slide (1) to clear chamber. If magazine is empty and slide open, a good deal of force will be neces-sary to remove the magazine because slide pressure tends to hold magazine in.

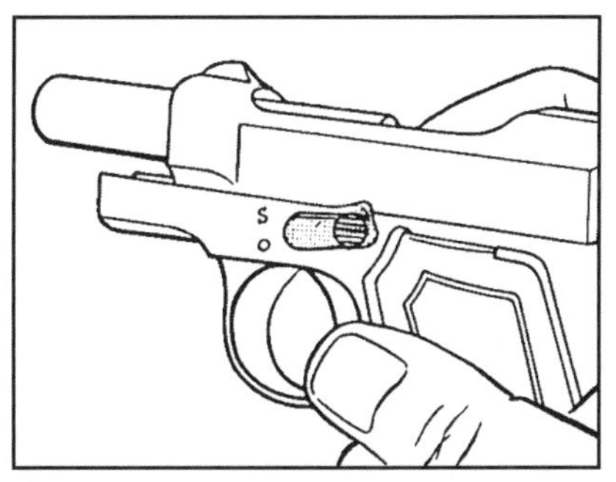

2 To remove barrel, rotate safety catch (30) to safe position and pull slide back as far as it will go. The safety catch will snap into hold-open notch on the slide. Push back or tap muzzle of barrel to free it from receiver grooves.

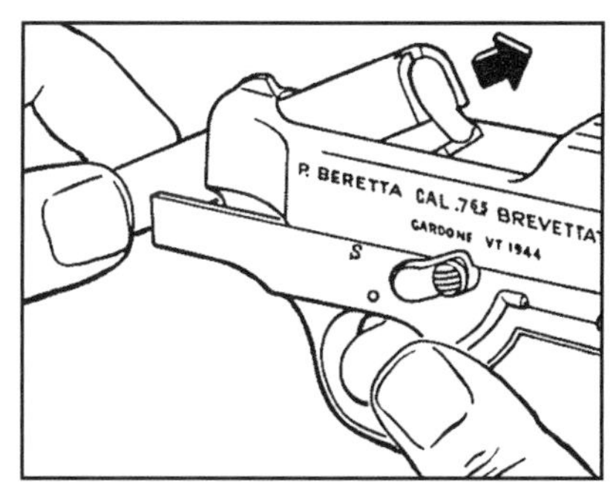

3 After barrel (36) is free of recesses in receiver, push it up and out, through open portion of slide as shown. Next, hold slide and release safety catch (30). Ease slide assembly off front of receiver (33).

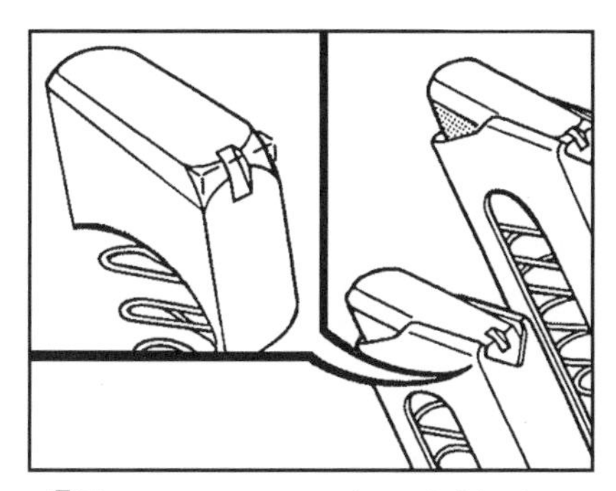

4 To prevent magazine being held in by slide, grind back edge of follower to a slight radius, removing sharp shoulder that holds slide open after last shot. Remove follower before grinding by depressing button on magazine floorplate. At same time, slide plate off to front.

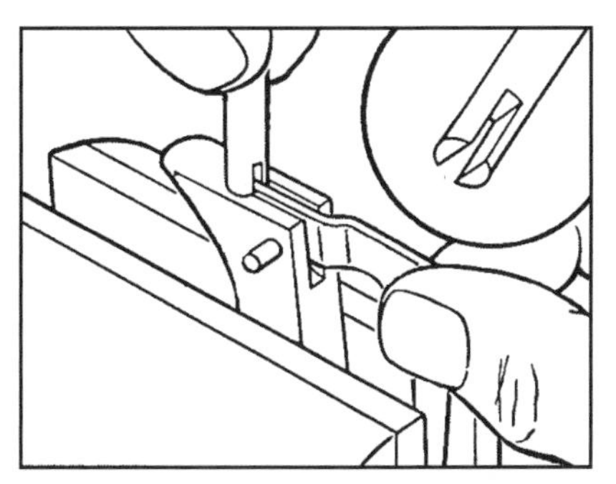

5 In general, the gun is simple to strip—it is merely a case of driving out retaining pins. When it comes to replacing trigger bar (20), the simple tool shown above will hold trigger spring plunger (25) depressed while trigger bar is pinned back into place.

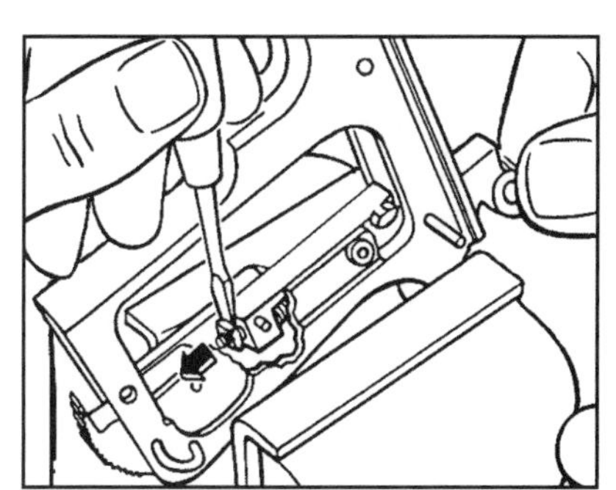

6 After replacing sear lever (12), hammer (10) can be easily lined up with hole in receiver (33) if hammer strut is out of way. To do this, first push hammer strut down from hammer opening. Use a screwdriver or piece of brass to hold it down, as shown, until hammer is pinned into place.

BERETTA MODEL 8000 COUGAR

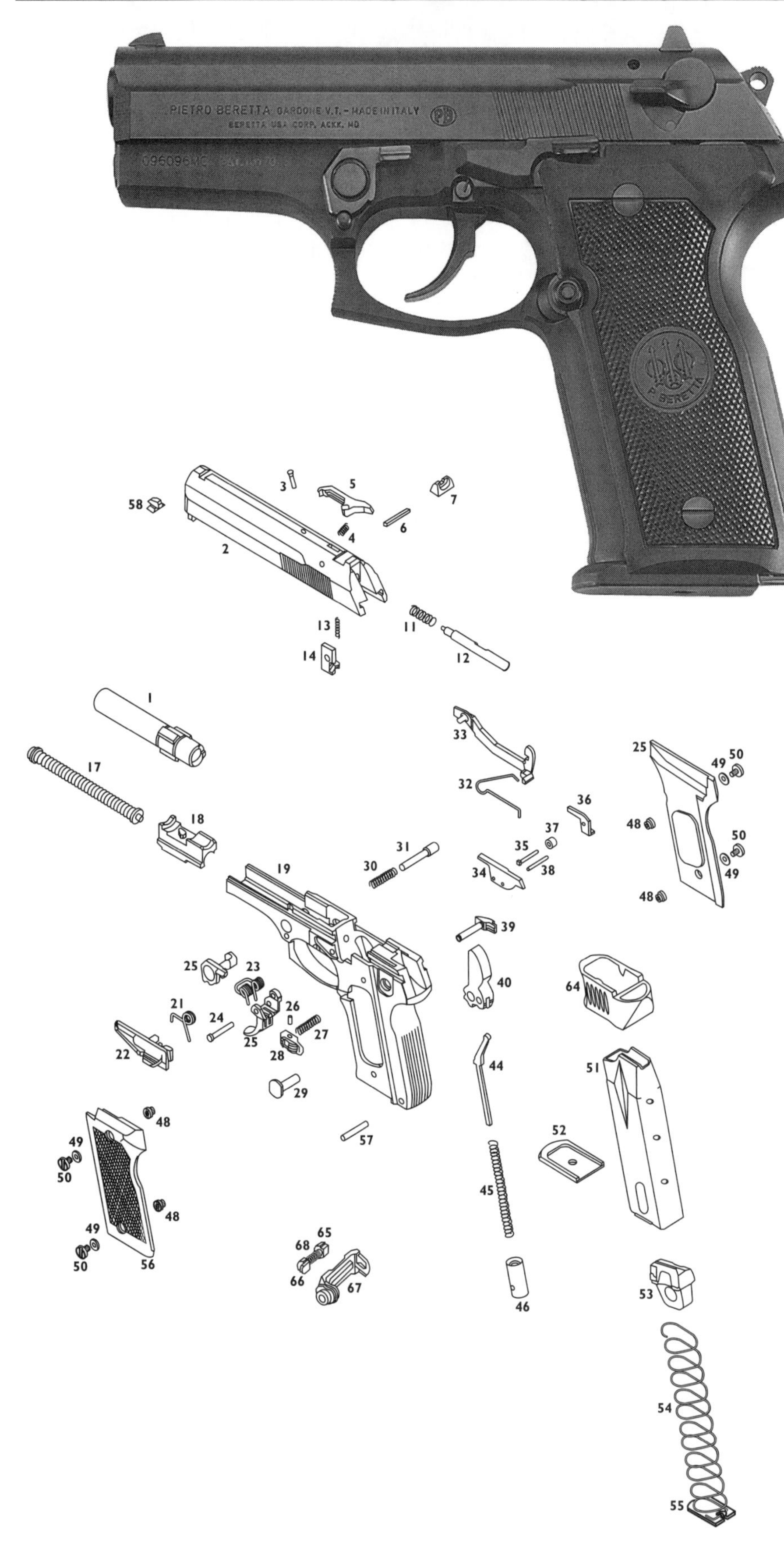

PARTS LEGEND

1. Barrel
2. Slide
3. Extractor pin
4. Extractor spring
5. Extractor
6. Firing pin catch spring pin
7. Rear sight
8. Safety spring pin
9. Safety spring
10. Firing pin spring
11. Firing pin catch
12. Firing pin
13. Firing pin catch spring
14. Firing pin catch
15. Safety
16. Firing pin plunger
17. Recoil spring & spring guide assembly
18. Central block
19. Frame
20. Disassembling latch
21. Slide catch spring
22. Slide catch
23. Trigger spring
24. Trigger pin
25. Trigger
26. Magazine release spring pin
27. Magazine release spring
28. Magazine release button
29. Hammer pin
30. Disassembling latch release button spring
31. Disassembling latch release button
32. Trigger bar spring
33. Trigger bar
34. Ejector
35. Hammer release lever pin
36. Firing pin catch lever
37. Hammer release lever
38. Ejector spring pin
39. Magazine release
40. Hammer
41. Sear
42. Sear spring
43. Sear pin
44. Hammer spring guide
45. Hammer spring
46. Hamme spring cap
47. Grip, right
48. Grip bush
49. Spring washer
50. Grip screw
51. Magazine
52. Magazine bottom
53. Magazine follower
54. Magazine spring
55. Magazine plate
56. Grip, left
57. Hammer spring cap pin
58. Black front sight, white dot
59. Trigger bar release plunger
60. Trigger bar release plunger spring
61. Safety ball spring
62. Safety ball
63. Magazine grip extension
64. Magazine release button spring bush
65. Magazine release button
66. Magazine release button spring

Beretta began to experiment with a turning-barrel pistol in the early 1990s, and it emerged in 1994 as the Model 8000 Cougar, chambered in 9mm Parabellum. Versions of the pistol in .40 S&W (Model 8040) and .45 ACP (Model 8045) were introduced in 1995 and 1998, respectively.

Unlike other locking systems, the rotating-barrel type seems to automatically adjust to loads of differing power. Because of the locking system, the traditional Beretta "open-barrel" slide design could not be used. The Cougar is smaller than the Model 92-Series pistols, and its grip frame shape is similar to that of the FN Hi-Power. The controls on the Cougar are in the same location as on the 92-series pistols.

The Model 8000 was initially made in three versions: the Model 8000F with conventional selective double- and single-action operation, the double-action-only 8000D with no manual safety and the 8000G with a decocking lever Instead of a safety. Other versions included the Type L, with a shortened grip frame, and the even more diminutive Mini Cougar. In 2004, an "Inox" (stainless steel) version was briefly placed on the market.

DISASSEMBLY

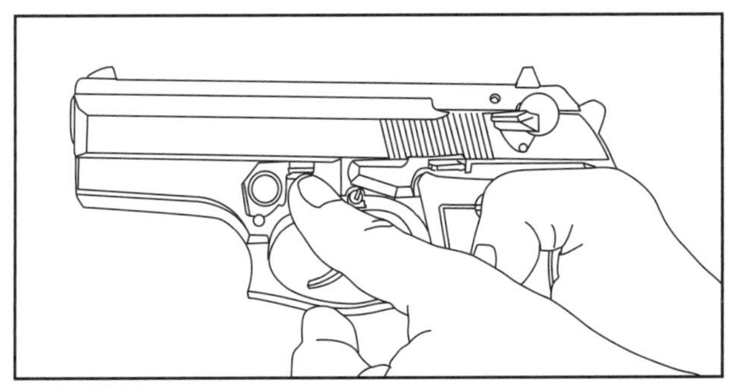

1 Remove magazine by depressing magazine release button. Hold pistol in the right hand; with left forefinger press disassembly latch release button and with left thumb rotate disassembly latch 45° downward

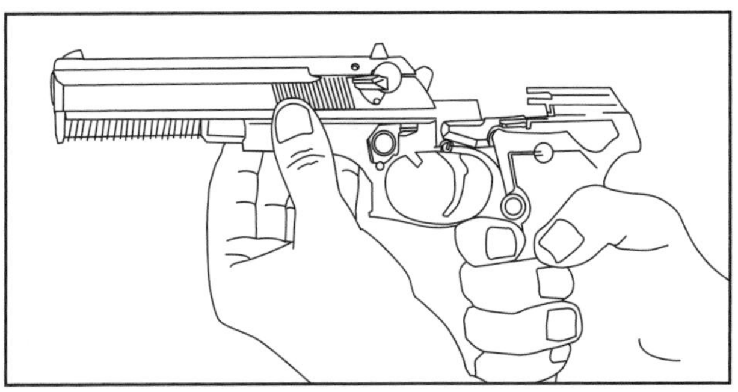

2 Pull the slide-barrel assembly with central block, recoil spring and spring guide forward. In case the hammer is in the half-cocked position, cock it in order to facilitate forward travel of slide barrel assembly.

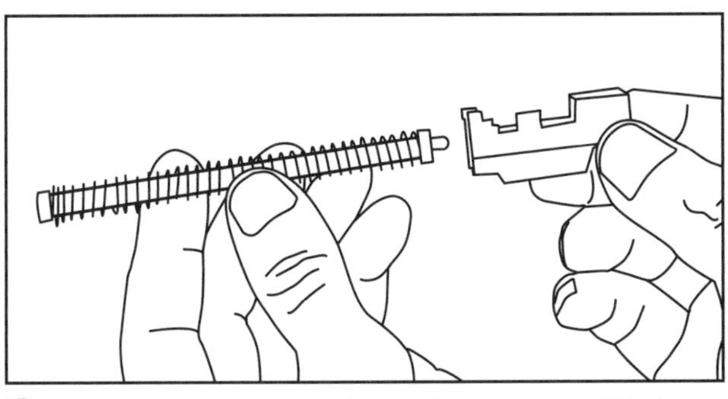

3 Pull out the recoil spring with guide from the central block.

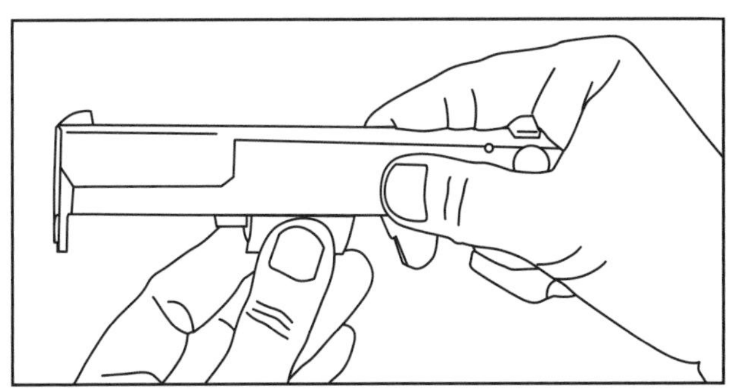

4 Take out the barrel from slide, rotating the barrel itself (counter clockwise looking at it from the rear). CAUTION: No further disassembly is recommended unless done by a competent gunsmith.

BERETTA MODEL 9000S PISTOL

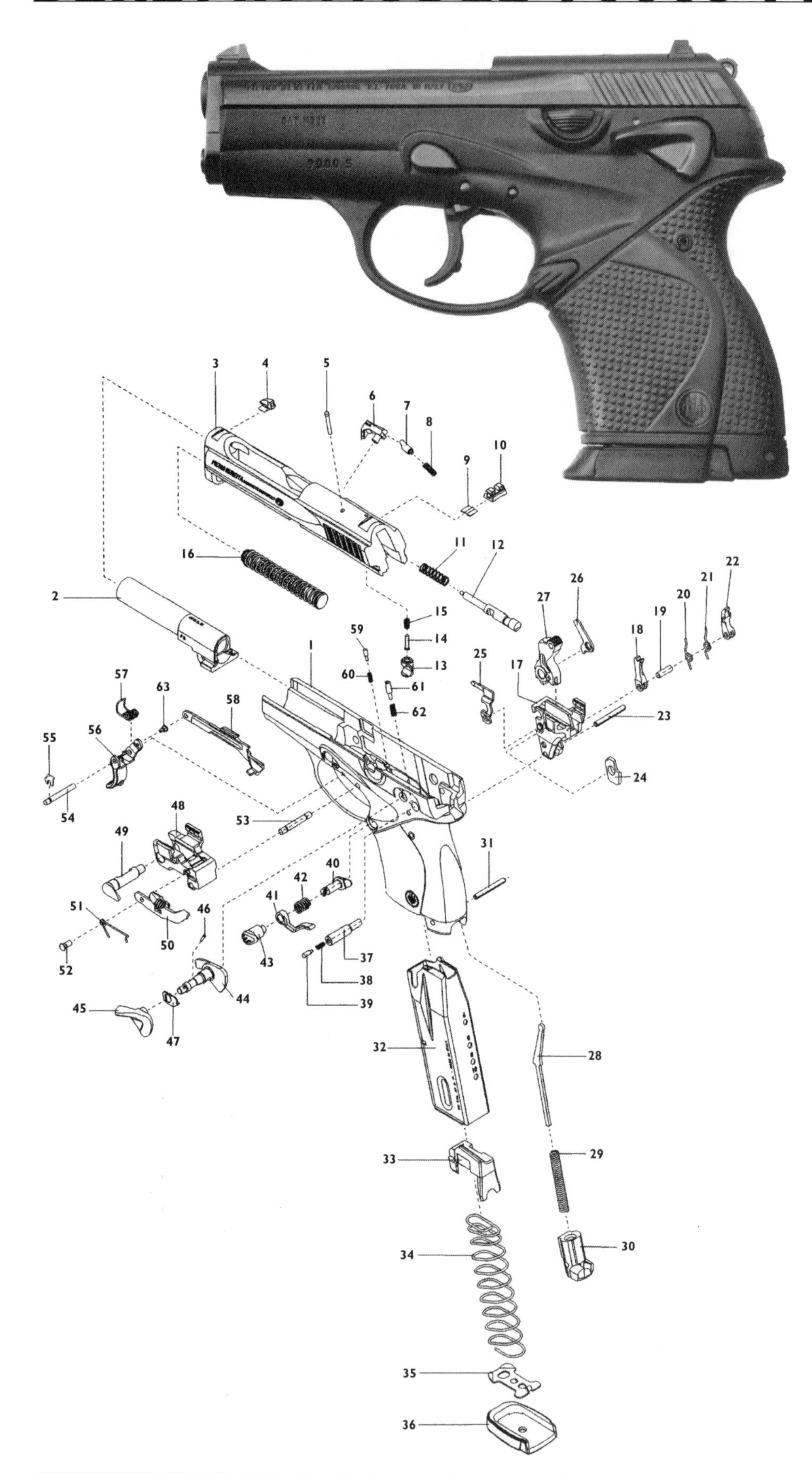

PARTS LEGEND

1. Frame
2. Barrel
3. Slide
4. Front sight
5. Firing pin retaining pin
6. Extractor
7. Extractor plunger
8. Extractor spring
9. Rear sight spring
10. Rear sight
11. Firing pin spring
12. Firing pin
13. Firing pin catch
14. Firing pin catch plunger
15. Firing pin catch spring
16. Recoil spring
17. Rear block
18. Sear, left
19. Sear pin
20. Left sear spring
21. Right sear spring
22. Sear, right
23. Rear block spring pin
24. Interceptor
25. Ejector
26. Firing pin catch lever
27. Hammer
28. Hammer spring guide
29. Hammer spring
30. Hammer spring cap
31. Hammer spring cap pin
32. Magazine
33. Follower
34. Magazine spring
35. Magazine plate
36. Magazine bottom
37. Hammer pin
38. Safety plunger spring
39. Safety plunger
40. Magazine catch pin
41. Magazine catch
42. Magazine catch spring
43. Magazine release button
44. Safety, right
45. Safety, left
46. Safety pin
47. Disconnector lever
48. Front block
49. Disassembly latch
50. Slide catch
51. Slide catch spring
52. Slide catch pin
53. Front block pin
54. Trigger pin
55. Spring clip – trigger pin
56. Trigger
57. Trigger spring
58. Trigger bar
59. Trigger bar plunger
60. Trigger bar plunger spring
61. Hammer drop plunger
62. Hammer drop plunger spring
63. Trigger bar pin

The Model 9000S Compact, Beretta's first polymer-frame pistol, was introduced in 2000. Beretta for the first time went to an outside firm, Guigiaro Design, to design the pistol's appearance and ergonomics. In addition to a swept-back grip, Guigiaro incorporated a snap-down finger-rest into the magazine floorplate.

The 9000S employs a classic falling-barrel locking system. Since the design featured a traditional Beretta exposed barrel, the pistol could not use top mounted locking lugs and the barrel was designed with a heavy lug on each side that engages recesses in the lower edge of the slide. The Model 9000S is produced in 9mm Parabellum and .40 S&W. The F model has a selective double- and single-action with a hammer spur and dual safety levers, while the D variant is double-action only with no hammer spur or safety levers.

The safety lever is turned upward to block the sear and disconnect the trigger. Pushed further upward, it drops the hammer to a safe, at-rest position. The magazine release is reversible for left-handers.

DISASSEMBLY

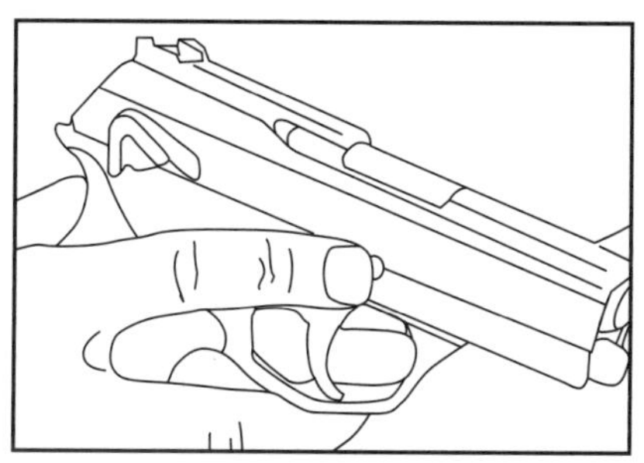

1 Remove the magazine by depressing the magazine release button.

Hold the pistol in the right hand and with the index finger press the disassembly latch that protrudes from the right side of the pistol.

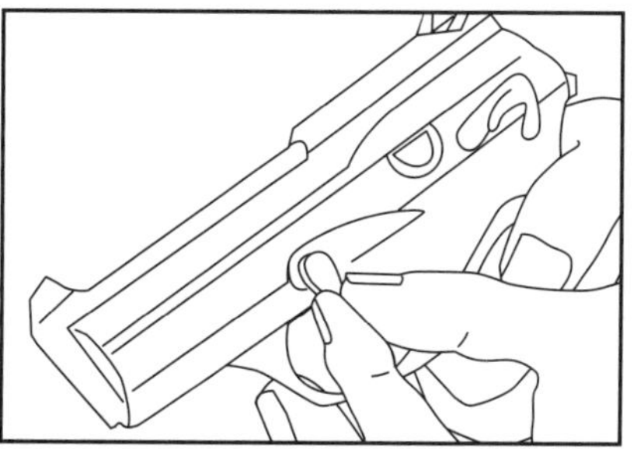

2 Simultaneously, with the thumb and the index finger of the other hand, rotate the disassembly latch approximately 90° downward to disengage the slide-barrel assembly with recoil springs.

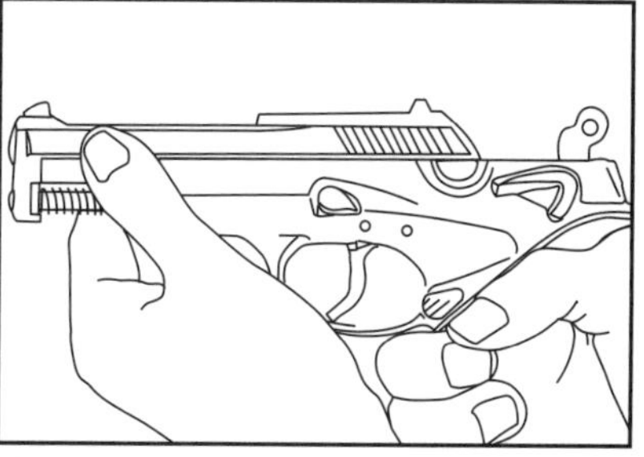

3 Pull the slide-barrel assembly with recoil springs forward.

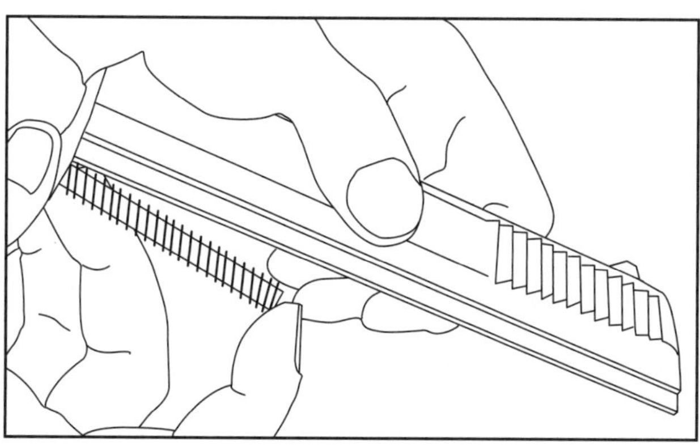

4 Pull out the recoil spring.

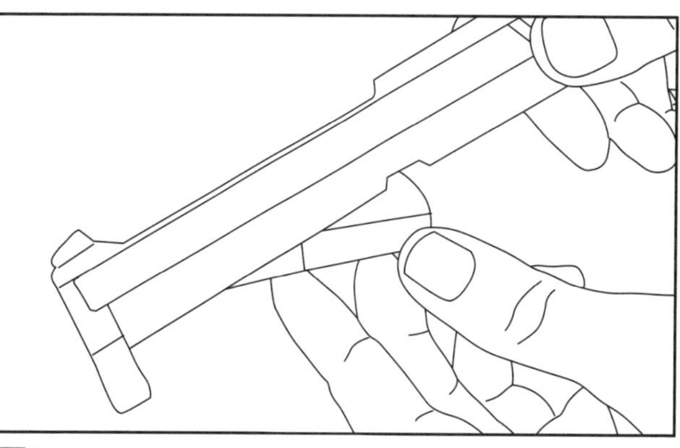

5 Remove the barrel from the slide.

BERGMANN SPECIAL PISTOL

PARTS LEGEND

1. Slide
2. Extractor pin
3. Extractor
4. Extractor spring
5. Housing plunger
6. Plunger spring
7. Firing pin housing
8. Firing pin spring
9. Firing pin
10. Safety catch
11. Detent retainer screw
12. Detent ball
13. Detent spring
14. Spring guide
15. Right grip
16. Retainer plate screw
17. Spring retainer plate
18. Trigger bar guide
19. Trigger bar
20. Spring retainer pin
21. Trigger bar spring
22. Pin retainer spring
23. Trigger
24. Trigger pin
25. Retainer spring pin
26. Trigger spring
27. Recoil spring
28. Frame and barrel
29. Hammer spring
30. Sear
31. Hammer strut
32. Sear spring
33. Hammer spring
34. Magazine catch
35. Magazine
36. Left grip
37. Grip screw
38. Sear stop pin
39. Hammer pin
40. Ejector
41. Hold-open spring
42. Hold-open catch
43. Takedown latch assembly
44. Takedown latch
45. Takedown latch pin

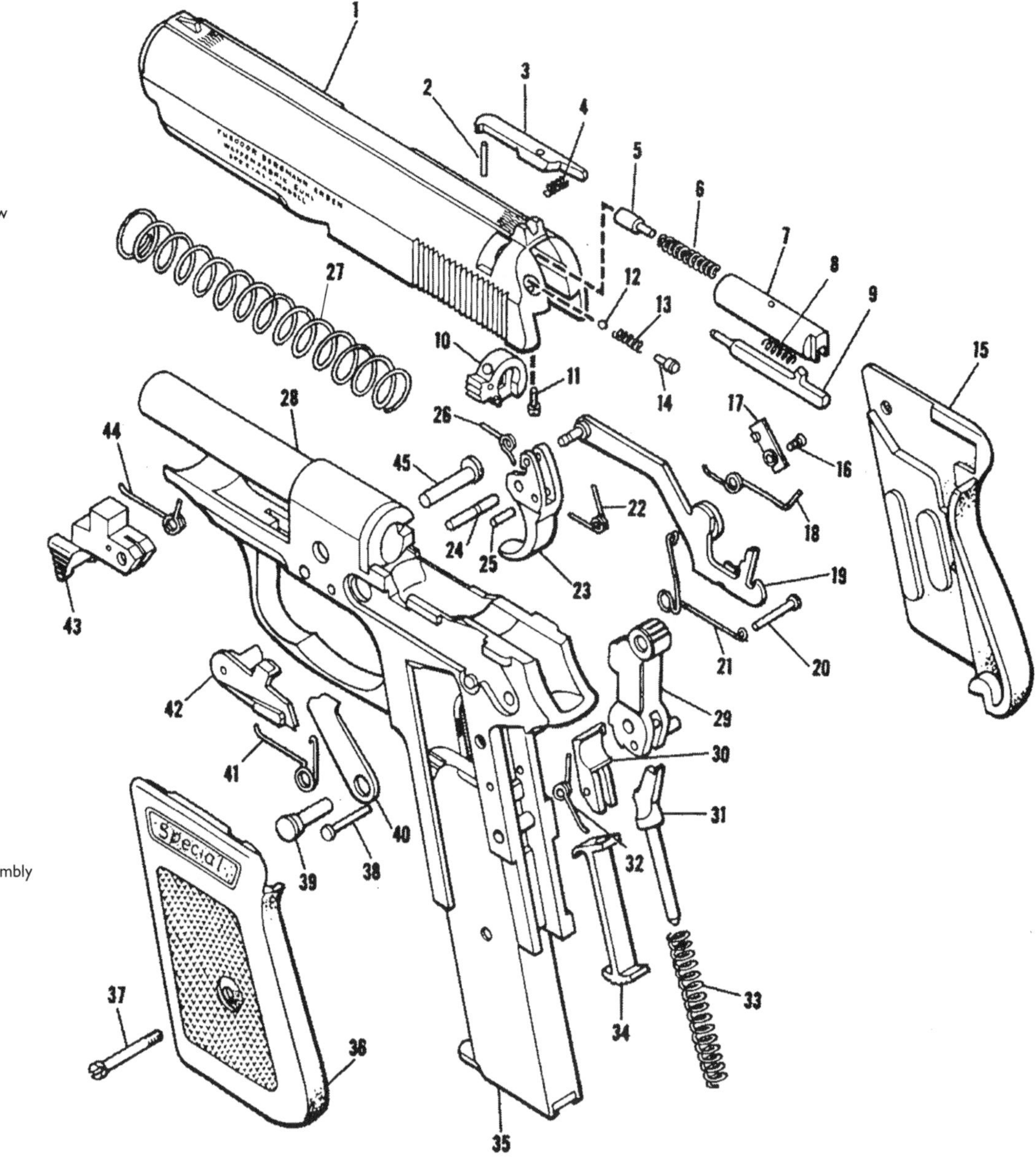

Theodor Bergmann was one of the earliest exponents of self-loading firearms. His firm, in Gaggenau and Suhl, Germany, turned out a wide variety of guns, ranging from automatic pistols to light machine guns.

Shortly before World War II, German gun firms were engaged in a double-action pistol race. Walther started the competition with the extremely successful PP and PPK models, followed by similar guns from Mauser and J.P. Sauer. Around this time the firm of August Menz started the design of a double-action blowback-operated pistol, which was ultimately produced under the Theodor Bergmann trade name.

While resembling the Walther PP, the Bergmann Special is different internally, being composed of many small springs and intricately-machined parts. Its double-action trigger was also unusual. On an ordinary double-action pistol, a steady pull on the trigger cocks and releases the hammer. On the Bergmann, a steady pull only brings the hammer to full cock, and holds it there. The trigger must then be released slightly and pulled again to fire the gun. Though facilitating accurate aimed fire, this trigger hinders rapid shooting.

Among other features, the gun remains open after the last round in the magazine is fired. The safety mechanism is unusual in that the safety catch rotates the firing pin, housed in a cylinder, out of alignment with the hammer but does not lock the sear. As the firing pin housing rotates, a projection on its end moves into position to absorb the hammer blow.

Sales of the cal. .32 Bergmann Special Model I began around 1938. The .380 caliber Model II was to be produced a short time later, but the onset of World War II put an end to these interesting pocket pistols in 1939.

DISASSEMBLY

1 To field strip the Bergmann, first remove magazine and clear chamber. Pull down takedown latch (43) at front of trigger guard. Pull slide to rear as far as it will go and lift it free of frame. Slide (1) can now be run forward off barrel.

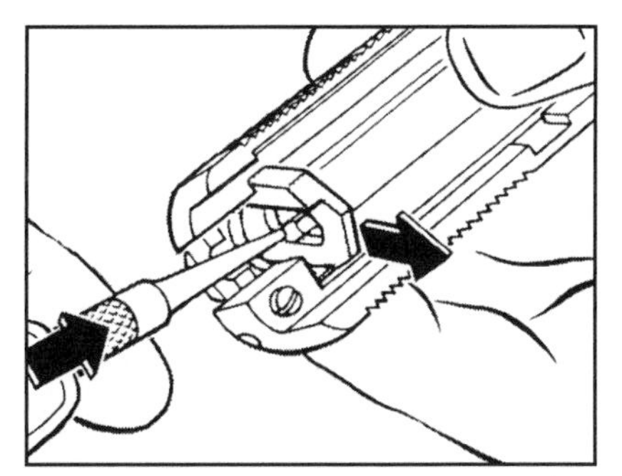

2 Safety catch (10) must be removed to get at firing pin (9). Loosen detent retainer screw (11) and carefully remove detent components. Hold firing pin housing (7) and firing pin forward and free of seat in safety catch, and push up safety catch.

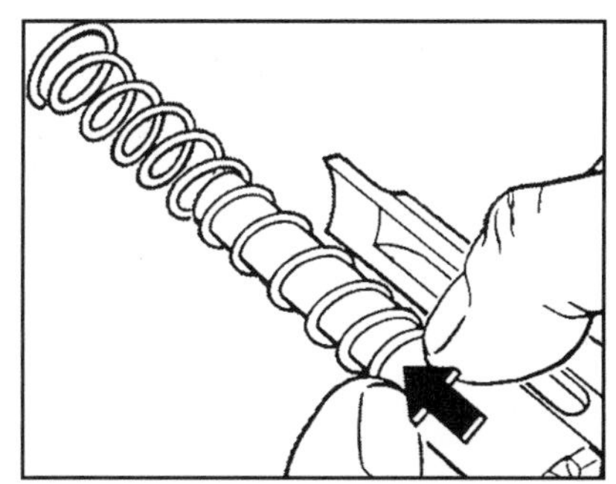

3 Last coil of recoil spring (27) fits barrel very snugly and must be pushed free as shown. When replacing spring, be sure large end protrudes off barrel; other-wise gun cannot be reassembled.

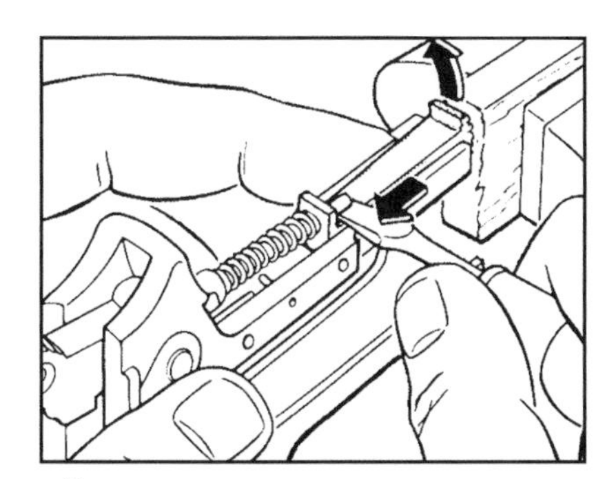

4 Magazine catch (34) hooks over a cross-pin in frame and must be pushed back and lifted up for removal. Use a screwdriver to ease it free and to prevent hammer spring (33) from throwing catch. Remove hammer spring and strut (31).

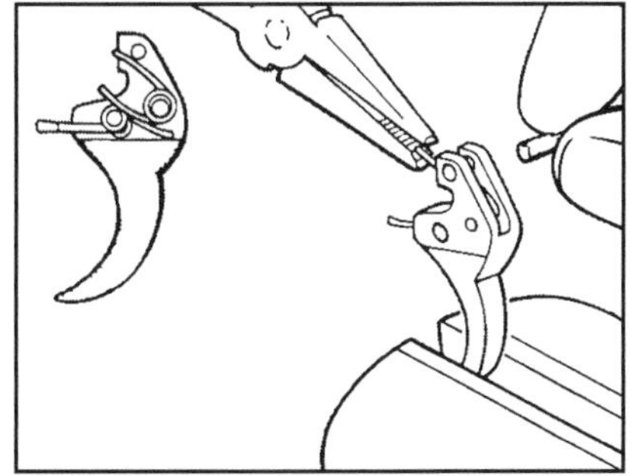

5 Trigger (23) houses two springs: the trigger spring (26) and pin retainer spring (22). When reassembling gun, use slave pins to hold springs in place. Slave pins should be only as wide as trigger and are pushed out when parts are pushed in.

BERNARDELLI MODEL 60 PISTOL

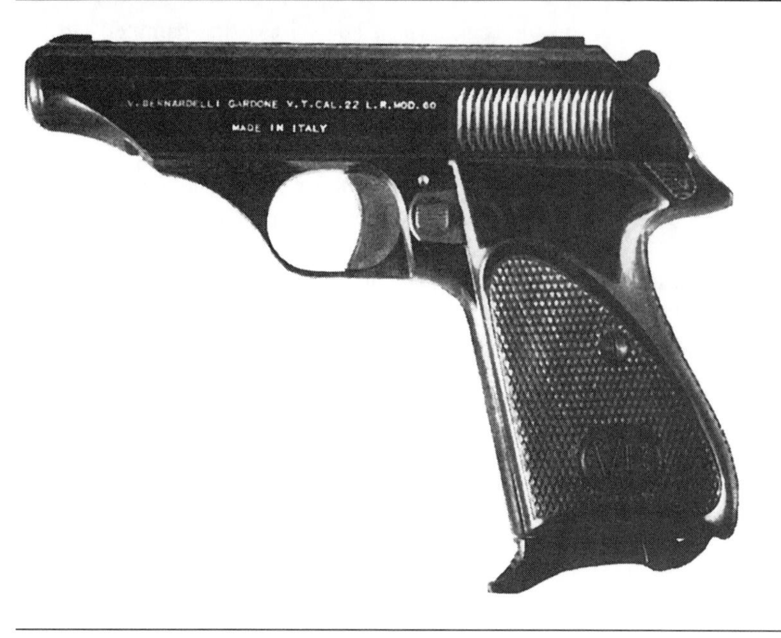

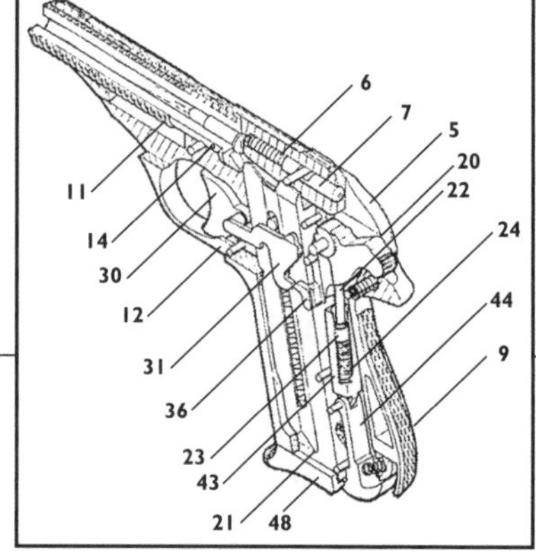

Cutaway indicates relationship between parts. Pistol is shown loaded and cocked. Parts are number keyed to parts legend

PARTS LEGEND

1. Extractor
2. Extractor spring
3. Extractor pin
4. Firing pin retainer
5. Slide button
6. Firing pin spring
7. Firing pin
8. Magazine follower
9. Right grip
10. Grip screw (2)
11. Recoil spring
12. Frame
13. Barrel pin
14. Barrel
15. Ejector
16. Ejector pin
17. Hammer pin
18. Takedown catch screw
19. Hammer spring housing stop
20. Hammer
21. Magazine body
22. Hammer strut
23. Hammer plunger
24. Hammer spring
25. Magazine follower
26. Left grip
27. Magazine safety
28. Magazine safety spring
29. Magazine safety pin
30. Trigger
31. Trigger bar
32. Trigger bar spring
33. Trigger bar spring screw
34. Sear spring
35. Sear pin
36. Sear
37. Takedown catch spring
38. Takedown catch
39. Manual safety
40. Manual safety screw
41. Magazine catch stop
42. Hammer spring housing pin
43. Hammer spring housing
44. Magazine catch
45. Magazine catch spring
46. Magazine spring
47. Magazine spring plate
48. Magazine base

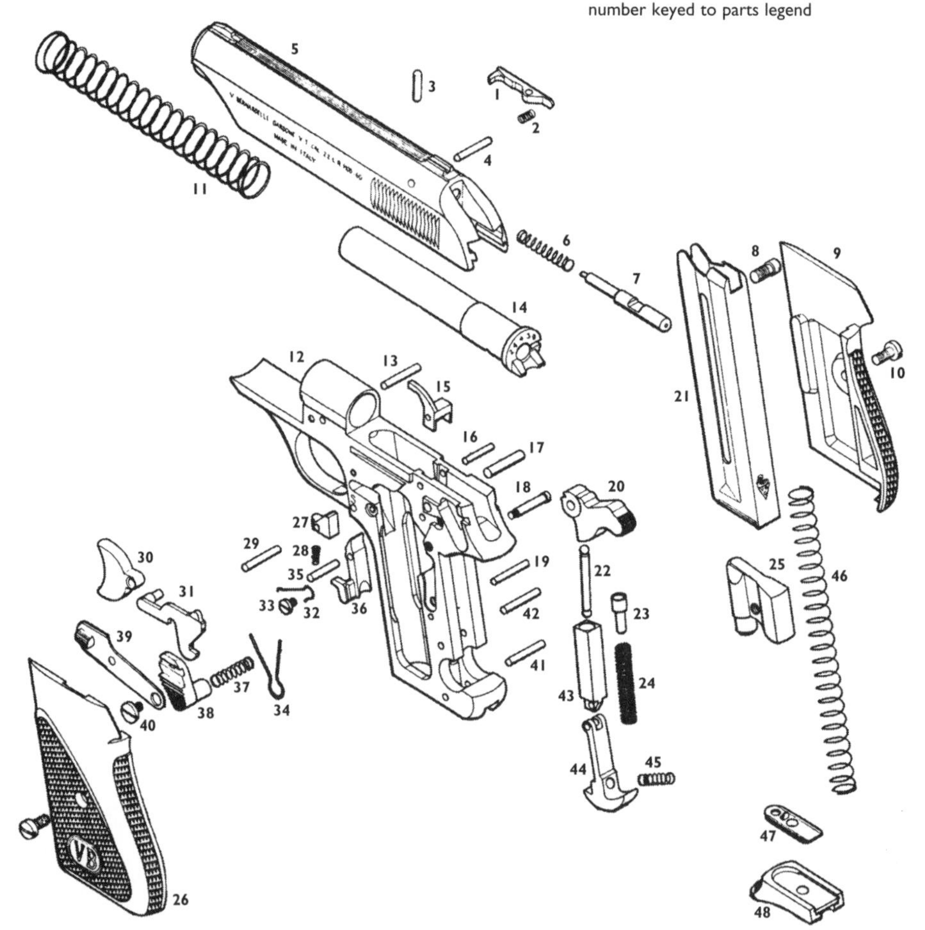

Produced by the firm of Vincenzo Bernardelli in Gardone, Italy, the Bernardelli Model 60 self-loading pistol was designed for informal target shooting and self-defense. Introduced in 1959 and discontinued around 1990, this single-action, blowback-operated pistol was offered in .22 Long Rifle, .32 ACP (7.65mm Browning) and .380 ACP (9mm Short).

The Model 60 features a blued-steel slide with integrally-machined sights, and a 3½-inch barrel that is attached rigidly to a black-finished light-weight alloy frame. The coil recoil spring encircles the barrel. The pistol's ergonomic black plastic grips are checkered on the sides and rear, and the magazine base incorporates a curved finger-rest.

A manual safety is located on the left side of the frame behind the trigger. Other safety features include a half-cock position of the exposed hammer and a magazine safety which prevents the pistol being fired when the magazine has been removed. At the rear of the frame, in the position normally occupied by a safety, is the takedown latch.

Though well-finished and reliable, the Model 60, along with numerous "pocket" designs, was made unimportable by the 1968 Gun Control Act, and was replaced by the Model 80, a similar pistol with modifications to allow its importation.

DISASSEMBLY

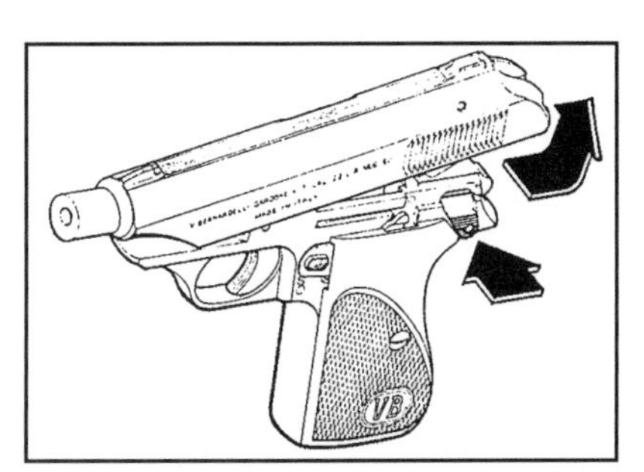

1 Begin field-stripping the Model 60 by moving manual safety (39) up to safe position. Push back magazine catch (44) and remove magazine. Draw slide (5) fully rearward to clear chamber. Hold takedown catch (38) depressed and pull slide rearward ⅝". Then, lift rear of slide and ease forward off frame (12). Remove recoil spring (11). This is sufficient take-down for normal cleaning. Position tightest coil of recoil spring to rear in reassembly.

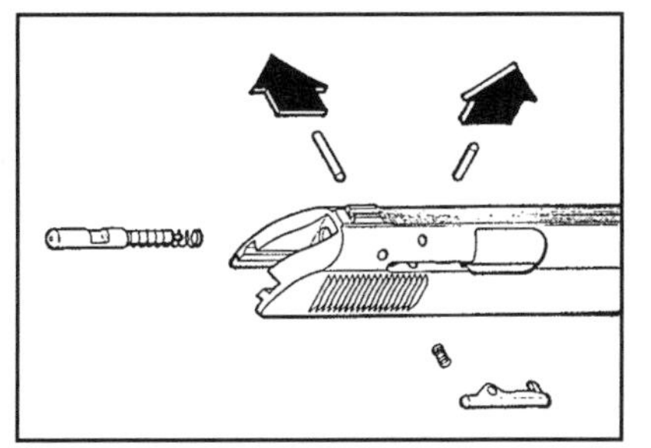

2 For further disassembly, drift out firing pin retainer (4) to release firing pin (7) and spring (6). Drift out extractor pin (3), and remove extractor (1) and its spring (2). Extractor pin must not protrude from bottom of slide on replacement.

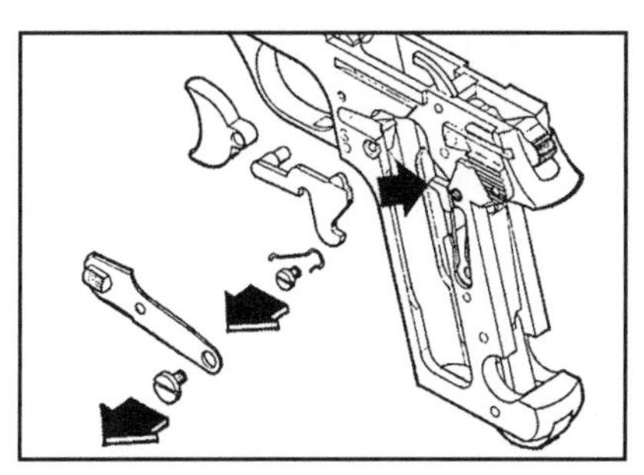

3 Unscrew grip screws (10) and remove grips (9) (26). Remove manual safety screw (40) and lift off manual safety. Unhook trigger bar spring (32) from trigger bar (31). Unscrew trigger bar spring screw (33) and remove trigger bar spring. Pull trigger bar from frame. Draw trigger (30) forward and remove through trigger guard. Grasp hammer (20) firmly and push arm of sear (36) to the rear. Ease hammer fully forward.

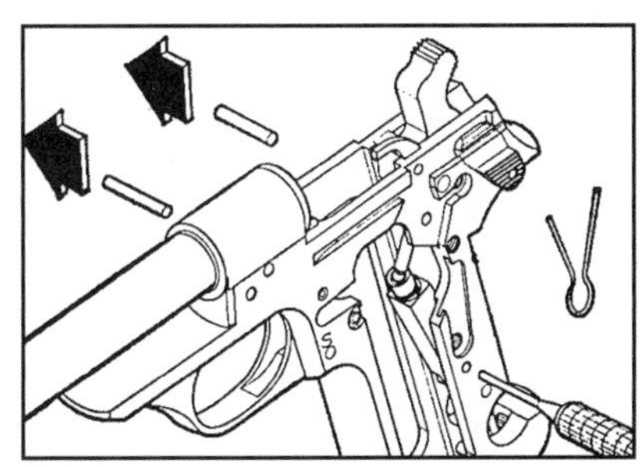

4 Unhook arms of sear spring (34) from sear and frame, and pry the spring upward out of its frame grooves. Drift out sear pin (35) and remove sear. Drift out hammer spring housing stop (19) with 1⁄16"-diameter pin punch. Hold hammer spring housing (43) to rear while removing punch, then allow housing to pivot slowly forward into the magazine well until spring tension is relieved. Remove hammer strut (22), plunger (23), and spring (24).

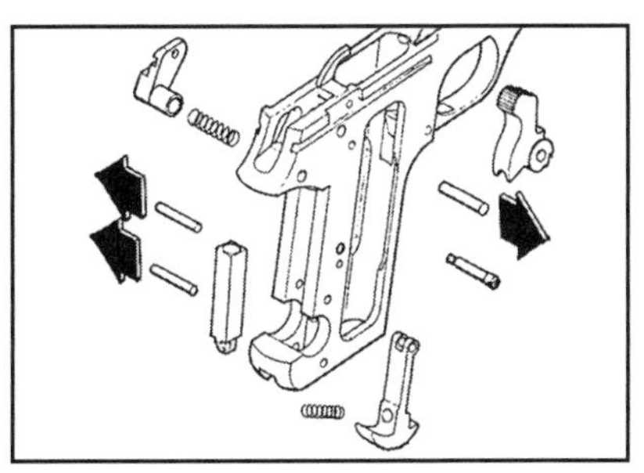

5 Drift out hammer pin (17) and remove hammer. Drift out magazine catch stop (41) and remove magazine catch spring (45). Hammer spring housing and magazine catch are released by removing hammer spring housing pin (42). Unscrew takedown catch screw (18) to release takedown catch and spring (37). Reassemble in reverse. Angled cut on spring housing faces toward rear of frame. Assembly of hammer group is eased if hammer spring is tensioned with hammer in full-cock position.

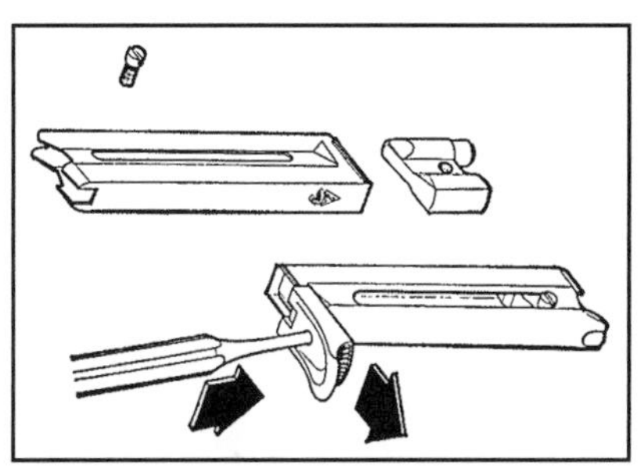

6 To dismount magazine, depress spring plate (47) with punch inserted through hole in magazine base (48). Slide base partially forward. Then, place thumb over spring plate as base is removed. Ease spring plate and spring (46) from magazine body (21). Unscrew follower button (8) and slide follower (25) out through bottom of magazine body.

BROWNING CAL. .25 VEST POCKET

PARTS LEGEND

1. Receiver
2. Trigger
3. Trigger spring
4. Connector
5. Sear
6. Sear spring
7. Sear pin
8. Safety
9. Magazine safety
10. Magazine latch
11. Magazine latch spring
12. Magazine latch pin
13. Magazine assembly
14. Grip, left (right grip not shown)
15. Grip screw
16. Grip escutcheon (contained in right grip)
17. Slide
18. Extractor
19. Extractor pin
20. Extractor spring
21. Barrel
22. Firing pin
23. Firing pin spring
24. Cocking indicator assembly
25. Recoil spring assembly

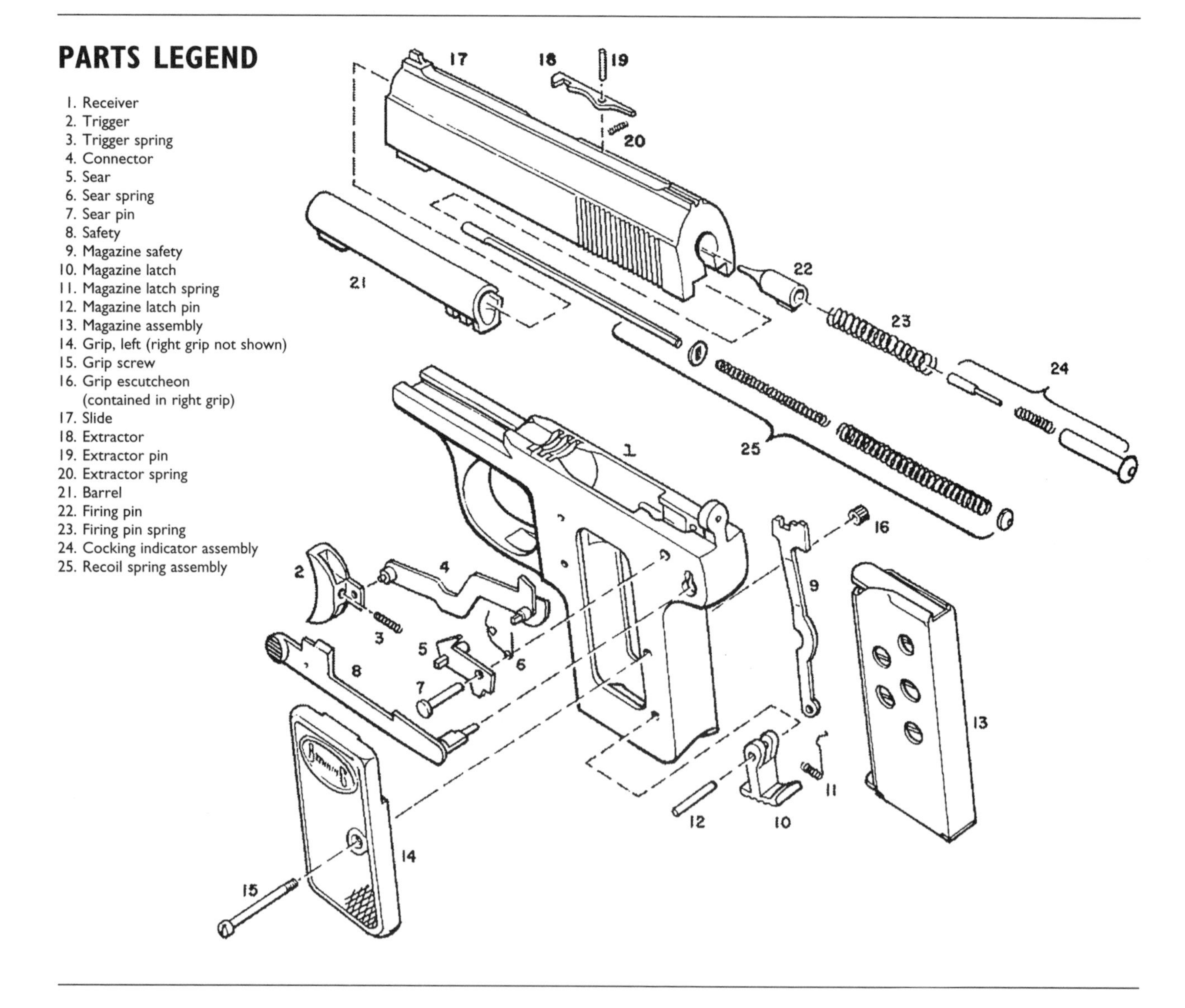

The .25 ACP (6.35mm Browning) "Vest Pocket" pistol was invented by John M. Browning, patented in Belgium in 1905, and manufactured beginning in 1906. It is thus sometimes called both the "Model 1905" and "Model 1906." Initial production was by the Belgian arms firm Fabrique Nationale d'Armes de Guerre (FN). Though equipped with a grip safety, the original Browning .25 lacked a slide-lock safety lever. Fabrique Nationale pistols manufactured after about 1908 were provided with this feature.

The U.S. patent covering this hammerless, blowback-operated, self-loading pistol was granted to Browning on January 25, 1910 (No. 947,478). U.S. production of this pistol was begun in 1908 by Colt's Patent Fire Arms Mfg. Co., under license from the inventor. In 1954, the Browning Arms Co. of St. Louis, Mo., introduced a redesigned model of this pistol, made in Belgium by FN. It featured a magazine disconnector, mechanical safety and cocking indicator, and weighed 10 ounces (standard), or 7¾ ounces (lightweight).

FN produced more than a million Browning .25 ACP pistols before ceasing production of the gun in 1959, and Colt made approximately 500,000 before discontinuing the model in 1946. A lighter, smaller version, the Browning "Baby," was made by FN from 1931-1983. Importation of the "Baby" was discontinued due to the 1968 Gun Control Act.

DISASSEMBLY

Pull back magazine latch (10) and remove magazine (13) from butt. Draw slide (17) back and check chamber to be sure pistol is unloaded. Replace empty magazine and pull trigger to uncock action. Remove magazine.

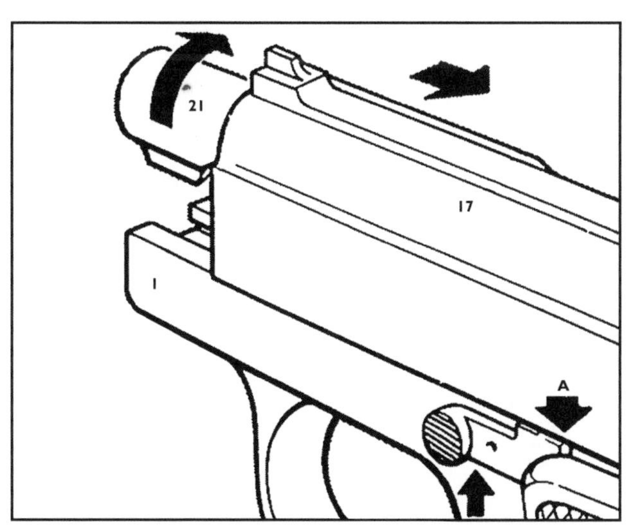

1 To separate slide (17) from receiver (1), pull slide back until forward nose of safety (8) can be pressed up into front notch of slide (17) as shown at "A", holding slide to rear. Turn barrel (21) ⅓-turn clockwise to unlock it from receiver. Push down on safety and draw slide forward off receiver.

Remove recoil spring assembly (25) from receiver. Turn barrel ⅓-turn counterclockwise and withdraw it from front end of slide (17). Firing pin (22), firing pin spring (23), and cocking indicator assembly (24) may be removed from rear of slide. Extractor (18) and extractor spring (20) may be removed by drifting out extractor pin (19). Reassemble in reverse.

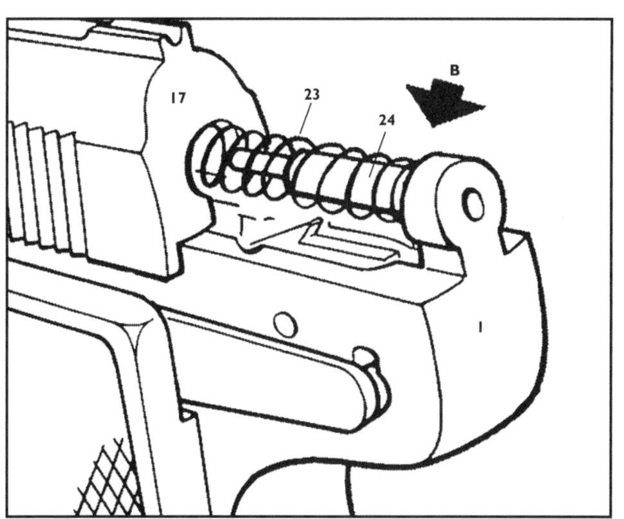

2 In reassembling pistol, replace barrel so that its ribs enter corresponding grooves in slide. Replace recoil spring assembly (25) in receiver and firing pin (22), spring (23), and cocking indicator assembly (24) in rear of slide. Replace slide on receiver so its lugs engage grooves in receiver. Be sure that rear of cocking indicator assembly (24) is seated against spur projecting upward from rear of receiver as shown at "B". Push slide rear-ward until forward nose of safety can be pressed up into front notch of slide. Turn barrel ⅓-turn counterclockwise, locking it in receiver. Disengage safety, release slide, and replace magazine, completing reassembly.

BROWNING .380 AUTO, POST '68

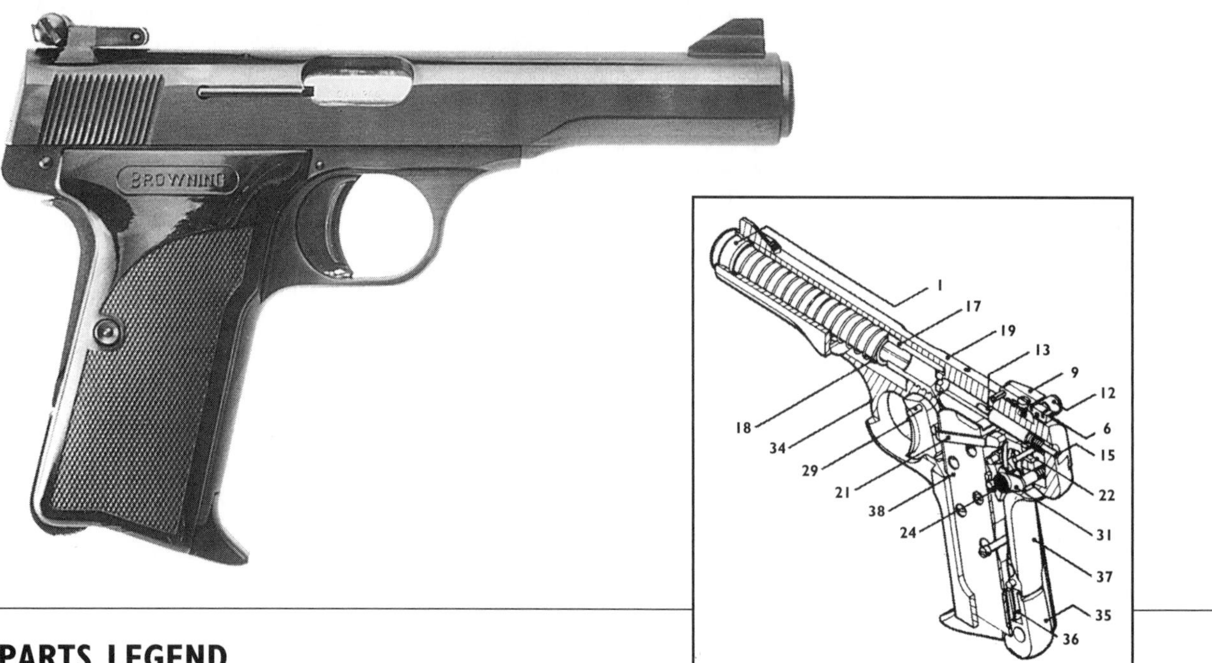

PARTS LEGEND

1. Slide ring
2. Extractor pin
3. Extractor spring
4. Extractor
5. Rear sight adjusting screw, elevation
6. Rear sight leaf
7. Rear sight spring, elevation
8. Rear sight leaf pin
9. Rear sight base
10. Rear sight detent spring, elevation
11. Rear sight adjusting screw, windage (2)
12. Rear sight aperture
13. Firing pin
14. Firing pin spring
15. Signal pin
16. Signal pin spring
17. Barrel
18. Recoil spring
19. Slide
20. Grip plate, right
21. Connector
22. Sear
23. Magazine safety spring
24. Magazine safety
25. Grip plate screw
26. Grip plate, left
27. Sear pin
28. Trigger pin
29. Trigger
30. Magazine safety pin
31. Safety
32. Safety spring
33. Grip safety pin
34. Frame
35. Magazine latch
36. Sear spring
37. Grip safety
38. Magazine

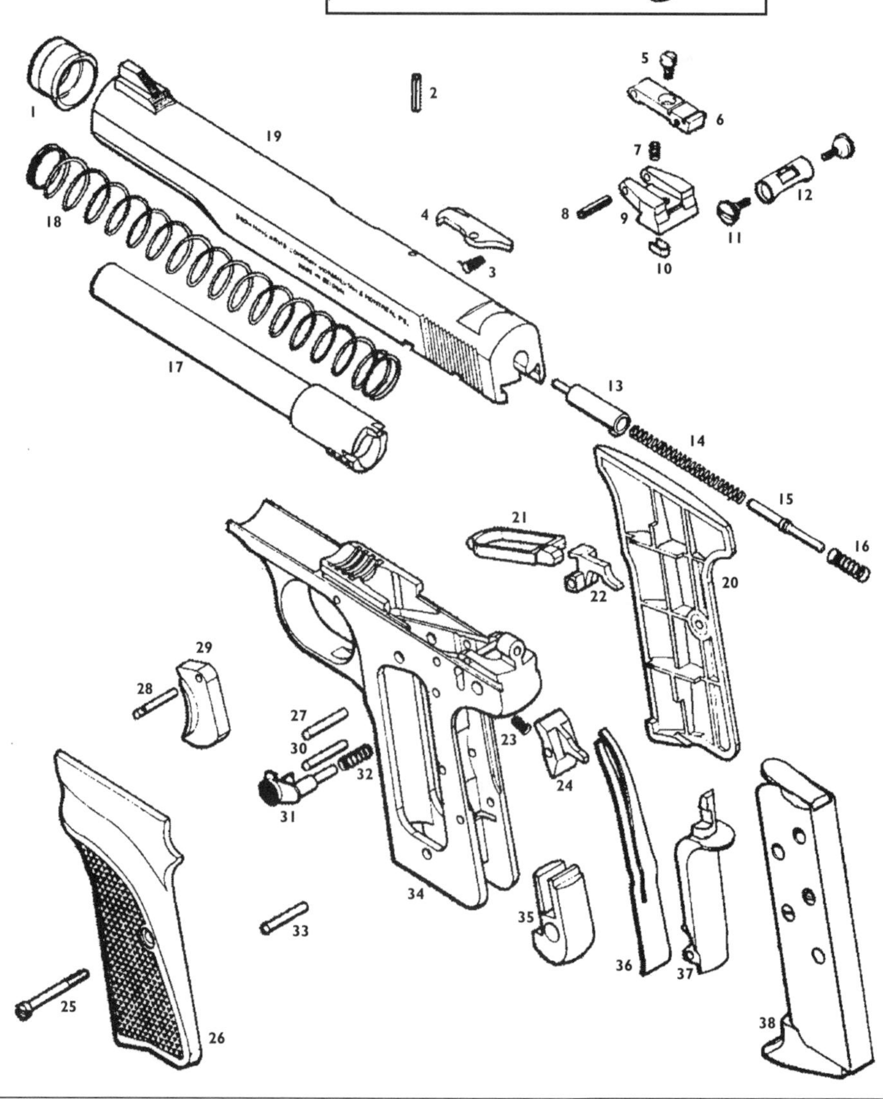

Among the most popular of the pistols designed by John Browning and produced by Fabrique Nationale (FN) was the Model 1910, a simple blowback-operated arm offered in .32 ACP and .380 ACP. In 1954 the Browning Arms Co. imported the .380 ACP version of this pistol into the U. S. where it was sold for many years as the "Browning .380 Caliber Automatic Pistol". This pistol failed to meet the requirements of the point system of the Federal Gun Control Act of 1968, and it was redesigned to qualify for importation under those regulations.

Called the Browning .380 Pistol, the redesigned version, introduced about 1970, incorporated the same mechanical design as its predecessor, but featured a number of modifications allowing it to comply with the new regulations, including a 4 7/16-inch barrel, adjustable target sights, and a curved extension on the six-round magazine floorplate serving as a finger rest. These changes enabled the pistol to meet the minimum size regulation, which specified that the combined length and height measurement must exceed 10 inches.

Safety features included a left-side frame-mounted manual safety, a grip safety, a magazine disconnector to prevent firing when the magazine is removed, along with both cocking and loaded-chamber indicators.

Well-made and nicely finished, the Browning .380 Auto was sold in the United States from about 1970-1975.

DISASSEMBLY

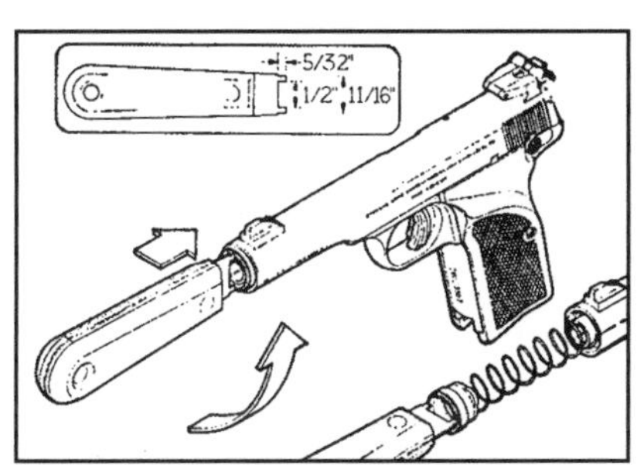

1 Ensure chamber is empty, and insert empty magazine. With slide (19) forward, pull trigger and engage safety (31). Use a tool to force the slide ring (1) rearward, and rotate ¼ turn. Hold slide ring tightly and ease it out of the slide. (Removal and replacement of the slide ring is aided by use of a spanner tool fitted to the index cuts, such as can be made from a thin-bladed putty knife.) Remove the recoil spring while turning it counterclockwise as viewed from the muzzle.

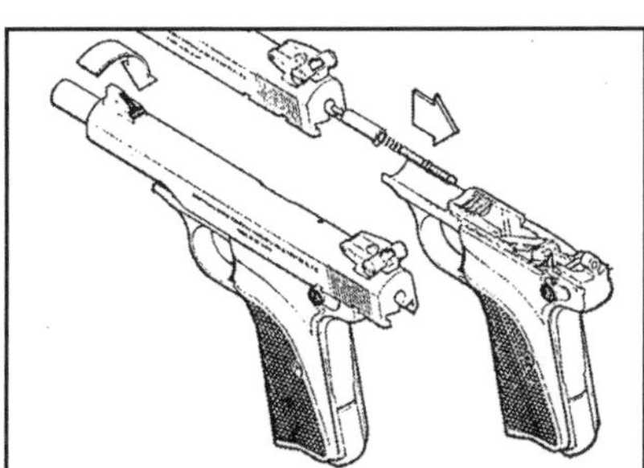

2 Remove the magazine. Release the safety and pull the slide back until the safety can be raised into the forward slide notch. Turn the barrel (17) to the right (viewed from the rear) as far as it will go. Release the safety and move the slide forward off the frame (34). Withdraw the firing pin and signal pin with springs (13) (14) (15) (16) from the rear of the slide. Turn the barrel fully to the left and remove through the front of the slide. This completes field-stripping for normal cleaning.

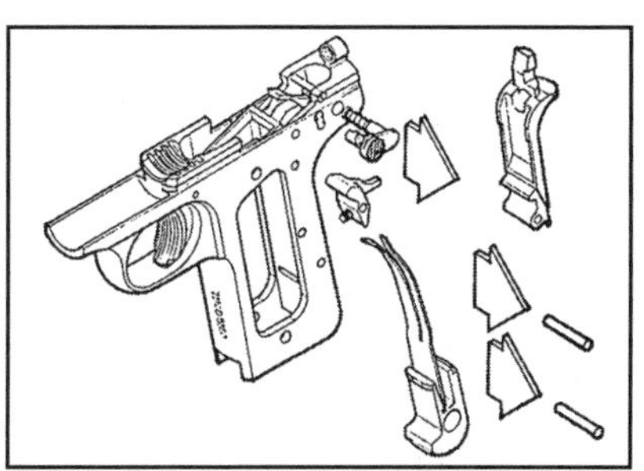

3 If necessary to disassemble further, rotate the safety upward and withdraw the safety and safety spring (32) to the left. Unscrew and remove the grip plate screw (25), and remove the grips (20) (26). Push out the grip safety pin (33) to release the grip safety (37), sear spring (36), and magazine latch (35). Push out the magazine safety pin, and remove the magazine safety (24), taking care to avoid loss of its spring (23). In reassembling these parts, seat the large end coil of the spring in the recess at the front of the magazine safety.

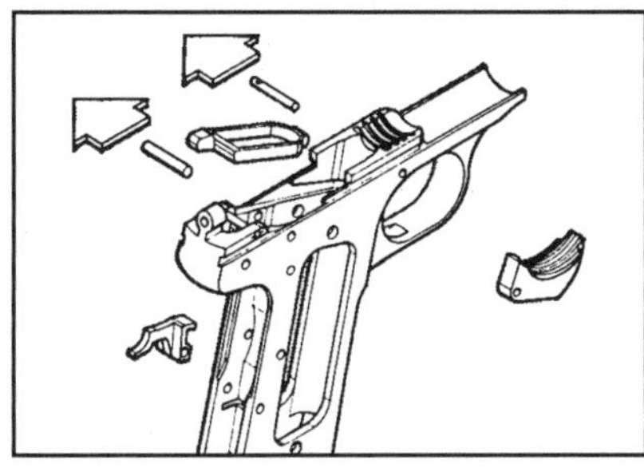

4 Push out the sear pin (27) and withdraw the sear (22) through the rear of the frame. Slide the connector (21) rearward, and lift it out of the frame grooves. After the trigger pin (28) has been driven out, the trigger can be rotated forward and removed through the guard.

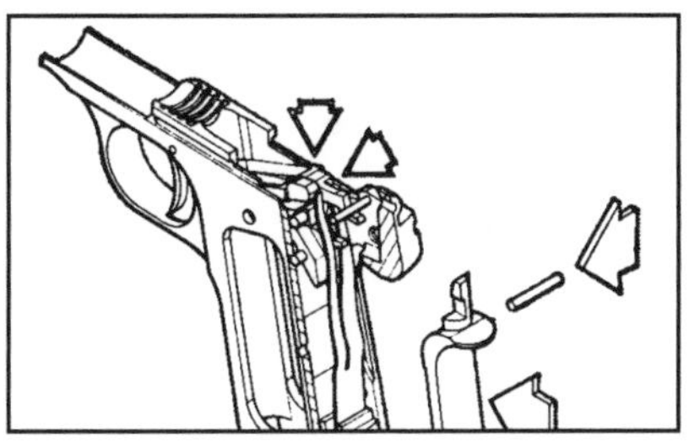

5 Reassemble the parts in the frame in reverse order, being careful to avoid deforming the magazine safety spring. The pins for the sear, magazine safety, and grip safety are interchangeable. Install the sear spring with its hooked end seated in the groove at the front of the magazine latch cutout (arrow), split fingers contacting the connector and sear (arrows). The spring is tensioned by insertion of the grip safety.

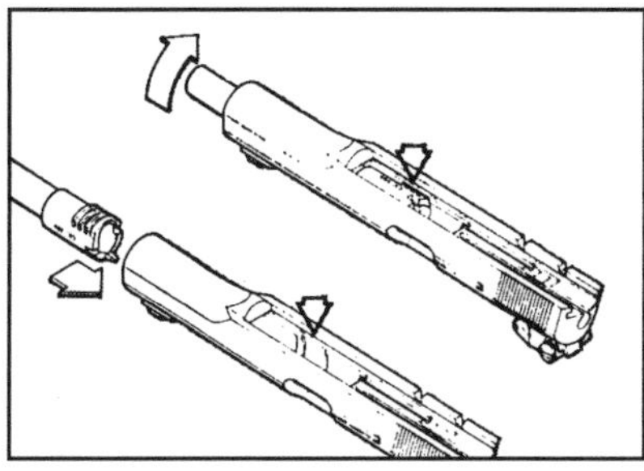

6 In reassembling the barrel and slide, hold the slide upside down. Insert the barrel with its multiple lugs up, and move the barrel rearward until the lugs align with the recess opposite the front of the ejection port (arrow). Rotate the barrel fully to the right to move its lugs into the slide recess (arrow). The rest of the reassembly is the reverse of field-stripping.

BROWNING MODEL 1900 PISTOL

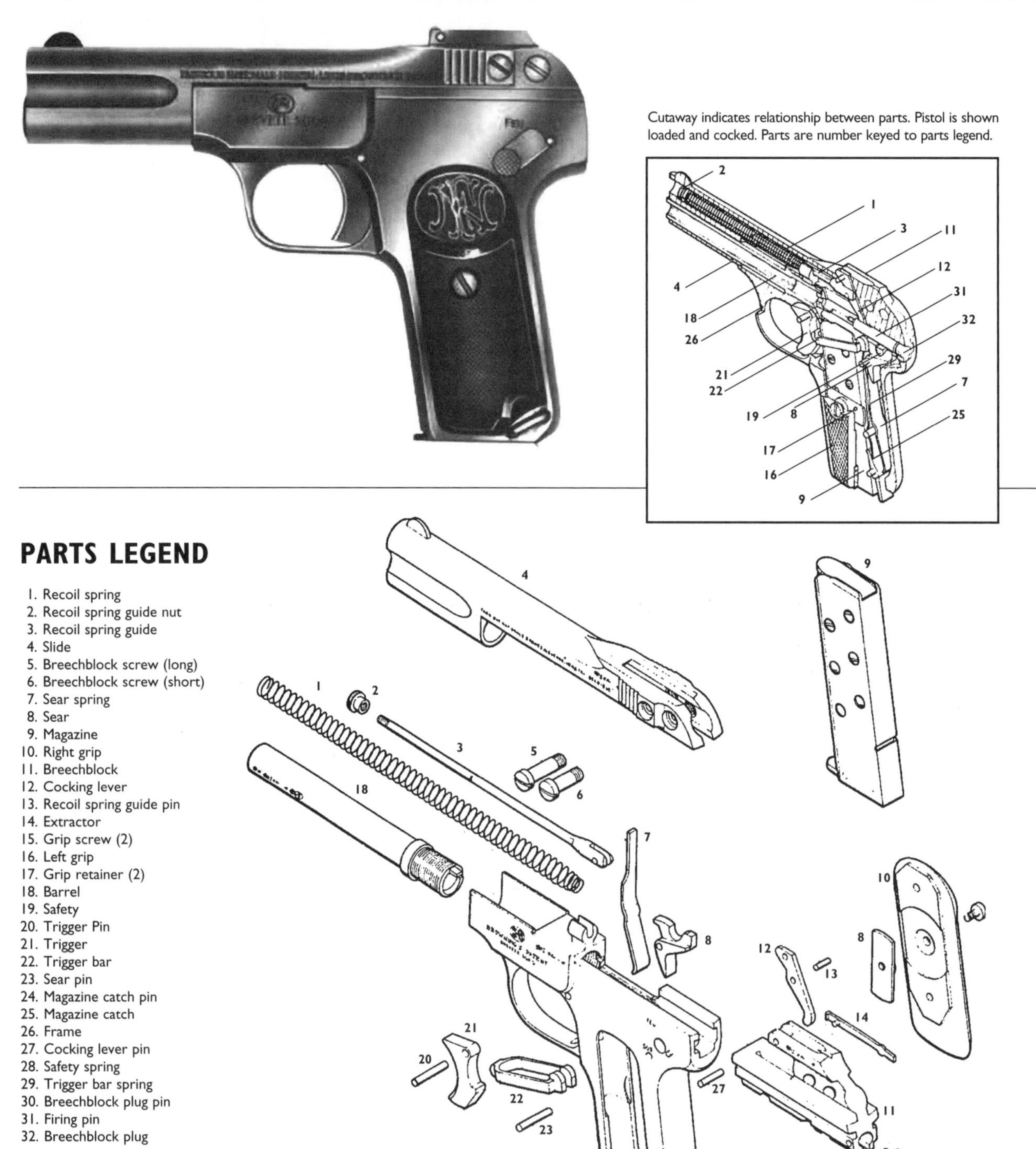

Cutaway indicates relationship between parts. Pistol is shown loaded and cocked. Parts are number keyed to parts legend.

PARTS LEGEND

1. Recoil spring
2. Recoil spring guide nut
3. Recoil spring guide
4. Slide
5. Breechblock screw (long)
6. Breechblock screw (short)
7. Sear spring
8. Sear
9. Magazine
10. Right grip
11. Breechblock
12. Cocking lever
13. Recoil spring guide pin
14. Extractor
15. Grip screw (2)
16. Left grip
17. Grip retainer (2)
18. Barrel
19. Safety
20. Trigger Pin
21. Trigger
22. Trigger bar
23. Sear pin
24. Magazine catch pin
25. Magazine catch
26. Frame
27. Cocking lever pin
28. Safety spring
29. Trigger bar spring
30. Breechblock plug pin
31. Firing pin
32. Breechblock plug

In April, 1897, John M. Browning of Ogden, Utah, met Hart O. Berg, commercial director of the Fabrique Nationale d'Armes de Guerre (FN) armsmaking firm of Herstal, Belgium, and began a relationship which resulted in that company producing a wide variety of Browning-designed small arms.

Browning's first FN-made pistol was the Model 1900, initially produced in January 1899. It was the first pistol chambered for the .32 ACP cartridge, also a Browning development. Immediately popular, the Model 1900 sold in large quantities, and was adopted by many European police forces.

The Model 1900 weighed 22 ounces and was 6⅜ inches long. A single-action, blowback-operated, striker-fired arm, it featured a fixed barrel, manual safety, cocking indicator, and seven-round magazine. It had such an excellent reputation that several of its features were used in other European pistols. It was discontinued about 1912 and supplanted by the Browning Model 1910.

DISASSEMBLY

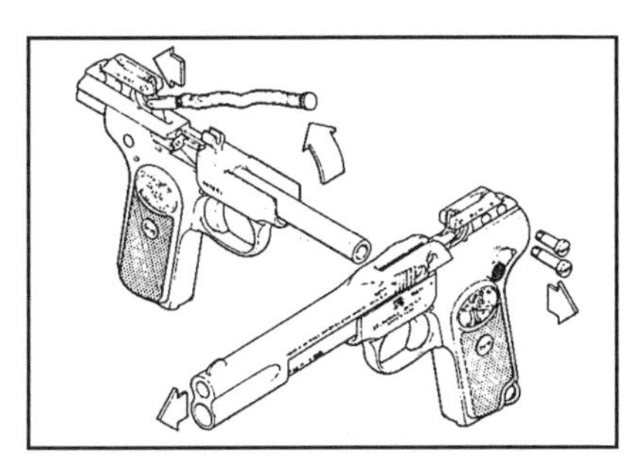

1 Push the magazine catch (25) forward and remove the magazine (9). Release the safety (19). Retract the slide (4) and check that the chamber is empty. Release the slide and pull the trigger. Remove the breechblock screws (5) (6), and move the slide forward off the frame (26). Lift the forward end of the recoil spring (1) until it snaps free of the frame. Withdraw the breech block (11) to the rear. This is sufficient disassembly for normal cleaning. Disassemble further only as required.

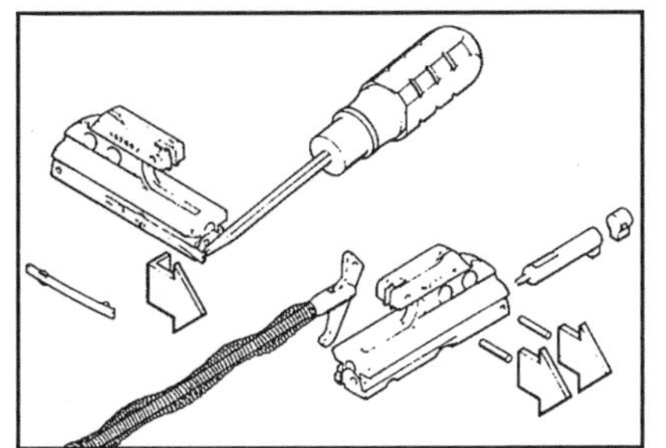

2 Insert a narrow screwdriver blade beneath the hook of the extractor (14). Push the extractor outward until its lug clears the side of the breechblock. Then, pry the extractor forward, bringing its wings into alignment with the disassembly hole. Drift out the cocking lever pin (27), and remove the recoil spring mechanism. Drift out the breechblock plug pin (30) to release the breechblock plug (32) and firing pin (31).

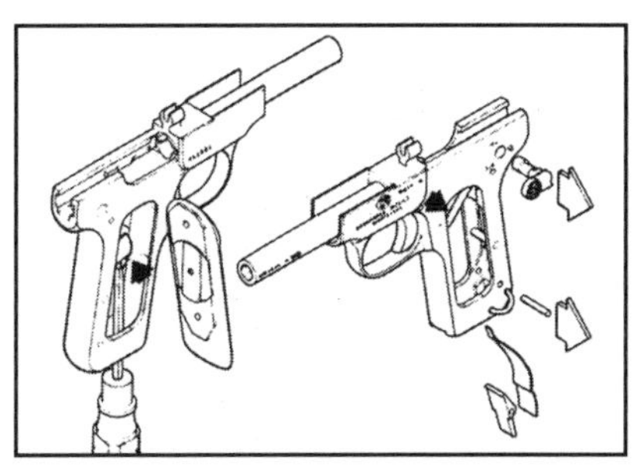

3 To release the grips (10 & 16), first loosen the grip screws (15) and turn the grip retainers (17) from horizontal to vertical with a screwdriver inserted into the magazine well. Drift out the magazine catch pin (24), and remove the magazine catch (25) and trigger bar spring (29). Pull the forward end of the trigger bar (22) downward into the magazine well and remove. Move the safety midway between "safe" and "fire" and push out with a punch.

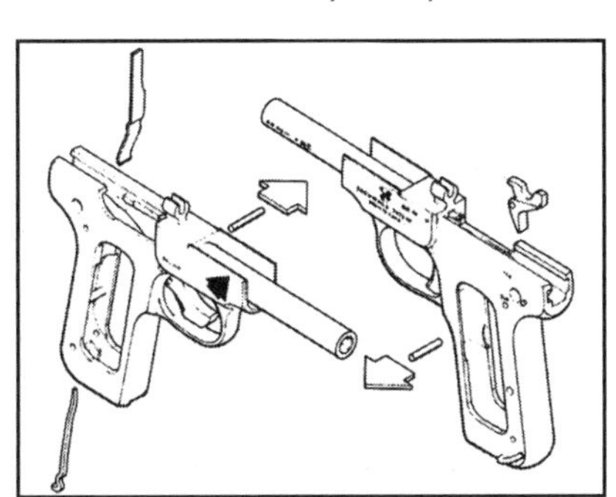

4 Drift out the sear pin (23) and lift out the sear (8), Push the safety spring (28) downward and remove through the underside of the frame. Center the sear spring (7) in the frame with a screwdriver blade, and push upward to remove. Drift out the trigger pin (20), roll the bottom of the trigger forward, and remove through the side of the trigger guard.

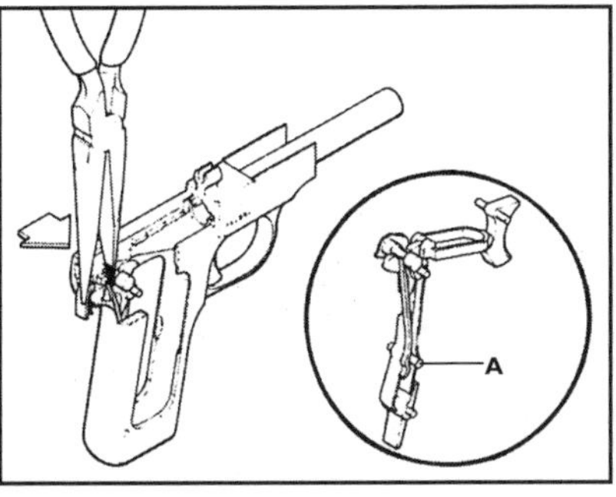

5 In reassembly, replace the trigger and trigger pin, and install the sear spring through the top of the frame. Align the spring vertically, and lever it horizontally against the left side of the frame. Insert the tail of the sear between the sear spring and frame backstrap, and replace the sear pin. Install the safety spring from below, sliding it upward against the right side of the frame and behind the sear. Flex the safety spring with padded long-nose pliers when in-stalling the safety. Inset shows proper location of springs in the frame. All seat upon the fixed frame pin (A), which is never removed.

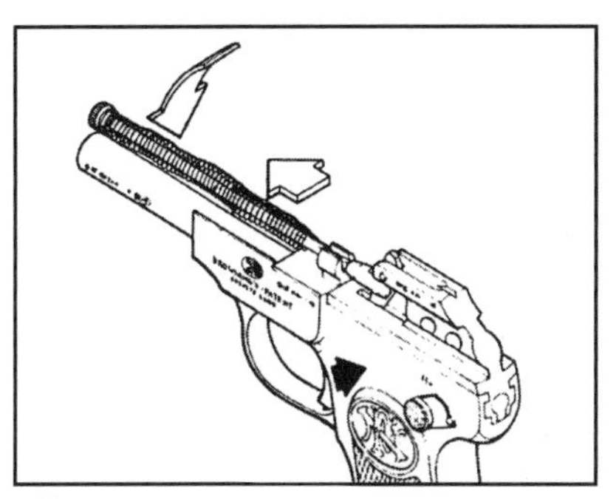

6 Safety must be disengaged to install the breechblock. Depress the trigger and start the breechblock assembly into the frame until resistance is felt, then release the trigger and push the breechblock fully home. Again depress the trigger and pull forward on the recoil spring to release the firing pin from the sear. Grasp the rear of the recoil spring tightly and pull forward over the recoil spring guide (3), until the assembly can be swung down within the frame fork.

BROWNING MODEL 1907 SWEDISH

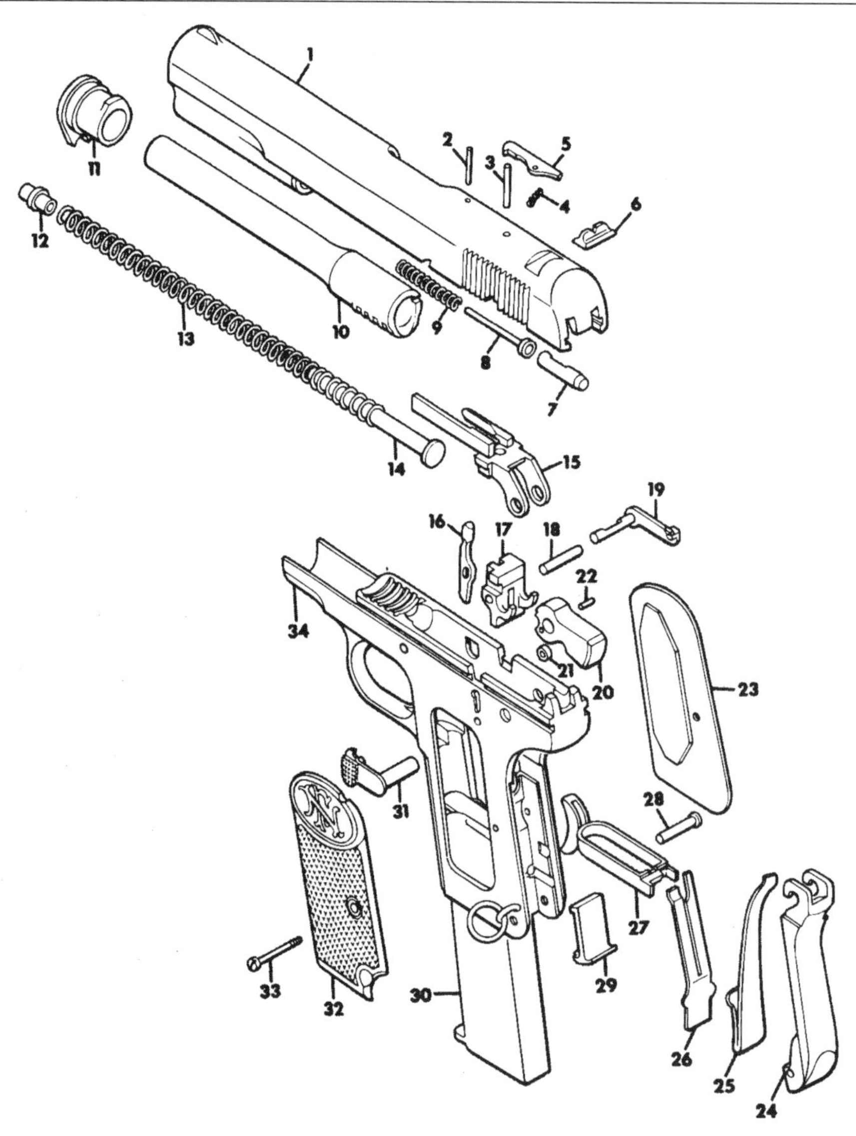

PARTS LEGEND

1. Slide
2. Extractor pin
3. Firing pin retainer pin
4. Extractor spring
5. Extractor
6. Rear sight
7. Firing pin extension
8. Firing pin
9. Firing pin spring
10. Barrel
11. Barrel bushing
12. Bushing stop
13. Recoil spring
14. Recoil spring guide
15. Ejector and cartridge guide
16. Disconnector
17. Sear
18. Sear pin
19. Slide stop
20. Hammer
21. Hammer roll
22. Roll axis pin
23. Right grip
24. Grip safety
25. Hammer spring
26. Sear spring
27. Trigger
28. Grip safety pin
29. Magazine catch
30. Magazine
31. Safety
32. Left grip
33. Grip screw
34. Receiver

The Swedish Model 1907 semi-automatic pistol was designed by American arms inventor John M. Browning. Chambered for the 9mm Browning Long cartridge, this well-made blow-back-operated pistol was produced by Fabrique Nationale (FN) in Belgium and Husqvarna Vapenfabriks Aktiebolag (Husqvarna Arms Factory, Inc.) in Sweden.

Of concealed-hammer type, the pistol is simple and compact, and has a good grip and balance. It has a detachable seven-round magazine, a manual safety, a grip safety, and a slide stop that holds the slide open after the last shot. The grip safety also serves as a cocking indicator, since it projects rearward only when the hammer is cocked.

During World War II, the Model 1907 was superseded in the Swedish Service by Walther and Lahti pistols chambered for the 9mm Luger cartridge. However, the Model 1907 was retained for several years as a substitute standard sidearm.

In the late 1950s, a quantity of Model 1907 pistols were imported into the U.S. and sold as military surplus. Many of these were converted to fire the .380 Automatic cartridge, and were stamped "CAL 380" on the left of the receiver. Converted specimens are accurate but give feeding and ejection mal-functions.

While the 9mm Browning Long cartridge is not produced in the United States, it has been imported by military surplus arms dealers in sufficient quantity for shooting. It has a semi-rimmed straight case slightly longer than that of the .380 Automatic cartridge, and is similar to that cartridge in power.

DISASSEMBLY

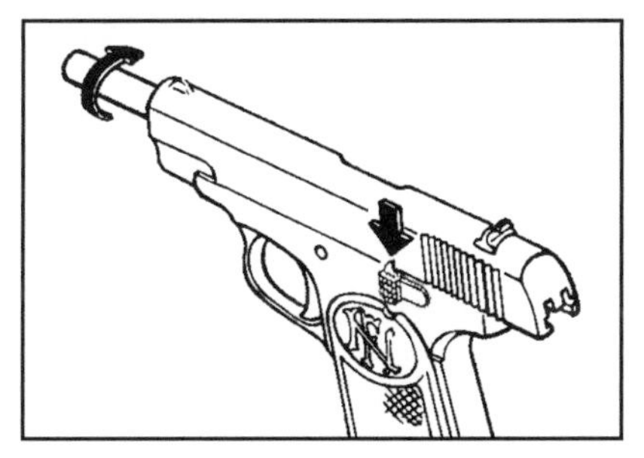

1 To disassemble the pistol, first remove the magazine (30) and clear the chamber. Pull back the slide (1) and push the safety (31) upward to engage it with the forward notch in the slide. Turn the barrel (10) 90° to lock it into the slide. While holding the slide, release the safety from the slide notch, and strip the slide, barrel, and recoil spring (13) off the front of the receiver (34). Also remove the slide stop (19) from the receiver.

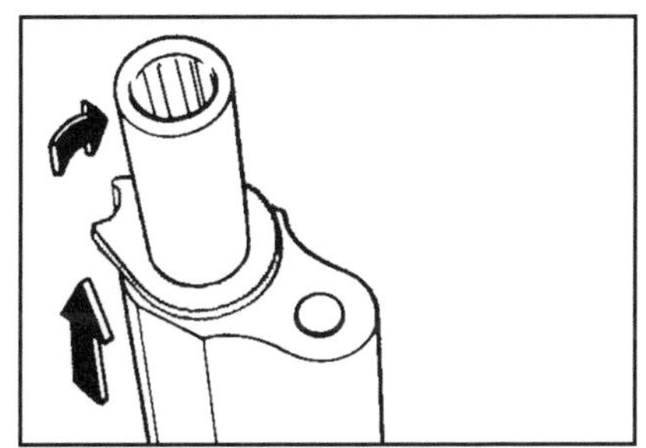

2 Remove the recoil spring guide (14), and bushing stop (12). To remove the barrel bushing (11), rotate it 180° as shown and lift it free of the slide. Rotate the barrel to free it from its recess in the slide. Then pull the barrel out forward.

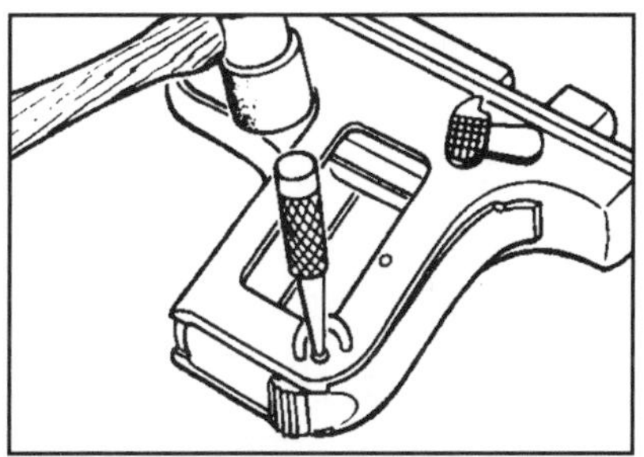

3 Unscrew the grip screw (33) and remove the grips (23) and (32). While holding the hammer (20) firmly, pull the trigger (27), and ease the hammer forward. Drift the grip safety pin (28) out to the right, cock the hammer, pivot the safety upward, and lift it from the re-ceiver. Remove the hammer, ejector (15), grip safety (24), hammer spring (25), sear spring (26), and magazine catch (29). Drift out sear pin (18); remove sear (17), disconnector (16). and trigger.

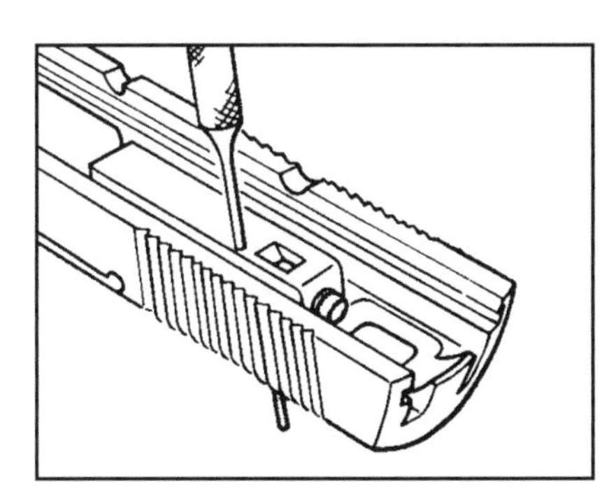

4 The firing pin (8) and firing pin extension (7) are retained by a long pin (3). Drive this pin out of the slide using the correct-size punch. The extractor (5) is retained by a shorter pin (2). When replacing the retaining pins, be sure they are driven in to proper depth so that they do not drag on the receiver and scar it.

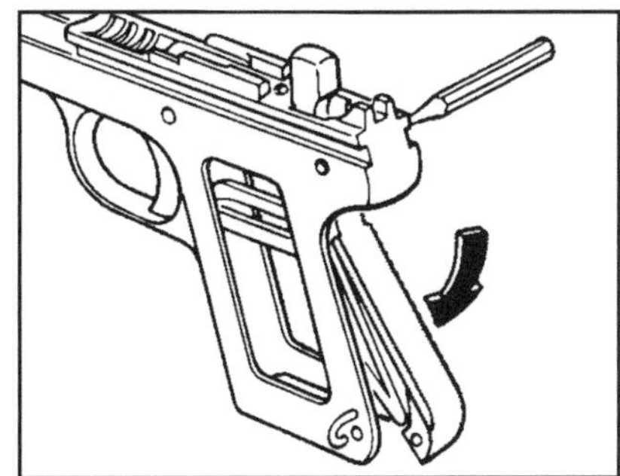

5 In reassembling the lock mechanism, replace the trigger, sear, disconnector, and sear pin. Then install the ejector, engaging the disconnector. Replace the magazine catch, sear spring, hammer spring, and grip safety, and put the hammer in position with the hammer roll behind the hammer spring.

Use a punch to align hole in hammer with hole in receiver. Then pull the trigger down, and insert the safety in the receiver part way. Pressing forward on grip safety, align holes in grip safety and receiver using punch and insert pin from right. Cock the hammer, and push safety in all the way.

BROWNING MODEL 1910 PISTOL

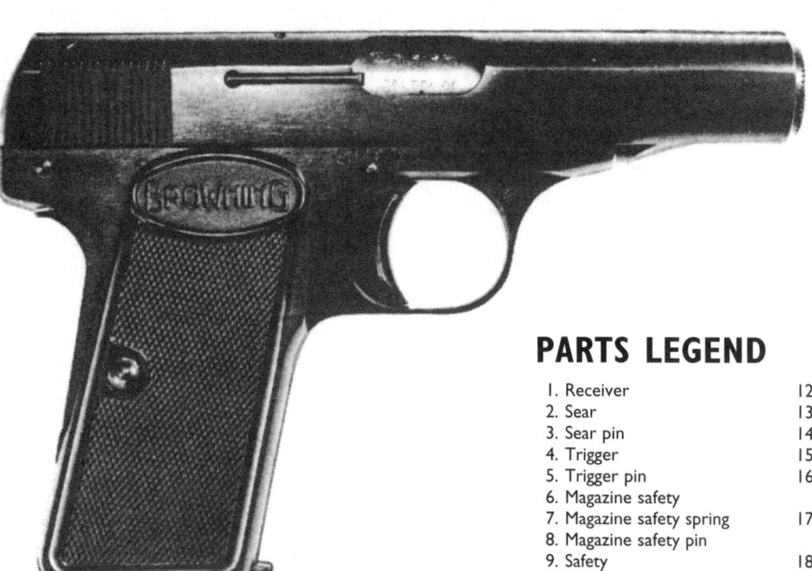

PARTS LEGEND

1. Receiver
2. Sear
3. Sear pin
4. Trigger
5. Trigger pin
6. Magazine safety
7. Magazine safety spring
8. Magazine safety pin
9. Safety
10. Safety spring
11. Connector
12. Sear spring
13. Grip safety
14. Magazine latch
15. Grip safety pin
16. Grips (right grip not shown)
17. Grip escutcheon, unthreaded
18. Grip escutcheon, threaded (contained in right grip)
19. Grip screw
20. Barrel
21. Recoil spring
22. Slide ring
23. Firing pin
24. Firing pin spring
25. Firing pin spring guide
26. Extractor
27. Extractor pin
28. Extractor spring
29. Slide
30. Magazine assembly

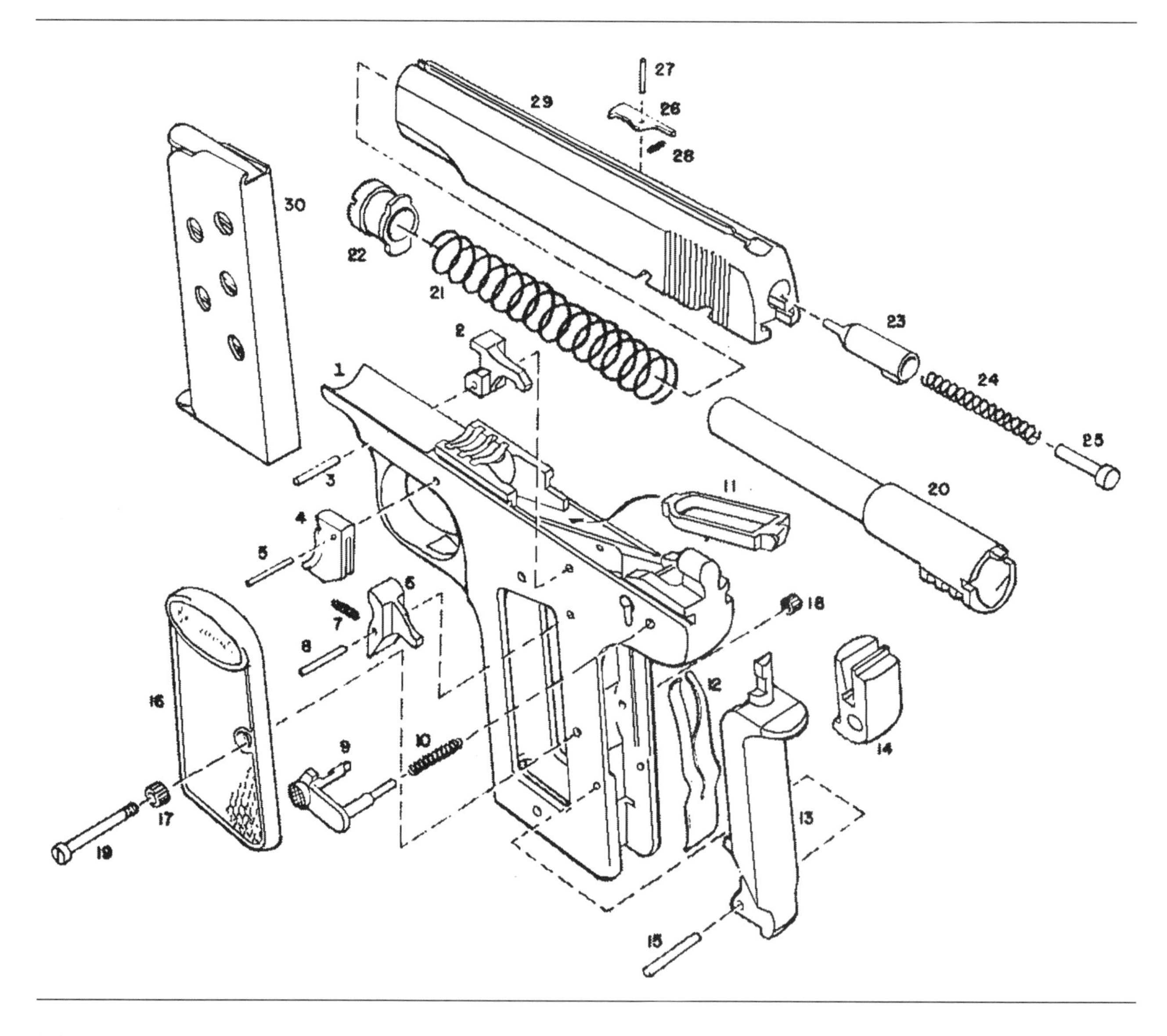

In 1910 John M. Browning obtained a Belgian patent for an improved version of his earlier Model 1900 self-loading pocket pistol. The new pistol, designated Model 1910, featured magazine, grip and manual safeties, and was striker fired. The recoil spring encircled the barrel giving the muzzle a streamlined appearance.

The Model 1910 was first produced by the Belgian firm of Fabrique Nationale d'Armes de Guerre in 1912, in both .32 ACP (7.65 mm) and .380 ACP (9mm Short). Up to the end of World War II, the pistol was extremely popular on the European market. In 1954, Browning Arms Co., of St. Louis, Missouri introduced the Model 1910 into the United States. Chambered for the .380 ACP cartridge, the pistol was known as the Browning .380 Auto.

Browning .380s sold before the 1968 Gun Control Act halted their importation had fixed sights and a magazine capacity of six rounds. They were offered in Standard and Renaissance grades, the latter having a hand-engraved, chrome-plated frame and slide, simulated mother-of-pearl grips and a gold-plated trigger. Standard-grade guns were blue-finished with black plastic grips.

Following implementation of GCA '68, the Browning .380 was re-engineered to meet import criteria. The barrel was lengthened by an inch to 4 7/16 inches; the magazine floorplate was redesigned to provide a finger extension; and the grips were modified to include a thumbrest. Additionally, the sights were changed to a target-style front blade and a windage and elevation adjustable rear notch. In that configuration Browning .380 Autos qualified for importation, and their sale was resumed.

Although the Model 1910/Browning .380 was well-made, accurate, good-handling and reliable, it was supplanted by later double-action designs. Production of the pistol ceased in 1980.

BROWNING

DISASSEMBLY

Remove magazine (30) and check to be sure it is empty. Check action to be sure pistol is unloaded. Replace magazine and pull trigger to release firing pin. Remove magazine.

Pull slide (29) to rear until nose of safety (9) enters front notch of slide. Turn barrel (20) 1/3-turn counterclockwise and press safety down to release slide. Draw slide assembly off receiver to front. Remove firing pin (23), firing pin spring (24), and guide (25) from rear of slide.

With slide upside down, turn barrel 1/3-turn clockwise until its lugs release from slide. Depress slide ring (22) slightly and rotate it 1/4-turn counterclockwise until its lugs release from slide. Take care as slide ring is under great pressure from recoil spring (21). Withdraw slide ring, barrel, and recoil spring from slide.

To assemble, replace barrel in slide and turn it so its lugs enter corresponding groove in rear of slide. Replace firing pin assembly in rear of slide. Replace slide on receiver and push back until safety nose engages front notch in slide. Turn barrel clockwise, release safety, and allow slide to move forward until nose of safety can be engaged in rear notch in slide. Replace recoil spring around barrel and place slide ring on spring and press spring back into slide. Position slide ring so its lugs enter corresponding slots in face of slide. When slide ring is firmly seated, rotate 1/4-turn clockwise to lock it in place.

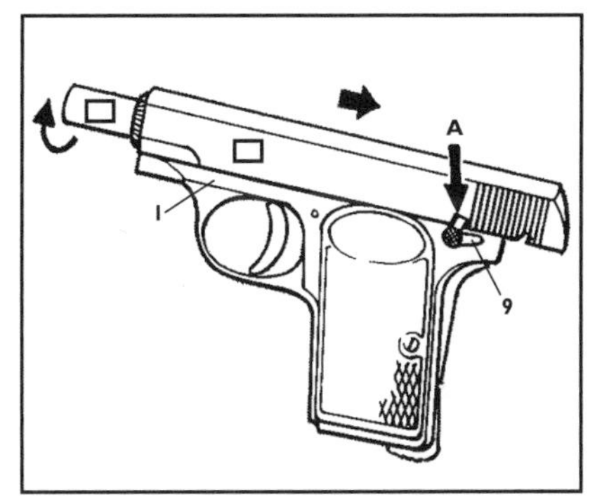

1 To remove slide (29) from receiver (1), pull slide back to position shown. Press nose of safety (9) up into front notch of slide as shown at "A". Turn barrel (20) 1/3-turn counterclockwise. Depress safety (9); draw slide off receiver to front.

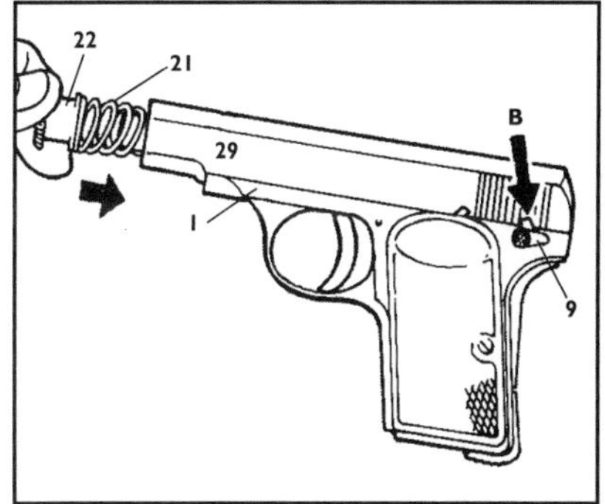

2 In reassembling pistol, after replacing slide assembly on receiver, lock in rear position with nose of safety (9) in forward notch of slide (29). Turn barrel (20) 1/3-turn clockwise and allow slide to go forward until nose of safety can be engaged in rear notch in slide as shown at "B". Replace recoil spring (21) on barrel (20). Place slide ring (22) over end of spring and press spring back into slide as shown. When slide ring is firmly seated against face of slide, turn 1/4-turn clockwise to lock in place.

BROWNING MODEL 1922 PISTOL

PARTS LEGEND

1. Slide extension
2. Slide extension spring
3. Slide extension catch
4. Slide
5. Extractor pin
6. Extractor
7. Extractor spring
8. Rear sight
9. Firing pin
10. Firing pin spring
11. Spring follower
12. Right grip
13. Grip safety
14. Magazine catch
15. Mainspring
16. Magazine safety
17. Magazine safety spring
18. Sear
19. Magazine safety pin
20. Trigger bar
21. Barrel
22. Recoil spring
23. Frame
24. Trigger
25. Trigger pin
26. Sear pin
27. Safety catch
28. Safety catch spring
29. Grip safety hinge pin
30. Magazine
31. Left grip
32. Grip screw

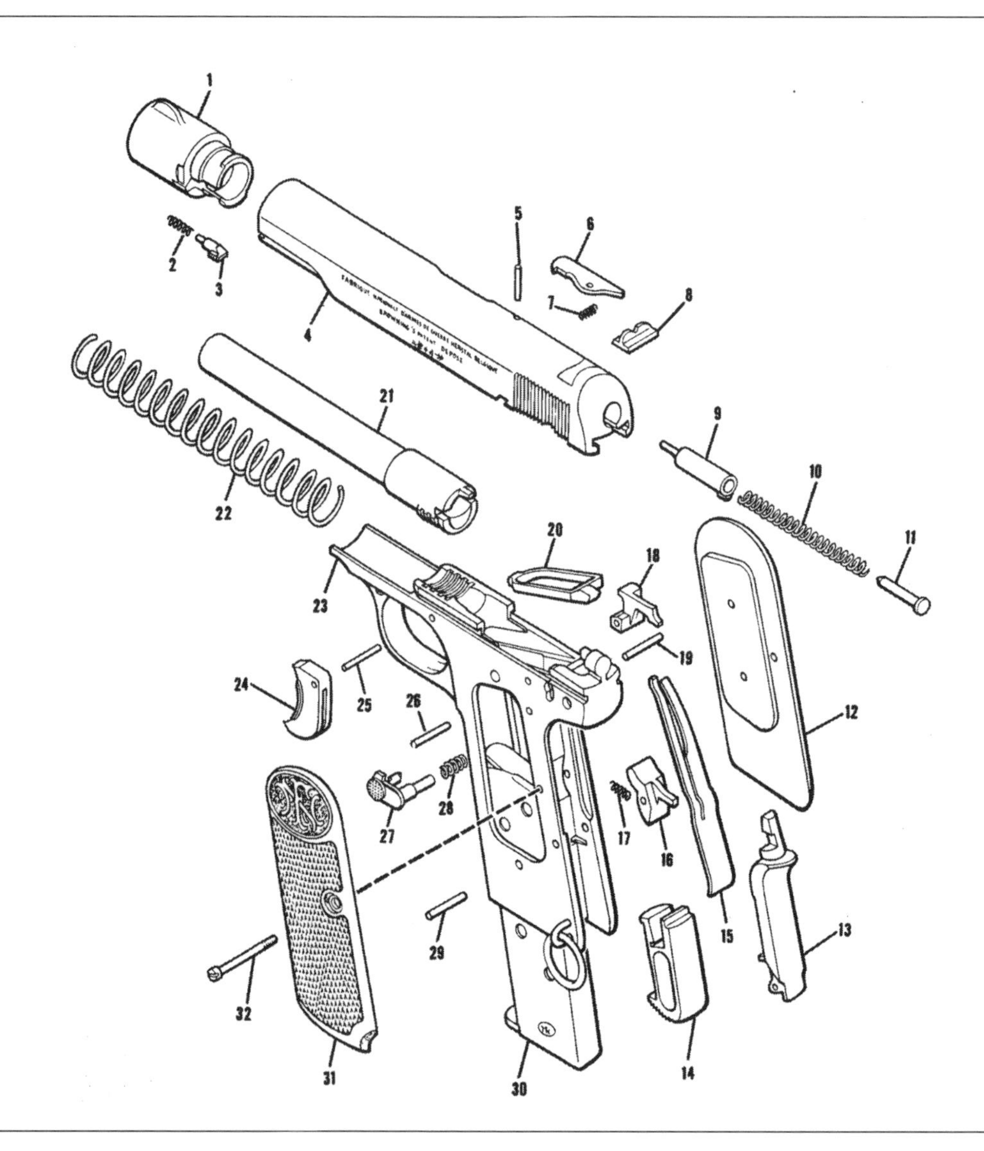

John Browning's reputation for designing reliable and compact pistols is well-known. In the early years of the 20th century, Fabrique Nationale d'Armes de Guerre (FN) found the market for Browning pocket pistols so great that over a million had been produced by the middle of 1912.

The compact Model 1910 was highly popular with police forces and was carried throughout Europe and South America. When the need for a larger military-type pistol arose, the Model 1910 was revised, with a longer barrel and grip frame. The new gun, commonly called the Model 1922, was, like its predecessor, available in both the 7.65mm. (.32 ACP) and 9mm Browning Short (.380 ACP) chamberings. The cal. .32 gun has a magazine capacity of 9 rounds and was issued to French, Belgian, Dutch, and Danish officers before World War II. The .380 caliber gun, with 8-round magazine capacity, was even more popular. It was issued to police and army officers in Poland, Czechoslovakia, Yugoslavia, Holland, Sweden, France, and Belgium, and was widely used in Central and South America.

The Model 1922 was a blowback-operated, striker-fired, single-action semi-automatic pistol. While not a true military arm by American standards, it was simple, reliable and good-handling. The gun's takedown procedure allows field-stripping in a matter of seconds.

Aside from the difference in calibers and national crests or markings, there are two Model 1922 variations: a pre-war gun with fine finish, and a crude revised gun made under German occupation. Apparently the Germans liked the Model 1922 and issued all that FN produced. As the war progressed, however, the gun was modified to save materials and speed production. The magazine safety and lanyard loop were dropped, internal parts were simplified, the hard rubber FN grips were replaced by crude wooden grips, and the commercial high-polish finish was eliminated. Although the Germans put their ordnance proofmarks on the guns, they also allowed FN to mark the pistols with their trade name and not the 'ch' code assigned to the company.

Manufacture of the Model 1922 was discontinued in 1983.

DISASSEMBLY

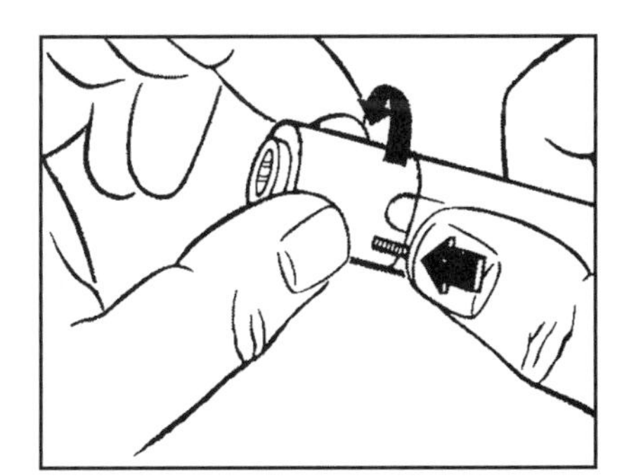

1 To strip the Model 1922, first remove the magazine and clear chamber. Push small serrated slide extension catch (3) forward, until it is clear of slide. Rotate extension about ¼ turn as shown, until it snaps free of slide.

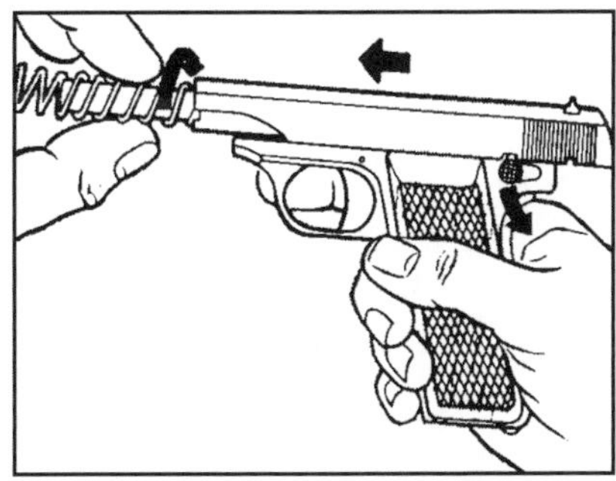

2 Pull back slide (4) until safety catch (27) can be engaged in forward notch. Rotating barrel (21) as shown will free it from recesses in frame. Release safety catch and pull slide and barrel off front of frame.

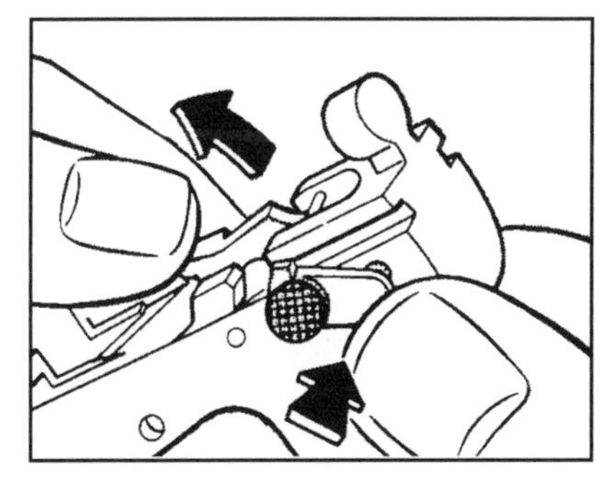

3 To remove safety catch (27), push up as far as it will go and it will snap out. To replace safety, push it in as far as it will go, then snap it down to "fire" position. Be sure sear (18) is pivoted clear before pushing safety all the way in.

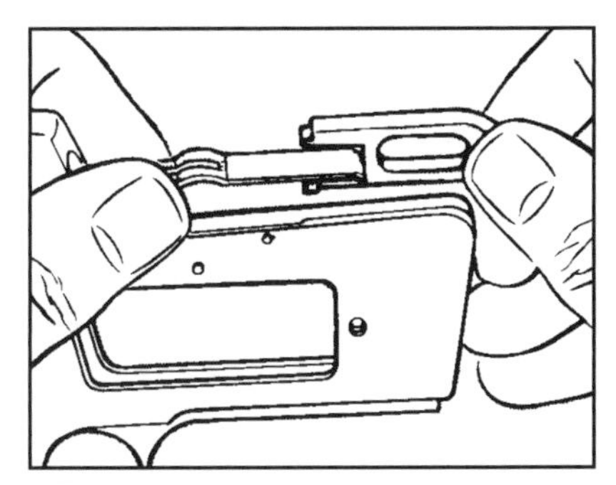

4 If gun is disassembled further, entire sear mechanism can be easily checked by removing the grips and pushing out grip safety hinge pin (29). When replacing mainspring (15), be sure tail is engaged in corresponding notch in magazine catch (14) as shown.

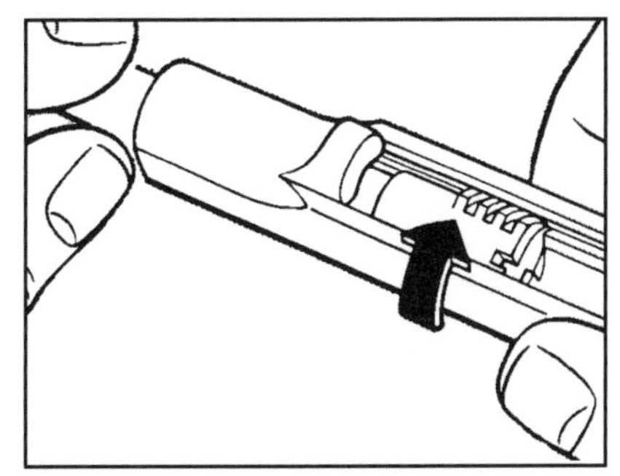

5 When reassembling gun, insert barrel into slide until barrel lugs line up with cut in slide. Then rotate barrel as far as it can go. It is now in position to allow slide to be assembled to frame.

BROWNING MODEL 1935 HI-POWER

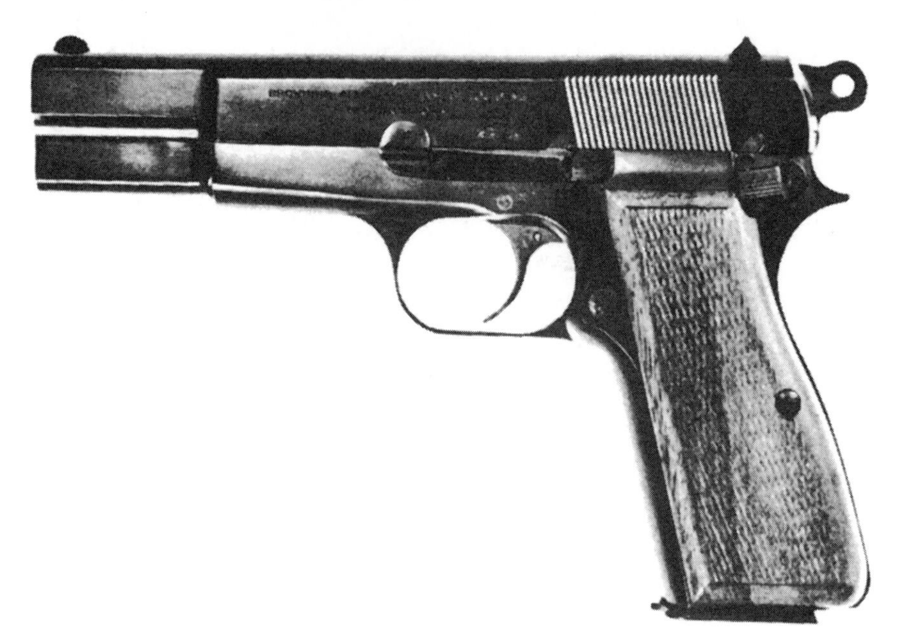

PARTS LEGEND

A. Slide
B. Sear lever retainer
C. Rear sight
D. Extractor
E. Firing pin spring
F. Firing pin
G. Magazine catch spring guide
H. Magazine catch spring
I. Magazine catch
J. Hammer
K. Hammer pin
L. Hammer strut
M. Hammer strut pin
N. Hammer spring
O. Hammer spring support
P. Magazine
Q. Sear spring
R. Left-hand grip
S. Grip screw
T. Slide stop
U. Trigger spring
V. Frame (receiver)
W. Recoil spring
X. Spring retainer
V. Detent ballspring
Z. Detent ball
AA. Recoil spring guide
BB. Barrel
CC. Sear Lever
DD. Firing pin retainer plate
EE. Sear
FF. Ejector
GG. Trigger pin
HH. Trigger spring pin
II. Trigger lever
JJ. Sear pin
KK. Safety catch
LL. Stud retainer pin
MM. Stud spring
NN. Stud
OO. Trigger

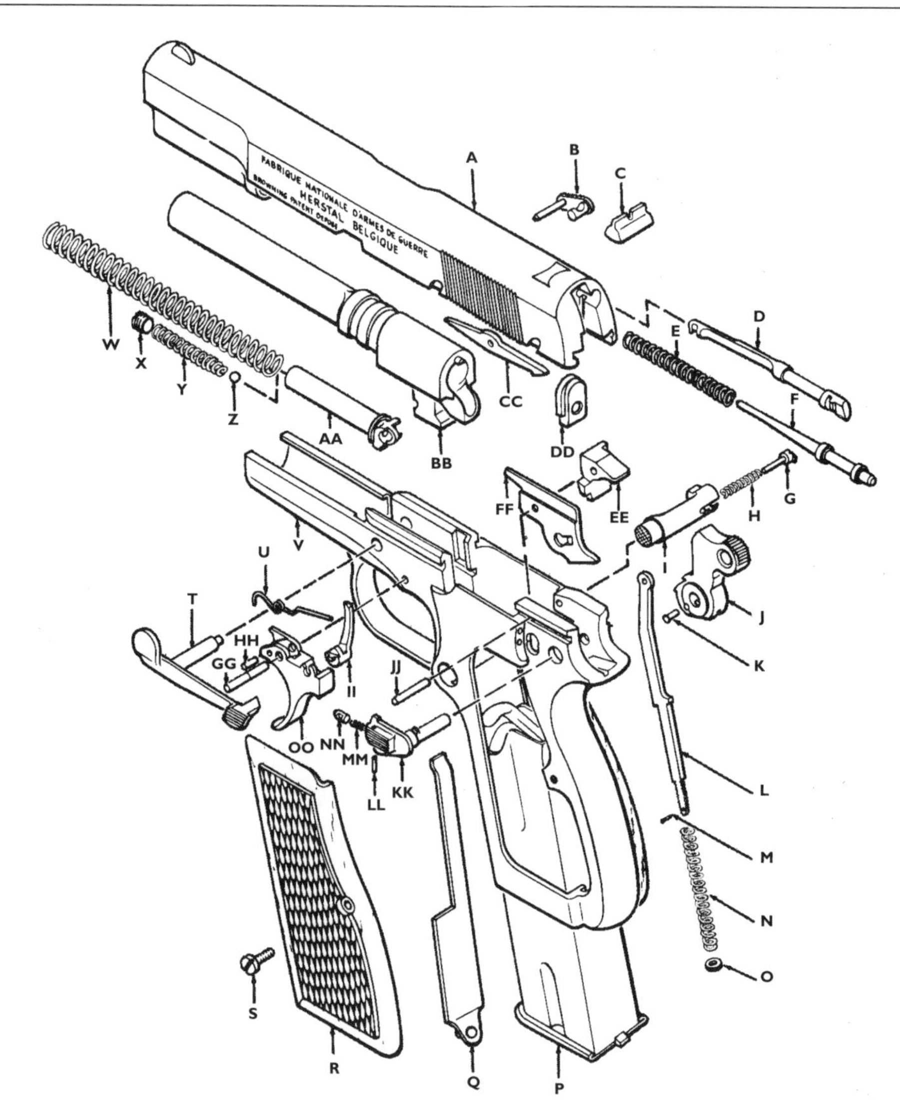

The Browning Model 1935 is considered an excellent example of what a military semi-automatic pistol should be: rugged, dependable, accurate, with a large magazine capacity.

Better known as the Browning Hi-Power, it was the last pistol designed by John Browning, and featured a double-row magazine holding 13 rounds of 9mm Luger ammunition, a 4⅛-inch barrel, a length of 7¾ inches, and a weight of approximately 2 lbs. Although patented in 1927, the gun was not produced until 1935, when it was manufactured by Fabrique Nationale for French Colonial troops. Later, a shorter 10-shot version was produced by FN for the Belgian government.

The Hi-Power was also manufactured, under license, by the John Inglis Co. of Canada, which made it in two versions during World War II for the Chinese Government. The first model was a standard holster gun with fixed sights; the second had an adjustable rear sight and could take a detachable shoulder stock for long-range shooting. The Hi-Power is still available in a variety of versions in both 9mm and .40 S&W.

DISASSEMBLY

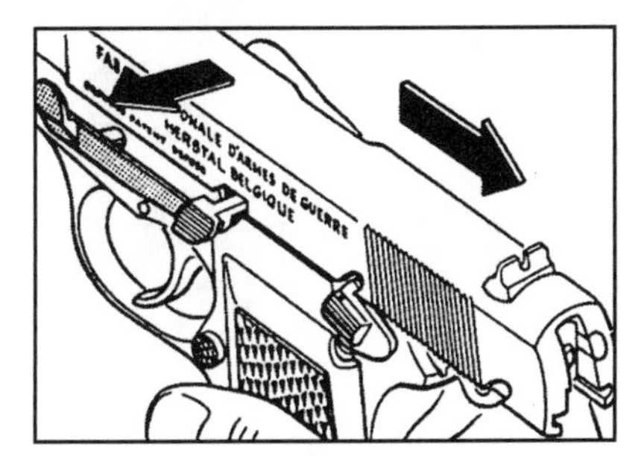

1 Remove the magazine. Pull back the slide and push the safety catch into the second notch. Push out the slide stop (T-see exploded drawing) from right to left, as shown. Release the safety catch and permit the slide to go forward and off the receiver rails.

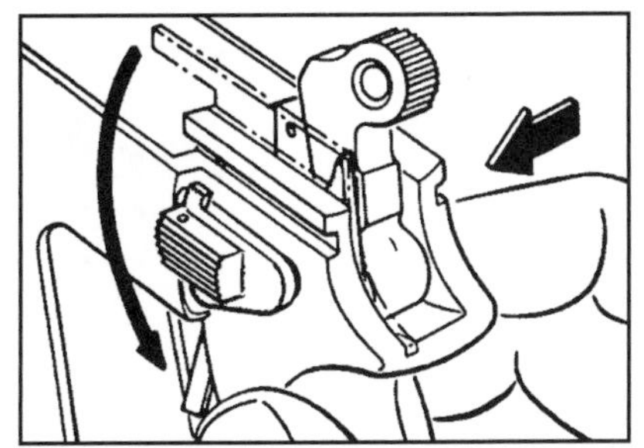

2 Push the safety catch dawn to "fire" position, then push sear pin (JJ) out from right to left. Allow the ejector (FF) to pivot down until it stops. With the ejector in this position, the safety catch (KK) can now be pushed out.

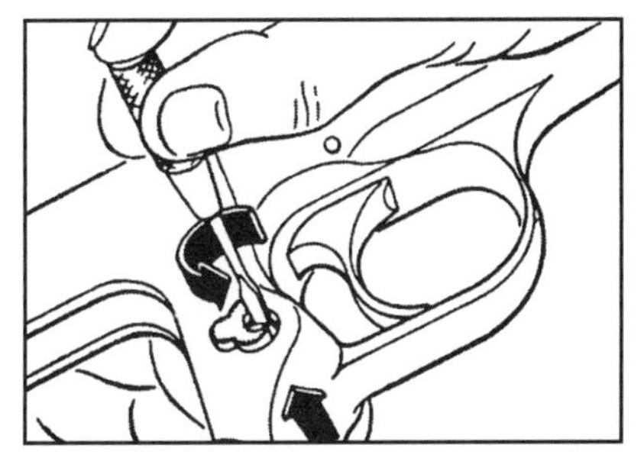

3 Hold the gun in the left hand and push in the magazine catch (I) until it is flush with frame. Using a ⅛"-wide screwdriver, turn the magazine catch spring guide (G) ¼ turn. This will lock the spring guide to the magazine catch. Then lift out the unit.

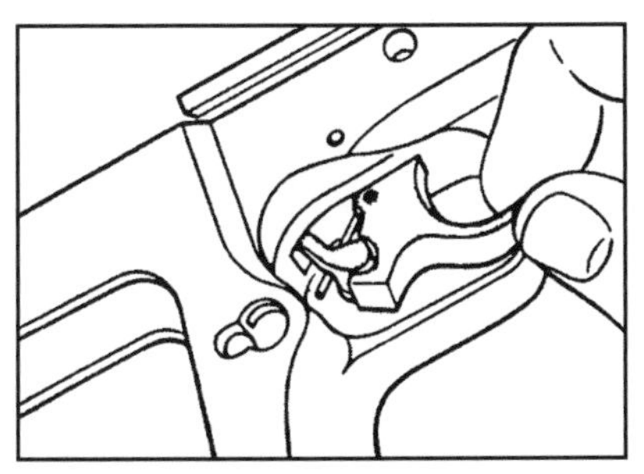

4 Push trigger pin (GG) out from right to left. Hold the gun with the right side up. With the right hand, pull the trigger forward and upward; this will allow removal of parts (U), (HH), (II), and (00) as a unit. These parts must be replaced as a unit when reassembling the gun.

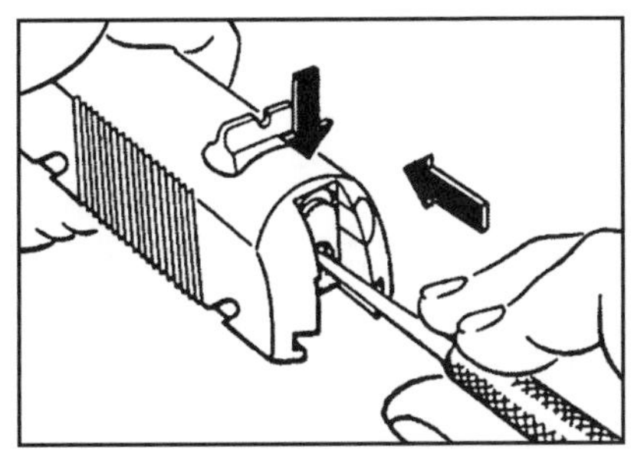

5 To remove firing pin (F) and spring (E), hold the slide in the left hand. With a ⅛" punch, push in the end of the firing pin; at the same time, push down on the firing pin retainer plate (DD). After firing pin and spring have been removed, pry out extractor (D).

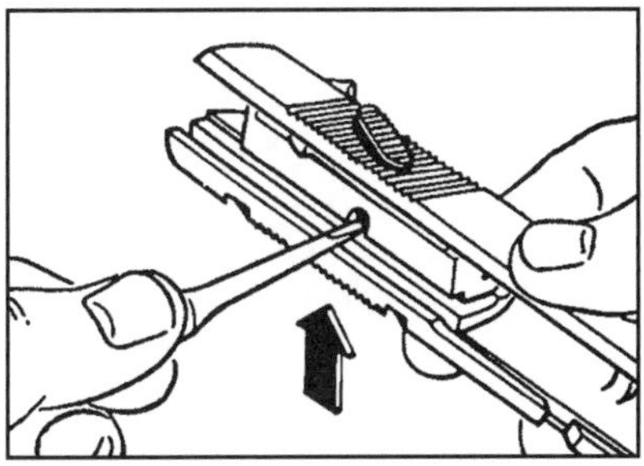

6 To remove the sear lever (CC), hold the slide upside down in the right hand. Using a small screwdriver, pry up the end of the sear lever retainer (be sure the extractor has been removed before doing this). When the head of the retainer is clear of the slide, pry it the rest of the way from the outside of the slide.

BROWNING MODEL 1936 PISTOL

This Browning handgun was never manufactured. Only a few were made, in French 7.65 Long automatic, in 1936 for French government trials.

The knurled plug in the base of the grip is a combination hammer spring guide and screwdriver.

The hammer and sear mechanism on the Browning Model 1936 is one unit.

The so-called "small version" of the Browning Model 1935 Hi-Power has come to be almost a legend among automatic pistol collectors.

The legend was that the gun was manufactured for the French by Fabrique Nationale of Belgium, and that it is a small-scale version of the Hi-Power. But that is where the story ended, at least until an original test model, serial #7, turned up on this side of the Atlantic.

The pistol pictured here was 'liberated' from the Fabrique Nationale company museum by either German or Allied troops. Ten years later, it turned up in a Washington, D. C., gun shop where it was purchased for a nominal sum by a pistol collector.

A letter to Fabrique Nationale via their American representative, the Browning Arms Co., brought a prompt informative reply:

"This model was actually never manufactured. There were a few made in 1936 for French government trials. The exact quantity is not known. It was designed for the French 7.65 Long automatic cartridge which, being considerably more powerful than the regular .32 caliber automatic pistol cartridge, required a locking system.

FN presented its models at the French trials through FN's subsidiary at that time which was known as the *Manufacture d' Armes de Paris* and explains the marking on the right-hand side of the pistol.

The tests were held at Versailles and Chalon; and according to FN, they clearly emerged the victor in the competition. In any case, the pistol gave good results; however, the French considered it too complicated. They then proceeded to make their own pistol at St. Étienne which in some respects was a copy of the FN model and which was never very successful as made by the French.

The changes made on the mechanism with respect to the present 9mm HP model were partly made to satisfy French specifications (caliber, single row magazine, front sight, and angle of grip), and partly for simplification and economy (recoil spring guide, ejector mounting, hammer and sear) and partly as necessary adaptation to the different caliber."

While the Model 1936 may look, operate, and field strip like the Hi-Power, the resemblance is only skin deep, for it has many unique and original features. Probably the greatest point of difference between the Models 1935 and 1936 is in the hammer and sear mechanism. This new mechanism is a removable assembly, similar to the Swiss Neuhausen SP47/8 or the Russian Tokarev. It is held in the frame by a large-headed pin and the safety catch. A cartridge case is the only tool necessary to remove the large-headed pin. When the pin is pried out, it frees the safety catch so that it can be removed. Then the entire sear mechanism can be lifted out of the frame. A simple, rugged and compact assembly, it also contains the magazine safety mechanism that prevents the gun from being fired when the magazine is out of the gun. Additionally, it holds the disconnector, which prevents full-auto firing, or firing before the gun is fully locked. The Model 1936 sear assembly encloses the hammer and sear in one block, in their relative operating positions for repair or adjustment.

Another interesting feature of the pistol is the inclusion of a small screwdriver in the butt. The large knurled plug doubles as a hammer spring guide and a screwdriver of just the right size to fit the screw slot in the magazine catch. However, another screwdriver is required to begin with to remove the walnut grips and get at the pin that retains the screwdriver in the butt.

Shooting this pistol is a distinct pleasure. The cartridge is not too powerful and the excellent grip shape gives the pistol an extremely comfortable feel. It weighs 28 ounces empty, is 8⅛ inches long, and has a magazine capacity of eight rounds. When compared to the Model 1935 Hi-Power, the so-called "small model" is actually 3⁄8 inch longer.

BROWNING BUCK MARK PISTOL

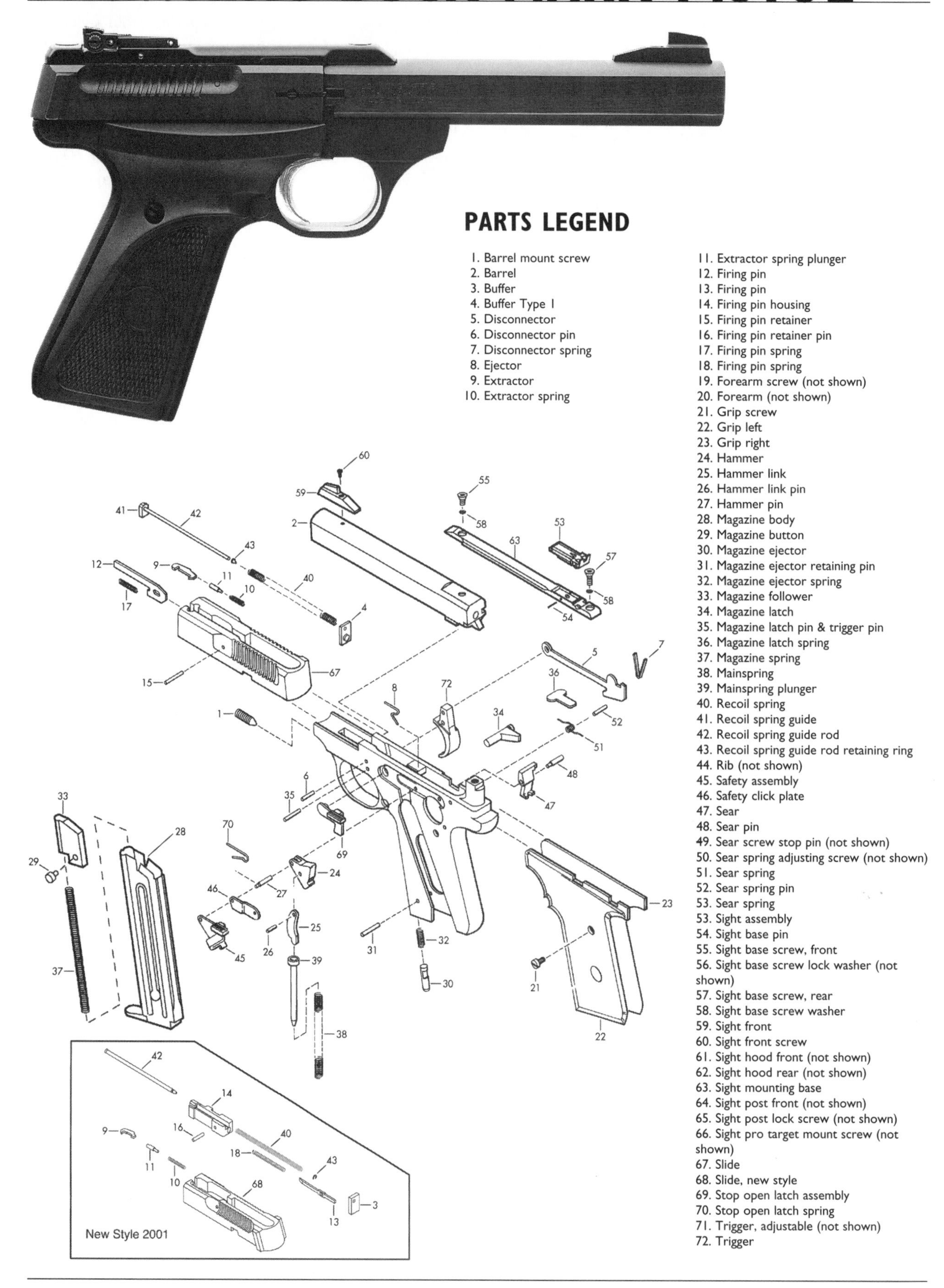

PARTS LEGEND

1. Barrel mount screw
2. Barrel
3. Buffer
4. Buffer Type I
5. Disconnector
6. Disconnector pin
7. Disconnector spring
8. Ejector
9. Extractor
10. Extractor spring
11. Extractor spring plunger
12. Firing pin
13. Firing pin
14. Firing pin housing
15. Firing pin retainer
16. Firing pin retainer pin
17. Firing pin spring
18. Firing pin spring
19. Forearm screw (not shown)
20. Forearm (not shown)
21. Grip screw
22. Grip left
23. Grip right
24. Hammer
25. Hammer link
26. Hammer link pin
27. Hammer pin
28. Magazine body
29. Magazine button
30. Magazine ejector
31. Magazine ejector retaining pin
32. Magazine ejector spring
33. Magazine follower
34. Magazine latch
35. Magazine latch pin & trigger pin
36. Magazine latch spring
37. Magazine spring
38. Mainspring
39. Mainspring plunger
40. Recoil spring
41. Recoil spring guide
42. Recoil spring guide rod
43. Recoil spring guide rod retaining ring
44. Rib (not shown)
45. Safety assembly
46. Safety click plate
47. Sear
48. Sear pin
49. Sear screw stop pin (not shown)
50. Sear spring adjusting screw (not shown)
51. Sear spring
52. Sear spring pin
53. Sear spring
53. Sight assembly
54. Sight base pin
55. Sight base screw, front
56. Sight base screw lock washer (not shown)
57. Sight base screw, rear
58. Sight base screw washer
59. Sight front
60. Sight front screw
61. Sight hood front (not shown)
62. Sight hood rear (not shown)
63. Sight mounting base
64. Sight post front (not shown)
65. Sight post lock screw (not shown)
66. Sight pro target mount screw (not shown)
67. Slide
68. Slide, new style
69. Stop open latch assembly
70. Stop open latch spring
71. Trigger, adjustable (not shown)
72. Trigger

Introduced in 1985, the Browning Buck Mark series of pistols evolved from John M. Browning's original Woodsman design using a blowback action with removable magazine. The rimfire semi-auto was designed as a medium-priced, general-purpose pistol, and, in the more than two decades since its introduction, Browning has used the Buck Mark frame as the basis for a wide variety of models ranging from weekend "plinkers" and camp guns to serious competition target models. As of this writing (2007), Browning catalogs around two dozen Buck Mark variants.

Among the Buck Mark's more interesting features is a cover that forms the rear sight base, running nearly the length of the action on top of the slide. The cover is fastened in place by two Allen-head screws, and when they are removed, the entire base, including the rear sight, can be lifted off. This exposes the top of the action and allows for easy removal the recoil rod and slide.

DISASSEMBLY

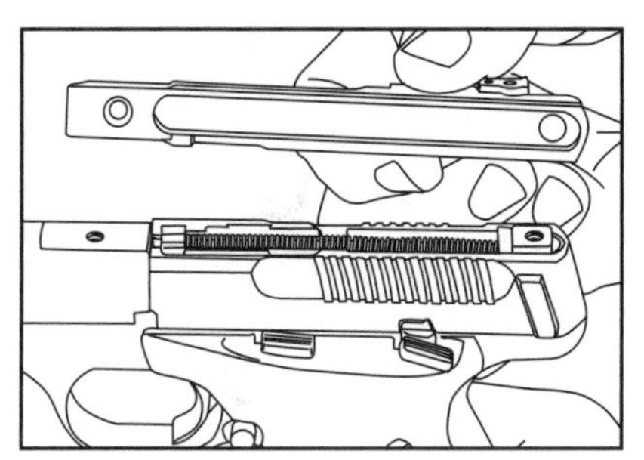

1 Remove the magazine. Draw the slide to the rear and lock it open with the slide stop open latch. Release the slide stop open latch and allow the slide to close. Remove the two sight base screws and lift the sight base – with sight attached – from the frame. Be careful not to lose the two lock washers.

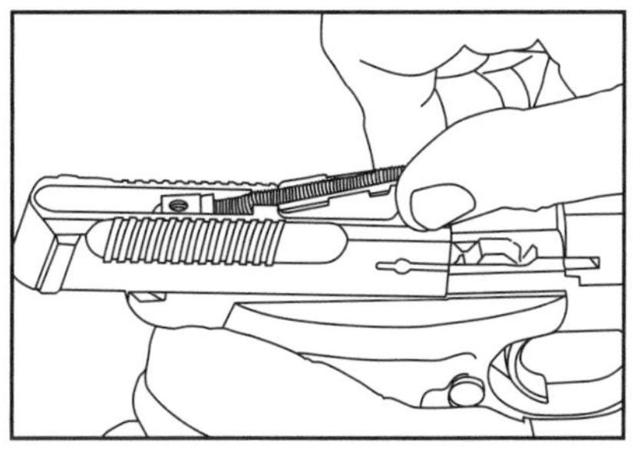

2 Pull the slide back approximately one inch and lift the recoil spring guide rod upward from the slide.

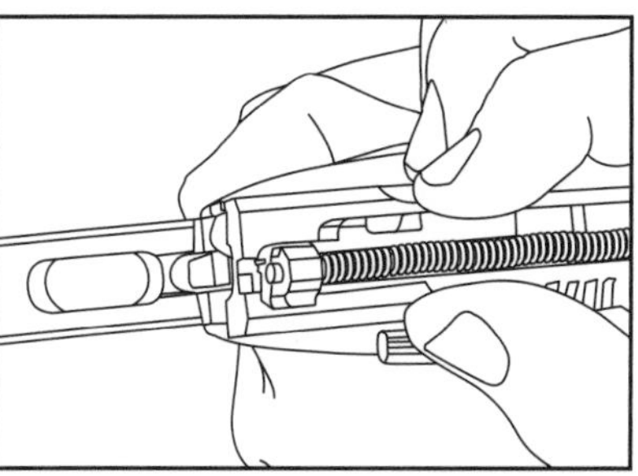

3 After lifting the recoil spring guide rod, the buffer will usually remain in place, in front of the recoil post; however, occasionally it may remain affixed to the end of the recoil spring guide rod.

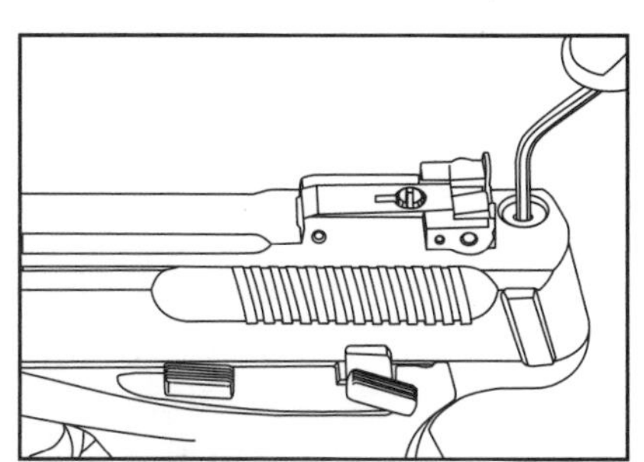

4 Remove the rear sight base screw located behind the rear sight. On Target models the sight hood may have to be removed by inserting an index finger inside the hood and pulling up and outward until it comes off. (Replace in reverse order). CAUTION: When reinstalling the rear sight base screws make certain to replace the lock washers. Always use the Browning sight base screw lockwashers supplied with the pistol.

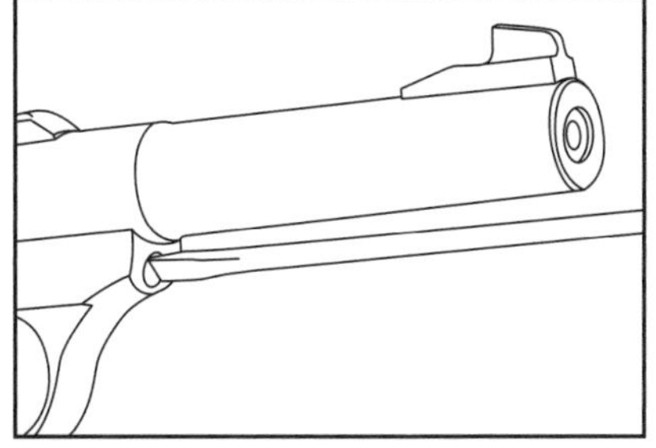

5 Loosen the barrel mounting screw – found below the barrel, at the front of the frame – approximately 3½ turns.

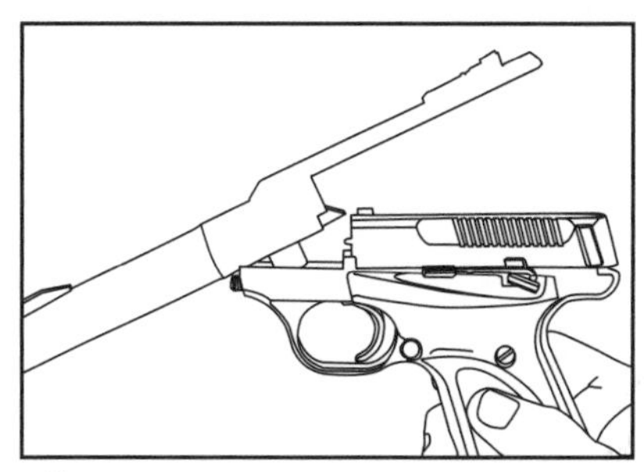

6 To remove the barrel, pull the slide back about 1 inch. Then pivot the barrel down and lift the barrel off of the frame.

BROWNING MEDALIST PISTOL

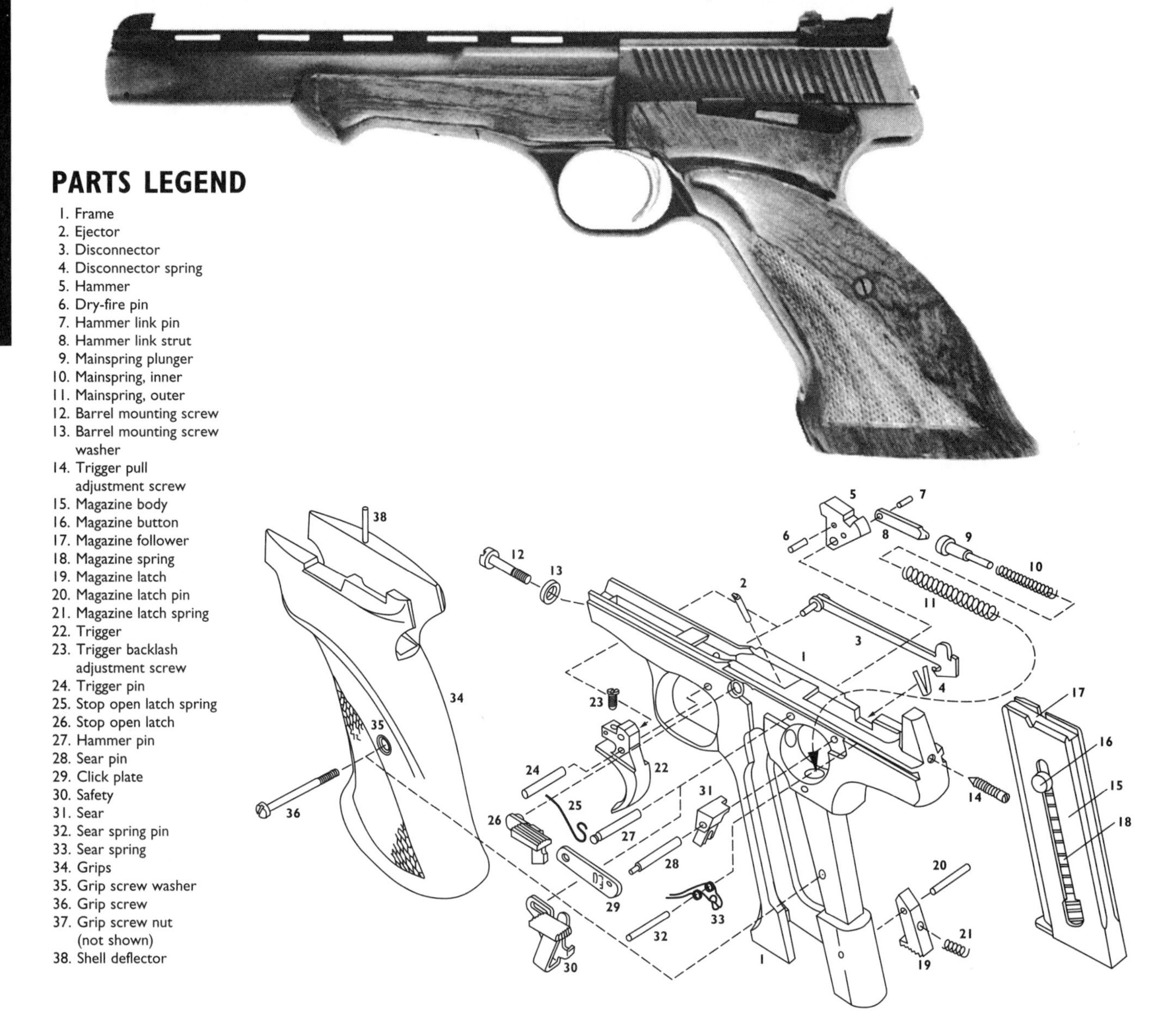

PARTS LEGEND

1. Frame
2. Ejector
3. Disconnector
4. Disconnector spring
5. Hammer
6. Dry-fire pin
7. Hammer link pin
8. Hammer link strut
9. Mainspring plunger
10. Mainspring, inner
11. Mainspring, outer
12. Barrel mounting screw
13. Barrel mounting screw washer
14. Trigger pull adjustment screw
15. Magazine body
16. Magazine button
17. Magazine follower
18. Magazine spring
19. Magazine latch
20. Magazine latch pin
21. Magazine latch spring
22. Trigger
23. Trigger backlash adjustment screw
24. Trigger pin
25. Stop open latch spring
26. Stop open latch
27. Hammer pin
28. Sear pin
29. Click plate
30. Safety
31. Sear
32. Sear spring pin
33. Sear spring
34. Grips
35. Grip screw washer
36. Grip screw
37. Grip screw nut (not shown)
38. Shell deflector

PARTS, BARREL ASSEMBLY

A. Barrel
B. Sight blade
C. Sight blade pin
D. Barrel guide pin
E. Rear sight base
F. Elevation screw
G. Detent plunger
H. Detent plunger spring
J. Windage screw
K. Windage screw detent plunger
L. Windage screw detent spring
M. Windage screw nut
N. Elevation spring
O. Fore-end
P. Fore-end screw
Q. Fore-end screw escutcheon (not shown)
R. Barrel weight support
S. Barrel weight screw
T. Barrel weights (3)

PARTS, SLIDE ASSEMBLY

1A. Slide
2A. Recoil spring
3A. Recoil spring guide
4A. Extractor
5A. Extractor spring plunger
6A. Extractor spring
7A. Firing pin
8A. Firing pin retaining pin
9A. Firing pin spring

The Browning Medalist, in .22 Long Rifle caliber, was a self-loading pistol introduced by Browning Arms Co., of St. Louis, Missouri, in 1962. The Medalist remained part of the company's sales lineup until 1974. Made in Belgium, the Medalist pistol was designed primarily for target shooting.

It was regularly furnished with a set of hand-filling, thumb rest target grips and three accessory barrel counterweights. The sight rib, which carries both front and rear sights, is permanently attached to the barrel. The rear sight is fully adjustable for elevation and windage.

There is a dry-fire device made in combination with the mechanical safety. By activating this device the shooter can conduct realistic dry-firing exercises without retracting the slide to cock the lock mechanism before each shot. Using the dry-fire device, the sear can be engaged with the hammer by a light downward thumb pressure against the safety latch. The dry-fire device must be inactivated before the pistol can be fired with live ammunition.

Another interesting feature of the Medalist pistol is the shell deflector pin installed on the upper right side of the grip opposite the breech. The Medalist's detachable box magazine holds 10 rounds of .22 Long Rifle ammunition. The trigger is adjustable for weight of pull and overtravel. The breech of the pistol remains open after firing the last shot.

DISASSEMBLY

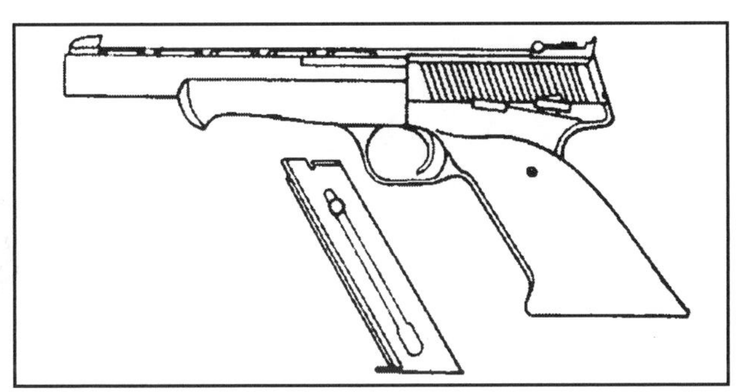

1 Check action to be sure pistol is unloaded and then remove the magazine. Pistol is shown assembled with the magazine removed.

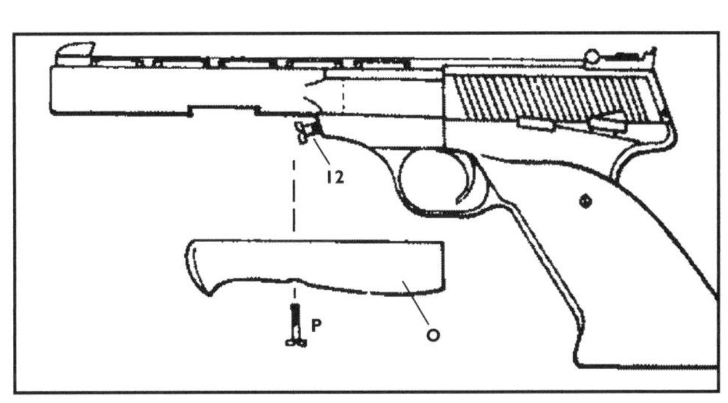

2 Loosen fore-end screw (P) and remove fore-end (0). Loosen barrel mounting screw (12) until it is felt to disengage from threads in barrel.

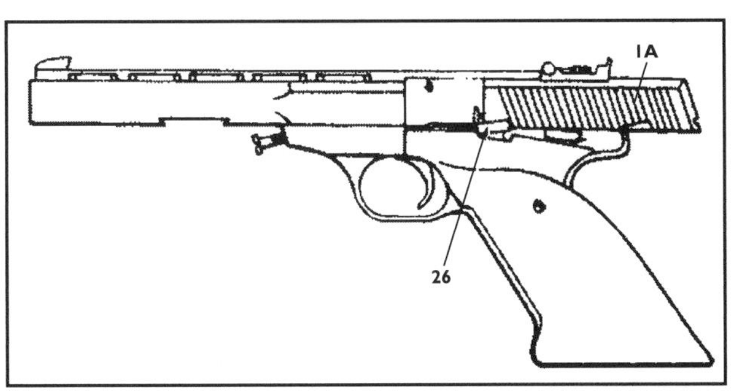

3 Pull slide (IA) all the way back and lock back by pressing up on stop open latch (26).

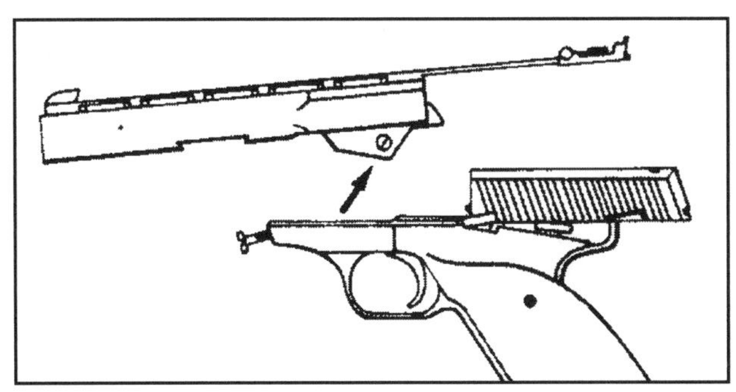

4 Slide barrel assembly rearward and upward to disengage it from the frame as shown.

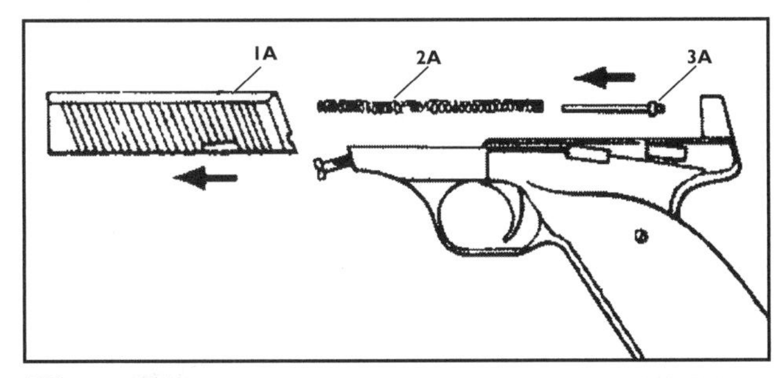

5 Press down on stop open latch (26), releasing slide (IA). Pull slide off front end of frame taking care not to allow compressed recoil spring (2A) to escape. Remove spring and recoil spring guide (3A). Further disassembly is not recommended.

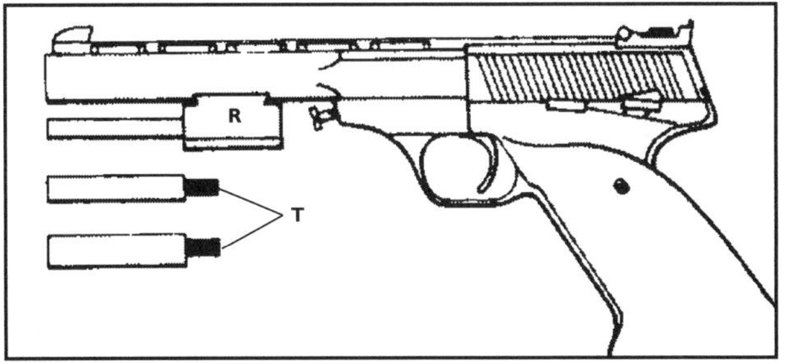

6 Pistol is shown with barrel weight support (R) fastened into dovetail under barrel with one of 3 barrel weights (T) assembled to support.

BROWNING NOMAD PISTOL

PARTS LEGEND

1. Barrel
2. Rear sight base *
3. Rear sight base mounting screw *
4. Rear sight adjusting screw, elevation
5. Rear sight adjusting screw nut
6. Rear sight
7. Rear sight adjusting screw, windage
8. Barrel guide pin
9. Slide
10. Extractor
11. Extractor plunger
12. Extractor spring
13. Firing pin spring
14. Firing pin
15. Firing pin retaining pin
16. Barrel mounting screw
17. Barrel mounting screw washer
18. Frame
19. Ejector *
20. Trigger pin
21. Trigger
22. Disconnector
23. Disconnector spring
24. Sear
25. Sear pin
26. Recoil spring
27. Recoil spring guide
28. Sear spring
29. Sear spring pin
30. Grip
31. Grip screw nut *
32. Grip screw washer *
33. Grip screw
34. Magazine latch spring
35. Magazine latch
36. Magazine latch pin
37. Magazine
38. Outer mainspring
39. Inner mainspring
40. Mainspring plunger
41. Hammer link strut
42. Hammer link pin
43. Hammer
44. Click plate
45. Safety
46. Hammer pin

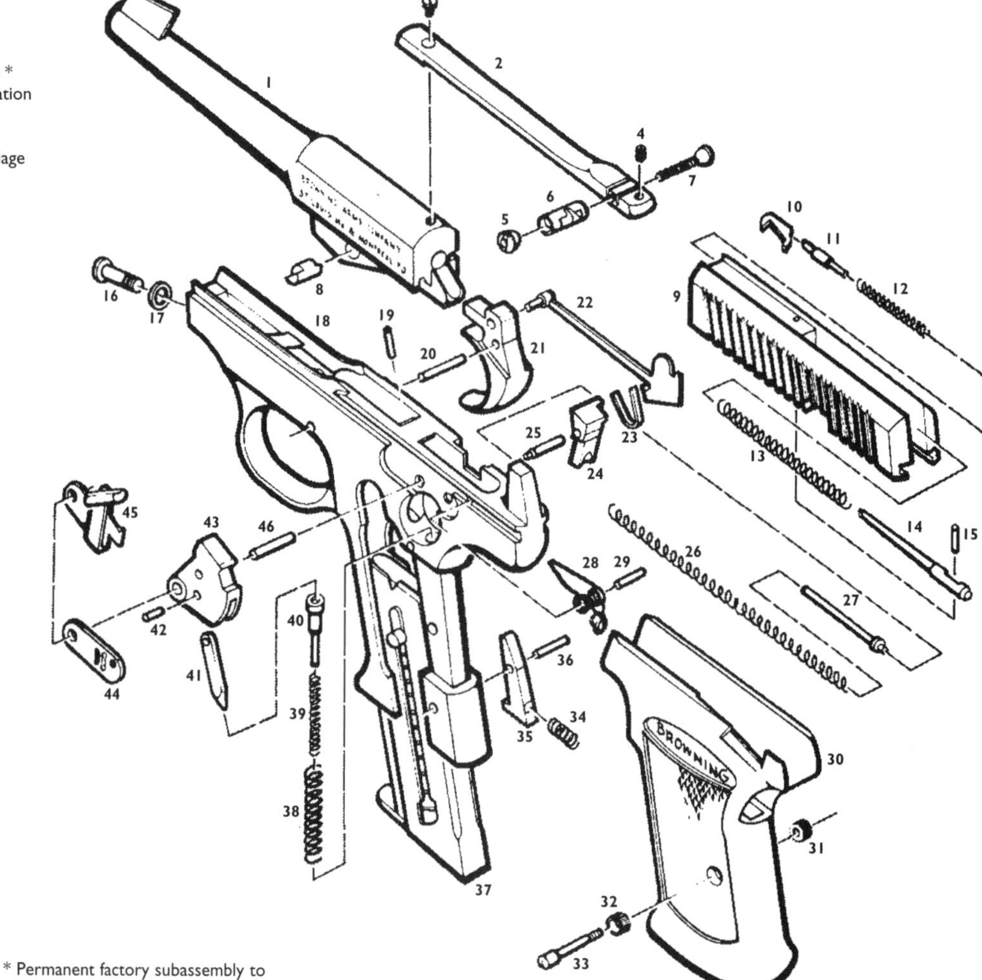

* Permanent factory subassembly to other major part.

The Belgian-made Browning Nomad self-loading pistol, chambered for the .22 Long Rifle cartridge (standard and high velocity), was introduced in 1962 and dropped in about 1973. It was blowback-operated and featured a concealed pivoting hammer.

The Nomad's frame was manufactured in lightweight alloy and other parts were steel. The black plastic grip was of one-piece construction and the side panels were sharply checkered. The detachable magazine held 10 rounds. The open rear sight was fully adjustable for elevation and windage.

The barrel was secured to the frame by a single screw and a unique wedge lock arrangement. The standard barrel was $4\frac{1}{2}$" long, but a $6\frac{3}{4}$-inch barrel was also offered. This pistol did not have an automatic slide stop or magazine disconnector.

The Browning Nomad was essentially a sport pistol, for the camper or the informal target shooter. It weighed 26 ounces and, with the standard barrel, was $8\frac{1}{8}$ inches overall.

DISASSEMBLY

1 Remove magazine (37) and coin-slotted barrel mounting screw (16) located under barrel (1) on front of frame (18). Pull slide (9) rearward and tap muzzle on a padded surface, while retaining slide in rearward position. Push barrel rearward and slightly upward to separate it from frame. Allow slide to move slowly forward and off front of frame, being careful not to lose control of recoil spring (26).

2 Remove firing pin (14) by inserting a small punch into hole on top of slide and drifting out firing pin retaining pin (15). Firing pin and firing pin spring (13) may then be removed from rear of slide. Perform this disassembly only when necessary. When replacing firing pin retaining pin, it is necessary to peen over the rim of the pin hole to keep the pin in place.

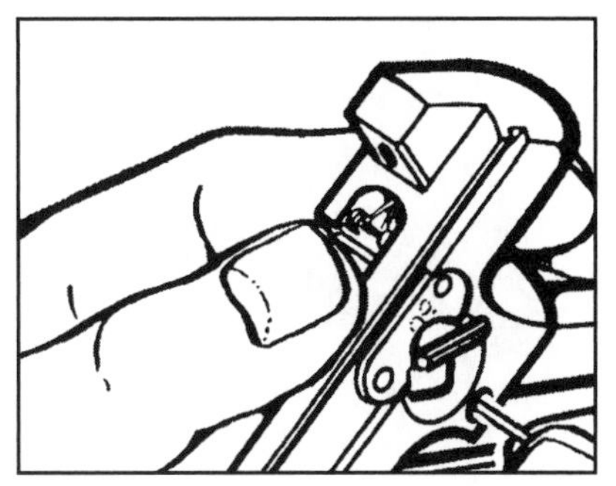

3 Remove grip screw (33) and grip (30). Depress hammer (43) with thumb until upper collar on mainspring plunger (40) is no longer visible through access hole in side of frame. Insert a long, $\frac{1}{16}$" diameter steel brad in this hole to retain mainsprings (38 and 39) fully compressed. Hammer will now move loosely.

4 Using tweezers, pluck out disconnector spring (23) from right side of frame and lift away disconnector (22). Drift out trigger pin (20, arrow) and remove trigger (21).

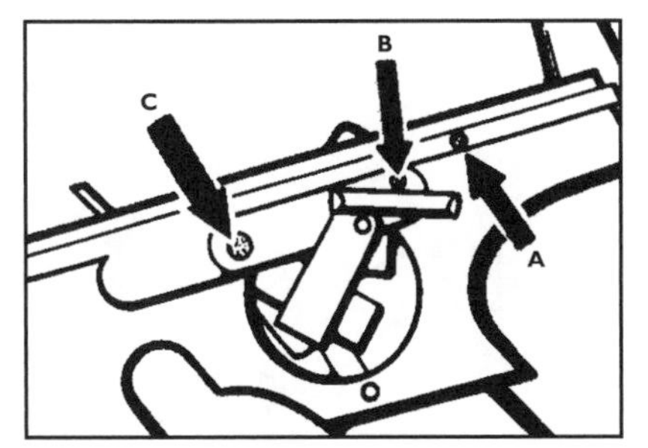

5 Continue by drifting out (A) sear spring pin (29) and remove sear spring (28). Tweezers will aid in lifting spring from slot in top of frame. Drift out (B) sear pin (25) from left to right and remove sear (24). Drift out (C) hammer pin (46) and remove hammer with attached link strut (41). The safety (45) and click plate (44) may now be removed.

6 Should it be necessary to remove mainsprings, grasp the frame using clean cotton waste to pad hand, placing thumb over slot in top of frame and over that area where springs will emerge. Withdraw steel brad inserted earlier. Springs and plunger will jump upward into padding. Reassemble arm in reverse.

BROWNING PRO-9 PISTOL

PARTS LEGEND

1. Backstrap
2. Backstrap retaining screw
3. Barrel
4. Block unlock
5. Decock lever
6. Decock lever safety detent
7. Decock rebound lever
8. Decock rebound lever spring
9. Ejector
10. Extractor
11. Extractor plunger
12. Extractor spring
13. Fire control housing
14. Fire control housing assembly
15. Fire control housing cover
16. Firing pin
17. Firing pin block
18. Firing pin block spring
19. Firing pin retainer
20. Firing pin spring
21. Frame
22. Hammer
23. Hammer bushing
24. Hammer link
25. Hammer link pin
26. Hammer pin (not shown)
27. Hammer spring, left
28. Hammer spring, right
29. Housing pin
30. Magazine catch
31. Magazine catch spring
32. Magazine disconnect assembly
33. Rail frame, left rear
34. Rail frame, left front
35. Rail frame, right front
36. Rail frame, right rear
37. Rail rear retaining spring
38. Recoil spring guide assembly
39. Sear
40. Sear actuator
41. Sear pin
42. Sear spring
43. Sight front
44. Sight rear
45. Slide
46. Slide stop lever sleeve assembly
47. Slide stop lever spring
48. Spreader horseshoe
49. Takedown lever
50. Trigger assembly
51. Trigger bar disconnect lever
52. Trigger pin

The 9mm Para Browning PRO-9 was the civilian version of the FNP9, designed by Fabrique Nationale of Belgium. Introduced in 2003, the PRO-9 was manufactured at the FN factory in Herstal, Belgium for the European market, and at FN Manufacturing, Inc. in Columbia, South Carolina for the U.S. market. The PRO-9, intended for police and security forces as well as for self-defense, was also cataloged in .40 S&W as the PRO-40.

The PRO-9 is a double-action, short-recoil-operated pistol with a SIG-Sauer-style tilting-barrel locking system, a black polymer frame, a 16-round magazine, and Walther-style interchangeable grip backstraps. Other features include an exposed hammer with an internal firing pin safety, an ambidextrous frame-mounted decocking lever, and a hammer/trigger module that detaches as a single unit. In addition, the front section of the frame under the barrel forms an integral accessory rail.

No longer carried in the Browning line, the pistol is listed in FN's U.S. catalog as the FNP-9. Also listed are the compact FNP-9M, the FNP-40 (.40 S&W) and the FNP-45 (.45 ACP).

DISASSEMBLY

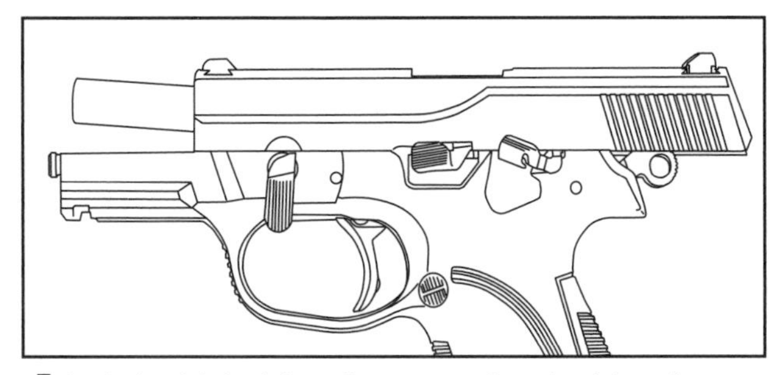

1 Lock the slide back by pulling rearward on the slide and engaging the slide release/stop latch into the notch on the slide. Rotate the takedown lever clockwise slightly more than 90° until it remains in place. If it is not rotated sufficiently it will jump back to its original position.

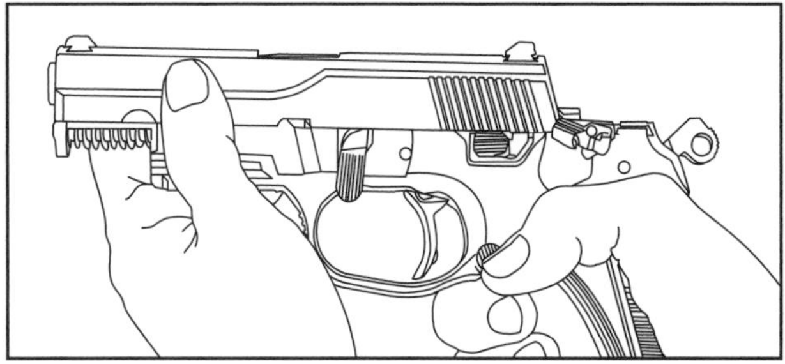

2 While holding the frame with one hand and the slide with the other hand, pull the slide slightly rearward to release the slide release/stop latch, then guide the slide forward off of the frame. The slide will be under spring pressure for part of its travel, then push it entirely off the frame and remove.

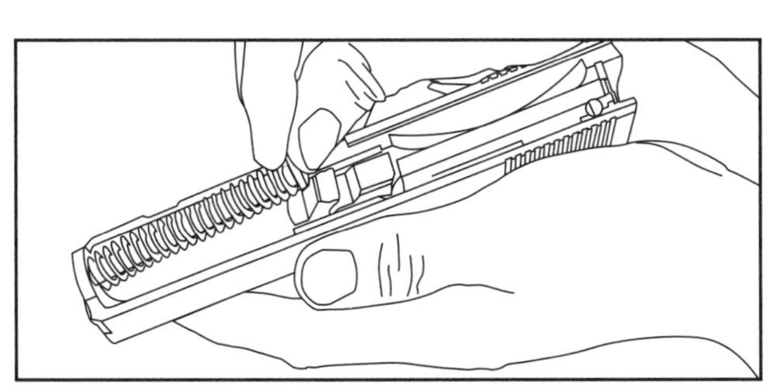

3 While holding the slide with one hand, grasp the spring guide assembly. Press the head of the recoil spring guide forward slightly to disengage the head of the recoil spring guide from the barrel lug. Then you can remove the recoil spring assembly. CAUTION: Never try to disassemble the recoil spring guide assembly.

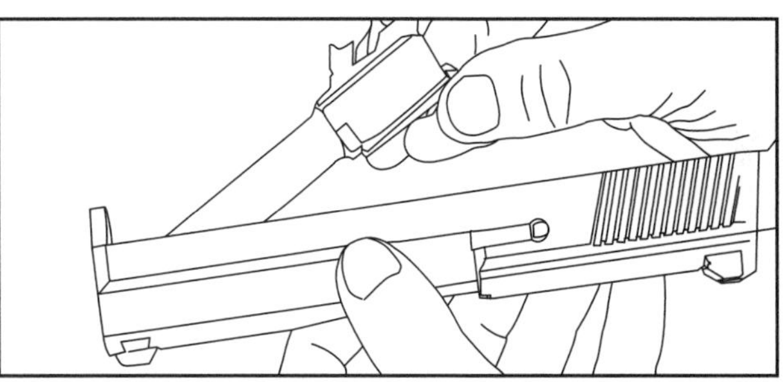

4 To remove the barrel from the slide, lift up the barrel lug and slide the barrel out rearward. Disassembly to this point is sufficient for normal maintenance of your pistol. Disassembly beyond this point is rarely necessary. WARNING: If further disassembly should become necessary it should be performed by an authorized Browning Service Center. Incorrect reassembly could render the Pro-9 inoperative or unsafe.

CHARTER ARMS POLICE BULLDOG

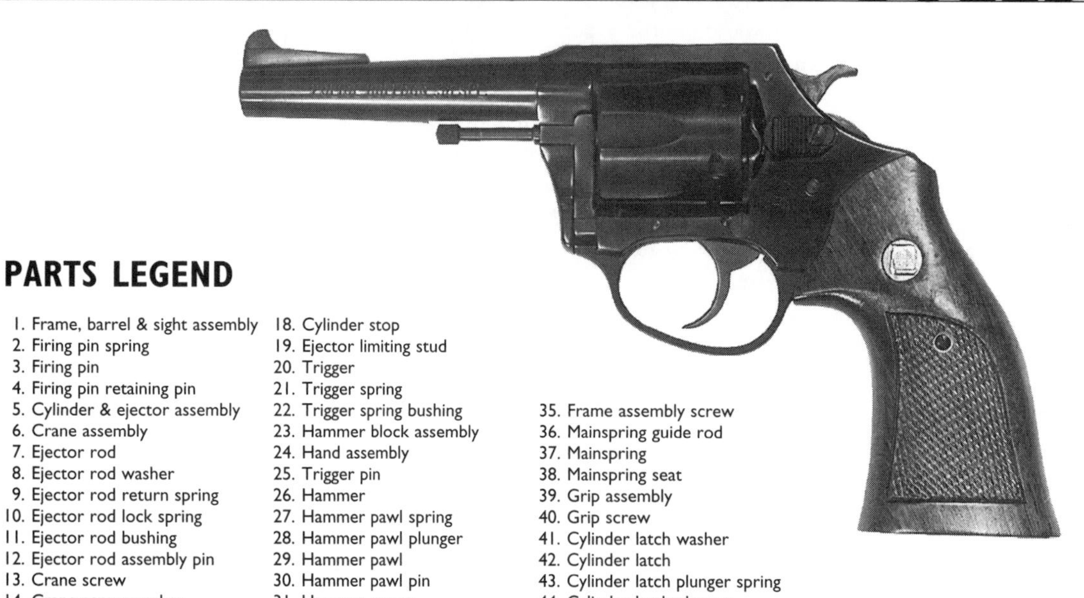

PARTS LEGEND

1. Frame, barrel & sight assembly
2. Firing pin spring
3. Firing pin
4. Firing pin retaining pin
5. Cylinder & ejector assembly
6. Crane assembly
7. Ejector rod
8. Ejector rod washer
9. Ejector rod return spring
10. Ejector rod lock spring
11. Ejector rod bushing
12. Ejector rod assembly pin
13. Crane screw
14. Crane screw washer
15. Cylinder stop bushing
16. Cylinder stop spring
17. Cylinder stop plunger
18. Cylinder stop
19. Ejector limiting stud
20. Trigger
21. Trigger spring
22. Trigger spring bushing
23. Hammer block assembly
24. Hand assembly
25. Trigger pin
26. Hammer
27. Hammer pawl spring
28. Hammer pawl plunger
29. Hammer pawl
30. Hammer pawl pin
31. Hammer screw
32. Grip frame
33. Cylinder stop retaining pin
34. Frame assembly pin
35. Frame assembly screw
36. Mainspring guide rod
37. Mainspring
38. Mainspring seat
39. Grip assembly
40. Grip screw
41. Cylinder latch washer
42. Cylinder latch
43. Cylinder latch plunger spring
44. Cylinder latch plunger
45. Cylinder latch cover plate
46. Cylinder latch retaining screw
47. Cylinder latch release screw

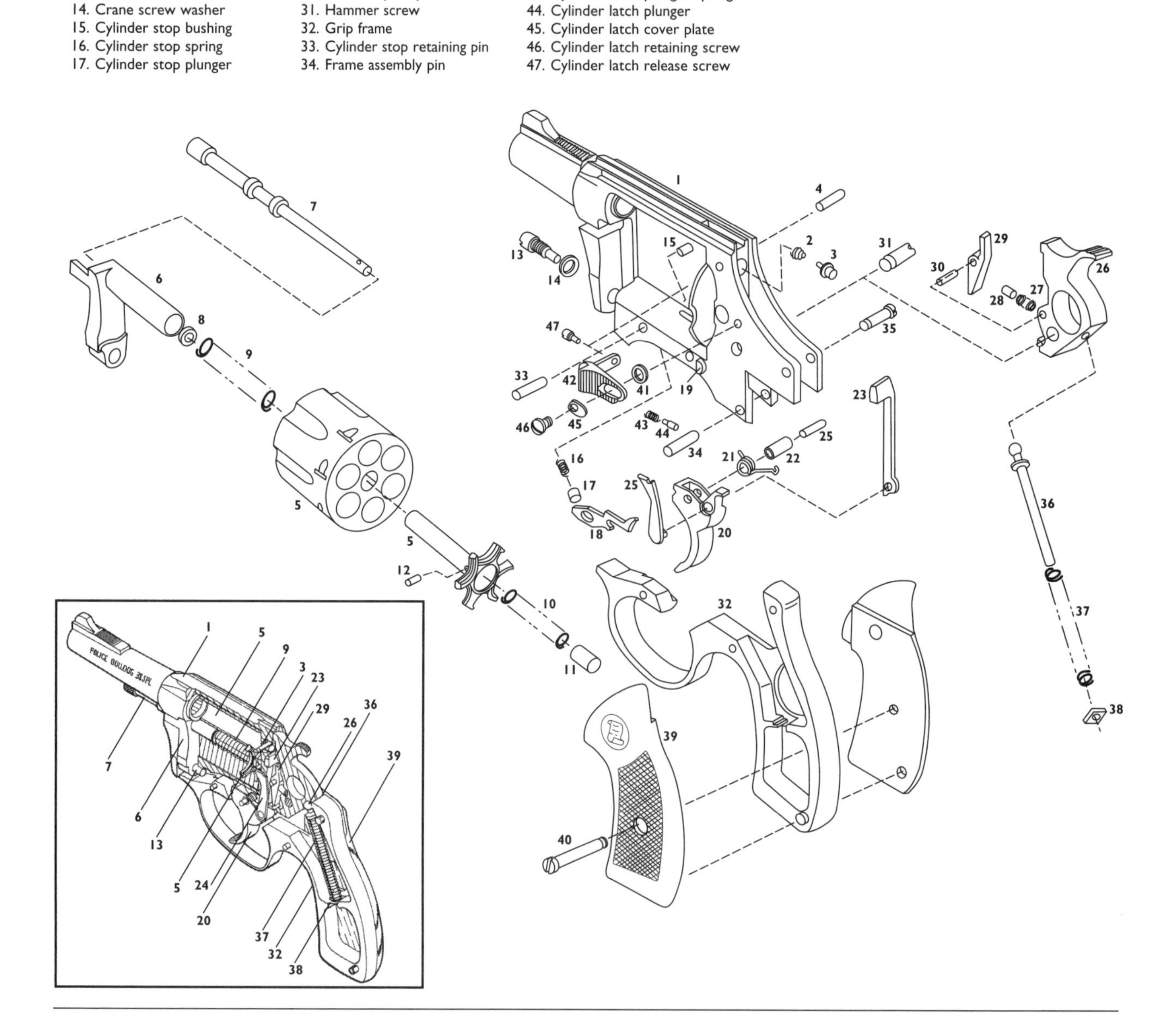

Charter Arms Corp., of Stratford, Connecticut was founded in 1964 and produced its first revolver, the Undercover, in 1965. A five-shot, .38 Spl. with a 2-inch barrel, it remained part of the Charter line for three decades.

Through the years, the company offered other revolvers in a variety of calibers. All incorporated characteristic Charter Arms design features: lightweight all-steel construction, beryllium copper firing pin, hammer block safety, and single- and double-action lockwork without a sideplate.

Built on a larger frame, the Police Bulldog was first produced in 1976 as a six-shot, fixed-sight revolver in .38 Spl., rated for +P ammunition. Later, .32 H&R Magnum, .357 Mag. and .44 Spl. chamberings were added, the last in a five-shot model. Barrels were 3½ and 4 inches. The Police Bulldog was discontinued in the early 1990s, but reintroduced in 2002, in .38 Spl. with a 4-inch barrel.

DISASSEMBLY

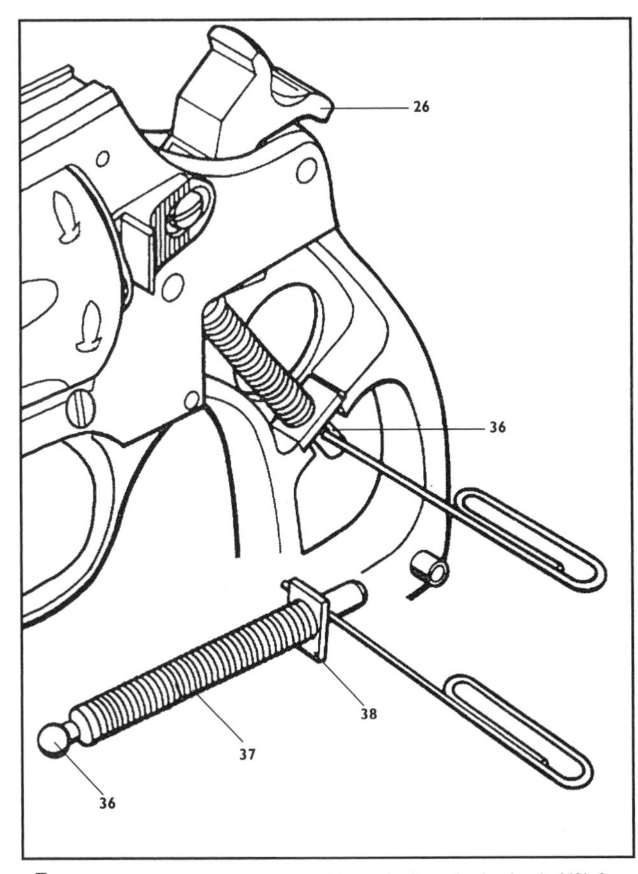

1 Before attempting any disassembly, push the cylinder latch (42) forward and swing the cylinder (5) out to be sure that it is unloaded.

To remove grip assembly (39), unscrew grip screw (40) until it protrudes above the left-hand grip surface or on larger grips is completely free. With screwdriver blade in screw slot, tap screwdriver handle inward to loosen right-hand grip. Remove screw (40) and grips (39).

Bring hammer (36) all the way back to cocked position. Insert paper clip or small pin through hole at bottom of mainspring guide rod (36). Gently lower hammer and remove entire guide rod (36), mainspring (37) and mainspring seat (38) assembly. CAUTION: If paper clip is removed from (36, 37, 39) assembly, components under compression could cause serious injury.

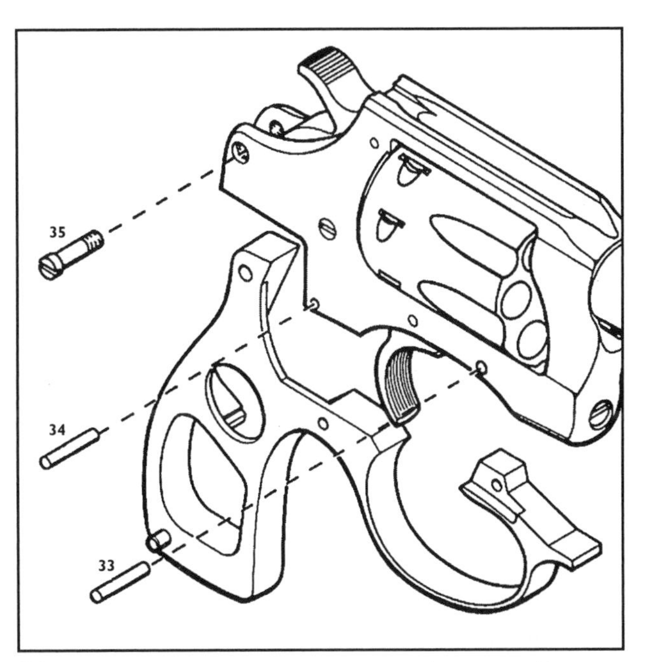

2 Disassemble grip frame (32) by removing frame assembly screw (35) from right side of frame. Then tap out frame assembly pin (34) and cylinder stop retaining pin (33). Carefully ease grip frame from bottom of frame group (1).

By removing hammer screw (31), from right side of revolver, hammer (26) can be disengaged from trigger (20) and lifted out of frame.

To remove cylinder group, remove crane screw (13) and nylon crane screw washer (14). Push forward on cylinder latch (42) and swing cylinder (5) out. Cylinder, crane assembly and the rest of cylinder group can now be removed from frame.

The preceding disassembly procedure allows for the occasional cleaning of the entire revolver. The factory does not recommend further disassembly. Reassemble in reverse order.

CHARTER ARMS UNDERCOVER

PARTS LEGEND

1. Frame and barrel assembly
2. Firing pin retaining pin
3. Firing pin spring
4. Firing pin
5. Hammer screw
6. Frame assembly pin
7. Frame assembly screw
8. Cylinder stop pin
9. Trigger pin
10. Right grip
11. Ejector rod head
12. Ejector rod collar spring
13. Ejector rod collar
14. Crane
15. Ejector rod washer
16. Ejector return spring
17. Ejector rod
18. Cylinder
19. Crane screw
20. Crane screw washer
21. Cylinder stop spring
22. Cylinder stop plunger
23. Ejector
24. Ejector rod lock spring
25. Cylinder stop
26. Ejector rod bushing
27. Ejector rod assembly pin
28. Round butt
29. Hammer pawl
30. Hammer pawl pin
31. Hammer pawl plunger
32. Hammer pawl spring
33. Hammer
34. Grip locating pin
35. Cylinder latch washer
36. Cylinder latch release screw
37. Cylinder latch
38. Cylinder latch cover plate
39. Cylinder latch retaining screw
40. Cylinder latch spring
41. Cylinder latch plunger
42. Mainspring guide rod
43. Mainspring
44. Left grip
45. Mainspring seat
46. Trigger spring
47. Hand
48. Trigger spring bushing
49. Trigger
50. Hammer block
51. Grip screw

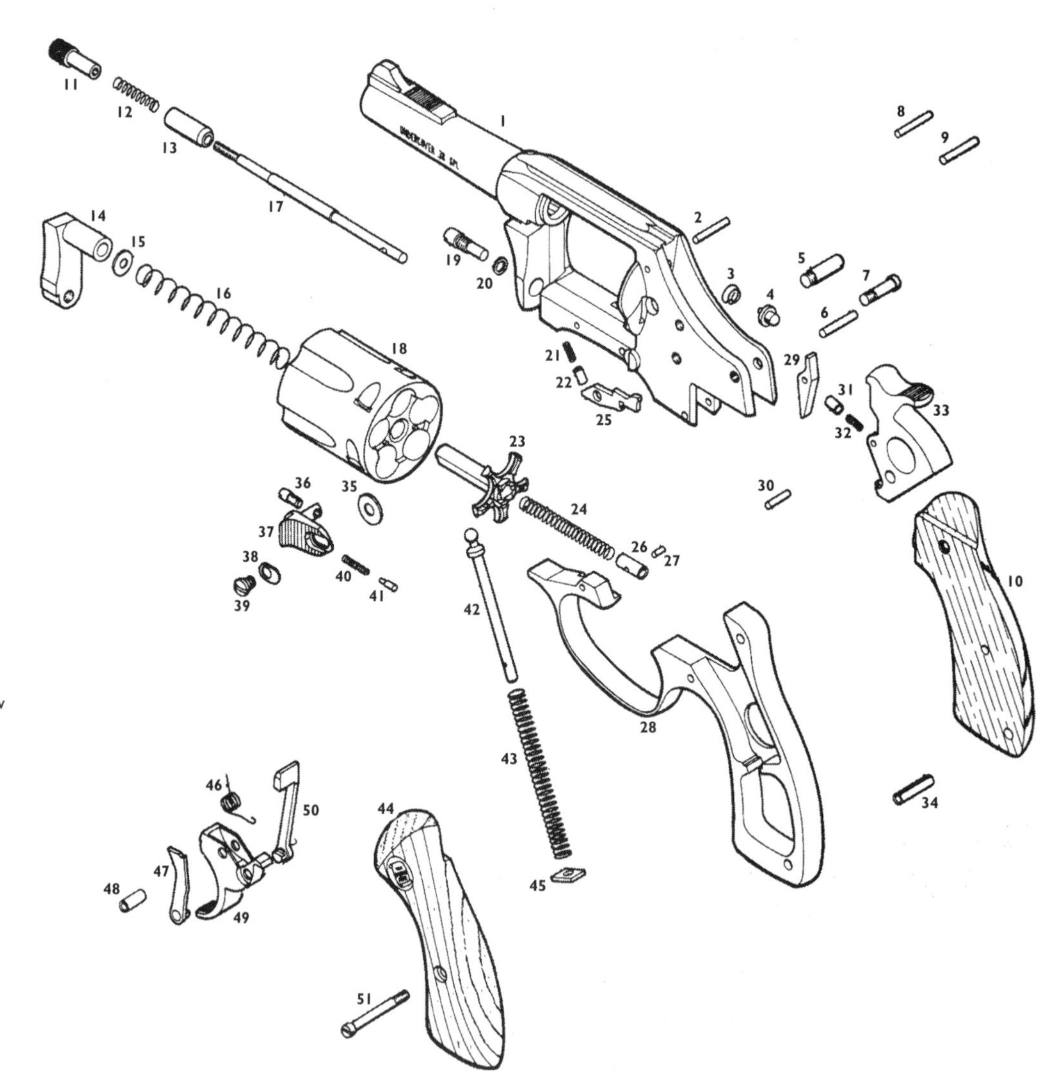

Civilians with carry permits and law-enforcement personnel alike desire a compact, lightweight, reliable and powerful handgun that can be carried concealed under clothing, either as a primary arm or as a backup. During the 1960s, most shooters felt that a short-barreled, small-frame .38 Special revolver best met these require-ments.

To satisfy this demand, in 1966 the Charter Arms Corp. of Bridgeport, Connecticut, brought out the double-action Undercover revolver. This .38 Spl. arm featured a small frame and rounded butt, a choice of 2- or 3-inch barrels, a weight (with 2-inch barrel) of only 16 ounces, an overall length of 6¼ inches and a five-shot cylinder which was smaller in diameter than a six-shot .38 Spl. cylinder. Most metal parts were of steel, except for the one-piece butt and trigger guard, made from aluminum alloy to save weight.

The Undercover lacks the sideplate typical of many modern double-action revolvers, and has simple lockwork. Coil springs are used throughout, except for the torsion-type trigger spring. Aiming is by way of a front post with a serrated ramp, and a square notch machined in the frame at the rear.

The Undercover utilizes a transfer bar safety system in which the bar (called a "hammer block" by Charter Arms) transmits the hammer blow to the frame-mounted firing pin only when the trigger is pulled to the rear. This prevents an accidental discharge if the revolver is dropped onto the hammer or the muzzle.

Later Undercover variants featured nickel plating, a pocket hammer, and a .32 S&W chambering. The original Undercover was discontinued in the mid-1990s. A new Undercover model was introduced in the late 1990s.

DISASSEMBLY

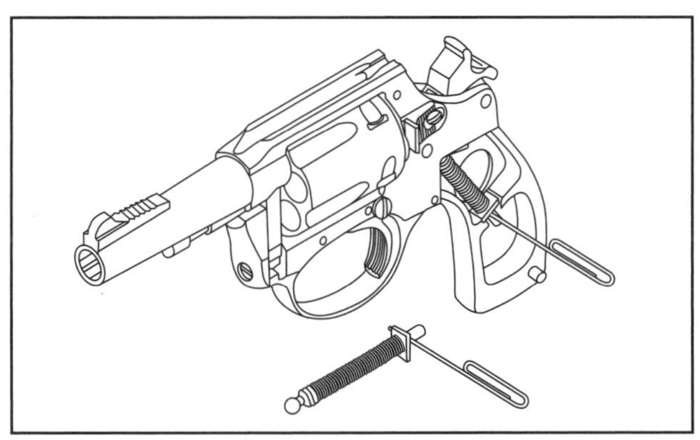

1 Press cylinder latch (37) forward and swing out cylinder (18). Make sure that gun is unloaded. Partially unscrew grip screw (51), and tap with screwdriver handle to loosen right grip (10). Remove both grips, then draw back hammer (33). Insert a straightened paper clip through hole in bottom of mainspring guide rod (42), pull trigger, and lower hammer gently with thumb. Remove mainspring (43), seat (45), and guide rod as an assembly.

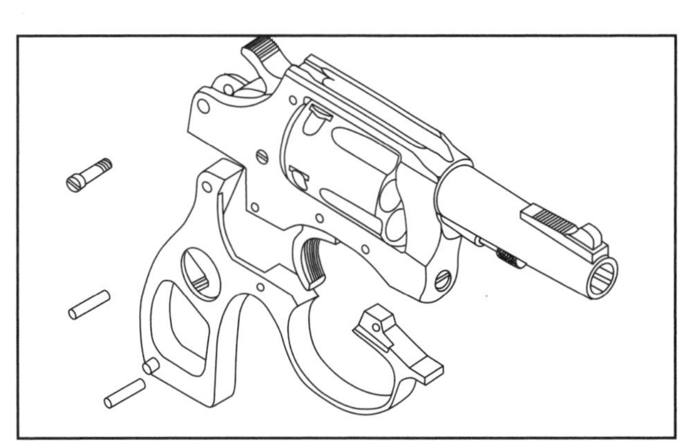

2 Unscrew frame assembly screw (7), and drift out frame assembly pin (6) and cylinder stop pin (8). Butt (28) can now be removed from frame (1).

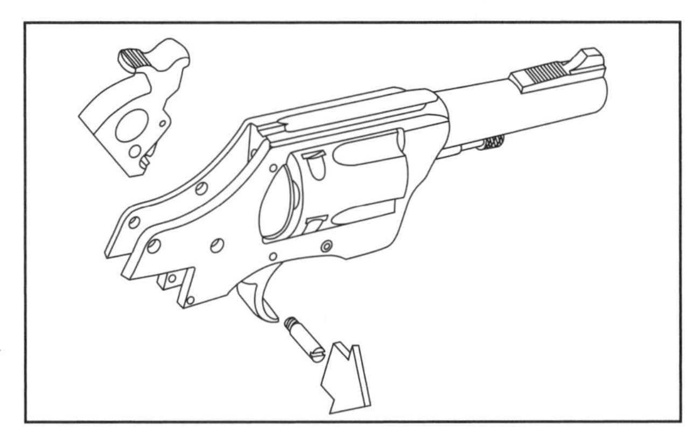

3 Unscrew hammer screw (5), and lift hammer from frame. All moving lock-work parts are now accessible for cleaning and lubrication.

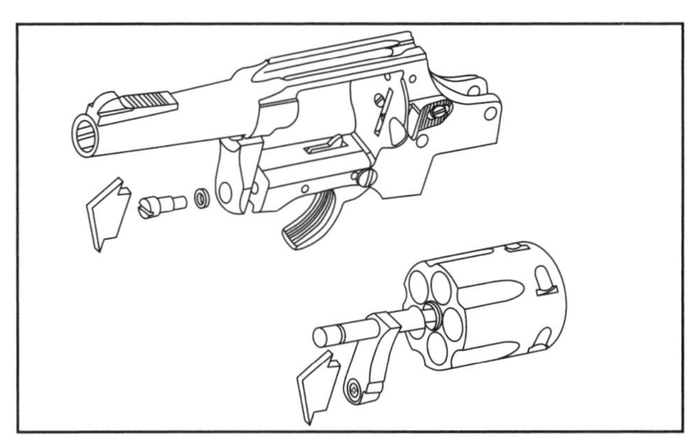

4 To remove fouling from bushing portion of crane (14), unscrew crane screw (19), and remove it along with its nylon washer (20). Then dismount cylinder from frame. Draw crane forward out of cylinder to clean the crane bushing. Further disassembly is not recommended. Reassemble in reverse.

COLT .22-.45 CONVERSION UNIT

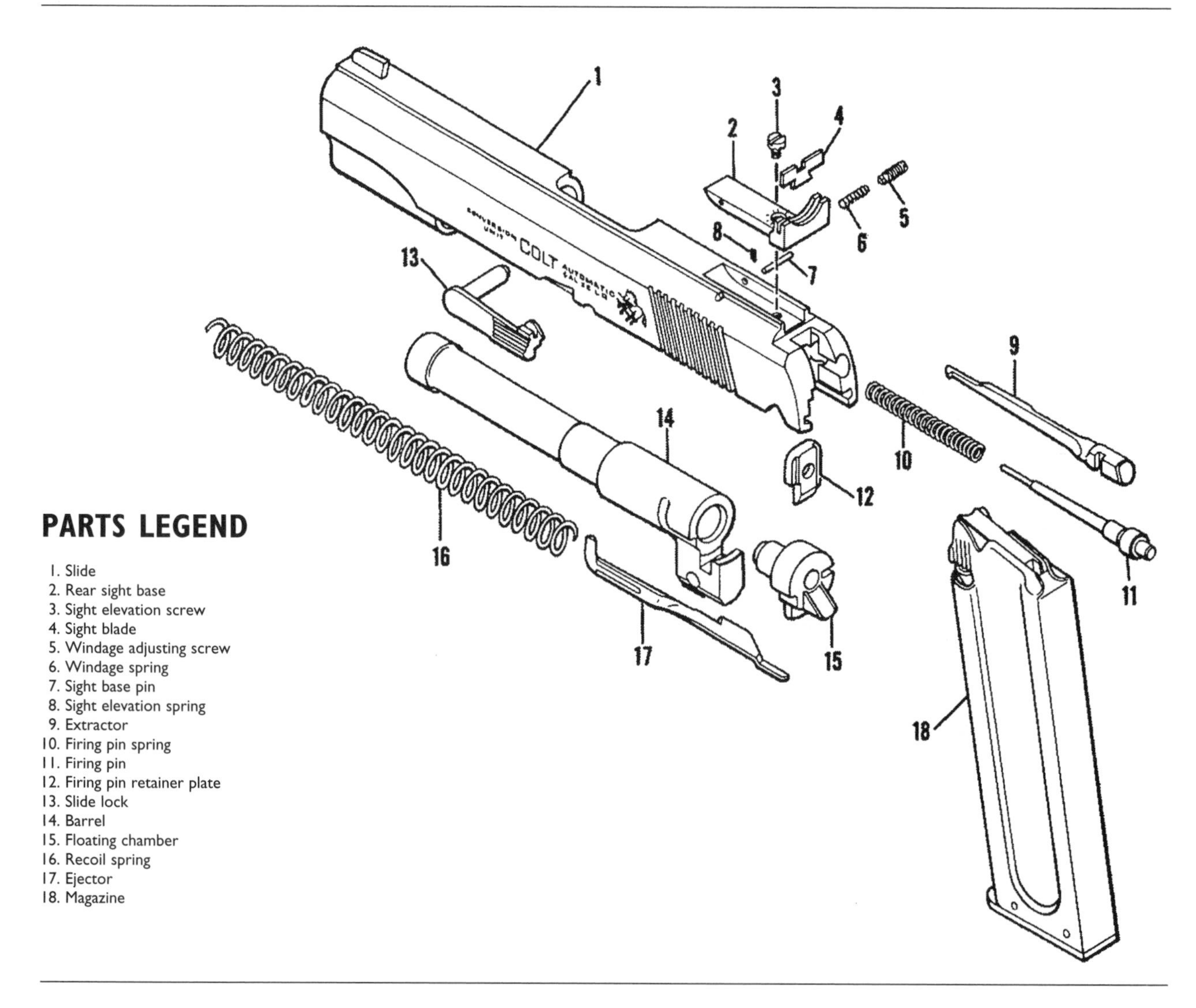

PARTS LEGEND

1. Slide
2. Rear sight base
3. Sight elevation screw
4. Sight blade
5. Windage adjusting screw
6. Windage spring
7. Sight base pin
8. Sight elevation spring
9. Extractor
10. Firing pin spring
11. Firing pin
12. Firing pin retainer plate
13. Slide lock
14. Barrel
15. Floating chamber
16. Recoil spring
17. Ejector
18. Magazine

In 1931, Colt's Patent Firearms Mfg. Co brought out the Ace, and in 1937, an improved version of this, known as the Service Ace. Both were rimfire pistols were built on an M1911 frame, and featured adjustable sights and approximately the same size, weight and appearance as a 5-inch barreled Government Model pistol. The Service Ace was best known for its "floating chamber," invented by David "Carbine" Williams and designed to give a recoil impulse like that developed by the .45 ACP cartridge. The floating chamber was effectively a movable piston attached to the rear of the barrel. Propellant gases trapped between the barrel and the floating chamber would impel the chamber rearward with enough force to operate the slide and thus simulate the recoil of the .45 ACP.

Colts has also produced a number of kits allowing conversion of .45 ACP pistols to .22 LR. The original unit was marked "Colt Service Model Conversion;" a later model was marked ".22-.45 Conversion" on the slide. The model shown here consists of a barrel with floating chamber, complete slide assembly with Micro adjustable rear sight, slide stop, recoil spring and magazine.

Several conversion units have been offered over the years, with models for installation on different Government Model pistols, such as the Series 70 and Series 80 guns.

DISASSEMBLY

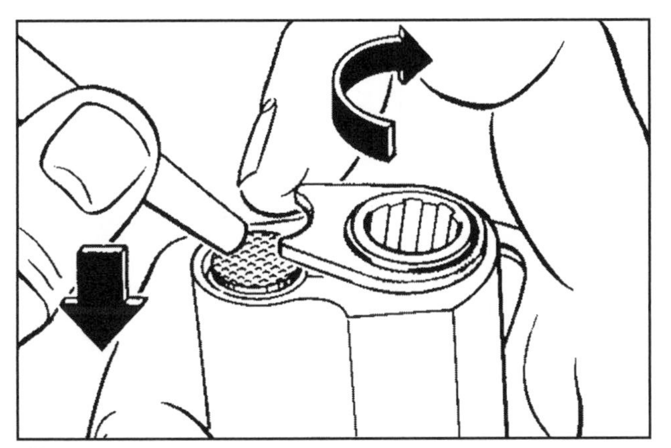

1 Centerfire slide assembly and magazine must be removed prior to installing conversion unit. First remove magazine and clear chamber. Push in knurled end of plug below barrel and rotate bushing ¼-turn clockwise. Ease out plug and recoil spring. Turn bushing counterclockwise until it can be eased off barrel.

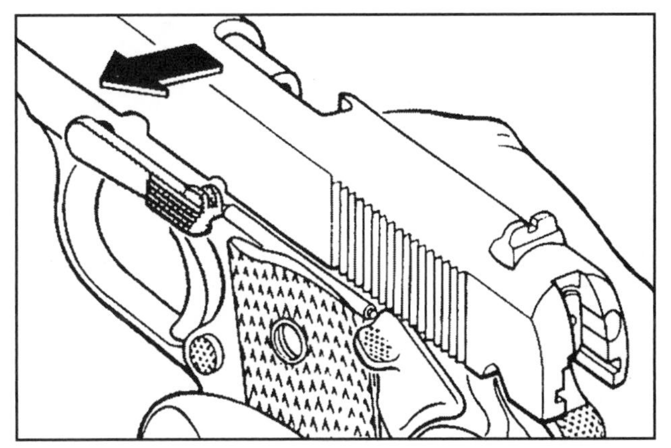

2 Pull slide to rear until smaller recess in lower edge of slide is even with end of slide stop. Press end of slide stop that projects from right side of frame and pull it free from left side. Ease slide and barrel forward off frame. Turn conversion unit upside down. Insert recoil spring guide in conversion unit recoil spring and place assembly in position on barrel. Slide conversion unit on frame. Install slide stop from the conversion unit and bushing of center-fire barrel. Place plug over recoil spring, then depress plug until bushing can be rotated ¼-turn clockwise to secure plug and recoil spring assembly in slide.

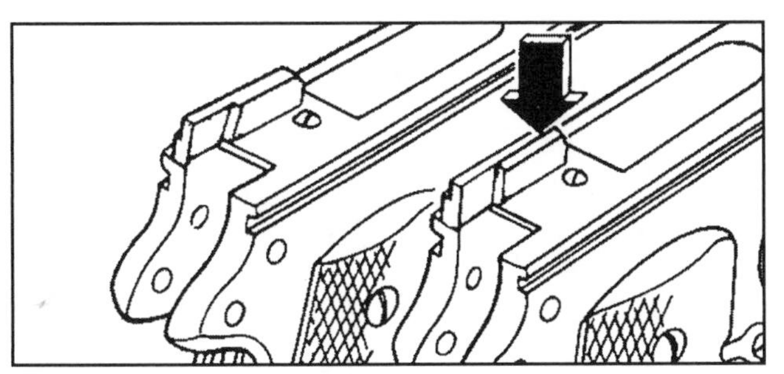

3 If conversion unit binds when installing it on a Super .38 pistol, the ejector may be at fault. To correct this, file a 1/32-inch wide bevel (arrow) along inside edge of ejector. This alteration to the gun will not affect its operation when firing .38 Super cartridges.

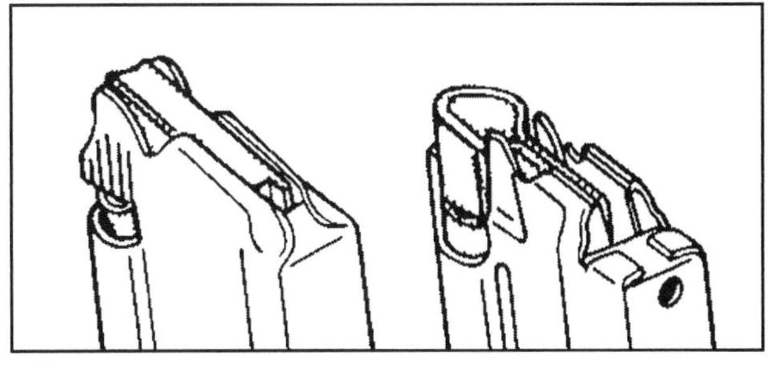

4 Colt Ace (right) and conversion unit (left) magazines are not interchangeable although they handle the same ammunition. Conversion unit magazines are usually marked as such on the base. If not, they can be recognized by the narrow follower as compared with hollow sheet metal follower of Ace magazine. Follower button on conversion unit magazine runs diagonally up the magazine, while follower button of Ace magazine runs parallel to back and front strap.

COLT AUTOMATIC CALIBER .25

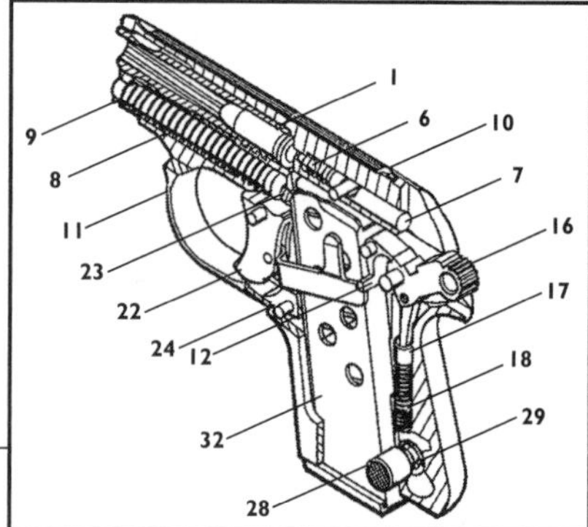

Cutaway indicates relationship between parts. Pistol is shown loaded and cocked. Parts are number keyed to parts legend.

PARTS LEGEND

1. Barrel
2. Extractor pin
3. Extractor
4. Extractor spring
5. Firing pin retaining pin
6. Firing pin spring
7. Firing pin
8. Recoil spring
9. Recoil spring guide
10. Slide
11. Frame
12. Sear
13. Sear pin
14. Sear spring
15. Hammer pin
16. Hammer w/strut & pin
17. Hammer spring guide
18. Hammer spring
19. Grip plate, right
20. Grip screw (2)
21. Trigger pin
22. Trigger w/disconnector
23. Thumb safety
24. Magazine safety
25. Magazine safety pin
26. Magazine safety spring
27. Grip plate, left
28. Magazine catch button
29. Magazine catch spring
30. Magazine catch pin
31. Magazine catch
32. Magazine

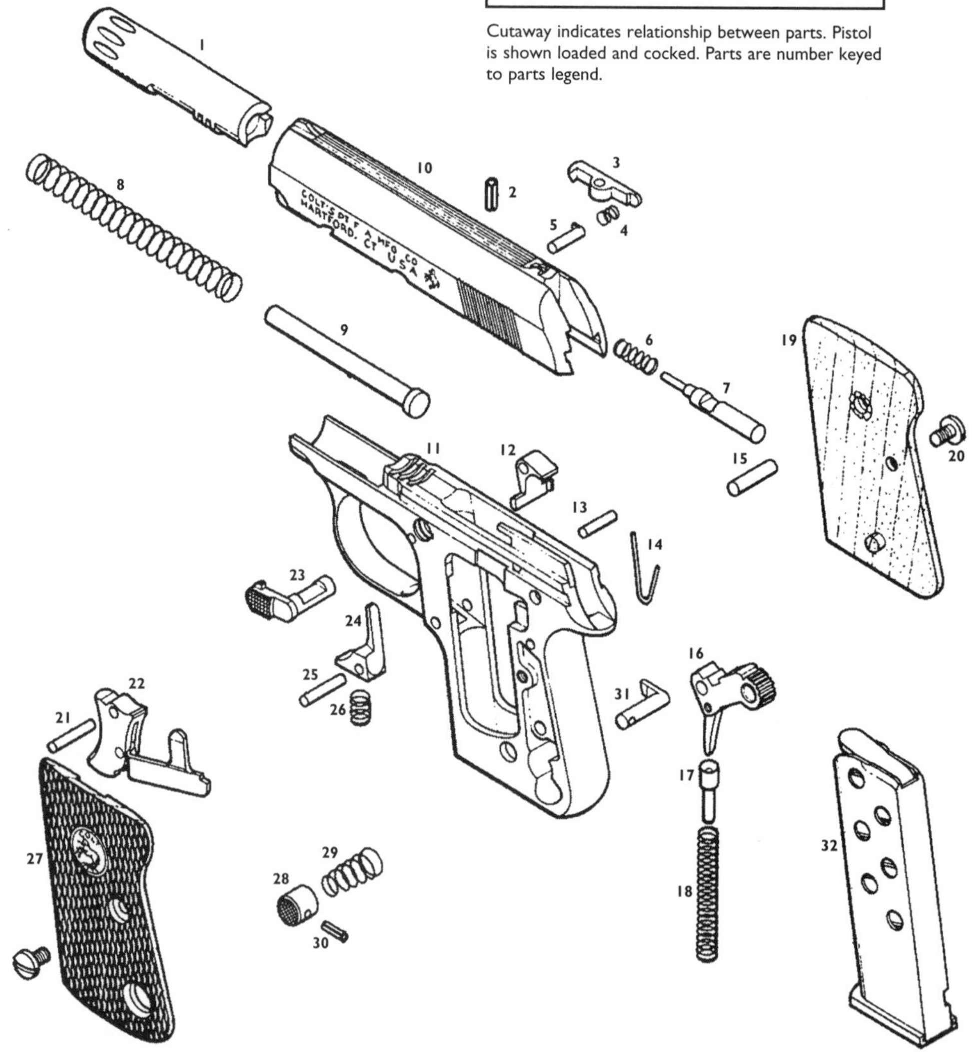

Colt's Patent Firearms Manufacturing Co., has a long history of producing .25 ACP pocket pistols, such as the Model 1908 Hammerless, developed by famed American arms designer John M. Browning, and the Colt Junior, introduced in 1958 and made by Unceta & Cia. in Spain.

The 1968 Gun Control Act stopped importation of the Junior, which Colt replaced in 1970 with the Colt Automatic Caliber .25, also made for the company by another manufacturer. This blowback-operated pistol weighed 12½ ounces and measured 4⅛ inches long, and featured integral fixed sights, a mechanical thumb safety/slide hold-open device, an exposed hammer, and a magazine disconnector that prevented firing when the six-shot magazine was removed.

The lack of a rebounding firing pin in the original Colt Junior and .25 Auto allowed the tip of the firing pin to contact the primer of a chambered cartridge when the hammer was fully lowered, making the pistol unsafe to carry with a round in the chamber and the hammer down. A recall issued in the mid-1980s allowed Colt to retrofit returned pistols with a rebounding firing pin.

The Colt Automatic Caliber .25 was discontinued in 1975.

DISASSEMBLY

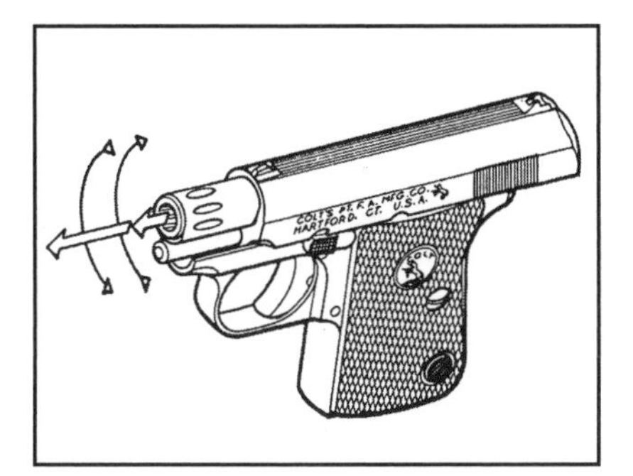

1 Begin takedown by moving safety (23) upward to safe position. Depress magazine-catch button (28) and remove magazine (32). Draw slide (10) fully rear-ward to clear chamber. Safety will engage slide, locking it open. Rotate barrel (1) ⅜ turn clockwise and pull forward as far as it will go. Then rotate it ⅜ turn counterclockwise and remove from slide.

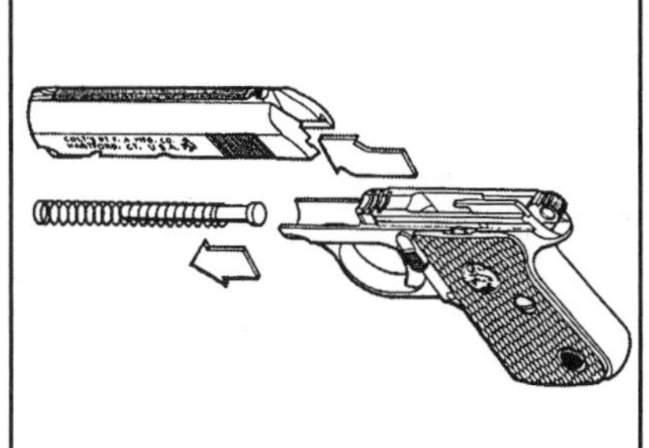

2 Grasp slide firmly and move safety downward to "fire" position. Ease slide forward off frame (11). Remove recoil spring (8) and guide (9) from frame tunnel. This is sufficient disassembly for normal cleaning.

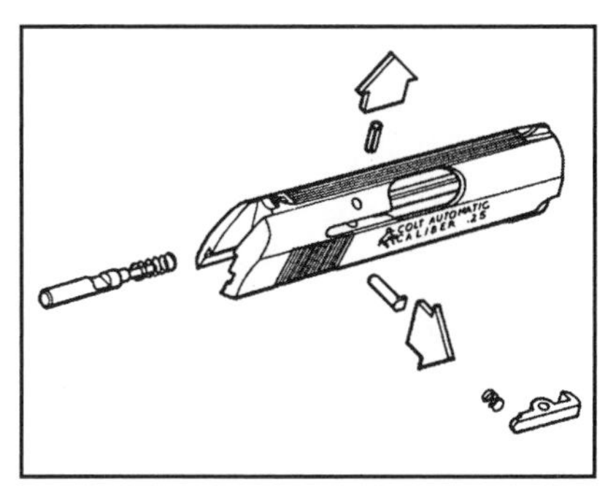

3 To disassemble further, drive out extractor pin (2) with a pin punch that closely fits hole in slide. Extractor (3) and its spring (4) may then be lifted out. Pry out firing pin retaining pin (5) with a narrow screwdriver blade inserted under its elongated head. Removal of the pin releases firing pin (7) and spring (6).

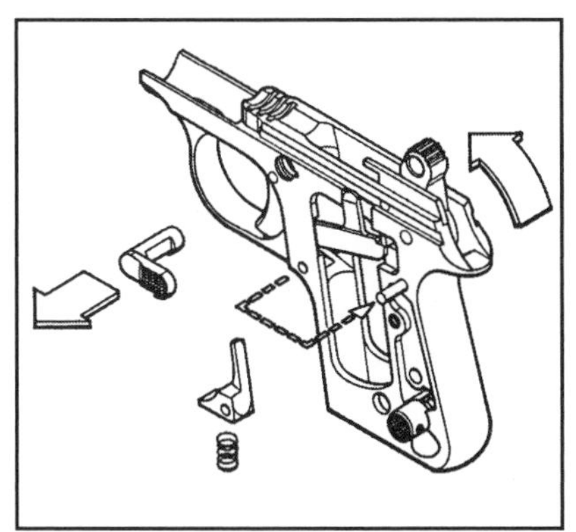

4 Unscrew grip screws (20) and re-move grips (19) (27). Rotate safety ½ turn from "safe" position and withdraw from frame. Drift out magazine safety pin (25) and remove magazine safety (24) and spring (26). Insert magazine safety pin in frame hole below disconnector (22). Pull trigger and lower hammer with thumb, until hammer spring guide (17) stops against the pin.

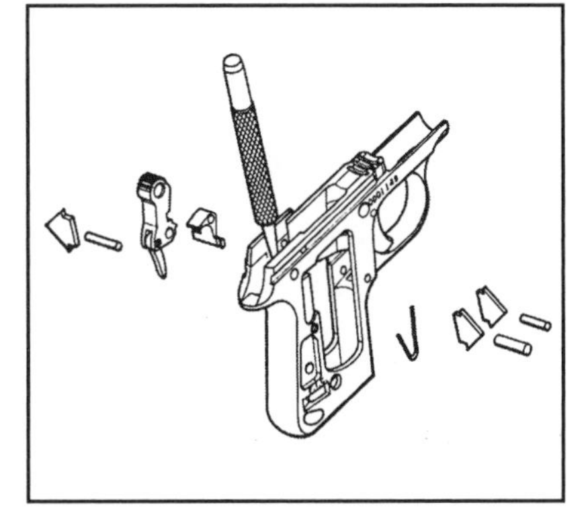

5 Unhook forward arm of sear spring (14) from sear (12), and remove spring. Drift out hammer pin (15) and lift hammer assembly (16) from frame. Drift out sear pin (13) and remove sear. Depress hammer spring guide with punch, and withdraw magazine safety pin. Then, ease out hammer spring (18) and guide.

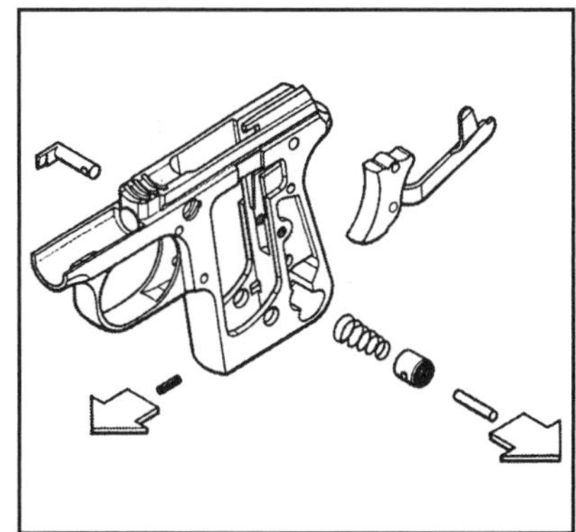

6 Drift out magazine catch pin (30) to free magazine catch (31), spring (29), and button. Drift out trigger pin (21), releasing the trigger assembly. Reassemble in reverse. Trigger must be rotated forward to fully compress its internally-located spring when the trigger pin is replaced.

COLT AUTO .32 AND .380 POCKET

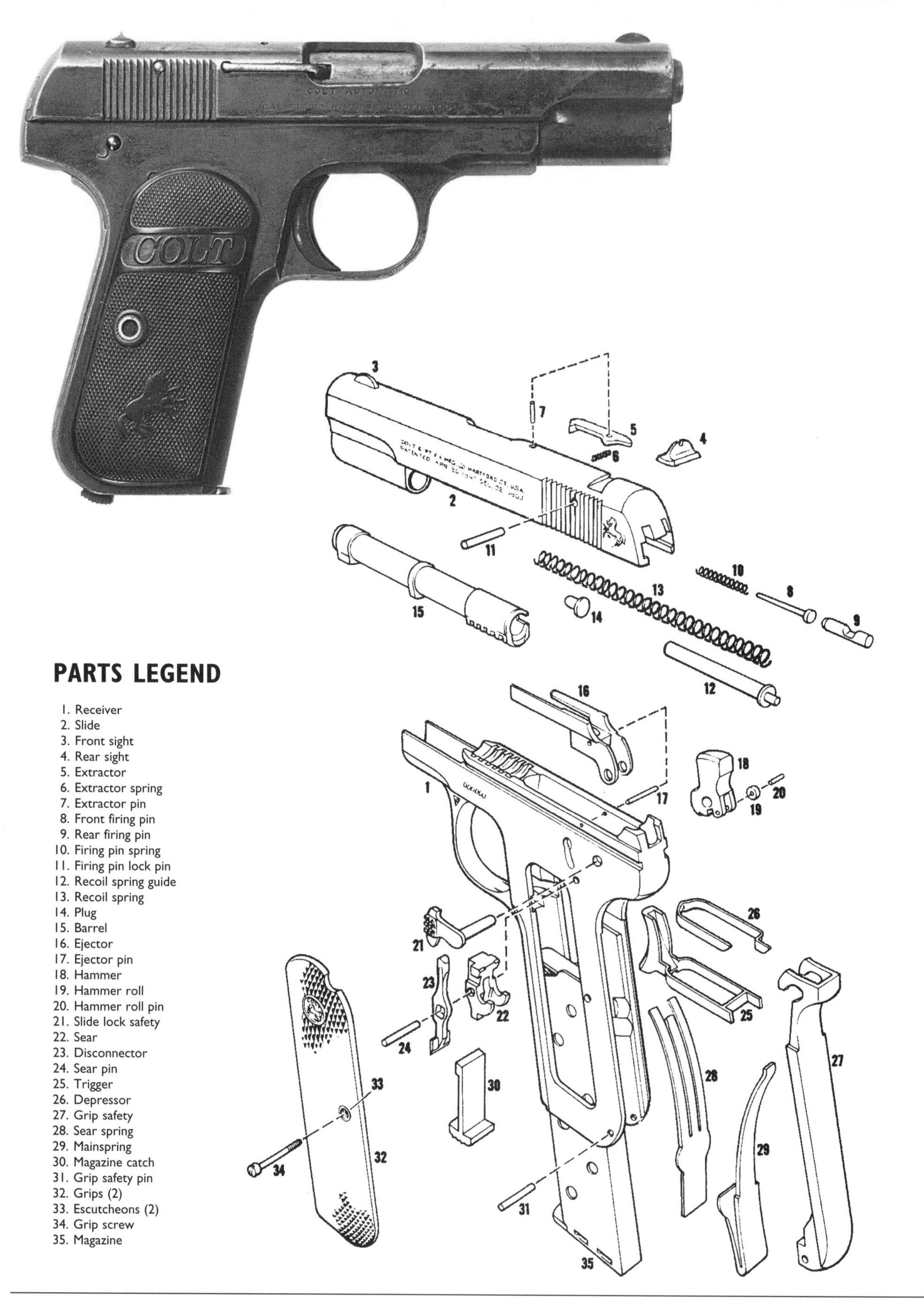

PARTS LEGEND

1. Receiver
2. Slide
3. Front sight
4. Rear sight
5. Extractor
6. Extractor spring
7. Extractor pin
8. Front firing pin
9. Rear firing pin
10. Firing pin spring
11. Firing pin lock pin
12. Recoil spring guide
13. Recoil spring
14. Plug
15. Barrel
16. Ejector
17. Ejector pin
18. Hammer
19. Hammer roll
20. Hammer roll pin
21. Slide lock safety
22. Sear
23. Disconnector
24. Sear pin
25. Trigger
26. Depressor
27. Grip safety
28. Sear spring
29. Mainspring
30. Magazine catch
31. Grip safety pin
32. Grips (2)
33. Escutcheons (2)
34. Grip screw
35. Magazine

Introduced in 1903, the Browning-designed .32 ACP Model 1903 Pocket was the first hammerless or concealed-hammer pistol produced by the Colt firm. Early models show the single patent date of April 20, 1897; later models bear the additional December 22, 1903, patent date. A .380 ACP pistol, derived from the Model 1903, was brought out in 1908, and is known as the Model 1908 Pocket.

Both pistols are single-action, blowback-operated guns, and share a common design. Among the safety features are a grip safety that blocks the sear unless depressed by the grip of the firing hand, and a left-side, hammer-blocking, frame-mounted manual safety. This manual safety also serves to lock the slide to the rear. Additionally, the grip safety functions as a cocking indicator, as it protrudes from the rear of the backstrap only when the hammer is cocked.

Later versions of both the .32 ACP and .380 ACP models also incorporate a magazine disconnect safety that keeps the gun from firing when the magazine is removed.

During the production life of both guns, Colt made slight design changes, including shortening barrel length, enlarging the extractor, eliminating the barrel bushing, and incorporating the previously-mentioned magazine disconnect safety.

It is possible to convert from one caliber to another by substituting the proper magazines and barrels. Colt discontinued production of both of these pistols in 1946.

DISASSEMBLY

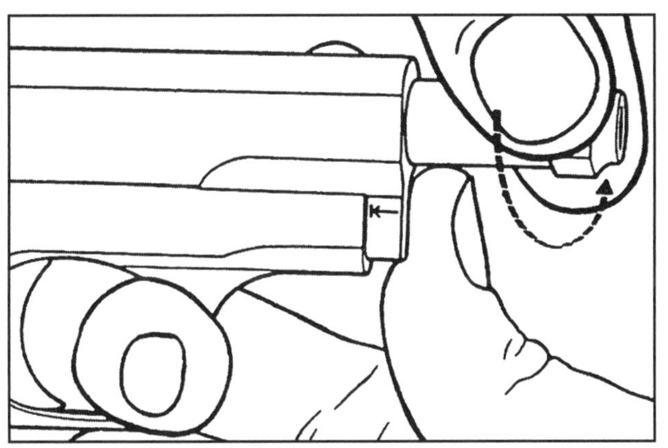

1 Remove magazine and check chamber to ensure that it is unloaded. Cock the pistol. Grasp the pistol as shown, lining up the mark and arrow stamped on right side of slide with forward edge of receiver. With fingers of left hand, twist barrel to left until its locking lugs disengage from receiver. Withdraw slide, barrel, recoil spring, and guide from receiver. Turn barrel and withdraw it from slide.

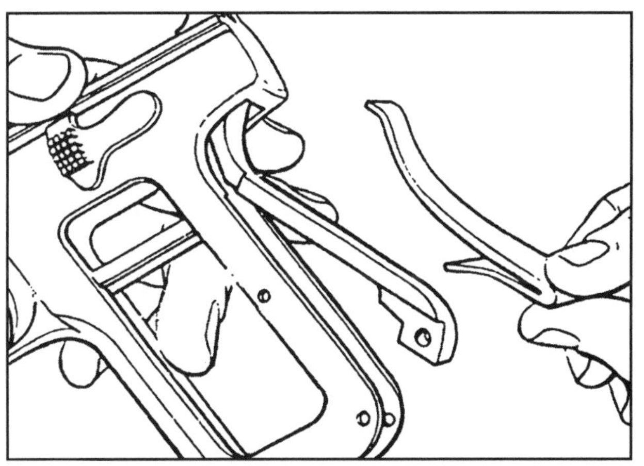

2 Remove stocks and drive out grip safety pin (31). Pull out lower end of grip safety (27) and withdraw the mainspring (29), sear spring (28), and magazine catch (30).

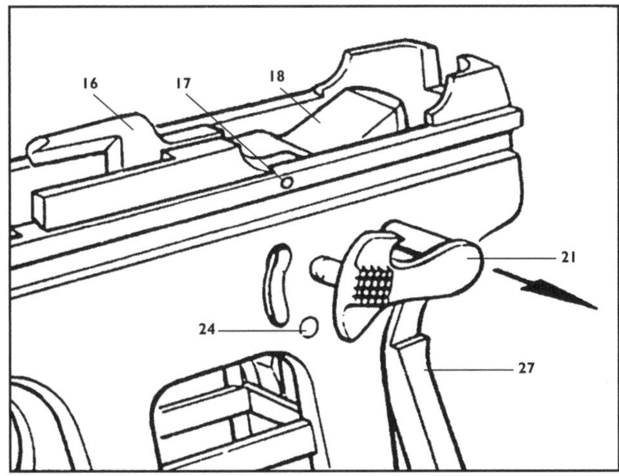

3 Put slide lock safety (21) in "safe" or up position and withdraw it from receiver as shown. Hammer (18), ejector (16), and grip safety (27) can now be removed. Sear (22) and disconnector (23) con be removed by driving out their retaining pin (24).

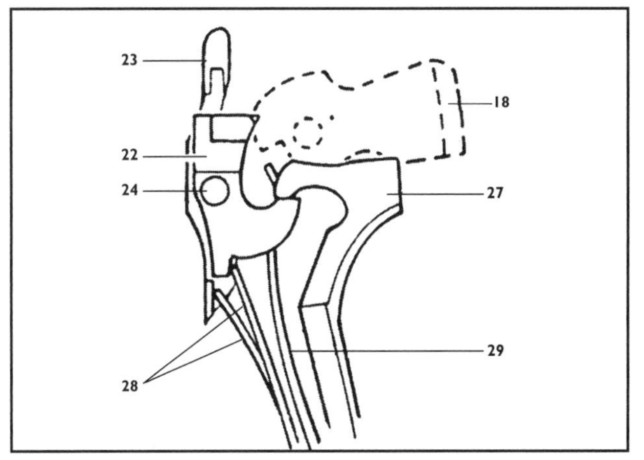

4 Parts may be reassembled in reverse order. Sear and disconnector are assembled in relationship as shown. Insert sear spring so that its leaves engage sear and disconnector. Insert mainspring so smaller leaf faces in toward the magazine well. Hammer must be in forward position to insert mainspring.

COLT MODEL 1851 NAVY REVOLVER

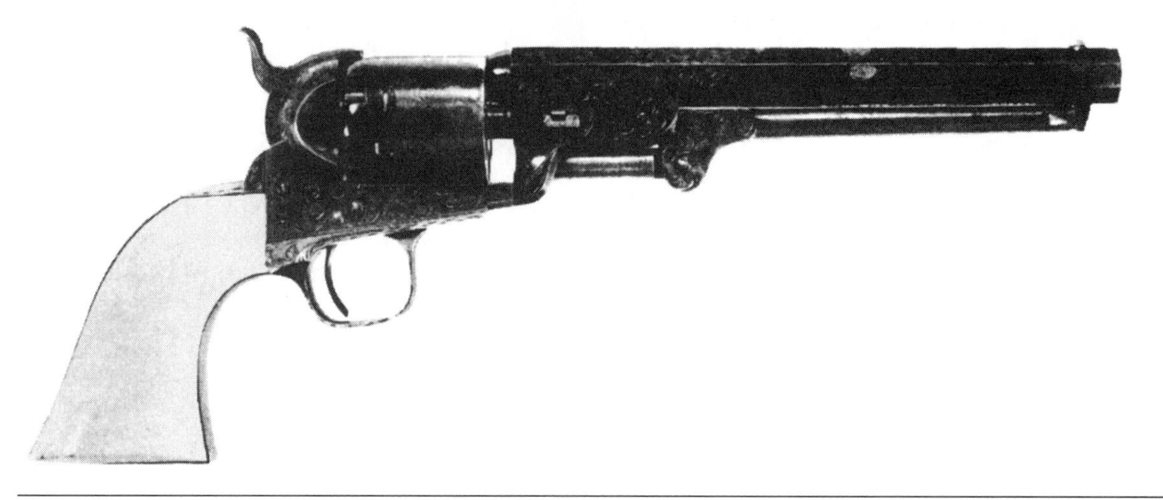

PARTS LEGEND

1. Front sight
2. Barrel
3. Loading lever latch
4. Loading lever latch spring
5. Loading lever latch spring retaining pin
6. Barrel stud
7. Loading lever
8. Loading lever screw
9. Loading plunger
10. Loading plunger screw
11. Barrel wedge (with spring)
12. Barrel wedge screw
13. Cylinder
14. Nipples (6)
15. Safety pins (6)
16. Cylinder pin
17. Cylinder pin lock pin
18. Lad frame
19. Cylinder locking bolt
20. Trigger and cylinder lading bolt screws (2)
21. Trigger
22. Trigger and cylinder locking bolt spring
23. Trigger and cylinder locking bolt spring screw
24. Hammer
25. Hammer roll
26. Hammer roll pin
27. Hand and hand spring
28. Hammer screw
29. Trigger guard
30. Front trigger guard screw
31. Rear trigger guard screws (2)
32. Mainspring
33. Mainspring screw
34. Butt screw
35. Backstrap
36. Backstrap screws (2)
37. Grip (one-piece)

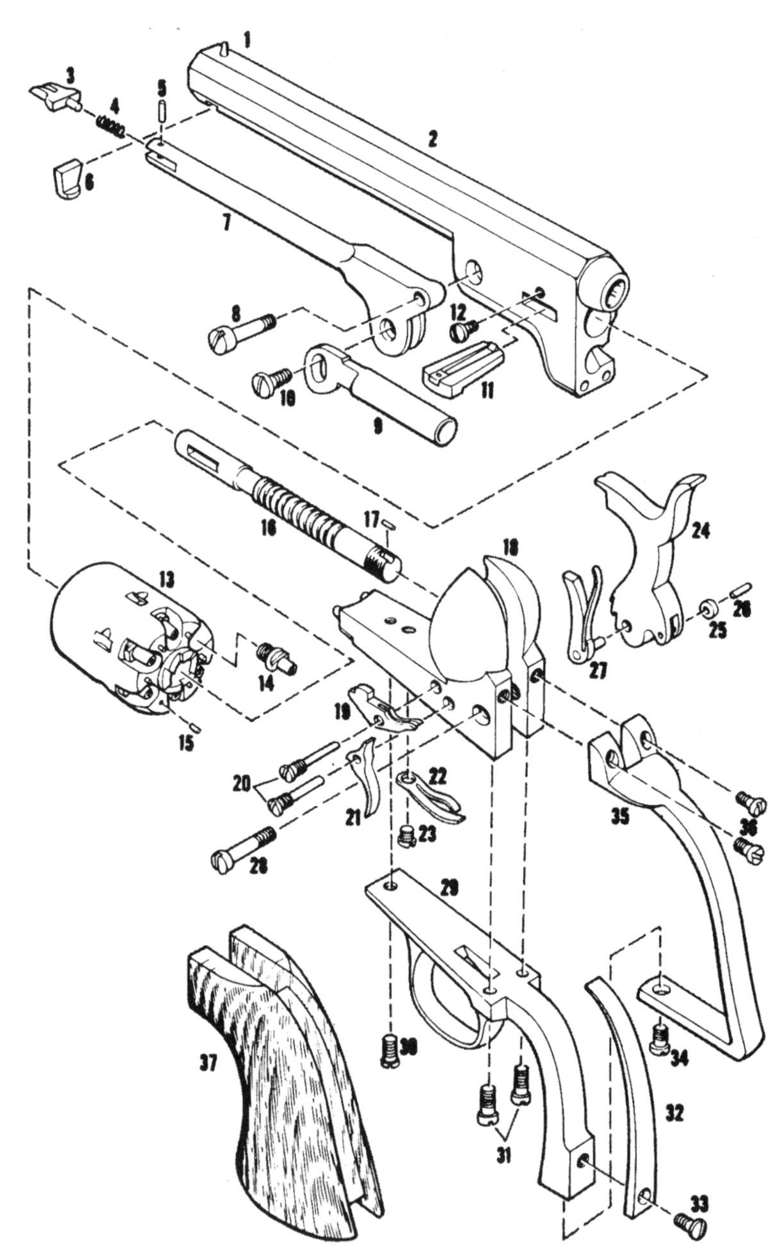

The Colt Model 1851 Navy, produced from 1850 to 1873, was a .36-caliber, six-shot percussion revolver with a 7½-inch octagonal barrel, and was produced in a variety of models differing mostly in the size, shape and materials of the grip frame and trigger guard. Mechanically, the Model 1851 Navy is typical of all Colt percussion-ignition open-top revolvers, regardless of caliber, and its disassembly and assembly procedures can generally be followed for all guns of this type.

When working with antique revolvers such as these, care should be taken to prevent damage to old and often hard-to-replace parts. Marring of the original finish must be avoided; screwdrivers should precisely fit the various screw-heads; and a plastic or fiber-head hammer should be used for any necessary tapping, such as is required for the removal of the barrel wedge.

Since original Colt nipple wrenches are brittle and easily broken, modern nipple wrenches are preferable and will prove more effective for the removal of old nipples, which often are rusted in place.

For normal cleaning purposes, separation of barrel from frame and removal of cylinder will usually suffice.

DISASSEMBLY

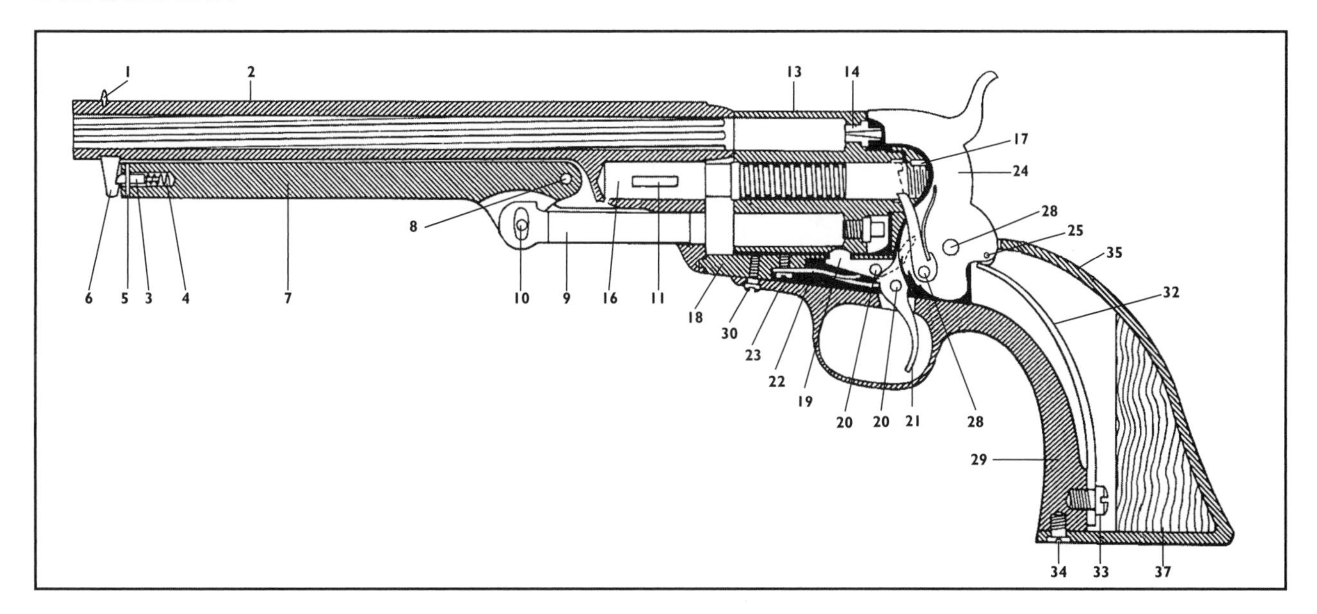

Separate barrel and frame assemblies by gently driving barrel wedge (11) as far as it will go to the left and pulling barrel (2) off the cylinder pin (16). If barrel wedge has a spring, the right-hand lip of the spring must be depressed where it protrudes from barrel before wedge can be moved. Wedge can be removed completely by unscrewing barrel wedge screw (12).

Remove loading lever screw (8) and pull loading lever (7) and plunger (9) free of barrel. The loading lever latch (3) and spring (4) may be removed by gently drifting out their retaining pin (5). Remove plunger screw (10) and separate loading lever and plunger. The barrel stud (6) is force-fitted in a dovetail milled on underside of barrel and should be removed only if replacement is necessary.

Slide cylinder (13) off cylinder pin (16). If removal of nipples (14) is necessary for replacement, care should be taken that a proper nipple wrench is used.

Removal of cylinder pin (16) from lock frame (18) is not recommended. This cylinder pin, or arbor, was very tightly fitted originally and the firm association of pin and frame over the years is further complicated by a lock pin (17) which is usually next to impossible to remove and generally must be drilled out, before cylinder pin can be unscrewed from frame.

Remove the two backstrap screws (36) and butt screw (34). Pull backstrap (35) and one-piece wood grip (37) free of lock frame (18) and trigger guard (29). If it is necessary to remove grip from backstrap, use care to avoid chipping or cracking grip since it is usually quite tightly fitted. If gun has two-piece grips held together by a screw, they should be removed before removing backstrap. Remove mainspring screw (33) and mainspring (32). Remove front trigger guard screw (30) and rear trigger guard screws (31) and drop trigger guard (29) off frame.

Remove trigger and cylinder locking bolt spring screw (23) and spring (22). Remove trigger and cylinder locking bolt screws (20) and drop trigger (21) and cylinder locking bolt (19) out of frame. Remove hammer screw (28) and pull hammer (24) and hand and spring (27) gently out bottom of frame. The hand can be lifted out of its hole in the hammer. If replacement is necessary, hammer roll (25) can be removed by gently drifting out its retaining pin (26).

COLT MODEL 1855 SIDEHAMMER

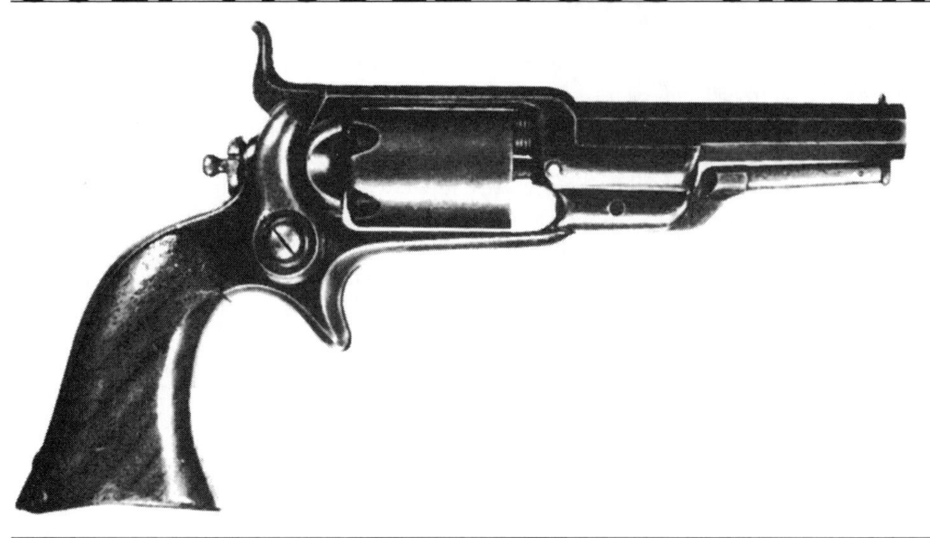

PARTS LEGEND

1. Barrel
2. Loading lever
3. Loading lever latch pin
4. Loading lever latch spring
5. Loading lever latch (ball type)
6. Rammer pin
7. Rammer
8. Frame
9. Cylinder (nipples integral)
10. Hammer
11. Hammer screw
12. Hand pin
13. Trigger spring
14. Trigger
15. Hand spring
16. Hand
17. Mainspring retaining pin
18. Grip screw
19. Grip
20. Mainspring tension screw
21. Cylinder arbor
22. Cylinder arbor sleeve
23. Mainspring
24. Stirrup
25. Cylinder stop
26. Cylinder stop spring
27. Trigger screw
28. Stirrup pin
29. Sear
30. Side-plate
31. Cylinder stop screw
32. Side-plate screw
33. Cylinder arbor retaining latch
34. Arbor retaining latch pin
35. Arbor retaining latch pin spring

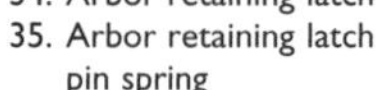

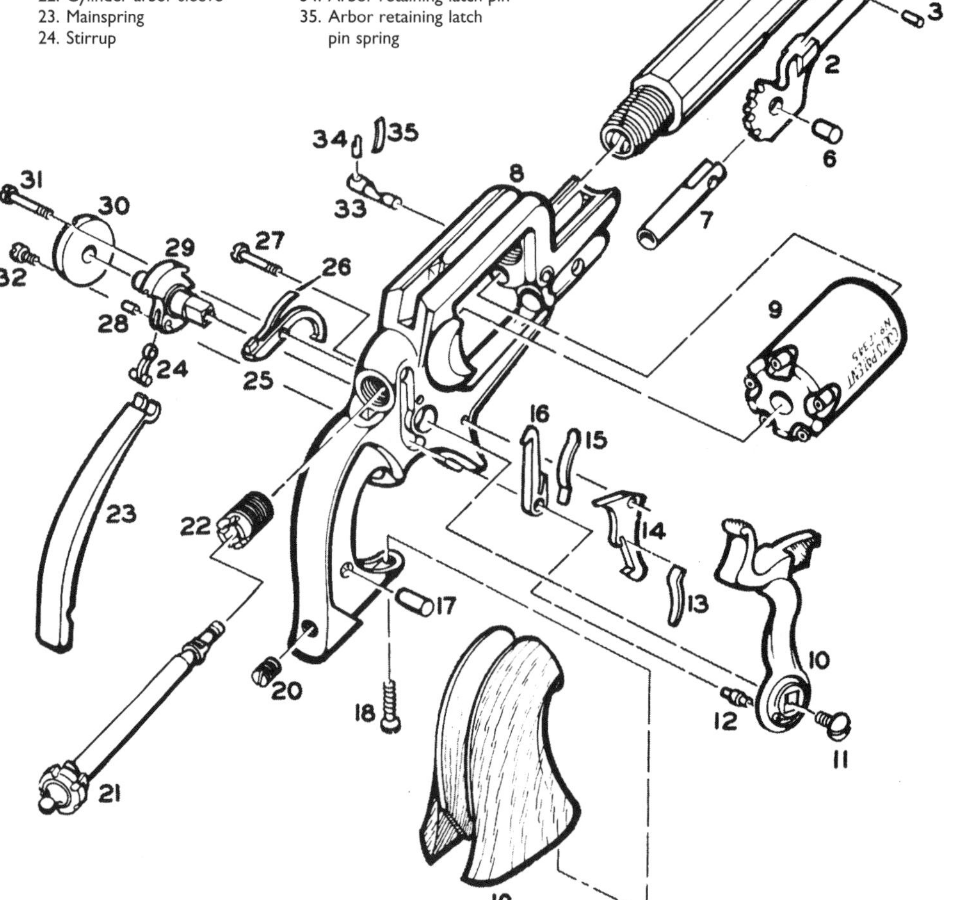

In terms of both design and serviceability, the Model 1855 spur-trigger sidehammer pocket revolver was inferior to other early percussion revolvers produced by Colt's Patent Fire Arms Mfg. Co., as its fragile internal components produced frequent mechanical failures. Nonetheless, many Model 1855s were sold.

The basic patent that covered the Model 1855 was granted to Elisha K. Root on Dec. 25, 1855 (No. 13,999). A gifted inventor, Root was involved in the design of many Colt firearms as well as the machines used for mass production, and eventually became President of Colt.

The Model 1855 revolver, commonly called Root Model by collectors, was made in .28 and .31 calibers only, at the Hartford, Conn. factory established in 1855. During its production life (1855-1870), the Model 1855 was made in a number of versions differing primarily in barrel length and profile, cylinder fluting and engraving, and stocks.

The Model 1855 was the first Colt revolver with a top strap over the cylinder and a screw-in barrel. It was also the first to use Colt's creeping-type loading lever.

DISASSEMBLY

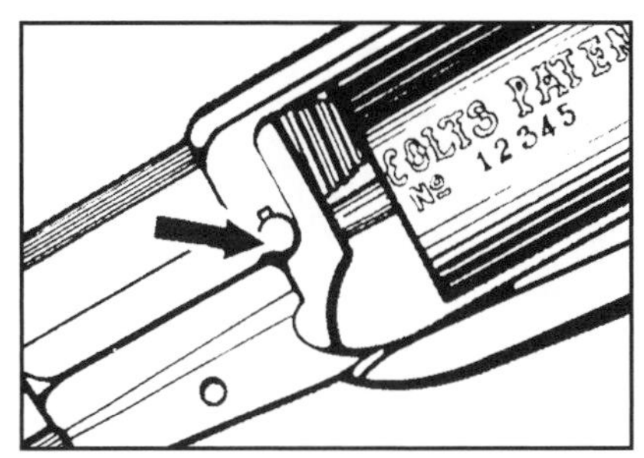

1 Disassembly of the Colt Root Model should not be attempted, due to the fragile and intricate nature of the parts, unless absolutely necessary. Should disassembly be required, commence by depressing the cylinder arbor retaining latch (33). On some models, a screw is used to retain the cylinder arbor (21). Withdraw arbor from rear of frame (8) and remove cylinder (9). Remove grip screw (18) and grip (19).

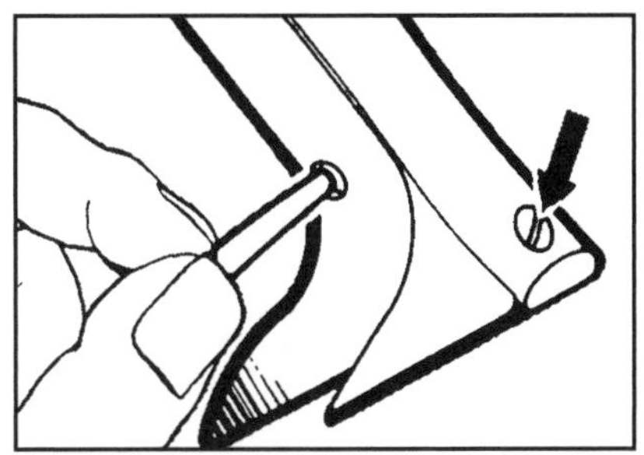

2 Next, remove mainspring tension screw (20-arrow) and drift out mainspring retaining pin (17). This will relieve spring tension on moving parts.

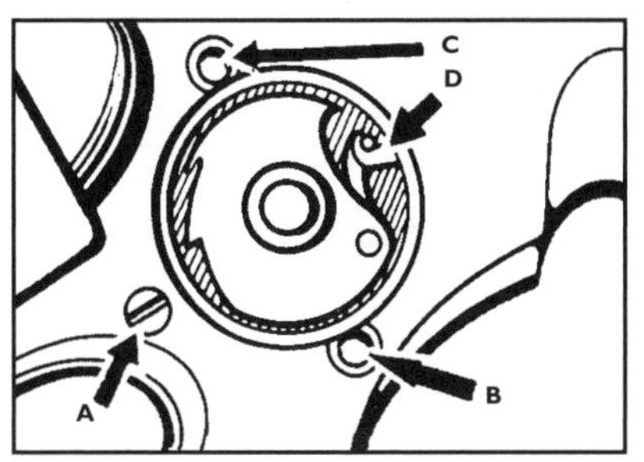

3 Continue by removing (A) trigger screw (27), (B) side-plate screw (32), and (C) cylinder stop screw (31). Tap out sideplate (30), then using a small screwdriver or punch as a lever, flick (D) mainspring free of stirrup (24).

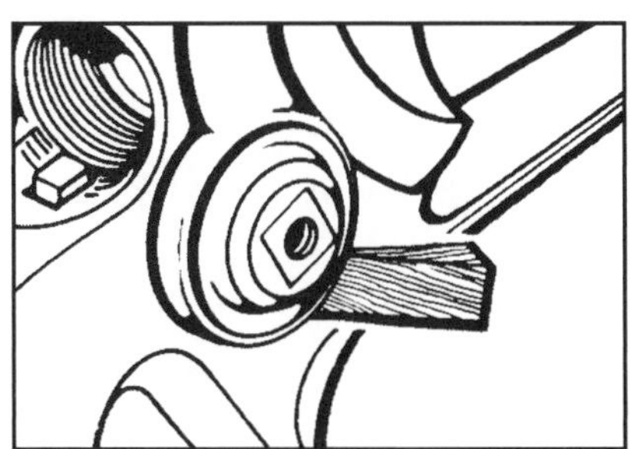

4 Remove hammer screw (11). Insert a narrow, hardwood wedge in small crevice between hammer (10) and frame, and tap gently. This will pry off hammer which is usually hard pressed in place on the sear (29), which may now also be removed from left side of frame. Trigger (14), trigger spring (13), cylinder stop (25), cylinder stop spring (26), hand (16), and hand spring (15) may be dismounted. Removal of these parts is obvious once the sideplate is off, but removal sequence is important.

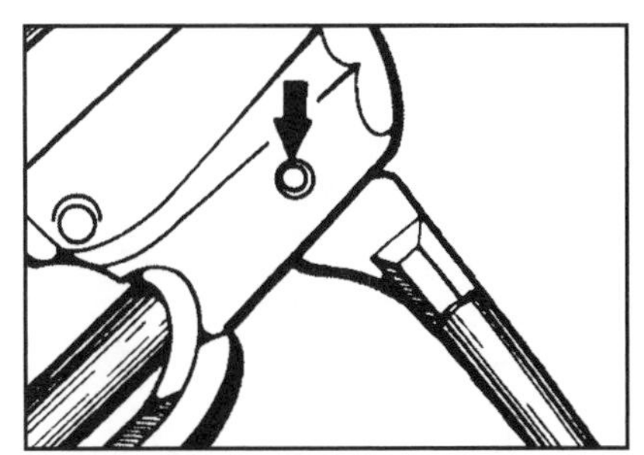

5 Unlatch loading lever (2) and push down until rammer pin (6) is seen through hole in front portion of frame (arrow). Drifting out of rammer pin will permit removal of loading lever assembly and rammer (7).

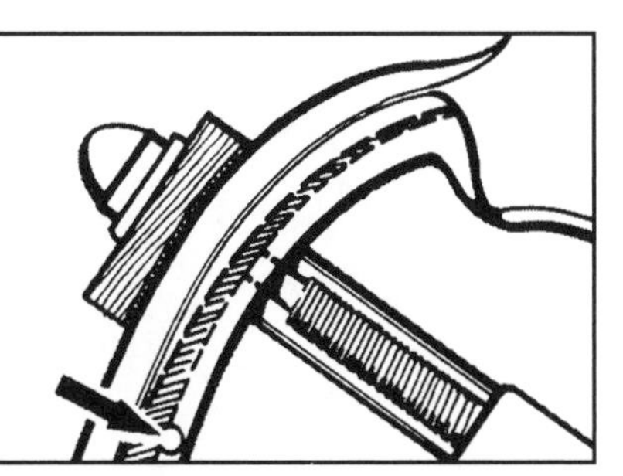

6 Reassemble in reverse order. When replacing mainspring retaining pin, it is necessary to compress mainspring to align groove in spring with pin hole in frame. Accomplish this by placing a small block of soft wood, shaped to contour of backstrap, and felt padded on surface which bears on backstrap. Using a woodworker's clamp, from which the button has been removed, apply to mainspring as shown and compress until pin hole (arrow) is clear, then insert mainspring retaining pin, and replace mainspring tension screw (20).

COLT MODEL 1877 DOUBLE-ACTION

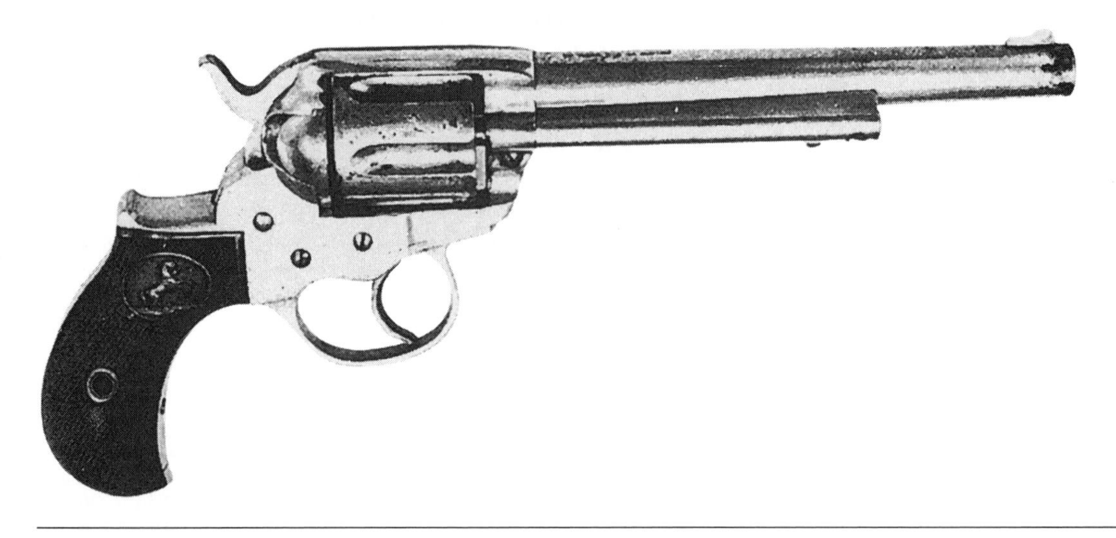

PARTS LEGEND

1. Barrel
2. Ejector housing
3. Ejector housing screw
4. Ejector rod
5. Ejector rod head
6. Ejector spring
7. Cylinder pin
8. Cylinder
9. Main frame
10. Cylinder pin lock screw
11. Cylinder pin lock screw spring
12. Cylinder pin lock nut
13. Loading gate
14. Loading gate catch
15. Loading gate catch spring
16. Loading gate catch screw
17. Hand
18. Trigger
19. Trigger screw
20. Trigger roller
21. Trigger roller pin
22. Trigger strut spring
23. Hand spring
24. Hand and strut spring screw
25. Trigger strut
26. Trigger strut pin
27. Sear
28. Sear screw
29. Hammer
30. Firing pin
31. Firing pin rivet
32. Hammer screw
33. Stirrup
34. Stirrup pin
35. Hand and cylinder stop tension spring
36. Trigger spring
37. Trigger spring screw
38. Cylinder stop
39. Mainspring
40. Mainspring screw
41. Back strap
42. Backstrap screws (2)
43. Butt screw
44. Trigger guard
45. Rear trigger guard screws (2)
46. Front trigger guard screw
47. Mainspring tension screw
48. Grip pin *
49. Grips, hard rubber (left hand only shown)
50. Escutcheon *
51. Escutcheon nut *
52. Grip screw *
53. Recoil plate

*Grip pin, grip screw, and escutcheons were not supplied on 'Lightning' revolvers with one-piece hardwood grips.

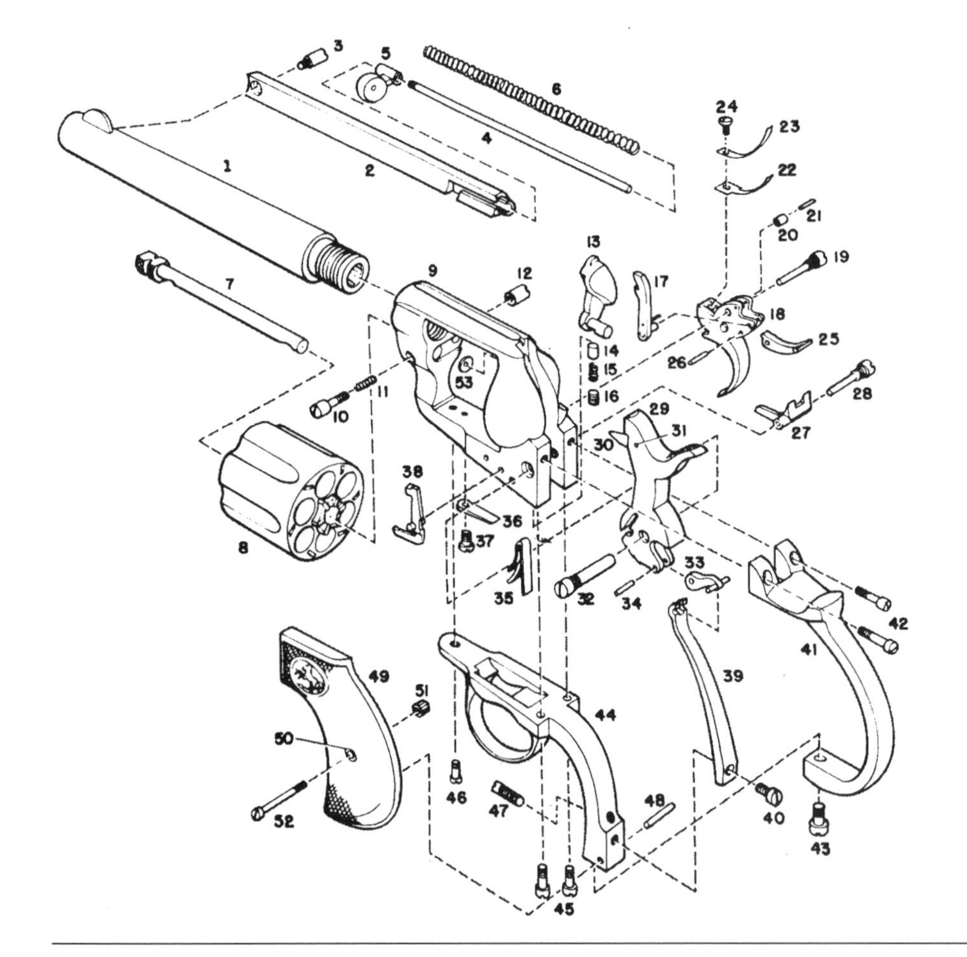

Although self-cocking revolvers had been in use for many years prior to 1877, it was not until that year that such an arm was offered by Colt's Patent Fire Arms Mfg. Co., of Hartford. Designed in 1876 by Colt employee William Mason, the Double-Action or DA model was initially introduced in .38 caliber only. Subsequently it was offered in .41 caliber, with a small quantity also made in .32 caliber. Distinctive features of the DA model are the double hand, birdshead grip, and the absence of the customary bolt locking notches on outer surface of the cylinder.

Collectors commonly refer to this model as the 'Lightning' although this was not a factory appellation, having been apparently coined by B. Kittridge & Co., of Cincinnati, Ohio, who used it in their arms catalogs to identify the original cal. .38 model. The name "Thunderer," applied to the later .41 caliber version, also stemmed from this firm and was likewise not an official Colt name.

The DA model was offered both with and without rod ejector and in various barrel lengths from 2" up to 7½", with the 7- and 7½-inch barrel lengths available on special order only. Manufacture of this model ceased in 1910.

DISASSEMBLY

Due to the intricacy of the lock mechanism of the Lightning Colt. special care should be taken in disassembling to note the exact relative positions of all parts to facilitate correct reassembly.

To remove cylinder (8), open loading gate (13) and press in cylinder pin lock screw (10). Draw cylinder pin (7) forward as far as it will go. Cylinder may be pushed out of main frame (9) after pulling hammer (29) back slightly. This is disassembly for normal cleaning purposes.

To disassemble lock mechanism, proceed as follows:

a) Remove grip screw (52) and grips (49). Remove backstrap screws (42) and butt screw (43) and drop backstrap (41) off main frame (9).

b) Loosen mainspring tension screw (47) and remove mainspring screw (40). Disengage top of mainspring (39) from stirrup (33) and remove.

c) Remove rear and front trigger guard screws (45 & 46), pull trigger (18) back slightly, and remove trigger guard (44) from main frame, exposing inside lock mechanism.

d) Remove sear screw (28) and drop out sear (27) hand and cylinder stop tension spring (35).

e) Remove hammer screw (32) and drop hammer (29) down out of main frame. Disengage trigger strut (25) from its seat in hammer and remove hammer

f) Loosen trigger spring screw (37) and remove trigger screw (19). Draw trigger (18) out of main frame with hand (17) intact. Cylinder stop (38) may be dropped out of its hole in left side of main frame. Trigger strut spring (22) and hand spring (23) may be removed from trigger (18) by unscrewing hand and strut spring screw (24). Trigger strut (25) and trigger roller (20) may be removed from trigger by drifting out their respective retaining pins (26 & 21).

g) Ejector assembly (2,3,4,5,6) may be removed by unscrewing ejector housing screw (3) and drawing ejector housing (2) forward out of its seat in main frame. Loading gate (13) may be removed by unscrewing loading gate catch screw (16) from underside of main frame. Drop out loading gate catch and spring (14 & 15). Swing loading gate down and pull forward out of main frame.

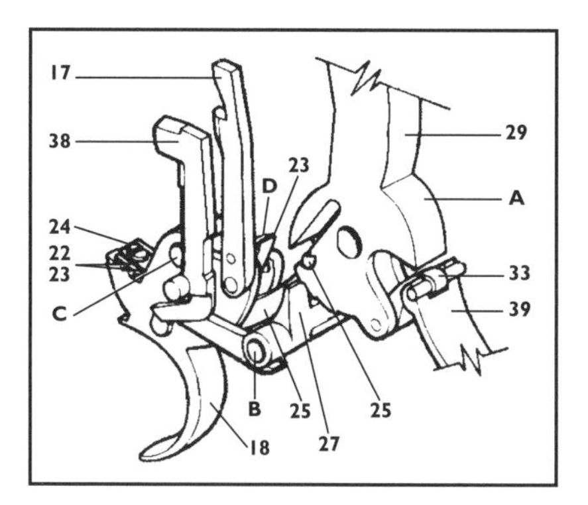

1 This perspective view shows lock mechanism with all parts in proper position as they are when assembled inside the main frame. For greater clarity of detail, hammer screw (32), trigger screw (19), and sear screw (28) are not shown but their respective centerlines are indicated at "A," "B," and "C." Also omitted for clarity is hand and cylinder stop tension spring (35) which is inserted into bottom of frame so its wider, flat arm presses against rear of hand cut in frame and its 2 forward, curving arms press against rear edges of hand and cylinder stop respectively. Trigger spring (36) is also omitted to avoid confusion. "D" indicates the pin of the hand against which hand spring (23) bears.

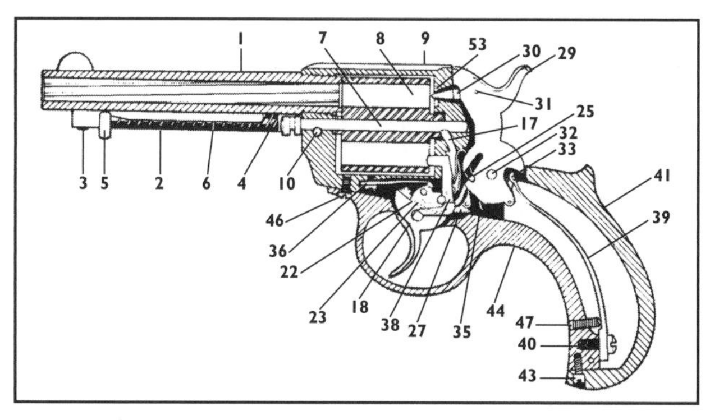

2 This drawing shows entire revolver in longitudinal section and demonstrates proper relationship of all interior parts. Note that hand and cylinder stop tension spring (35) is shown here with its long arm behind hammer for clarity only. In assembling the lock mechanism in this position, this spring is on the left side of hammer.

COLT MODEL 1878 DA REVOLVER

More than 50,000 of the Colt Model 1878 (above) and Model 1902 revolvers were produced by 1905. The Model 1902, sometimes erroneously called the "Alaskan" model, was for Filipino police use.

PARTS LEGEND

1. Barrel
2. Ejector tube
3. Ejector tube screw
4. Ejector rod and head
5. Ejector spring
6. Base pin
7. Cylinder bushing
8. Cylinder
9. Frame
10. Base pin catch screw
11. Base pin catch spring
12. Base pin catch
13. Loading gate
14. Loading gate spring
15. Loading gate spring screw
16. Hand
17. Hand/strut spring
18. Trigger
19. Trigger pin
20. Strut
21. Trigger spring
22. Trigger stirrup
23. Trigger stirrup pin
24. Sear
25. Sear pin
26. Hammer
27. Firing pin
28. Grip plate screw
29. Hammer screw
30. Sideplate
31. Hammer stirrup
32. Hammer stirrup pin
33. Mainspring
34. Mainspring screw
35. Trigger saddle
36. Lanyard ring
37. Lanyard ring pin
38. Trigger guard
39. Front guard screw
40. Rear guard screw
41. Grip plate pin
42. Grip plates, pair
43. Sear spring

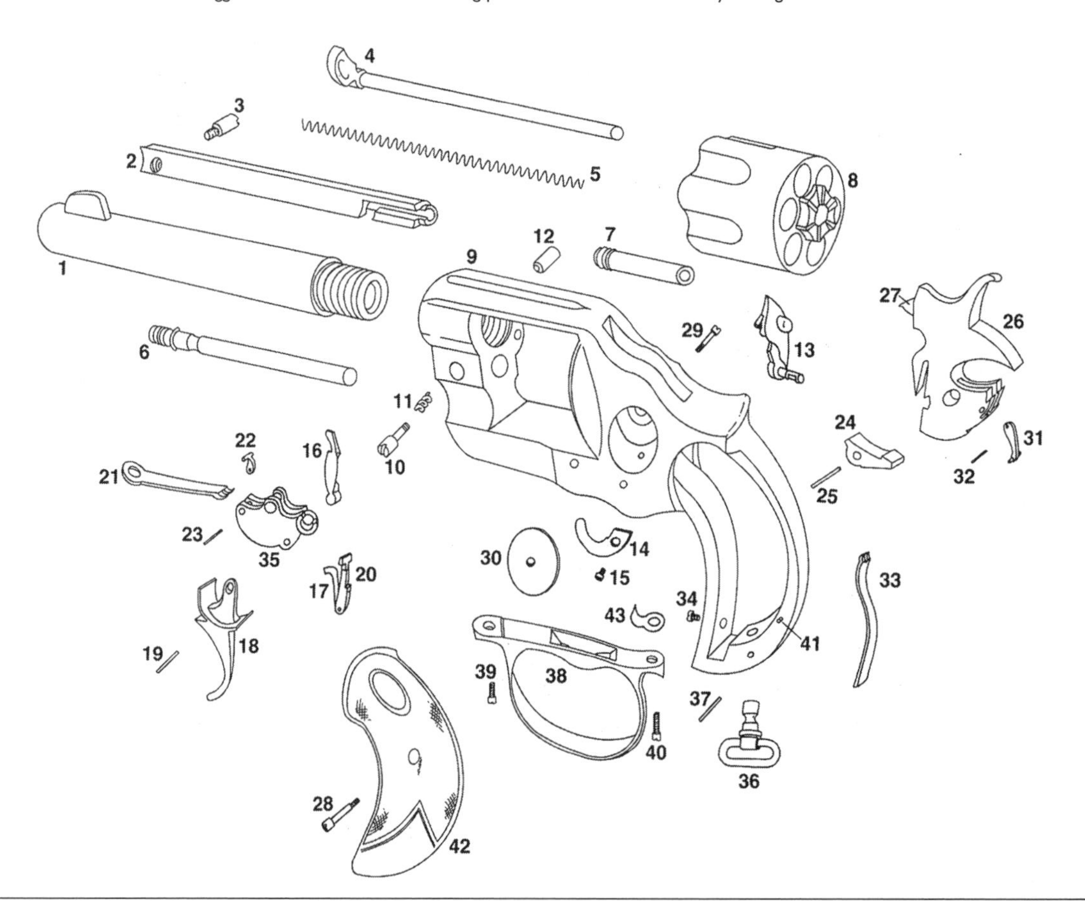

COLT

Colt's first heavy-frame double-action revolver was, in some respects, an evolution of its smaller 1877 "Lightning" that was made for cartridges ranging only from .32 to .41 caliber.

In contrast to the Model 1877, the Model 1878 had an integral grip frame and was primarily made for the .45 Colt or .44-40 Win. cartridges. Lesser quantities were made in .32-20 and .38-40 for domestic use, and in .450, .455 and .476 calibers for the British trade.

Other chamberings, perhaps made on a special-order basis, have been reported, ranging from the .22 rimfire through the 11mm German Ordnance cartridge. Cataloged barrel lengths ran from 3½ to 7½ inches.

A removable circular plate on the left side of the frame allowed access to the internal parts, an important consideration due to the intricate construction of the solid-framed Model 1878. Lockup was effected by indexing cuts on the ratchet rather than the periphery of the cylinder, but ejection of spent cartridges still relied on the proven ejector-rod system of Colt's Single-Action Army revolver.

The first Model 1878s had checkered walnut grip panels, but later examples left the factory with checkered hard rubber panels embossed with the traditional Colt device in an oval cartouche. Checkered walnut, ivory or pearl grip panels were available as options.

Produced from 1878 to 1905, the majority of these revolvers went to the civilian market, but an order for 5,000 units for the Philippine Constabulary in 1901 (in .45 Colt with a 6-inch barrel and hard rubber grips), resulted in production of a modified revolver with lengthened trigger and a larger trigger guard. Only 4,600 are estimated to have been actually produced. The total production for the Models 1878 and 1902 is estimated at about 51210 before manufacture ceased in 1905.

DISASSEMBLY

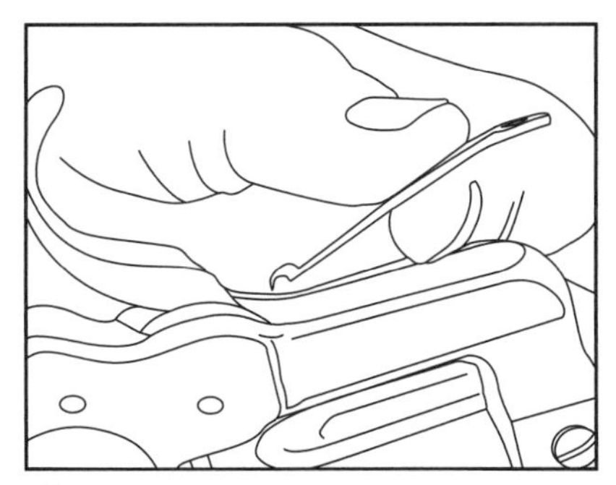

1 Open the loading gate (13) and pull back the hammer (26) to the half-cock position. Rotate the cylinder (8) and check that each of the chambers is empty.

To remove the cylinder, open the loading gate and press in on the base pin catch screw (10). Draw the base pin (6) forward for removal. The cylinder can be pushed out of the frame (9) after pulling the hammer back slightly. For cleaning purposes, no further disassembly is required or advised.

To disassemble the lock mechanism, remove the grip plate screw (28) and the grip plates (42). Remove the mainspring screw (34). Disengage the top of the mainspring (33) from the hammer stirrup (31). Take out the front and rear trigger guard screws (39 & 40). In reassembly, be sure the longer of the two screws is replaced in the front trigger guard screw hole.

Pull the trigger guard (38) down and out of the frame. To remove the trigger spring (21), disengage the top of the spring from the trigger stirrup (22) and tilt the spring up and out.

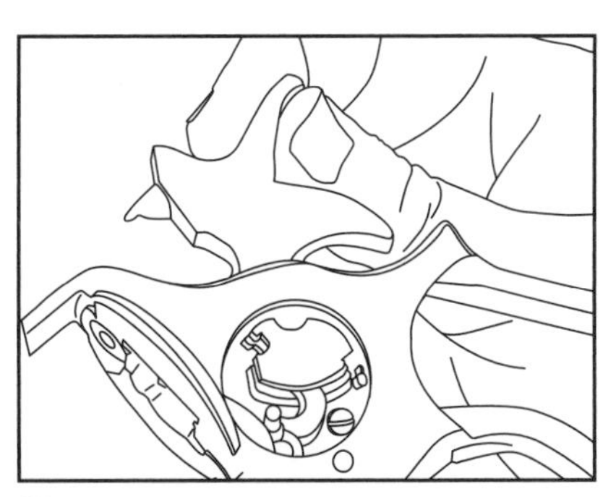

2 Remove the hammer screw (29) to detach the sideplate (30). Pull the hammer back and out through the frame opening.

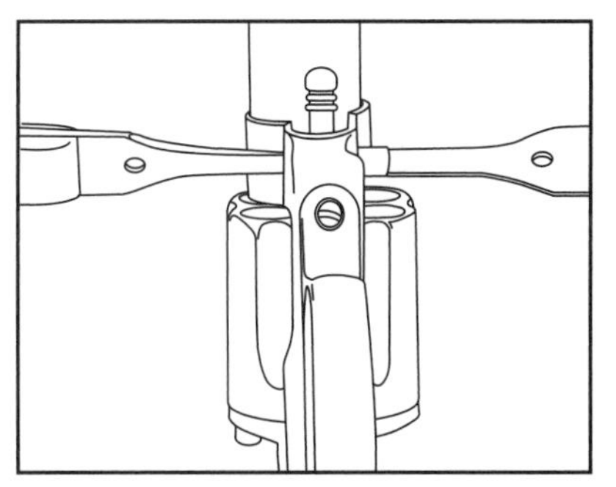

3 To remove the trigger (18), drive out the trigger pin (19) to the left, then push the trigger up into the frame to free the hand (16). The hand can be pulled up and out through the sideplate hole. Depress the front of the trigger and pull downward for removal.

Drive out the sear pin (25) to the left and lift out the sear (24). To remove the loading gate (13), loosen the loading gate spring screw (15) and using a screwdriver, pry up the loading gate spring (14). Pull the loading gate out toward the barrel for removal.

Note that the firing pin (27) is held in place by a staked-in rivet and should not be removed except for replacement.

The ejector assembly can be removed by unscrewing the ejector tube screw (3) and drawing the ejector tube (2) forward out of its seat in the frame.

To remove the base pin catch screw (10), use two screwdrivers (above) to hold the base pin catch (12) and unscrew the lock screw.

COLT MODEL 1902 MILITARY .38

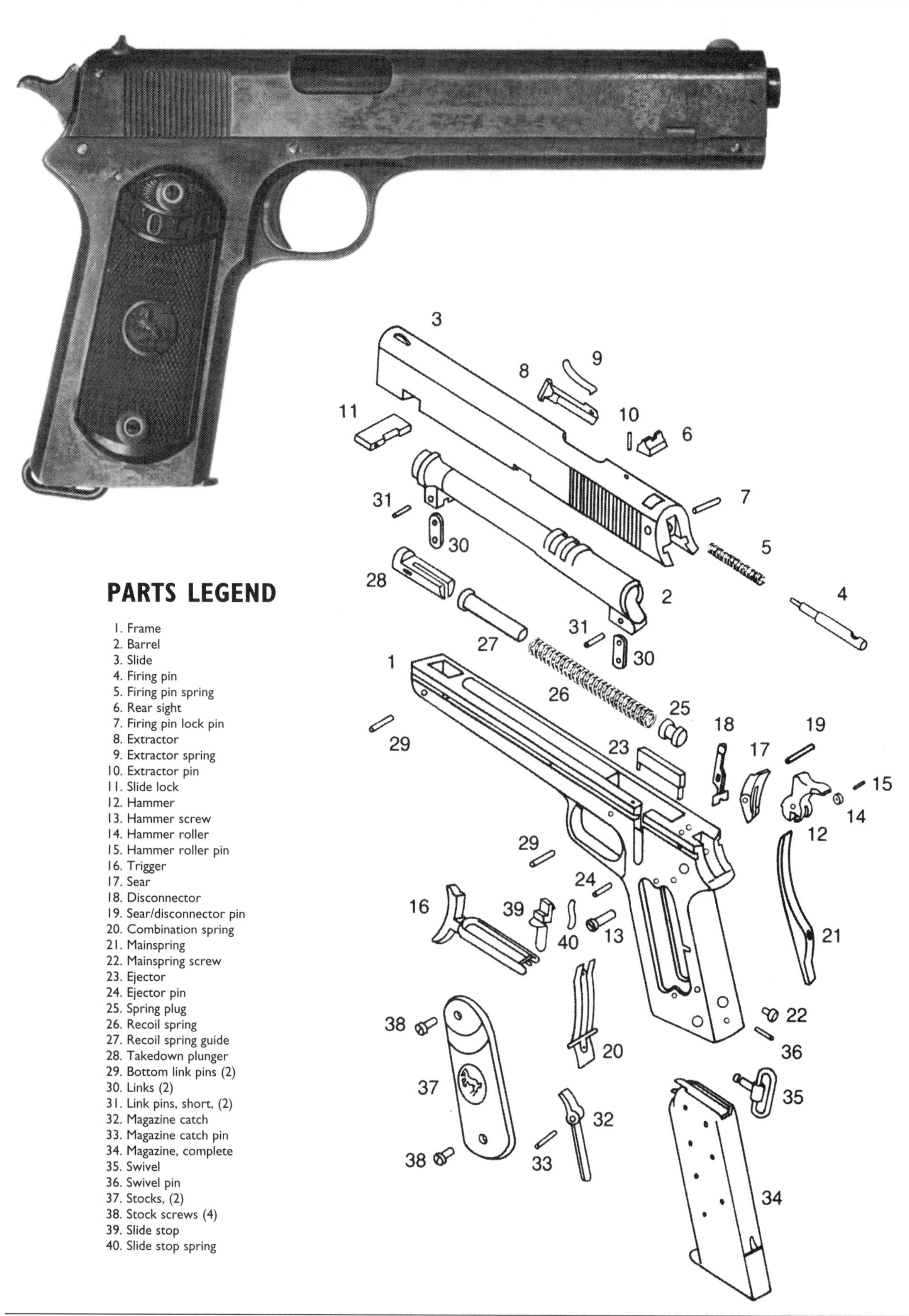

PARTS LEGEND

1. Frame
2. Barrel
3. Slide
4. Firing pin
5. Firing pin spring
6. Rear sight
7. Firing pin lock pin
8. Extractor
9. Extractor spring
10. Extractor pin
11. Slide lock
12. Hammer
13. Hammer screw
14. Hammer roller
15. Hammer roller pin
16. Trigger
17. Sear
18. Disconnector
19. Sear/disconnector pin
20. Combination spring
21. Mainspring
22. Mainspring screw
23. Ejector
24. Ejector pin
25. Spring plug
26. Recoil spring
27. Recoil spring guide
28. Takedown plunger
29. Bottom link pins (2)
30. Links (2)
31. Link pins, short, (2)
32. Magazine catch
33. Magazine catch pin
34. Magazine, complete
35. Swivel
36. Swivel pin
37. Stocks, (2)
38. Stock screws (4)
39. Slide stop
40. Slide stop spring

The Model 1902 Military .38, a locked-breech, 6-inch barrel pistol in .38 ACP, was introduced in 1902. It was one of several early Browning-designed Colt arms that used the "parallel-rule" locking system, in which front and rear swinging links maintained the bore axis constantly parallel to the slide's centerline.

Disassembly instructions for the Model 1902 Military are also useful for the Model 1900, which featured a combination rear sight and firing pin safety but no slide lock; the 1902 Sporting Model, a shorter-gripped seven-shot version of the eight-shot Military; and the 1903 Pocket Model, which was similar to the 1902 Sporting except for a shorter barrel and slide. All chambered for the .38 ACP cartridge, these guns should never be fired using higher-pressure .38 Super or .38 Super + P ammunition. The Model 1902's takedown procedure also applies to the later .45 cal. Colt Model 1905 pistol.

The Model 1902 and its variants had half-cock hammer notches and disconnectors (called "safeties" by Colt), but lacked conventional manual safeties. Early versions had a rounded hammer instead of the spur hammer shown.

The Model 1902 was discontinued after the introduction in 1929 of Colt's Super .38 pistol with its more powerful .38 Super chambering.

DISASSEMBLY

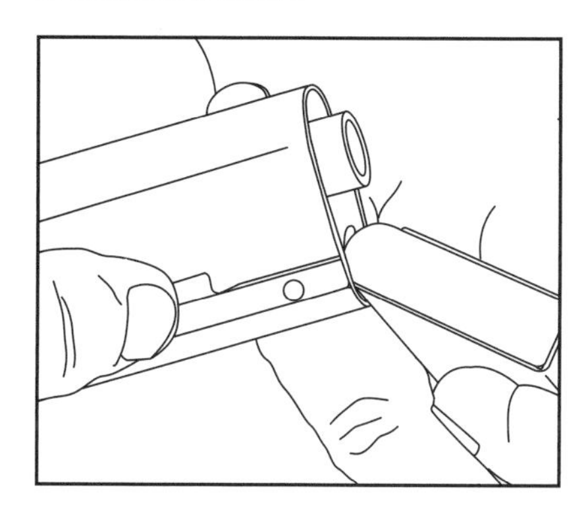

1 Push magazine catch (32) forward and remove magazine (34). Retract slide (3), check that chamber is empty and allow slide to close.

Grasp mid-portion of slide/receiver in right hand. With left hand, use toe of magazine's floorplate to depress takedown plunger (28). With right index finger push out slide lock (11) from its seat. After complete removal of the slide lock, the slide can be withdrawn from the rear of the receiver.

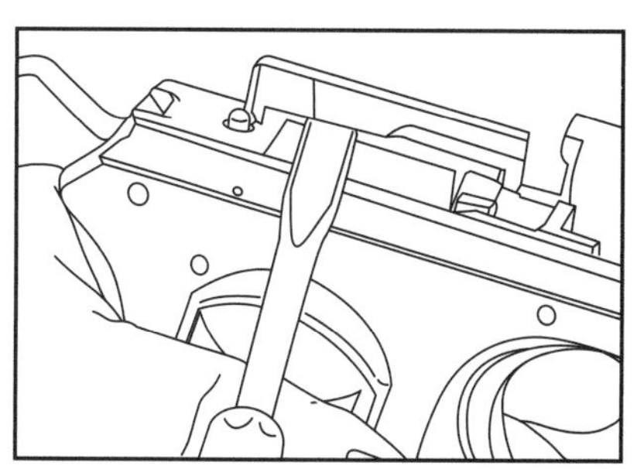

2 The barrel (2) and its dual links (30) are removed by drifting out the long front and rear bottom link pins (29). Note that when the front link pin is fully removed, it frees the takedown plunger (28), and the recoil spring (26) with its guide (27) that are under compression and will be released with considerable force. Separation of barrel, links and their short retaining pins is straightforward.

Receiver stripping, if required, is accomplished by first removing the four stock screws (38) and both stocks (37). After drifting out the ejector pin (24), carefully pry up the ejector (23) from its seat. This frees the slide stop (39) that is removed as a unit with its friction spring (40).

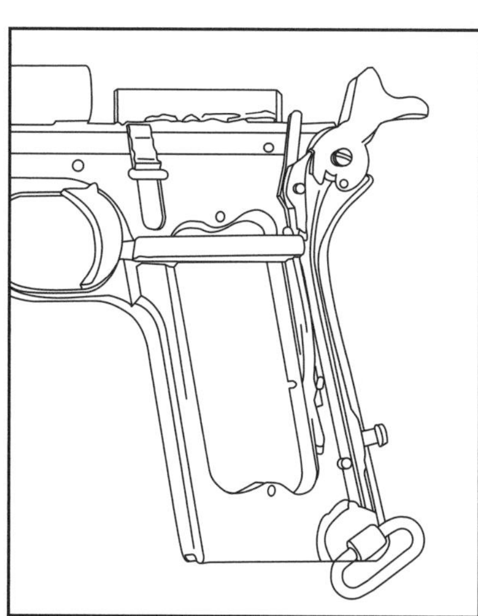

3 When the magazine catch pin (33) is driven out, the catch will drop from the magazine well together with the combination sear/disconnector/trigger spring (20). The trigger itself (16) may now be removed.

A single pin (19), when removed, frees the sear (17) and disconnector (18), and it is wise to keep their relative positions in mind for reassembly.

Removal of the mainspring screw (22), located on the backstrap, releases the mainspring (21). Removal of the hammer screw (13) and hammer (12) with its roller (14) and pin (15) completes receiver stripping except for the swivel (35) that is held by a pin (36) at the bottom of the backstrap.

The slide may be completely stripped, if required, by first drifting out the rear sight (6) from left to right. The inertial firing pin and its spring (4 and 5) are held by a lateral pin (7) that is also driven from the left and the extractor with spring (8 and 9) are fixed with a small vertical pin (10) that can be drifted down through the top of the slide by a small punch.

Once the extractor pin is removed, the extractor and spring, by means of a small screwdriver, may be pried away from the firing pin hole and forward until they are free of the slide. The spring should not be removed from the extractor unless replacement is necessary.

Reassembly is done in reverse order, with, of course, the rear sight firing pin retainer and slide lock being inserted from right to left.

Various parts are shown where they are placed on top of the receiver for clarity.

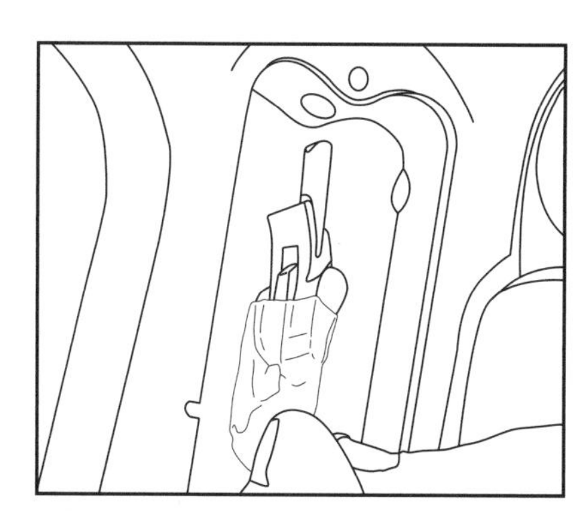

4 A piece of tape is used as an insertion aid for the sear and disconnector.

COLT MODEL 1908 HAMMERLESS .25

PARTS LEGEND

1. Receiver
2. Slide
3. Extractor
4. Extractor pin
5. Extractor spring
6. Firing pin
7. Mainspring
8. Mainspring guide
9. Recoil spring
10. Recoil spring guide
11. Barrel
12. Connector
13. Depressor
14. Trigger
15. Trigger pin
16. Sear
17. Sear and grip safety pin
18. Sear stop pin
19. Slide lock safety
20. Slide lock safety plunger
21. Slide lock safety plunger spring
22. Magazine catch
23. Sear spring
24. Grip safety
25. Grip safety pin
26. Magazine
27. Stocks (2)
28. Escutcheons (2)
29. Stock Screw

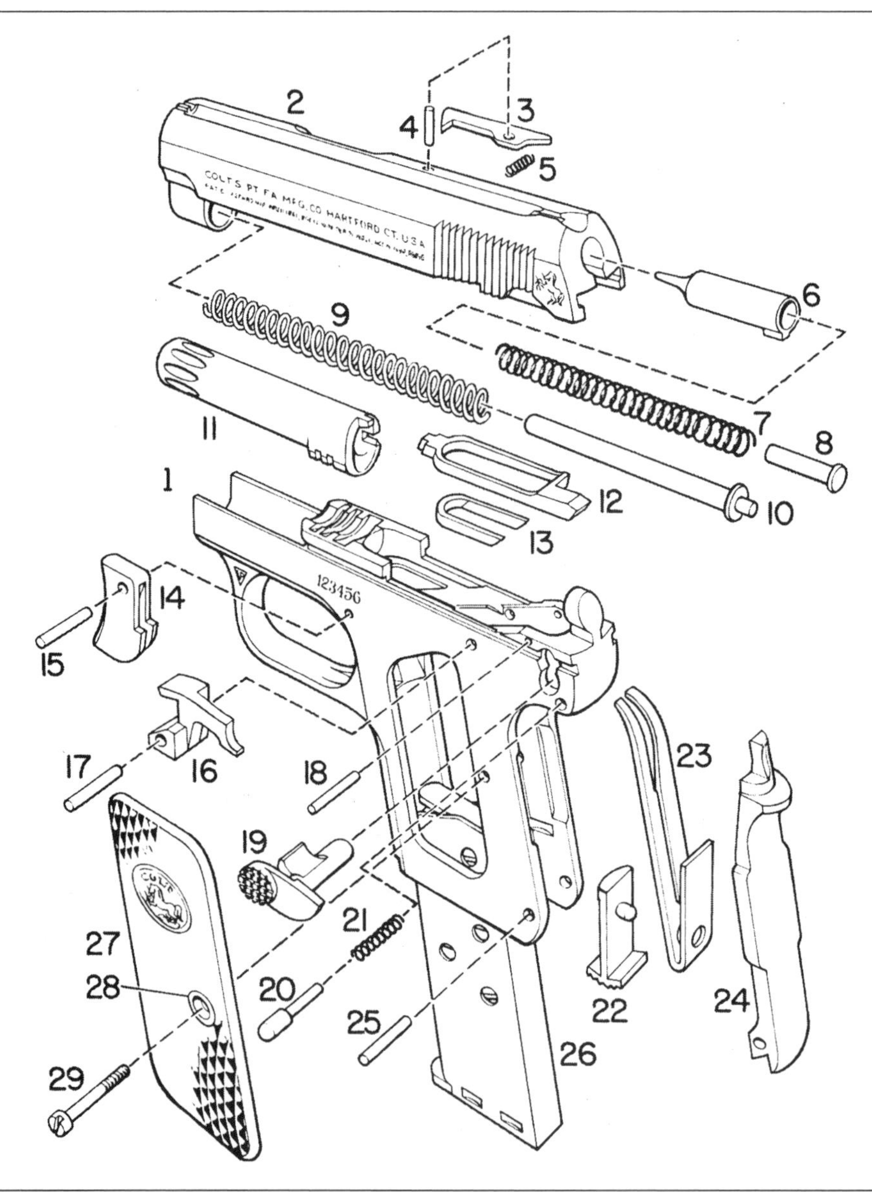

Colt's Patent Firearms Manufacturing Co., has a long history of producing .25 ACP pocket pistols, such as the Model 1908 Hammerless, developed by famed American arms designer John M. Browning, and the Colt Junior, introduced in 1958 and made by Unceta & Cia. in Eibar, Spain.

The 1968 Gun Control Act stopped importation of the Junior, which Colt replaced in 1970 with the Colt Automatic Caliber .25, also made for the company by another manufacturer. This blowback-operated pistol weighed 12½ ounces and measured 4⅛ inch long, and featured integral fixed sights, a mechanical thumb safety/slide hold-open device, an exposed hammer, and a magazine disconnector that prevented firing when the six-shot magazine was removed.

The lack of a rebounding firing pin in the original Colt Junior and .25 Auto allowed the tip of the firing pin to contact the primer of a chambered cartridge when the hammer was fully lowered, making the pistol unsafe to carry with a round in the chamber and the hammer down. A recall issued in the mid-1980s allowed Colt to retrofit returned pistols with a rebounding firing pin.

The Colt Automatic Caliber .25 was discontinued in 1975.

DISASSEMBLY

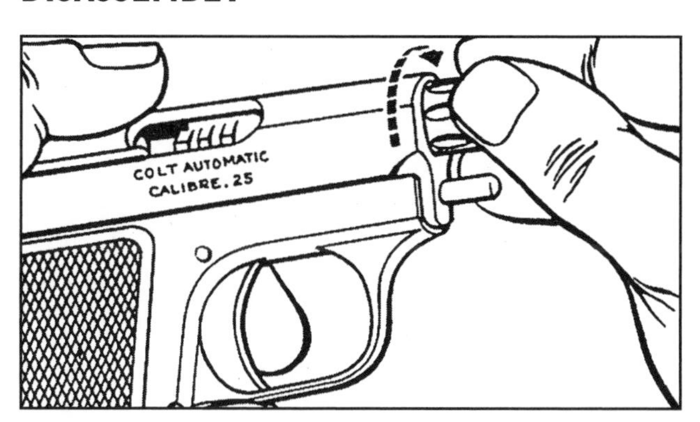

1 Check the pistol to be sure it is unloaded. Insert magazine and pull the trigger. (Caution: Do not attempt to disassemble this gun with the action cocked.) Remove magazine. Holding the pistol as shown, draw the slide back until its front edge is about 1/16 of an inch from the front edge of the receiver. Turn the barrel ¼-turn to the right. The slide may now be drawn forward and off the receiver. Turn the barrel back ¼ turn to the left and drop it out of the receiver from the rear. The firing pin, mainspring, and guide are easily withdrawn from the slide as are the recoil spring and guide from the receiver. The extractor and extractor spring can be removed from the slide by drifting out their retaining pin.

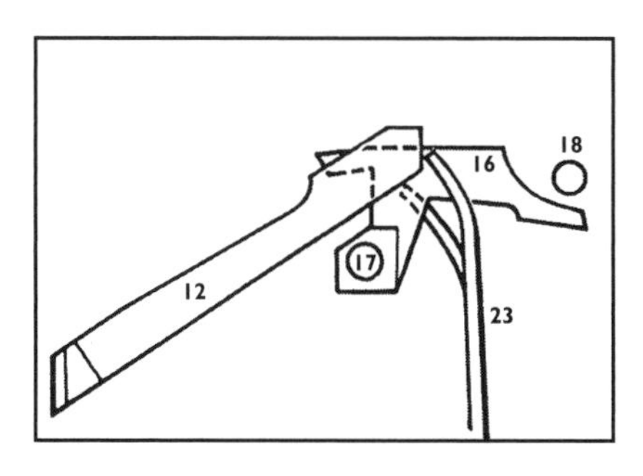

2 Remove the stocks. Drift out the grip safety pin (25) and remove the grip safety (24) from the receiver. Remove the sear spring (23). Note that the short leaf of the sear spring faces toward the rear of the pistol. Remove the magazine catch (22). Turn the slide lock safety (19) to the "up" position and withdraw it from the receiver. Remove the slide lock safety plunger and spring (20 and 21) from their hole beneath the slide lock safety. Drift out the sear and grip safety pin (17) and remove the sear through the bottom of the receiver behind the magazine well. Normally there is no need to withdraw the sear stop pin (18). The trigger may be withdrawn by drifting out its retaining pin (15). Withdraw the connector (12) from its grooves in the receiver. The depressor (13) is not normally removed but can be withdrawn toward the rear through the connector grooves. Reassemble in reverse order, ensuring that the sear, connector, sear spring, and sear stop pin are in the proper relationship as shown by the diagram.

COLT MODEL 1911/1911A1 PISTOL

PARTS LEGEND

1. Barrel
2. Barrel bushing
3. Barrel link
4. Barrel link pin
5. Disconnector
6. Ejector
7. Ejector pin
8. Extractor
9. Firing pin
10. Firing pin spring
11. Firing pin stop
12. Front sight
13. Grip safety (1911A1)
14. Hammer
15. Hammer pin
16. Hammer strut
17. Hammer strut pin
18. Magazine assembly
19. Magazine catch
20. Magazine catch lock
21. Magazine spring
22. Mainspring
23. Mainspring cap
24. Mainspring cap pin (1911A1)
25. Mainspring housing (1911A1)
26. Mainspring housing pin
27. Mainspring housing pin retainer (1911A1)
28. Plunger spring assembly
29. Plunger tube
30. Plunger spring
31. Rear sight
32. Recoil spring
33. Recoil spring guide
34. Recoil spring plug
35. Safety lock
36. Safety lock plunger
37. Sear
38. Sear/disconnector pin
39. Sear spring
40. Slide
41. Slide stop
42. Slide stop plunger
43. Grip assembly
44. Grip screws (4)
45. Grip screw bushing
46. Trigger
47. Frame
48. Lanyarg loop (1911A1)

The fact that the U.S. Pistol, Caliber .45, Model of 1911, was the official American military handgun for more than 70 years, speaks well for both the Colt firm and the board of U.S. Army officers involved in the pistol's selection. This selection board, convened by a special order of the Secretary of War dated December 28, 1906, considered .45 caliber semi-automatic pistol designs from Colt, Luger, Savage, Knoble, Bergmann, and White-Merrill; double-action .45 caliber revolvers from Colt and Smith & Wesson; and the unique British Webley-Fosbery semi-automatic revolver.

The evaluation program instituted by the board was designed to simulate rigorous service conditions as much as possible and included endurance, dust, rust, accuracy, functioning, and numerous other tests calculated to reveal design flaws and general service capabilities of the various guns submitted.

By 1907 the board had completed its work and all but the Colt and Savage entries had been eliminated from consideration. After testing of these two guns involving two troops of U.S. Cavalry, additional improvements, and a series of further experiments and informal tests, a new selection board, convened in March of 1911, issued a report which began:

"Of the two pistols, the board was of the opinion that the Colt is superior, because it is more reliable, more enduring, more easily disassembled when there are broken parts to be replaced, and the more accurate."

That, in short, explains why the Browning-Colt .45 Automatic pistol was eventually adopted as an official U.S. service arm and formally designated as the U.S. Pistol, Caliber .45, Model of 1911. Colt reportedly made up nearly 200 experimental pistols before producing the model finally accepted.

Serviceably accurate, readily disassembled without the use of tools, and extremely rugged in every detail, the Government Model pistol achieved a reputation for combat serviceability equaled by few, if any, military handguns. To address difficulties some shooters reported with the pistol, during the early 1920s, several changes were made to improve its handling, including an arched mainspring housing, shorter hammer

continued on page 95

DISASSEMBLY

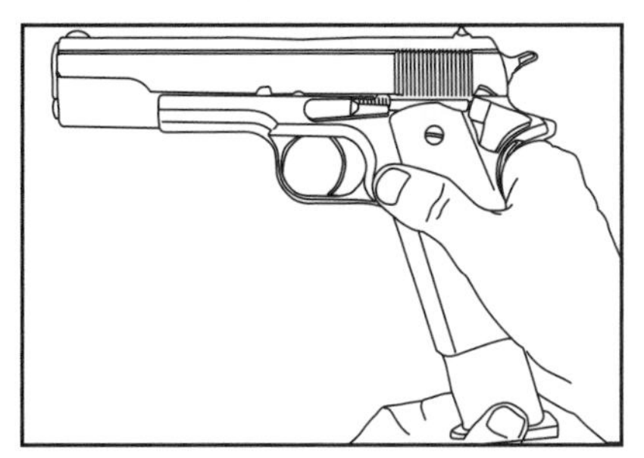

1 Press magazine catch with right thumb and, at same time, withdraw magazine from receiver. Pull slide to rear and look in chamber to see that gun is not loaded. Close slide and pull trigger so hammer is down.

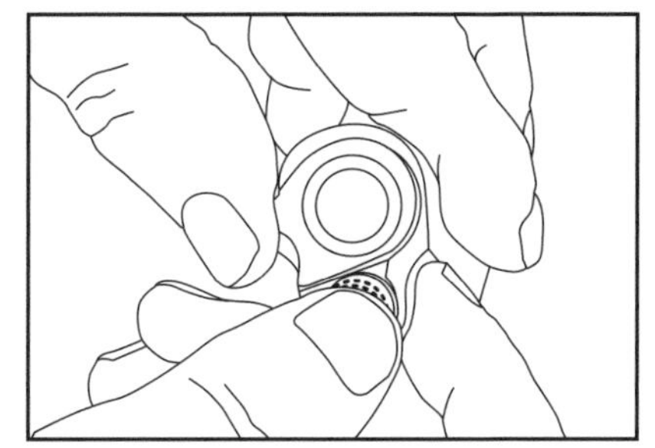

2 With thumb, press inward on knurled end of plug, at same time rotating barrel bushing ¼-turn clockwise to free plug and recoil spring assembly. Rest heel of gun on table so both hands may be used.

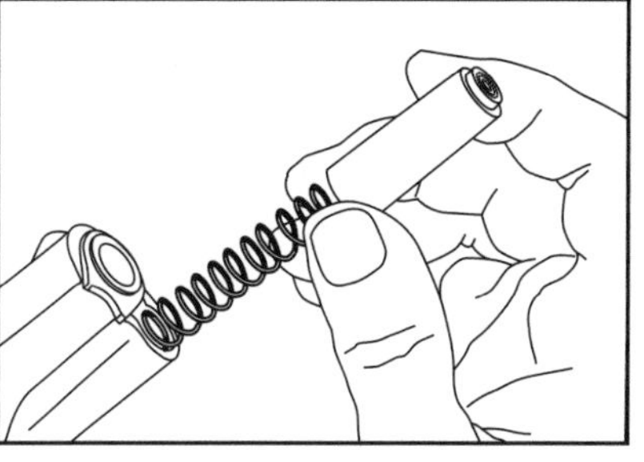

3 Remove plug and recoil spring. If spring does not come free easily, rotate plug in counterclockwise direction to separate plug from recoil spring.

4 Rotate barrel bushing counter-clockwise until disengaged from slide. Remove barrel bushing.

5 Pull slide to the rear until lug on slide stop is aligned with disassembly notch in slide. Using the left hand, push rounded end of slide stop pin protruding on right side of receiver inward, disengaging slide stop from slide.

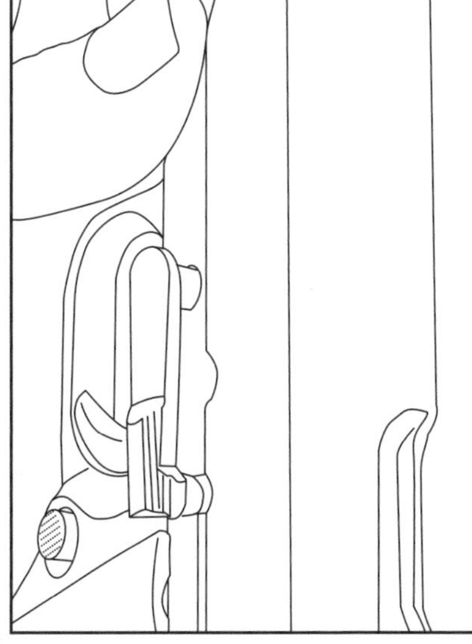

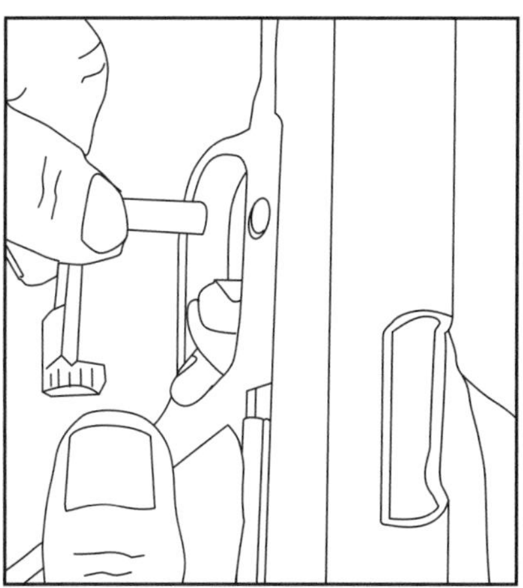

6 Remove slide stop out of left side of frame.

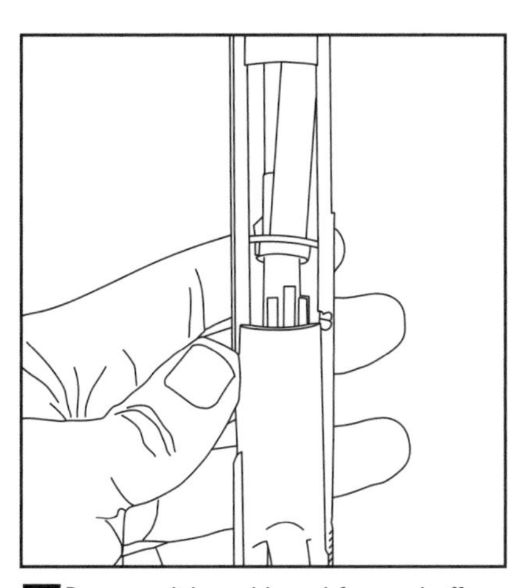

7 Remove slide and barrel forward off frame.

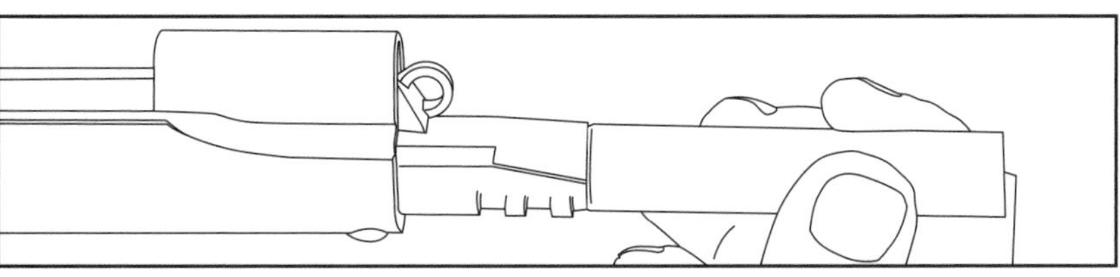

8 Rotate barrel link down, against barrel, and pull barrel forward out of frame.

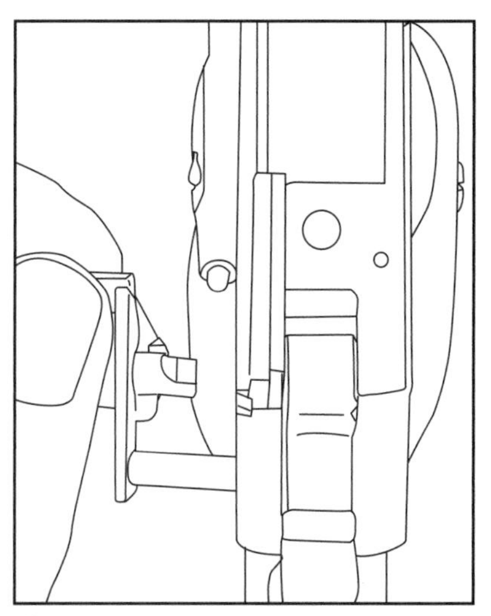

9 With hammer cocked, rotate safety lock almost to "safe" position. It can now be pulled to left and away from frame.

COLT MODEL 1911/1911A1 PISTOL

DISASSEMBLY CONTINUED

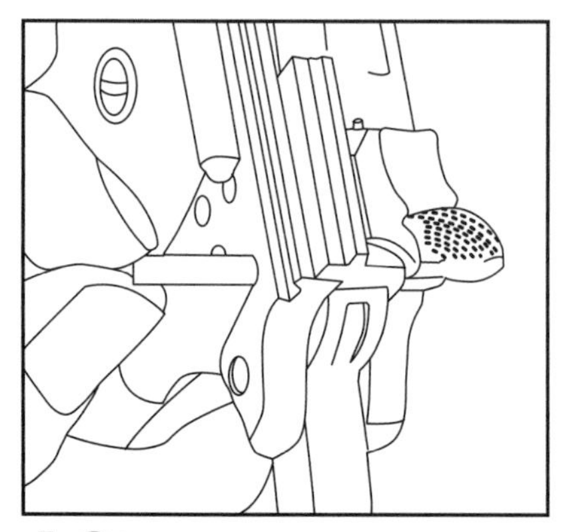

10 Remove hammer pin from left side of frame.

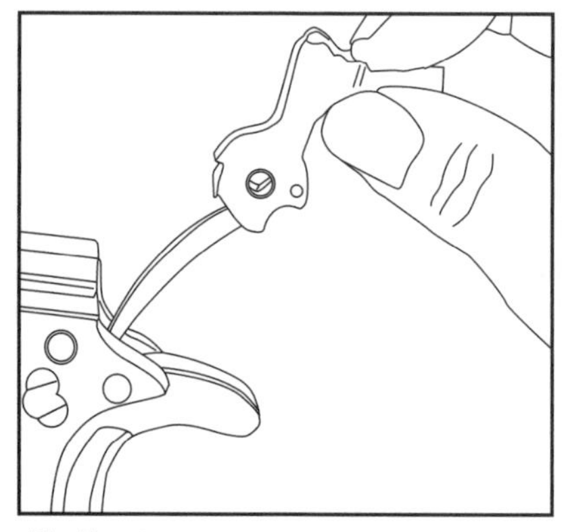

11 Lift out hammer assembly.

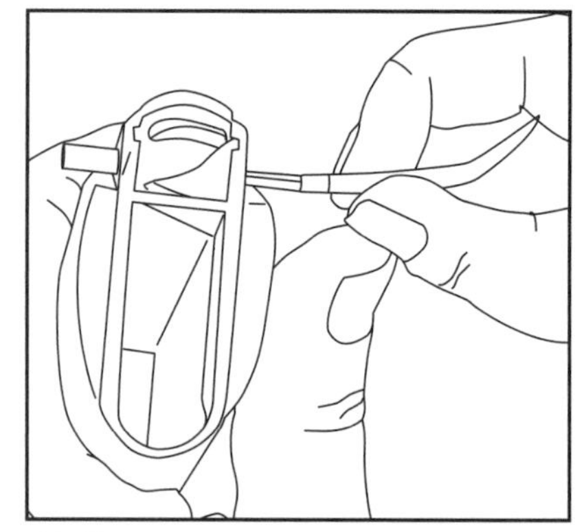

12 Using hammer strut, punch out mainspring housing pin.

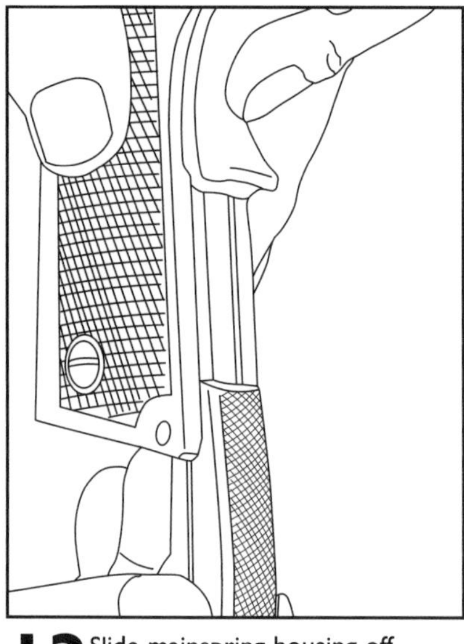

13 Slide mainspring housing off receiver.

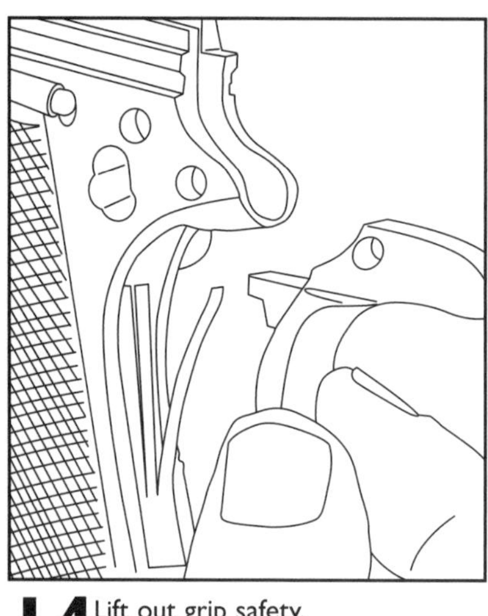

14 Lift out grip safety.

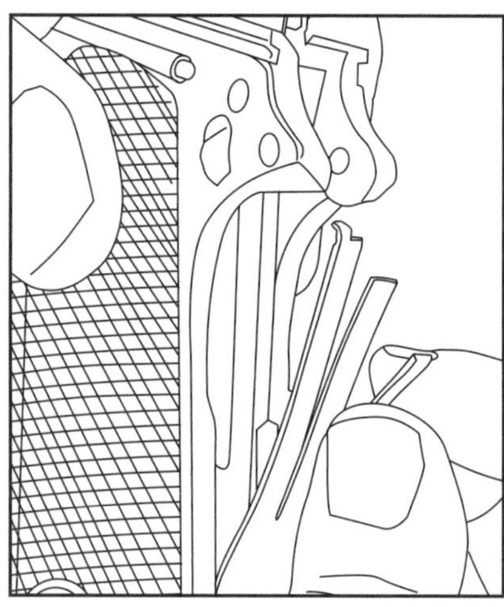

15 Lift out sear spring.

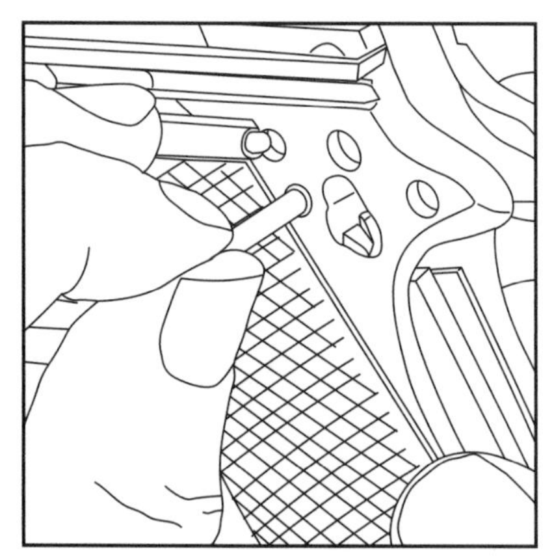

16 Remove sear pin from left side of frame.

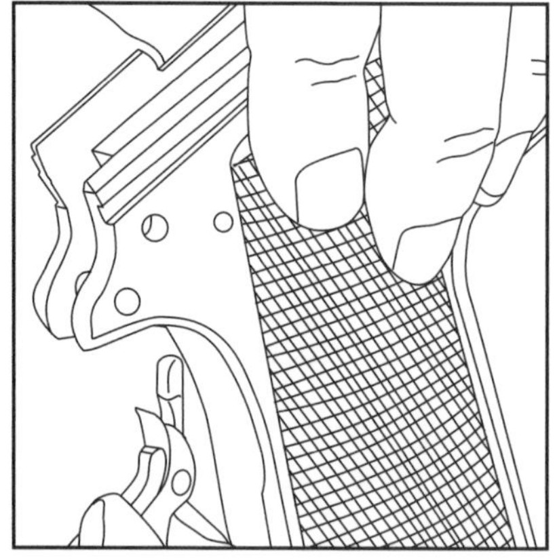

17 Lift out sear and disconnector. Note relationship of these parts to facilitate reassembly.

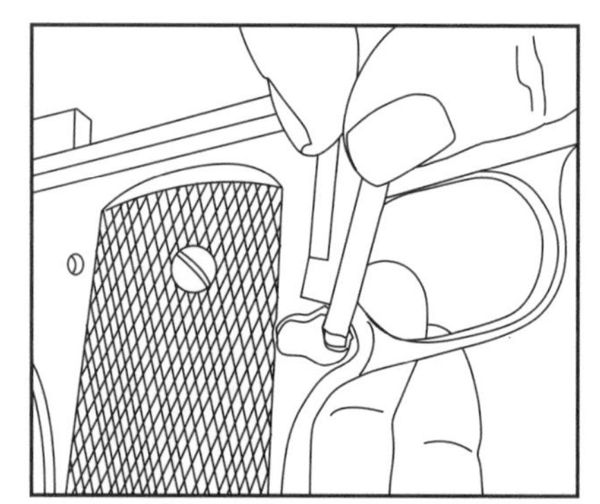

18 Depress magazine catch from left side; at same time rotate magazine catch lock ¼-turn counterclockwise using lip of sear spring as screwdriver. Magazine catch assembly is then removed from right side of receiver. Catch assembly can be reduced to components by turning lock clockwise ¼-turn. Spring and lock will come out.

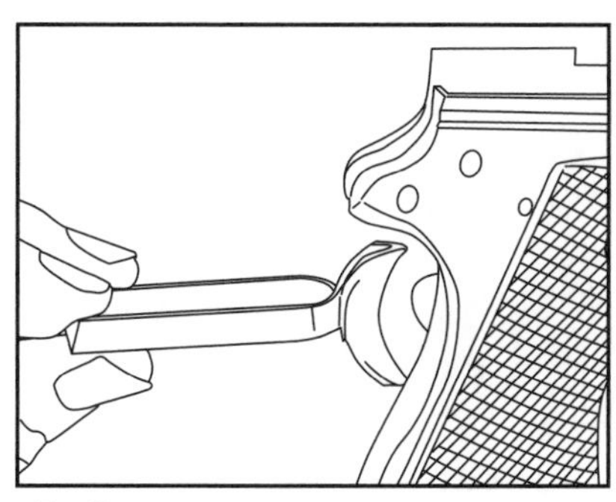

19 Pull trigger out the rear of the frame.

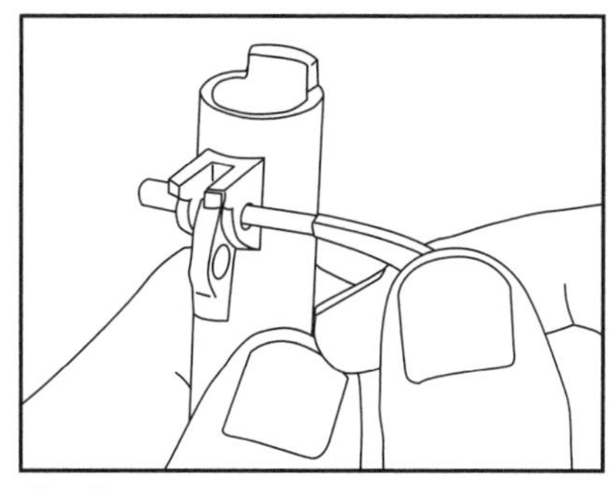

20 With hammer strut, push out link pin, separating link from barrel.

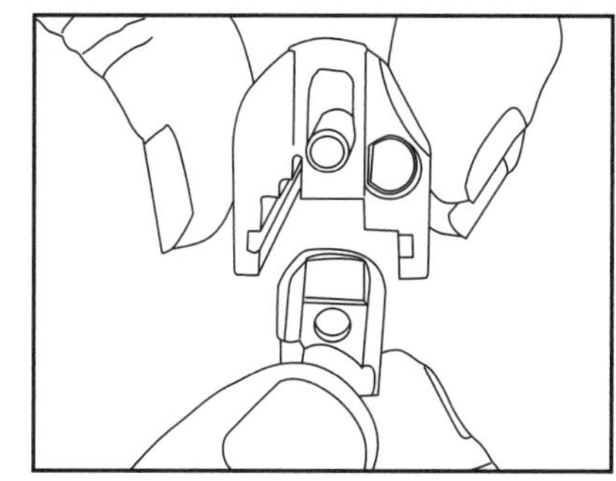

21 With hammer strut, push in on firing pin. At same time place fingernail against top edge of firing pin stop and push downward, freeing firing pin stop from recess in slide.

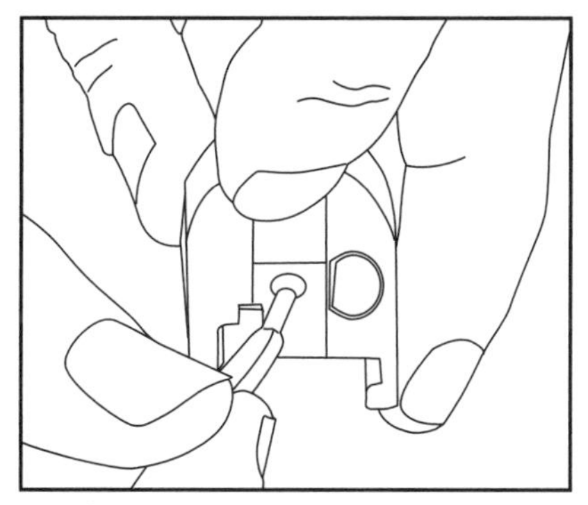

22 Remove firing pin stop. Firing pin assembly can now be re-moved from slide.

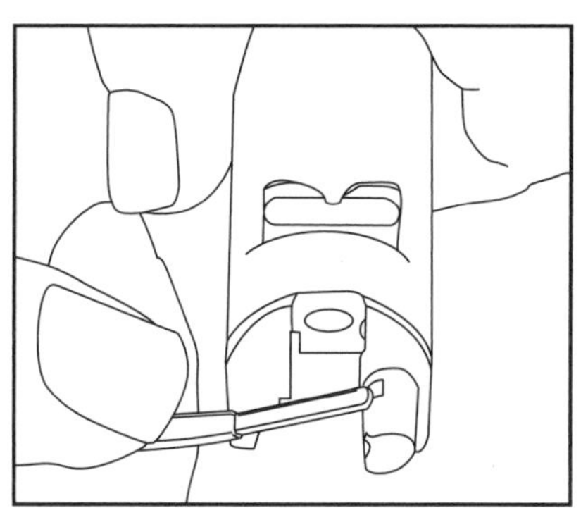

23 With hammer strut, pry out and remove extractor.

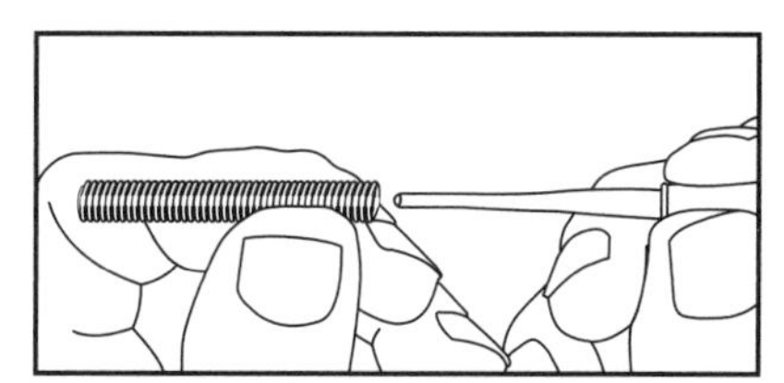

24 Separate firing pin from firing pin spring.

continued from page 92

spur, Patridge-type sights, short trigger, and longer grip safety horn. The modifications to the hammer spur and grip safety eliminated 'pinching' of the thumb web, and shooters with short fingers or small hands welcomed the shorter trigger. The better sights also improved the sight picture for target shooting purposes. This improved model was designated as the Model 1911-Al.

To function reliably with a good deal of foreign matter in its mechanism, the M1911 was made with generous clearances between its moving parts. Desirable in a military arm, this was not conducive to target-grade accuracy. Colt, in 1933, introduced the National Match .45, which is the same basic pistol machined to closer tolerances, with a specially-selected barrel and optional adjustable rear sight, and precision-fitted lock work. Although popular, it was discontinued during World War II. It was reinstated in the Colt line in 1957 as the Colt Gold Cup National Match model.

Contemporary target shooters using the M1911 have their commercial or military .45's "accurized" by specialized pistolsmiths, or avail themselves of accurate commercial Government Model pistols that come with match barrels, target sights, numerous ergonomic improvements and precision-fitted components.

Colt later produced a number of variations on the basic M1911 theme. The Colt Commander, introduced in 1950, featured a ¾-inch shorter barrel and an aluminum alloy frame which afforded a 26 ½-ounce weight. A steel-frame model, the Combat Commander, was later added. In 1985, the Officer's Model was brought out, with a 3½-inch barrel and a shorter grip frame which reduced the magazine capacity to six rounds of .45 ACP ammunition. Even smaller was the Defender, a 3-inch barrel M1911 pistol with a weight of 22½ ounces, first cataloged in 1998. In the 1980s, Colt also incorporated a new passive firing-pin safety that prevented the firing pin from striking a cartridge primer unless the trigger was pulled. This was done to prevent an accidental discharge should the pistol fall muzzle-down onto a hard surface.

In recent years, the resurging popularity of the M1911 design has given rise to a number of gunmakers offering Government Model clones, in different lengths and frame materials, and with a wide variety of features and options.

COLT DEFENDER PISTOL

PARTS LEGEND

1. Slide
2. Front sight
3. Rear sight screw
4. Rear sight
5. Extractor
6. Firing pin spring
7. Firing pin
8. Firing pin stop
9. Plunger spring F/P
10. Firing pin plunger
11. Recoil spring bushing
12. Outer recoil spring
13. Recoil spring guide rod
14. Recoil spring cap
15. Inner recoil plunger
16. Recoil spring guide cap
17. Recoil cap retainer
18. Barrel
19. Barrel link
20. Barrel link pin
21. Receiver
22. Ejector
23. Magazine catch
24. Magazine catch spring
25. Magazine catch lock
26. Plunger tube
27. Slide stop plunger
28. Plunger spring
29. Safety lock plunger
30. Grip safety
31. Disconnector
32. Sear
33. Trigger bar lever
34. Plunger lever
35. Hammer
36. Hammer strut pin
37. Hammer strut
38. Main spring cap
39. Main spring
40. Housing pin retainer
41. Main spring housing
42. Main spring cap pin
43. Trigger assembly
44. Sear spring
45. Main spring housing pin
46. Stock screw bushing (4)
47. Safety lock
48. Slide stop
49. Ejector pin
50. Hammer pin
51. Sear pin
52. Stock set
53. Stock screw
54. Magazine
55. Magazine follower
56. Magazine spring

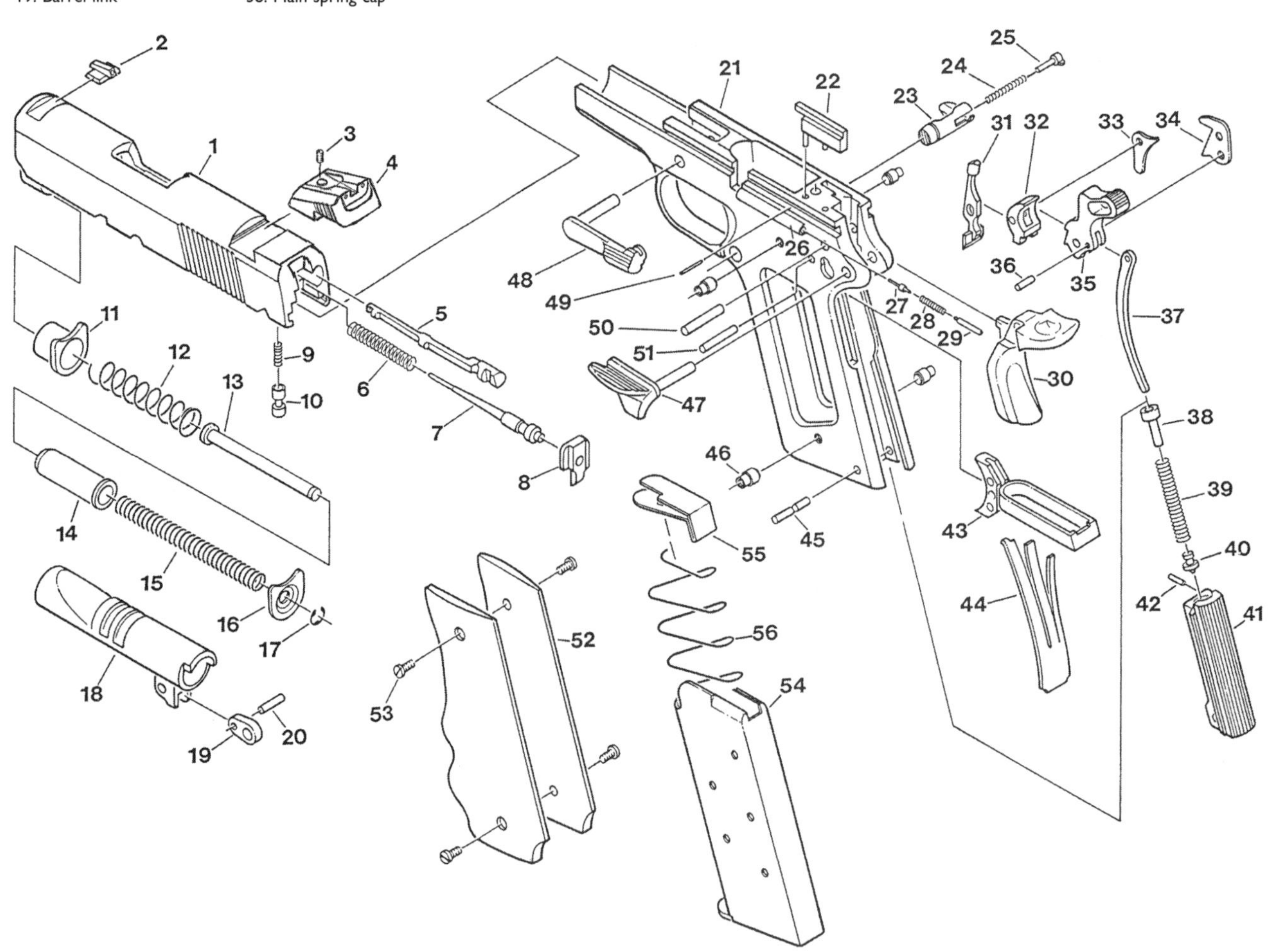

In 1972, the U.S. Army adopted the M15 General Officer's Model pistol developed by the Rock Island Arsenal as a self-defense weapon for high-ranking officers. This was a compact, lightweight version of the original M1911A1 Pistol. The Colt Defender, introduced in 1997, is a commercial descendant of the General Officer's Model, with a shorter grip, barrel and slide than the Government Model pistol.

One of Colt's Series 90 semi-automatic pistols, the Defender features an aluminum alloy frame — a concept pioneered by Colt as early as 1948 — a brushed stainless slide, a 3-inch bull barrel with no bushing, a lightweight aluminum trigger and a Commander-style hammer. Magazine capacity is six rounds of .45 ACP ammunition.

Sighting is by way of a front post dovetailed into the slide, and a fixed rear sight resembling the Novak Low-Mount sight. Both front and rear sights are marked with white dots. The pistol features the traditional M1911A1 thumb and grip safeties, as well as the Colt Series 80 passive firing pin safety.

DISASSEMBLY

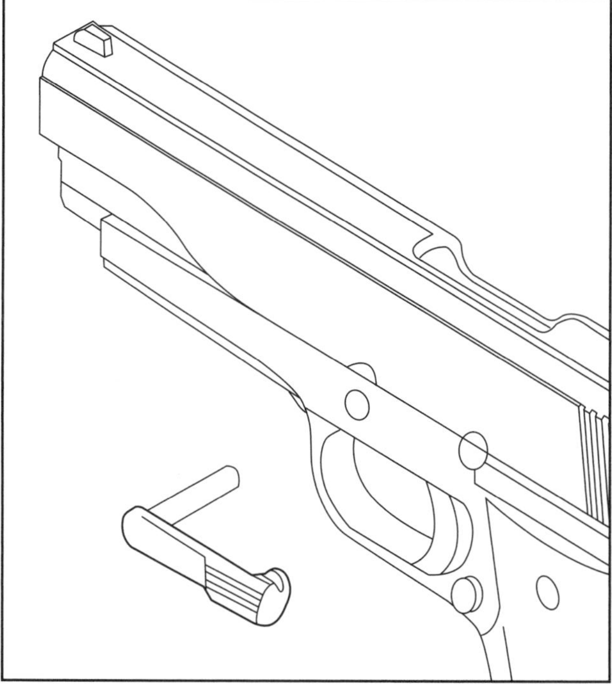

1 Ensure magazine is removed and pistol is not loaded. Cock hammer by pulling back on hammer spur. Pull slide to rear until lug on slide stop is opposite disassembly notch and push rounded end of pin of slide stop (on right side of receiver) inward and through receiver to disengage slide stop from slide. Remove slide stop and push slide forward off the receiver.

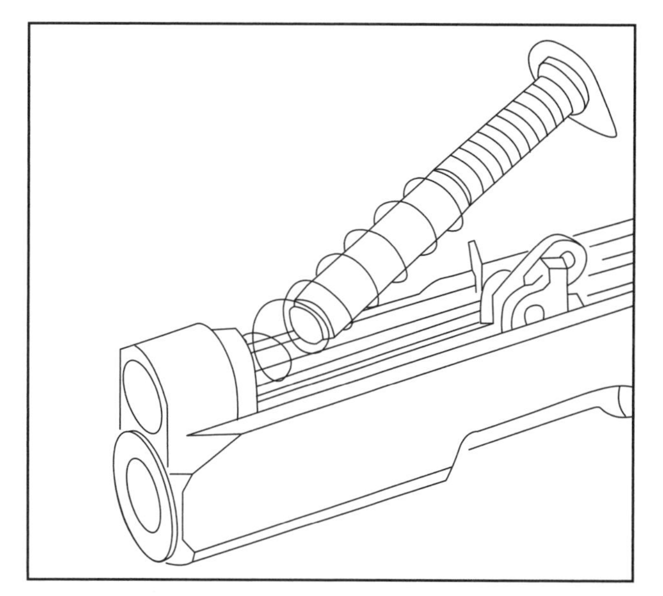

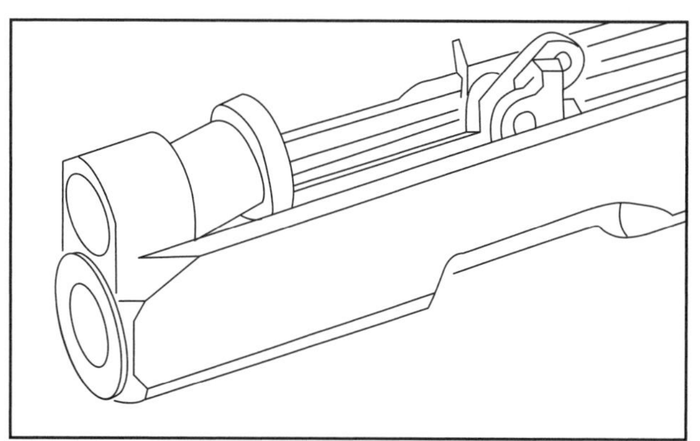

2 Compress and remove recoil spring assembly, then separate outer spring from it. Lift out recoil spring bushing. Push link forward and remove barrel from slide. CAUTION: Do not strip your pistol further than previously described. Do not remove or alter parts, particularly safety parts. If additional maintenance is required, see "Service and Repair" in the instruction manual.

COLT FRONTIER SCOUT REVOLVER

PARTS LEGEND

1. Barrel
2. Ejector tube plug
3. Ejector rod tube
   3a. Ejector tube screw
4. Nylon washer, small (8)
5. Backstrap screw, bottom (2)
6. Ejector rod
7. Ejector spring
8. Stock screw
9. Stock, left
10. Stock pin
11. Mainspring
12. Backstrap
13. Stock, right
14. Stock screw nut
15. Backstrap screw, top (3)
16. Gate spring
17. Gate detent
18. Hand and post
19. Hammer
20. Hand spring
21. Gate
22. Trigger
23. Bolt
24. Bolt and trigger spring
25. Bolt spring screw
26. Hammer screw
27. Bolt and trigger screw
28. Nylon washer, large (2)
29. Recoil cup pin
30. Base pin screw
31. Base pin
32. Recoil cup
33. Firing pin spring
34. Firing pin
35. Cylinder bushing
36. Cylinder
37. Frame

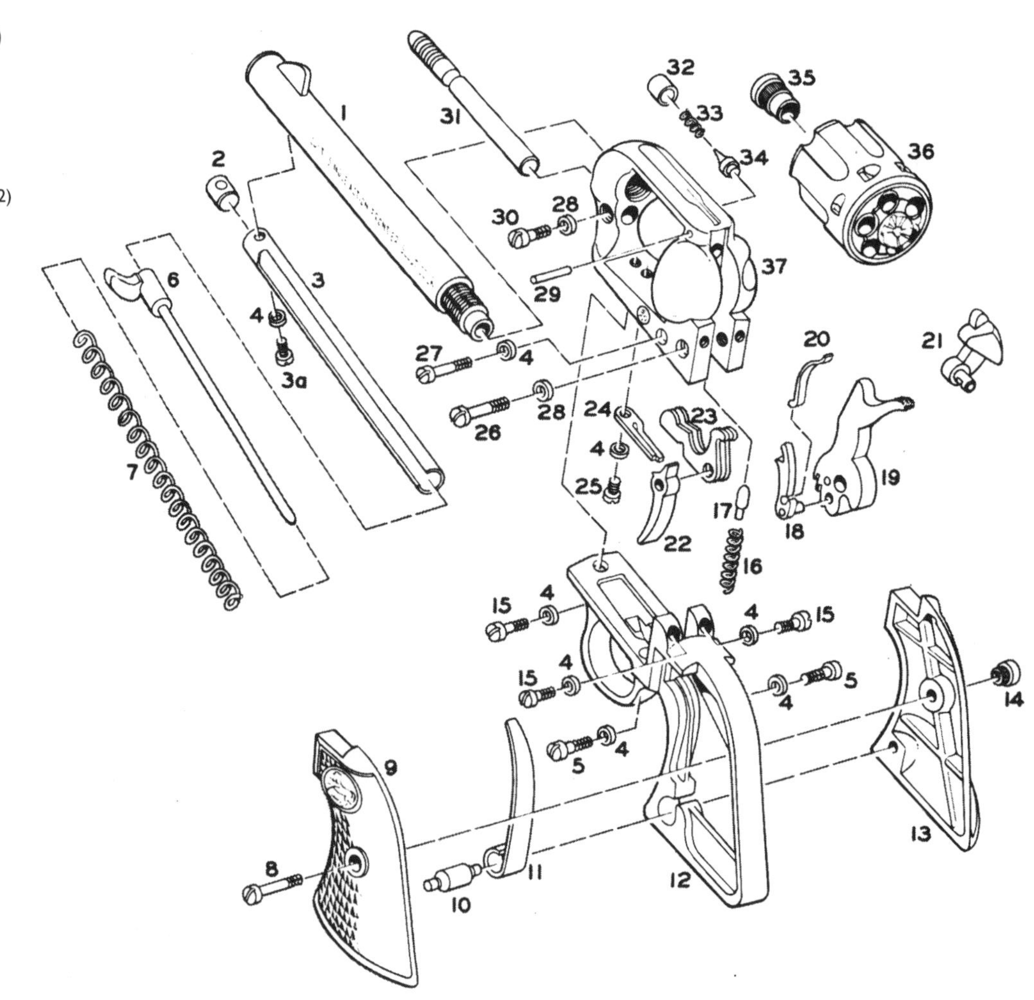

In late 1957 Colt's Patent Firearms Mfg. Co. announced production of a new .22 Long Rifle single-action revolver patterned after the famed Model P Single Action Army revolver. Designated the Frontier Scout, it was about 4/5 the size of its progenitor and featured a one-piece aluminum alloy grip frame. The upper frame, containing the cylinder and lockwork, was also of aluminum, but the barrel and cylinder were of steel. Barrel length was originally 4¾ inches, and is empty weight was 23 ounces. Initially the Frontier Scout was furnished in a dual-tone finish, in which the grip and cylinder frames were bright and the barrel and cylinder were blue. An all-blue version was announced in September 1958.

The 9½-inch barrel, Buntline Frontier Scout was introduced in July 1958, available in blue finish only. In July 1959 Colt began delivery of Frontier Scout revolvers chambered for the then-new .22 Winchester Magnum Rimfire cartridge.

Colt Industries terminated production of the Frontier Scout revolver in 1970, replacing it with the Peacemaker and New Frontier models.

DISASSEMBLY

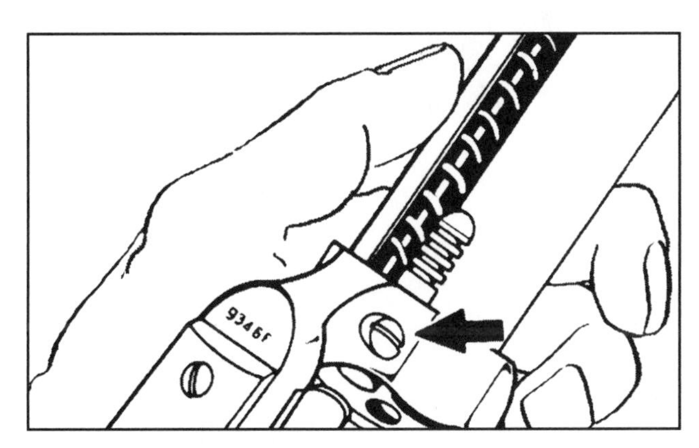

1 To remove cylinder (36), first ensure that the hammer (19) is in half-cock position with cylinder free to rotate. Open loading gate (21). Next, using screwdriver, remove base pin screw (30) and washer (28). Withdraw base pin (31). Cylinder may now be removed from loading gate side of arm.

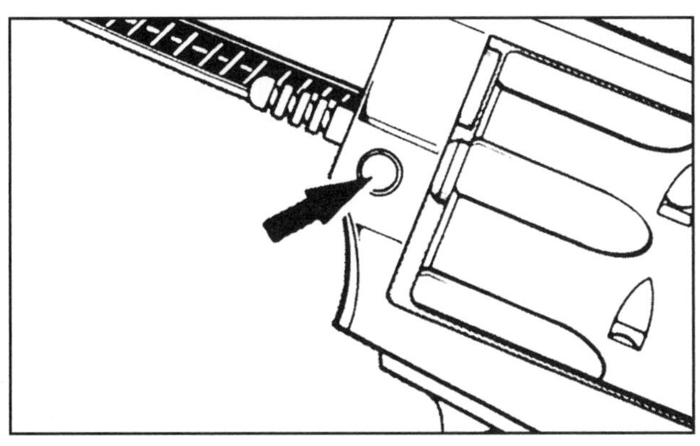

2 Reassemble cylinder into revolver in reverse order. Locking notch in base pin must be properly aligned with base pin screw hole in left side of frame (37), otherwise screw cannot be replaced.

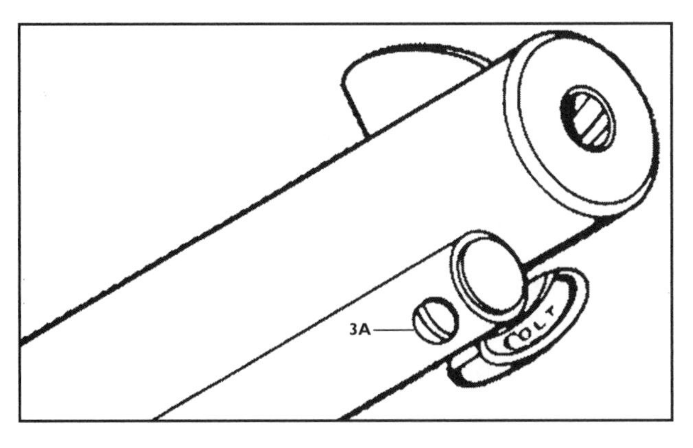

3 To remove ejector rod tube (3) and assembly, including ejector rod (6) and ejector spring (7), unscrew ejector tube screw (3a) holding assembly to right lower side of barrel (l). Entire assembly may now be removed. Reassemble in reverse order, ensuring that small nylon washer (4) is replaced.

COLT GOLD CUP NATIONAL MATCH

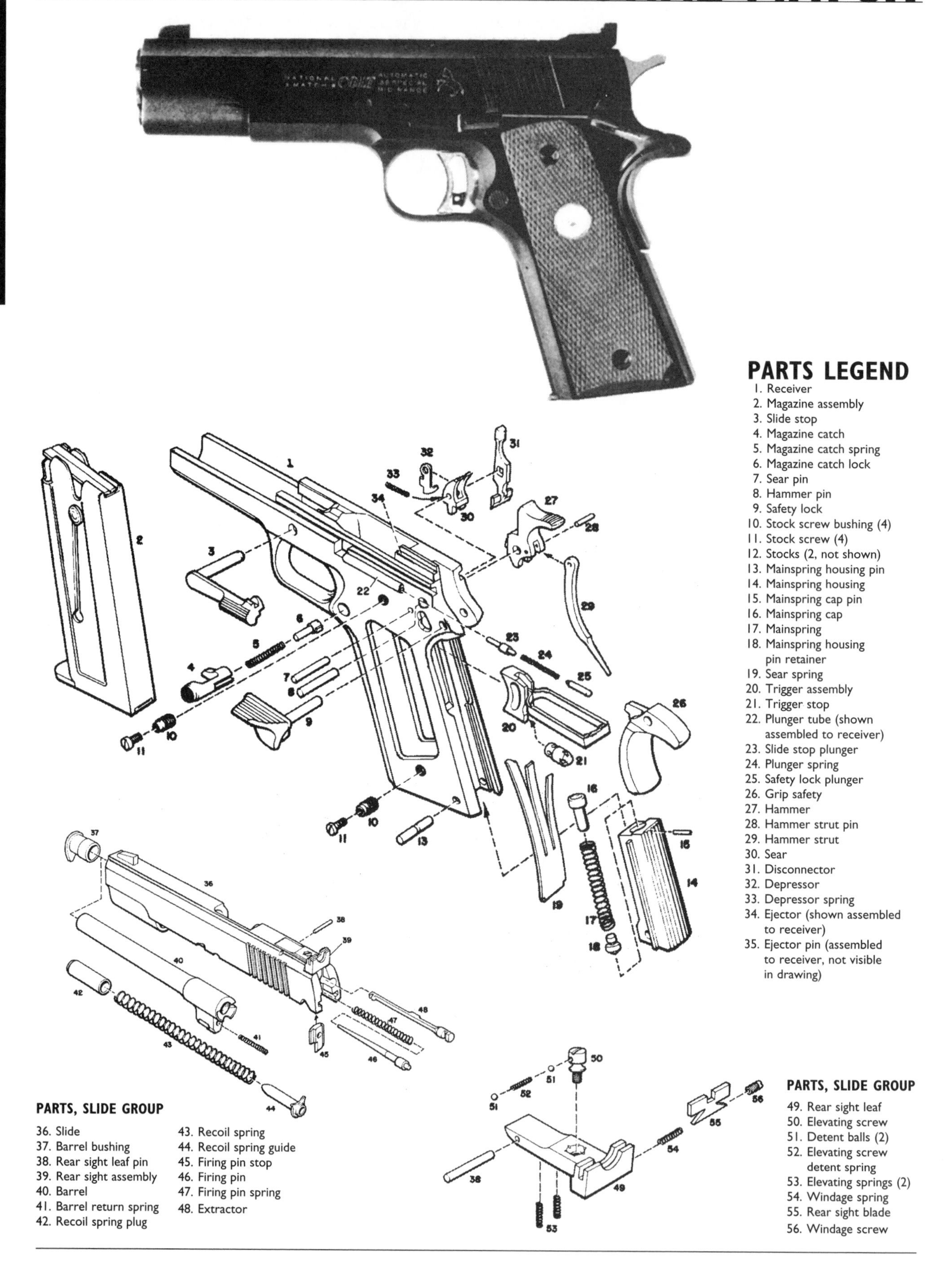

PARTS LEGEND

1. Receiver
2. Magazine assembly
3. Slide stop
4. Magazine catch
5. Magazine catch spring
6. Magazine catch lock
7. Sear pin
8. Hammer pin
9. Safety lock
10. Stock screw bushing (4)
11. Stock screw (4)
12. Stocks (2, not shown)
13. Mainspring housing pin
14. Mainspring housing
15. Mainspring cap pin
16. Mainspring cap
17. Mainspring
18. Mainspring housing pin retainer
19. Sear spring
20. Trigger assembly
21. Trigger stop
22. Plunger tube (shown assembled to receiver)
23. Slide stop plunger
24. Plunger spring
25. Safety lock plunger
26. Grip safety
27. Hammer
28. Hammer strut pin
29. Hammer strut
30. Sear
31. Disconnector
32. Depressor
33. Depressor spring
34. Ejector (shown assembled to receiver)
35. Ejector pin (assembled to receiver, not visible in drawing)

PARTS, SLIDE GROUP

36. Slide
37. Barrel bushing
38. Rear sight leaf pin
39. Rear sight assembly
40. Barrel
41. Barrel return spring
42. Recoil spring plug
43. Recoil spring
44. Recoil spring guide
45. Firing pin stop
46. Firing pin
47. Firing pin spring
48. Extractor

PARTS, SLIDE GROUP

49. Rear sight leaf
50. Elevating screw
51. Detent balls (2)
52. Elevating screw detent spring
53. Elevating springs (2)
54. Windage spring
55. Rear sight blade
56. Windage screw

In 1957, Colt introduced the Gold Cup National Match model, a version of the standard .45 ACP M1911 Government Model specially modified for target shooting. The National Match featured a hand-fitted slide, match-grade barrel, collet-type barrel bushing, long trigger with overtravel stop, flat mainspring housing, enlarged ejection port and adjustable target-type sights. Additionally, the sear had a spring-loaded depressor to prevent hammer follow.

The Colt Gold Cup National Match Mark III, made from 1961 through 1974, was a variation of the original National Match pistol, and was chambered in .38 Spl. and chamber dimensions were optimized for accuracy, and other modifications made to allow the pistol to reliably function with .38 Spl. wadcutter ammunition. Additionally, a new magazine was developed to feed the rimmed .38 Spl. cartridge.

An interesting mechanical change from the .45 ACP National Match model was the use, in the Mark III, of a barrel lacking the characteristic M1911 swinging link. Instead, the Mark III barrel featured an under-lug with a longitudinal slot that engaged the slide stop pin. This allowed the barrel to recoil rearward a short distance with the slide, with the bore axis remaining parallel to the slide centerline. A small barrel return spring assisted the barrel to go back forward.

The Mark III pistol was fitted with Colt "Accro" rear sights and a Patridge front. Later Colt Gold Cup pistols — the Series 70 and Series 80 — have used Colt-Eliason target sights.

DISASSEMBLY

Press in magazine catch (4) at left side of receiver and drop magazine assembly (2) out butt of pistol. Draw slide to rear and check chamber to be sure pistol is unloaded. Return slide forward, pull trigger and let hammer down with thumb. Press inward on knurled end of recoil spring plug (42) and turn barrel bushing approximately ¼ turn clockwise. (Due to close fit of bushing to slide, a wrench fitted to bushing should be employed to loosen it.) Remove plug (42) and recoil spring (43) from front of slide. Rotate barrel bushing counter-clockwise until it disengages from slide and remove to front.

Draw slide to rear until lug at rear end of slide stop (3) lines up with clearance cut on lower left hand edge of slide. Press in rounded end of slide stop pin which protrudes from right-hand side of receiver.

Remove slide stop from left side of receiver. Pull slide forward off receiver and remove recoil spring guide (44). Remove barrel from front of slide, taking care not to lose barrel return spring (41).

Slide group disassembly: Press in on rear end of firing pin (46) with a small punch until it clears firing pin stop (45). Remove firing pin stop from bottom of slide. Firing pin and firing pin spring (47) may be removed from rear of slide. Extractor (48) may be pried from rear of slide with small screw-driver. Removal of rear sight assembly (39) is accomplished by drifting out rear sight leaf pin (38). Complete disassembly of rear sight assembly is not recommended except when necessary for repair. Reassemble in reverse.

Receiver group disassembly: With hammer at full-cock position, rotate safety lock (9) toward its "on" position until it can be pulled out of left side of receiver. Drift out hammer pin (8) and remove hammer (27) and hammer strut (29) from top rear of receiver. Hammer strut can be removed from hammer by drifting out hammer strut pin (28). Drift out mainspring housing pin (13) and slide mainspring housing (14) out of grooves at rear of receiver. Mainspring (17), mainspring cap (16), and mainspring housing pin retainer (18) are removed from housing after drifting out mainspring cap pin (15). Lift grip safety (26) out rear of receiver and remove sear spring (19) from rear of receiver. Drift out sear pin (7); drop sear (30) and disconnector (31) with depressor (32) and depressor spring (33) out of receiver.

Remove stock screws (11) and stocks (12-not shown in exploded drawing) from sides of receiver. Depress magazine catch (4) from left side of receiver and, using a small screwdriver, turn magazine catch lock (6) ¼ -turn counterclockwise from right side of receiver. Remove entire magazine catch assembly from right side of receiver NOTE: Magazine catch assembly parts are shown at left side of receiver in exploded drawing for clarity. They are assembled in the receiver from hole in right side. Turn magazine catch lock (6) ¼ -turn clockwise to separate catch lock, spring (5), and catch (4). Remove trigger assembly (20) with trigger stop (21) from rear of receiver. Reassemble receiver group parts in reverse.

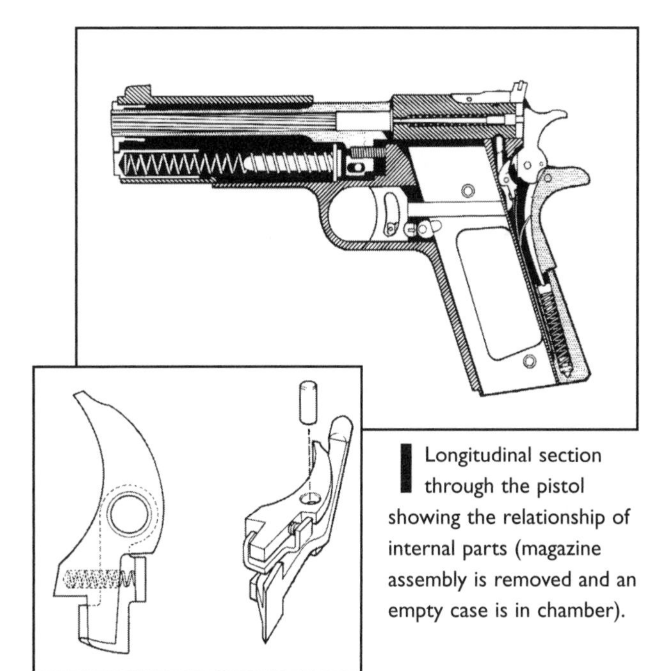

1 Longitudinal section through the pistol showing the relationship of internal parts (magazine assembly is removed and an empty case is in chamber).

2 The sear (30), disconnecter (31), depressor (32), and depressor spring (33) are shown above assembled in correct relationship. In the view to the left the disconnector has been omitted for clarity. In the view to the right, sear, disconnector, depressor, and depressor spring are shown assembled.

To facilitate reassembly of this assembly in receiver, it is suggested that a short slave pin having a length equal to the width of the sear be employed to hold the parts together correctly. The slave pin will be drifted out when sear pin is replaced through frame.

COLT DA NEW ARMY AND NAVY

PARTS LEGEND

1. Frame
2. Barrel
3. Cylinder
4. Ejector & ratchet
5. Ejector rod
6. Ejector spring
7. Crane bushing
8. Crane
9. Ejector head
10. Latch
11. Latch pin
12. Latch spring
13. Hammer
    13A. Hammer pin
14. Stirrup
15. Stirrup pin
16. Strut pin
17. Strut spring
18. Strut
19. Mainspring
20. Mainspring tension screw
21. Crane lock screw
22. Crane lock
23. Recoil plate
24. Locking lever
25. Locking lever screw
26. Trigger
    26A. Trigger pin
27. Hand
28. Hand spring
29. Bolt
30. Bolt spring
31. Rebound lever
    31A. Rebound lever pin
32. Rebound lever spring
33. Rebound lever spring pin
34. Sideplate
35. Sideplate screws (2)
36. Stock pin
37. Stock screw
38. Escutcheons (2), right only shown
39. Stocks (2), right only shown

Cutaway indicates relationship between parts.

In 1889, Colt's Patent Fire Arms Mfg. Co., of Hartford, Connecticut, offered its first double-action revolver with a swing-out cylinder. Chambered for the .38 Short and Long Colt and .41 Short and Long Colt, the revolver, known as the Model 1889 Navy, featured a solid frame and barrel lengths of 3, 4½ and 6 inches. The revolver was adopted by the U.S. Navy, which ordered 5,000 units chambered for .38 Long Colt.

The Army, in 1892, also adopted the revolver, but with some changes. Modifications to the Model 1889 found in the new model, called the Model 1892 New Army & Navy (or, variously, New Navy, 2nd Issue), included double cylinder notches, a double cylinder locking bolt, and shorter cylinder flutes. As with the earlier Navy order, the Army's Model 1892 revolvers were in .38 Long Colt.

Subsequently, the Model 1892 underwent a number of manufacturing and design changes, which led to a succession of models, all in .38 Long Colt. The Model 1894 incorporated the most significant mechanical modification, a locking lever that prevented the hammer from being cocked unless the cylinder was completely closed and locked-something that could not be done on the Model 1892. Later variations of the Model 1892 included the Models 1896, 1901 and 1903.

Commercial models of the New Army & Navy were offered in 3-, 4½-, and 6-inch barrel lengths and in several calibers, including .38 Short and Long Colt, .41 Short and Long Colt, .32-20 WCF, and .38 Special. In 1904, Colt's offered a target version of the Model 1892, the Officer's Model, in .38 Spl. and with adjustable sights. Another variant of the Model 1892 was the Model 1905 Marine Corps, which differed primarily in having a round butt.

In 1908, production of all versions of the New Army & Navy ceased, and in their stead, Colt's introduced an improved revolver, the Colt Army Special.

DISASSEMBLY

To remove cylinder and crane assembly, unscrew crane lock screw (21) and withdraw crane lock (22). Press latch (10) back and swing out cylinder. Grasp crane (8) and pull forward out of frame (1). Further disassembly of cylinder and crane is not recommended. However, if disassembly is absolutely necessary, note that, after pressing in ejector rod (5) and clearing ratchet from cylinder, ejector and ratchet (4) must be unscrewed from ejector rod clockwise. A special wrench or spanner will be necessary to remove crane bushing (7).

To disassemble lock mechanism, unscrew stock screw (37) and remove stocks (39). Remove sideplate screws (35). Loosen sideplate (34) by turning revolver over and tapping frame with a fiber or wooden mallet. If it is necessary to pry out the sideplate to any extent, do so most gently and gradually to avoid burring edges of sideplate cut in frame. Remove sideplate, exposing lock mechanism.

Lift hand (27) out of trigger. Loosen mainspring tension screw (20). Pull hammer to full cock and slip a ½" wooden dowel or handle of a small screwdriver between mainspring (19) and rear strap of frame. Pull trigger, releasing hammer and allowing stirrup (14) to rise clear of its seat in end of mainspring as shown at "A" in Drawing 1. Remove dowel and pull mainspring up out of its seat in frame. Rebound

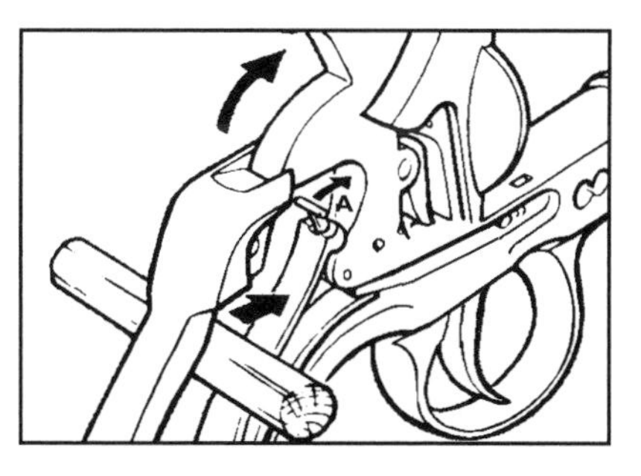

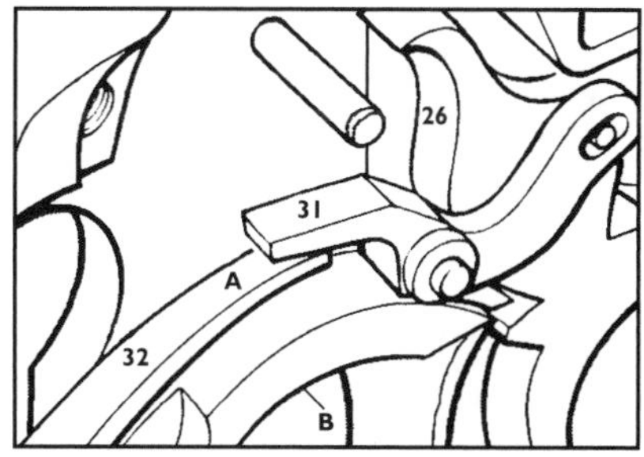

lever spring (32) may be removed by drifting out its pin (33). Pull hammer back to almost full-cock position and lift out of frame. With the blade of a small screwdriver, lift bolt (29) up off its pin and remove. Rebound lever (31) and trigger (26) may now be lifted out of frame. Locking lever (24) is removed by unscrewing locking lever screw (25). Latch may be removed by drifting out latch pin (11) with a very thin punch, withdrawing latch (10) and spring (12) toward the front.

Removal of hammer pin (13A), trigger pin (26A), or rebound lever pin (31A) from frame is not recommended and is seldom if ever necessary.

In reassembling lock mechanism, replace latch assembly, locking lever, and trigger first. Replace rebound lever spring and pin. Compress tip of rebound lever spring with pliers, the jaws of which have been taped or otherwise covered to protect the finish of the arm, applied at A and B as shown in Drawing 2. Drop rebound lever into place while holding spring compressed fully. A little juggling will be necessary when replacing bolt (29), and bolt spring (30) must be pressed down with blade of small screwdriver or other small tool to clear forward arm of rebound lever before bolt can be pressed all the way down into position on trigger pin (26A).

Pull trigger back and replace hammer. Replace mainspring in its seat and compress with a dowel as previously described. Pull stirrup back until it is in position over its seat in tip of mainspring. Pull trigger releasing hammer and withdraw dowel. Replace hand and push forward into its slot. When replacing sideplate, be sure hand spring slips into the recess milled into reverse of sideplate. Replace sideplate screws and stocks. Replace cylinder and crane assembly. Place crane lock and crane lock screw together and press into frame, tightening crane lock screw as it engages its threads.

COLT OFFICIAL POLICE REVOLVER

PARTS LEGEND

1. Hammer
2. Hammer pin
3. Hammer stirrup
4. Hammer stirrup pin
5. Strut
6. Strut spring
7. Strut pin
8. Firing pin
9. Firing pin rivet
10. Safety
11. Safety lever
12. Hand
13. Trigger
14. Trigger pin
15. Mainspring
16. Bolt
17. Bolt spring
18. Bolt screw
19. Rebound lever
20. Rebound lever pin
21. Crane lock
22. Crane lock screw
23. Sideplate
24. Sideplate screws (2)
25. Latch
26. Latch spring
27. Latch spring guide
28. Latch pin
29. Cylinder
30. Cylinder bushing
31. Ejector and ratchet
32. Ejector rod
33. Ejector rod head
34. Ejector spring
35. Crane bushing
36. Crane
37. Barrel
38. Stock pin
39. Stock screw
40. Stocks (2)
41. Escutcheons (2)
42. Recoil Plate
43. Frame

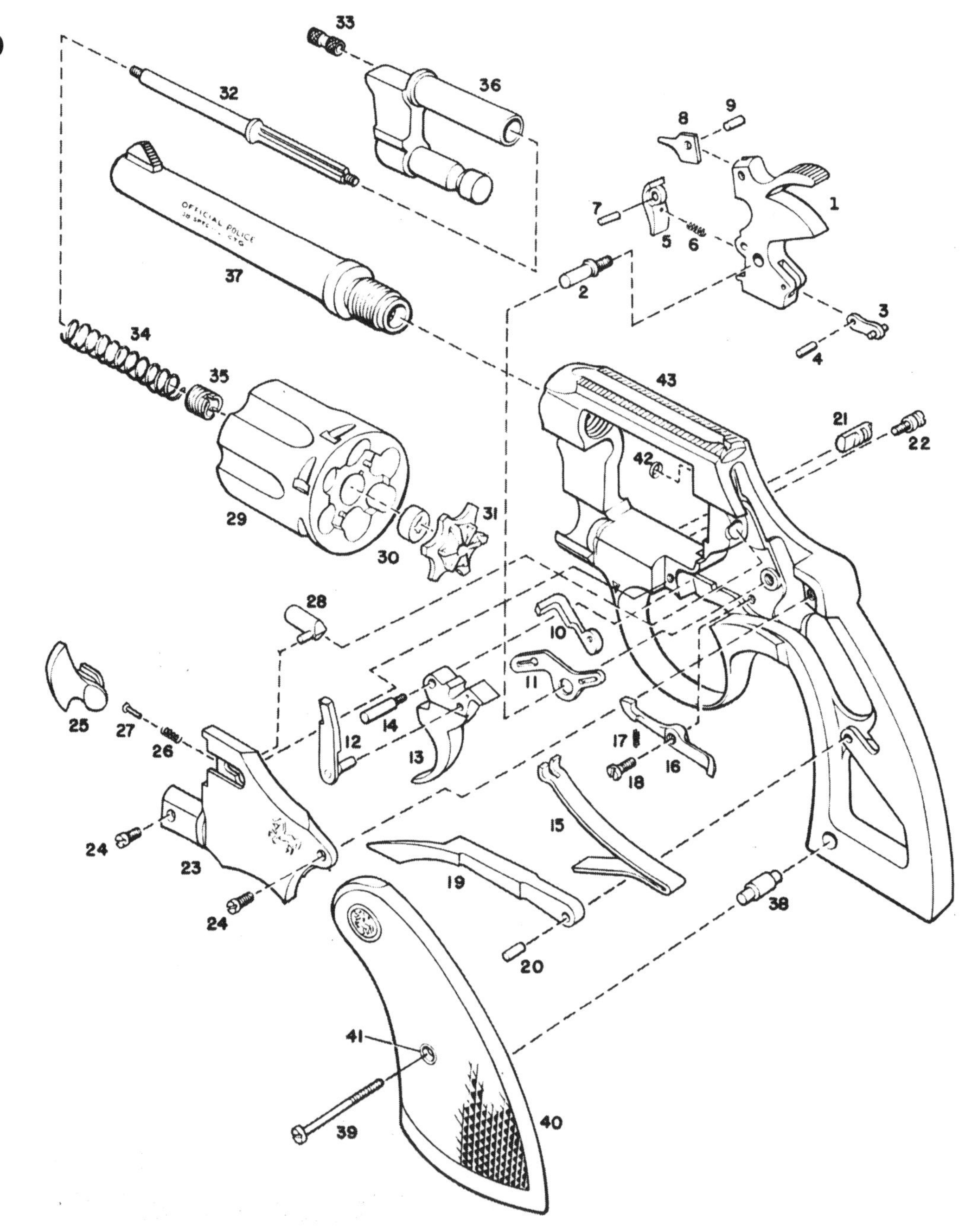

Colt's Official Police Revolver was introduced in 1908, as an improvement over the New Army and Navy revolvers. Originally known as the "Army Special," the Official Police was given its most recent name in 1928. Production of Army Special/Official Police revolvers continued without any interruption in serial number sequence.

From its introduction until 1935, Army Special/Official Police models were offered in .32-20, .38 Special and .41 Colt. In 1930 the Official Police was offered chambered for .22 rimfire ammunition, and in 1935, the .32-20 and .41 Colt versions were discontinued. Over its production life, the Army Special/Official Police was offered with grips of black hard rubber, walnut and reddish-brown plastic. Late-production guns had checkered walnut grips.

During World War II, Colt produced a Parkerized, .38 Spl. version of the Official Police revolver for use by defense plant security officers and other emergency personnel. Known as the Commando model, it was discontinued at the war's end. In addition, Colt Officer's Model revolvers, in .22 rimfire, .32 S&W Long and .38 Special were made using the Official Police frame and mechanism, as were the round-butt, .38 Spl. Marshal model guns made from 1954 to 1956.

Army Special and Official Police revolvers were serially numbered beginning at "1." The change in designation came at about number 526000 — there being an overlap between 513276 and 540000. Marshal models were numbered concurrent with the Official Police production. Rimfire Official Police revolvers, Commando Models and Officer's Models were numbered separately, beginning with "1."

The Official Police revolver was discontinued in 1969.

DISASSEMBLY

Remove crane lock screw (22) and crane lock (21). Swing out cylinder and remove cylinder and crane assembly by pushing to the front. Disassembly of the cylinder and crane assembly should be undertaken only by a competent gunsmith.

Remove stock screw (39) and stocks (40).

Remove side plate screws (24). Do not attempt to pry out the sideplate (23) but tap the frame and sideplate with the wooden handle of a tool until the plate loosens and can be lifted out. Remove the latch (25) and latch spring and guide (26 and 27) from the sideplate.

To remove the mainspring (15), lay the pistol flat and push the hammer back about ¼" with the left forefinger. Holding a screwdriver in the right hand, press down on the mainspring near the stirrup (3) with the fiat tip of the screwdriver. Push the hammer forward to disengage the stirrup from the mainspring and lift out the mainspring with the fingers.

Remove hand (12) from trigger (13). Drive out the rebound lever pin (20) with a punch or drift pin and remove the rebound lever (19). Remove the trigger by lifting it up off the trigger pin (14). Draw the hammer (l) to its rearmost position and lift it up off the hammer pin (2). Drive out the strut pin (7) from the hammer with a small punch and remove the strut (5) and strut spring (6). Drive out the hammer stirrup pin (4) and remove the hammer stirrup (3).

Remove the safety lever (ll) from its pivot around the base of the hammer pin (2) and remove the safety (10) from its slot in the frame. Remove the bolt screw (18) and remove the bolt (16), using care not to lose the bolt spring (17). The latch pin (28) can be dropped out of its hole in the frame.

Removal of the barrel, firing pin, recoil plate, stock pin, trigger pin, or hammer pin should be attempted only by an experienced gunsmith.

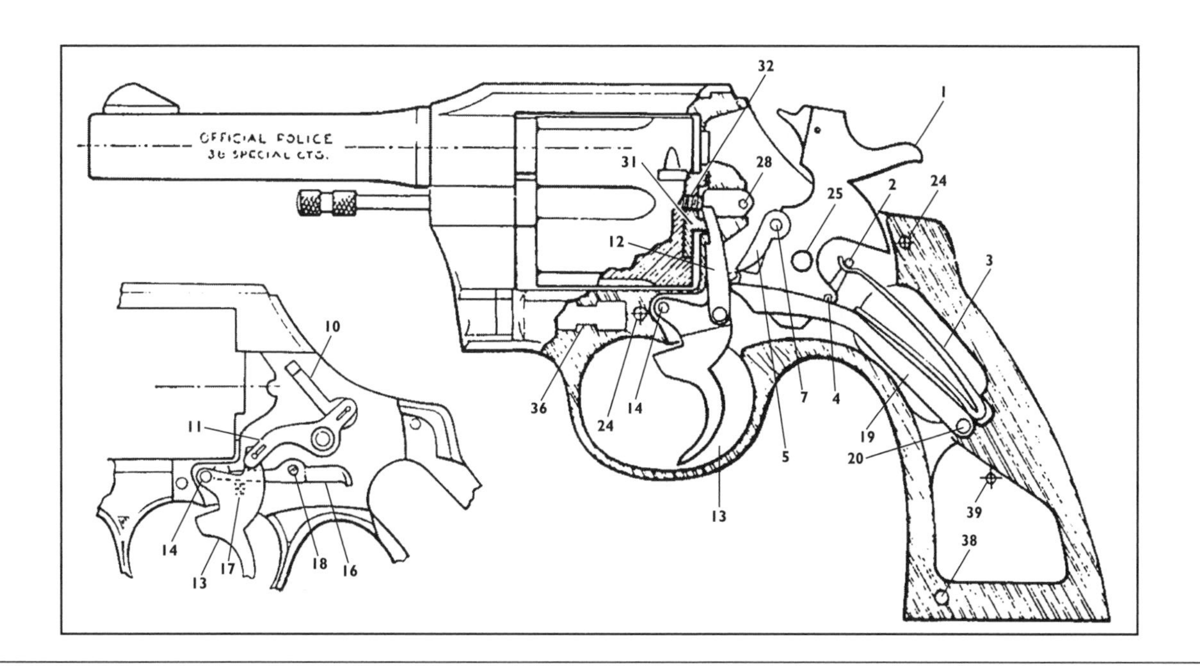

COLT PATERSON REVOLVING PISTOL

PARTS LEGEND

1. Barrel
2. Wedge screw
3. Cylinder
4. Nipple (5)
5. Ratchet retaining collar pin
6. Ratchet retaining collar
7. Ratchet
8. Wedge
9. Cylinder arbor
10. Recoil shield
11. Frame
12 Bolt
13. Upper trigger spring screw
14. Upper trigger spring
15. Trigger actuating bar
16. Trigger
17. Frame plate
18. Bolt and trigger spring
19. Bolt and trigger spring screw
20. Frame plate screw (2)
21. Trigger screw
22. Bolt screw
23. Actuating bar screw
24. Hammer screw
25. Mainspring
26. Hand spring
27. Hand spring screw
28. Hand
29. Hammer
30. Stirrup
31. Stirrup pin
32. Recoil shield retaining screw (2)
33. Grip
34. Backstrap screw (2)
35. Backstrap
36. Butt screw

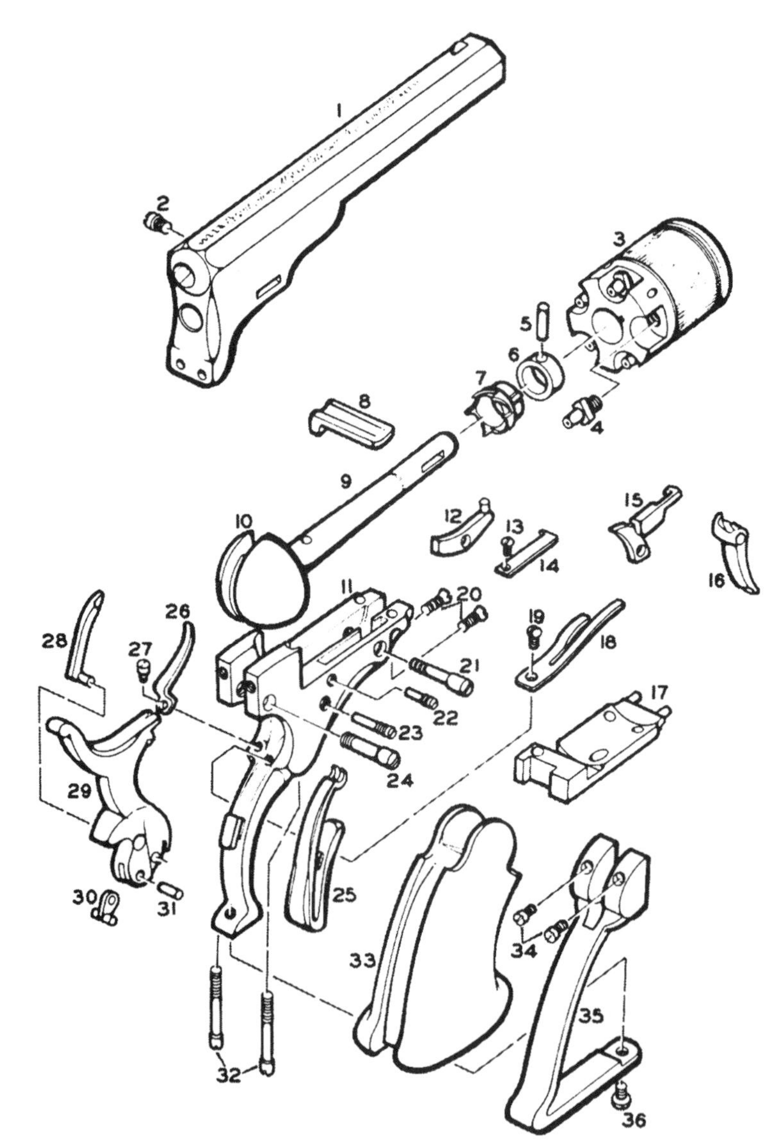

In 1836 a group of financiers in Paterson, N.J. organized the Patent Firearms Manufacturing Co. for the purpose of making percussion-ignition, revolving-cylinder, repeating firearms under patents held by Samuel Colt, a young inventor from Hartford, Connecticut. The group, led by its president, Elias B.D. Ogden, established a factory in Paterson. Dudley Selden, Colt's cousin, was secretary and general manager.

Except for a limited number of revolving rifles, very few arms were produced in 1836. The first government trial of the rifles was held in 1837 and the results were unfavorable. In 1838, however, Colt succeeded in selling 125 rifles to the United States Army for use in the Seminole campaign. A number of the officers of the campaigning force also purchased a few of the pistols.

An additional order, for both carbines and pistols, was obtained from the Republic of Texas, in 1839.

During this time Colt did everything possible to promote the sale of his guns, including presentation of a pistol to President Andrew Jackson. Some of his promotional methods may have seemed unorthodox to his conservative cousin Dudley Selden, as friction between the two eventually caused Selden to resign. John Ehlers took over Selden's duties as secretary and general manager.

In 1841, Colt, dissatisfied with the distribution of royalty payments by Ehlers, undertook legal action against the firm. Colt's suit resulted in the company's bankruptcy in 1842 despite a last-minute order from the Army's Ordnance Department for 160 carbines. Luckily for Colt, he retained ownership of his patents.

Though short-lived, the Patent Firearms Manufacturing Co. made a wide variety of guns: rifles, carbines, pistols, and shotguns. Pistols were sold in calibers from .28 to .36 and with barrels ranging from 2½ to 9 inches in length. By virtue of their place of manufacture, these early Colt firearms are referred to as "Paterson Colts," or "Patersons."

Paterson guns, especially the pistols, are much sought after by collectors. This desirability plus their relative rarity causes them to be ranked among the most valuable of antique arms.

DISASSEMBLY

Remove wedge screw (2) and tap out wedge (8) from right side using a plastic or rubber hammer. Remove barrel (1) and cylinder (3). Next, remove frame plate screws (20) and lift away frame plate (17). Remove butt screw (36) and backstrap screws (34). Lift away backstrap (35) and grip (33), which may then be separated. All internal working parts are exposed at this point.

Should further disassembly be required, continue by removing hand spring screw (27) and hand spring (26). With the left hand, compress mainspring (25) slightly to relieve tension on stirrup (30) and hammer (29), and remove hammer screw (24) and hammer together with hand (28). Remove bolt and trigger spring screw (19) and spring (18), then remove trigger screw (21), bolt screw (22), and actuating bar screw (13). This permits removal of the upper trigger spring (14). Drifting out the ratchet retaining collar pin (5) permits removal of the ratchet retaining collar (6) and ratchet (7).

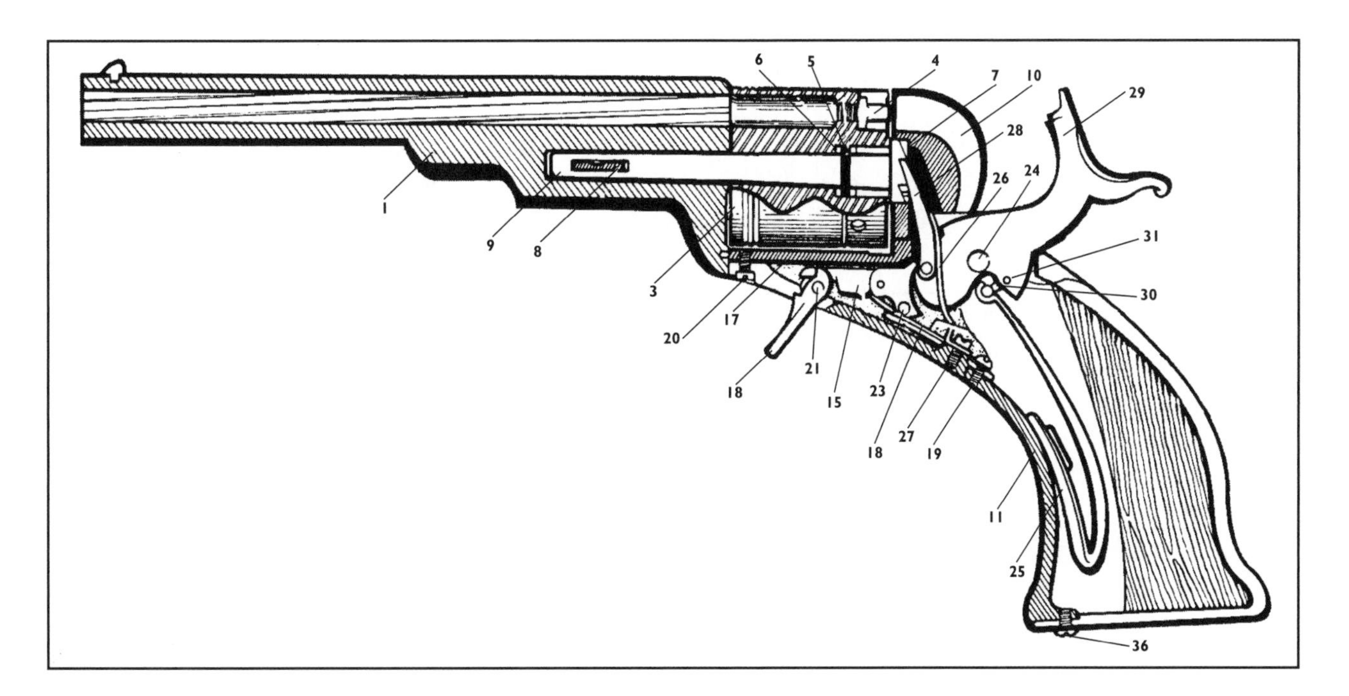

COLT SINGLE-ACTION ARMY

PARTS LEGEND

1. Barrel
2. Ejector tube
3. Ejector tube screw
4. Ejector spring
5. Ejector rod
6. Ejector rod head
7. Base pin
   7A. Base pin screw (old style)
8. Base pin screw
9. Base pin spring
10. Base pin nut
11. Base pin bushing
12. Frame
13. Recoil plate
14. Cylinder
15. Gate
16. Hammer
17. Firing pin
18. Firing pin rivet
19. Hammer roll
20. Hammer roll pin
21. Hand (with hand spring)
22. Gate catch
23. Gate spring
24. Gate catch screw
25. Bolt
26. Trigger & bolt screws
27. Trigger
28. Sear & bolt spring
29. Bolt spring screw
30. Hammer screw
31. Trigger guard
32. Front trigger guard screw
33. Rear trigger guard screws (2)
34. Stock pin
35. Front backstrap screw
36. Mainspring screw
37. Mainspring
38. Backstrap
39. Backstrap screws (2)
40. Escutcheons
    (2, left-hand only shown)
41. Stock screw
42. Stocks (left-hand only shown)

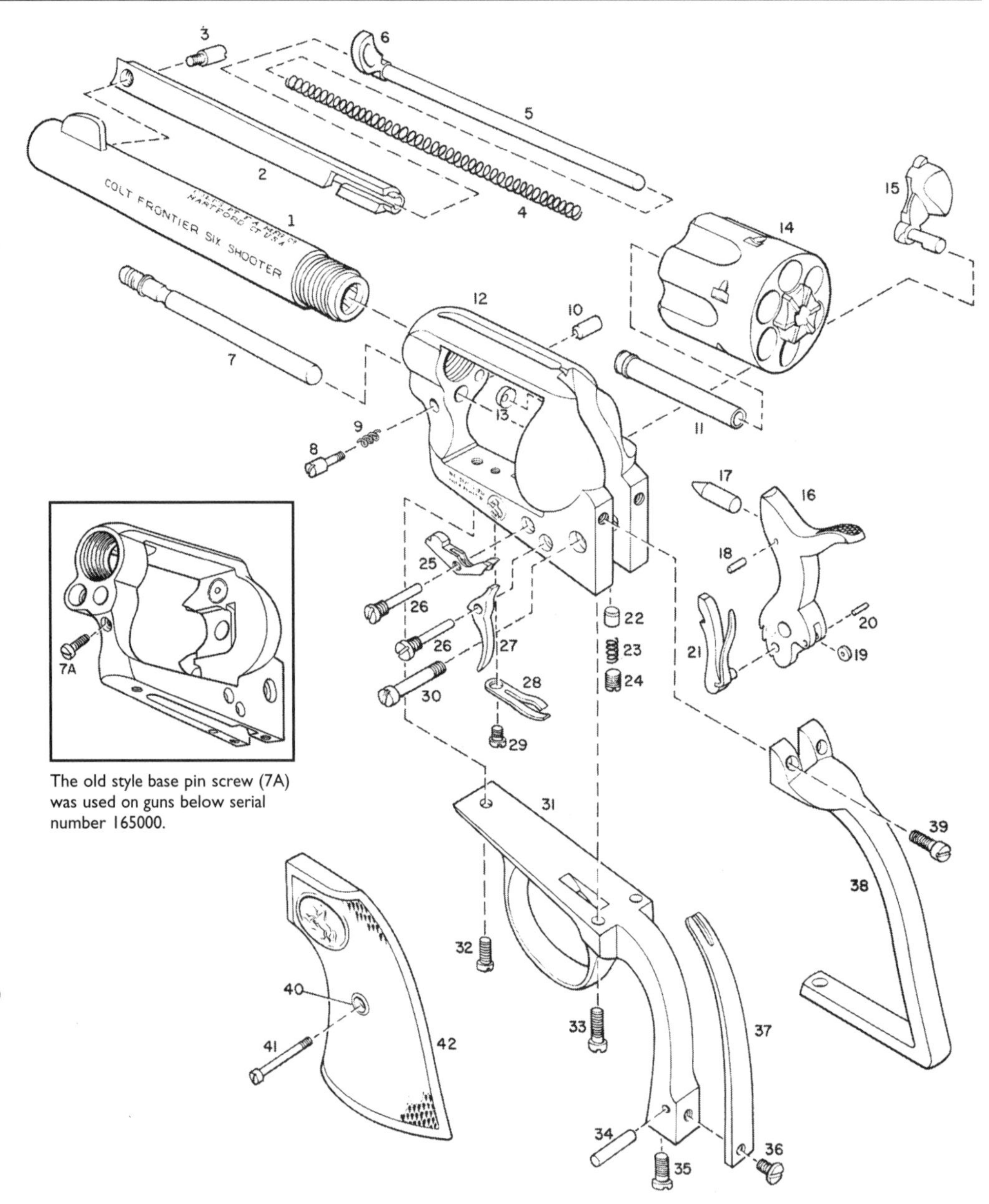

The old style base pin screw (7A) was used on guns below serial number 165000.

"A military weapon extracting the discharged shells singly; combining strength and simplicity of action; not liable to get out of order; readily taken apart and easily cleaned; having entire exchangeability of parts, with a high order of finish. Commended for durability and actual service in the hands of a soldier . . ."

The above succinct report, by the judges of the Centennial Exposition held in Philadelphia in 1876, is as relevant today as it was over 130 years ago. It is a striking fact indeed that the revolver referred to remains in production as of this date, and has also inspired a large number of copies from various manufacturers. As such, it can claim the longest production period of any revolver, if not any cartridge firearm, ever commercially produced. Introduced in 1873 as the Single Action Army, it is also known as the Single Action Army and Frontier, Frontier Six-Shooter, Peacemaker, and Model "P."

It enjoyed continuous production from 1873 until 1940 when reduced sales and pressure of defense contracts terminated its manufacture. The guns manufacturerd during this period are generally known as "First Generation" SAAs. After World War II the demand for Colt Single-Action revolvers skyrocketed to the point where collectors often paid from three to four times the pre-war price. In light of this strong demand, Colt's Patent Firearms Mfg. Co. in 1955 decided to resume limited production, yielding the "Second Generation" guns, which continued to be made through 1975. Colt's "Third Generation" Peacemakers were produced from 1976 through the present.

Early guns with serial numbers below 165000 are in the so-called black powder category, whereas those with higher numbers were manufactured after the advent of smokeless powder. The change-over, which occurred in 1896, was reflected in reduced headspace tolerances to accommodate the higher pressures developed by smokeless powder cartridges. The substitution of the spring release for the screw originally used to retain the base pin occurred about the same time as the changes related to the use of smokeless powder.

The barrels of early Single-Action revolvers were rifled with comparatively narrow lands, whereas those made later had wider lands, of equal width to the grooves. Some were furnished smooth-bored for use with shot cartridges. Barrel lengths varied from three inches up to 16 and 18 inches for the special-order Buntline models.

Over the course of its long production life, the SAA has been made in some 36 different calibers, and in a dazzling variety of models with different barrel lengths, grip frame designs, stocks, finishes and degrees of ornamentation. It is significant that only minor design changes have been effected during the entire time the Colt Single-Action has been produced. At present, the Colt SAA is enjoying a resurgence in popularity, due in large part to the growth of the sport of Cowboy Action Shooting.

DISASSEMBLY

Unload revolver. Remove cylinder (14) by opening loading gate (15) and withdrawing base pin (7) and, with hammer at half-cock, pressing cylinder out of frame to right. The base pin is removed by pressing in base pin screw. On older models below serial number 165000, base pin is held in place by base pin screw (7A) in front of frame; loosening this screw will free base pin.

Remove stocks (42). Remove backstrap (38) by unscrewing two upper backstrap screws (39) and front backstrap screw (35). Remove mainspring screw (36) and drop out mainspring (37). Remove front trigger guard screw (32) and two rear trigger guard screws (33) and lift trigger guard (31) from frame. Unscrew bolt spring screw (29) and remove sear and bolt spring (28) from underside of frame. Remove hammer screw (30) and trigger and bolt screws (26) and remove trigger (27), bolt (25), and hammer (16) with attached hand and spring (21) from inside of frame.

The loading gate (15) is removed by unscrewing gate catch screw (24) from its hole in underside of frame and dropping out gate spring (23) and gate catch (22). The base pin screw (8), base pin spring (9), and base pin nut (10) can be removed from frame by unscrewing screw from nut.

The ejector assembly is removed by unscrewing ejector tube screw (3) from barrel (l). Lift ejector tube (2) free of ejector stud in barrel and push tube toward front of gun, disengaging rear of tube from its seat in frame. The ejector rod (5) and ejector rod head (6) and ejector spring (4) may be withdrawn from ejector tube from rear.

This completes disassembly. Reassembly is accomplished in reverse order. Removal of barrel or replacement of either barrel or cylinder should only be attempted by an experienced person equipped with proper tools. The accompanying longitudinal section shows relationship of all parts with revolver assembled.

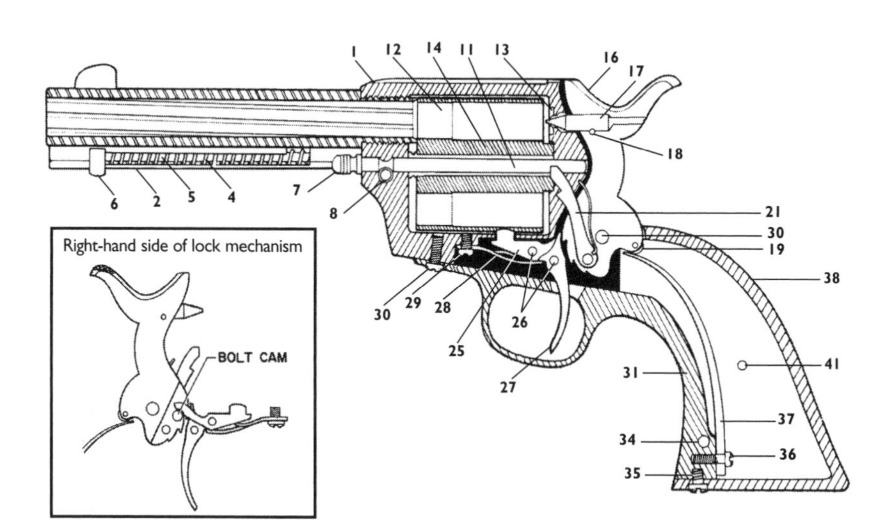

COLT THIRD MODEL DERRINGER

PARTS LEGEND

1. Frame
2. Barrel screw
3. Barrel latch bushing
4. Barrel
5. Front sight
6. Barrel stop pin
7. Barrel latch release pin
8. Barrel latch & ejector screw
9. Barrel latch & ejector spring
10. Barrel latch & ejector
11. Hammer
12. Hammer screw
13. Mainspring
14. Trigger
15. Trigger screw
16. Trigger spring (flat or coil type)
17. Grip pin
18. Escutcheon (2, right & left)
19. Grip screw
20. Grip (2, right & left)

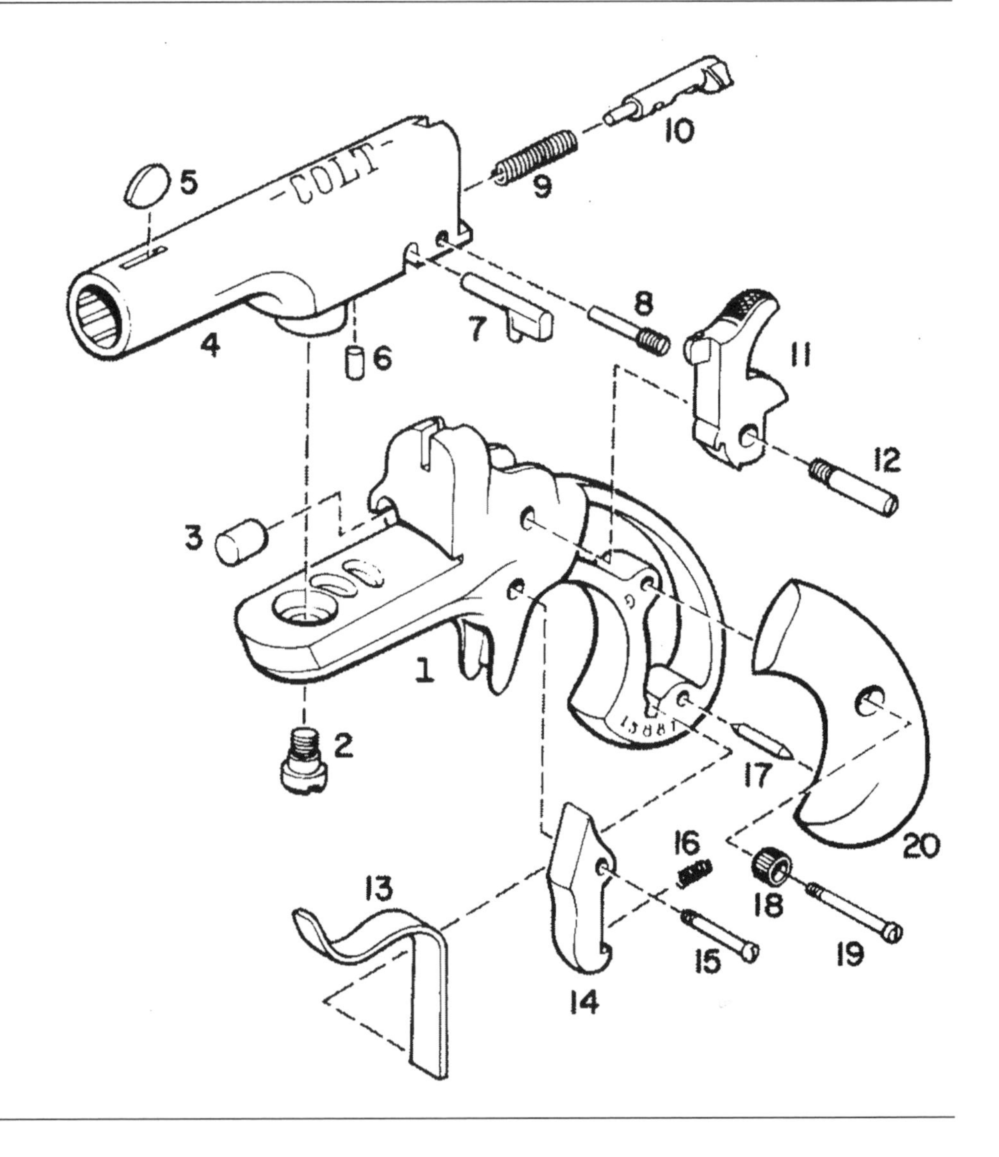

Colt's Patent Fire Arms Mfg. Co., of Hartford, Conn., began manufacture of single-shot cartridge pistols about 1872 after the acquisition of patents and other assets of the National Arms Co. of Brooklyn, New York. The National Arms Co., formed about 1863, was the successor to the Moore Patent Fire Arms Co., manufacturer of the single-shot cartridge pistol patented (No. 31,473) on Feb. 19, 1861, by Daniel Moore.

As made by Colt's, the National derringer (Moore patent) was offered with both metal and wood stocks in .41 rimfire only. At about the same time Colt's also began production of a small .41 rimfire single-shot pistol based upon a patent granted July 12, 1870, to an employee, F. Alexander Thuer.

The Thuer pistol was of side-swinging barrel type, similar in appearance to side-swing single-shot pocket pistols manufactured at the time by J. M. Marlin, Hopkins & Allen, Forehand & Wadsworth, and others. The unique patented feature of the Thuer pistol was the automatic ejector which eliminated the necessity for manual case extraction after opening of the breech. As stated in a Colt advertisement of 1872, "The exploded shell need not be touched by the fingers."

The Thuer pistol weighed 6½ oounces compared to 10 ounces for the Colt-National derringer with metal grips. It was available with silver-plated frame and blued barrel, or with silver-plated frame and barrel. Stocks were optionally of walnut, rosewood, ivory, or pearl. There was a change made in the barrel marking and in the shape of the hammer and frame during the gun's period of manufacture, which extended to 1912. The frames of all variants were of bronze, with other parts of iron.

Collectors designate the Thuer-designed pistol as the Third Model Derringer, whereas the Colt-National metal-grip and wood-grip pistols are designated as First Model and Second Model Derringers, respectively.

In late 1959, Colt introduced the Colt Derringer No.4, chambered for the .22 Short cartridge. A non-firing model of this gun was also produced. Both were primarily offered to interest the collector of Colt arms, and were close replicas of the original Thuer model.

COLT

DISASSEMBLY

To disassemble barrel assembly, remove barrel screw (2) from underside of frame (1). With hammer at half-cock or safety position, swing rear of barrel (4) to right and remove barrel from frame. Remove barrel latch and ejector screw (8) from left side of barrel while pressing barrel latch and ejector in. Withdraw barrel latch & ejector (10) and spring (9) from rear of barrel. Draw barrel latch release pin (7) from left side of barrel. Removal of barrel stop pin (6) is seldom necessary and should not be attempted during normal disassembly.

To disassemble lock mechanism, first remove grip screw (19) and grips (20) The Mainspring (13) may be tapped out of its seat in frame and removed. Remove hammer screw (12) from left side of frame and withdraw hammer (11) from top of frame while pressing back on trigger. Remove trigger screw (15) from left side of frame and drop trigger (14) and trigger spring (16) out bottom of frame. NOTE: Trigger spring shown in exploded drawing is of the coil type which rests in a shallow hole at rear of trigger. Earlier types are provided with a flat, V-shaped trigger spring, shown in longitudinal-section drawing. The barrel latch bushing (3) may be removed only by drilling.

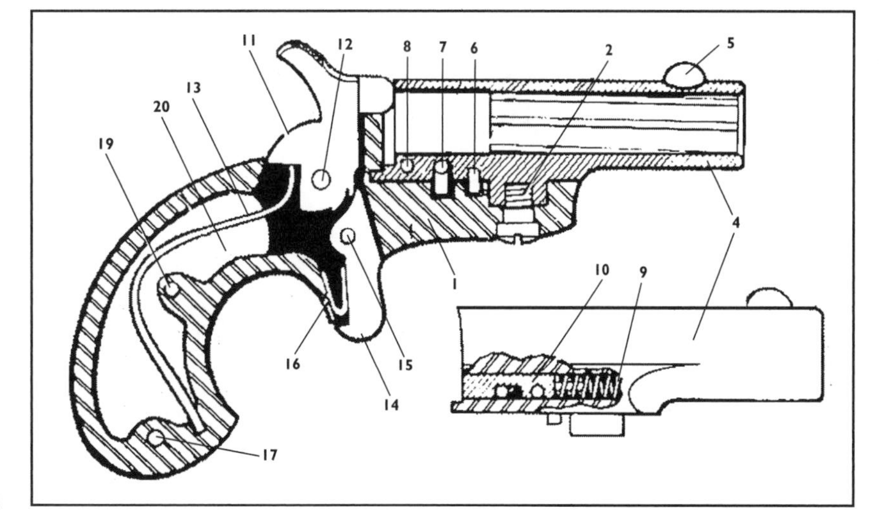

COLT WOODSMAN PISTOL

PARTS LEGEND

A Barrel
B Front sight blade
C Sight blade pin
D Recoil spring
E Firing pin spring
F Firing pin
G Extractor
H Firing pin stop
I Recoil spring guide
J Assembly lock
K Assembly lock plunger
L Rear sight
M Sight windage screw
N Windage screw detent spring
O Windage detent
P Slide
Q Sear
R Hammer
S Hammer strut pin
T Hammer strut
U Bushing
V Trigger pin
W Ejector
X Ejector pin
Y Magazine catch
Z Magazine catch spring
AA Magazine catch lock
BB Ejector pin
CC Ejector spring
DD Ejector plunger
EE Mainspring cap (not shown)
FF Mainspring
GG Mainspring housing
HH Mainspring cap pin
II Sear spring
JJ Grip adapter screw
KK Magazine
LL Housing lock pin
MM Left hand grip
NN Grip screw
OO Safety catch
PP Upper housing lock pin
QQ Sideplate screw
RR Slide stop
SS Trigger bar
TT Slide stop spring
UU Trigger
VV Trigger spring
WW Frame (receiver)
XX Sideplate

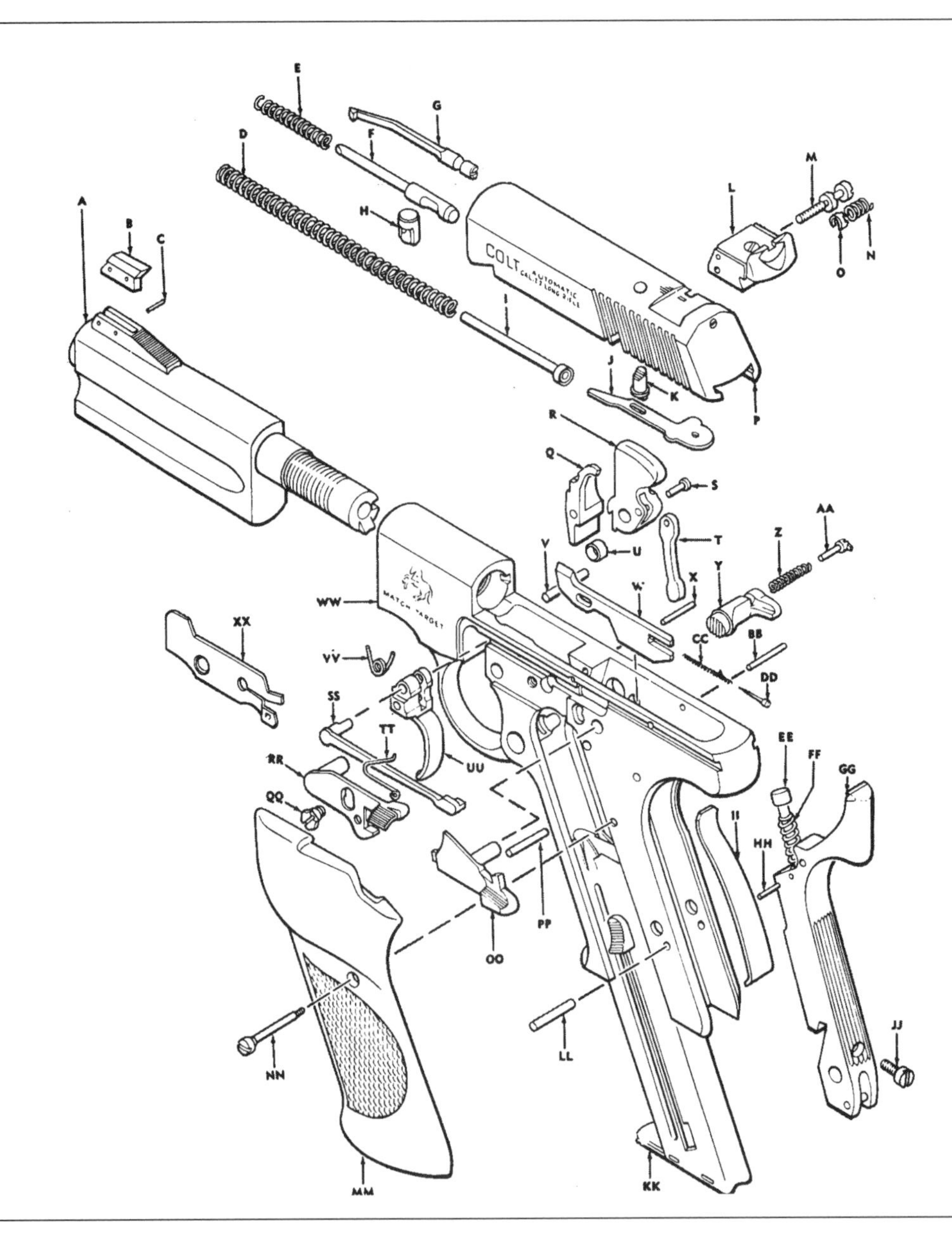

From its introduction in 1915, as the "Colt Automatic Cal. .22 Long Rifle", to its discontinuance in 1977, the "Woodsman" (so named in 1927) was the pistol by which other .22 semi-automatic handguns were judged.

Pistols with se-rial numbers below 83790 should not be fired with high-velocity ammunition unless their original checkered mainspring housings have been replaced with the later, stronger, horizontally-grooved housings. In the Woodsman's heyday, Colt offered these stronger housings as replacement parts. Older housings are safe only with standard-velocity ammunition.

The Match Target version shown is only one of many heavy and light-barrel target and sporting models made. Produced shortly after World War II, it had a disconnector (incorporated from 1948 to 1955) and an M1911-style magazine release. Earlier and later versions had a magazine release at the bottom of the grip frame. Other post-war changes included an internal extractor and an automatic slide stop. This last feature was not installed in the Colt Challenger (1950-1955) or the Huntsman (1955-1976) pistols, essentially less-expensive versions of the Woodsman.

Pre-World War II "Colt Automatic" and "Woodsman" pistols are prized by collectors. They are distinguished by their short mainspring housings, which give a "pocket pistol" look to the grip frame.

Pistols made from 1948-1955 have a housing lock pin (LL) that must be pushed out of the frame to remove the mainspring housing. This was requested by Marine Corps shooters to prevent the back strap from moving inward and pinching the web of the hand.

DISASSEMBLY

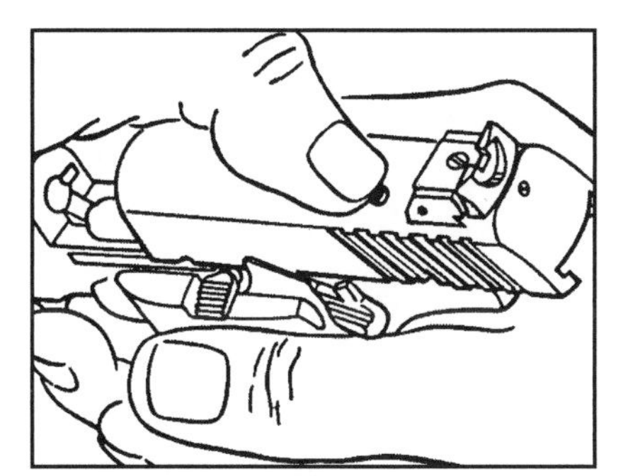

1 Check the magazine and chamber to be sure the gun is empty. Pull the slide back as far as it will go. Press down the assembly lock plunger (K), depress the slide stop (RR), and push the slide closed by hand, since the recoil spring is locked and cannot return the slide.

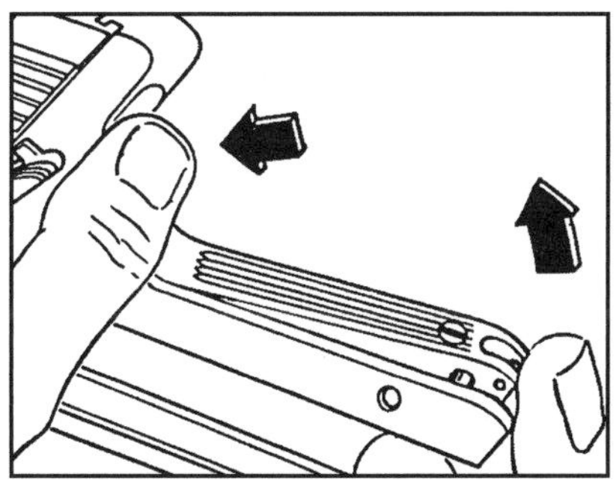

2 Remove the grips and push out the upper hous-ing lock pin (PP). Pull the trigger to release hammer. Retract the slide about ⅛ inch, then press inward and upward as shown. The main spring housing (GG) will snap out. Remove the slide (P) and magazine (KK).

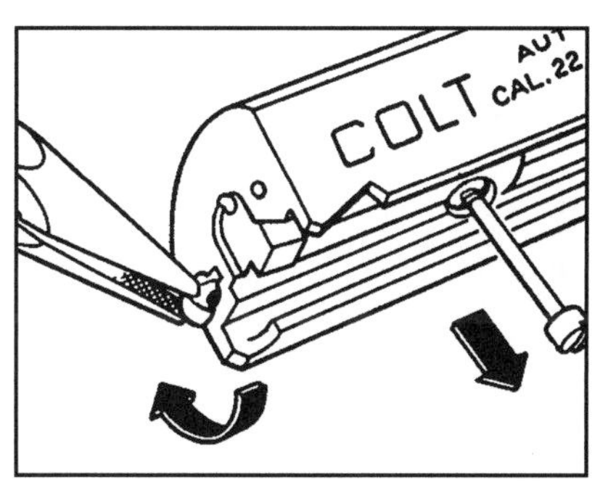

3 Grasp the end of the extractor (G) with pliers and rotate 180° then pull it forward. Thread grip screw (NN) into the firing pin stop (N). Pull it out. The firing pin (F) and firing pin spring (E) may then be removed through the rear of the slide.

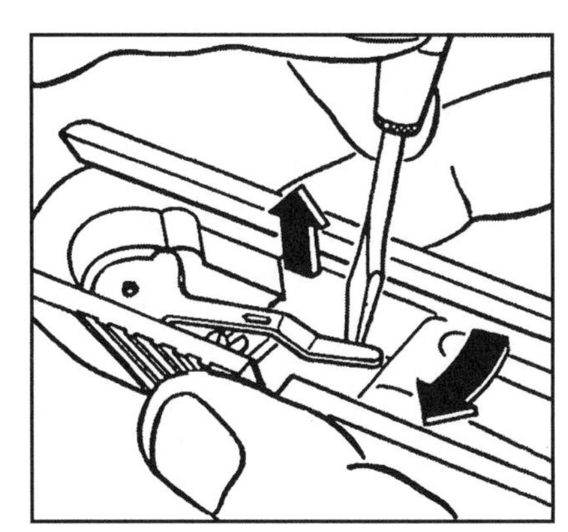

4 Press forward on recoil spring guide (I) with small screwdriver assembly. Assembly lock (J) will disengage. Ease recoil spring (D) and guide (I) out of the slide. Lift end of assembly lock (J) up and turn lock plunger (K) 90°. Work the assembly lock forward out of its grooves in slide.

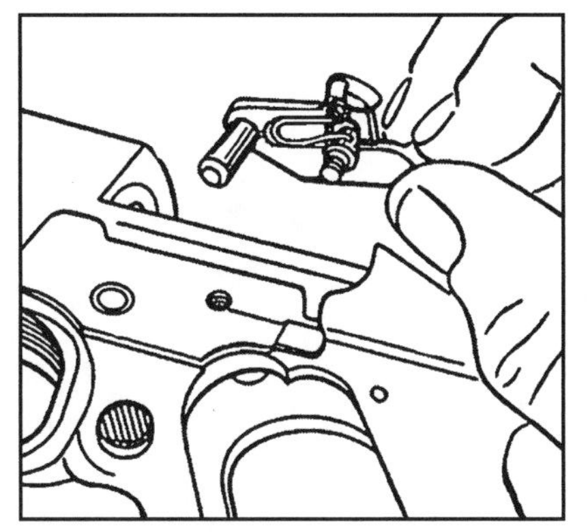

5 The Woodsman goes back together again easily except for the slide stop spring (TT). A great deal of effort will be saved if the slide stop (RR), the plate screw (QQ), and spring (TT) are assembled as shown before attempting to install them when reassembling the gun.

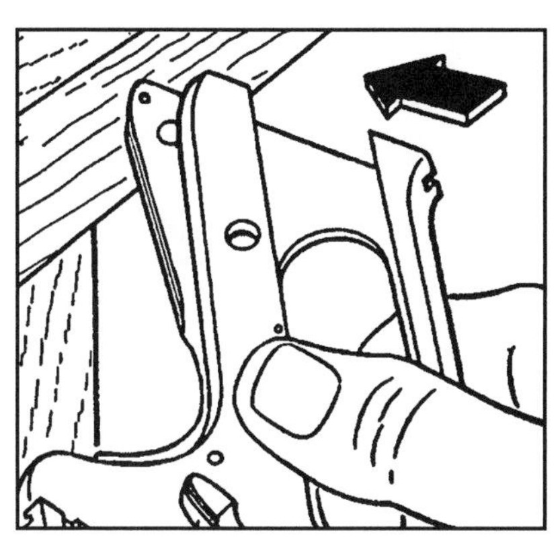

6 After all parts, with the exception of the housing (GG) and grips, have been reassembled into the slide (P) and receiver (WW), assemble the frame and slide together. Then insert housing into the receiver, and press firmly against a table. The housing will snap into place.

CROSMAN MODEL 130/137 PISTOLS

PARTS LEGEND

1. Barrel
2. Lock pin
3. Grip screw (2)
4. Tube plug
5. O ring (breech bolt)
6. Breech bolt
7. Loading sleeve
8. Breech bolt screw
9. Breech plug
10. Sight screw
11. Rear sight
12. Right grip
13. Left grip
14. Front sight
15. Sear block stop
16. Sear spring (for sear block)
17. Tube
18. Breech gasket
19. Front sight pin
20. Valve cap assembly
    21a. O ring (valve cap assembly)
    22a. Quad ring
    23a. Exhaust valve washer
24. Exhaust valve ring
25. Exhaust valve body
26. Check valve spring
27. Check valve
28. O ring (check valve)
29. Check valve body
30. O ring (check valve body, front)
31. Compression head
32. Cup washer
33. Felt retainer
34. Felt washer
35. Piston
36. O ring (not shown)
37. Pump lock nut
38. Pump guide
39. Pump guide pin
40. Lever link
41. Lever
42. Lever rivet
43. Trigger
44. Takeup spring
45. Safety spring
46. Safety ball
47. Sear
48. Front frame screw lockwasher
49. Front frame screw
50. Grip frame
51. Trigger pin
52. Safety
53. Sear pin
54. Sear spring head
55. Sear spring (for sear)
56. Frame screw
57. Sear block
58. Bumper
    (a) Components of permanent factory valve cap assembly (20)
    (b) Permanently assembled to piston (35) at factory

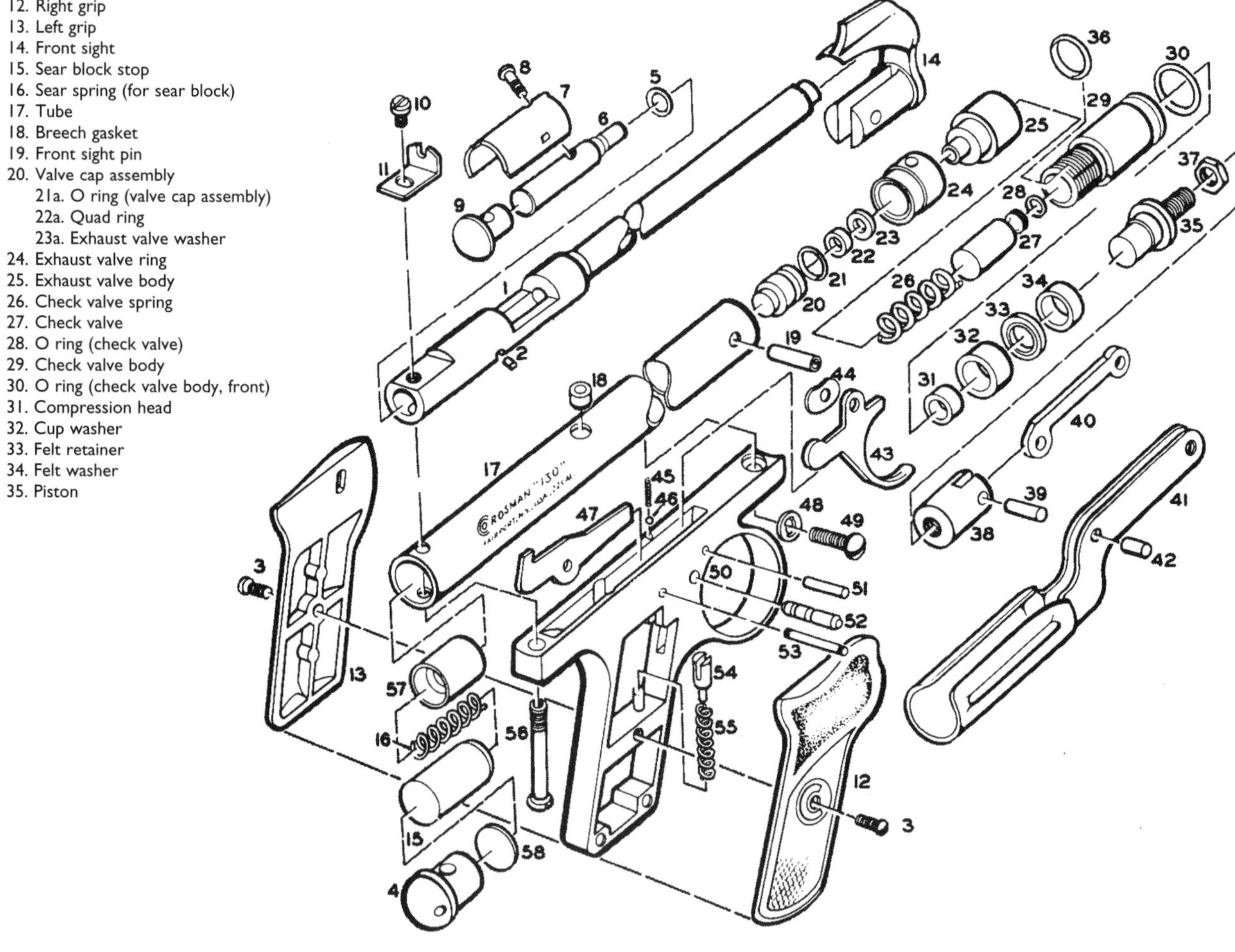

In 1952, Crosman Arms Co., of E. Bloomfield, New York., introduced its Model 130 .22-caliber pneumatic single-shot pistol. A .177-caliber version was designated the Model 137. Both guns had rifled barrels and shot skirted lead pellets.

The Models 130 and 137 pistols were well-suited for indoor target practice as they developed relatively low power and made very little noise. They were less expensive to shoot than CO_2 pistols as they required no gas cylinders. However, these guns had to be pumped up before each shot, requiring considerable effort on the part of the shooter. About six strokes were needed for shooting at 25 feet, and up to 10 strokes were needed when additional power was desired.

Over the years, there were several changes made to this pistol, yielding a number of model variations during its production life.

DISASSEMBLY

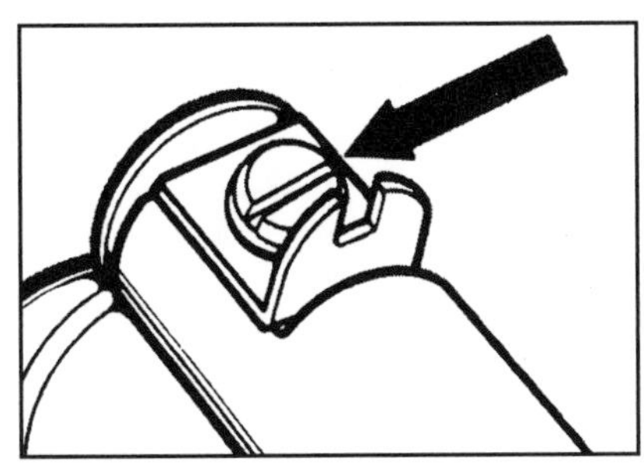

1 Remove sight screw (10), rear sight (11), and frame screw (56).

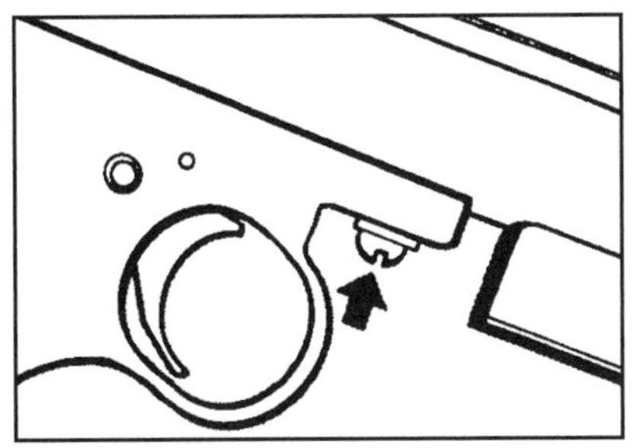

2 Remove front frame screw (49) and front frame screw lock washer (48). Grip frame (50) may now be separated from barrel and tube.

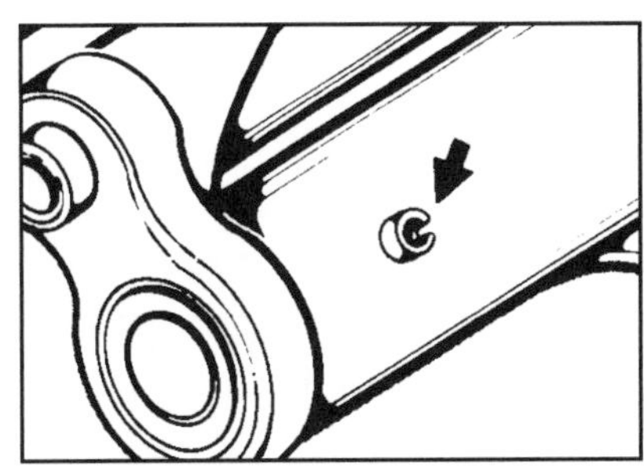

3 Drift out front sight pin (19) and remove front sight (14). The entire pump assembly, from lever (41) back to and including piston (35), may now be withdrawn from front of tube (17). From rear of tube, withdraw tube plug (4), bumper (58), and sear block stop (15). Sear spring (16) and sear block (57) may also be removed. Insert a ⅜" dowel into rear of tube and push out exhaust valve body assembly.

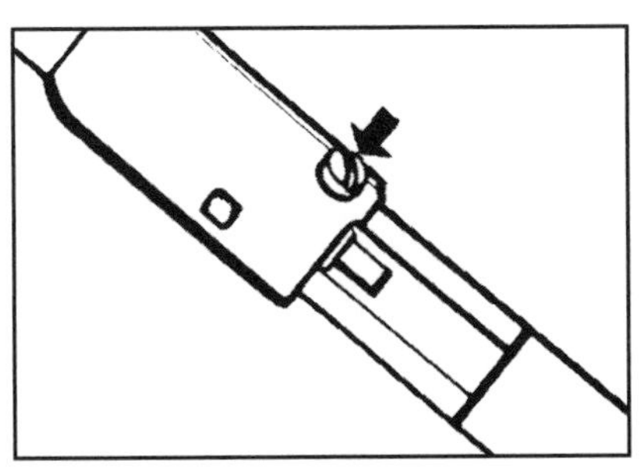

4 Remove breech plug (9) from rear of barrel (1). Remove breech bolt screw (8) and loading sleeve (7). Breech bolt (6) may now be removed from rear of barrel.

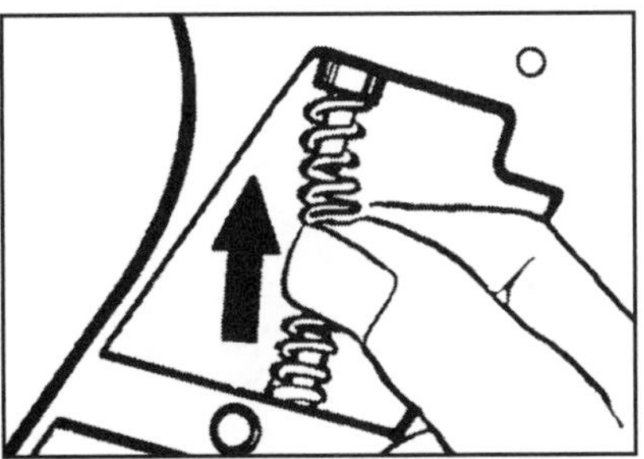

5 Remove grip screws (3) and grips (12 and 13). With thumb and forefinger, lift up on sear spring (55) and remove it. Sear spring head (54) will drop out. Drift out sear pin (53) from right to left and remove sear (47). Drift out trigger pin (51) from right to left, and remove trigger (43) and takeup spring (44). Reassemble in reverse.

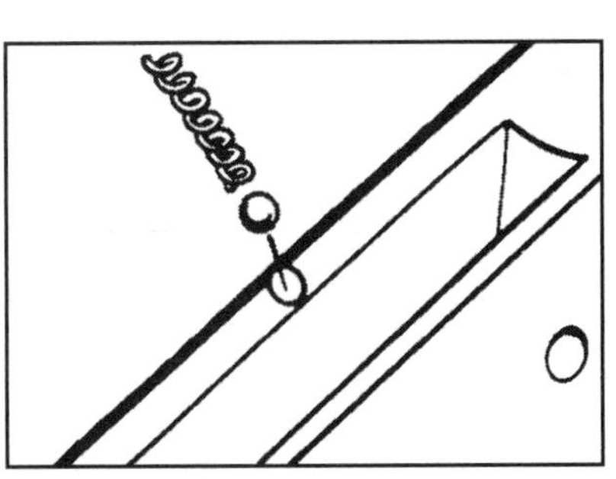

6 When working with grip frame assembly, be careful not to lose safety spring (45) and safety ball (46).

CROSMAN MODEL 150/157 PISTOLS

PARTS LEGEND

1. Barrel
2. Lock pin
3. Front sight
4. Front sight screw
5. Rear sight
6. Rear sight screw
7. Breech plug
8. Sight blade
9. Elevation screw
10. Breech bolt screw
11. Loading sleeve
12. Breech bolt
13. O-ring (breech bolt)
14. Tube
15. Hold-down screw
16. Breech gasket
17. Small tube plug
18. Hammer plug*
19. Cocking rod*
20. Cocking spring*
21. Hammer*
22. Hammer spring*
23. Tube plug*
24. Cocking cap*
25. Frame screw, rear
26. Sear spring
27. Sear spring head
28. Grip frame
29. Sear pin
30. Safety
31. Trigger pin
32. Frame screw, front
33. Trigger
34. Take-up spring
35. Sear
36. Safety spring
37. Safety spring ball
38. Exhaust valve
39. O-ring (exhaust valve)
40. Valve stem
41. Exhaust valve washer
42. Exhaust nut
43. Piercing pin
44. Check valve spring
45 Spacer
46. Washer
47. Screen
48. Filter
49. Piercing body
50. O-ring (piercing body)
51. O-ring (rest block)
52. Rest block
53. Tube cap
54. Connecting screw
55. Grip screw (2)
56. Grip, right
57. Grip, left
58. Thrust pin

* Permanent factory assembly

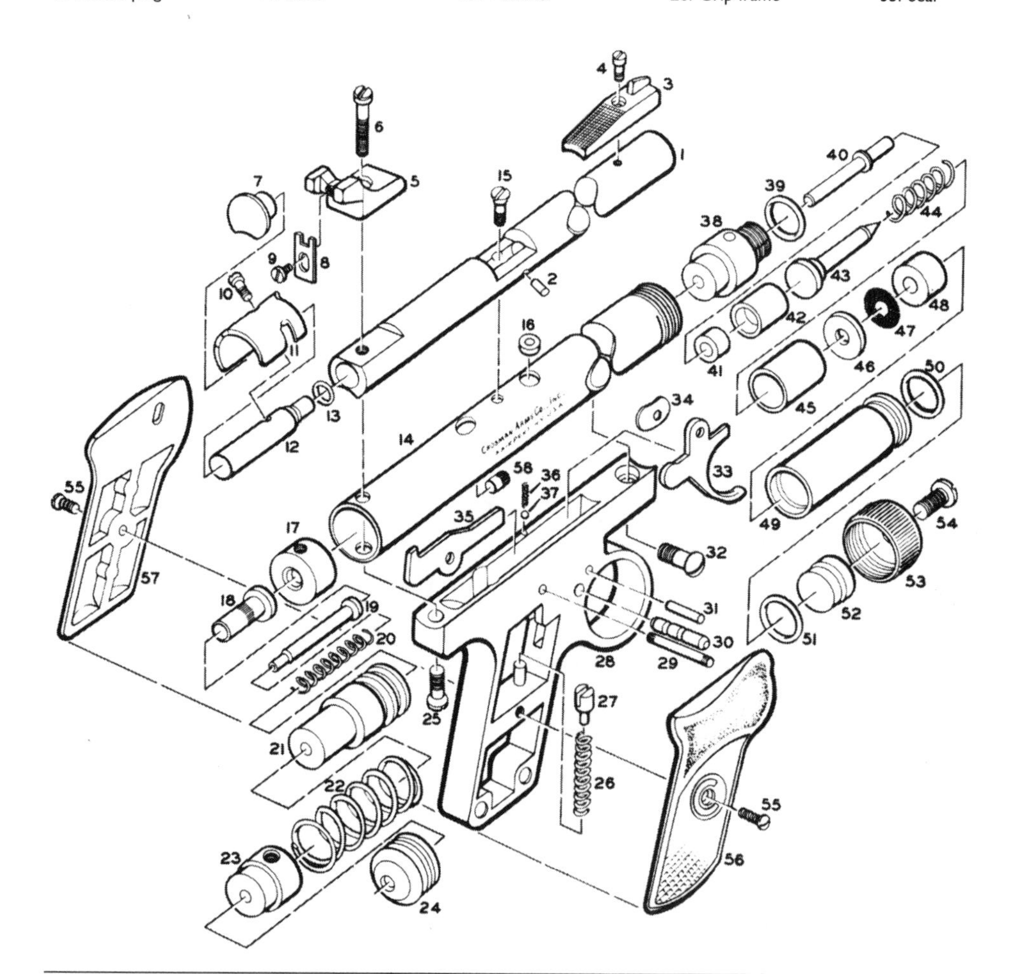

The .22-caliber Model 150 air pistol, and its .177-caliber twin, the Model 157, were produced by Crosman Arms Co. These models were the first Crosman arms to use the company's carbon dioxide (CO_2) "Powerlets." The Models 150 and 157 single shots featured rifled barrels and fired skirted lead pellets. Called "Pellguns," this design was introduced in 1954.

Unlike pneumatic and spring-type air guns, these pistols lacked a pump or cocking mechanism. Liquid CO_2 was contained in the "Powerlet," which was inserted into a tube beneath the barrel. Pulling the trigger released the hammer, and actuated a valve that metered a fixed amount of gas into the barrel to propel the pellet. As soon as gas was released from the Powerlet, more liquid CO_2 turned to gas, keeping the pressure constant from shot to shot until the Powerlet was almost empty. The Crosman Models 150 and 157 underwent numerous changes during their production history, and were sold under several brand names, including J.C. Higgins and Montgomery Ward.

DISASSEMBLY

1 Before disassembly, exhaust all gas from pistol by successive cocking and firing. Then remove tube cap (53) and take out gas cylinder. Remove the rear and front frame screws (25 & 32). The barrel and tube assembly may now be separated from the grip frame (28).

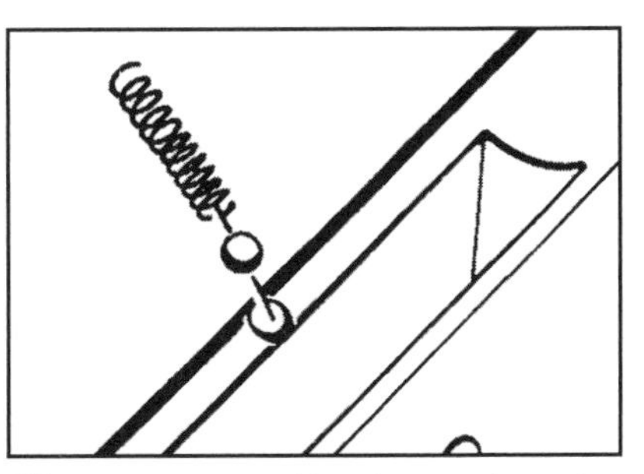

2 During disassembly, take care that safety spring (36) and safety spring ball (37) do not drop out of the grip frame and become lost.

3 Remove rear sight screw (6), rear sight (5), and breech plug (7). Remove the breech bolt screw (10) and slide the breech bolt (12) and the loading sleeve (11) off to the rear.

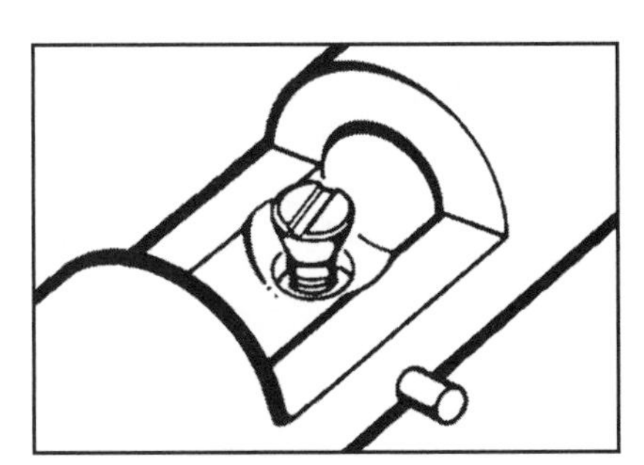

4 Remove hold-down screw (15) and lift barrel (1) off tube (14).

5 From rear of tube, remove hammer assembly consisting of cocking cap (24), tube plug (23), hammer spring (22), hammer (21), cocking spring (20), cocking rod (19), and hammer plug (18). Using a ⅛" rod from rear of tube, push valve assembly out forward. Through screw hole in top of tube, drive out thrust pin (58) and then remove small tube plug (17).

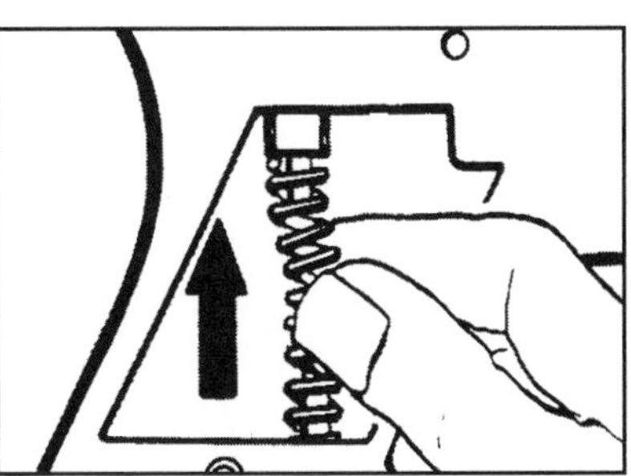

6 Remove grip screws (55) and right and left grips (56 & 57). Lift sear spring (26) off its guide in grip frame, and remove sear spring head (27). Drift out sear pin (29) from right to left, and remove sear (35). Drift out trigger pin (31) from right to left, and remove trigger (33) and take-up spring (34). Prior to reassembly, clean and oil all o-rings.

CROSMAN SINGLE-ACTION 6

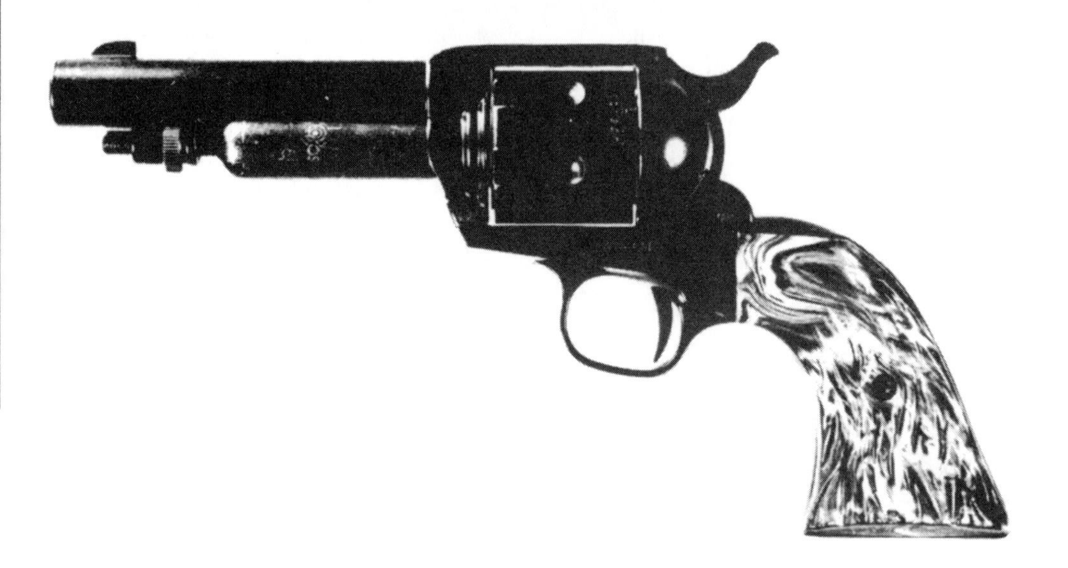

PARTS LEGEND

1. Barrel
2. Frame, left
3. Frame, right
4. Frame screw, long
5. Frame screw, short (2)
6. Lock washer
7. Hammer screw
8. Grip insert
9. Grip, right
10. Hammer*
11. Index spring*
12. Index hand*
13. Index pin*
14. Hammer spring
15. Trigger pin
16. Trigger spring
17. Trigger
18. Cylinder spring
19. Cylinder ball
20. Retaining nut
21. Retaining screw
22. Grip screw
23. Grip, left
24. Cylinder
25. Plate
26. Pell spring
27. O-ring (rear valve body)
28. Valve body
29. O-ring (front valve body)
30. Valve stem
31. Exhaust nut washer
32. Exhaust nut
33. Valve return spring
34. Spacer
35. Screen
36. Filter
37. Piercing body
38. CO_2 seal

* Factory subassembly

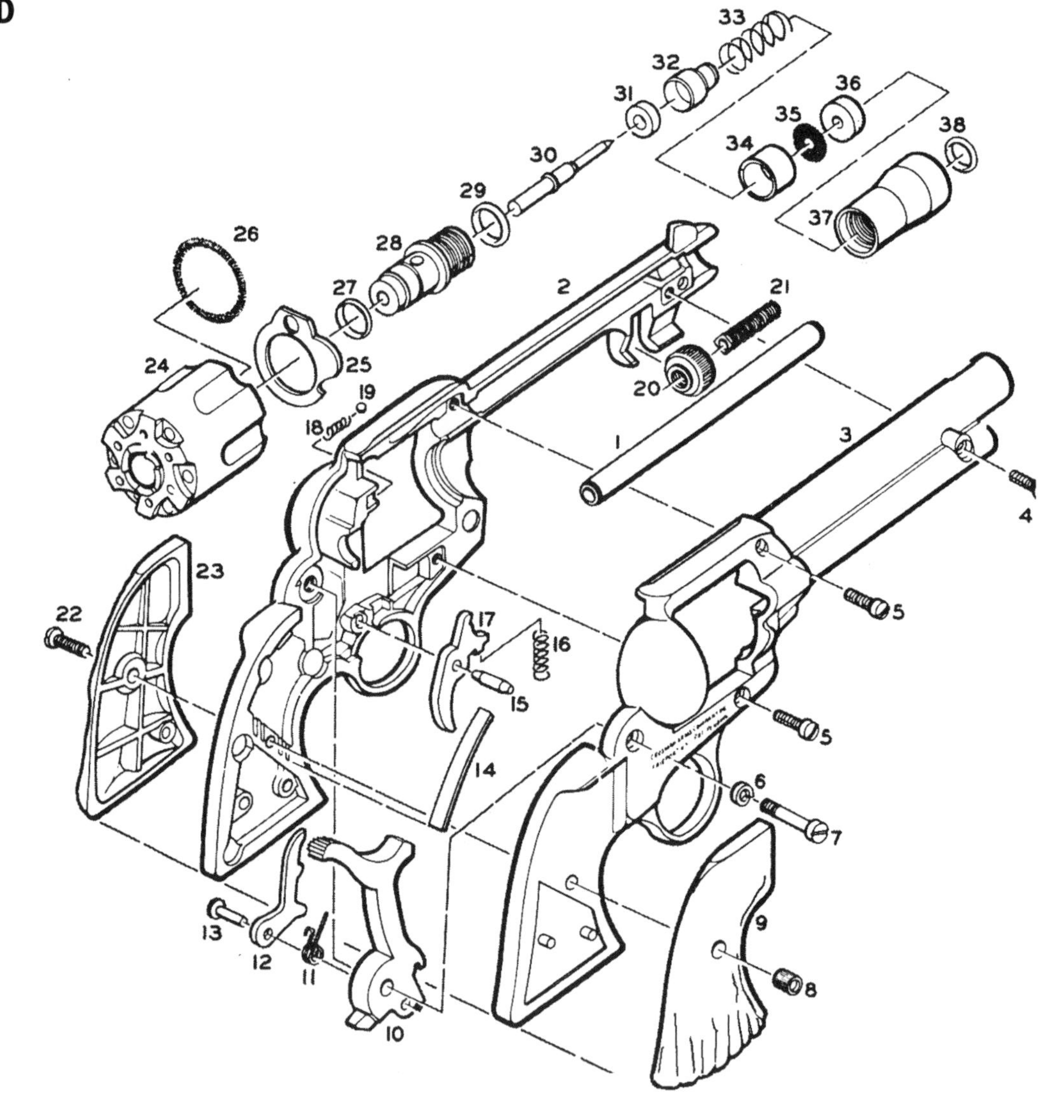

The Crosman Single-Action 6 .22-caliber gas-powered revolver was introduced in 1959. Bearing a strong resemblance to the Colt Single-Action Army, it utilized Crosman Powerlet CO_2 gas cylinders to propel .22-caliber skirted pellets, or Pells, which were contained in the pistol's six-shot revolving cylinder. The mechanism was of single-action type, requiring hand cocking of the hammer before each shot.

Velocity was about 245 feet-per-second with the 14.3-grain skirted pellet, which gave a penetration of 1 inch in hard laundry soap at 5 feet., indicating that the pistol was quite capable of inflicting a serious wound at close range.

The Crosman Single-Action was discontinued in 1969.

DISASSEMBLY

1 To disassemble the Crosman Single Action, first exhaust CO_2 gas by pushing hammer (10) forward with thumb and remove empty gas cylinder. Remove grip screw (22) and right and left grips (9 & 23). Support butt and muzzle of gun on wooden blocks to free cylinder (24). Place hammer at half cock and remove hammer screw (7) with lock washer (6), two short frame screws (5), and long frame screw (4). Insert a screwdriver in slot behind trigger (17) and pry off right frame (3). CAUTION: Use care when removing right frame as internal parts are under spring tension. All internal parts may now be lifted away. Oil and clean all o-rings and seals before reassembly.

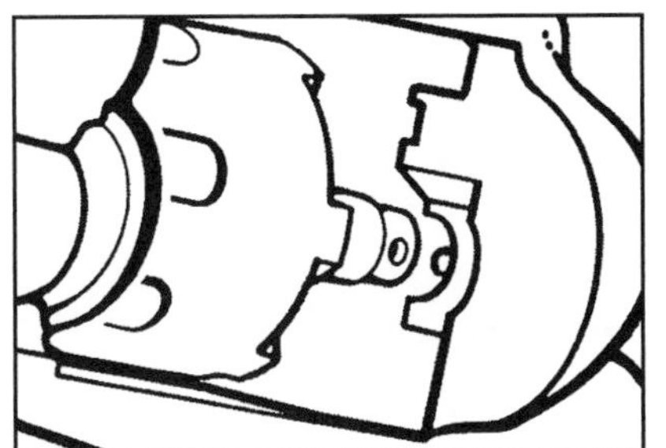

2 Commence reassembly by first assembling plate (25) onto valve assembly, then place valve, with plate in position, into cylinder. Install valve and cylinder assembly into left frame (2). Spot hole in valve fits over pin in frame casting. Place barrel (1) in left frame and locate shoulder of barrel in plate.

3 Place cylinder spring (18) and ball (19) into depression in casting. Hold ball and spring lightly with left thumb, then rotate cylinder forward until ball raises slightly and back end of spring drops into depression in casting. Holding ball and spring firmly, turn cylinder backward until spring compresses and lies flat in depression. CAUTION: Cylinder must not be moved or disturbed after ball and spring are in place.

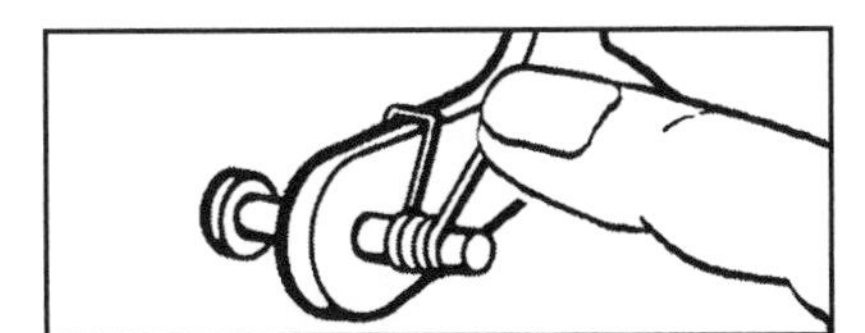

4 Index hand (12) should not normally be disassembled from the hammer (10), since that disturbs the riveted end. Should it be necessary, the hammer group may be reassembled by placing index pin (13) through its hole in index hand (12), and placing index spring (11) over pin and hooking it to hand as shown. Next, place other end of index pin in its hole in left side of hammer and catch index spring on hammer boss. Re-rivet or peen end of index pin against right side of hammer. When placing hammer assembly in right frame, hold index hand away from indexing lugs on cylinder lest it be disturbed. Hammer assembly may be held in place with a ⅛" slave pin.

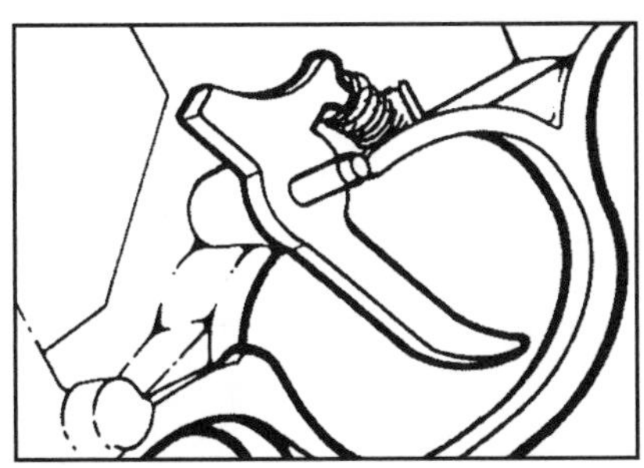

5 Assemble trigger pin (15), trigger (17), and trigger spring (16).

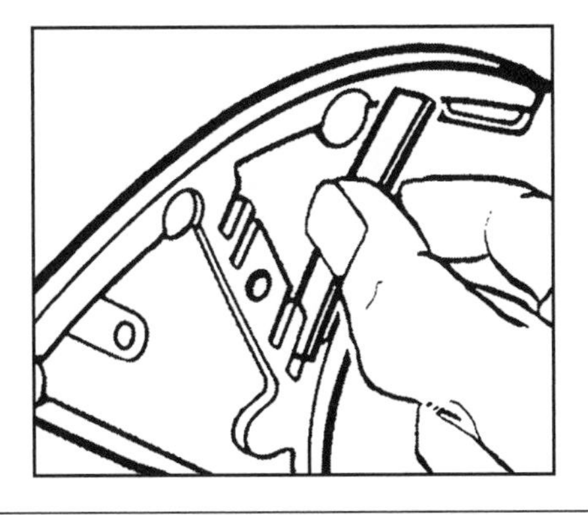

6 Put hammer spring (14) into lower slot in left frame. Place retaining screw and nut (21 & 20) in notch at muzzle end, then place right frame over left and press halves together. Replace frame screws (4 & 5), hammer screw and lock-washer (7 & 6), grips (9 & 22), and grip screw (22).

CZ MODEL 27 PISTOL

PARTS LEGEND

1. Barrel bushing
2. Barrel
3. Slide
4. Extractor pin
5. Extractor
6. Extractor spring
7. Rear sight
8. Firing pin retainer
9. Firing pin spring
10. Firing pin
11. Barrel retainer
12. Recoil spring
13. Recoil spring guide
14. Sideplate
15. Sideplate screw
16. Ejector
17. Ejector pin
18. Safety and trigger bar spring
19. Hammer spring
20. Spring retaining screw
21. Magazine catch
22. Grip screw (2)
23. Grip
24. Magazine
25. Safety catch
26. Disconnector
27. Disconnector spring
28. Hinge pin
29. Trigger bar
30. Trigger
31. Trigger spring
32. Hammer
33. Safety release
34. Magazine disconnector
35. Disconnector hinge pin
36. Takedown catch spring
37. Takedown cross pin
38. Takedown catch
39. Frame

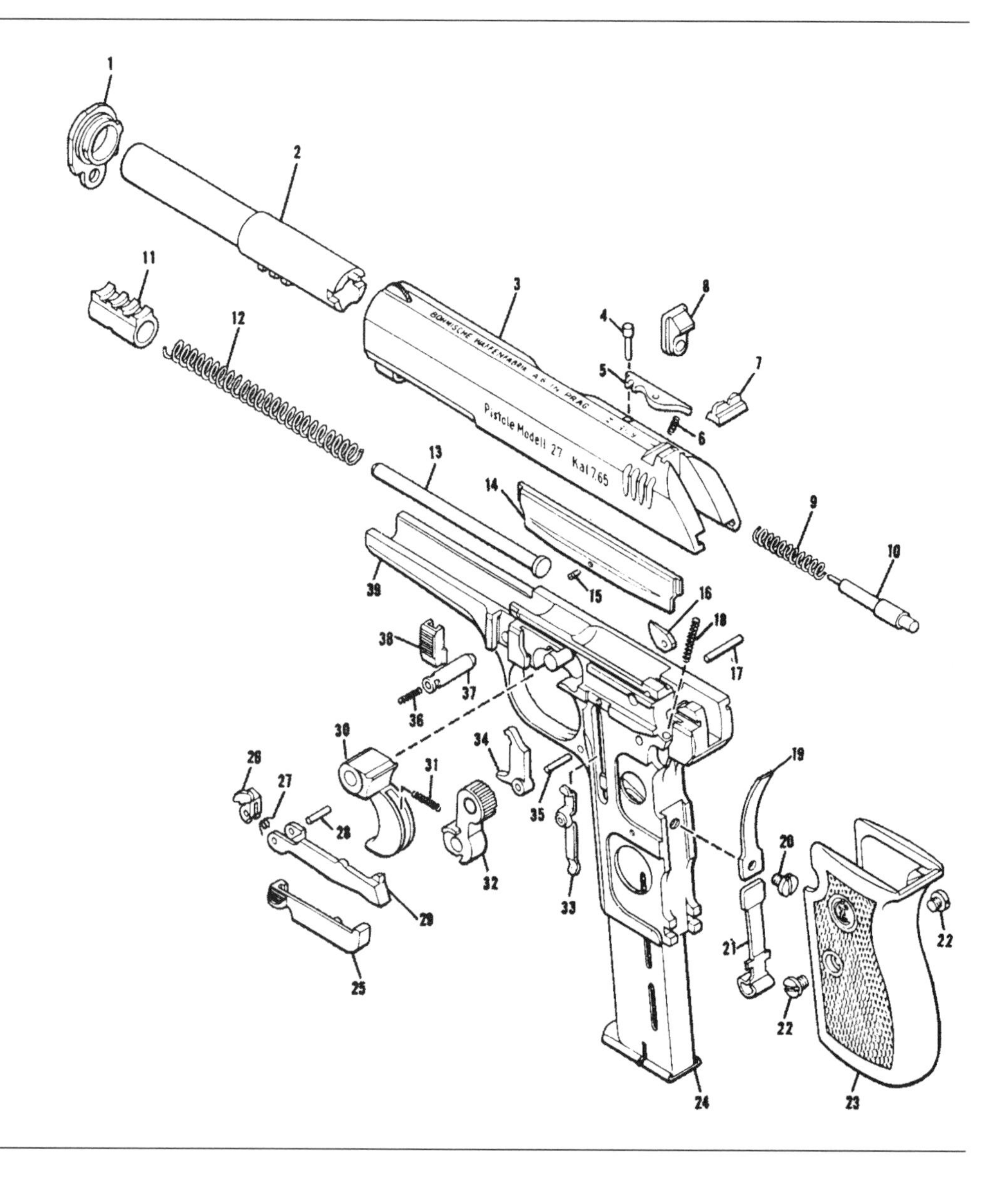

The Czech Model 27 pistol was developed in the 1920s for the newly-formed Czech army, then seeking a military sidearm. A blowback-operated, single-action semi-automatic handgun chambered for the .32 ACP, the Model 27 featured fixed sights, a Mauser-type safety catch, a 4" barrel, an overall length of 6" and a weight of 23½ ounces. The Model 27, with its fixed barrel, should not be confused with the earlier CZ Model 24, which has a rotating-barrel locking system, but is similar in appearance.

The Model 27 saw wide service before, during, and after World War II, with production continuing during German occupation. Thousands were brought back from Europe by U.S. soldiers. Late prewar and early war-time guns are usually blued and well-finished, while in later war-production units, stampings were substituted for machined parts such as the side-plate, safety arm, magazine catch, and firing pin retainer, and Parkerizing replaced the prewar blued finish.

Although simple, compact, reliable and easy to field-strip, the Model 1927 nonetheless had drawbacks from a military point of view. The small exposed hammer rowel made cocking difficult with greasy or wet fingers, and the magazine safety precluded firing, even in the single-shot mode, with the magazine removed. Furthermore, since the magazine follower held the action open after the last shot, the magazine had to be removed against the slide's spring pressure, slowing magazine changes. The Czechs realized these shortcomings and replaced the Model 27 with the double-action Model 50.

DISASSEMBLY

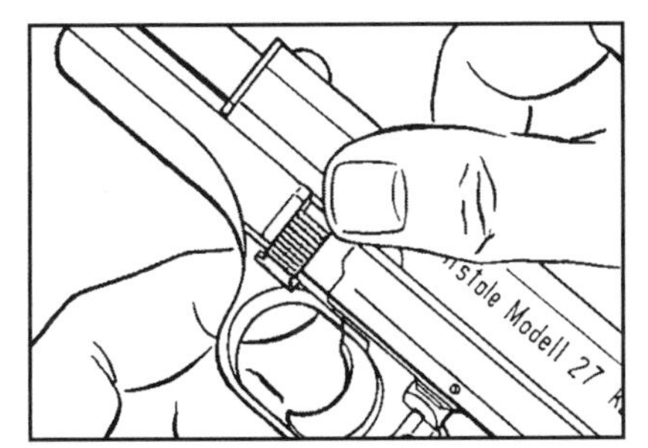

1 To strip the Model 27, pull slide back over an empty magazine. Slide will stay open and relieve tension on barrel retainer (11). Push in protruding end of take-down cross pin (37), and at same time slide take-down catch (38) down and free of frame.

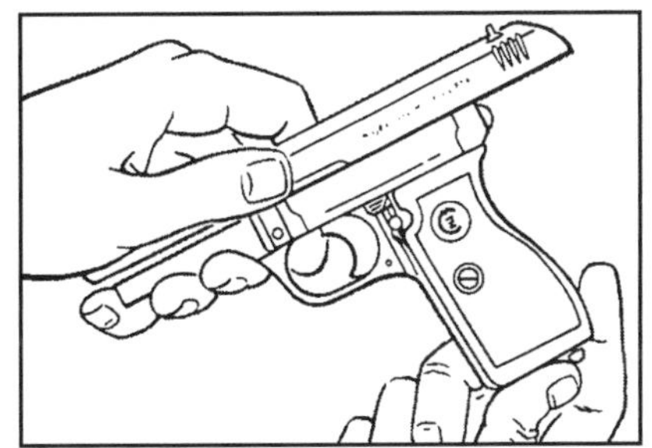

2 After takedown catch assembly has been removed, pull out magazine as shown and ease slide assembly off frame. Magazine is difficult to remove because it holds the slide open, and must be removed against pressure of recoil spring.

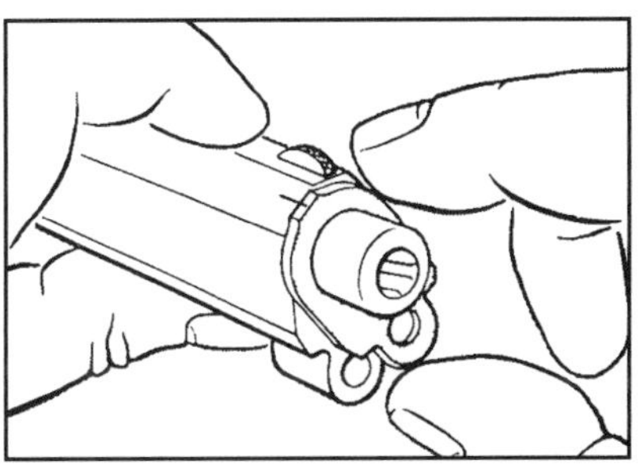

3 Barrel is retained by barrel bushing (1). First step in removing barrel, is to turn bushing about 30° until line on bushing coincides with line on slide (3). Then bushing can be pulled out of slide and off barrel.

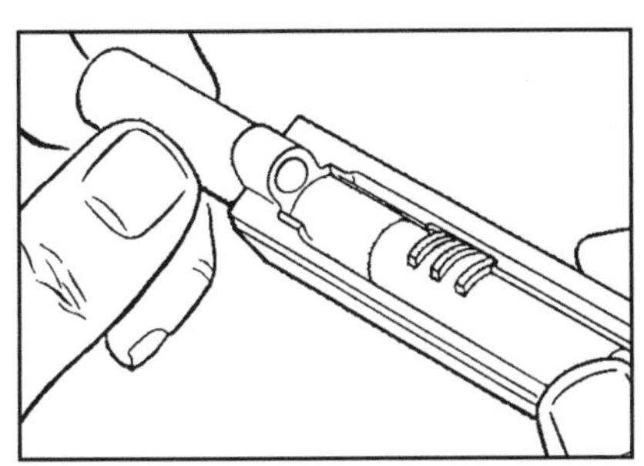

4 To get barrel (2) out of slide, pull it forward until the three barrel lugs line up with cut in slide as shown. Rotate lugs into cutout and pull barrel free of slide.

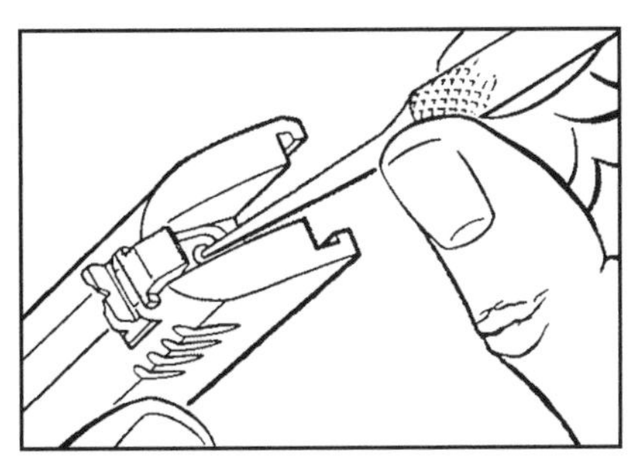

5 Firing pin (10) is retained by a small machined block in early guns, and by a sheet metal stamping in wartime models. To remove pin, simply push protruding end of it below surface of firing pin retainer (8), and pry retainer up and out as shown.

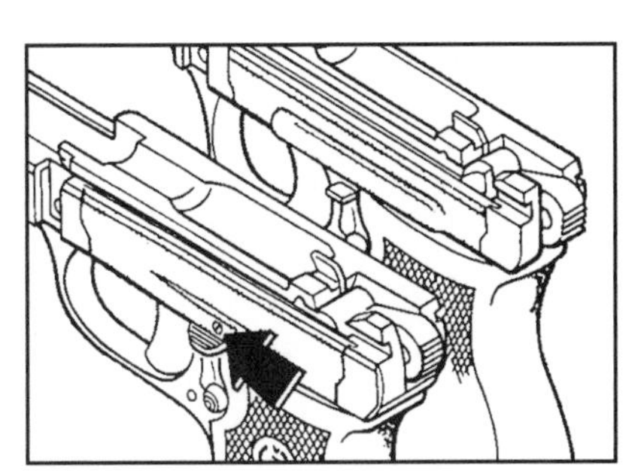

6 With sideplate (14) and grip (23) removed, operating parts can be easily removed. Early guns have a small sideplate screw (15) which must be loosened before plate can be slid up. Screw, if overly tightened, will bend sideplate and bind parts.

CZ MODEL 50 PISTOL

PARTS LEGEND

1. Slide
2. Extractor pin
3. Cartridge indicator
4. Rear sight
5. Extractor spring
6. Extractor
7. Firing pin
8. Firing pin lock spring
9. Firing pin lock
10. Recoil spring
11. Hold-open latch spring
12. Hold-open latch and ejector
13. Hold-open hinge pin
14. Left grip
15. Grip screw
16. Safety
17. Safety plunger
18. Safety spring
19. Hammer bolt
20. Sear spring
21. Sear
22. Hammer strut pin
23. Hammer
24. Hammer strut
25. Hammer spring
26. Spring retainer
27. Right grip
28. Trigger bar
29. Trigger spring
30. Trigger
31. Trigger pin
32. Trigger bar pin
33. Takedown catch spring
34. Takedown catch screw
35. Takedown catch
36. Magazine catch
37. Magazine catch spring
38. Sear pin
39. Sideplate
40. Hammer bolt nut
41. Receiver
42. Magazine
43. Barrel

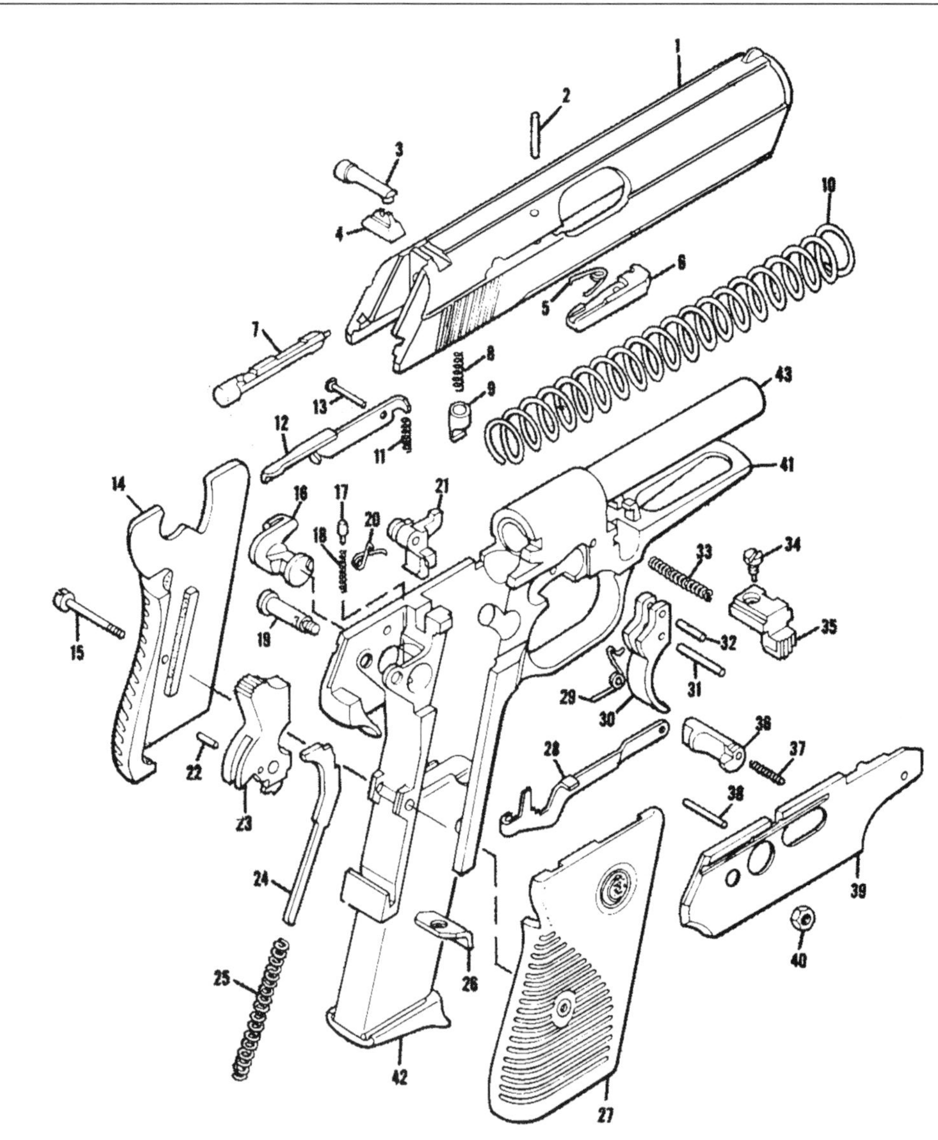

In 1948, the Czech arms factories were nationalized, and shortly thereafter various new Czech commercial arms were introduced. One of these new guns was the CZ Model 50 self-loading pistol, developed in 1947-48 by Jan and Jaroslav Kratochvil and produced by Ceska Zbrojovka — Narodni Podnik, Strakonice (Czech Arms Factory, National Corporation, in Strakonice). Besides being sold commercially, this pistol (designated as the Vz.50) was used by the Czechoslovakian national police.

A conventional double-action blowback-operated pistol chambered for the .32 ACP cartridge, the CZ Model 50 featured a 3⅛-inch barrel, an overall length of 6½ inches, and a weight of 24½ ounces. Most parts of the gun were of blued steel, and the grips were grooved black plastic.

In appearance and basic construction, the Model 50 is similar to the Walther Model PP, but nonetheless differs mechanically in a number of ways. Rather than the Walther's slide-mounted safety, the Model 50's safety is located on the frame. Moreover, the Model 50 lacks the Walther's hinged trigger guard, and also features a loaded-chamber indicator.

The eight-round steel box magazine is released by way of a magazine catch just to the rear of the trigger guard on the left side of the frame. A combination hold-open latch and ejector holds the slide of the Model 50 to the rear when the last shot is fired. Disassembly is by way of a right-side takedown catch.

The CZ Model 50 was discontinued In 1970.

DISASSEMBLY

1 To field-strip the CZ Model 50, first remove the magazine (42) and clear the chamber. While pressing the take-down catch (35) to the left, pull the slide (1) back and lift it upward at the rear. Then ease the slide forward off the barrel (43) and remove the recoil spring (10).

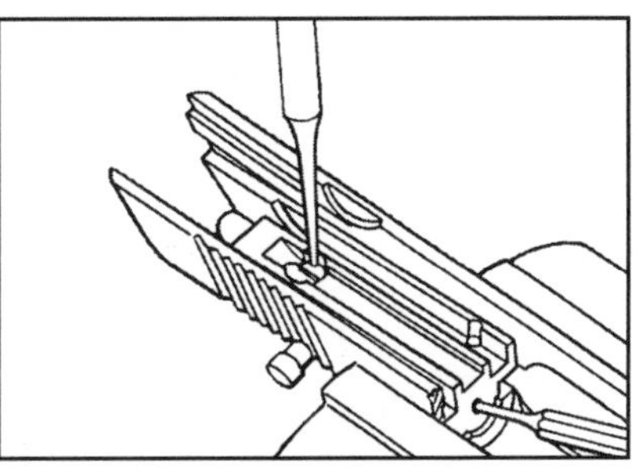

2 Hold the slide bottom-side-up in a vise. Depress the firing pin lock (9) with a punch and use a long thin punch from the front to push the firing pin (7) out. After the firing pin lock and spring are removed, drive out the extractor pin (2), and remove the extractor (6), extractor spring (5), and cartridge indicator (3).

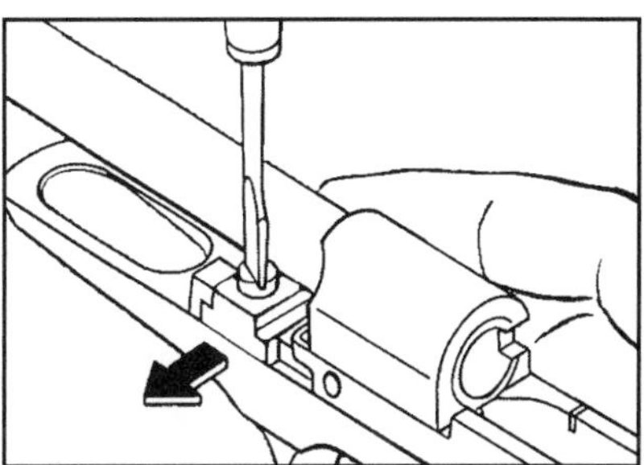

3 Push the takedown catch all the way to the left, and unscrew the takedown catch screw (34). In doing this, a screwdriver with a thin shank is required to clear the barrel. After removing the screw, take out the catch and spring to the right. The hold-open latch and ejector (12) and latch spring (11) can be removed by driving out the hold-open hinge pin (13) to the left. Do not remove these unless necessary.

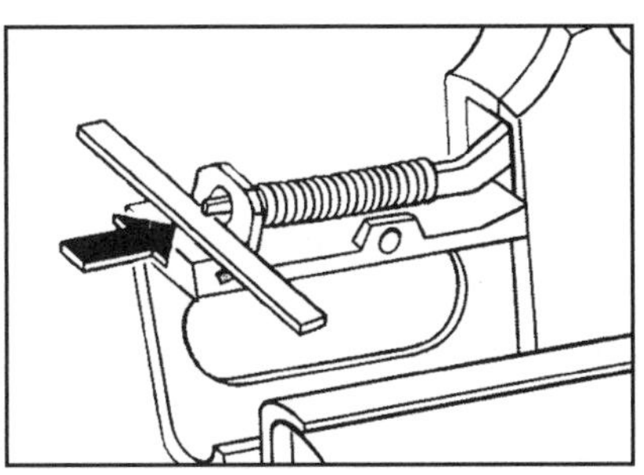

4 Before attempting disassembly of the lock mechanism, remove the grip screw (15) and grips (14) (27). Then carefully clamp the receiver (41) in a vise with padded jaws. Place a thin metal bar against the bottom of the spring retainer (26), and push on the bar until the retainer is free of the receiver. Then ease the bar back to its original position and remove the hammer spring (25) from the hammer strut (24).

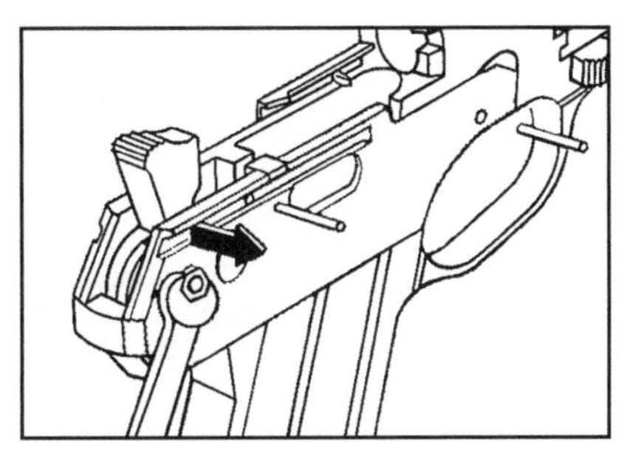

5 Continue disassembly of the lock mechanism by driving out the trigger pin (31) and sear pin (38), and use a small wrench to remove the nut (40) from the hammer bolt (19). Then push out the hammer bolt, lift the sideplate (39) from the receiver, and remove the trigger bar (28), trigger (30), hammer (23), and other lock parts.

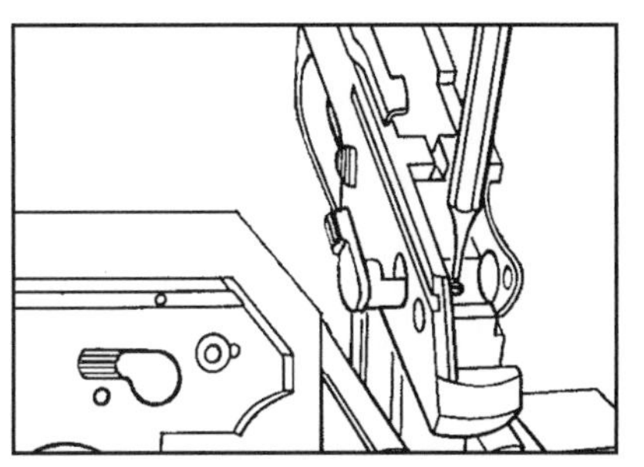

6 After removing the hammer, push the safety (16) out to the left without rotating. Take care not to lose the safety plunger (17) and safety spring (18). Reassemble in reverse. In replacing the safety, use a small punch to hold the safety plunger depressed. In replacing the hammer bolt nut, do not use excessive force and strip the threads.

CZ MODEL 75 PISTOL

PARTS LEGEND

1. Frame
2. Slide stop
3. Slide stop spring
4. Slide stop spring pin
5. Trigger
6. Trigger pin
7. Trigger bar
8. Trigger spring
9. Pin (3x)
10. Ejector
11. Sear
12. Sear spring
13. Sear pin
14. Firing pin block lever
15. Firing pin block lever spring
16. Hammer
17. Disconnector
18. Hammer pin
19. Hammer pin retaining peg
20. Main spring strut
21. Main spring
22. Main spring plug
23. Main spring plug pin
24. Magazine brake
25. Magazine brake pin
26. Grip panel – left
27. Grip panel – right
28. Grip panel screw (2)
29. Safety
30. Safety detent plunger
31. Safety detent plunger spring
32. Magazine catch
33. Magazine catch spring
34. Trigger bar spring
35. Magazine catch spring screw
36. Magazine body
37. Magazine base
38. Magazine base lock
39. Magazine spring
40. Follower
41. Recoil spring
42. Recoil spring guide
43. Barrel
44. Slide with barrel bushing
45. Front sight
46. Front sight pin
47. Loaded chamber indicator
48. Loaded chamber indicator Spring
49. Loaded chamber indicator nut
50. Extractor
51. Extractor pin
52. Extractor spring
53. Rear sight
54. Firing pin
55. Firing pin spring
56. Firing pin stop
57. a) Firing pin roll pin
    b) Firing pin roll pin
58. Firing pin block stop
59. Firing pin block stop spring
60. Hammer decocking lever controller
61. Decocking lever
62. Decocking lever spring
63. Fixing insert
64. Securing screw

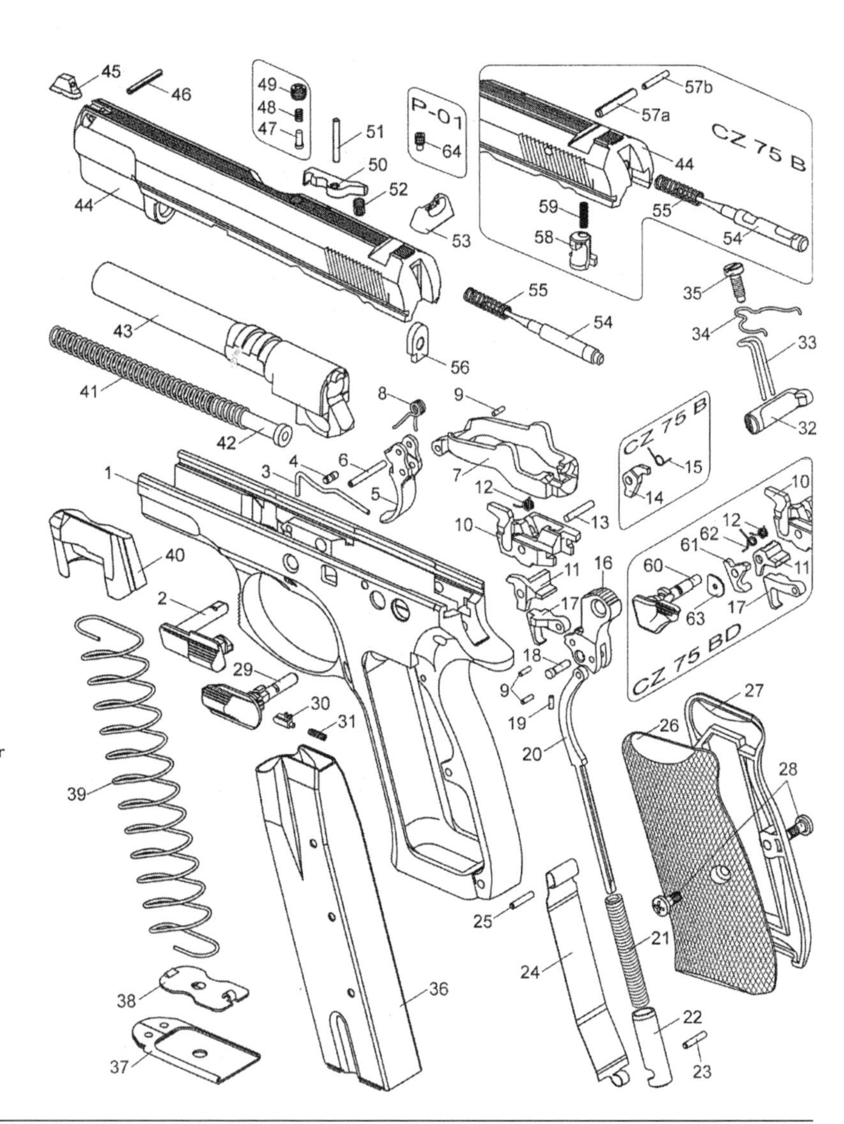

CZ was established by the Czechoslovakian National Defence Council in 1936 to produce military and civilian arms including aircraft machine guns, military pistols and hunting rifles. Under German occupation during World War II, the plant was forced to produce and repair military arms. In 1950 the company became the Presne Strojirenstvi Uhersky Brod (The Precision Machine Tooling Company) and in the 1970s it was merged with Agrozet Brno. In 1992, the new Czech Republic privatized the plant under the name Ceska Zbrojovka A.S., Uhersky Brod (CZ).

The CZ 75, introduced in 1975, is a short-recoil, locked breech pistol, originally offered only in 9mm Para. A .40 S&W chambering was later brought out. The pistol has a double-action trigger, as well as an exposed hammer and frame-mounted manual safety. This permits carry with the hammer down (the first shot being fired by way of a double-action trigger pull), or in "condition one," with the hammer cocked and the manual safety engaged. Because of this versatility, as well as its ruggedness, accuracy, excellent ergonomics and high-capacity magazine, the CZ 75 is widely considered one of the world's premier combat pistols.

Since the 1980s, all CZ 75 pistols have had internal firing-pin safeties, and carry the "CZ 75B" designation. There are numerous CZ 75 models, varying in size, safety mechanisms, finish, and frame material (steel, aluminum and polymer). The pistol was upgraded in the mid 1980s with an ambidextrous slide release and safety (CZ 85) and in 1997 with a .45 ACP chambering (CZ 97B).

DISASSEMBLY

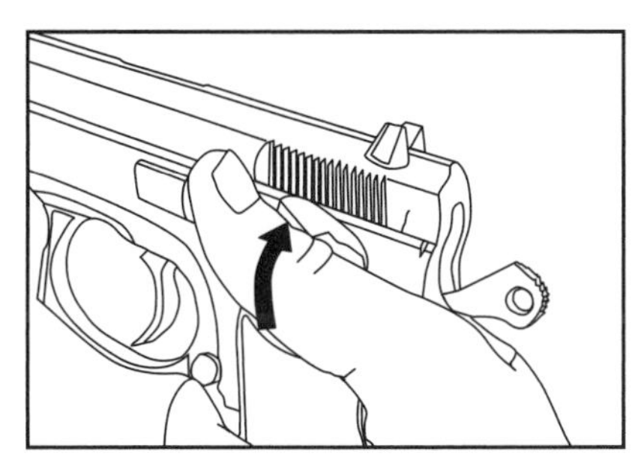

1 Remove the magazine. The pistol must not be disassembled with the magazine inserted.

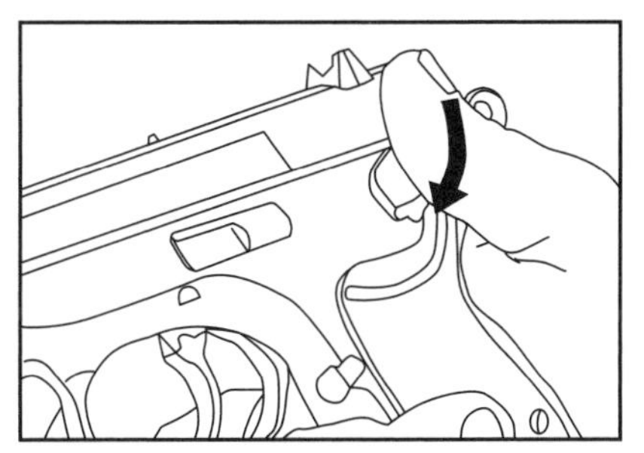

2 Place the safety to "off" position, in order to allow movement of the slide (for models with manual safety only).

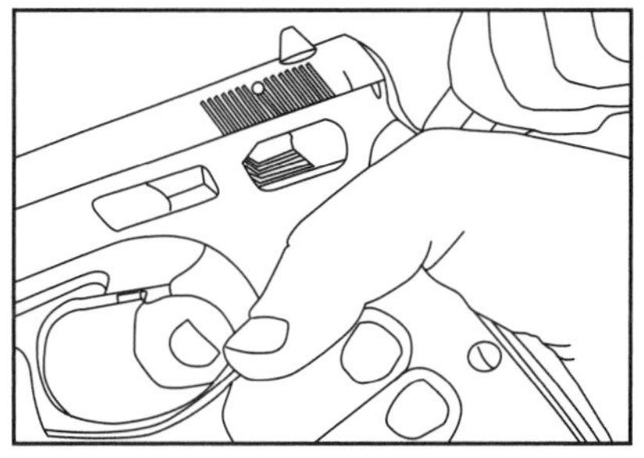

3 Pull the hammer back part of the way and release it to the half-cock position. This will make disassembly easier.

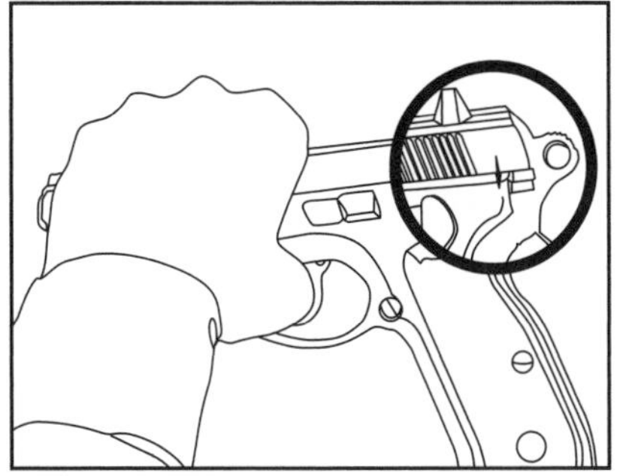

4 Put your left thumb through the trigger guard and grasp the front part of the slide firmly. Push the slide slightly back until the two vertical lines engraved on the rear part of the frame and slide are aligned.

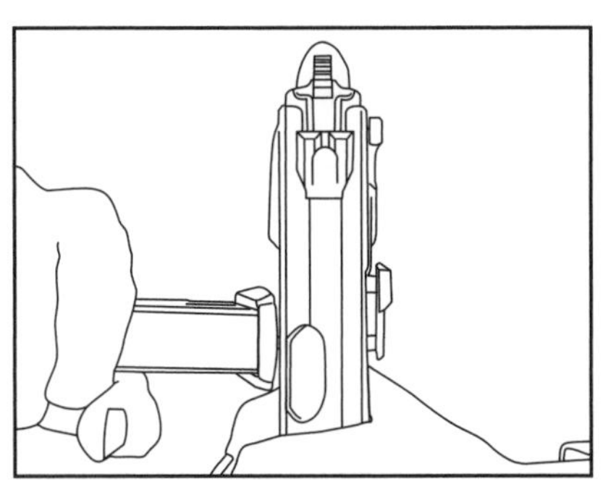

5 Keeping the lines aligned, push out the slide stop from the right hand side of the frame, using the magazine base. Remove the slide stop from the left. Pull the slide and barrel forward off of the frame. Remove recoil spring, guide and, lastly, the barrel.

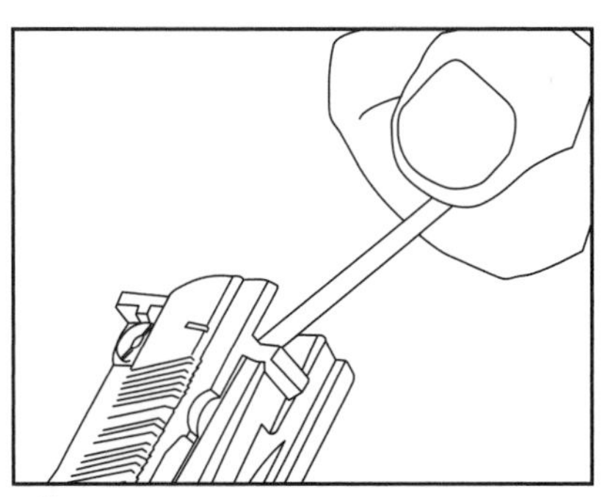

6 Using a suitable tool, push the rear end of the firing pin in below the level of the firing pin stop and shift the firing pin stop approximately 1/16-inch down. Cover firing pin stop with your thumb to retain the spring-loaded firing pin and, with the other hand, pull the firing pin stop completely off the slide. Caution: Firing pin is under tension and could fly out. Consult gunsmith for pistols with firing pin block.

CZ MODEL 83 PISTOL

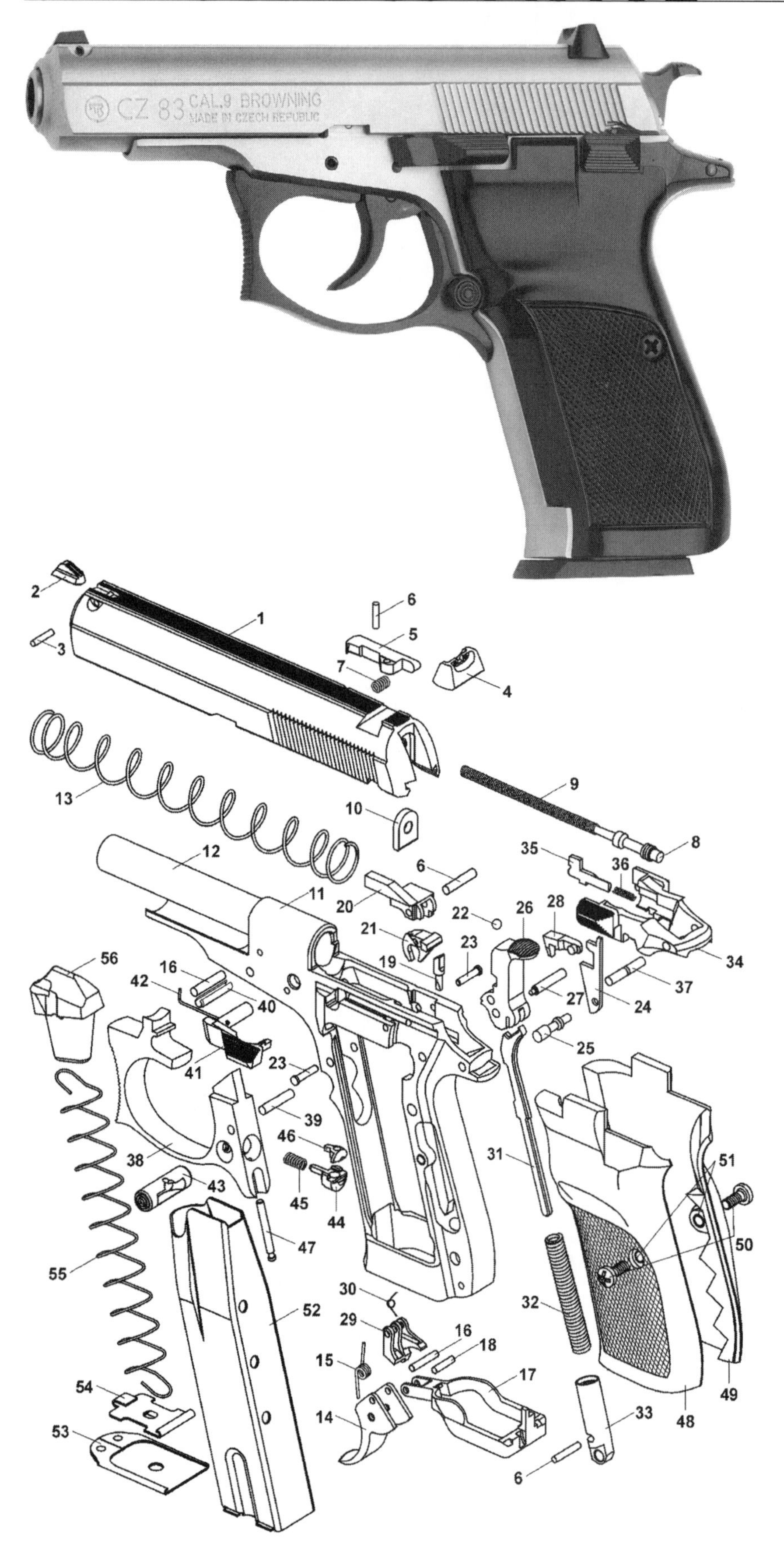

PARTS LEGEND

1. Slide
2. Front sight
3. Front sight pin
4. Rear sight
5. Extractor
6. Pin (3)
7. Extractor spring
8. Firing pin
9. Firing pin spring
10. Firing pin stop
11. Frame
12. Barrel
13. Recoil spring
14. Trigger
15. Trigger spring
16. Pin (2)
17. Trigger bar
18. Trigger bar pin
19. Disconnector
20. Ejector
21. Automatic safety
22. Steel ball
23. Pin (2)
24. Trigger bar disconnector
25. Trigger bar disconnector rivet
26. Hammer
27. Hammer pin
28. Hammer lever
29. Sear
30. Sear spring
31. Main spring strut
32. Main spring
33. Main spring plug
34. Safety
35. Safety latch
36. Safety latch spring
37. Safety pin
38. Trigger guard
39. Pin
40. Trigger guard pin
41. Slide stop
42. Slide stop spring
43. Magazine catch push button
44. Magazine catch
45. Magazine catch spring
46. Magazine catch lever
47. Magazine catch lever pin
48. Left grip panel
49. Right grip panel
50. Grip panel screw (2)
51. Grip panel insert (2)
52. Magazine body
53. Magazine base
54. Magazine base lock
55. Magazine spring
56. Magazine follower

During the early 1980s, the Czechoslovak army, under pressure from the USSR, replaced their existing 7.62x25mm ammunition with the 9x18mm Makarov cartridge. However, instead of adopting the Russian Makarov PM pistol, the Czechs developed their own weapon, the Vz.82, at the CZ factory in Uhersky Brod., which became the standard sidearm of the Czech army in 1982.

Recognizing the commercial potential of the design, CZ introduced a version of the pistol, the CZ 83, to the European civilian market in the mid-1980s, followed by importation into the U.S.

Currently available in .32 ACP (7.65mm Browning), .380 ACP and 9mm Makarov, the CZ 83 is a compact, double-action, blowback-operated high-capacity semi-automatic pistol. Features include a fixed 3.8"-long barrel, a steel frame and slide, an external hammer, an ambidextrous frame-mounted safety, a length of 6.8 inches and a weight of 26 ounces. The sear- and slide-locking safety allows carry in the cocked-and-locked condition. Capacity of the double-column magazine is 12 rounds in .380 ACP and 15 rounds in .32 ACP. Aiming is by way of fixed sights with a three-dot pattern.

DISASSEMBLY

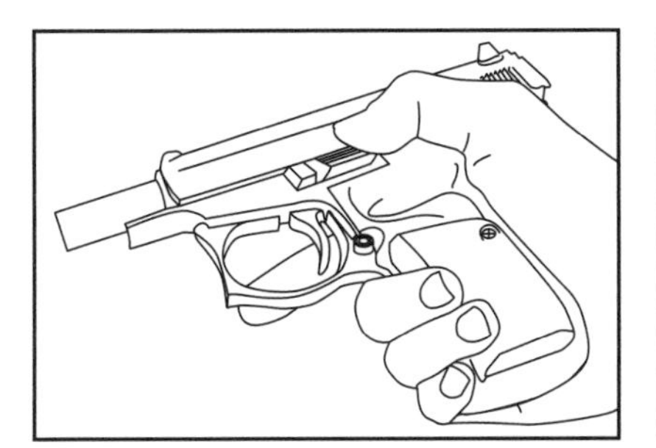

1 Remove the magazine. The pistol must not be disassembled with the magazine inserted.

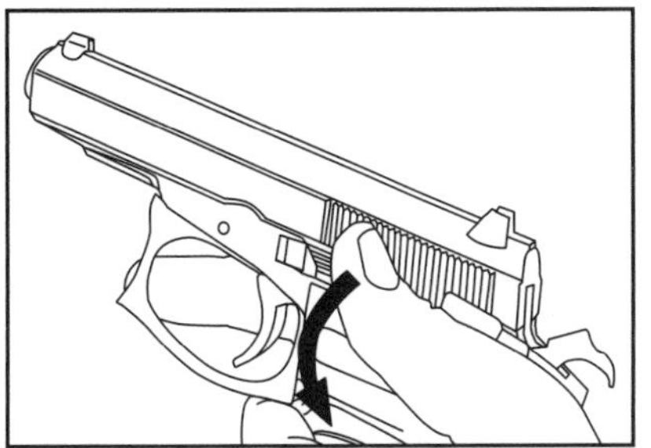

2 Place the safety in the "off" position, in order to allow movement of the slide. Pull the hammer back part way and release it to the half-cock position.

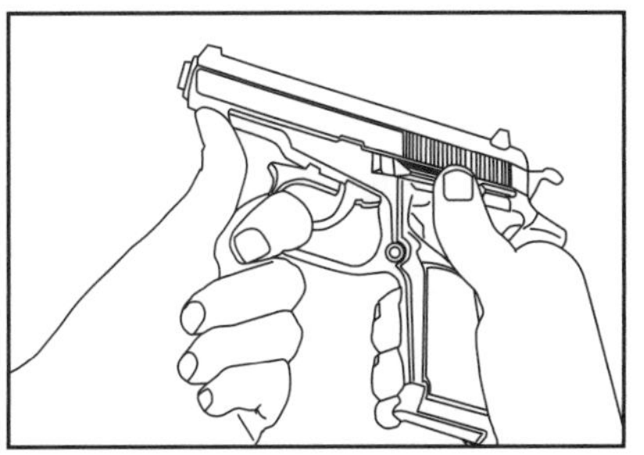

3 Hold the pistol grip with one hand. Place the index finger of your other hand through the trigger guard, support your thumb against front lower part of the slide and pull straight out and down to rotate the trigger guard downward.

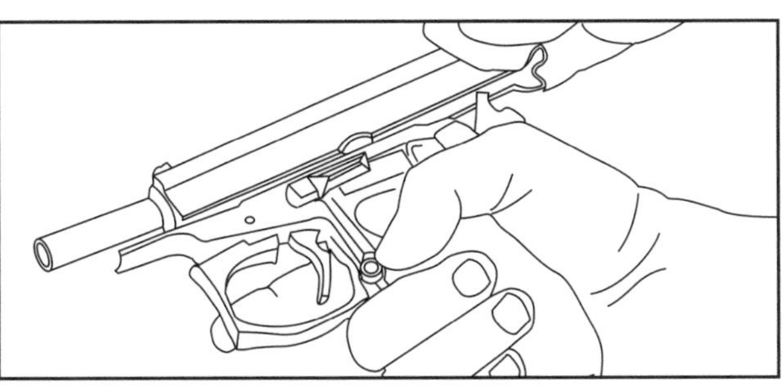

4 Pull the slide back all the way. Lift the rear end of the slide and move it forward to separate it from the barrel and frame.

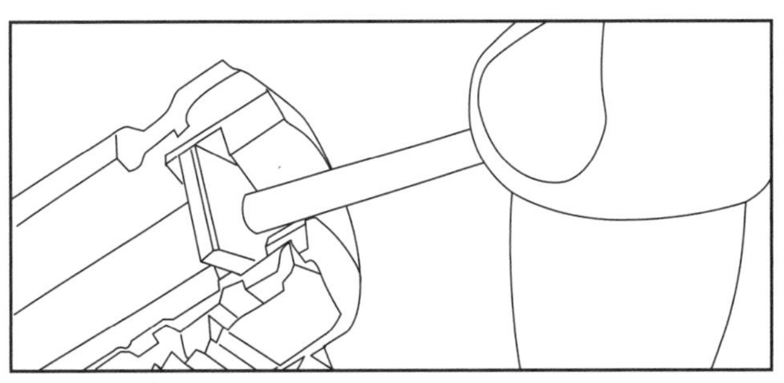

5 Push in the rear end of firing pin using a suitable tool, below the level of the firing pin stop, and shift the firing pin stop approximately 2mm down. Then cover the firing pin stop with your thumb in order not to lose the spring-loaded firing pin and with the other hand pull the firing pin stop completely off the slide. CAUTION: Be very careful at this stage of the disassembly procedure, as the firing pin spring is under tension.

DAN WESSON MODEL W-12

PARTS LEGEND

1. Front sight
2. Front sight pin
3. Shroud
4. Elevation screw
5. Elevation click plunger
6. Elevation tension
7. Elevation tension
8. Rear sight body
9. Hinge pin
10. Windage tension spring
11. Plunger spring
12. Windage click plunger
13. Windage screw
14. Elevation nut
15. Firing pin
16. Firing pin spring
17. Firing pin
18. Frame
19. Barrel nut
20. Barrel
21. Latch retaining pin
22. Latch
23. Latch spring
24. Crane
25. Firing pin connector
26. Strut
27. Hammer
28. Strut plunger
29. Strut spring
30. Cylinder aligning ball
31. Aligning ball spring spring
32. Aligning ball screw
33. Grip screw plunger
34. Grip
35. Hand
36. Bolt spring
37. Bolt plunger (2)
38. Bolt
39. Hand spring
40. Trigger
41. Trigger stop screw
42. Sideplate screw retaining pin
43. Trigger return spring
44. Mainspring guide
45. Mainspring
46. Sideplate
47. Sideplate screw
48. Ejector rod
49. Ejector rod bushing
50. Cylinder
51. Ejector spring
52. Extractor

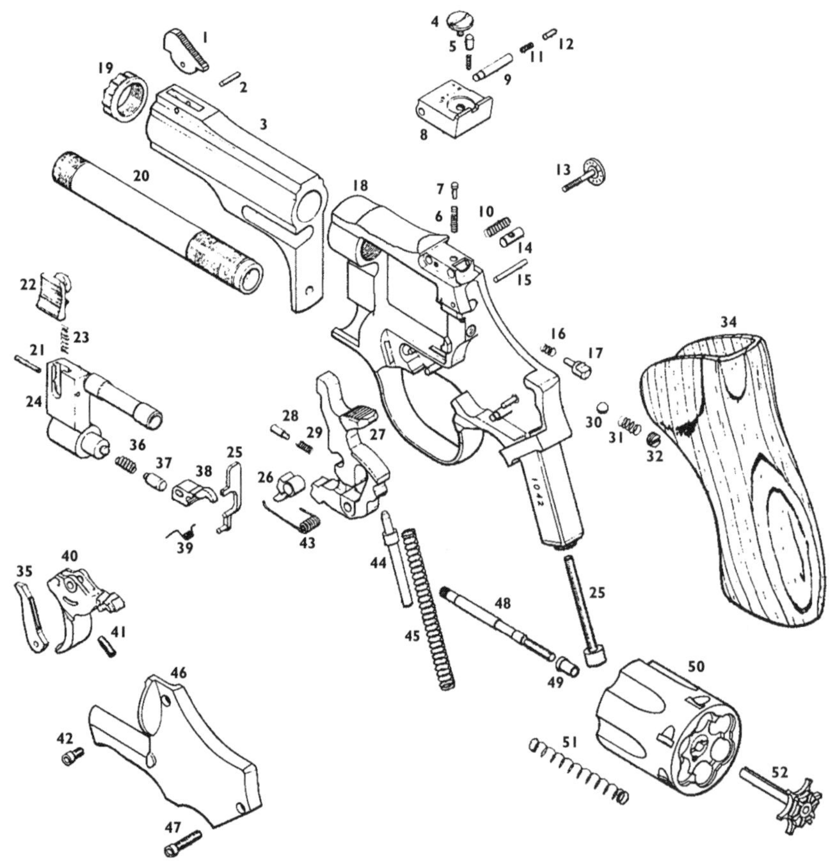

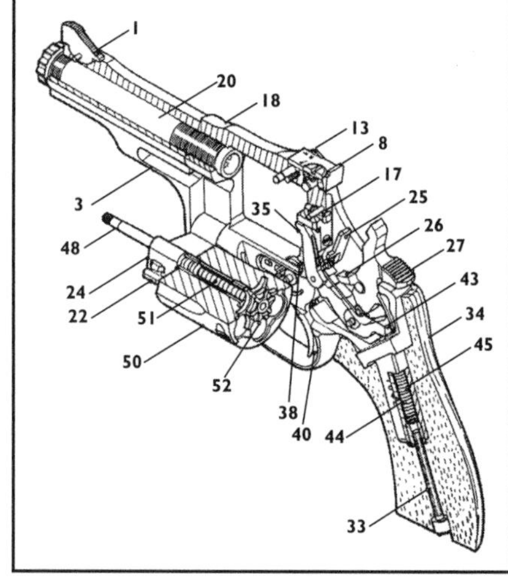

The Model W-12, .357 Magnum, solid-frame revolver was produced by Dan Wesson Arms, which was organized in 1968 at Monson, Massachusetts. The late Daniel B. Wesson, the founder and president of the firm, was a great-grandson of Daniel B. Wesson of Smith & Wesson.

The W-12's barrel can be easily interchanged for others of different lengths. A combination tool is used to unscrew the barrel nut. After the shroud is removed, the barrel can be unscrewed by hand. Interchangeable barrels of six-, four- and 2½-inch lengths are available for the Model W-12. When installing a replacement barrel, a shim is used to obtain the proper clearance between the barrel and cylinder. The one-piece grip can also be interchanged. The Model W-12 was dropped by Dan Wesson Arms in about 1974.

DISASSEMBLY

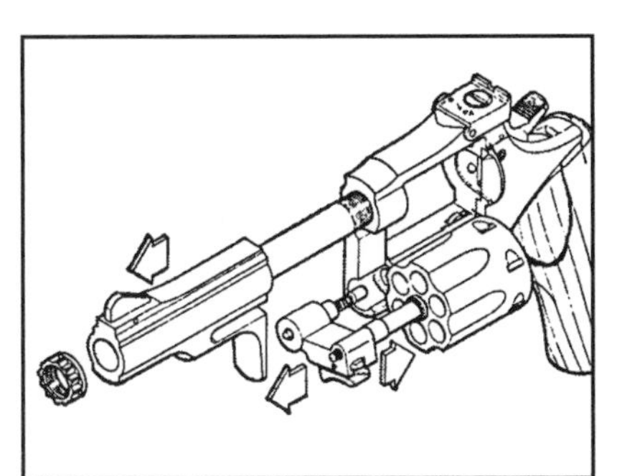

1 Before attempting disassembly, unload cylinder (50), and lower hammer (27). Use Wesson combination tool (or ⅝-inch double-hex box wrench) to unscrew and remove barrel nut (19). Slide off shroud (3), and unscrew barrel (20). Depress latch (22), and swing out crane (24) and cylinder. Pull cylinder-crane assembly forward from frame (18), and detach cylinder from crane. This is sufficient takedown for normal cleaning.

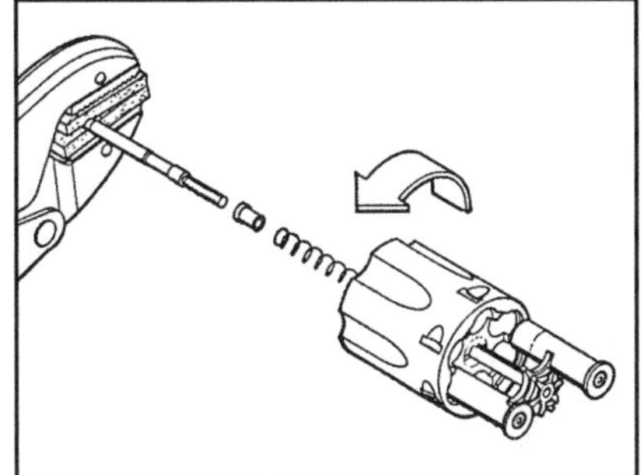

2 To disassemble cylinder parts, clamp knurled tip of ejector rod (48) between wooden blocks in vise or locking jaw pliers. Insert two empty cartridge cases in opposite chambers, and use cases to unscrew cylinder from rod. This releases extractor (52), ejector rod bushing (49), and ejector spring (51).

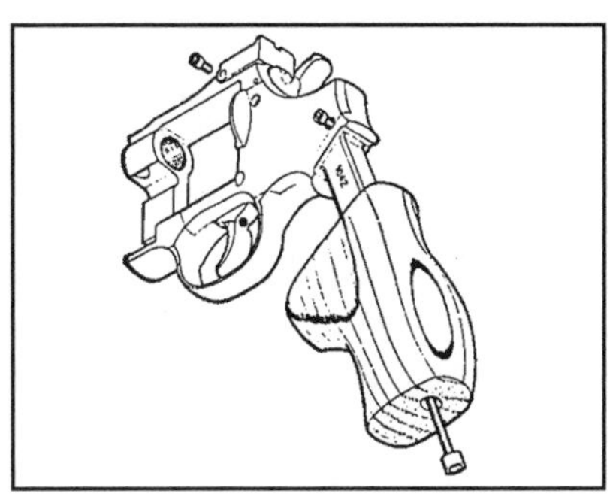

3 Hole in underside of grip (34) gives access to grip screw (33). Remove screw with combination tool (5/32" Allen wrench), and pull grip downward from frame spike. Unscrew and remove sideplate screws (42 & 47) with combination tool (5/64" Allen wrench). Lift sideplate (46) carefully; hand (35) is under spring tension and is easily displaced.

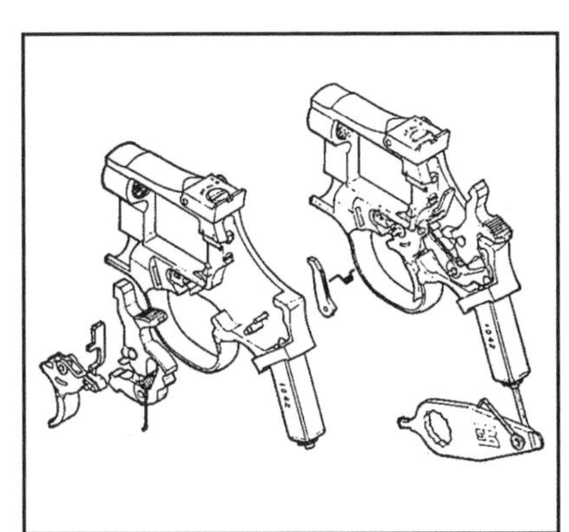

4 Unhook hand spring (39) from groove in rear of hand, and remove hand and spring. Cock hammer. Then tighten long sideplate screw into mainspring guide (44), through hole at bottom of frame spike. Pull trigger (40), and lower hammer with thumb. Draw long arm of trigger return spring (43) outward from trigger, and allow it to arc downward until the tension is relieved. Trigger and firing pin connector (25), hammer, trigger spring, and bolt (38) can then be lifted from frame.

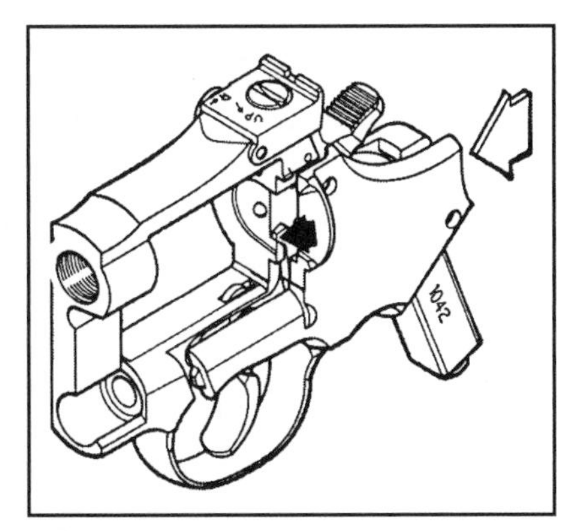

5 Assemble in reverse. Stub arm of trigger spring must be positioned to rear of frame-mounted hammer pivot pin. Install hand spring with shorter arm bearing on forward surface of firing pin connector and longer arm hooked into hand groove. Maintain fingernail pressure against tip of hand to prevent its escape while replacing sideplate. Hold sideplate flat against frame and slide forward into place.

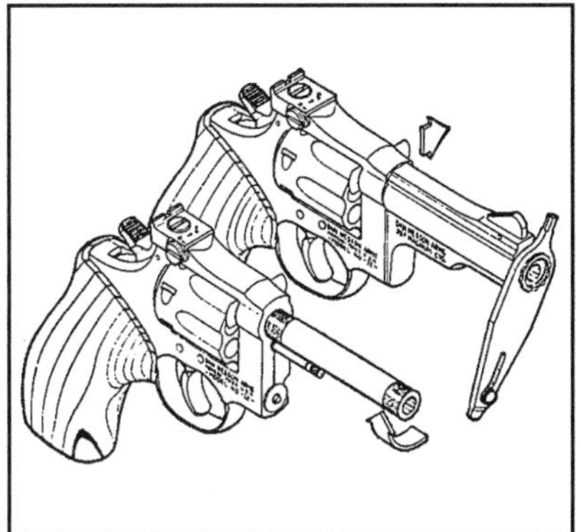

6 Clean barrel threads, rear barrel face, and forward face of cylinder before adjusting clearance. Place .006" shim gauge on cylinder face, and screw barrel inward until a very light drag is felt on shim, just enough to hold shim in position. Install shroud and barrel nut with shim in place, rechecking clearance after barrel nut has been tightened.

DERINGER POCKET PISTOL

PARTS LEGEND

1. Barrel
2. Front sight
3. Cone
4. Breech plug & tang
5. Breech plug tang screw
6. Stock
7. Wedge plates (2)
8. Stock tip
9. Escutcheon
10. Wedge
11. Trigger guard plate
12. Trigger guard
13. Trigger guard screw
14. Trigger
15. Trigger pivot pin
16. Buttplate (with trapdoor)
17. Rear buttplate screw
18. Front buttplate screw
19. Back-action lock
20. Hammer
21. Hammer screw
22. Lockplate screw
23. Side-plate
24. Side-plate screw

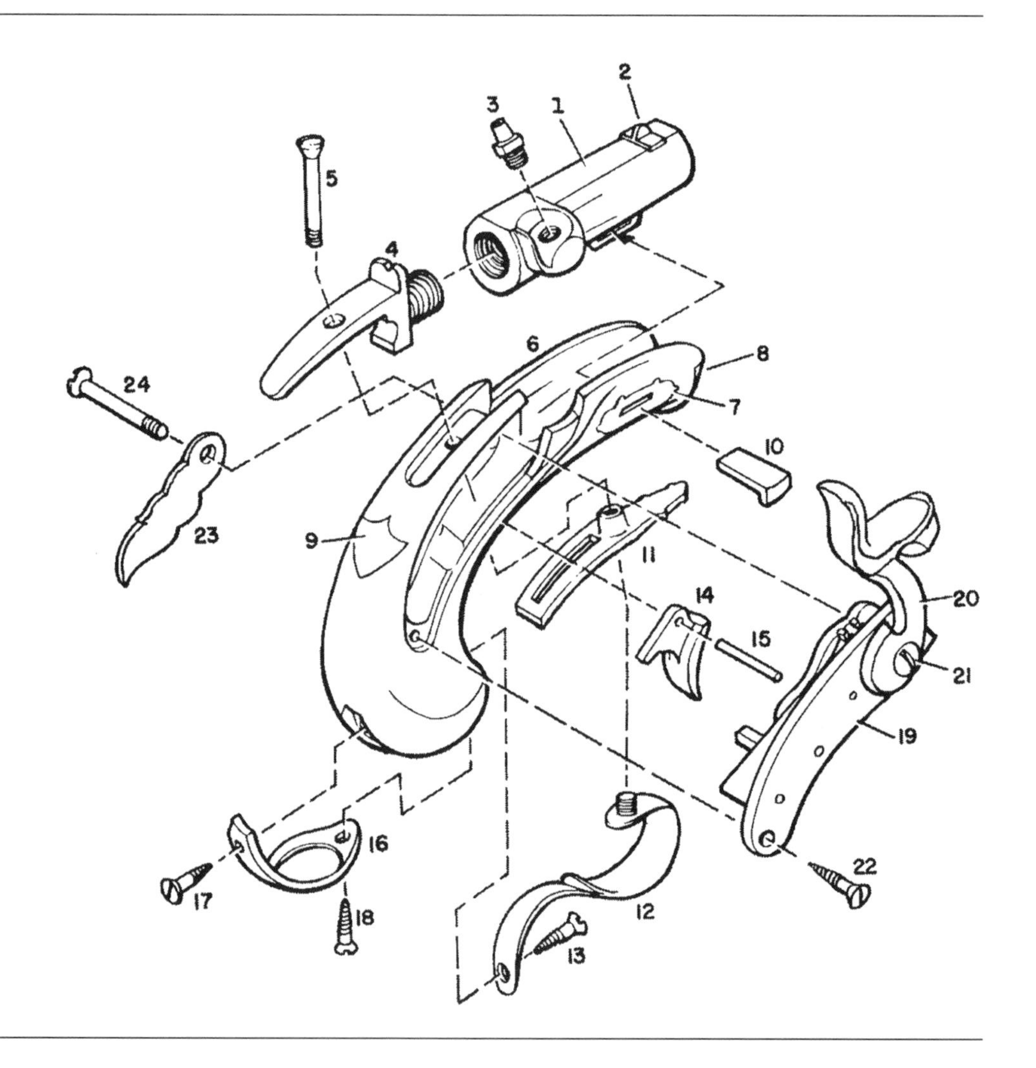

Henry Deringer, Jr., of Philadelphia, Pa., began manufacture of his famed single-shot muzzle-loading percussion pocket pistols in 1825 and limited production continued even after his death in 1868, when the firm was operated for a time by a son-in-law, Dr. Jonathan Clark.

However, the demand for all types of percussion pistols fell off sharply following the Civil War when the self-contained metallic cartridge came into common use. The Deringer was but one of many erstwhile popular percussion arms doomed by this development. In its heyday, the Deringer pistol was favored by individuals from all walks of life who desired a powerful yet easily concealed handgun. It was made in several calibers from .33 to .51, and with barrels ranging in length from less than 1" to more than 4".

Commonly sold in matched pairs, the genuine Deringer pistols had rifled barrels of wrought iron. Some were fitted with single-set triggers. The 2-line trademark DERINGER PHILADELA was invariably stamped on the lockplate and breech. These pistols were not serially numbered, but the various parts were stamped with matching assembly numbers or letters. Like most well-made products, the Deringer pistols were subject to counterfeiting and some of this was done by former employees of the Deringer firm. This resulted in litigation successful to Deringer, but the fact remains that the word Deringer (or Derringer) is today a proper noun commonly applied to any easily concealable short barrel pocket pistol of non-automatic type.

Deringer pistols figured in many notable homicides, the most famous being the assassination of President Abraham Lincoln by John Wilkes Booth.

The full story of the Deringer pistol is given in the book entitled *Henry Deringer's Pocket Pistol*, by John E. Parsons, published in 1952 by William Morrow & Co.

DISASSEMBLY

Place hammer (20) at half-cock position and unscrew side-plate screw (24) from left side of stock. Unscrew lockplate screw (22) and tap left side of stock gently to loosen lock plate. Lift lock assembly out right side of stock. To remove barrel (1), drift wedge (10) out of stock. Unscrew breech plug tang screw (5) and lift barrel and breech plug assembly up out of stock. Trigger guard (12) and plate (11) can be removed from underside of stock after removing trigger guard screw (13). Trigger (14) is removed by drifting trigger pivot pin (15) out of stock. Buttplate is removed by unscrewing rear and front buttplate screws (17 & 18).

Removal of wedge plates (7), stock tip (8), escutcheon (9), and side-plate (23) from stock (6) is not recommended.

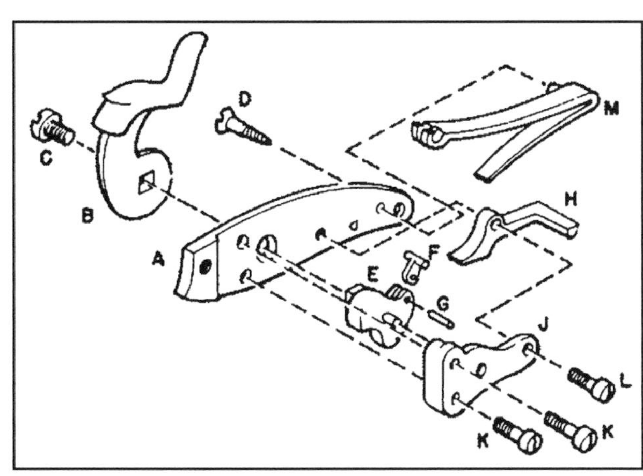

1 The conventional back-action lock is easily disassembled after removal from the stock. The lower end of the V mainspring (M) bears directly on the sear (H) and no sear spring is employed.

A) Lockplate
B) Hammer (20)
C) Hammer screw (21)
D) Lockplate screw (22)
E) Tumbler
F) Stirrup
G) Stirrup pin
H) Sear
J) Bridle
K) Bridle screws (2)
L) Sear screw
M) Mainspring

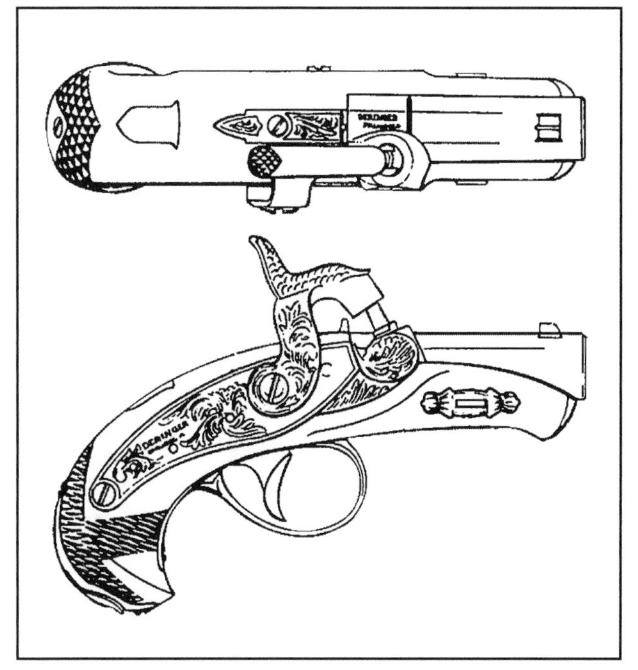

2 The scale drawing shows right side and top detail of the assembled Deringer pistol and is a reference in identifying genuine H. Deringer pistols of this type. Minor variations in style of engraving occur; however, the engraving shown is most typical of this arm.

DREYSE MODEL 1907 PISTOL

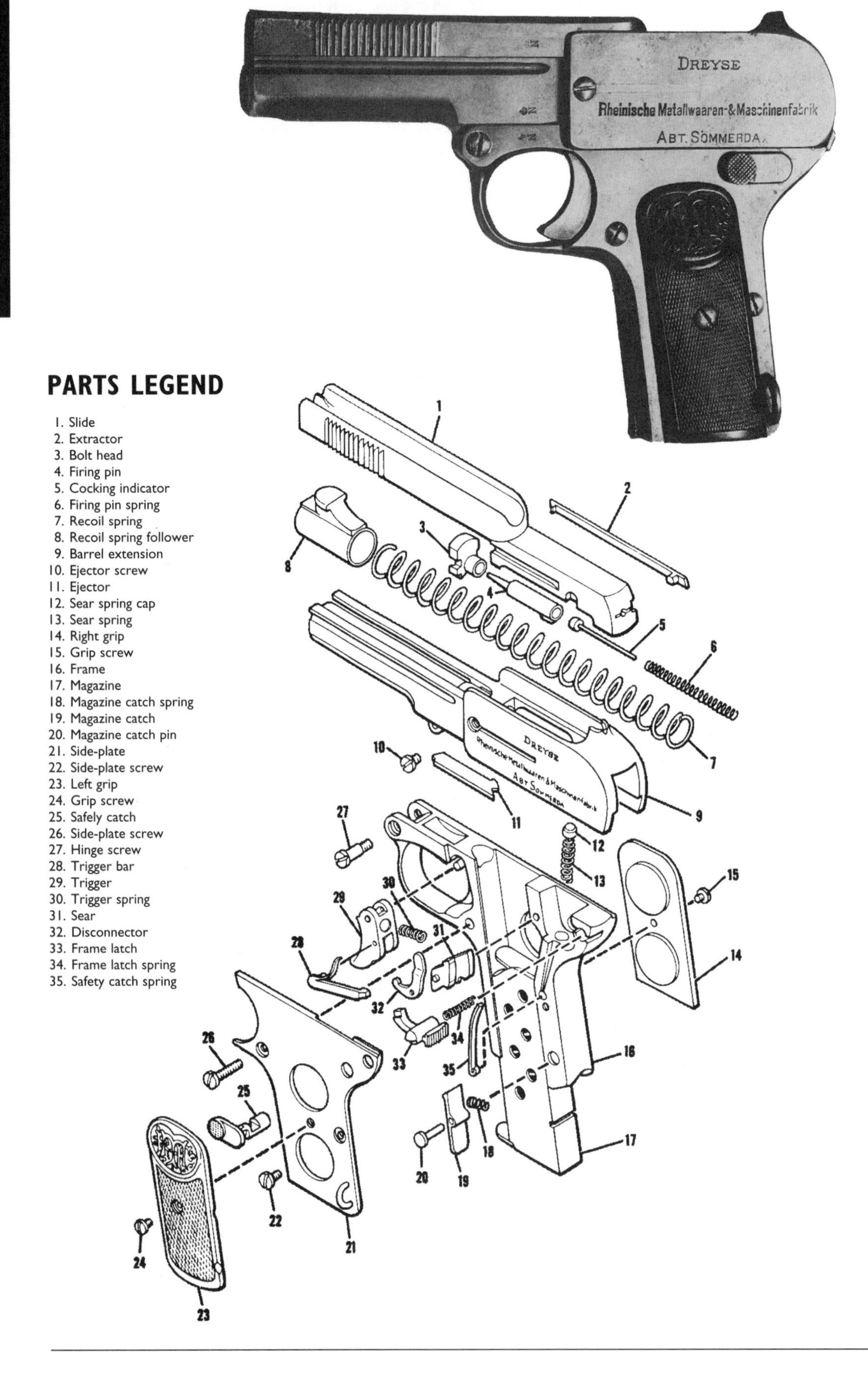

PARTS LEGEND

1. Slide
2. Extractor
3. Bolt head
4. Firing pin
5. Cocking indicator
6. Firing pin spring
7. Recoil spring
8. Recoil spring follower
9. Barrel extension
10. Ejector screw
11. Ejector
12. Sear spring cap
13. Sear spring
14. Right grip
15. Grip screw
16. Frame
17. Magazine
18. Magazine catch spring
19. Magazine catch
20. Magazine catch pin
21. Side-plate
22. Side-plate screw
23. Left grip
24. Grip screw
25. Safely catch
26. Side-plate screw
27. Hinge screw
28. Trigger bar
29. Trigger
30. Trigger spring
31. Sear
32. Disconnector
33. Frame latch
34. Frame latch spring
35. Safety catch spring

There was a period in Germany when any schoolboy could tell you that Nikolaus von Dreyse invented the famous Prussian needle gun. Though he died in 1867, his name was revered up through World War I and numerous guns designed long after his death carried his name. One is the Schmeisser-designed Dreyse Model 1907 pistol, manufactured by the *Rheinische Metallwaren and Maschinenfabrik* of Sömmerda, Germany.

The Dreyse is an awkward pistol, due in part to the fact that it was developed near the beginning of the automatic pistol era. A few years after the gun was first marketed, Europe was swamped by the 1910 series of Browning, Mauser, Sauer, and Walther pocket pistols. The better designs of these weapons soon overshadowed the Dreyse. Although it was manufactured up to World War I, the Model 1907 was superseded by the Rheinmetall pistol after World War I. During the short time it was in production, numerous machining changes were made. Around 1912 the gun was redesigned and scaled up to handle the 9mm Luger cartridge. The 9mm pistol was used to a limited extent during World War I, but the German Army never liked a blow-back-operated gun for such a powerful cartridge.

Although the grip design and general outline of the Model 1907 leave a great deal to be desired, it has a few interesting features. The most notable is the frame design. Unlike most common automatics, the sear mechanism can be inspected by removing a large side-plate.

The frame is hinged and can be tipped up by moving a button at the back of the receiver. This action does not expose the barrel as in the Smith & Wesson and Le Français pistols. It is helpful in clearing a jam, but unfortunately it does not simplify the cleaning problem.

When the gun is cocked, a pin that can be easily seen or felt as it protrudes from the end of the slide. In spite of its seemingly complicated exterior, the operating parts are simple and fairly rugged.

DISASSEMBLY

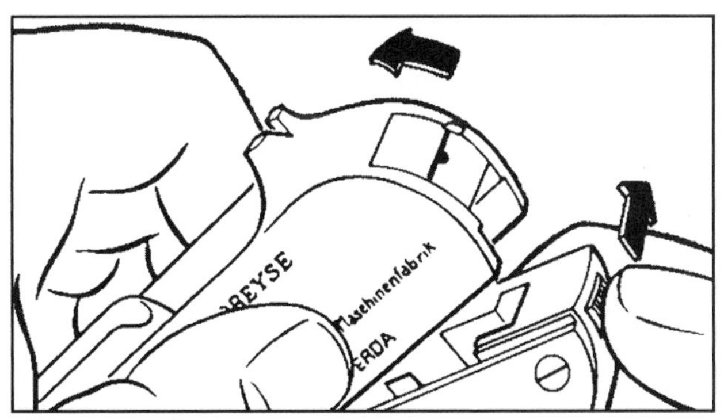

1 To disassemble: Remove magazine and clear chamber. Open action by pushing frame latch (33), on end of frame, to right and lifting up barrel extension (9) as shown. The gun will not come apart as it is hinged by a screw above the trigger guard

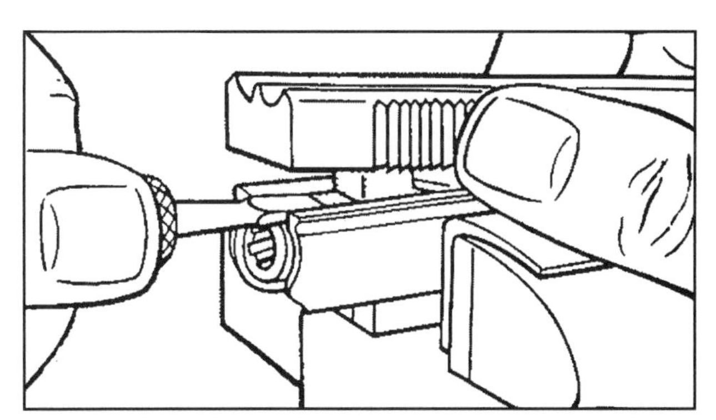

2 To avoid injuring knuckles it is best to clamp barrel extension of pistol in vise to simplify removal of slide. Depress recoil spring follower (8) with blade of small screwdriver until lug on follower clears notch in slide. Lift up serrated end of slide as shown, then ease follower off barrel, remembering it is under extremely heavy spring tension

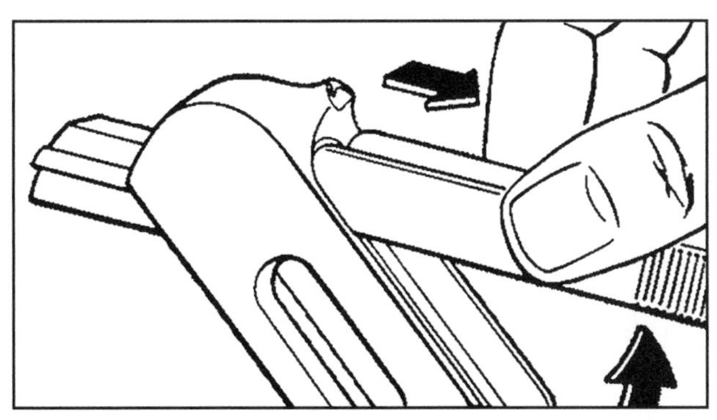

3 After recoil spring follower (8) and recoil spring (7) have been removed, push slide back as far as possible. Lift serrated portion and slide it free of barrel extension

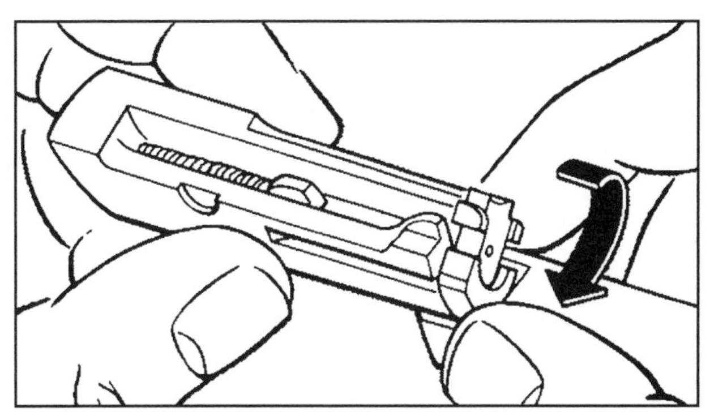

4 To remove firing pin (4) first lift out extractor (2), then rotate bolt head (3) as shown until rounded portion is free of retaining cut in slide. It may be necessary to tap the bolt head with a soft hammer to start it.

ENFIELD NO. 2 MK I AND MK I*

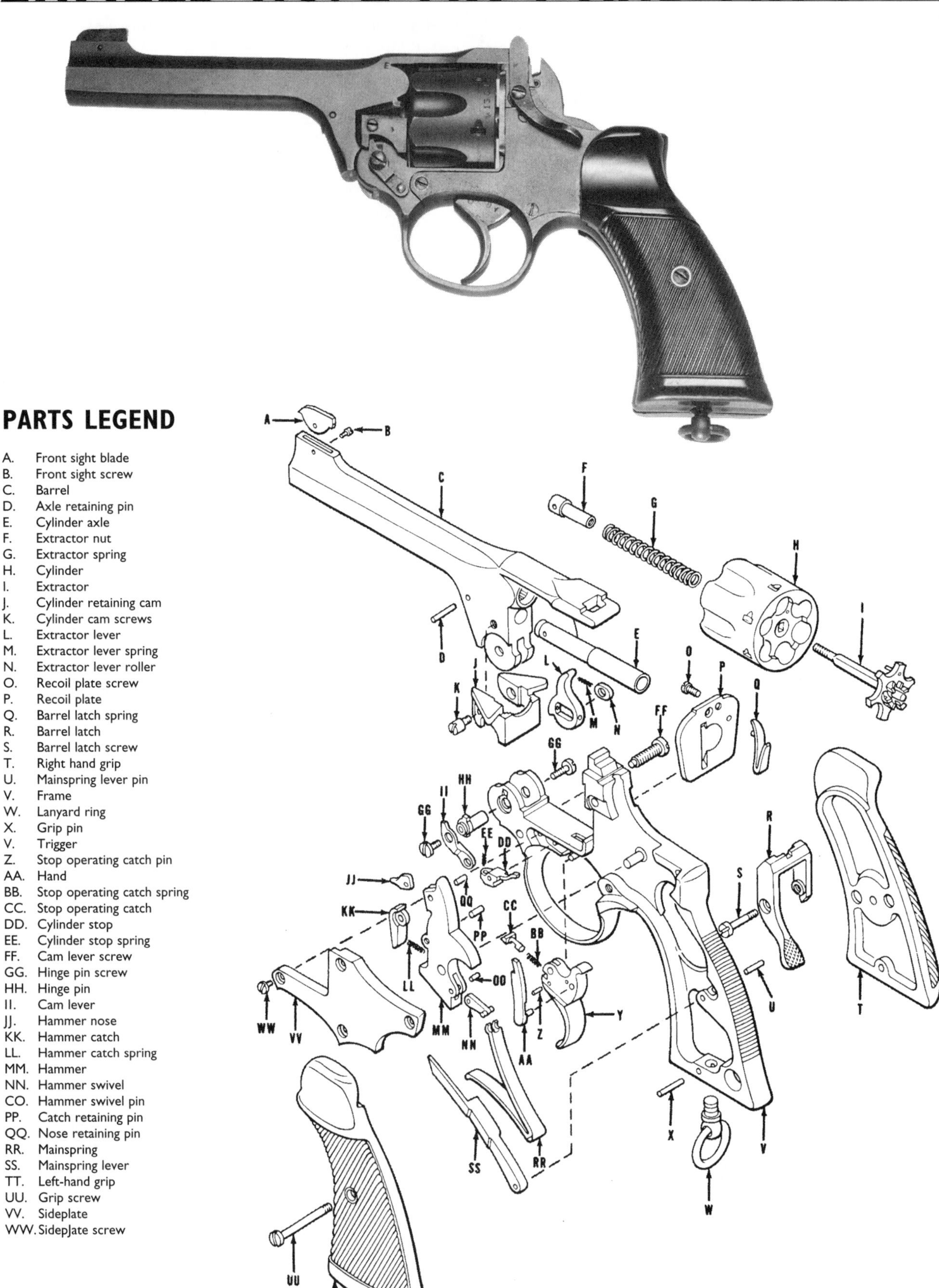

PARTS LEGEND

A. Front sight blade
B. Front sight screw
C. Barrel
D. Axle retaining pin
E. Cylinder axle
F. Extractor nut
G. Extractor spring
H. Cylinder
I. Extractor
J. Cylinder retaining cam
K. Cylinder cam screws
L. Extractor lever
M. Extractor lever spring
N. Extractor lever roller
O. Recoil plate screw
P. Recoil plate
Q. Barrel latch spring
R. Barrel latch
S. Barrel latch screw
T. Right hand grip
U. Mainspring lever pin
V. Frame
W. Lanyard ring
X. Grip pin
V. Trigger
Z. Stop operating catch pin
AA. Hand
BB. Stop operating catch spring
CC. Stop operating catch
DD. Cylinder stop
EE. Cylinder stop spring
FF. Cam lever screw
GG. Hinge pin screw
HH. Hinge pin
II. Cam lever
JJ. Hammer nose
KK. Hammer catch
LL. Hammer catch spring
MM. Hammer
NN. Hammer swivel
CO. Hammer swivel pin
PP. Catch retaining pin
QQ. Nose retaining pin
RR. Mainspring
SS. Mainspring lever
TT. Left-hand grip
UU. Grip screw
VV. Sideplate
WW. Sidepjate screw

The Enfield No. 2, Mk 1 revolver, chambered for the .38-200 (or .38 S&W) cartridge, was adopted by the British army in 1932 to replace the older .455, Mk VI Webley-pattern revolver. The more recent No. 2, Mk 1*, a double-action only modification, was introduced in 1938.

Enfield No.2 revolvers, the mainstay service handgun of British armed forces during World War II, were originally devised, as a simplification of a Webley and Scott design, by the Royal Small Arms Factory at Enfield Lock.

The No.2, Mk 1 and Mk 1* are basically the same revolver. The major difference between them is that the Mk 1* has a double-action only mechanism, and lacks the full-cock notch and thumbcocking hammer spur of the Mk I.

Webley & Scott "Mark IV" revolvers are often mistaken for Enfield No. 2 guns (particularly the No.2, Mk I), but they are actually quite different both in design and in method of manufacture. While both were used during World War II, Enfields were made at the government arsenal at Enfield and Mark IV revolvers were made by Webley & Scott in their Birmingham plant. The Enfield is the simpler of the two from a repair standpoint. By removing the sideplate, the operation of the parts can be studied. Not so with the Webley, as the parts are installed through openings in the frame.

These top-break revolvers are faster to load and extract than any other type of revolver, but there are drawbacks. The cylinder can be knocked out of line should the gun be dropped while in the open position.

Enfield revolvers remained in service until 1957, when the British armed forces adopted a version of the Belgian, 9mm GP-35 (the Browning Hi-Power) designated L9Al.

DISASSEMBLY

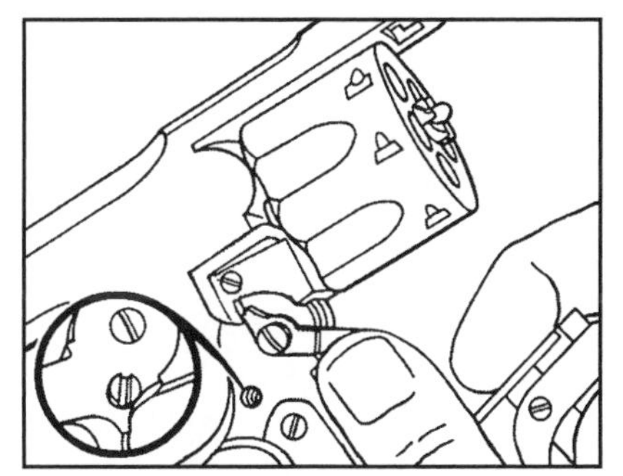

1 The first point in stripping the No. 2 revolver is to remove the cylinder (H). Remove the cam lever screw (FF). The screw slot is wide enough for a coin. Open the gun as far as it will go and push up on the cam lever (II) as shown. Lift the cylinder off the axle.

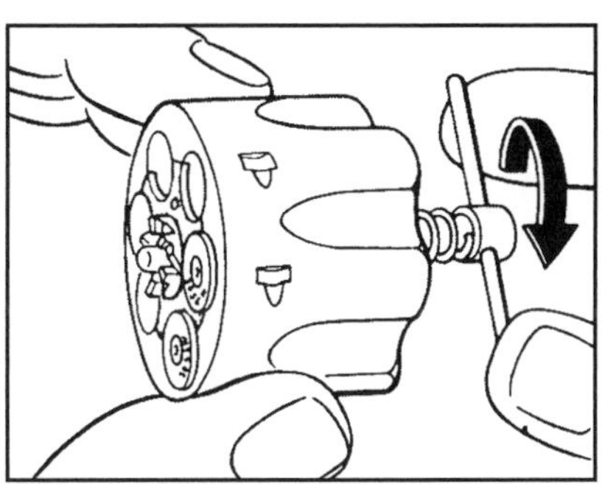

2 Before removing the extractor (I), put a few empty cartridges in the cylinder (H) to prevent the tiny locating pin from shearing off. Run a nail or punch through the hole in extractor nut (F) and unscrew it as shown. Lift out the extractor (I) and extractor spring (G).

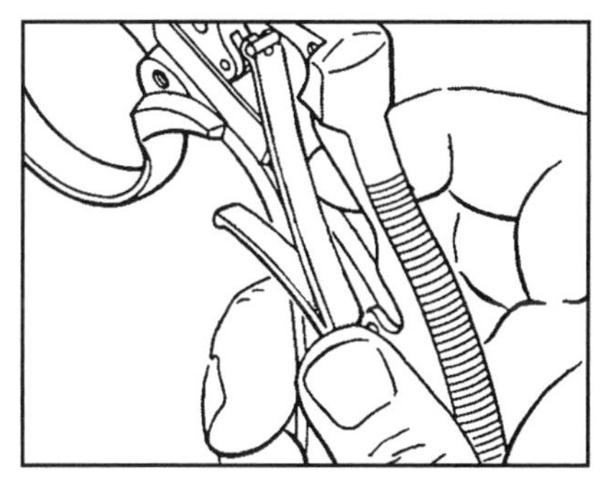

3 After the barrel latch (R), the sideplate (VV), and the grips have been removed. the mainspring (RR) may be pushed out of its seat as shown and unhooked from the hammer swivel (NN). Needless to say, this should not be attempted with the hammer at full cock (Mk I only).

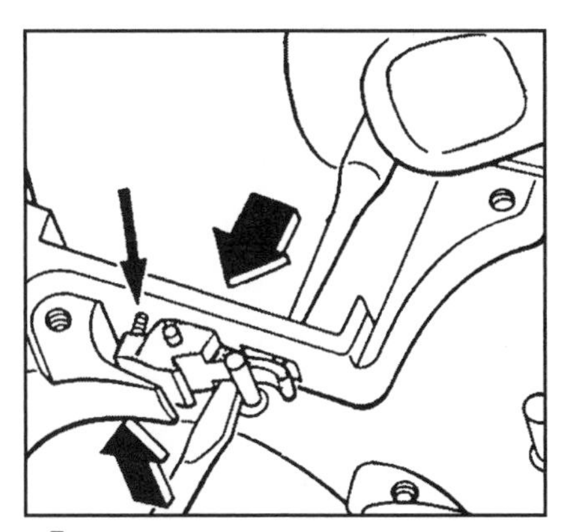

4 The only other delicate part in this gun is the cylinder stop spring (EE). Care must be taken not to deform it when removing the cylinder stop (DD). To remove the stop, it is necessary to depress it below the surface of the frame while prying it up off its pin.

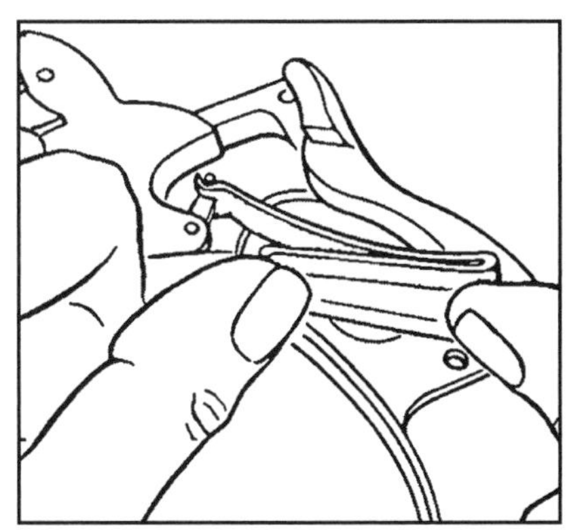

5 When re-assembling the gun, the mainspring is the only part that presents any difficulty. Squeeze the mainspring as shown. Insert the closed end into its seat in the frame. Then push the hammer swivel (NN) into its cutout in the mainspring (RR).

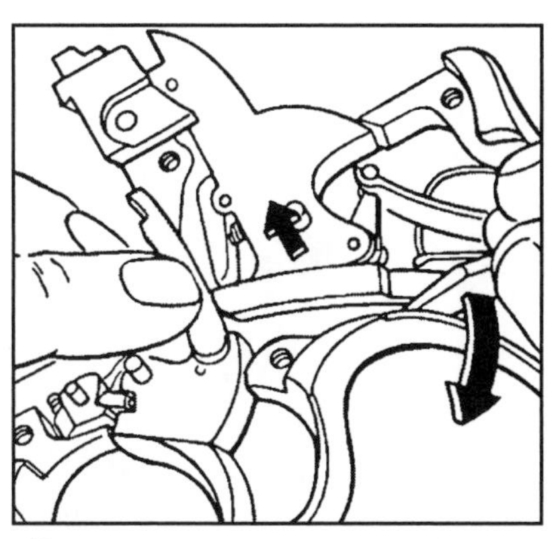

6 The hand (AA) is kept forward by the pressure of the mainspring lever (SS). To replace the hand (AA), it is necessary to pry the mainspring lever up until it is opposite its notch in the hand. Then push the hand in over the mainspring lever.

ERMA .22 PISTOL

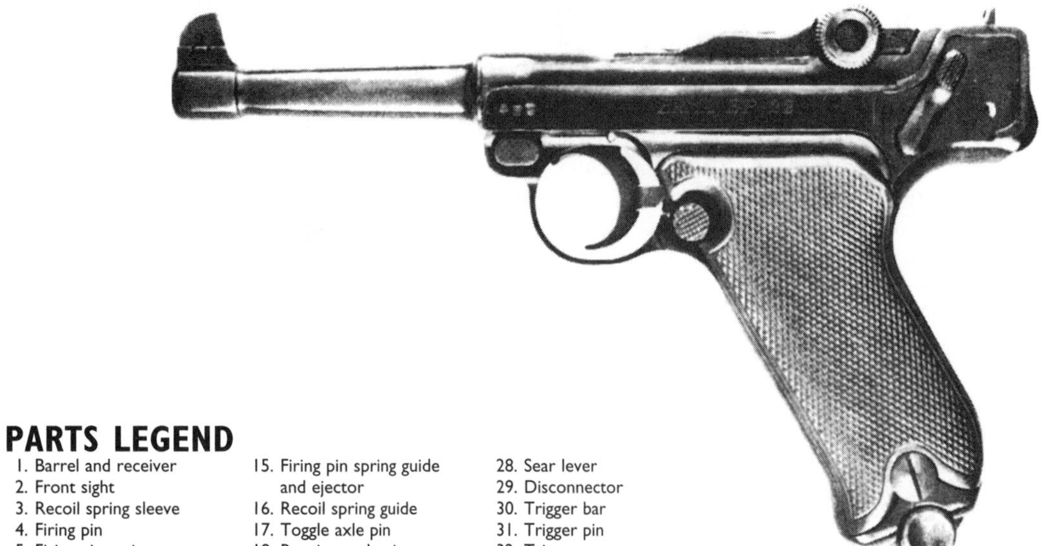

PARTS LEGEND

1. Barrel and receiver
2. Front sight
3. Recoil spring sleeve
4. Firing pin
5. Firing pin spring
6. Extractor pin
7. Extractor
8. Extractor spring
9. Breechblock
10. Breechblock pin
11. Front toggle link
12. Recoil spring
13. Toggle axle lockwasher
14. Rear toggle link
15. Firing pin spring guide and ejector
16. Recoil spring guide
17. Toggle axle pin
18. Receiver axle pin
19. Magazine catch
20. Magazine
21. Safety ball
22. Safety spring
23. Safety
24. Grip screws (2)
25. Magazine catch spring
26. Safety bar
27. Sear housing screws (2)
28. Sear lever
29. Disconnector
30. Trigger bar
31. Trigger pin
32. Trigger
33. Trigger plunger
34. Trigger spring
35. Sear housing
36. Sear spring
37. Sear
38. Locking bolt
39. Frame

NOTE: Grips are not shown

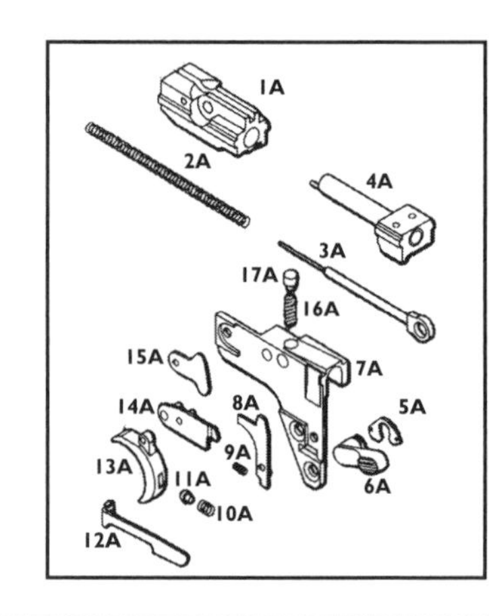

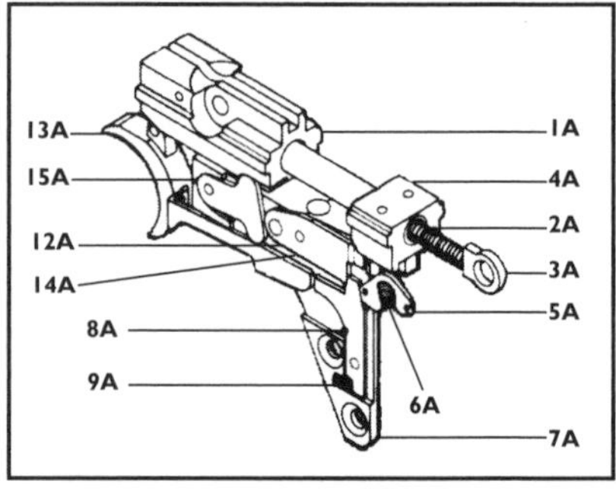

PARTS USED IN MODELS EP AND NAVY ET ONLY

1A. Breechblock
2A. Firing pin spring
3A. Ejector
4A. Firing pin assembly
5A. Safety ring
6A. Safety
7A. Sear housing
8A. Sear release
9A. Sear release spring
10A. Trigger bar plunger spring
11A. Trigger bar plunger
12A. Trigger bar
13A. Trigger
14A. Sear
15A. Disconnector
16A. Sear spring
17A. Sear plunger

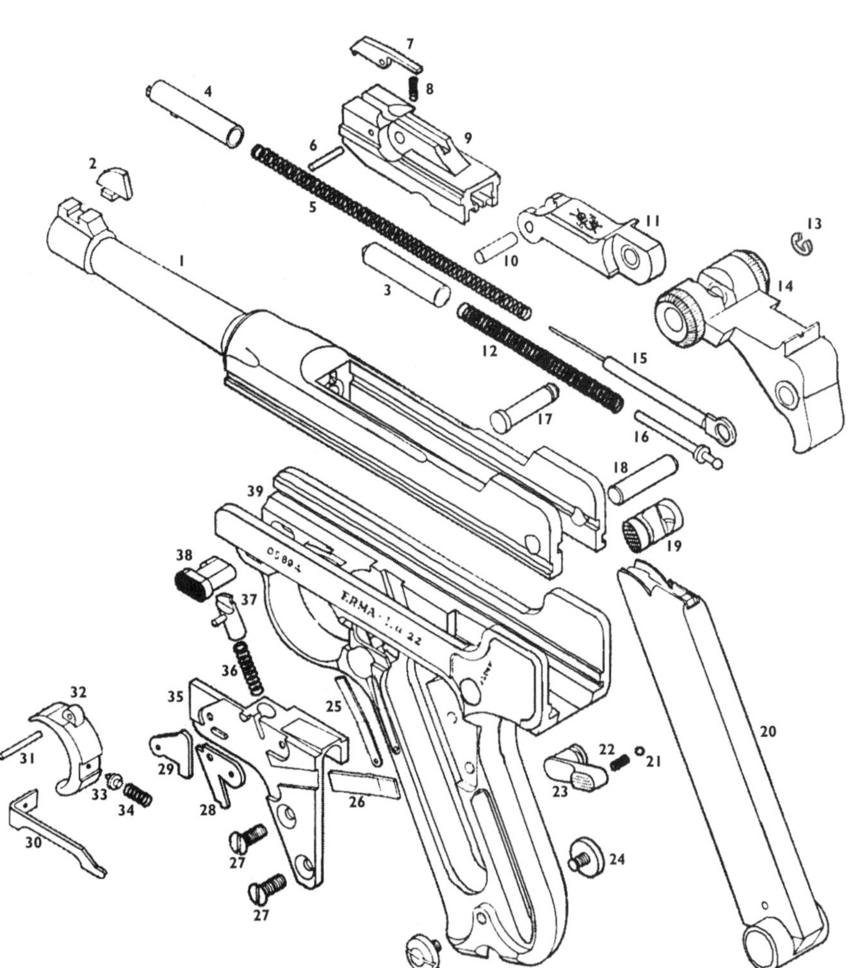

In 1964 Erma brought out a .22 pistol that has the same general size and appearance as the popular German Model 1908, 9mm Luger. However, these pistols differ from each other mechanically and in several other respects.

Chambered for the .22 Long Rifle, the Erma weighs 36 ounces and has a $4\frac{9}{16}$-inch barrel. Its toggle-joint breech mechanism resembles that of the Luger, but the barrel does not recoil. The toggle mechanism retards the opening of the breech, and the pistol is thus of retarded-blowback type.

A manual safety on the left of the frame is pivoted down for engagement. With the safety in this position the word "GESICHERT" (safe) on the frame is exposed. The magazine holds eight rounds and can be removed by depressing the magazine catch on the left side behind the trigger. Many metal parts, including the frame, are die-cast non-ferrous alloy with a black finish. The breechblock, barrel liner and small parts are steel and the grips are checkered brown plastic.

In 1967, a redesigned pistol, the Model EP, was introduced. It featured checkered walnut grips and an improved trigger and firing mechanism. Unlike the older version made for use with high-speed ammunition only, the improved pistol fires both high speed and standard velocity cartridges.

A long-barrel version of the Erma, brought out in 1967, was called the Navy Model ET. It had an $11\frac{3}{16}$-inch barrel and fired high speed and standard velocity .22 Long Rifle cartridges. It is equipped with a fully adjustable rear sight, checkered walnut grips and fore-end, and an improved trigger mechanism and firing mechanism.

An improved version, the KGP-22 was introduced in 1978, and the last model, the KGP-69, was discontinued in 1969.

DISASSEMBLY

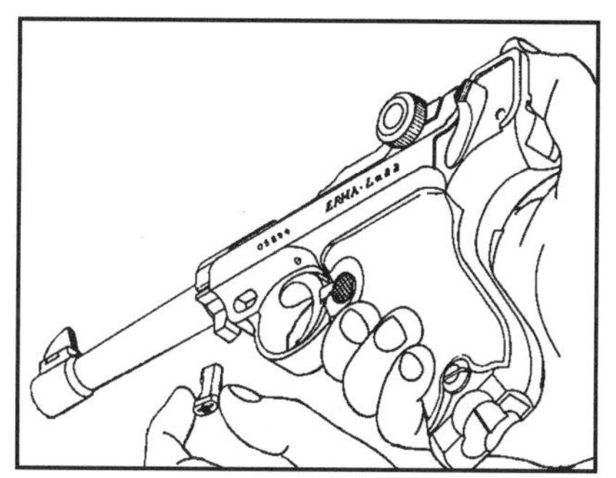

1 To field strip the Erma pistol, remove the magazine (20) and clear the chamber. Cock the pistol by pulling the rear toggle link (14) up and to the rear. Push the barrel and receiver assembly forward with the thumb as shown, and remove the locking bolt (38) to the left.

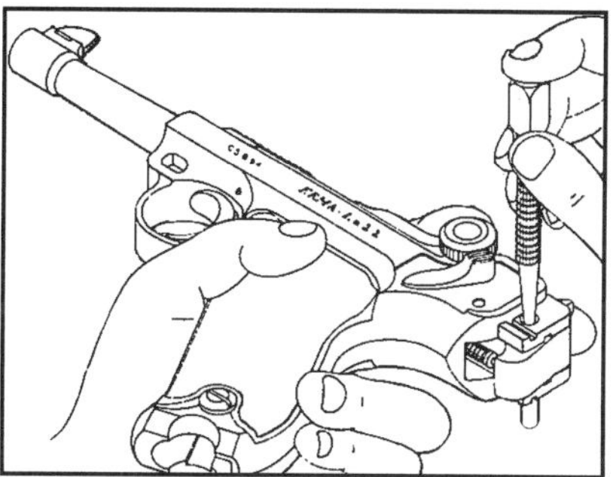

2 Release thumb pressure on rear toggle link, and allow the barrel and receiver assembly to spring rearward. Drift out the receiver axle pin (18).

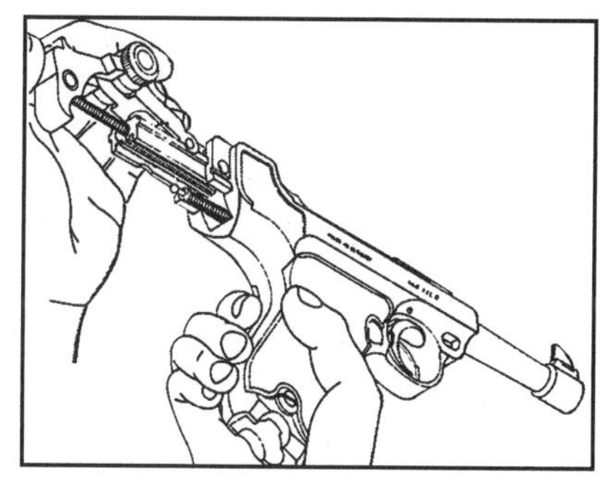

3 Remove toggle link and breechblock assembly to the rear. Take the recoil spring (12), recoil spring guide (16), and recoil spring sleeve (3) from rear of frame (39).

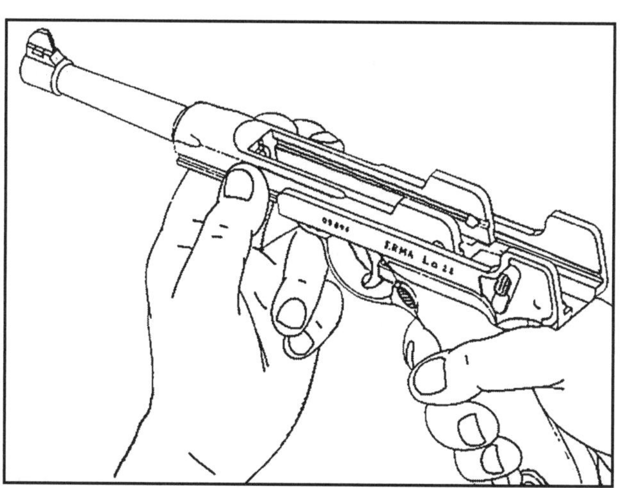

4 Slide the barrel and receiver (1) forward off the frame. Remove the firing pin spring (5), firing pin spring guide and ejector (15), and firing pin (4) from the breechblock (9). This completes fieldstripping.

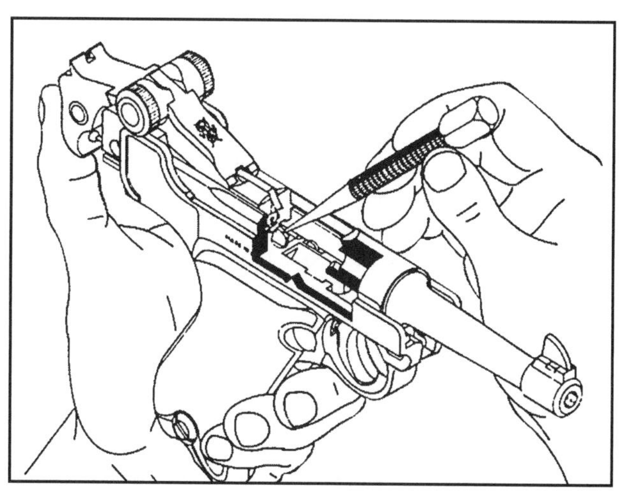

5 Reassemble in reverse. In replacing the toggle link and breechblock assembly of the older-version pistol, depress tip of sear with a punch.

FEINWERKBAU MODEL 65 PISTOL

Manufactured by Feinwerkbau Westinger & Altenburger G.m.b.H., of Oberndorf/Neckar, Germany, the FWB M-65 air pistol is favored by world championship record holders. It was imported by Daisy from 1967 to 1978 and then by Beeman, of San Raphael, Calif., who sold the M-65, Mk II. Feinwerkbau ceased production of the Model 65 in 1998, having made approximately 145,000 units.

With fully adjustable sights and trigger, the M-65 action is manipulated by a side lever. Two features permit the shooter to fire this gun either as a normal air gun or with the characteristics of a cartridge-firing pistol. A trigger adjustment can give a light or a relatively heavy pull at will, and a recoil stop can be activated to increase felt recoil. A safety mechanism prevents the gun from being discharged when the action is open.

DISASSEMBLY

Make sure pistol is not cocked. Remove grip screws (78), grips (79,80) and the two front grip attachment screws (77). With a short or ball-type 3mm (.118") Allen wrench, remove both rear grip frame attachment screws (75) and lock washers (76). The grip frame (74) containing the trigger assembly may now be separated from the barrel and piston housing (1).

Remove the two trigger assembly retaining screws (62). Lift the trigger assembly housing plate (63) from the grip frame (74). Reassemble in reverse manner.

Further takedown is not necessary or recommended for ordinary cleaning. Should it be required, proceed as follows:

Free the slot of the cocking lever pivot screw (30) and remove. Depress the cocking lever latch (9) and unhook the front of the cocking lever (29). Swing the cocking lever assembly with retracting lever (27) and pin (28) from the rear of the mainspring retainer (31) sufficiently to allow the front of the retracting lever (27) to be removed from its seat in the compression chamber (19). With barrel and piston housing (1) gripped in a padded vise, loosen the main spring retainer screw (12). Carefully take up the spring strain with a block of wood held against the main spring retainer (31) while lifting the retainer screw (12) from the assembly. Ease the mainspring retainer (31) containing the rear sight assembly and the outer piston spring(s) (25 & 26) from the barrel and piston housing.

To remove the rear recoil guide (13), the piston (22) with ring (23) and buffer (24), take the rear "E" ring (16) and spacing washer(s) (14) from the rear recoil guide pin (15) and drift it toward the muzzle enough to free the front "E" ring. Remove this "E" ring, slide the rear recoil guide pin (15) out to the rear. Use caution not to distort the front spacing washers (14), and note sequence for reassembly.

Further disassembly of the shooting mechanism is accomplished by clamping the inverted barrel and piston housing (1) in a padded vise. Remove all the "E" rings from one side of the assembly. Remove the front locking slide retaining pin (47) with attached "E" ring. Unhook the locking slide spring (46) from the locking slide (45). With a .450" long slave pin of less than .118" dia., push the retaining pin (47) for the compression chamber pawl (49) and trigger pull change lever (50) from the assembly. When the slave pin is in place, these parts with associated springs (46 & 53), plunger (54), detent and screw (52 & 51), will spring free and may be removed as a unit. Push out the trigger pull connector (55), retaining pin (47) with its "E" ring and remove the trigger pull connnector (55). Push out sear connector (56) and retaining pin (47) with its "E" ring. A small pick may be used to lift the locking slide (45) enough to slide it forward and free of the assembly. The sear connector (56) may now be picked free of the assembly in a similar manner. Disconnect piston sear catch spring (60) where it attaches to the recoil release pawl (61). With a .450" long slave pin, push out the interlock (57) and recoil release pawl retaining pin (47). Make sure that the interlock tension spring (58) is caught by the slave pin. Using another slave pin of similar size, push the retaining pin (47) for the piston sear catch (59) from the assembly. Now the interlock (57), piston sear catch (59), recoil release pawl (61) and the two springs may be removed from the assembly as a unit. The compression chamber (19) can now be slid rearward and removed.

PARTS LEGEND

1. Barrel and piston housing
2. Front sight base
3. Front sight insert
4. Front sight insert retaining screw
5. Front sight base retaining pin
6. Recoil guide (front)
7. Recoil guide pin (front) (2 required)
8. Recoil guide pin "E" ring (4 required)
9. Cocking lever latch
10. Cocking lever latch retaining screw
11. Cocking lever latch spring
12. Main spring retainer screw
13. Recoil guide (rear)
14. Recoil guide spacers (as required)
15. Recoil guide pin (rear)
16. Recoil guide pin "E" rings (2 required)
17. Recoil lock
18. Recoil lock screw
19. Compression chamber
20. Barrel seal
21. Compression chamber buffer
22. Piston
23. Piston ring
24. Piston buffer
25. Piston spring, outer
26. Piston spring, inner (not present in all models)
27. Piston retracting lever
28. Piston retracting lever pin
29. Cocking lever
30. Cocking lever pivot screw
31. Mainspring retainer
32. Windage adjustment screw
33. Windage adjustment "E" ring
    33A. Thrust washer
34. Windage adjustment screw detent ball
35. Windage adjustment screw detent ball tension spring
36. Rear sight base
37. Rear sight depth adjustment plate
38. Rear sight elevation adjustment spring
39. Rear sight elevation adjustment spring retaining screw
40. Elevation adjustment screw
41. Elevation adjustment detent ball spring
42. Elevation adjustment detent ball
43. Elevation adjustment screw limiting clip
44. Rear sight depth adjustment screw
45. Locking slide
46. Locking slide spring
47. 3mm x 21.5mm pin (6 required)
48. "E" rings for above (12 required)
49. Compression chamber pawl
50. Trigger pull change lever
51. Change lever fine adj. screw
52. Change lever spring seat
53. Change lever spring
54. Change lever spring plunger
55. Change lever connector
56. Sear connector
57. Interlock
58. Interlock tension spring
59. Piston sear catch
60. Piston sear catch spring
61. Recoil release pawl
62. Trigger assembly retaining screws (2 required)
63. Trigger assembly housing plate
64. Pull-off adjustment screw
65. Pull-off adjustment/trigger sear housing
66. Trigger sear
67. Trigger sear spring
68. Trigger sear retaining pin
69. Trigger sear/pull-off adjustment housing retaining pin
70. Trigger spring
71. Trigger retaining pin
72. Trigger
73. Trigger stop adjustment screw
74. Grip frame
75. Grip frame attachment screws (rear) (2 required)
76. Grip frame attachment screws (rear) lock washer (2 required)
77. Grip frame attachment screws (front) (2 required)
78. Grip screws (2 required)
79. Grip panel, left
80. Grip panel, right

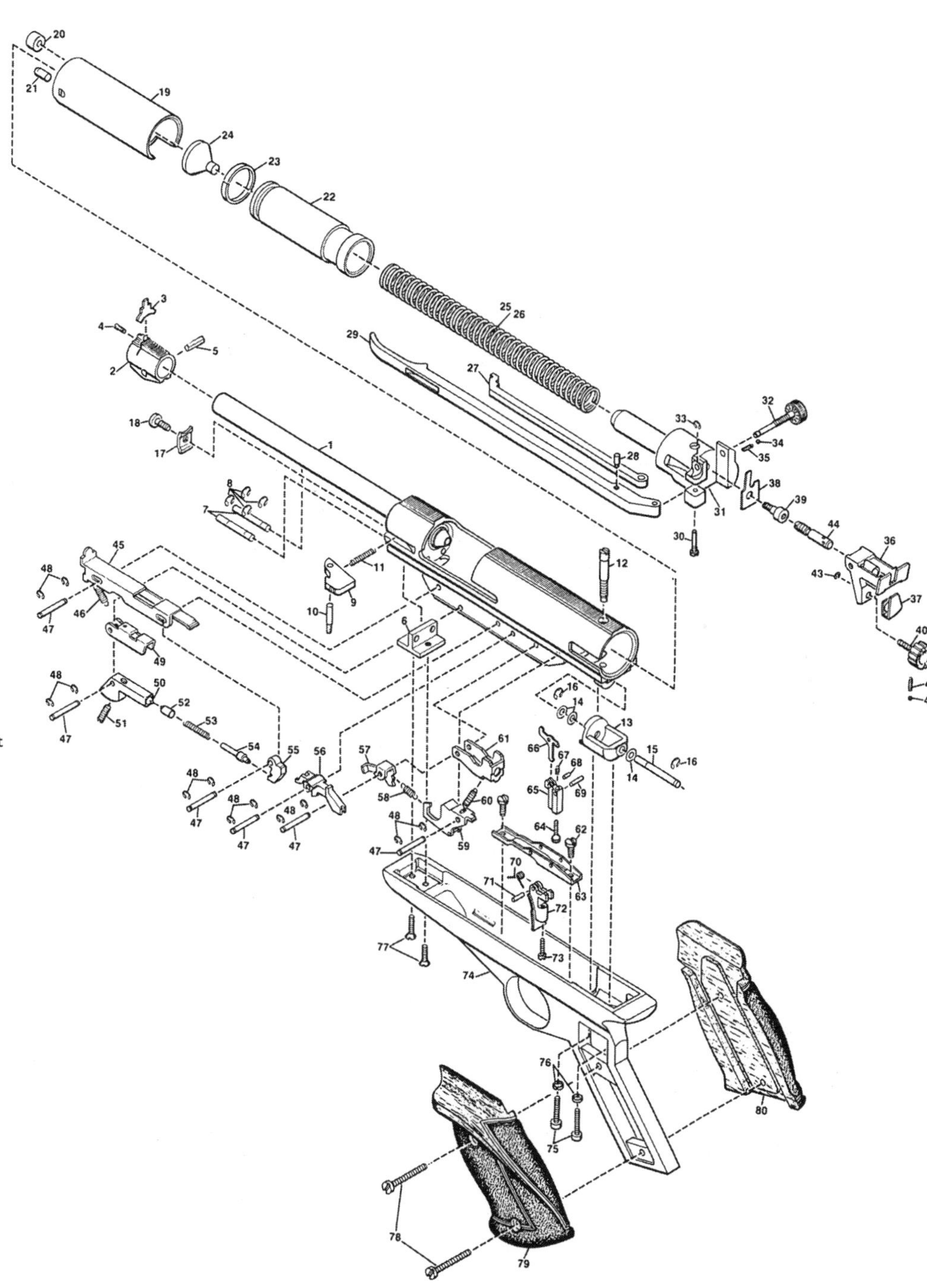

FRENCH MODEL 1935-A PISTOL

PARTS LEGEND

1. Front sight
2. Cartridge indicator
3. Cartridge indicator spring
4. Cartridge indicator pin
5. Extractor pin
6. Extractor
7. Extractor spring
8. Slide
9. Safety
10. Barrel link pin
11. Barrel link (2)
12. Barrel
13. Firing pin spring
14. Firing pin
15. Right grip
16. Grip screw bushing (4)
17. Grip screw (4)
18. Trigger
19. Trigger bar pin
20. Trigger bar/disconnector
21. Trigger bar spring
22. Trigger pin
23. Magazine safety
24. Magazine safety screw
25. Magazine catch
26. Hammer strut
27. Hammer pin
28. Hammer strut pin
29. Hammer
30. Magazine
31. Sear
32. Sear pin
33. Sear housing/ejector
34. Sear pressure plate
35. Hammer spring
36. Hammer strut nut
37. Left grip
38. Frame
39. Magazine catch spring
40. Magazine catch nut
41. Slide stop catch
42. Slide stop
43. Recoil spring guide tip
44. Recoil spring ring
45. Recoil spring
46. Recoil spring guide pin
47. Recoil spring guide

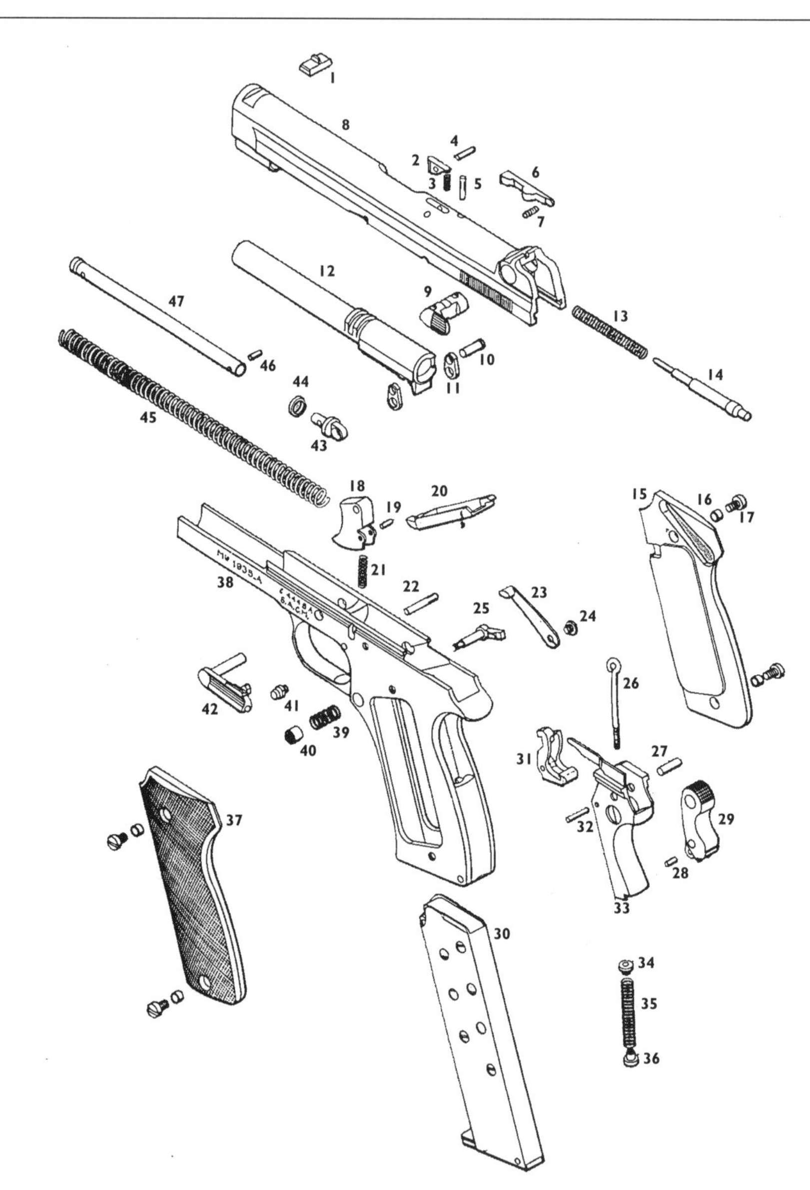

Between the World Wars, the French experimented with several different automatic pistols in an effort to find a suitable replacement for their 8mm Model 1892 Service revolver. This culminated in adoption of the 7.65mm Model 1935 automatic pistol. The Model 1935-A was a modification produced in 1937 by the *Manufacture d'Armes de St. Étienne.*

Based on the Browning short-recoil system and the designs of French engineer Charles Petter, this pistol was developed and produced by the *Société Alsacienne de Constructions Mécaniques*, better known as S.A.C.M. It has an 8-round magazine, weighs 26 ozs., and fires a 7.65mm Long cartridge. The pistol can be field-stripped quickly and easily without use of tools. Instead of the recoil spring being separate, it is of captive type and forms an assembly with the spring guide. This greatly facilitates field-stripping and reassembly. The hammer, sear, and several other lock parts are also combined in an assembly that can be easily removed from the frame.

This well-designed pistol was used by France during World War II, and some were used as substitute standard weapons by Germany during the occupation. In the 1950's it was replaced by a new French pistol in 9mm Parabellum caliber.

The black painted finish applied to protect the metal parts gives the Model 1935-A a cheap appearance. Despite its appearance, the pistol is both well-made and reliable.

DISASSEMBLY

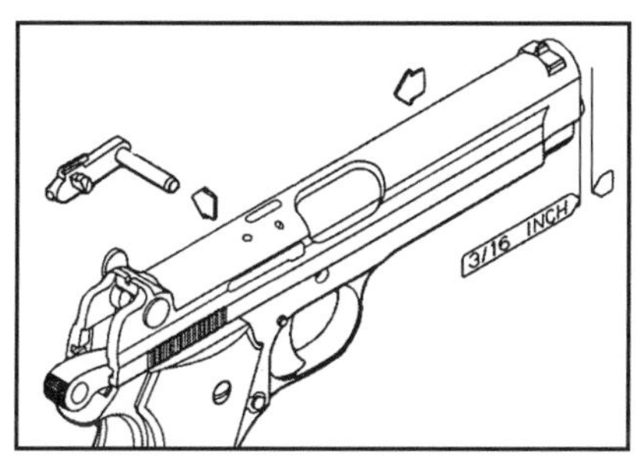

1 To field strip the French Model 1935-A pistol, remove the magazine (30) and clear the chamber. Pull the slide (8) 3⁄16" to the rear, and remove the slide stop (42) to the left. Push the slide forward off the frame (38).

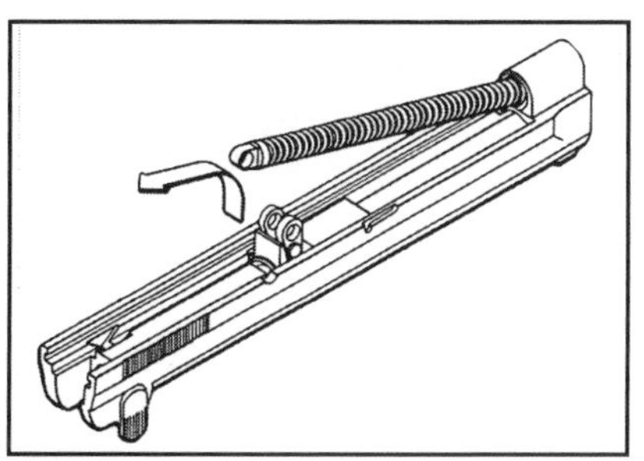

2 With the slide held bottom up, grasp the recoil spring and guide assembly, and remove it up and to the rear. Remove the barrel (12) in a similar manner. This completes field stripping.

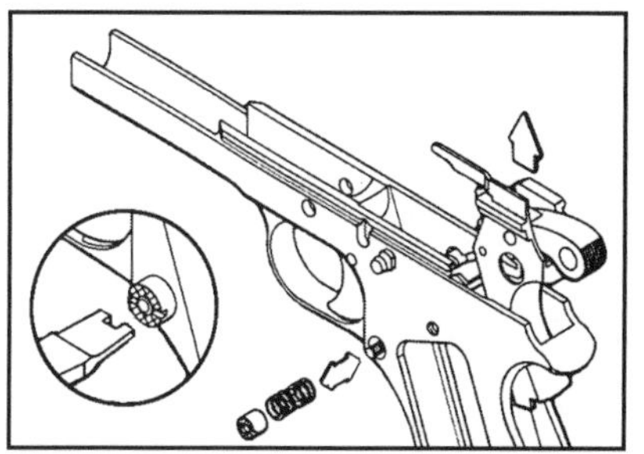

3 For further disassembly, grasp the upper part of the lock assembly, and lift it upward out of the frame. Remove the grip screws (17), grip screw bushings (16), and grips (15), (37). Grind a square notch in a screwdriver blade, and use this tool to unscrew the magazine catch nut (40). The magazine catch spring (39) comes out to the left, the magazine catch (25) to the right.

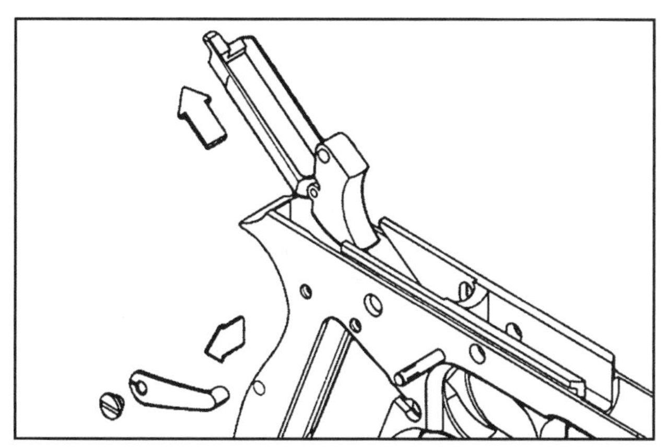

4 Remove the magazine safety screw (24) and magazine safety (23). Drift out the trigger pin (22) to the right. Then lift the trigger and trigger bar assembly from the top of the frame.

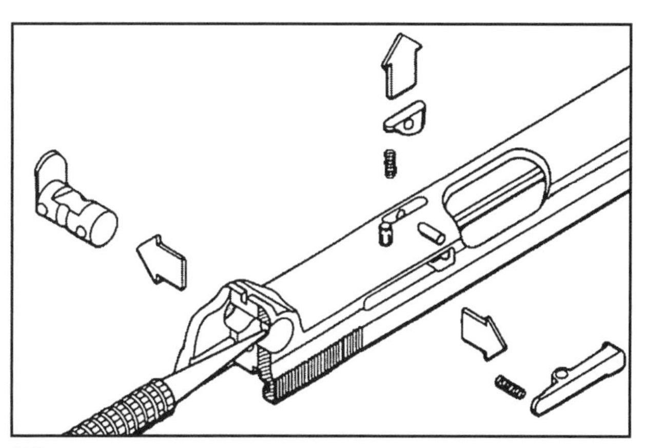

5 Push firing pin (14) forward with a thin punch, and pull the safety (9) from the left of the slide. Ease firing pin and firing pin spring (13) rearward out of the slide. Drift out the cartridge indicator pin (4) to the right, and remove the cartridge indicator (2) and indicator spring (3). Drift extractor pin (5) out through top of slide, and remove extractor (6) and extractor spring (7). Reassemble in reverse taking care that the extractor pin does not project from the lower surface of the slide.

FROMMER STOP AUTOMATIC PISTOL

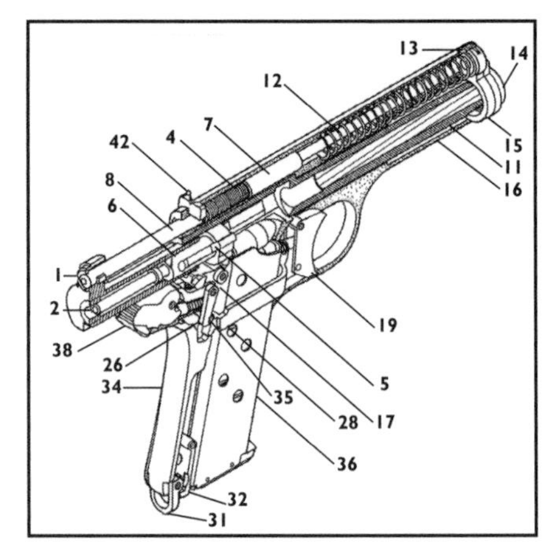

PARTS LEGEND

1. Bolt body
2. Firing pin
3. Firing pin spring
4. Bolt return spring
5. Extractor
6. Bolt head pin
7. Recoil spring guide sleeve
8. Recoil spring guide
9. Ejector spring
10. Ejector
11. Barrel and extension
12. Recoil spring
13. Barrel nut retainer
14. Barrel nut
15. Barrel guide
16. Frame
17. Bolt catch
18. Bolt catch pin
19. Trigger
20. Trigger pin
21. Grip screw
22. Right grip
23. Trigger bar pin
24. Sear spring
25. Sear pin
26. Sear
27. Trigger spring
28. Trigger bar
29. Magazine catch pin
30. Grip safety pin
31. Lanyard loop
32. Magazine catch
33. Grip safety spring
34. Grip safety
35. Disconnector pin
36. Magazine
37. Hammer pin
38. Hammer
39. Hammer plunger
40. Hammer spring
41. Left grip
42. Rear sight

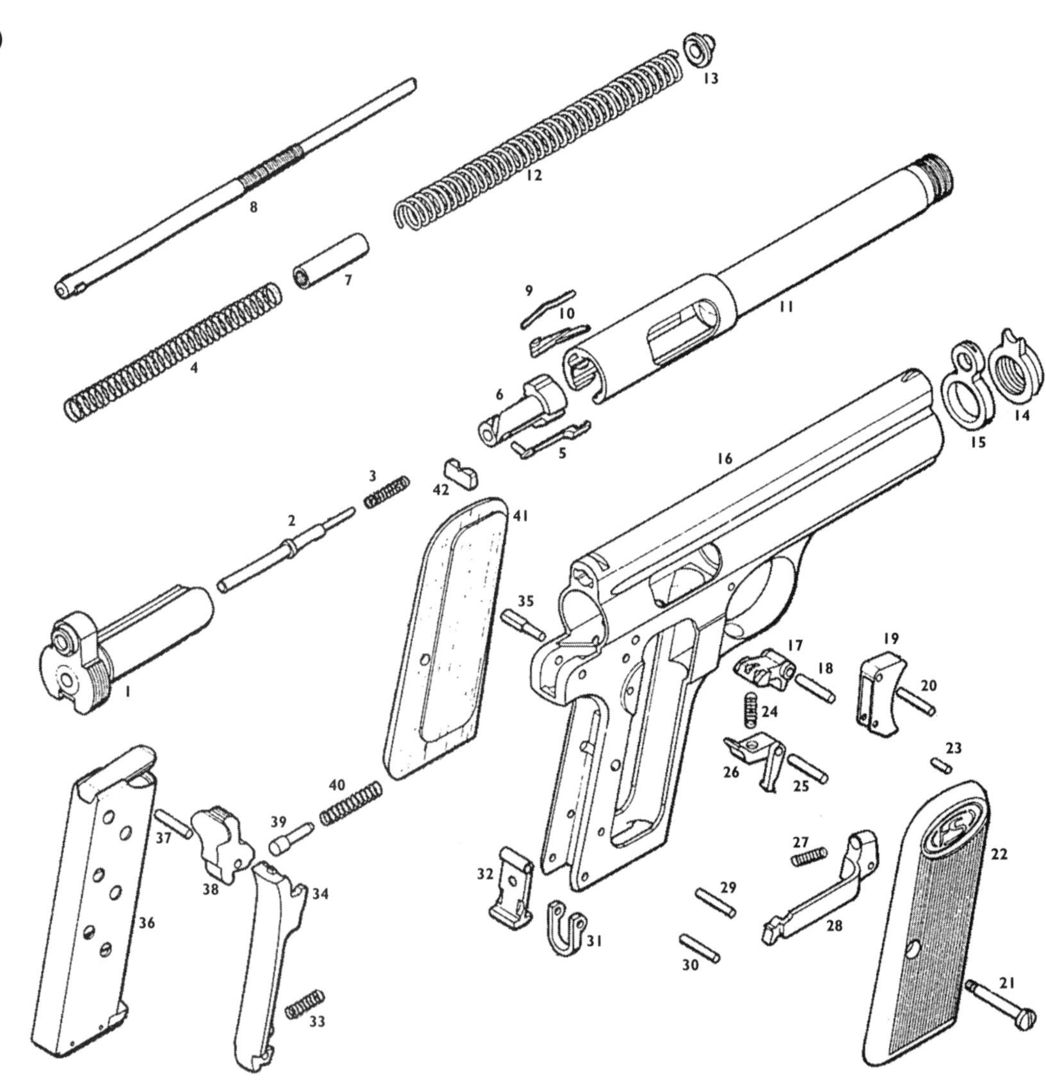

Pistols chambered for the .32 Automatic cartridge are commonly of blowback design. An exception is the Frommer Stop automatic pistol which operates on the long-recoil system. Developed by Rudolf Frommer, a Hungarian arms designer, this pistol was produced by the Small Arms and Machine Works, Inc., Budapest, Hungary. It was introduced in about 1911 or 1912, and was offered in .380 and .32 Automatic calibers. During World War I, it was extensively used in .32 Automatic caliber by the Austro-Hungarian services.

The Frommer long-recoil system is rather complex. During firing, the bolt mechanism and barrel are locked together and recoil as a unit. This compresses the recoil spring and bolt return spring above the barrel. At the end of recoil, the bolt is held to the rear by a catch. The barrel then unlocks from the bolt and is driven forward by the recoil spring. As the barrel nears its front position, the bolt is released and is pushed forward by the bolt return spring.

The seven round magazine (.32 caliber) is retained by a magazine catch on the lower rear of the handle. The only safety is the grip safety projecting from the rear of the handle.

There is a small version of the long-recoil Frommer pistol called the Frommer Baby. It is mechanically similar to the Stop model. Both the Stop and Baby models gave way in the 1920's to a Frommer pistol based on Browning's blowback system.

DISASSEMBLY

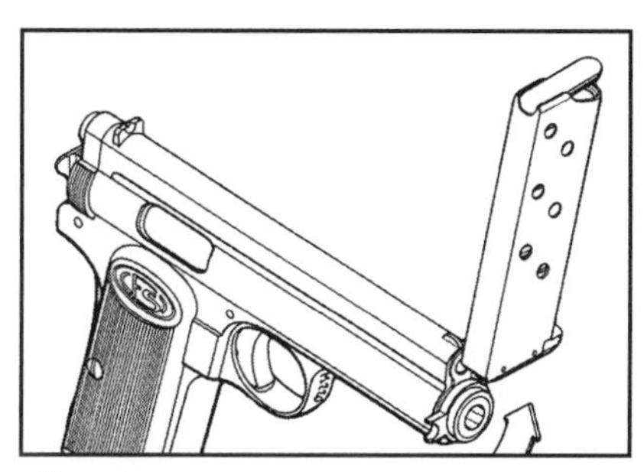

1 To field-strip the Frommer, remove magazine (36) and clear the chamber. Depress barrel nut retainer (13) with a corner of the magazine and unscrew barrel nut (14). Ease off pressure on barrel nut retainer and barrel guide (15) and remove them. Remove recoil spring (12).

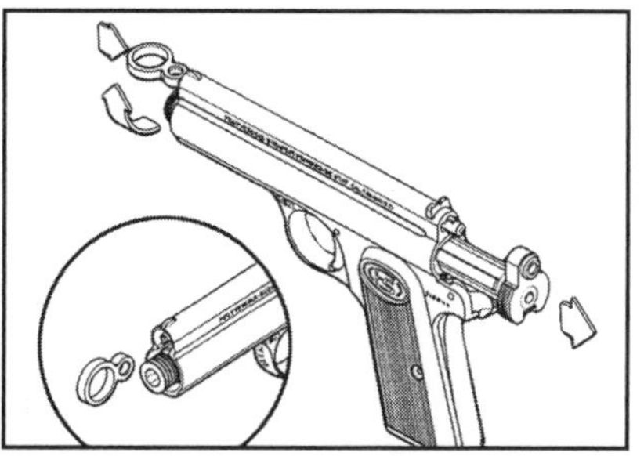

2 Top of barrel guide is slotted for use as a tool. Fit slot over cross lug at end of recoil spring guide (8). Push guide rearward, and rotate ¼ turn. Cock hammer (38) and pull bolt body (1) out to rear. Rotate bolt head (6) clockwise to separate from body.

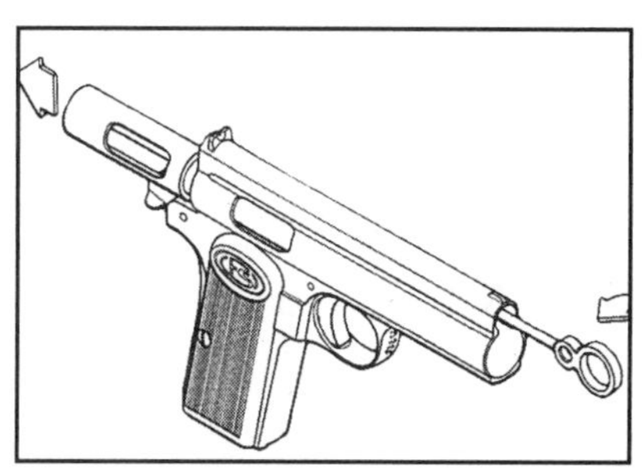

3 Again making use of barrel guide, rotate recoil spring guide an additional ¼ turn to release it from frame (16). Ease guide out forward. Push barrel (11) rearward to remove from frame. This completes field-stripping.

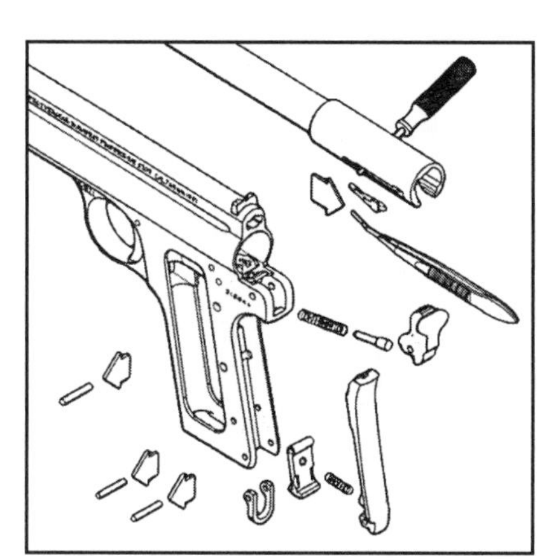

4 For further disassembly, use a small screwdriver to flex ejector spring (9) outward slightly. Grasp spring with a tweezers and slide out rearward; then, remove ejector (10). Unscrew grip screw (21) and remove grips (22, 41). Lower hammer. Drive out hammer pin (37) to release hammer with its plunger (39) and spring (40). Remove grip safety (34), spring (33), and lanyard loop (31), by driving out the grip safety pin (30). Drive out magazine catch pin (29) to free the catch (32).

Bolt catch (17) and trigger with trigger bar (19, 28) can now be removed by driving out pins (18, 20). Both disconnector pin (35) and sear pin (25) must be driven out to detach sear (26). Remove these parts only where necessary, as sear and trigger springs (24, 27) are difficult to reinsert.

Bolt head (6) is staked on both sides of extractor (5). The mushroomed edges must be filed down to disassemble these parts and the bolt head restaked on assembly. This should not be attempted without good cause.

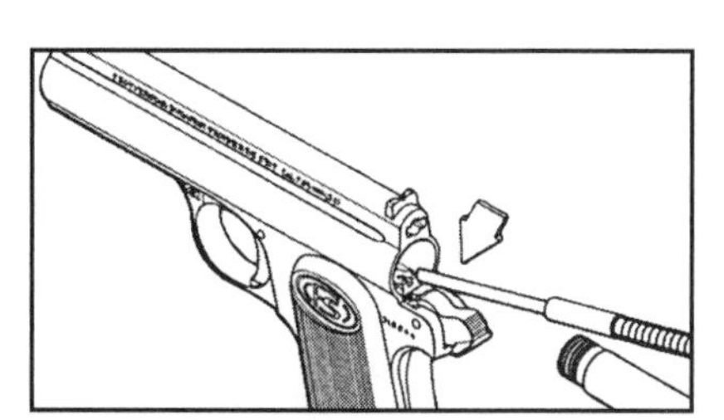

5 Reassemble in reverse. Depress bolt catch with tip of recoil spring guide when inserting barrel so that catch clears barrel threads.

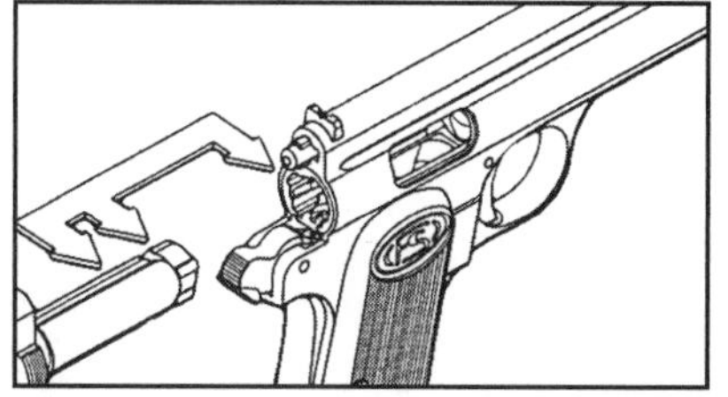

6 Bolt head must be turned so that its smaller locking lug aligns with rib on bolt body and groove in barrel extension when these parts are reassembled.

GLISENTI MODEL 1910 PISTOL

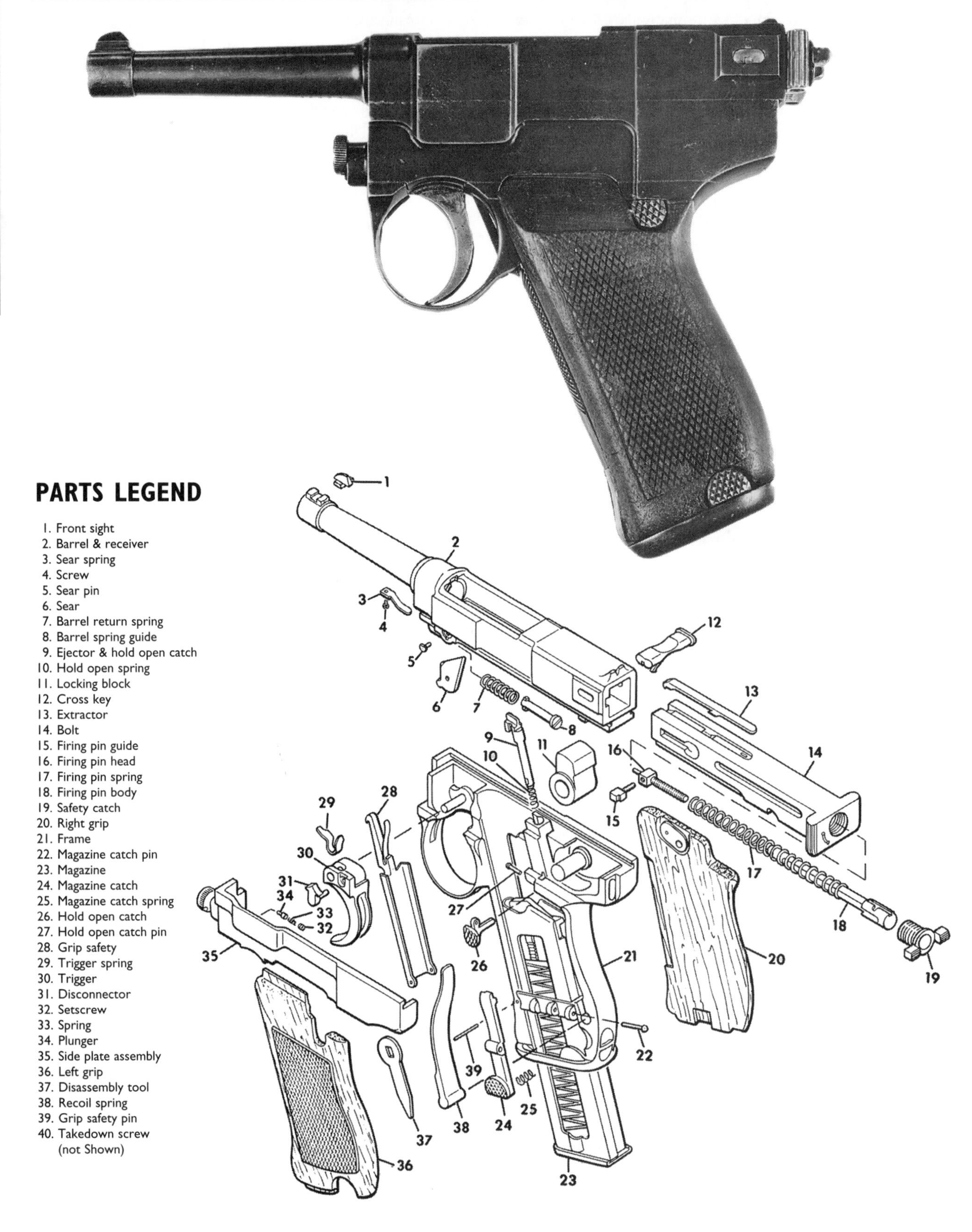

PARTS LEGEND

1. Front sight
2. Barrel & receiver
3. Sear spring
4. Screw
5. Sear pin
6. Sear
7. Barrel return spring
8. Barrel spring guide
9. Ejector & hold open catch
10. Hold open spring
11. Locking block
12. Cross key
13. Extractor
14. Bolt
15. Firing pin guide
16. Firing pin head
17. Firing pin spring
18. Firing pin body
19. Safety catch
20. Right grip
21. Frame
22. Magazine catch pin
23. Magazine
24. Magazine catch
25. Magazine catch spring
26. Hold open catch
27. Hold open catch pin
28. Grip safety
29. Trigger spring
30. Trigger
31. Disconnector
32. Setscrew
33. Spring
34. Plunger
35. Side plate assembly
36. Left grip
37. Disassembly tool
38. Recoil spring
39. Grip safety pin
40. Takedown screw (not Shown)

The Glisenti pistol was originally patented in 1905 by the *Societa Siderurgica Glisenti* in Brescia, Italy. Early pistols were chambered for the .30 Luger (7.63mm) cartridge, but in 1909 the gun appeared in 9mm caliber, was adopted by the Italian Military and eventually named the Pistola Automatica M910.

The Glisenti will chamber conventional 9mm Parabellum ammo, but was not designed to handle it. The 9mm ammo as made in Italy developed considerably less pressure than 9mm German-made ammo of the same period, and the usage of commonly available 9mm Parabellum ammo in the Glisenti is not recommended.

In 1911 a simplified version was put out by *Metallurgica Bresciana Tempini* (which accounts for the MBT molded into the grips of some guns). While the Brixia, as the revised gun was called, and the Glisenti are similar in appearance, their parts are not interchangeable.

DISASSEMBLY

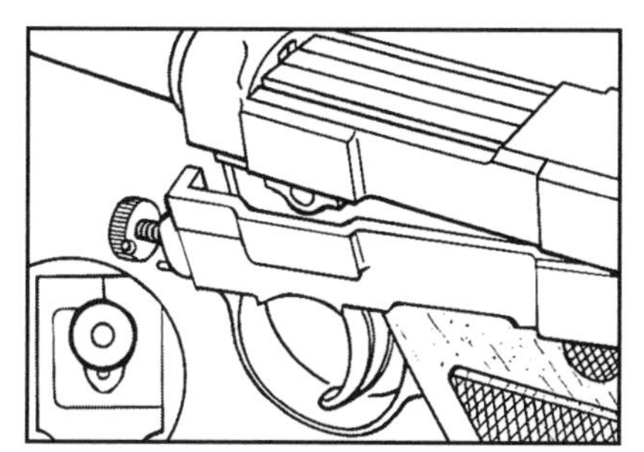

1 Exposing the operating mechanism only requires removing the side plate (35). To do this, first remove the magazine (23) and clear the chamber. Push in the plunger (34), turn the large knurled screw (40) until it stops, then lift off the side plate, the left grip (36) and the disassembly tool (37). Push the barrel and receiver assembly to the left until it is free of the guide rib in the frame, then lift it up.

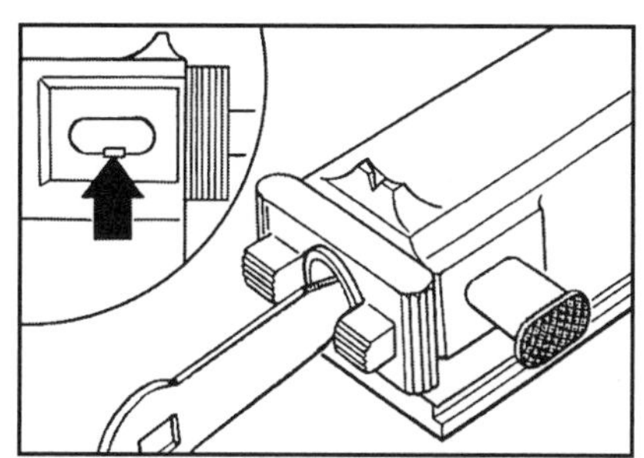

2 The bolt assembly (14) is held in the receiver (2) by a cross key (12). To remove it, push up on the small spring (shown in the inserted drawing), push the key out from left to right and withdraw the bolt (14). To replace the bolt, push the firing pin in as far as it can go. It may be necessary to trip the sear to get it far enough forward to allow the cross key to clear the firing pin spring (17). Use a screwdriver or the disassembly tool to push the firing pin (18) forward.

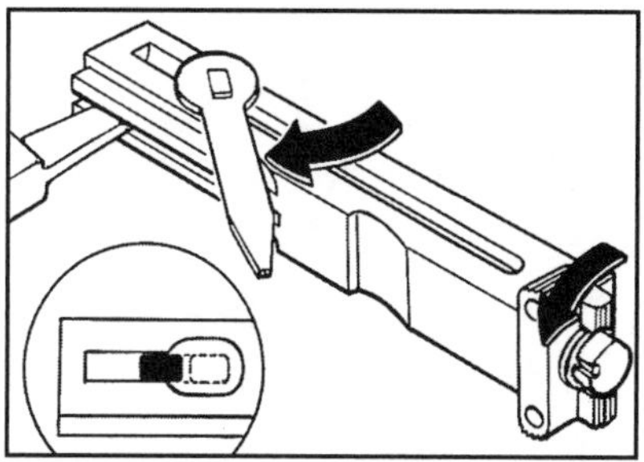

3 The firing pin guide (15) also acts as the sear and must be removed before removing the firing pin (18). It has a left hand thread and must be turned in the direction indicated by the arrow, using the disassembly tool as a wrench. Before attempting to remove the guide, insert a thin blade into the bolt and push back the firing pin until the guide is centered in the wide opening (note inserted drawing). When the guide is out, unscrew the safety catch (19) as shown and remove the firing pin (18), firing pin head (16) and firing pin spring (17).

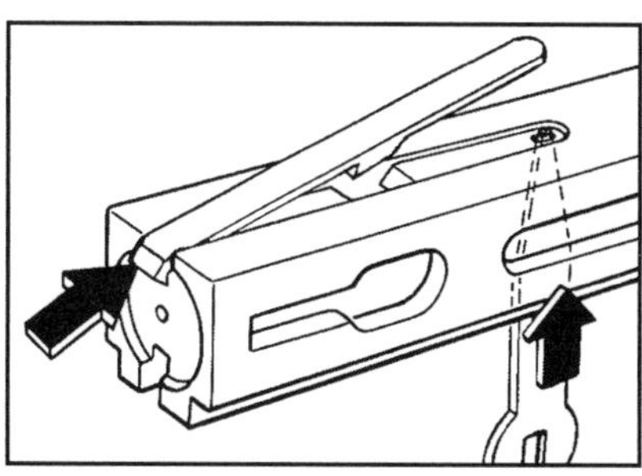

4 The disassembly tool is used to remove the extractor (13). After the firing pin has been removed, insert the tool into the small elongated slot in the bolt as shown. Push the tail of the extractor up slightly until it is just clear of the bolt (14); then tap it lightly on the front or claw end and it will spring free of the bolt.

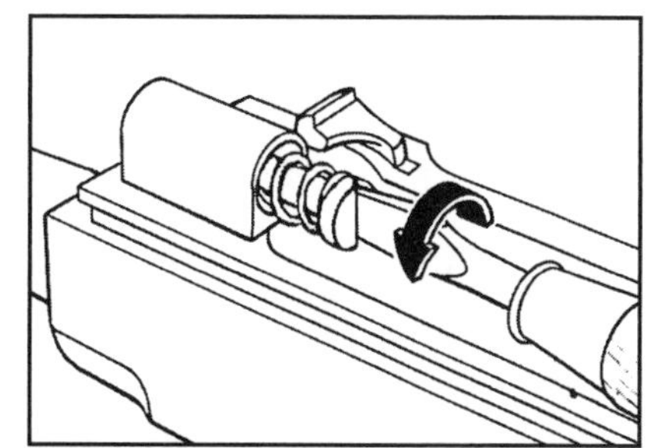

5 A separate barrel return spring (7) is incorporated into the underside of the receiver. The spring is rigidly assembled to the spring guide (8) so the assembly must be removed as a unit by inserting a small screwdriver into the screw slot on the spring guide. Push the plunger forward, rotate it 90° and ease the assembly out.

6 To remove the right grip (20), first remove the magazine and rotate the small plate on the grip as shown. When the plate is free of the cut in the frame, the right hand grip can be lifted off.

GLOCK 17 PISTOL

PARTS LEGEND

1. Slide
2. Barrel
3. Recoil spring
4. Recoil spring tube
5. Firing pin
6. Spacer sleeve
7. Firing pin spring
8. Spring cups (2)
9. Firing pin safety
10. Firing pin safety spring
11. Extractor
12. Extractor plunger
13. Extractor plunger spring
14. Spring-loaded bearing
15. Slide cover plate
16. Rear sight
17. Receiver
18. Magazine catch spring
19. Magazine catch
20. Locking slide spring
21. Locking slide
22. Locking block
23. Mechanism housing with ejector
24. Connector
25. Trigger spring
26. Trigger with trigger bar
27. Slidestop lever
28. Trigger pin
29. Mechanism housing pin
30. Follower
31. Magazine spring
32. Magazine floorplate
33. Magazine tube
34. Front sight

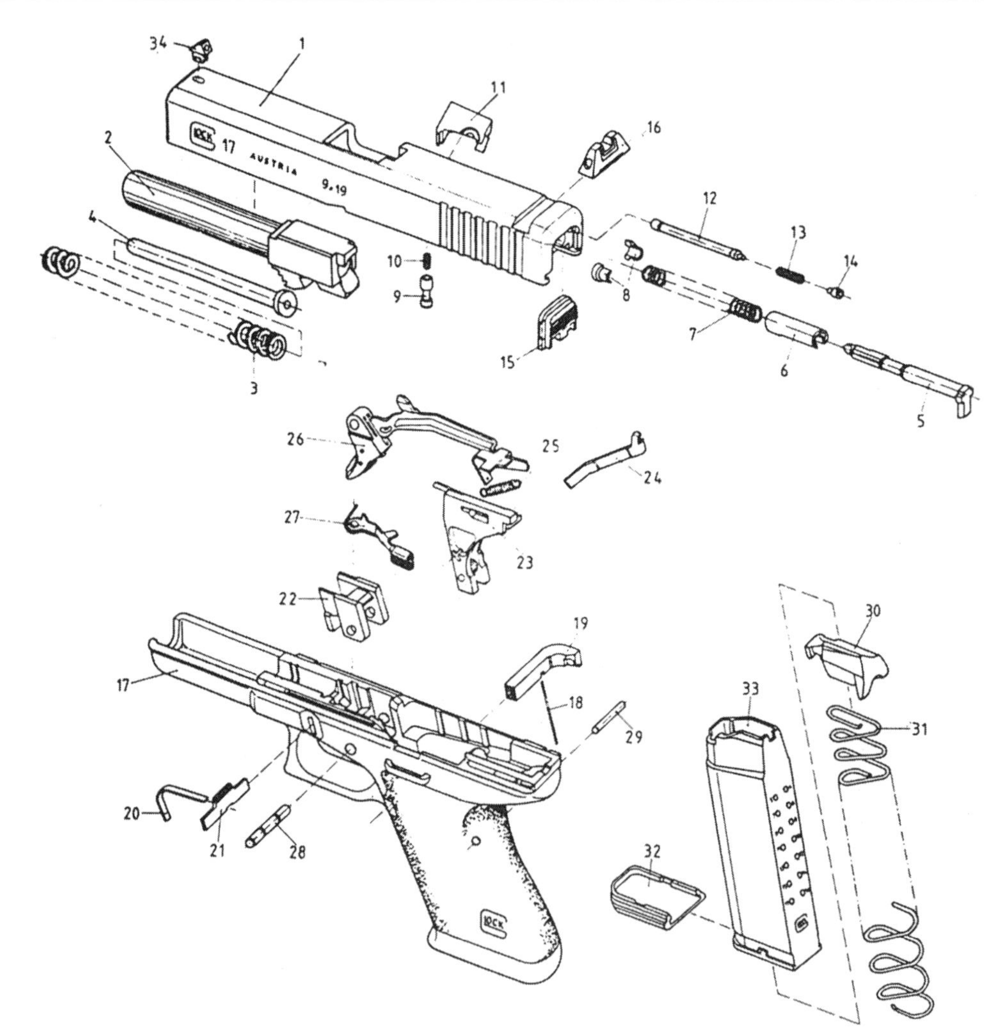

The Glock 17 was introduced in the early 1980s for Austrian Army weapons trials and was adopted as the P80. Since its introduction the Glock 17 and its variants have been adopted by law enforcement agencies and military organizations worldwide, and are standard-issue sidearms for the armies of many nations. Glocks are also in use among many U.S. police departments as well as numerous federal agencies, such as the FBI and the Drug Enforcement Administration.

The Glock 17 is a locked-breech, short-recoil semi-automatic pistol using a modified Petter/Browning barrel locking system. It is chambered for the 9mm Parabellum. Utilizing a steel slide and a polymer frame, the Glock design features a "safe action" semi-double-action trigger system. There is no manual safety other than a pivoting lever that protrudes through the face of the trigger. When the trigger finger depresses the trigger, the safety lever pivots, allowing its rear section to move freely out of contact with the frame. The trigger may then rotate through its full range of motion, discharging the pistol.

Ignition is by way of a striker instead of a hammer and firing pin. A spring-loaded firing pin safety plunger blocks firing pin movement and prevents accidental discharge if the pistol is dropped and lands muzzle-first.

DISASSEMBLY

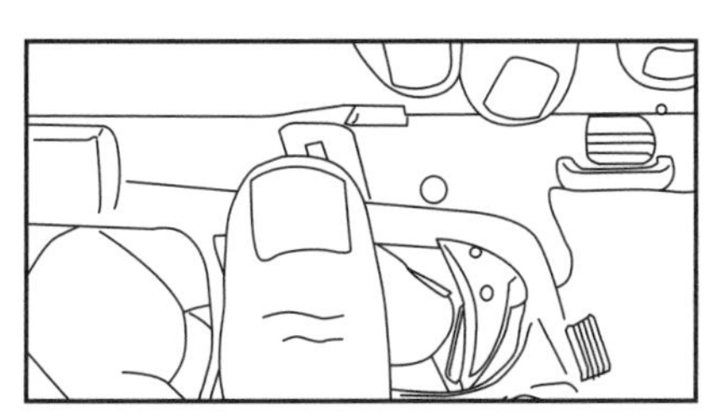

1 To determine that the pistol is unloaded, lock the slide open by pushing up on the slide stop lever while pulling the slide to the rear with your other hand. Pull back the slide to release the stop lever and close the action. Hold the pistol in either hand so that four fingers grasp the top of the slide as shown above. With these four fingers, pull and hold the slide back approximately 1/10 of an inch. Simultaneously pull down and hold both sides of the slide lock using the thumb and index finger of your free hand.

Push the slide forward until it is fully separated from the receiver. While removing the slide, always use care to control the recoil spring, which is under tension.

Push the recoil spring assembly slightly forward while lifting it away from the barrel.

Remove the recoil spring assembly. This will allow you to lift the barrel from the slide. CAUTION: With the pistol field stripped, the trigger should not be manually reset to its forward position and pulled. Also, do not manually pull the firing pin to the rear and allow it to snap forward. This can damage the firing pin assembly.

Further disassembly is not recommended by Glock, Inc., unless performed by a competent, factory-trained gunsmith.

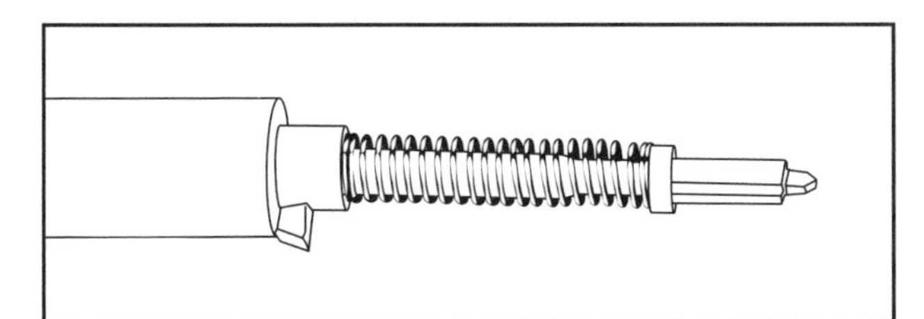

2 Slide disassembly: Using a pin punch, push down the spacer sleeve (6) towards the muzzle end of the slide and pull the slide cover plate (15) down, restraining the spacer sleeve and the spring-loaded bearing (14) within. The firing pin assembly and extractor plunger (12) with its spring (13) can then be pulled out. To break down the firing pin assembly, use the muzzle of the barrel to hold the spacer sleeve (Fig. 2). Depress the firing pin spring (7) and remove the spring cups (8) and the spacer sleeve.

To remove the extractor (11), push down on the firing pin safety (9) and pry out the extractor. The firing pin safety can then be lifted out with its spring (10).

The elevation-adjustable or fixed rear sight (16) can be removed by drifting out with a non-marring punch. The front sight (34) is factory staked in place and should not be removed except for replacement.

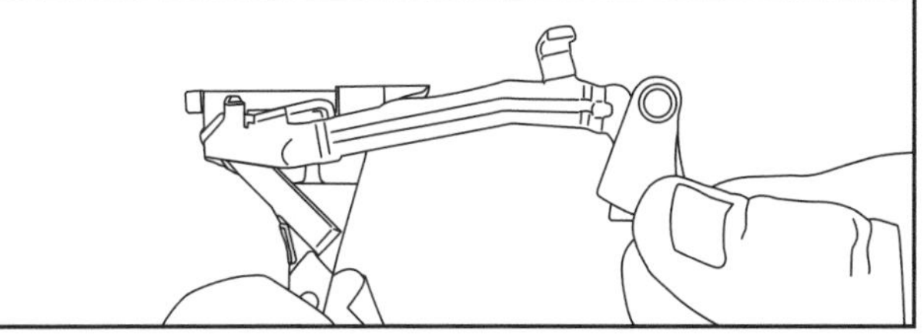

3 Frame disassembly: Using a pin punch, remove the trigger pin (28) and the mechanism housing pin (29), pushing from left to right. Pull the slide stop lever (27) with its spring to the rear for removal. Prying up on the mechanism housing (23), lift it out with the attached trigger (26) and trigger bar. Twist the trigger bar extension forward and up to detach from the mechanism housing. Separate the trigger spring (25) from the housing. Pry up on the locking block (22) for removal. Press the locking slide spring (20) down and push the locking slide (21) to the left or the right to remove. The locking slide spring can then be lifted out.

To remove the magazine catch (19), use a screwdriver to raise the magazine catch spring (18) out of its groove in the magazine well and pull the spring out from the top using a pair of pliers. The magazine catch can be then pushed out to the right.

Disassemble the Glock 17 magazine by squeezing the magazine tube (33) in the center part of each side near the magazine floorplate (32). Simultaneously, push the floorplate off the tube, holding a finger over the top of the opening to prevent the spring from escaping.

HAENEL-SCHMEISSER MODEL I

PARTS LEGEND

1. Barrel guide
2. Extractor pin
3. Extractor
4. Extractor spring
5. Slide
6. Firing pin
7. Mainspring
8. Right grip
9. Grip screw
10. Recoil spring guide
11. Recoil spring
12. Frame
13. Sear
14. Sear pin
15. Magazine safety
16. Magazine safety spring
17. Sear spring
18. Sear spring plunger
19. Sear spring housing
20. Magazine
21. Signal pin
22. Signal pin spring
23. Grip escutcheon
24. Left grip
25. Trigger pin
26. Trigger
27. Trigger bar
28. Safety
29. Trigger bar spring
30. Magazine catch pin
31. Magazine catch
32. Magazine catch spring

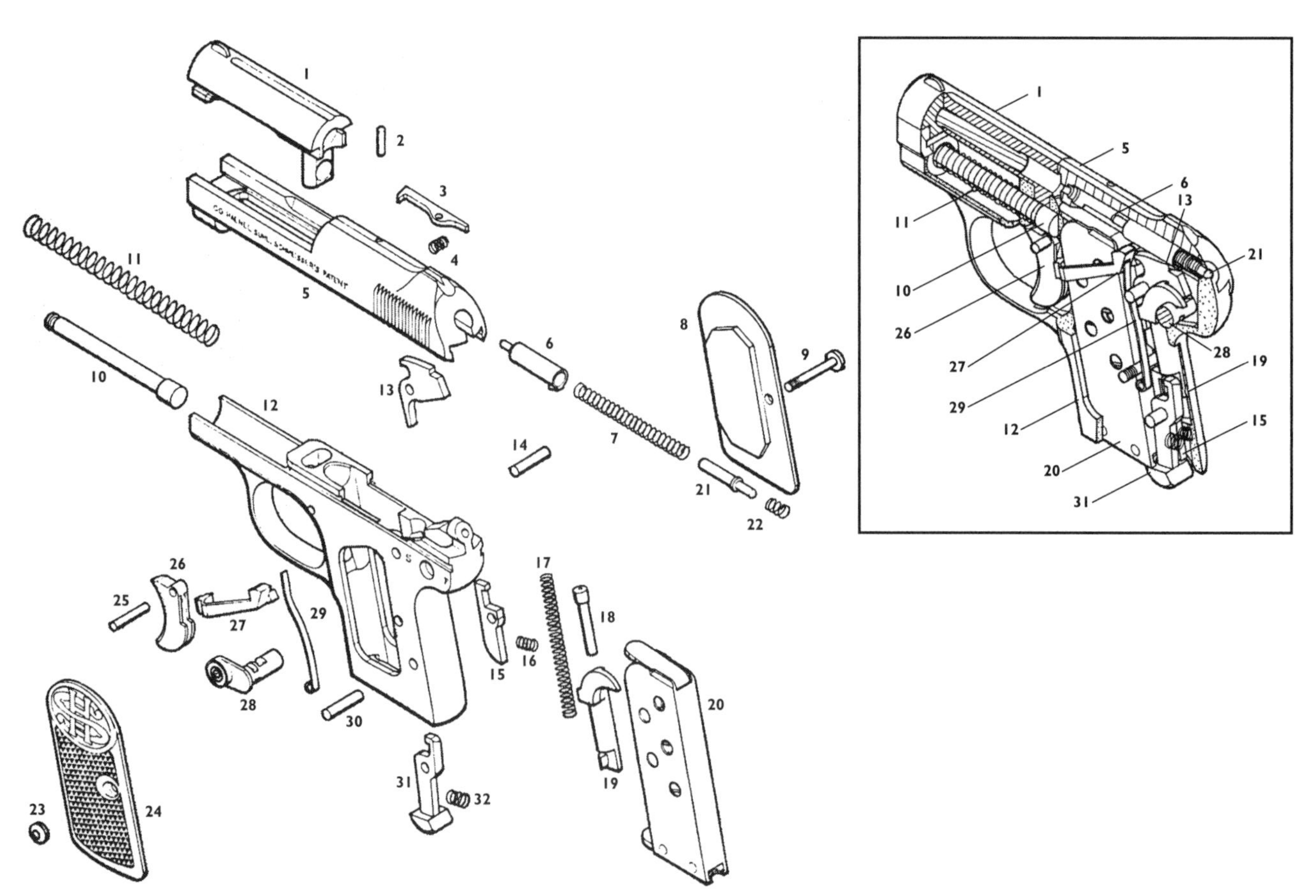

The great success of John Browning's compact .25 ACP semi-automatic vest pocket pistol produced by Fabrique Nationale in 1906, resulted in the development of many other semi-automatic pocket pistols.

Among these was the Haenel-Schmeisser Model I. Designed by Hugo Schmeisser, new pistol was produced by the C. G. Haenel firm, Suhl, Germany. The blowback-operated .25 ACP handgun was introduced in the early 1920's.

The Haenel-Schmeisser Model I has a spring-driven firing pin that firing also serves as the ejector. When the pistol is cocked, a signal pin projects from the rear of the frame. The upper front of the slide is cut away so that the breech is exposed when the slide is to the rear.

Overall length of the pistol is 4½ inches, and the weight unloaded is 13½ ozs. The magazine holds six rounds. The pistol was discontinued at about the time of World War II.

DISASSEMBLY

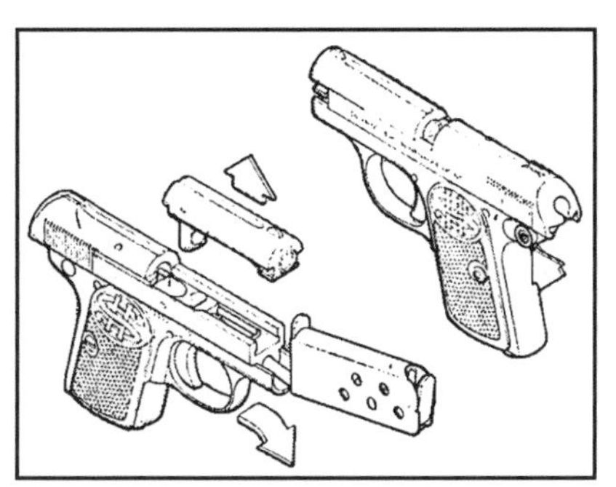

1 To field-strip the pistol, engage safety (28) on safe, and remove and unload magazine (20). Replace magazine and disengage safety. Draw slide (5) fully rearward to clear chamber. Pull trigger (26), and re-engage safety on safe. Lock slide half open by pulling it back and lifting safety into slide notch. Remove magazine, and engage cutout on its bottom rear with annular groove on exposed tip of recoil spring guide (10). Pull guide forward and down until it locks. Lift out barrel (1).

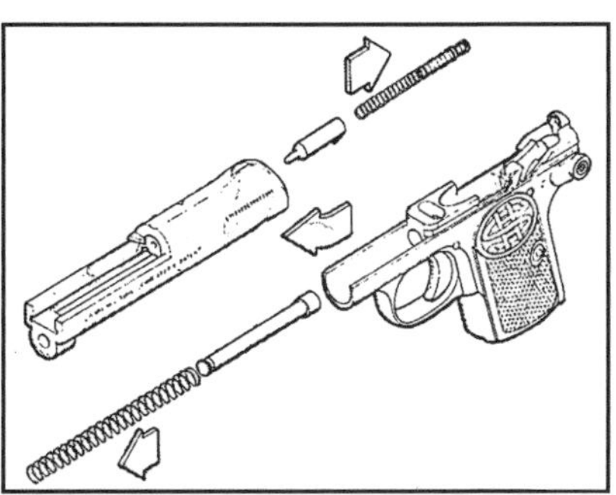

2 Grasp recoil spring guide from below, maintaining contact between magazine and guide with thumb pressure from above. Raise guide into alignment and ease to rear. Draw slide slightly rearward to unlock from safety and ease slide forward off frame (12). Remove recoil spring (11) and guide from frame. Then, remove firing pin (6), mainspring (7), signal pin (21), and spring (22) from slide. This completes field-stripping for normal cleaning.

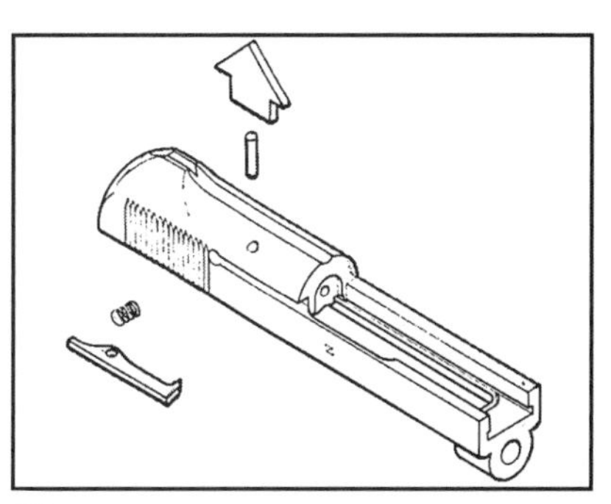

3 To disassemble further, drift extractor pin (2) upward out of slide, releasing extractor (3) and spring (4).

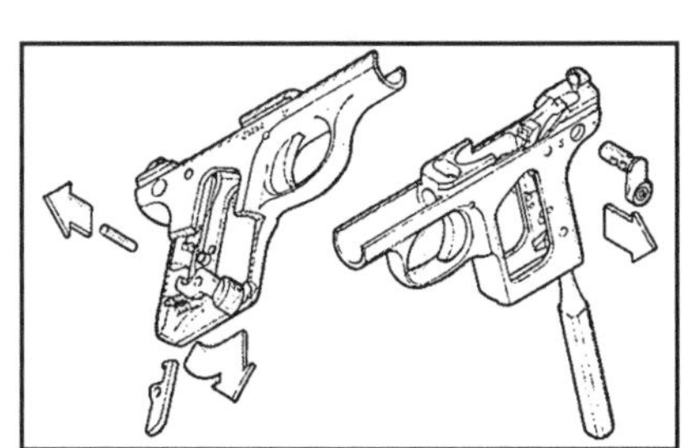

4 Unscrew grip screw (9), and remove grips (8) (24). Drift out magazine catch pin (30), and remove magazine safety (15). Rotate magazine catch (31) forward into magazine well to unhook from sear spring housing (19). Remove magazine safety, magazine safety spring (16), and magazine catch spring (32) from their frame recesses with tweezers. Raise sear spring housing with flat punch to allow removal of safety. (During reassembly, safety must be installed in engaged position.)

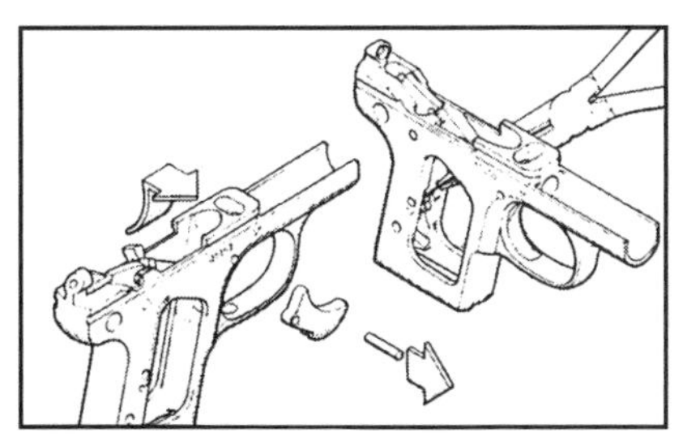

5 Drift out trigger pin (25), rotate bottom of trigger forward into guard, and remove. Twist trigger bar (27) slightly, so that its upper surface clears top of frame. Pull bar out of its frame recess into magazine well, and remove. Rotate trigger bar spring (29) forward into magazine well, and remove from its fixed frame pin with long-nose pliers.

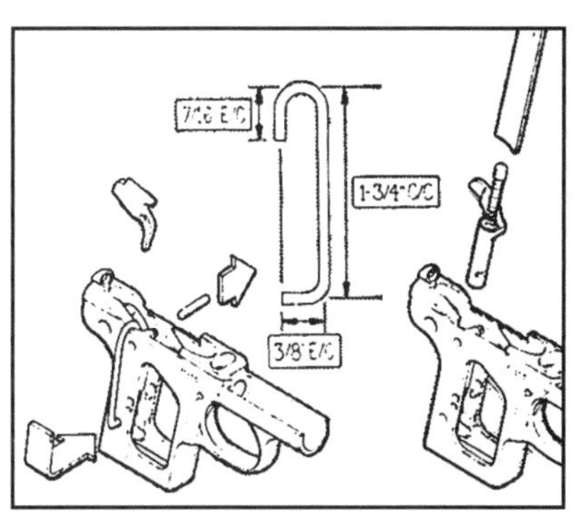

6 Bend a piece of 3⁄32" brazing rod as shown. Place upper end of rod atop head of sear spring plunger (18), depressing the plunger so that lower end of rod may be inserted into frame hole for magazine catch pin. Drift out sear pin (14), and remove sear (13). If necessary to remove spring housing, make a concave cut at end of 3⁄16" wide flat wood stick, and use stick to depress sear spring plunger. Remove brazing rod tool, and then ease out plunger and sear spring (17). Wear glasses and keep face clear.

HÄMMERLI FREE-PISTOL

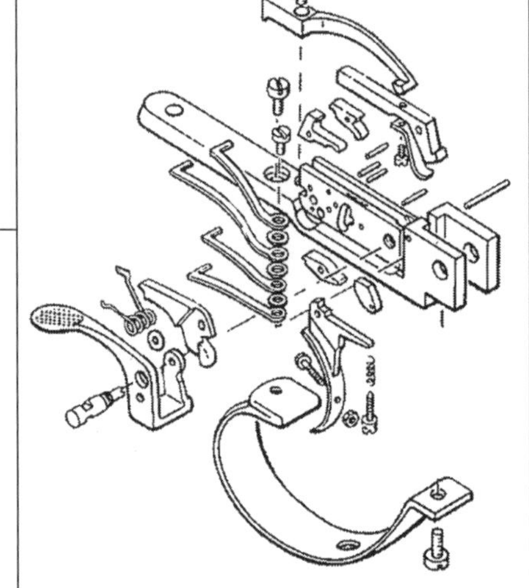

The trigger mechanism is the heart of the cal. .22 Hämmerli free-pistol. It is carefully adjusted at the factory and can be adjusted to a very light pull. The exploded view gives some idea of the complexity and why it should be disassembled and adjusted only by factory trained gunsmiths.

PARTS LEGEND

1. Barrel
2. Front sight blade
3. Front sight latch
4. Sight latch spring
5. Latch hinge pin
6. Barrel lug
7. Forestock
8. Bushing
9. Frame
10. Breechblock
11. Firing pin spring
12. Firing pin
13. Firing pin retaining pin
14. Breechblock hinge pin
15. Hinge pin retaining spring
16. Spring retaining screw
17. Cross pin
18. Right extractor screw
19. Left extractor screw
20. Extractor
21. Extractor spring
22. Extractor spring screw (2)
23. Front guard screw
24. Lever
25. Hammer
26. Spring roller
27. Roller pin
28. Mainspring retaining screw
29. Mainspring
30. Lever latch
31. Latch spri ng
32. Latch pin
33. C-washer
34. Washer
35. Spring
36. Nut
37. Sight retainer screw
38. Retainer plate
39. Sight base
40. Sight leaf spring
41. Sight leaf
42. Retainer pin
43. Sight blade screw
44. Sight elevating screw
45. Windage screw
46. Sight leaf hinge
47. Sight blade
48. Detent spring
49. Detent (2)
50. Right grip
51. Heel support screw
52. Washer
53. Heel support
54. Elongated washer
55. Nut
56. Left grip
57. Grip screw
58. Bushing
59. Trigger assembly

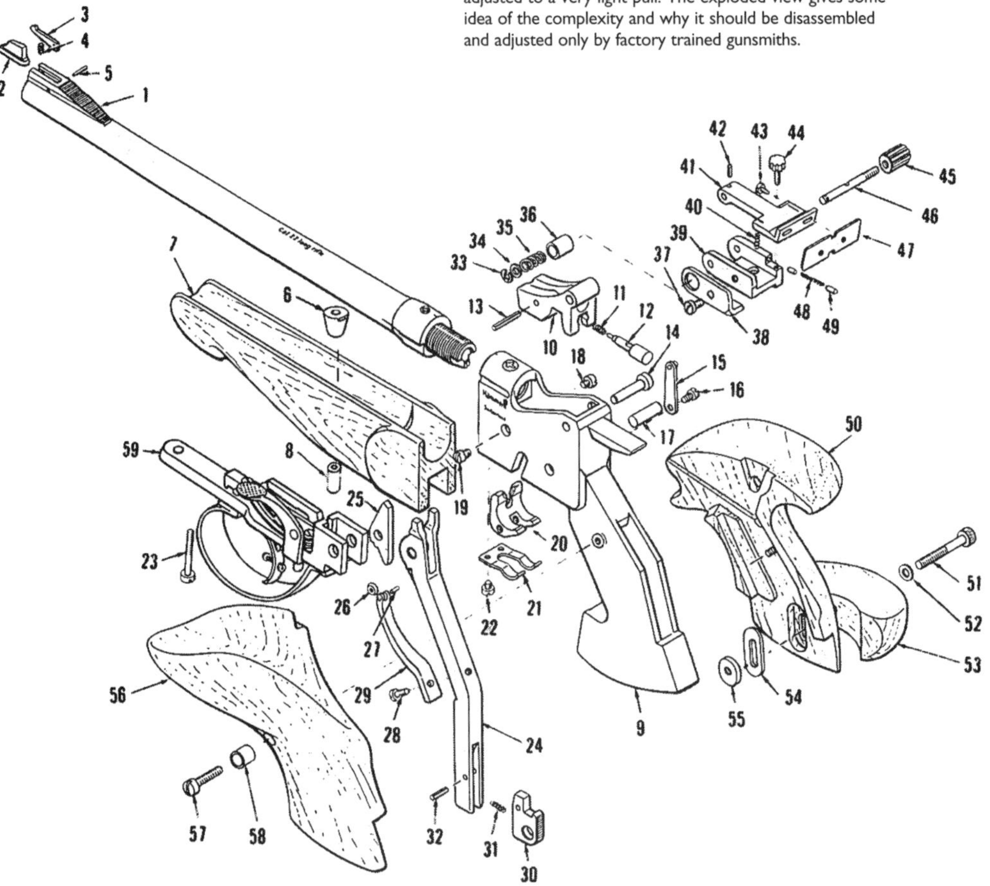

The free-pistol, offered in various models by the venerable Swiss firm of Hämmerli, is designed specifically for precision slow-fire target shooting in international 50-meter singleshot pistol events. As "free pistols," there are few limitations and the choice of barrel length, sight radius, trigger pull, weight and grip-shape are nearly unlimited.

Hämmerli Models 101, 102 and 103 (103 shown here) were replaced in February 1963 by the Models 104 and 105. Mechanical refinements and changes made since then have led to the Models 150 (with mechanical set trigger) and 152 (with electric trigger). Both the 150 and 152 featured floating barrels and under-barrel floating fore-ends. The updated Models 160 and 162 were introduced in the 1990s with either mechanical (160) or electronic trigger (162), and synthetic fore-ends. The frames of early production free-pistols were machined from bar stock, but later models are investment cast.

The Hämmerli free pistols are .22 caliber rimfire, singleshot Martini-action pistols. All have set triggers and the factory will fit the grips to the shooter's hand, based on physical measurements and shooting style

The Martini-type action of the Hämmerli gives the rigidity and short hammer throw necessary in any super-accurate gun. The action also allows for easy loading and has a powerful extraction system.

DISASSEMBLY

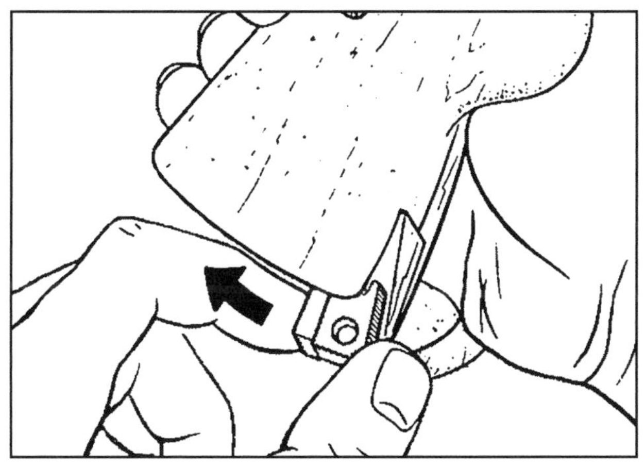

1 The Hämmerli has a miniature Martini action. To drop the breechblock (10), squeeze the lever latch (30) at rear underside of the grip. When the lever (24) is moved forward, it cocks the hammer (25), drops the breechblock, and actuates the extractor (20).

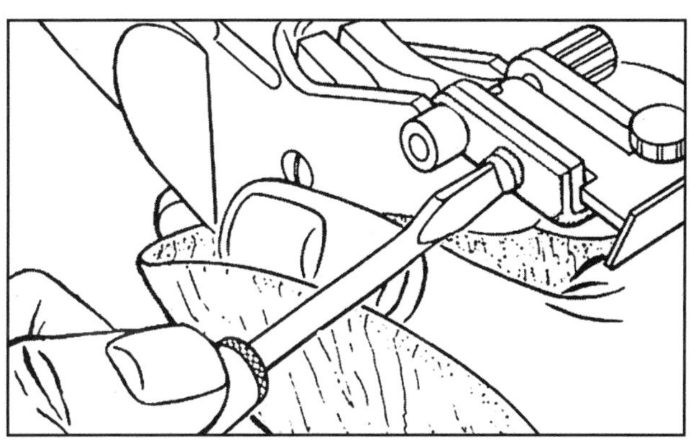

2 Two methods of rear sight attachment are used by Hämmerli. The later type shown here is attached by a sight retainer screw (37) and a retainer plate (38). When the screw is loosened, the rear sight slides off the integral sight mount. The earlier type uses 2 screws to retain the sight. These are under the leaf and tapped into the sight mount. The leaf must be raised upright to get at these screws.

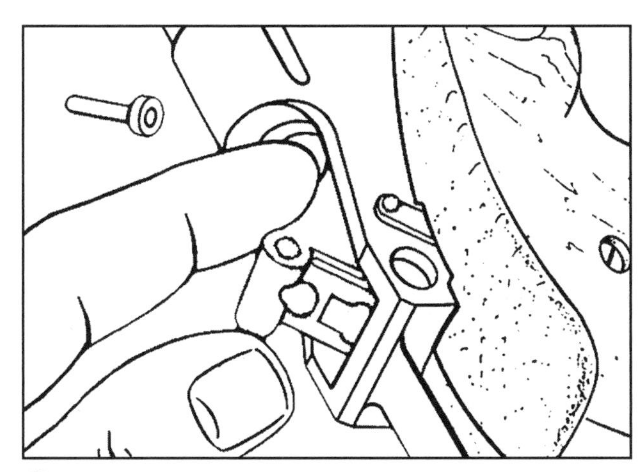

3 Occasionally it is necessary to remove the breechblock (10) for cleaning. To remove it, lift the hinge pin retaining spring (15) slightly and push it forward and clear of the breechblock hinge pin (14). Push out the hinge pin. Depress front of the breechblock (10) and lift it out. It may be necessary to move the loading lever a bit to free it from the breech block.

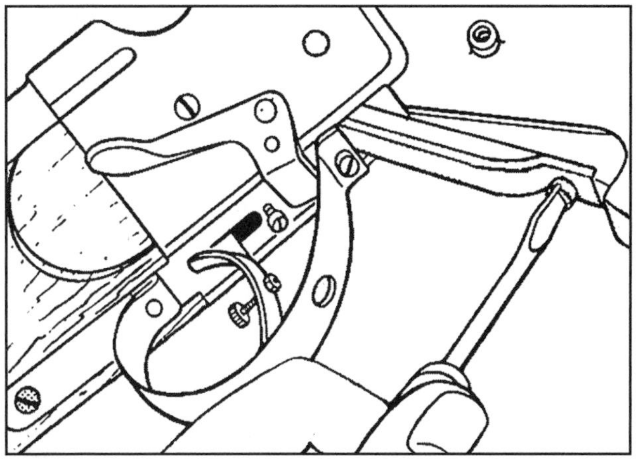

4 The cross pin (17) retains the rear of the trigger guard, the lever (24), and the hammer (25). Before attempting to remove it, loosen the mainspring retaining screw (28); this relieves tension on the cross pin (17). When cross pin is out, the trigger mechanism can be removed intact by removing front guard screw (23).

HÄMMERLI WALTHER OLYMPIA

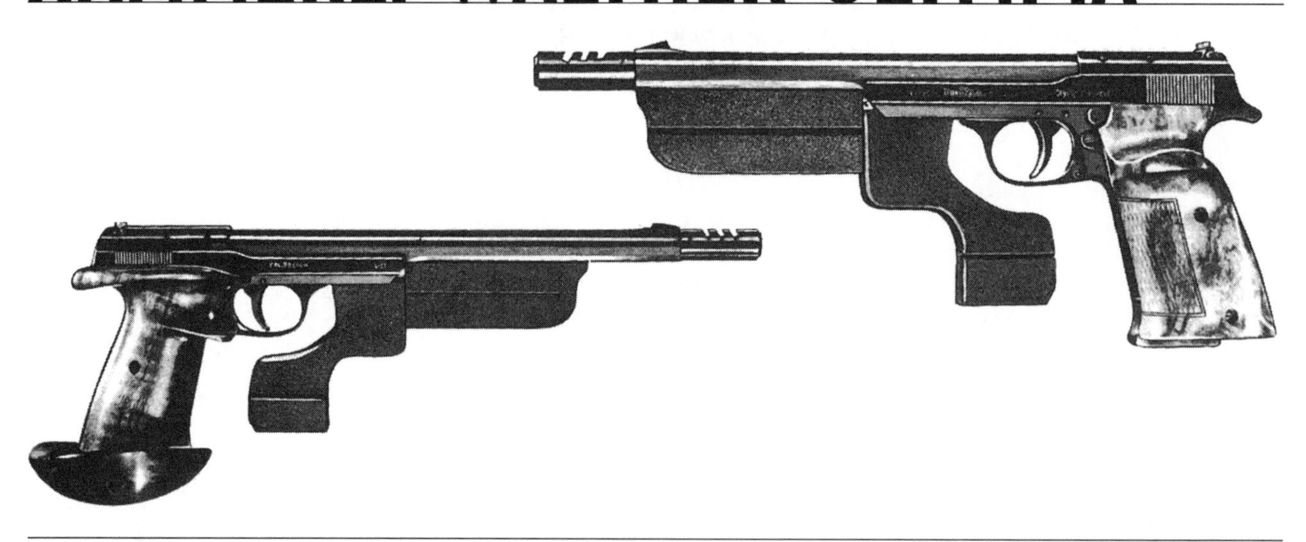

PARTS LEGEND

A. Slide
B. Extractor
C. Extractor plunger
D. Extractor spring
E. Firing pin housing pins
F. Firing pin retaining pin
G. Rear sight
H. Rear sight adjusting screws
I. Rear sight base
J. Firing pin housing
K. Firing pin spring
L. Firing pin
M. Right-hand grip
N. Muzzle brake
O. Muzzle brake set screw
P. Front sight
Q. Front sight set screw
R. Weight retaining screws
S. Barrel and receiver
T. Ejector
U. Trigger stop set screw
V. Trigger spring
W. Trigger
X. Trigger bar
V. Hammer
Z. Hammer strut pin
AA. Sear pin
BB. Sear
CC. Sear spring
DD. Sear spring pin
EE. Hammer strut
FF. Hammer spring
GG. Hammer spring seat
HH. Magazine
II. Trigger guard plunger
JJ. Plunger spring
KK. Trigger guard pin
LL. Safety catch
MM. Trigger guard
NN. Magazine catch
OO. Magazine catch spring
PP. Trigger pin
QQ. Trigger stop pin
RR. Trigger stop screw
SS. Recoil spring
TT. Front weight
UU. Recoil spring guide
VV. Secondary weight
WW. Weight retaining screws (long)
XX. Small weight
YY. Grip screw
ZZ. Left-hand grip

At the 1936 Olympic games in Berlin, the top five shooters in the Olympic rapid-fire matches all used the new Walther Olympia .22 rimfire self-loading pistol. From then until it was eclipsed by Italian designs and by newer guns from Walther, the Olympia was the overwhelming choice of International and Olympic target shooters.

After World War II Fritz Walther moved to Switzerland. working as design engineer and consultant and sold rights to the Olympia to Hämmerli Arms Co., of Lenzburg. From the end of World War II until about 1963, two models of the Hämmerli/Walther Olympia were made. One, the Special Olympia, had a 9½-inch barrel and a trigger pull of 1½ pounds. The other, the Standard Olympia had a 7½-inch barrel and a trigger pull of at least 33 ounces.

Like its Walther predecessor, the Hämmerli Olympia was made for either .22 Short or .22 Long Rifle ammunition. A muzzle brake and weights was added to combat recoil.

On the early model Hämmerli Olympia pistols the front sight is adjustable for elevation and rear sight is adjustable for windage. More recent versions, the rear sights are fully adjustable for elevation and windage.

Since the pistol is blowback operated, there is no locking mechanism to make the takedown procedure involved. The only point in the takedown that might be called unorthodox is the method used to remove the recoil spring and recoil spring guide. The front end of the receiver has to be sprung away from the barrel. This is accomplished driving a brass wedge or screwdriver between the barrel and the front of the receiver.

DISASSEMBLY

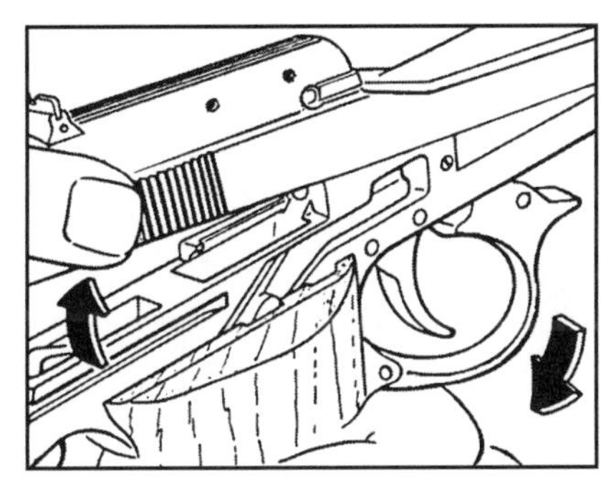

1 Remove the magazine and check chamber to be sure the gun is empty. Remove the weights. Pull down on the front of the trigger guard (MM), push it to the side until it catches on a lip in the receiver (S). Draw the slide to the rear, lift it up off the receiver, and ease it forward over the barrel

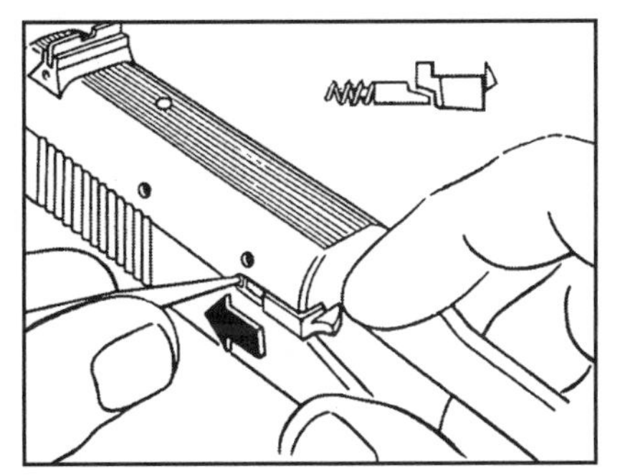

2 The extractor (B) is retained by a spring-loaded plunger (C). Using a small screwdriver, push the plunger back into the slide (A). If the slide is turned on its side, the extractor will then drop out. Ease up on the plunger (C) and it will come out with its spring (D).

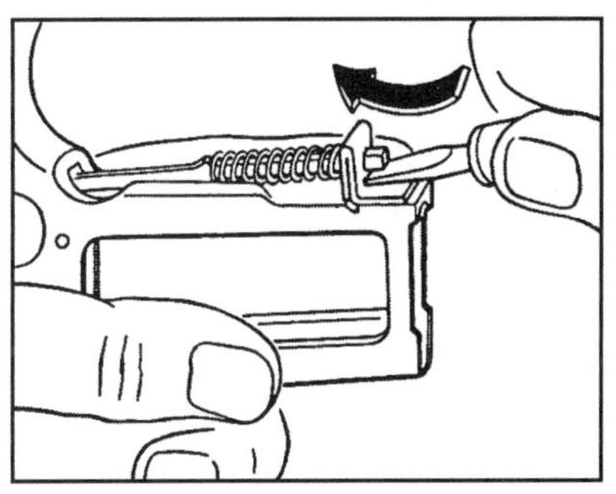

3 Removing the hammer spring seat (GG) is a bit tricky. First pull the trigger and ease the hammer to fired position, to take the tension off the hammer spring (FF). Push up hard as shown at the same time; lift the seat free from its notch in the receiver.

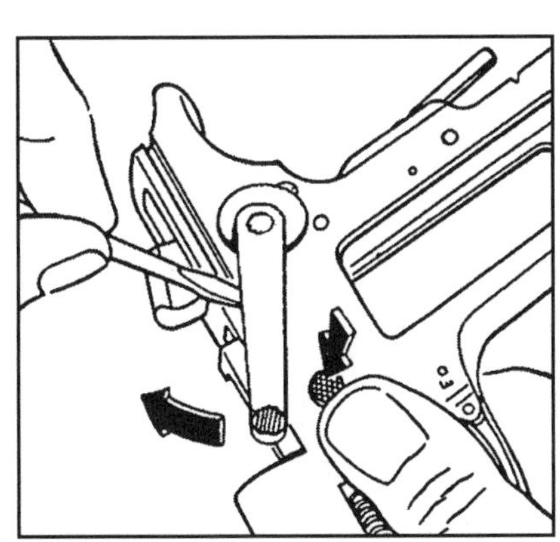

4 To remove the safety, lower the hammer (Y) to fired position. Depress the magazine catch (NN), lift the catch (LL) a bit as shown, to prevent it scratching the finish, and rotate it up over the edge of the receiver to the position illustrated. The catch will then spring free of the receiver.

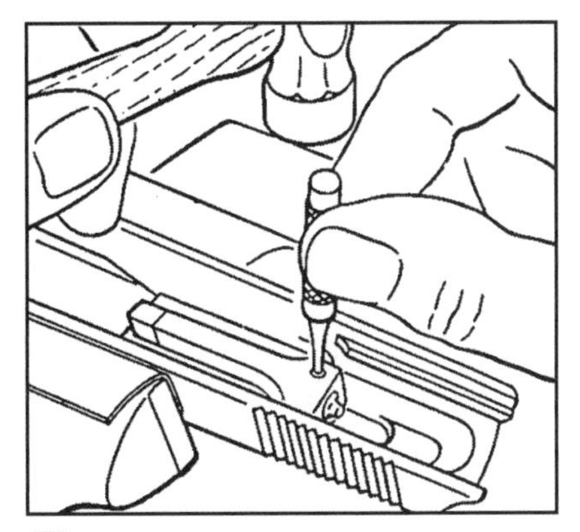

5 A spare firing pin (L) and firing pin spring (K) are supplied with each new gun. To remove the old parts, hold the slide (A) upside down in a vise, and tap the firing pin retaining pin (F) out, as shown. The firing pin and spring can then be lifted out of the slide.

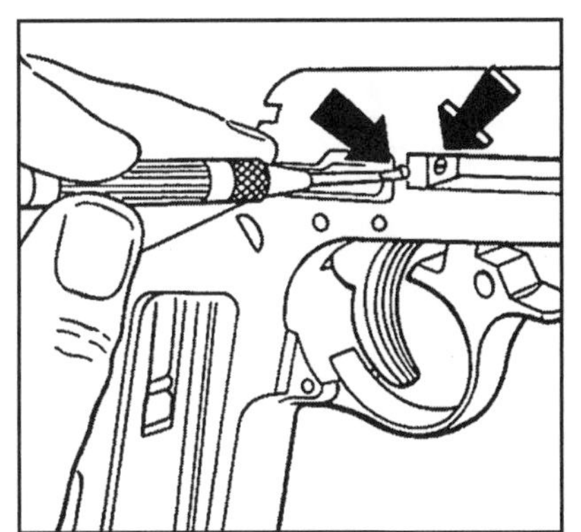

6 The trigger pull on the Olympia is not adjustable, but the amount of travel can be limited. The trigger stop screw (RR) can be reached only with a long thin screwdriver, but its set screw (U) can be reached from the outside, as shown.

H&R MODEL 922 REVOLVER

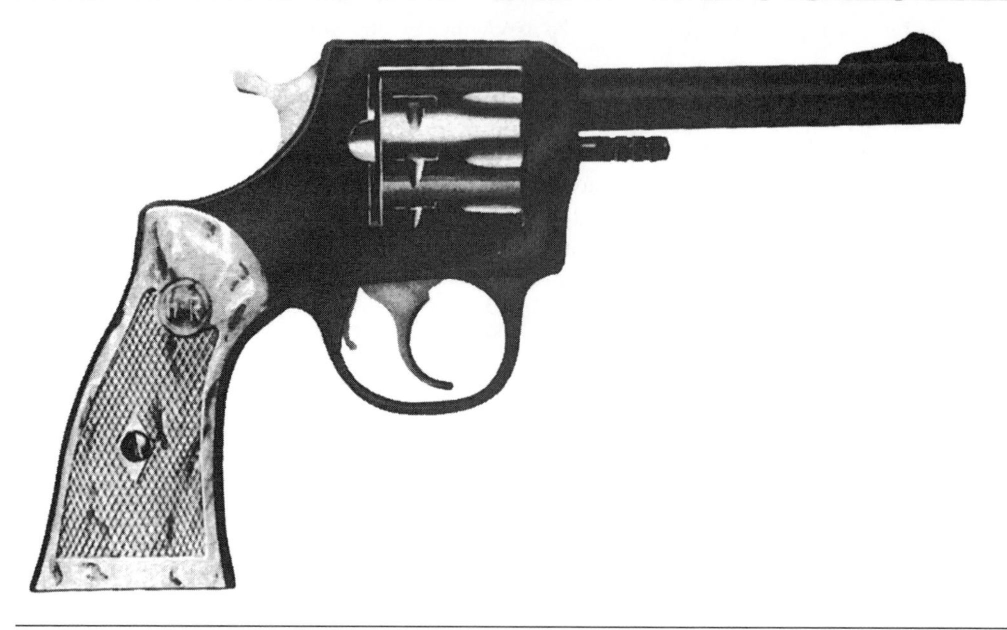

PARTS LEGEND

1. Center pin
2. Cylinder
3. Extractor
4. Guard and sear pin
5. Trigger guard
6. Sear spring
7. Sear
8. Cylinder stop
9. Cylinder stop spring
10. Center pin plunger spring
11. Center pin plunger
12. Trigger and front guard pins (2)
13. Trigger
14. Lifter
15. Lifter pin
16. Lever and spring assembly
17. Trigger spring
18. Grip screws (2)
19. Grips (2)
20. Mainspring
    20a. Mainspring assembly
21. Mainspring guide
22. Mainspring seat
23. Hammer screw
24. Hammer screw stud
25. Hammer
26. Barrel retaining pin
27. Barrel
28. Front sight
29. Mainframe
30. Grip pins (2)

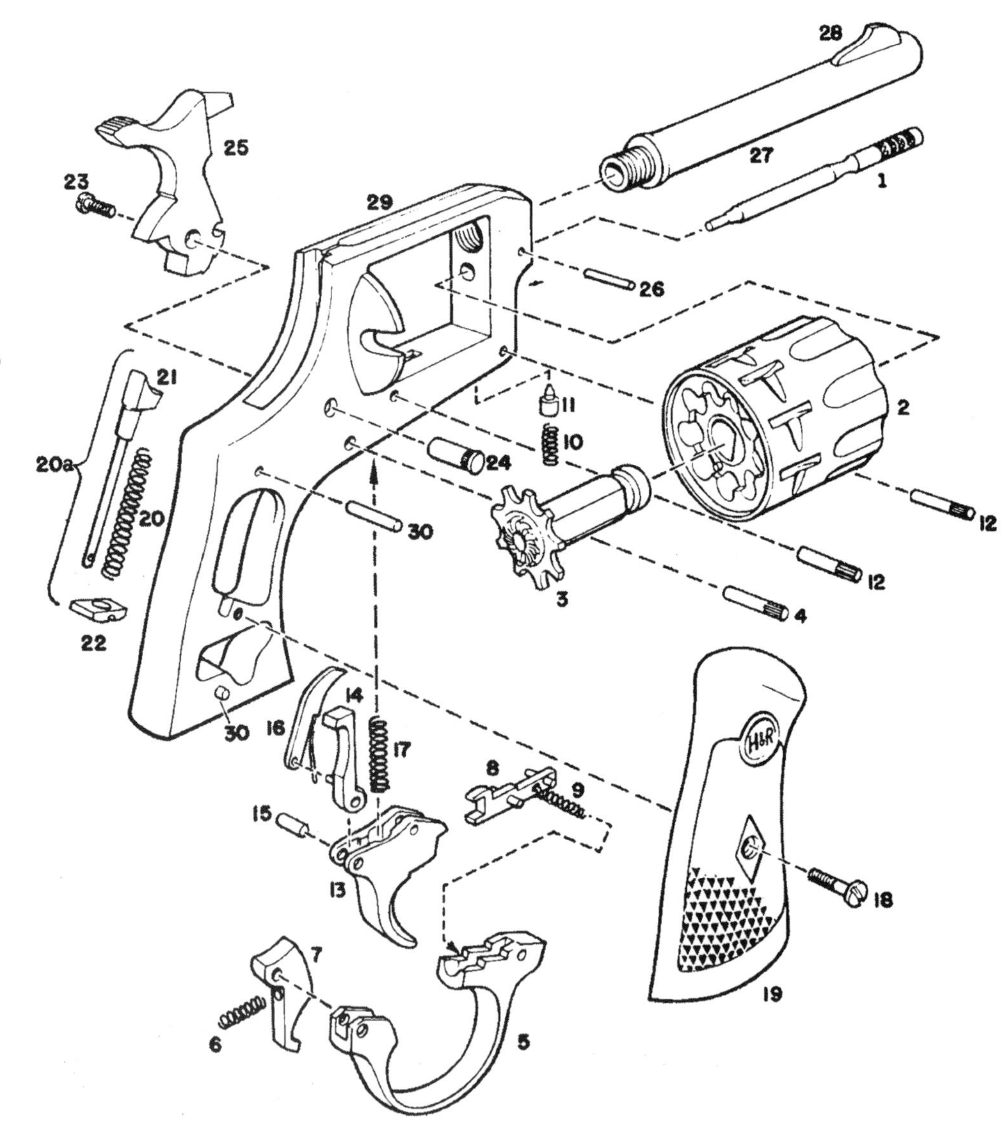

DISASSEMBLY

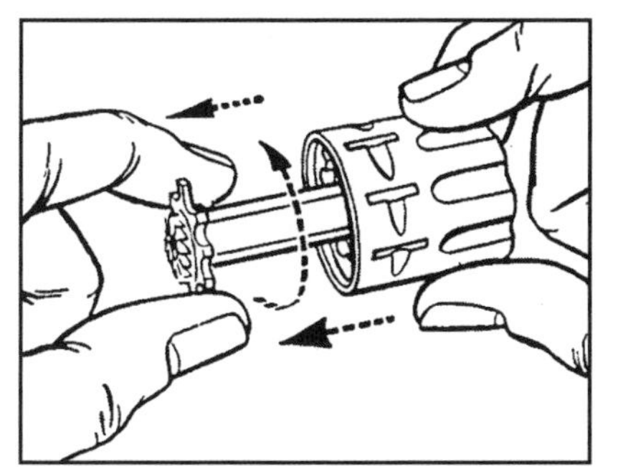

1 Remove center pin (1) and cylinder (2) from frame. Remove extractor (3) after pushing it out of cylinder as far as possible with center pin and rotating it ½ turn in either direction, then withdrawing.

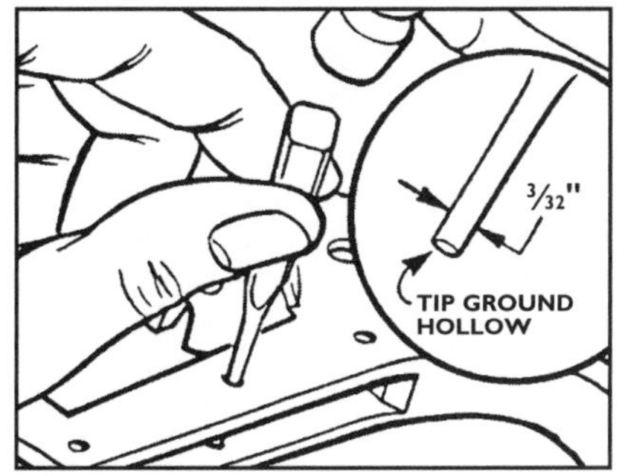

2 Drive out guard and sear pin (4) and front guard pin (12). These pins are knurled on one end and care should be taken to drive them out from the left and replace them from the right. Use proper size punch to avoid burring pin holes.

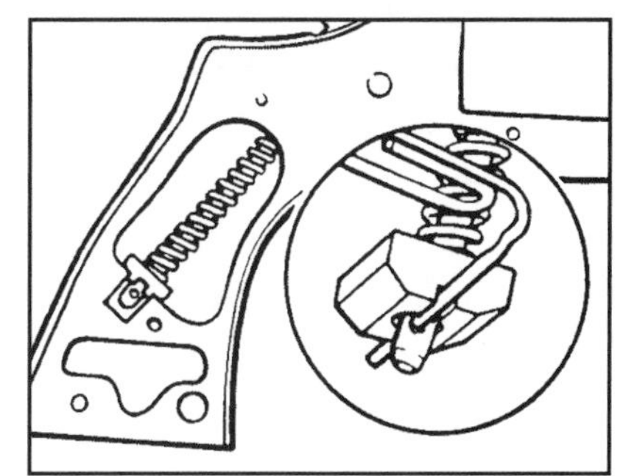

3 Remove grip screws (18) and grips (19). Remove mainspring assembly (20a) by moving hammer back toward cocked position until hole at bottom of mainspring guide (21) protrudes beneath mainspring seat (22). Secure mainspring by placing piece of wire through hole. Release hammer and drop out mainspring.

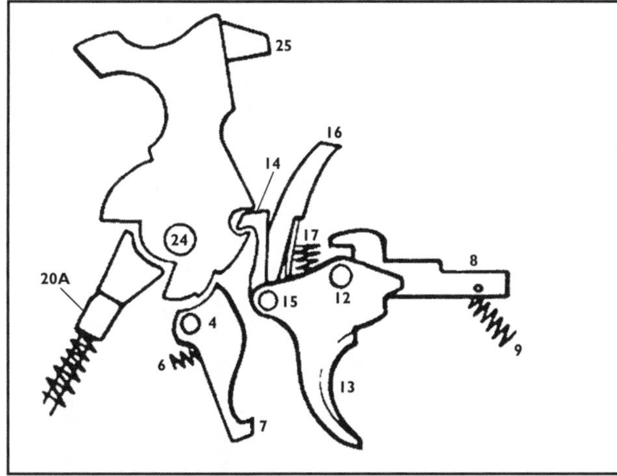

4 Remove trigger guard (5), cylinder stop (8), and stop spring (9), sear (7), sear spring (6), center pin plunger spring (10), plunger (11), from mainframe. Drive out trigger pin (12) and remove trigger assembly [trigger (13), trigger spring (17), lifter (14), lifter pin (15), lever and spring assembly (16)]. Diagram shows relative position of these parts assembled. Remove hammer screw (23) and gently drive out hammer screw stud (24) using care not to damage stud threads. Remove hammer (25). Removal of barrel should not be attempted except by a gunsmith.

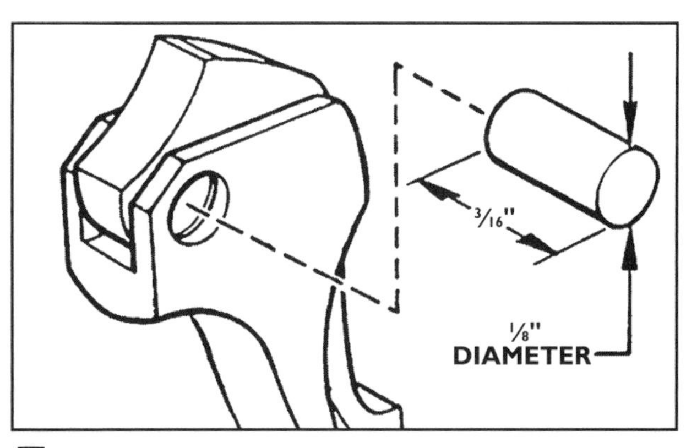

5 In reassembling, replace hammer first. Sear spring, sear, and trigger guard must be assembled before installation in frame, using slave pin through sear and trigger guard. Length of slave pin should not exceed width of trigger guard. Cylinder stop spring must be inserted into stop spring hole in trigger guard before assembling guard to frame.

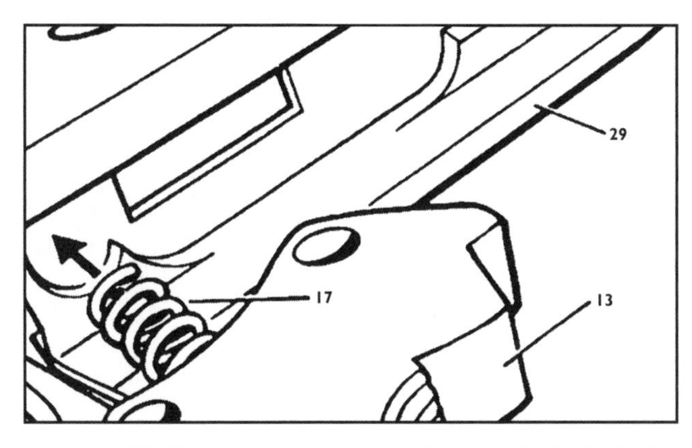

6 When reinstalling trigger assembly, end of trigger spring must be in line with spring seat in bottom of trigger guard slot in frame. Guide lifter into position between hammer and frame with small screwdriver and press trigger assembly up into frame until pin holes line up. Secure by replacing trigger pin (12). Trigger guard, sear, and cylinder stop assembly is secured by replacing front guard pin (12) and guard and sear pin (4). The slave pin holding sear and guard for assembly should be driven out when replacing guard and sear pin (4). Note: By making extra long slave pins with finger loops it is possible to speed up preliminary assembly and disassembly operations when adjustments are required. When functioning is satisfactory, install permanent pins.

H&R MODEL 929 "SIDE-KICK"

PARTS LEGEND

1. Frame
2. Barrel
3. Front sight
4. Barrel retaining pin
5. Rear sight leaf
6. Rear sight screws (2)
7. Front trjgger guard pin
8. Trigger pjn
9. Rear trigger guard and sear pin
10. Hammer screw stud
11. Hammer screw
12. Hammer
13. Mainspring guide
14. Mainspring
15. Mainspring seat
16. Trigger
17. Lever and spring assembly
18. Lifter
19. Lifter pin
20. Sear
21. Sear spring
22. Trigger spring
23. Cylinder stop assembly
24. Trigger guard
25. Swingout arm assembly
26. Center pin spring
27. Extractor spring
28. Center pin
29. Center pin guide
30. Center pin head
31. Center pin head pin
32. Swingout arm pivot pin
33. Cylinder
34. Extractor

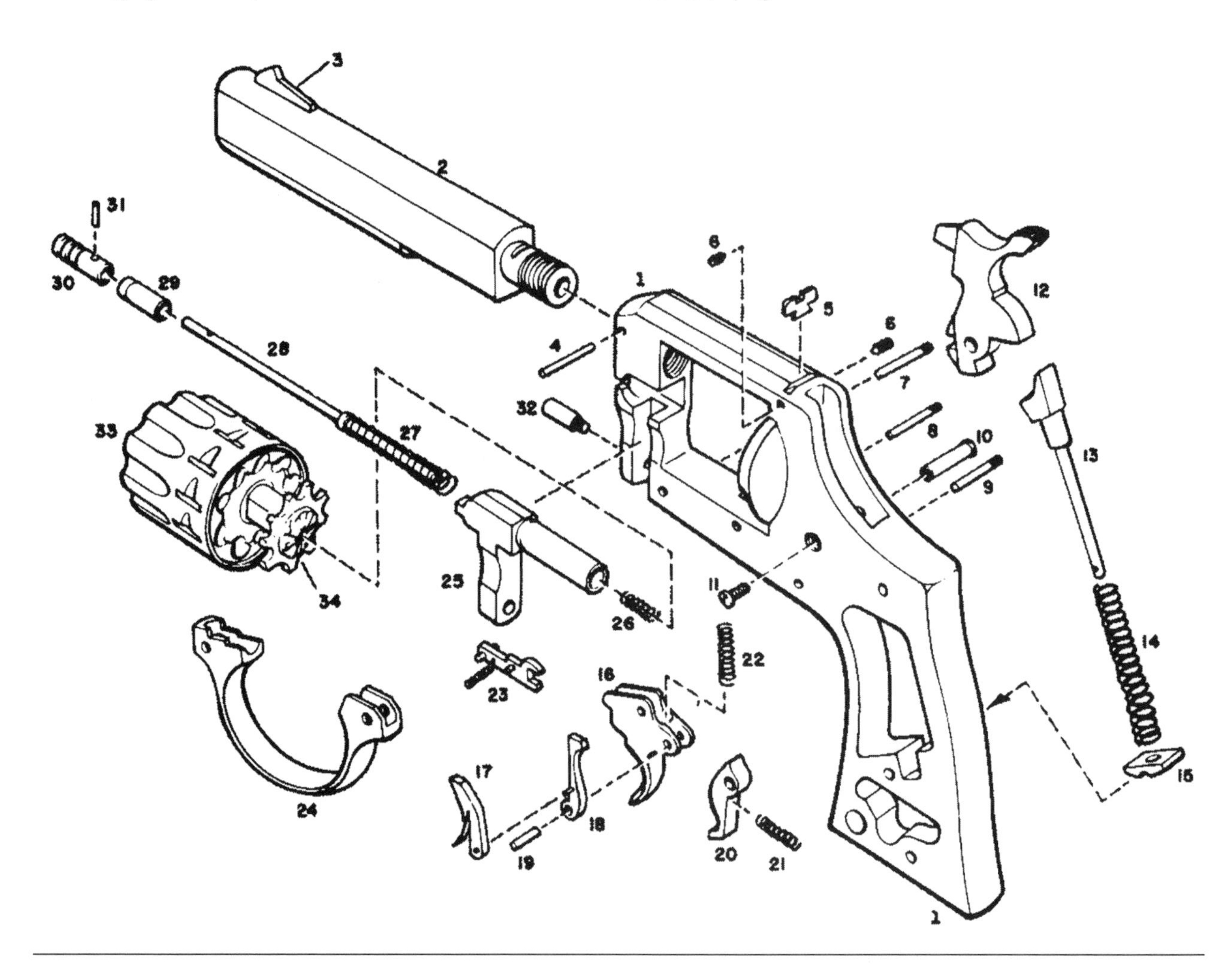

The Harrington & Richardson Model 929, "Side-Kick," double-action revolver was introduced in 1956. A solid frame design, with a swing-out cylinder, the Model 929 is chambered for .22 Short, Long or Long Rifle ammunition. Cylinder capacity is nine cartridges. There were minor changes in the design of the revolver, made before Harrington & Richardson closed its doors in 1986. In 1988, a new firm, New England Firearms Co., resumed production of many of Harrington & Richardson's old products, including a revolver similar to the Model 929.

DISASSEMBLY

Check revolver to be sure it is unloaded. Remove swingout arm pivot pin (32) from front end of frame (1). Pull hammer (12) back to lower cylinder stop, swing out cylinder and extractor assembly (33 & 34) with swingout arm assembly (25). Disassembly of extractor (34) from cylinder is not recommended and is unnecessary for normal cleaning.

Drift out front trigger guard pin (7) and rear trigger guard and sear pin (9) from *left to right.* Remove trigger guard (24) with cylinder stop assembly (23) and sear (20) with sear spring (21).

Remove grip screws and grips (not shown). Cock hammer (12) and place a nail or small pin through hole in lower end of mainspring guide (13) where it protrudes through mainspring seat (15). Release hammer and drop mainspring, guide, and seat assembly out of frame.

Drift out trigger pin (8) from *left to right* and drop trigger (16), trigger spring (22), lever and spring assembly (17), lifter (18) and lifter pin (19) out of frame. Remove hammer screw (11) and drift hammer screw stud (10) out of frame from *left to right.* Remove hammer (12) from top of frame. Reassemble in reverse. Note that all pivot pins are knurled at their right ends and should be replaced in frame from right to left with knurls at right.

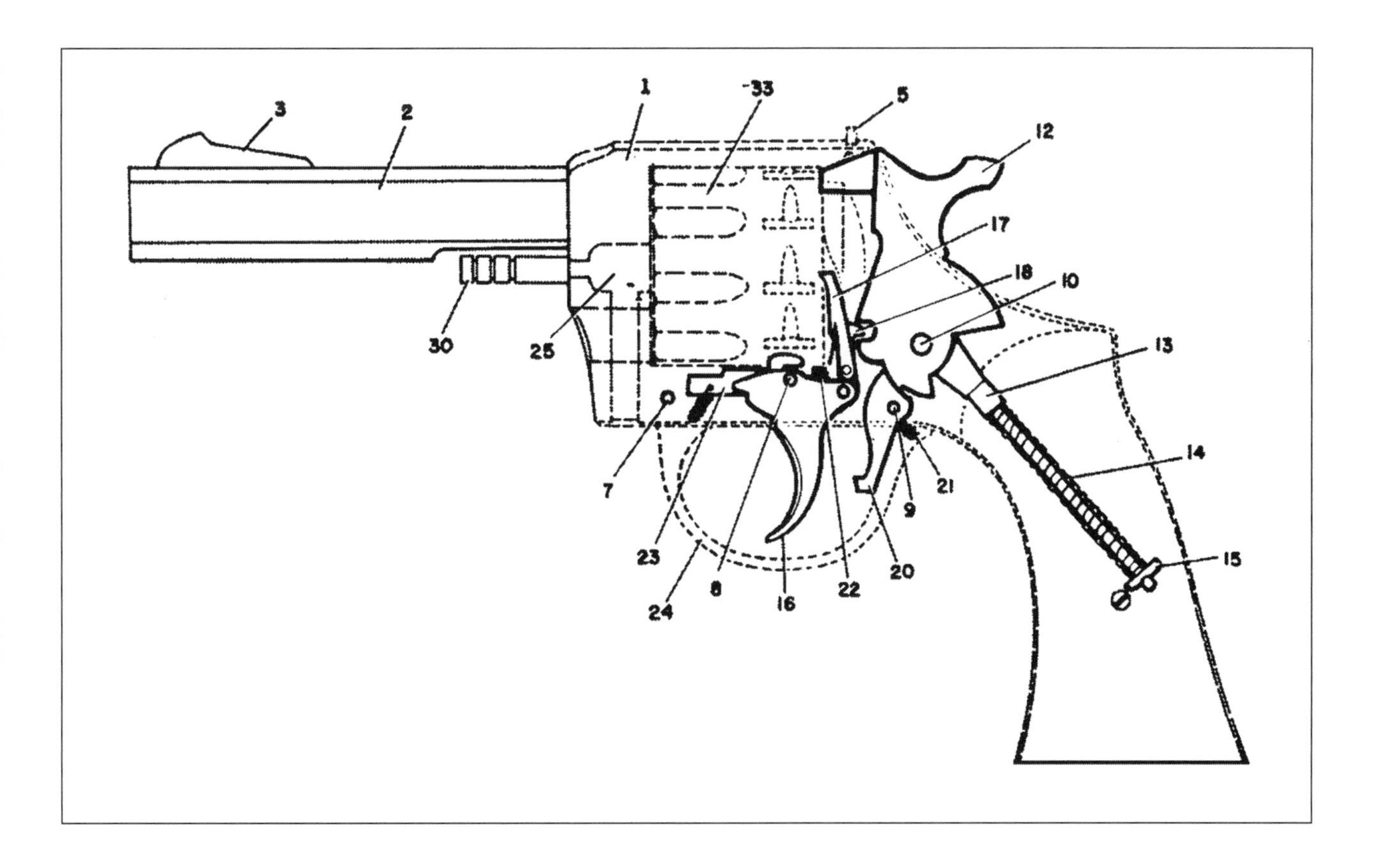

HARRINGTON & RICHARDSON

H&R PREMIER REVOLVER

PARTS LEGEND

1. Frame
2. Barrel
3. Trigger guard
4. Cylinder
5. Extractor
6. Front guard pin
7. Guard/sear pin
8. Stocks (pr.)
9. Barrel catch
10. Barrel catch spring
11. Catch spring screw
12. Catch screw
13. Quill
14. Quillpin
15. Extractor extension
16. Extractor spring
17. Hammer
18. Hammer screw
19. Trigger
20. Lifter
21. Lifter pin
22. Hand
23. Handspring
24. Cylinder stop
25. Cylinder stop screw
26. Trigger spring
27. Trigger pin
28. Sear
29. Sear spring
30. Extractor hook
31. Hook spring
32. Hinge screw
33. Mainspring
34. Stock pin
35. Stock screw

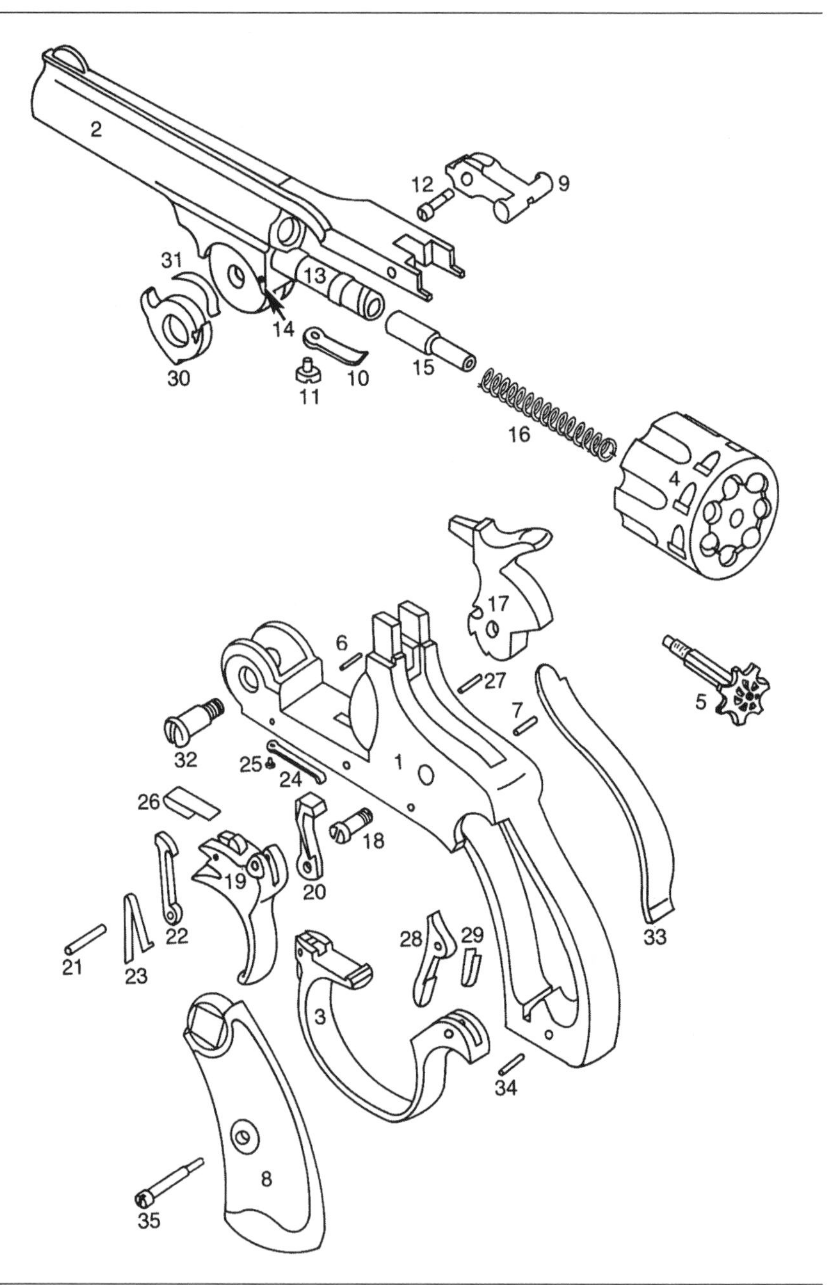

The history of Harrington & Richardson's Premier revolvers is a bit hazy despite their popularity. The revolver was first noted in this research in the 1895 Montgomery Ward catalog, where it already had the Premier name but was offered (at $4) only in .32 S&W caliber with 3-inch barrel and nickel plating. It continued in production at least until World War II in the five-shot .32 version, joined by a seven-shot .22 Long Rifle model. Both calibers could be had with blue or nickel finishes in 2-, 3-, 4-, 5- and 6-inch barrels.

At one time or another, there were variants available such as the "Police Premier," (the illustrated standard model), and the "Hammerless," that actually had a semi-circular hammer concealed by the addition of a contoured plate that was pinned into the top rear of the frame.

The disassembly/assembly guide given here can be applied to all the above models and will be also useful for disassembly of the larger-framed Harrington & Richardson break-open pocket revolvers of the period.

Most of these larger revolvers were made for the .32 S&W Long (six-shot) or .38 S&W (five-shot), with various barrel lengths and spurred, spurless and concealed hammers. Many names were applied to them, including "Automatic," "Automatic Ejecting," "Auto Ejecting," "Police Automatic," "Hammerless" and "Heavy Hammerless."

DISASSEMBLY

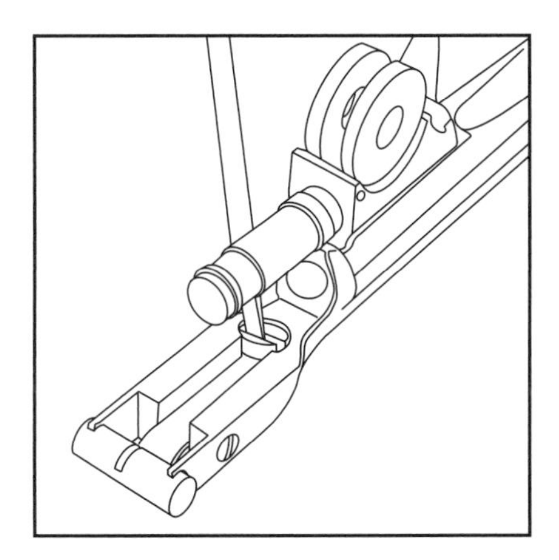

1 Lift up the barrel catch (9), swing the barrel unit fully down and unscrew the cylinder counterclockwise.

Remove the hinge screw (32) to separate barrel and frame units and free the extractor hook (30) and its spring (31).

The barrel catch (9) and its screw (12) are removed after first taking out the catch spring (10) and spring screw (11) from the underside of the top strap. This is done with an angled or thin-shanked screwdriver bypassing the cylinder quill (13) that should be left in place.

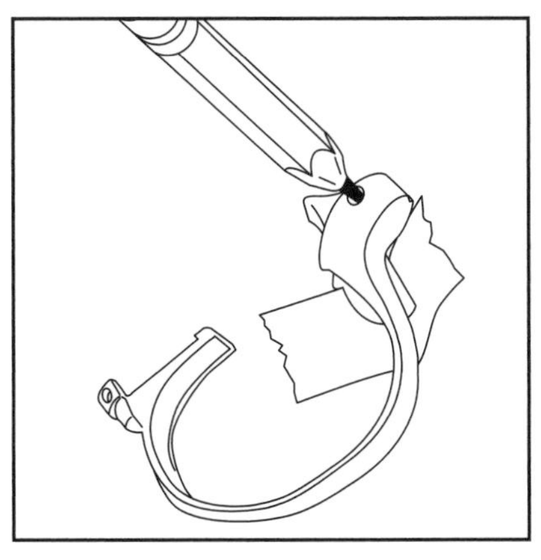

2 If quill removal is necessary, its pin (14) must be drifted out and great care taken in removing the fragile quill with padded pliers.

The cylinder can be stripped by grasping the extractor extension (15) with padded pliers and turning counterclockwise. This releases the extractor (5) and its spring (16).

For frame stripping, remove the stocks (8) and, with the hammer down, push the mainspring (33) out from its seat in the butt. Drift out front and rear guard pins (6 & 7) and remove trigger guard (3), noting the position of the trigger spring (26) in front of the guard and the sear and its spring (28 & 29) that are positioned in the rear slot of the guard.

It is probably well to prepare the guard/sear/sear spring for reassembly at this point, as these components will require a "slave pin." A common lead pencil can be trimmed with a knife so that its lead is exposed for about ½". The lead is carefully pushed in to pin guard and sear together, and then trimmed flush with the guard sides. The sear should now be pushed down into the rear of the guard and held there with a strip of tape.

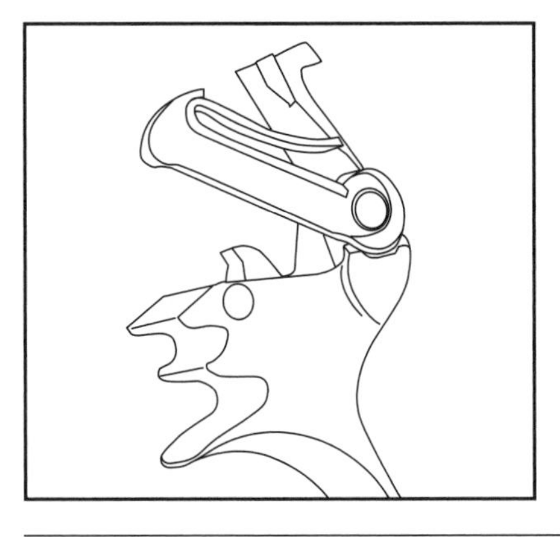

3 The trigger pin (27) is drifted out and the hammer screw (18) removed to permit removal of the trigger assembly and hammer. Position of the trigger, lifter, lifter pin, hand and hand spring (19-23) should be noted if these parts are to be separated.

Finally, the cylinder stop and screw (24 & 25) are removed from the front of the trigger guard slot in the frame.

H&R SELF-LOADING PISTOL

PARTS LEGEND

1. Barrel
2. Slide
3. Bolt face retainer pin
4. Slide endplate
5. Detent spring
6. Endplate detent
7. Firing pin
8. Spring guide
9. Firing pin spring
10. Right grip
11. Slide return block
12. Recoil spring
13. Spring guide
14. Bolt face
15. Extractor
16. Extractor spring
17. Front guard pin
18. Trigger pin
19. Trigger guard hinge screw
20. Sear
21. Sear pin
22. Sear stop pin
23. Grip safety stop pin
24. Sear spring follower
25. Sear spring
26. Grip safety hinge pin
27. Grip safety
28. Spring plunger
29. Magazine safety spring
30. Trigger bar detent
31. Magazine safety pin
32. Magazine safety
33. Magazine
34. Magazine catch
35. Magazine catch spring
36. Magazine release button
37. Magazine catch pin
38. Trigger bar
39. Left grip
40. Grip screw
41. Thumb safety
42. Safety catch detent
43. Detent spring
44. Trigger spring plunger
45. Trigger spring
46. Trigger
47. Trigger stop pin
48. Trigger guard
49. Frame

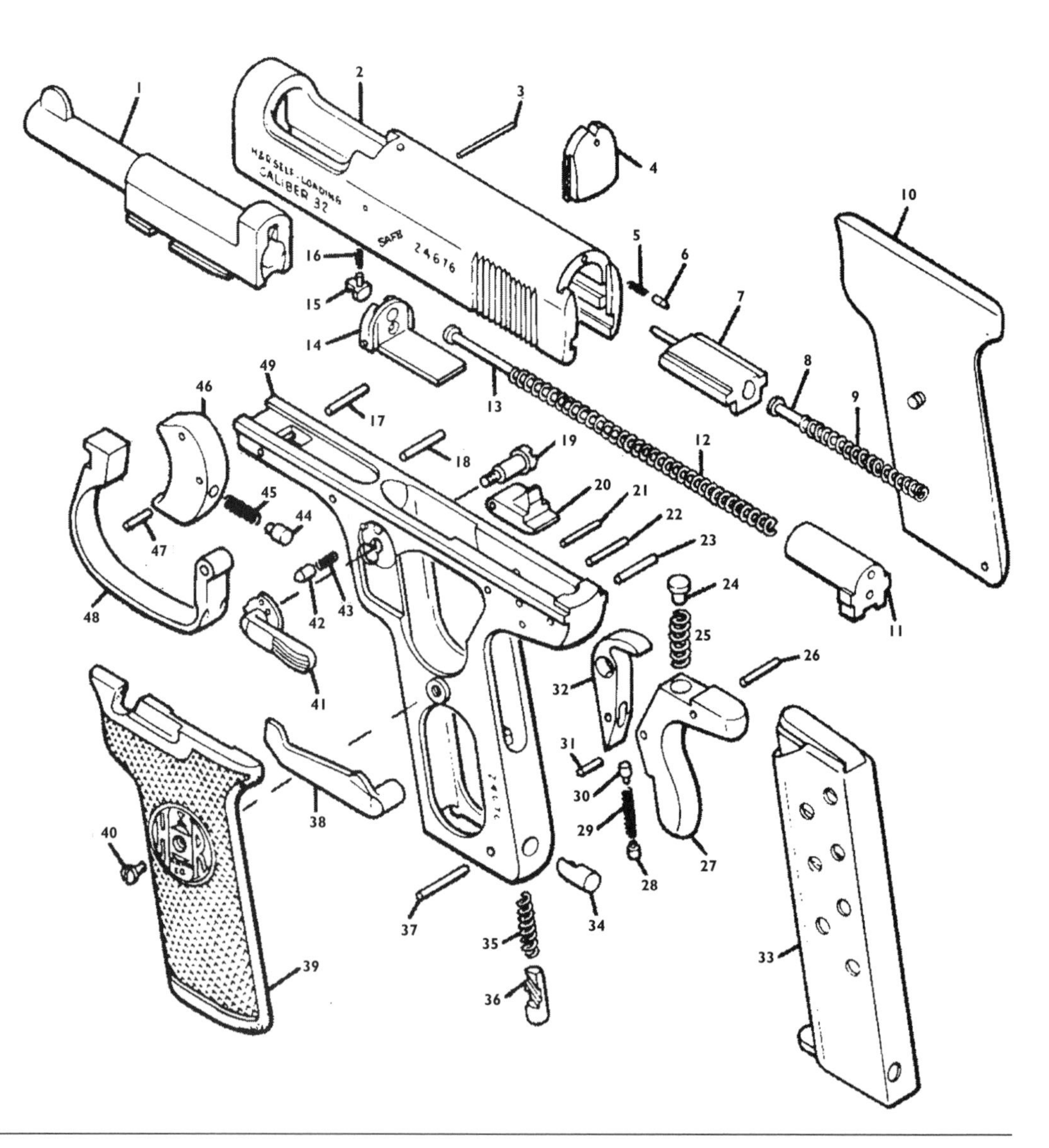

Introduced in 1916 by Harrington & Richardson of Worcester, Massachusetts, the H&R .32 caliber self-loading pistol was based on design patents held by the English gunmaking firm of Webley & Scott. The Webley & Scott version of this pistol featured an outside hammer, but the model offered by H&R was a true hammerless, striker-fired arm.

The H&R cal. .32 pistol was one of the first American-made pocket pistols to have a magazine safety or disconnector to prevent firing of the gun when the magazine was removed. However, this feature was subsequently abandoned, so H&R pistols of this type will be found both with and without the magazine safety device.

Mechanical details of interest in this pistol include the cartridge indicator pin on the extractor which extends above the top of the slide when there is a cartridge in the chamber and the thumb safety which is pushed upward rather than downward to disengage it. The latter procedure is contrary to usual practice in pocket automatic pistols.

Production of the H&R .32 caliber self-loading pistol was discontinued in 1939. Approximately 40,000 were made.

DISASSEMBLY

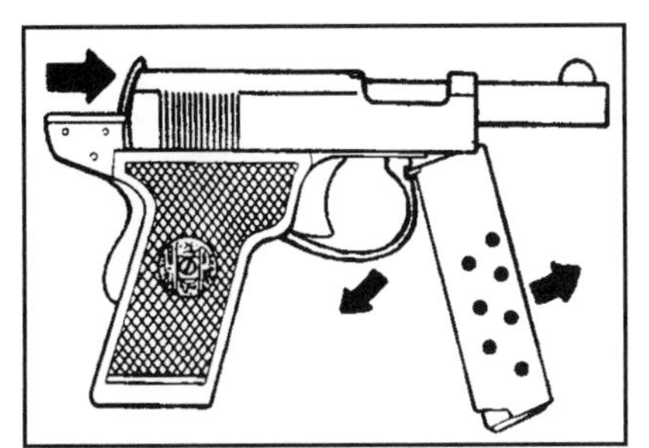

1 Takedown of the cal. .32 H&R pistol is not difficult. The barrel (1) is retained by the front of the trigger guard (48). The guard has a notch to allow the toe of the magazine floorplate to be used as a lever in disassembly. Pull trigger guard down slightly as shown, and push barrel and slide off. When reassembling, it is not necessary to pull down the guard. The cam on the underside of the barrel will push the trigger guard down.

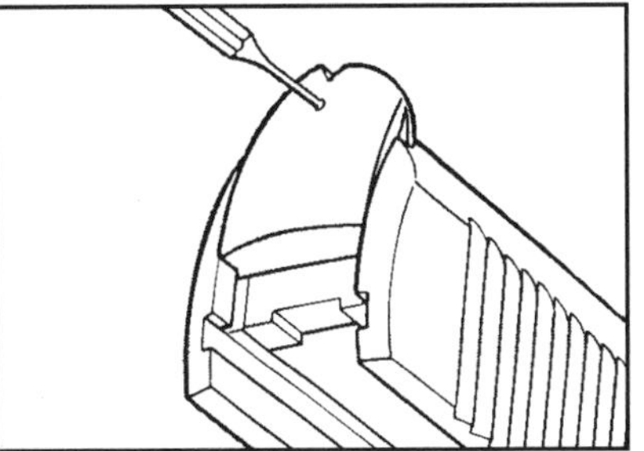

2 Once the slide endplate (4) is removed, the firing pin (7) and recoil spring (12) can be removed. To remove slide endplate, the endplate detent pin (6) must be depressed with a thin punch while the endplate is pushed up. Take care when the endplate is removed to prevent the slide return block (11) from flying out.

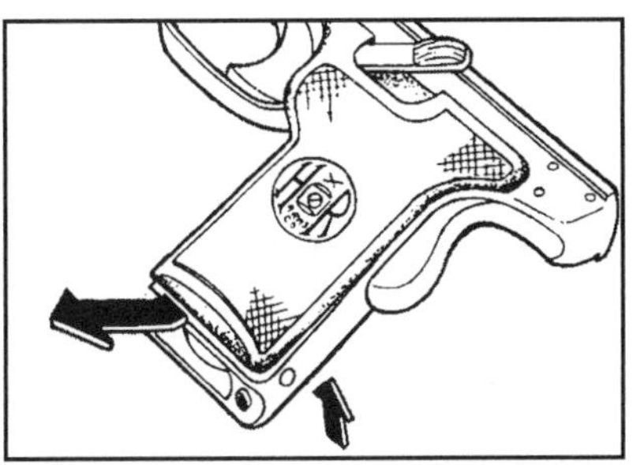

3 The left hard rubber grip (39) is easily broken if removed improperly. First remove the grip screws (40). Remove the right grip (10) and the magazine (33). Put thumb safety (41) in up or "off" position. Through the magazine well, push the lower end of the left grip. When free of the magazine catch pin (37), slide it down and out from under the edge of the thumb safety. Do not force.

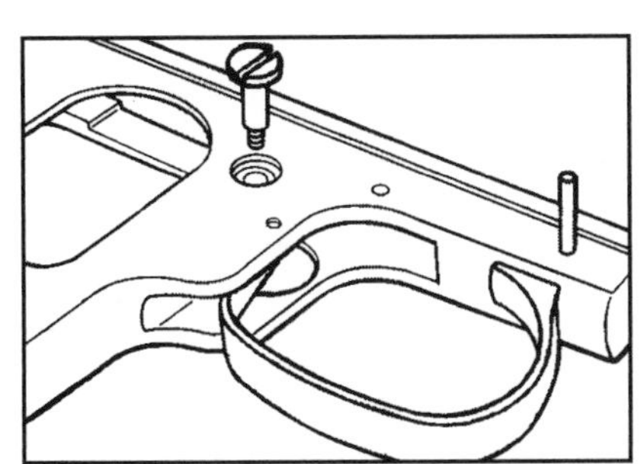

4 The H&R sear mechanism is unique in that there is no mechanical connection between trigger (46) and trigger bar (38). To remove the trigger, it is first necessary to remove the trigger stop pin (47). There is a small hole in the right side of the frame. If a thin punch is inserted through the frame hole when the trigger is at rest, the trigger stop pin can be driven out. Then the trigger pin (18) can be removed.

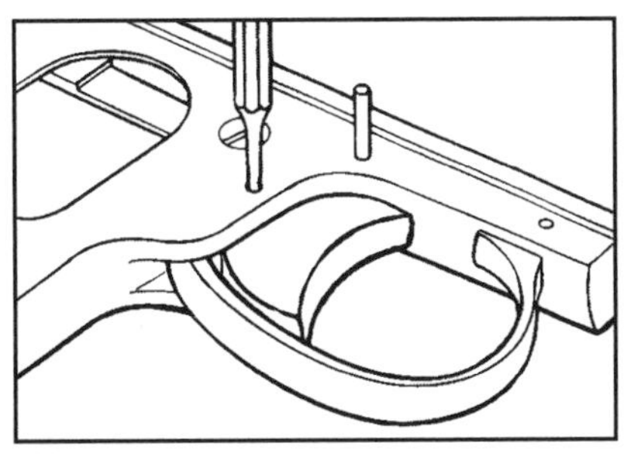

5 When reassembling trigger guard (48), insert the front tang into the frame with the front guard pin (17) out. Push the rear end of the guard into place and insert the trigger guard hinge screw (19) through the frame and through the hole in the trigger guard. Then pull the front tang down slightly and drive the front guard pin (17) into place.

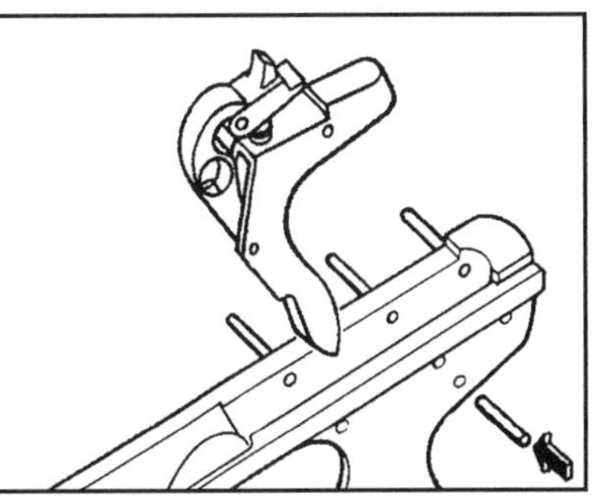

6 The sear (20), sear spring (25), sear spring follower (24), grip safety (27), magazine safety (32), and magazine safety spring assembly parts (28) (29) (30), must all be assembled together as shown and held together with the magazine safety pin (31). This assembly can then be easily installed in the frame as a unit. Line up the grip safety hinge pin (26) and then drive in the others.

HECKLER & KOCH P9S PISTOL

PARTS LEGEND

1. Receiver
2. Catch
3. Spring for catch
4. Trigger
5. Trigger spring
6. Cylindrical pin
7. Barrel clamp
8. Compression spring for barrel clamp
9. Insert piece
10. Trigger guard
11. Lens head countersunk screw
12. Elastic buffer
13. Buffer housing
14. Support
15. Threaded insert
16. Safety latch
17. Catch lever, assembled
18. Pull bar
19. Trigger bar
20. Hammer
21. Indicator pin
22. Disconnector, assembled
23. Axle for hammer
24. Compression spring for shank
25. Magazine catch
26. Angle lever
27. Cocking lever
28. Bearing plate, left
29. Countersunk screw for bearing plate
30. Intermediate lever
31. Bearing plate, right
32. Elbow spring for cocking lever, angle lever and intermediate lever
33. Spring for pull bar
34. Slide with sights
35. Front sight
36. Safety catch
37. Barrel
38. Compression spring for barrel
39. Bolt head, complete
40. Bolt head carrier
41. Catch bolt
42. Compression spring
43. Set screw
44. Compression spring for locking catch
45. Pressure pin
46. Pin
47. Compression spring for locking catch
48. Locking catch
49. Cylindrical pin
50. Firing pin
51. Compression spring
52. Grip
53. Lens head countersunk screw
54. Lens head countersunk screw
55. Magazine housing
56. Follower
57. Follower spring
58. Support for follower spring
59. Magazine floor plate

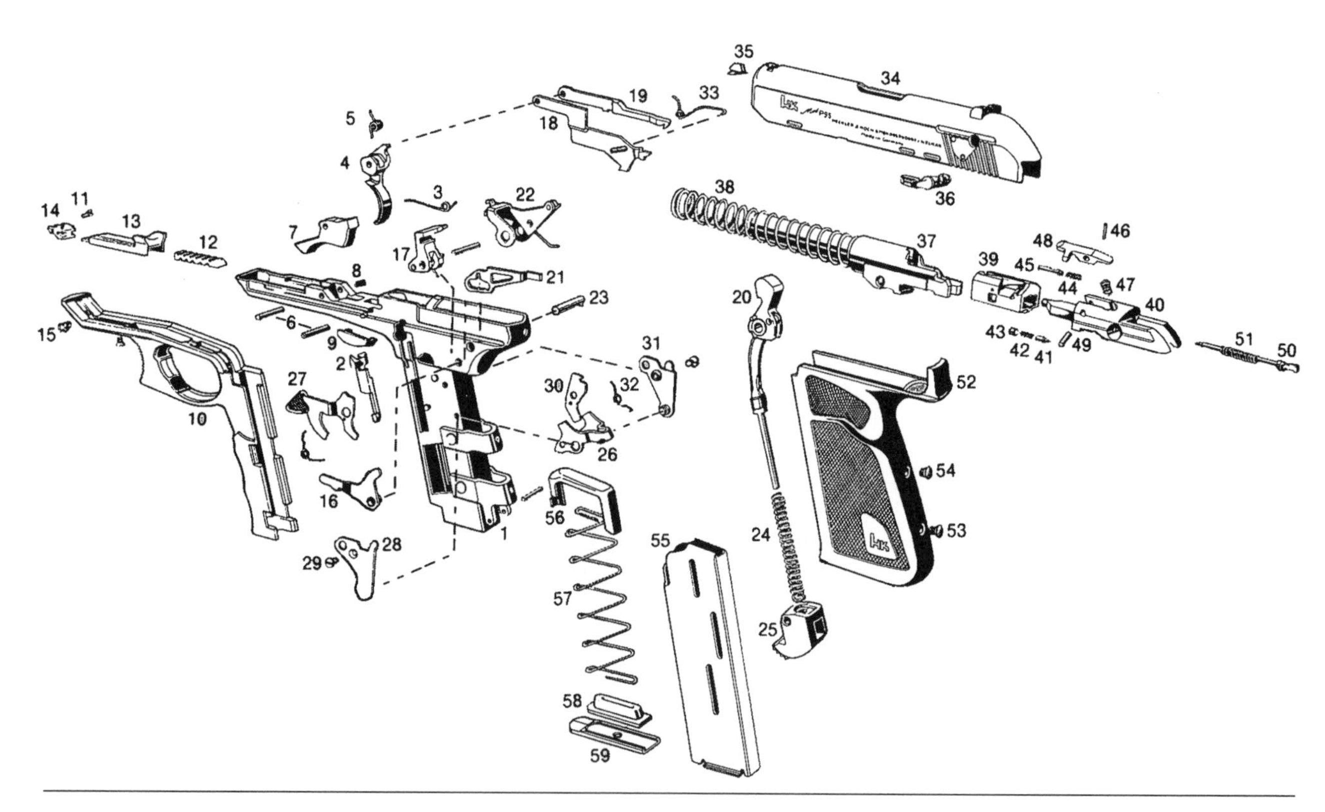

The introduction of Heckler & Koch's P9S in 1972 helped open the U.S. market to a new kind of pistol — the modern military/police semiautomatic. The manufacturing techniques used to construct the P9S and its successors, the P7 and VP 70Z, were vastly different from those used in making familiar sidearms like the M1911 Colt or Walther P38.

The P9S is made almost entirely of precision steel stampings by automatic machinery. Hand fitting is minimized by extensive use of alloy stampings and plastic parts.

Like most H&K products, the P9S operates on the delayed blowback principle, with the delay provided by roller bearings which protrude through two holes on either side of the bolt. The bearings rest in recesses in the barrel extension. The barrel is fixed to the frame and does not move during firing.

When the P9S is fired, the bearings hold the action shut until they are rolled from their recesses. This keeps the slide forward until the bullet has left the barrel. The bolt and slide assembly continues fully to the rear, ejecting the spent case and cocking the hammer. As the slide moves forward, it strips a cartridge from the magazine and chambers it for firing.

When the breech closes, the bolt face stops on contact with the rear of the chamber and the slide continues forward a short distance, causing the angled surfaces of the locking piece to force the bearings into the recesses in the barrel extension.

Among the P9S's advanced features is a lever on the left side of the grip, which performs several functions. The lever is raised to lock the slide open, and pressed down to release the slide. When the pistol is uncocked, it can be cocked for a single-action shot by firmly pressing down on the same lever. The gun can be uncocked by pressing down on the lever, pulling the trigger while maintaining pressure on the lever and gradually releasing the lever. This operation should be performed only with the safety applied.

The P9S has two added "safety" features. When the pistol is cocked, a small pin protrudes from the end of the slide. A loaded chamber is indicated by a raised extractor. The pin and extractor can be seen by day or felt at night, making it easy to determine the condition of the P9S at any time.

The safety on the P9S is located on the left-hand side of the slide. When it is pulled down, a white dot shows, indicating the gun is safe. When the safety lever is pushed up, a red dot shows that the gun is ready to be fired.

DISASSEMBLY

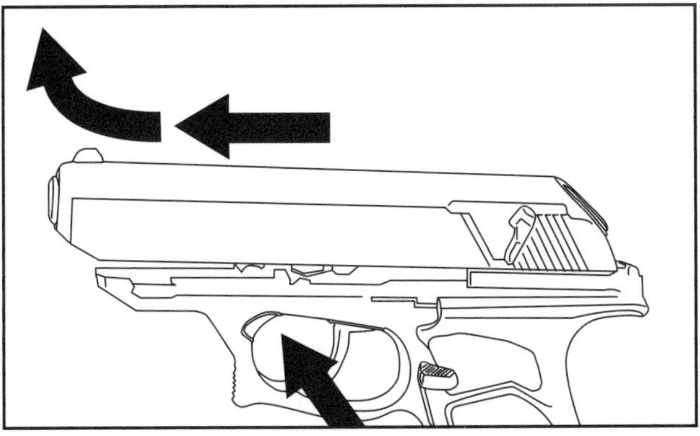

1 Remove the magazine by pressing the magazine catch to the rear and withdrawing the magazine. Retract the slide to ensure the chamber is empty.

Release the slide, allowing it to return to the forward position. Hold the pistol in one hand, using the thumb of the other hand to press the barrel clamp inside the trigger guard upward and push the slide/barrel assembly forward and lift it up and off the receiver. This may be done while the pistol is cocked or uncocked, on safe or off.

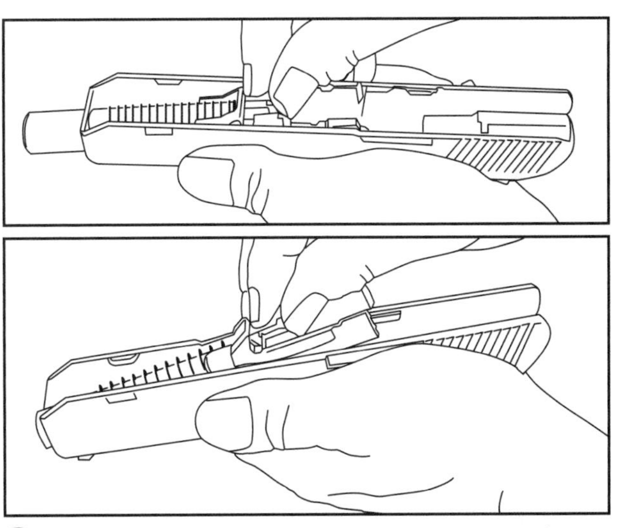

2 The barrel may be removed from the slide by pushing it forward against the pressure of the recoil spring, then lifting the rear of the barrel when it comes free of engagement with the bolt head. The barrel can then be allowed to come to the rear and out.

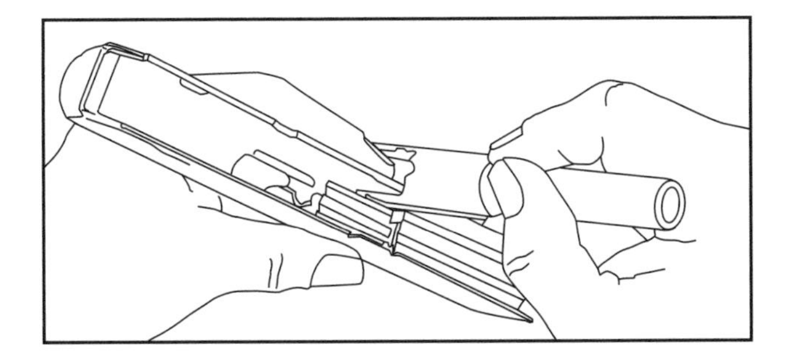

3 The bolt head may be removed by using the barrel extension tang as a tool. The tang is inserted at the right rear of the bolt head, between the bolt head and the slide rail. The bolt head locking catch is depressed, freeing the bolt head from the bolt proper.

The bolt head may now be lifted out of the slide. Further disassembly for cleaning or maintenance is not required.

HECKLER & KOCH USP 40 PISTOL

PARTS LEGEND

1. Exterior spring
2. Extractor
3. Roll pin
4. Front sight
5. Front sight (7.4mm) (not shown)
6. Rear sight
7. Barrel
8. Slide
9. Firing pin spring
10. Firing pin
11. Firing pin block spring
12. Firing pin block
13. Recoil spring
    13A. Front recoil spring retainer
    13B. Snap ring
14. Buffer spring retainer
15. Buffer spring
16. Recoil spring retainer
17. Recoil spring guide rod
    17A. Recoil/buffer spring assembly
18. Roll pin
19. Slide release
20. Trigger bar
21. Trigger bar detent
22. Trigger bar detent spring
23. Disconnector
24. Sear axle
25. Catch
    25A. Control latch
26. Detent plate
27. Shaped spring (slide release)
28. Flat spring
29. Hammer
30. Hammer, bobbed
31. Cyl. pin
32. Hammer axle
33. Control lever
34. Sear
    34A. Tube
35. Roll pin
36. Detent slide
37. Compression slide
38. Frame
39. Trigger rebound spring
40. Trigger axle
41. Trigger
42. Magazine release
43. Magazine release spring
44. Hammer strut
45. Hammer spring
46. Lanyard loop insert
47. Lanyard loop insert pin

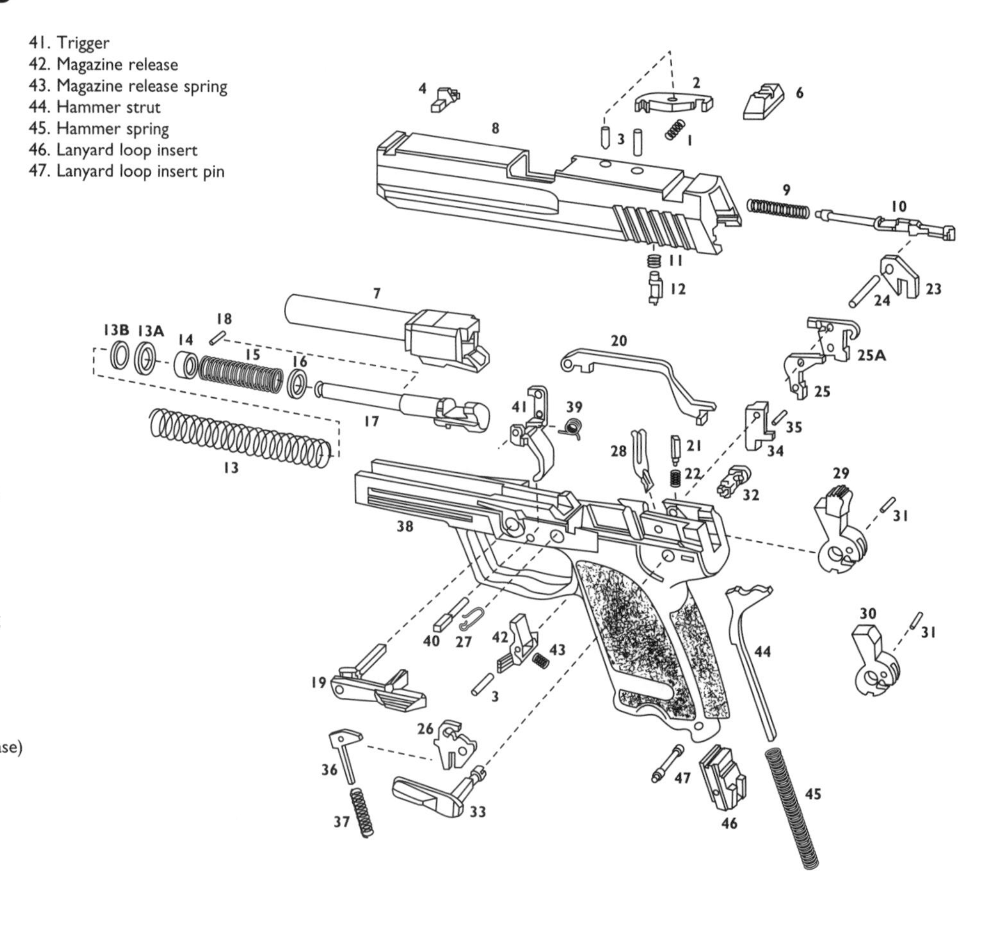

The Hechler & Koch USP (Universal Self-Loading Pistol), designed by H&K engineer Helmut Weldle, was designed to incorporate features required by potential U.S. law enforcement and military customers. The USP's controls were influenced by American designs such as the Government Model 1911 pistol.

USPs are manufactured with a fiber-reinforced polymer frame which is reinforced by stainless steel inserts at areas that must withstand friction and stress. The barrel features a polygonal bore and the pistol's one-piece, machined steel slide incorporates universal mounting grooves to permit easy installation of accessories. The USP is made with a modified Browning-type action with a special recoil reduction system that accepts a wide range of ammunition types and requires no special adjustments. The control lever, a combination safety and de-cocking lever, is frame mounted. The internal components of the USP are designed on a modular concept that allows the control lever function to be switched from the left to the right side of the frame. The firing mode can be switched from combination double-action and single-action to double action only. The USP is available in three calibers: 9mm, .40 S&W and .45 ACP.

DISASSEMBLY

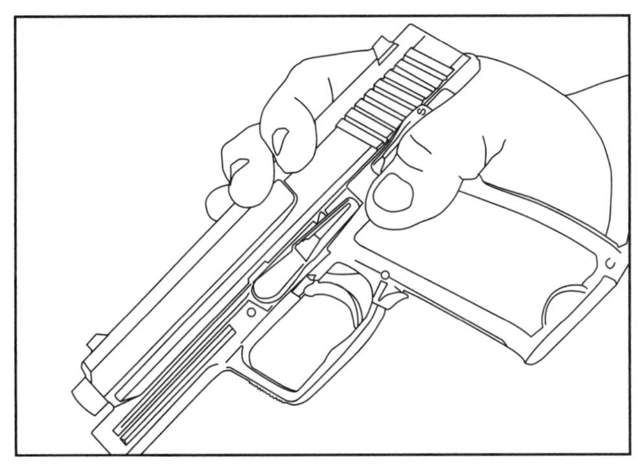

1 Depress the slide release and allow the slide to move forward. Using the firing hand, retract and hold the slide to the rear so that he axle of the slide release is visible through the recess in the left side of the slide.

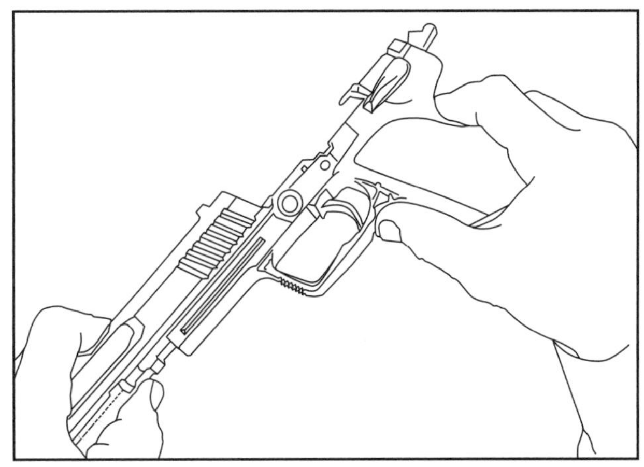

2 With the non-firing hand, completely remove the slide release from the left side of the frame by pressing on it from the side of the frame. CAUTION: Hold the recoil/buffer assembly in place while removing the slide from the frame. If not, this assembly could be released under spring tension and could possibly cause injury to personnel, or become damaged or lost. Remove the slide with barrel and recoil/buffer spring assembly by sliding it forward off of the frame.

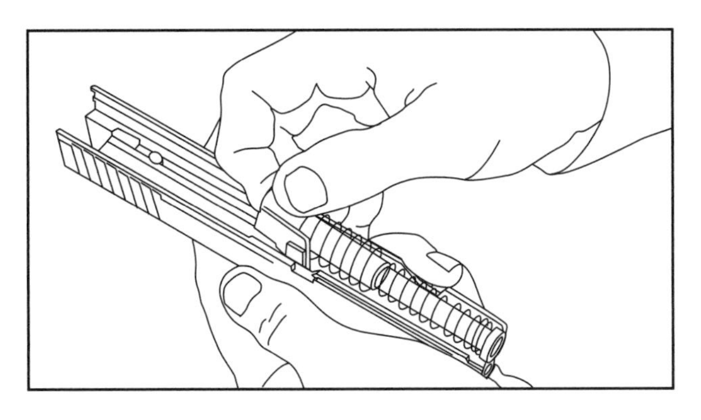

3 CAUTION: Carefully remove the recoil/buffer spring assembly from the barrel and slide by lifting up on the rear of the recoil spring guide rod. The entire assembly can now be lifted out of the slide. Remove the recoil spring from around the recoil spring guide rod. On USP models with "captive" recoil springs, disassembly is not recommended. Lift the rear of the barrel by the locking block and withdraw it from the slide. NOTE: Disassembly of the pistol is now complete. Only HK certified armorers should disassemble the pistol further.

HIGH STANDARD DURA-MATIC

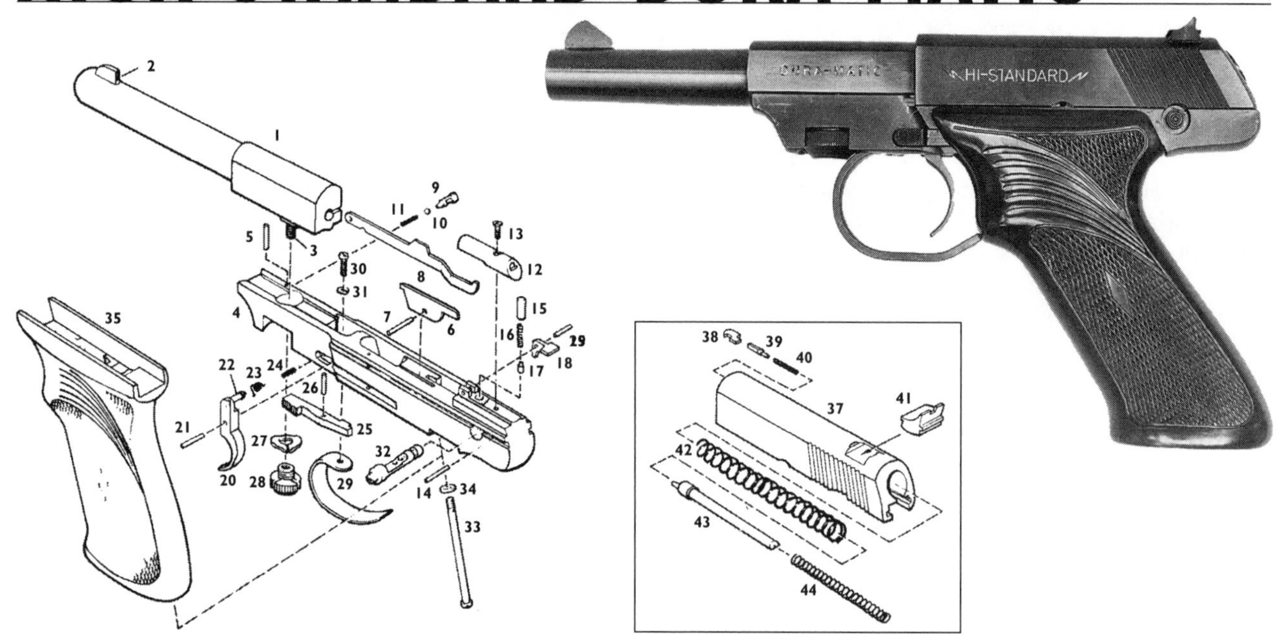

PARTS LEGEND

1. Barrel*
2. Front sight
3. Barrel set screw
4. Frame*
5. Barrel lock plunger pin *
6. Ejector
7. Ejector pin
8. Sear bar
9. Barrel lock plunger*
10. Barrel lock ball *
11. Barrel lock ball spring*
12. Striker sleeve
13. Striker sleeve screw
14. Striker sleeve screw locking pin
15. Sear plunger
16. Sear spring
17. Safety detent
18. Sear
19. Sear pin
20. Trigger
21. Trigger pin
22. Trigger pull pin
23. Trigger spring
24. Magazine catch spring
25. Magazine catch
26. Magazine catch pin
27. Barrel nut lock washer*
28. Barrel nut*
29. Trigger guard
30. Trigger guard screw
31. Trigger guard screw lock washer
32. Safety*
33. Grip bolt
34. Grip bolt washer
35. Grip
36. Magazine (not shown)
37. Slide
38. Extractor
39. Extractor plunger
40. Extractor spring
41. Rear sight
42. Slide spring
43. Striker pin (firing pin)*
44. Striker spring

Parts marked * are not interchangeable between M-100 and M-101 models.

DISASSEMBLY

Press in magazine catch (25) and withdraw magazine from grip (35). Draw slide (37) rearward and lock open by moving safety (32) to left. Safety acts as slide lock [safety is "on" when red enamel on right end of safety is not visible—safety locks striker pin (43) and slide]. Check chamber to be sure pistol is unloaded before proceeding with disassembly.

To remove barrel (1), depress barrel lock plunger (9) on front right side of frame (4). Unscrew barrel nut (28) and pull barrel up and out of its seat in frame. Slots in barrel nut permit use of coin or screwdriver for tightening or loosening nut. Barrel of M-101 is removed by unscrewing nut (28). A barrel lock is not provided in this model.

Move safety (32) to right, or "off" position, to release slide (37) and draw slide forward until its rear end is about ½" forward of rear of frame. Then, while holding the slide, pull the trigger to disengage sear plunger (15) from striker pin (43). Draw slide off frame and remove slide spring (42), striker pin (43), and striker spring (44) from rear of slide. Note striker pin and spring rest inside of slide spring and that flat surface of striker pin faces slot in bottom of slide.

To remove grip from frame, unscrew grip bolt (33), and remove bolt and its washer (34) from bottom of grip.

The above constitutes sufficient disassembly for normal cleaning purposes. Lock parts within frame are easily removed, but disassembly further than that given here is not recommended except for repair or replacement of parts.

The High Standard Model M-100 Dura-Matic pistol was introduced in 1954 by the High-Standard Manufacturing Corp., and was dropped from production in 1969.

Made to sell at a moderate price, this pistol was a blowback-operated, striker-fired pistol chambered for regular or high speed .22 Long Rifle contained in a 10-round magazine. It was designed for informal target shooting or plinking. A choice of 4½- and 6½-inch barrel lengths was available, The sights were fixed but the rear sight could be drifted to the right or left to adjust for windage.

The Dura-Matic's cross-bolt safety locks the slide, immobilizing the striker. When the striker is cocked, a red dot is visible on the rear of the striker at the end of the striker sleeve.

An improved barrel locking system for this pistol was introduced in 1957, designated M-101. Sears & Roebuck's J.C. Higgins Model 80 was mechanically identical to the M-101.

HIGH STANDARD MODEL D-100

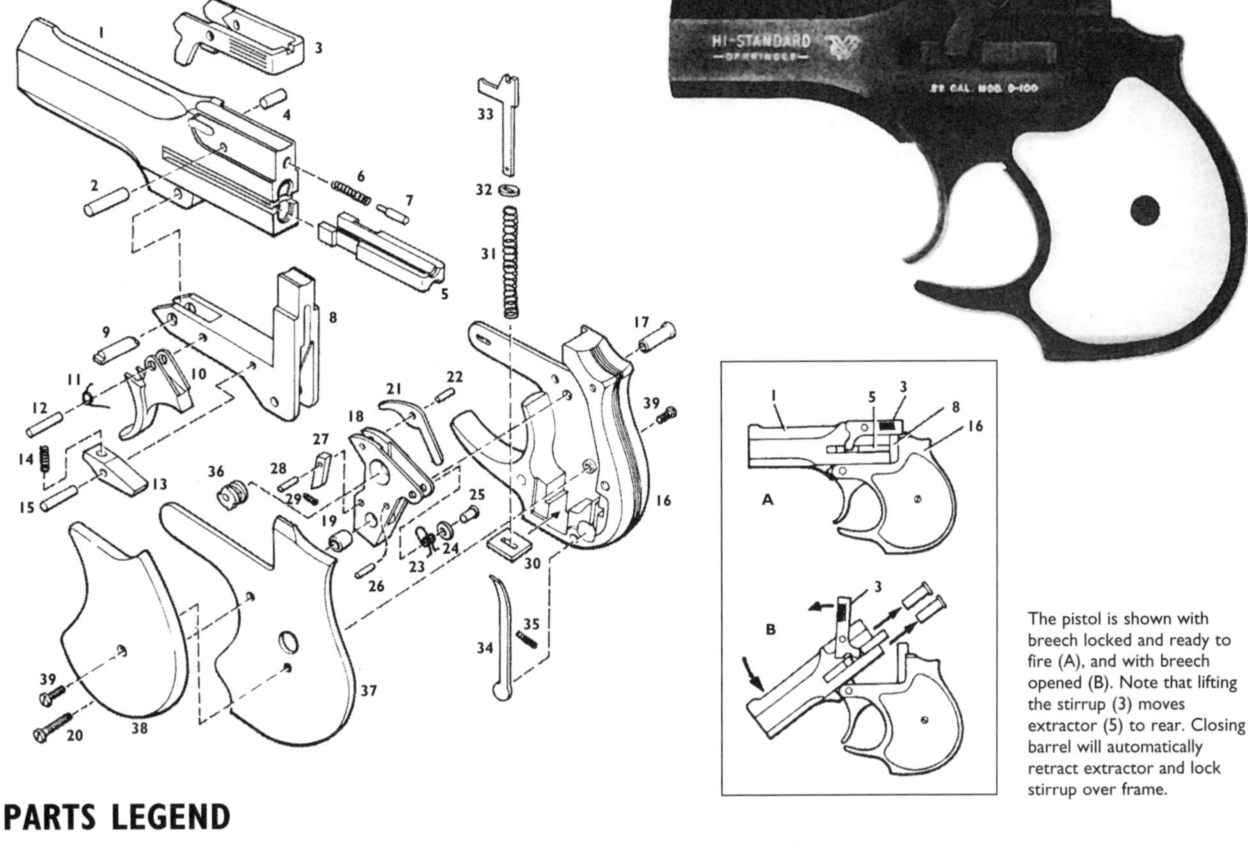

The pistol is shown with breech locked and ready to fire (A), and with breech opened (B). Note that lifting the stirrup (3) moves extractor (5) to rear. Closing barrel will automatically retract extractor and lock stirrup over frame.

PARTS LEGEND

1. Barrel
2. Stirrup pivot pin
3. Stirrup
4. Stirrup roller
5. Extractor
6. Stirrup plunger spring
7. Stirrup plunger
8. Frame
9. Barrel pivot pin
10. Trigger
11. Trigger spring
12. Trigger pivot pin
13. Hammer safety block
14. Hammer safety block spring
15. Hammer safety block pin
16. Housing
17. Hammer pivot screw
18. Hammer
19. Hammer pivot sleeve
20. Cover plate screw
21. Striker
22. Striker pivot pin
23. Striker spring
24. Striker spring spacer washer
25. Striker spring retaining pin
26. Hammer strut pin
27. Hammer pawl
28. Hammer pawl pin
29. Hammer pawl spring
30. Hammer spring abutment
31. Hammer spring
32. Hammer strut washer
33. Hammer strut
34. Actuator
35. Actuator spring
36. Ratchet
37. Cover plate
38. Grips (2) (left grip only is shown.)
39. Grip screws (2)

DISASSEMBLY

Lift stirrup (3) and tip barrel (I) to expose breech. Be sure pistol is unloaded.

Remove grip screws (39) and grips (38). Cover plate (37) over left side of housing (16) is removed by removing cover plate screw (20). Action is then exposed and is readily disassembled. Lift out actuator (34), taking care not to lose actuator spring (35). Compress hammer spring (31) to permit removal of spring, hammer strut (33), and abutment (30) assembly from housing. Hammer (18) assembly may be removed intact from housing.

Barrel (1) assembly can be removed from frame (8) by removing barrel pivot pin (9). Extractor (5) is removed from barrel to rear. Remove stirrup pivot pin (2) and remove stirrup (3) from barrel.

Due to simplicity of design of Model D-100, removal of grips and cover plate is sufficient disassembly for normal cleaning. Disassembly of hammer components from housing is not recommended unless for repairs.

The High Standard Model D-100 pistol was introduced in 1962. Manufactured by the High Standard Manufacturing Corp., of Hamden, Connecticut, the Model D-100 has two, over-under, enbloc barrels that tip down for loading. It is chambered for the .22 Long Rifle cartridge and the lock mechanism is of hammerless, trigger cocking type with a ratchet to discharge the cartridges alternately. The breech of the D-100 is opened by lifting the stirrup hinged at the top of the barrel assembly. The barrels can then be tipped down to expose the breech. Lifting the stirrup to its upward limit cams the extractor to the rear and if done smartly throws the cartridges cases clear. The D-100 and its .22 WMR stablemate, D-101 remained in production until High Standard ceased manufacturing operations in 1985.

HIGH STANDARD MODEL HB PISTOL

PARTS LEGEND

A. Recoil spring stop
B. Recoil spring
C. Recoil spring guide
D. Extractor
E. Extractor plunger
F. Extractor spring
G. Recoil spring stop pin
H. Extractor pin
I. Slide
J. Assembly lock screw
K. Firing pin spring
L. Firing pin
M. Rear sight
N. Assembly lock plunger
O. Assembly lock
P. Firing pin retaining screw
Q. Mainspring guide
R. Mainspring
S. Slide stop
T. Slide stop plunger
U. Slide stop spring
V. Takedown latch
W. Sear pin
X. Hammer pin
V. Hammer strut pin
Z. Hammer
AA. Hammer strut
BB. Sear plunger
CC. Sear spring
DD. Frame
EE. Magazine
FF. Magazine catch
GG. Magazine catch spring
HH. Magazine catch pin
II. Safety catch screw
JJ. Safety catch
KK. Side plate
LL. Trigger bar spring
MM. Trigger bar
NN. Sear
OO. Trigger
PP. Trigger pin
QQ. Pull pin
RR. Trigger spring plunger
SS. Trigger spring
TT. Barrel pin
UU. Barrel
VV. Grip screw
WW. Left-hand grip

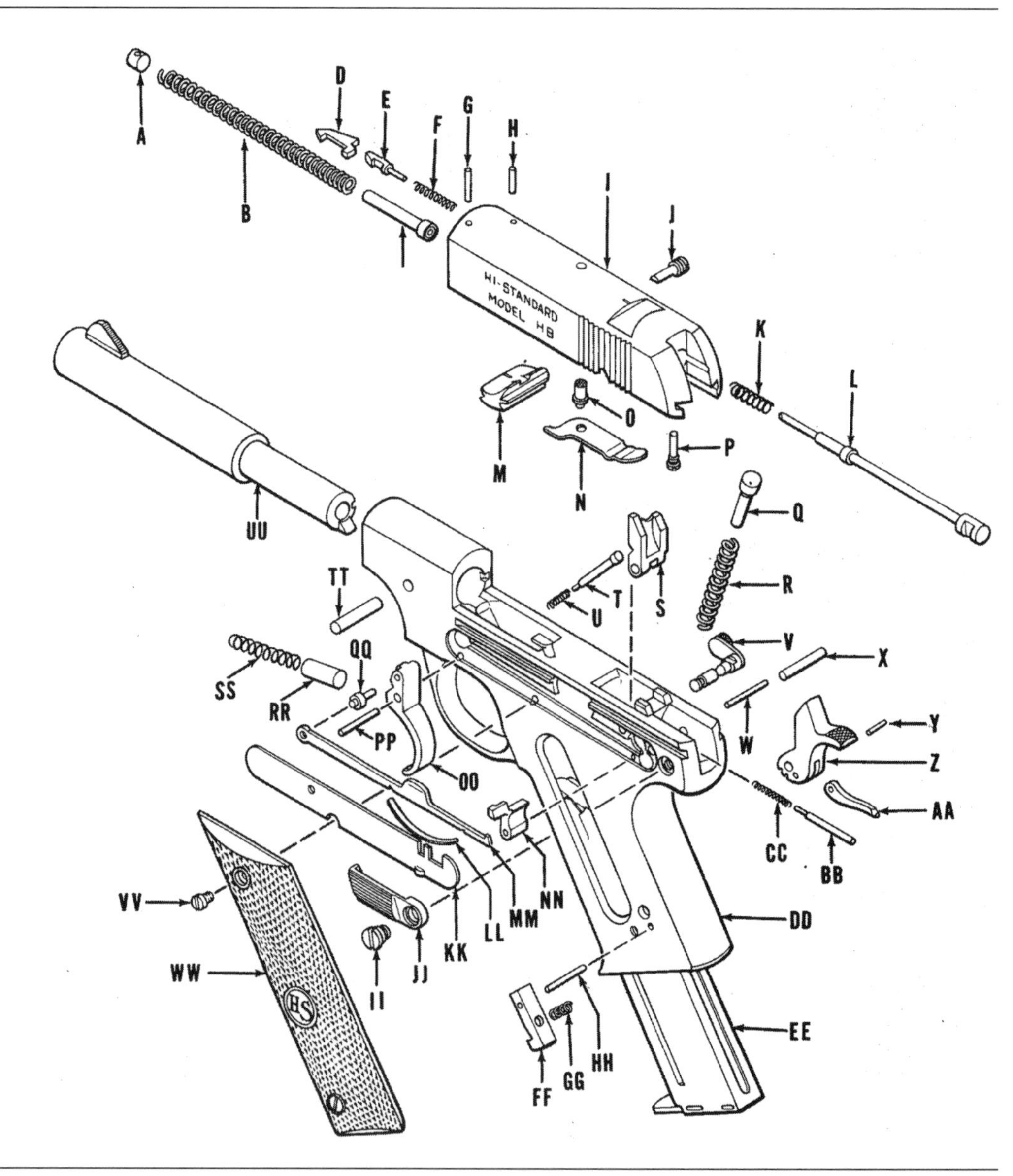

For years, until shortly before the firm closed its doors in 1985, High Standard manufactured the widest range of .22 rimfire self-loading pistols of any handgun maker.

Not only did High Standard produce a great variety of guns, they kept pace with the times and demands of shooters and handgun enthusiasts.

High Standard started production of their first pistol during the great depression. This gun, the Model B, looked a great deal like the defunct Hartford pistol produced between 1929 and 1930. But, it was well made and priced a good deal below its competitors, so it caught on.

Following the Model B, High Standard kept up a steady stream of variations to delight the market and confuse the gunsmith.

The Model HB, shown here, is really the original Model B with a external hammer added. It makes an ideal plinking pistol for it is comparatively small and compact. Its external hammer is an excellent safety feature, since you can tell at a glance whether the gun is cocked. As a target gun it suffers from a short grip, but as a fishing or hunting companion the reverse angle on the grip makes for easy removal from a coat or trouser pocket. With a 4½-inch barrel it weighs only 31 ounces, light enough to stick in your pocket and forget about. Like other, current, .22 caliber pistols, High Standards are blowback operated, since the .22 cartridge does not develop enough pressure to require a more involved lock breech mechanism, High Standard pistols are generally well made and finished. While they are easy to repair, care must be taken in ordering parts, since in the hammer gun series there are three different hammers and five different sears.

In 1993, the High Standard Manufacturing Company, Inc. of Houston, Texas acquired the company's assets and resumed production of High Standard pistols in 1994.

DISASSEMBLY

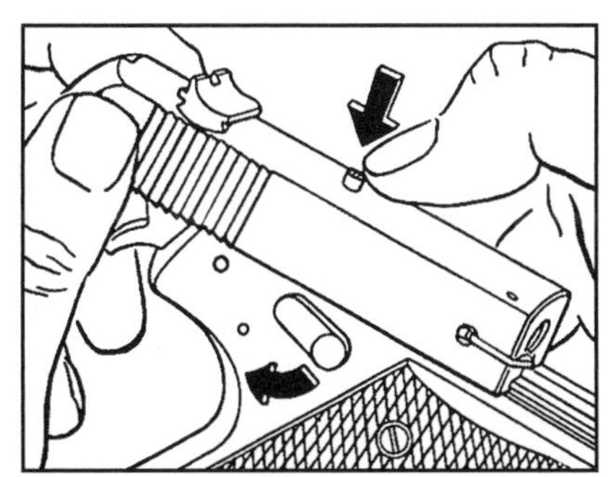

1 Remove the magazine, check the chamber to be sure it is empty. Pull the slide (I) to the rear until it stops. Depress the assembly lock plunger (N) and push the slide forward. Now depress the takedown latch (V) and pull the slide back off the frame.

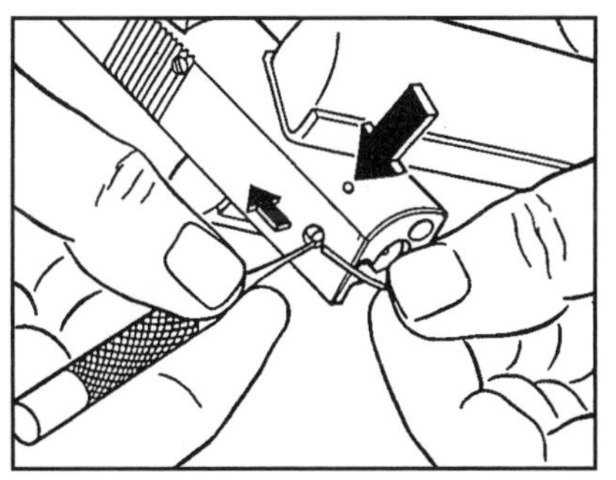

2 To remove the extractor (D), first remove the extractor retaining pin (H). Then insert a thin screwdriver or pointed tool, as shown. Push the extractor plunger (E) back into the slide. Now remove the extractor (D) by rotating it in toward the firing pin.

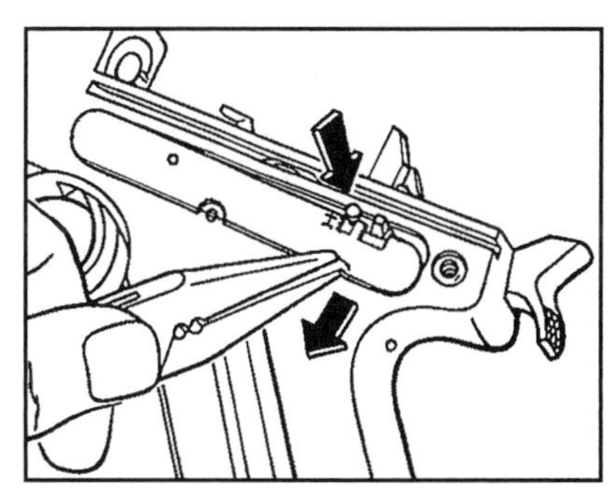

3 Never remove the takedown latch (V) while the slide (I) is on the frame, as it would cause a condition that is difficult to remedy. The side plate (KK) retains the takedown latch (V) on some models and must be removed as shown, to free the latch.

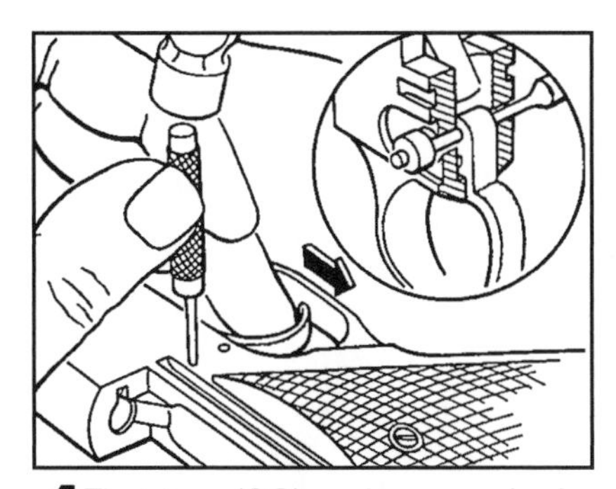

4 The trigger (OO) can be removed only after the pull pin (QQ) has been driven out. Insert a thin drift pin into the hole above the trigger pin. Move the trigger a bit until the drift is seated in the hole in the trigger. Drive out the pull pin (QQ), then the trigger pin (PP).

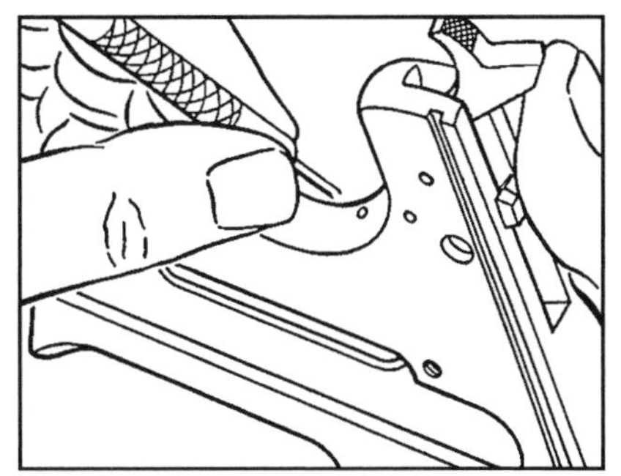

5 Because the mainspring is powerful, it must be kept in check when removing the hammer (Z) and sear (NN). To do so, cock the hammer and insert a thin pin into the hole in the back strap. Release the hammer and drive out the hammer in (X) and the sear pin (W).

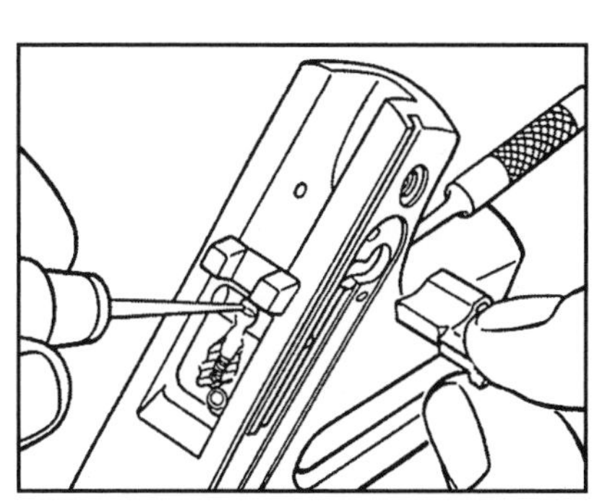

6 To replace the sear, push the sear spring (CC) and plunger (BB) back into the frame far enough to be caught through the opening for the takedown lever. While holding the plunger as shown, replace the sear (NN) and sear pin (W).

HIGH STANDARD SENTINEL PISTOL

PARTS LEGEND

1. Barrel
2. Frame
3. Rear sight
4. Front sight set screw
5. Front sight
6. Barrel pin
7. Ejector rod
8. Crane
9. Hammer pivot pin
10. Cylinder bushing
11. Cylinder
12. Cylinder lock plunger spring
13. Cylinder lock plunger
14. Cylinder lock plunger pin
15. Link pivot pin
16. Cylinder stop spring
17. Cylinder stop
18. Hand spring
19. Hand
20. Trigger
21. Hammer safety stop
22. Trigger pivot pin
23. Ejector alignment dowel
24. Ejector
25. Grip
26. Trigger guard
27. Grip lock washer
28. Grip screw
29. Hammer
30. Hammer pawl spring
31. Hammer pawl
32. Hammer pawl pin
33. Hammer sleeve
34. Trigger spring
35. Hammer spring guide
36. Hammer spring
37. Hand
38. Hammer
39. Hand spring
40. Trigger spring plunger
41. Trigger spring
42. Trigger

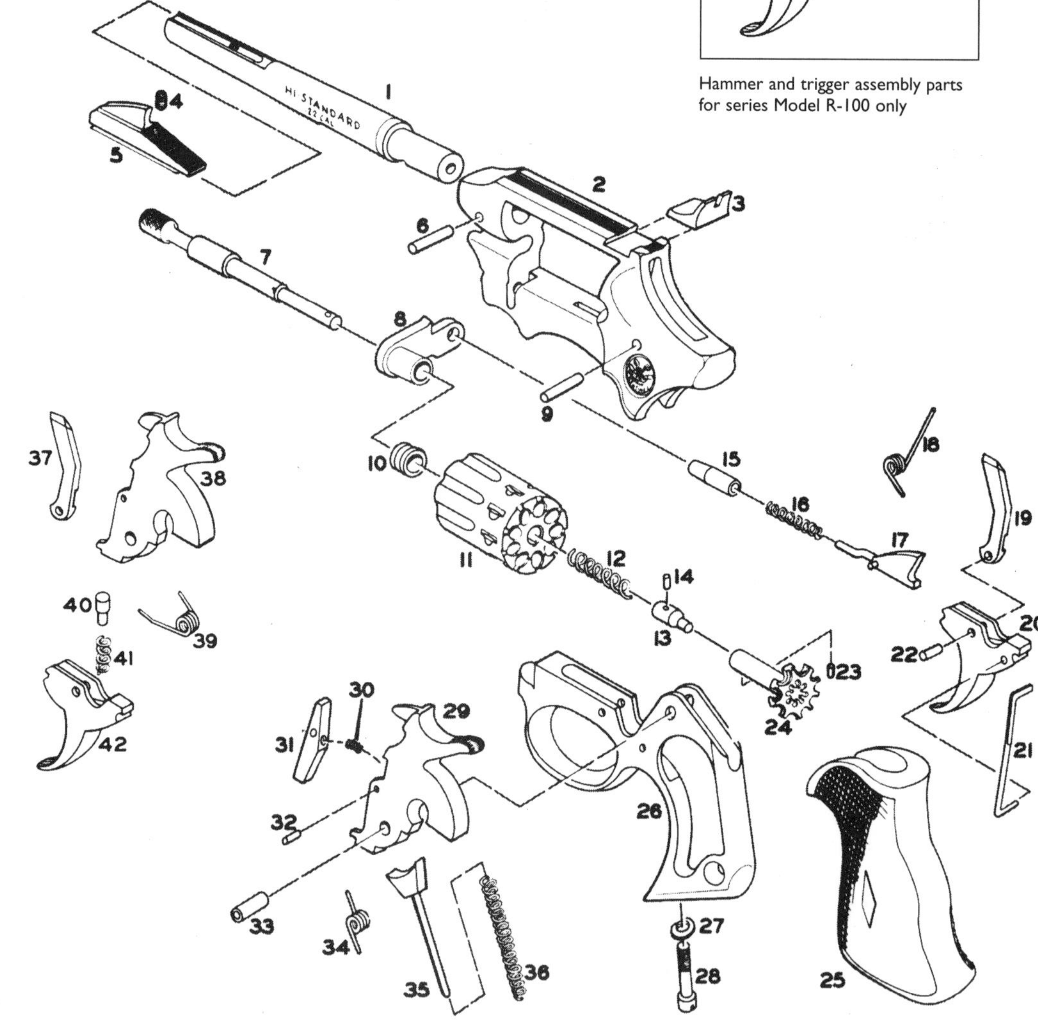

Hammer and trigger assembly parts for series Model R-100 only

The High Standard Sentinel, introduced in 1955 by the High Standard Manufacturing Corp., of Hamden, Connecticut, met the demand for an moderately priced, 9-shot, swing out cylinder, double-action revolver chambered for economical .22 rimfire cartridges. The Sentinel remained in High Standard's line until about 1974.

Modern in concept when introduced, the Sentinel featured a light weight frame of aluminum alloy with a barrel and cylinder of steel. It was designed for use with either regular or high-speed .22 Short, Long or Long Rifle cartridges, with chambers counterbored to surround the cartridge rims. Hammer and trigger are of case-hardened steel and virtually unbreakable coil springs are used throughout.

The hammer is of the rebounding type and the lock mechanism incorporates an automatic safety block to prevent accidental discharge should the gun be dropped on a hard surface.

The front sight is of the square-blade Patridge pattern. The square-notch rear sight can be adjusted for windage by tapping it from side to side in its transverse slot.

The Sentinel was offered with 2⅜-, 4-, and 6-inch barrel lengths and in several finishes including nickel plate and anodized turquoise, gold and pink as well as the traditional blue. Grips were of brown or white checkered plastic, with the latter also available in smooth finish to simulate ivory.

For several years, Sears, Roebuck & Co. sold a variant of the Sentinel under its own brand name.

DISASSEMBLY

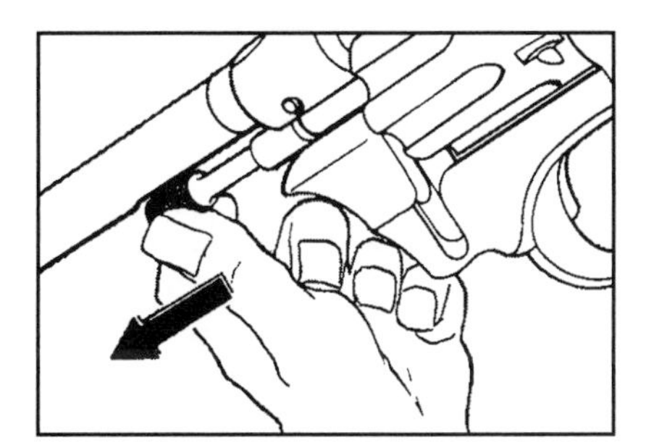

1 To swing out cylinder (11) as for for loading. Pull ejector rod (7) forward and thence left. Check cylinder to ensure that the revolver is not loaded.

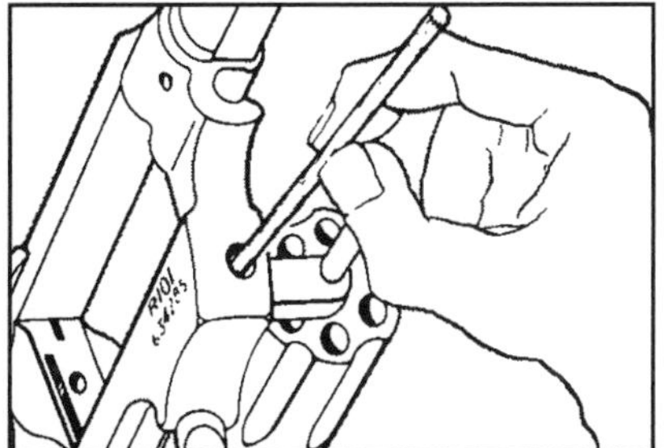

2 Next insert a small hardwood dowel into hole in front portion of frame (2) to depress link pivot pin (15). Pull cylinder assembly left until wood dowel prevents any further movement left. Withdraw dowel and place thumb over hole in frame. This will prevent cylinder stop spring (16) and link pivot pin from flying out of the hole as cylinder assembly is separated from the frame

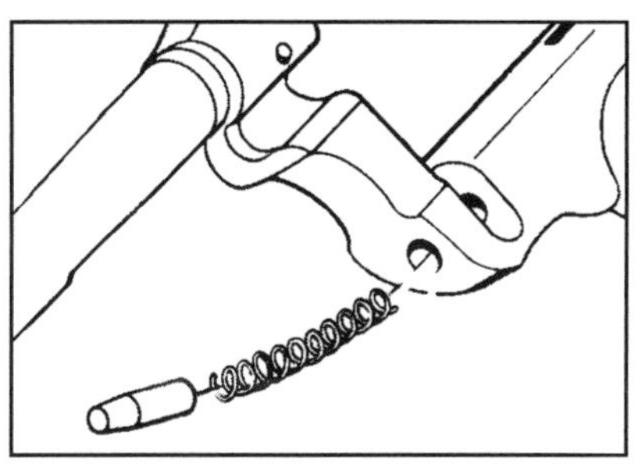

3 Up-end the revolver and shake out the link pivot pin and cylinder stop spring

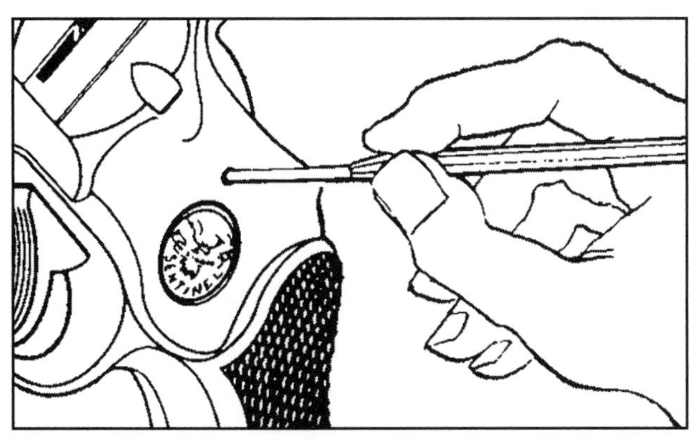

4 Loosen or remove grip screw (28) and drift out hammer pivot pin (9) with small flat-nosed punch. Entire trigger guard (26) and assembly may now be removed from frame. All internal parts are now exposed. Exercise care when executing this portion of the disassembly that cylinder stop (17) does not drop out and become lost

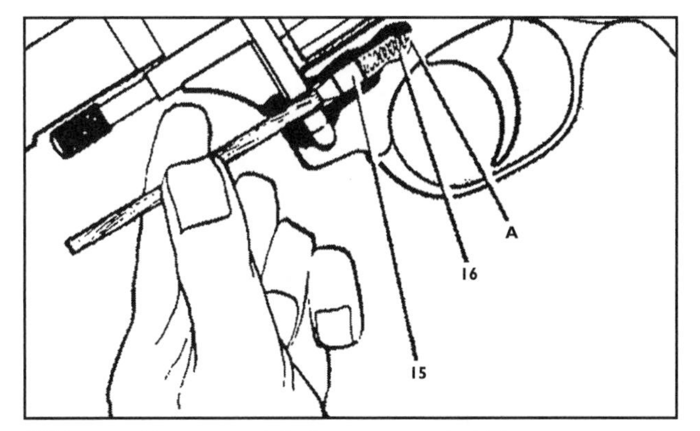

5 Reassembly is accomplished in reverse order. When reinserting the cylinder stop spring (16) ensure that it slides onto arm portion (A) of cylinder stop; otherwise it becomes jammed and may be deformed

HIGH STANDARD SUPERMATIC TROPHY

PARTS LEGEND

1. Stabilizer
2. Stabilizer set screw (2)
3. Front sight
4. Front sight screw
5. Barrel
6. Driving spring plug
7. Driving spring
8. Extractor plunger
9. Extractor spring
10. Driving spring plunger
11. Driving spring plunger pin (2)
12. Extractor
13. Slide
14. Firing pin spring
15. Firing pin
16. Sear spring
17. Sear
18. Slide lock lever
19. Slide lock spring
20. Hammer
21. Hammer strut pin
22. Anti-backlash screw
23. Adjustable rear sight
24. Right bracket, short barrel weight
25. Right bracket, long barrel weight
26. Left bracket, short barrel weight
27. Left bracket, long barrel weight
28. Long barrel weight
29. Short barrel weight
30. Barrel weight screw (2)
31. Barrel takedown plunger
32. Barrel takedown plunger spring
33. Anti-backlash detent washer
34. Frame
35. Barrel takedown plunger pin
36. Trigger
37. Trigger pin
38. Sear bar and trigger pull pin assembly
39. Safety
40. Side plate
41. Side plate screw
42. Hammer strut anchor pin
43. Magazine catch pin
44. Magazine catch
45. Magazine catch spring
46. Right hand grip
47. Sear pin
48. Hammer pin
49. Sear bar spring
50. Safety spacer washer
51. Magazine
52. Sear adjustment screw plunger
53. Sear adjustment screw
54. Hammer spring
55. Hammer strut ring
56. Hammer strut
57. Grip screw (2)
58. Left handgrip

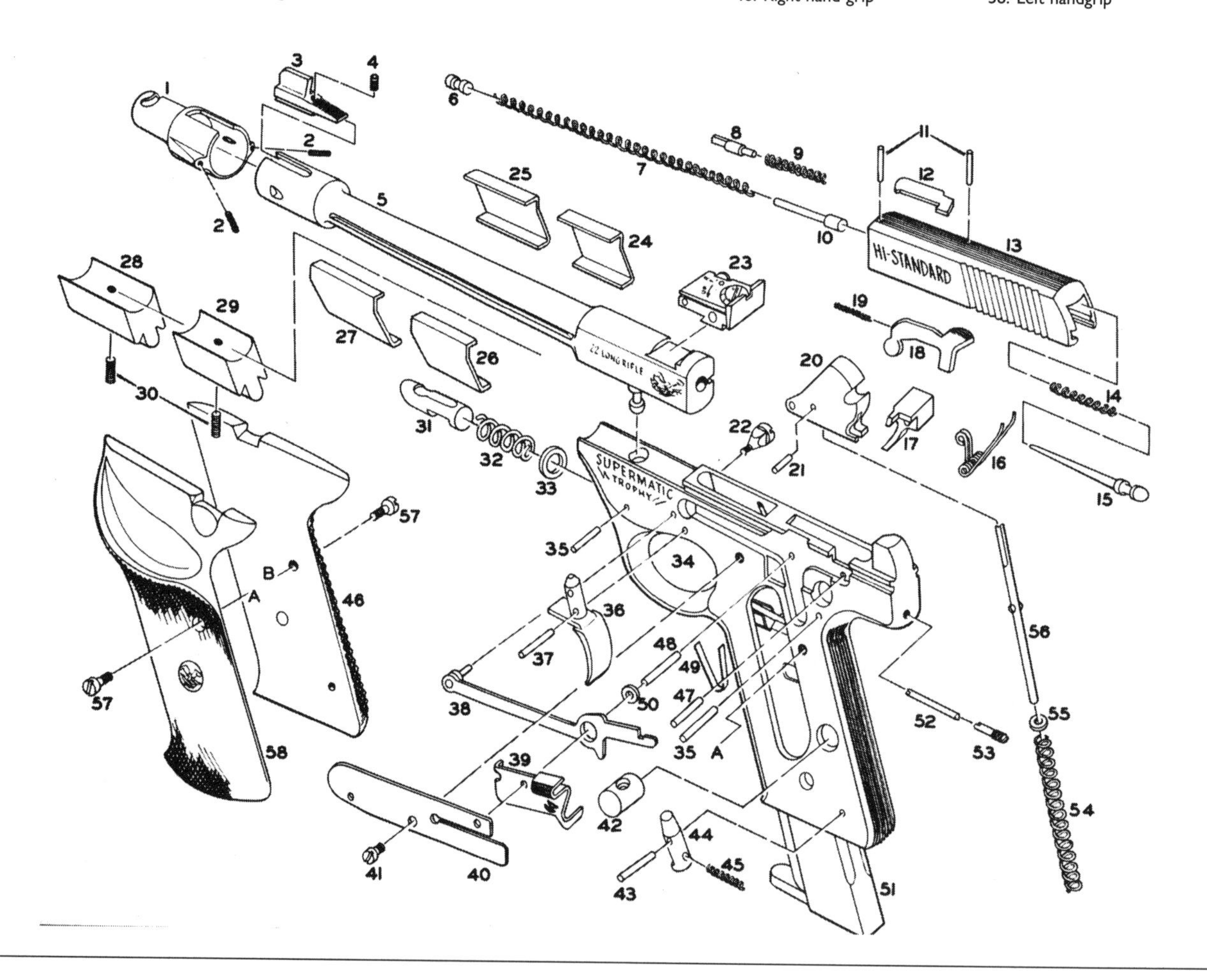

In the late summer of 1958 High Standard Manufacturing Corp. introduced four, 10-shot detachable magazine, .22 rimfire, self-loading pistols with detachable barrels and improved lockwork to provide crisp and uniform sear disengagement. These guns were designated Supermatic Trophy, Supermatic Citation, Olympic Citation and Supermatic Tournament.

The first three guns were available with 10-, 8- and 6¾-inch barrels. A fully adjustable rear sight was mounted on the slide of the 6¾-inch-barreled version and mounted on the breech ring of the 8- and 10-inch barrels. The detachable barrel stabilizer minimizes muzzle jump. The trigger is screw adjustable. The frame straps are grooved.

The Supermatic Trophy and Citation models were chambered for the .22 Long Rifle cartridge and conversion units was available to permit use of .22 Short cartridge. The Olympic Citation is chambered for .22 Short and is convertible to .22 Long Rifle by means of a factory installed conversion unit. The Supermatic Trophy is the deluxe model, featuring high polish blue finish, checkered walnut grips and gold plated trigger and safety button. Lettering is gold inlaid. The other models have checkered plastic grips, and triggers, and safety buttons are finished blue. Walnut grips are available at extra cost in lieu of the plastic grips.

The Supermatic Tournament, (.22 Long Rifle only), was available with 4½- or 6¾-inch barrel. The lockwork is nearly identical to that of the other models, but does not incorporate trigger pull adjustment. The barrels are not equipped with integral or detachable stabilizers. The fully adjustable rear sight is mounted on the slide. Grips are of checkered plastic.

Disassembly procedure for the four guns, all of which had been discontinued in favor of more advanced models by the 1970s, is substantially the same. High Standard ceased manufacturing operations in 1985 but, in 1993, High Standard Manufacturing Company, Inc. of Houston, Texas acquired the company's assets and resumed production of High Standard pistols in 1994.

DISASSEMBLY

1 To disassemble Supermatic Trophy pistol, first press magazine catch (44) and withdraw magazine (51). Pull back slide (13) and lock it in place by pushing up slide lock lever (18). At same time inspect gun to ensure that no cartridge remains in chamber. Next, move safety (39) to "On" position. This locks hammer (20) and sear (17), disconnects trigger (36), and completely separates sear bar (38) from sear. Grasp pistol as shown (left-handed persons should use a reversed grip) and depress barrel takedown plunger (31) with thumb. Lift barrel (5) out of its bedding with a straight upward motion. If, after extensive shooting, it becomes difficult to remove barrel by thumb pressure alone, press takedown plunger against a padded but solid object.

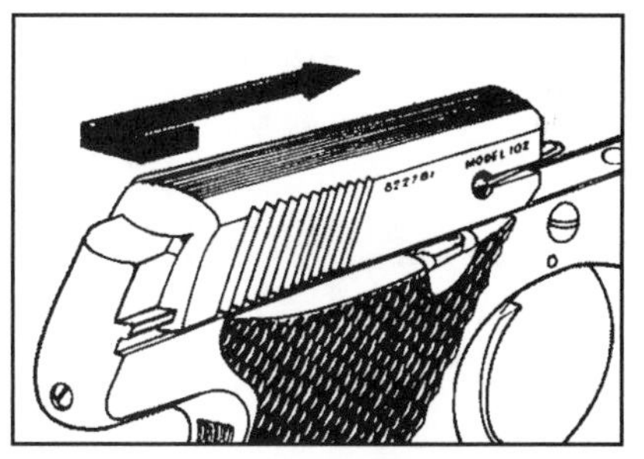

2 Continue disassembly by pulling back slide a short distance to release slide lock and ease slide forward off frame (34).

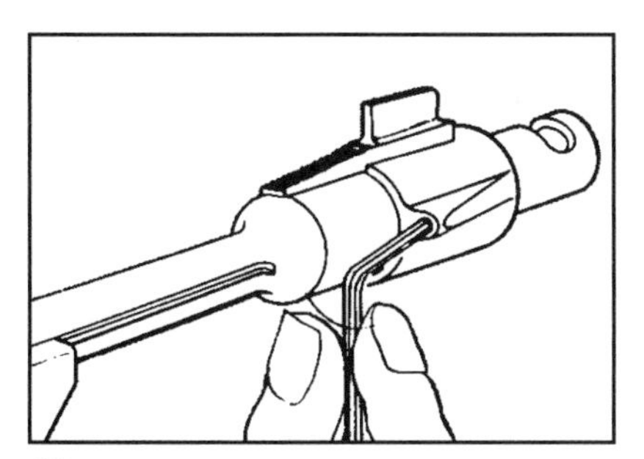

3 For top performance, stabilizer (1) should be removed and cleaned every 300 rounds. Clean with tool fumished by manufacturer. Remove stabilizer by inserting proper-size Allen wrench (provided with gun) into stabilizer set screws (2) and back them off until they are clear of engaging slots in muzzle end of barrel. Stabilizer will then slide off.

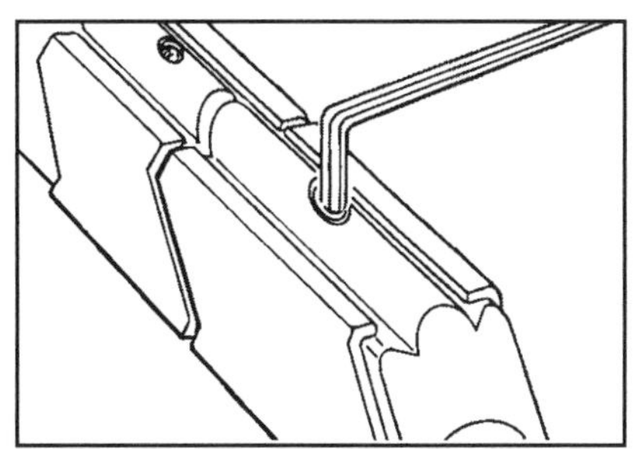

4 Forward weight and balance of gun may be adjusted by inserting proper-size Allen wrench (also provided with gun) into barrel weight set screw or screws (30) and loosening until either or both weights are movable within brackets (24 through 27). The weight may then be moved forward or backward as barrel groove permits. When optimum balance is achieved, tighten set screws with the wrench into detents provided.

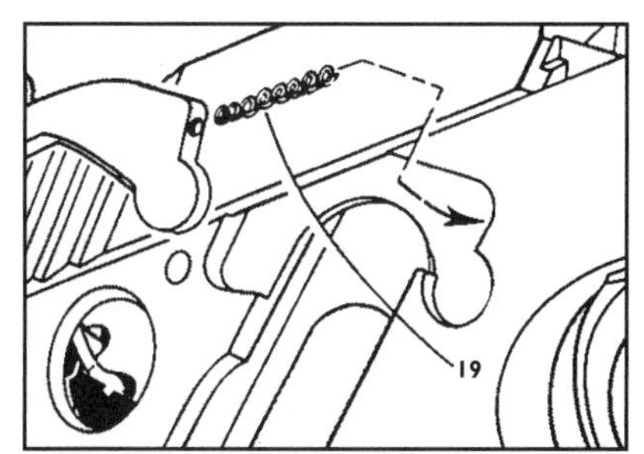

5 Should it become necessary to remove right grip (46) for replacement or exposure of working parts, slide lock lever (18) comes out very easily. Care must be exercised not to lose slide lock spring (19) as it is very small and hardly noticeable. When reinserting slide lock, make sure that this spring is properly seated in its hole in frame (34).

HIGH STANDARD VICTOR PISTOL

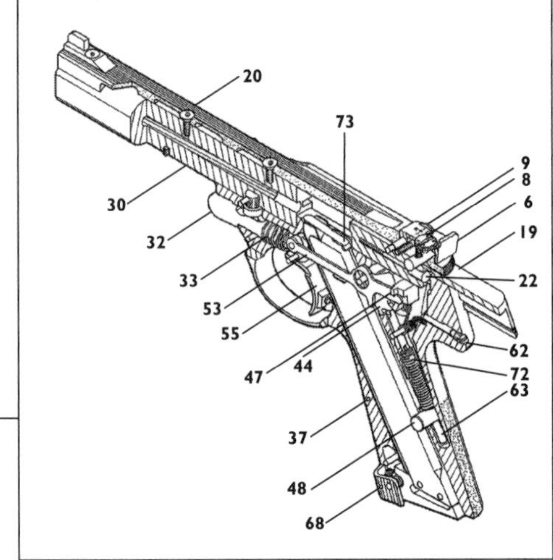

PARTS LEGEND

1. Rib screw, short (2)
2. Sight elevation spring (2)
3. Elevation plunger
4. Elevation detent plunger
5. Elevation ball (2)
6. Sight leaf
7. Windage spring
8. Elevation adjustment screw
9. Windage screw
10. Rib screw, long
11. Driving spring plug
12. Driving spring
13. Driving spring plunger
14. Extractor
15. Extractor plunger
16. Extractor spring
17. Driving spring plug pin
18. Firing pin retaining pin
*19. Slide
*20. Rib
21. Firing pin spring
22. Firing pin
23. Grip, right
24. Sight leaf pivot pin
25. Windage detent plunger spring
26. Windage detent plunger
27. Sight, rear cross member
28. Grip washer (2)
29. Grip screw (2)
*30. Barrel
31. Barrel filler screw (2)
32. Barrel takedown plunger
33. Barrel takedown plunger spring
34. Barrel stud retaining pin
35. Barrel takedown plunger pin
36. Barrel stud
37. Frame
*38. Ejector
39. Slide lock spring
40. Slide lock lever
41. Hammer strut pin
42. Sear pin
43. Sear pin retaining ring
*44. Hammer
45. Sear spring, adjustable
46. Sear spring leg retainer
*47. Sear
48. Hammer strut anchor pin
49. Magazine follower
50. Magazine button
51. Magazine spring
*52. Safety
*53. Sear bar and trigger pull pin assy.
54. Trigger stop screw
*55. Trigger
56. Trigger pin
57. Hammer pin
*58. Sear bar spring
59. Sear spring pin
60. Grip alignment pin
*61. Sear adjustment screw plunger
*62. Sear adjustment screw
63. Hammer strut
64. Hammer strut ring
65. Side plate screw
66. Side plate
67. Grip, left
68. Magazine catch
69. Magazine catch roller pin
70. Magazine catch spring
71. Magazine catch roller and spring guide assy.
72. Hammer spring
73. Magazine, complete

* High Standard recommends factory fitting of replacement part.

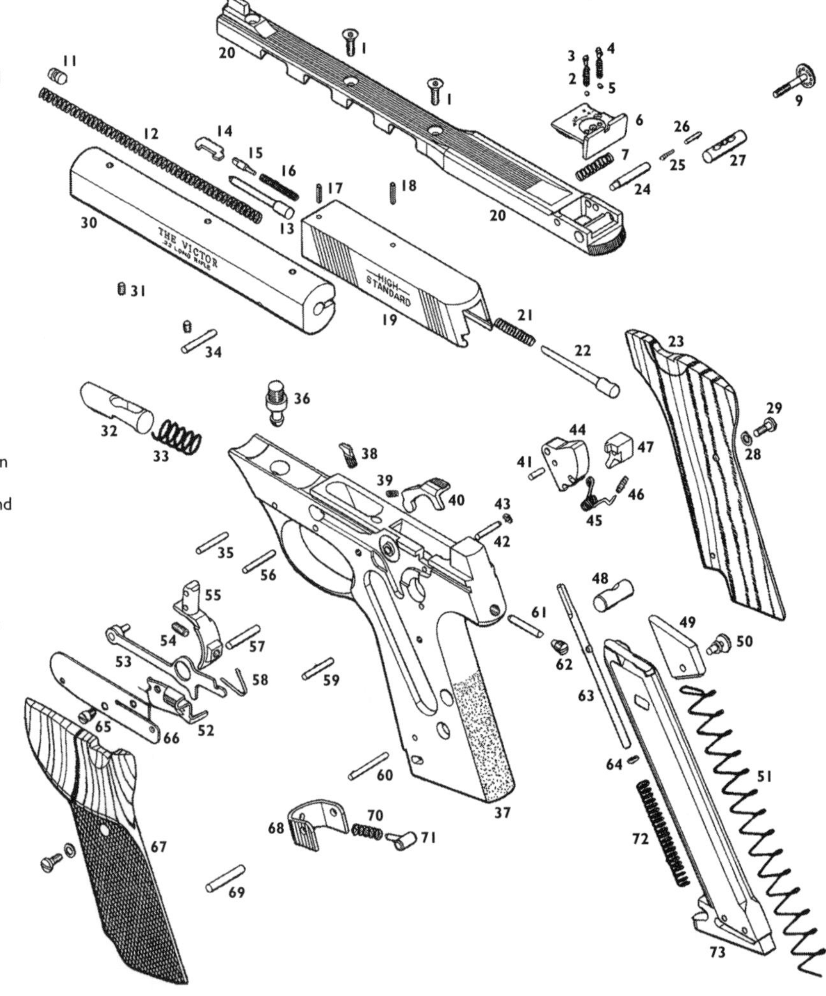

The High Standard Victor self-loading pistol, one of several pistols in High Standard's "Military" Model 107 series, was a well balanced target pistol chambered for the .22 Long Rifle rimfire cartridge. The Victor weighed 50 ounces unloaded, a feature intended to aidin steady holding.

The Victor was introduced in 1972. Optionally available with 5½- or 4½-inch barrels, the blowback operated Victor had an internal hammer, two-stage trigger and a 10-shot detachable magazine. Both front and rear target-style sights are mounted on a ventilated rib which extends from the muzzle to the upper rear of the pistol, above the slide.

Placed out of production when High Standard ceased operations in 1985, the Victor has been re-issued by the High Standard Manufacturing Company, Inc. of Houston, Texas.

DISASSEMBLY

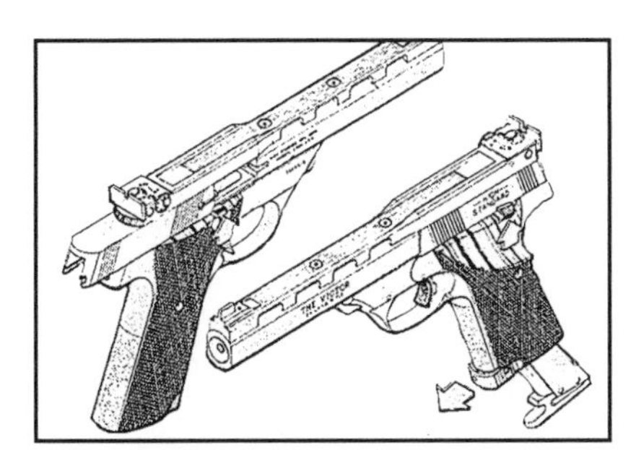

1 Begin disassembly by pushing safety (52) upward into safe position. Pull magazine catch (68) forward and remove magazine (73). Draw slide (19) fully to rear, checking visually that chamber is empty. Raise slide lock lever (40), and ease slide forward slightly until held open by slide lock.

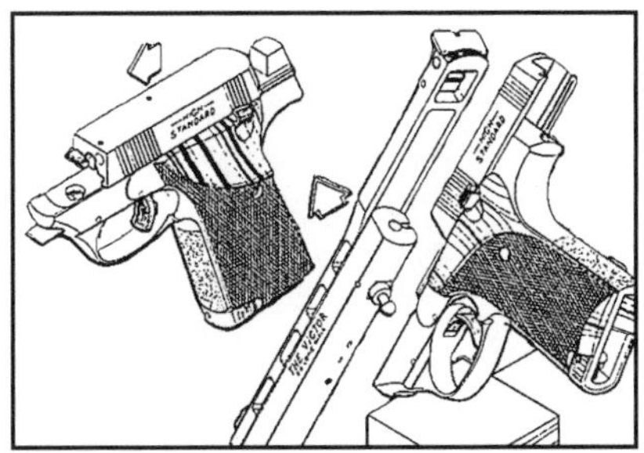

2 Depress barrel take down plunger (32) against a stable wooden block, holding gun muzzle down with barrel at a 45-degree angle to block. Grasp pistol firmly with one hand on barrel and the other on grip. With takedown plunger fully depressed, pull barrel assembly upward out of frame. Draw slide slightly rearward to release slide lock, and guide slide forward off the frame.

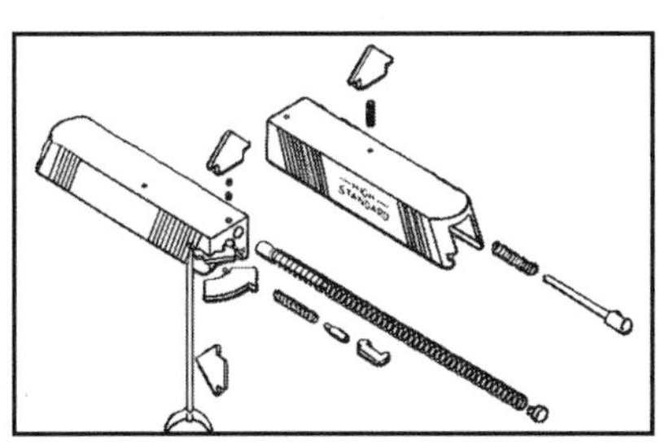

3 To disassemble further, drift out firing pin retaining pin (18) through top of slide to release firing pin (22) and firing pin spring (21). Insert point of ice pick or awl between the extractor (14) and extractor plunger (15), and depress the plunger well into the slide. Rotate forward end of extractor toward center of breech face and remove. Then, ease out plunger and extractor spring (16). Drift out driving spring plug pin (17) through top of slide. Place thumb against driving spring plug (11) in breech face and withdraw punch. Ease plug, driving spring (12), and plunger (13) from slide. On replacement, face notch in firing pin head to right side of slide.

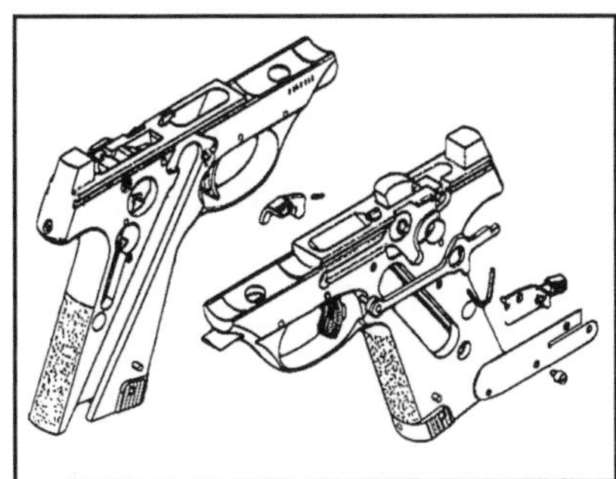

4 Unscrew grip screws (29), and remove grips (23 & 67). Use caution in removing right grip to avoid dislocation of slide lock lever and loss of its spring (39). Remove slide lock lever and spring. Move safety to fire position, pull trigger (55) while holding hammer (44), and ease hammer fully forward with thumb. Unscrew and remove side plate screw (65), side plate (66), and safety. Unseat and remove sear bar spring (58). Push down rear end of sear bar (53) to disconnect it from sear (47). Hold frame left side down, and shake out sear bar.

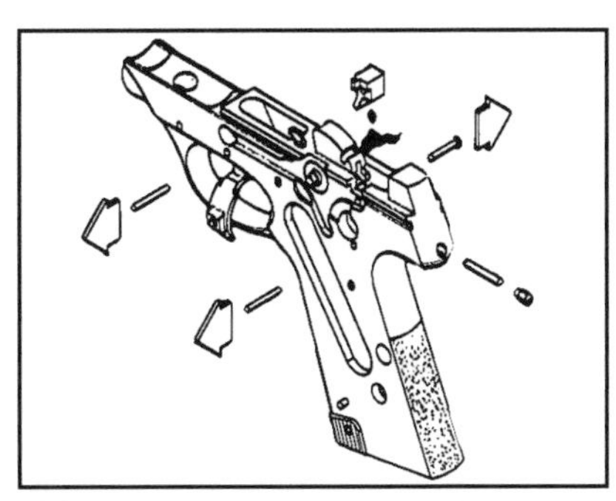

5 Unscrew and remove sear adjustment screw (62), and shake out its plunger (61). When replacing plunger, its notched end must straddle legs of sear spring (45). Drift sear pin (42) out to right and remove sear. Drift out sear spring pin (59) and remove sear spring. Drift out trigger pin (56), rotate trigger ¼ turn, and pull downward from the frame.

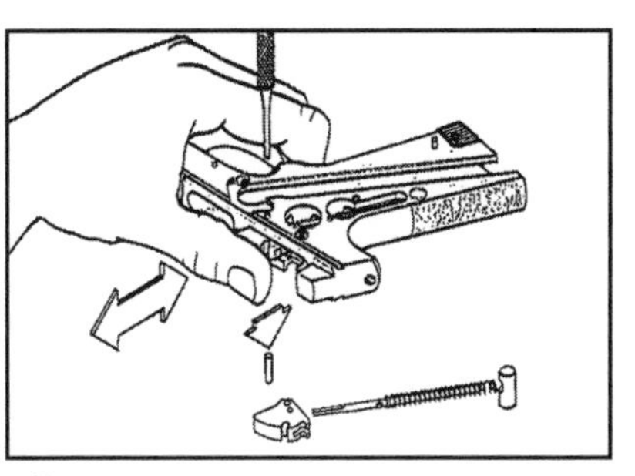

6 Drift out hammer pin (57) with a 3/16" pin punch. Grasp frame as shown, and apply pressure to hammer with thumb. Withdraw punch, and ease hammer outward. Remove hammer strut (63), ring (64), and hammer spring (72). Push hammer strut anchor pin (48) out through side of frame. In reassembling these parts, ensure that offset hammer spring seat in the anchor pin lies toward right side of frame, and that hammer strut contacts the hammer strut pin (41) contained within hammer.

HUNGARIAN MODEL 1937 PISTOL

PARTS LEGEND

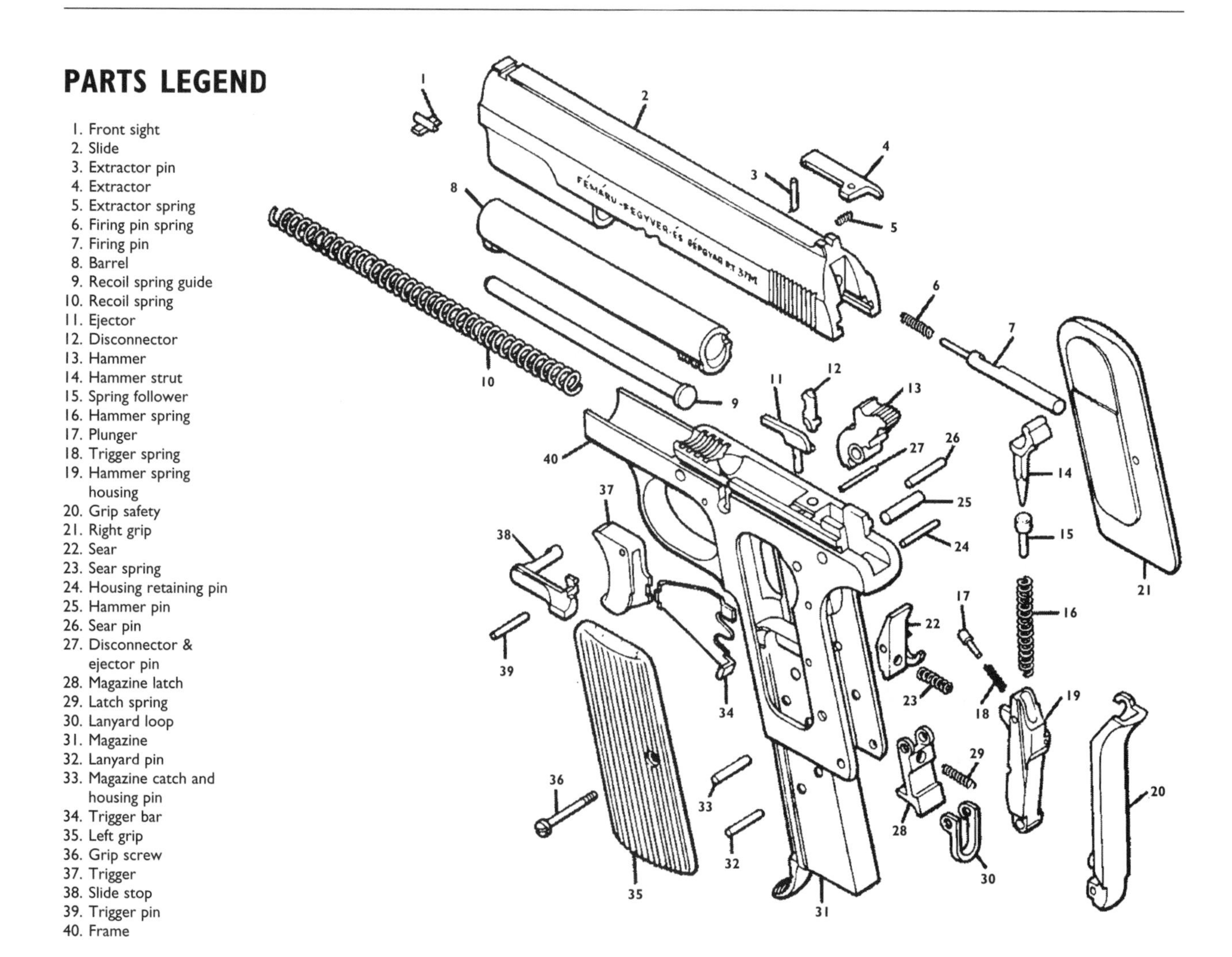

1. Front sight
2. Slide
3. Extractor pin
4. Extractor
5. Extractor spring
6. Firing pin spring
7. Firing pin
8. Barrel
9. Recoil spring guide
10. Recoil spring
11. Ejector
12. Disconnector
13. Hammer
14. Hammer strut
15. Spring follower
16. Hammer spring
17. Plunger
18. Trigger spring
19. Hammer spring housing
20. Grip safety
21. Right grip
22. Sear
23. Sear spring
24. Housing retaining pin
25. Hammer pin
26. Sear pin
27. Disconnector & ejector pin
28. Magazine latch
29. Latch spring
30. Lanyard loop
31. Magazine
32. Lanyard pin
33. Magazine catch and housing pin
34. Trigger bar
35. Left grip
36. Grip screw
37. Trigger
38. Slide stop
39. Trigger pin
40. Frame

Introduced in 1937, the Hungarian Model 1937 (M37) automatic pistol was chambered for either the .32 ACP or the .380 ACP. The Model 1937's action is a Browning blowback design with an exposed hammer and detachable magazine.

The pistol was designed by arms designer Rudolf Frommer as an improved version of his Model 29M, the older Hungarian service pistol. The slides of prewar M37 pistols are generally marked "FEMARU-FEGYVERES. GEPGYAR R.T. 37M." Translated this means Metalware, Small Arms and Machine Works, Inc. Model 37. Following the German occupation, this Budapest firm was integrated into the German war economy and the M37 pistol, in .32 ACP, was adopted by the Germans as a substitute standard military pistol. Slide markings were changed to "Pistole M37, Cal. 7.65mm." plus the "jhv" code and a 2-digit numeral to indicate year of manufacture. On many guns the inscription "Kal." is found instead of "Cal."

M37 pistols made under German supervision have a manual safety in addition to the Hungarian model's grip safety.

DISASSEMBLY

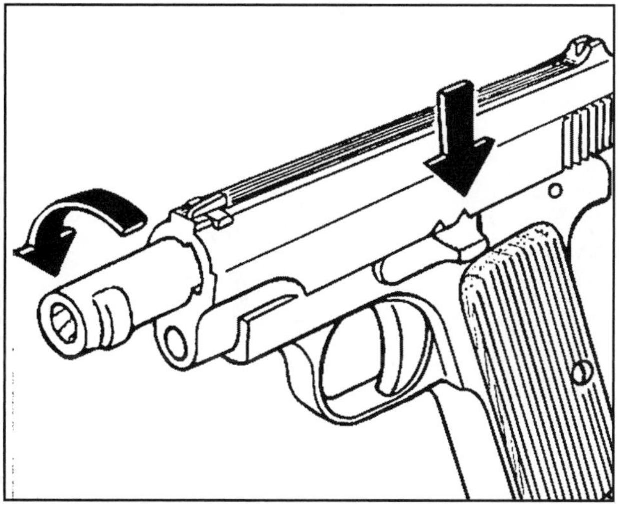

1 To strip the M37, first step is to be sure gun is unloaded. Pull slide (2) to rear until slide stop (38) engages rear notch as shown. Rotate barrel (8) and pull it out of slide. Then release slide stop, ease slide off frame, and remove magazine.

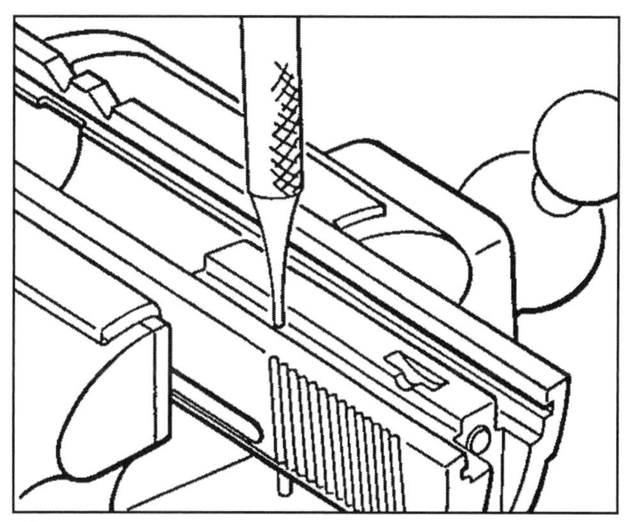

2 A single pin (3) retains firing pin in slide and acts as extractor hinge pin. Hold slide in padded vise as shown and drive pin out. Remove firing pin (7), firing pin spring (6), extractor (4) and extractor spring (5).

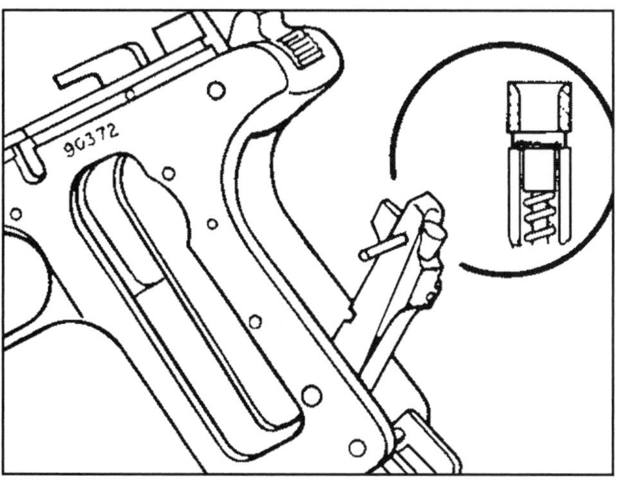

3 Only difficult piece to reassemble is hammer spring (16). A slave pin is employed to retain the hammer spring (16) and plunger (15). This slave pin is a short wire or nail that holds assemblies in place until proper pin is inserted. Correct pin (24) is driven through frame and knocks out slave pin.

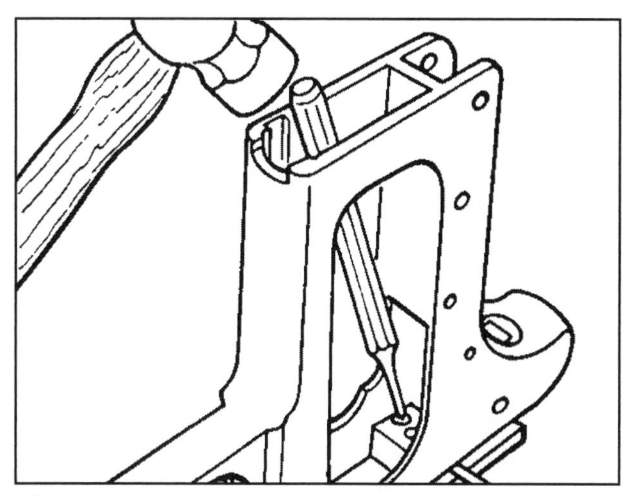

4 Disconnector (12) and ejector (11) are retained by cross pin (27) through frame. Remove pin and disconnector will drop out; however, ejector must be driven out as shown. When reinstalling cross pin, be sure it is in slightly below the surface to prevent retarding slide motion.

I.J. MODEL 50 REVOLVER

PARTS LEGEND

1. Frame
2. Barrel
3. Front sight blade
4. Ejector assembly
5. Ejector tube screw
6. Ejector lock screw
7. Cylinder
8. Center pin
9. Center pin catch nut
10. Center pin catch spring
11. Center pin catch screw
12. Loading gate
13. Loading gate screw
14. Trigger guard
15. Trigger guard pins (2)
16. Cylinder friction stud
17. Cylinder friction stud spring
18. Sear
19. Sear spring
20. Trigger
21. Trigger pin
22. Trigger spring
23. Lever
24. Lever spring
25. Lifter
26. Hammer
27. Hammer screw
28. Mainspring
29. Mainspring plunger
30. Mainspring adjusting screw
31. Grip screw
32. Grip, one-piece (not shown)

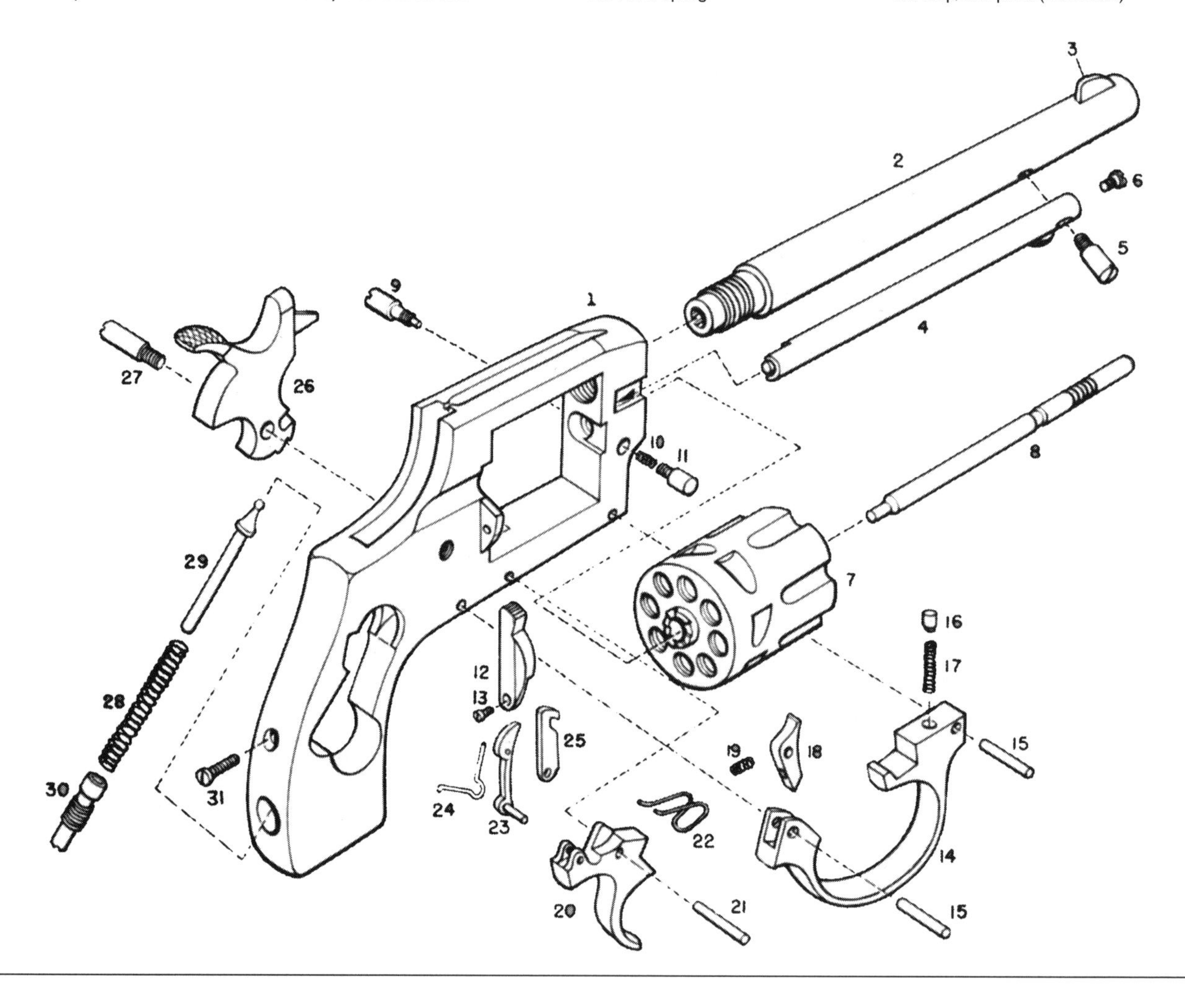

Introduced in 1961, and produced until 1980, the Iver Johnson Model 50, "Sidewinder," was a .22 rimfire revolver designed for informal target shooting. The Sidewinder was chambered for .22 Long rifle or .22 Magnum calibers.

A solid frame, double-action, the Model 50 features rod ejection, a hinged loading gate and a western style walnut grip. Barrel length is 4¾ or 6 inches. Sights are fixed or adjustable. The eight-shot capacity cylinder has counterbored chambers to enclose the cartridge heads. A flash shield on the front of the cylinder diverts powder gases forward and away from the shooter. The trigger mechanism includes a half-cock safety which permits cylinder rotation for loading and unloading.

DISASSEMBLY

The basic mechanism of Models 50, 55A, 55S-A, 56A, and 57A is the same and disassembly for all Model 50 series Iver Johnson revolvers is essentially the same.

Press in center pin catch screw (11) at right of frame and withdraw center pin (8). Open loading gate (12). Rotate cylinder (7) until rear end of barrel can slip through slot in flash control rim at front of cylinder. Remove cylinder to right. Remove grip screw (31) and pull off one-piece grip. In revolvers with small, 2-piece grips remove transverse grip screw.

Unscrew mainspring adjusting screw (30) until it stops. Remove hammer screw (27). Hold trigger (20) back and remove hammer (26) through top of frame. Remove mainspring (28) and mainspring plunger (29) through top of frame. Remove mainspring adjusting screw through cutout in frame.

Drift out trigger guard pins (15) and pull trigger guard (14) from bottom of frame with sear (18), sear spring (19), cylinder friction stud (16) and cylinder friction stud spring (17). Drift out trigger pin (21) and remove trigger (20) with lifter (25), lever (23), and springs (22, 24).

Remove loading gate after unscrewing loading gate screw (13). Ejector assembly (4) is removed from barrel by removing ejector tube screw (5) and ejector lock screw (6), then sliding forward to disengage slotted rear end of tube from frame.

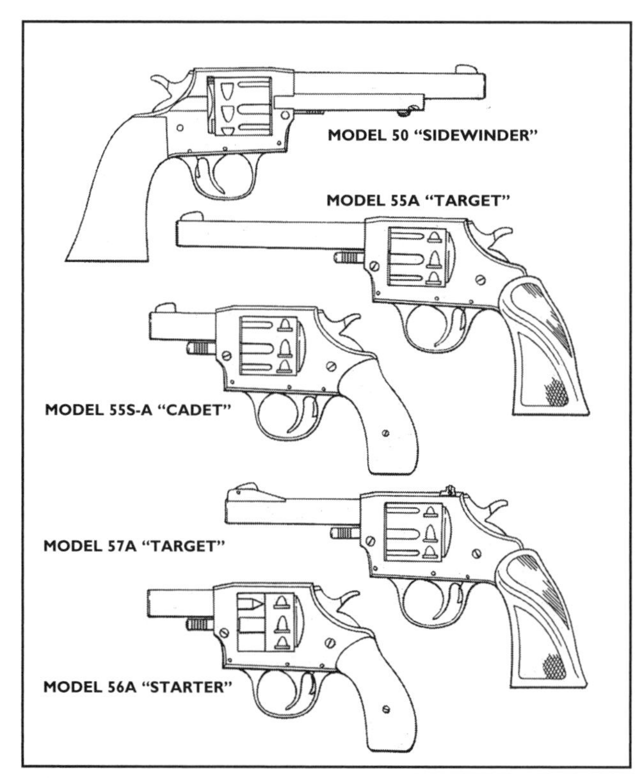

1 All Iver Johnson revolvers in the Model 50 series are shown here for comparison. Basic mechanism of all versions is the same and main differences in parts are in barrels, calibers, cylinders, sight arrangements, and grip styles.

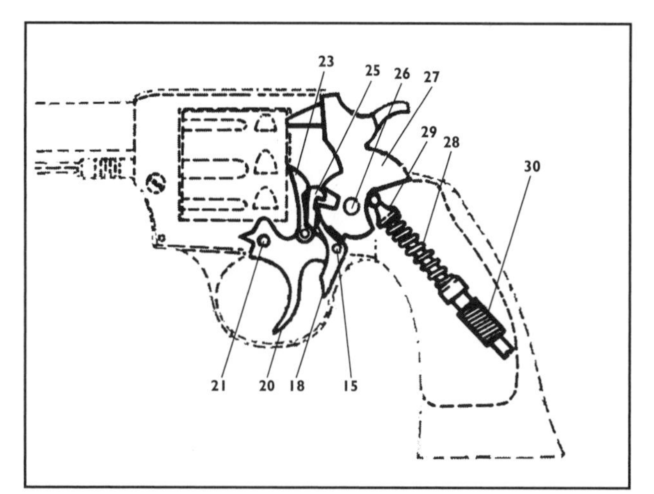

2 Basic lock mechanism of the Model 50 Sidewinder and other Model 50 series Iver Johnson revolvers is shown in this phantom view. The small trigger spring (22), sear spring (19), and lever spring (24) are omitted for clarity.

I.J. MODEL 66 REVOLVER

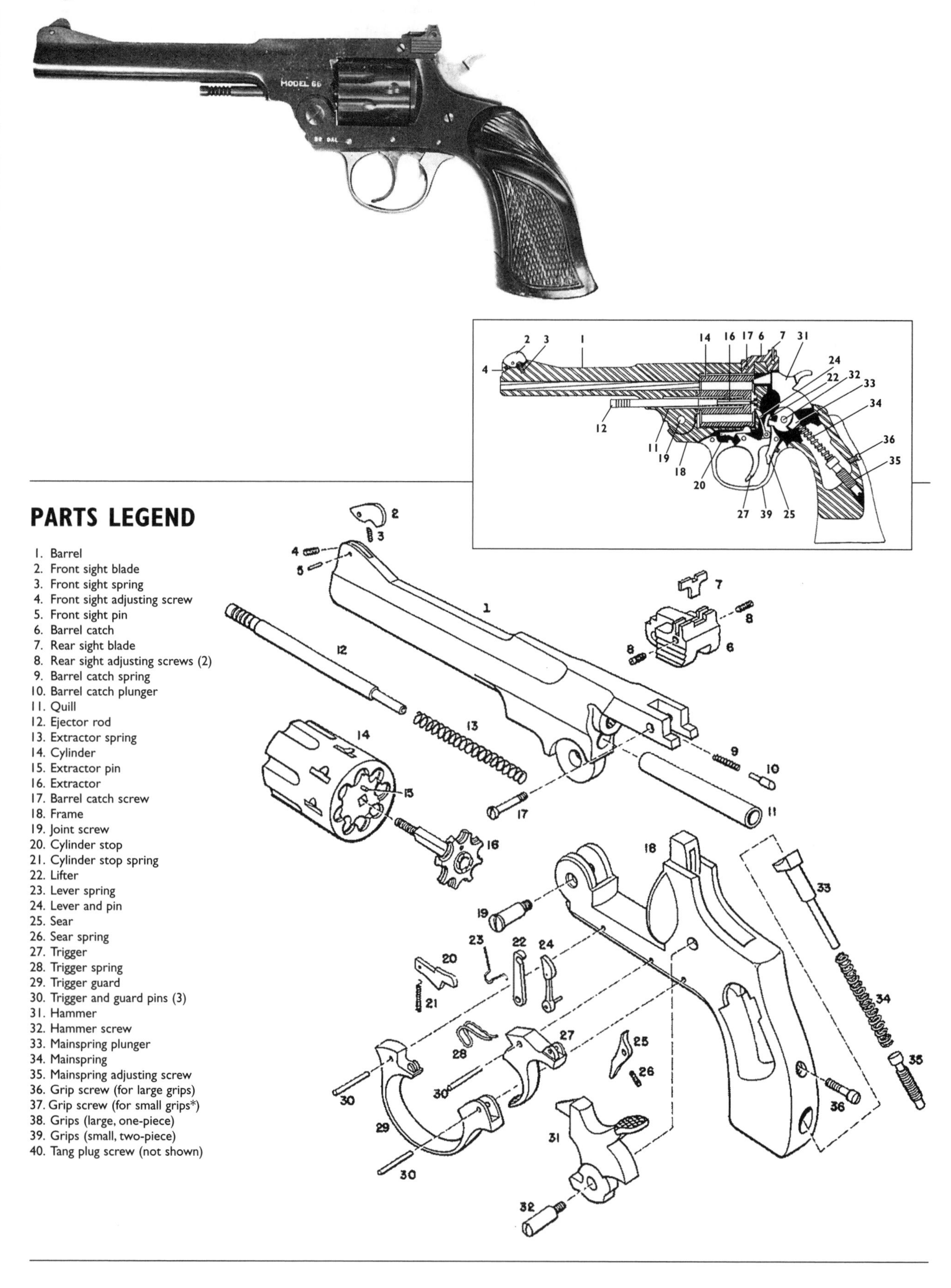

PARTS LEGEND

1. Barrel
2. Front sight blade
3. Front sight spring
4. Front sight adjusting screw
5. Front sight pin
6. Barrel catch
7. Rear sight blade
8. Rear sight adjusting screws (2)
9. Barrel catch spring
10. Barrel catch plunger
11. Quill
12. Ejector rod
13. Extractor spring
14. Cylinder
15. Extractor pin
16. Extractor
17. Barrel catch screw
18. Frame
19. Joint screw
20. Cylinder stop
21. Cylinder stop spring
22. Lifter
23. Lever spring
24. Lever and pin
25. Sear
26. Sear spring
27. Trigger
28. Trigger spring
29. Trigger guard
30. Trigger and guard pins (3)
31. Hammer
32. Hammer screw
33. Mainspring plunger
34. Mainspring
35. Mainspring adjusting screw
36. Grip screw (for large grips)
37. Grip screw (for small grips*)
38. Grips (large, one-piece)
39. Grips (small, two-piece)
40. Tang plug screw (not shown)

The Model 66 "Trailsman" revolver was manufactured by Iver Johnson Arms in Fitchburg, Massachusetts., beginning in 1958 until it was discontinued in 1980. The Trailsman was a single-shot, double-action revolver with a 6-inch-barrel and was chambered for the .22 Long Rifle cartridge.

Of top-break, or tipping-barrel, design, the Trailsman featured fully adjustable sights and a rebounding hammer. The chambers were counterbored to enclose cartridge heads and the front face of the cylinder had a flash shield to divert powder gases forward and away from the shooter. Cartridges or fired cases were ejected manually by depressing the ejector rod under the barrel. The 6-inch-barrel Model 66 was optionally available with one piece plastic, or walnut, grip.

From 1960 until 1964 the Model 66 was offered with a 2¾-inch barrel under the designation "Trailsman-Snub" (Model 66S). The Model 66S was chambered for the .32 S&W and .38 S&W, centerfire cartridges (cylinder capacity, five rounds) as well as in .22 rimfire.

From 1962 until 1964 the Trailsman .22 was offered with a 4½-inch barrel in addition to the standard 6 inch length.

DISASSEMBLY

To separate barrel assembly (1) from frame (18), remove joint screw (19) and pull barrel off joint. Rear sight and barrel catch assembly (6) can be removed by unscrewing barrel catch screw (17) from left side of top strap of barrel, taking care not to allow ejection of barrel catch spring (9) and plunger (10). Cylinder (14) can be removed by holding up barrel catch and pulling cylinder to rear off quill (11). Complete disassembly of cylinder, extractor (16) and ejector rod (12) assembly is unnecessary for normal cleaning purposes and is not recommended.

Remove grip screw (36) and pull grip off frame. Unscrew mainspring adjusting screw (35) until it stops. Remove hammer screw (32). Hold trigger (27) back and remove hammer (31) through top of frame. Remove mainspring plunger (33) and mainspring (34) through top of frame. Unscrew and remove mainspring adjusting screw through cutout in frame. Drift out trigger guard and trigger pins (30). Remaining lock parts are easily removed from frame. Reassemble in reverse order. Be sure that barrel catch is held up in unlocked position when replacing cylinder on quill to avoid damaging cylinder finish.

Note: Hammer must be in fired position when opening or closing revolver or lever will be damaged.

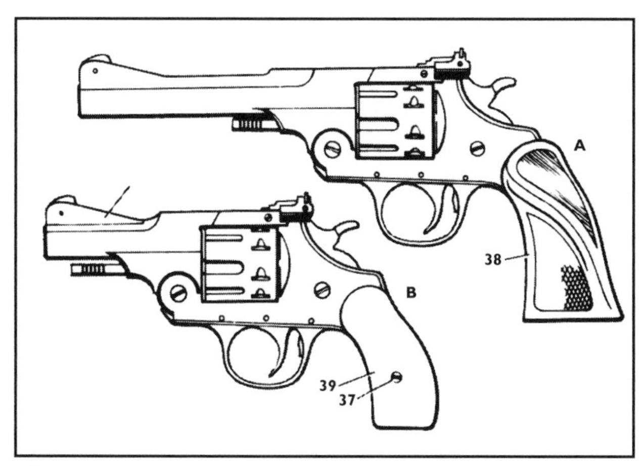

1 Note that the 2¾" barrel Snub Model 66S (B) is provided with the smaller two-piece grips (39) and single transverse grip screw (37). The standard model (A) with 6" barrel has one-piece grip with thumb rest (38). Grip is secured by a single screw (36).

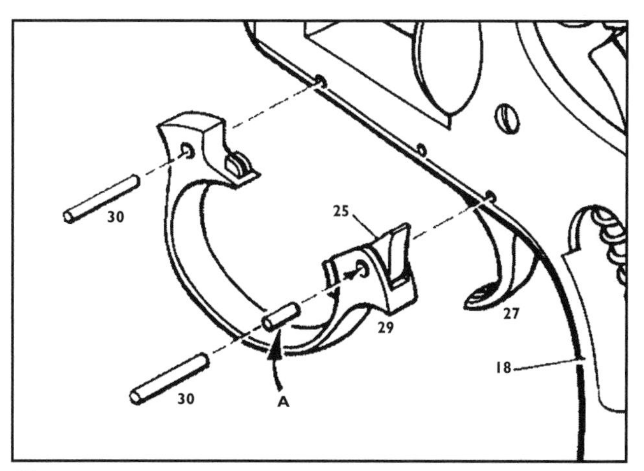

2 In reassembling lock mechanism, replacing trigger guard (29) in frame is facilitated by using a small slave-pin (as shown at 'A') to secure sear and sear spring (25, 26) in rear of trigger guard. Make the slave-pin of brass rod or wood, slightly shorter than width of trigger guard. With slave-pin in place, trigger guard can be replaced in frame (18) with sear and spring and trigger guard pins (30) replaced. As rear trigger guard pin is drifted into frame, it will push slave-pin out.

I.J. MODEL 1900 AND U.S. REVOLVERS

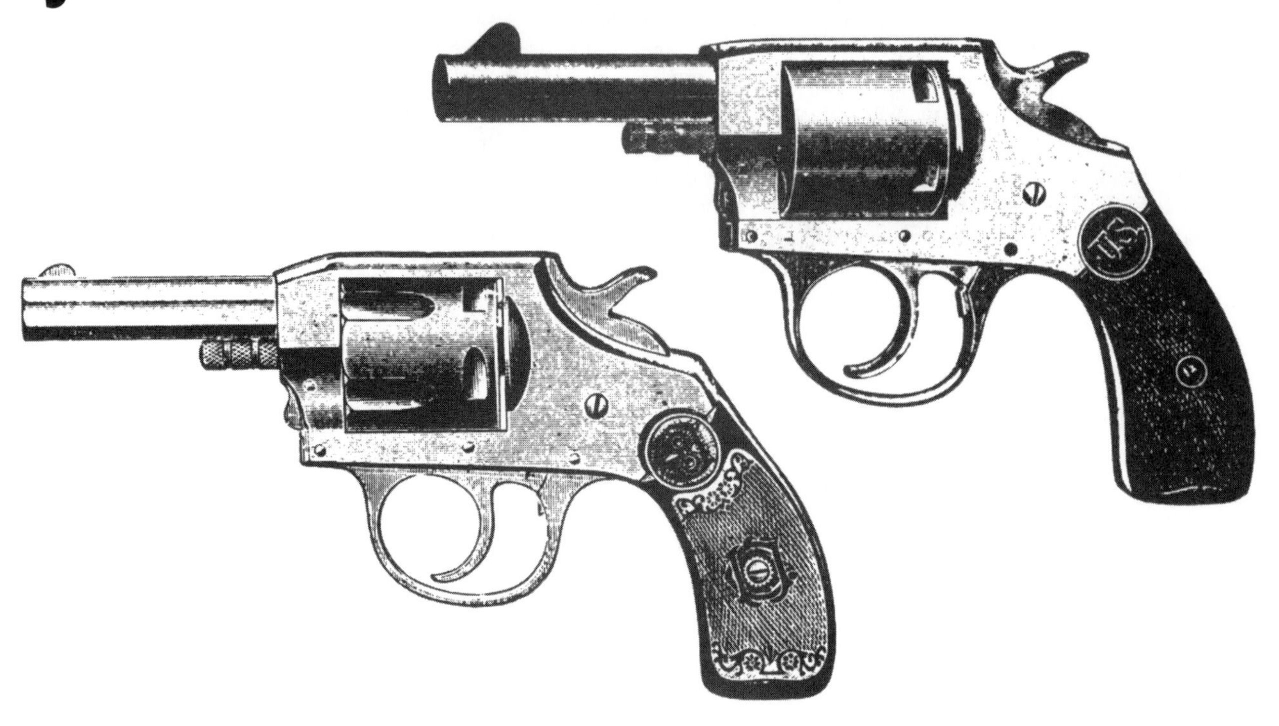

PARTS LEGEND

1. Barrel
2. Cylinder
3. Cylinder pin/ejector
4. Cylinder pin latch
5. Cylinder pin latch pin
6. Cylinder pin latch spring
7. Frame
8. Friction spring
9. Friction stud
10. Guard
11. Guard pin, front
12. Guard/sear pin
13. Hammer
14. Hammer screw
15. Hand
16. Hand spring
17. Lifter
18. Mainspring
19. Sear
20. Sear spring
21. Sight
22. Trigger
23. Trigger pin
24. Trigger spring

(Stocks not illustrated)

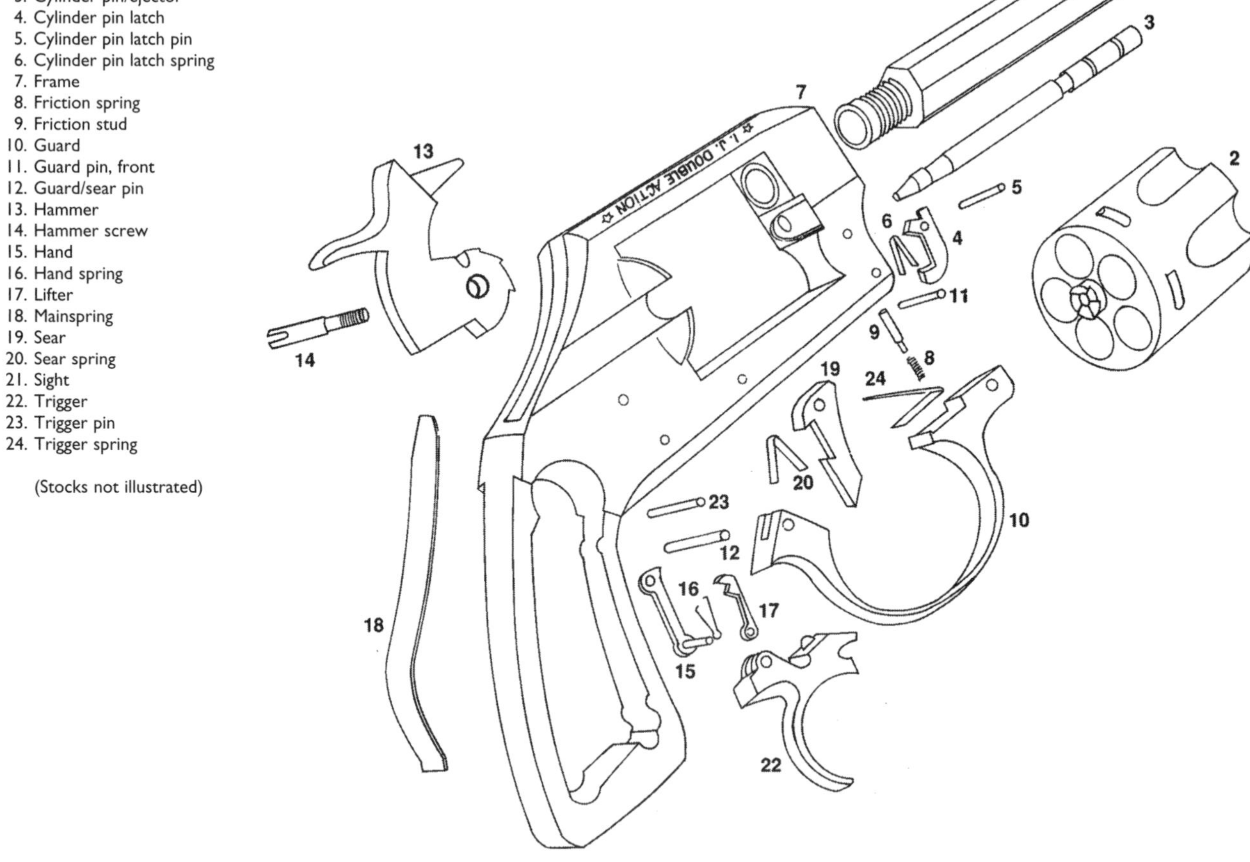

Iver Johnson's Arms & Cycle Works of Fitchburg, Massachussets made the Model 1900 as an improved successor to its double-action "Bulldog" revolver line that had started in the 1880s. It was made from the model date until just after World War II and, for much of that time, was run concurrently with a mechanically identical version intended for catalog houses and others demanding a lower price.

The Iver Johnson "MODEL 1900" (so-marked with the address on the top-strap) had an octagonal barrel and fluted cylinder with the familiar Owl Head logo on the grips; its cheaper running mate was round-barrelled and lacked the flutes. It bore no Iver Johnson identification, and its top-strap was marked only "U.S. REVOLVER CO. MADE IN U.S.A." with the initials "U.S." in a circle on its hard rubber grips.

The 1900 and U.S. models were produced by the millions, but the total quantity is not known. The factory claimed an annual output of nearly half a million in good years, and the low price insured sales even through the Great Depression. After the war, the remaining parts of the 1900 were assembled, but the last of them seem to have been completed and sold by 1946.

The tremendous popularity of the small, solidframed "pin-ejectors" lay in their simplicity and affordability. The prices ran from $2 or $3 at the tum of the century through $5 or $6 during the depression to $11 for the postwar "cleanup," and the U.S. versions were usually somewhat cheaper.

A surprising number of nickel-plated or blued variations of the two brands were available during the manufacturing span. The original caliber choices were: .22 Long Rifle (seven shots), .32 rimfire (five), .32 S&W (five) and .38 S&W (five). In time the .32 rimfire was dropped, and a larger six-shot version chambered for the .32 S&W Long was added. The standard barrel length for all calibers was 2½ inches, but 4½- or 6-inch barrels were also regularly offered, as were oversized hard rubber "target" grips or pearl grips and hinged loading gates, all at extra cost.

The 1900-series solid-framed revolvers were succeeded in the early 1960s by the similar Model 50 Iver Johnson that took advantage of formed wire springs and employed a rod ejector and a loading gate as standard equipment.

DISASSEMBLY

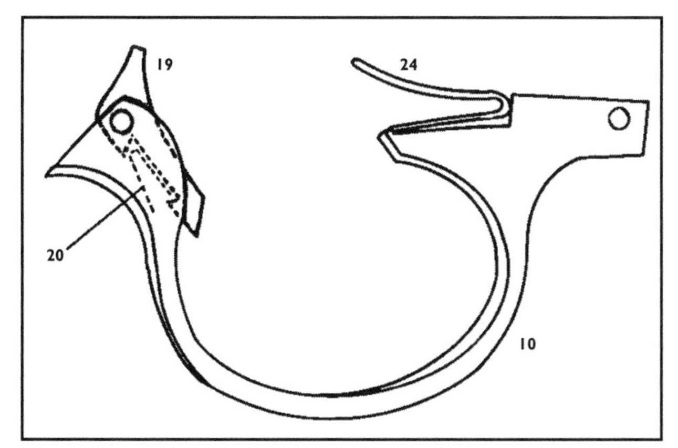

1 Depress the cylinder latch (4); withdraw the cylinder pin (3) and remove the cylinder (2) from the right side of the frame (7).

Drift out rear guard/sear pin (12) and front guard pin (11). Work trigger guard (10) out of frame carefully, noting position of sear (19) and sear spring (20) at the rear of the trigger guard and the trigger spring (24) at the front.

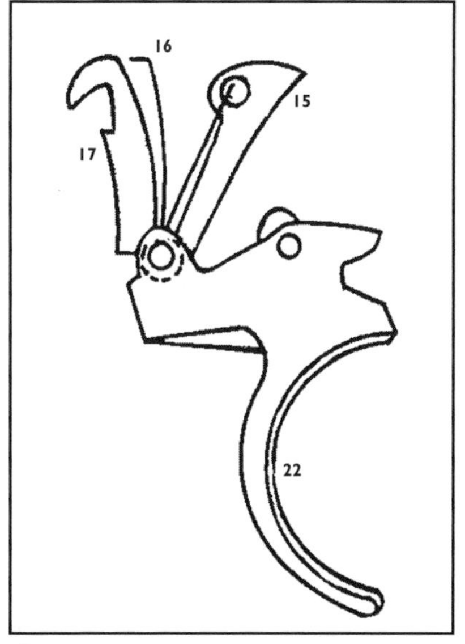

2 The end of the revolver's only coil spring, the cylinder friction spring (8) will appear in the now-exposed frame recess ahead of the trigger.

The friction spring and stud (9) can be withdrawn, and drifting out the cylinder latch pin (5) will permit removal of the latch and its spring (6).

Remove the stock screw and stocks and pry out the bottom of the mainspring (18). Then remove the hammer screw (14) and drift out the trigger pin (23).

Work the trigger assembly (15, 16, 17 & 22) and the hammer down through the frame and push forward on the lifter (17) to disengage it from the hammer (13); then lift the hammer from the top of the frame. Note carefully the position of the trigger assembly components.

I.J. TOP-BREAK REVOLVER

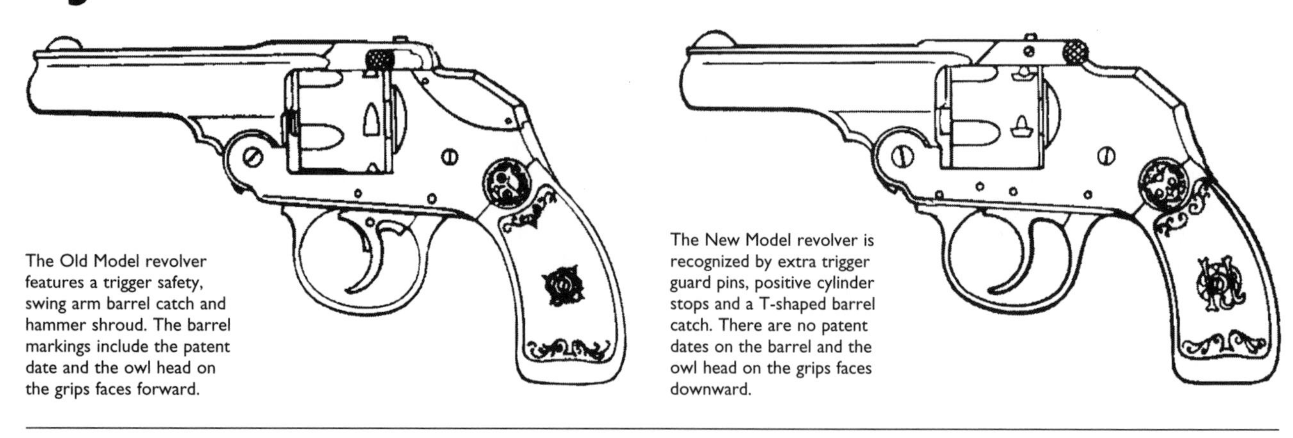

The Old Model revolver features a trigger safety, swing arm barrel catch and hammer shroud. The barrel markings include the patent date and the owl head on the grips faces forward.

The New Model revolver is recognized by extra trigger guard pins, positive cylinder stops and a T-shaped barrel catch. There are no patent dates on the barrel and the owl head on the grips faces downward.

PARTS LEGEND

1. Barrel assembly
2. Barrel catch screw
3. Barrel catch
4. Barrel catch spring cover
5. Barrel catch spring
6. Extractor stem
7. Cylinder friction spring
8. Extractor spring
9. Cylinder
10. Extractor
11. Hammer
12. Hammer spring
13. Right grip
14. Frame
15. Trigger guard
16. Left grip
17. Grip screw
18. Sear
19. Sear spring
20. Trigger spring
21. Trigger guard pin
22. Hammer screw
23. Lifter
24. Trigger
25. Hand
26. Hand spring
27. Trigger pin
28. Hinge screw
29. Firing pin
30. Trigger guard screw
31. Firing pin spring
32. Firing pin bushing
33. Extractor spring
34. Extractor bushing
35. Extractor cam

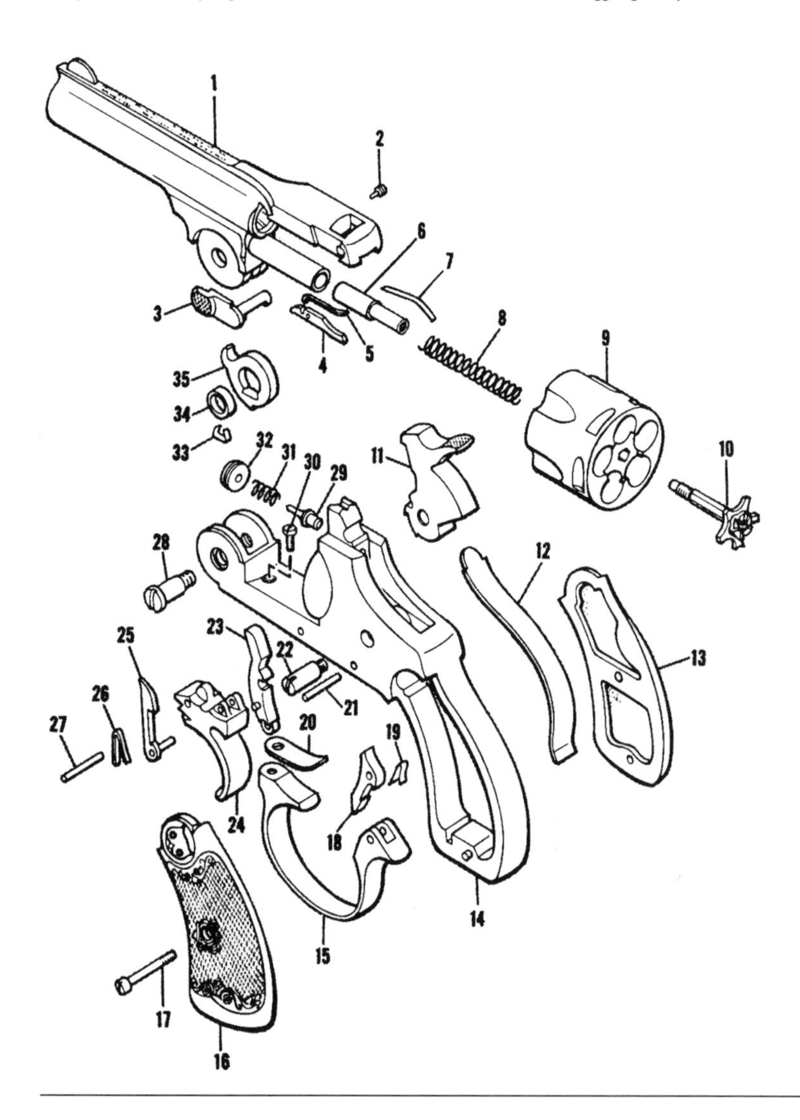

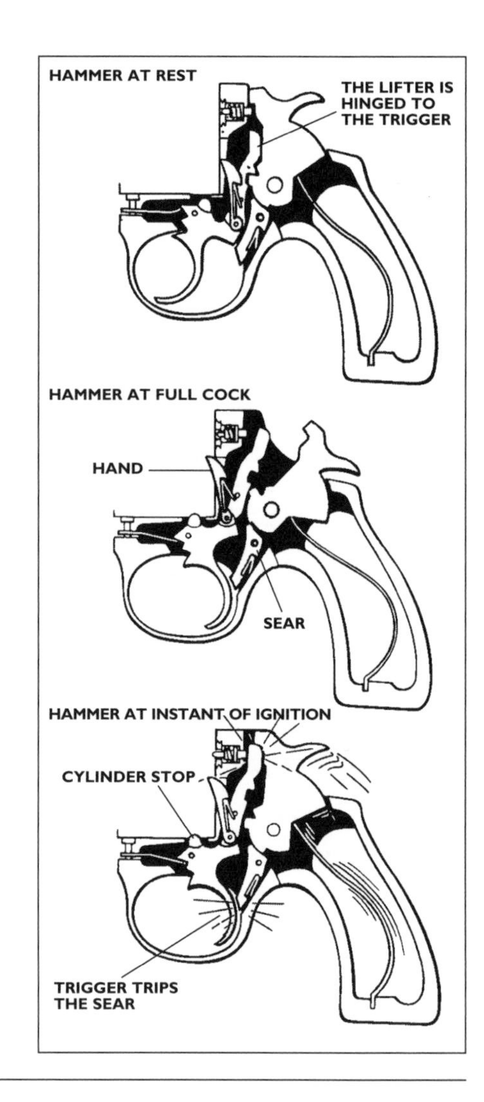

Around the turn of the 20th century top-break revolvers were as common, in the average American home, as can openers are today. For less than $2.00, a person could buy a solid frame revolver in .22, .32 or even .38 (usually rimfire) caliber. In 1902, Sears, Roebuck & Co., offered the more sophisticated Iver Johnson top-break revolvers at $3.50 for a .32 or .38 S&W, blue-finish, exposed hammer model, and $4.00 for the hammerless version of the same gun.

Iver Johnson top-break revolvers were made in barrel lengths from 2 to 6 inches with several styles of grip, all available at added cost. Iver Johnson also made a less expensive line of top-breaks, marked "U.S." For years Iver Johnson advertisements pictured the hammering of a top-break hammer to prove its safety. While this sort of safety test is not particularly good for the gun, it was an effctive selling point.

There are considerable design differences between "new" and "old" Iver Johnson top-break models. Both feature the safety hammer, but most of the internal parts are unique to each model. The gun illustrated is a visible-hammer model of the "old" model. New models are recognized by the round barrel catch and the two additional frame pins. Internally the new model features a separate cylinder latch that allows a more positive stop. The flat hammer spring was changed to an adjustable coil spring. The extractor cam was made more reliable by replacing the fragile flat spring with a coil spring.

The greatest source of trouble in the old model was the lack of a positive cylinder stop which resulted in lead being shaved from the bullet as it passed from the cylinder to the barrel. This difficulty was overcome in the new model.

Production of Iver Johnson top-break revolvers, both visible hammer and hammerless models, had all but ceased by the time of World War II.

DISASSEMBLY

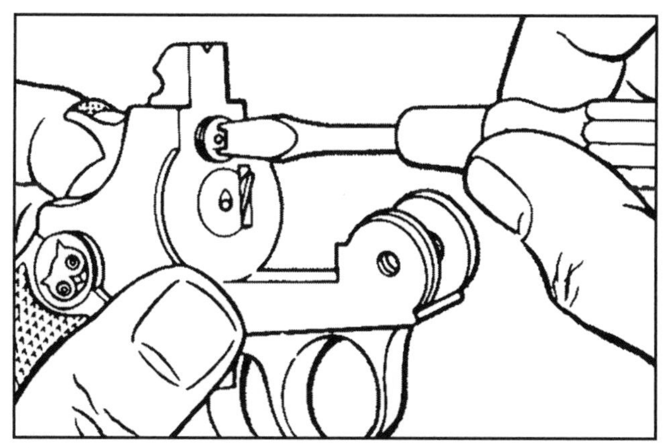

1 To remove cylinder (9) of the old model, open gun sufficiently for the extractor to snap back into cylinder. Pull back on cylinder and revolve it counterclockwise to free it from the barrel.

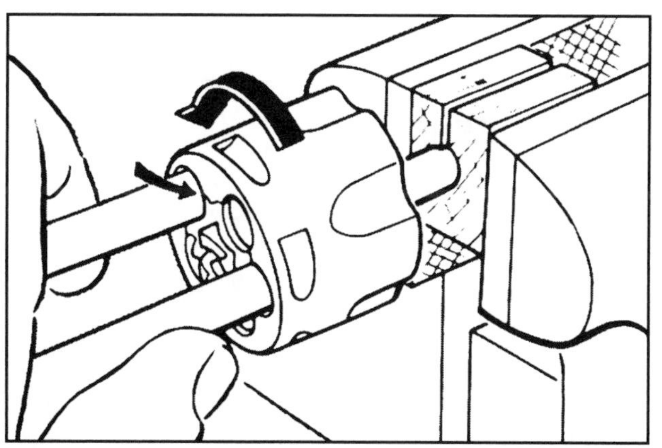

2 To remove extractor (10), hold extractor stem (6) in a padded vise. Insert a few empty cases part way into chambers and turn cylinder counterclockwise. It may be necessary to insert a pair of brass rods as shown to afford a better grip on cylinder.

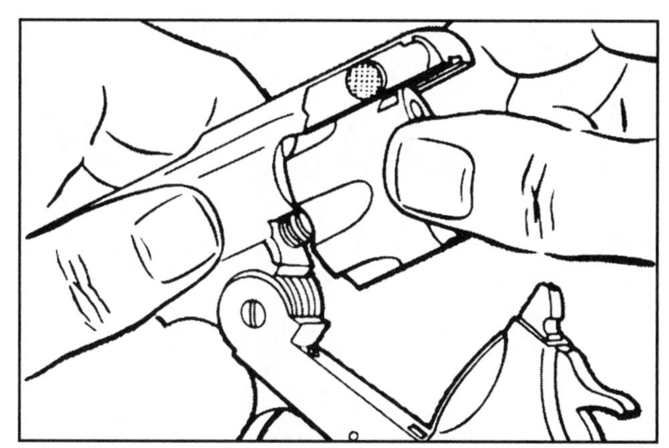

3 To remove firing pin (29), grind an old screwdriver into a 2-pronged tool. Hone prongs to fit into holes in firing pin bushing (32). Screw out bushing and remove firing pin and firing pin spring (31.)

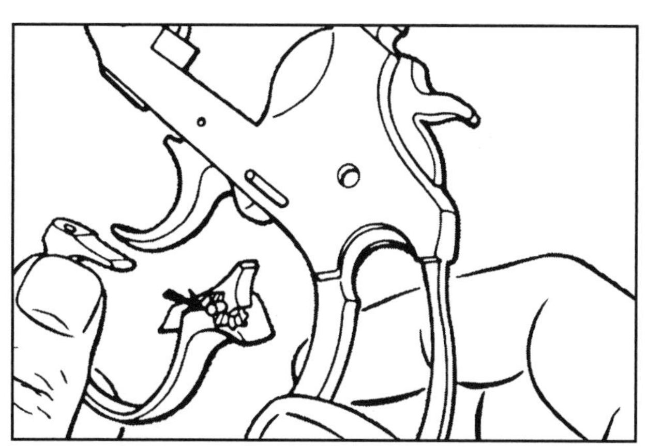

4 Reassembling the top-break can be simplified by using slave pin. Assemble ports outside gun with pin (arrow) slightly shorter than trigger guard width. Insert assembly in frame and drive pin through frame, to drift slave pin out other side.

JAPANESE TYPE 14 PISTOL (NAMBU)

PARTS LEGEND

1. Front sight
2. Barrel and barrel extension
3. Extractor
4. Bolt
5. Recoil springs
6. Cocking piece
7. Firing pin extension
8. Firing pin spring
9. Firing pin
10. Locking block spring
11. Locking block
12. Trigger bar hinge pin
13. Magazine safety
14. Magazine safety spring and plunger
15. Trigger sear
16. Sear spring
17. Trigger
18. Trigger sear pin
19. Trigger guard
20. Trigger hinge pin
21. Receiver (frame)
22. Safety catch
23. Magazine safety hinge pin
24. Magazine catch
25. Magazine catch spring
26. Magazine
27. Trigger bar
28. Trigger bar spring
29. Left grip
30. Grip screw

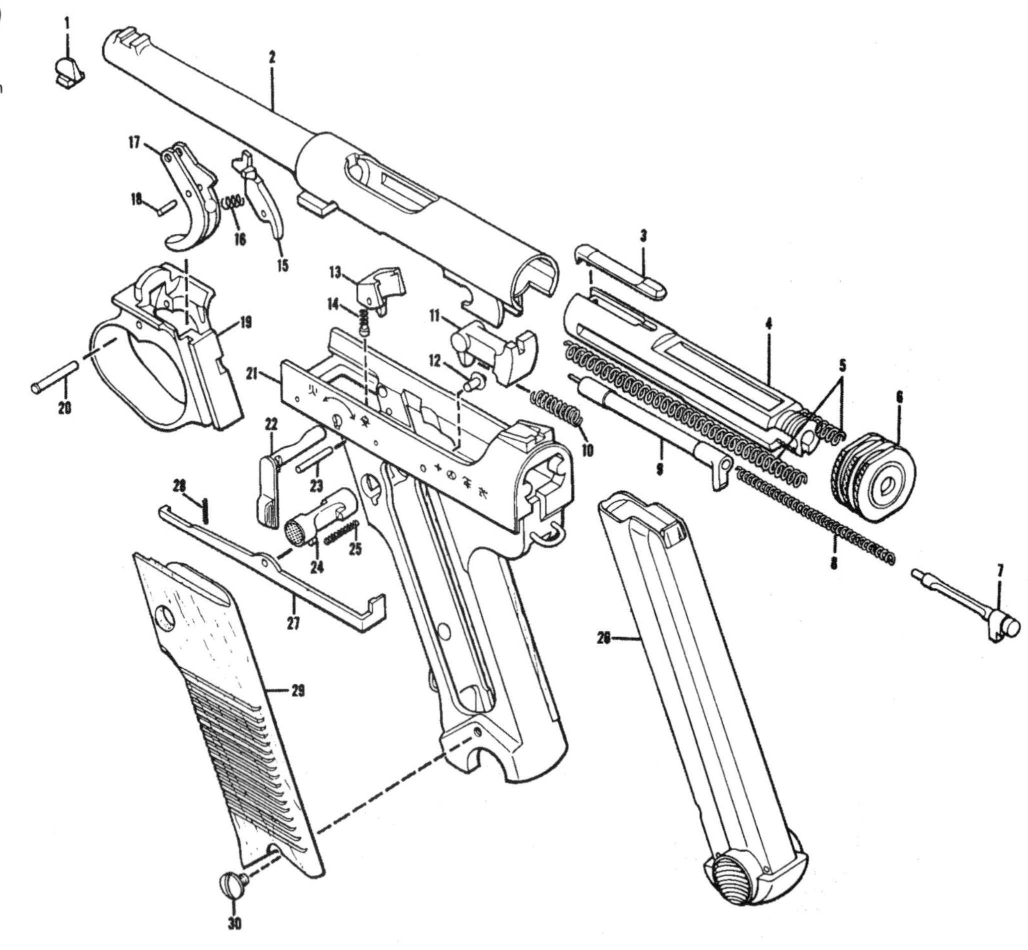

Seven years before we adopted the Model 1911 Colt Automatic, the Japanese high command issued a directive permitting Japanese officers to purchase and carry the Nambu pistol. While Colonel Kijiro Nambu's pistol physically resembled the Luger pistol, it was an original design and not a direct copy of an existing arm. This early model, with its characteristic offset recoil spring and front-operated grip safety, was eventually modified.

The revised design, known as the Type 14 (1925), is far more common, for it was widely used by the Japanese during World War II and by Chinese troops in Korea. There are two common varieties of the Type 14. The early model has a small trigger guard and usually lacks a magazine safety. The later model, with the large, cold weather trigger guard, has a magazine safety.

While the two Type 14s may look alike, many of the working parts are not interchangeable. For instance, the breech bolt on the early model is machined to take a long firing pin that stops short of the bolt lock, while the large trigger guard model has a short firing pin that passes through a notch in the bolt lock. Many round-type trigger guards do not have the cutouts in the back strap or trigger projection necessary to operate in a frame equipped with a magazine safety.

The Type 14 Nambu is a locked breech, recoil-operated pistol. It fires an 8mm bottleneck cartridge that looks a great deal like the .30 caliber Luger cartridge but has a larger base.

The Type 14 has several bad features. First is the awkward position of the safety catch, which cannot be operated with the shooting hand. Second, the magazine follower holds the breech open, making magazine removal difficult. The magazine of the late model is harder to remove due of a friction spring in the front strap. This prevents the magazine from dropping out if the magazine catch is accidentally released. The gun's worst feature is the fact that it can be assembled without the locking block. If fired in this condition, it might injure the shooter and damage the gun. The quality of workmanship varies considerably. Prewar guns were generally well made and finished, but wartime guns are often poorly finished.

DISASSEMBLY

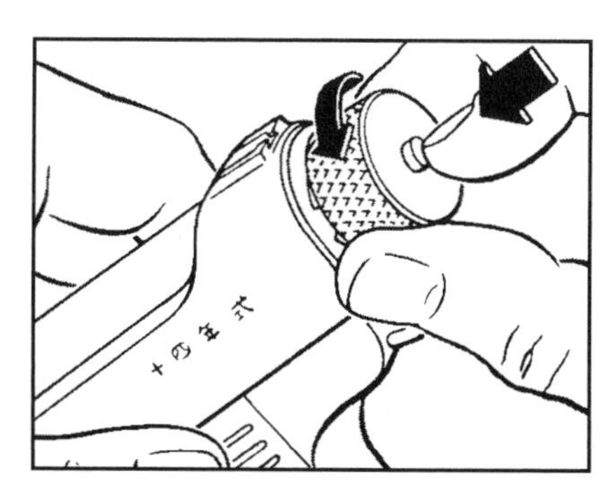

1 To field strip gun, first remove magazine. Then pull back bolt (4) to clear chamber, but not enough to cock the weapon. Ease bolt forward. Press in firing pin extension (7) protruding through cocking piece (6) and unscrew cocking piece. Shake out firing pin spring (8).

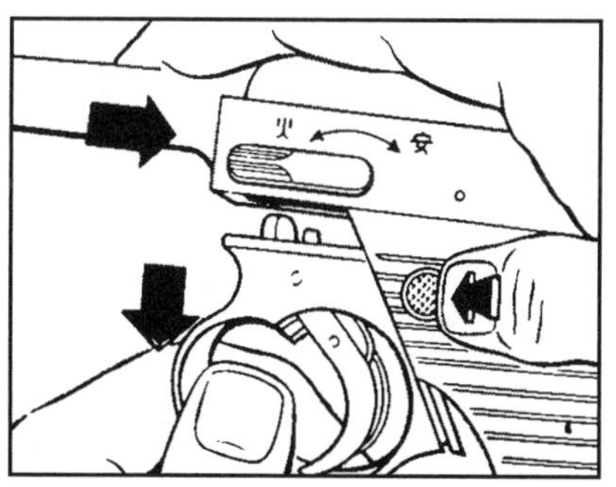

2 Rotate safety catch (22) to fire position as shown. Press magazine catch (24) in as for as it will go. Hold back barrel extension (2) or press muzzle against a solid surface. Pull down hard on trigger guard (19) until it is free of frame. Lift barrel extension (2) out of frame.

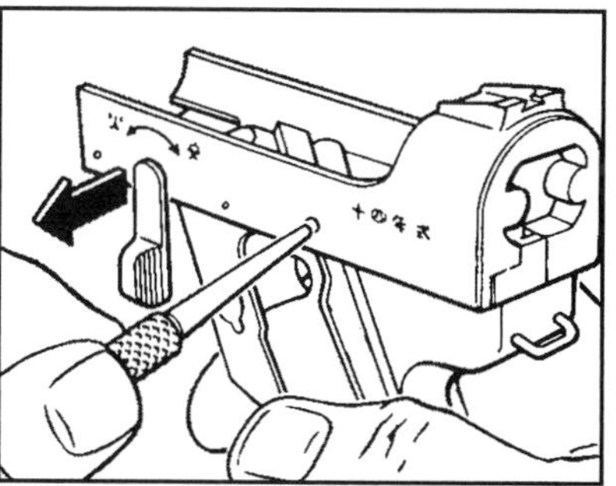

3 To remove safety catch (22) first remove left grip (29). Use a small punch to push out trigger bar hinge pin (12). This will allow trigger bar (27) and trigger bar spring (28) to drop out. Rotate safety catch to down position and pull it out of frame.

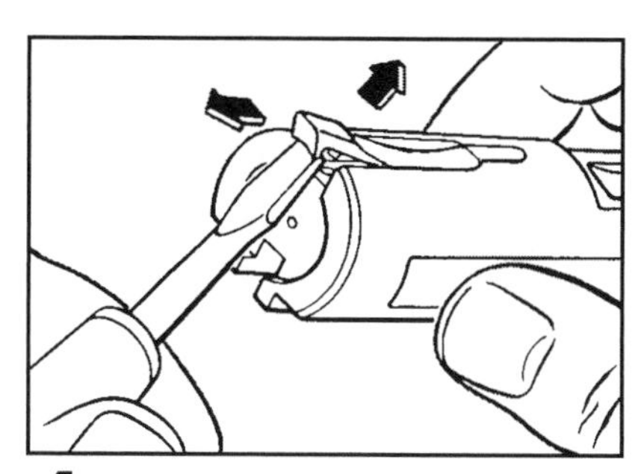

4 The method of retaining the extractor is a great deal like that of the Model 1900 Luger. To remove extractor (3), use a small screwdriver to push front free of retaining hole in bolt (4), then pry it forward, out of bolt.

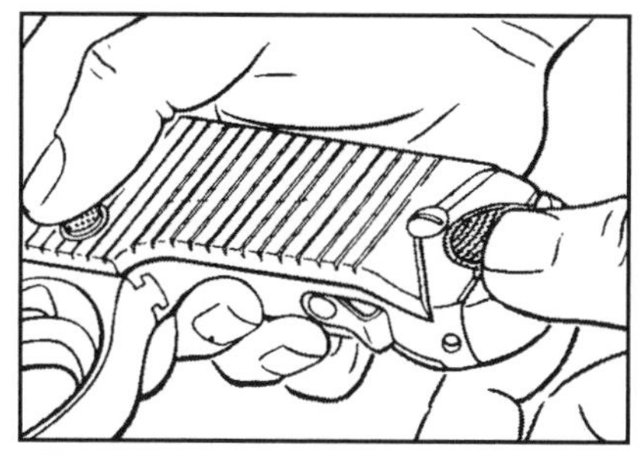

5 On early Type 14 pistols a loaded magazine will drop out of the gun if magazine catch is accidentally pushed. To prevent this, a friction spring was riveted to front strap of grip. This spring bears on magazine and holds it until deliberately pulled out.

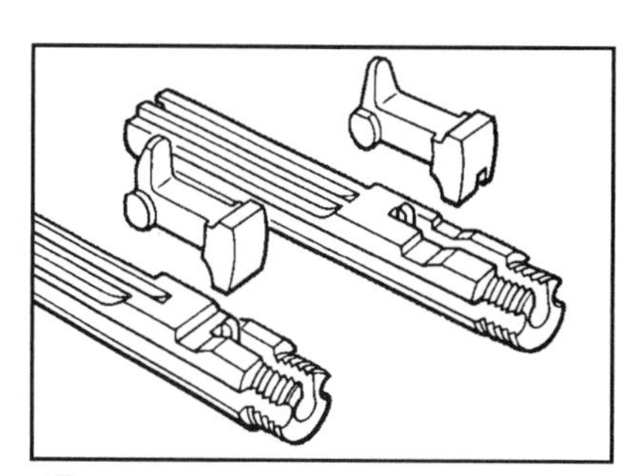

6 Although early and late Type 14's may look alike, parts are not necessarily interchangeable. The early type has a solid bolt lock and a long firing pin. The later, more common type, has a much shorter firing pin (9) and a grooved locking block (11) that allows the short firing pin to pass through it.

JAPANESE TYPE 26 REVOLVER

PARTS LEGEND

1. Front sight
2. Front sight pin
3. Barrel
4. Latch
5. Extractor bearing
6. Extractor bearing pin
7. Extractor spring
8. Cylinder
9. Extractor
10. Barrel hinge pin
11. Latch spring
12. Latch spring plunger
13. Latch screw
14. Hinge pin screw
15. Extractor cam
16. Extractor release
17. Release tension spring
18. Hammer
19. Strut
20. Strut spring
21. Strut screw
22. Hammer stirrup
23. Rebound lever
24. Rebound lever screw
25. Right grip screw (2)
26. Sideplate hinge screw
27. Right grip
28. Frame
29. Mainspring
30. Left grip
31. Sideplate
32. Trigger guard
33. Trigger
34. Hand
35. Hammer stirrup pin

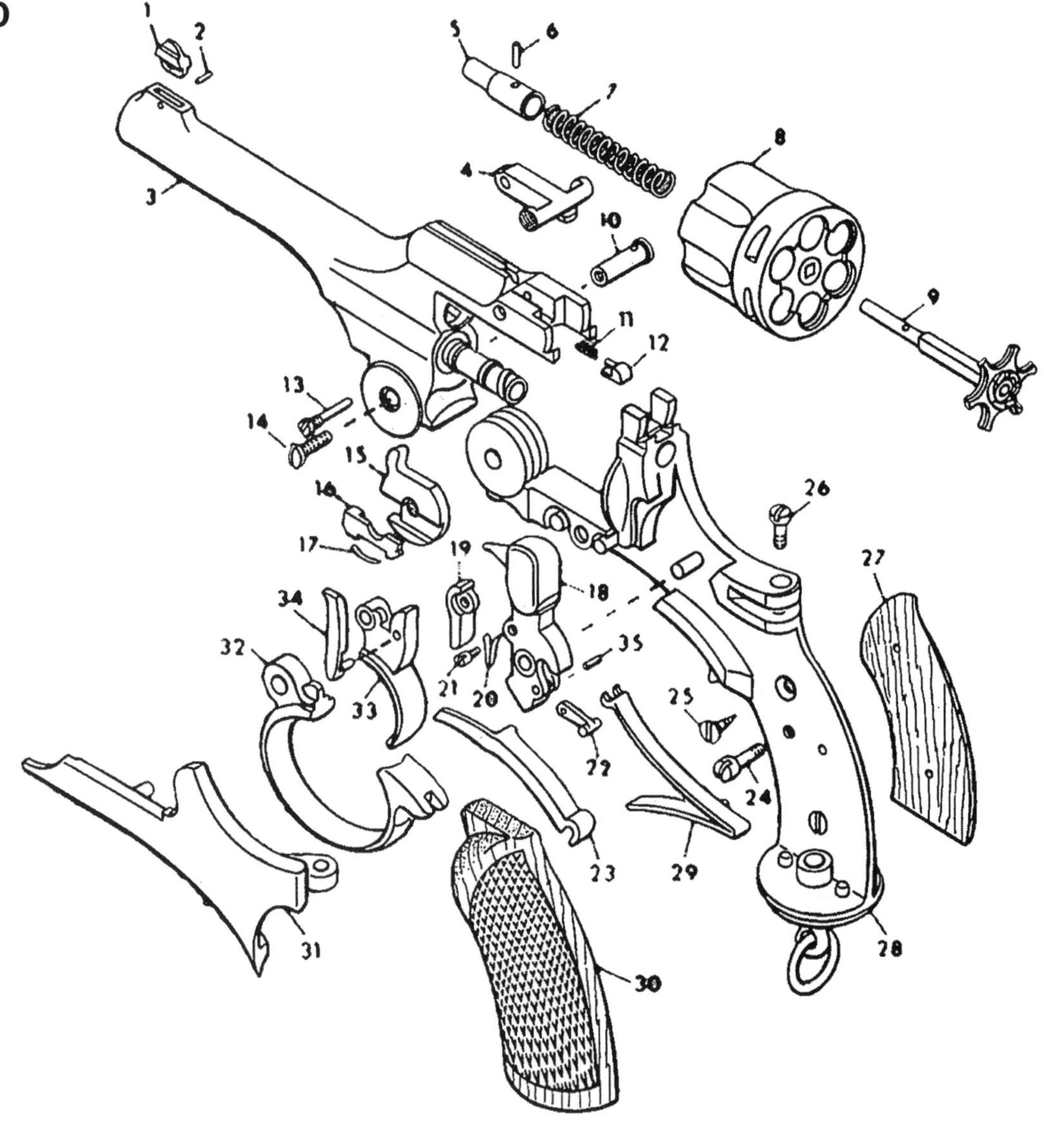

During the 26th year of Emperor Meiji's reign (1893), the Japanese Army adopted the Type 26 9mm revolver. Designed and produced at Japan's Koishikawa Arsenal, this weapon was the standard Japanese Army handgun until replaced about 1914 by the Nambu automatic pistol. It was used in combat during the Russo-Japanese War and in China in the 1930s and remained in service as substitute standard (for cavalry issue) after the Nambu was adopted. The Type 26 was used to some extent during World War II.

The top-break system of the Type 26 is similar to that of several older Smith & Wesson revolvers. To open for loading and unloading, the latch at the top rear of the barrel is lifted, and the barrel is pivoted down. As the barrel pivots down, all 6 cartridges are extracted and ejected automatically and simultaneously.

In lockwork design, the Type 26 closely resembles the Austro-Hungarian Rast & Gasser Model 98 revolver. An excellent feature is that the sideplate can be pivoted open easily to expose the mechanism, and the lock parts can be removed for cleaning and lubrication without use of tools. Firing requires a long pull of the trigger. The hammer has no full-cock notch and thus lacks a spur for thumb-cocking. This system, satisfactory for military purposes, is also used in the British No. 2 Mark I* Enfield service revolver.

Simple and well made, this revolver has checkered wood grips and a lanyard swivel. It is marked on the right of the frame with the serial number, symbol of the manufacturing arsenal, and Japanese numerals and letters which stand for "26 Year Type."

After World War II, the Type 26 was brought to the United States by returning servicemen in considerable numbers and is encountered frequently. The 9mm cartridge for it, however, is rare. Of straight-case rimmed type, it has a round-nose, lead bullet, propelled by smokeless powder. Other identifying features are the lack of a headstamp and the unusually thin rim.

The takedown of the revolver is illustrated; the assembly is in reverse order.

DISASSEMBLY

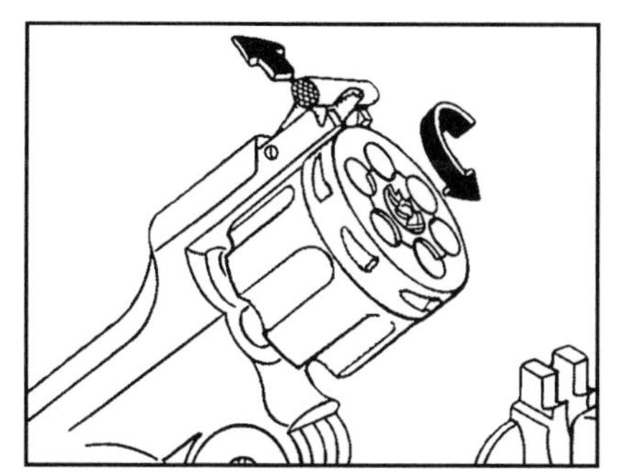

1 To disassemble, first lift the latch (4), and pivot the barrel (3) down, and remove any cartridges from the cylinder (8). Then, while holding latch up, unscrew the cylinder (8) counterclockwise.

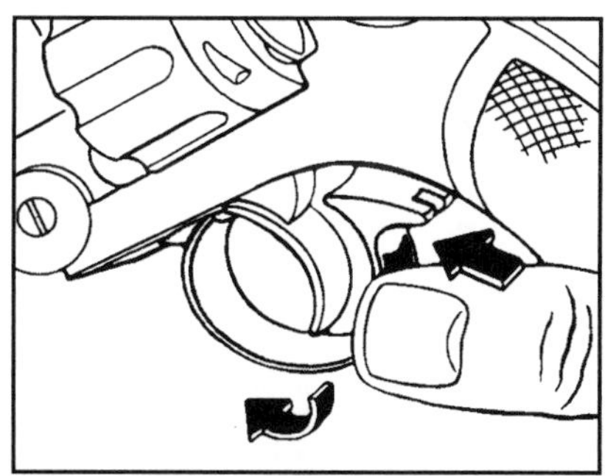

2 Push forward slightly on the rear of the trigger guard (32) to unlatch it, and then pivot the trigger guard down. This unlocks the sideplate (31) so it may be opened.

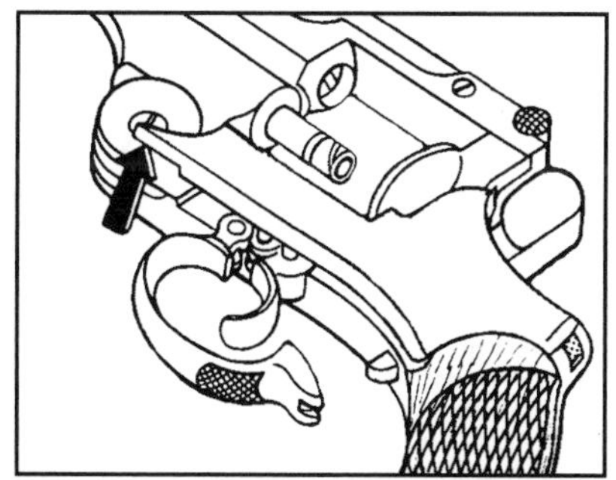

3 Grasp the lower front of the sideplate where it is knurled and pivot it rearward to expose the lock mechanism. Lift off the left grip (30) and remove the trigger guard.

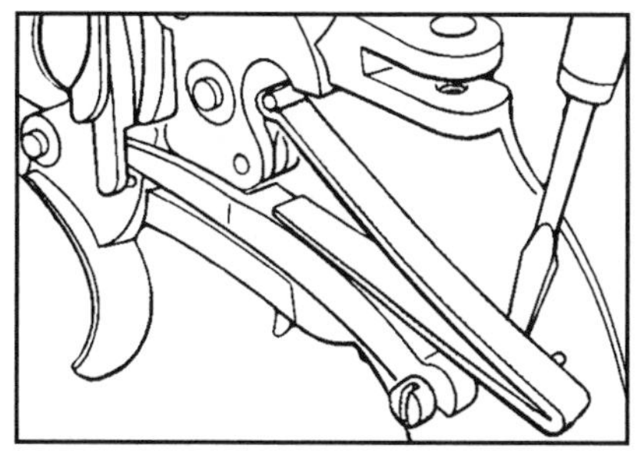

4 Hold the rear of the mainspring (29) firmly, lift it away from the frame (28) slightly or pry outward gently with a small screwdriver. Ease it upward and disengage it from the hammer stirrup (22). Lock parts can now be easily removed.

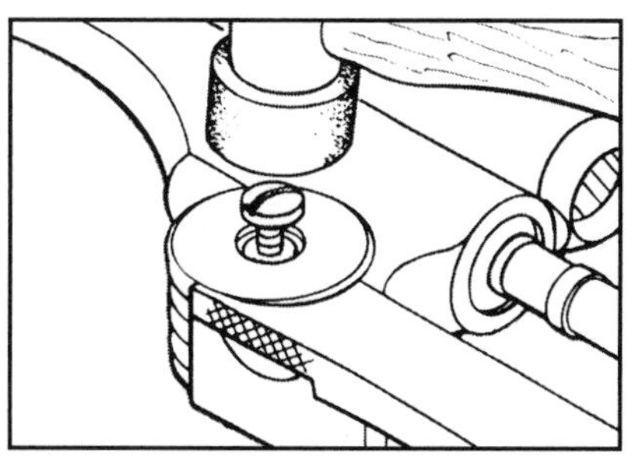

5 Unscrew the hinge pin screw (14) about ⅛ inch and tap it lightly with a mallet to partially drive out the barrel hinge pin (10). Then completely remove the screw and hinge pin, separate the barrel from the frame, and take out the extractor cam (15), extractor release (16), and release tension spring (17).

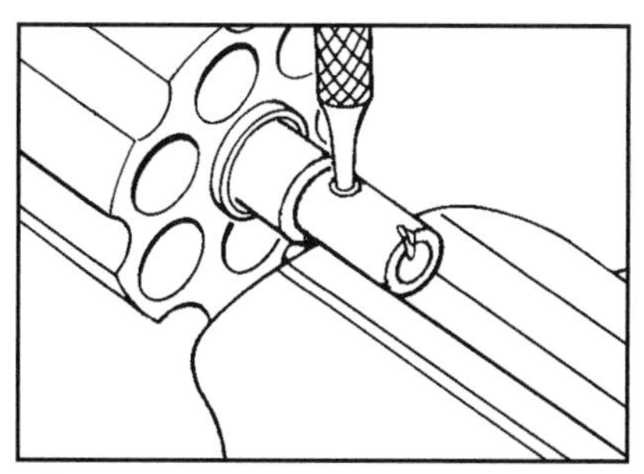

6 Locate the extractor bearing pin (6). Rest the bearing on vise jaws and drive out the pin with a drift punch and hammer. Then remove the bearing, extractor spring (7), and extractor (9) from the cylinder. The latch, latch spring (11) and latch spring plunger (12) can be removed from the barrel after turning out the latch screw (13).

JAPANESE TYPE 94 PISTOL

PARTS LEGEND

1. Front sight
2. Slide
3. Extractor
4. Breechbolt
5. Firing pin spring
6. Firing pin
7. Recoil spring
8. Recoil spring collar
9. Barrel
10. Crossbolt
11. Locking block
12. Hammer
13. Hammer roller pin
14. Hammer roller
15. Hammer spring
16. Sear hinge pin
17. Magazine catch
18. Right grip
19. Grip screw
20. Disconnector
21. Disconnector pin
22. Disconnector spring
23. Trigger spring
24. Trigger
25. Trigger screw
26. Sear spring
27. Sear and trigger bar
28. Magazine catch nut
29. Magazine catch spring
30. Magazine operated safety
31. Magazine safety spring
32. Hammer screw
33. Safety catch
34. Frame
35. Magazine
36. Left grip
37. Grip screw

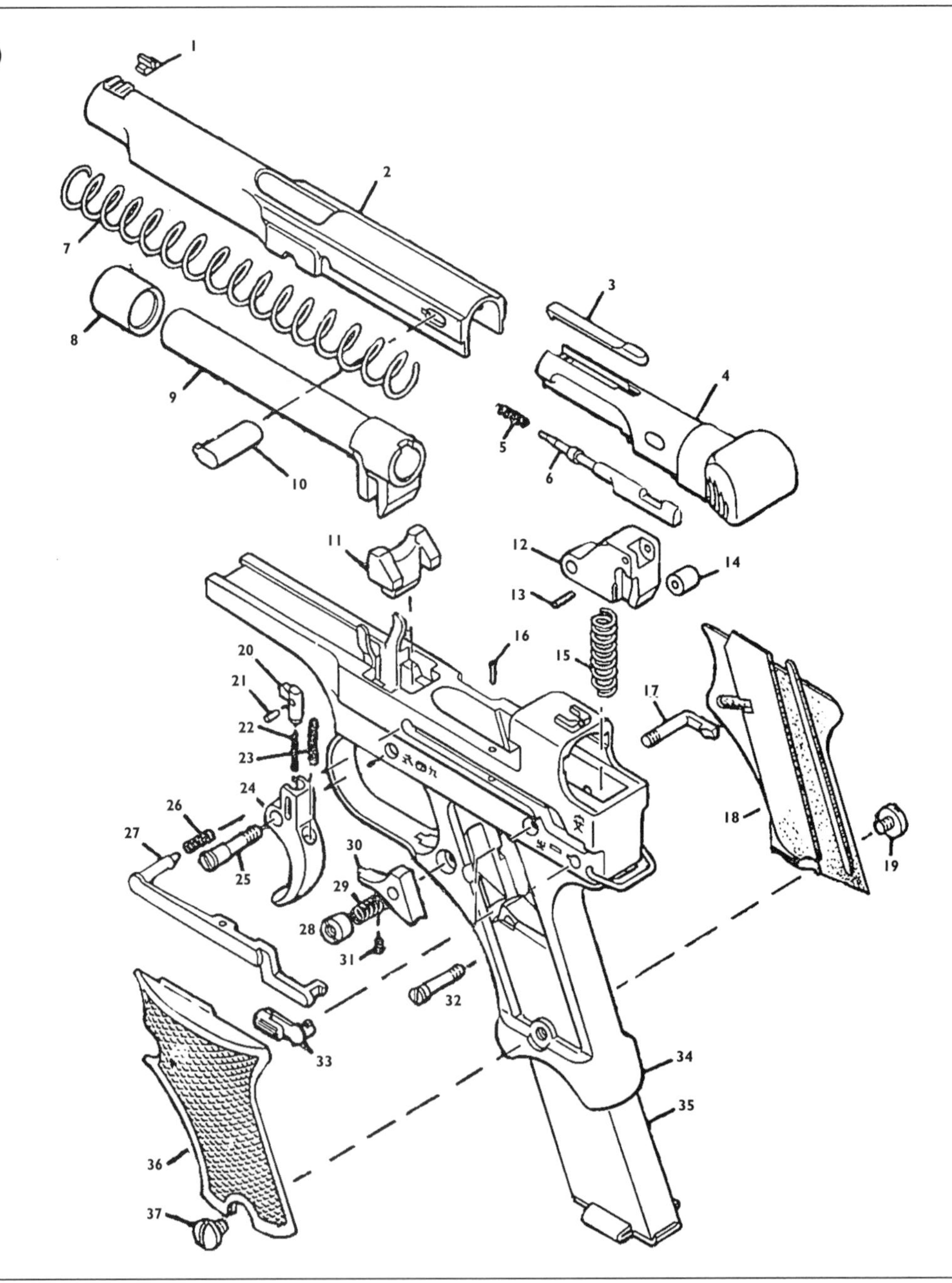

Designed by Kijiro Nambu, the Type 94 (1934) Japanese Service pistol was chambered for the rimless, 8mm Nambu Japanese service cartridge. This bottleneck cartridge was also used in Japanese Type 14 (1925) semi-automatic Service pistols and in Japanese submachine guns.

The recoil-operated Type 94 has a device to lock barrel and slide together until the bullet has cleared the barrel. The detachable magazine housed in the grip holds 6 cartridges.

The Type 94 has two safety devices; a manual safety which locks the external sear and trigger bar and a safety activated by the magazine catch mechanism. When the magazine catch button on the left side of the frame is depressed and the magazine is withdrawn from the grip, a bar rises to engage a detent notch in the rear of the trigger to block rearward movement of the trigger. These safeties are not particularly reliable.

Other mechanical features of note in the Type 94 pistol include an independent spring-loaded firing pin, an internal, concealed hammer and a lanyard ring attached to the rear of the frame. Grip plates are commonly of coarsely checkered black plastic, but smooth wood grips are also found on this arm.

A potentially dangerous feature of the Type 94 pistol is that it can be fired by accidentally depressing the front end of the external sear and trigger bar which lies exposed in a slot milled in the left side of the frame.

The average Type 94 pistol is roughly machined and poorly finished, showing hasty wartime manufacture.

DISASSEMBLY

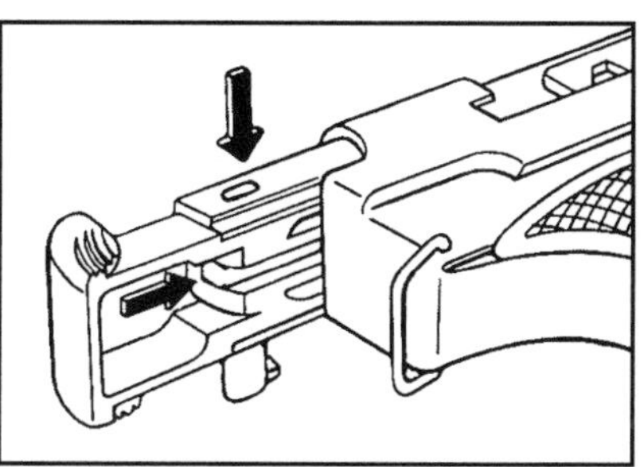

1 The first step in disassembling the Type 94 pistol is to pull the slide to the rear over an empty magazine. The slide (2) and the breechbolt (4) will be held to the rear. Push the firing pin (6) forward until it is flush with the shoulder in the slide; this will free the crossbolt (10). The crossbolt can then be pushed out of the slide from right to left as shown.

2 After the breechbolt has been removed, the slide may stay in place. To remove the breechbolt first take out the magazine (35). Then, holding the gun as shown, push the barrel (9) back while holding the slide. This action unlocks the slide and permits it to be eased off the front of the frame (34).

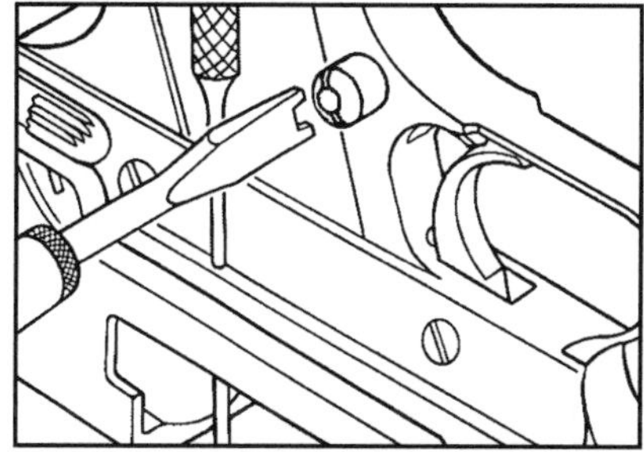

3 The magazine catch nut (28) is some times peened or riveted to the shaft of the magazine catch (17). It can be unscrewed with a screwdriver ground to the shape shown or, if difficulty is encountered, with the aid of pliers or a vise.

After removing left grip screw (37) and left grip (36), drift out sear hinge pin (16) from bottom. Remove trigger screw (25) and disengage trigger (24).

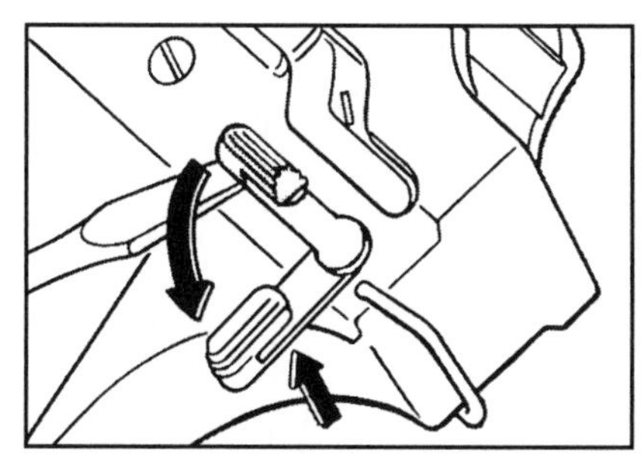

4 The safety catch has a detent on the inner face which retains the catch in the "on" or "off" position. The safety catch (33) blocks only the sear. To remove the safety catch, remove the left grip (36), lift the catch out of engagement with frame, and swing it down. The safety catch can then be lifted out.

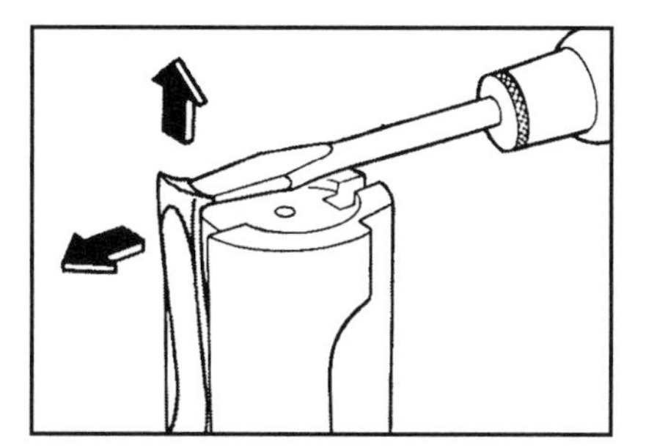

5 The extractor (3) is of simple design. The tail is dove-tailed into the top of the breechbolt. To remove the extractor, with a screwdriver push the front of the extractor outward far enough for the projection on the extractor to clear its seat in the bolt. When it is free, pry the extractor out as shown.

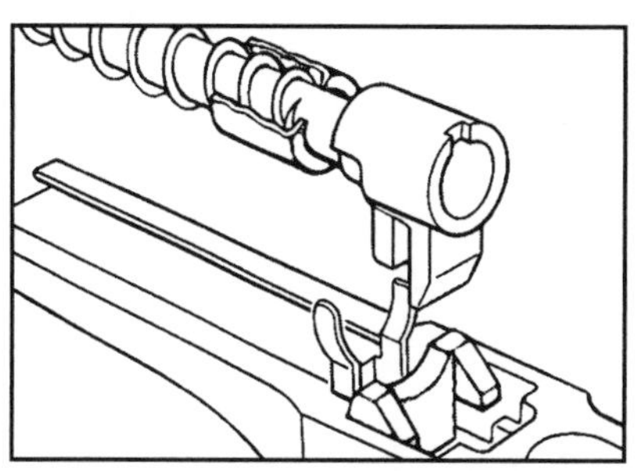

6 When reassembling the gun, place the locking block (11) in the frame correctly so that the yoke on the barrel can fit over the curved surface of it. The barrel must be installed in the frame before putting the slide back on. The recoil spring collar (8) must be installed with the solid face toward the chamber.

KAHR P-9 PISTOL

PARTS LEGEND

1. Polymer frame
2. Barrel
3. Slide
4. Slide back
5. Recoil spring
6. Recoil spring guide
7. Striker block
8. Striker block spring
9. Trigger
10. Trigger spring
11. Trigger spacer
12. Trigger pivot pin
13. Trigger bar
14. Trigger bar spring
15. Cocking cam
16. Cocking cam spring
17. Magazine catch body
18. Magazine catch leaf spring
20. Sriker
21. Striker spacer
22. Striker spring
23. Striker spring guide
24. Extractor
25. Extractor pin – front
26. Extractor spring
27. Extractor pin– back
28. Slide stop
29. Slide stop spring
30. Slide stop spring screw & washer
31. Ejector
32. Cocking cam pivot pin
33. Rear sight
34. Front sight
35. Magazine tube
36. Magazine spring
37. Magazine base lock
38. Magazine base
39. Magazine follower
40. Side panel pin
41. Side panel

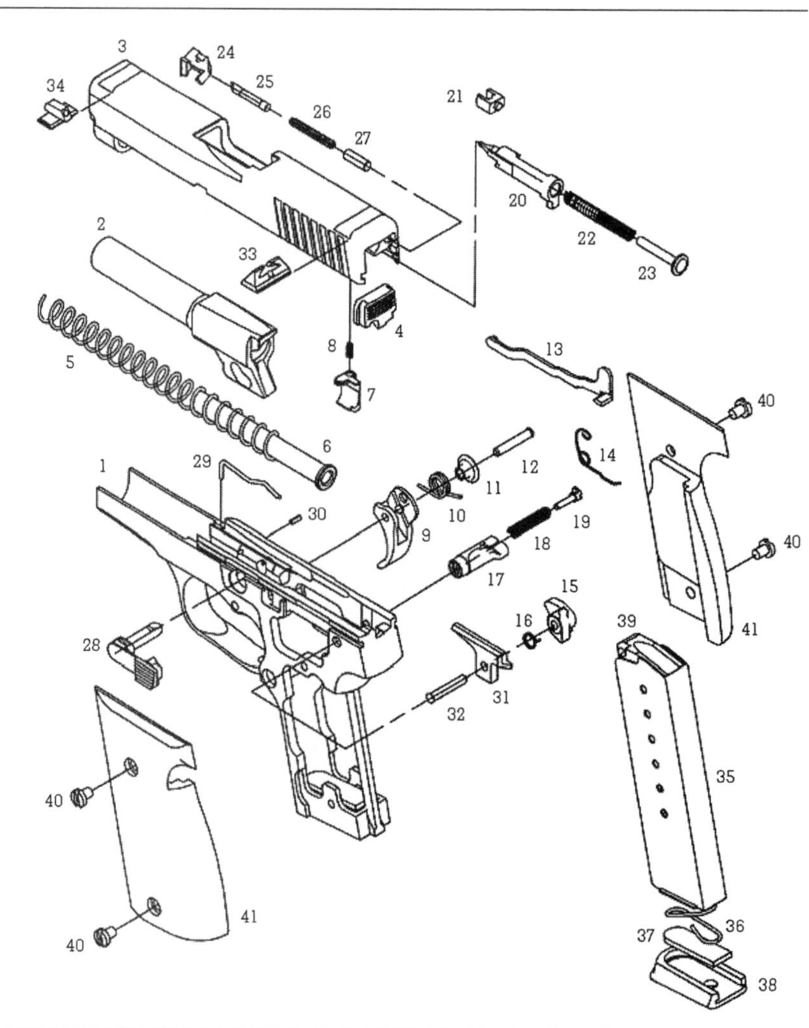

The initial product of Kahr Arms, founded in 1986, was the K9, a compact, all-steel double-action pistol in 9mm Parabellum. Under the direction of Kahr head designer Justin Moon, a polymer-frame version of this gun, the P9, was created and introduced at the 1999 SHOT Show.

The Kahr P9 is a Browning-inspired, short-recoil-operated, striker-fired, double-action only semi-automatic utilizing a polymer frame with steel inserts in the frame rails. A long double-action trigger pull retracts and then releases the striker, obviating the need for an external safety. Lockup is by a rectangular block around the chamber end of the barrel that engages the ejection port. A kidney-shaped cutout in the bottom of the block engages the slide stop to raise and lower the barrel during cycling.

Variants of the basic Kahr design are offered in different sizes, frame materials and calibers (9mm Parabellum and .40 S&W). Disassembly is essentially the same for all models.

DISASSEMBLY

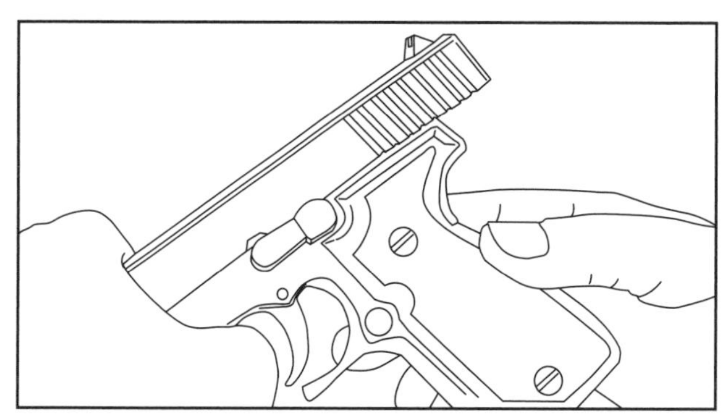

1 Draw the slide about ¼ inch to the rear so that the relief cut in the slide aligns with the slide stop.

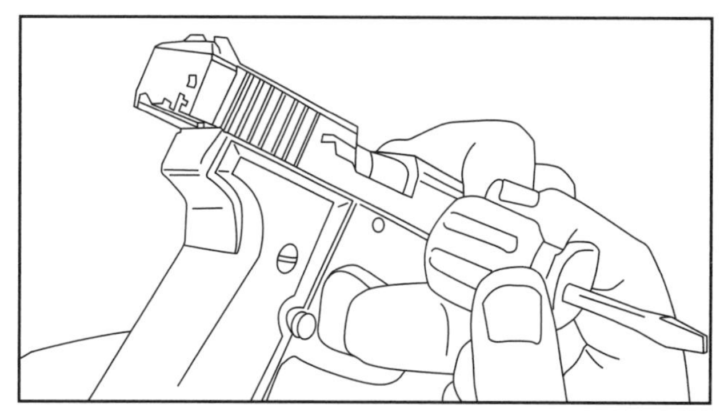

2 Tap the slide stop out of the pistol from right to left with a light, non-marring hammer or plastic screwdriver handle. Ease the slide forward under recoil spring tension. With the slide stop removed, pull the trigger to release the striker, then relax pressure on the trigger and push the slide forward off of the frame.

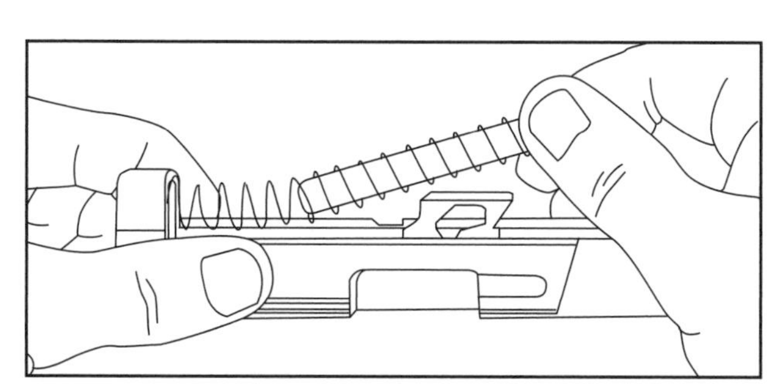

3 Push the rear of the recoil spring guide slightly forward with the thumb and lift it clear of the recoil lug. CAUTION: *protect eyes when removing the recoil spring guide. Recoil spring is under tension and may fly off guide and cause injury. Carefully remove recoil spring guide with recoil spring from slide.* NOTE: *Do not attempt to dismantle this recoil spring assembly. This is a factory-assembled component. The recoil spring is designed to work one way only. The smaller-diameter closed end must be against the flange on the rear of the recoil spring guide. Improper reassembly will cause damage to the firearm and cause injury to the user.*

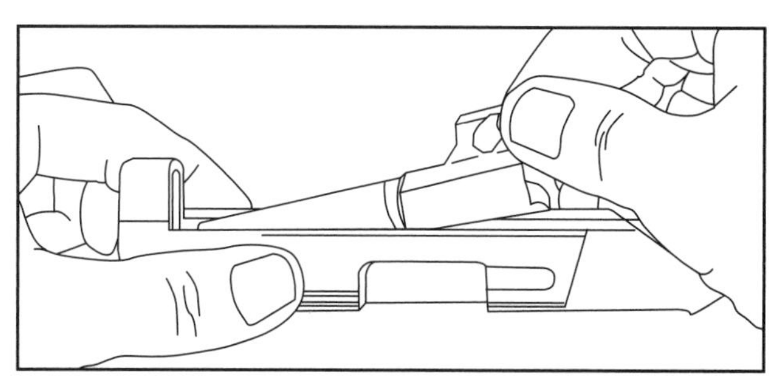

4 Grasp recoil lug of barrel and push it slightly forward, then lift and pull it rearward out of the slide. Removal of the barrel is carried out as follows: Push the rear of the recoil spring guide (6) slightly forward with the thumb and lift it clear of the recoil lug. Carefully remove recoil spring guide with recoil spring from slide. Grasp recoil lug of barrel and push it slightly forward, then lift and pull it rearward out of the slide.

KIMBER ULTRA CARRY PISTOL

PARTS LEGEND

1. Frame
2. Ejector
3. Ejector pin
4. Plunger tube
5. Slide stop plunger
6. Plunger spring
7. Thumb safety plunger
8. Grip screw bushings (4)
9. Grip, right
10. Grip, left
11. Grip screws (4)
12. Magazine catch
13. Magazine catch spring
14. Magazine catch lock
15. Disconnector
16. Sear
17. Sear pin
18. Push rod
19. Hammer
20. Hammer pin
21. Hammer strut
22. Hammer strut pin
23. Mainspring housing
24. Mainspring housing pin Retainer
25. Mainspring
26. Mainspring cap
27. Mainspring cap pin
28. Mainspring housing pin
29. Trigger assembly
30. Trigger stop screw
31. Sear spring
32. Grip safety
33. Thumb safety, port side
34. Slide
35. Front sight
36. Rear sight fixed
37. Rear sight screw
38. Firing pin
39. Firing pin spring
40. Extractor
41. Firing pin stop
42. Firing pin block
43. Firing pin block spring
44. Barrel
45. Barrel link
46. Barrel link pin
47. Slide stop
48. Recoil spring bushing**
49. Outer recoil spring**
50. Recoil spring assembly**
51. Recoil spring rod**
52. Head guide**
53. Inner recoil spring
54. Recoil spring sleeve
55. Magazine assembly
56. Magazine tube*
57. Magazine spring*
58. Magazine follower*
59. Takedown tool

*Parts of an assembly (not shown)
** Detail

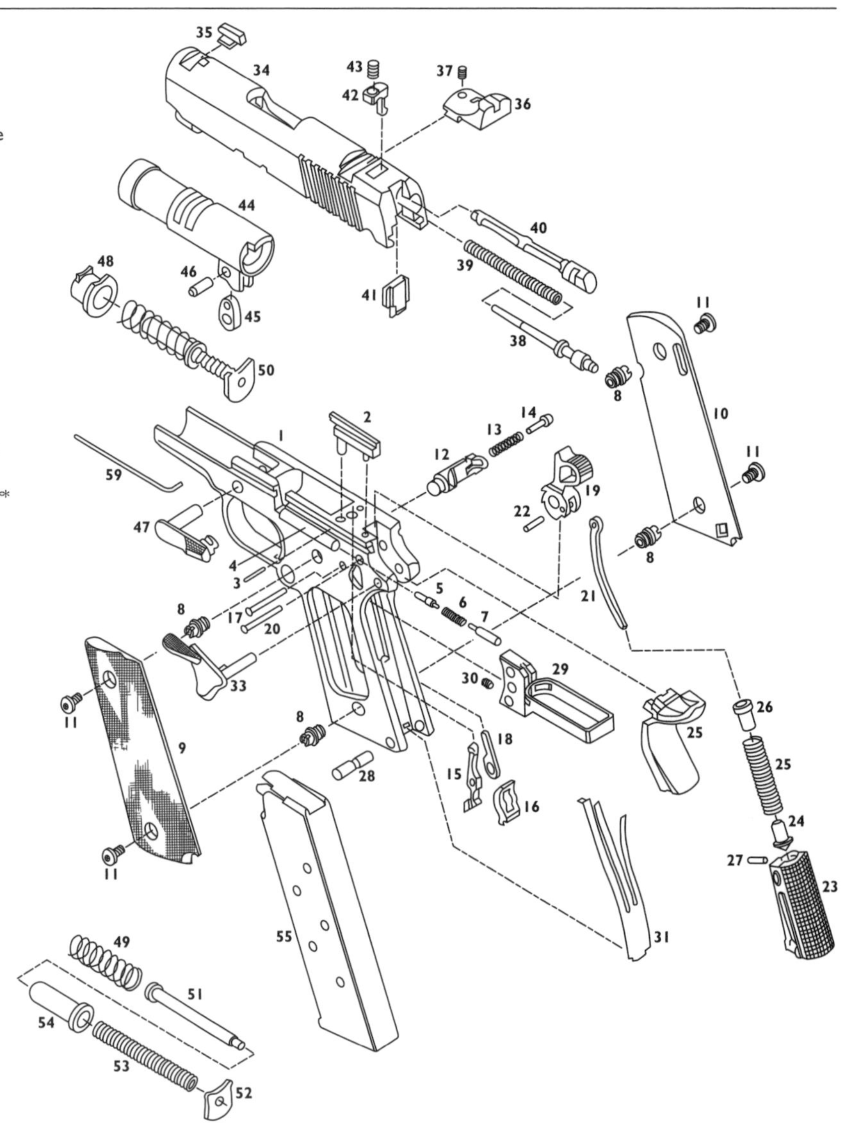

Kimber was founded in 1979 in Colton, Oregon by brothers Greg and Jack Warner, under the name "Kimber of Oregon." The company initially produced a line of .22-caliber rimfire rifles and expanded to include a manufacturing plant in the nearby city of Clackmas, Oregon.

After a series of financial difficulties, however, Kimber closed its Oregon facilities in 1997. Under new management, the firm purchased Jerico Precision Manufacturing in Yonkers, New York, and the new company was renamed Kimber of America and expanded its product line to include M1911-style handguns. Kimber's manufacturing facility is currently located in Ridgefield, New Jersey. As Kimber Mfg., Inc, the company manufactures 1911-style handguns, shotguns and high-powered rifles.

The Kimber Ultra Carry, introduced in 1999, is a compact, lightweight M1911-style semi-automatic handgun built on a machined aluminum frame with a steel slide. The Ultra-Carry weighs 25 ounces and has a 3-inch barrel, beavertail grip safety, extended thumb safety, lightweight, match grade trigger and slotted hammer.

The Ultra Carry's design does not use a barrel bushing like a conventional 1911, but the barrel engages the bore of the slide directly. The Ultra Carry is offered in .45 ACP and .40 S&W, loaded with a seven-shot, single-column magazine.

DISASSEMBLY

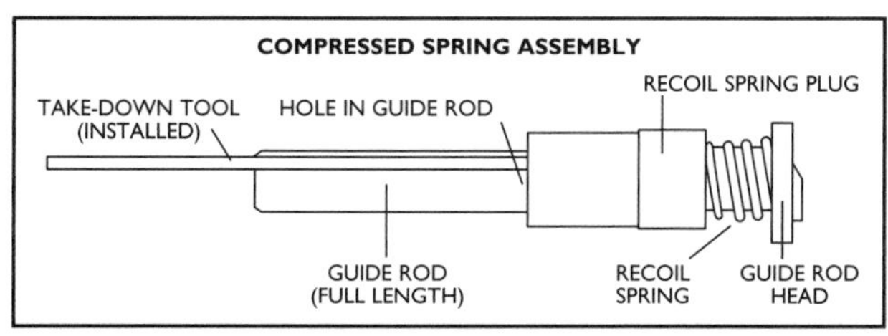

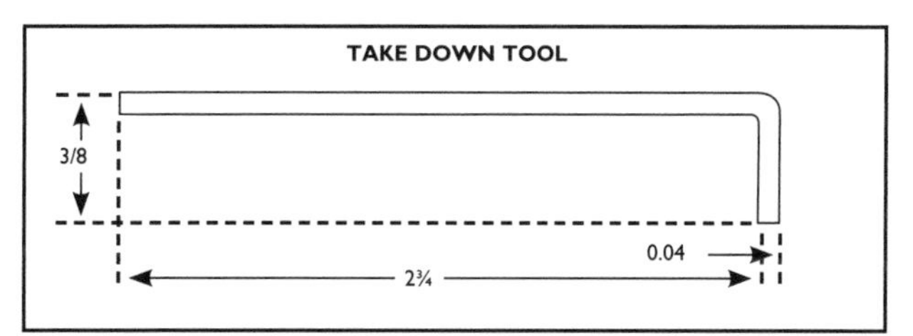

1 With the pistol unloaded and the magazine removed, retract and lock back the slide. Locate the exposed small hole in the recoil spring guide rod. Insert the take down tool in the hole in the guide rod and carefully release the slide stop.

With hammer still cocked, push the slide forward until the semi-circular tab on the back of the slide stop aligns with the semi-circular disassembly notch in the bottom of the slide.

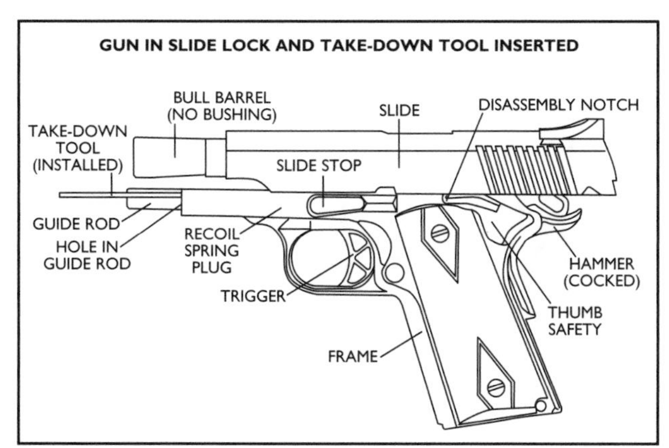

2 Push inward on the end of the slide stop shaft on the right side of the pistol and remove the slide stop form the left side.

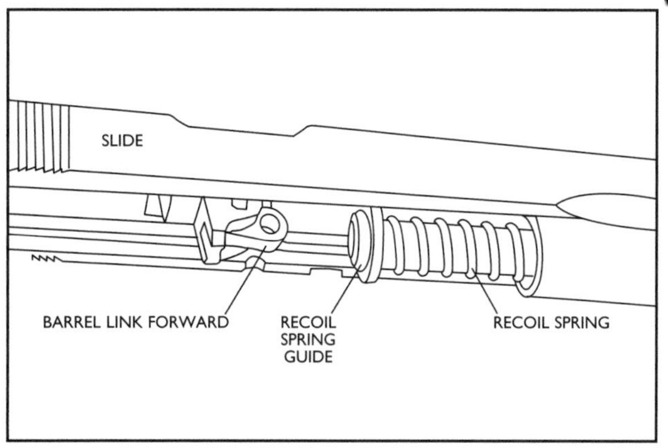

3 Remove the slide by sliding it forward off the frame. Tip the barrel link forward to clear the recoil spring tunnel. Then pull the barrel clear of the slide. The pistol is now disassembled for cleaning purposes (field stripped). CAUTION: *Do not drop the hammer while slide is removed from the pistol.*

LAHTI M40 PISTOL

PARTS LEGEND

1. Front sight
2. Barrel and barrel extension
3. Accelerator stop pin
4. Accelerator retainer
5. Accelerator retainer spring
6. Accelerator
7. Ejector
8. Locking block
9. Extractor
10. Slide
11. Right grip
12. Grip screw
13. Firing pin retainer pin
14. Firing pin spring
15. Firing pin
16. Disconnector
17. Trigger pin
18. Trigger
19. Trigger spring pin
20. Trigger spring
21. Trigger bar
22. Trigger bar pin
23. Sear spring
24. Sear
25. Hammer strut pin
26. Hammer
27. Hammer strut
28. Hammer spring plunger
29. Hammer spring
30. Spring guide nut
31. Trigger bar spring
32. Frame
33. Magazine
34. Magazine catch
35. Magazine catch spring
36. Magazine catch pin
37. Left grip
38. Grip screw
39. Safety catch
40. Sear pin
41. Hammer pin
42. Takedown catch
43. Takedown catch spring
44. Recoil spring
45. Recoil spring guide
46. Hold-open catch
47. Hold-open catch spring

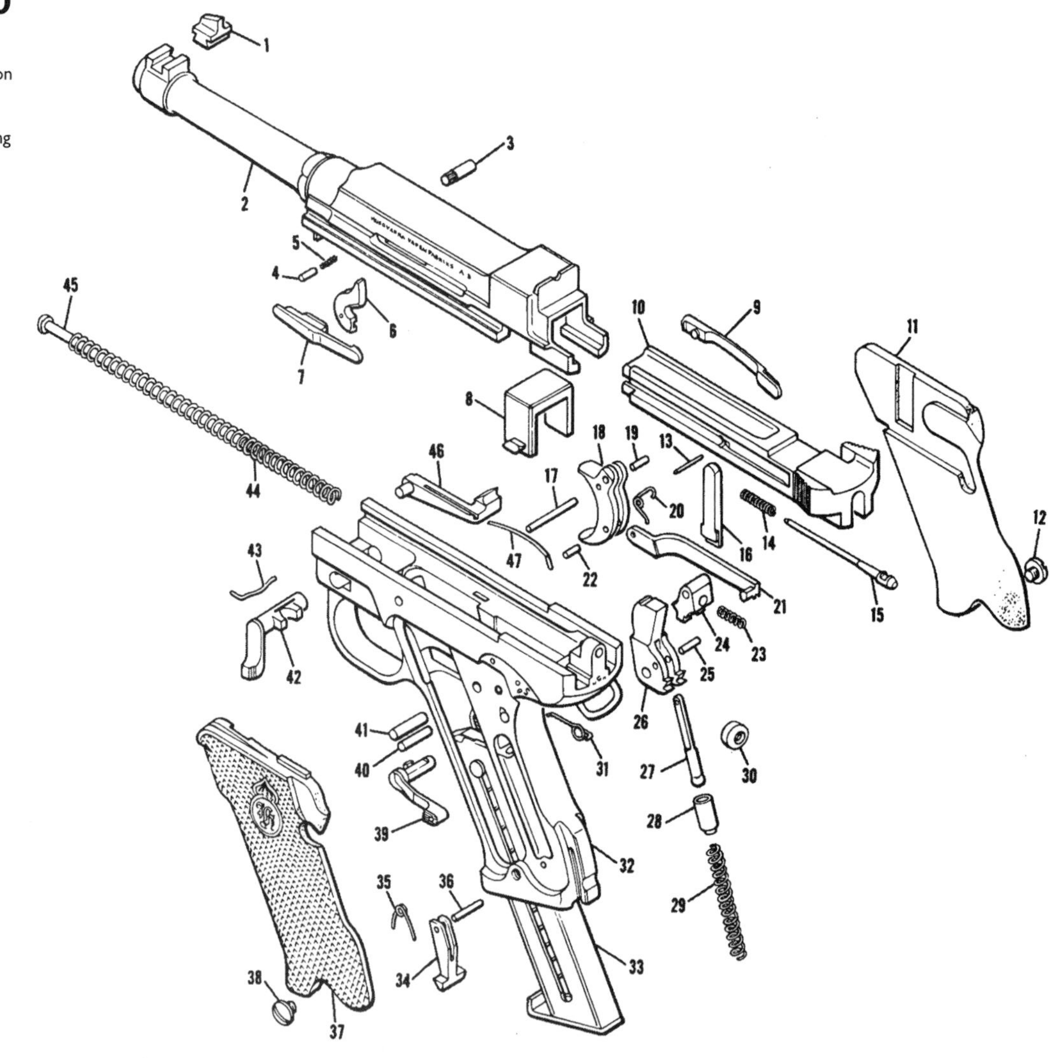

Gun designer Aimo Johannes Lahti of Finland developed a wide range of firearms for his native land — from automatic pistols to aircraft cannons. Today he is best known for an automatic pistol adopted as the L35 by Finland and, in slightly modified form, as the M40 by Sweden.

While the Finnish L35 Lahti is virtually unknown here, the Swedish M40 version is far more common. A number of these guns, marked Husqvarna Vapenfabriks A. B., were imported and sold in the United States around 1949 and 1950.

The Lahti is a heavy, rugged gun and mirrors the conditions it was designed for. The operating parts are strong and well designed for the extreme cold encountered along the Finnish and Swedish frontiers. The serrations on the slide are deep and tapered so that the slide can be retracted easily with a heavily gloved hand. The large trigger guard and protruding safety catch were also designed for gloved-hand operation. The cold weather also influenced mechanism design.

Even though the gun shoots the powerful 9mm Luger cartridge, Lahti added an accelerator to aid the operating mechanism. The accelerator in L35 and M40 pistols is a lever pivoted to the barrel extension. As the barrel, barrel extension, and slide recoil to the rear, the locking block is cammed free of the slide. At this instant the lower portion of the accelerator strikes the receiver wall and this blow is transmitted to the unlocked slide, throwing it back with great force. When the slide counter-recoils, it pushes the accelerator back into place.

An excellent grip and a long, fixed sighting radius make the gun a fine shooter. When equipped with its Luger-type shoulder stock, it becomes a formidable carbine.

An unfavorable feature of this pistol is that it will fire with its locking block removed. A check should therefore be made before firing to make sure locking block is present.

Under an excellent blue job, the Swedish-made Lahti shows a great deal of rough machining and hand finishing. Fortunately this does not detract from the reliability and accuracy of the gun. since critical operating parts and bore are well finished.

DISASSEMBLY

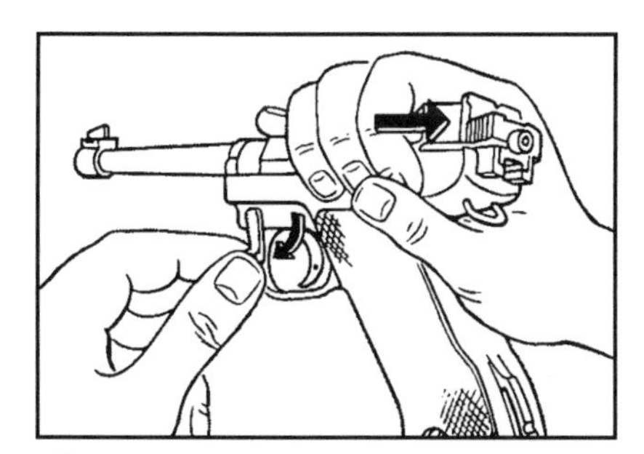

1 The Lahti takedown is simple. First remove magazine and clear chamber. Hold barrel extension (2) back as shown, or push the muzzle against a hard surface; at same time rotate takedown catch (42). Barrel assembly is now slid forward off receiver.

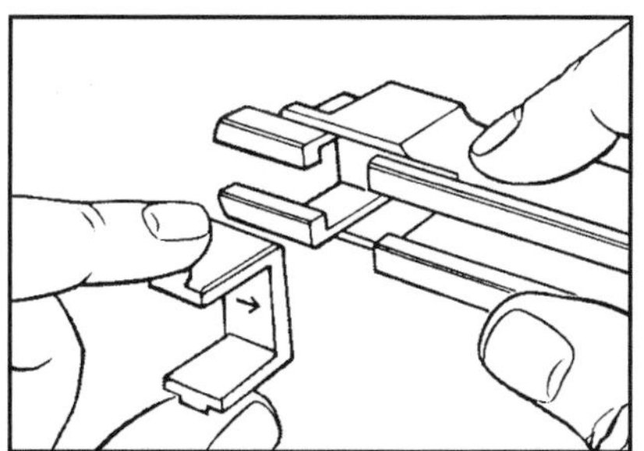

2 After barrel and barrel extension are free of receiver, push locking block (8) up and withdraw slide (10). When replacing locking block, be sure arrow on underside of block is facing forward toward barrel.

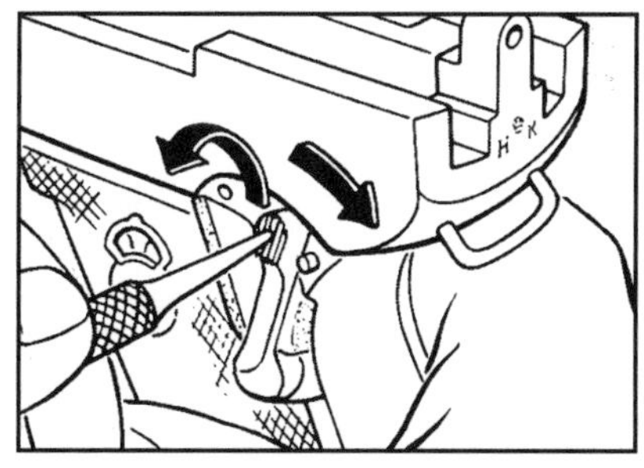

3 Safety catch (39) must be removed before attempting removal of left grip. Insert a thin punch into hole in serrated portion of safety. Pry it back slightly, enough to swing it over stop pin in frame. Rotate it to horizontal position and pull it out.

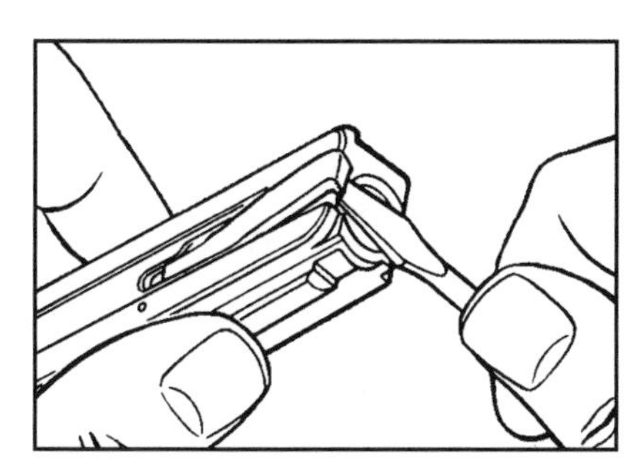

4 Extractor (9) is long and flexible. It is removed by inserting a small screwdriver under lip to push it free of locking hole in slide (10), then prying it out of its seat.

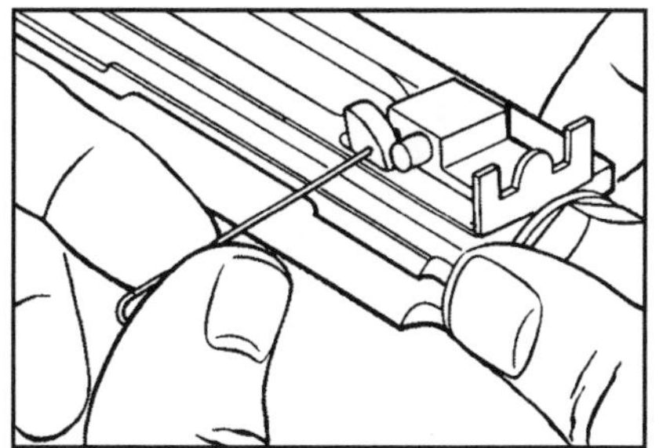

5 The accelerator (6) is designed for easy removal. Simply rotate accelerator until small hole in its side lines up with spring-loaded retainer pin (4). Push a thin piece of wire or paper clip through hole to depress spring. Lift out accelerator.

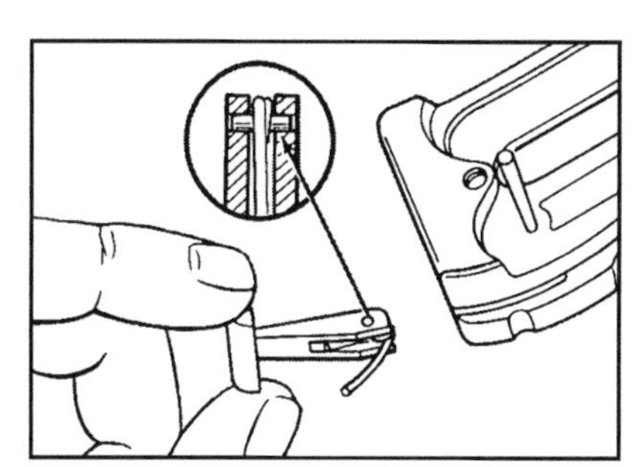

6 Some Lahti parts are difficult to reassemble without the aid of short slave pins. To replace magazine catch (34) and spring (35), use a short pin to hold them together until in position. Incoming magazine pin will drive short pin out other side and spring will remain in its place.

LE FRANÇAIS 9MM BROWNING LONG

PARTS LEGEND

1. Barrel
2. Slide
3. Firing pin rebound spring
4. Mainspring
6. Firing Pin
6. Slide cap
7, Frame
8. Barrel lever
9. Right grip
10. Barrel lever spring
11. Right recoil lever
12. Left recoil lever
13. Magazine
14. Recoil spring guide
15. Trigger strut
16. Recoil lnik pin
17. Recoil link
18. Recoil spring
19 Left grip
20 Trigger spring
21. Trigger spring washer
22. Trigger strut pin
23. Trigger
24. Trigger guard
25. Barrel hinge pin

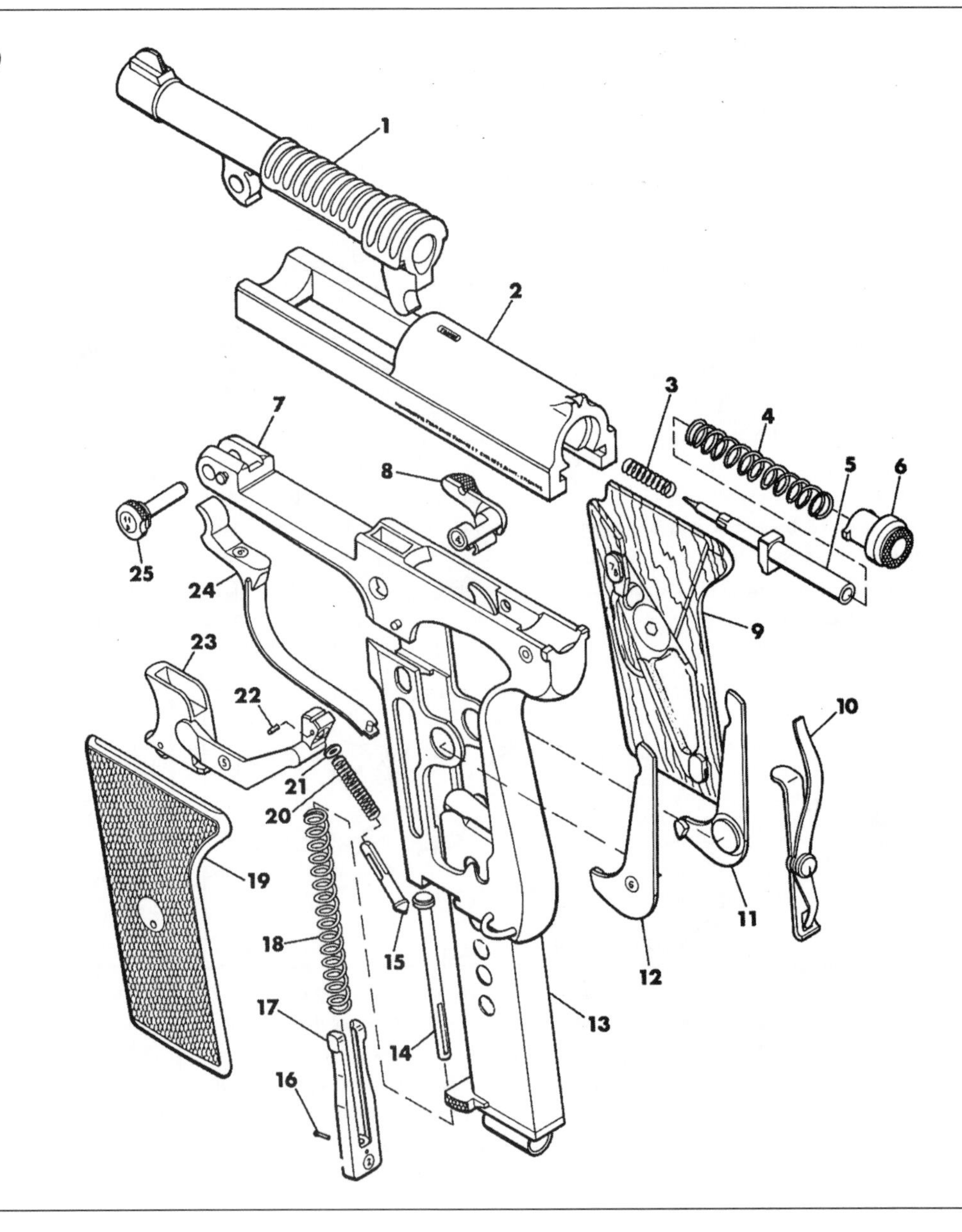

Variously known as the Model 1928, the Armée Model V and the Le Français Military Model, this pistol was made by Manufrance of Saint-Étienne, France from 1928 to 1938 to a quantity of around 4000 pistols. The *Armée Model*, M/1928. despite its name, ingenious design and high quality, was never officially adopted by the French military.

The Le Français is blowback operated and quite similar in appearance and function to the more common and smaller Manufrance-made Le Français pistols in 6.35mm (.25 ACP) and 7.65 (.32 ACP).

The 9mm Browning Long cartridge is more impressive in nomenclature than in ballistics, being little more effective than the standard .380 ACP. By modern standards it would be considered underpowered for a military load.

The M28 operates on the double-action only system and a long trigger pull is necessary to cock and release the striker. It is impossible to avoid this long pull and fire the pistol in single-action mode. The pistol lacks any manual safety.

Another significant design feature of the Le Français is the "pop-up" barrel which is activated by a lever on the right side of the frame (or by the removal of the magazine). This makes loading the chamber easy, and eliminates the need for an extractor or slide serrations. The clip on the bottom of the magazine is designed to hold a single cartridge which is available for quick chamber loading.

Disassembly of the M28 is simple, once the procedures are known, and requires no tools. The M28 is one of those few pistols that utilizes no screws in its construction — not even a grip screw.

DISASSEMBLY

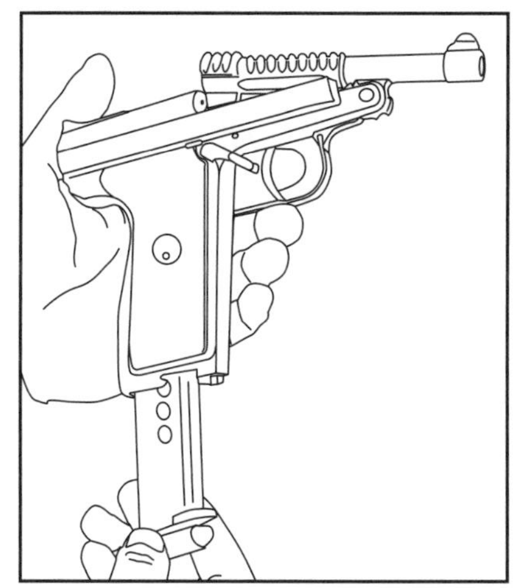

1 Remove magazine (13) by pushing serrated wings of floorplate forward and down. Magazine removal automatically opens the barrel (1).

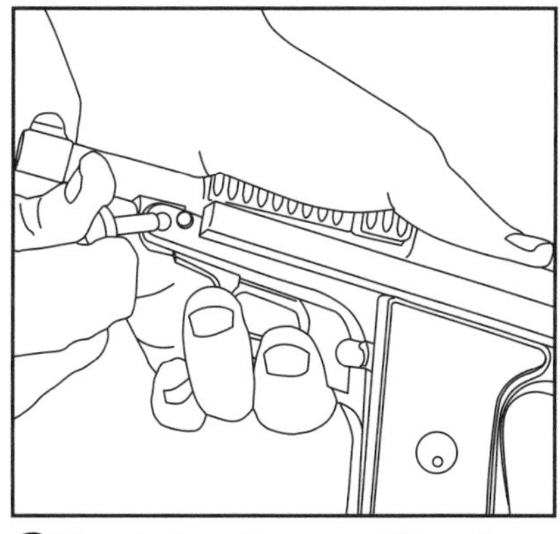

2 Turn the barrel hinge pin (25) until its notch mates with the frame lug. Holding the barrel firmly down in its closed position, remove the barrel hinge pin. Release the barrel slowly and remove it and the trigger guard (24) from the frame (7).

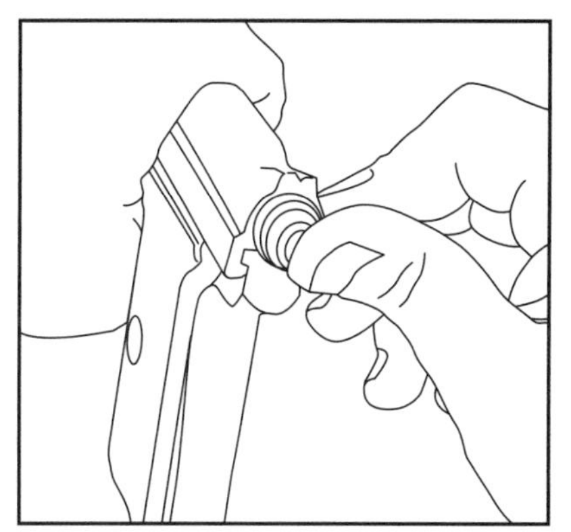

3 Push the slide cap (6) in and turn it counterclockwise one-quarter turn. Remove slide cap, firing pin (5), main spring (4) and firing pin rebound spring (3). Slide (2) may now be removed by pulling its front end upward slightly.

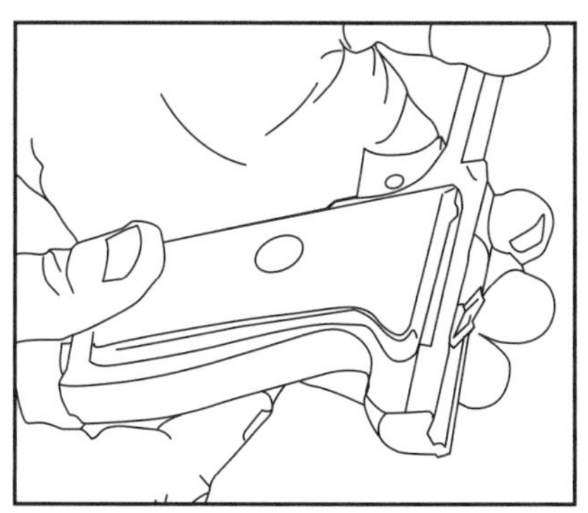

4 Slide right and left grips (9 & 19) straight up and remove them.

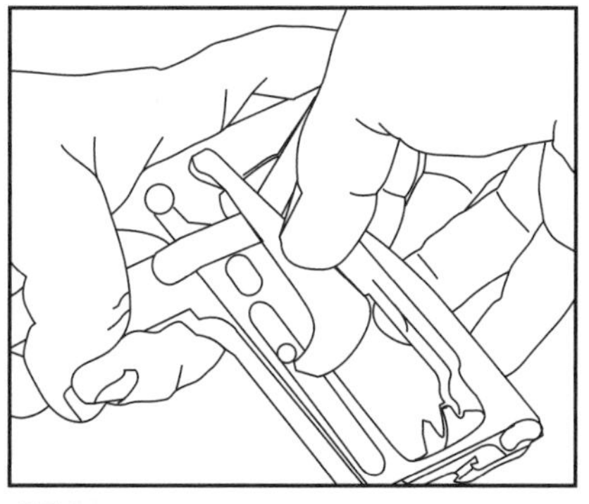

5 Push the frame down with the recoil link (17), which protrudes from the bottom front of the grip, bearing on a hard surface. With pressure on the recoil link, the recoil levers (11 & 12) can be removed. The trigger assembly (23) can now be lifted from the frame, as can the barrel lever spring (10).

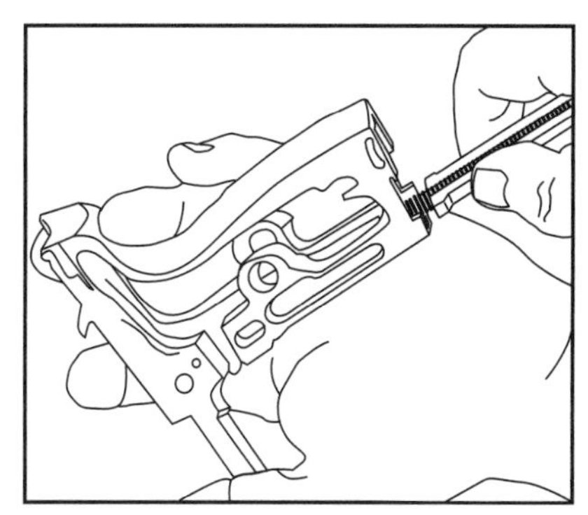

6 By pressing the sides of the recoil link together, it and the recoil spring assembly (18) can be withdrawn. The barrel lever (8) will now be free and can be removed, thus completing disassembly. Reassemble in reverse order.

LE FRANÇAIS POCKET MODEL PISTOL

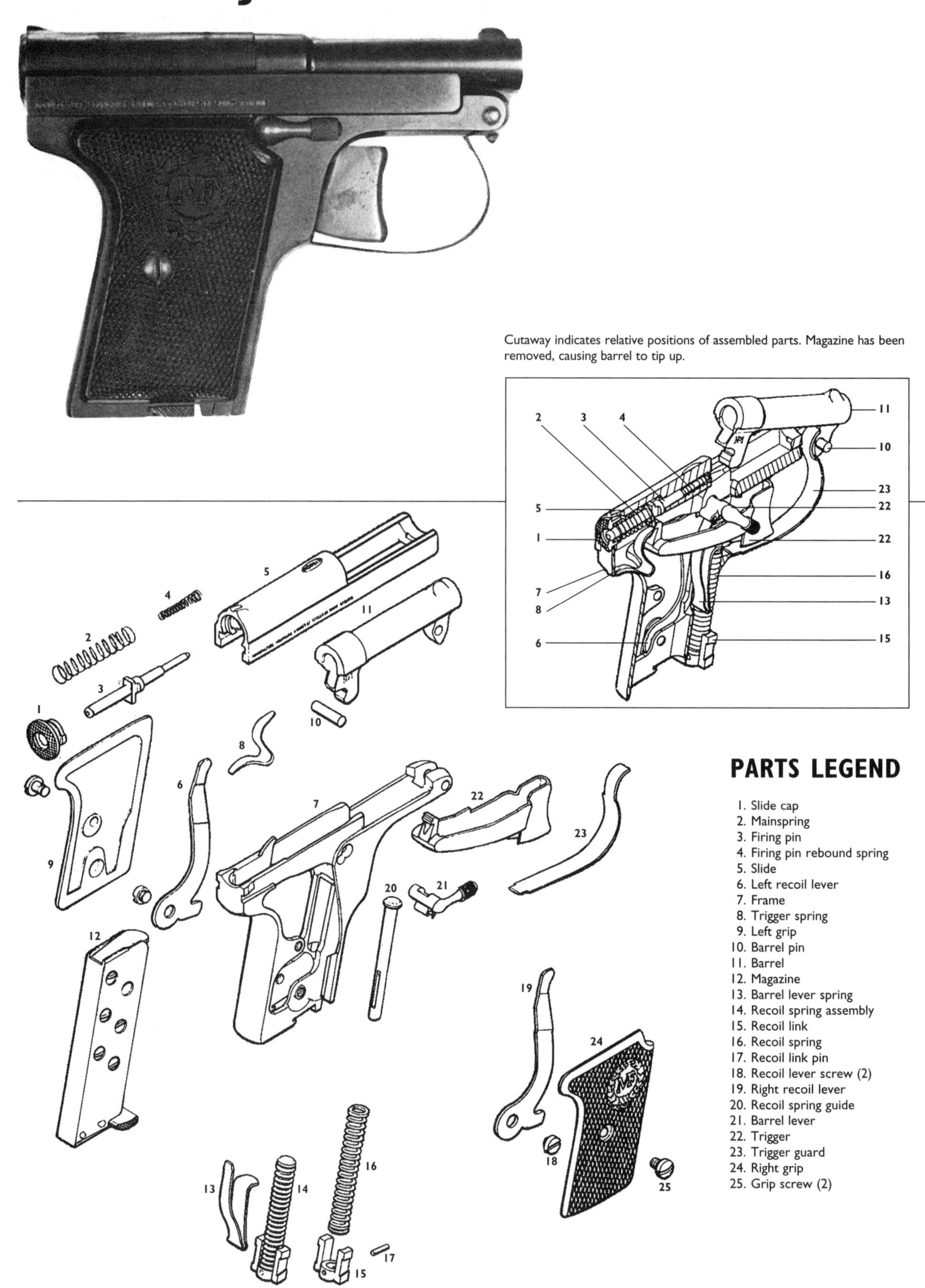

Cutaway indicates relative positions of assembled parts. Magazine has been removed, causing barrel to tip up.

PARTS LEGEND

1. Slide cap
2. Mainspring
3. Firing pin
4. Firing pin rebound spring
5. Slide
6. Left recoil lever
7. Frame
8. Trigger spring
9. Left grip
10. Barrel pin
11. Barrel
12. Magazine
13. Barrel lever spring
14. Recoil spring assembly
15. Recoil link
16. Recoil spring
17. Recoil link pin
18. Recoil lever screw (2)
19. Right recoil lever
20. Recoil spring guide
21. Barrel lever
22. Trigger
23. Trigger guard
24. Right grip
25. Grip screw (2)

The Le Français Pocket Model .25 ACP semi-automatic pistol, introduced in about 1914 by Manufrance (*Manufacture Française d'Armes et Cycles de Saint-Étienne*), St. Étienne, France, was an early double action, blowback operated, semi-automatic pistol. There was no extractor.

The double-action mechanism is simple and ingenious. Pulling the trigger forces back the firing pin and compresses the mainspring. As it moves back, the upper rear of the trigger follows a cam surface in the frame. This causes the trigger to move down near the end of its rearward travel and releases the firing pin to fire the cartridge. The design also featured a tip-up barrel which permited loading and unloading the chamber without retracting the slide.

Well made and finished, this compact arm weighs only 11¾ ounces and has a seven-round magazine. In early versions, the magazine is detached by pulling it forward and down. Later versions had a thumb-operated magazine release.

Le Français pistols were also made in .25 and .32 ACP. The Police Model, in .25 ACP, has a domed mainspring housing and a longer barrel than the Pocket Model. A Military Model in 9mm Browning Long was introduced about 1928, but was discontinued shortly before World War II.

DISASSEMBLY

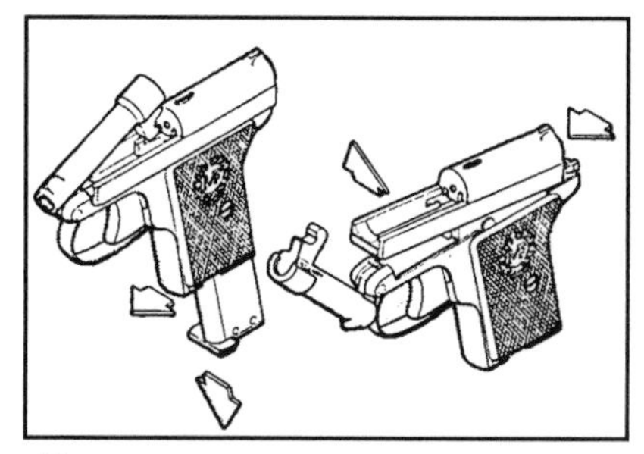

1 Takedown of the Le Francais begins by removing the magazine (12). To do this, pull forward and down on the knurled wings extending from sides of magazine bottom. Barrel (11) automatically tips up as magazine is withdrawn. Pivot the barrel fully upward, and lift the slide (5) up and forward off frame (7). Later versions of this pistol have a conventional butt-mounted magazine catch, but takedown procedures are similar to above.

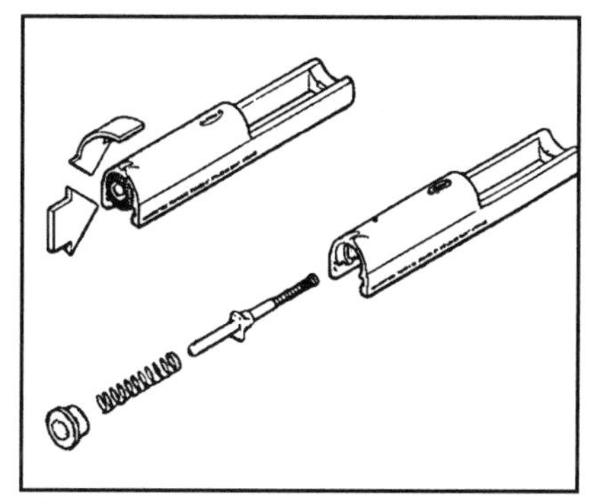

2 Press the slide cap (1) forward into the slide, rotate it ¼ turn counterclockwise, and ease it out to the rear. Remove mainspring (2), firing pin (3), and rebound spring (4). This completes field stripping for normal cleaning.

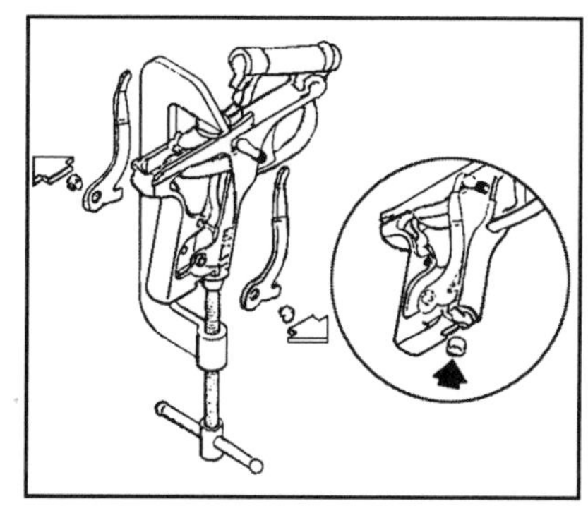

3 To disassemble further, unscrew grip screws (25) and remove grips (9 & 24). Cut a short section of ¼" copper tubing, and tighten against recoil link (15) with clamp or vise to slightly compress recoil spring (16). Unscrew recoil lever screws (18), and remove recoil levers (6 & 19). These levers are offset slightly to provide clearance for trigger (22), and must be replaced with offsets facing outward.

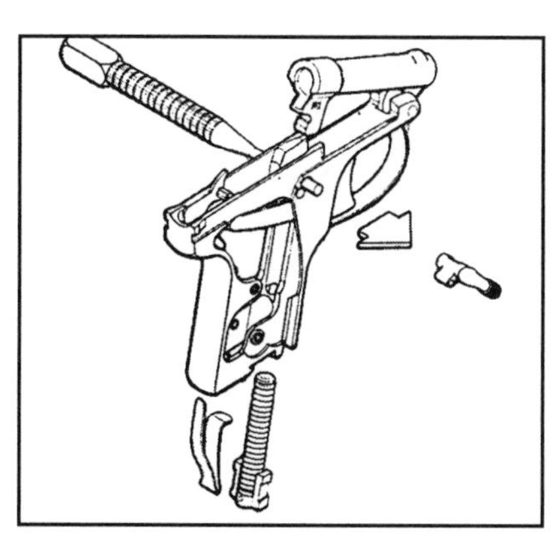

4 Release clamp, and remove recoil spring assembly (14) and barrel lever spring (13). Move barrel lever (21) to down (released) position, and push out of frame with punch. The straight leaf of the barrel lever spring must seat within the barrel lever's notched lug during reassembly.

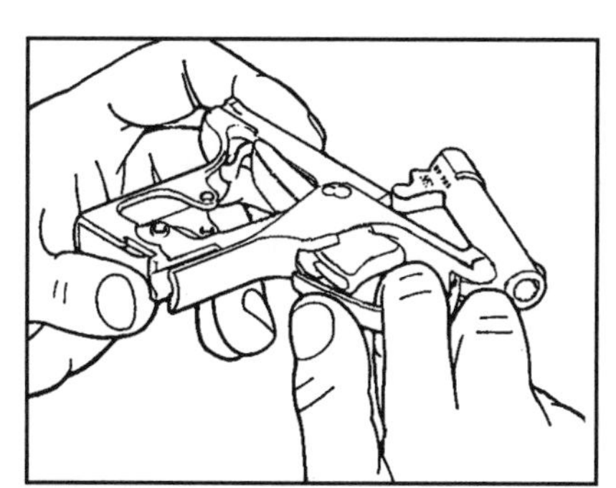

5 Holding the pistol in your left hand, pull the rear of trigger guard (23) out of the frame with the right forefinger, keeping the guard bowed with pressure from the right thumb and middle finger.

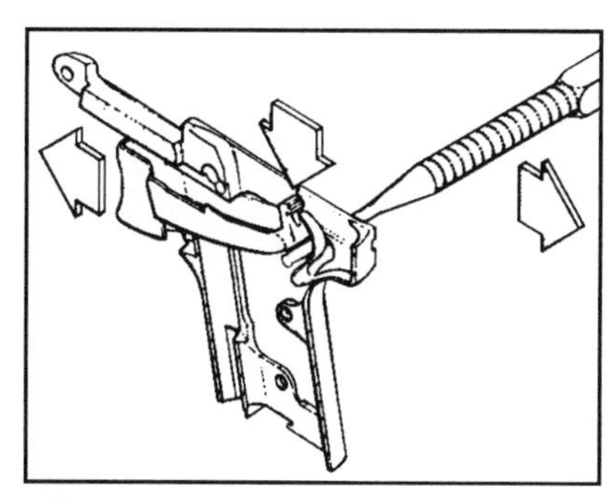

6 Insert a punch between trigger and trigger spring (8), and flex the spring rearward to disengage from trigger. Press down on rear of trigger to unlatch from frame and slide trigger forward and out. Remove trigger spring. The late version of this pistol has a coil-type trigger spring.

LILIPUT 4.25MM AUTOMATIC PISTOL

PARTS LEGEND

A. Slide
B. Extractor
C. Extractor retaining pin
D. Spring guide retaining screw
E. Firing fin
F. Firing pin spring
G. Firing pin spring guide
H. Recoil spring guide
I. Recoil spring
J. Sear
K. Sear spring
L. Safety catch spring
M. Safety catch plunger
N. Trigger
O. Trigger spring
P. Trigger bar pivot screw
Q. Grip screw
R. Right-hand grip
S. Trigger bar
T. Trigger bar spring
U. Rear operating lever
V. Magazine catch spring
W. Magazine catch
X. Magazine
Y. Magazine catch pin
Z. Left-hand grip
AA. Safety catch
BB. Trigger pin
CC. Frame

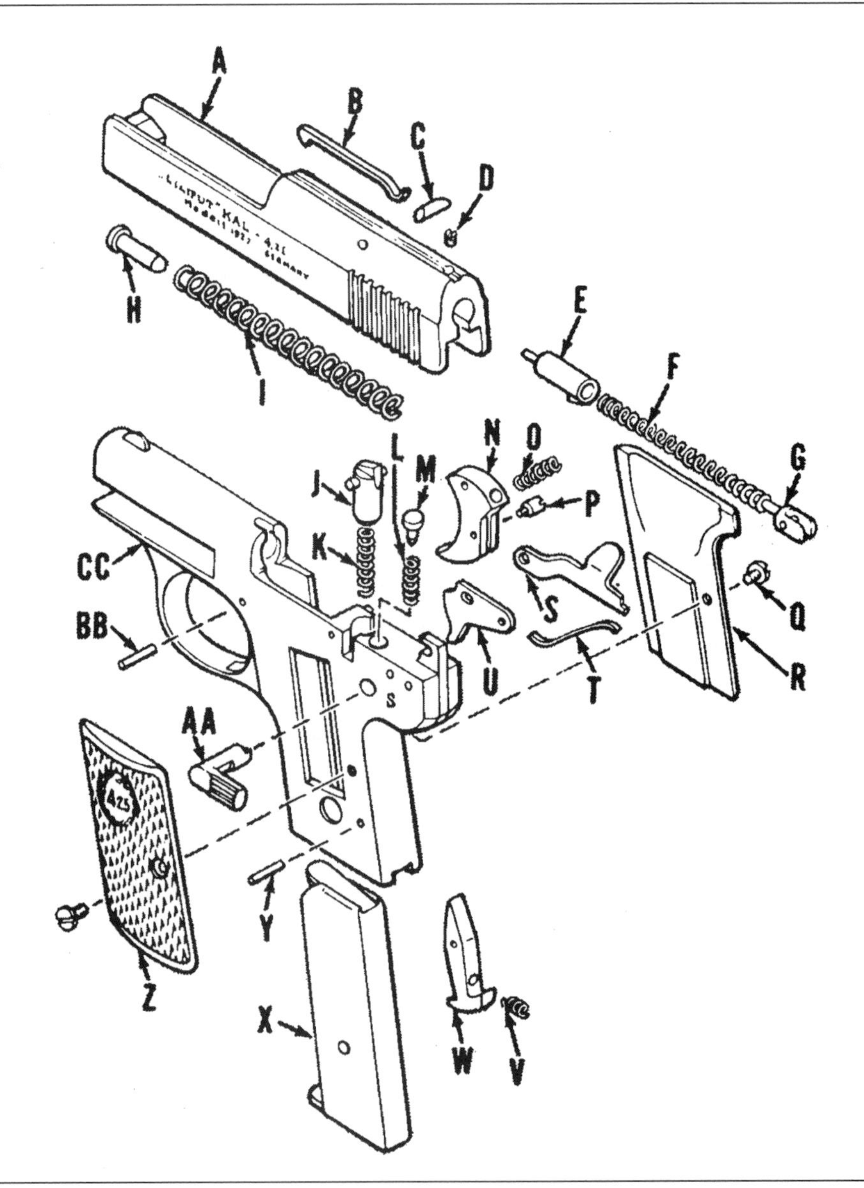

The Liliput pistols were first manufactured in 1920 by the firm of August Menz (*Waffenfabrik August Menz*) of Suhl, Germany. The diminutive Liliput, as befits its name, was one of the smallest semiautomatic handguns ever made — only 3½ inches long with a weight of only six ounces. The Liliput's barrel length was 1¾ inches.

In spite of its eye appeal, not too many were sold, partly due to the post-World War I economic troubles in Germany, and partly due to the fact that its tiny cartridge was not a very potent one. Yet the gun was not a toy, for it fired a 14-grain jacketed bullet at approximately 800 feet-per-second and will penetrate about 1½ inches of soft pine. The report is almost as loud as that of a .25 automatic pistol cartridge. August Menz ceased production of the Liliput in 1927.

Like most pistols less than 9mm, the Liliput is a straight blow-back operated firearm, which means that the slide and barrel are not locked together at the instant of firing. When the cartridge is fired, the slide is driven back, ejecting the empty cartridge case and chambering a fresh round from the magazine on the return trip.

These tiny automatics were well made, and finely finished, and the design is simple and reliable. All metal parts were made from steel. The barrel was machined as an integral part of the frame. The rest of the operating parts are simple shapes that can be easily reproduced in case of loss or breakage. The repair procedure is simple. Since the open rating parts are not inside the frame, they can be removed by simply taking off the right-hand grip.

DISASSEMBLY

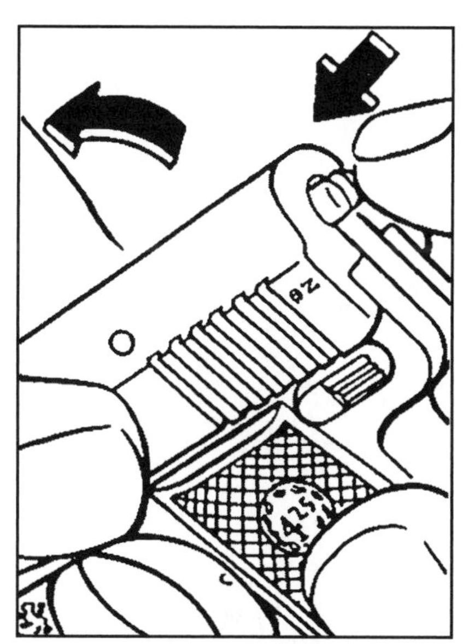

1 When "taking down" the Liliput, first remove the magazine (X). Then check to be sure that the gun is empty, pull back the slide as far as it will go, and push in on the end of the firing pin spring guide (G). Lift the rear end of the slide and run it forward off the receiver.

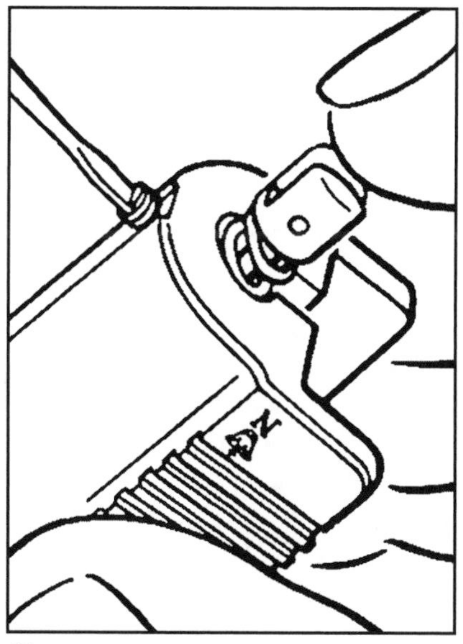

2 The only part that presents any problem is the firing pin. The spring guide retaining screw (D) is all that holds it in. Remove it and you get the spring guide, the firing pin spring (F), and firing pin (E). The other parts can be lifted off frame after removal of right-hand grip.

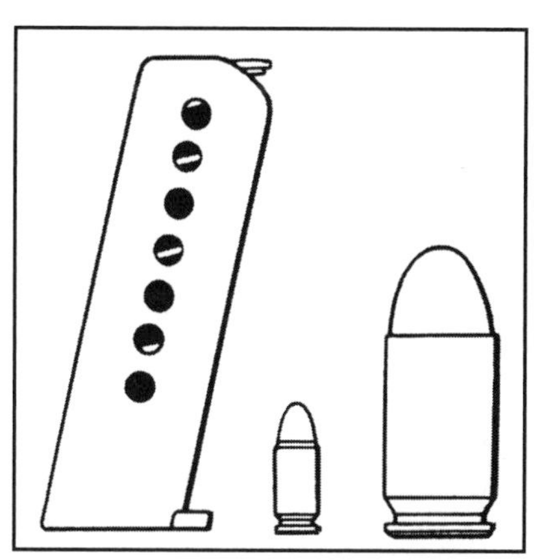

3 Some idea of the Liliput s size can be gained by comparing the magazine and a cartridge with a standard .45 caliber automatic pistol cartridge.

LUGER P-08 PISTOL

PARTS LEGEND

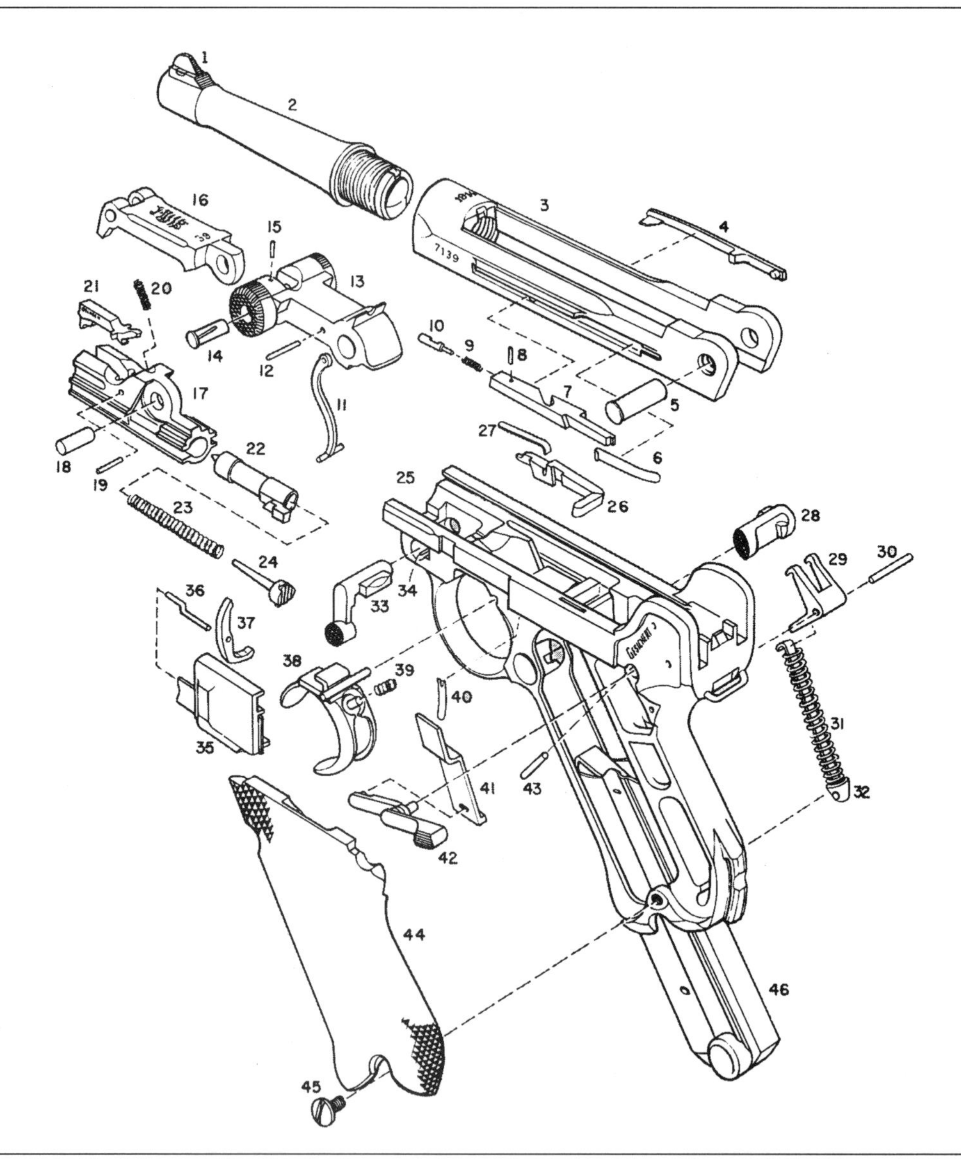

1 Front sight
2. Barrel
3. Receiver
4. Ejector
5. Receiver axle
6. Trigger bar spring
7. Trigger bar
8. Trigger bar plunger pin
9. Trigger bar plunger spring
10. Trigger bar plunger
11. Coupling link
12. Coupling link pin
13. Rear toggle link
14. Toggle axle
15. Toggle axle pin
16. Forward toggle link
17. Breechblock
18. Breechblock pin
19. Extractor pin
20. Extractor spring
21. Extractor
22. Firing pin
23. Firing pin spring
24. Firing pin spring guide
25. Frame
26. Hold-open latch
27. Hold-open latch spring
28. Magazine catch
29. Recoil lever
30. Recoil lever pin
31. Mainspring
32. Mainspring guide
33. Locking bait
34. Locking bolt spring
35. Trigger plate
36. Trigger lever pin
37. Trigger lever
38. Trigger
39. Trigger spring
40. Magazine catch spring
41. Safety bar
42. Safety catch
43. Safety pin
44. Grip (2—right-hand grip not shown)
45. Grip screw (2)
46. Magazine (shown partially withdrawn)

In 1900, German inventor Georg Luger patented a series of major design improvements to the toggle-breech Borchardt pistol manufactured by the German firm of Ludwig Loewe. Luger preserved the Borchardt's toggle-breech and removable-clip magazine, producing a pistol that was lighter and easier to manufacture. The first production model, the Model 1900, was in 7.65mm with a grip-safety. The following year, Switzerland, adopted the Luger as a service arm.

In 1902 the Luger's manufacturer, *Deutsche Waffen und Munitionsfabriken* (DWM), offered the pistol chambered for the new 9mm Parabellum cartridge and an improved model was adopted by the German Navy in 1904. In 1906 DWM offered the Model 1906, the first of the so-called "New Models," with coiled rather than flat mainsprings. The Model 1906 was equipped with a grip safety but lacked the toggle-locking device found on earlier models.

In 1908 the German Army adopted the Luger as the *Pistole 08* (P 08). The P 08 was in 9mm Parabellum and lacked the grip safety. An additional manufacturing facility was established at the Royal Arsenal in Erfurt, Germany. Luger pistols issued to German forces during World War I were manufactured by DWM or at Erfurt.

After World War I, Simson & Company of Suhl, furnished Luger pistols to the Reichswehr. In 1930, Luger production was begun by Mauser in Oberndorf and the firm of Heinrich Krieghoff produced Luger pistols for the *Luftwaffe* during the 1930s. German production of Luger pistols was terminated after World War II.

DISASSEMBLY

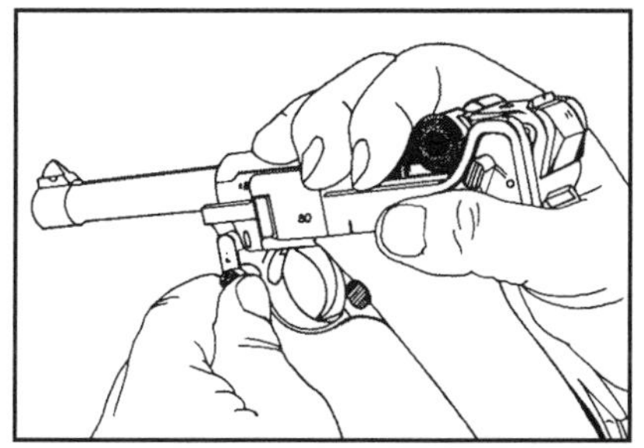

1 Push the barrel and receiver assembly to the rear about ¼-inch to relieve tension on the recoil spring. Hold it in position with the right hand, (above). With the left hand rotate the locking bolt (33) 90 degrees clockwise to free the trigger plate.

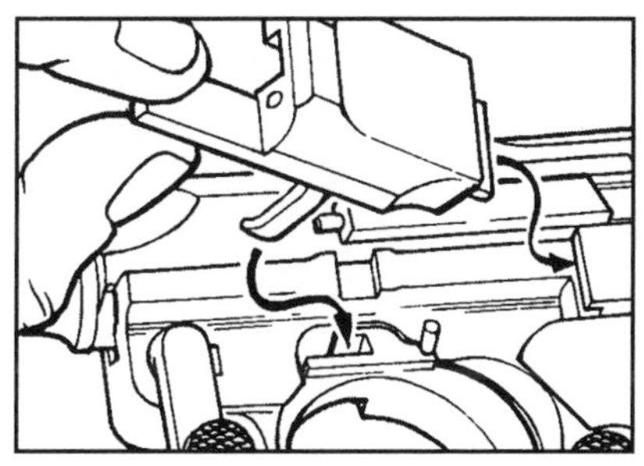

2 Lift trigger plate assembly (35) from frame. When reassembling pistol, trigger lever (37) in trigger plate must fall into its slot in trigger (38) and small lip at rear of trigger plate must be inserted underside of frame in recess provided.

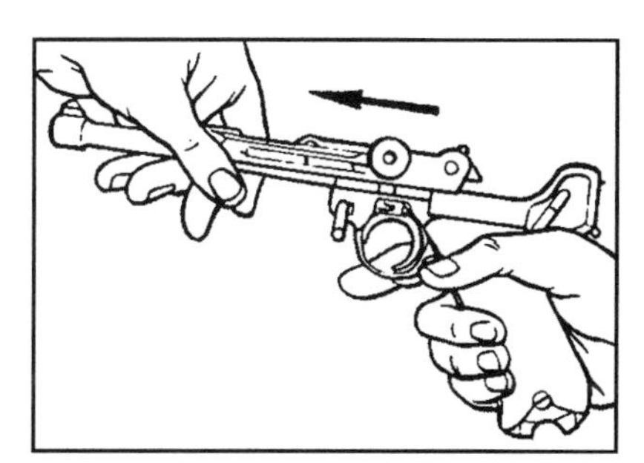

3 Slide complete barrel, receiver and breech assembly forward and out of frame as shown. Note the position of the coupling link (11) with relation to the recoil lever (29) for reference in reassembly.

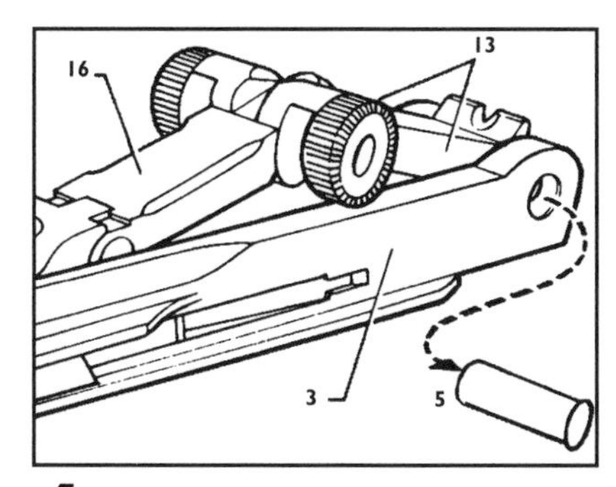

4 Grasp knurled knobs of rear toggle link (13) and pull upward buckling raer and forward toggle links (13 & 16) to relieve tension. Press receiver axle (5) from right to left out of the receiver. Toggle and breechblock assembly can now be withdrawn from rear of receiver.

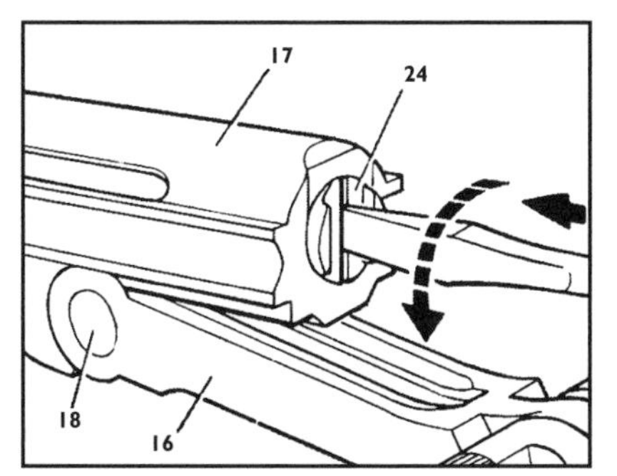

5 Insert a screwdriver blade in slot in firing pin spring guide (24) in rear of breechblock (17). Press guide in about 1/16-inch and turn counterclockwise ¼ turn and ease out firing pin spring guide and firing pin spring (23), without allowing firing pin spring to escape. Drop out firing pin (22). Remove extractor (21) by holding thumb over top of breechblock and extractor and drift out extractor pin (19), allowing extractor to pop up. Lift out extractor and extractor spring (20).

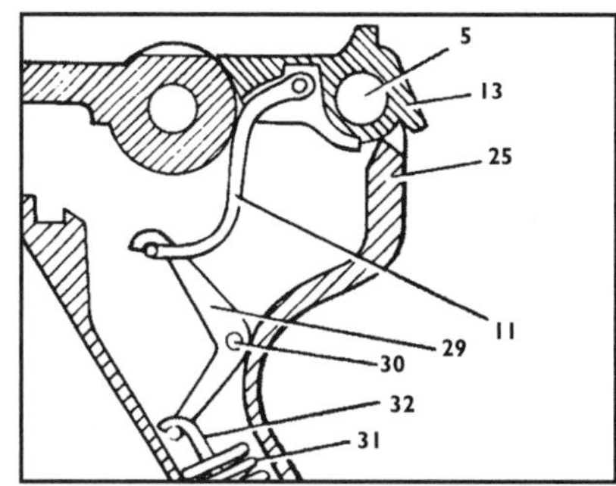

6 The above steps complete normal field stripping necessary for cleaning and lubrication. Reassembly is accomplished in reverse order. When replacing barrel, receiver and breech assembly on frame, be sure coupling link (11) drops into its proper place in front of inclined upper arms of recoil lever (29). The proper relationship of these parts, when assembled is shown here.

MAGNUM RESEARCH DESERT EAGLE VII

PARTS LEGEND

1. Barrel
2. Front sight
3. Gas piston
4. Bolt stabilizer pin
5. Bolt stabilizer spring
6. Bolt stabilizer guide pin
7. Ejector
8. Slide
9. Ejector spring
10. Extractor pin
11. Ejector pin
12. Extractor
13. Extractor spring
14. Bolt
15. Rear sight
16. Safety screw
17. Right safety lever
18. Safety spring
19. Safety
20. Firing pin
21. Firing pin spring
22. Left safety lever
23. Bolt guide pin
24. Firing pin stop
25. Recoil spring assembly *
26. Trigger assembly *
27. Barrel lock
28. Barrel lock spring
29. Barrel lock pin
30. Hammer pin
31. Sear pin
32. Adjustable trigger assembly
33. Magazine catch
34. Frame
35. Magazine catch spring
36. Magazine catch pin
37. Slide catch spring
38. Slide catch assembly
39. Magazine assembly
40. Grip
41. Grip pin spring
42. Grip pin
43. Retaining rng (C-clip)

Magnum Research, Inc. patented the basic design of their gas-operated Desert Eagle in 1980, and the prototype was completed in 1981. Final refinements of the Desert Eagle design were made by Israel Military Industries, under contract to Magnum Research and a .357 Magnum production model was produced in an edition of just over 1,000 pistols. In 1985, the barrel design was modified to incorporate polygonal rifling to improve accuracy.

In 1986 Magnum Research marketed a potent .44 Magnum version of the Desert Eagle, the first commercial .44 Magnum semi-automatic pistol. By 1989, the Mark VII model became standard with enlarged safety levers, larger slide release and a two-stage trigger. Magnum Research introduced the .50 Action Express Desert Eagle Pistol in 1996, and shortly afterward the basic design was upgraded to Mark XIX specifications with the adoption of one frame size for all calibers. This allowed the use of barrels of different caliber on same frame.

Desert Eagle is a gas operated, locked-breech semi-automatic pistol with a stationary, removable barrel. The trigger is single-action, with an exposed hammer and ambidextrous safety. Magazines are single stack, with different configuration for each major caliber. Sights are either fixed or adjustable, both front and rear are dovetailed into the barrel and slide respectively.

DISASSEMBLY

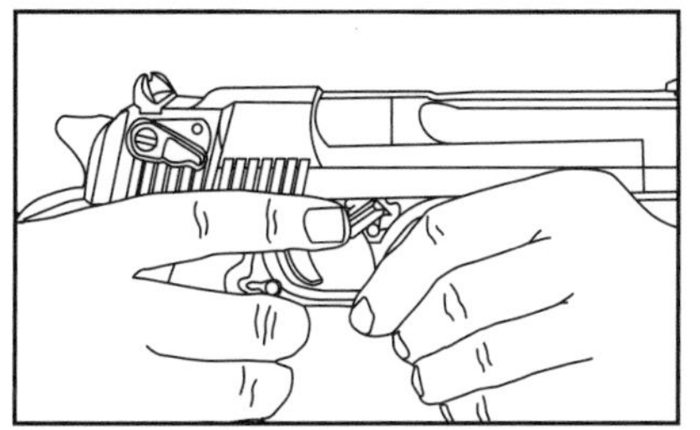

1 Pull the hammer slightly to the rear until a click is heard; the hammer is now in semi-cocked position. Move the front end of the safety catch lever down into its "SAFE" position. Press the barrel lock pin in on the left side of the pistol and at the same time swing the barrel lock on the other side of the pistol counter clockwise.

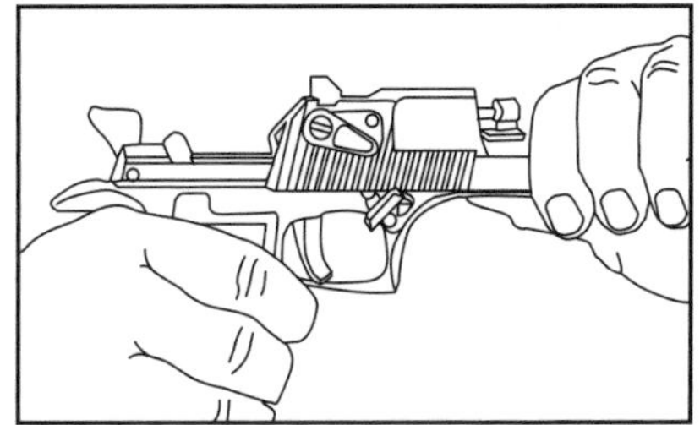

2 Pull the barrel slightly forward to release it and lift it out. Draw the slide forward and remove it. This allows the recoil springs assembly to be pulled forward and easily removed (.357). On .41, .44, .440 and .50 the recoil spring comes out with slide assembly.

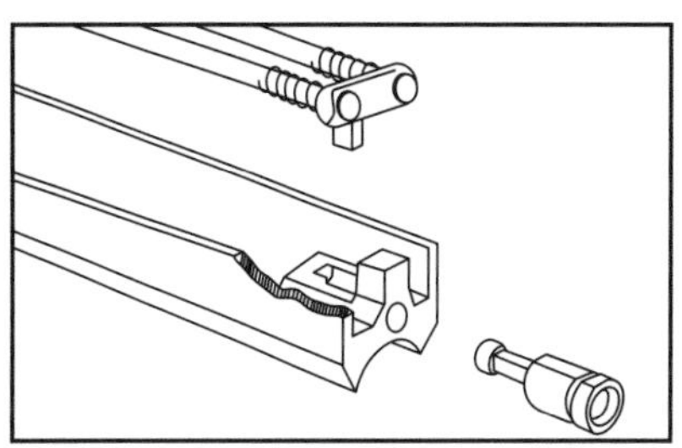

3 Turn the slide upside down and place it on a level surface. Insert the piston into place. Make sure the piston shaft recess is facing the slide recess. The other piston shaft recess will face up. Engage piston shaft with recoil spring plate lug and the slide. Use your thumb to push the base of the spring plate assembly against the slide, supporting the slide all the way to align the spring assembly in parallel with the slide. Keeping the spring assembly parallel to the slide, draw the frame all the way into the slide (do not compress the spring).

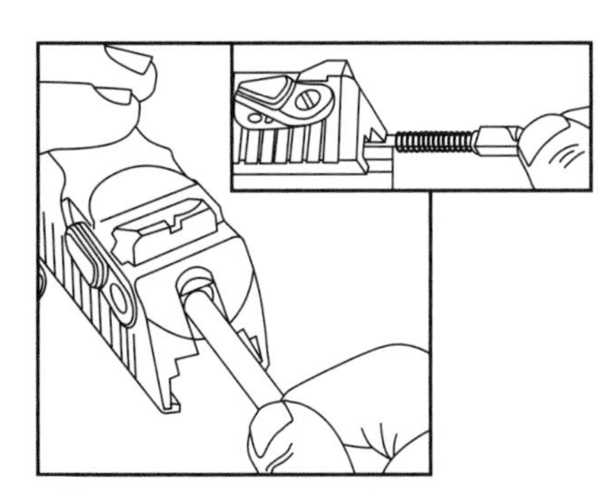

4 Make sure the safety catch lever is in the "FIRE" position. Push the rear end of the firing pin in with the combination tool and slide the firing pin stop down. The firing pin is now free to be pushed out by its spring. Remove the firing pin and its spring.

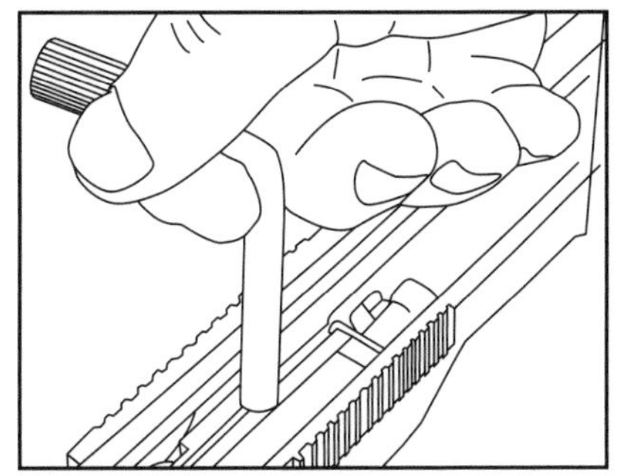

5 Hold the slide upside down and push back with your thumb. Now remove the bolt guide pin with the combination tool. Release the bolt slowly and remove the bolt assembly, bolt stabilizer pin, spring and pin.

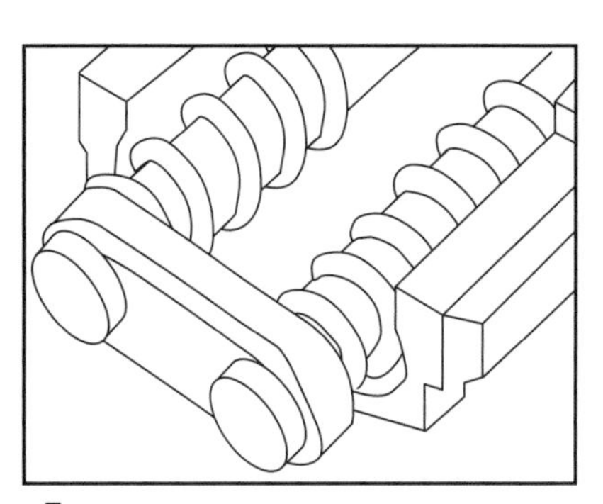

6 Place the return springs on end with the crossplate down. Pull down on one return/recoil spring and hold down. Pry C-clip from end of spring rod (C-clip is under tension and will "fly" off if not held under control while moving). Slowly release tension on return/recoil spring and remove. Remove spring rod from crossplate.

MAKAROV 9MM PISTOL

PARTS LEGEND

1. Slide
2. Extractor
3. Extractor plunger
4. Extractor spring
5. Rear sight
6. Firing pin
7. Safety
8. Safety detent spring
9. Recoil spring
10. Ejector and slide stop
11. Hammer
12. Sear
13. Sear and slide stop spring
14. Trigger bar assembly
15. Receiver and barrel assembly
16. Trigger
17. Trigger guard
18. Trigger guard pin
19. Trigger guard spring
20. Spring plunger
21. Magazine
22. Hammer and trigger spring
23. Spring retainer
24. Grip
25. Grip screw detent bushing
26. Grip screw

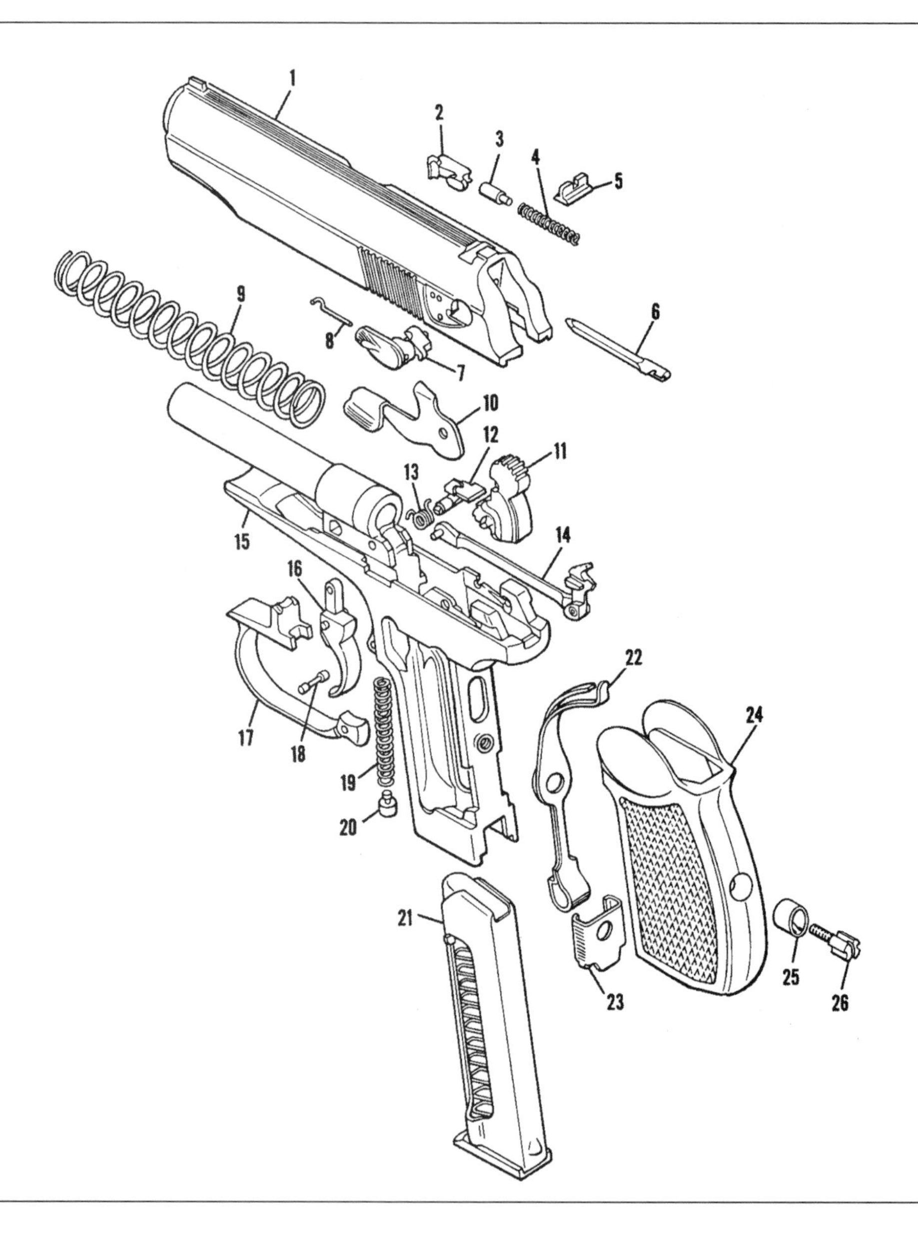

The Makarov PM, is a semi-automatic pistol with a straight blowback action designed by Russian firearms designer Nikolai F. Makarov. Makarov also designed a new round for the PM, the 9x18mm PM cartridge, based on the Browning .380 ACP. The pistol was adopted in 1951 and designated the *Pistolet Makarova* (PM). It was intended to replace the Red Army's venerable Tokarev TT-33 semi-automatic pistol. The Makarov became the standard firearm of the Soviet Union's armed forces and of several former Soviet-bloc allies.

The PM remained in service with Soviet military and police forces until about 1991. A commercial version of the PM, the Baikal IJ-70 pistol, was produced in Russia by the *Ishevsky Mechanichesky Zavod* arms and ammunition plant.

Based on the Walther PP (Police Pistol), the PM has a double-action/single-action operating system. The Makarov employs a free-floating firing pin with no firing pin spring or block. The slide stop doubles as the ejector and the mainspring powers both the hammer and the trigger.

DISASSEMBLY

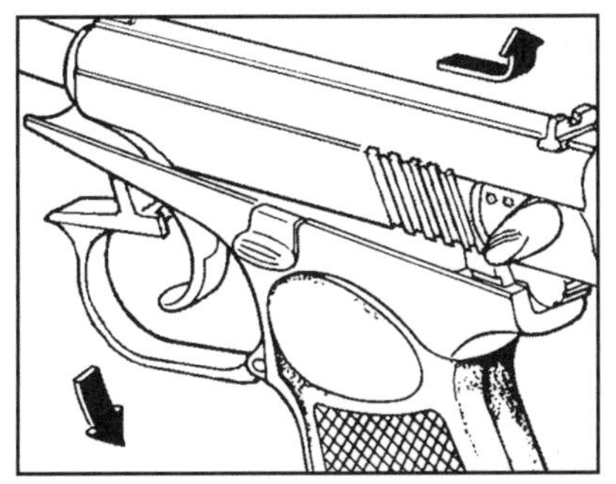

1 To field strip, first remove the magazine and clear the chamber. Put the safety (7) in fire position. Pull down on the front of the trigger guard (17) until it clears the receiver (15). Pull the slide (1) to the rear, lift the slide up, and ease it forward off the receiver.

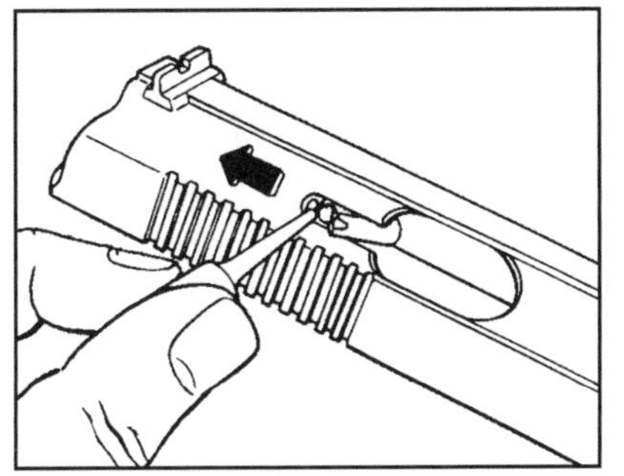

2 To remove the extractor (2), use a thin punch to push the plunger (3) back into the slide. Turn the slide on its right side. Extractor should drop out. If not, rotate the extractor in toward the firing pin hole or in such a way as to remove the tail section from the slide first.

3 The firing pin (6) is retained by the safety (7). To remove the safety, push it up beyond the safe position. It can be rotated as shown only when the slide is held to the rear or off the gun completely.

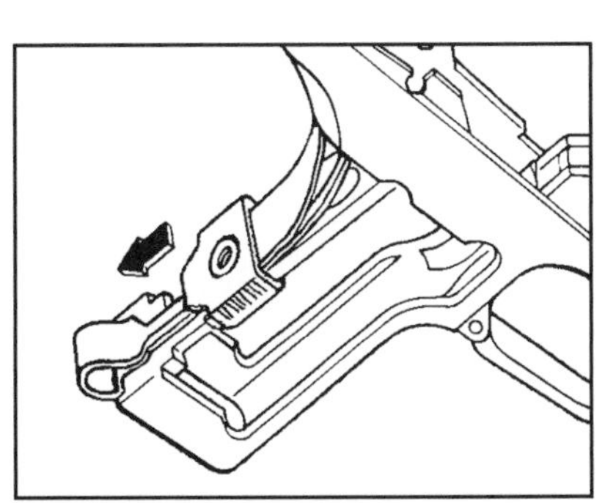

4 Remove grip screw (26). Grip (24) can be slid off receiver. This will expose the hammer and trigger spring (22). This spring acts as the magazine catch, hammer spring, and trigger spring. To remove, pull down on spring retainer (23) until free; then lift spring off boss in receiver.

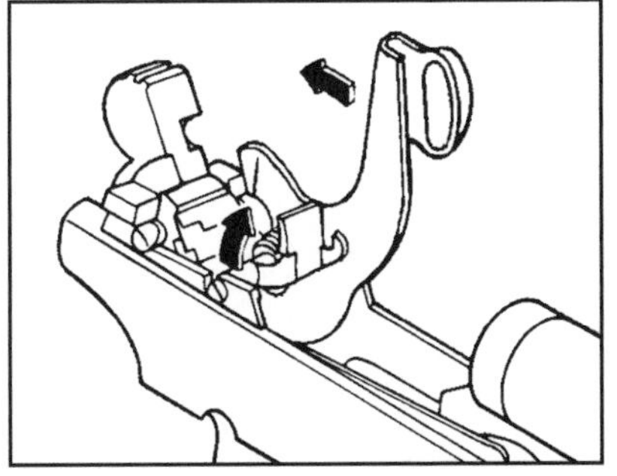

5 The next step is to unhook the tail of the sear and slide stop spring (13) from the ejector and slide stop (10). After the spring is free, rotate the slide stop up as shown. Then use it as a lever to lift the sear (12) out of its hole in the right of the frame.

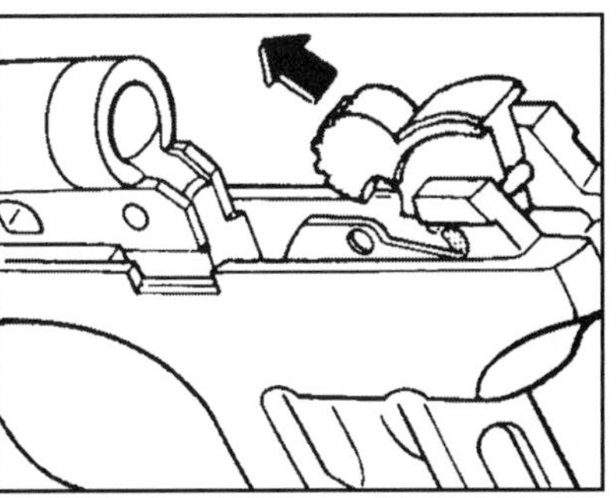

6 The hammer (11) is one of the last parts to be removed. It can be removed in only one position. Rotate the hammer forward as shown, and pull it forward free of the receiver.

MAUSER MODEL 96 PISTOL

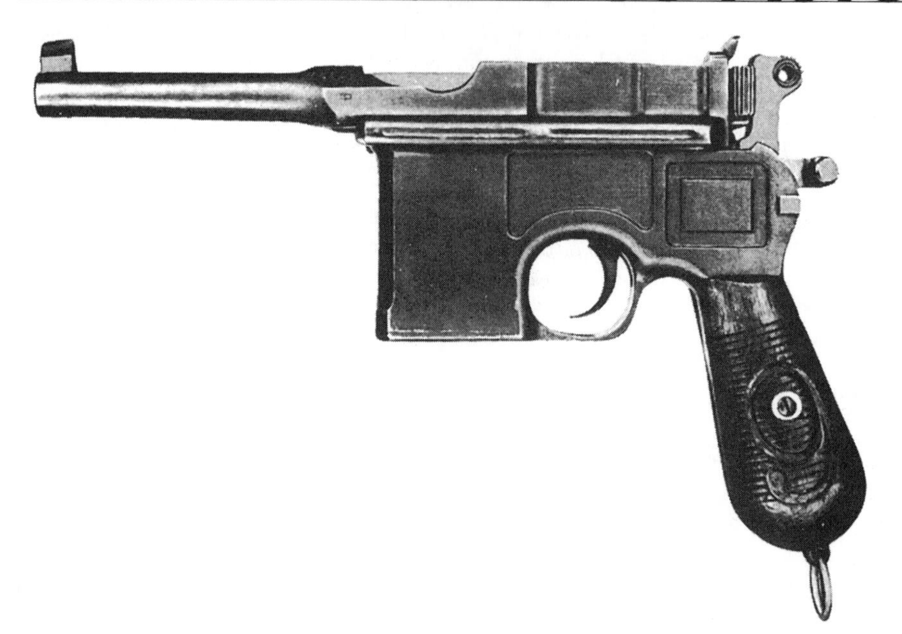

PARTS LEGEND

1. Barrel and barrel extension
2. Extractor
3. Bolt
4. Bolt stop
5. Firing pin spring
6. Firing pin
7. Recoil spring
8. Trigger spring
9. Magazine plunger
10. Trigger
11. Rocker plunger
12. Mainspring
13. Mainspring plunger
14. Bolt locking block
15. Sear arm
16. Sear
17. Sear spring and hammer pivot
18. Hammer
19. Lock mechanism frame
20. Lock frame stop
21. Safety
22. Rocker coupling
23. Receiver
24. Lanyard ring
25. Left-hand grip
26. Grip screw
27. Follower spring
28. Follower
29. Magazine floorplate

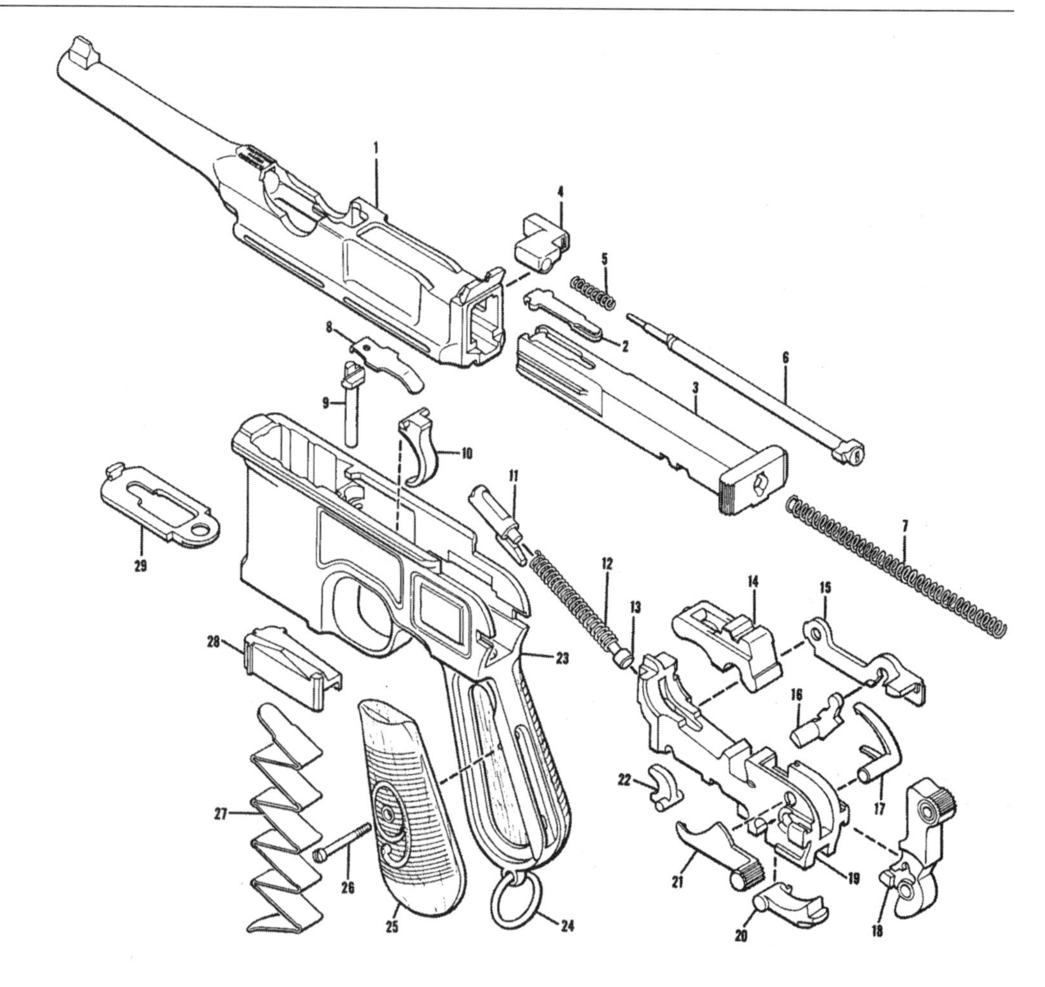

The 1890's can rightly be called the beginning of the automatic pistol era. During these years, gun designers such as Borchardt, Mannlicher, Schwarzlose, Browning, and Mauser focused their mechanical ingenuity on self-loading pistols. Probably the most remarkable of these early designs was Paul Mauser's Model 1896 Military Pistol. Few handguns can match its remarkable success and world-wide distribution. This unique design contains no pins and only one screw, the grip screw. All internal parts that require a pin or pivot are machined from solid stock so the pin is integral with the part.

During the half century that the gun was in production, several models were offered. These range from the odd 6-shot pistol to the selective-fire Model 712. Although never officially adopted by the German Army, Mauser pistols were widely carried by German officers during World War I, and to a limited degree in World War 11. The World War I pistol is the most common; it has a 5½" barrel and is chambered for the 7.63mm Mauser cartridge. To simplify wartime ammunition problems, these guns were also chambered for the 9mm Luger (Parabellum) cartridge. These can be recognized by the big red "9" carved into the grips.

In 1930 Mauser made a change in the safety catch operation. On previous pistols it was necessary to pull back the hammer with one hand and engage the safety with the other. The new universal safety of 1930 made it possible to apply the safety with the gun hand only. The only other major change came when Mauser dropped the rifle-style magazine and changed to a removable sheet-metal magazine which can be loaded in the gun from a stripper clip like a military rifle, or outside the gun like any normal pistol magazine. The sear mechanism was changed to incorporate a selector switch that allowed optional semi- or full-automatic fire. Manufacture was eventually stopped because the gun became too expensive to produce. It was subsequently replaced by cheaper and more modern designs.

Mauser military pistols were widely copied in Spain and China. Some are excellent copies and operate reliably. Others reflect only the distinctive Mauser outline with lock mechanism differing from the original.

DISASSEMBLY

1 Using a screwdriver or point of a bullet, press up magazine plunger (9) and slide floorplate (29) forward. Remove follower (28) and spring (27). Cock hammer. Press up lock frame stop (20). Pull barrel extension assembly (1) off rear of receiver (23).

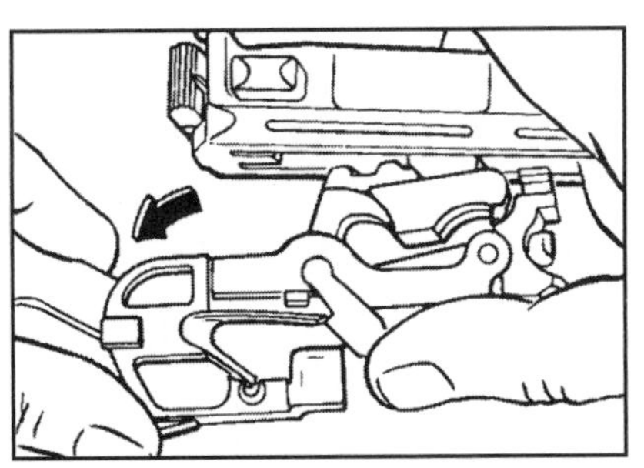

2 After barrel extension assembly is free of frame, pull down on rear of lock mechanism frame (19) to free it from barrel extension. Remove locking block (14). Handle lock work carefully to prevent frame stop (20) and sear (16) dropping out of place.

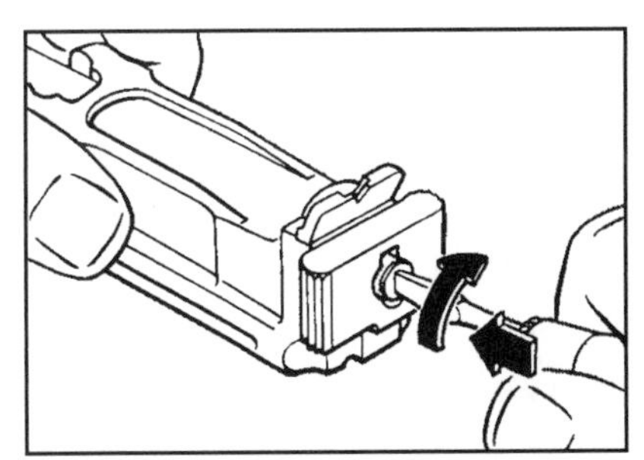

3 To remove firing pin (6), use a small screwdriver to push in firing pin as for as it will go and give it a ¼-turn clockwise. Remove pin and push bolt stop (4) forward and out to right. Recoil spring (7) con now be removed.

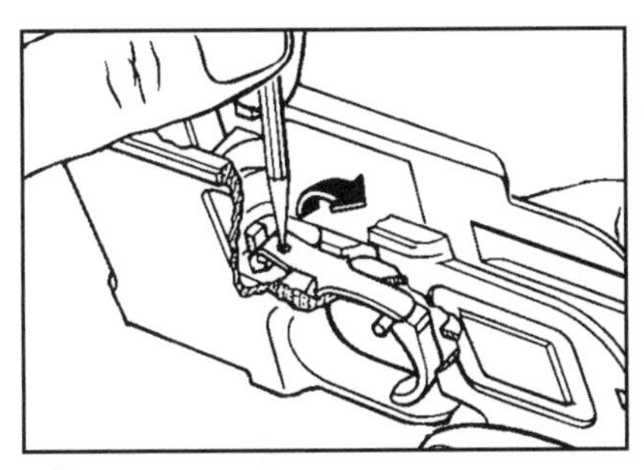

4 To remove trigger (10) and magazine plunger (9), trigger spring (8) must be removed first. To do this, use a tool with a small hook to lift spring free of plunger (9). At same time, push it toward butt until free.

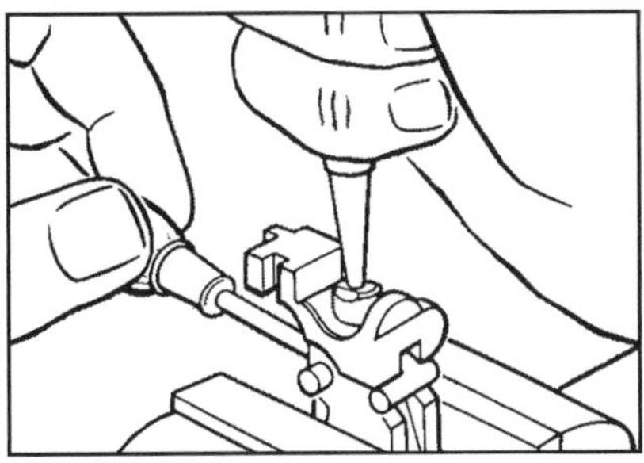

5 Care must be taken when removing rocker coupling (22) since it is under heavy spring tension. First lower hammer. Hold lock mechanism in a vise and press down on plunger (11). At same time push rocker coupling (22) through as shown.

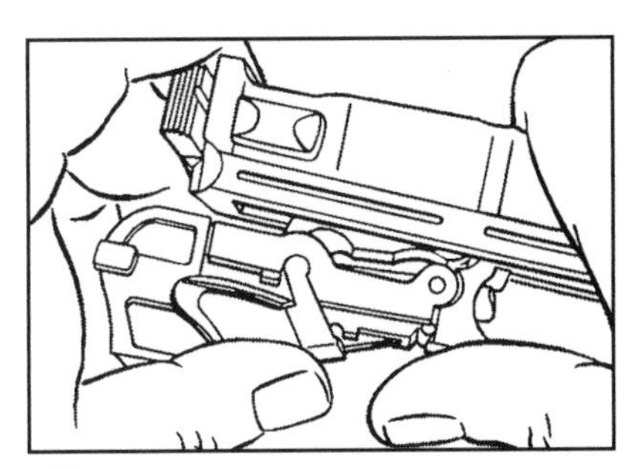

6 To reassemble gun, install bolt (3) and firing pin, etc. Turn barrel extension upside down and drop locking block (14) over its projection. Cock hammer and press down on forward end of lock mechanism until the tail of locking block (14) snaps into rocker coupling (22).

MAUSER MODEL 1910 POCKET PISTOL

MAUSER

PARTS LEGEND

1. Slide
2. Extractor
3. Rear sight
4. Firing pin
5. Firing pin spring
6. Takedown rod
7. Barrel
8. Recoil spring
9. Takedown rod catch
10. Receiver
11. Grip
12. Grip screw
13. Magazine catch
14. Magazine
15. Side-plate
16. Safety catch release
17. Safety catch
18. Trigger bar spring
19. Trigger bar
20. Trigger
21. Trigger spring
22. Disconnector
23. Trigger sear
24. Trigger sear spring
25. Trigger sear pin
26. Elector and hold open catch
27. Recoil spring guide

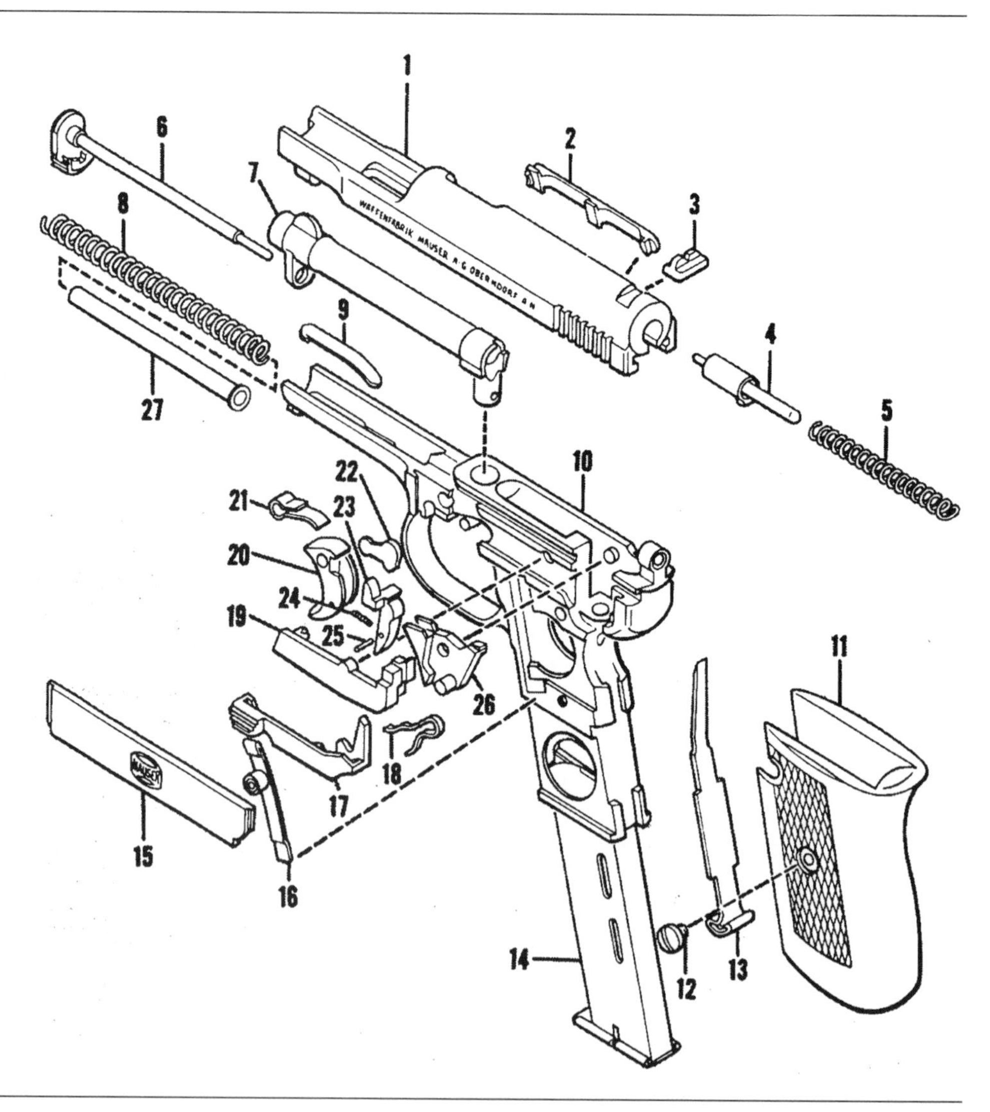

The Mauser 1910 — though never officially assigned this name by Mauser — was a self-loading pocket pistol chambered for 6.35mm (.25 ACP) cartridge. It was introduced in 1910, and more than 61,000 were produced by 1913. Various minor design changes, such as an improved extractor and a wrap-around walnut grip, were applied to the 6.35mm pocket model between 1910 and 1913.

A second model, chambered for 7.62mm (.32 ACP), was introduced in 1914 and production continued until 1940 when the introduction of the double-action HSc model and WWII ended production. A version introduced in 1934 featured a curved back grip and has been dubbed the Model 1934.

The 1910 contains some interesting features. For instance, when the firing pin is cocked, the end of it protrudes from the back of the slide. It can be easily seen in the daytime or felt in the dark. Another feature is the magazine disconnector that prevents the gun firing when the magazine is not in the gun. The thumb safety has a rather novel method of operation in that it locks the slide closed and also prevents it being accidentally released while the gun is being taken from the pocket. To engage the thumb safety, simply push the thumbpiece down toward the button in the grip. To release it, press the button and the safety will snap back to fire position.

When the last shot is fired, the slide remains open, and if a loaded magazine is inserted, the slide will automatically run forward and chamber the first round in the magazine.

While the gun features the usual fine Mauser workmanship, its internal design leaves a bit to be desired. The flat trigger spring and trigger bar spring are the source of some trouble, since they break easily if not carefully removed. Another bad feature is the strong magazine catch spring. This spring is usually so stiff that it causes the magazine catch to score the magazine when it is inserted. It also at times causes damage to the magazine floorplate.

DISASSEMBLY

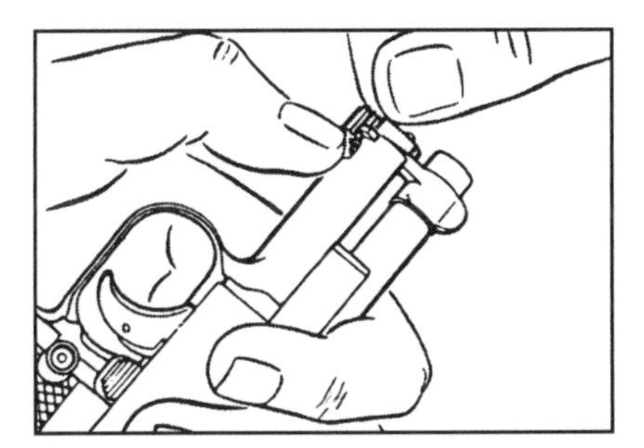

1 To field strip the gun, first remove the magazine and pull back the slide until it stays open. Depress the protruding portion of the takedown rod catch (9) and turn the takedown rod (6) until it is free of the lug on the receiver.

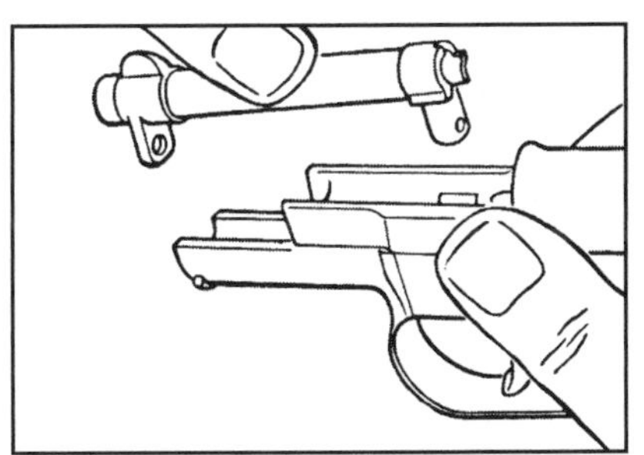

2 Withdraw the takedown rod (6) from the receiver (10). The barrel (7) can now be lifted out of its seat in the receiver. Replace the magazine and ease the slide (1) off the front of the receiver. Pull the trigger while easing the slide off to release the firing pin spring.

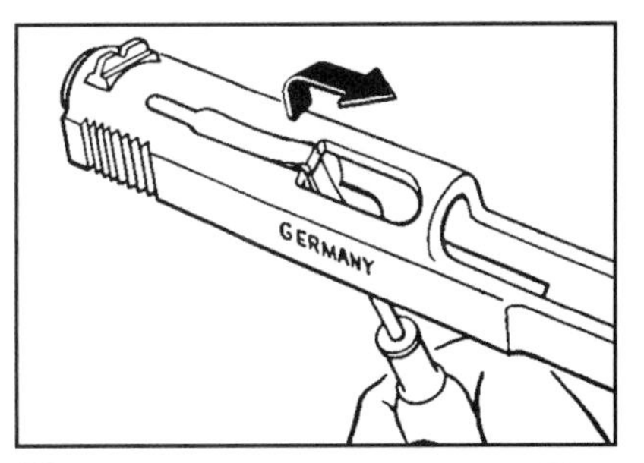

3 There are two types of extractors. The early type shown narrows down a short distance from its tail. This tail fits into a T-slot in the slide. Use a small screwdriver to lift the projection on the front end of the extractor free of the slide before attempting to pry it forward as shown.

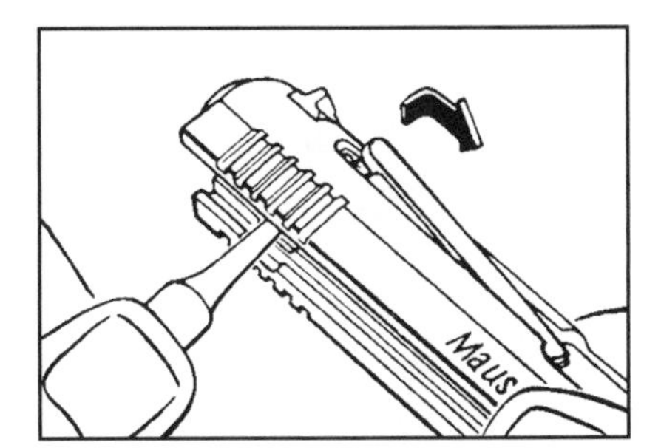

4 The later type extractor can be recognized by its straight outline and by the hole in the underside of the slide. The tail of the extractor must be pushed out of this hole with a thin punch and then pushed forward as shown.

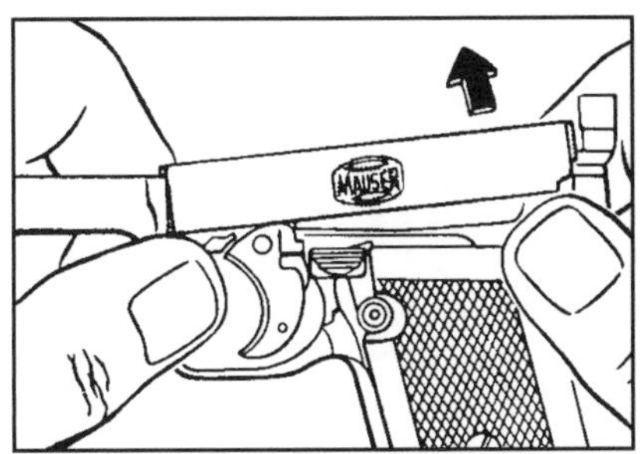

5 To observe the operating parts, the side-plate (15) can be pushed up and out of it grooves in the receiver. To remove the operating parts, it is necessary to remove the grip (11). Do this carefully to prevent the safety catch parts (16, 17 & 18) jumping out when they are free of the grip.

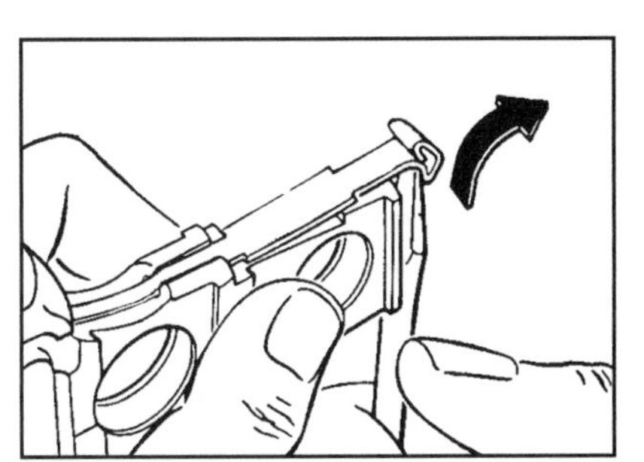

6 When the side-plate (15) and grip (11) have been removed, all the operating parts can be easily removed except the hold-open catch (26). The hold-open catch can be removed after the magazine catch (13) is removed. To remove the magazine catch, push it up clear of the receiver and pry it forward as shown.

MAUSER HSC POCKET PISTOL

PARTS LEGEND

1. Slide
2. Extractor
3. Extractor plunger
4. Extractor spring
5. Safety detent plunger
6. Rear sight
7. Firing pin spring
8. Firing pin
9. Safety catch
10. Recoil spring
11. Barrel
12. Takedown latch
13. Takedown latch spring
14. Magazine safety
15. Sear
16. Sear spring
17. Cartridge feed cam
18. Magazine safety spring
19. Sear hinge pin
20. Hammer hinge pin
21. Hammer
22. Strut pin
23. Hammer strut
24. Hammer spring
25. Magazine catch
26. Magazine
27. Magazine catch pin
28. Disconnector
29. Trigger bar
30. Trigger pin
31. Trigger
32. Trigger spring
33. Frame
34. Left grip
35. Grip screw
36. Right grip
37. Grip screw

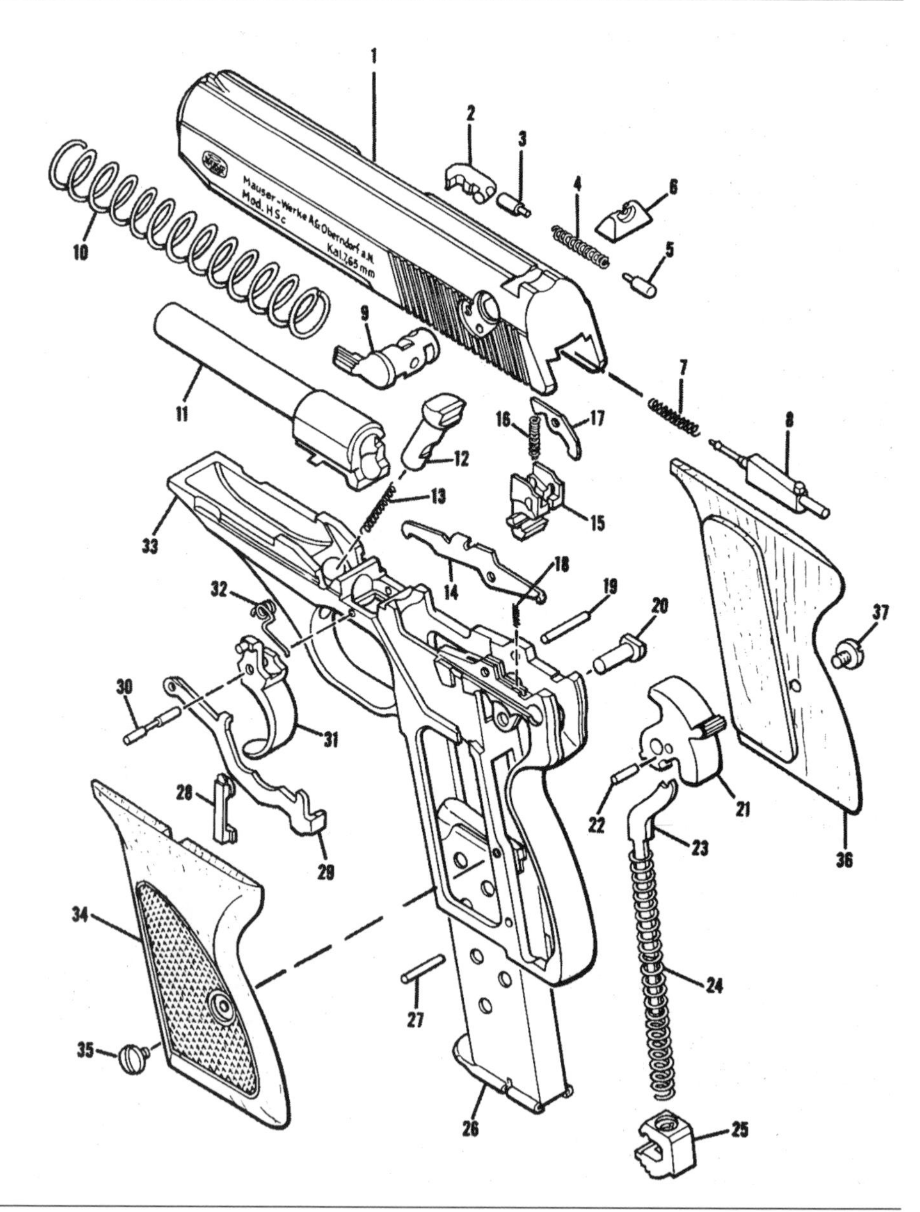

The Mauser HSc was a late-1930s vintage attempt by the Mauser firm to produce a pistol to compete with the Walther Model PP. Far from simply building on the earlier Mauser Model 1910 pistols, the HSc was an entirely new design that featured a double-action trigger mechanism.

In that same respect, the HSc is a far cry from Mauser's earlier, intricate and carefully machined military pistols. Internal parts were stamped wherever possible and music wire springs replace expensive and forged types. The result was a simple, rugged pistol, well suited for mass production and salable at a competitive price.

The HSc is a natural pocket pistol with no sharp edges to hang up in the user's clothing. The gun has an excellent grip and a fairly good double-action trigger pull. Many of the operating parts perform two or more functions. For instance, a simple, stamped bar, pinned to the frame, acts as a magazine safety, slide hold-open device and ejector. Another part, the cartridge feed cam, positions the top round in the magazine for chambering, puts tension on the sear spring, and acts as a retainer for the hammer hinge pin.

The slide release system is a carryover from the 1910 pocket pistol. When the last shot is fired, the slide stays locked to the rear. It can be released to return to battery only by partially withdrawing the magazine and pushing it back into place — again the presumption being that this would be done when exchanging an empty magazine for a full one. Thus, if a loaded magazine is inserted with the slide to the rear, the slide will automatically run forward, chambering a cartridge.

Mauser/Oberndorf ceased production of the HSc at the end of World War II. The French, however, assembled a few using captured machinery and Heckler & Koch made a variant of the HSc, the HK4, from the mid-1960s until about 1984.

DISASSEMBLY

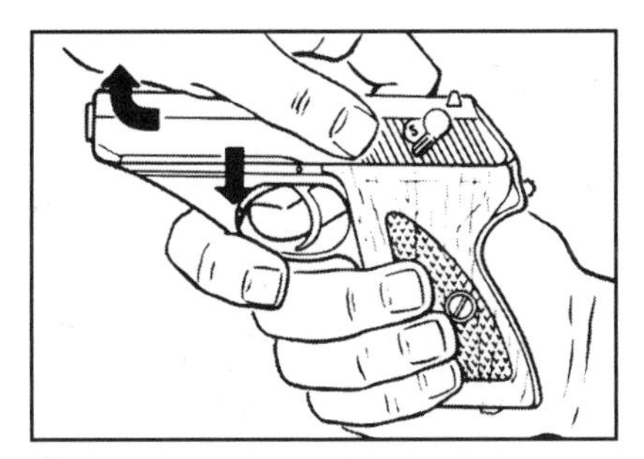

1 To take down the HSc, remove magazine and clear chamber. Pull hammer back to full cock and put safety catch down over red dot. Hold down notched catch inside front of trigger guard. At same time pull slide forward and upward until it is free of frame.

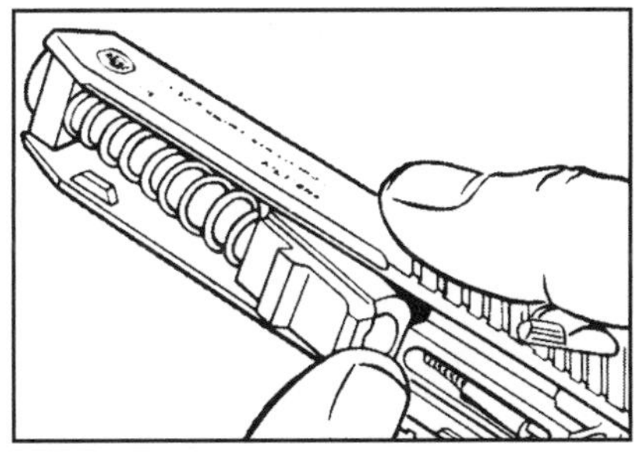

2 To remove barrel, hold slide as shown. Push chamber end of barrel forward and upward until it clears bolt face. If barrel is held too tightly in slide, use a block of wood or magazine floorplate to lever it out.

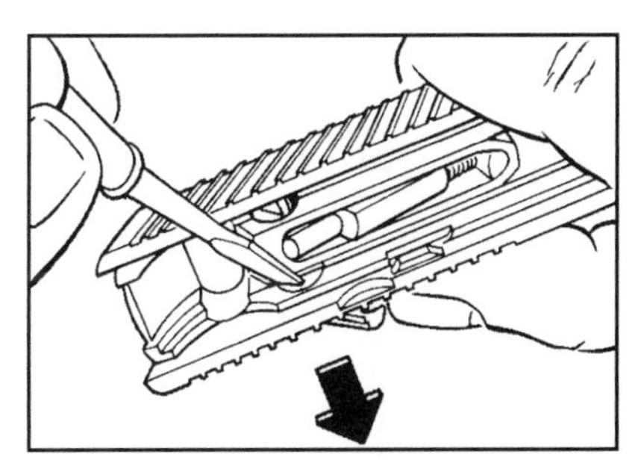

3 The safety catch (9) is held in place by a detent (5) and spring (4) that also actuate extractor. To remove firing pin (8) or safety catch, lift end of firing pin to position shown. Turn safety to a position half way between on and off positions and push safety out with a screwdriver as shown. Remove extractor and detent parts.

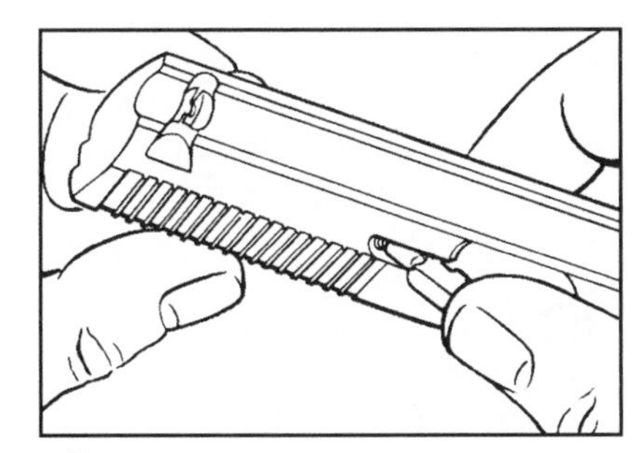

4 To replace safety catch, back firing pin (8) and spring (7) into slide. Lift firing pin tail as in disassembly. Install safety and push firing pin down into place. Replace detent part and push extractor in and back until it seats itself properly in slide.

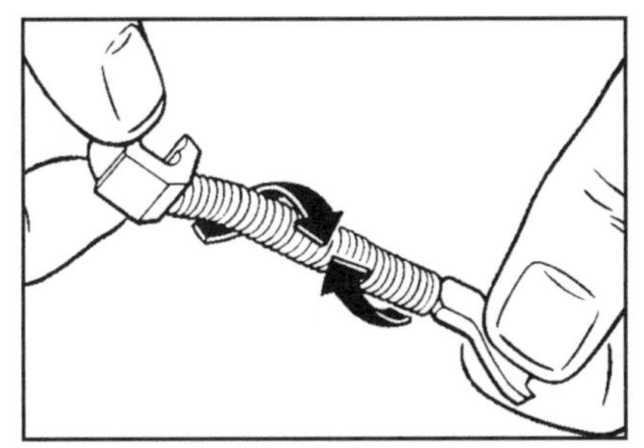

5 When magazine catch pin (27) is removed, magazine catch (25), hammer strut (23), and spring (24) come out as an assembly. This assembly can be taken apart by giving magazine catch a quarter turn. Great care must be taken when assembling or disassembling these pieces since they are under heavy spring tension.

6 To remove takedown launch (12), hold frame as shown. Use a screwdriver or black of wood to push down latch and rotate it clockwise 180 defgrees. Care must be taken to prevent latch from flying out since it is under heavy spring tension.

MAUSER W.T.P. OLD MODEL

PARTS LEGEND

1. Slide
2. Extractor pin
3. Extractor
4. Firing pin retainer
5. Firing pin
6. Firing pin spring
7. Firing pin spring guide
8. Barrel
9. Recoil spring guide rod
10. Recoil spring
11. Disconnector
12. Magazine disconnector
13. Disconnector spring
14. Sear pin
15. Sear spring
16. Sear
17. Trigger lever
18. Trigger bar
19. Magazine catch
20. Grip
21. Grip screw
22. Frame
23. Magazine
24. Takedown catch
25. Takedown catch
26. Safety catch
27. Trigger pin
28. Trigger

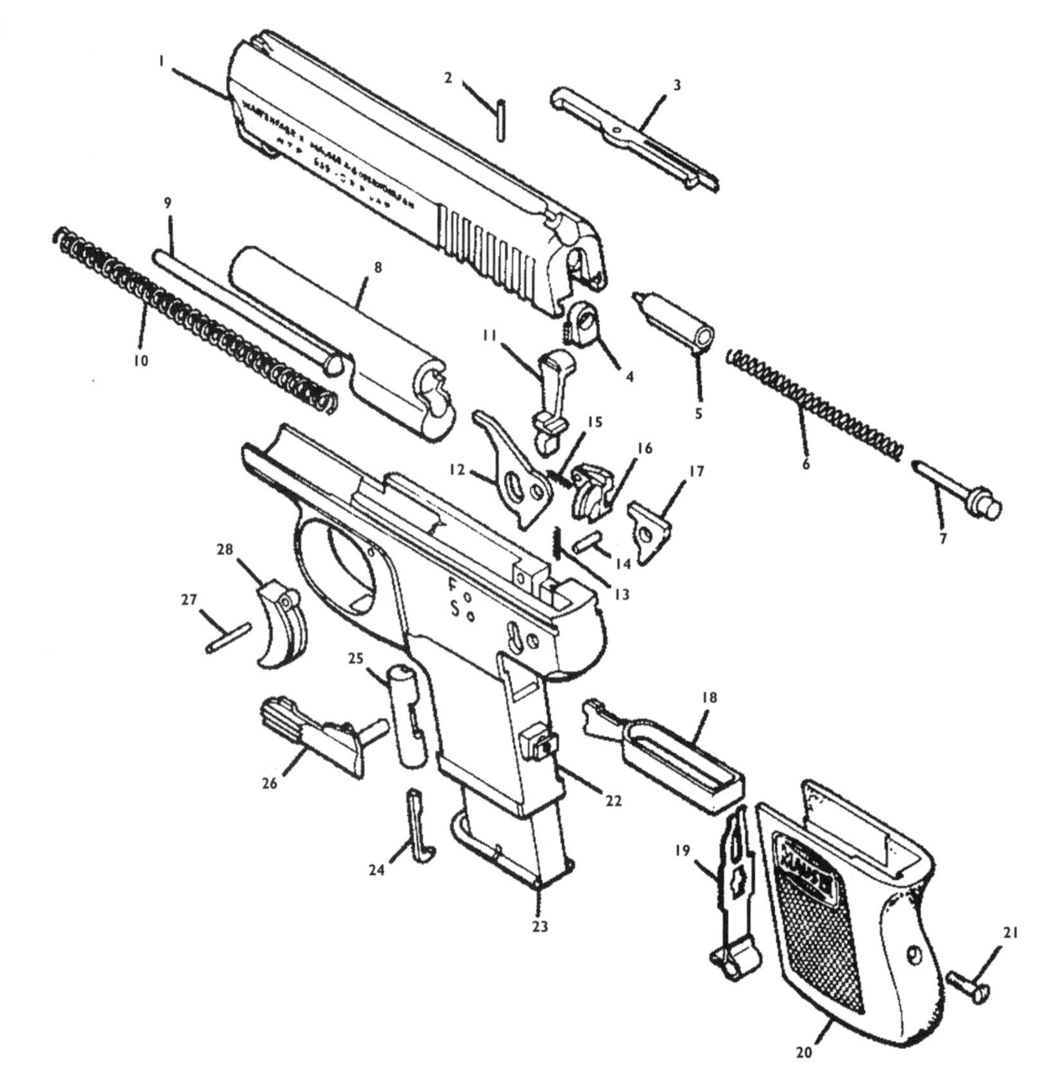

In the 1920s all major German gun companies and many minor ones turned out vest-pocket pistols. Mauser brought out their W.T.P. or *WestenTaschen-Pistole* (vest-pocket pistol), but it was not the most popular. The average German shopping for a vest-pocket gun usually chose the smallest and least expensive. Mauser was neither.

The W.T.P. is well made and finished. While not the smallest of its type, it is very compact. The grip is comfortable, and the safety catch is convenient and locks both sear and slide. Frame grip section is square and a thick hard rubber grip is used to fill out the area to a comfortable shape. This made the frame easier to machine but also made the grip susceptible to breakage. When the new model was introduced in 1938, the frame was forged to proper contour and conventional fiat grips were screwed to the sides.

The W.T.P. has a magazine safety that prevents the gun from being fired with magazine removed. The firing pin spring guide projecting from the back of the slide locks the firing pin retainer and serves as a cocking indicator. It cannot be pressed inward when the gun is cocked.

When the last shot has been fired, the slide is held open by the magazine follower. When the magazine is removed, the slide snaps closed. Unfortunately this means that the magazine must be removed against the resistance of recoil spring tension. While the old model is a reliable gun, the new model that replaced it is a far better design.

DISASSEMBLY

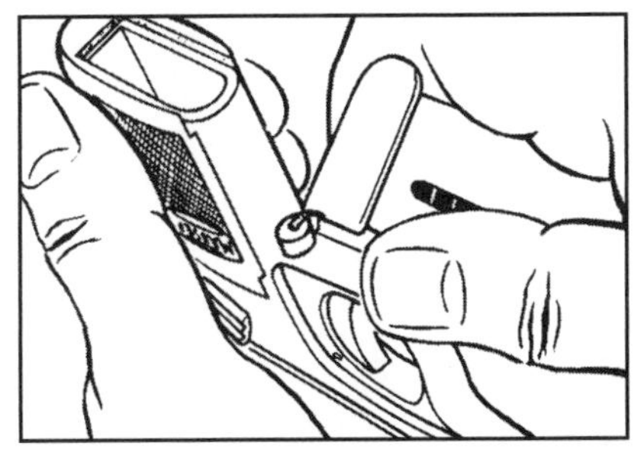

1 The takedown catch (25) runs through frame and locks barrel to frame. To strip gun, simply push in and down on takedown catch spring (24). This will disengage barrel and allow barrel and slide to be stripped off front of frame.

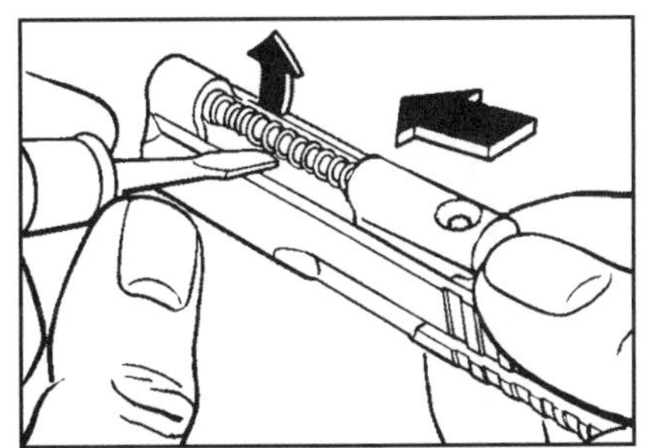

2 To remove barrel (8) and recoil spring (10) from slide, push barrel forward and upward. Ease it out of slide since it is under spring tension. When reassembling barrel and recoil spring, it may be necessary to lift spring and recoil spring guide rod (9) as shown to help align the rod.

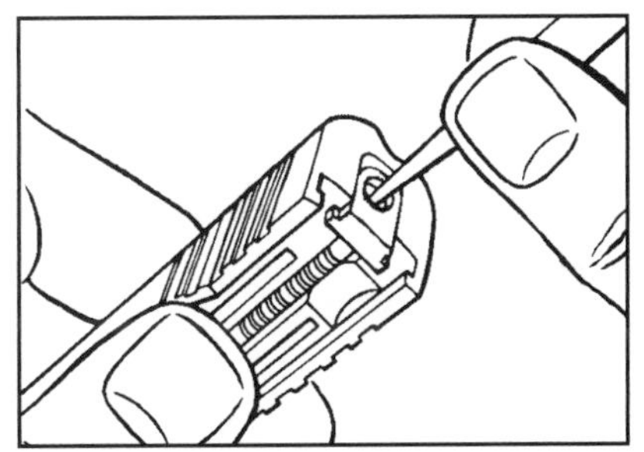

3 To remove firing pin (5), push firing pin spring guide (7) in with a punch. When it is clear of the firing pin retainer (4), push the retainer down as shown and ease out firing pin spring, and spring guide.

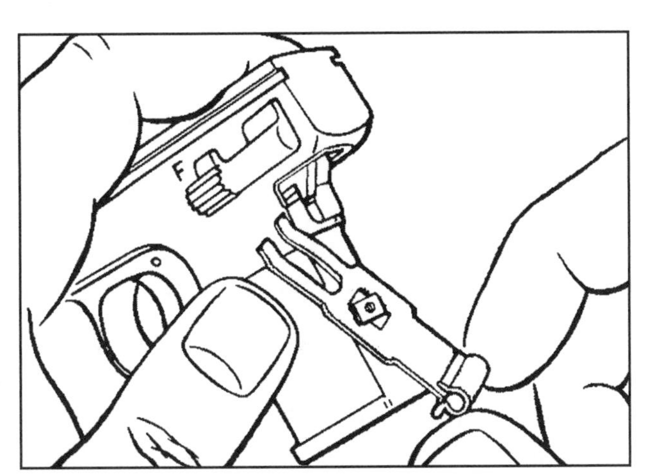

4 After grip (20) has been removed, the combination magazine catch (19) must be removed to expose sear parts. To do this, rotate the spring 90 degrees until square cutout on spring lines up with lug on frame, and lift off spring spring.

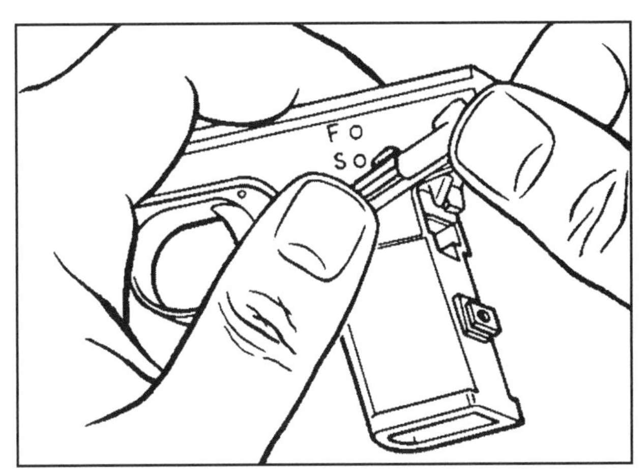

5 When safety catch (26) is removed it frees sear parts. To remove safety, it is necessary to first remove the grip. Safety can then be pushed down lower until it snaps free of frame. To reassemble, push it in until it is flat against frame, then push it up toward "Fire" position.

ORTGIES POCKET PISTOL

PARTS LEGEND

1. Slide
2. Extractor pin
3. Extractor
4. Extractor spring
5. Firing pin spring guide
6. Firing pin spring
7. Firing pin
8. Right grip
9. Grip safety
10. Magazine catch
11. Magazine catch spring
12. Grip latch
13. Magazine
14. Grip safety hinge pin
15. Magazine and grip latch hinge pin
16. Left grip
17. Takedown catch
18. Takedown catch spring
19. Trigger spring plunger
20. Trigger spring
21. Trigger
22. Trigger pin
23. Frame
24. Barrel
25. Recoil spring
26. Disconnector
27. Disconnector spring
28. Sear
29. Sear spring

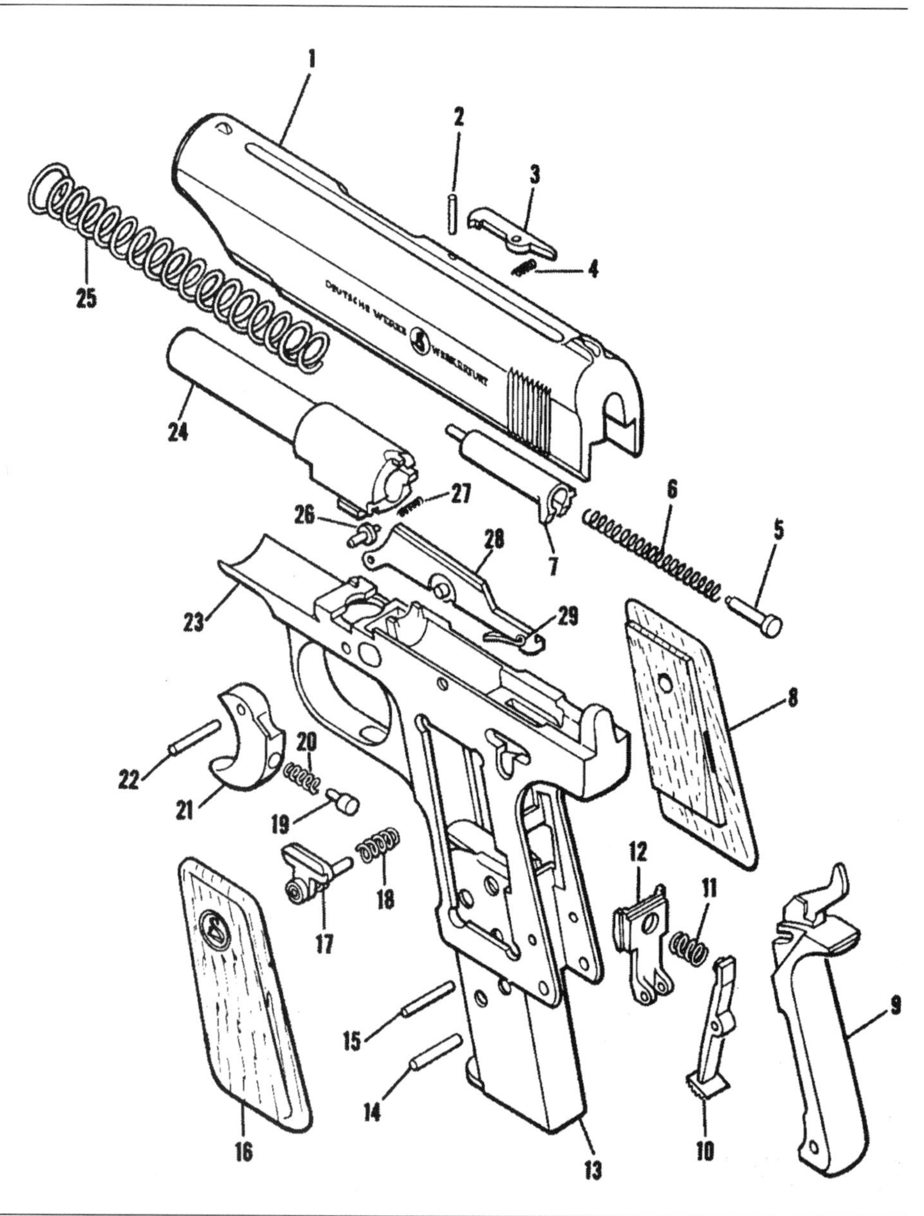

Ortgies pistols are among the most common of the early German pocket pistols. They were extremely popular in Germany and central Europe in the 1920s-30s and large numbers were exported to the Americas during this period.

Heinrich Ortgies set up shop during 1919 in Erfurt, Germany. His guns, produced within the framework of the Versailles Treaty, were not classified as military weapons. The .32 caliber model was well received because of its compact design and low price. In 1920, the Deutsche Werke of Erfurt took over the production of the Ortgies. The 32 caliber pistol was followed by the smaller scale .25 caliber model. Around 1922 Deutsche Werke brought out the caliber .380. At this point the design changed a bit and many of the .380 (9 mm. short) Ortgies will be found with an additional thumb-operated safety catch. Somewhere around 1926, production ceased.

Although the design contains 4 hinge pins, there is not a screw in the gun. The grips are retained by a clever spring-loaded catch. The barrel is rigidly fixed to the frame but can be easily removed for cleaning or replacement. It is interesting to note that the Ortgies does not have a fixed ejector. After the extractor has pulled the case from the chamber, the firing pin protrudes through the bolt face to eject it.

The .25 and .32 calibers, and some models of the .380 have only one safety catch. This safety is of the squeeze type and protrudes only when the firing pin is cocked. Although the disconnector design is very clever it subjects the end of the disconnector to appreciable wear.

Due to the simple blowback action, takedown procedure is easy and uncluttered. The gun can be reassembled just as easily once the trick of restraining the firing pin assembly is known.

DISASSEMBLY

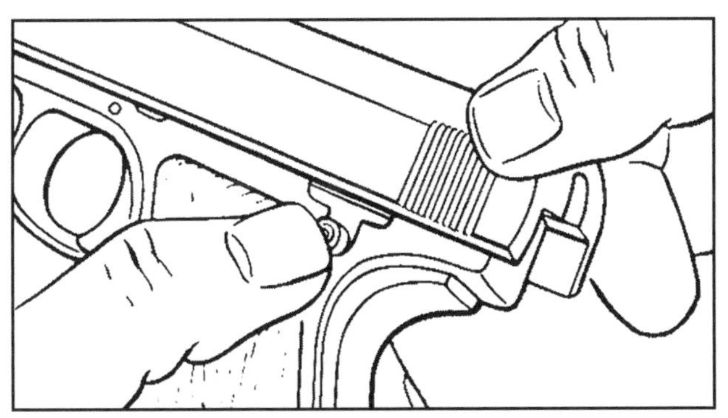

1 Remove magazine (13). Pull slide (1) back until slide serrations line up approximately with end of frame as shown. Push in takedown catch (17) and lift end of slide free of frame. Push slide forward off barrel.

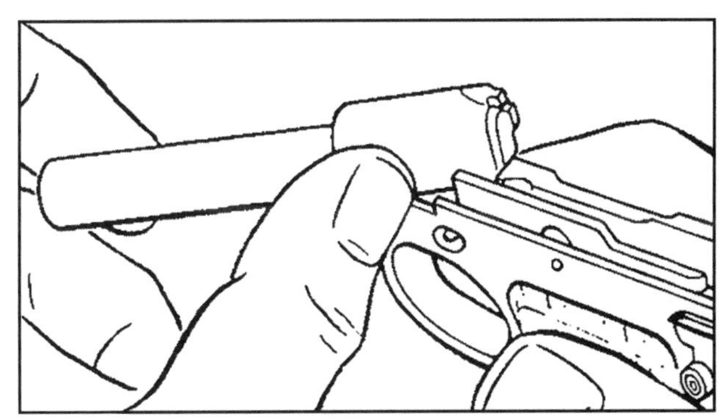

2 To remove barrel (24) for cleaning or repair, grasp barrel (24) and frame (23) as shown. Twist barrel counterclockwise until it is at right angles to frame and lift up.

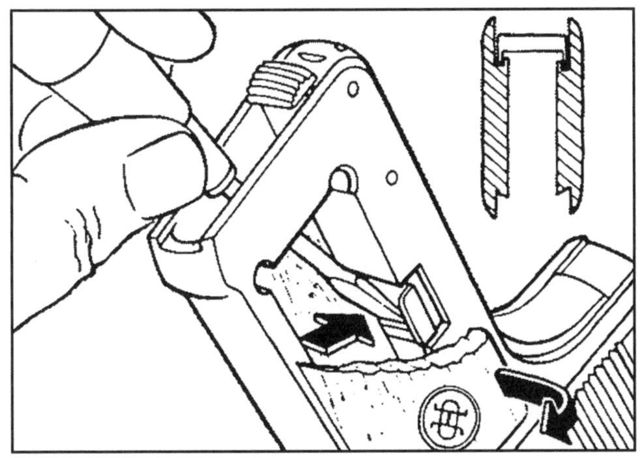

3 To remove grips, insert a screwdriver into magazine well and push grip latch (12) in toward backstrap. At same time pry or push up bock edge of grips and rotate them free of undercut on front edge of grip.

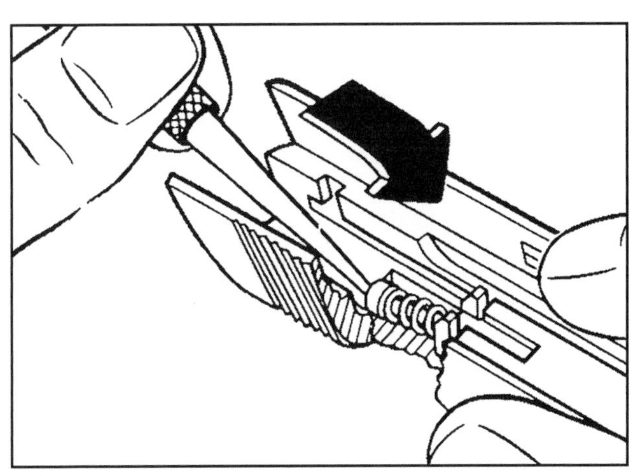

4 Ortgies reassembles easily once firing pin (7) is held in check. Push firing pin spring (6) and guide (5) into firing pin until end of guide can be pushed into its notch in top of slide. Hook slide over barrel, pull it to rear and downward.

PARA ORDNANCE PXT LDA PISTOL

PARTS LEGEND

1. Barrel
2. Barrel bushing
3. Barrel link
4. Barrel link pin
5. Drawbar
6. Ejector
7. Ejector pin
   8a. Extractor claw
   8b. Extractor body
   8c. Extractor plunger
   8d. Extractor spring
9. Firing pin
10. Firing pin plunger
11. Firing pin spring
12. Firing pin stop
13. Front sight
14. Front sight (limited)
15. Fixed rear sight
16. Adjustable rear sight
17. Grip safety
18. Grip (set)
19. Grip screws (4)
    19a. Grip screw locking rings
    19b. Grip screw bushing
20. Hammer
21. Hammer pin
22. Hammer strut
23. Cocking cam pin
24. Magazine assembly
25. Magazine catch
26. Magazine catch lock
27. Magazine catch spring
28. Magazine follower
29. Magazine spring (not shown)
30. Main spring
31. Main spring cap
32. Main spring cap pin
33. Main spring housing
34. Main spring housing pin
35. Main spring housing pin retainer
36. Plunger lever
37. Plunger spring
38. Plunger spring F/P
39. Receiver
40. Recoil spring
41. Recoil spring guide
42. Recoil spring plug
43. Slide lock safety
44. Safety lock plunger
45. Sear
46. Sear pin
47. Sear spring
48. Slide
49. Slide (limited)
50. Slide stop
51. Slide stop plunger
52. Trigger
53. Straddle
54. Trigger pin
55. Trigger return spring
56. Cocking cam
57. Hammer return spring
58. Safety lock lever
59. Grip safety lever
60. Drawbar platform spring
61. Hammer assembly pin
62. Drawbar platform
63L/R. Ambidextrous slide lock safety (left/right)

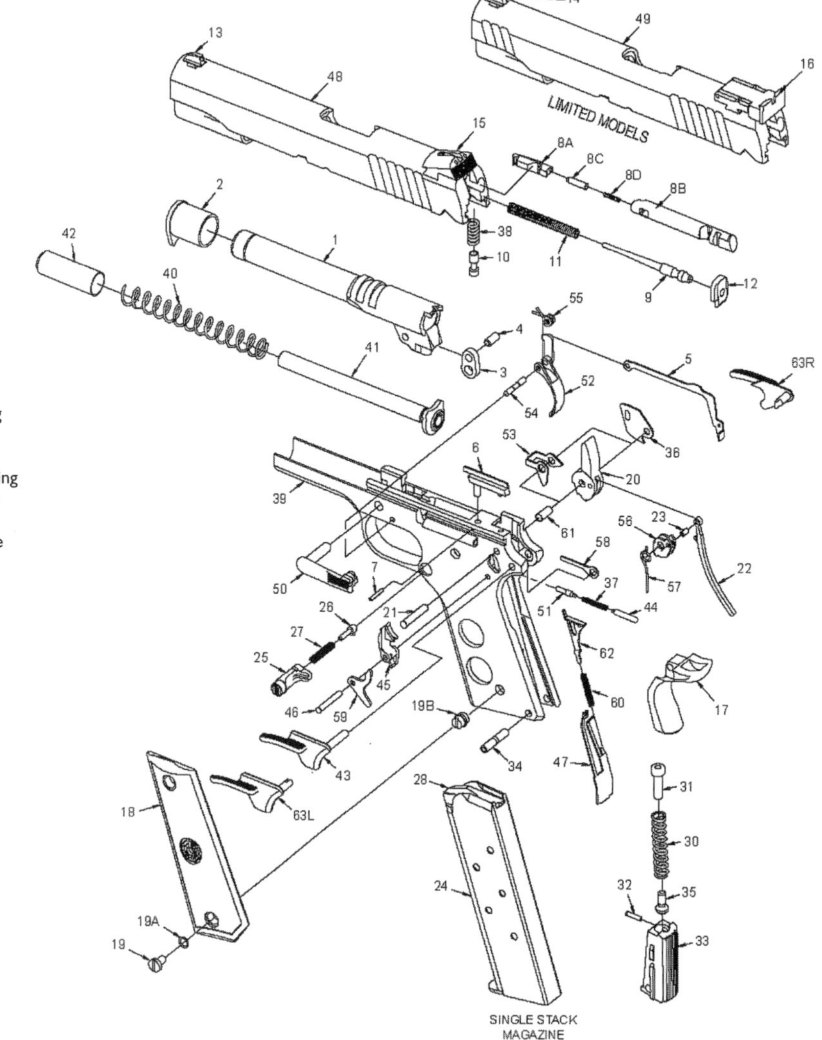

Para-Ordnance Mfg. Inc. of Ontario, Canada, founded in 1985, was the brainchild of engineer and designer Ted Szabo. In 1987 Para-Ordnance released their first product, a selective-fire paint ball gun intended as a law enforcement and military training device.

Szabo focused then on the Model 1911 Automatic design and by 1988, Para-Ordnance had introduced an innovative high-capacity frame and magazine for John Browning's classic. Szabo also developed a light double-action (LDA) trigger system that eliminated the heavy double-action trigger pull and allowed the gun to be safely carried with a round in the chamber and the hammer down. He also added a larger extractor claw, the "Power Extractor"(PXT) in 2004, for controlled feeding and positive extraction of empty cases.

In the late 1980s, Para Ordnance introduced a high capacity conversion kit for M1911A1 pistols, consisting of a thick frame that accepted a double-stack magazine which doubled the number of rounds. Para Ordnance eventually introduced their own line of M1911A1-style pistols with high capacity magazines in 9mm, .40 S&W and .45 ACP.

In 1999, the company introduced a line of Lightweight Double Action (LDA) pistols. The Para Ordnance LDAs are short-recoil operated, locked-breech weapons with a classic Browning two-lug locking system.

DISASSEMBLY

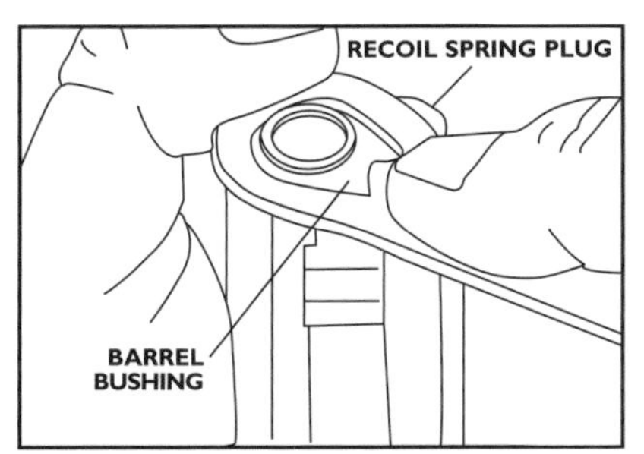

1 With barrel pointing upward and away from your face, place the pistol with the back (heel) of the receiver and the grip safety testing on a table or bench.

Using the barrel bushing wrench provided, press down the recoil spring plug (located below the muzzle) while at the same time, rotating the barrel bushing clockwise for about a quarter (¼) turn so as to free the plug and recoil spring.

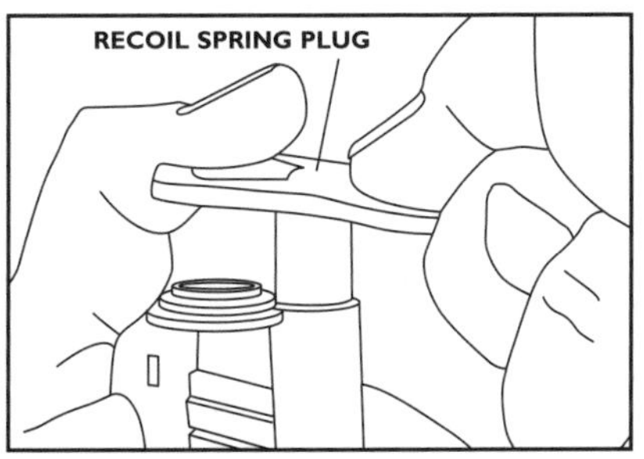

2 Continue to apply pressure on the recoil spring plug to prevent ejection of it and the spring. Then gently and gradually allow the spring and the recoil spring plug to extend out of the slide.

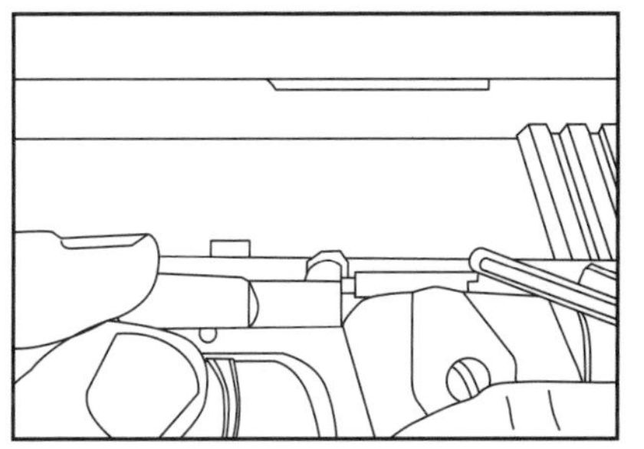

3 With the grip safety depressed, push the slide back to the point that the slide stop lug is directly opposite the disassembly notch. Then push the rounded end of the slide stop pin, on the right side of the receiver, inward and through the receiver and out the left side.

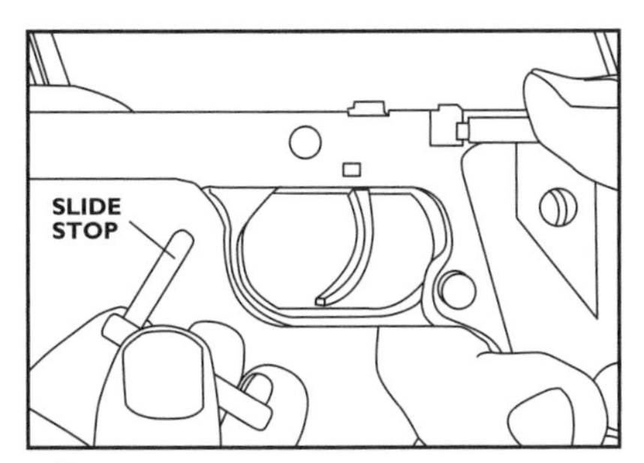

4 Disengage slide stop from the slide by removing slide stop completely from the receiver.

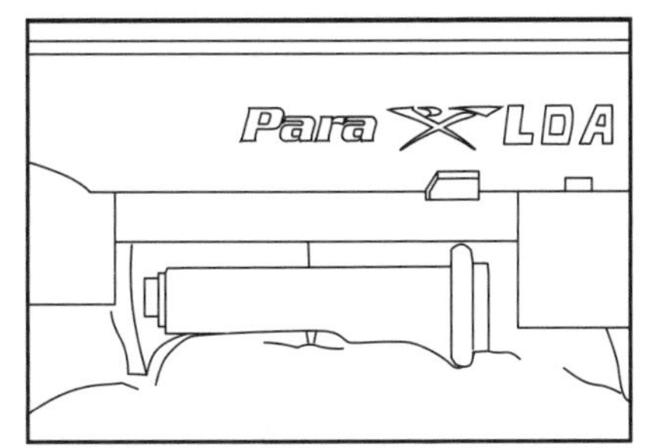

5 Push slide forward and remove slide from receiver. On all models with recoil spring guide rods: pull recoil spring guide rod. Lift recoil spring guide rod and pull to rear and out of the slide. On all other LDA pistols: when you remove the recoil spring, the recoil spring guide will drop out of the slide.

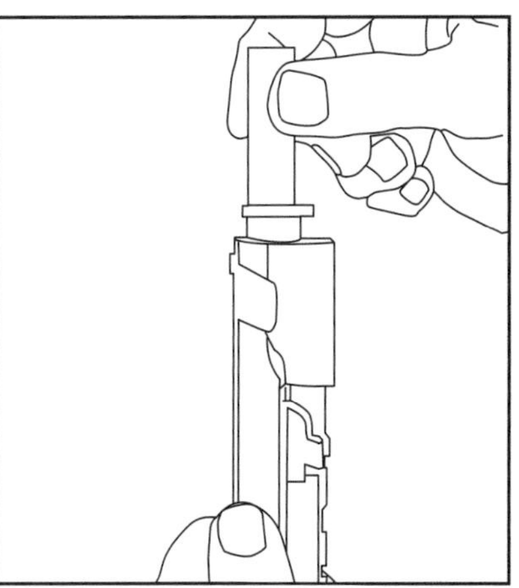

6 To remove the barrel bushing from the barrel, turn the bushing counterclockwise and then push the barrel and bushing forward to the point that the bushing is clear of the slide and can be removed from the barrel.

PARA ORDNANCE WARTHOG PISTOL

PARTS LEGEND

1. Barrel
2. Barrel link
3. Barrel link pin
4. Drawbar
5. Ejector
6. Ejector pin

7A. Extractor claw
7B. Extractor body
7C. Extractor plunger
7D. Extractor spring

8. Firing pin
9. Firing pin plunger
10. Firing pin spring
11. Firing pin stop
12. Front sight
13. Rear sight
14. Grip safety
15. Grip (Set)

16A. Grip screw (4)
16B. Grip screws locking rings
16C. Grip screw bushing

17. Hammer
18. Hammer pin
19. Hammer strut
20. Cocking cam pin
21. Magazine assembly
22. Magazine catch
23. Magazine catch lock
24. Magazine catch spring
25. Magazine follower
26. Magazine spring (not shown)
27. Main spring
28. Main spring cap
29. Main spring cap pin
30. Main spring housing
31. Main spring housing pin
32. Main spring housing pin retainer
33. Plunger lever
34. Plunger spring
35. Plunger receiver
36. Receiver

37A. Recoil spring, outer
37B. Recoil spring, inner
38A. Recoil spring guide rod, inner
38B. Recoil spring guide plate
38C. Recoil spring guide rod, outer

39. Recoil spring plug
40. Slide lock safety
41. Safety lock plunger
42. Sear
43. Sear pin
44. Sear spring
45. Slide
46. Slide stop
47. Slide stop plunger
48. Trigger
49. Straddle
50. Trigger pin
51. Trigger return spring
52. Cocking cam
53. Hammer return spring
54. Safety lock lever
55. Grip safety lever
56. Drawbar platform spring
57. Hammer assembly pin
58. Drawbar platform

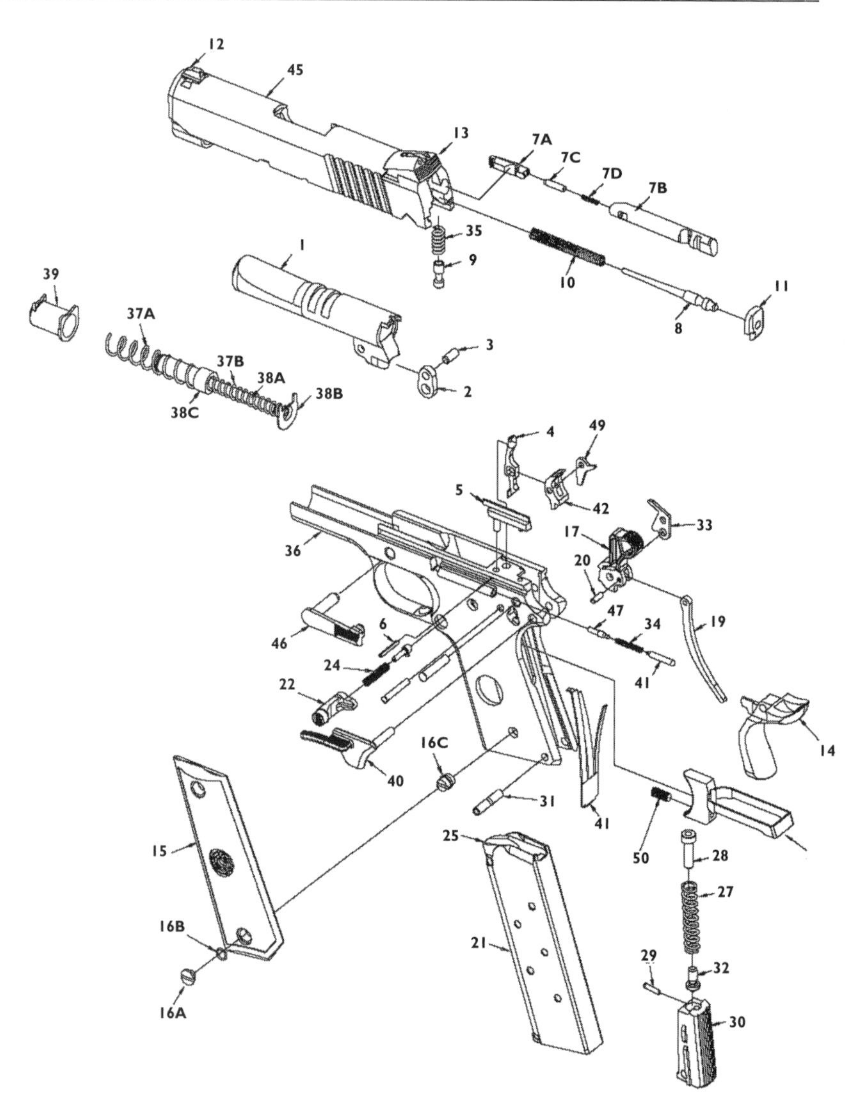

Para-Ordnance Mfg. Inc. of Ontario, Canada manufactures the Warthog semi-automatic pistol. Introduced to the market in 2005, the Para Warthog is among the smallest .45 ACP semi-automatics currently manufactured and is best described as a "super-compact."

The Warthog is an upgraded version of the Para-Ordnance's original compact, single action P-10 semi-automatic pistol with the addition of an enlarged beaver-tail safety grip, 3-inch stainless conical barrel and improved extractor. The Warthog's "Para-Power" extractor consists of a sub-assembly containing a control arm, pin, spring and extra-wide extractor. The wide extractor claw is intended to provide better purchase on the rim of the cartridge during extraction. Like the P-10, the Warthog weighs 24 ounces and is 6.5 inches in long. The pistol carries ten-rounds of .45 ACP cartridges in a stainless, double-column magazine. Total capacity is 10+1 rounds.

Variants of the Warthog include the Slim Hawg, a 6+1-round single stack model; the Nite Hawg with non-reflective finish and tritium night sights; and the 9mm, 12-round Hawg 9 with a lightweight alloy frame.

DISASSEMBLY

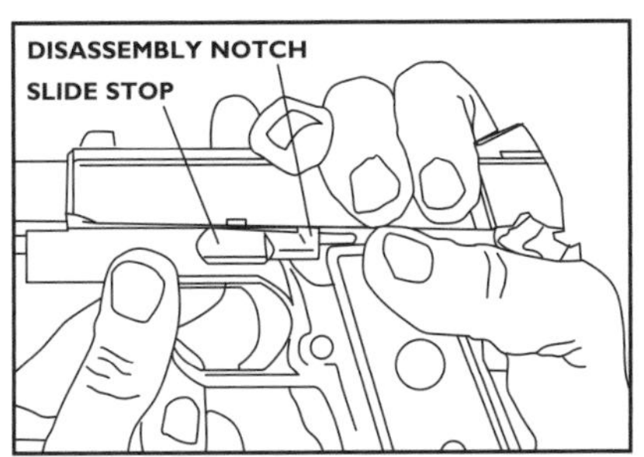

1 With the pistol unloaded and the muzzle pointing in a safe direction, depress the grip safety while pushing the slide back to the point that the slide stop lug is directly opposite the disassembly notch. Then push the rounded end of the slide top pin, on the right side of the receiver, inward and through the receiver and out the left side. CAUTION: the recoil spring is partially compressed during and after this step.

2 While holding the slide firmly, disengage the slide stop from the slide by removing it completely from the receiver. Carefully allow the slide to move forward. This allows the recoil spring to decompress.

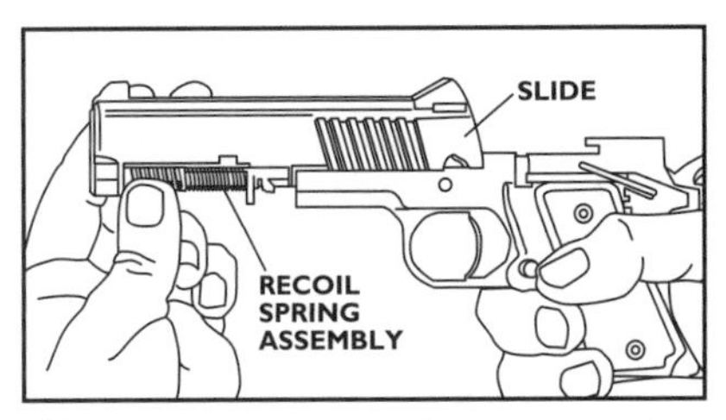

3 Push the slide forward and remove the slide from the receiver. The recoil spring is partially compressed. Use care to prevent the recoil spring assembly from becoming disengaged from the slide.

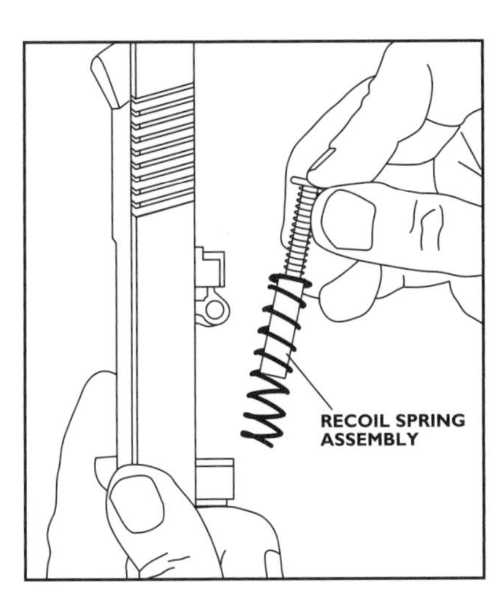

4 Carefully lift the rear of the recoil spring assembly from the slide and allow it to fully decompress.

Lift the decompressed recoil spring assembly and pull it toward the rear and out of the slide.

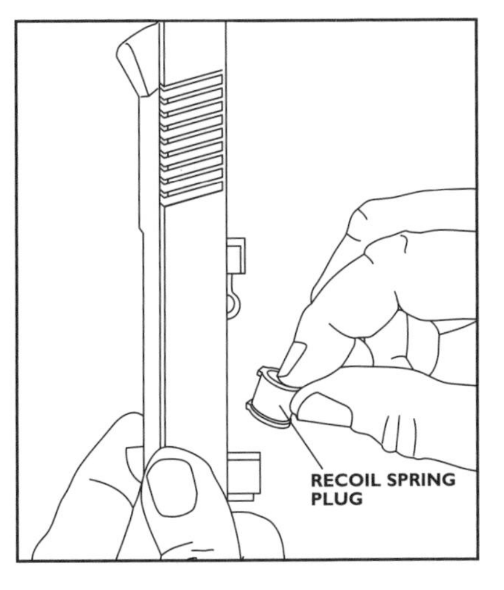

5 To remove the recoil spring plug, push the plug from the front of the slide to the rear and remove it completely from the slide.

With the recoil spring plug already removed, push the barrel link forward and remove it through the front of the slide.

If your pistol requires further work it should be done at an Authorized Service Center or at Para-Ordnance's Customer Service Center.

POLISH RADOM P35 PISTOL

PARTS LEGEND

A. Slide
B. Rear sight
C. Extractor
D. Firing pin spring
E. Firing pin
F. Magazine catch spring guide
G. Magazine catch spring
H. Magazine catch
I. Hammer strut pin
J. Hammer
K. Hammer strut
L. Grip safety
M. Trigger
N. Sear spring
O. Main spring cap
P. Main spring
Q. Main spring retainer pin
R. Main spring housing
S. Magazine
T. Main spring housing pin
U. Grip screw bushing
V. Left-hand grip
W. Grip screw
X. Take-down latch
Y. Sear and disconnector pin
Z. Hammer pin
AA. Slide stop
BB. Frame (receiver)
CC. Recoil spring
DD. Slotted recoil spring guide
EE. Spring guide retainer pin
FF. Auxiliary recoil spring
GG. Recoil spring stop
HH. Recoil spring guide
II. Barrel
JJ. Hammer lowering catch
KK. Hammer catch operating spring
LL. Firing pin retainer plate
MM. Disconnector
NN. Sear

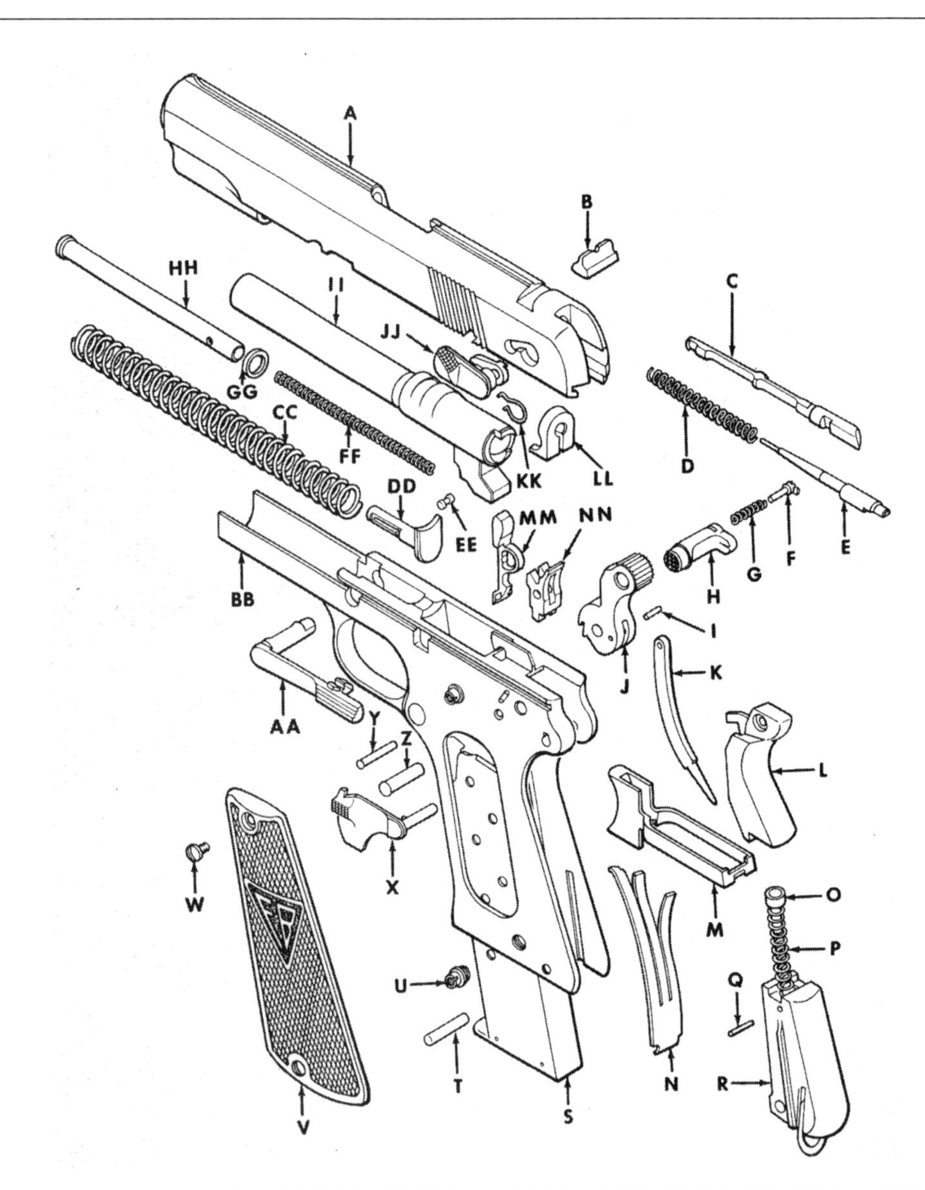

In 1935, with the help of Belgian Fabrique Nationale engineers, Poland began production of what might be termed a modernized version of the Colt 1911 automatic pistol. The guns, designated the the P 35 pistol, were manufactured at the government arsenal at Radom in central Poland.

The P 35 weighed 2 pounds, 3 ounces, and was 8 1/32 inches long. Pre-war P 35s were well made and finely finished and can be easily recognized by the Polish eagle crest engraved on the slide. Wartime pistols, manufactured in Polish plants under German occupation, are less finely finished and often show tool marks. In addition, many of the occupation guns were manufactured without a take-down latch.

The main mechanical difference between the Radom and the Colt 1911 is the use of a captive recoil spring and different barrel locking device. The action is unlocked by recoil, but in place of a link at the breech, a cam projection unlocks the barrel from the slide. Another feature is the hammer lowering device. A thumb catch on the left side of the slide drops the hammer but will not fire a chambered round because the thumb catch shifts the firing pin aside before tripping the hammer.

DISASSEMBLY

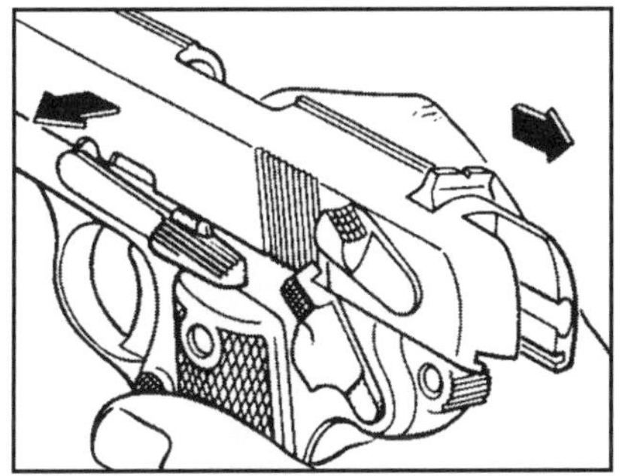

1 Remove the magazine, draw back the slide far enough to put on the take-dawn latch (X). Pull forward on the exposed end of the recoil spring guide (HH) to relieve the tension on the slide stop (AA). At the same time, push out the slide step. Release the take-down latch and draw the slide assembly off the front of the receiver. (If pistol has no take-down latch, retract the slide, depress hammer-lowering catch, and ease slide forward until catch engages notch on hammer.)

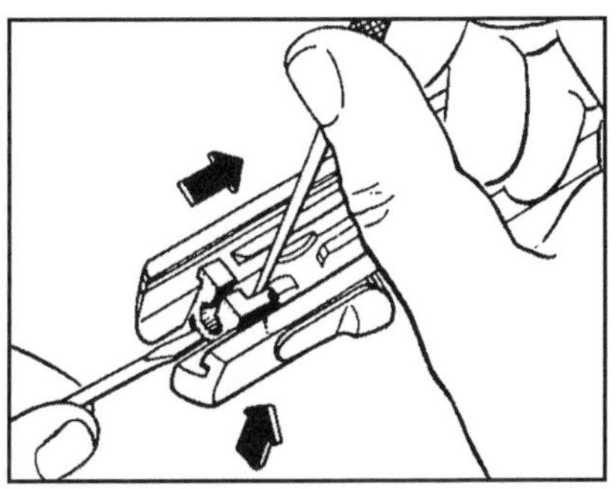

2 To remove the firing pin (E), first remove the firing pin retainer plate (LL). Due to the split construction, the retainer plate sometimes gets wedged into the slide. So, insert a thin-bladed screwdriver as shown. Push in the firing pin (E) with a thin punch far enough to catch the shoulder on the pin and hold it out of the bushing, while prying the retainer plate down and out of the slide.

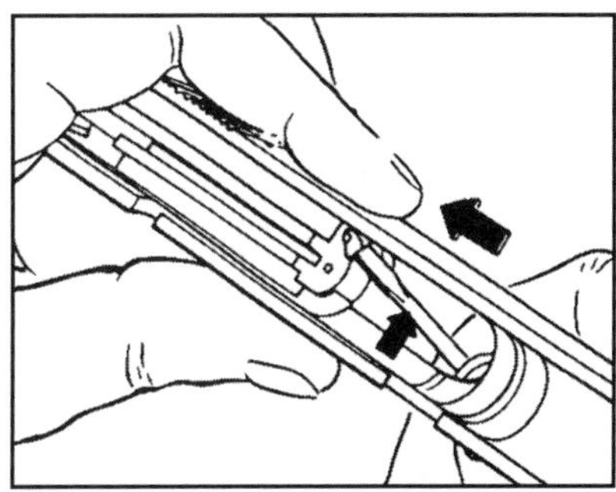

3 To remove the extractor (C), pull out the recoil spring assembly (CC through HH) and disengage the barrel (II) from the slide. Remove the firing pin retainer plate (LL). Using a small screwdriver, press the extractor (C) outward toward the outside of the slide, pressing rearward at the some time. Remove the extractor through the rear of the slide.

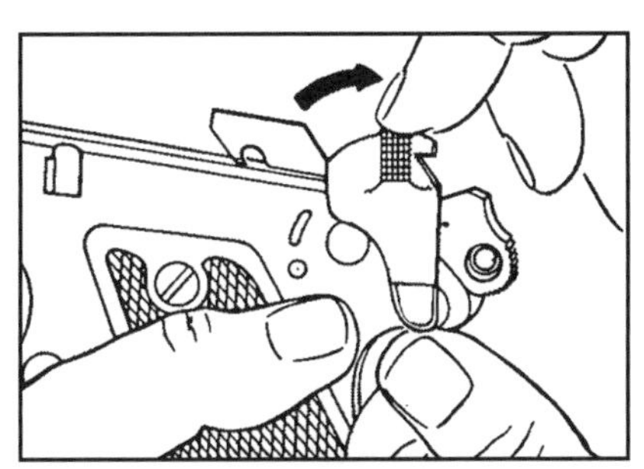

4 To remove the take-down latch (X), first cock the hammer, Hold the receiver (BB) as shown to depress the grip safety (L). Pull the take-down latch out slightly and turn it up as shown. To remove the latch, it may be necessary to wiggle it or move the safety slightly to free the pin. When the latch is removed, the grip safety (L) will drop free.

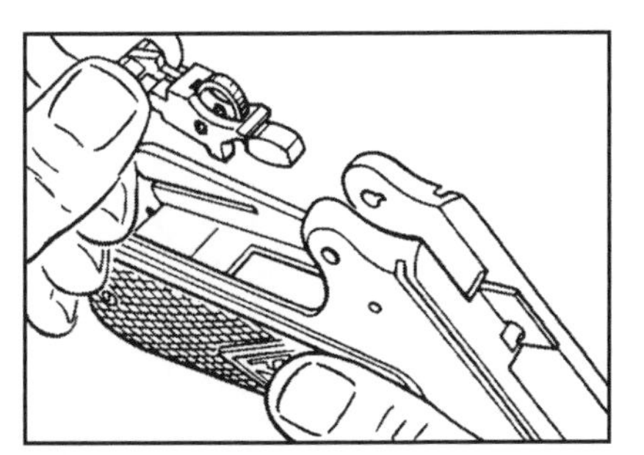

5 The sear (NN) and disconnector (MM) will drop out when the sear and disconnector pin (Y) is removed. To reassemble, place the pieces together as shown. Drop the tail of the disconnector into the hole in the receiver (BB). If the bearing holes in the parts do not line up with the hole in the receiver, pull the trigger a bit. This will usually line up the holes.

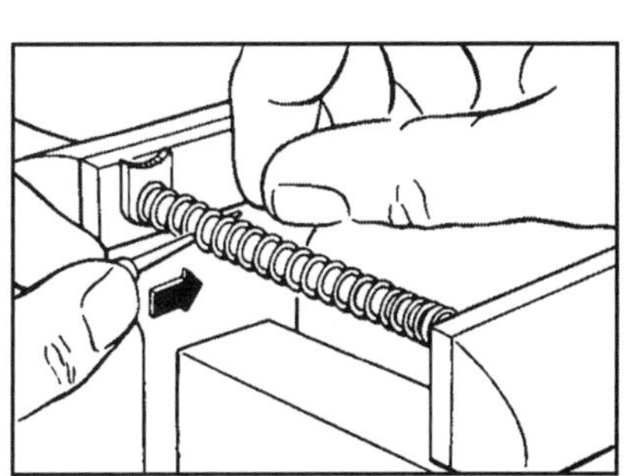

6 The recoil spring on this gun must be removed as an assembly. To disassemble the recoil spring group (CC through HH), squeeze the assembly slowly in a vise until the slotted recoil spring guide (DD) is in as far as it can go. Now, using a thin punch, push out the spring guide retainer pin (EE). It may be necessary to spread the coils of the spring to remove the pin.

REMINGTON MODEL 51 PISTOL

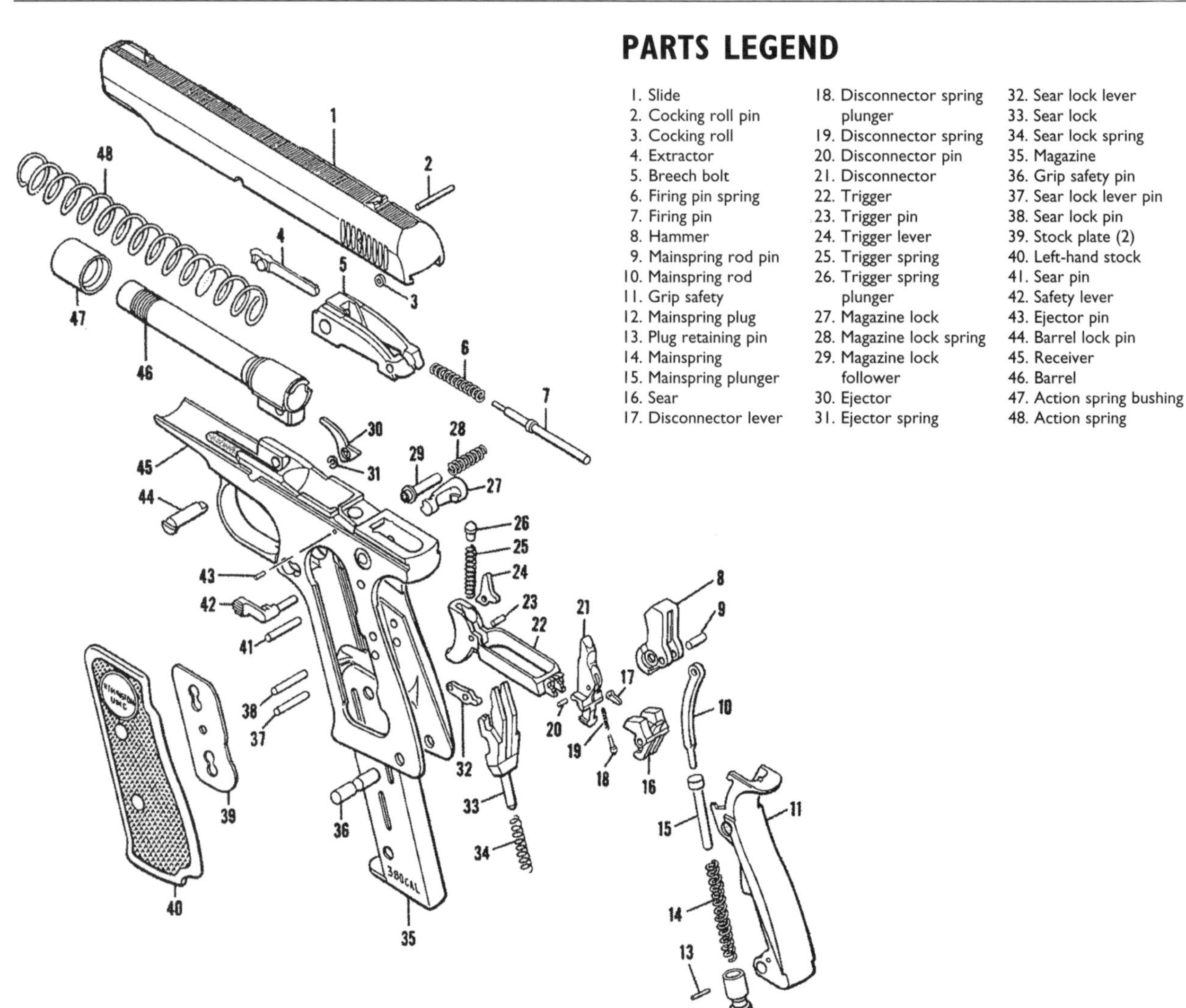

PARTS LEGEND

1. Slide
2. Cocking roll pin
3. Cocking roll
4. Extractor
5. Breech bolt
6. Firing pin spring
7. Firing pin
8. Hammer
9. Mainspring rod pin
10. Mainspring rod
11. Grip safety
12. Mainspring plug
13. Plug retaining pin
14. Mainspring
15. Mainspring plunger
16. Sear
17. Disconnector lever
18. Disconnector spring plunger
19. Disconnector spring
20. Disconnector pin
21. Disconnector
22. Trigger
23. Trigger pin
24. Trigger lever
25. Trigger spring
26. Trigger spring plunger
27. Magazine lock
28. Magazine lock spring
29. Magazine lock follower
30. Ejector
31. Ejector spring
32. Sear lock lever
33. Sear lock
34. Sear lock spring
35. Magazine
36. Grip safety pin
37. Sear lock lever pin
38. Sear lock pin
39. Stock plate (2)
40. Left-hand stock
41. Sear pin
42. Safety lever
43. Ejector pin
44. Barrel lock pin
45. Receiver
46. Barrel
47. Action spring bushing
48. Action spring

The Model 51 was developed by John D. Pedersen, designer of the "Pedersen Device" of World War I fame, and the Pedersen semi-automatic rifle. The design incorporates a number of noteworthy features, best of which is the grip outline. This shape was settled on only after hundreds of experiments had been carried out to determine the best grip for the average hand.

The Model 51 has a full set of safety features. It has a grip safety, a thumb safety, and a magazine safety. The grip safety acts as a cocking indicator and as a hold-open device. When the slide is pulled all the way back, and the grip safety is not interfered with, the disconnector is held up in front of the breech bolt, preventing the slide running forward. When the grip safety is squeezed, it allows the disconnector to drop out of the path of the slide. If there is a cartridge in the magazine, it will chamber it but will not fire it until the trigger is pulled.

Unlike most common pocket automatics, the gun is not a true blowback. It is operated by cartridge setback or by what is sometimes called impinging action. The breech bolt is separate and not a fixed part of the slide. It is locked into a recess in the frame but can recoil in a straight line for a short distance. When the cartridge is fired, the bolt recoils at a high speed, striking the slide. The slide moves to the rear, lifting the breech bolt free of the locking recess in the frame.

Model 51 pistols were first marketed in .32 and .380 ACP calibers around 1918 and discontinued by 1935. Even with its outstanding design, a Model 51 could be purchased for $15.75 when the Colt Pocket Model sold for $20.50.

DISASSEMBLY

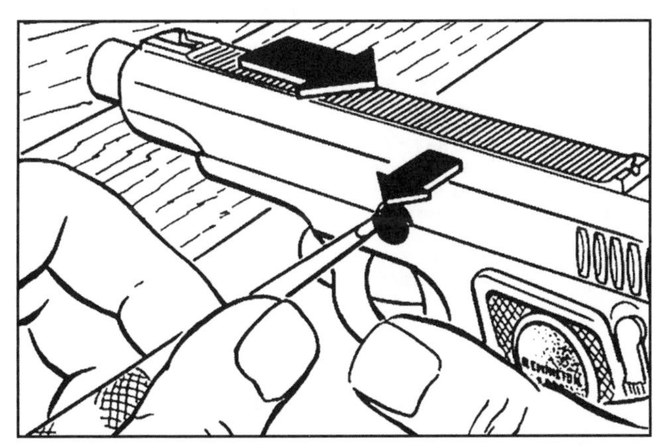

1 To field-strip the Remington, first remove the magazine and empty the chamber. Then push the slide (1) back far enough to align the cut in the slide with the head of the barrel lock pin (44). Push on the end of the pin to start it and pry it out the rest of the way with a screwdriver or the magazine floorplate tip.

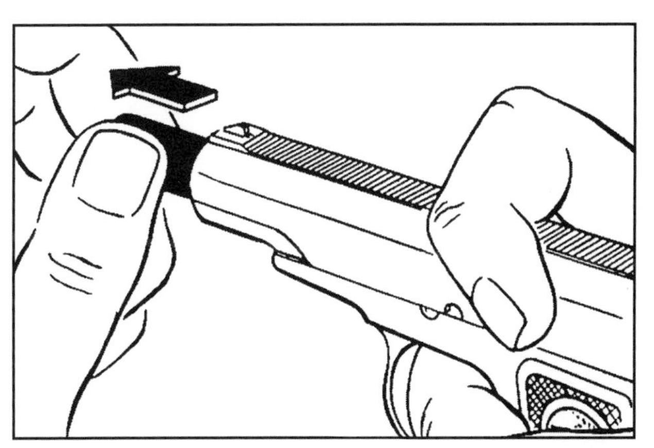

2 Pull back the slide again as shown, and at the same time pull the muzzle of the barrel forward. This will release the slide and barrel (46) from the receiver (45). To reassemble, push the slide assembly back on the receiver until it is stopped by the disconnector (21). Pull the trigger, depress the disconnector, and the slide can be pushed into final position.

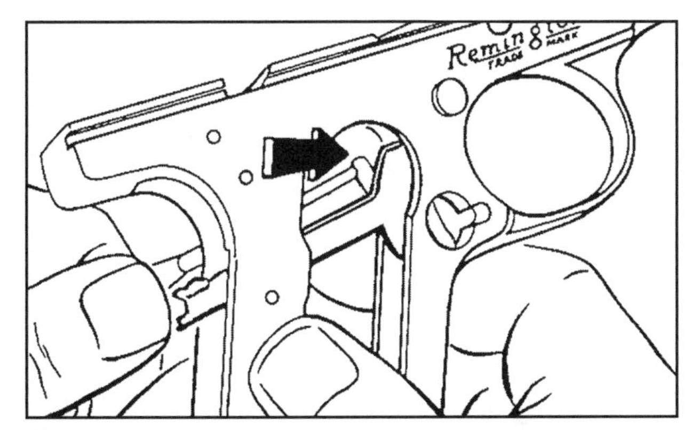

3 The trigger (22) will come out easily during disassembly, but putting it back requires the aid of a small screwdriver. Put the trigger assembly into the frame as shown. Then depress the trigger lever (24) until it can pass under the top surface of the trigger opening in the receiver.

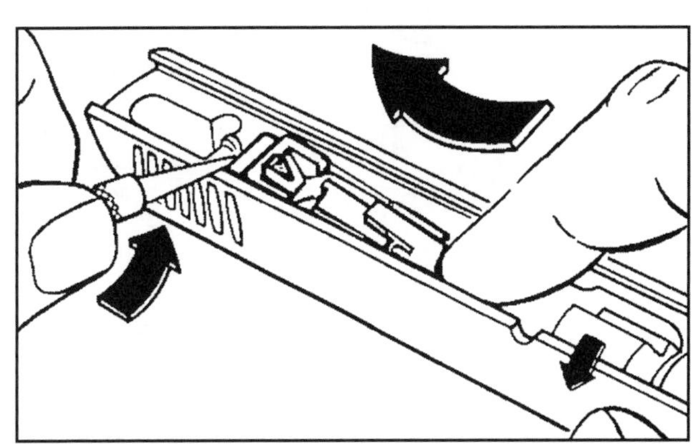

4 To remove the breech bolt (5) and firing pin (7), pull the barrel forward about ⅝ inch. Rotate it counterclockwise until it locks into the slide. Push the breech bolt to the rear and lift up the end as shown. Lift it free of the slide and the firing pin, and the firing pin spring (6) will drop down through the barrel.

REMINGTON MODEL XP-100 PISTOL

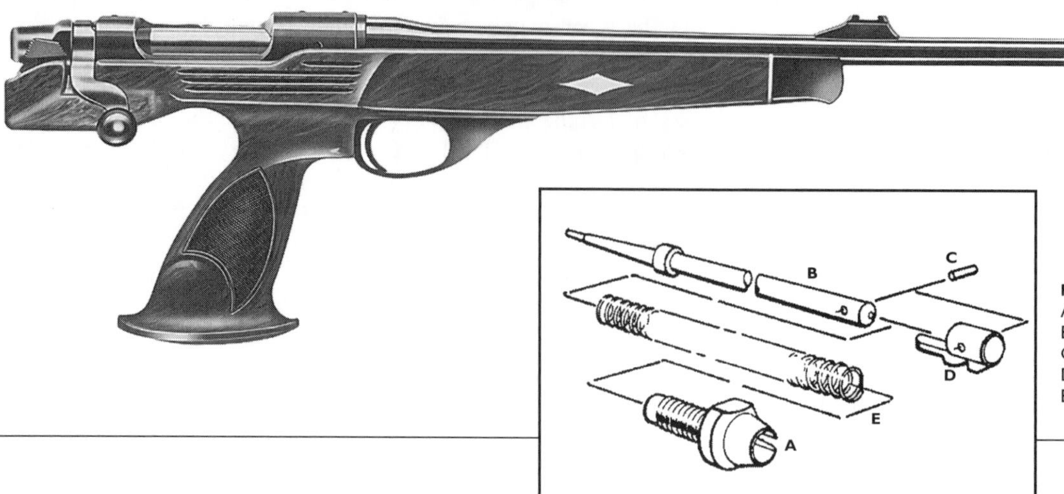

FIRING PIN ASSEMBLY
A. Bolt plug
B. Firing pin
C. Firing pin cross pin
D. Firing pin head
E. Mainspring

PARTS LEGEND

1. Barrel assembly
2. Bolt assembly
3. Bolt stop
4. Bolt stop pin
5. Bolt stop spring
6. Ejector
7. Ejector pin
8. Ejector spring
9. Extractor
10. Extractor rivet
11. Firing pin assembly
12. Forward receiver screw
13. Forward receiver screw washer
14. Front sight
15. Rear receiver screw
16. Rear receiver screw washer
17. Rear sight base
18. Rear sight elevation screw
19. Rear sight eyepiece
20. Rear sight leaf
21. Rear sight nut
22. Rear sight windage screw
23. Receiver plug screw (3)
24. Rib
25. Rib screw (2)
26. Safety assembly
27. Safety detent ball
28. Safety detent spring
29. Safety pivot pin
30. Safety snap washer
31. Sear block assembly
32. Sear block pin
33. Sear block spring
34. Sear block stop screw
35. Sear housing
36. Sear pin (2)
37. Sear safety cam
38. Sight screw (4)
39. Sight washer (4)
40. Stock assembly
41. Trigger
42. Trigger adjusting screw
43. Trigger balance
44. Trigger balance pin
45. Trigger balance spring
46. Trigger housing
47. Trigger housing screw (2)
48. Trigger link
49. Trigger link pin (2)
50. Trigger link roller (2)
51. Trigger pin

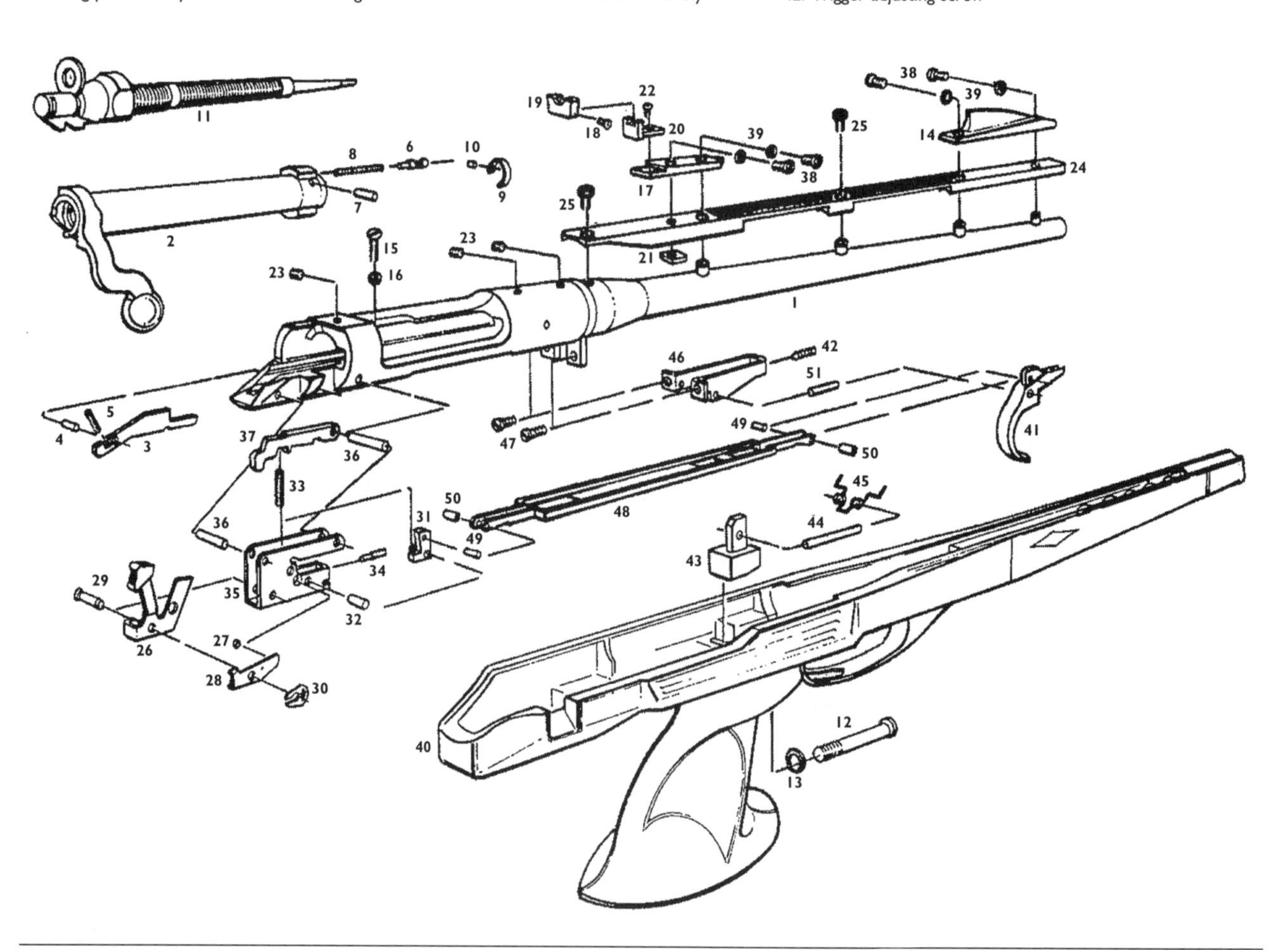

REMINGTON

Introduced in 1963, the Remington Model XP-100 single shot pistol was designed for hunting varmints and small game. It fired the .221 Remington Fire Ball center-fire cartridge loaded with a 50-grain, pointed soft-point bullet. The muzzle velocity is 2650 feet per second and the muzzle energy is 780 ft.-lbs.

Chiefly responsible for the unique appearance of this pistol is the rear position of the action, mostly behind the grip. Other features contributing to the unusual appearance are the ventilated barrel rib, long fore-end extending almost to the muzzle of the 10¹³⁄₁₆ barrel, peculiar forward bend of the bolt handle, and the large flare around the base of the grip.

As with many modern bolt-action rifles, the bolt of the XP-100 has dual-opposed, integral locking lugs which engage shoulders in the receiver ring. The extractor and plunger-type ejector are in the bolt head. The trigger is single-stage and is screw-adjustable for sear engagement and overtravel after removing the stock. A long bar, the "trigger link," connects the trigger assembly with the sear mechanism.

The barrel rib is fitted with a flat-top blade front sight and a fully-adjustable, square-notch open rear sight. The receiver top is drilled and tapped for scope mounts and the thumb-operated safety is on the right side of the receiver tang where it does not interfere with low mounting of a scope.

The stock is made of DuPont "Zytel" structural nylon.

DISASSEMBLY

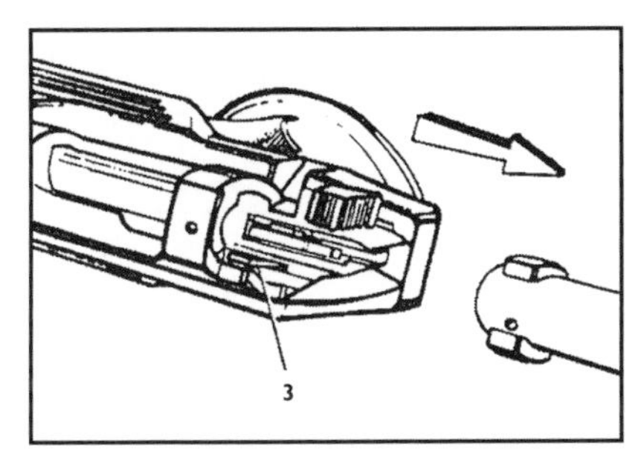

1 To disassemble the pistol, push safety (26) forward, open bolt (2), and remove any cartridge from chamber. Pull bolt rearward until bolt stop (3) is engaged. Push bolt stop downward with small screwdriver or similar tool. Then, pull bolt rearward out of pistol.

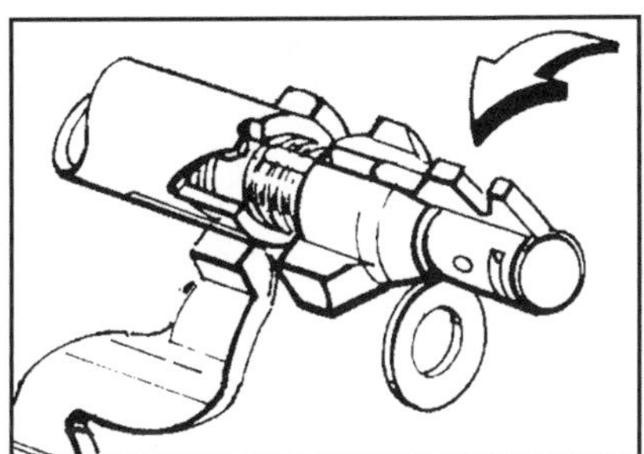

2 Hold firing pin head (D) in padded vise. Pull bolt forward and insert washer between firing pin head and bolt plug (A). Then, unscrew firing pin assembly from bolt. Place a metal sleeve (3/8"diameter, 7/8", long, with 3/16" hole through it lengthwise) over front of firing pin (B), and screw bolt plug back into bolt until washer is released. Drive out firing pin cross pin (C) with close-fitting drift punch, and remove firing pin head. Unscrew bolt plug carefully as it is under force of mainspring (E). Remove bolt plug and mainspring from firing pin.

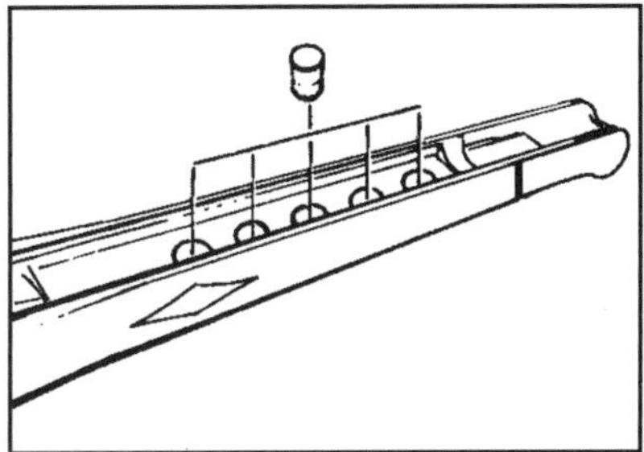

3 Unscrew forward receiver screw (12) and rear receiver screw (15). Remove stock (40). With stock removed, cal. .38 lead bullets can be placed in holes in fore-end to increase weight of pistol. Reassemble in reverse. During reassembly of firing mechanism, place metal sleeve over front of firing pin, reassemble mainspring and bolt plug on firing pin, and screw bolt plug into bolt. Then, replace firing pin head and firing pin.

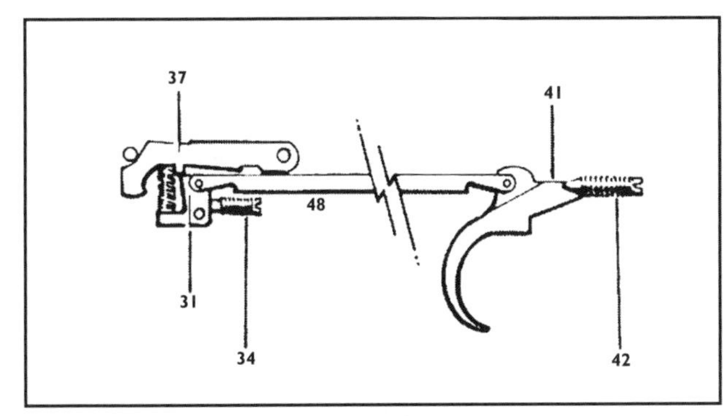

4 Sear block stop screw (34) adjusts engagement of sear block (31) to sear safety cam (37). This engagement should be about .020 inch. Trigger adjusting screw (42) on forward end of trigger housing (46) can be screwed in or out to regulate play of trigger

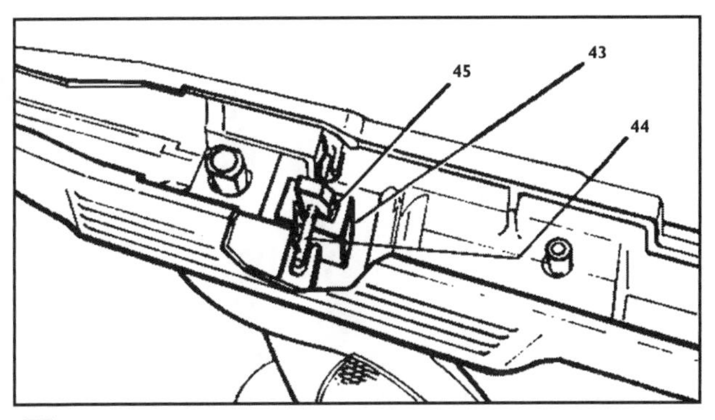

5 Trigger balance (43) must be positioned with large angle on bottom pointing forward. Both ends of trigger balance pin (44) must seat in slots of stock. Trigger balance spring (45) encircles pin on both sides of balance. Ends of spring engage against stock wall to hold balance under tension forward and central in stock. Trigger balance engages through opening in trigger link when stock is reassembled to action.

REMINGTON DOUBLE DERRINGER

PARTS LEGEND

1. Frame
2. Mainspring screw
3. Firing pin ratchet spring screw
4. Mainspring
5. Firing pin ratchet spring
6. Hammer
7. Hammer pin
8. Hammer stirrup
9. Hammer stirrup pin
10. Firing pin ratchet
11. Firing pin
12. Firing pin spring
13. Barrel lock screw
14. Barrel lock
15. Trigger
16. Trigger pin
17. Trigger spring
18. Barrels
19. Ejector
20. Ejector screw
21. Barrel hinge screw
22. Grips (2)
23. Escutcheons (2)
24. Grip screw

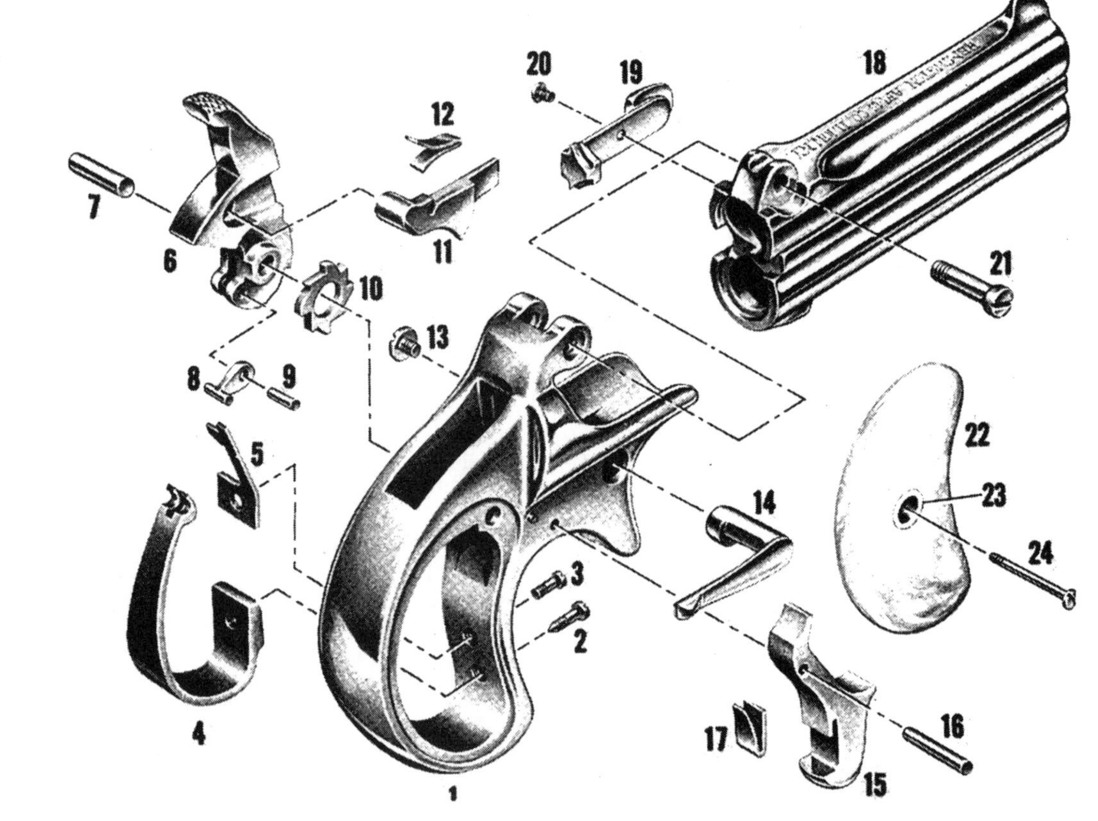

The fact that over 150,000 were eventually manufactured attests to the long-time popularity of the famous .41 caliber Remington Double Derringer pistol. Patented on December 12, 1865, and first offered in 1866, this stubby little 11-ounce three-inch barrel gun was invented in 1864 by William Elliot, a gun designer employed by Remington in 1861.

The pistol was not designed by Henry Deringer (note the one "r" in Henry's name), inventor of the equally famous single-shot Deringer pistol. Like the original muzzle-loading Deringer, Elliot's superposed-barrel breech-loading gun owed its effectiveness to its relatively large caliber. The .41 rimfire cartridge with its blunt-nosed 130-grain lead bullet backed by ten grains of blackpowder was more than adequate.

The Remington Double Derringer is of particular interest to arms collectors since it was offered in an extraordinary assortment of finishes. These ran the gamut from plain blue with hard rubber grips to elaborately engraved versions with ivory, walnut, or pearl grips. Guns plated with silver, gold, or nickel are also encountered in both standard and elabrate custom "presentation grades." Production of the Double Derringer was discontinued in 1935.

Early Remington Double Derringers are marked (in capital letters) on top of barrel: "E. Remington & Sons, Ilion, N.Y., Elliot's Patent Dec. 12, 1865." Later models are marked (in capital letters): "Remington Arms Co., Ilion, N.Y." or "Remington Arms-UMC Co., Ilion, N.Y."

DISASSEMBLY

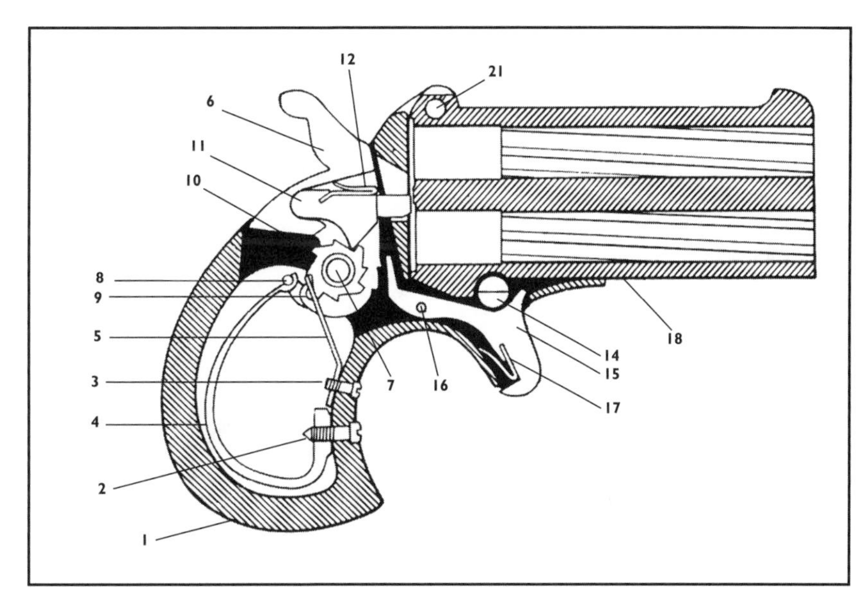

Turn barrel lock (14) to forward position and swing barrel up to determine that pistol is unloaded. Remove barrel hinge screw (21) and separate barrel (18) from frame (1). Ejector (19) may be slid out of its slot on left-hand side of barrel after first removing ejector screw (20).

Unscrew grip screw (24) and remove grips (22) from frame. Pull hammer (6) all the way back to cocked position and slip blade of screwdriver between mainspring (4) and inside of frame. Holding mainspring compressed with blade of screwdriver, release hammer slowly at same time shaking or tapping frame slightly to allow hammer stirrup (8) to fall free of its seat at end of mainspring. Unscrew mainspring screw (2) and firing pin ratchet spring screw (3) and remove mainspring (4) and firing pin ratchet spring (5) from frame.

The hammer (6), with firing pin ratchet (10) and firing pin and spring (11 & 12) intact, can be removed from top of frame after drifting out hammer pin (7). The ratchet (10), firing pin and spring (11 & 12) are easily pulled free of hammer with the fingers. Although not normally disassembled except for replacement, hammer stirrup (8) can be removed by drifting out its retaining pin (9).

Unscrew barrel lock screw (13) and remove barrel lock (14) from right-hand side of frame. Drift out trigger pin (16) and remove trigger (15) and spring (17) intact from top of frame.

Reassemble pistol in reverse order. To reinstall mainspring, replace mainspring and mainspring screw in frame. Replace hammer assembly through top of frame and fit hammer stirrup (8) to end of mainspring (4). Compressing mainspring by use of a screwdriver blade between mainspring and rear of frame will allow hammer to be pressed into position and will line up hammer pin hole in hammer and frame, permitting reentry of hammer pin.

The pistol (above), is shown with action in fired position. When hammer (6) is drawn all the way back, the sear end of trigger (15) engages lower notch on hammer holding it in cocked position until trigger is depressed. As hammer is drawn back, the firing pin ratchet spring (5) holds the firing pin ratchet (10) in a fixed position. At the hammer's rear-most position, the lower arm firing pin arm (11) drops into the deeper cut in ratchet (10). Firing pin drops into lower barrel chamber on firing. As hammer falls, ratchet (10) turns one notch clockwise by forward movement of lower arm of firing pin. On re-cocking hammer the process is repeated except that arm of firing pin now rests in shallow cut in ratchet, raising firing pin so that it will drop into upper chamber.

REMINGTON-ELLIOT REPEATERS

PARTS LEGEND

1A. Barrel cluster.22
1B. Barrel cluster .32
2. Firing pin
3. Firing pin spring
4. Frame
5A. Front sight bead .22
5B. Front sight bead .32
6. Grip panel (left)
7. Grip panel (right)
8. Grip panel escutcheons (2)
9. Grip panel retainer
10. Grip panel screws (2)
11. Hammer
12. Hammer connecting hard
13. Hammer screw
14. Mainspring
15. Mainspring front cover
16. Pawl
17. Pawl spring
18A. Ratchet .22
18B. Ratchet.32
19A. Recoil plate .22
19B. Recoil plate .32
20. Recoil plate screws (2)
21. Ring trigger
22. Sear connecting link
23. Sear rivet
24. Sear spring
25A. Sliding latch .22
25B. Sliding latch .32
26A. Sliding latch pin.22
26B. Sliding latch pin .32
27. Trigger screw

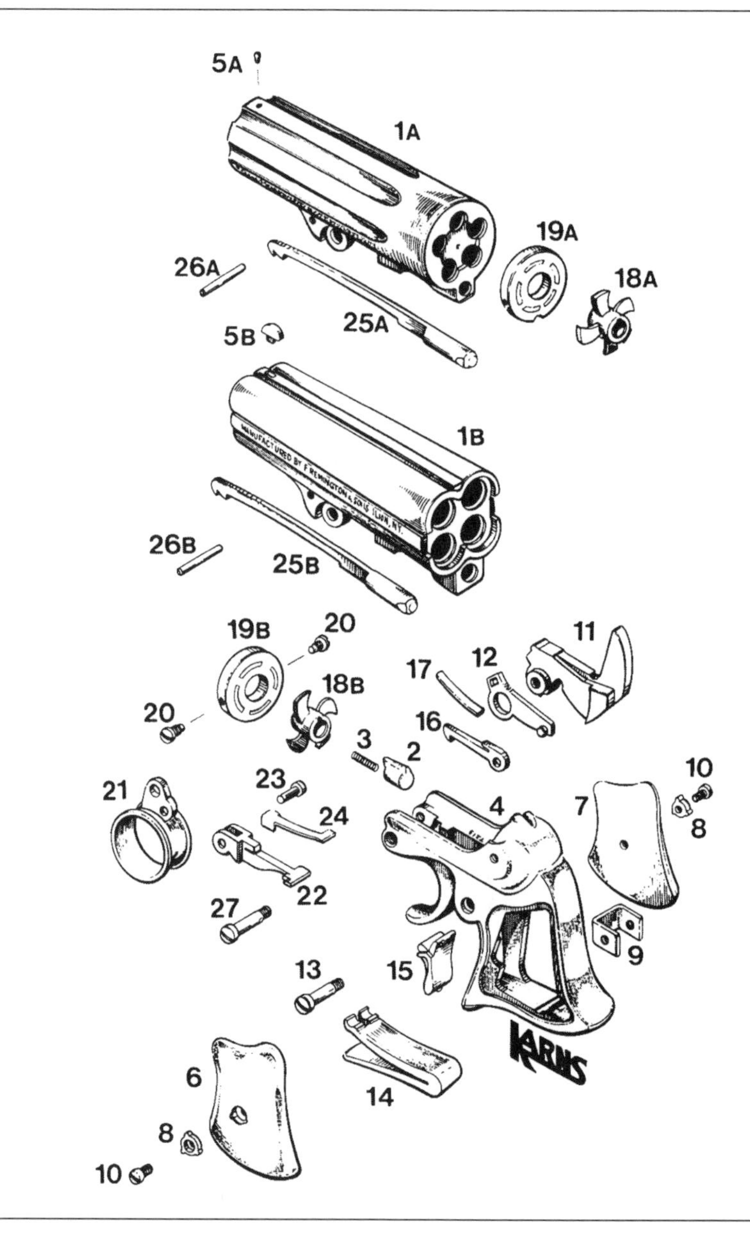

In 1861 the firm of E. Remington & Sons brought out its first fixed cartridge handgun. Dubbed the "Zig-Zag" derringer by collectors, it was a six-shot .22 Short ring-trigger pepperbox with straight index slots and diagonal grooves on the rear of its revolving barrel cluster. The grooves guided the cluster in its rotation and account for the pistol's name.

This was only the first of three William H. Elliott-patented ring-trigger pistols that Remington made, and it was soon replaced by the more common Remington-Elliot derringers with non-rotating barrels here described.

The "new" .22 and .32 Remington rimfires, advertised as Elliot's Pocket Repeaters, were introduced in 1863 and differed from the Zig-Zag in that their barrel clusters did not revolve but depended on a rotating firing pin assembly for repetitive firing.

Production is said to have continued until 1888 (Flayderman estimates a total production of about 25,000 pieces in both calibers), but the last factory listing noted in this research appeared in an 1876 flyer. There, in very small print, the five-shot .22 was listed at $8 (blue), $8.50 (nickel-plated frame) and $9 (full plate). Engraving was available for $4 extra and ivory or pearl stocks could be had, instead of the standard hard rubber, at premiums of $4 and $6 respectively. The four-shot .32 caliber version was listed in the same finishes at $.50 more, with engraving and fancy grip options priced the same.

The .22 and .32 both work in the same way. Sliding the barrel latch forward allows the barrels to be tipped down for loading or manual extraction. A forward stroke of the index finger in the trigger ring sets the mechanism for firing with a double-action trigger pull. As the trigger is pulled, the hammer rotates down, compressing the mainspring as the pawl engages and rotates the firing pin assembly to the next chamber.

As the trigger nears full stroke, the connecting link lifts the hand and releases the hammer. The trigger, when back in the ready position, can be be retracted to its rearward position for safe carrying by depressing the connecting link located between the ring-trigger and the guard spur.

DISASSEMBLY

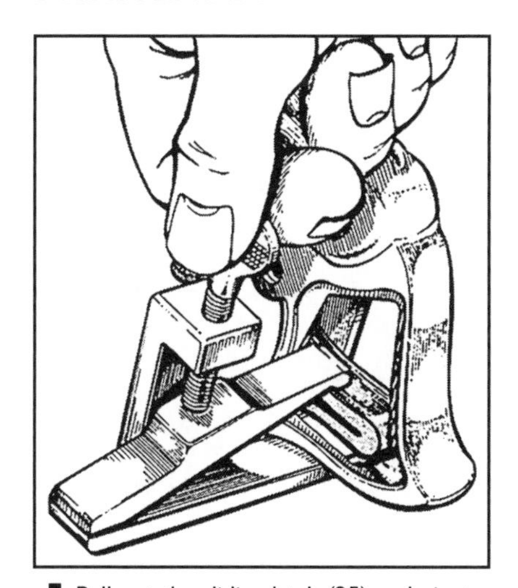

1 Pull out the sliding latch (25) and pivot the barrel cluster down to insure the gun is not loaded. Remove the left grip panel screw (10) to detach both panels (6 & 7) and their retainer (9).

Remove the trigger screw (27) to free the barrel cluster (1A or 1B) from the frame (4). To remove the sliding latch (25) drift out its retaining pin (26) and slip the latch forward out of its recess in the barrel cluster.

Remove both recoil plate screws (20) and invert the gun to cause the recoil plate (19), ratchet (18), firing pin (2), and its spring (3), to be displaced.

Next depress the mainspring (14). NOTE: This "V" style spring is very strong and a mainspring vise (above) or locking grip pliers may be required to accomplish this.

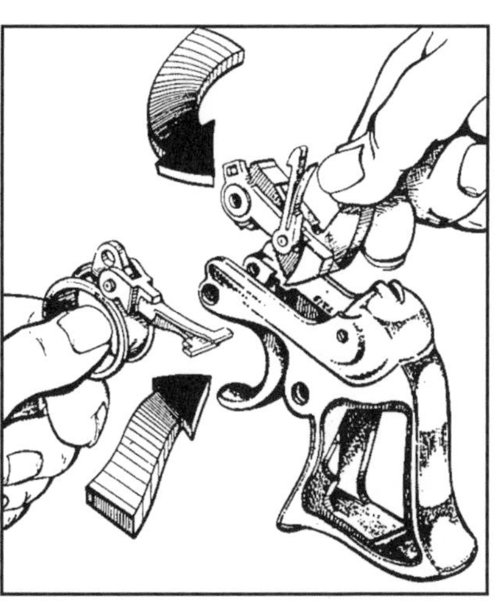

2 With the mainspring (14) depressed, disengage the front cover plate (15) from the mainspring hooks and remove it from the grip frame. Slowly release both the hammer and trigger link assemblies. Raise the hammer assembly (11, 12, 16 & 17) to disengage the lug of the sear connecting link (22) from the hand (12) and withdraw the trigger assembly (21-24) down and out. Lift the hammer assembly out of the frame. This completes disassembly.

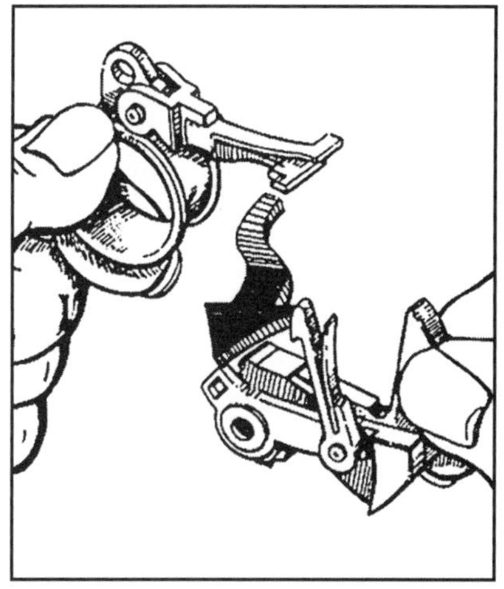

3 Reassembly: Both the hammer and trigger sub-groups must be assembled and installed in the frame together. First insert the hammer into the frame from the top and hold the pivot area above the barrel channel. Now position the pawl with its spring over the elevated pivot area on the left side of the hammer and lower it into the recess in the frame. Next insert the trigger assembly into the frame from the bottom and engage the lug on the connecting link in the hole in the hand as it is lowered into the frame. Now insert the hammer and trigger screws to retain their respective sub-assemblies in position to facilitate further reassembly.

REMINGTON NEW MODEL ARMY

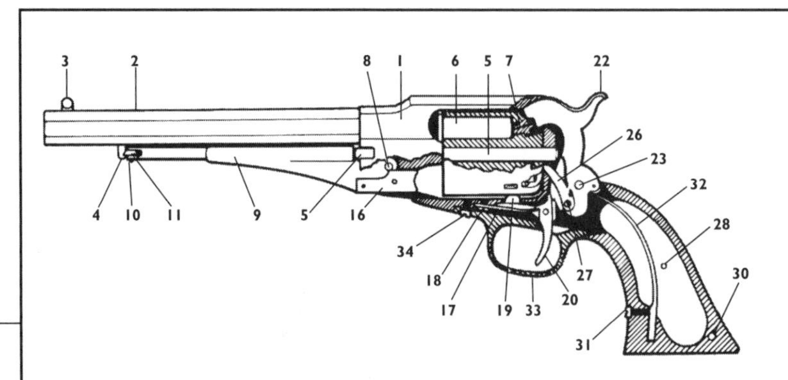

PARTS LEGEND

1. Main frame
2. Barrel
3. Front sight
4. Barrel stud
5. Cylinder pin
6. Cylinder
7. Nipples (6)
8. Loading lever screw
9. Loading lever
10. Latch pin
11. Latch
12. Latch spring
13. Front plunger link pin
14. Plunger link
15. Rear plunger link pin
16. Plunger
17. Trigger and cylinder stop spring
18. Trigger and cylinder stop spring screw
19. Cylinder stop
20. Trigger
21. Trigger and cylinder stop screw
22. Hammer
23. Hammer screw
24. Hammer roll
25. Hammer roll pin
26. Hand and hand spring assembly
27. Hand screw
28. Grip screw
29. Grips (2)
30. Grip pin
31. Mainspring set screw
32. Mainspring
33. Trigger guard
34. Trigger guard screw

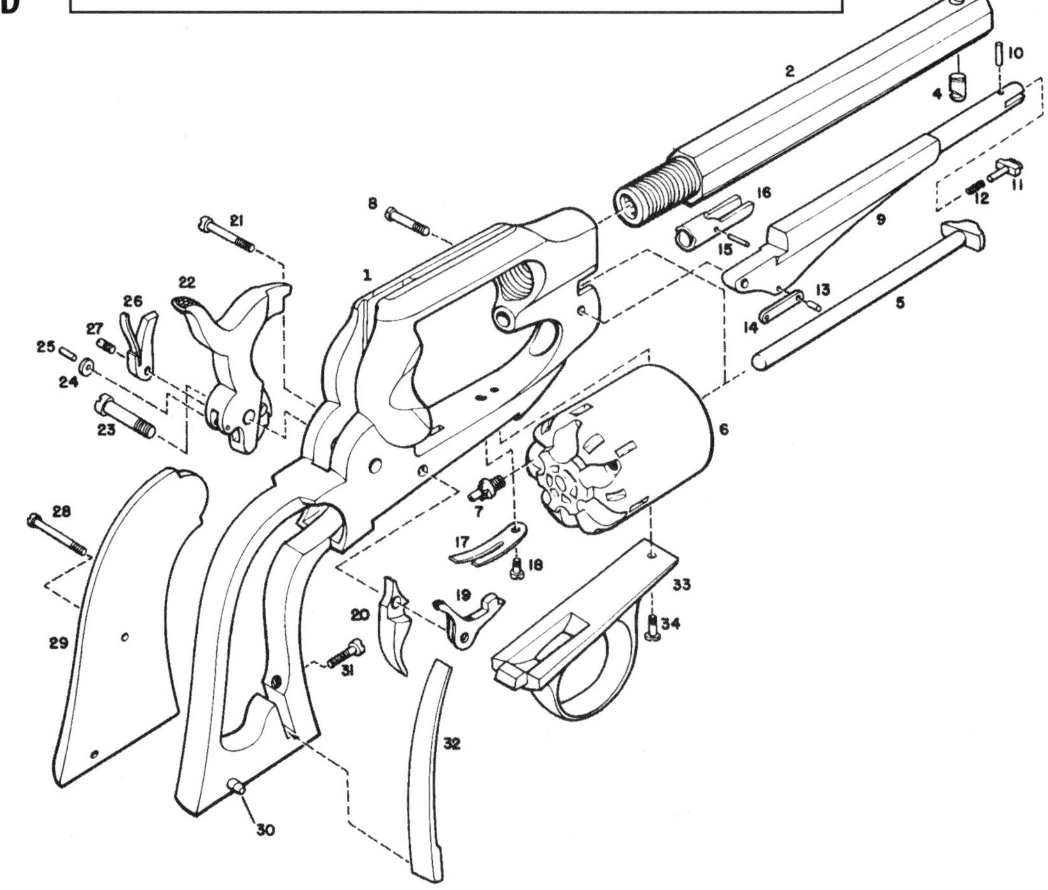

The .44 caliber, 6-shot Remington New Model Army percussion revolver, introduced in 1863, was a Civil War U.S. martial arm second only to the Colt in importance. A total of more than 140,000 had been manufactured by the time production ceased in 1875. For the military issue it was furnished in blue finish, with casehardened hammer and oil-finished walnut grips. The oval trigger guard is of brass. The commercial version of the New Model was blue finished with varnished walnut grips. It was also available plated or engraved and with pearl or ivory grips at extra cost.

With its 8-inch octagonal barrel, the New Model weighed 2 lbs. 14 ozs. It represents one of the highest developments of the percussion revolver. A noteworthy design feature is the provision of hammer recesses between the nipples which permitted it to be carried safely fully loaded with hammer down. It was regularly used with combustible cartridges but was also conveniently loaded with loose powder and ball.

The .36 caliber, 6-shot Remington New Model Navy revolver, also introduced in 1863, is mechanically similar and was regularly furnished with 7⅜-inch full octagon barrel. Its total weight was 2 lbs. 10 ozs. Military and commercial versions were finished to same specifications as the Army revolver. Over 32,000 of the .36 caliber revolvers were produced from 1863 until its discontinuance in 1888.

DISASSEMBLY

Pull backward on latch (11) and drop the loading lever (9) down. Draw the cylinder pin (5) out to front. The cylinder (6) may be withdrawn from main frame (1) to right by pulling back on the hammer slightly. Remove loading lever screw (8) and pull loading lever (9) and plunger (16) assembly to front and out of main frame.

Remove the grip screw (28) and grips (29). Loosen mainspring set screw (31) and tap mainspring (32) out of its seat in frame. Remove trigger guard screw (34) and drop trigger guard (33) out bottom of frame. Trigger and cylinder stop spring screw (18) and spring (17) may be removed from bottom of frame. Remove trigger and cylinder stop screw (21) and pull trigger (20) and cylinder stop (19) out from bottom of frame. Remove hammer screw (23) and pull hammer down from bottom of frame far enough so that head of hand screw (27) on left side of hammer is exposed. Remove hand screw and pull down and out bottom of frame. Hammer may now be removed from top of frame.

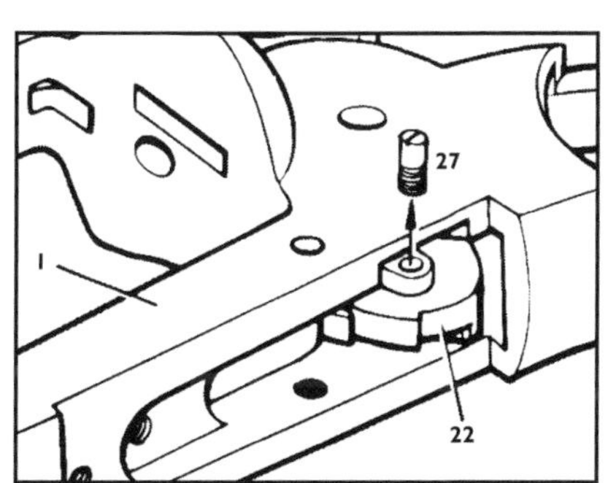

1 To remove hammer and hand assembly from main frame, remove hammer screw (23) and pull hammer (22) down and out bottom of frame until head of hand screw (27) is exposed. Removal of the hand screw will allow removal of hand and spring assembly (26) from the bottom of the frame. Pull hammer back up into frame and remove from top of frame.

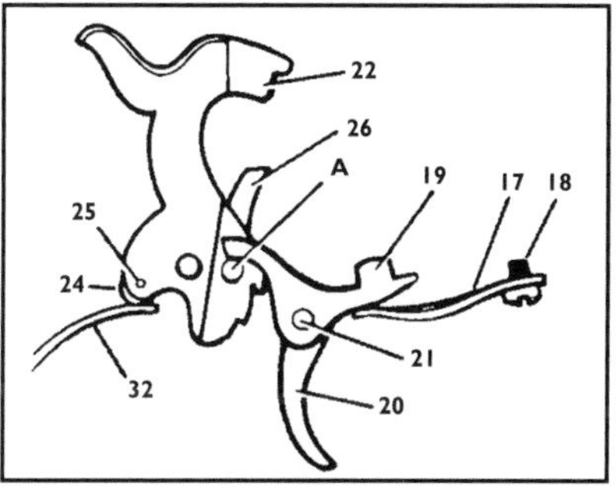

2 The drawing shows the relationship of lock mechanism parts from right when assembled inside frame. Note that cylinder stop cam (A) is integral with hammer and removal should not be attempted.

REMINGTON NEW MODEL POCKET

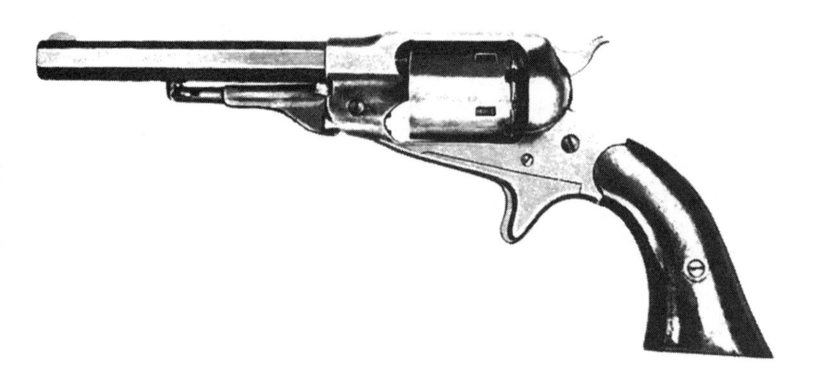

PARTS LEGEND

1. Barrel
2. Rammer latch
3. Cylinder pin
4. Frame
5. Cylinder
6. Cylinder back-plate
7. Right grip
8. Hammer
9. Roller pin
10. Roller
11. Hand
12. Hand retaining screw
13. Mainspring
14. Trigger guard
15. Trigger guard screw
16. Trigger
17. Cylinder stop
18. Trigger spring screw
19. Trigger spring
20. Hammer screw
21. Trigger screw
22. Left grip
23. Grip screw
24. Loading lever latch
25. Latch spring
26. Latch pin
27. Loading lever
28. Lever screw
29. Lever link pin
30. Link
31. Rammer
32. Rammer link pin

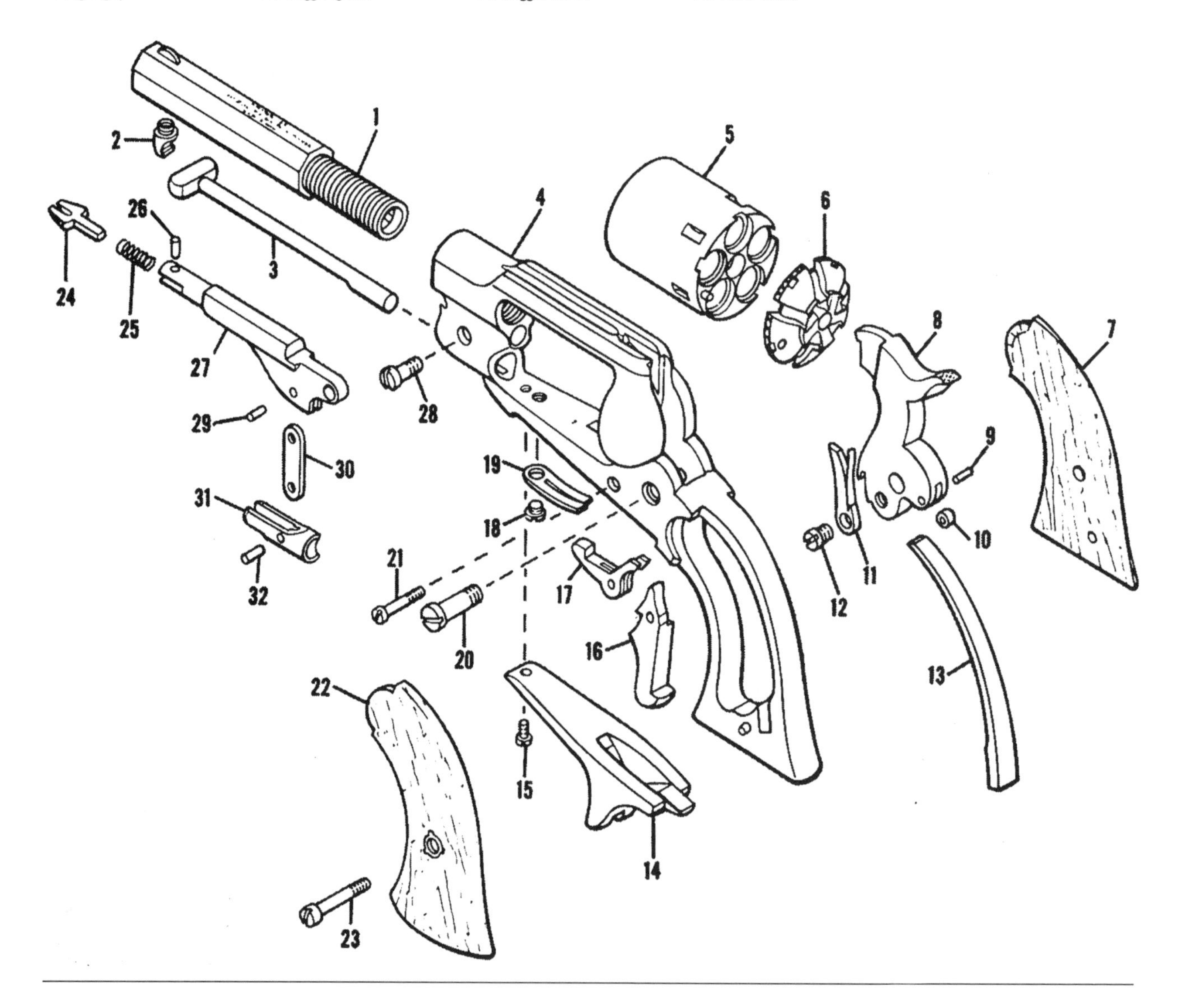

The Civil War proved the effectiveness of the metallic cartridge over the cap-and-ball system. Not long afterward, most major gun companies revised their lines and adopted the new rimfire cartridges. Remington began by converting their military revolvers to handle metallic cartridges as early as 1868. In most cases the conversions were such that the gun could not be readily converted back to shoot loose powder and ball or combustible cartridges.

The Remington New Model Pocket Revolver conversion is unique in this respect. It started out as a .31-caliber percussion arm. For conversion to metallic cartridges, a clever 2-piece cylinder was designed. It consisted of a 5-shot cylinder bored through from end to end, and a back-plate. The cylinder was counter-bored to recess the heads of the cartridges. A back-plate that contained the cylinder rotating ratchet was loosely pinned to the end of the cylinder. The plate was machined to allow the hammer to hit only the rim of the cartridge. Safety notches were provided between the firing notches. When the gun was loaded, the hammer rested on one of the safety notches.

Since the conversion retained the rammer assembly, it was a simple matter to switch back to cap-and-ball loading. The shape of the hammer was such that the lower portion fired the percussion caps, while the upper lip fired the metallic cartridge, depending on which cylinder was installed.

The New Model Pocket Revolver was first marketed around 1863 and proved fairly popular. The conversion system worked so well that the gun was offered as a combination gun until around 1888.

DISASSEMBLY

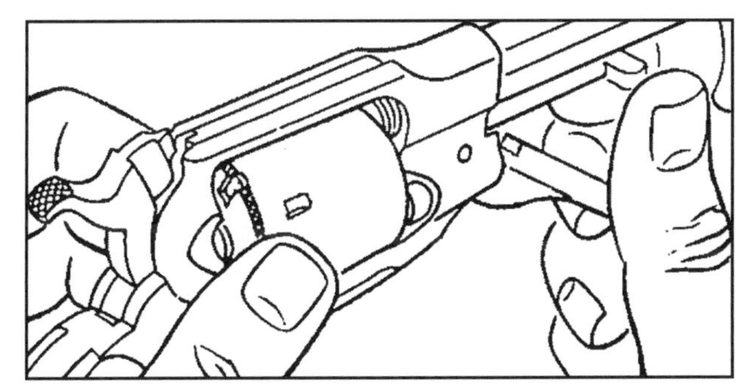

1 The Remington New Model Pocket Revolver is relatively easy to disassemble; but before attempting it, it is wise to place a few drops of penetrating oil on the screws. To remove the cylinder (5) pull hammer back to half cock position. Pull loading lever (27) down far enough to allow cylinder pin (3) to be withdrawn. When pin is all the way forward, push cylinder out from left to right. If cylinder will not come out, check to see if loading lever is down too far. If it is, it may have pushed the rammer into one of the chambers.

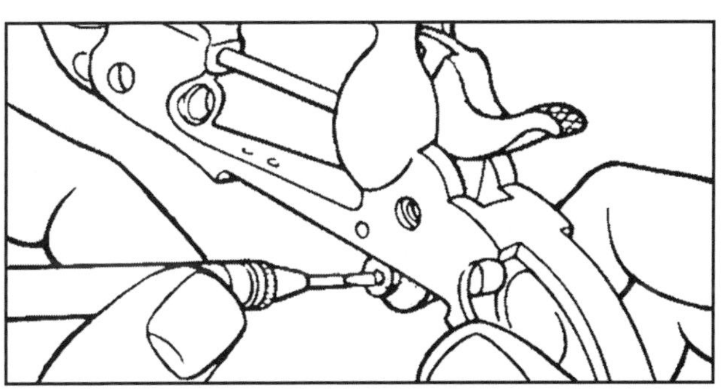

2 After trigger guard (14), hammer screw (20), and mainspring have been removed, push hammer down. This will expose screw (12) that retains hand (11). Remove this screw and hand, then hammer can be removed through top of frame (4).

LOADING

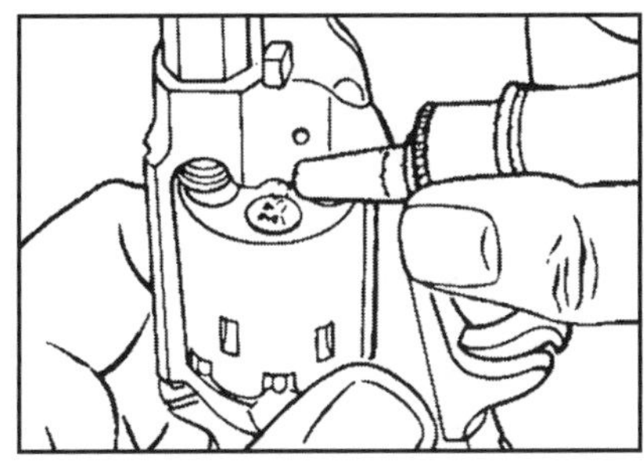

1 To load the cap-and-ball model, first fire a cap on each nipple to clear it. Then hold gun as shown, and throw a charge of FFg blackpowder into the chamber; place a cal. .31 ball on top and rotate the chamber under the rammer. Never, under any circumstances, load the gun with smokeless powder.

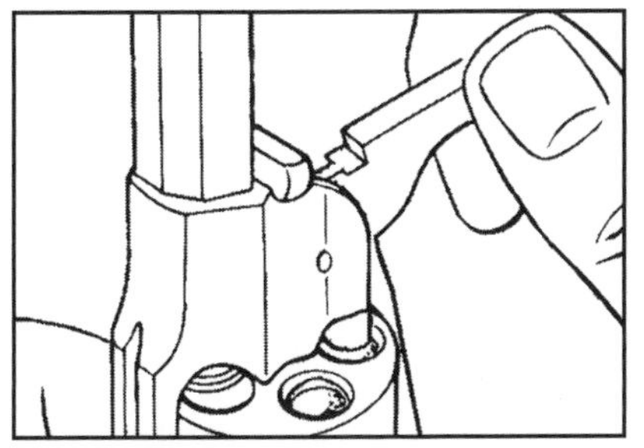

2 When the ball is under rammer (31), pull down loading lever (27) until it presses ball well below edge of chamber. If ball protrudes it will interfere with rotation of cylinder. After all balls are in place, fill remaining area around balls with heavy grease. This will act as a lubricant and prevent a flashover from setting off adjoining chambers. When all is ready, put caps on nipples and drop hammer until it rests in safety notch.

The cartridge version was loaded by removing back-plate (6) and inserting 5 rimfire cal. .32 cartridges. The plate was then replaced and cylinder put back in frame.

ROSSI PRINCESS REVOLVER

PARTS LEGEND

1. Frame
2. Barrel
3. Side-plate
4. Front plate screw
5. Top plate screw
6. Bottom plate screw
7. Rear plate screw
8. Cylinder lock
9. Cylinder lock spring
10. Cylinder lock cap
11. Extractor rod cap
12. Yoke
13. Extractor rod
14. Cylinder pin
15. Cylinder pin spring
16. Extractor spring
17. Cylinder
18. Extractor
19. Grip screws (2)
20. Left grip plate
21. Right grip plate
22. Grip plate spacer
23. Mainspring plate
24. Mainspring stop
25. Mainspring
26. Mainspring collar
27. Mainspring rod
28. Firing pin cup
29. Firing pin
30. Firing pin spring
31. Sear
32. Sear spring
33. Cylinder stop
34. Cylinder stop spring
35. Barrel pin
36. Hammer
37. Trigger plunger
38. Plunger spring
39. Plunger spring seat
40. Trigger
41. Transfer bar pin
42. Transfer bar
43. Hand
44. Hand spring

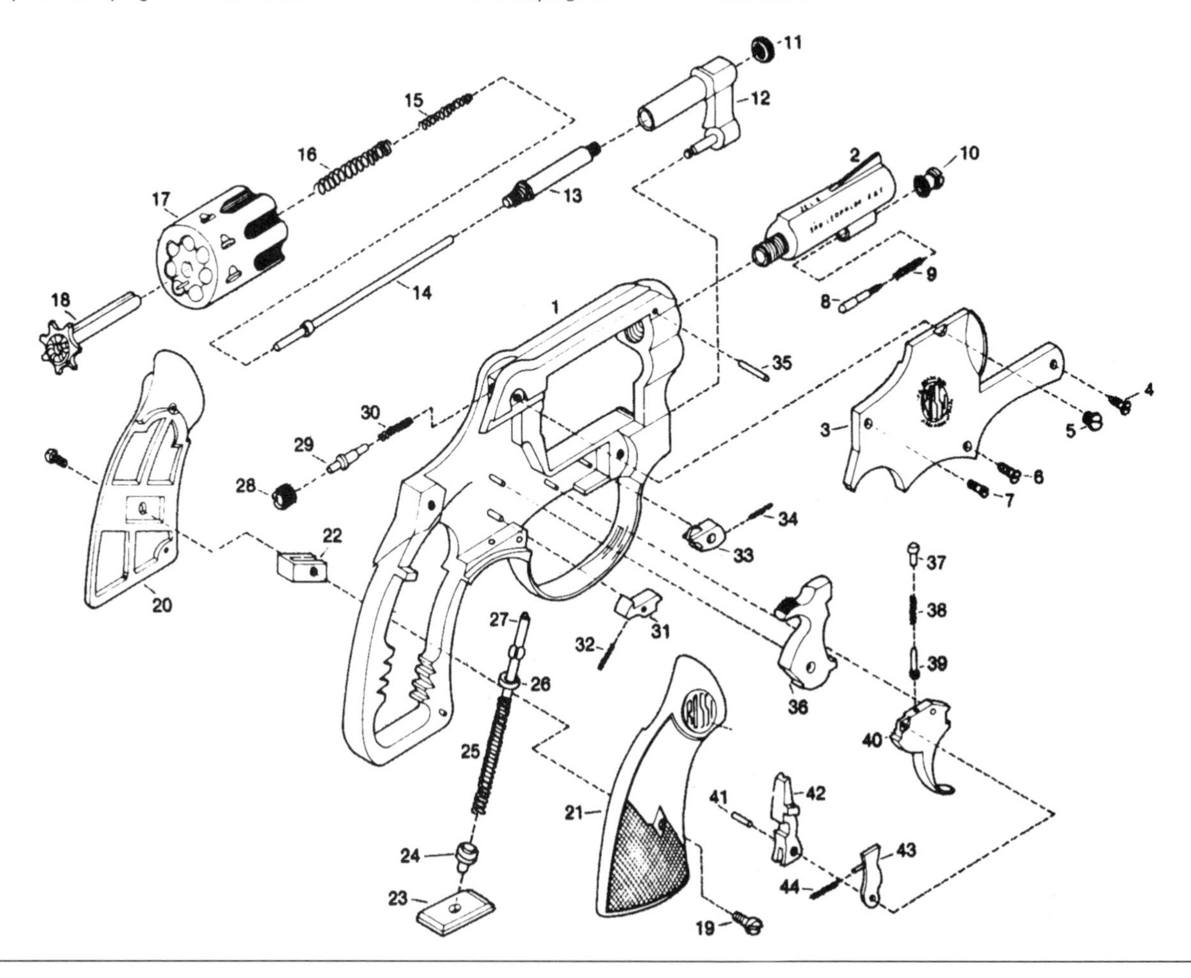

Close to a million Rossi .22 caliber Princess revolvers have been made by Amadeo Rossi S.A., of Sao Leopoldo, Brazil, since 1957. The prime market for these seven-shot double-actions has been Brazil and some Central American countries, but when they were imported from late 1965 through 1968 by the now defunct firm of Firearms International Corp., almost 60,000 came into the United States.

Because of its size, importation of the Rossi "Ladysmith," as is was known in the United States, ceased after the passage of the 1968 Gun Control Act. The Act prohibited importation of any revolver frame of less than 4 inches, when measured lengthwise, parallel to the bore line. The Rossi came up ¼-inch short.

Even with a longer frame the Princess would still not have met the BATF's criteria which stipulated that a revolver must accrue 45 "points" to qualify for importation and must have certain safety standards. The Rossi easily met the safety standards, but it fell far short on point system. United States importers were furious, but Rossi couldn't have cared less. The firm had already tried to discontinue the Princess in order to concentrate on more profitable and conventional steel-framed Rossis. South and Central American customers simply wouldn't permit the Princess to die.

The Princess was an excellent product for its price and purpose. In 1968 it sold for $38.25, complete with presentation case. Externally it resembled the Smith & Wesson "Ladysmith" (Hand Ejector, Third Model), which accounted for its sales appeal, but inside it employed coil springs, a floating firing pin and an Iver Johnson-type transfer bar safety system.

DISASSEMBLY

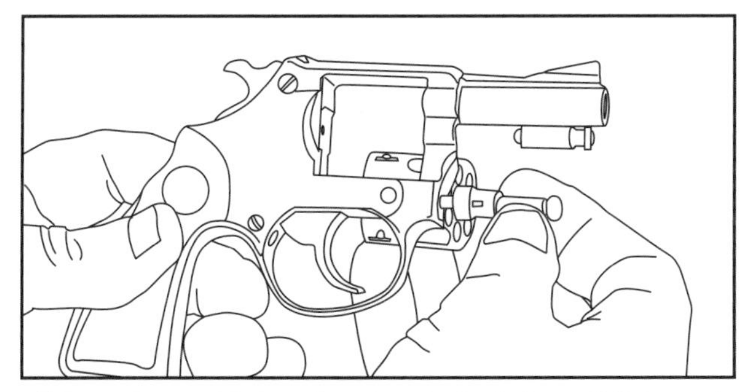

1 Begin disassembly by pulling the cylinder lock cap (10) forward and swing the cylinder out to the left. Remove the front side-plate screw (4) which serves to retain the cylinder yoke (12).

Slide the yoke, which holds the cylinder (17) and its parts, forward out of the frame (1).

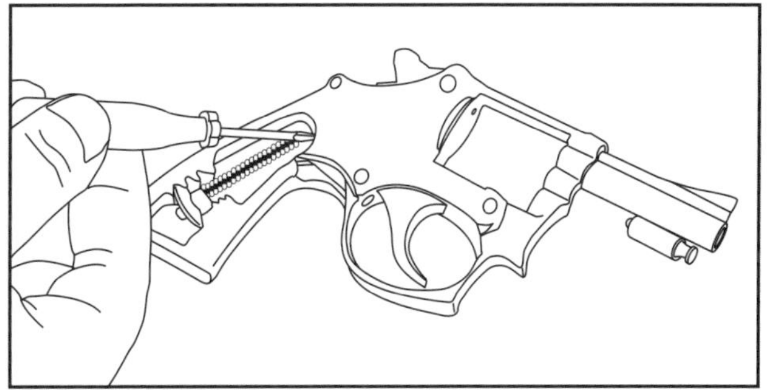

2 Remove both the grip screws (19) and grip plates (20 & 21). Now the three remaining side-plate screws (5, 6 & 7) can be taken out and the side-plate itself (3) will be free. If it is relatively loosely fitted to the frame, it may fall free or may be dislodged by holding the revolver right-side-down and tapping on the grip portion of the frame with a plastic mallet. If it is tightly fitted, it may be necessary to pry it from its seat with a suitable bar.

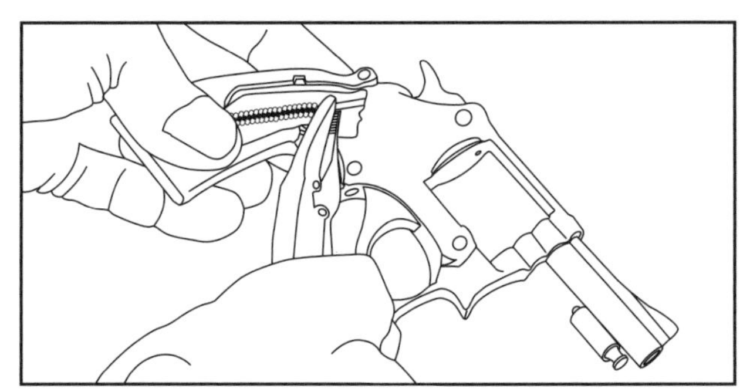

3 Removing the side-plate will expose all the parts of the firing mechanism for cleaning and maintenance, no further stripping of the frame is necessary. To remove the hand (43), simply lift it and its spring (44) straight off its permanently mounted frame stud.

To remove the hammer, push the mainspring rod (27) down, against spring pressure, to free it from its seat in the hammer. It is then lifted from the frame.

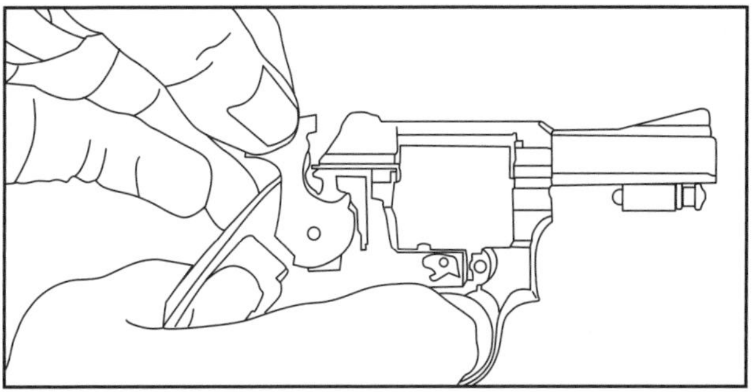

4 Then the hammer (36) can be partially retracted and lifted from its frame stud.

The firing pin (29) may be removed by unscrewing the slotted firing pin cup (28), which will free the firing pin and its spring. Other frame parts removal is obvious.

RUGER .22 AUTOMATIC PISTOL

PARTS LEGEND

A Front sight retaining pin
B Front sight blade
C Barrel and receiver assembly
D Micro rear sight
E Hammer
F Hammer bushing
O Hammer strut
H Hammer strut pin
I Safety catch
J Bolt stop pin
K Main spring housing
L Bolt stop pivot pin
M Housing latch
N Main spring plunger
0 Main spring
P Detent ball
Q Housing latch pivot pin
R Magazine catch
S Magazine catch spring
T Magazine
U Magazine catch pivot pin
V Magazine catch stop pin
W Left hand grip
X Grip screw
Y Sear spring stop pin
Z Sear pivot pin

AA Sear
BB Sear spring
CC Disconnector
DD Trigger
EE Trigger pivot pin
FF Trigger pin lock washer
GG Trigger spring
HH Trigger spring plunger
II Frame
JJ Recoil spring
KK Recoil spring guide pin
LL Hammer pivot pin
MM Extractor
NN Extractor plunger
OO Extractor spring
PP Recoil spring support
QQ Firing pin
RR Rebound spring support
SS Rebound spring
TT Firing pin stop
UU Bolt

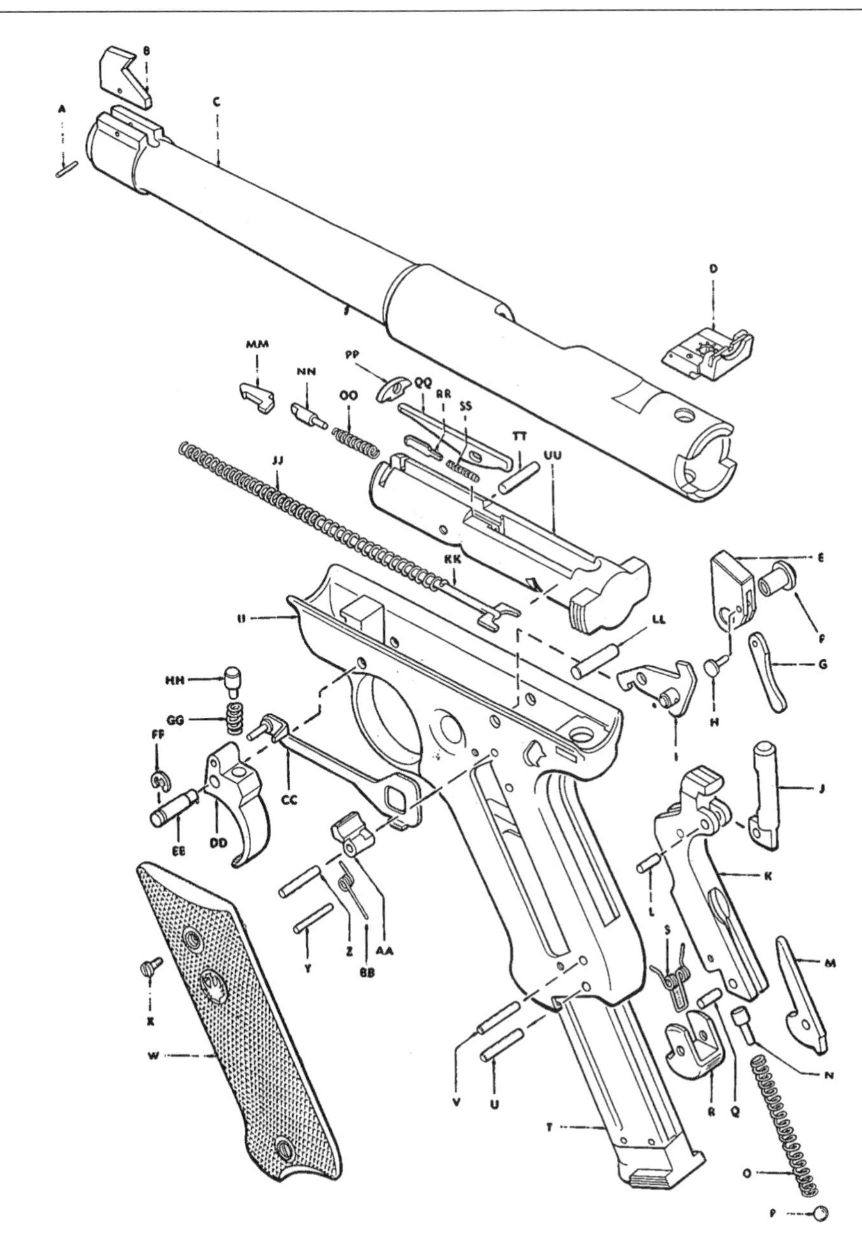

In late January 1949, Southport, Connecticut saw the birth of a new gun company. It was the result of a collaboration between designer Bill Ruger and the late Alex Sturm, business man. The result was the new Ruger .22 blow-back operated automatic. Production began in a small shop in Southport and the first guns were shipped in October 1949 with a production run of about 1,000 guns.

About 2,500 pistols were manufactured before the first change of any significance was made. Somewhere between serial number 2,500 and 2,800, the bolt and firing pin were changed to facilitate production. This change ended the hand fitting that was necessary in the early guns. In 1950, after the standard model had won its spurs, the firm introduced a target model, the Mark I. It was basically the same as the standard model with the addition of a heavy barrel and target sights.

The Ruger was designed with modern mass production methods in mind. The gun made use of numerous well-designed stamped and screw machined parts. The two sides of the frame were stamped and pressed to shape, then welded together to form a complete unit. This procedure made for a lightweight receiver and kept costly machinery time to a minimum. The barrel and receiver were treated as a single assembly. The barrel was screwed tightly against the face of a receiver blank and the assembly was machined as a unit. The Mark I was discontinued in 1981.

A few points must be observed when stripping the gun; be sure the hammer is down resting on the firing pin and the hammer strut (G) is in position to engage the main spring plunger (N) in the main spring housing (K). If strut is not in place, bolt cannot be drawn back.

DISASSEMBLY

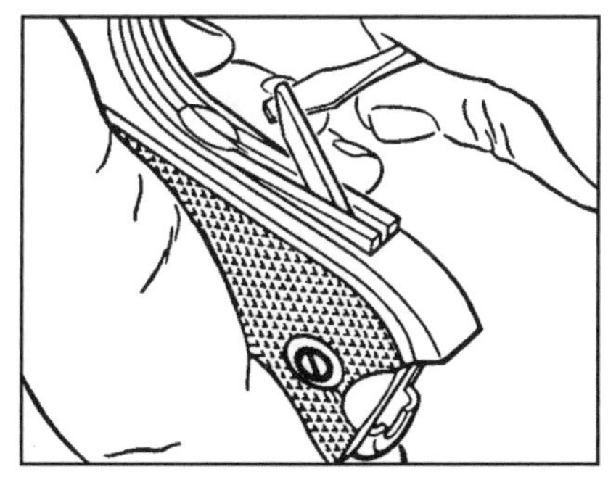

1 Remove magazine, pull bolt all the way back, release it and snap the trigger to uncock the hammer before attempting disassembly. Use a piece of plastic or a screw driver to pry the housing latch (M) open fully, then swing main spring housing (K) outward.

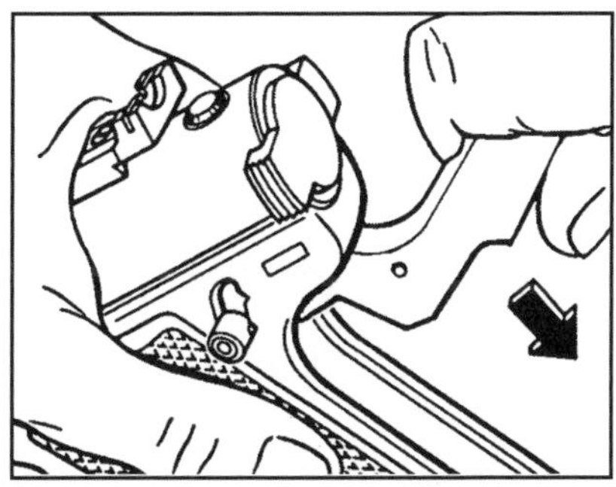

2 Pull main spring housing (K) down hard to disengage bolt stop pin (J) from the receiver. With bolt stop pin removed, the bolt assembly may be withdrawn. To disengage barrel and receiver (C) from the frame (II), grasp the barrel and pull it forward.

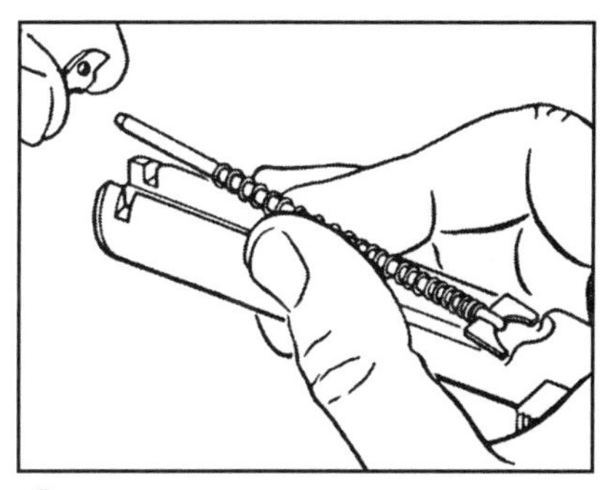

3 The recoil spring (JJ) can easily be pried out. Reassembly of the bolt requires care, as the recoil spring is heavily compressed. To replace bolt, hold the recoil spring compressed on spring guide pin (KK), as shown. Slip recoil spring support (PP) on the spring guide and ease it down into belt.

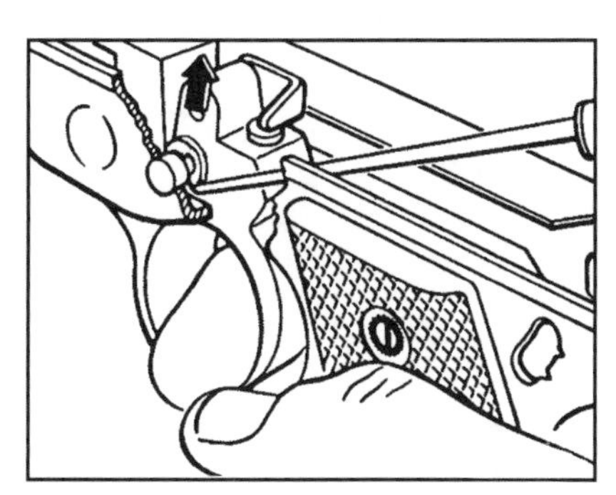

4 All pins except the staked pins in the main spring housing and the trigger pivot pin (EE) can easily be removed. Before removing the trigger pin, we must pry out the lock washer (FF) that holds the pin in place. Use a long thin rod to pry it upward. The pin can now be pushed out from left to right.

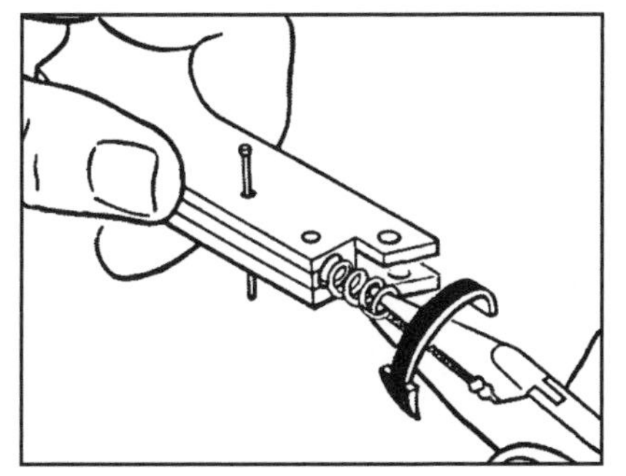

5 The simplest way to replace the main spring (O) or main spring plunger (N) without special tools is to drill an .062-inch hole through the main spring housing (K). Insert a wire nail and wind the spring in around it, below the surface, to support the detent ball (P) while pinning the housing latch (M) into place.

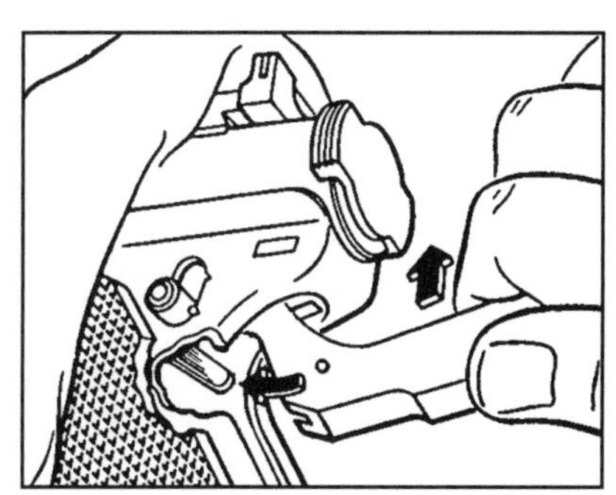

6 To reassemble, replace bolt. Lay receiver on the frame, ends flush. Push receiver back until it locks into the frame. Hold gun so that hammer rests on firing pin; push the bolt step pin up through bolt and receiver. Swing main spring housing (K) down to engage the hammer strut. Snap the housing latch shut.

RUGER BEARCAT REVOLVER

PARTS LEGEND

1. Barrel
2. Front sight
3. Ejector housing
4. Ejector housing screw
5. Ejector rod assembly
6. Ejector spring
7. Base pin latch body
8. Base pin latch nut
9. Base pin latch spring
10. Base pin
11. Frame
12. Gate assembly
13. Gate detent plunger
14. Gate detent spring
15. Gate retaining screw
16. Hammer
17. Hammer pivot
18. Hammer strut
19. Hammer spring
20. Hammer spring seat
21. Hammer plunger
22. Hammer plunger pin
23. Hammer plunger spring
24. Pawl
25. Pawl spring
26. Pawl screw
27. Pawl spring plunger
28. Firing pin
29. Firing pin rebound spring
30. Recoil plate
31. Recoil plate cross pin
32. Trigger
33. Trigger pivot
34. Trigger spring
35. Trigger spring plungers
36. Cylinders
37. Cylinder latch
38. Cylinder latch Plunger
39. Cylinder latch spring
40. Grip panel
41. Grip panel screw
42. Trigger guard
43. Trigger guard Screw

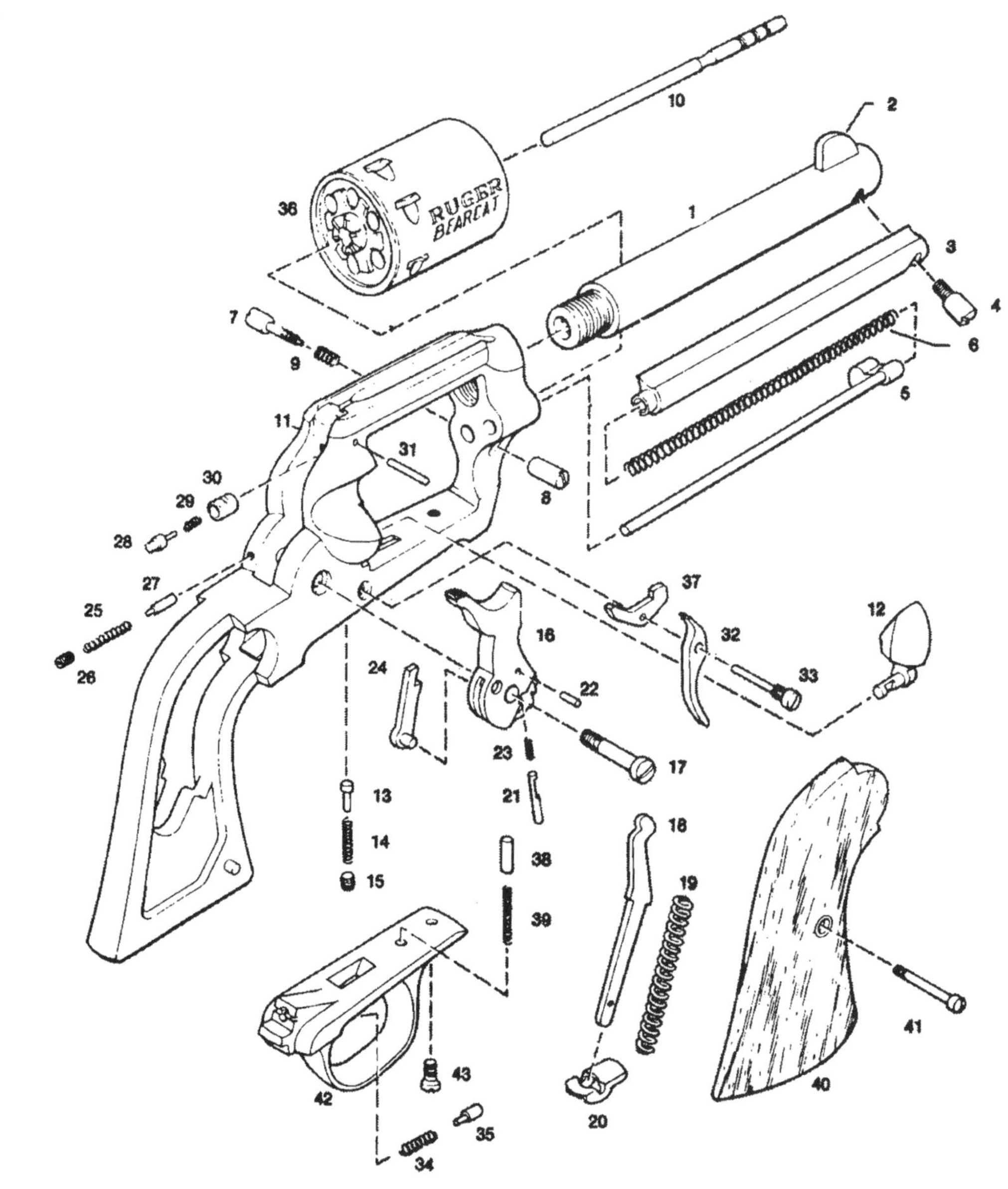

Introduced in 1958, the Bearcat revolver was a significant departure from earlier Ruger single-action models. The Bearcat's one-piece cylinder and grip-frame construction recalled the design of the 1861 Remington Army revolver.

The lockwork of the Bearcat was, however, typically Ruger and incorporates the piano wire coil springs and Ruger patent coil spring/plunger cylinder latching mechanism found in the Single-Six and Blackhawk revolvers. Designed for use with standard .22 rimfire cartridges, the Bearcat revolver was dimensioned accordingly.

During its 15-year (1958 to 1973) production history, the design remained virtually unchanged. The major difference between the 1958 Bearcat and its final evolution, the Super Bearcat, lies in the frame material. The Bearcat frame was made of aircraft-quality aluminum while the Super Bearcat frame was constructed of a chrome molybdenum steel alloy.

Disassembly of the Bearcat revolver is simple and straightforward. With the exception of steps, which require the compression of springs, no force is required to take apart or reassemble these guns.

DISASSEMBLY

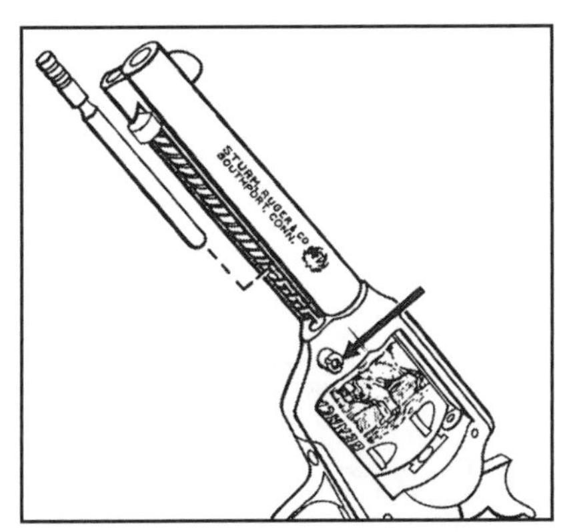

1 Check that revolver is unloaded by retracting hammer (16) two clicks to loading notch, opening loading gate (12) and, while manually rotating cylinder (36), examining each chamber.

Depress base pin latch body (7-arrow) and remove base pin (10) and cylinder (36).

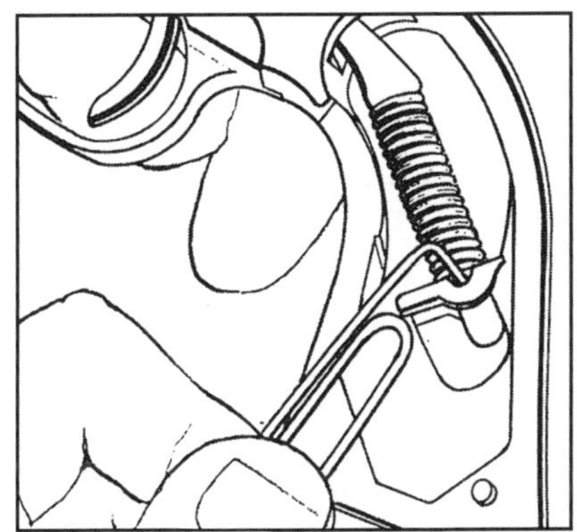

2 Remove ejector housing screw (4), ejector housing (3), rod assembly (5) and spring (6).

Remove grip panels (40). Bring hammer (16) to full cock and insert small wire or pin in hole in hammer strut (18). Depress trigger (32) and push hammer fully forward. Do not remove hammer strut (18) and hammer spring (19) at this time.

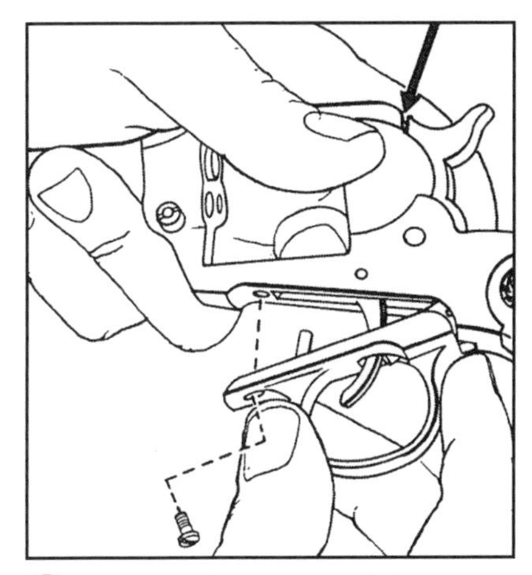

3 Retract the hammer two clicks, remove trigger guard screw (43) and pull trigger guard (42) down and forward until free of trigger. Note position of trigger (32), cylinder latch spring (39) and plunger (38).

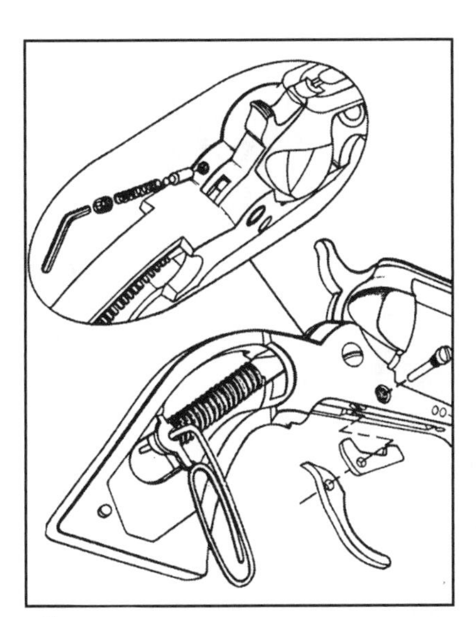

4 With ¹⁄₁₆-inch hex wrench, remove pawl screw (26), spring (25) and plunger (27) (see insert). Remove trigger pivot (33), trigger (32) and cylinder latch (37).

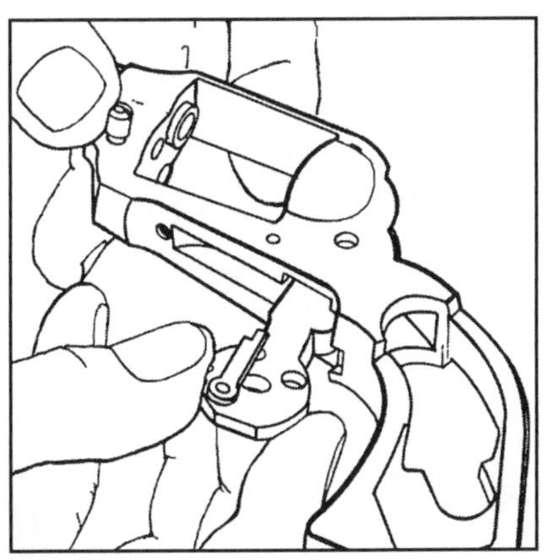

5 Remove the hammer pivot (17) and (without removing the pin or clip holding them together) take from the grip frame the hammer strut (18), spring (19) and seat (20) assembly. Remove hammer (16) and pawl (24).

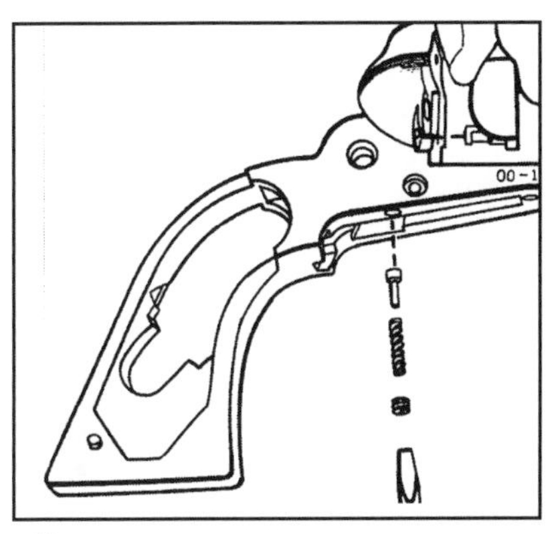

6 Remove gate retaining screw (15), gate detent spring (14) and gate detent plunger (13). This will free the gate assembly (12) which can be pulled forward from its seat in the frame.

Further disassembly should be attempted only by a competent gunsmith. Reassembly is accomplished by reversing the above procedures.

RUGER BLACKHAWK REVOLVER

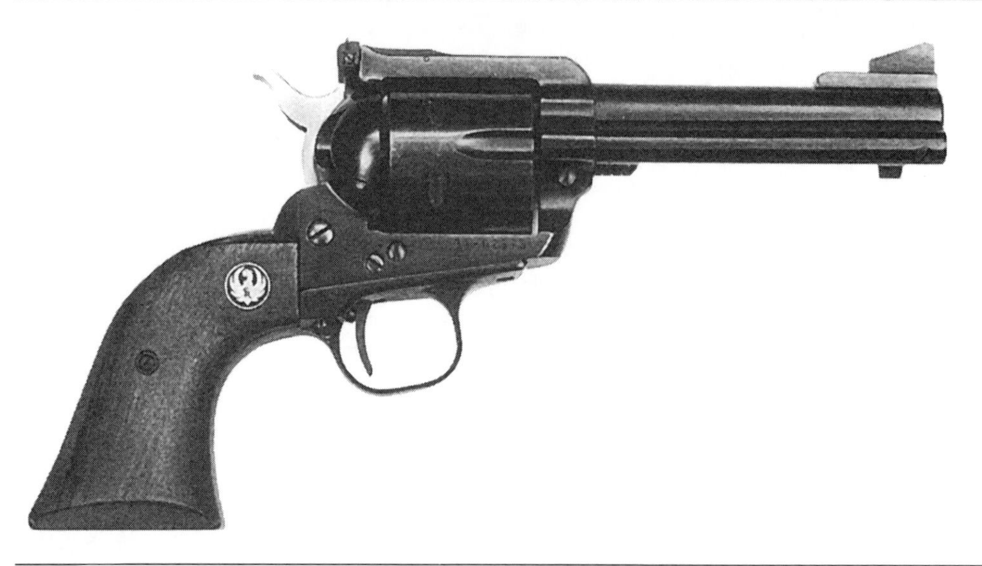

PARTS LEGEND

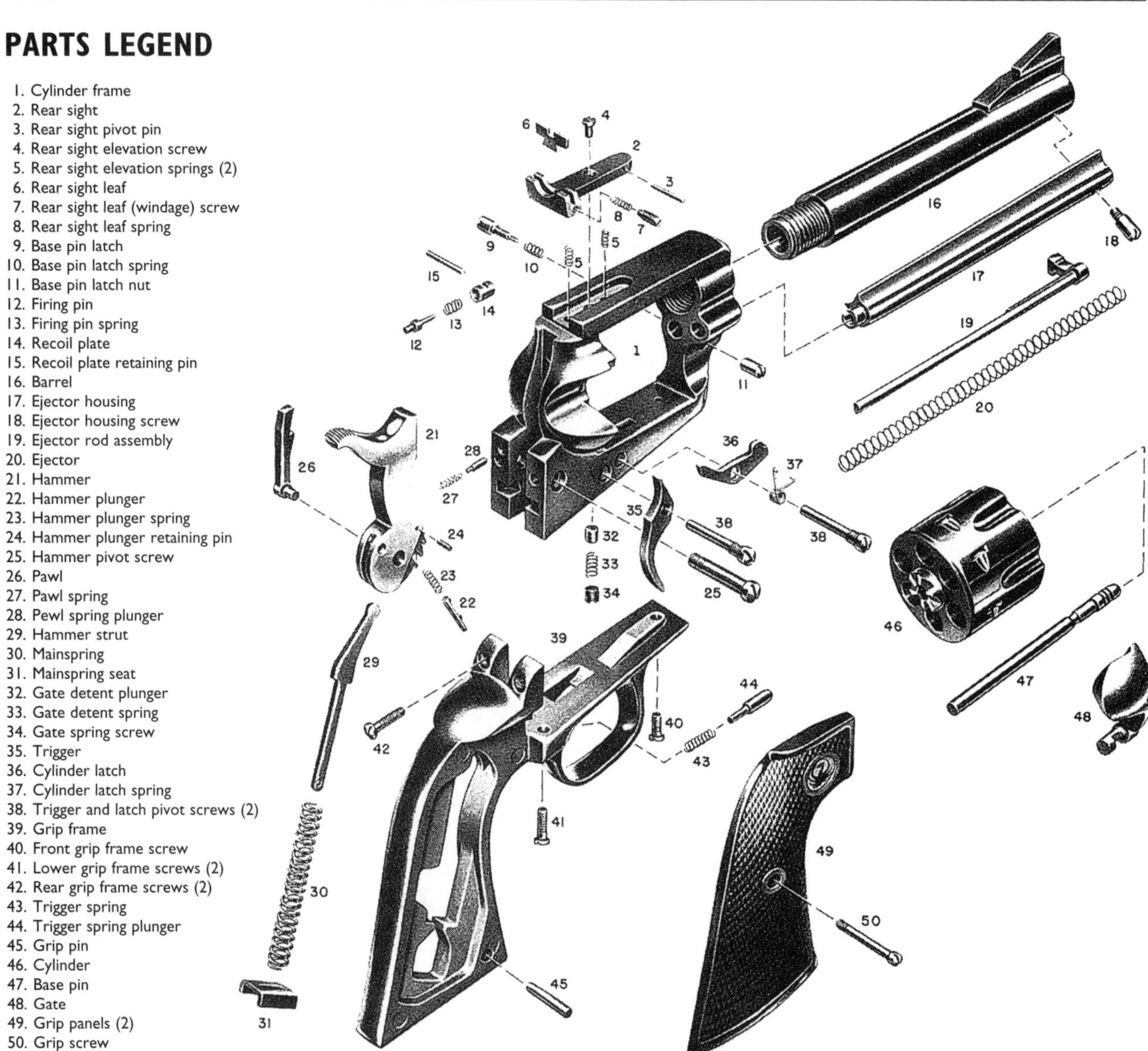

1. Cylinder frame
2. Rear sight
3. Rear sight pivot pin
4. Rear sight elevation screw
5. Rear sight elevation springs (2)
6. Rear sight leaf
7. Rear sight leaf (windage) screw
8. Rear sight leaf spring
9. Base pin latch
10. Base pin latch spring
11. Base pin latch nut
12. Firing pin
13. Firing pin spring
14. Recoil plate
15. Recoil plate retaining pin
16. Barrel
17. Ejector housing
18. Ejector housing screw
19. Ejector rod assembly
20. Ejector
21. Hammer
22. Hammer plunger
23. Hammer plunger spring
24. Hammer plunger retaining pin
25. Hammer pivot screw
26. Pawl
27. Pawl spring
28. Pewl spring plunger
29. Hammer strut
30. Mainspring
31. Mainspring seat
32. Gate detent plunger
33. Gate detent spring
34. Gate spring screw
35. Trigger
36. Cylinder latch
37. Cylinder latch spring
38. Trigger and latch pivot screws (2)
39. Grip frame
40. Front grip frame screw
41. Lower grip frame screws (2)
42. Rear grip frame screws (2)
43. Trigger spring
44. Trigger spring plunger
45. Grip pin
46. Cylinder
47. Base pin
48. Gate
49. Grip panels (2)
50. Grip screw

RUGER

First announced in August 1955, the Ruger Blackhawk single-action revolver in .357 Magnum caliber bears a strong resemblance to the original Colt Single Action Army and Frontier revolver, Model of 1873. Designwise, however, the Blackhawk is a modernized version of its Colt counterpart. The incorporation of virtually unbreakable coil springs in the lockwork is a significant improvement. The ingenious one-piece grip frame of lightweight alloy, massive frame and fully adjustable rear sight are features to delight any shooter. Simplicity of the original Colt design was a strong selling point with the Frontiersman and the same holds true for the modem Blackhawk.

In 1973 the original Blackhawk was replaced by a "New Model Blackhawk." The new revolver featured a transfer-bar between the hammer and the firing pin. Subsequently the Ruger factory undertook a program to modify older Blackhawk models to incorporate the new mechanism.

DISASSEMBLY

Pull hammer (21) to half-cock, press in base pin latch (9) from left, and withdraw base pin (47) from cylinder frame (1). Open loading gate (48) and withdraw cylinder (46).

Remove grip panels (49) and cock hammer fully. Insert a nail or pin into the small hole at the lower end of the hammer strut (29). This pin will confine the mainspring (30) when the hammer is released. Remove the five grip frame screws (40, 41, 42) which fasten the grip frame (39) to the cylinder frame. In separating the grip frame from the cylinder frame, take care to prevent loss of the pawl spring (27) and plunger (28), which are located in a hole in the rear of the cylinder frame, adjacent to the upper left rear grip frame screw hole.

Remove the hammer pivot screw (25) and the hammer from the cylinder frame. Remove the trigger pivot screw (38) and trigger (35). With a small screwdriver free the fixed leg of the cylinder latch spring (37). Remove the cylinder latch pivot screw (38), cylinder latch (36), and spring (37). Remove trigger spring (43) and plunger (44) from hole in grip frame, taking care not to deform the spring. Hammer plunger (22) and spring (23) may be removed from the hammer by drifting out the small retaining pin (24). Unscrew base pin latch (9) and remove base pin latch nut (11) and spring (10). The gate (48) may be removed from the cylinder frame by removing the gate spring screw (34) and dropping out the gate detent spring (33) and gate detent plunger (32).

To disassemble the rear sight assembly drift out the rear sight pivot pin (3) and remove the rear sight elevation screw (4). Remove the rear sight (2) from the cylinder frame using care not to lose the elevation springs (5). The rear sight leaf (6) and spring (8) may be removed by unscrewing the rear sight leaf windage screw (7).

Remove the ejector housing screw (18) and withdraw the ejector assembly from the barrel (16) and cylinder frame. The ejector rod assembly (19) may now be removed from the ejector housing (17).

The recoil plate (14), firing pin (12), and firing pin spring (13) are held in the cylinder frame by the recoil plate retaining pin (15). Disassembly of the recoil plate and firing pin is not recommended and should be attempted only by an experienced gunsmith. Removal of the hammer plunger (22) and spring (23) from the hammer is likewise not recommended. Although the above is a complete stripping procedure, it should be emphasized that, due to the rugged simplicity of the Ruger design, such a complete dismantling is seldom if ever necessary.

RUGER GP-100 REVOLVER

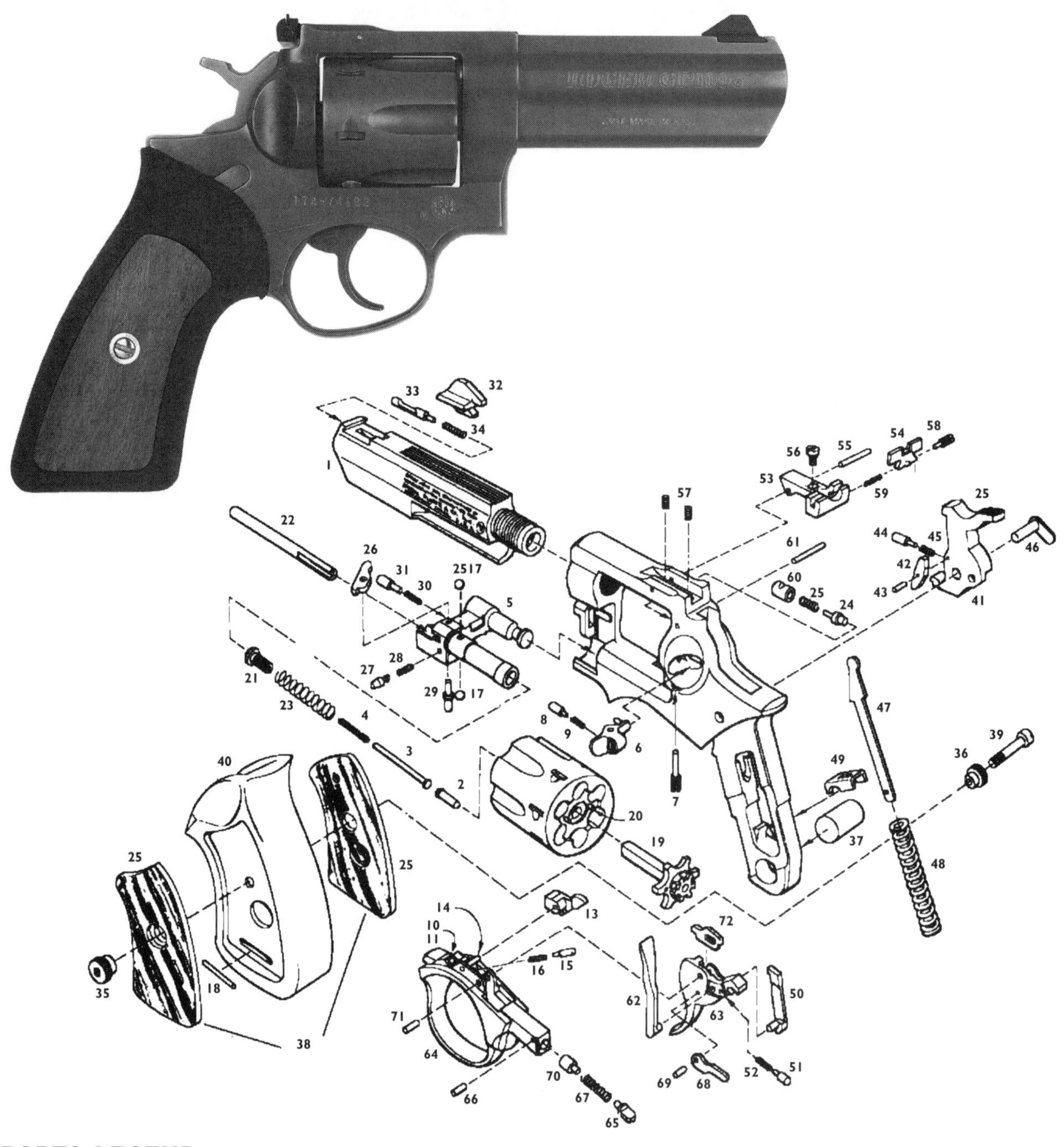

PARTS LEGEND

1. Barrel*
2. Center pin lock
3. Center pin rod
4. Center pin spring
5. Crane & crane pivot assembly
6. Crane latch
7. Crane latch pivot
8. Crane latch plunger
9. Crane latch spring
10. Crane pivot lock plunger
11. Crane pivot lock spring
12. Cylinder
13. Cylinder latch
14. Cylinder latch pivot
15. Cylinder latch plunger
16. Cylinder latch spring
17. Cylinder retaining ball
18. Disassembly pin
19. Ejector
20. Ejector alignment pins (2)
21. Ejector retainer
22. Ejector rod
23. Ejector spring
24. Firing pin
25. Firing pin rebound spring
26. Front latch
27. Front latch pivot lock
28. Front latch pivot Lock Spring
29. Front latch pivot pin
30. Front latch spring
31. Front latch spring plunger
32. Front sight
33. Front sght plunger
34. Front sight plunger spring
35. Grip ferrule, left
36. Grip ferrule, right
37. Grip panel locator
38. Grip panel inserts
39. Grip panel screw
40. Grip, one-piece rubber
41. Hammer*
42. Hammer dog*
43. Hammer dog pivot pin
44. Hammer dog plunger
45. Hammer dog spring
46. Hammer pivot assembly
47. Hammer strut
48. Hammer strut mainspring
49. Hammer strut seat
50. Pawl
51. Pawl plunger
52. Pawl plunger spring
53. Rear sight base
54. Rear sight blade, high (white outline notch)
55. Rear sight cross pin
56. Rear sight elevation screw
57. Rear sight elevation spring, (2)
58. Rear sight windage adjustment screw
59. Rear sight windage spring
60. Recoil plate
61. Recoil plate cross pin
62. Transfer bar
63. Trigger
64. Trigger guard
65. Trigger guard latch
66. Trigger guard latch pin
67. Trigger guard latch spring
68. Trigger link
69. Trigger link pin
70. Trigger link plunger
71. Trigger pivot pin
72. Trigger plunger

* Parts must be factory fitted.

In about 1985 the Security-Six was dropped from production in favor of the Ruger GP100, a firearm that includes many features found in Ruger's Redhawk and Security-Six revolvers. Ruger designed the GP100 as a rugged medium-framed, double action revolver that could withstand repeated firing of the potent .357 Magnum cartridge.

Designed with a heavy barrel with a full-length under-lug, the GP100 is manufactured in blued or stainless steel with barrel lengths of 3, 4, or 6 inches. The grip was designed using a frame extension and wrap-around rubber and wood grip.

The crane and cylinder assembly locks into the frame at the rear of the cylinder and the front of the crane. Ejection of spent cartridges is by an ejector rod that does not rotate with the cylinder. All of the cylinder mechanism is removable without tools and dismantles, along with the cylinder/crane group, into a subassemblies for inspection and cleaning.

DISASSEMBLY

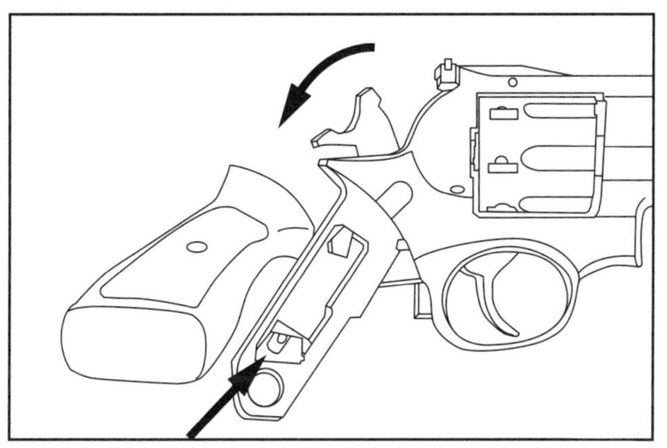

1 Using a properly fitting screwdriver, remove grip screw. Remove pistol grip inserts from grips. Grip panel locator may then be removed. Pull grip downward off frame. Take care not to lose the disassembly pin, which may fall free when the grip is removed.

Cock the hammer. Insert disassembly pin about one half its length into the hole at the rear of the mainspring strut. Lacking a disassembly pin, any similar instrument will serve.

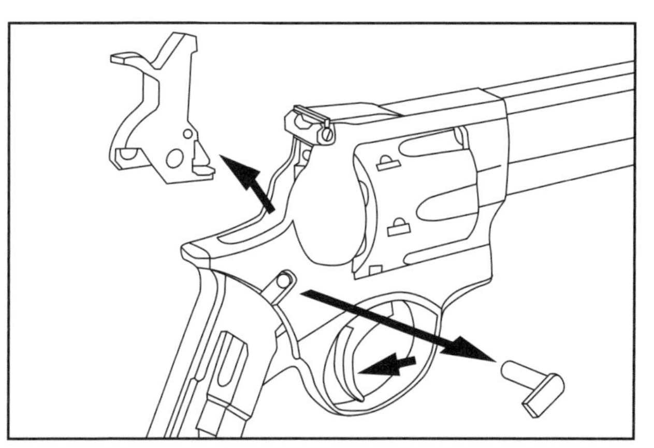

2 With thumb on hammer spur, squeeze trigger, allowing hammer to go fully forward. Lift out mainspring assembly. CAUTION: Do not remove the disassembly pin until the mainspring assembly is reinstalled in the revolver at the time of reassembly. This will permit the mainspring to fly off its strut with great force.

Pull trigger and remove hammer pivot while holding trigger in a rearward position. Lift hammer out of the top of the frame while trigger is held in a rearward position.

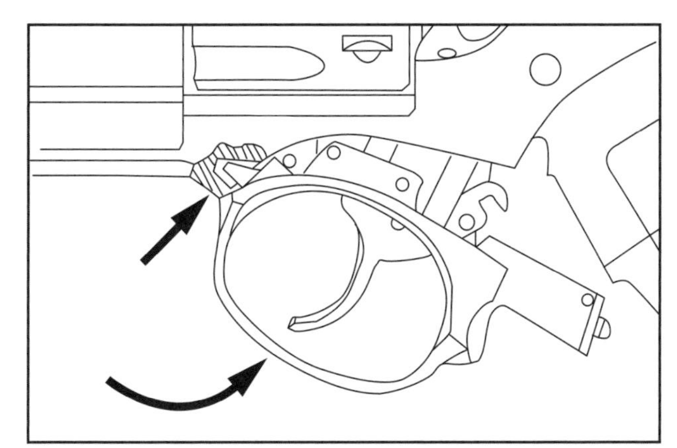

3 Use mainspring assembly to depress trigger guard lock plunger located inside frame at rear of trigger guard. Simultaneously pull down and remove trigger guard assembly. NOTE: If you cannot supply sufficient force to the plunger using the mainspring assembly as a "tool," then use a screwdriver of appropriate size and insert through hole in frame. It may be necessary to slightly depress the trigger while removing the trigger guard assembly.

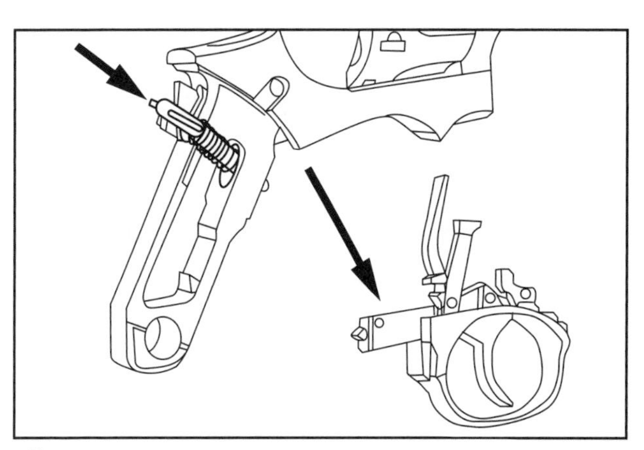

4 Cradle the revolver frame in your left hand and with the thumb of your right hand press cylinder latch button, swing out cylinder assembly and remove it forward from the frame.

Further disassembly is not essential for normal cleaning purposes. Any further disassembly should only be undertaken by factory service personnel.

RUGER HAWKEYE SINGLE SHOT

PARTS LEGEND

1. Barrel
2. Front sight
3. Ejector housing
4. Ejector housing screw
5. Ejector rod assembly
6. Ejector
7. Ejector thumb piece
8. Ejector thumb piece retaining pin
9. Ejector spring
10. Breechblock
11. Base pin
12. Firing pin
13. Firing pin spring
14. Breechblock lock plunger
15. Breechblock lock plunger spring
16. Cylinder frame
17. Base pin latch
18. Base pin latch spring
19. Base pin latch nut
20. Detent plunger
21. Detent plunger spring
22. Rear sight body
23. Rear sight pivot pin
24. Rear sight springs (2)
25. Rear sight elevation screw
26. Rear sight blade
27. Rear sight windage screw
28. Rear sight windage screw spring
29. Trigger
30. Trigger pivot screw
31. Hammer
32. Hammer pivot screw
33. Grip frame
34. Lower grip frame screws
35. Front grip frame screw
36. Rear grip frame screws (2)
37. Trigger spring plunger
38. Trigger spring
39. Mainspring seat
40. Mainspring
41. Hammer strut
42. Grip panel
43. Grip panel screw
44. Escutcheon (in right grip panel)

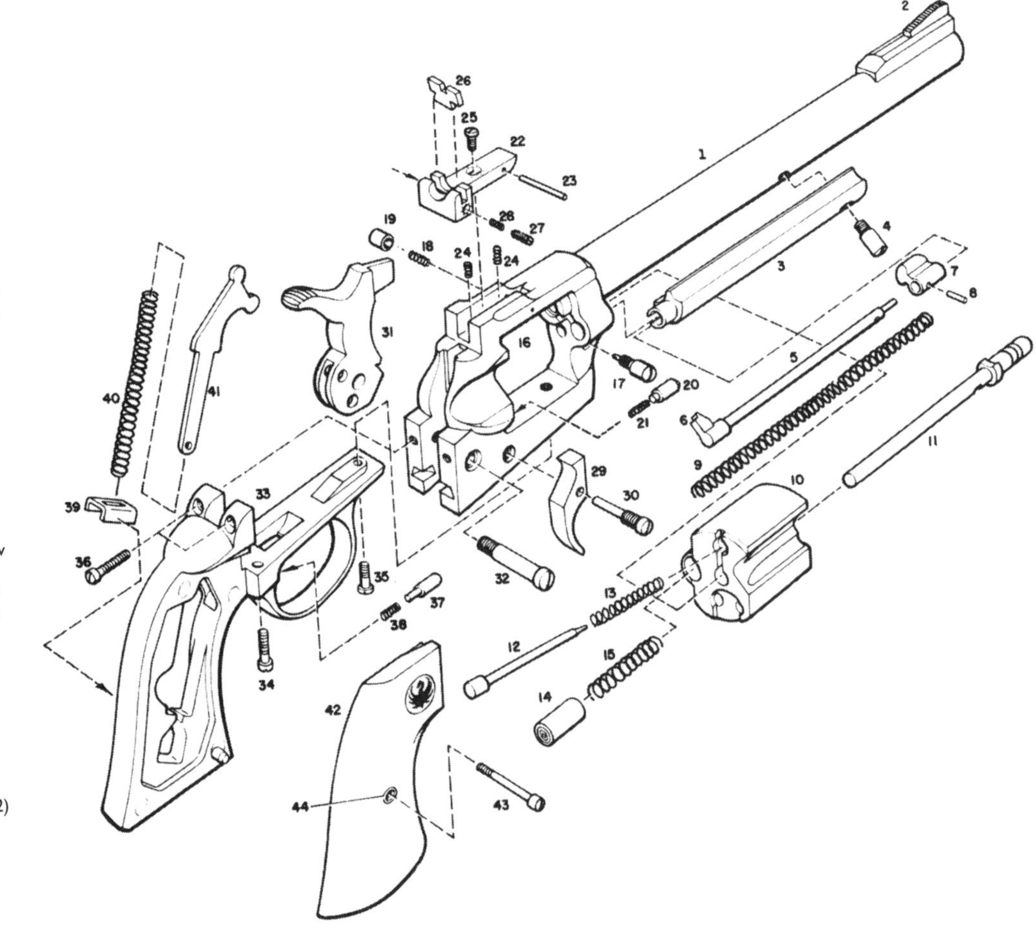

Ruger introduced the Hawkeye, rotating block, single shot pistol in 1963, in response to the rapid growth of handgun hunting in the United States. Desiring an inexpensive entry into the hunting handgun market, Ruger modified a single-action revolver, replacing the cylinder with a latched, rotating breechblock fitted with an internal firing pin.

The Hawkeye was chambered for the .256 Winchester Magnum cartridge, Its 8⅜-inch barrel was drilled and tapped at the factory for telescopic sight mounts. Although the Hawkeye was well designed and constructed, neither it nor the cartridge gained much popularity with American hunters. The Hawkeye was discontinued after only one year of production.

DISASSEMBLY

To open breechblock (10), press in breech-block lock plunger (14) at left of cylinder frame (16) and rotate breechblock counter-clockwise. Check chamber to be sure pistol is unloaded. To remove breechblock (10) from cylinder frame (16), press in base pin latch (17) at left of cylinder frame and pull base pin (11) forward as far as possible. Roll breech-block (10) out to left side of cylinder frame taking care to prevent firing pin and breech-block lock plunger (14) from being ejected forcibly by their compressed springs.

To remove ejector assembly, remove ejector housing screw (4) and withdraw ejector housing (3) with ejector rod (5), ejector (6), ejector spring (9) and ejector thumb piece (7) toward front of pistol.

Remove grip panel screw (43) and grip panels from grip frame (33). Pull hammer (31) back to a fully cocked position and insert a small close-fitting nail or pin through hole in lower end of hammer strut (41) where it protrudes below the main-spring seat (39). Release hammer (31).

Remove grip frame screws (34, 35, 36) and drop grip frame (33) from cylinder frame (16), taking care not to lose trigger spring (38) and trigger spring plunger (37).

Remove compressed mainspring (40), hammer strut (41) and mainspring seat (39) as a unit from grip frame (33). Remove hammer pivot screw (32) and remove hammer (31) from cylinder frame (16). Remove trigger pivot screw (30) and drop out trigger (29). Reassemble in reverse order.

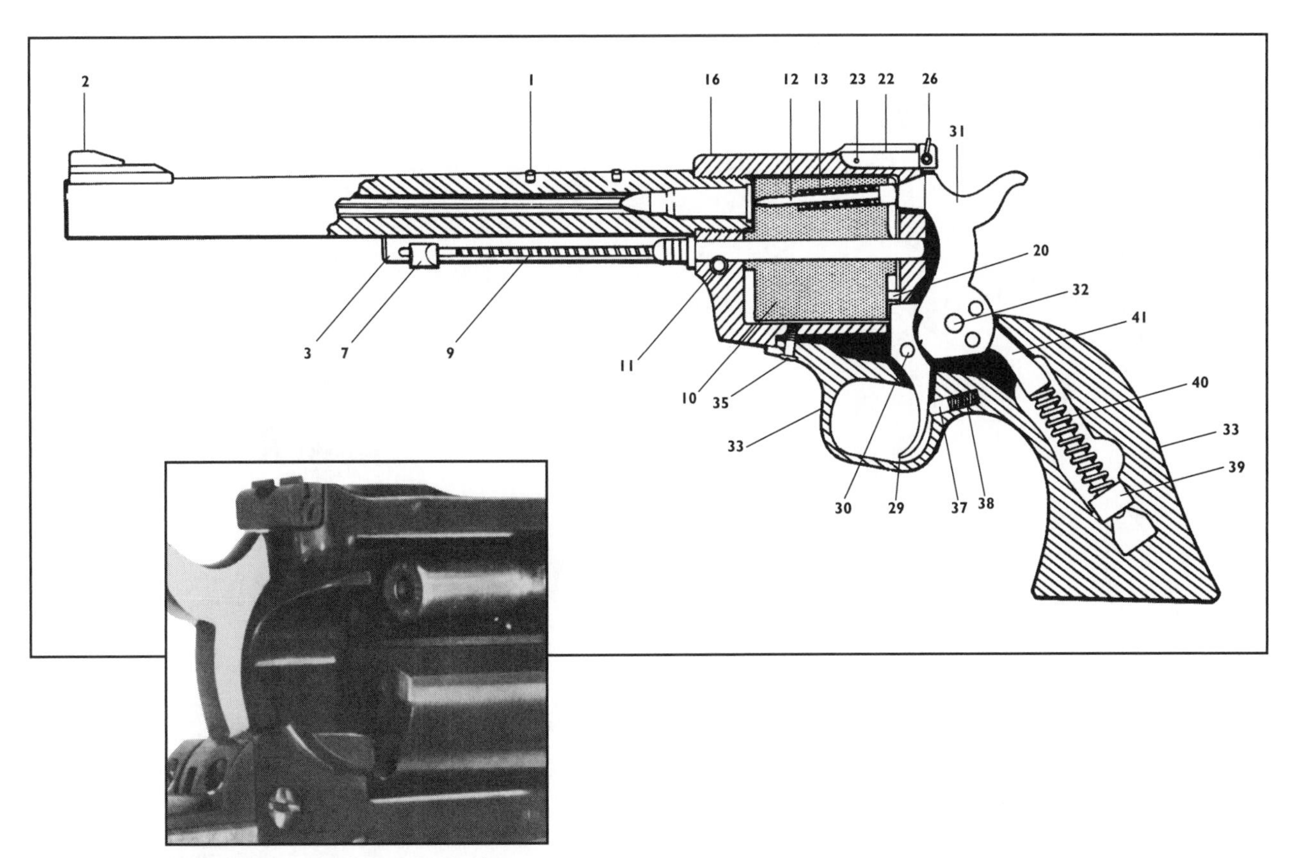

Standard Ruger revolver frame is fitted with a rotating breech-block, which has an inertia firing pin. After rotating breech-block, cartridge is loaded directly into the barrel.

RUGER NEW VAQUERO REVOLVER

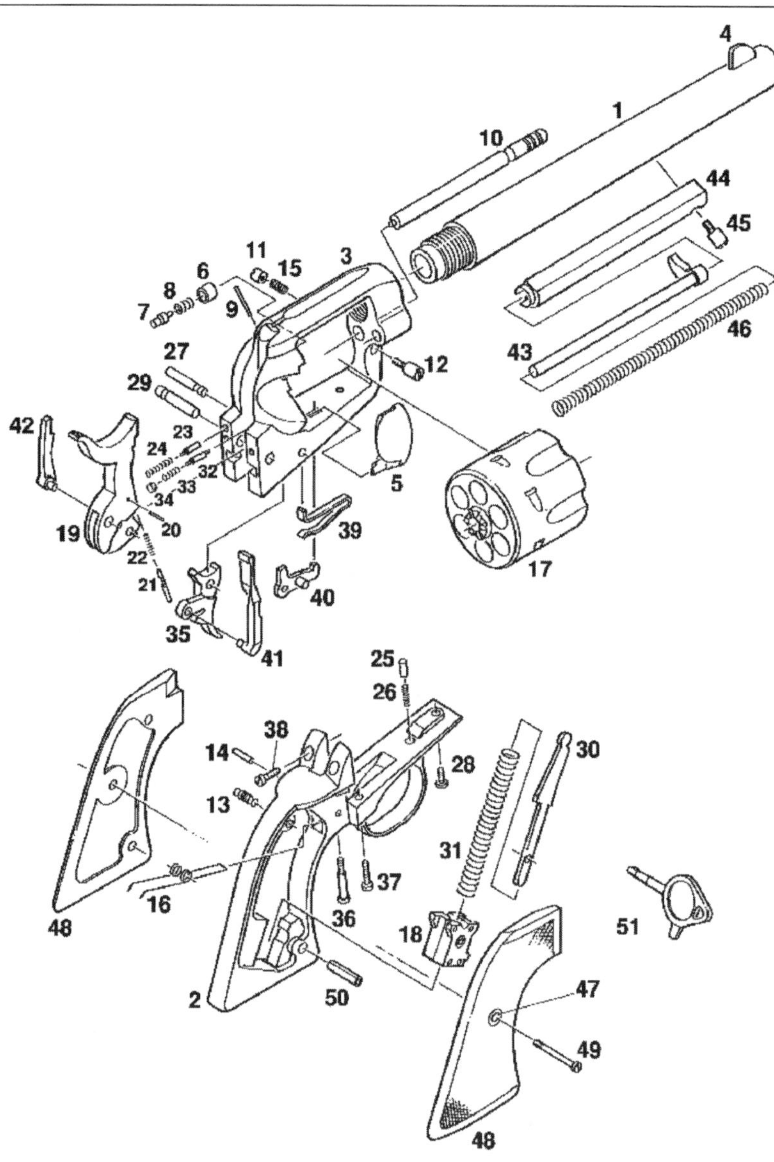

PARTS LEGEND

1. Barrel
2. Grip frame
3. Cylinder frame
4. Front sight blade
5. Loading gate
6. Recoil plate
7. Firing pin
8. Firing pin rebound spring
9. Recoil plate cross pin
10. Base pin assembly
11. Base pin latch nut
12. Base pin latch body
13. Trigger spring retaining pin
14. Trigger spring pivot pin
15. Base pin latch spring
16. Trigger cylinder
17. Cylinder *
18. Internal lock assembly
19. Hammer
20. Hammer plunger cross pin
21. Hammer plunger
22. Hammer plunger spring
23. Pawl spring plunger
24. Pawl spring
25. Cylinder latch spring plunger
26. Cylinder latch spring
27. Trigger pivot pin
28. Grip frame screw, front
29. Hammer pivot pin
30. Hammer strut
31. Mainspring
32. Ejector alignment pawl
33. Cylinder rotation stop spring
34. Cylinder rotation stop screw
35. Trigger
36. Grip frame screw & pivot lock
37. Grip frame screw, bottom
38. Grip frame screws, back (2)
39. Gate detent spring
40. Cylinder latch assembly
41. Transfer bar
42. Pawl
43. Ejector rod assembly
44. Ejector housing
45. Ejector housing screw
46. Ejector housing spring
47. Grip panel ferrule, right
48. Grip panels
49. Grip panel screw
50. Grip panel dowel
51. Internal lock key

Ruger introduced the Vaquero single-action in 1993. The Vaquero was a fixed-sight version of the Blackhawk revolver and was available in blue and case-colored finish or stainless steel in 4⅝-, 5½-, or 7½-inch barrel lengths. The Vaquero was offered in .44 Magnum and .45 Colt with the later addition of versions in .357 Magnum and .44-40.

The Ruger New Model Vaquero, introduced in 2005, incorporates a transfer bar that makes a safety notch unnecessary. The bar is raised into firing position as the trigger is pulled transmitting the blow of the hammer to the firing pin.

The loading gate on the New Model Vaquero can be opened only when the the hammer and trigger are fully forward. Opening the gate immobilizes the trigger, hammer and transfer bar and unlatches the cylinder allowing it to be turned for loading or ejection. When the gate is closed, the cylinder latch functions in the normal manner.

DISASSEMBLY

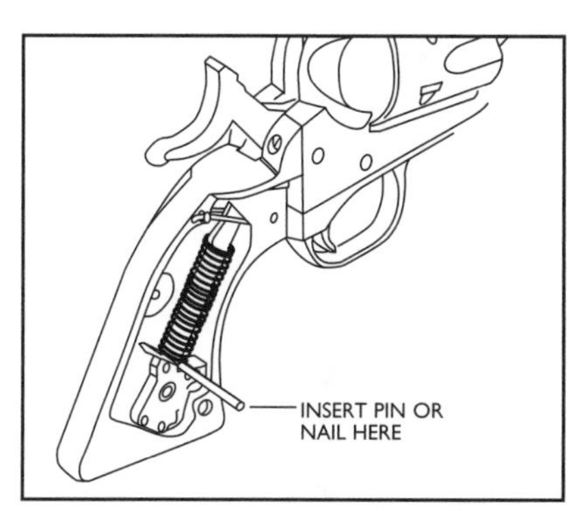

1 Remove the grip panel screw and remove grip panels. Unlock the internal lock.

Draw the hammer rearward to full cock position. Insert a short length (about 1 inch) of nail or pin into the small hole at the lower end of the hammer strut. The hole is visible between the mainspring and the top of the internal lock assembly. The purpose of inserting the pin or nail is to confine the mainspring when the hammer is released.

While maintaining the thumb pressure on the hammer spur, squeeze the trigger and ease hammer down to full forward position.

Remove the five (5) screws that fasten the grip frame to the cylinder frame.

Pull the grip frame rearward and downward to separate it from the cylinder frame. (If the grip frame does not readily separate from the cylinder frame, draw the hammer rearward a short distance.) Remove the mainspring assembly and internal lock assembly from the grip frame, but do not remove the small pin that is confining the mainspring. (The mainspring assembly will later be reassembled into the frame as it is.) The internal lock assembly is removed from the grip frame by lifting it up and then out.

Do not 'lose' the pawl spring and plunger (located in a hole in the rear of the left side of the cylinder frame, just above the grip frame screw hole) or the cylinder latch spring and plunger (located in the hole above front of the trigger guard bow in the grip frame).

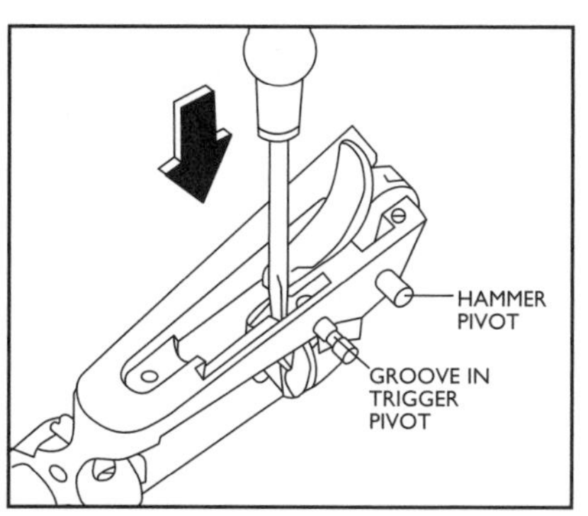

2 Remove the trigger pivot (pin) as follows: using a screwdriver as shown-above, depress the gate detent spring so that the end of the spring which rests in one groove of the trigger pivot is free of the groove. Then, use a drift and hammer to push the pivot completely out of the frame.

Remove cylinder latch, gate detent spring, and gate.

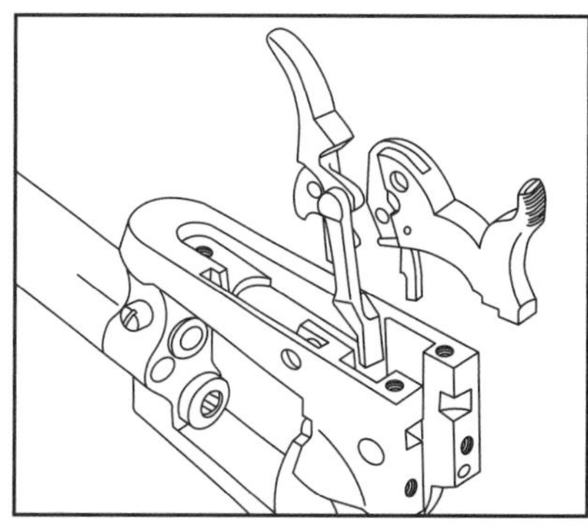

3 Remove hammer pivot. Then remove the hammer/pawl assembly and the trigger/transfer bar assembly (Note that the hammer is attached to the pawl and the transfer bar is attached to the trigger.)

The revolver is now disassembled as far as it needs to be for major cleaning and maintenance. If it is necessary to go beyond the above steps, the following cautions and suggestions should be useful:

Ejector/Ejector Housing: Wrap one hand firmly around barrel and housing when loosening the screw. Remove screw, then carefully lift housing (which contains compressed spring and ejector rod) away from the barrel.

Base Pin Latch/Nut and Spring: The nut must be held firmly (with jaw-protected pliers) while the latch is being unscrewed. Don't lose the spring. When reassembling, be certain the nut and spring are on the left side of the frame.

CAUTION: The preload on the cylinder rotation stop is factory set. Do not alter the position of the cylinder rotation stop screw.

RUGER P95 PR PISTOL

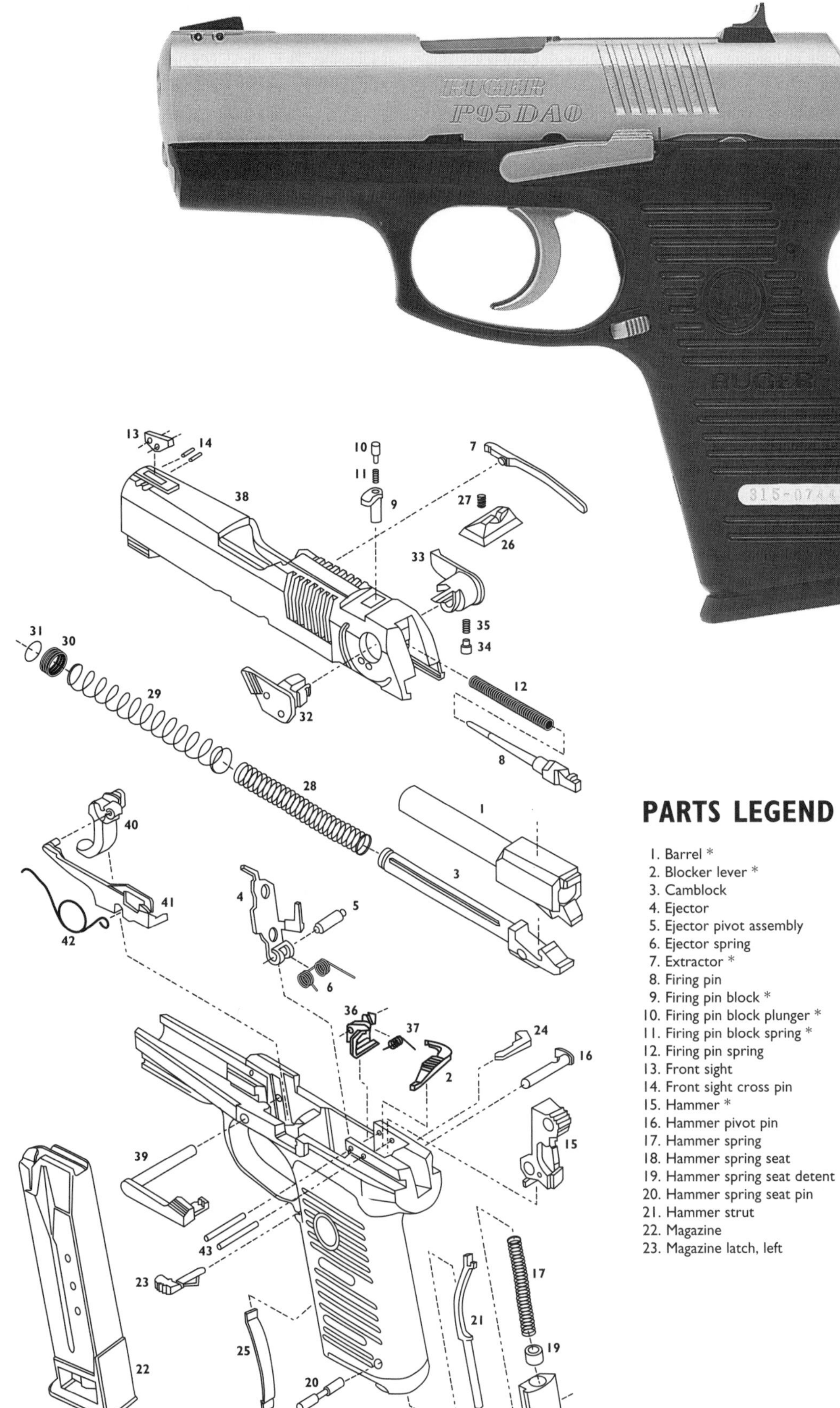

PARTS LEGEND

1. Barrel *
2. Blocker lever *
3. Camblock
4. Ejector
5. Ejector pivot assembly
6. Ejector spring
7. Extractor *
8. Firing pin
9. Firing pin block *
10. Firing pin block plunger *
11. Firing pin block spring *
12. Firing pin spring
13. Front sight
14. Front sight cross pin
15. Hammer *
16. Hammer pivot pin
17. Hammer spring
18. Hammer spring seat
19. Hammer spring seat detent
20. Hammer spring seat pin
21. Hammer strut
22. Magazine
23. Magazine latch, left
24. Magazine latch, right
25. Magazine latch spring
26. Rear Sight
27. Rear sight lock screw
28. Recoil spring, inner
29. Recoil spring, outer
30. Recoil spring collar
31. Recoil spring collar retainer
32. Safety, left
33. Safety assembly, right
34. Safety detent plunger
35. Safety detent plunger spring
36. Sear *
37. Sear spring
38. Slide *
39. Slide stop assembly
40. Trigger
41. Trigger bar *
42. Trigger bar spring
43. Sear pivot pin

* Parts so marked must be factory fitted

Sturm, Ruger & Co. entered the centerfire semi-automatic pistol market in 1987 with the P85, a short-recoil-operated 9 mm Para pistol with a conventional double-action/single-action trigger. Though robust and reliable, the gun seemed to lack the ergonomic refinements and accuracy expected by the shooting public, and in 1991 Ruger replaced it with the P89. This pistol was available in three firing modes: double-action with a manual safety (as with the P85), double-action with an ambidextrous de-cocker, or double-action-only. A shorter, lighter version of the 9mm P89, the P93, came out in 1994.

In 1996, Ruger unveiled a polymer-frame version of the P93, named the P95. Like its predecessors, the P95 utilized a SIG-Sauer-type locking system, in which a shoulder on the enlarged chamber end of the barrel locks into the forward edge of the ejection port. Unlike the previous P-series pistols, however, in which an M1911-style swinging link tilted the barrel out of and into lockup with the slide, the P95 employed a cam surface on the barrel underlug which engaged a cam-block in the head of the recoil spring guide.

Currently cataloged by Ruger, the P95 has a 3.9-inch barrel, weighs 27 ounces, and has a magazine capacity of 15 rounds of 9mm Para ammunition.

DISASSEMBLY

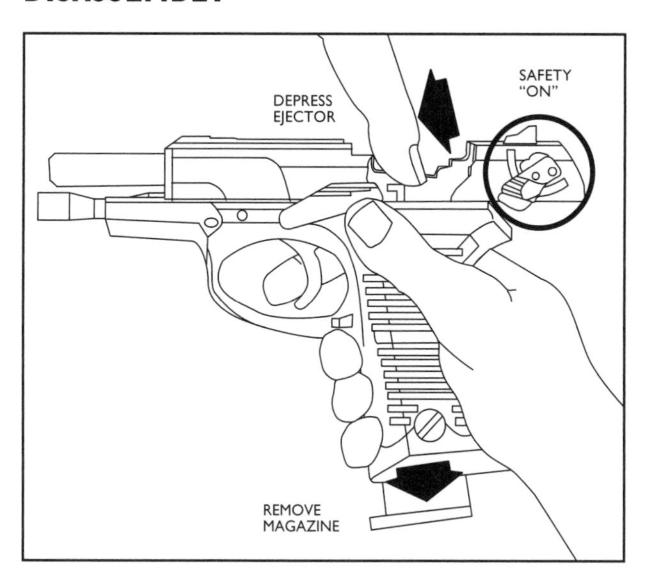

1 Place either safety lever in the "safe" position (leer fully down, white dot and the letter "S" exposed). Press forward on either magazine latch and withdraw magazine from butt of pistol.

Pull slide to rear and lock in open position by pressing upward on rear end of slide stop.

Keep upward pressure on slide stop to prevent forward movement of slide. Open slide is under strong spring tension and could injure fingers if allowed to slam shut. Insert finger through top of slide and push ejector downward and forward until it locks in its lower position. This will permit forward movement of slide. Further disassembly is impossible unless this is done.

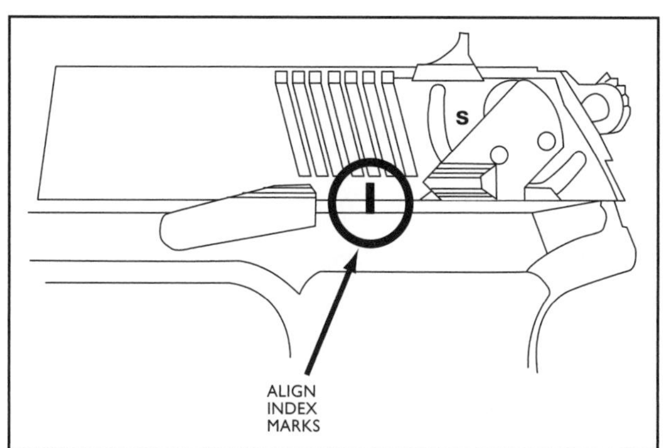

2 Remove fingers from ejection port. Grasp slide tightly. Now press down on slide stop and allow slide to move slowly forward until the vertical disassembly line on the frame is aligned with the vertical disassembly line on the slide.

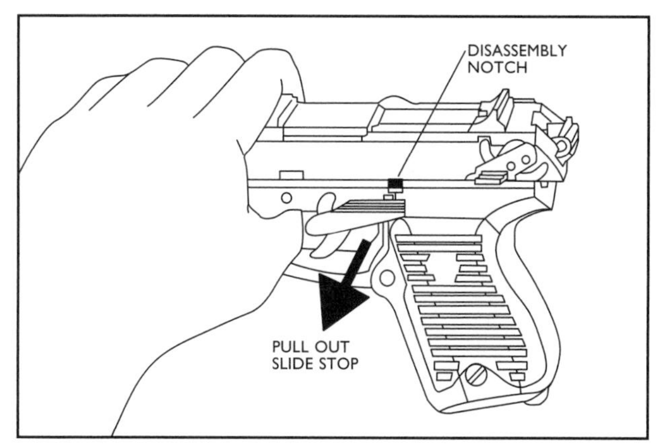

3 Press in on right-hand end of slide stop and pull slide stop out of frame to the left until it is withdrawn completely out of the frame. Push slide forward and remove entire slide assembly to the front.

With slide held upside down, lift rear end of camblock/recoil spring assembly to disengage it from its seat against the barrel lug. Withdraw the camblock/recoil spring assembly to the rear of the slide.

RUGER SECURITY-SIX REVOLVER

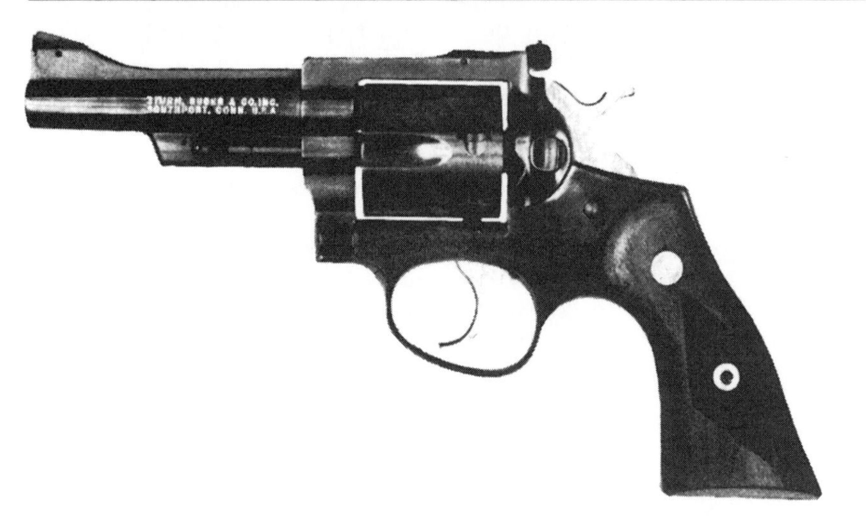

Cutaway indicates relationship between assembled parts. Gun is shown unloaded, with all springs at rest. Crane latch has been omitted for clarity; its crossbar would lie between center pin lock and transfer bar. Parts are number keyed to parts legend.

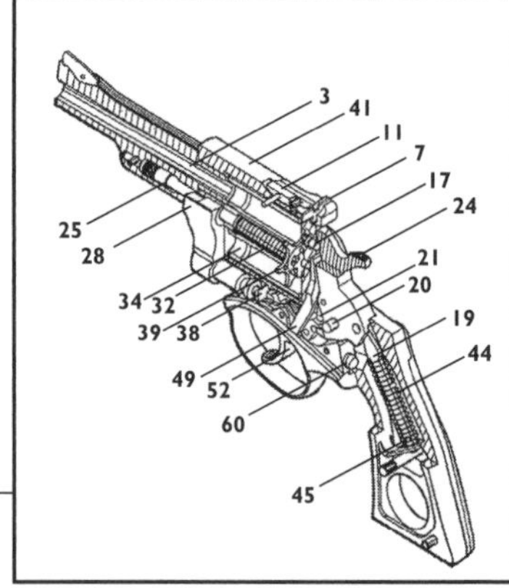

PARTS LEGEND

1. Front sight
2. Front sight cross pin
3. Barrel
4. Front latch cross pin
5. Front latch spring
6. Front latch
7. Rear sight blade
8. Rear sight elevation screw
9. Rear sight pivot pin
10. Rear sight elevation spring (2)
11. Rear sight
12. Rear sight windage spring
13. Rear sight windage screw
14. Recoil plate cross pin
15. Recoil plate
16. Firing pin rebound spring
17. Firing pin
18. Hammer dog pivot pin
19. Hammer strut
20. Hammer pivot assembly
21. Hammer dog
22. Hammer dog spring plunger
23. Hammer dog spring
24. Hammer
25. Ejector rod
26. Center pin spring
27. Center pin rod
28. Crane and crane pivot assembly
29. Cylinder latch spring
30. Cylinder latch plunger
31. Ejector rod washer
32. Ejector spring
33. Center pin lock
34. Cylinder
35. Crane latch spring plunger
36. Crane latch spring
37. Crane latch
38. Cylinder latch
39. Ejector
40. Crane latch pivot
41. Frame
42. Grip panel (left) complete
43. Disassembly pin
44. Mainspring
45. Mainspring seat
46. Grip panel dowel
47. Grip panel (right) complete
48. Grip panel screw
49. Transfer bar
50. Trigger spring
51. Trigger bushing
52. Trigger
53. Trigger pivot pin
54. Pawl spring
55. Pawl plunger
56. Pawl
57. Trigger guard
58. Trigger guard plunger cross
59. Trigger guard plunger spring
60. Trigger guard plunger

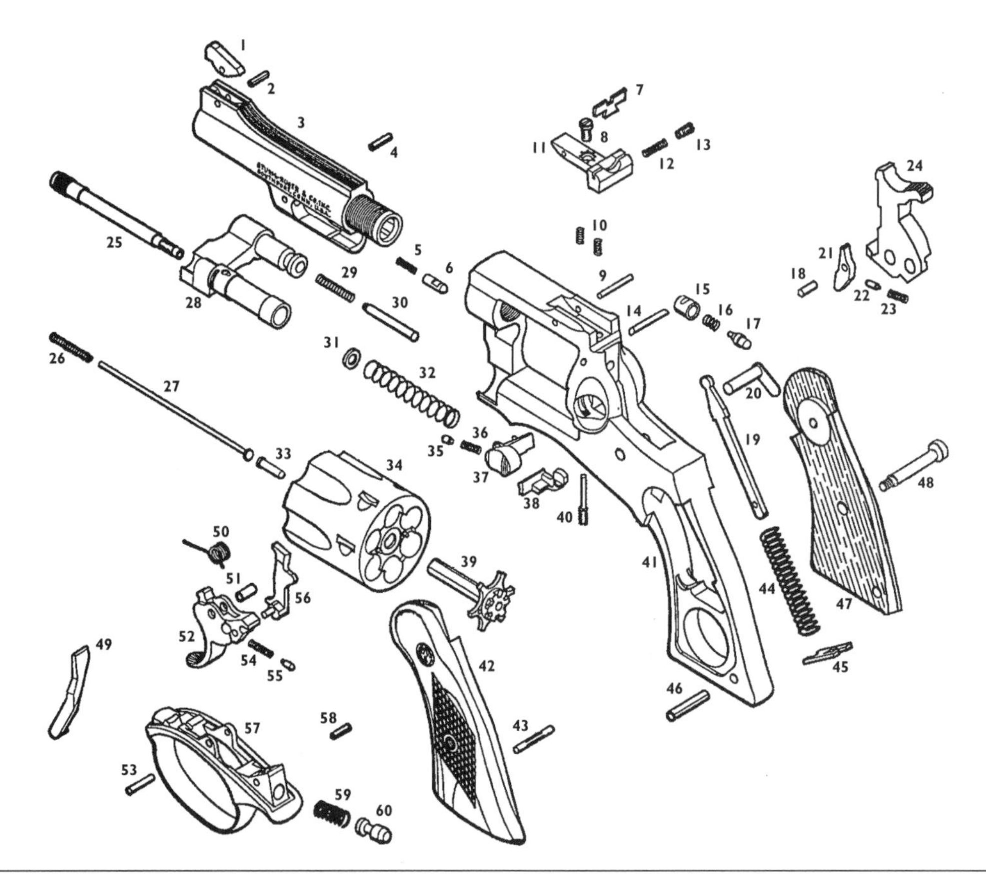

The Security-Six was Ruger's first double-action revolver. Introduced in 1970, the new revolver was a 33 oz., solid-frame revolver with side-swing cylinder and simultaneous ejection. The Security-Six was designed to take advantage of manufacture using investment casting and coiled springs.

The Security-Six was offered first in .357 Magnum but was soon available in 9mm (using "half-moon clips) and .38 Special. Over the years, versions of the Security-Six were offered in blued or stainless steel and with 2¾-, four- or six-inch barrels. Models of the Security-Six in .38 Spl. with fixed sights were marketed as the Speed-Six, Service-Six or the Police Service-Six. Some models featured rounded butts and a few Speed-Six Models came with factory bobbed triggers.

In the 1970s the U.S. Army purchased a new supply of .38 caliber revolvers from several commercial suppliers, including an order of Service-Six Revolvers with a 4-inch barrel. Service-Sixes were also issued to Air Force Police and Marine Embassy Security personnel. These were Parkerized and fitted with lanyard loops. Ruger discontinued the revolver in 9mm in 1984 and production of the Security-Six line ended in 1985.

DISASSEMBLY

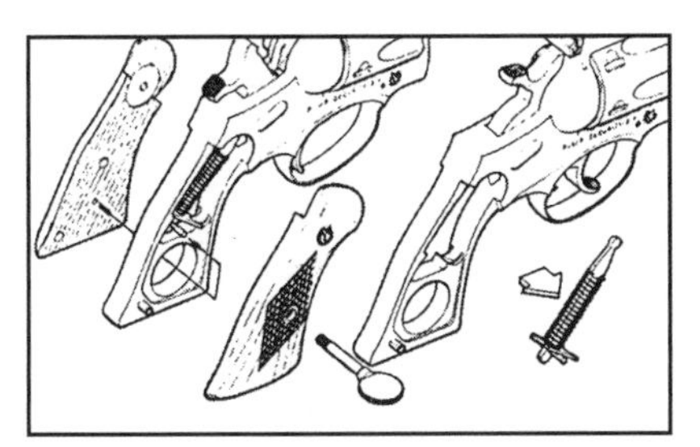

1 Determine that revolver is unloaded before attempting disassembly. Unscrew grip screw (48) with coin or cartridge rim, and remove grips (42 & 47). Cock hammer (24) with thumb. Insert disassembly pin (43), stored in left grip, through hole at bottom of hammer strut (19). Pull trigger, lower hammer with thumb, and remove mainspring/hammer strut assembly from grip frame.

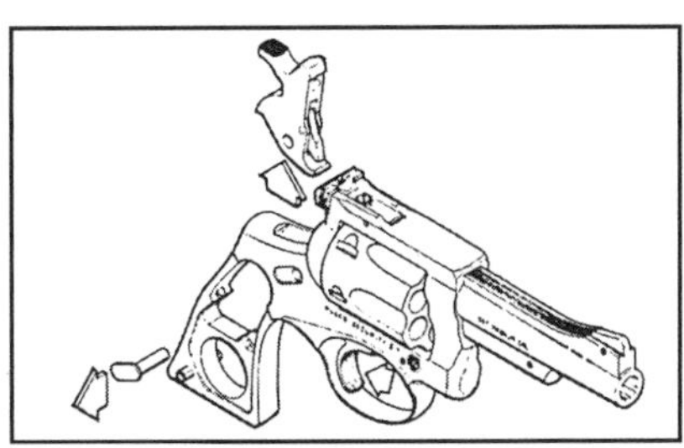

2 Pull trigger fully to rear and remove hammer pivot assembly (20). Keeping trigger fully depressed, roll hammer forward and lift straight upward from frame.

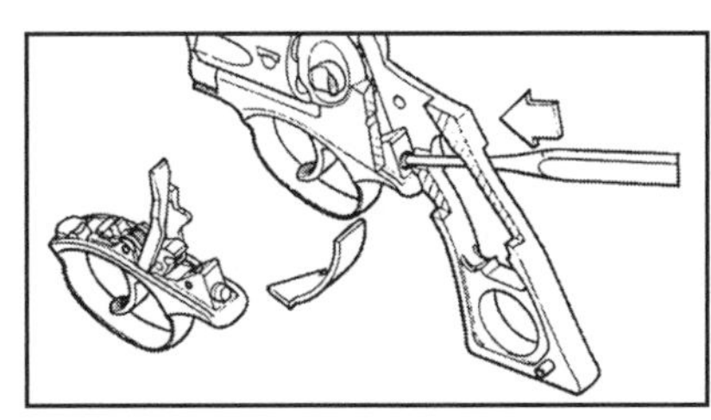

3 Working through frame opening, depress trigger guard plunger (60) with punch. Pull rear of trigger guard (57) downward and remove from frame. In the field, trigger guard plunger may be depressed by rounded head of hammer strut.

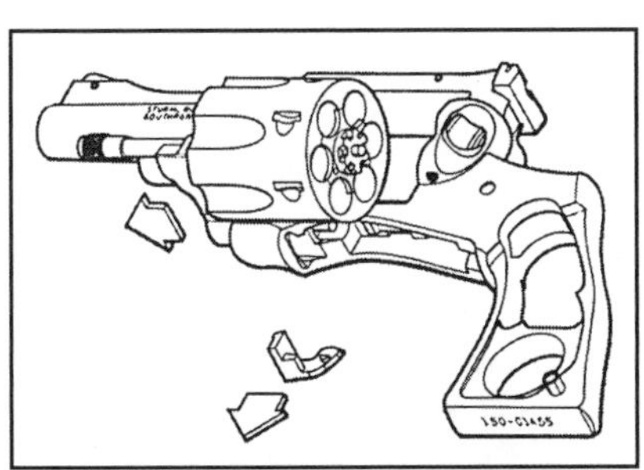

4 With the gun on its right side, press crane latch (37) and open cylinder (34). Draw cylinder/crane assembly forward and out of frame. Remove cylinder latch (38).

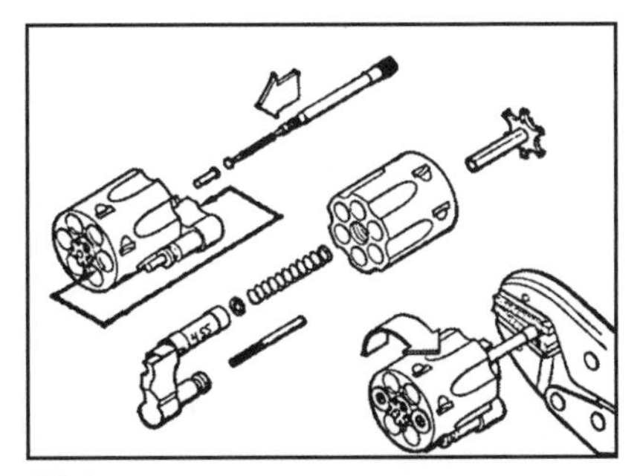

5 If cylinder/crane assembly must be taken down, clamp knurled head of ejector rod (25) between wood blocks in vise or locking jaw pliers. Insert empty cartridge cases in opposite chambers and unscrew cylinder, turning clockwise. (Assembly is secured with left-hand threads.) When cylinder is fully unscrewed, squeeze crane (28) and cylinder together and remove from ejector rod. All parts may then be separated.

To reassemble cylinder/crane assembly, replace cylinder latch spring and plunger (29 & 30) within crane pivot. Insert ejector rod washer (31) and ejector spring (32) within cylinder axle, making sure that the washer seats squarely upon its shoulder. Assemble ejector (39), cylinder, and crane. Slide center pin spring (26) over center pin rod (27) and insert through threaded end of ejector rod. Holding cylinder/crane assembly tightly together, replace center pin lock (33) and ejector rod assembly, turning ejector rod counter-clockwise to start its thread. Tighten in vise, as before.

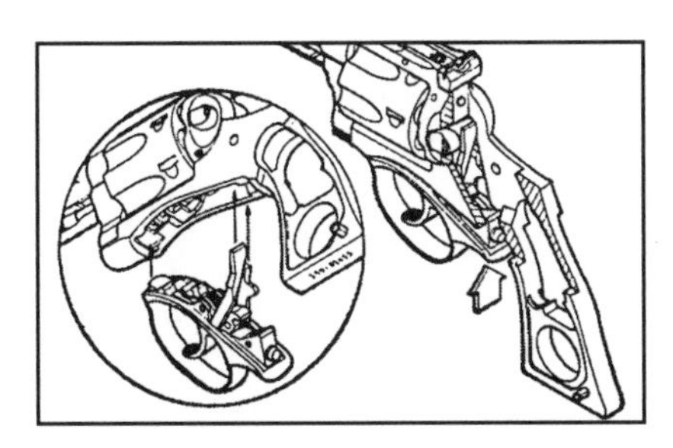

6 Assemble rest of gun in reverse order. When installing trigger guard assembly, locate transfer bar (49) and pawl (56) ahead of their internal frame shoulders, and enter lug at front of guard within its frame seat. Pivot assembly upward into contact with frame. Determine that transfer bar is situated to rear of internal crossbar of frame latch, and snap guard home. Pulling trigger will cycle cylinder, if assembly is correct. When replacing mainspring assembly, position mainspring seat (45) with offset hammer strut hole to rear.

RUGER SINGLE-SIX REVOLVER

PARTS LEGEND

1. Barrel
2. Front sight
3. Base pin
4. Ejector housing
5. Ejector housing screw
6. Cylinder frame
7. Recoil plate
8. Rebound spring
9. Firing pin
10. Recoil plate pin
11. Pawl spring
12. Pawl plunger
13. Pawl
14. Hammer
15. Hammer plunger pin
16. Hammer plunger spring
17. Hammer plunger
18. Base pin nut
19. Base pin nut latch spring
20. Base pin latch
21. Gate assembly (contoured)
22. Cylinder latch spring
23. Cylinder latch
24. Pivot screw (2)
25. Gate spring screw
26. Gate detent spring
27. Gate detent plunger
28. Ejector spring
29. Ejector rod assembly
30. Cylinder
31. Trigger
32. Trigger plunger
33. Trigger spring
34. Grip frame screw, front
35. Grip frame screw, lower (2)
36. Grip frame screw, rear (2)
37. Hammer pivot screw
38. Grip frame
39. Grip panel, left
40. Grip panel, right
41. Grip panel screw
42. Mainspring seat
43. Hammer strut
44. Mainspring
45. Rear sight

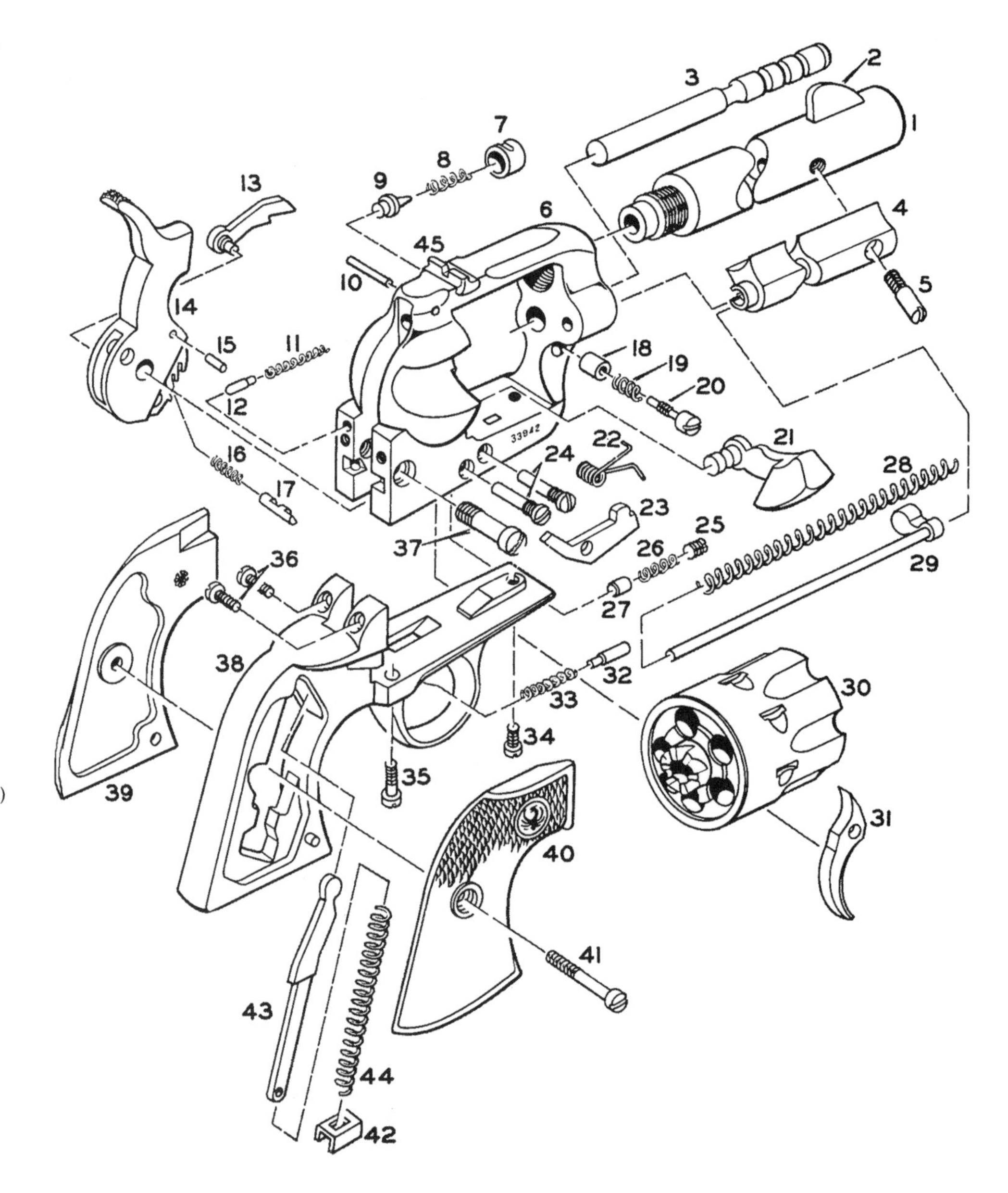

In early 1954 Strum, Ruger & Co., of Southport, Connecticut, began production of their Single-Six, a .22 rimfire, six-shot, single-action rod ejecting revolver. Patterned after the Colt Single Action Army, the Ruger Single-Six answered the demand for a high-quality, western style, single-action revolver chambered for the economical .22 rimfire cartridge.

It was not designed for competitive shooting, but rather for plinking at informal targets of opportunity. This is not to disparage the accuracy of the Single-Six, as it is quite capable of target accuracy within the limitations of its sights. The blade front sight is fixed but the rear sight can be adjusted for windage by tapping it sideways in its dovetail slot. There is no provision for adjusting elevation. The salient design feature of the Single-Six is the use of durable coil springs throughout the lock mechanism.

For a short period in the mid-1950s, the Single-Six was made with a lightweight, 22-oz., alloy frame that gave a considerable weight saving over the 35-oz. steel frame guns. There was also a "Buntline," 9½-inch barrel version. Single-Sixes were first offered in .22 Winchester Magnum Rimfire in 1959 followed by interchangeable cylinder models.

In 1973 the Single-Six underwent a major change with the incorporation of a transfer bar, to preclude accidental discharge. Ruger changed the model's name to "Super Single-Six" and undertook a program to convert existing Single-Sixes to the new lock mechanism.

DISASSEMBLY

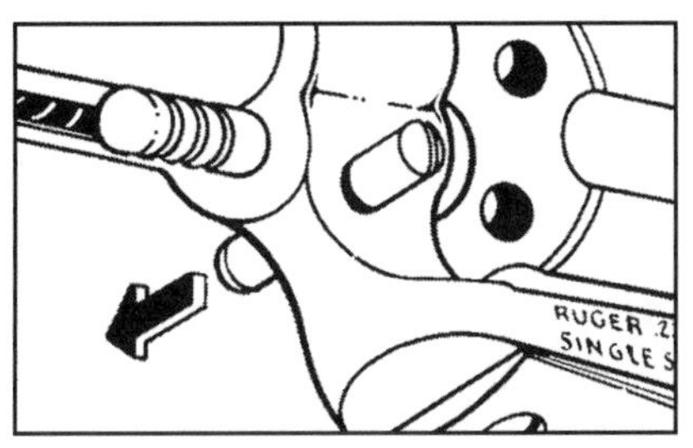

1 To remove cylinder (30), first remove any cartridges, position hammer on loading notch, and open gate (21). Next, press base pin nut (18) on left side and withdraw base pin (3). Cylinder may now be removed from right side.

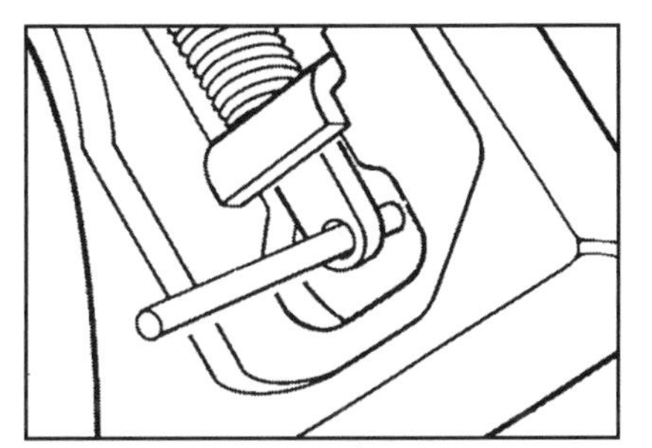

2 To further disassemble, remove grip panel screw (41), and lift grip panels (39) and (40) away from grip frame (38). Bring hammer to full cock and insert nail or pin into small hole in lower end of hammer strut (43). Next, depress trigger and move the hammer forward. The nail will keep mainspring (44) compressed.

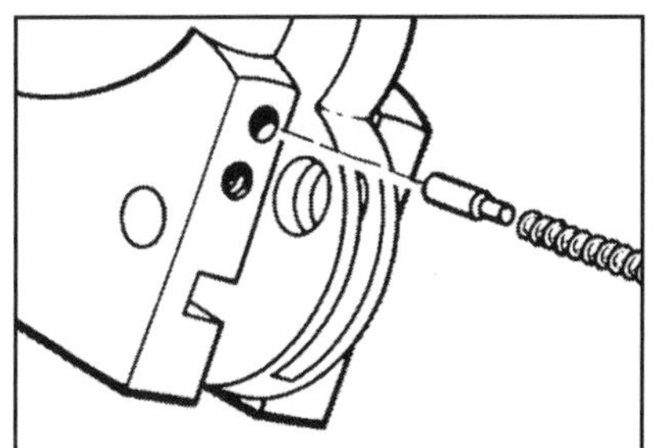

3 Continue disassembly by removing the 5 screws—2 (35), 2 (36), and (34)—which hold grip frame to cylinder frame (6). In separating grip and cylinder frames, take care to prevent loss of pawl spring (11) and plunger (12). These parts are located in a hole drilled in left rear face of cylinder frame, adjacent to rear left grip frame screw hole.

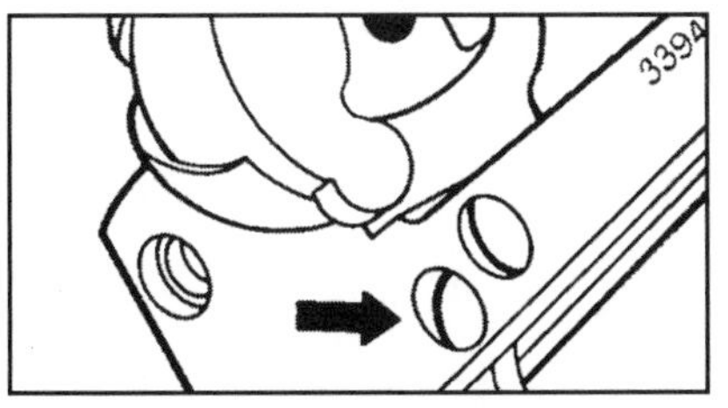

4 Remove hammer pivot screw (37) and hammer. Remove trigger pivot screw (24-arrow) and trigger (31).

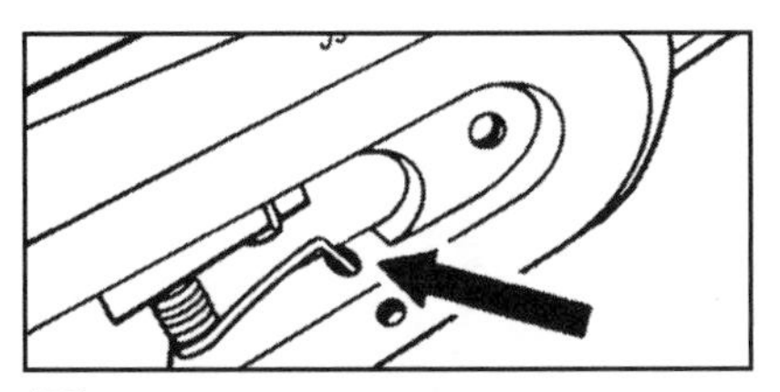

5 With a small screwdriver, free fixed leg of cylinder latch spring (22) from its anchoring hole in left inside wall of cylinder frame. Remove cylinder latch pivot screw (24), cylinder latch (23), and cylinder latch spring (22).

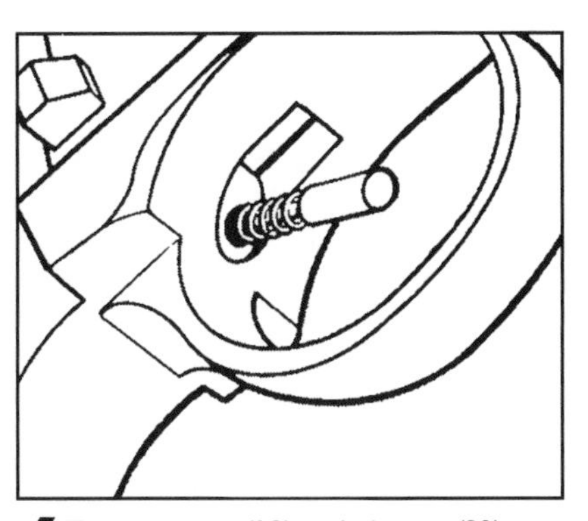

6 Trigger spring (33) and plunger (32) are positioned in a hole in grip frame at rear of trigger guard bow. Innermost coil of trigger spring is enlarged to prevent loss during disassembly and reassembly. Care should be exercised in removing plunger and spring to prevent deformation of spring.

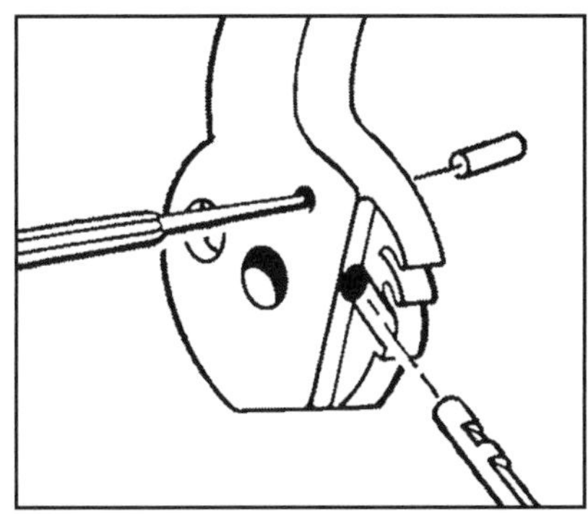

7 Hammer plunger (17) is retained in hammer by a small pin (15) which may be removed by means of a small flat-nosed punch. Reassembly of arm is accomplished in reverse order.

SAUER MODEL 1930 PISTOL

PARTS LEGEND

1. Slide
2. Rear sight and latch
3. Pin
4. Slide cap
5. Firing pin spring
6. Firing pin
7. Breechblock
8. Extractor
9. Extractor pin
10. Trigger
11. Trigger bar and sear
12. Mechanism housing
13. Sear pin
14. Sear cam pin
15. Sear cam
16. Mainspring follower
17. Mainspring
18. Mainspring cap
19. Magazine catch
20. Magazine catch pin
21. Frame
22. Magazine
23. Grip, left
24. Grip screws (2)
25. Lower mechanism pin
26. Upper mechanism pin
27. Safety catch detent pin
28. Detent spring
29. Safety catch
30. Trigger pin
31. Recoil spring guide
32. Recoil spring
33. Grip, right

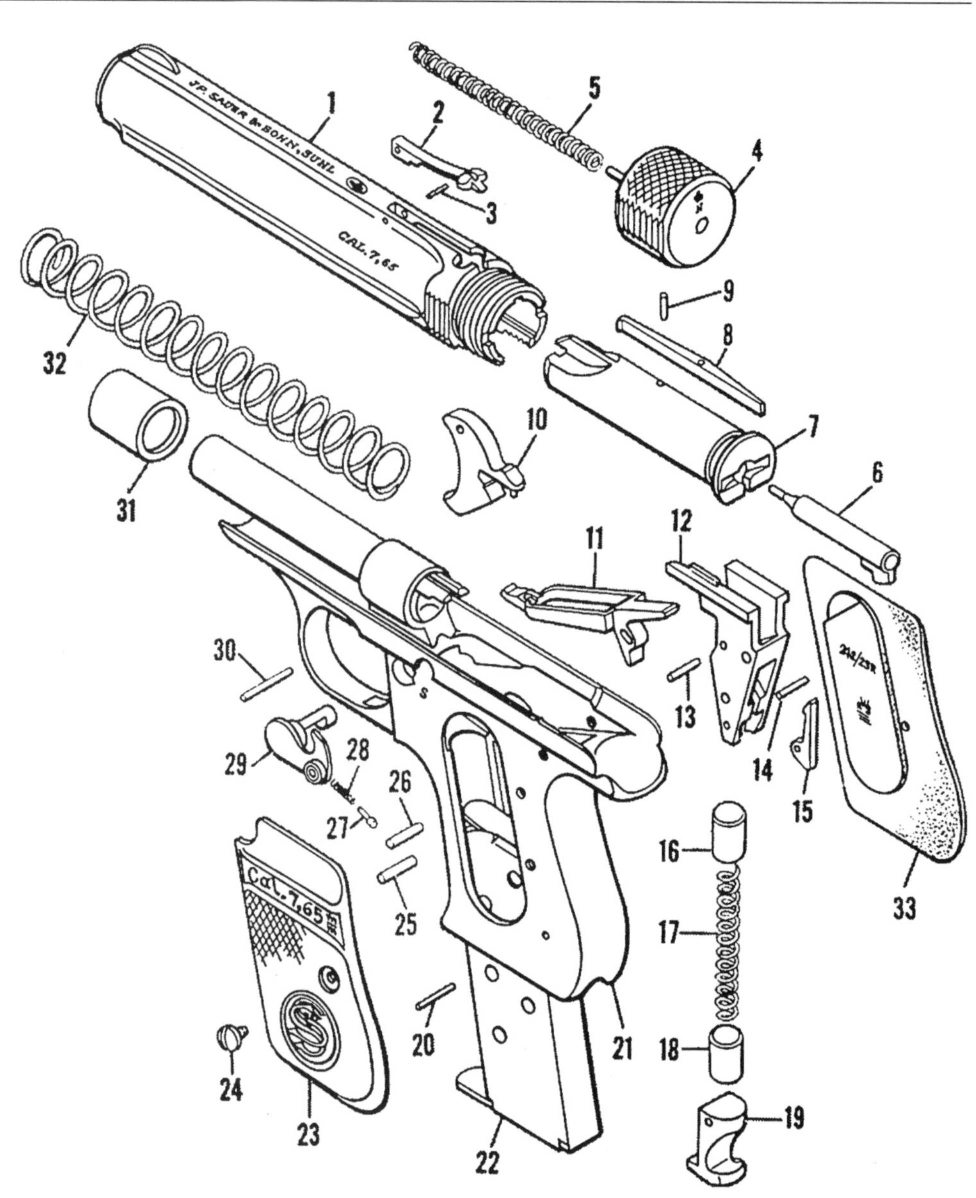

Manufactured by the German arms firm of J. P. Sauer & Sohn, the Sauer Model 1930 caliber .32 ACP pistol was first offered in 1930. Of simple blowback-operated, striker-fired design, the Model 1930 pistol is a development of an earlier Sauer pistol introduced in 1913. Detachable magazine of the Model 1930 pistol holds 7 cartridges.

There is a close resemblance between the earlier version and the Model 1930 pistol, but they can be readily distinguished by differences in frame design. Front grip strap of the earlier pistol is straight, whereas that of the Model 1930 curves forward at the base to provide a support for the little finger. The frame of the Model 1930 pistol extends beyond the rear face of the slide cap, whereas the slide cap of the earlier model overhangs the frame.

As a further refinement of the Model 1930 pistol, the Sauer firm introduced their Behörden Model (Authority Model), also chambered for the .32 ACP cartridge. Apparently aimed at possible municipal government markets, the Behörden Model featured a trigger safety, magazine safety, manual safety, and optional cartridge signal pin device in the slide cap. With the exception of the manual safety, none of these auxiliary safety devices are present in the Model 1930 pistol. Model 1930 and Behörden Model pistols were optionally available with steel or aluminum frames and slides. Minor changes were made in their internal mechanisms during course of manufacture. Sauer Model 1930 and Behörden Model pistols were superseded by the Sauer Model 38 double-action pistol.

DISASSEMBLY

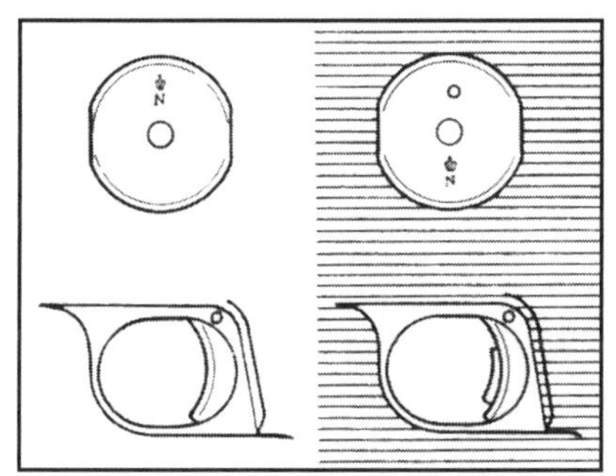

1 Slide cap and trigger details of Model 1930 (left) and Behorden Model pistols. Trigger safety of Behorden Model pistol extends from face of trigger. Cartridge signal pin protrudes from upper hole in slide cap of Behorden Model pistol when cartridge is in chamber.

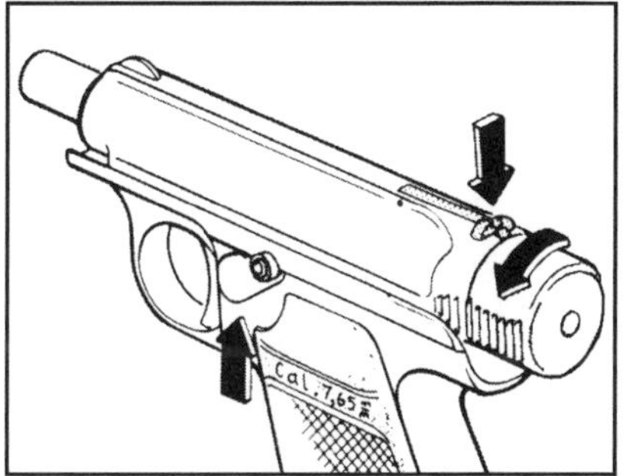

2 To disassemble Model 1930 pistol, first remove magazine and be certain chamber is unloaded. Pull back slide (1) about an inch until safety catch (29) engages slide. Depress rear sight and unscrew slide cap (4) from slide. Remove breech-block assembly (7). Then release safety and ease slide off front of frame.

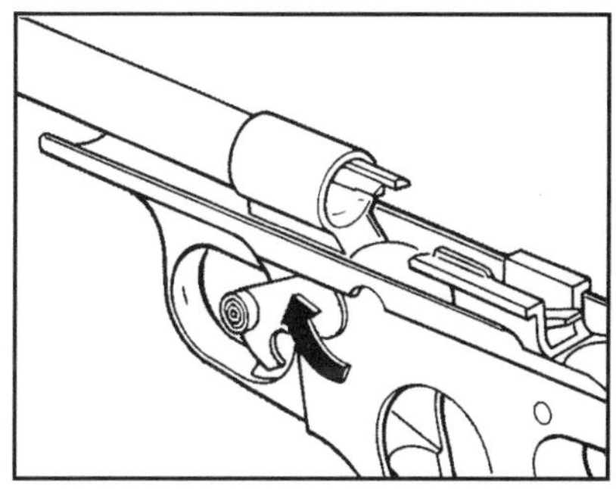

3 Safety catch should be removed before disassembling gun internally. First remove grips, then rotate safety catch 180 degrees until hinge pin portion is clear of undercut in frame. Do not let safety catch detent pin (27) and detent spring (28) fly out when safety catch is withdrawn. To replace, depress the safety catch detent pin with thin piece of brass and push into frame.

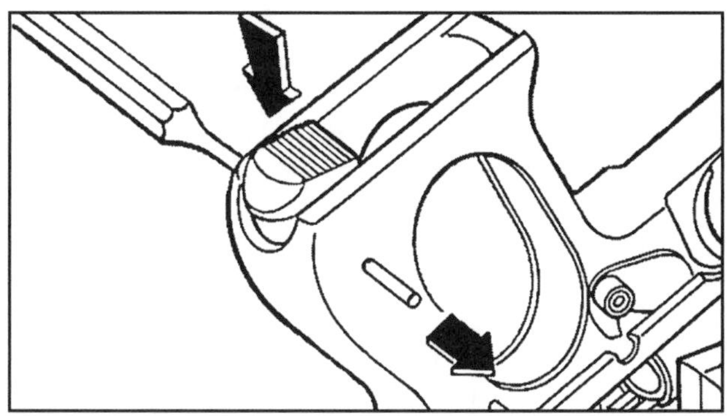

4 The pins in the Model 1930 Sauer pistol are tapered and should be removed from right to left. In reassembly, install mainspring (17), mainspring follower (16) and mainspring cap (18) last. Hold pistol in padded vise jaws and push in magazine catch. Use a thin punch to hold and align magazine catch (19) in frame while inserting magazine catch pin (20).

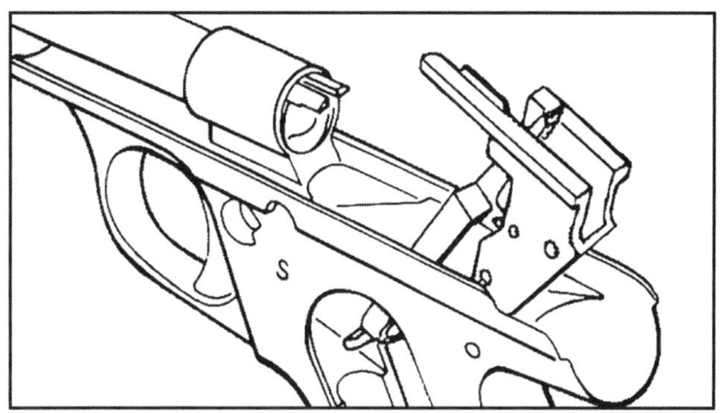

5 Mechanism housing (12) has several functions: ejector, cartridge guide, slide guide, and it also contains the sear mechanism. To remove unit, drive out lower and upper mechanism pins (25, 26) and lift free of trigger. Take care to prevent mainspring assembly (16, 17, 18) from flying out. To replace, be sure trigger bar and sear (11) are pointing down.

SAUER MODEL H (38) PISTOL

PARTS LEGEND

1. Slide
2. Rear sight
3. Breechblock
4. Cartridge indicator
5. Indicator spring
6. Spring retainer
7. Extractor
8. Block retainer pin
9. Safety catch
10. Safety detent spring
11. Safety detent
12. Firing pin
13. Firing pin spring
14. Right grip
15. Grip screw
16. Recoil spring
17. Trigger bar
18. Magazine safety retainer
19. Magazine safety bar
20. Safety spring
21. Hammer
22. Hammer strut
23. Hammer spring
24. Sear spring
25. Sear
26. Sear disconnector
27. Disconnector spring
28. Spring retainer
29. Frame
30. Magazine
31. Sear hinge pin
32. Hammer extension
33. Cocking lever spring
34. Hammer lever
35. Cocking lever
36. Lever hinge screw
37. Retainer ring
38. Left grip
39. Grip screw
40. Magazine catch screw
41. Magazine catch
42. Magazine catch spring
43. Trigger pin
44. Trigger bushing
45. Trigger
46. Trigger spring
47. Spring retainer
48. Detent spring
49. Takedown detent
50. Takedown latch
51. Latch crosspin

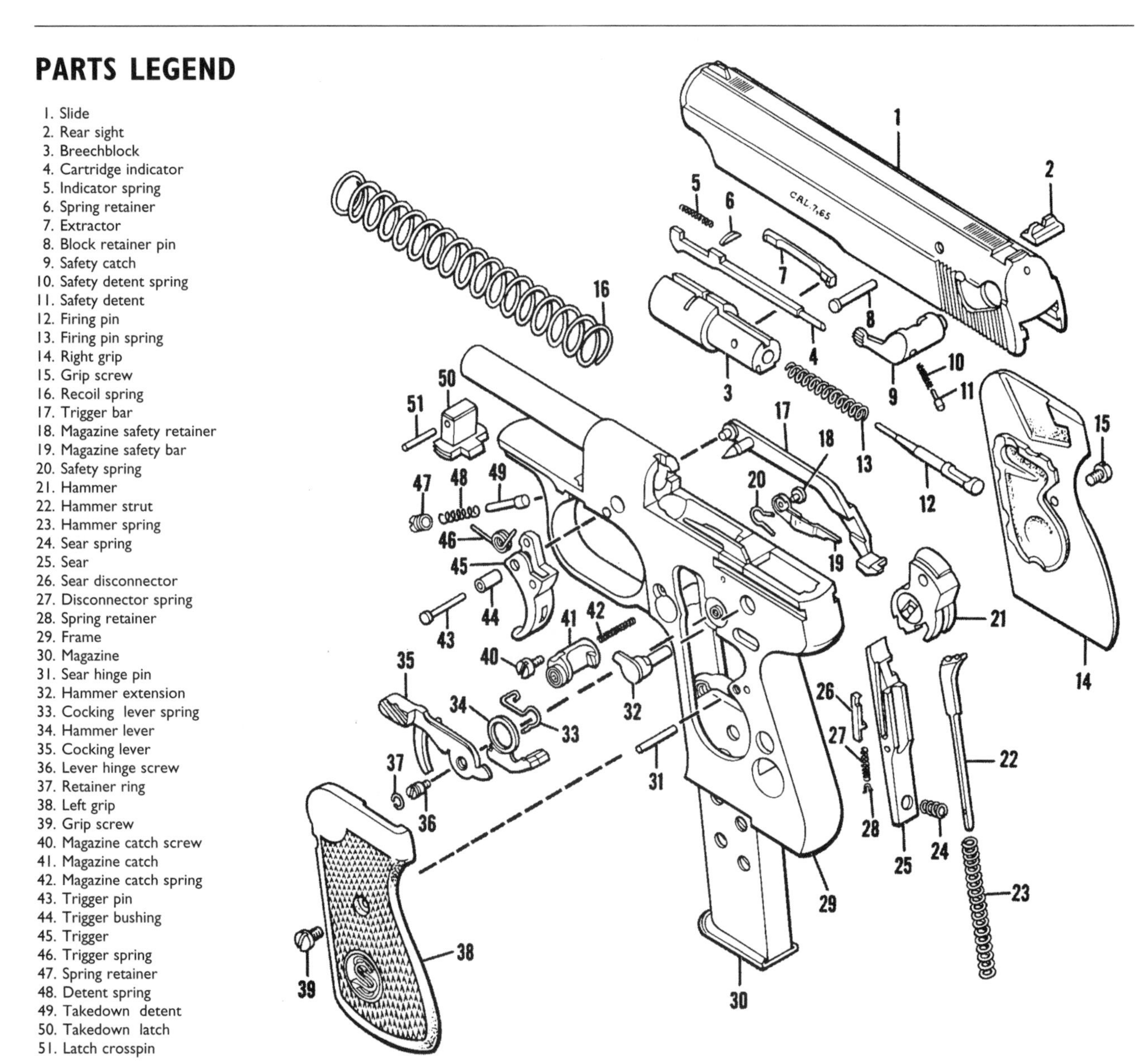

Except for short periods between wars, the German firm of J. P. Sauer & Sohn has been making fine guns continuously for more than 200 years. Beginning wth flintlock fowling pieces in 1751, they ended up in 1945 producing semi-automatic pistols and Mauser military rifles.

When the Russians occupied the German firearms manufacturing center of Suhl, they turned arms manufacture over to the Eastern Zone authorities. Production was resumed under a state cooperative called MEWA. The firms were given new names such as *Ernst-Thalmann-Werk* (C.G. Haenel), *Jagdgewehr-und Lehrenbau* (Greifelt & Co.), *Fortuna-Werk* (J.P. Sauer & Sohn). The Sauer management finally left the East Zone, and in March 1951, set up shop in Dusseldorf and Eckernforde in West Germany. They are currently making business machines, shotguns, and 3-barrel guns.

During the early 1930s, Walther startled the German gun trade with their double-action pistols. Not to be outdone, Sauer began work on the Model H. While retaining some of the lines of the old Sauer Behörden model, the new gun was designed for mass production. Many of the operating parts were stampings or die castings and machining of the slide was simplified by making the breech a separate piece and pinning it to the slide.

Unlike its contemporaries, the Model H, or Model 38 as it is better known, features an enclosed hammer. The internal hammer can be cocked for single-action fire. A lever allows the hammer to be eased down from full cock. If the lever is depressed when the hammer is cocked, it releases the hammer, allowing it to be lowered. Another feature is the indicator pin, which protrudes from the end of the slide when a cartridge is chambered. The Model 38 has two safeties: a magazine safety and a slide safety. The slide safety blocks the hammer and locks the trigger mechanism.

Like most late German pocket pistols, the Sauer Model 38 is found in two types — the pre-war gun with very fine finish and excellent workmanship, and the crudly finished but serviceable wartime product.

DISASSEMBLY

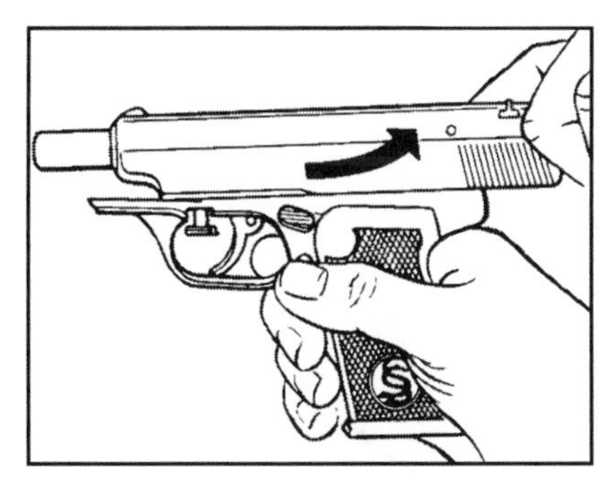

1 To disassemble, remove magazine and clear chamber. Pull down latch (50) in upper portion of trigger guard. Pull slide (1) to rear and lift it up. Ease slide forward off barrel.

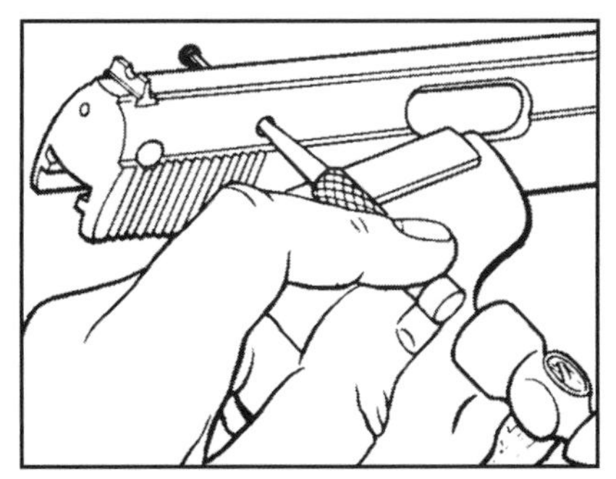

2 To remove breechblock assembly, drive out retainer pin (8). It must be driven from right to left. Breechblock can now be driven forward out of slide exposing firing pin (12), extractor (7), and cartridge indicator (4).

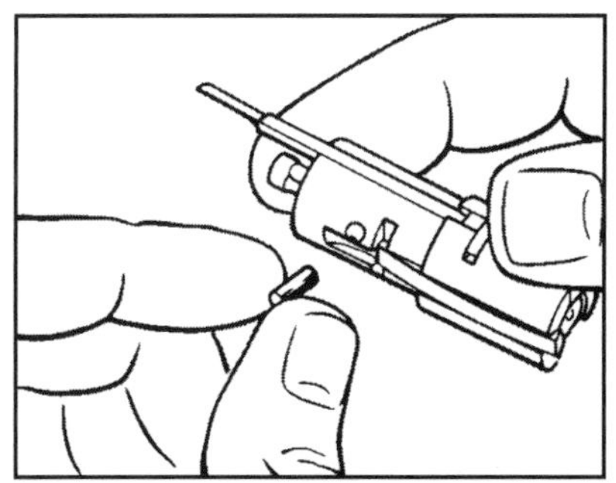

3 When reassembling breechblock, install extractor and indicator pin. Firing pin should be held in place by a short slave pin which is pushed out when retainer pin is driven in. This will prevent damage to spring and firing pin.

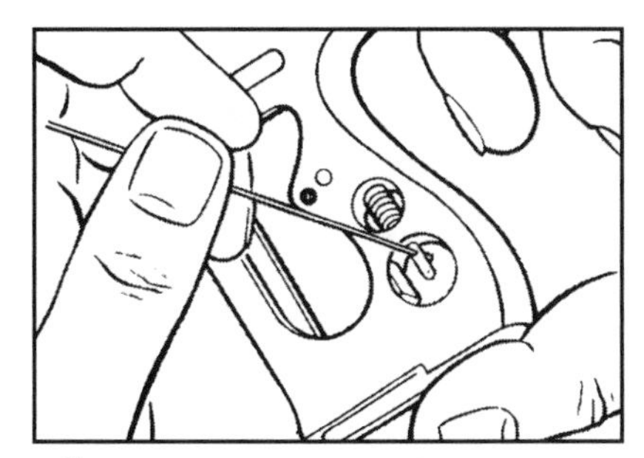

4 To disassemble sear mechanism, bring hammer back to full cock. Hammer strut (22) will extend through hole in frame exposing a small cross-drilled hole. Slip a piece of wire through to hold hammer strut and hammer spring. Sear mechanism can now be easily removed.

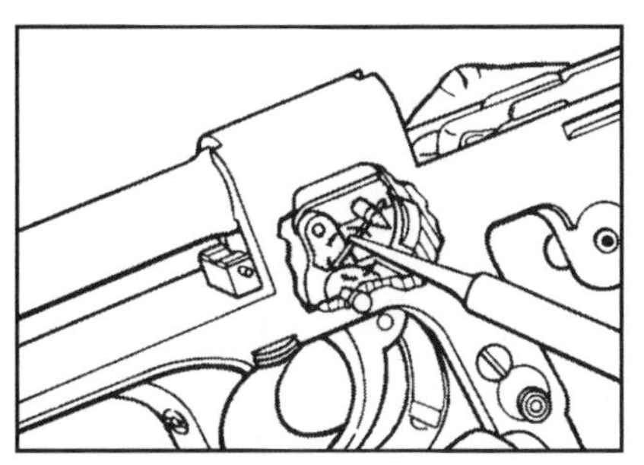

5 When trigger bar (17) is reinstalled, long tail of trigger spring (46) must push up on pointed pin on trigger bar. To do this, hold spring down with a thin punch thrust through large hole on left side of frame (29).

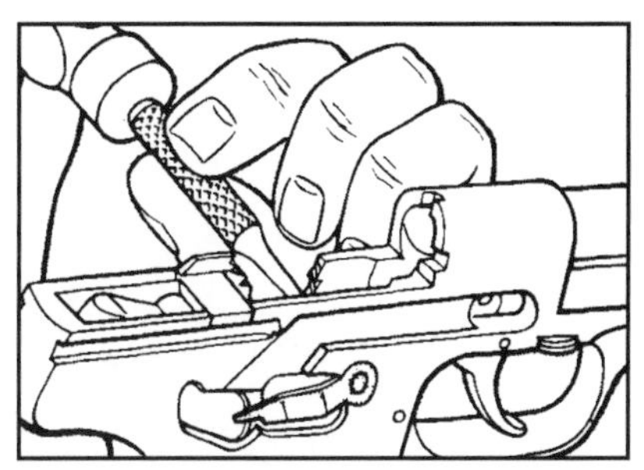

6 Magazine safety retainer (18) is staked to frame but sometimes it is necessary to remove it. To do this, hold gun in a vise and tap out from inside. It must be restaked when replaced.

SAVAGE MODEL 101 REVOLVER

PARTS LEGEND

1. Frame
2. Barrel & cylinder assembly
3. Front sight
4. Cylinder pivot pin
5. Detent housing
6. Detent plunger spring
7. Detent plunger
8. Cylinder pivot pin bushing
9. Firing pin
10. Firing pin spring
11. Recoil plate
12. Recoil plate retaining pin
13. Rear sight
14. Hammer
15. Hammer pin
16. Mainspring plunger
17. Mainspring
    17A. Mainspring trunion
18. Trigger spring plunger
19. Trigger spring
20. Trigger
21. Trigger pin
22. Ejector assembly
23. Ejector spring
24. Ejector rod assembly
25. Ejector tube
26. Ejector tube guide
27. Ejector tube plug
28. Ejector tube screw
29. Grip, right
    (left grip not shown)
30. Grip screws (2)
    (right screw only shown)

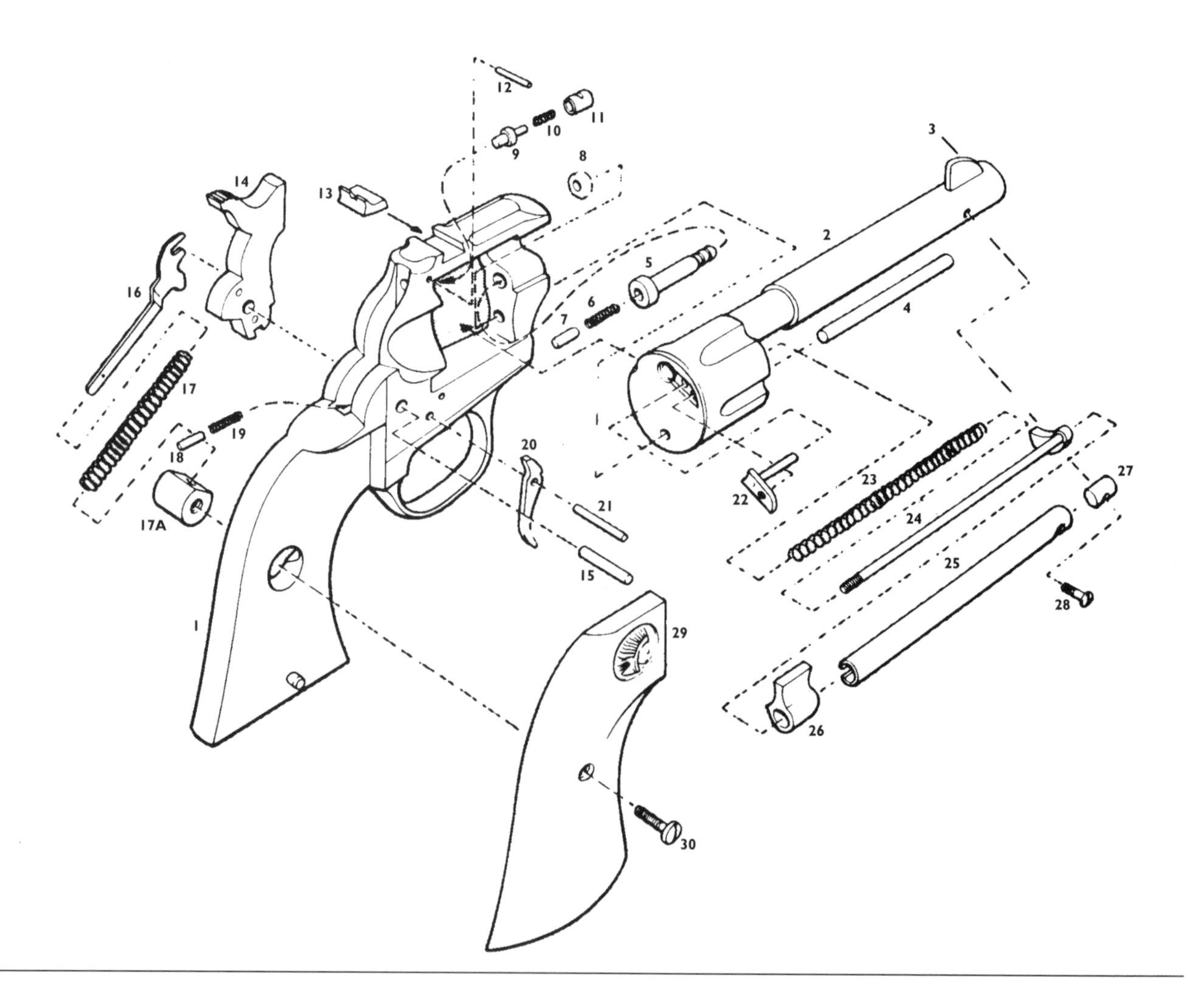

This inexpensive single-shot, .22 caliber pistol was introduced in 1960 and remained in production until 1969. It generally resembles the traditional frontier-type Colt Single-Action Army revolver, but the cylinder is actually a dummy and merely shrouds the rear end of the barrel. The barrel and dummy cylinder swing to the right to expose the breech for loading or ejection. The rod ejector is actuated by pressing a thumb button under the left side of the barrel near the muzzle. The hammer is of rebounding type. The Independent spring-loaded firing pin is pinned in the rear of the frame. The mainspring is of coil type.

The frame and dummy cylinder of the Model 101 are of die-cast alloy. The barrel and other parts are steel. The grips are laminated, walnut-colored wood, impregnated with plastic.

DISASSEMBLY

Check action to be sure pistol is unloaded. Remove grip screws (30) and grips (29) from frame (1). Drift out hammer pin (15) from left to right and drive mainspring trunnion (17A) out of frame from left to right. Remove mainspring (17), pull back on trigger (20), and lift hammer (14) out top of frame with mainspring plunger (16). Drift out trigger pin (21) from left to right, taking care not to allow escape of compressed trigger spring (19) and trigger spring plunger (18). Trigger (20) may now be removed from frame.

With barrel and cylinder assembly (2) in firing position, drift out cylinder pivot pin (4) toward muzzle by inserting punch through hammer slot in rear of frame. Remove cylinder pivot pin bushing (8).

To remove barrel and cylinder assembly from frame, follow procedure carefully. Do not rotate cylinder in frame after removing cylinder pivot pin. Take care to guide cylinder to allow detent plunger (7) to pass between dummy chamber holes in front face of cylinder. With detent plunger clear of cylinder, remove entire assembly from frame. Follow same procedure in reassembly of barrel and frame.

NOTE: If detent plunger (7) is allowed to enter any of the dummy chamber holes in front face of cylinder, it will be impossible either to complete disassembly or to reassemble barrel and cylinder assembly to frame without cutting or drilling out detent housing (5) in order to remove detent plunger (7) from front of cylinder.

After removing barrel and cylinder assembly from frame, withdraw detent plunger (7), detent plunger spring (6), and detent housing (5) to rear. Removal of firing pin assembly is accomplished by drifting out recoil plate retaining pin (12) and removing firing pin (9), firing pin spring (10), and recoil plate (11) to front. Ejector assembly is removed by unscrewing ejector tube screw (28) and separating ejector components after unscrewing ejector assembly (22) from ejector rod assembly (24). Reassemble pistol in reverse.

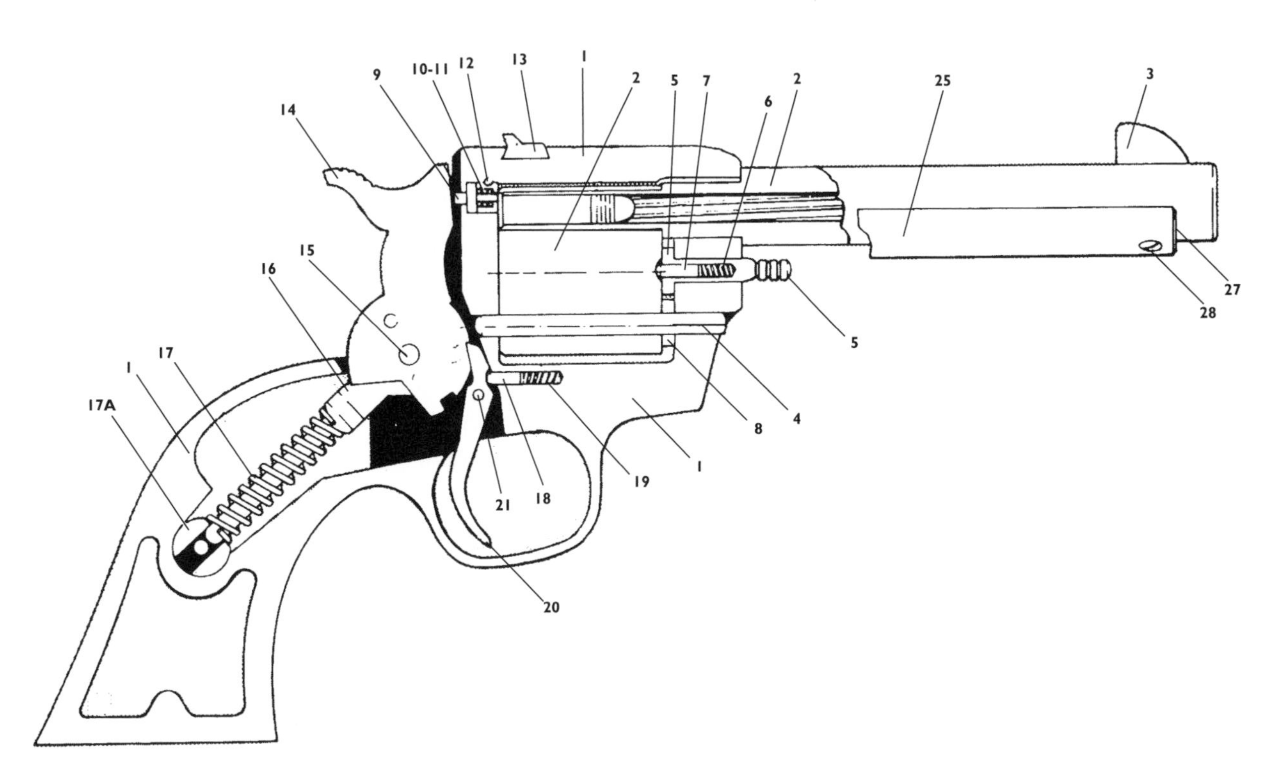

Principal components of the Model 101 single shot pistol are shown assembled in this sectional view. Note arrangement of detent housing(5), detent plunger spring (6) and detent plunger (7) through frame (1) with plunger bearing on detent depression in the front face of the cylinder (2).

SAVAGE MODEL 1910 PISTOL

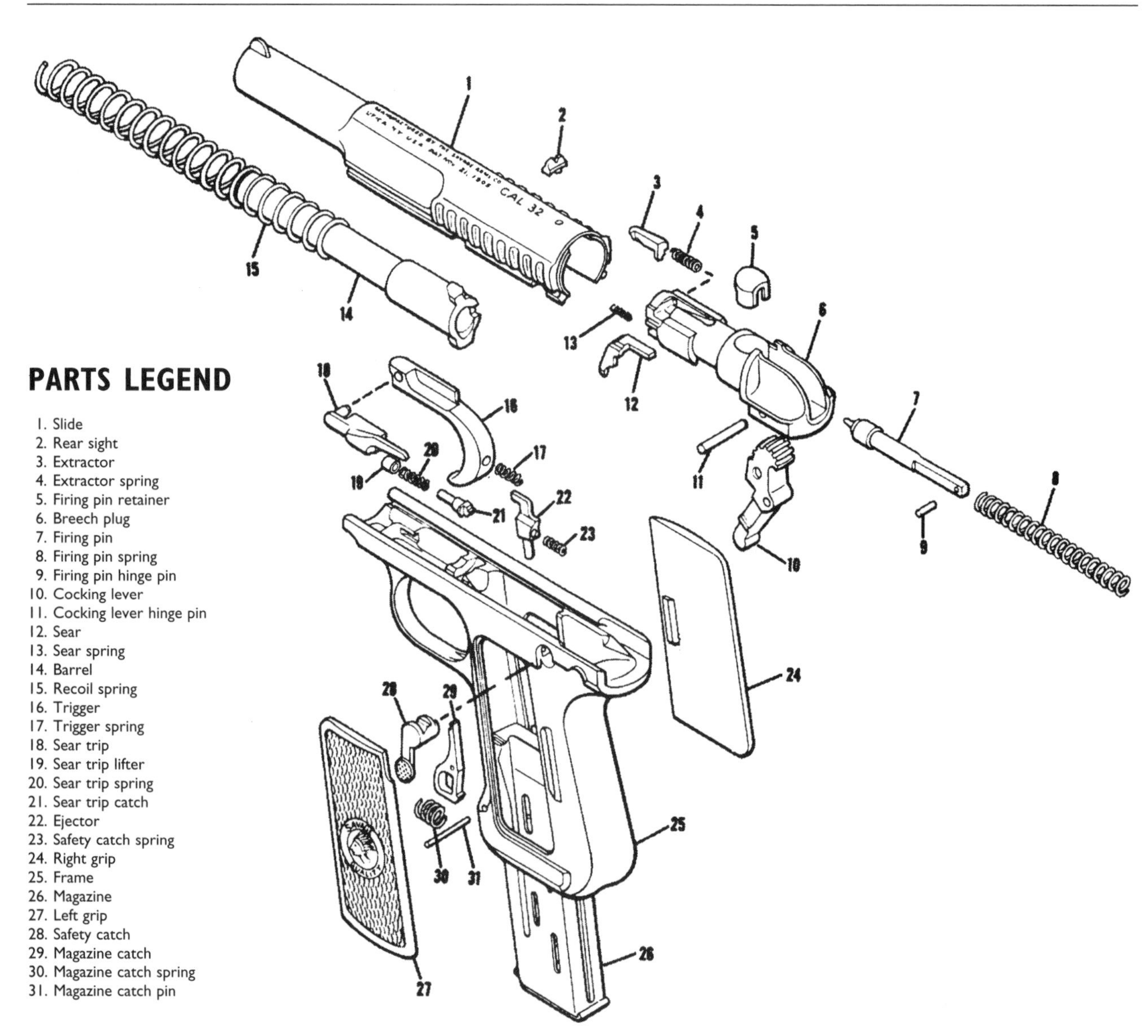

PARTS LEGEND

1. Slide
2. Rear sight
3. Extractor
4. Extractor spring
5. Firing pin retainer
6. Breech plug
7. Firing pin
8. Firing pin spring
9. Firing pin hinge pin
10. Cocking lever
11. Cocking lever hinge pin
12. Sear
13. Sear spring
14. Barrel
15. Recoil spring
16. Trigger
17. Trigger spring
18. Sear trip
19. Sear trip lifter
20. Sear trip spring
21. Sear trip catch
22. Ejector
23. Safety catch spring
24. Right grip
25. Frame
26. Magazine
27. Left grip
28. Safety catch
29. Magazine catch
30. Magazine catch spring
31. Magazine catch pin

The early 1900s was the golden age of automatic pistol development, with all leading American and European companies experimenting with both military and pocket types. The Savage Arms Co. was no exception, their first effort being a .45 ACP caliber pistol for the U.S. Army trials of 1907. At the same time they adapted E.H. Searle's locking system to a pocket pistol permitting the development of a light compact gun that lies low in the hand.

With the Searle system, the barrel has to turn as the breechblock moves to the rear. But while the bullet is going through the barrel, the work of spinning the bullet resists this rotation of the barrel, which helps to hold the breech closed until the bullet has left the barrel. In the .32 and .38 models there is no true mechanical lock.

The Savage has the largest magazine capacity of any early pocket pistol. The .32 model has a 10-round magazine capacity while the .380 has a 9-round capacity. The magazines hold the cartridges in a staggered double row, and are very strongly made.

In spite of its features and excellent workmanship, the Savage has its drawbacks. The unusual sear mechanism built into the breech plug does not have a half-cock position. Thus, the firing pin is either all the way forward or at full cock. This makes it, for practical considerations, impossible to carry the gun with a cartridge in the chamber and hammer down as the hammer is directly connected to the firing pin and the firing pin contacts the cartridge primer when the hammer is down.

If there is a round in the chamber, the only safe way to carry the gun is at full cock with safety catch on. Even though the trigger mechanism has a disconnector, if the trigger pull is lightened too much, or dirt and fouling build up between the sear and the breechblock, these pistols have been known to fire as the slide slams forward.

The gun illustrated is the 1908 type, more popularly called the Model 1910. It was made in .32 ACP and .380 ACP, in a number of variations. There were hammerless models, models with grip safeties and some with hold-open devices. In 1917 the gun was revised and the grip and hammer reshaped. These pistols are notable for their unsurpassed workmanship.

DISASSEMBLY

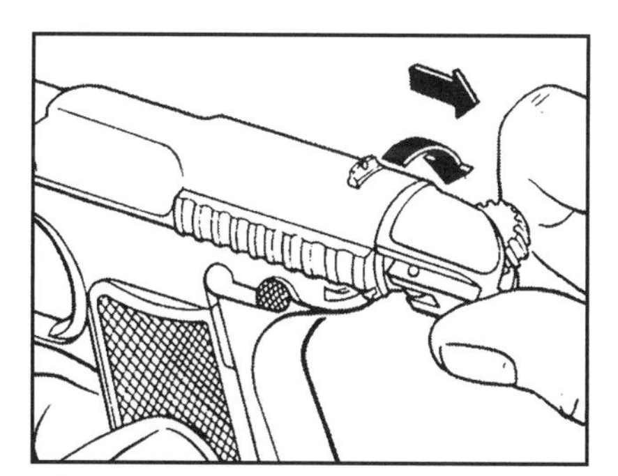

1 To take down the Savage, first remove magazine and clear chamber. Pull back slide and put safety catch (28) on. Grasp cocking lever and breech plug as shown, squeeze, and rotate plug ¼ turn. Plug assembly can now be pulled free of slide.

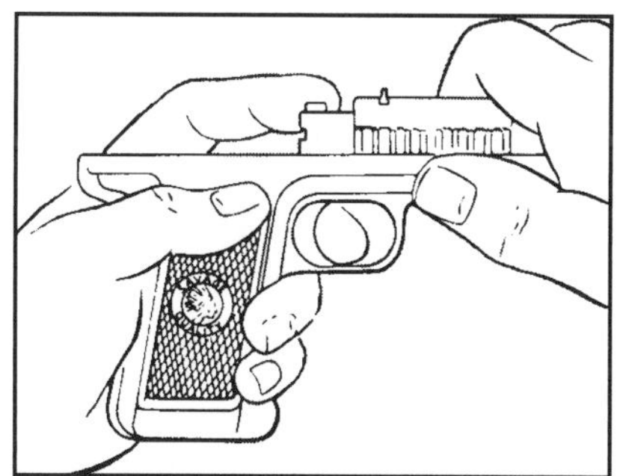

2 After removing breech plug (6), hold back trigger and release safety. Ease slide off front of frame (25); when reassembling, hold barrel as shown and push slide to rear until it can be held back by safety catch (28).

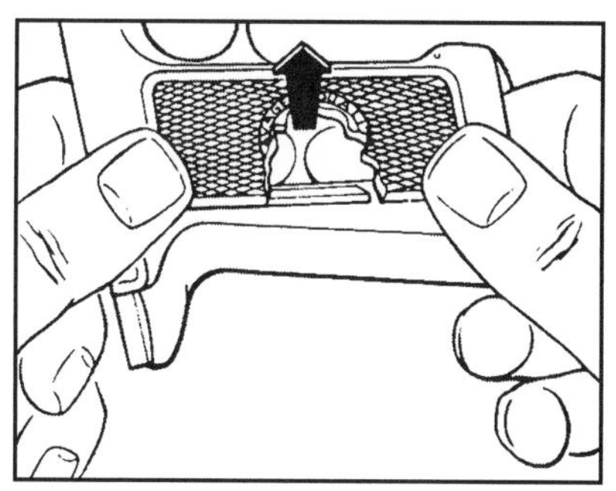

3 Grips are retained by dovetail slots in top and bottom of frame. To remove them, insert the first finger of each hand into magazine well as shown and push at center of grip. The resiliency of the hard rubber grip should allow it to snap out.

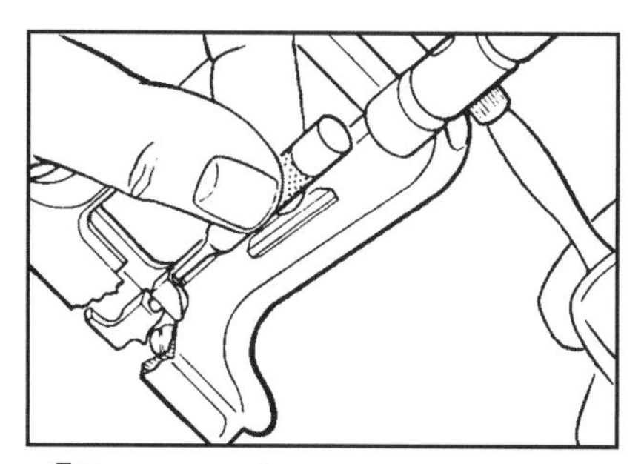

4 To remove safety catch (28), it is necessary to first drive out ejector (22). After grips are removed, insert a thin punch or nail set as shown, and gently tap ejector stem out. Put safety catch in "fire" position to prevent damage to safety catch spring (23).

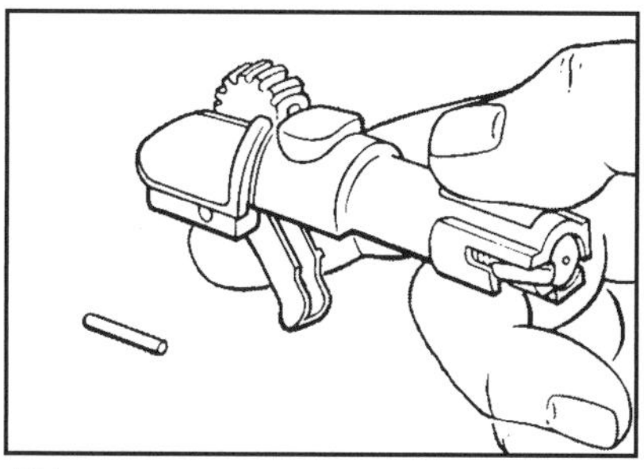

5 To disassemble breech plug (6), drive out cocking lever hinge pin (11). Then cock cocking lever (10) to raise firing pin retainer (5). Remove retainer and pull out cocking lever and firing pin assembly.

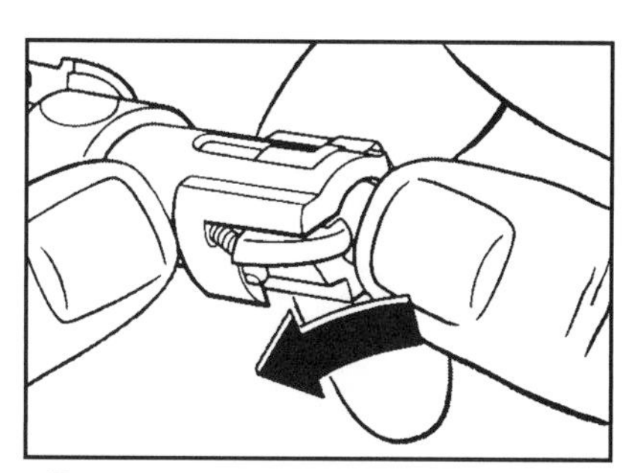

6 After cocking lever and firing pin assembly have been removed, rotate sear (12) upward so that its tail drops into breech plug hollow far enough to lift it out. Extractor (3) can easily be pushed out as shown.

SIG P-210 (M/49) PISTOL

PARTS LEGEND

A Front sight
B Slide
C Extractor
D Extractor spring
E Rear sight
F Firing pin spring
G Firing pin
H Firing pin retainer plate
I Extractor hinge pin
J Barrel
K Recoil spring assembly
L Slide stop operating spring
M Trigger spring
N Trigger hinge pin
O Trigger
P Trigger bar pin
Q Trigger bar
R Sear
S Sear pressure plate
T Sear and hammer housing
U Sear spring
V Hammer hinge pin
W Hammer
X Hammer strut pin
Y Hammer strut
Z Hammer spring
AA Spring retainer nut
BB Spring retainer lock nut
CC Sear hinge pin
DD Pressure plate stop pin
EE Magazine disconnector screw
FF Magazine disconnector
GG Grip screw
HH Grip, right
II Magazine catch pin
JJ Magazine catch
KK Magazine
LL Grip, left
MM Safety catch
NN Slide stop
OO Receiver

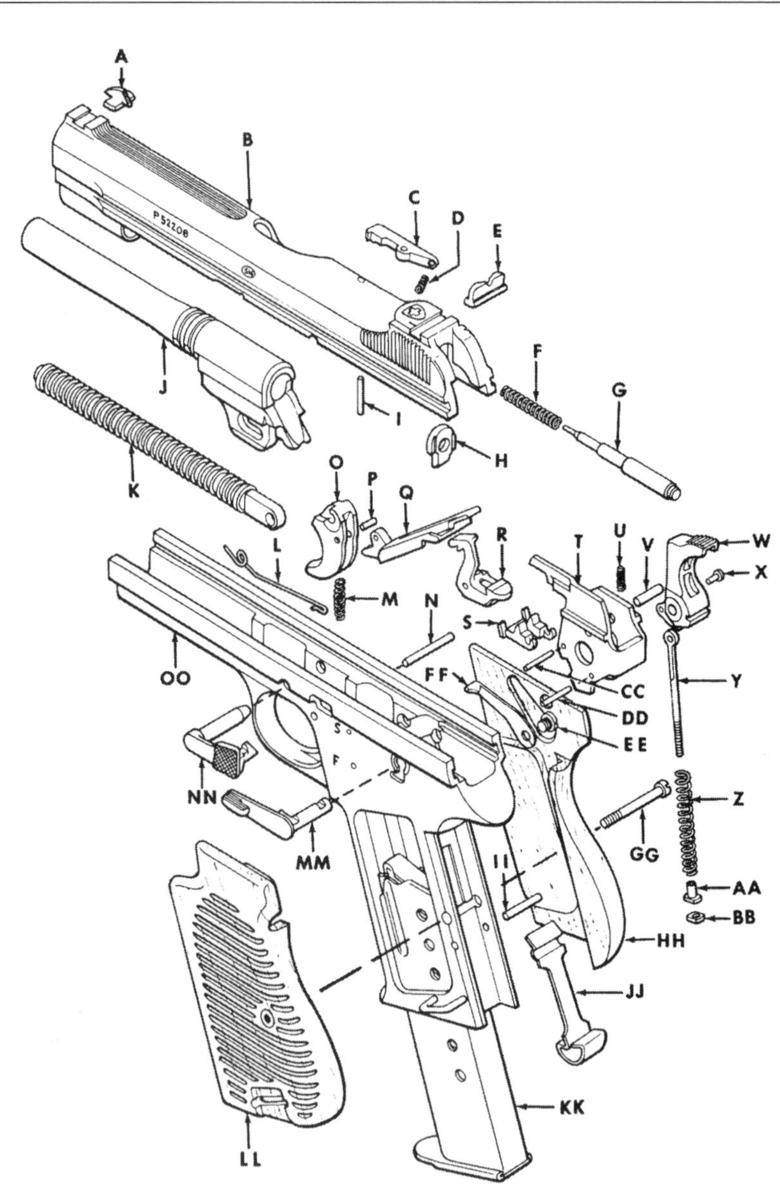

The same workmanship displayed in Swiss watches and machinery is carried over into the firearms they make. One of the most interesting of the latter is the SP47/8 SIG, known now as the SIG P-210. It was intended to replace earlier Luger pistols, revolvers, and other SIG designs. The pistol was designed by *Schweitzerische Industrie-Gesellschaft* (SIG) in Neuhausen/Rheinfalls, Switzerland. By the 1970s, SIG firearms had aquired the Swiss firm of Hämmerli Target Arms and J.P. Sauer & Sohn, of Eckernförde, West Germany and manufacture of the P-210 was transferred to a new firm, SIG-Sauer in the mid-1980s.

In 1949, the SIG P-220 was selected as the service sidearm of the Swiss Army (SIG M/49) and was adopted by the West German *Grenzschutz* (border patrol). The pistol was adopted for military and police use by Japan, Thailand, Nigeria and several other countries and was imported to the United States by Browning Arms and sold as the Browning BDA. Early SIG pistols were made in 9 mm Parabellum or 7.65 mm Luger. Small-bore conversion kits, consisting of a barrel, recoil spring, magazine, and lightened slide were available in 4 mm and .22 rimfire.

A quick glance at the P-210 suggests the Browning and P38 lines. An overall length of 8½ inches and a weight of 34½ ounces make the P-210 feel like a target pistol and it was noted for its accuracy. It is single-action with a magazine capacity of 8 rounds of 9 mm. The grips resemble those of the P-38 and the gun uses the Browning type of locked breech.

The sear, hammer and trigger mechanisms are entirely different from Browning or P-38 designs. A number of novel features are incorporated into this pistol. The slide is guided back and forth rigidly and accurately on long tracks that run the full length of the top of the receiver and the hammer and sear mechanism can be removed as an assembly for cleaning or repair.

The magazine release is located on the butt and is a simple, spring-loaded latch that holds the bottom of the magazine.

DISASSEMBLY

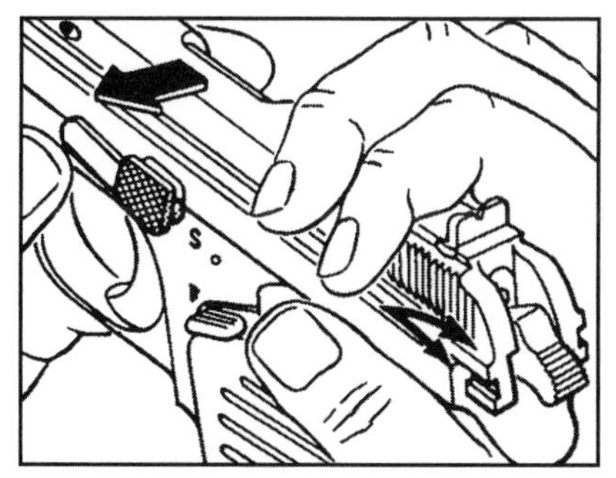

1 Remove the magazine (KK) and put the gun on safe. Grasp the gun with the right hand as shown, move the slide back enough to line up the first serration on the slide (B) with the edge of the receiver (OO). Now push the slide stop (NN) through from right to left.

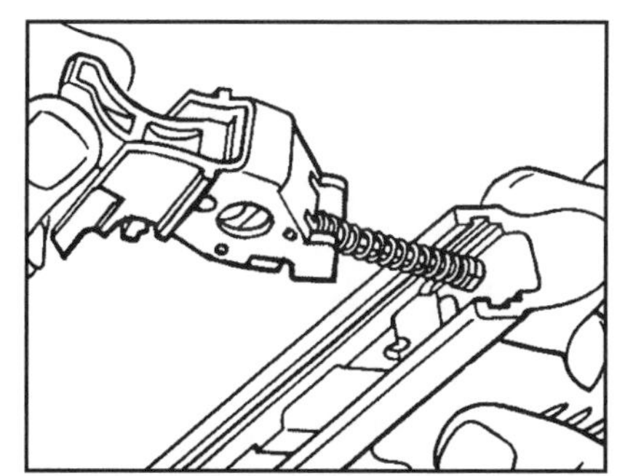

2 Strip the slide assembly off the receiver (OO). The sear and hammer assembly can now be lifted out as a unit. To strip this assembly, remove the hammer spring retainer (AA) and lock nut (BB) to relieve the tension on the hammer (W). Now pins (CC & DD), and (V) may be driven out if necessary.

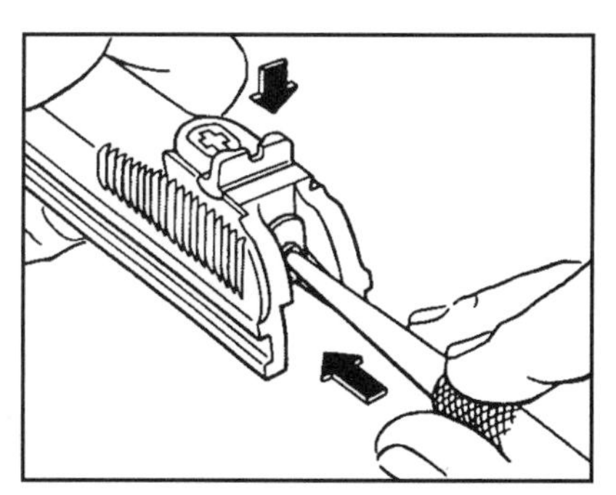

3 To remove the firing pin (G) and spring (F), it is necessary to depress the end of the firing pin below the surface of the firing pin retainer plate (H). Use the slide stop or a small diameter punch to depress the firing pin, then push the retainer plate down as shown.

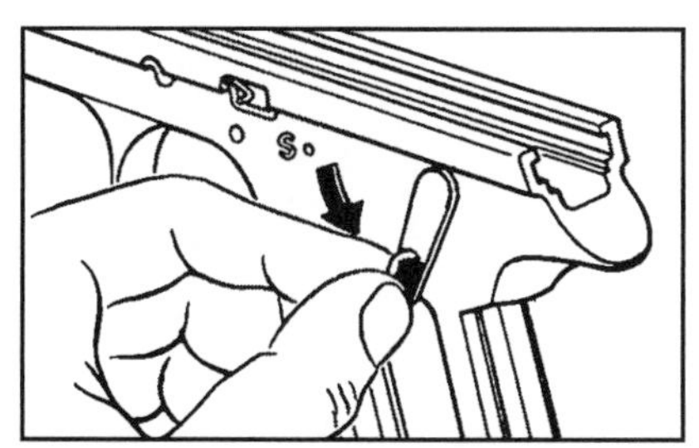

4 After removing the grips, (LL & HH), the safety (MM) can be rotated below the "F" engraved in the receiver until it springs free. It may be necessary to lift the safety out of the detent hole alongside the "F." before attempting to rotate it downward.

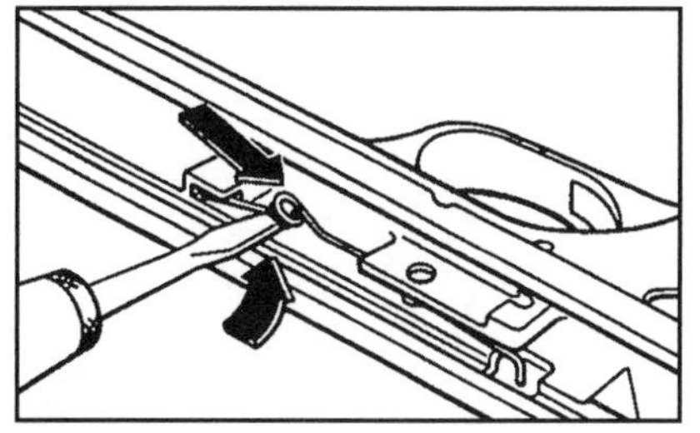

5 The slide stop spring (L) is the only part that is difficult to remove. It is necessary to pry it up and over the pin in the receiver as shown. Then push it toward the hammer until the end of the spring is out of its notch in the receiver.

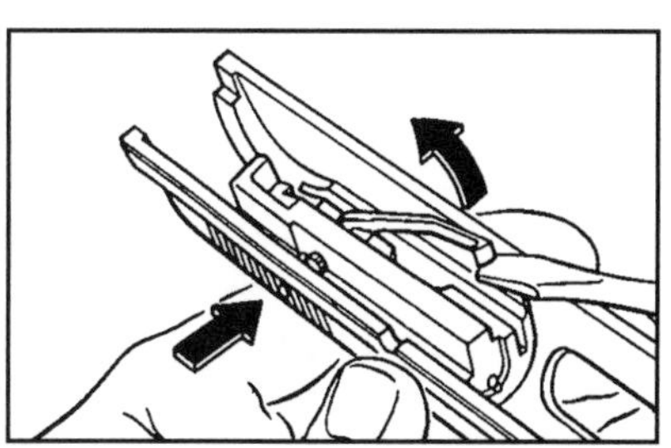

6 The extractor in the 9 mm. or 7.65 mm. can be removed by driving out pin (I). To remove the .22 conversion unit extractor, it is necessary to pry it up to a vertical position, as shown, to free it. With the aid of a thin punch, push the loose pin across the slide into the hole left by the extractor and the firing pin can be removed.

SIG SAUER P 226 PISTOL

PARTS LEGEND

1. Barrel
2. Recoil spring guide
3. Recoil spring
4. & 4B Slide
5. Front sight 05/06/07/08/09
6. Rear sight 05/06/07/08/09/10
   6B. Micrometre rear sight
7. Firing pin bolt
   7° Roll pin, heavy
8. Extractor spring
   8° Roll pin, heavy
9. Extractor bolt
   9° Breechblock
10. & 10° Extractor
11. Firing pin
12. Firing pin spring
13. & 13° Safety lock
14. & 14° Safety lock spring
15. Frame
16. Takedown lever
17. Locking insert
18. Slide catch lever
19. Slide catch lever spring
20. Trigger
21. Trigger pivot
22. Trigger bar
23. Trigger bar spring
24. Sear
25. Sear spring
26. Pivot, sear and safety lever
27. Roll pin, heavy
28. Safety lever
29. & 29C Hammer
30. Hammer strut pin
31. Hammer pivot pin
32. Ejector
33. Hammer strut
34. Mainspring
36. Mainspring seat
37. Hammer stop
38. Reset spring
39. Hammer stop pin
40* Decocking lever
41* Decocking lever bearing
42* Decocking lever spring
43. Magazine catch
44. Support plate
45. Magazine catch spring
46. Magazine catch stop
47. Catch stop spring
48. Grip plate, right
49. Grip plate, left
50. Grip plate screw
51. Magazine tube
52. Magazine spring
53. Feeder
54 Magazine floorplate
55. Floorplate insert

B = P 266 Sport
C = P 226 DAO
* = not for P 226 DAO
° = sheet metal slide

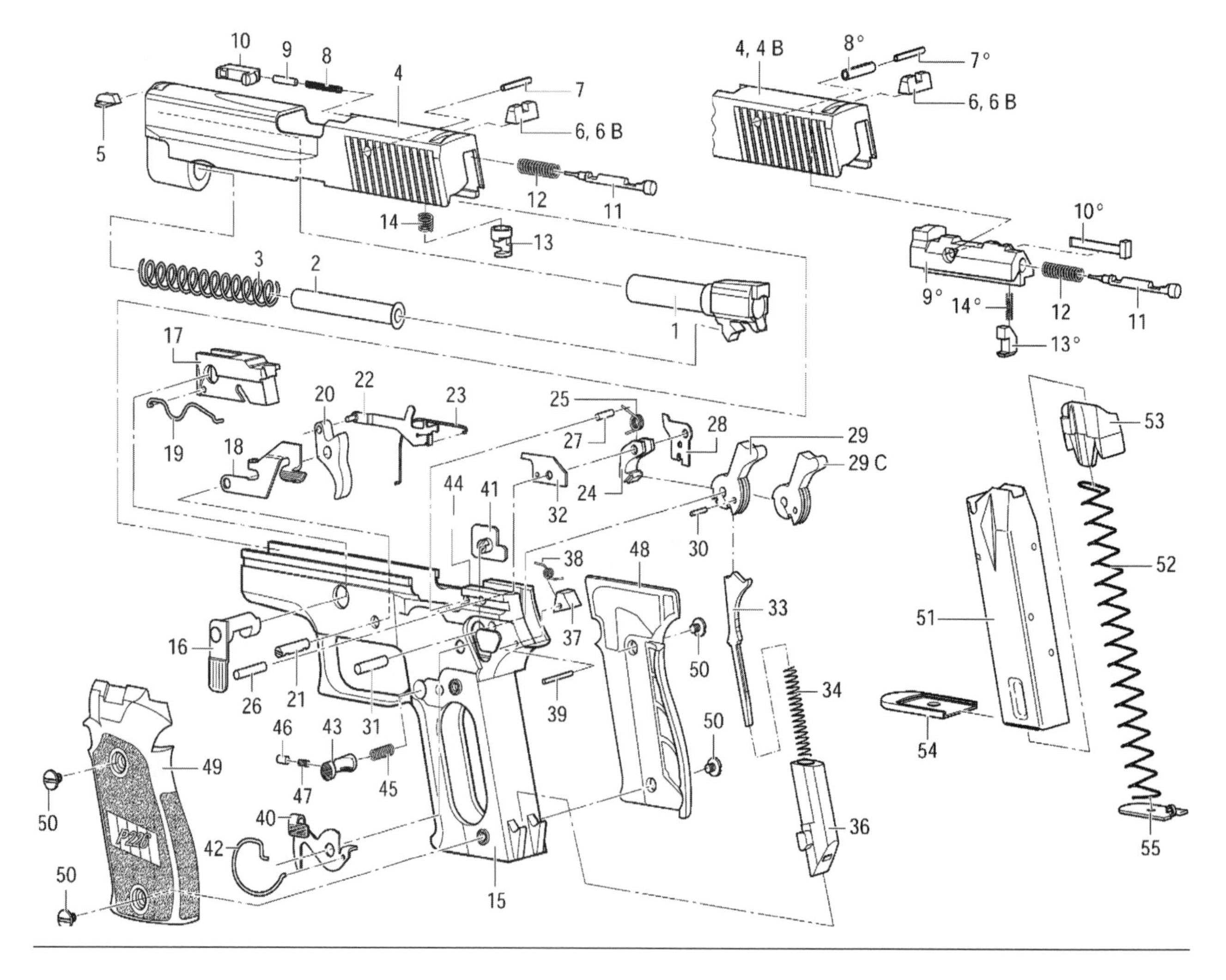

After twenty years of manufacturing the 9mm Parabellum SIG 210 series, directors of the *Schweizerische Industrie Gesellschaft*, (SIG) decided that manufacturing costs were becoming excessive and directed SIG designers to begin development of a new pistol. The new design would be primarily intended for export and was designed to be manufactured at lower cost using modern technology and extensive use of stamped and welded parts.

The new pistol, designated the P-220, was a double-action locked-breech semi-automatic, employing a de-cocking lever instead of a safety. SIG management entered into collaboration with the German firm of J.P. Sauer & Son in Eckernfoerde, Germany to manufacture the P-220 and the first pistols were produced in the mid-1970s.

The P-226 is basically the P-220 modified to accept a 15-round, double-column magazine. It pistol measures 7.7 inches overall and weighs 29 ounces.

The P-226 was planned for entry into the US Army's XM9 Service Pistol Trials in 1984. Only the Beretta 92F and the P226 satisfactorily completed the trials, but Beretta was ultimately awarded the contract for the new service pistol due to overall cost considerations. The P-226 is widely used by special forces world wide, including the British SAS and US Navy SEAL teams and by various police agencies.

DISASSEMBLY

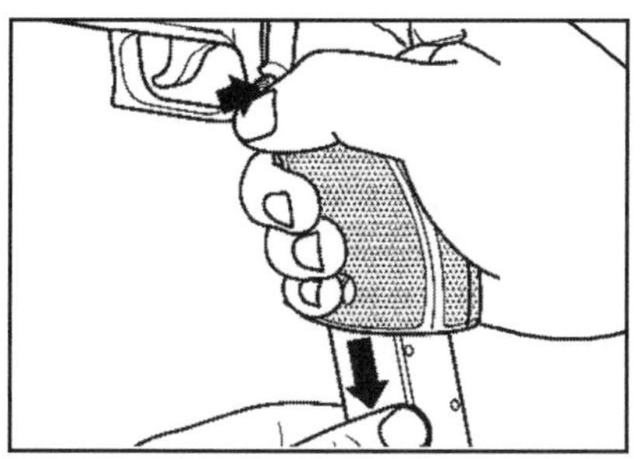

1 Press the magazine catch. Remove the magazine.

2 Pull back the slide (4) as far as it will go and hold it in the open position by pushing up the slide catch lever (18) with your thumb. Check carefully to ensure that the chamber is empty and the magazine well is clear.

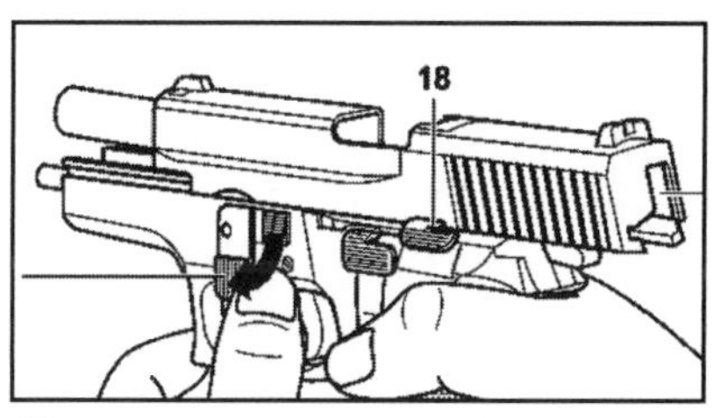

3 Turn the take-down lever (16) to a vertical (6 o'clock) position.

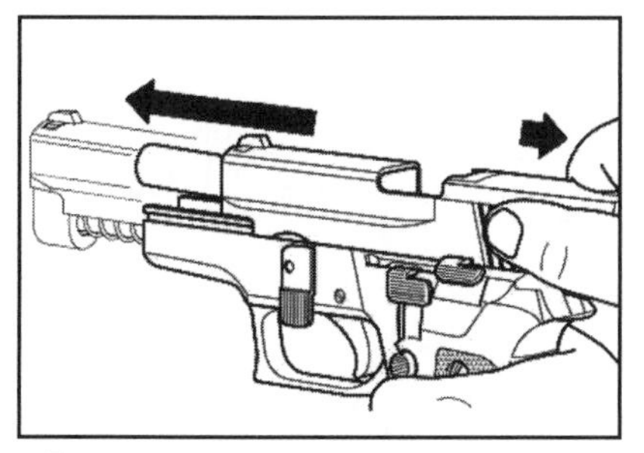

4 Pull back the slide slightly to disengage the slide catch lever. Hold the slide firmly and allow it to move forward slowly. Now slip the complete assembly, (slide, barrel, recoil spring and guide), forward and off the frame.

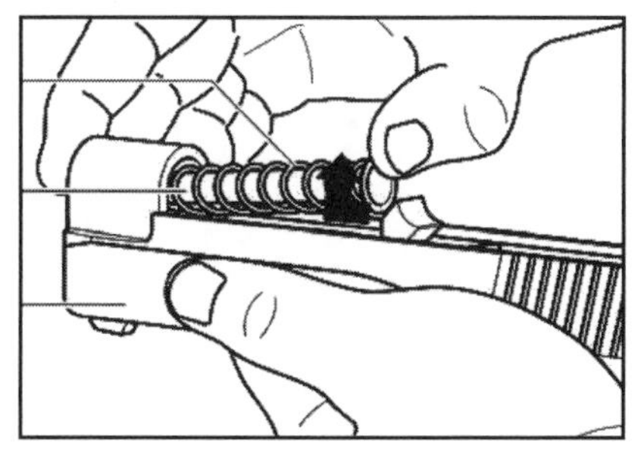

5 Remove the recoil spring (3) and guide (2), taking care to control the release of spring tension while pointing the assembly in a safe direction. Recoil spring is under tension – use care to control spring during removal!

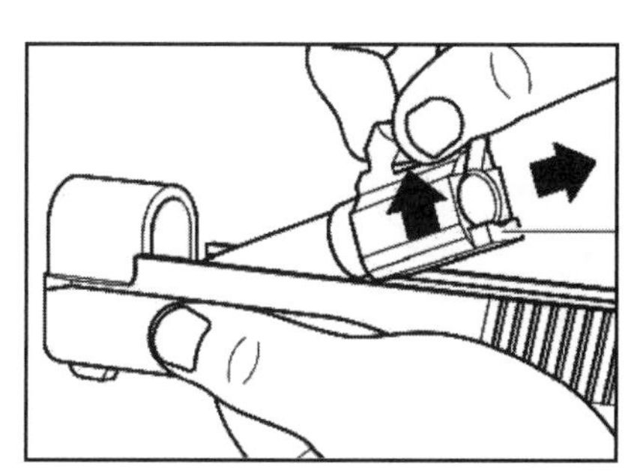

6 Remove the barrel (1) from the slide. CAUTION: Do not attempt to disassemble your pistol beyond this point.

SMITH & WESSON .35 AUTO PISTOL

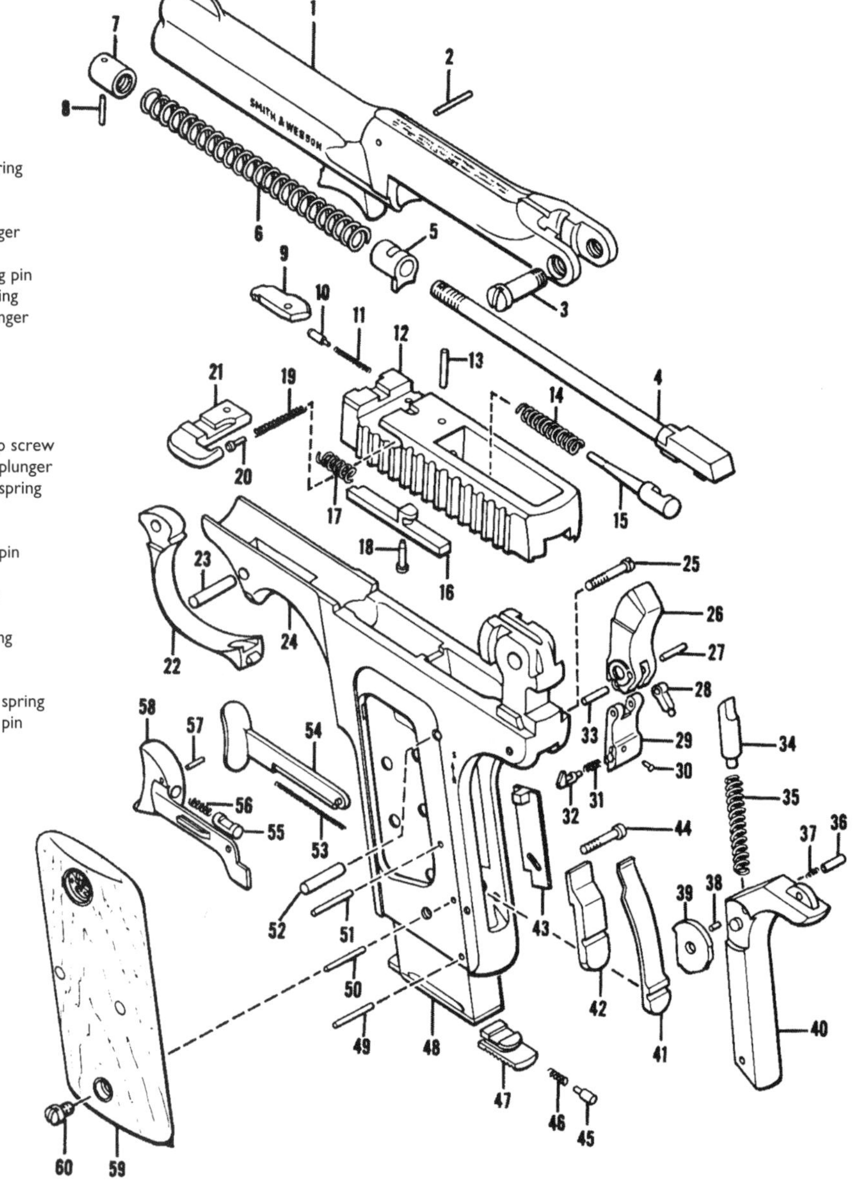

PARTS LEGEND

1. Barrel
2. Bushing retaining pin
3. Pivot screw
4. Recoil spring rod
5. Spring rod bushing
6. Recoil spring
7. Recoil spring cop
8. Cap retaining pin
9. Extractor
10. Extractor plunger
11. Extractor spring
12. Bolt (slide)
13. Firing pin retaining pin
14. Firing pin spring
15. Firing pin
16. Ejector
17. Ejector spring
18. Extractor pin
19. Bolt release catch spring
20. Bolt release catch spring plunger
21. Bolt release catch
22. Trigger guard
23. Trigger guard pivot
24. Frame
25. Upper backstrap screw
26. Hammer
27. Hammer strut pin
28. Hammer strut
29. Sear
30. Sear plunger pin
31. Sear plunger spring
32. Sear plunger
33. Sear hinge pin
34. Mainspring plunger
35. Mainspring
36. Plunger retaining pin
37. Safety catch spring
38. Safety catch plunger
39. Safety catch
40. Backstrap
41. Sear spring
42. Notch plate
43. Safety slide
44. Lower backstrap screw
45. Magazine catch plunger
46. Magazine catch spring
47. Magazine catch
48. Magazine
49. Magazine catch pin
50. Sear spring pin
51. Notch plate pin
52. Hammer pin
53. Grip safety spring
54. Grip safety
55. Trigger plunger
56. Trigger plunger spring
57. Trigger plunger pin
58. Trigger
59. Left-hand grip
60. Grip screw

In the early 1900s, pocket pistols were selling like "hotcakes." Most of the larger American gun companies were producing a variety of -25, .32, and .380 caliber automatics. About 1913, Smith & Wesson brought out not only a new gun, but a new cartridge, as well. The pistol was based on a patent by C. P. Clement of Belgium, and, like other Smith & Wesson products, was beautifully made and finished.

Unfortunately, the design had less to recommend it than those of its foreign and American contemporaries. For instance, while the gun had numerous safety features, the two main safeties were awkwardly placed. The manual safety is a small wheel which projects from the backstrap, making it almost impossible to remove or apply when the pistol is held in firing position.

The recoil spring disconnecting catch is novel but cumbersome. Since the slide is very light, a heavy recoil spring is needed to snub its high recoil speed. This makes the gun very difficult to cock. Therefore the gun was so made that by pressing the catch on the slide crosswise, the recoil spring is disconnected from the slide. Then the internal hammer can be cocked and a fresh cartridge chambered without working against the heavy recoil spring. In spite of its famous name, and the flawless workmanship, only a little over 8,000 pistols were sold between 1913 and 1921, when production ended.

DISASSEMBLY

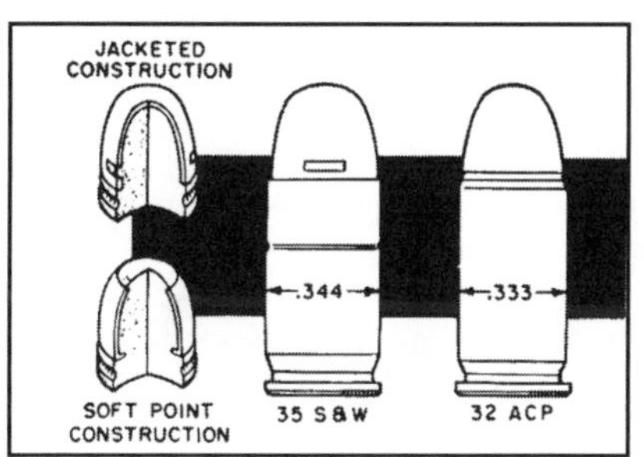

1 Except for the unusual construction of the bullets and the few thousandths increase in diameter, the .35 Smith & Weson cartridge could pass for a .32 automatic. The idea was to make a jacketed bullet that would operate through a magazine without deforming, yet have only the lead touch the rifling to decrease barrel wear. Ballistically, the .32 ACP is a bit more powerful.

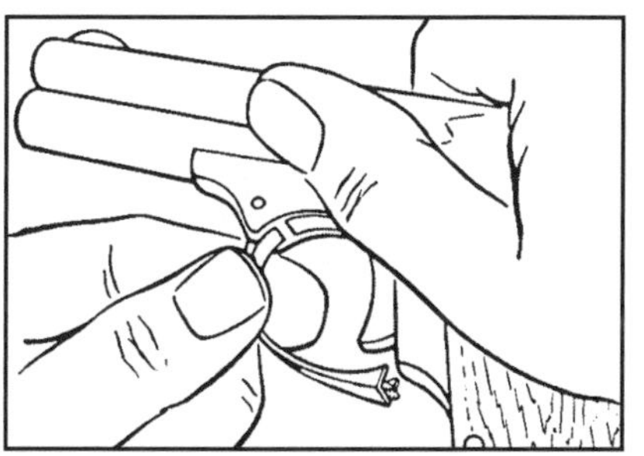

2 The takedown system is the best feature of the Smith & Weston .35 automatic. Simply pull down on the rear of the trigger guard as shown. When free, swing it forward and lift up the front end of the barrel. The gun can then be cleaned from the breech without fear of losing any parts.

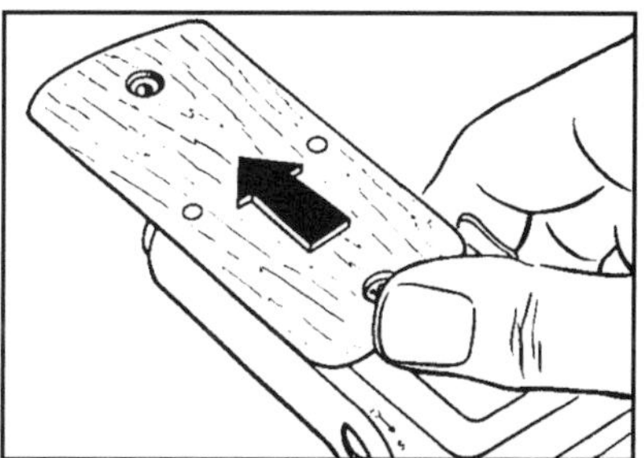

3 Unlike most pocket pistols, when the grip screws (60) are removed, the grips (59) remain fixed tightly to the frame. Since they are riveted to a metal plate that is dove-tailed into the frame, the grip (59) must be pushed off as shown. Never try to pry them free; it will ruin them.

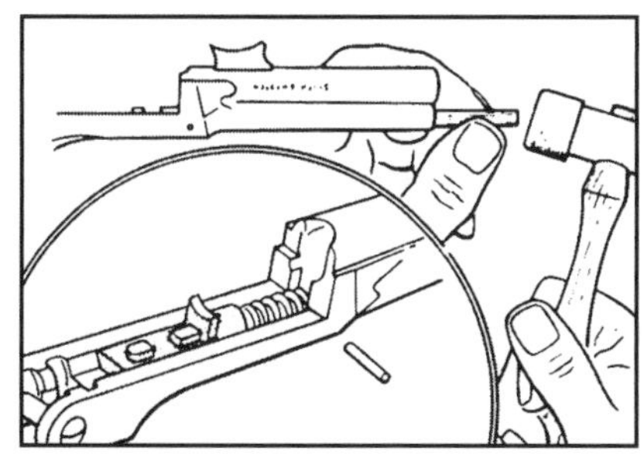

4 Since the recoil spring (6) is part of a captive assembly, it cannot fly out when the bushing retaining pin (2) is removed. When removing the spring rod bushing (5), replace the pivot screw (3) to prevent the assembly being damaged when it is driven out. Then, with a wooden dowel, drive the assembly out as shown.

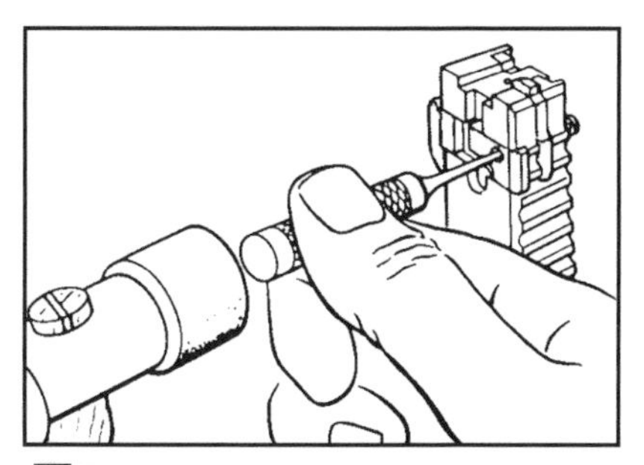

5 The extractor pin (18) is the key to the bolt (12) takedown. It must be driven out through the hole in the bolt release catch (21) with a thin punch. With this pin out, the extractor (9), its spring (11) and plunger (10), and the bolt release catch (21) with its spring (19) and plunger (20), will be free.

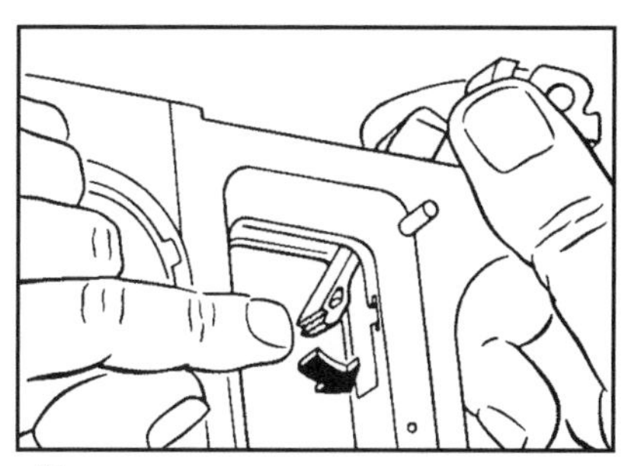

6 After the hammer (26) and sear (29) have been pinned together, insert the hammer into the frame through the magazine opening. Insert the hammer pin (52) and swing the sear back into the frame as shown. Do not try to insert the assembly through the backstrap opening.

SMITH & WESSON MODEL 29

PARTS LEGEND

1. Escutcheon
2. Escutcheon nut
3. Rear sight slide
4. Rear sight assembly
5. Sear pin
6. Rebound slide
7. Bolt plunger spring
8. Extractor pin
9. Extractor rod collar
10. Extractor spring
11. Hammer nose rivet
12. Hammer nose bushing
13. Hand pin
14. Locking bolt spring
15. Mainspring
16. Plate Screw, crowned
17. Hand spring pin
18. Hand spring torsion pin
19. Stirrup pin
20. Trigger lever pin
21. Sear spring
22. Stirrup
23. Stock pin
24. Strain screw
25. Thumbpiece nut
26. Trigger lever
27. Rebound slide spring
28. Trigger stud
29. Cylinder stop stud
30. Rebound slide stud
31. Rebound slide pin
32. Plate screw, flat head
33. Rear sight elevation nut
34. Rear sight spring clip
35. Rear sight elevation stud
36. Rear sight windage nut
37. Rear sight windage screw
38. Hammer stud
39. Sear
40. Hand spring
41. Rear sight leaf screw
42. Rear sight leaf
43. Trigger stop rod
44. Cylinder stop
45. Bolt plunger
46. Hammer nose
47. Hammer
48. Hammer block
49. Hand
50. Locking bolt
51. Side plate
52. Locking bolt pin
53. Extractor
54. Extractor rod
55. Center pin spring
56. Frame
57. Yoke
58. Bolt
59. Thumbpiece
60. Hammer nose spring
61. Barrel pin
62. Trigger
63. Cylinder
64. Barrel
65. Gas ring
66. Right stock
67. Left stock
68. Frame lug
69. Cylinder stop spring
70. Rear sight plunger
71. Rear sight plunger spring
72. Center pin
73. Stock screw

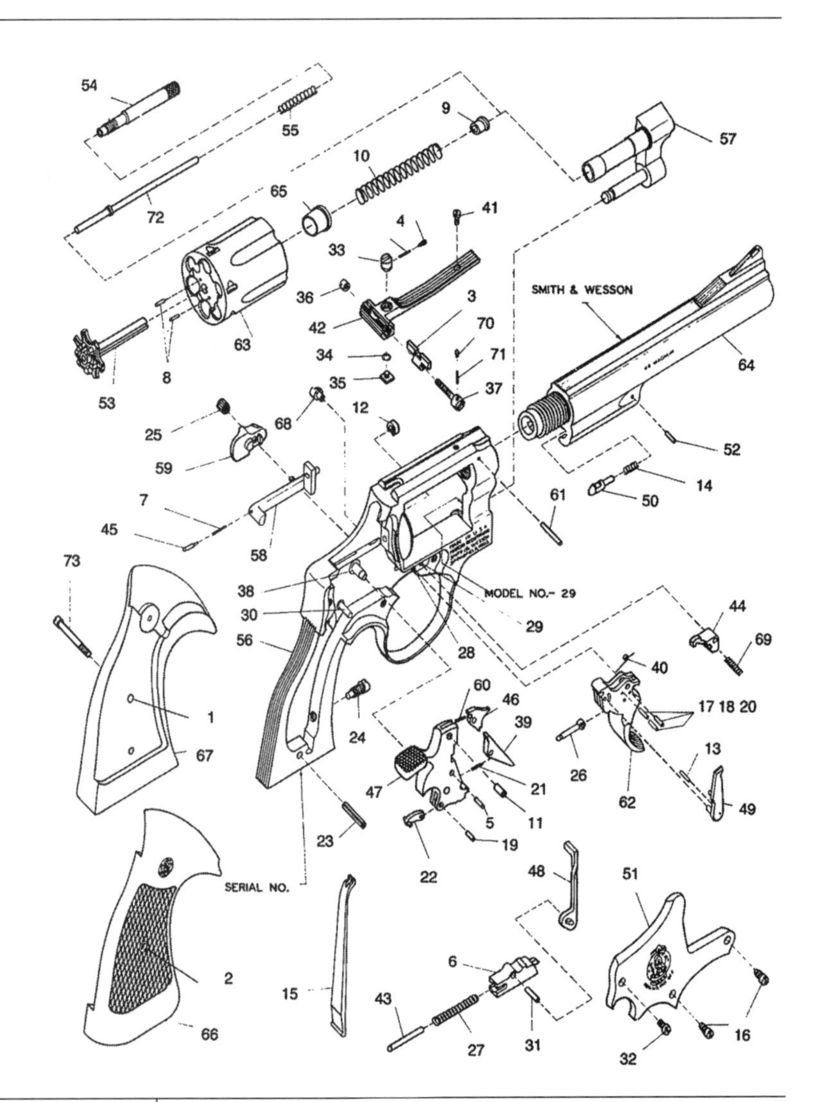

Shortly after World War II, experimenters developed ever more powerful loads for the .44 Spl. cartridge. It was natural that a more powerful counterpart to that round should emerge, just as the .357 Mag. had evolved from the .38 Spl.

Smith & Wesson and Remington agreed to take the plunge, and on December 29, 1955, the first .44 Magnum revolver was completed. The earliest models were available in blue or nickel finish, with 4- or 6-inch barrels. S&W was flooded with requests for a long-barreled .44 Mag., and in 1958, a drawing for an 8-inch barrel was completed. Production on the long-barrel version started soon thereafter.

The Model 29 commanded premium prices during the mid l970s after it was featured in the popular film *Dirty Harry*, making it among the most popular of S&W's many revolvers.

DISASSEMBLY

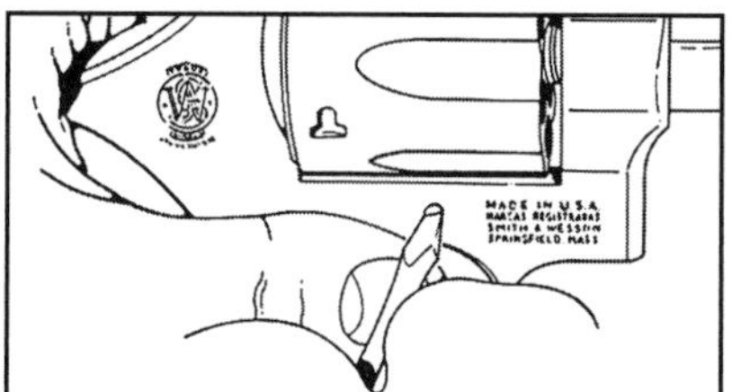

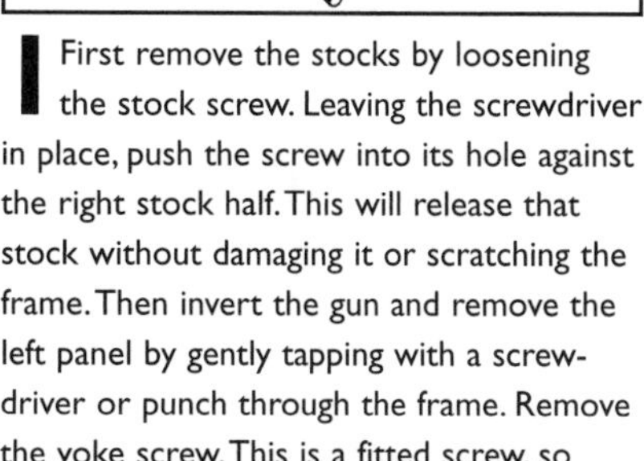

1 First remove the stocks by loosening the stock screw. Leaving the screwdriver in place, push the screw into its hole against the right stock half. This will release that stock without damaging it or scratching the frame. Then invert the gun and remove the left panel by gently tapping with a screwdriver or punch through the frame. Remove the yoke screw. This is a fitted screw, so keep it separate by placing it in a hole in one of the stock halves.

Remove yoke and cylinder by opening the cylinder and placing the gun on its right side. Hold the cylinder in its open position while drawing the yoke forward out of the frame.

2 Insert a dummy cartridge in one of the charge holes to protect the extractor pins, then grasp the extractor rod in a vise. Now turn the cylinder clockwise to unscrew the extractor rod. Model 29s and other N-frame revolvers made before 1960 have a right-hand thread, so the cylinder should be turned counterclockwise.

Remove round head side-plate screw and flat head side-plate screw. The flat head screw fits under the stocks. Then loosen the side-plate by tapping the side of the backstrap with a nylon hammer. Hold the front of the side-plate to prevent dropping it.

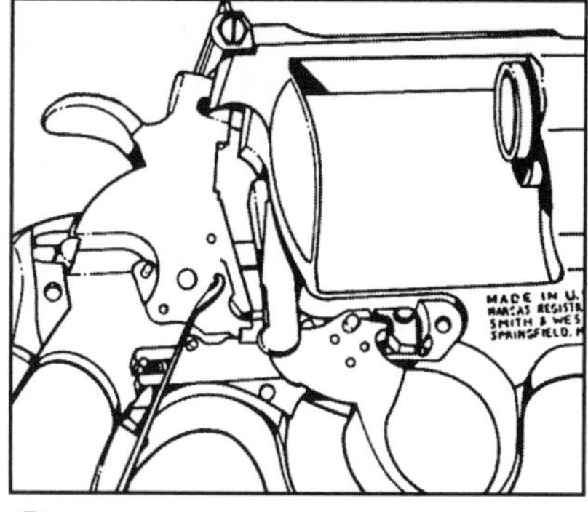

3 The hammer block will likely drop out when you remove the side-plate, as it rides in a slot on the side-plate. If it doesn't, remove it. Loosen the mainspring strain screw in the frontstrap. Then the foot of the mainspring can be pushed to the right and removed (Fig. 3).

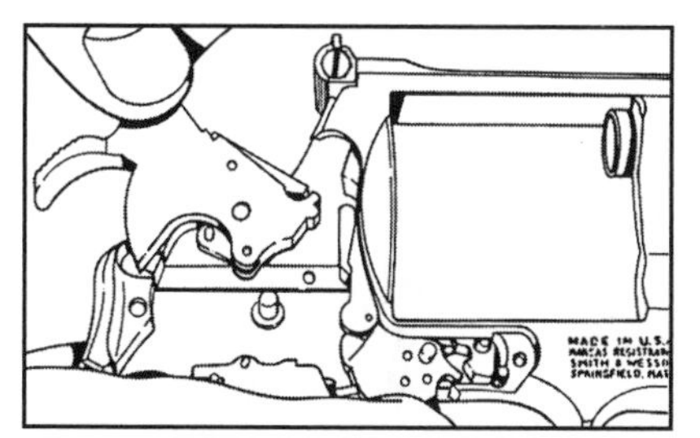

4 Push the thumbpiece bolt to the rear and pull the trigger to its full rearward position. This will cock the hammer. While holding the trigger rearward, lift the hammer straight out of the frame (Fig. 4).

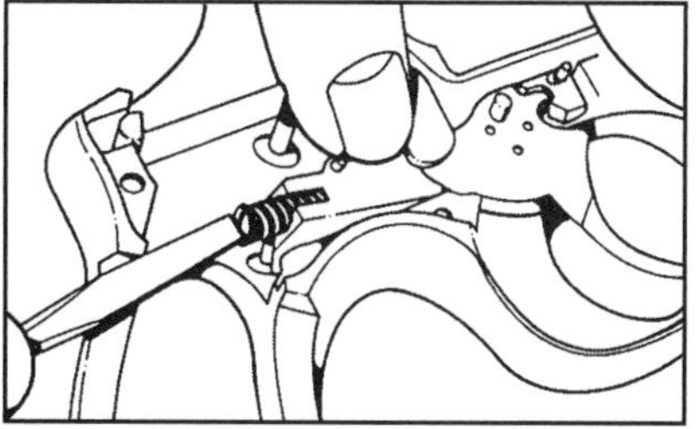

5 Remove the rebound slide and spring by raising the slide halfway up on the stud with a screwdriver. Change the position of the screwdriver to the flat edge and push in on the spring. Allow the spring to release slowly. Note that the screwdriver and finger prevent the spring from flying off.

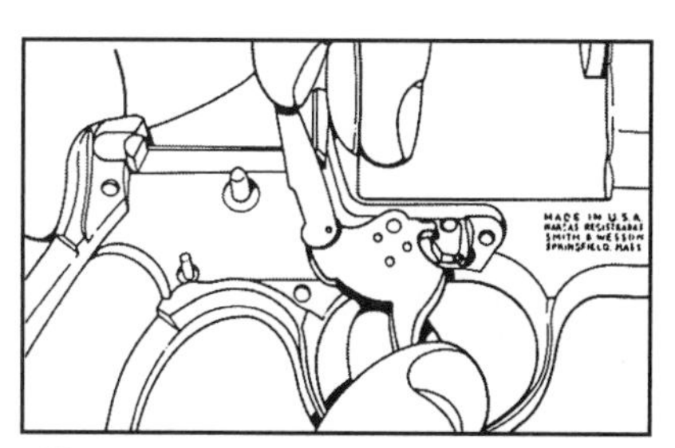

6 To remove the trigger and hand, use the left index finger to hold the hand out of the slot in the frame while the thumb and middle finger of the right hand lift the trigger straight off the trigger pin.

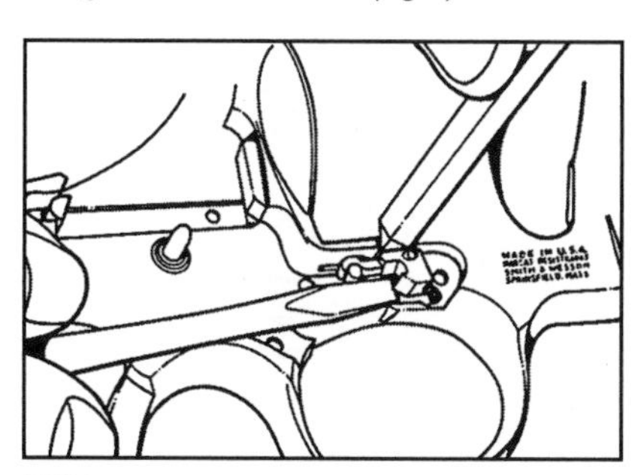

7 Push the cylinder stop down from the top, then use a drift pin to hold it down while the screwdriver lifts it straight up off its pin. Be careful to keep the spring from flying off. The adjustable sight can be removed by removing the screw at the front of the sight leaf and sliding the assembly to the rear.

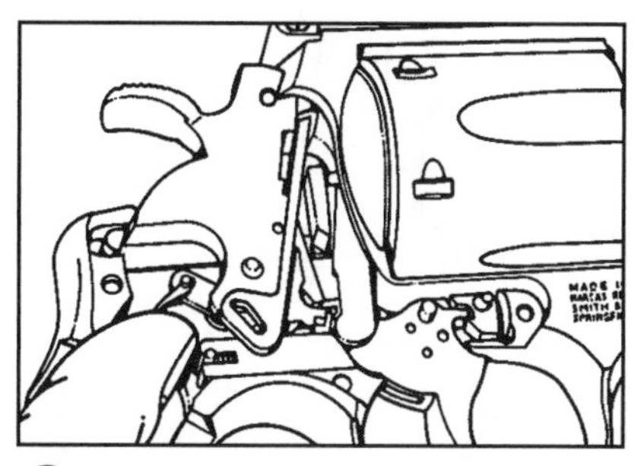

8 Reassemble in reverse order. Be sure the trigger lever is inside the frame and can be inserted into the front of the rebound slide assembly. Hold the trigger rearward when installing the hammer. Hook the top of the mainspring on the hammer stirrup first, then slide its foot into the frame and tighten the strain screw. Be sure the hammer block is in its up position. Install the side-plate front and top undercuts first, then seat it by tapping lightly with a nylon hammer on the screw holes.

SMITH & WESSON MODEL 39

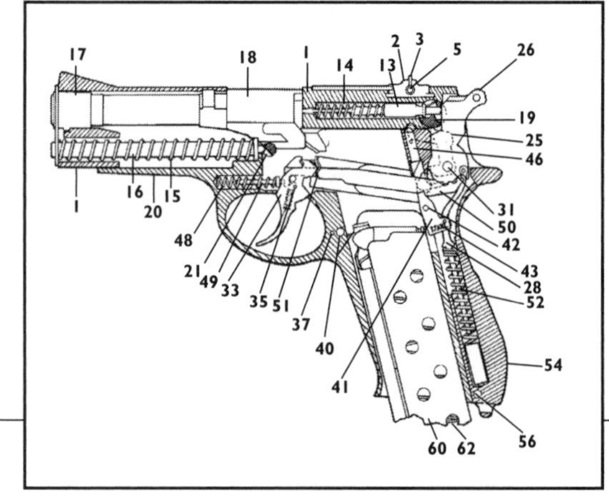

PARTS LEGEND

1. Slide
2. Rear sight leaf
3. Rear sight
4. Rear sight windage nut
5. Rear sight windage screw
6. Rear sight windage screw plunger
7. Rear sight windage screw plunger spring
8. Extractor
9. Manual safety plunger spring
10. Manual safety plunger
11. Ejector depressor plunger spring
12. Ejector depressor plunger
13. Firing pin
14. Firing pin spring
15. Recoil spring
16. Recoil spring guide assembly
17. Barrel bushing
18. Barrel
19. Manual safety
20. Frame assembly
21. Slide stop
22. Slide stop plunger pin
23. Slide stop plunger spring
24. Slide stop plunger
25. Sear release lever
26. Hammer
27. Stirrup pin
28. Stirrup
29. Elector
30. Elector spring
31. Side-plate assembly
32. Trigger pin
33. Trigger
34. Trigger plunger pin
35. Trigger plunger
36. Trigger plunger spring
37. Magazine catch plunger
38. Magazine catch plunger spring
39. Magazine catch nut
40. Magazine catch
41. Sear
42. Sear pin
43. Sear plunger
44. Sear plunger spring
45. Sear plunger pin
46. Disconnector
47. Disconnector pin
48. Draw-bar plunger spring
49. Draw-bar plunger
50. Draw-bar
51. Trigger play spring
52. Mainspring
53. Mainspring plunger
54. Insert
55. Insert pin
56. Frame studs (4—assembled to frame)
57. Slide stop button (assembled to frame)
58. Stocks (right hand not shown)
59. Stock screws (4)
60. Magazine tube
61. Magazine follower
62. Magazine spring
63. Magazine buttplate catch
64. Magazine buttplate

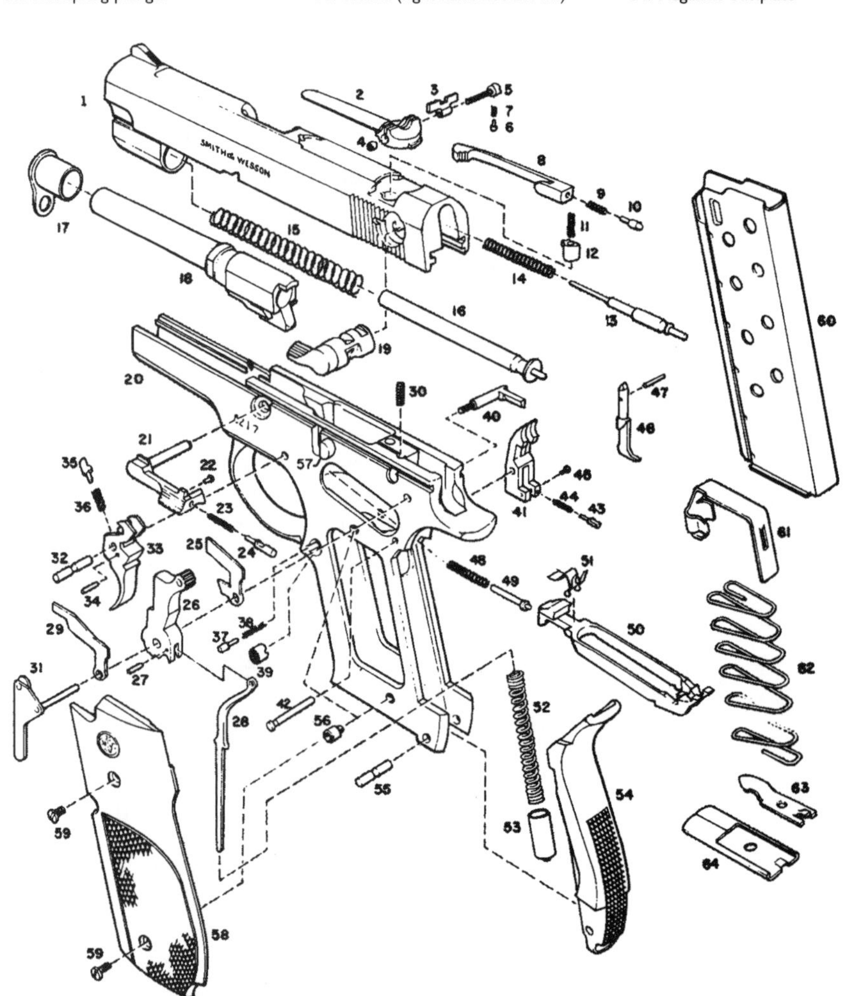

The Model 39 Smith & Wesson, introduced in 1955, was the first centerfire, self-loading double-action pistol produced and made for the commercial market by an American firm.

Developed for the U.S. Army service pistol trials of 1949, it was inspired by the German Walther 9mm *Heeres* (Army) Pistol designed in 1937 and subsequently adopted as an official German Service pistol, the *Pistole 38.*

The Model 39 design was directed by Smith & Wesson engineer Joe Norman. The design, in 9mm. Parabellum, was compleated in 1948 but was not adopted by the Army and a decision was made by Smith & Wesson to offer it commercially.

The commercial Model 39 was an aluminum-framed 9mm pistol with a curved backstrap and blued carbon steel slide. It was fitted with a manual safety and had the magazine release located at the rear of the trigger guard. A steel-framed model, also in 9mm. was manufactured in 1966.

The Model 39 sold slowly with less than 400 sold in 1957. In 1968 the pistol was purchased by the Illinois State Police, the first 9mm double-action auto issued by any United States police organization. General production of the Model 39 was discontinued in 1981, when it was replaced by the steel-framed Model 52. Another of the Model 39's descendants is the high-capacity 14-round Model 59 introduced in 1971.

DISASSEMBLY

Remove magazine and verify that pistol is unloaded. Put safety in "fire" (upper) position. While pressing in on right hand end of slide stop (21), draw slide (1) to rear until recess in lower left side is aligned with forward end of slide stop. Pull slide stop out of frame from left and pull slide forward off the frame (20). With slide upside down, compress recoil spring (15) and lift out recoil -spring guide assembly (16) with spring. Remove barrel bushing (17) by rotating its lower portion to left side of slide and draw it forward out of slide. Remove barrel (18) by grasping rear bottom end of barrel and drawing up and outward from slide to the rear. Further disassembly is not recommended as pistol may be properly cleaned and lubricated when thus field-stripped.

To reassemble pistol, replace barrel in slide and replace barrel bushing. Replace recoil spring and recoil spring guide assembly, making sure that recoil spring guide bushing is engaged in small radius cut in barrel lug and properly centered. Failure to center properly will leave recoil spring guide protruding from barrel bushing after assembly. Replace slide on frame, depressing ejector (29) and sear release lever (25) in turn so slide will travel to the rear over them. When slide stop cut on slide is aligned with slide stop hole in frame, insert slide stop and allow slide to return to forward position. Replace magazine. The numbered illustrations at right detail the steps in field-stripping the pistol.

To disassemble slide assembly, press rear end of firing pin (13) in as far as possible with a small punch and grasp forward end of firing pin with a pair of pliers and hold. Turn manual safety thumbpiece (19) half way between "fire" and "safe" positions and press right end of manual safety into slide, withdrawing it from slide from the left. Hold thumb over rear end of firing pin and release grip on pliers. Remove firing pin (13) and firing pin spring (14). Manual safety plunger (10) and spring (9) may be removed from rear end of extractor (8). Extractor may be removed by lifting it forward to clear hook and pressing to rear.

To disassemble frame assembly, remove stocks (58) by removing the four stock screws (59). Drive out insert pin (55) and remove insert (54) and mainspring. Lift out sideplate assembly (31). Lift out hammer (26) and stirrup (28). Remove ejector (29) and ejector spring (30) and sear release lever (25). Push sear pin (42) out from right side of frame, allowing sear (41) to drop out. Drive trigger pin (32) out from left side, allowing draw-bar (50) to slide back toward rear of frame. Let disconnected (46) drop out and pull drawbar out from rear. Tip frame to vertical position butt down, allowing drawbar plunger (49) and spring (48) to drop out. Push trigger (33) upward and forward out of frame. Place frame on right side so magazine catch body is supported. Using a drift pin or small punch, press down on magazine catch plunger (37) and hold. Turn magazine catch nut (39) counterclockwise and remove.

1 Slide is held rearward firmly with slide stop hole in frame aligned with cut in slide to allow removal of the slide stop (21).

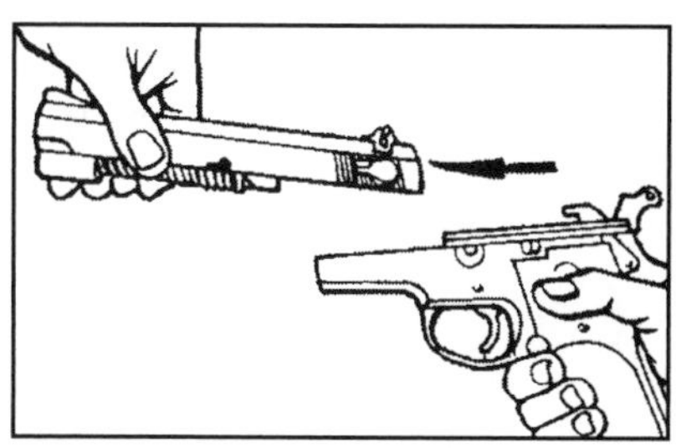

2 Slide assembly is withdrawn toward front and off frame assembly.

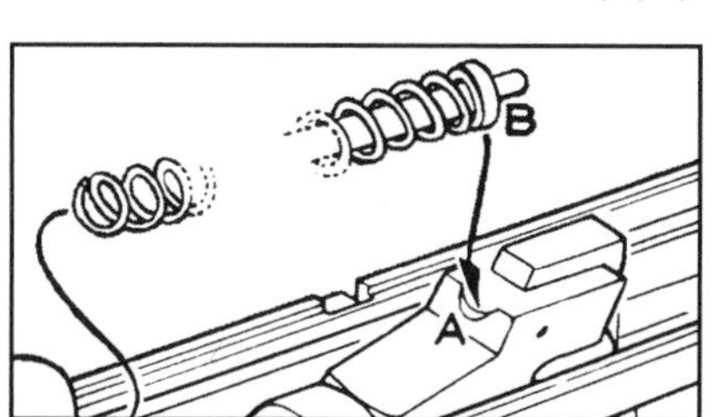

3 Remove recoil spring and guide assembly from underside of slide. Note radius cut in barrel lug at "A" which receives rim of recoil spring guide "B."

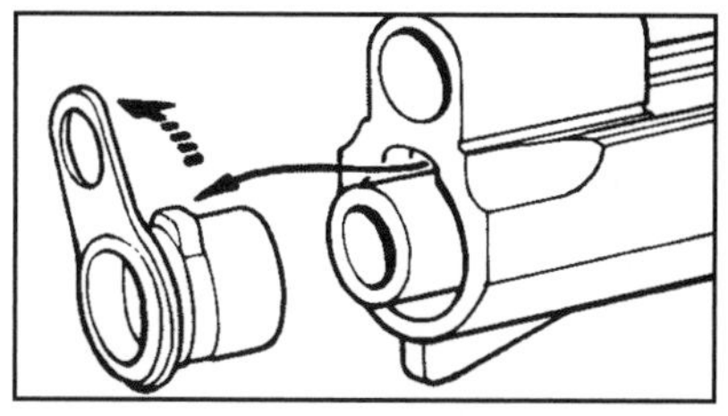

4 With slide upside down, turn barrel bushing (17) counterclockwise about 45° and withdraw from front of slide. Lift barrel lug upward and draw barrel out of slide to rear.

SMITH & WESSON MODEL 41-46

PARTS LEGEND

1. Barrel assembly
2. Muzzle brake
3. Muzzle brake screw
4. Barrel weight
5. Rear sight
6. Rear sight elevating nut
7. Rear sight elevating nut plunger spring
8. Rear sight elevating nut plunger
9. Rear sight windage screw plunger spring
10. Rear sight windage screw plunger
11. Rear sight windage screw
12. Rear sight slide
13. Rear sight windage nut
14. Rear sight elevating spring
15. Rear sight spring clip
16. Rear sight elevating stud
17. Rear sight pivot pin
18. Rear sight pivot clip
19. Slide
20. Extractor plunger
21. Extractor spring
22. Extractor
23. Bolt
24. Bolt pin
25. Firing pin spring
26. Firing pin
27. Trigger bar
28. Trigger bar spring
29. Magazine catch
30. Magazine disconnector assembly
31. Magazine disconnector spring
32. Indicator
33. Indicator spring
34. Hammer
35. Stirrup pin
36. Stirrup
37. Mainspring
38. Mainspring retainer
39. Mainspring retainer pin
40. Sear pin
41. Sear spring
42. Sear
43. Manual safety assembly
44. Pawl cam plunger
45. Pawl cam spring
46. Pawl cam
47. Manual safety spring plate
48. Manual safety spring plate screw
49. Magazine catch nut
50. Magazine catch plunger
51. Magazine catch spring
52. Pawl pin
53. Pawl & trigger spring
54. Pawl
55. Trigger pull adjusting lever
56. Slide stop & ejector assembly with slide stop spring
57. Recoil spring guide
58. Recoil spring
59. Frame
60. Trigger
61. Trigger pin
62. Trigger stop screw
63. Trigger guard
64. Trigger guard pin
65. Magazine follower
66. Magazine pin
67. Magazine tube
68. Magazine spring
69. Magazine spring plunger
70. Magazine buttplate
71. Grips (2)
72. Grip screws (2)

REMOVABLE BARREL COUNTERWEIGHTS

A. Counterweight upper section, steel or aluminum
B. Counterweight middle section
C. Counterweight nut
D. Counterweight lower section
E. Counterweight screws

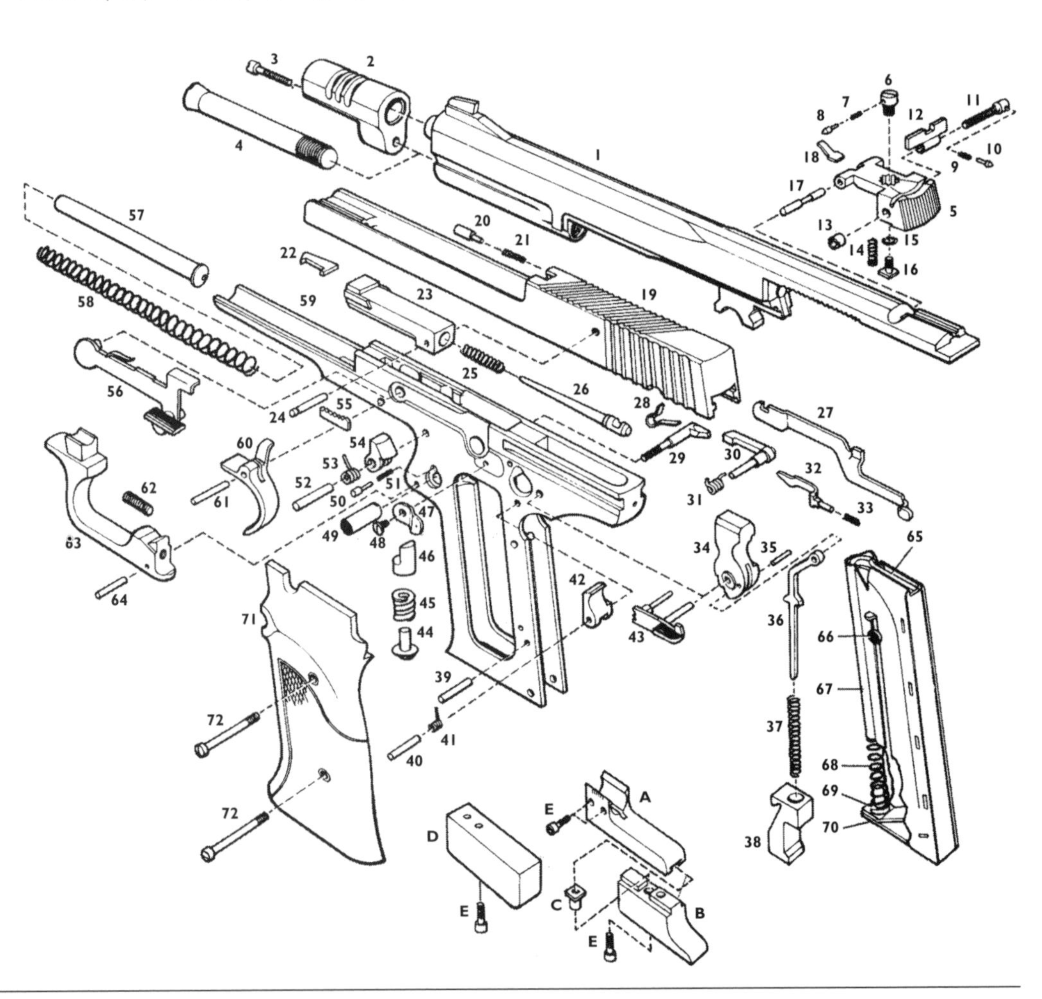

The Smith & Wesson Model 41, .22 Long Rifle semi-automatic target pistol, introduced in 1957, was the culmination of a development program begun in 1941. A pilot model was shown that year to shooters at Camp Perry, but United States entry into World War II halted further work on this project which was not resumed until after the war.

Production was eventually scheduled for 1950, but the outbreak of the Korean War in that year again resulted in a postponement, and it was not until late 1957 that Model 41's finally began coming off the assembly line.

Designed to be shot on an out-of-the-box basis, the Model 41 has all the extra refinements appreciated by topflight competitive shooters. These include a wide trigger adjustable for weight of pull, adjustable trigger stop, fully adjustable rear sight, cocking in-dicator pin, muzzle brake, and checkered walnut target grips with thumb-rest. Both front and rear sights are mounted on the barrel assembly to eliminate the possibility of a sight alignment error which is sometimes present in guns having the rear sight mounted on a separate breechblock.

The Model 41 was initially made with 7⅜-inch barrel only. The total weight is 43½ ounces with muzzle brake, barrel weight, and magazine in place. A set of three, accessory counterweights were offered. These totaled 16½ ounces and attached to the barrel assembly.

In the fall of 1959 an interchangeable five-inch barrel was offered so that the Model 41 could be purchased with either barrel length. Currently the Model 41 comes with either the original barrel length or an optional 5½-inch, heavy barrel. Weight of the short-barreled Model 41 is 44-1/2 ounces.

From late 1959 until 1968, a lower-price and somewhat simplified version of the Model 41, known as the Model 46, was offered. The Model 46 was made without the muzzle brake, cocking indicator and integral trigger adjusting device, and with plain rather than high-luster blue finish. Also, the Model 46 lacked the grooving on top of the barrel and on the front strap, and checkering on the head of the magazine release. Standard Model 46 grips were of Nylon rather than walnut. A detachable, two-ounce counterweight for attachment under the barrel was furnished as an extra. Disassembly for the Model 46 is the same as for the Model 41.

DISASSEMBLY

1 Pull slide (19) all the way back until it locks open. Press in magazine catch nut (49) and remove magazine. Pull trigger guard (63) down while holding finger over top of barrel assembly to prevent it falling off when trigger guard is down. Remove barrel assembly (1) from frame (59).

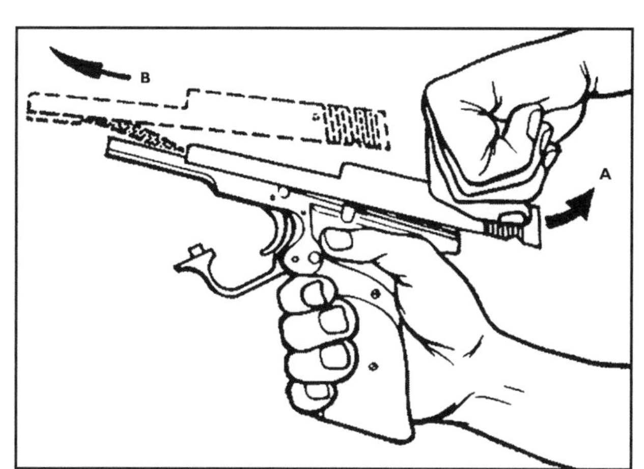

2 Pull slide (19) backward and raise rear of slide slightly. Slide may now be moved forward and off receiver and recoil spring (58) may be removed. This is sufficient disassembly for normal cleaning purposes. Removal of grip screws (72) and grips (71) will allow complete disassembly of parts inside frame. After reassembling slide (19) to frame (59), lock slide in its rearward position by holding back while pressing upward on slide stop (56). Barrel is then easily added.

SMITH & WESSON MODEL 52

PARTS LEGEND

1. Slide
2. Barrel bushing
3. Barrel bushing plate
4. Barrel bushing plunger
5. Barrel bushing plunger spring
6. Barrel
7. Recoil spring
8. Recoil spring guide assembly
9. Extractor
10. Extractor spring
11. Extractor spring plunger
12. Rear sight assembly (see detail)
13. Ejector-depressor plunger
14. Ejector-depressor plunger spring
15. Firing pin spring
16. Firing pin
17. Manual safety
18. Double action lockout screw
19. Ejector spring
20. Magazine catch
21. Sear
22. Sear plunger pin
23. Sear plunger spring
24. Sear plunger
25. Sear pin
26. Disconnector
27. Disconnector pin
28. Frame
29. Barrel bushing wrench
30. Slide stop
31. Slide stop plunger pin
32. Slide stop plunger spring
33. Slide stop plunger
34. Trigger
35. Trigger plunger
36. Trigger plunger spring
37. Trigger pin
38. Trigger plunger pin
39. Ejector & magazine depressor
40. Hammer
41. Stirrup pin
42. Stirrup
43. Side plate assembly
44. Magazine catch spring
45. Magazine catch plunger
46. Magazine catch nut
47. Frame stud (4)
48. Insert pin
49. Stock, left (Right stock not shown)
50. Stock screws (4)
51. Mainspring
52. Mainspring plunger
53. Insert
54. Drawbar
55. Trigger play spring
56. Drawbar plunger
57. Drawbar plunger spring
58. Trigger stop screw
59. Slide stop button
60. Magazine tube
61. Magazine follower
62. Magazine pin
63. Magazine spring
64. Magazine buttplate catch
65. Magazine buttplate

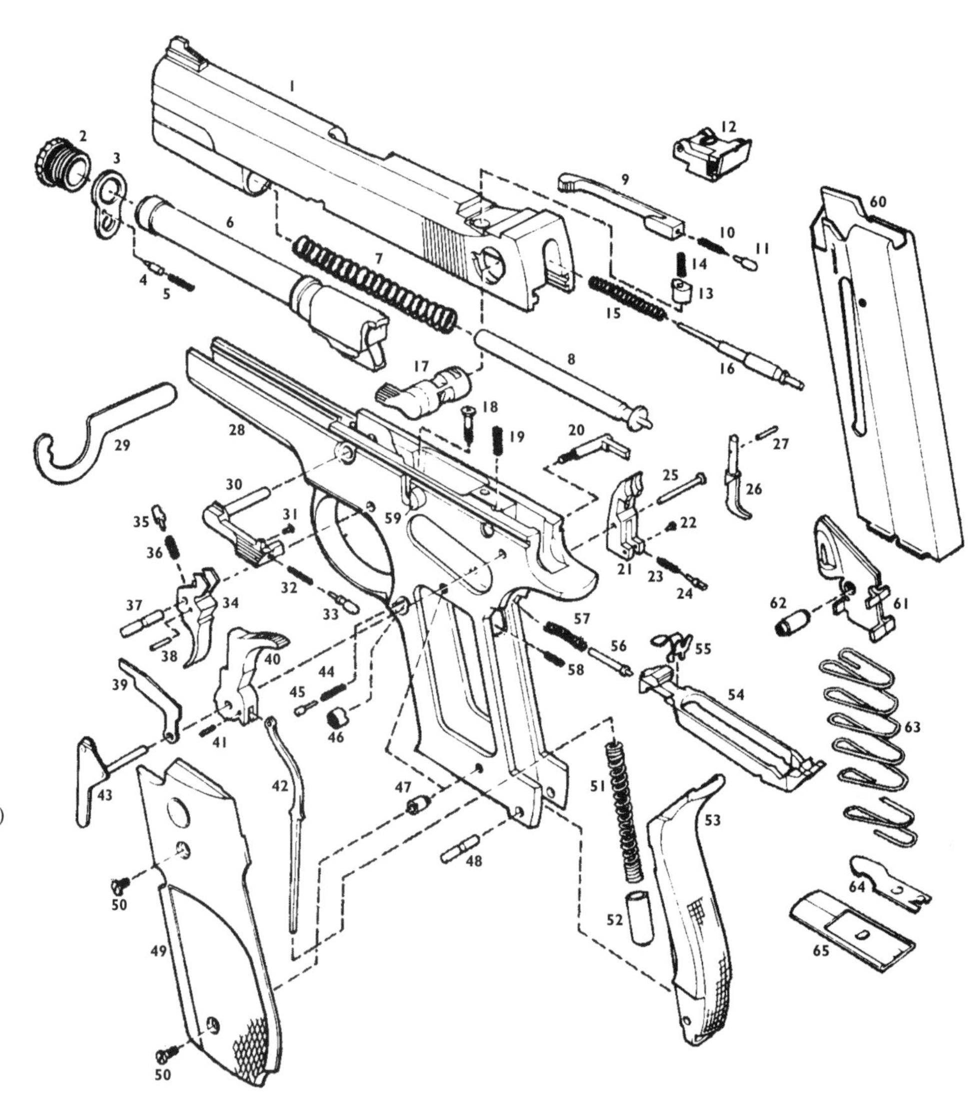

Designed expressly for target shooting, the Smith & Wesson Model 52 semi-automatic pistol was introduced in 1962. It is chambered for the .38 S&W Special cartridge loaded with flush-seated wadcutter bullet. The magazine will not accept cartridges that are longer than 1.19 inches, and capacity of the magazine is limited to 5 rounds only.

The Model 52 is of locked-breech type and its basic design stems from the Model 39 double-action pistol introduced by the same maker in 1954. The lock mechanism of the Model 52 can be adjusted for double-action use by tightening the double-action lockout screw. This pistol will not fire with magazine removed. A feature of interest to the target shooter is that this pistol may be dry-shot without risk of damage as the engagement of the safety interposes a solid block between hammer and firing pin.

The rear sight features click adjustments for both windage and elevation. Each click moves point of impact approximately ¾ inches in elevation and ½ inch in windage at 50 yards.

DISASSEMBLY

Press in magazine catch nut (46) on left side of frame (28) and withdraw magazine (60) from butt. Check chamber to be sure pistol is unloaded. Place manual safety (17) in fire or upper position.

While pressing to left on right end of slide stop (30), pull slide (1) rearward until recess on lower left side of slide is lined up with forward end of slide stop. Pull slide stop out of frame to left and draw slide forward off frame.

Invert slide and, while compressing recoil spring (7) with fingers, lift out recoil spring guide assembly (8). Place barrel bushing wrench (29) over notches on barrel bushing (2), depressing barrel bushing plunger (4). Turn bushing counterclockwise, removing it from slide. Lift rear end of barrel (6) and withdraw barrel from slide to rear.

To reassemble, replace barrel in slide. Replace barrel bushing and plate, turning bushing to a firm fit aligning closest notch to plunger. When replacing recoil spring guide assembly and spring, be sure that guide bushing part of guide. assembly (8) is engaged in small radius cut in barrel lug and properly centered. Replace slide in frame, depressing ejector (39) so slide will travel over it to rear. Align slide stop cut in slide with slide stop hole in frame and insert slide stop from left side of frame. Return slide to forward position and replace magazine, completing the reassembly procedure.

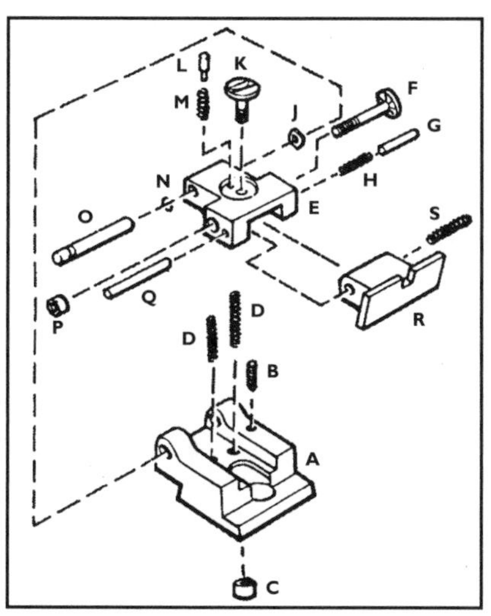

1 To elevate rear sight, turn top elevating screw (K) to left (counterclockwise). To depress, turn screw (K) to right (clockwise). To move sight to right, turn windage screw (F) to right (clockwise). To move sight to left, turn windage screw (F) to left (counterclockwise).

2 Hold slide (1) rearward in position shown with recess in slide aligned with forward end of slide stop (30) as shown at A. Press right end of slide stop into frame and withdraw slide stop from the left side.

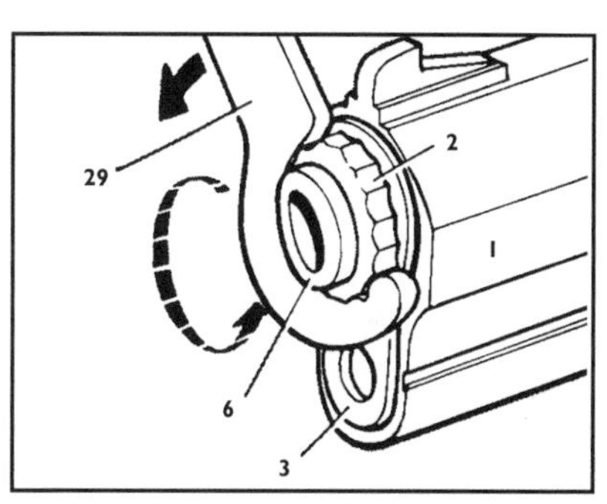

3 Place wrench (29) over notches on barrel bushing (2), compressing barrel bushing plunger (4) with wrench simultaneously. Turn bushing to left to unscrew from the slide.

REAR SIGHT ASSEMBLY PARTS LEGEND

A. Base
B. Lock screw
C. Elevation nut
D. Elevation springs
E. Body
F. Windage screw
G. Windage plunger
H. Windage plunger spring
J. Wavy washer
K. Elevation screw
L. Elevation plunger
M. Elevation plunger spring
N. Spring clip
O. Pivot pin
P. Windage nut
Q. Traverse pin
R. Slide
S. Windage spring

SMITH & WESSON MODEL 59

S&W's Model 59 is most commonly found with the rear sight as illustrated but recently the sight has been changed to include protective wings on either side.

PARTS LEGEND

1. Rear sight windage nut
2. Barrel
3. Barrel bushing
4. Trigger plunger pin
5. Ejector-depressor plunger
6. Ejector-depressor plunger spring
7. Ejector
8. Ejector spring
9. Firing pin
10. Firing pin spring
11. Magazine catch spring
12. Magazine catch plunger spring
13. Manual safety
14. Manual safety plunger
15. Rear sight leaf
16. Recoil spring
17. Rear sight slide
18. Extractor pin
19. Manual safety plunger spring
20. Extractor spring
21. Slide stop plunger
22. Slide stop plunger spring
23. Slide
24. Rear sight windage screw
25. Sear release lever
26. Disconnector
27. Disconnector pin
28. Drawbar plunger
29. Drawbar plunger spring
30. Trigger plunger
31. Trigger plunger spring
32. Trigger play spring rivet
33. Trigger play spring
34. Hammer
35. Mainspring
36. Stirrup
37. Stirrup pin
38. Trigger
39. Mainspring plunger
40. Drawbar
41. Frame
42. Frame stud
43. Insert
44. Insert pin
45. Trigger pin
46. Magazine follower
47. Magazine buttplate
48. Magazine catch
49. Stock screw
50. Magazine spring
51. Magazine tube
52. Sear pin
53. Slide stop
54. Stock
55. Sideplate
56. Sear spring retaining pin
57. Extractor
58. Slide stop plunger rivet
59. Sear
60. Recoil spring guide
61. Magazine buttplate catch
62. Magazine release button
63. Sear spring
64. Slide stop button
65. Windage screw plunger
66. Windage screw plunger spring

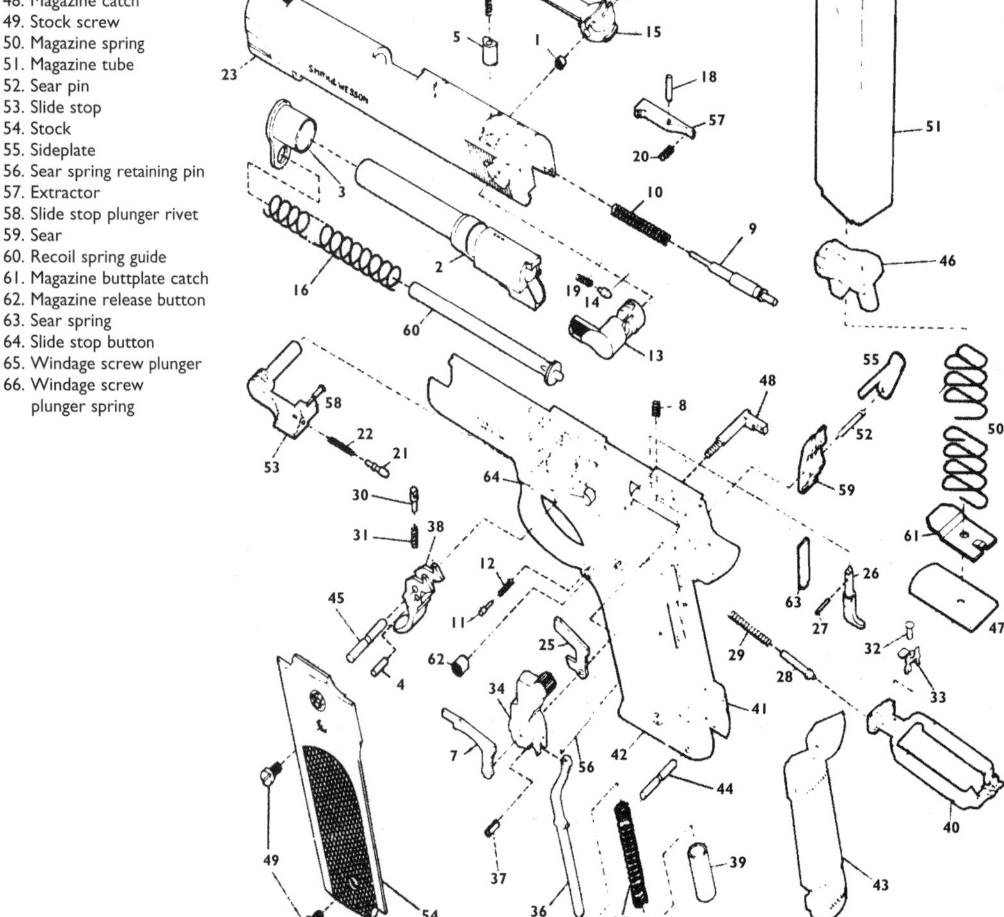

The prototype for the Smith & Wesson Model 59 was designed around 1965 for the U.S. Navy as a high-capacity (13-round) version of the Model 39 as part of the Navy's Mark 22 "Hush Puppy" silenced pistol program. The prototype, however, was not adopted by the Navy and Smith & Wesson brought out a commercial version in 1970.

The Model 59 was produced in 9mm Parabellum. It featured a wide anodized aluminum frame. To accommodate the larger magazine, the grip contour of the Model 59 was made straighter than the somewhat curved grip of its predecessor, the Model 39. The grip material was changed from walnut to relatively thin nylon to keep the total grip thickness down to a reasonable size and yet remove any chance of splitting. The Model 59 has a magazine safety (it cannot be fired without the magazine), and manual safety on the slide. The magazine release is located behind trigger guard, similar to the M1911A1. Production of the Model 59 ceased in 1980 when an improved version, the Model 459, was introduced.

DISASSEMBLY

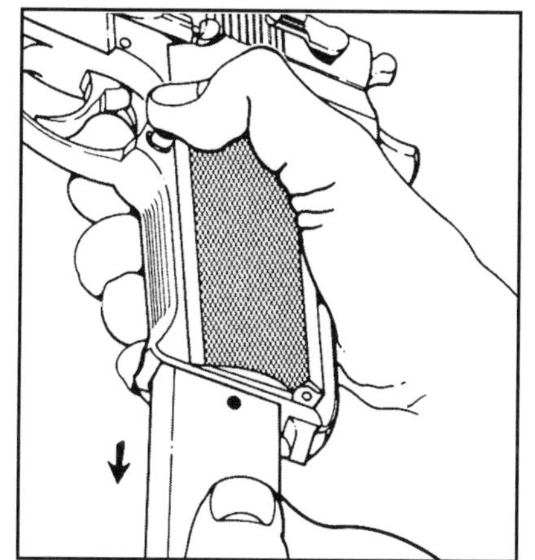

1 Place the manual safety (13) in low or "safe" position; remove the magazine by pressing the magazine release button (62) on the left side of the frame at the rear of the trigger guard and draw the magazine from the butt. Retract the slide (23) and inspect the chamber to make sure the pistol is not loaded, then put the safety in the "fire" position.

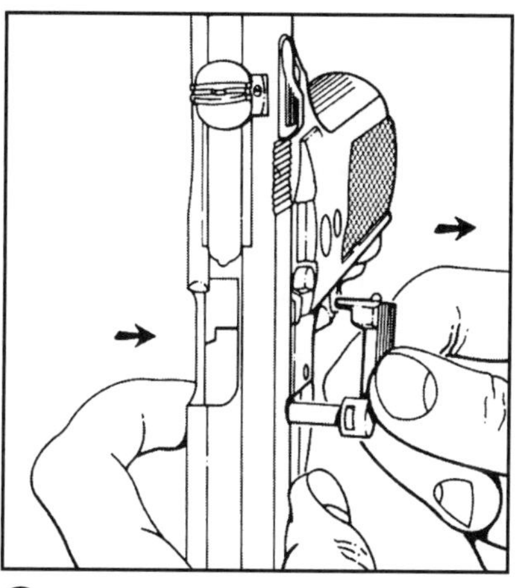

2 While pressing the protruding shaft of the slide stop (53), draw the slide (23) back until the recess in the lower left side of the slide is lined up with the forward end of the slide stop. Pull the slide stop completely from the frame.

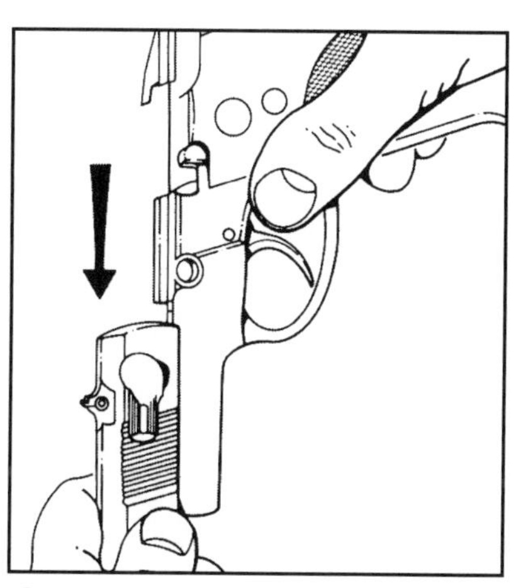

3 Remove the slide by pulling it forward and off the frame (41).

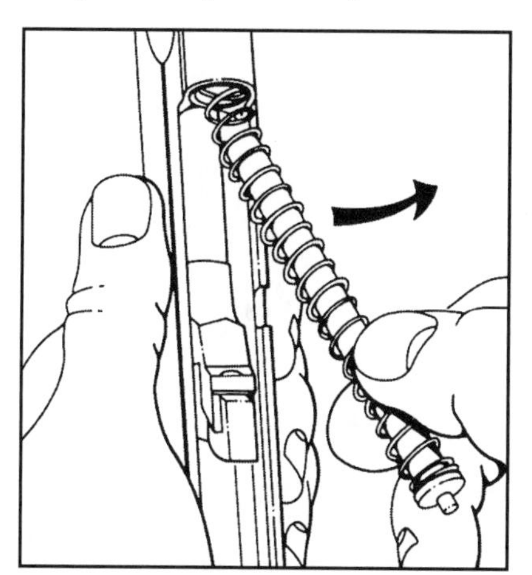

4 Hold the slide upside down, compress the recoil spring (16) and lift it out along with the recoil spring guide (60).

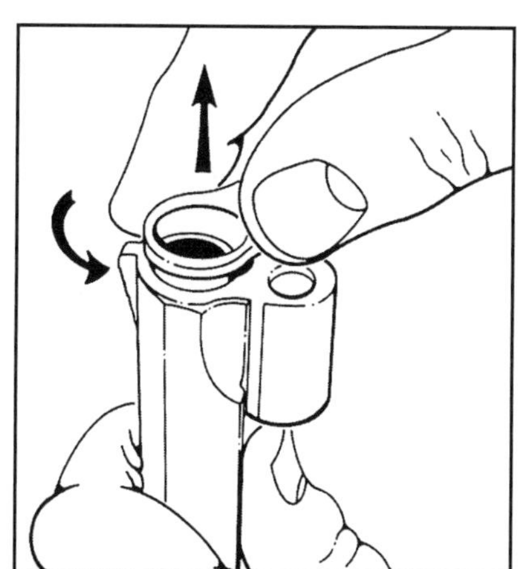

5 Remove the barrel bushing (3) by rotating its lower portion toward the left side of the slide and pulling it forward from the slide.

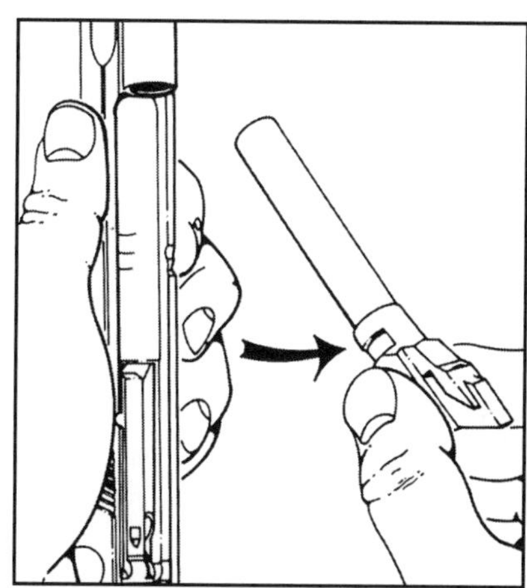

6 Remove the barrel (2) by lifting its rear end back and out of the slide. No further disassembly is recommended by the factory. Reassembly is accomplished in reverse order.

SMITH & WESSON BODYGUARD

The aluminum-frame Model 38 Bodyguard was introduced in mid-1955. Its heavier twin, the steel-frame Model 49, came along in 1959.

PARTS LEGEND

1. Cylinder pin
2. Cylinder pin spring
3. Extractor rod
4. Extractor
5. Extractor pin (2)
6. Cylinder
7. Extractor spring
8. Yoke
9. Stock screw
10. Stock, left
11. Stock pin
12. Escutcheon
13. Thumbpiece
14. Thumbpiece nut
15. Frame lug
16. Hammer nose bushing
17. Barrel
18. Locking bolt pin
19. Locking bolt spring
20. Locking bolt
21. Bolt
22. Bolt plunger spring
23. Bolt plunger
24. Barrel pin
25. Cylinder stop
26. Cylinder stop spring
27. Trigger stud
28. Rebound slide stud
29. Hammer stud
30. Frame
31. Escutcheon nut
32. Stock, right
33. Mainspring rod swivel
34. Mainspring
35. Mainspring rod
36. Hammer
37. Stirrup pin
38. Sear pin
39. Hammer nose rivet
40. Sear spring
41. Sear
42. Hammer nose
43. Trigger lever
44. Trigger
45. Hand
46. Hand pin
47. Torsion spring pin (2)
48. Hand spring pin
49. Torsion spring
50. Rebound slide spring
51. Rebound slide pin
52. Rebound slide
53. Hammer block
54. Side-plate
55. Flat plate screw
56. Round plate screw
57. Yoke screw

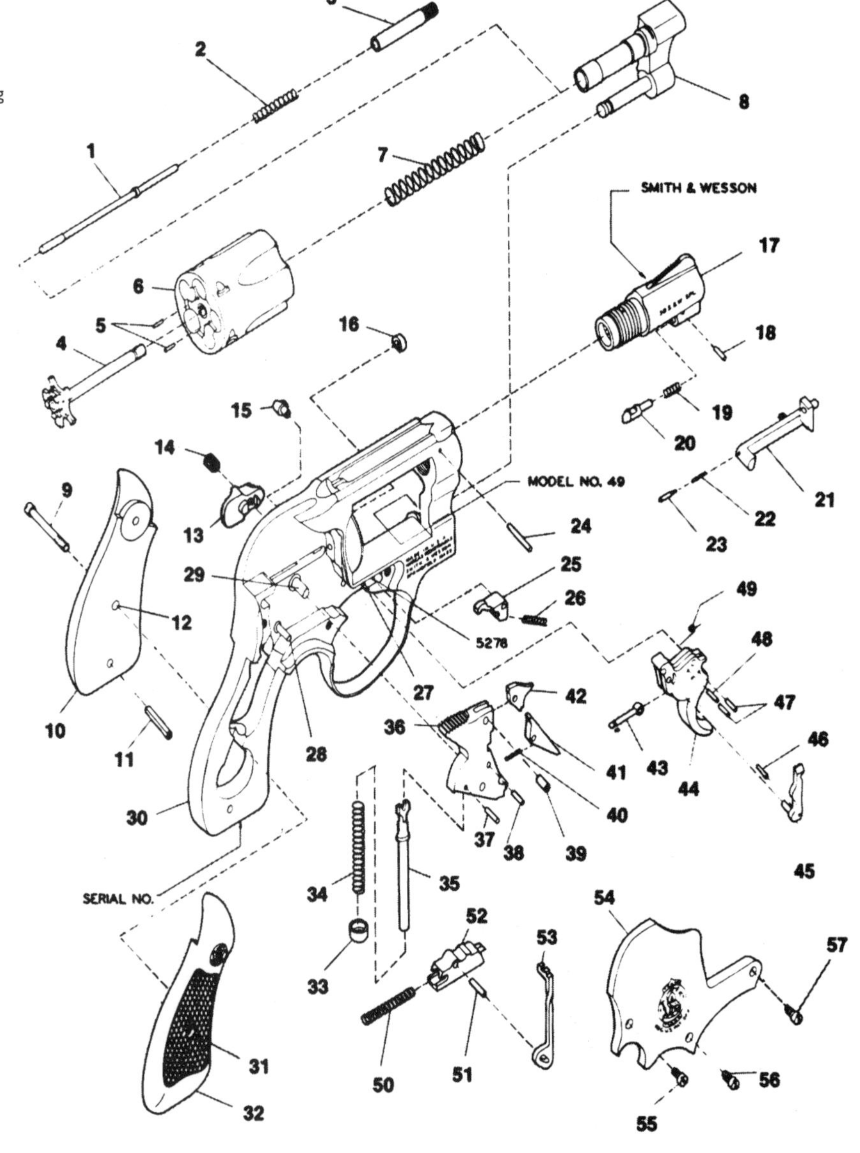

The S&W Bodyguard was developed for law enforcement I agencies that required a revolver with a protected hammer that would not catch on clothing but would be exposed enough for single-action cocking. To accomplish this, the factory designed a new J frame that extended even with the hammer spur, and a new low-profile hammer with more surface area.

The first Bodyguard (Model 38 Airweight) was made with an aluminum frame. Since the revolver was to be carried in the pocket by law enforcement personnel, the factory felt it was important to keep the weight to a minimum. This was the first airweight model made by S&W.

The first Model 38s were made in August, 1955, beginning at serial number 66,000 in the J-frame series. The first-year production revolvers (2,422 units) were manufactured in what the collectors classify as the four-screw side-plate variation, i.e., an additional screw on the upper area of the plate.

In 1959, after receiving an inquiry from the Massachusetts State Police, S&W began to produce the Model 49 with steel frame. Production began in July, 1959, with serial number 163,051.

The Models 38 and 49 are now available in blue or nickel finish with 2-inch barrels. In the past, a few Model 49s were manufactured with a 3-inch barrel, and a stainless steel cylinder Model 49 was once produced to meet the requirements of the Michigan State Police.

DISASSEMBLY

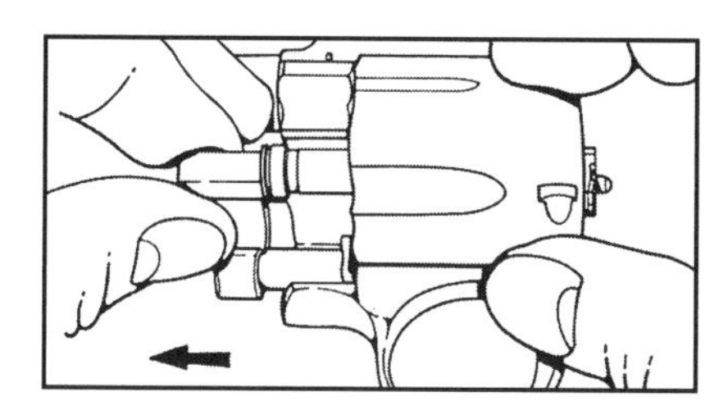

1 Remove stocks by loosening stock screw (9). Leaving screwdriver in place, push the screw in against the right stock (32). This will release that stock without damaging the frame. Remove left-hand stock (10) by tapping gently with screwdriver through the frame (30). Remove yoke screw (57). Hold cylinder (6) in open position and draw the yoke (8) forward out of the frame. Insert a dummy or empty cartridge in one of the chambers to protect extractor pins, then grasp the extractor rod (3) in a vise. Never put the knurled end into the vise. Now turn the cylinder clockwise to unscrew the extractor rod.

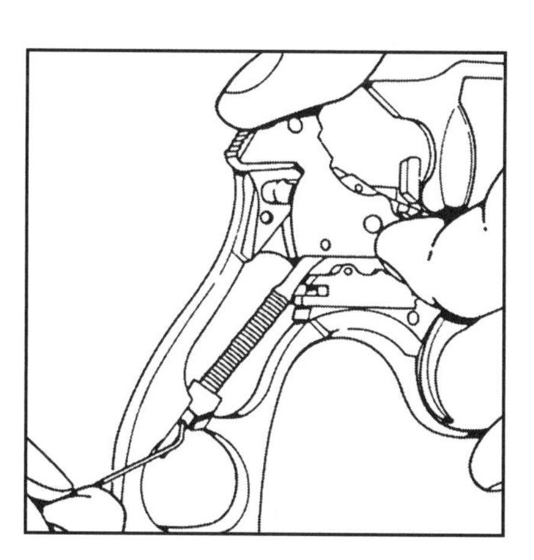

2 Remove round head side-plate screw (56) and flat head side-plate screw (55). Loosen side-plate (54) by tapping the side of the backstrap with a nylon hammer. Hold the front of the side plate to prevent dropping it. The hammer block (53) may drop out when you remove the side-plate, as it rides in a slot in the plate. If it does not, remove it. Cock the hammer (36) and insert a paper clip through the hole in the mainspring rod (35). Release hammer so compressed mainspring (34) and rod can be removed as shown.

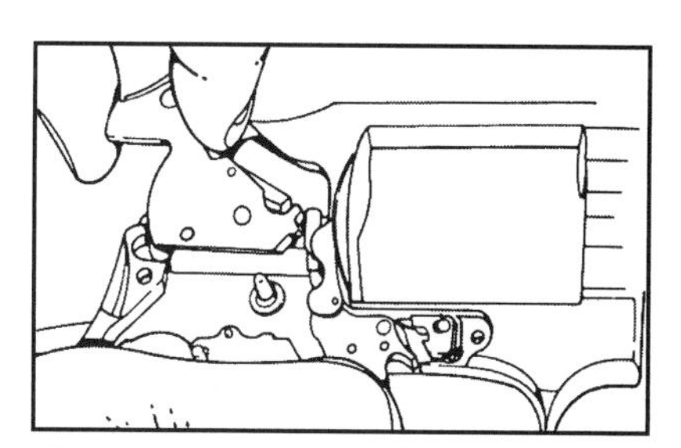

3 Push thumbpiece (13) to the rear and pull trigger (44) to its full rearward position. This will cock the hammer. While holding the trigger rearward, lift the hammer straight out of the frame as shown.

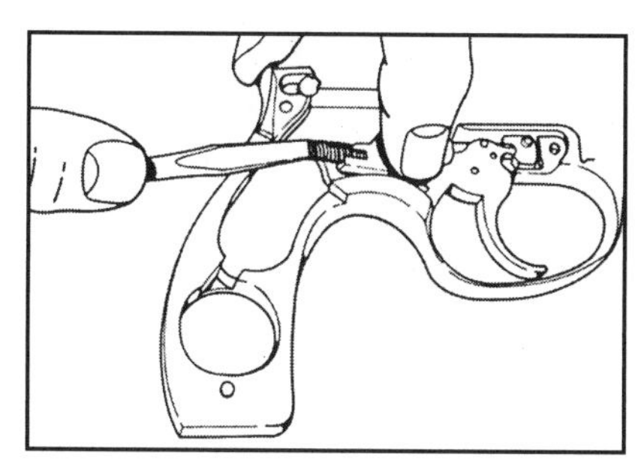

4 Remove rebound slide (52) and spring (50) by raising slide halfway up on stud (28) with screwdriver as shown. Change position of screwdriver to flat edge and push in on spring. Allow spring to release slowly. Note that the screwdriver and finger prevent spring from flying off.

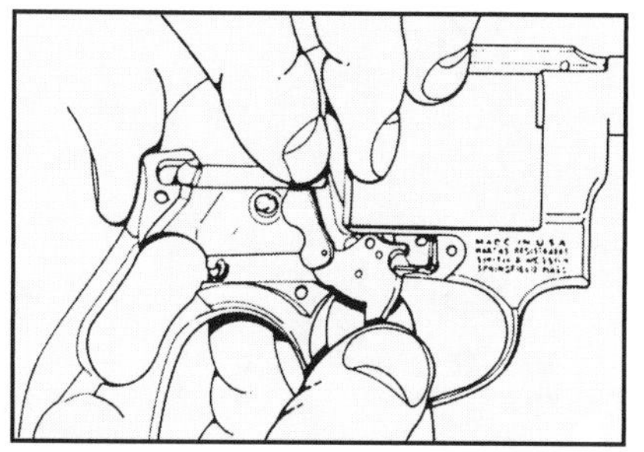

5 To remove trigger (44) and hand (45), use left index finger to hold the hand out of the slot in the frame while the thumb and middle finger of the right hand lift trigger straight off the trigger stud (27).

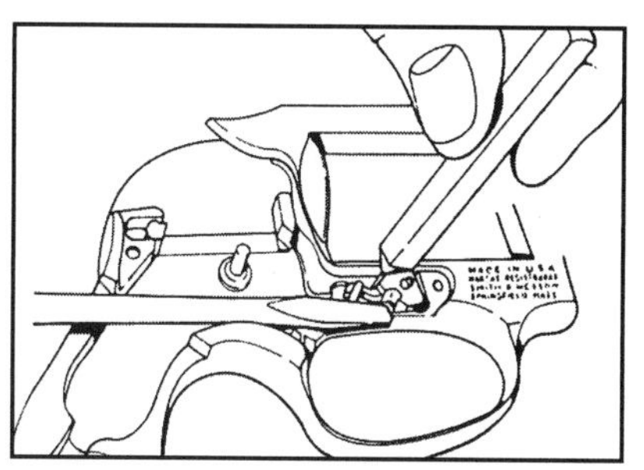

6 Push cylinder stop (25) down from the top, then use a drift pin to hold it down while the screwdriver lifts it straight up off its pin. Be careful to contain the spring to prevent loss.

SMITH & WESSON CENTENNIAL

PARTS LEGEND

1. Frame
2. Bolt
3. Bolt plunger
4. Bolt plunger spring
5. Thumbpiece
6. Thumbpiece screw
7. Extractor
8. Cylinder
9. Dowel pin (2)
10. Extractor spring
11. Center pin
12. Center pin spring
13. Yoke
14. Extractor rod
15. Locking bolt
16. Locking bolt spring
17. Locking bolt pin
18. Barrel
19. Barrel pin
20. Safety lever
    20A. Safety lever pin
    20B. Safety lever lock pin (in storage hole)
21. Safety lever spring
22. Stock pin
23. Safety latch
24. Safety latch pin
25. Rebound slide spring
26. Rebound slide
27. Cylinder stop
28. Hammer
29. Hammer nose rivet
30. Hammer nose
31. Sear
32. Sear pin
33. Sear spring
34. Mainspring rod
35. Mainspring
36. Mainspring swivel
37. Trigger
38. Trigger lever
39. Hand
40. Hand torsion spring
41. Hand torsion spring pins (2)
42. Trigger lever pin
43. Side-plate
44. Flat head side-plate screw (1)
45. Large head side-plate screw
46. Small head side-plate & yoke screws (2)
47. Stock screw
48. Stock (2)

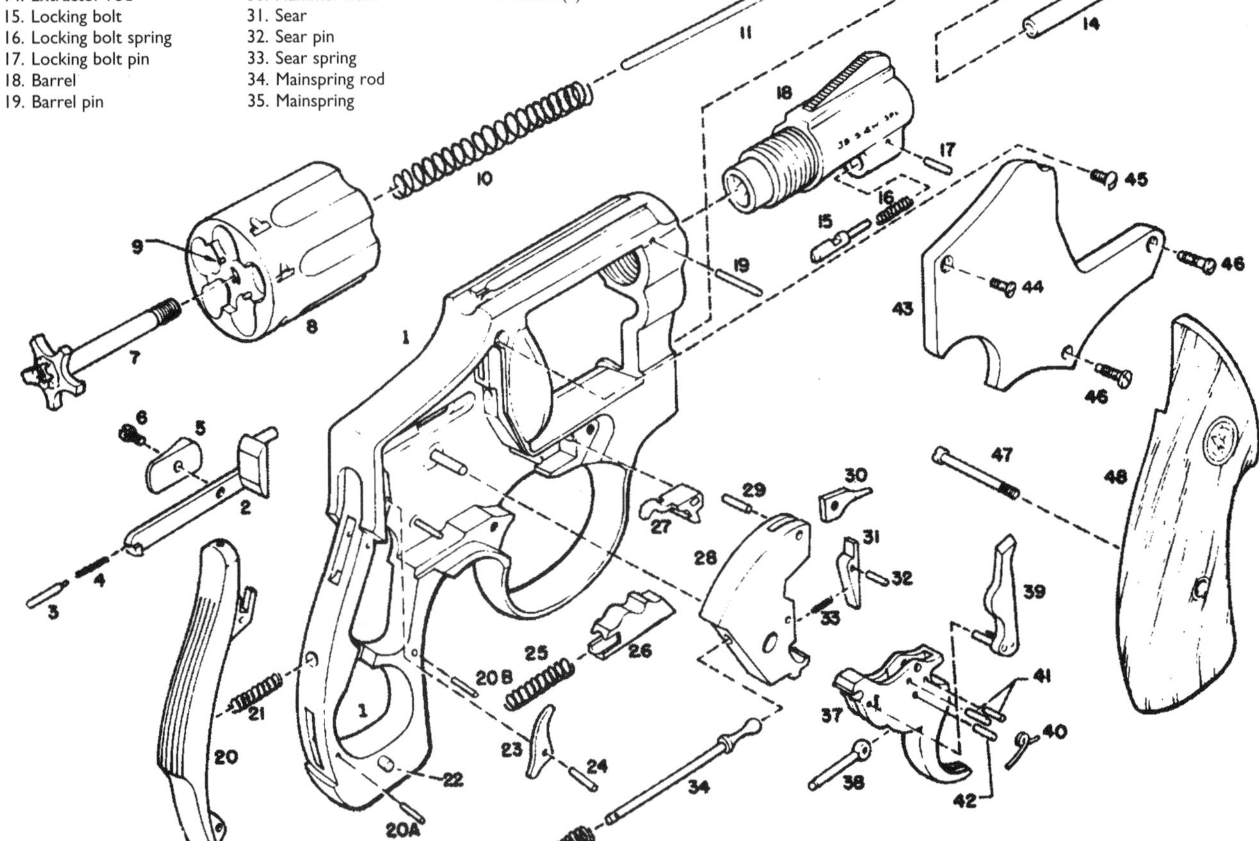

In 1953, S&W introduced the Centennial revolver, so named because the date of its introduction closely coincided with the company's 100th anniversary. Its design was inspired by the internal hammer, double-action, hinged frame Safety Hammerless "New Departure" revolver of 1888, but chambered for modern smokeless powder cartridges.

The Centennial was of solid frame design, capable of handling .38 Special cartridges. It was available in steel or lightweight (Centennial Airweight) alloy frame versions.

The Centennial was enthusiastically accepted by law enforcement officers, especially detectives who found it an excellent sidearm for undercover use, and private individuals who wanted a safe, effective handgun for personal defense. The Centennial remained in production until 1974.

DISASSEMBLY

Disassembly of the S&W Centennial follows generally that of other S&W revolvers. Remove the stock screw (47), stocks, and side-plate screws (44, 45, 46) and, holding the gun with the side-plate up, tap the frame gently with a wooden or fiber hammer until the side-plate works loose. Prying off the side-plate usually results in burring its edges and damaging the finish. The cylinder and yoke assembly are removed by swinging out the cylinder and pulling the yoke forward and out of the frame.

Remove the mainspring assembly as detailed below. Remove the rebound slide (26) and spring (25) by lifting the rear of the slide up and free of the pin in the frame. Care should be taken in this operation to prevent the compressed spring escaping once it is free from its pin.

The remaining interior parts of the revolver are easily removed. The safety lever (20) and spring (21) may be removed by gently drifting out the safety lever pin (20A). The safety latch (23) may be removed by drifting out its pin (24) also. Note that all S&W Centennial revolvers are supplied with a lock pin (20B) carried in a recess in the frame adjacent to the base of the mainspring. Installation of the lock pin in order to deactivate the safety lever is detailed in Step 3.

LONGITUDINAL SECTION

1 The working parts of the Centennial revolver. This mechanism is basically the some as that of other Smith & Wesson revolvers with the exception of hammer and the safety lever feature. This revolver also differs from other S&W arms in that it does not hove a hammer block. In order to fire the revolver, the grip must be held firmly enough to depress the safety lever (20) as shown by the arrow. Depressing the safety lever moves the upper arm of the safety latch back and out of the path of the rear face of the hammer as it is retracted when the trigger is pulled. If the safety lever is not fully depressed, its interlocking lug, which engages the lower arm of the safety latch (23) will hold the upper arm of the latch under the hammer, preventing the hammer from coming bock to a firing position. The drawing shows the safety lever extended (not depressed) with the safety latch blocking the hammer. Note that this arm is fired only double-action.

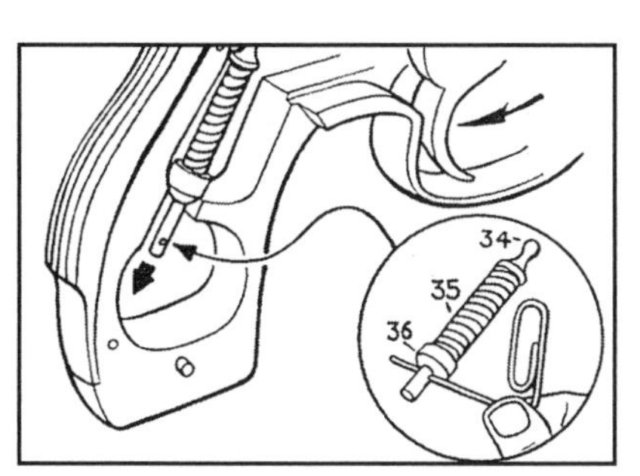

2 The mainspring can be removed by pulling back on the trigger until the small hole at the base of the mainspring rod (34) clears the mainspring swivel (36). Insert a straightened paper clip or other small pin in this hole, holding the mainspring (35) compressed and lift the entire mainspring assembly clear of the frame.

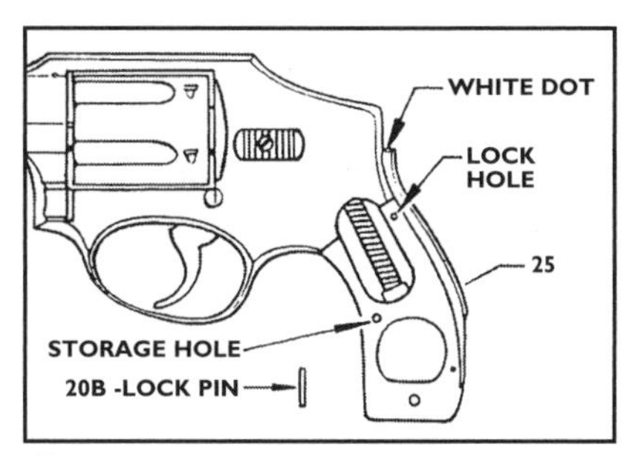

3 To deactivate the safety lever (20), remove the lock pin (20B) from storage hole in frame, and insert in lock hole in the frame above the lug of the safety lever while pressing the lever in to its depressed position. There is a white dot on the top of the safety lever which is visible when the lever is in its "safe" position. The dot is not visible when the lever is pressed in for firing or locked in by the lock pin.

SMITH & WESSON ESCORT PISTOL

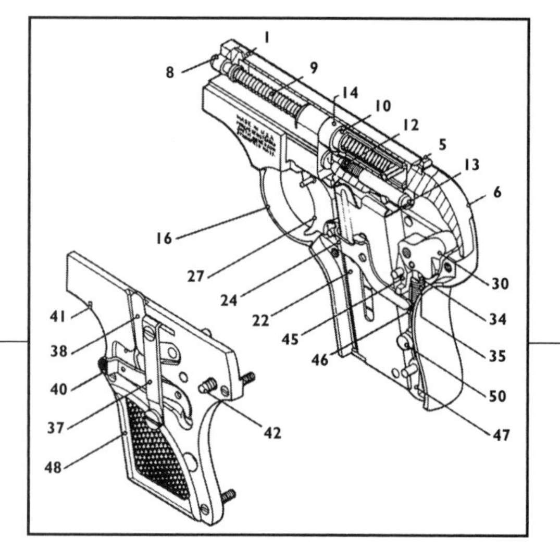

PARTS LEGEND

1. Front sight
2. Extractor spring
3. Extractor pin
4. Extractor
5. Rear sight
6. Slide
7. Stock screw (2)
8. Recoil spring guide
9. Recoil spring
10. Recoil spring guide tube
11. Firing pin retaining pin
12. Firing pin spring
13. Firing pin
14. Retainer tube
15. Recoil spring stop pin
16. Frame
17. Stock-right hand
18. Magazine buttplate
19. Magazine spring plate
20. Magazine spring
21. Magazine follower
22. Magazine tube
23. Magazine follower pin
24. Trigger bar
25. Trigger bar pin
26. Trigger bar spring
27. Trigger
28. Trigger pin
29. Hammer pin
30. Hammer
31. Trigger block
32. Trigger block rivet
33. Stirrup pin
34. Stirrup
35. Mainspring
36. Ejector screw
37. Ejector
38. Disconnector
39. Side-plate screw (3)
40. Manual safety lever
41. Side-plate
42. Indicator plunger
43. Indicator plunger spring
44. Sear pin
45. Sear
46. Spring, magazine catch and sear
47. Magazine catch
48. Stock-left hand
49. Magazine catch pin
50. Mainspring retainer

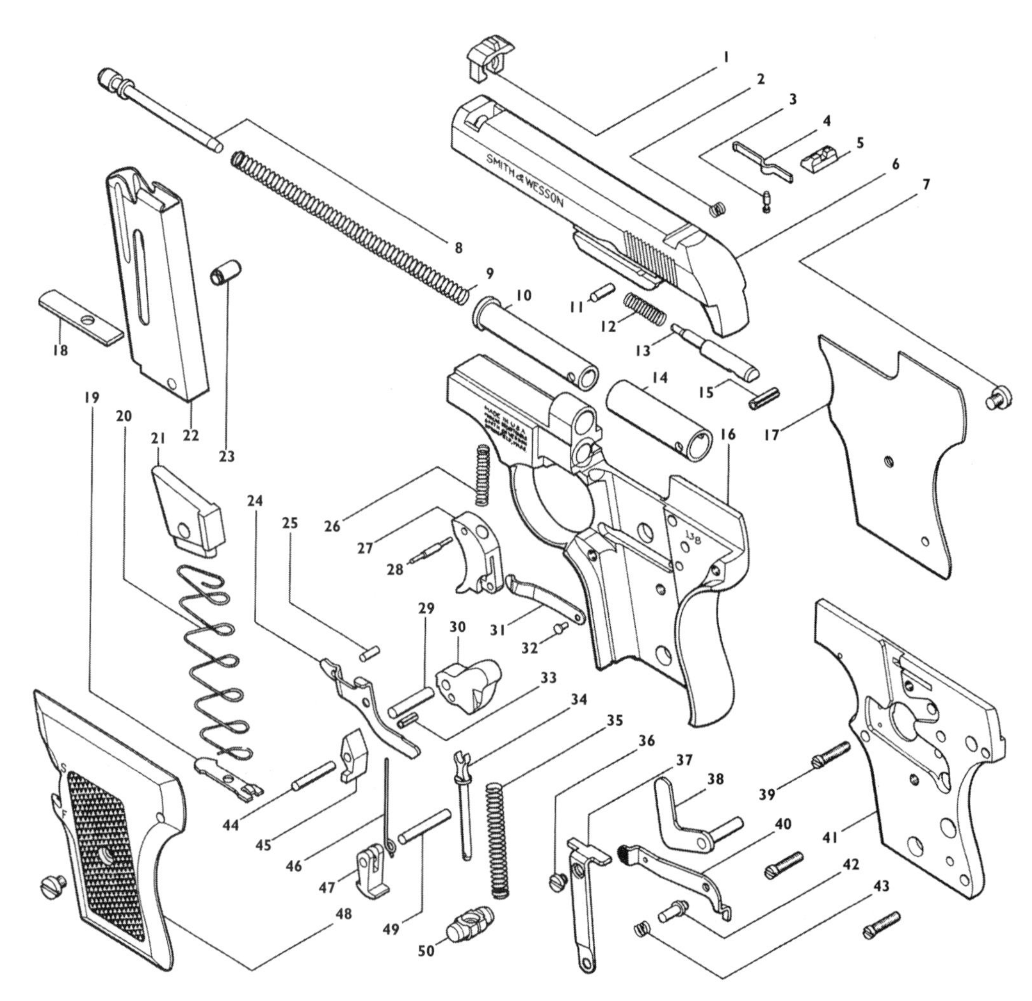

SMITH & WESSON

Introduced in March, 1970, the Model 61 Smith & Wesson Escort is a small, lightweight autoloading pistol for the .22 LR cartridge. It is blowback operated with a 2¼-inch barrel fixed in its aluminum frame. The grips and follower for the five-round magazine are made of molded plastic. The pistol is 4¾ inches long and weighs 14 ozs.

There are four versions. The original Model 61 carries serial numbers from B1001 to B7800. In May, 1970, a trigger block magazine safety was added and the result called the Model 61-1. The serial number range of this version is B7801—B9850. One lot was made with serial numbers from B1—B500. These low-numbered guns are not first production of the Model 61 but a special run of the Model 61-1. In September, 1970, Smith & Wesson engineers added a nut to secure the muzzle end of the barrel in the frame. This is the Model 61-2. Serial numbers range from B9850—B40000. In July, 1971, a forged aluminum frame which extends upward to hold the recoil spring guide tube replaced the earlier cast frame. The serial number range is B40001—B65438. This final version, the pistol illustrated here, is known as the Model 61-3. The four versions are identified by the model number stamped at the bottom of the grip behind the serial number.

The Model 61 was officially discontinued in March, 1973. Limited quantities were assembled from existing parts until February, 1974. Total production of all versions came to nearly 65000 pistols.

DISASSEMBLY

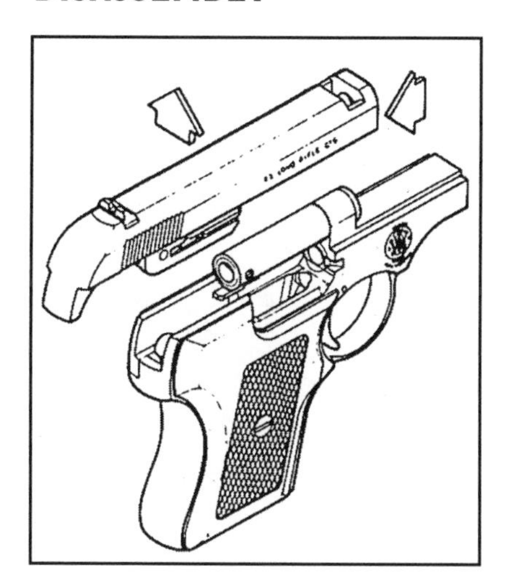

1 The Model 61 may be field stripped without tools. The front sight (1) is the key to disassembly. Remove the magazine and pull back the slide (6) to insure there is no cartridge in the chamber. Release the slide and press inward on the end of the recoil spring guide (8) which projects above the muzzle. Lift out the front sight while holding the spring guide in.

Pull the recoil spring (9) and guide out of the slide. The slide may then be removed by moving it to its extreme rearward position, then lifting it straight up off the frame. Further disassembly is not required for routine cleaning.

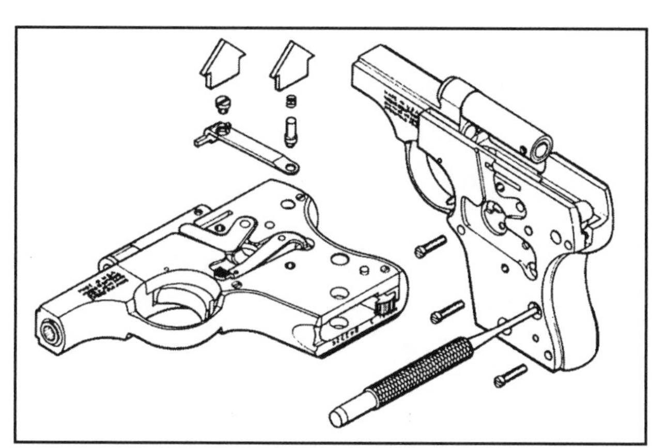

2 To strip the frame, place the assembly right side down on a bench. Remove the left stock screw and lift off the stock. Withdraw the indicator plunger (42) and spring (43). Unscrew the ejector screw (36) and lift off the ejector (37). Remove the disconnector (38) and safety lever (40). Unscrew the side-plate screws (39) and remove side-plate (41) by grasping at the top and bottom, working it off slowly and evenly. Do not allow the four frame pins or the mainspring retainer (50) to come out. It may be necessary to hold them down with a punch.

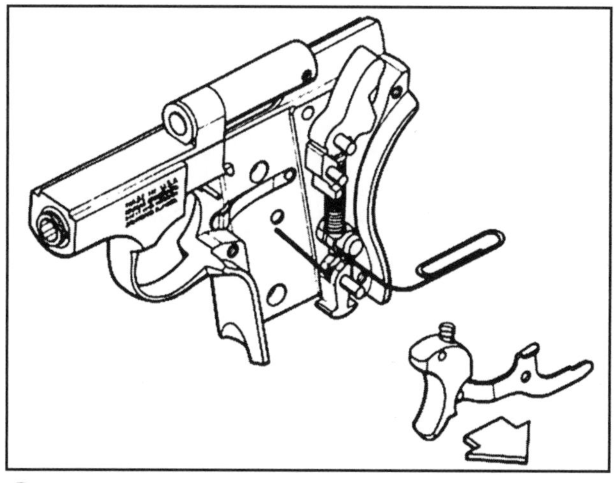

3 To disassemble the trigger mechanism, insert a straightened paper clip through the hole near the tip of the stirrup pin (33). Thumb back the hammer (30) and trip the sear (45), using the paper clip to check the mainspring (35). Pull out the trigger (27), trigger bar (24), and spring (26) as an assembly. Unhook the torsion spring (46) from the sear. The remaining parts are easily removed from the frame.

S&W K38 HEAVYWEIGHT REVOLVER

PARTS LEGEND

1. Extractor
2. Cylinder
3. Extractor spring
4. Extractor rod collar
5. Extractor rod
6. Yoke
7. Center pin spring
8. Center pin
9. Sight slide
10. Sight elevating nut
11. Sight leaf plunger spring
12. Sight leaf plunger
13. Sight leaf screw
14. Windage screw nut
15. Sight leaf
16. Windage screw spring clip
17. Sight elevating stud
18. Barrel
19. Locking bolt pin
20. Locking bolt spring
21. Locking bolt
22. Barrel pin
23. Sight leaf plunger
24. Sight leaf plunger spring
25. Windage screw
26. Cylinder stop plunger
27. Cylinder stop plunger spring
28. Cylinder stop screw
29. Cylinder stop
30. Hammer nose rivet
31. Hammer
32. Hammer nose
33. Sear
34. Sear pin
35. Sear spring
36. Trigger
37. Trigger pins
38. Sideplate
39. Large head plate screw
40. Small head plate screw
41. Small head plate screw
    41a. Small flat head plate screw
42. Stock, right-hand
43. Trigger lever
44. Hand
45. Hand spring
46. Hammer stirrup
47. Hammer stirrup pin
48. Rebound slide pin
49. Rebound slide
50. Rebound slide spring
51. Strain screw
52. Hammer block
53. Mainspring
54. Frame
55. Stock screw
56. Bolt plunger
57. Bolt plunger spring
58. Bolt
59. Thumbpece
60. Thumbpiece nut
61. Trigger stop
62. Trigger stop screw

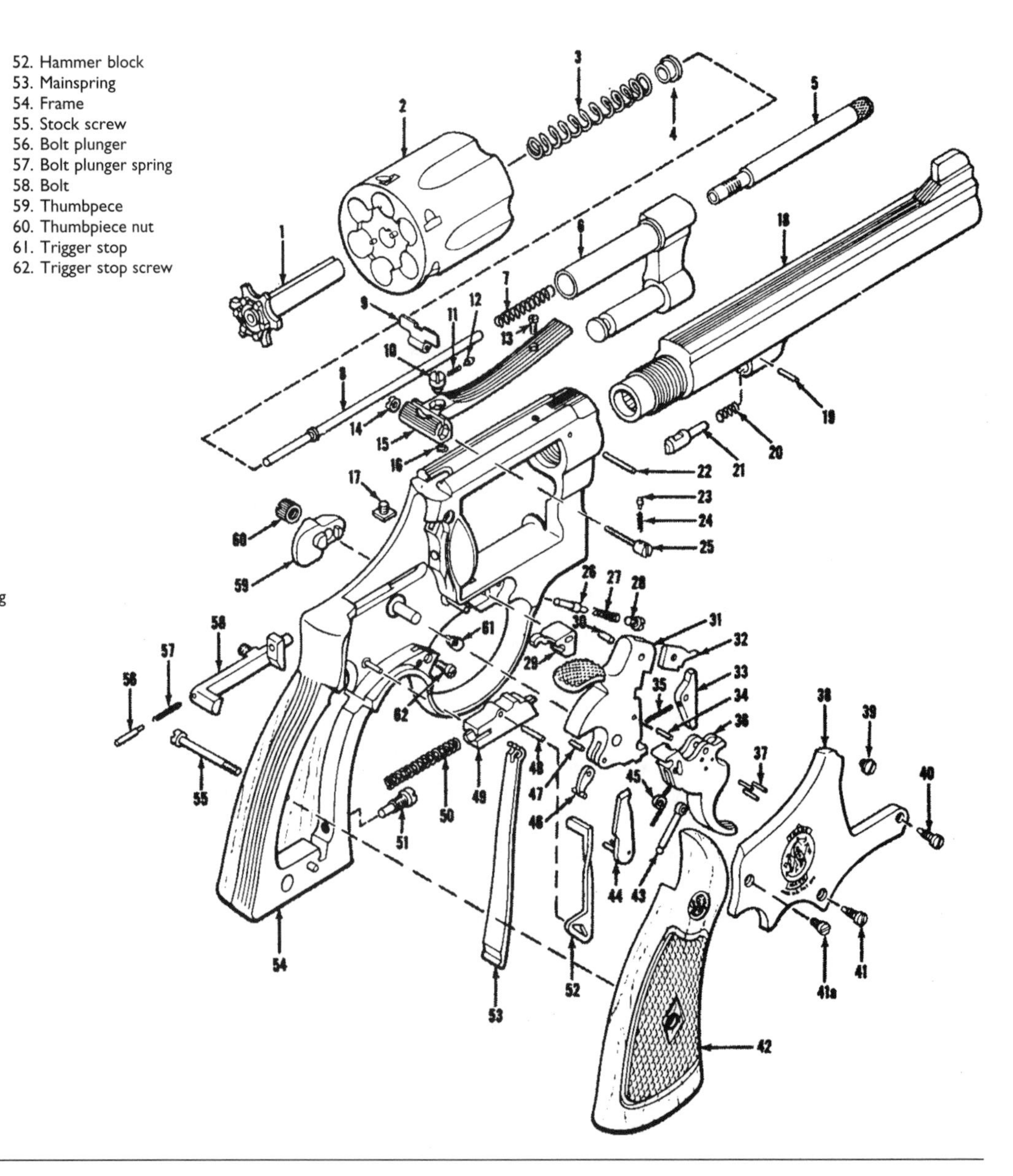

The first Smith & Wesson "Masterpiece", the K-22, was introduced in 1940, just in time to have its production suspended during World War II.

In 1947, the Masterpiece line was reintroduced, in .22 rimfire, .32 S&W Long and .38 Special, designated K-22, K-32 and K-38. In 1949, in answer to demands from target shooters, the K-38 was offered in a heavyweight version featuring a cylindrical, ribbed barrel of 6-inch length. The revised design brought the weight of the .38 Special revolver up to that of its .22 and .32 stablemates so that a shooter could switch from one gun to another without a change in the feel and handling qualities. Target stocks and target hammers were available at added cost.

The Masterpieces were fine revolvers, but were overtaken by technology, particularly the introduction of self-loading pistols to the country's target ranges. The K-32 was discontinued in 1974, the K-38 was dropped in 1981, and the .22 Magnum version of the K-22 disappeared in 1986. In 1992, only a cosmetically much-changed version of the .22 rimfire retains the Masterpiece name.

Smith & Wesson revolvers are comparatively simple to repair, mainly because they will operate without the sideplate, allowing a full view of what makes them tick. Malfunctions can then be seen and corrected. But, removing the sideplate can be difficult at times. The factory recommends that the gun be held with the sideplate up and the rear tang of the frame tapped lightly with a wooden or leather-faced mallet until the sideplate is jarred free.

Of course the grips must be removed before attempting this. These, too, must not be pried off. Instead, loosen the grip screw until the head clears the stock. Then use the screw to push the right-hand stock free. The left-hand stock can then be removed by tapping lightly through the frame from the right.

DISASSEMBLY

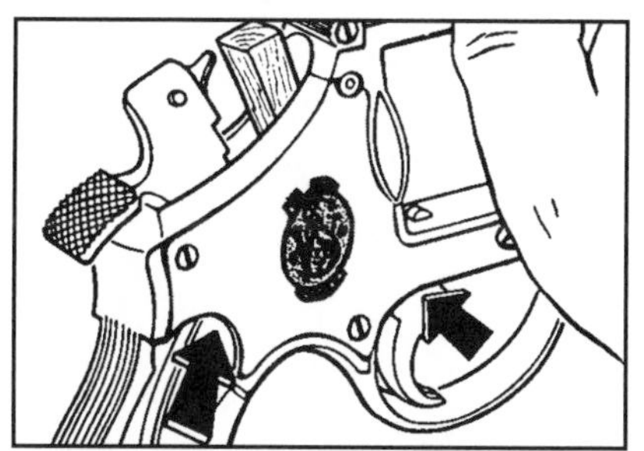

1 After removing the sideplate screws (39, 40, 41, 41a), tap the frame lightly with a wood or leather mallet to jar the sideplate (38) loose. If it is rusted in, it must be wedged up with a hard wood wedge and pried out evenly to prevent damage to plate or frame pins.

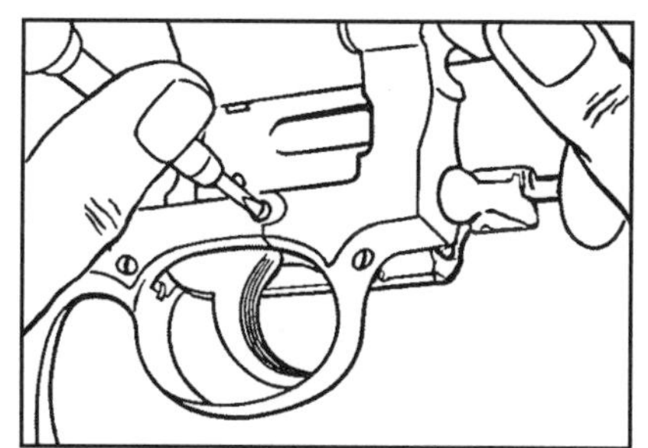

2 To remove the cylinder assembly, unscrew the small head plate screw (40). Then swing out the cylinder assembly and ease it forward out of the frame. This screw is sometimes filed on the end to give a close fit; be sure to replace it in the same position when reassembling.

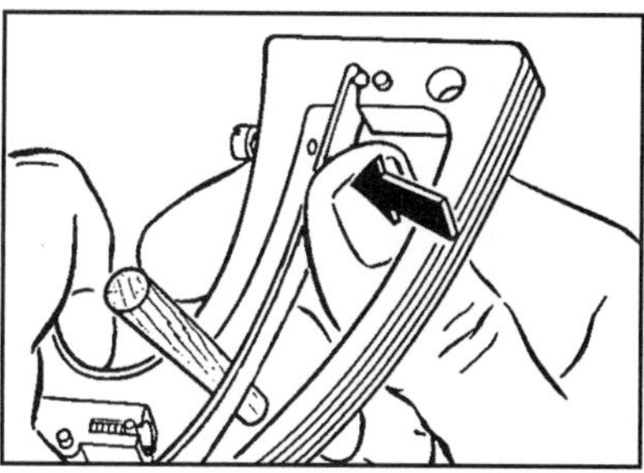

3 When removing the mainspring (53), remove the strain screw (51) and push the spring out of its slot. To replace the mainspring, hook it to the hammer stirrup (46), and spring it into place over a piece of 1/4-inch dowel as shown and tighten the strain screw (51).

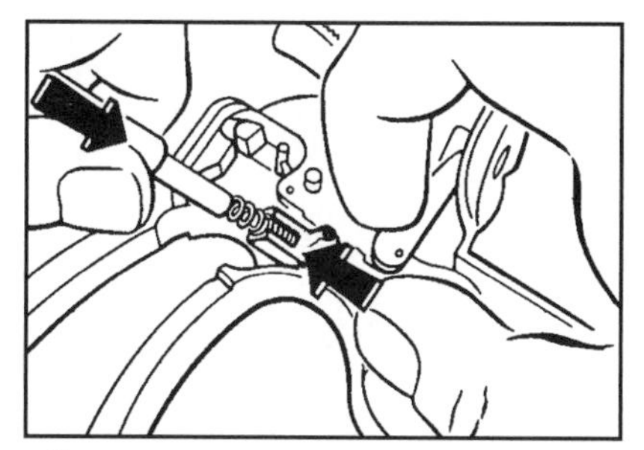

4 The rebound slide (49) and spring (50) can be removed by lifting the rear section free of the stud in the frame. Keep acloth over the gun to trap the spring and prevent injury. Replace it by pushing the spring (50) inside the rebound slide (49) and down behind the frame stud.

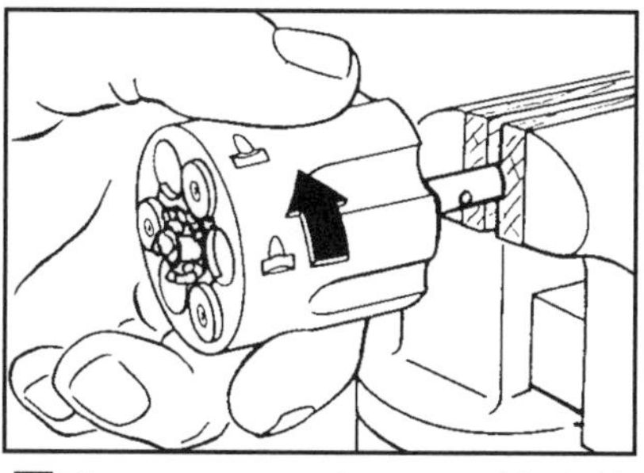

5 The extractor may be removed by holding the extractor rod (5) between wooden jaws in the vise and turning the cylinder as shown. Keep a few empty cartridges in the chamber to prevent strain on the cylinder spline and extractor-guide pins, Post-1959 guns have a left-hand thread.

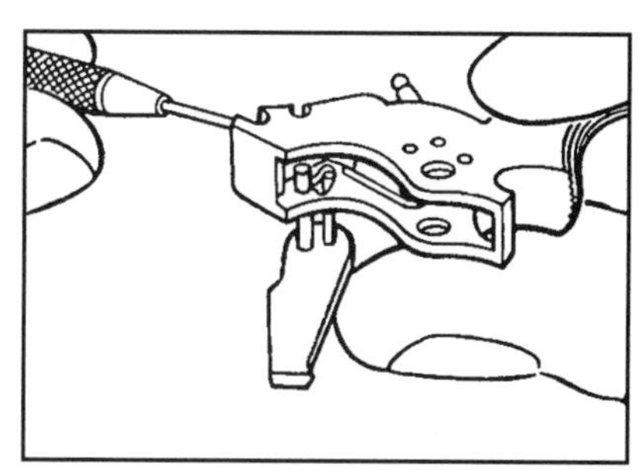

6 When replacing the hand (44) in the trigger (36), it is necessary to hold up the toil of the hand spring (45) with a small screwdriver while the hand pin is pushed into place as shown. The trigger and hand are then put in the gun as an assembly.

S&W MILITARY & POLICE REVOLVER

PARTS LEGEND

1. Frame
2. Barrel
3. Barrel pin
4. Yoke
5. Extractor rod
6. Center pin spring
7. Center pin
8. Extractor rod collar
9. Extractor spring
10. Cylinder
11. Extractor
12. Bolt
13. Bolt plunger spring
14. Bolt plunger
15. Thumbpiece
16. Thumbpiece nut
17. Locking bolt
18. Locking bolt spring
19. Locking bolt pin
20. Side-plate
21. Side-plate screws, roundhead (2)
22. Side-plate screw, large head (discontinued)
    22A. Side-plate screw, flathead
23. Cylinder stop plunger
24. Cylinder stop plunger spring
25. Cylinder stop screw
26. Cylinder stop
27. Strain screw
28. Stock pin
29. Rebound slide spring
30. Rebound slide
31. Rebound slide pin
32. Mainspring
33. Hammer block
34. Hammer
35. Hammer nose
36. Hammer nose rivet
37. Stirrup
38. Stirrup pin
39. Sear
40. Sear pin
41. Sear spring
42. Trigger
43 Trigger lever
44. Trigger lever pin
45. Hand spring torsion pins (2)
46. Hand torsion spring
47. Hand
48. Stocks
49. Stock screw

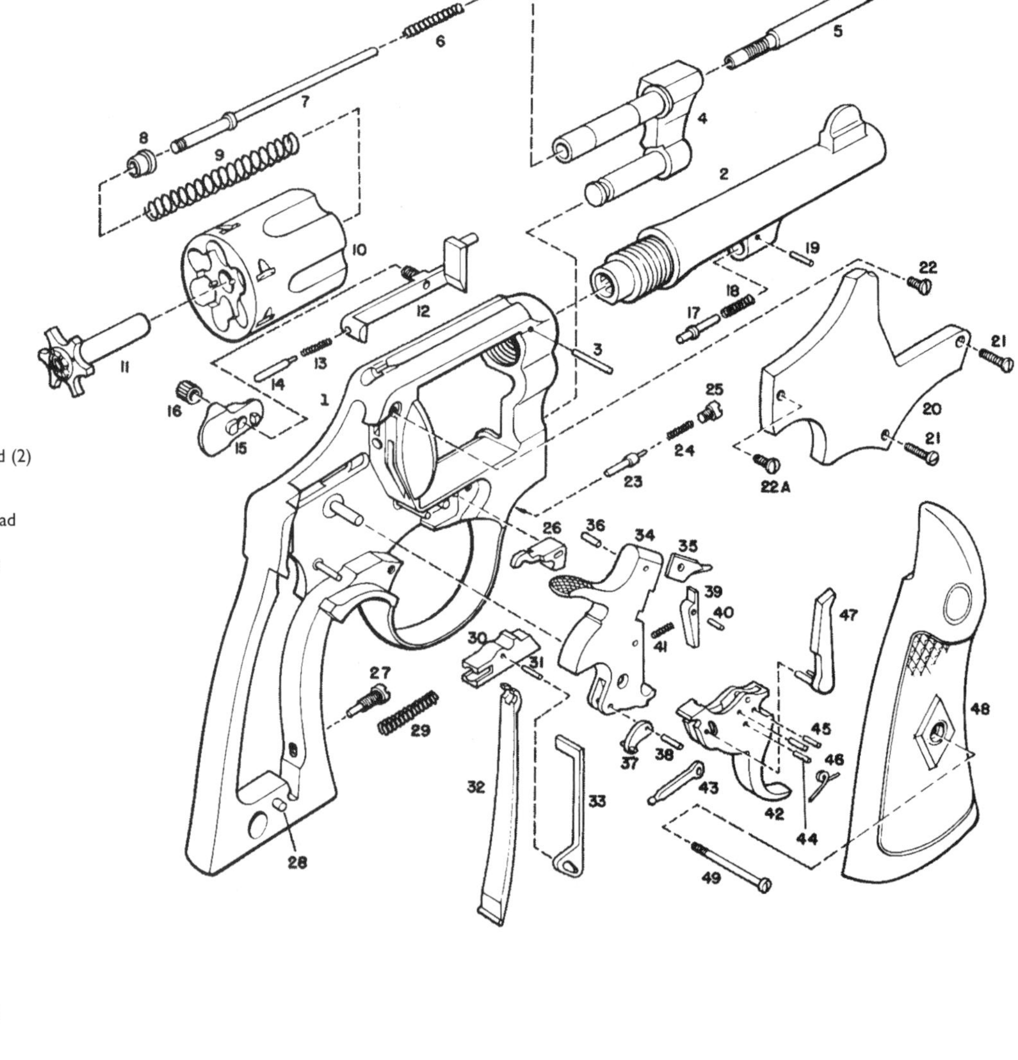

In 1899, Smith & Wesson, introduced their double-action "Hand Ejector, Military & Police" revolver, based on a design developed for the U.S. military during the Spanish American War. The Military & Police was the first .38 caliber, side-swing model to be made by Smith & Wesson. It was chambered for the .38 S&W and .32 Winchester cartridges and was sold with hard rubber grips and 4-inch barrel.

The improved Model 1902 M&P, introduced in that year, was chambered for the new .38 S&W Special cartridge and featured a front lock for the extractor rod. Its successor, the Model 1905, was available with 4-, 5-, 6-, and 6½-inch barrels. By 1942 more than 1 million M&P's had been manufactured. Beginning in 1942, Smith & Wesson began production of the "Parkerized" Victory Model for the armed forces. In December 1944 an improved hammer block was instituted.

After the war, Smith & Wesson resumed production of commercial M&Ps, producing a total of perhaps three million M&P models by 1967. The current S&W Military & Police revolver is known as the Model 10. Its variants include the Model 13, in .357 Magnum, and the stainless Model 65.

DISASSEMBLY

Swing out cylinder, then loosen forward side-plate screw (21) and withdraw cylinder and yoke assembly from frame. Withdraw yoke (4) from cylinder assembly. On older guns with knobbed extractor rod, yoke cannot be removed from cylinder assembly until extractor rod has been removed as in next step.

To disassemble cylinder assembly insert several empty cases in cylinder to prevent strain on extractor (11), then grip extractor rod (5) with pliers (pad jaws) and turn cylinder until extractor rod is free of extractor. Guns made from 1899 to 1960 have a right-hand thread; those after 1961 a left-hand thread. Withdraw extractor rod, yoke, extractor rod collar (8), extractor spring (9), center pin (7) with center pin spring (6), and extractor.

Remove stock screw (49) and stocks (48).

Remove side-plate screws (21 [2], 22, 22A). Side-plate (20) is loosened by tapping opposite surface of frame sharply with a wood or fiber hammer until it can be removed from frame. Attempts to pry out side-plate will deform its edges and those of frame cut.

Mainspring (32) is easily removed by loosening strain screw (27). All interior parts of lock mechanism are now easily removed for cleaning or replacement. However, for normal cleaning purposes, it is seldom necessary to carry disassembly beyond removal of side-plate. The accompanying drawings point Out some methods for further disassembly.

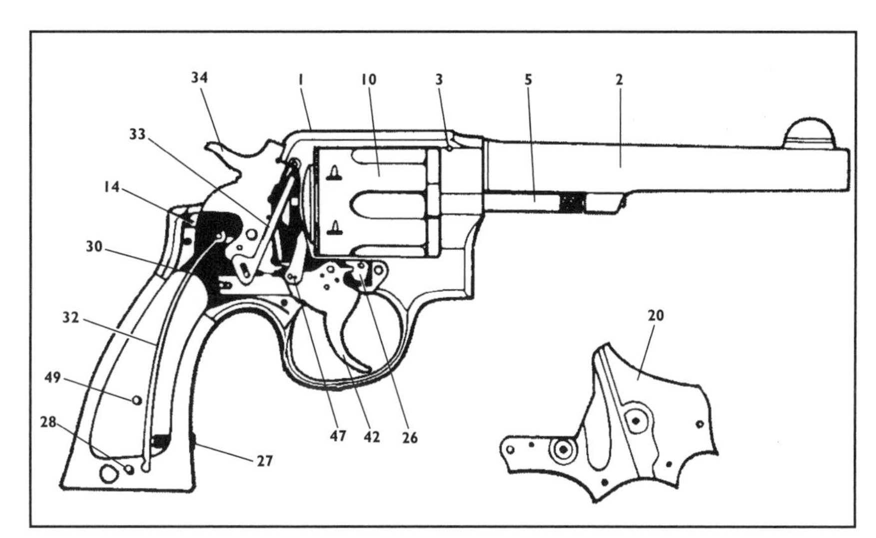

Drawing of revolver with side-plate removed shows proper relationship of interior parts.

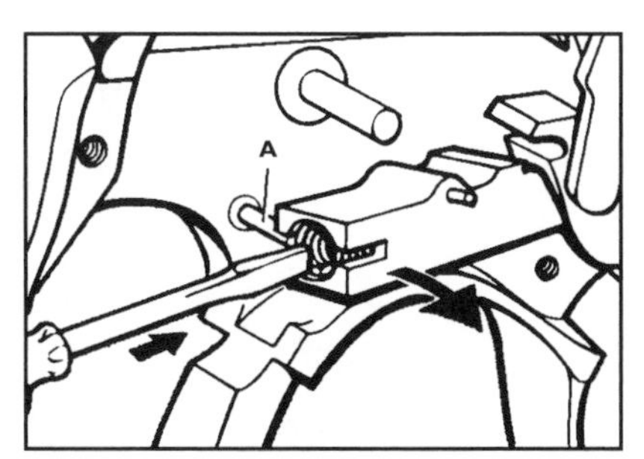

1 To remove rebound slide (30), pry up rear end of slide with blade of small screwdriver but do not allow spring to clear end of rebound slide stud (A) in frame. Compress rear end of rebound slide spring (29) with screwdriver blade as shown and draw rebound slide up off stud (A), taking care not to let compressed spring escape. In replacing rebound slide in frame, spring must again be compressed inside slide so that it will clear stud before slide can be pressed down into position. Note that the stud (A) and other pivot studs in frame are permanently installed and their removal should not be attempted.

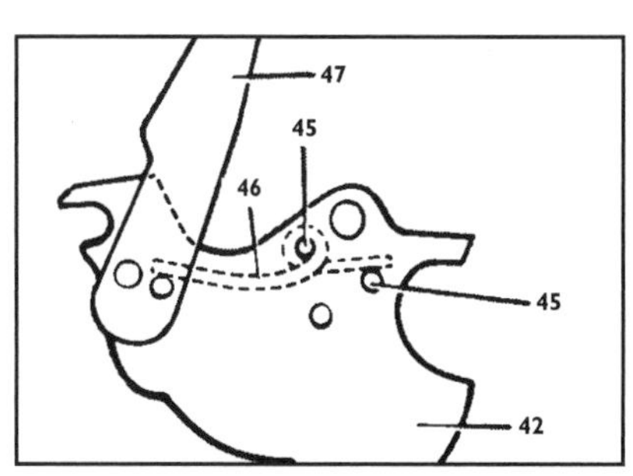

2 The drawing shows proper position of hand (47) installed in trigger (42). Hand can be removed from trigger by pulling it free. When replacing hand in trigger, take care that hand torsion spring (46) is in correct position with respect to hand spring torsion pins (45) in trigger and small torsion pin installed in hand.

S&W NUMBER 1 REVOLVER

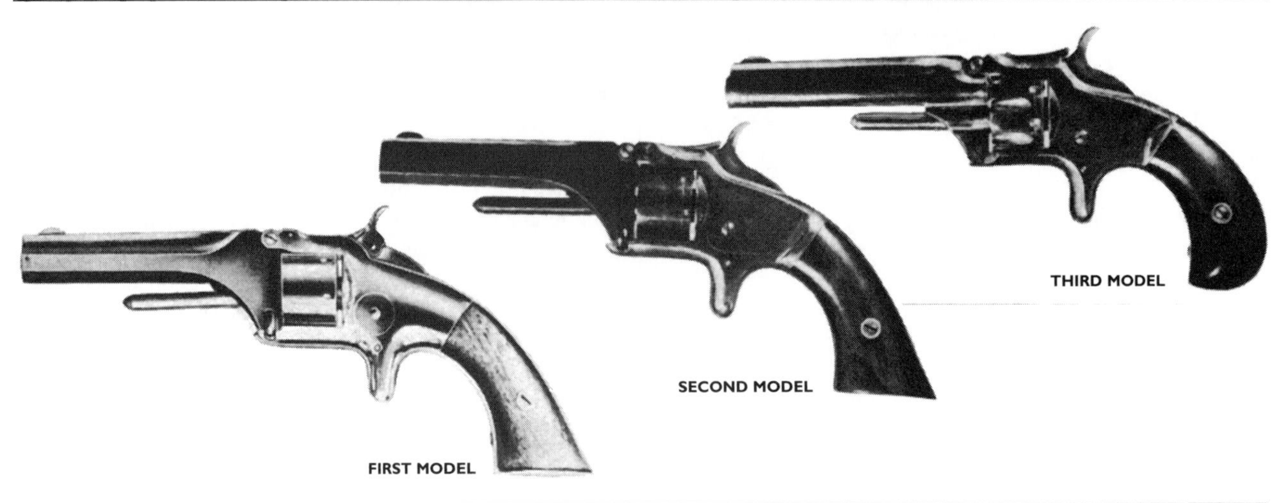

PARTS LEGEND

1. Frame
2. Cylinder stop
3. Cylinder stop screw
4. Cylinder stop striker
5. Cylinder stop spring
6. Cylinder stop spring pin
7. Cylinder stop pin
8. Barrel pivot screw
9. Cylinder
10. Cylinder stud
11. Hammer stud
12. Hammer
13. Hand spring
14. Hand pin
15. Hand
16. Stirrup
17. Stirrup pin
18. Sideplate
19. Sideplate screw (screws into hammer stud)
20. Trigger
21. Trigger pin
22. Trigger spring
23. Mainspring
24. Mainspring strain screw
25. Stock pin
26. Stock, left hand
27. Stock, right hand
28. Stock screw
29. Escutcheon
30. Escutcheon nut
31. Barrel
32. Ejector pin
33. Ejector pin screw
34. Barrel latch
35. Barrel latch spring
36. Barrel latch screw

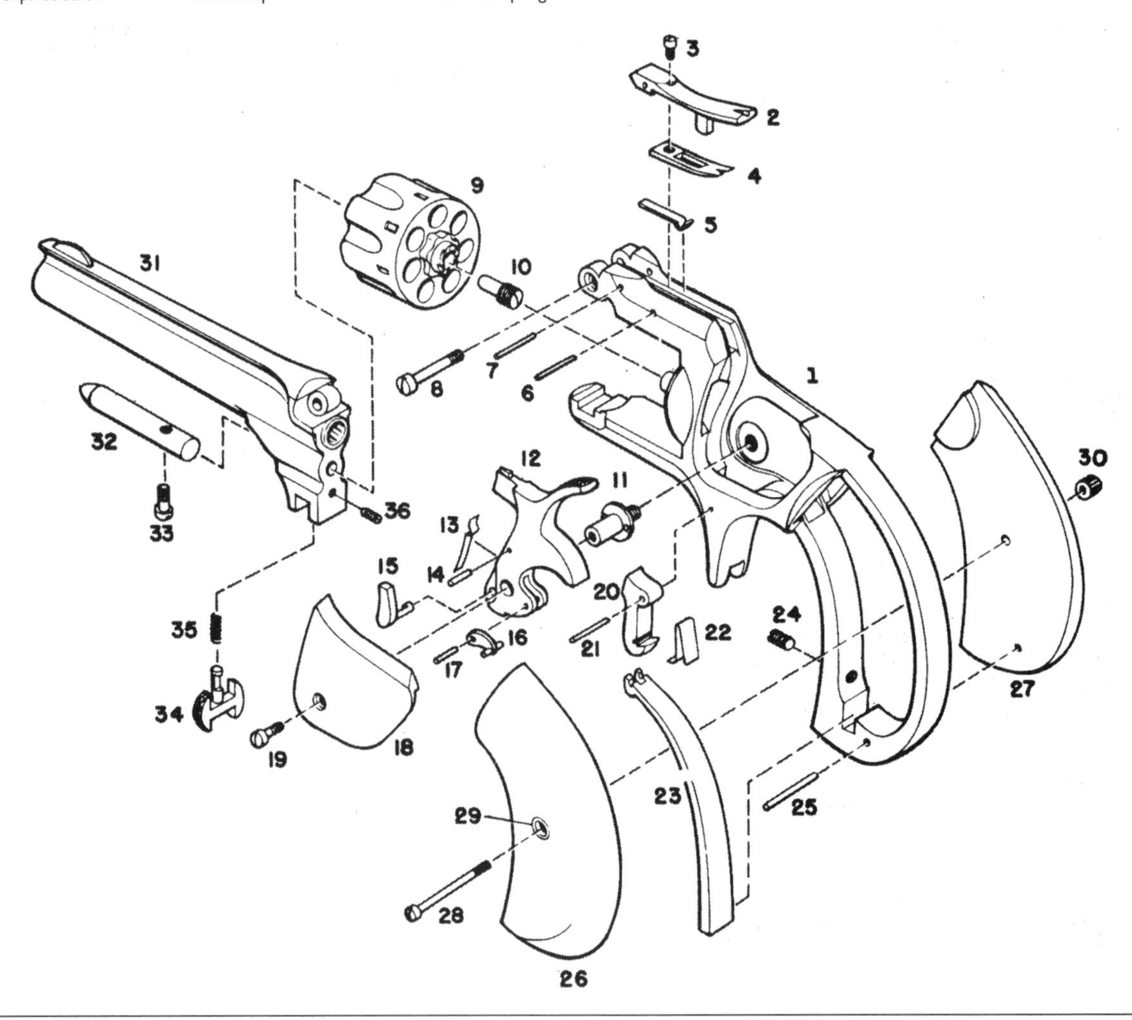

In 1857 Smith & Wesson of Springfield, Massachusetts, introduced the first American metallic cartridge revolver. It was also the first American revolver with chambers bored completely through the cylinder under the Rollin White's patent of 1855.

The 7-shot, brass framed revolver was designated the Number 1 and featured a 3¼-inch, tip-up octagonal barrel and no trigger guard. It's frame was round-sided and the revolver had a hinged hammer spur.

The Number 1 was chambered for the Smith & Wesson .22 caliber rimfire cartridge (.22 Short). The early round was loaded with a 3-grain powder charge behind a 30-grain lead bullet. While ballistically poor, this cartridge and revolver combination proved immediately popular. The 2nd Model of the Number 1 revolver, introduced in 1860, had a flat-sided frame and $3^{3}/_{16}$-inch barrrel. In 1868 the 3rd Model, Number 1 revolver was issued with a fluted cylinder and round barrel with a raised rib. Production was discontinued in 1879. All told, 254,958 Number 1 revolvers were manufactured, with the Third Model accounting for 128,528 of this total.

A note of caution regarding old S&W revolvers. While the cylinder is too short to chamber modern .22 Long or Long Rifle cartridges, a .22 Short will usually fit. However, these revolvers were manufactured for black powder and it would be unwise to fire them with modern smokeless loads.

DISASSEMBLY

While there are several minor variations in No. 1 S&W revolvers, disassembly procedure for all is substantially the same.

To tip up barrel, raise latch (34) and swing barrel (31) upward. Cylinder (9) is removed by drawing it straight forward.

To remove barrel from frame, unscrew barrel pivot screw (8). Ejector pin (32) is removed by unscrewing its screw (33). Remove barrel latch screw (36) and drop latch (34) out bottom of barrel lug. Barrel latch spring (35) will drop out after latch.

To disassemble lock mechanism, first remove stock screw (28) and stocks (26 & 27). Remove sideplate screw (19). Hold frame with sideplate (18) downward and tap frame sharply with a wooden or plastic hammer until sideplate works loose and drops out of frame. Do not attempt to pry sideplate out. Unscrew mainspring strain screw (24) and press top end of main spring (23) down with tip of screwdriver or similar tool until it disengages from stirrup (16). Mainspring (23) may be easily lifted out of frame. While holding tip of hand (15) back and clear of its slot in frame with tip of small screwdriver, work hammer (12) up off hammer stud (11) and out of frame (1) with fingers. Hammer will frequently fit quite snugly to its stud and a few drops of penetrating oil may help in lifting it free. Hand and hand spring (13) as well as stirrup rarely need be removed from hammer except for replacement. Either of these parts may be easily removed by drifting out their respective pins (14 & 17). Inasmuch as a special spanner wrench will be required to remove hammer stud from frame, such removal is not recommended and should seldom if ever be necessary. Cylinder stop assembly and spring (2, 3, 4, 5) can be removed from top of frame by drifting out cylinder stop pin (7) and spring pin (6). Trigger (20) and spring (22) are easily removed from frame by drifting out trigger pin (21).

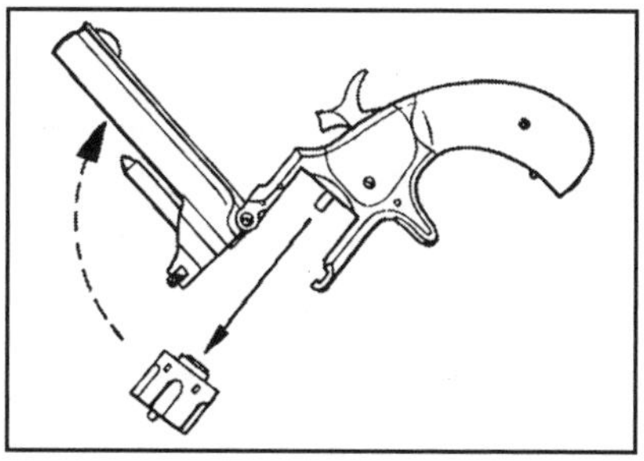

1 Pressing upward on barrel latch (34) releases barrel, which tips upward as shown. Cylinder can be withdrawn from frame toward the front.

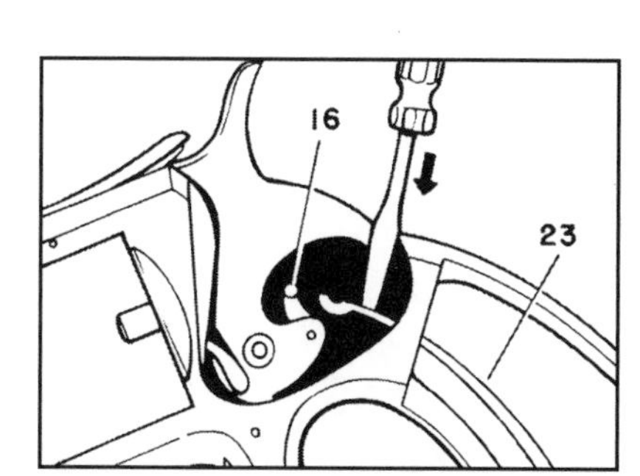

2 After loosening mainspring strain screw (24), mainspring (23) may be removed by pressing down an top end of spring at point shown to disengage stirrup (16) and lifting from frame with the fingers.

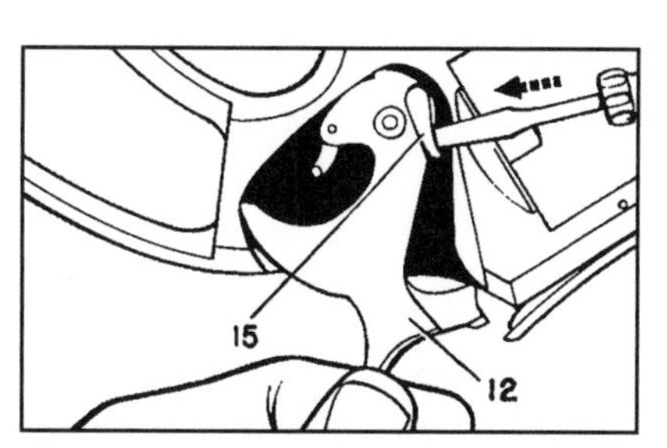

3 To remove hammer (12) from frame, hold hand (15) back and clear of its slot in frame with the tip of a small screwdriver or similar implement as shown and work hammer up off hammer stud.

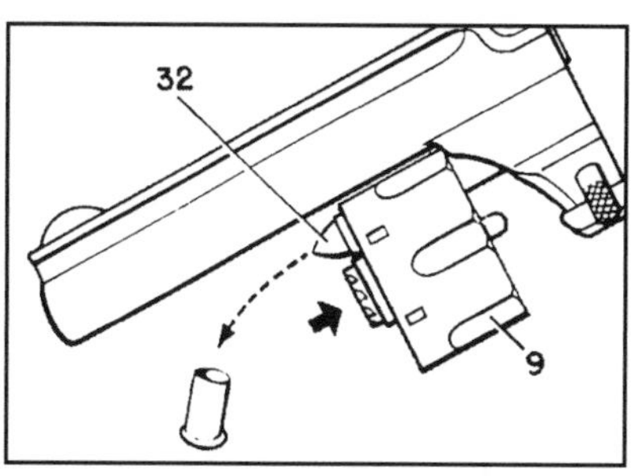

4 Empty cartridge cases are ejected by pressing reversed cylinder onto ejector pin (32).

S&W SAFETY HAMMERLESS

PARTS LEGEND

1. Frame
2. Barrel
   2a. Front sight
   2b. Front sight pin
3. Base pin
4. Extractor cam
5. Extractor cam latch
6. Extractor cam latch spring
7. Joint pivot screw
8 Joint pivot
9. Trigger guard
10. Trigger spring
11. Cylinder catch
12. Cylinder catch spring
13. Cylinder catch pin
14. Barrel catch
15. Barrel catch thumbpiece
16. Barrel catch spring
17. Barrel catch pin
18. Barrel catch thumbpiece screw
19. Barrel catch plate
20. Barrel catch plate spring
21. Barrel catch plate pin
22. Firing pin bushing
23. Firing pin
24. Firing pin spring
25. Extractor post
26.. Extractor spring
27. Extractor rod
28. Cylinder
29. Extractor
30. Extractor stud
31. Safety lever
32. Safety lever pin
33. Stock pin
34. Mainspring
35. Strain screw
36. Latch spring
37. Latch spring pin
38. Latch
39. Latch pin
40. Hammer stud
41. Hammer
42. Stirrup
43. Stirrup pin
44. Trigger
    44a. Trigger stop pin
45. Sear
46. Trigger pin
47. Hand & hand spring
48. Cylinder stop
49. Cylinder stop spring
50. Cylinder stop spring pin
51. Cylinder stop pin
52. Split spring
53. Split spring pin
54. Side-plate
55. Side-plate screw
56. Hammer stud nut

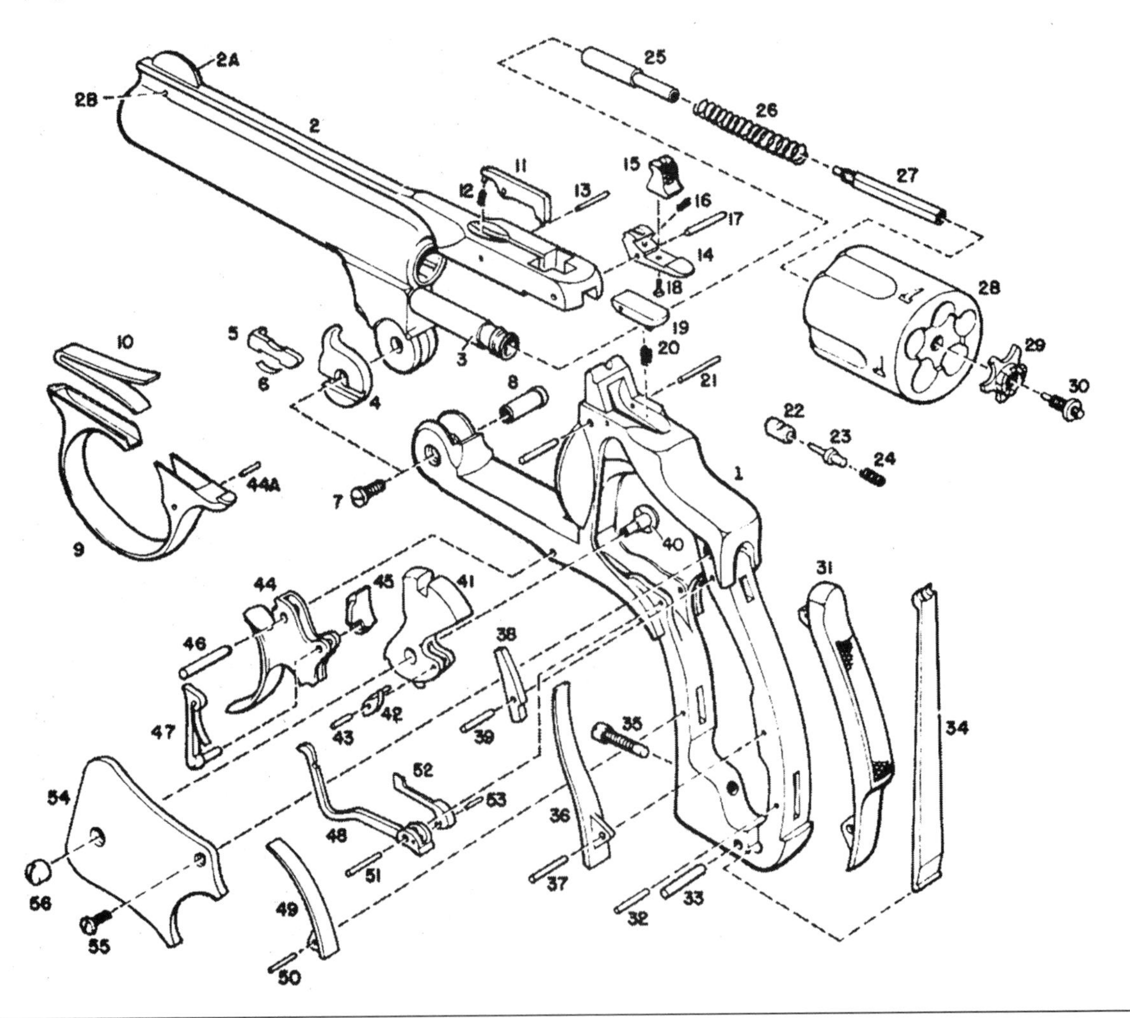

In 1887, Smith & Wesson announced a new 5-shot hammerless top-break revolver. An article in the April 1887 issue of the NRA's, *The Rifle*, stated that it represented a "new departure" in revolver design. The phrase appealed to Smith & Wesson and was used as the designation for this model.

First marketed in February 1888, the New Departure Safety Hammerless revolver was offered in .32 and .38 caliber S&W with choice of 3- and 3½-inch barrels with a 2-inch "bicycle" model available. The mechanical features of the Safety Hammerless included a grip safety that prevented cocking and firing of the gun until the safety lever had been depressed. S&W claimed that the revolver's heavy trigger pull made the gun safe around small children who lacked the strength to fire the gun. Production of the .32 caliber Safety Hammerless ended in about 1937, and the .38 caliber version was discontinued in 1940.

DISASSEMBLY

To dismount barrel from frame, break action and remove joint pivot screw (7). Punch out joint pivot (8) to right. Pull barrel (2) free of frame (1). Extractor cam (4) and extractor cam latch (5) can now be slipped free of joint. Remove cylinder (28) by pressing cylinder catch (11) on top strap of barrel and unscrewing cylinder and extractor assembly from base pin (3). (Note: Not all S&W Safety Hammerless revolvers have this cylinder catch.) Removal of base pin (3) from barrel is not recommended. Cylinder catch assembly (11) and barrel catch assembly (14-20) are removed by drifting out the respective pins (13, 17, 21). Remove barrel catch thumbpiece screw (18) to separate catch assembly.

To disassemble lock mechanism, remove grips and unscrew side-plate screw (55) and hammer stud nut (56). Ease side-plate (54) up out of frame gradually by prying gently and tapping reverse side of frame with a fiber or wooden hammer. Unscrew strain screw (35) and withdraw mainspring (34) from frame. Safety lever (31), latch (38) and latch spring (36) are removed by drifting out pins (32, 37, 39). Drift out trigger pin (46). Trigger guard (9) is removed by springing rear portion of guard toward the front and pulling it downward and out of frame. Drift out cylinder stop pin (51) and work hammer (41) back out of frame. Manipulate trigger and cylinder stop assembly in frame until hand (47) can be lifted out of frame. Drop trigger and cylinder stop out bottom of frame. Remove sear (45) through side-plate hole in frame.

1 This drawing shows the 4 major variations of the Safety Hammerless revolver: A: 1st Model with Z-bar barrel catch operated by pushing bar in top strap from left to right. B: 2nd Model, opened by pushing down on checked thumbpiece protruding from rear of top strap of barrel (this is the model illustrated in the exploded drawings). C: 3rd Model, opened by pushing down on checked flat thumbpiece on top of strap. D: 4th Model, opened by lifting T-shaped barrel catch with knurled buttons on each side. The 5th Model is identical with the fourth except that the front sight is forged integrally with the barrel rather than a separate piece.

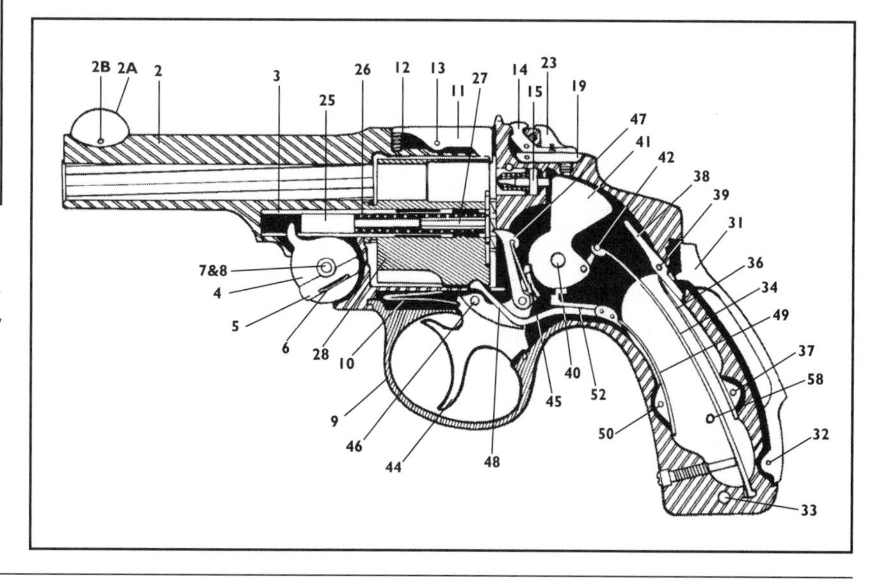

2 The revolver is shown with the lock mechanism in fired position. Note that the safety lever (31) is out, allowing the top end of the latch (38) to stand out in the way of the hammer (41), preventing the hammer from coming back far enough to fire. When the safety lever is pressed in, the top of the latch moves back against the inner wall of the frame, leaving the hammer clear to come all the way back to fire.

SMITH & WESSON SIGMA SERIES

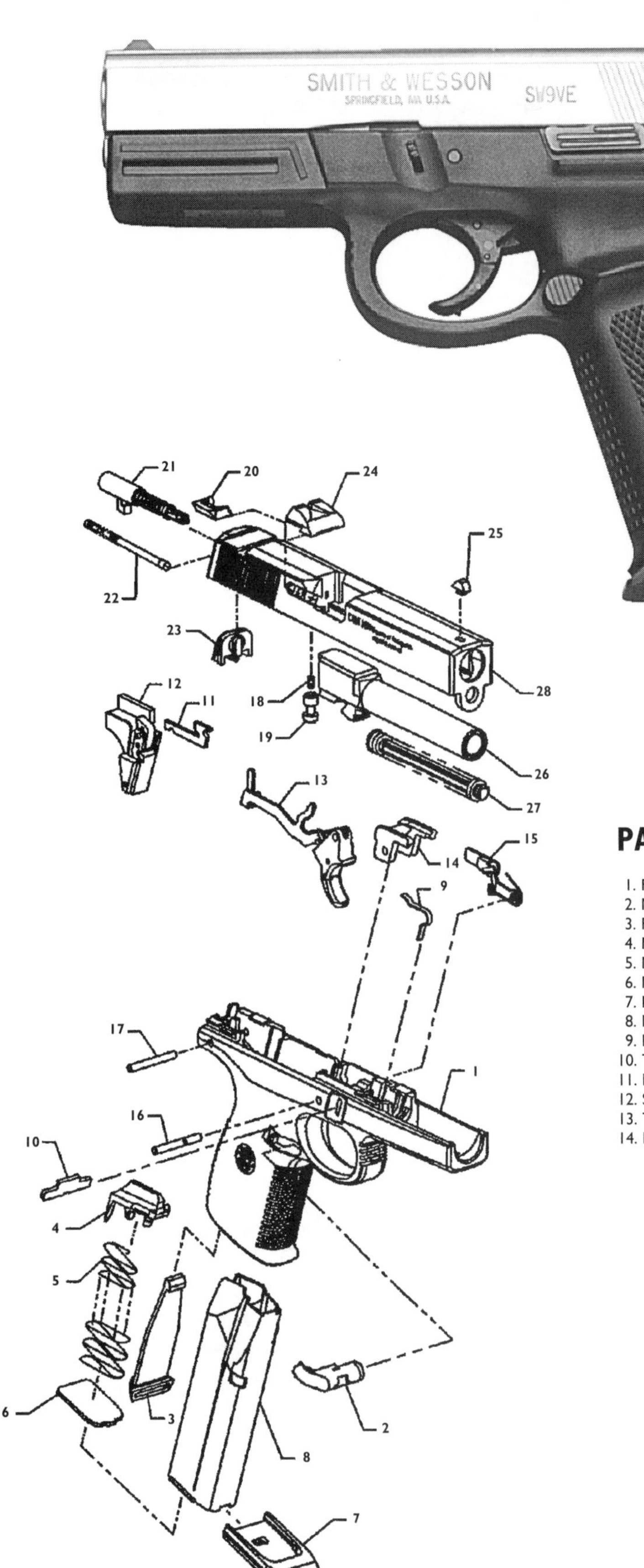

PARTS LEGEND

1. Frame
2. Magazine catch
3. Frame plug
4. Magazine follower
5. Magazine spring
6. Magazine Butt plate catch
7. Magazine butt plate
8. Magazine tube
9. Barrel stop spring
10. Take down catch/barrel stop
11. Ejector
12. Sear housing block assembly
13. Trigger bar assembly
14. Locking block
15. Slide stop lever assembly
16. Trigger pin
17. Sear housing block assembly pin
18. Safety plunger spring
19. Striker safety plunger
20. Extractor
21. Striker assembly
22. Extractor spring assembly
23. Slide end cap
24. Rear sight
25. Front sight
26. Barrel
27. Recoil spring assembly

Smith & Wesson introduced their Sigma series of polymer framed semi-automatic pistols in 1994 with the Sigma 40 (.40 S&W), followed by the Sigma 9 (9mm). The Sigma was Smith & Wesson's first foray into the manufacture of polymer plastic framed pistols.

The new Sigma semi-automatics were intended to compete with the Austrian Glock pistols and shared considerable design similarities. In early 1994, Glock sued Smith & Wesson for patent infringement. Ultimately the dispute was settled out of court and Smith & Wesson agreed to modify the Sigma's trigger mechanism and pay Glock an undisclosed sum.

The Sigma is a locked-breech, recoil-operated semi-automatic built on a modified Browning short recoil system. The barrel and slide are machined from either stainless or carbon steel. The pistol is striker fired and is reset by the slide after each pull of the trigger. The safety is integrated into the trigger, which must be deliberately pulled to fire the weapon and the Sigma has an internal firing pin block that prevents firing unless the trigger is held back.

The Sigma employs a plastic double stack magazine carrying between fifteen and seventeen rounds of 9mm ammunition depending upon its caliber. The Sigma is also produced in two other models, the 357V (.357 Sig) and Sigma 380 (.380 ACP).

DISASSEMBLY

Depress the magazine release, and remove the magazine. With the barrel pointing in a safe direction, and with your finger off the trigger and outside the trigger guard, grasp the serrated sides of the slide and from the rear with the thumb and fingers while holding the firearm in an upright position, and briskly draw the slide fully rearward in order to extract any cartridge from the barrel chamber and clear it from the pistol.

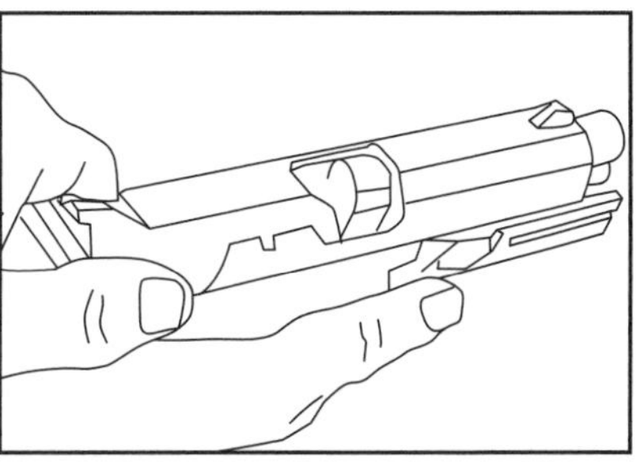

1 Make certain that the chamber is clear. With the pistol still pointing in a safe direction and the slide closed, pull the trigger once and remove your finger from the trigger and out of the trigger guard.

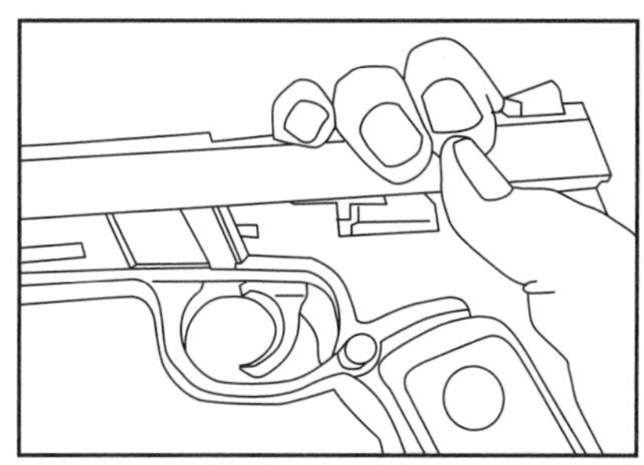

2 Move the slide approximately ⅛" to the rear and depress the takedown catch/barrel stop on both sides of the frame with your thumb and forefinger.

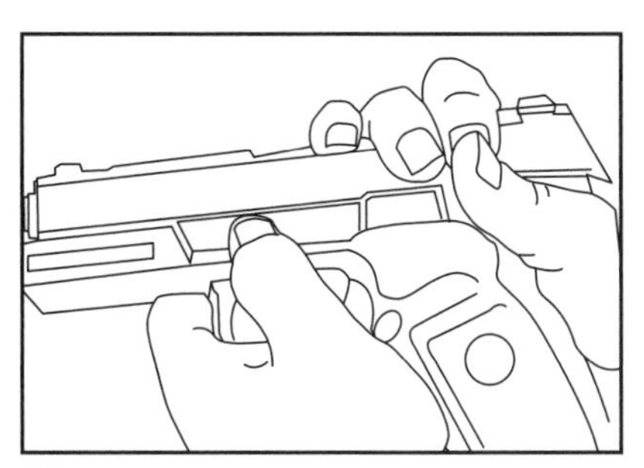

3 Allow the slide to return forward while depressing the takedown catch/barrel stop.

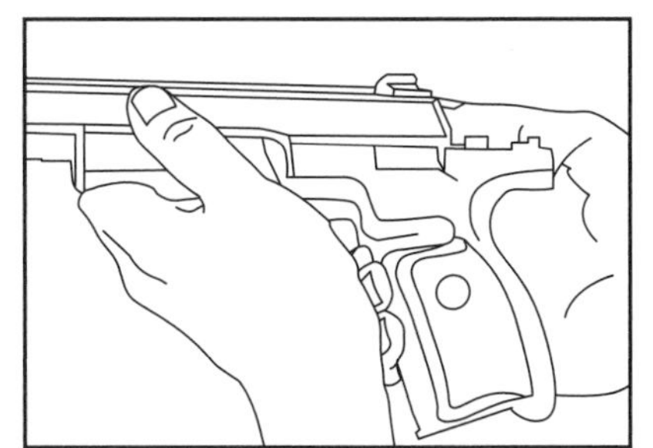

4 Grasp the slide from the top, just behind the front sight and remove the slide by pulling it forward while being careful to retain the recoil spring and guide rod assembly. WARNING: The recoil spring is under pressure. Control the recoil spring and the guide so that they do not fly out and cause injury.

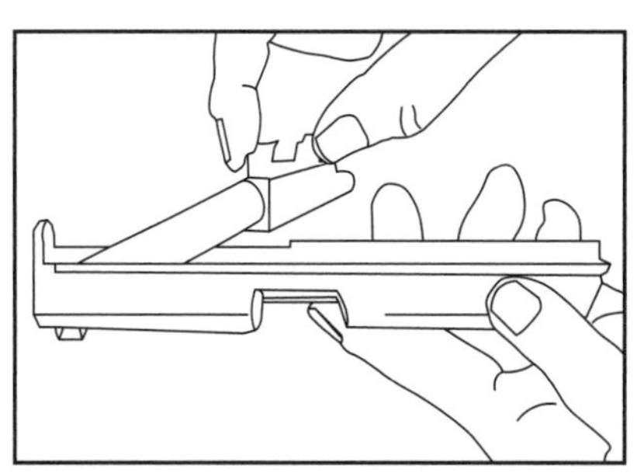

5 Remove the recoil spring and barrel. NOTE: No further disassembly is recommended, as the pistol may be properly cleaned and lubricated when field-stripped as described above.

SPRINGFIELD ARMORY XD PISTOL

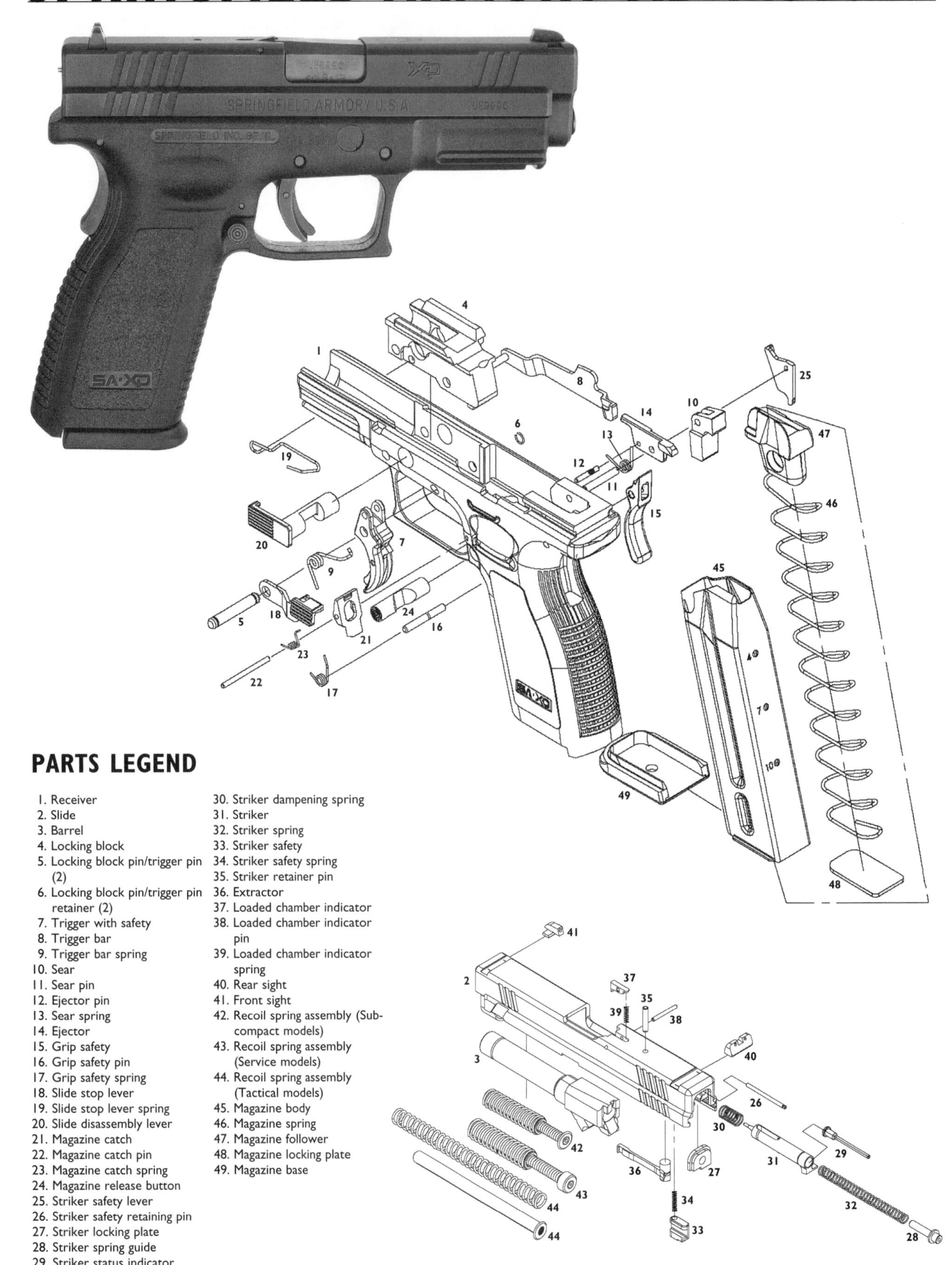

PARTS LEGEND

1. Receiver
2. Slide
3. Barrel
4. Locking block
5. Locking block pin/trigger pin (2)
6. Locking block pin/trigger pin retainer (2)
7. Trigger with safety
8. Trigger bar
9. Trigger bar spring
10. Sear
11. Sear pin
12. Ejector pin
13. Sear spring
14. Ejector
15. Grip safety
16. Grip safety pin
17. Grip safety spring
18. Slide stop lever
19. Slide stop lever spring
20. Slide disassembly lever
21. Magazine catch
22. Magazine catch pin
23. Magazine catch spring
24. Magazine release button
25. Striker safety lever
26. Striker safety retaining pin
27. Striker locking plate
28. Striker spring guide
29. Striker status indicator
30. Striker dampening spring
31. Striker
32. Striker spring
33. Striker safety
34. Striker safety spring
35. Striker retainer pin
36. Extractor
37. Loaded chamber indicator
38. Loaded chamber indicator pin
39. Loaded chamber indicator spring
40. Rear sight
41. Front sight
42. Recoil spring assembly (Sub-compact models)
43. Recoil spring assembly (Service models)
44. Recoil spring assembly (Tactical models)
45. Magazine body
46. Magazine spring
47. Magazine follower
48. Magazine locking plate
49. Magazine base

Well-known for its M1A semi-automatic rifles and M1911 variations, Springfield Armory entered the polymer-frame pistol market in 2002 with the introduction of its XD pistol.

Manufactured in Ozalj, Croatia by HS Produkt, the XD originated with the PHP pistol designed in 1991 by the Croatian firm of I.M. Metal. An improved version, the HS95, led to the HS2000 in 1999. Springfield Armory marketed the HS2000 in the U.S. as the XD or Xtreme Duty.

XD pistols are polymer-framed semi-automatic handguns with high-capacity magazines. The trigger design features a pivoting arm in the trigger face that prevents trigger movement unless the arm is depressed.

The XD is available in various models, in 9 mm Parabellum, .357 SIG, .40 S&W, .45 GAP and .45 ACP with a choice of barrel lengths that include 3- (Sub-Compact), 4- (Compact & Service models), 5- (Tactical) and 4-inch Ported barrels.

DISASSEMBLY

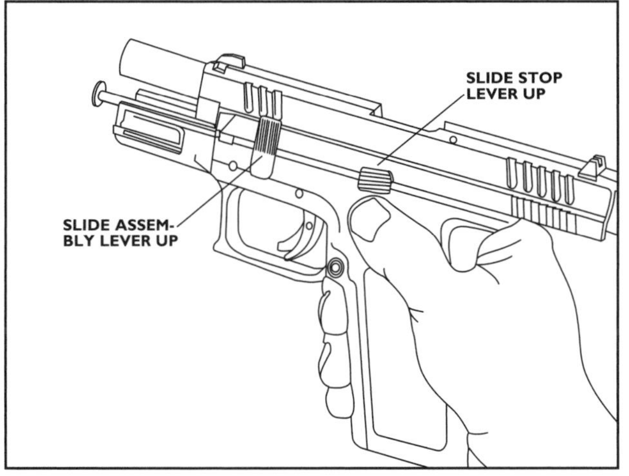

1 Draw back the slide to the rear stop position and lock it open, thumbing up the slide stop lever.

Visually inspect the chamber to confirm the pistol is unloaded.

Rotate the slide disassembly lever clockwise to a vertical 12 o'clock position.

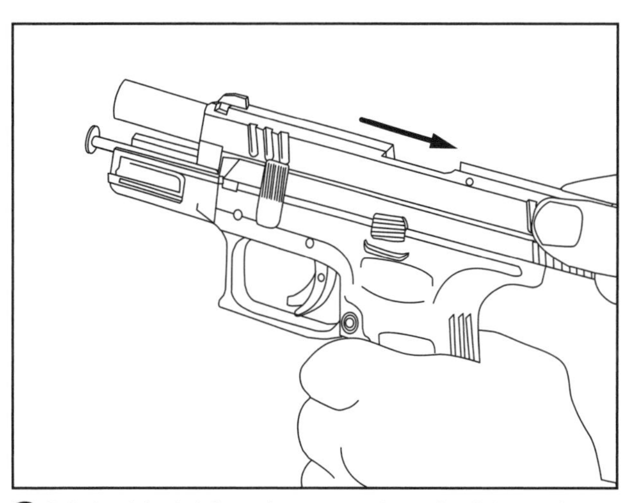

2 Pull the slide slightly to the rear to release the slide stop lever. Then allow the slide to slowly move forward until the spring tension is released. Pull the trigger with the pistol pointed in a safe direction to fully unlock the slide from the frame.

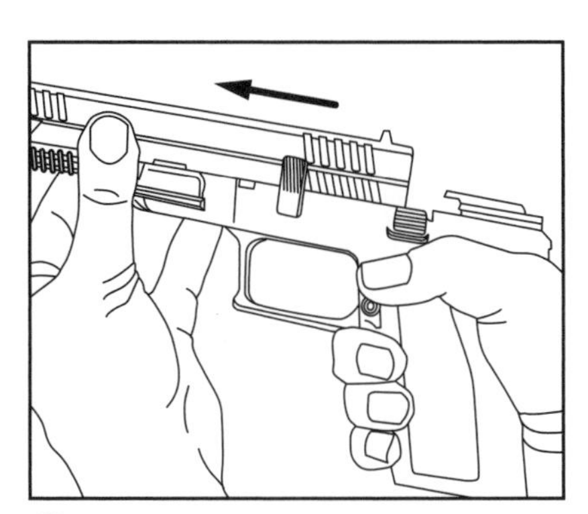

3 Move the complete slide assembly forward and off the frame.

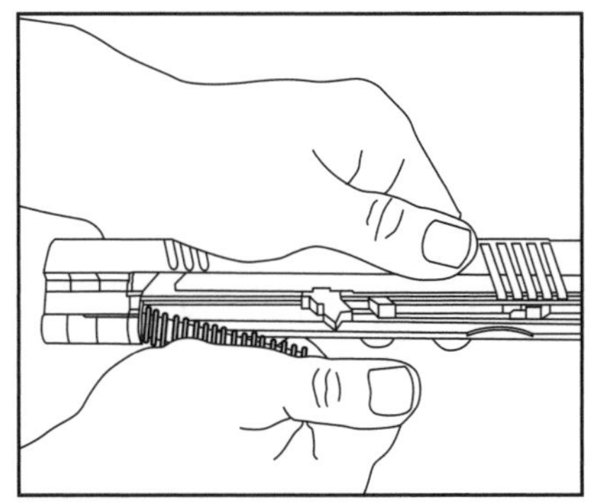

4 Remove the recoil spring assembly, from the slide. NOTE: The 5-inch Tactical models do not have a captive recoil system. Therefore, care should be taken when disassembling and reassembling the pistol.

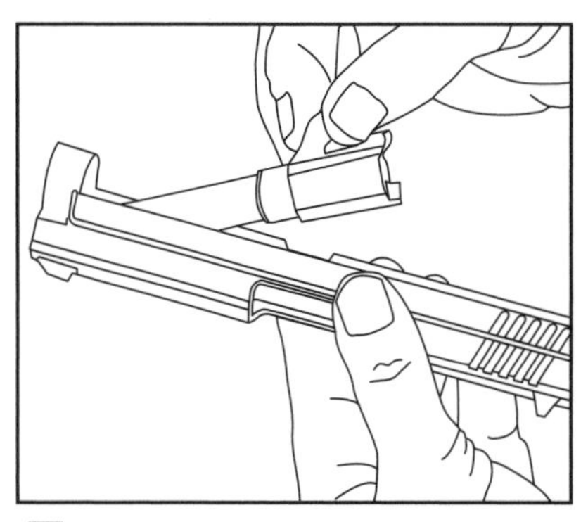

5 Remove the barrel from the slide.
The pistol is now fully field stripped and ready for cleaning. Further dismantling is not necessary and should only be done by Springfield Armory or a qualified gunsmith.

STAR MODEL F PISTOL

PARTS LEGEND

1. Slide
2. Extractor
3. Extractor plunger
4. Extractor spring
5. Firing pin retainer
6. Firing pin spring
7. Firing pin
8. Rear sight lock screw
9. Rear sight
10. Ejector
11. Hammer spring plunger
12. Hammer spring
13. Magazine catch
14. Magazine catch spring
15. Magazine catch retainer
16. Sear pin
17. Hammer
18. Sear
19. Sear spring
20. Frame and barrel
21. Magazine
22. Grip, left
23. Safety catch
24. Hammer hinge pin
25. Plunger spring
26. Safety catch detent plunger
27. Takedown catch
28. Takedown spring
29. Ejector retaining pin
30. Trigger pin
31. Trigger bar
32. Trigger spring
33. Trigger
34. Trigger bar pin
35. Recoil spring
36. Front sight
37. Front sight screw
38. Grip screws (4)
39. Grip, right

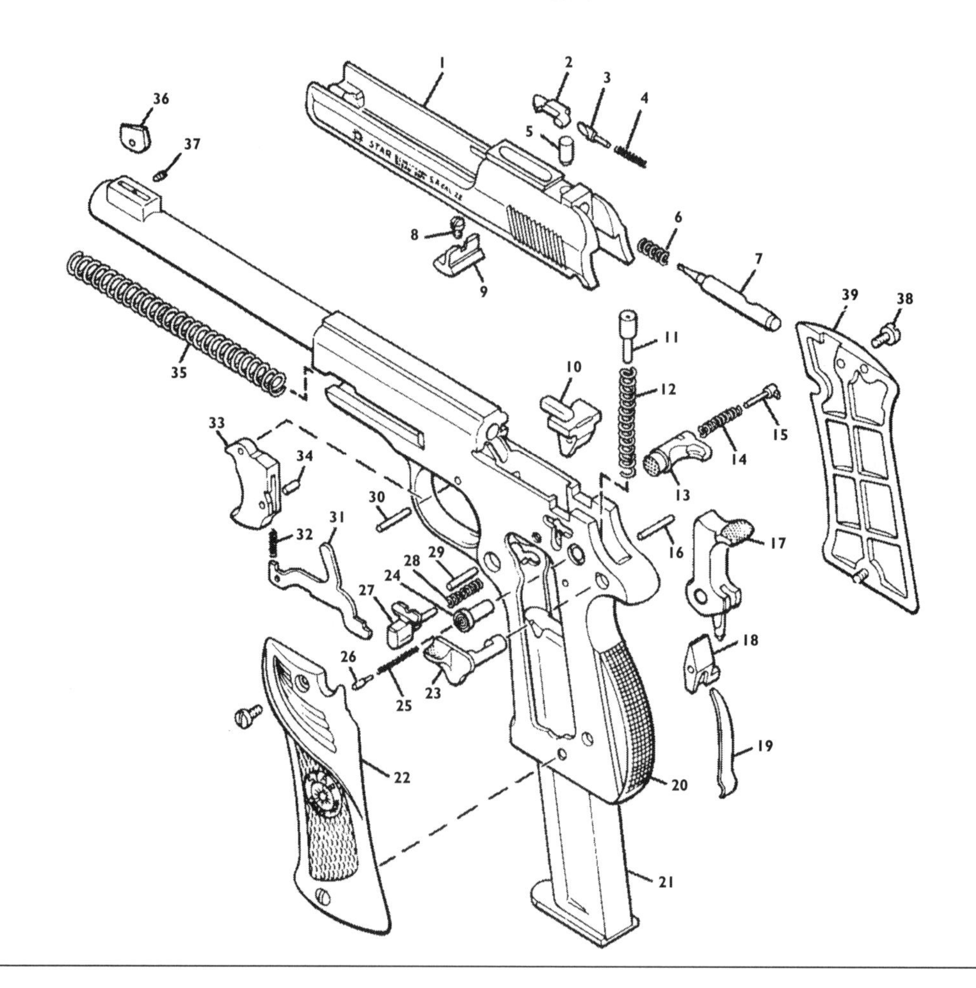

Since 1905 the firm of Bonifacio Echeverria of Eibar, Spain, has produced a wide variety of handguns, most of which have been sold under the "Star" brand name. Star guns range from small .25 ACP pistols up to a full-size, full-automatic version of the Colt M 1911.

Firearms International Corp. began importing the Star Model F, .22 Rimfire Series to the United States in 1948. Three barrel lengths were available, 4¼, 6, and 7 inches, plus a so-called "Olympic" model, with weights and muzzle brake.

Well-made and accurate, the Model F had only one design drawback, the lack of a slide hold-open device to lock the slide to the rear following the last shot. Thus, those who would use the pistol on a target range had to develop the habit of carrying a block of wood or plastic to hold the slide back in compliance with the safety rules in force on most ranges. This lack continued to plague the design until it was discontinued in 1967. The problem was corrected, however, when the follow-on FM, FR and FRS models were introduced, with slide hold-open devices.

The Model F was an excellent design, that incorporated a number of interesting features, The takedown system, for example, is truly clever — press a button and lift off the slide. The Model F had a sturdy and well-designed magazine. The follower was an aluminum casting and the floorplate was removable. Except for one or two small stamped parts, Model Fs were machined from steel. Internal parts such as the hammer, sear and ejector are case-hardened for durability. The external finish is excellent, but some of the internal parts are not well finished. The Model F was well suited for small-game hunting or informal target shooting.

DISASSEMBLY

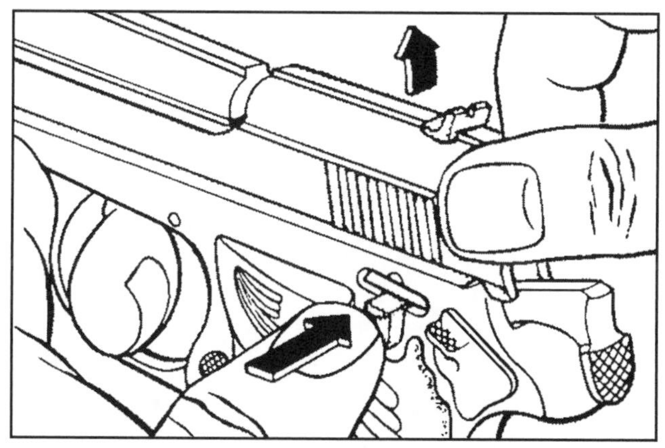

1 The Star Model F pistol has a comparatively simple takedown system. To strip the pistol, begin by first removing the magazine and clearing the chamber. Next push in the takedown catch (27—lower arrow) and lift the rear of the slide upward (upper arrow). The slide (1) can now be stripped off the front of the barrel.

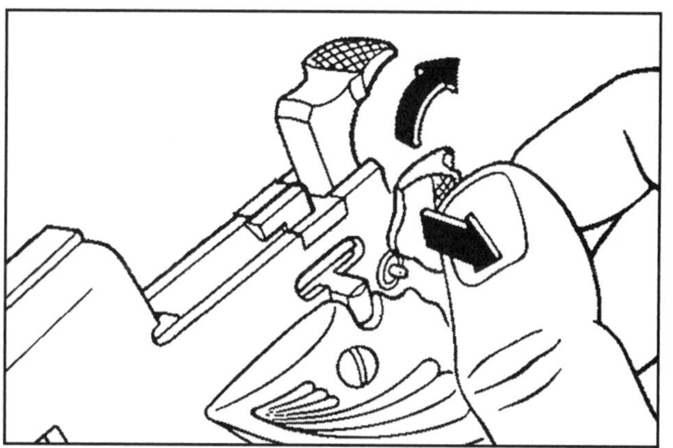

2 The safety catch (23) can best be removed when the hammer (17) is in fired position. Rotate the safety catch to vertical position and wiggle it free of the frame (20). If in the right position, the catch will come out easily; never force it out. Do not let safety catch detent plunger (26) and spring (25) fly out when catch is removed.

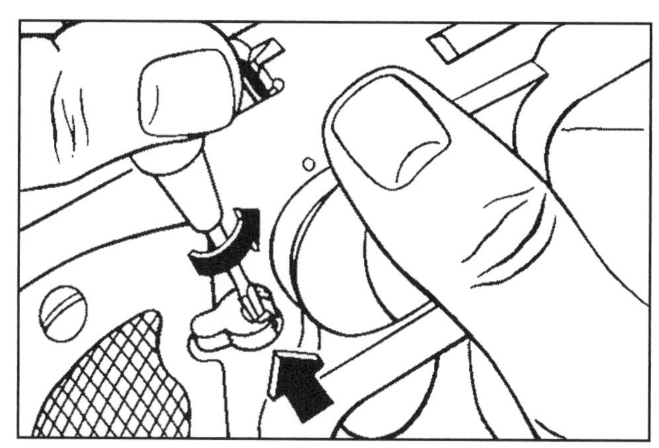

3 The magazine catch (13) is retained in exactly the same manner as in the Colt M1911 pistol. To remove the magazine catch, push it in as if removing the magazine. At the same time turn the magazine catch retainer (15) until it locks into the catch. Then the magazine catch, retainer, and spring can be removed as a single assembly.

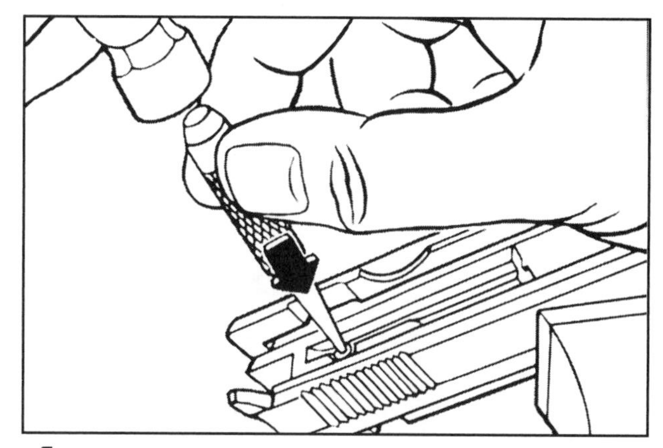

4 The firing pin (7) is retained by pin(5). Since this retainer pin is located under the rear sight (9), the rear sight must be removed in order to get at the pin. Simply loosen the sight lock screw (8) and push out the rear sight. Then, hold the slide in a vise padded to prevent marring finish and drive out the pin (5) as shown in the illustration.

STAR BM/BKM PISTOLS

PARTS LEGEND

1. Barrel bushing
2. Slide
3. Extractor pin
4. Firing pin retaining pin
5. Extractor
6. Extractor spring
7. Rear sight
8. Firing pin spring
9. Firing pin
10. Magazine catch lock spring
11. Magazine catch
12. Magazine catch lock
13. Recoil spring guide
14. Recoil spring guide washer
15. Recoil spring
16. Barrel w/ link and pin
17. Recoil spring guide head
18. Ejector
19. Interuptor
20. Trigger, assembly
21. Magazine safety
22. Sear
23. Sear spring
24. Hammer w/ strut and pin
25. Hammer spring plunger
26. Hammer spring
27. Grip, right
28. Magazine, complete
29. Frame
30. Grip screws
31. Grip left
32. Slide stop assembly
33. Trigger pin
34. Ejector pin
35. Safety thumb
36. Safety plunger
37. Safety plunger spring
38. Hammer pin
39. Sear pin

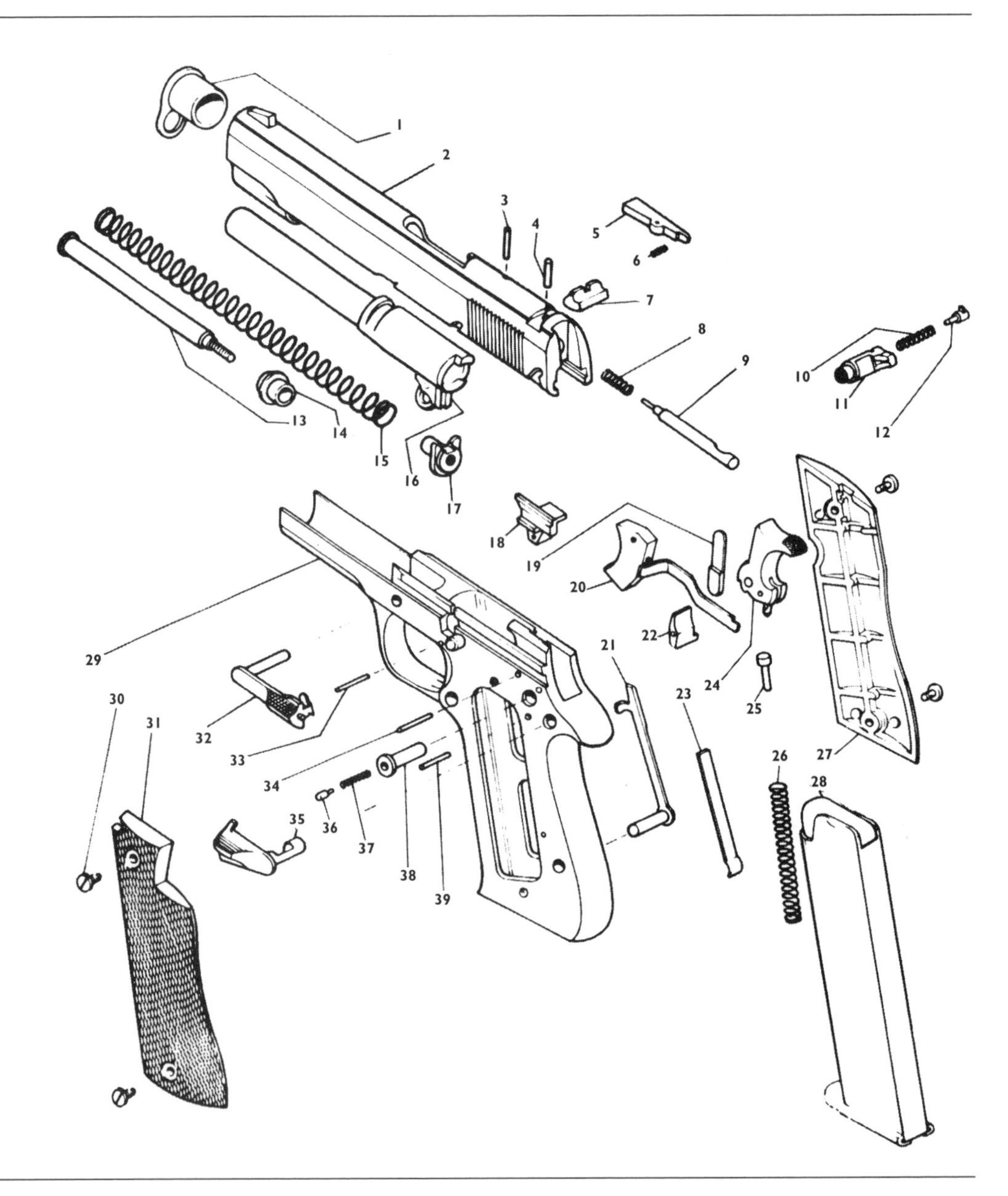

Bonifacio Echeverria, S.A., was founded in 1905 in Eibar by the brothers Bonifacio D. and Julian Echeverria-Orbea. In actuality, the company was a continuation of their father's small gunmaking firm Txantoya of that same city. The brand name Star, which is now the commonly used term for the firm, was used on some of their early blowback pistols, as were the names Izarra and Estrella, which mean Star in Basque and Spanish, respectively.

Star's first locked breech pistol, the Modelo Militar, was introduced in 1920 and adopted by the Spanish *Guardia Civil.* Star pistols in various models have been used by the Spanish military and police forces since that time.

In the early 1970s, while Star was developing their commercially successful PD .45, the Spanish Government showed interest in the concept of the PD —an ultra-compact pistol for a powerful cartridge. They were not, however, interested in the .45 ACP cartridge or the fully adjustable sights of the PD. They pressed Star to develop a 9 mm handgun smaller than the already small Model BKS, and in 1976 the Star BM was produced to meet their needs. The steel-framed BM became the official handgun of the Spanish Navy, the Guardia Civil and the Cuerpo General de Policia. It and a variation with aluminum frame, the Model BKM, were distributed in the United States by Interarms of Alexandria, Virginia.

DISASSEMBLY

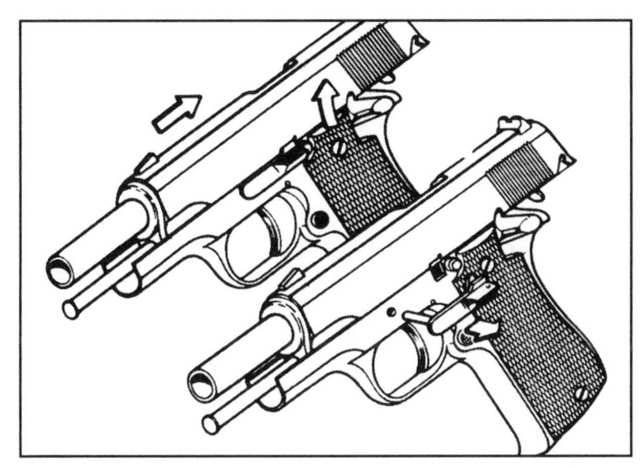

1 Check to be sure gun is unloaded by depressing magazine catch (11), removing magazine (28), retracting slide (2) and examining chamber to be sure it is empty. With slide still retracted, push up on the thumb safety (35) so that its hook engages in the slide notch just forward of the finger serrations. The slide will now remain in its rearward position and the slide (32) can be removed by pushing on its rod, which protrudes from the right side of the frame.

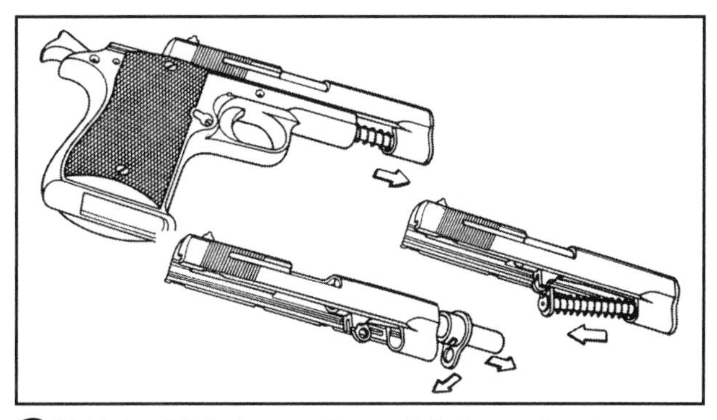

2 Hold the slide by its serrations to limit the recoil spring pressure and depress the thumb safety to allow the slide to ride forward off the frame (29). Lift recoil spring assembly (13, 14, 15 & 17) and remove it from the slide. Turn barrel bushing (1) counter-clockwise and pull it and the barrel (16) forward from the slide.

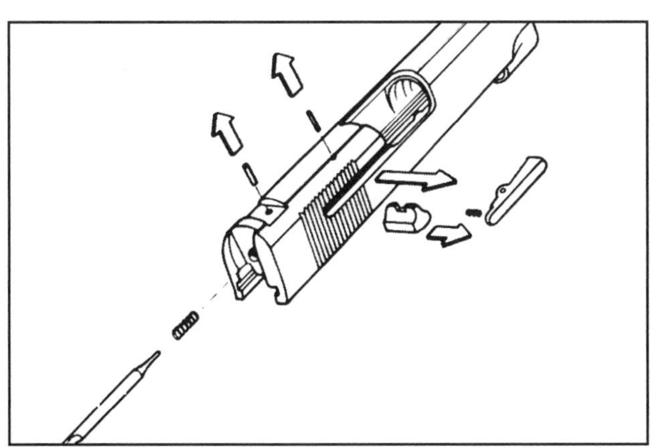

3 The slide itself can be stripped by using a brass punch to drift out the rear sight (7) from left to right. From the underside of the slide, using a suitable punch, drive up the firing pin retaining pin (4) and remove it, the firing pin (9) and its spring (8). Using the same punch, drift the extractor pin (3) up through the slide and remove the extractor (5) and extractor spring (6).

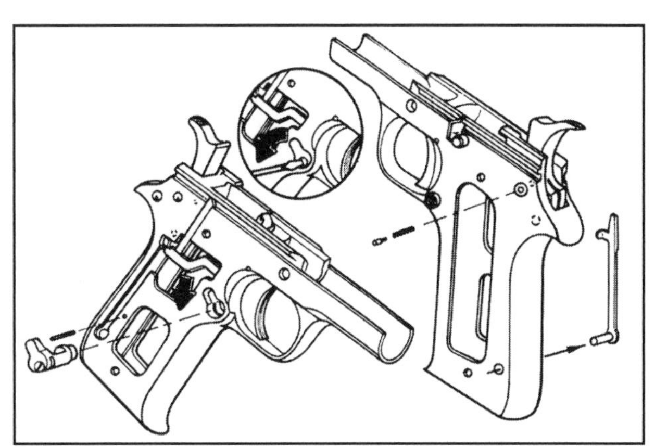

4 Remove grip screws (30) and grips (27 & 31). The magazine safety (21) may be temporarily or permanently removed, if desired, by driving out its lower arm from the frame. Lower the hammer (the magazine must be inserted to do this if the magazine safety is present) to simplify thumb safety removal. Rotate the thumb safety (35) to its vertical position and carefully "wiggle" it from the frame, being careful not to lose its plunger (36) and spring (37), which are small and under pressure. The magazine catch is taken out by depressing its knurled button and, with a small screwdriver, turning the magazine catch lock (12) counter clockwise out of its seat in the frame. The catch with its lock and spring may now be removed as an assembly (10, 11 & 12).

STAR PD PISTOL

PARTS LEGEND

1. Barrel bushing
2. Slide
3. Extractor pin
4. Firing pin retaining pin
5. Extractor
6. Extractor spring
7. Sight elevation spring
8. Sight windage spindle plunger
9. Sight windage spindle plunger spring
10. Sight windage spindle retaining pin
11. Sight slide
12. Sight windage spindle
13. Sight
14. Sight elevation screw
15. Magazine catch
16. Magazine catch lock spring
17. Magazine catch lock
18. Recoil spring
19. Recoil spring guide plug
20. Recoil spring guide washer
21. Recoil spring guide
22. Recoil spring guide washer
23. Recoil spring guide buffer
24. Recoil spring guide head
25. Firing pin spring
26. Ejector
27. Firing pin
28. Trigger assembly
29. Sear
30. Sear spring
31. Disconnector
32. Hammer spring plunger
33. Hammer assembly
34. Hammer spring
35. Grip, right
36. Magazine assembly
37. Frame
38. Slide stop assembly
39. Trigger pin
40. Slide stop button
41. Ejector pin
42. Safety plunger
43. Safety
44. Safety plunger spring
45. Hammer pin
46. Sear pin
47. Grip, left
48. Grip screw
49. Barrel with link and pin

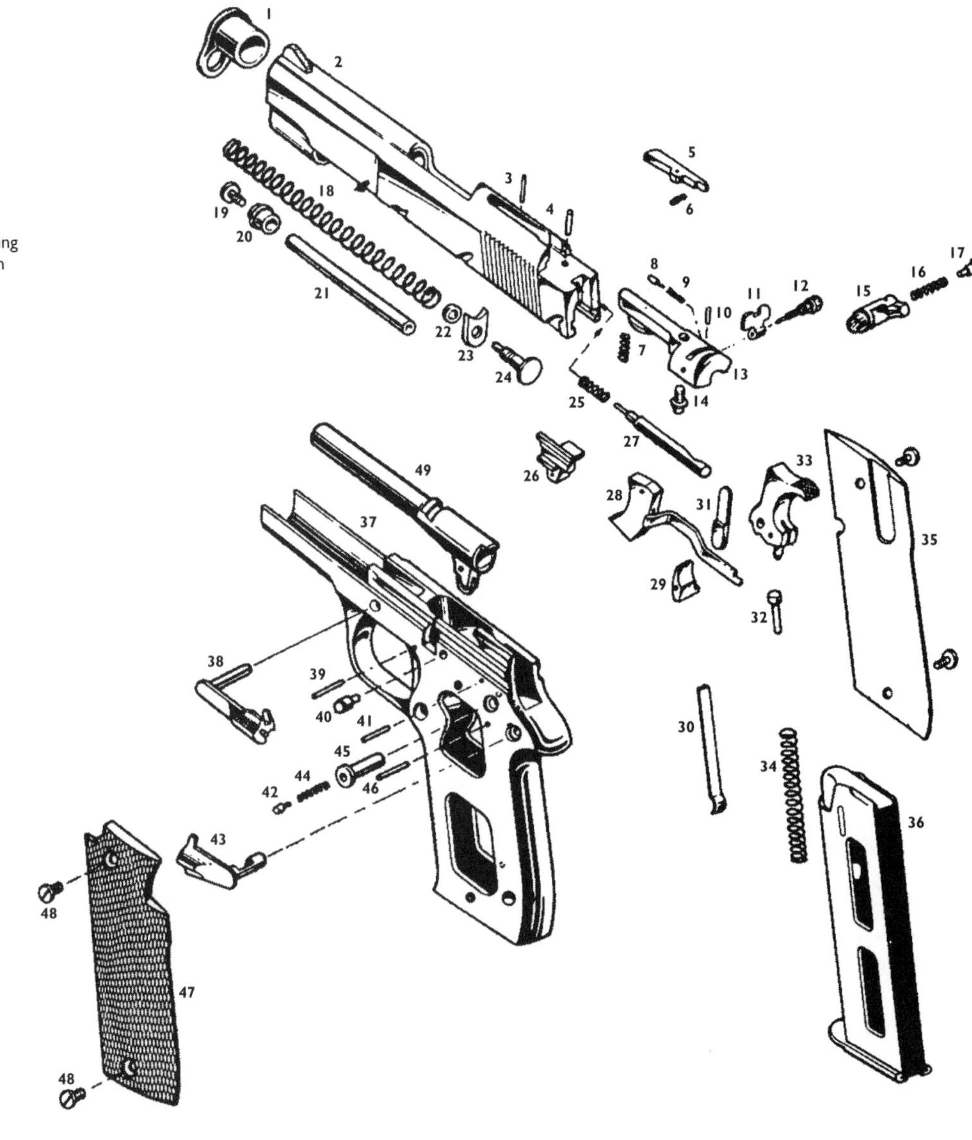

Manufacture of .45 ACP pistols is not a new undertaking for Star Bonifacio Echeverria of Eibar, Spain. In the 1920s, they made .45 ACP versions of their *Modelo Militar* pistols for export. Their Model A pistol was made in that caliber, and by the 1950s they had produced a selective-fire pistol complete with wooden shoulder stock/holster (Model MD) and three P Series pistols.

In 1975, after several years of development, the PD was introduced. With an aluminum alloy frame, the PD was considerably lighter, shorter and more compact than any of the other Star .45s, and was well received by police and civilian buyers. The PD led the field in a trend toward compact 1911-style pistols.

The PD was fitted with an internal plastic buffer to protect the alloy frame from the effects of recoil. and was equipped with a fully adjustable rear sight. It was imported into the United States by Interarms of Alexandria,Virginia. The Star PD was discontinued in 1983 and replaced by the Firestar M45.

DISASSEMBLY

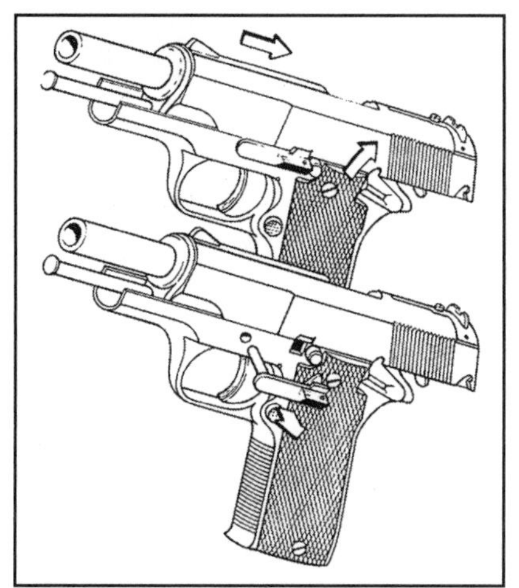

1 Check to be sure gun is unloaded by depressing magazine catch (15), removing magazine (36), retracting slide (2) and examining chamber to be sure it is empty. With slide still retracted, push up on the thumb safety (43) so that its hook engages in the slide notch just forward of the finger serrations. The slide will now remain in its rearward position, and the slide stop (38) can be removed by pushing on its rod, which protrudes from the right side of the frame.

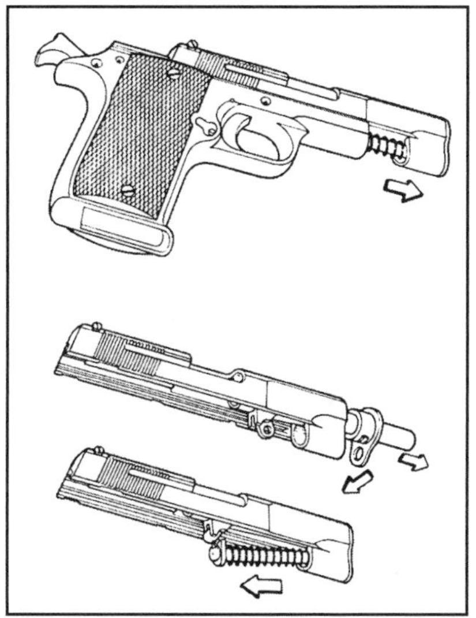

2 Hold the slide by its serrations to limit the recoil spring pressure and depress the thumb safety to allow the slide to ride forward off the frame (37). Lift recoil spring assembly (18 to 24) and remove it from the slide. Turn barrel bushing (1) counterclockwise and pull it and the barrel (49) forward from the slide.

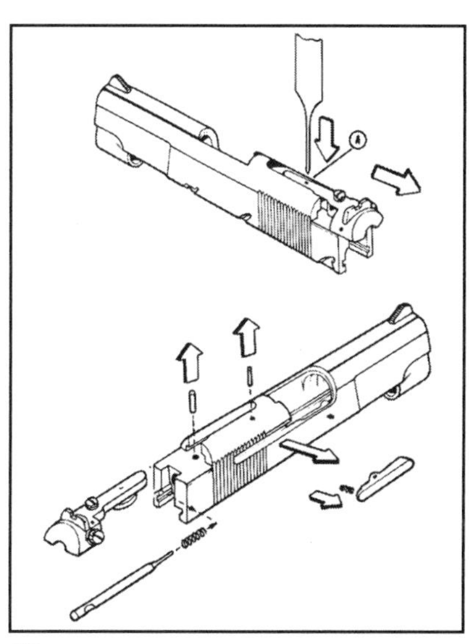

3 To strip the slide, first remove the rear sight assembly (7 to 14) by unscrewing the elevation screw (14) to its limit and then Inserting a small punch in hole A. The entire sight assembly may now be pushed out to the rear. From the underside of the slide, using a suitable punch, drive up the firing pin retaining pin (4) and remove it, the firing pin (27) and its spring (25). Using the same punch, drift the extractor pin (3) up through the slide and remove the extractor (5) and extractor spring (6).

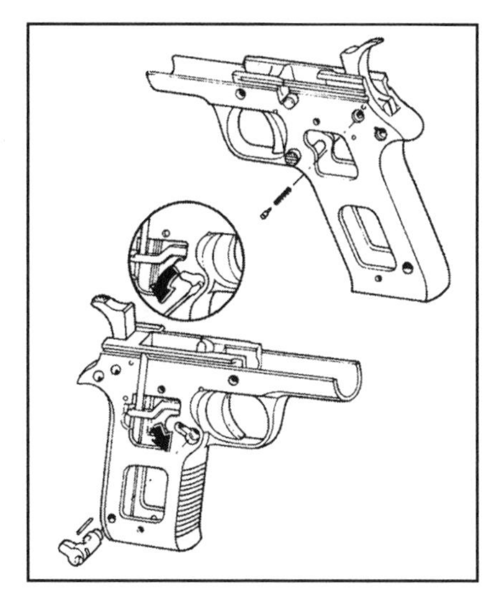

4 Remove grip screws (48) and grips (35 & 47). Lower the hammer to simplify thumb safety removal. Rotate the thumb safety (43) to its vertical position and carefully "wiggle" it from the frame, being careful not to lose its plunger (42) and spring (44), which are small and under pressure. The magazine catch is taken out by depressing its knurled button and, with a small screwdriver, turning the magazine catch lock (17) counterclockwise out of its seat in the frame. The catch with its lock and spring may now be removed as an assembly.

STAR "SUPER" MODEL PISTOL

PARTS LEGEND

1. Frame
2. Ejector
3. Ejector pin
4. Hammer
5. Hammer strut
6. Hammer strut pin
7. Hammer spring
8. Hammer spring plunger
9. Hammer pin
10. Sear
11. Sear pin
12. Sear spring
13. Sear spring pin
14. Trigger
15. Trigger pin
16. Trigger plunger spring
17. Trigger plunger
18. Sear bar
19. Sear bar pin
20. Interrupter
21. Magazine catch
22. Magazine catch lock
23. Magazine catch lock spring
24. Magazine safety
25. Magazine safety lock
26. Magazine safety lock spring
27. Thumb safety
28. Thumb safety plunger
29. Thumb safety plunger spring
30. Slide stop
31. Slide stop plunger
32. Slide stop plunger spring
33. Slide stop plunger retaining screw
34. Takedown lever
35. Magazine
36. Magazine follower
37. Magazine spring
38. Magazine floorplate
39. Magazine floorplate catch
40. Barrel
41. Slide
42. Extractor
43. Extractor pin
44. Extractor spring
45. Firing pin
46. Firing pin retaining pin
47. Firing pin spring
48. Live round indicator
49. Rear sight blade
50. Rear sight sight screw
51. Rear sight base
52. Rear sight spring
53. Barrel bushing
54. Recoil spring button
55. Recoil spring guide
56. Recoil spring
57. Front sight
58. Grip plate, right
59. Grip plate, left
60. Grip screws (4)

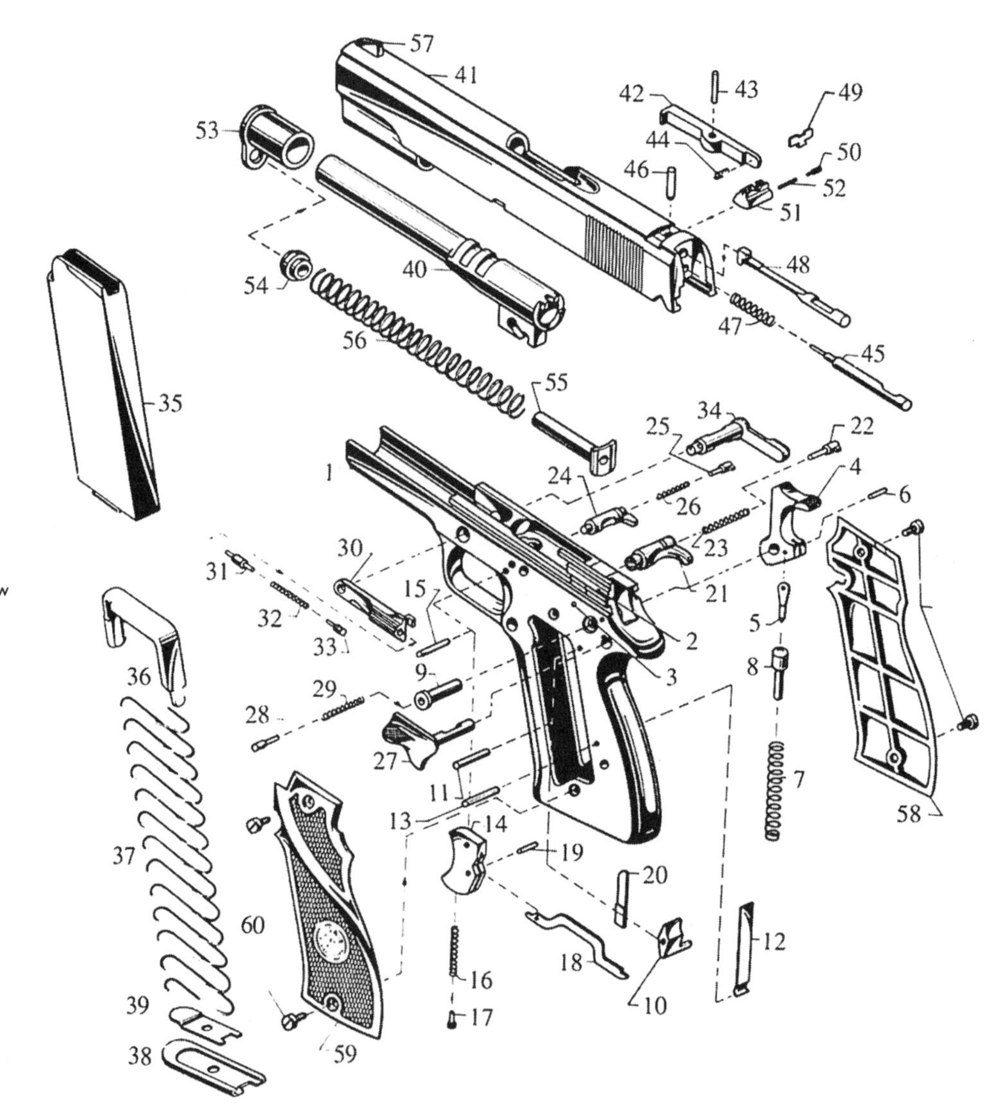

From 1946 until 1983, Star Bonifacio Echeverria of Eibar, Spain, made "Super" variations of its standard Colt M1911-type pistols in various sizes. The standard Stars differed from the M1911 design, having hammer-blocking thumb safeties, no grip safety and external extractors. The Super Models added a quick takedown feature, a magazine safety and a loaded chamber indicator.

Super Models were made for seven different cartridges. The Model Super M was chambered for the Spanish service cartridge, the 9 mm. Bergmann Bayard and also accepted .38 ACP or .38 Sup er ACP ammunition. Soon the thinner-slided Model Super A, the 9 mm Parabellum Model Super B and 9 mm Browning Long Super C were under poduction along with the smaller .32 ACP Super SI and .380 Super S. All save the Super C, continued in manufacture until 1983. In 1950 a smaller .380, the Super D, was made on a trial basis, and in 1958, a very few .45 ACP Super Ps were produced.

In 1989, Star shipped its final inventory of new Super B 9 mm Parabellum pistols to its United States importer, Interarms of Alexandria, Virginia.

DISASSEMBLY

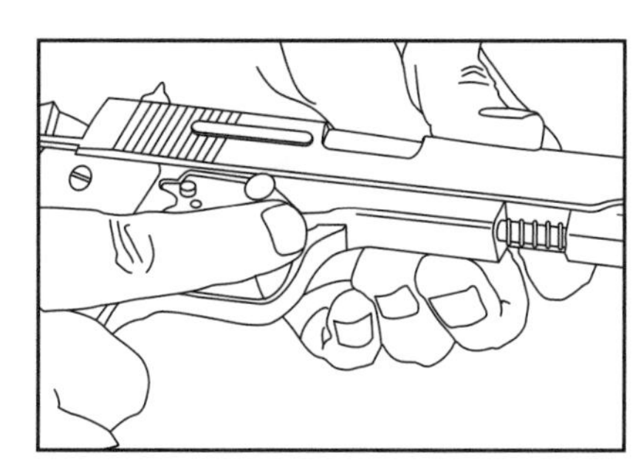

1 Depress the magazine catch (21) and remove the magazine assembly (35-39). Retract and release the slide (41) and ensure that the chamber is empty. Turn the takedown lever (34) counterclockwise and remove the slide assembly from the front of the frame (1).

The slide assembly can be stripped by lifting out the recoil spring (56) with its button and guide (54 & 55). This frees the barrel bushing (53) that is turned 45 degrees to the left of the slide and pulled out, allowing the barrel (40) to be removed from the front of the slide. No further dismantling is necessary for normal cleaning or inspection

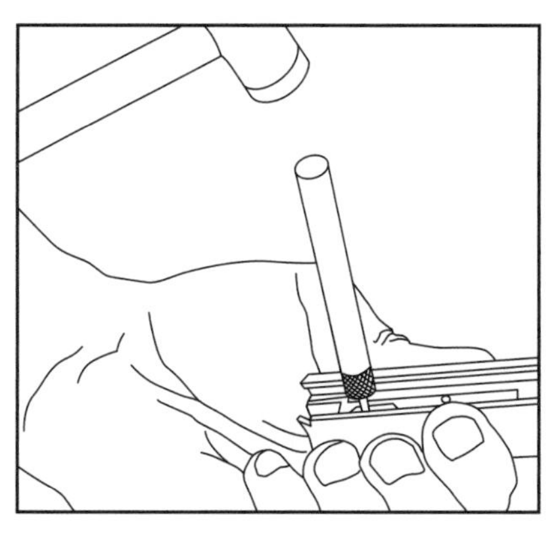

2 With a brass or plastic punch, drift out the rear sight or, in the case of the Super SM, the rear sight assembly (49-52). This will free the live-round indicator (48) and expose the top of the firing pin retaining pin (46). Now, with the slide inverted, drift out the firing pin retaining pin (46) as shown (Fig. 2). The firing pin (45) and its spring (47) can now be removed. With the slide inverted, drift out the extractor pin (43), whose bottom is exposed about an inch forward of the firing pin retaining pin hole. It too is drifted from the bottom of the slide through the top. The front sight is staked in place and should not be removed.

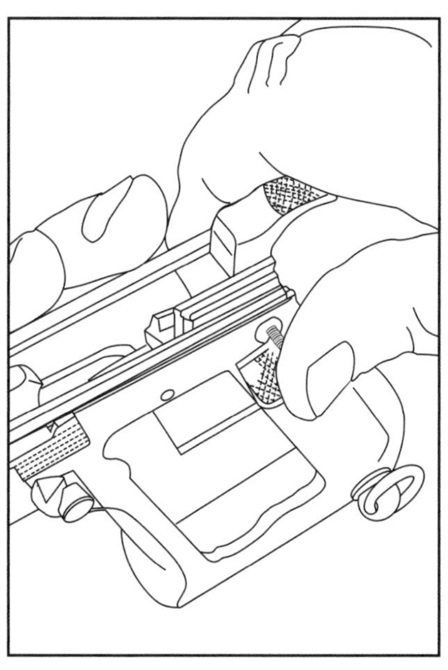

3 Remove the four grip screws (60) and the grip plates (58 & 59); depress the magazine catch (21) and turn the slotted magazine catch lock (22) 90 degrees counterclockwise. Remove the magazine catch assembly (21-23).

Removal of the thumb safety (27) requires special care, as its plunger (28) is under pressure from its spring (29) and is easily lost. Hold the frame (1) left side up in the left hand and, placing the right thumb on the top of the thumb safety's platform, push it down until the plunger pops up to be retained by the thumb. Swing the thumb safety up and, while pulling the hammer (4) back past its full-cock position, out of its recess. Rotate the takedown lever (34) so that it points straight down and pull it from its seat, freeing it and the slide stop (30), plunger, spring and retaining screw (31-33).

To remove the magazine safety and its lock and spring (24-26), temporarily reinsert the magazine. Then turn the slotted magazine safety lock (25) a quarter turn counterclockwise and remove the magazine, permitting the magazine safety to fall out.

Drift out the trigger pin (15) from left to right and remove the trigger (14) with its attached plunger spring, plunger and sear bar (16-18) to the rear. This permits removal of the interrupter (20) from its slot.

With the hammer (4) fully down and firmly retained by the thumb, drive out the hammer pin (9) and carefully remove the hammer that will be under pressure of its spring and plunger (7 & 8).

This is followed by the removal of the sear pin (11), the sear (10), the sear spring pin (13) and the sear spring (12).

STAR MODEL SUPER B PISTOL

Cutaway shows how the parts interrelate. Barrel is shown locked to slide, hammer is at half-cock, and manual safety is disengaged. Parts are number keyed to the parts legend.

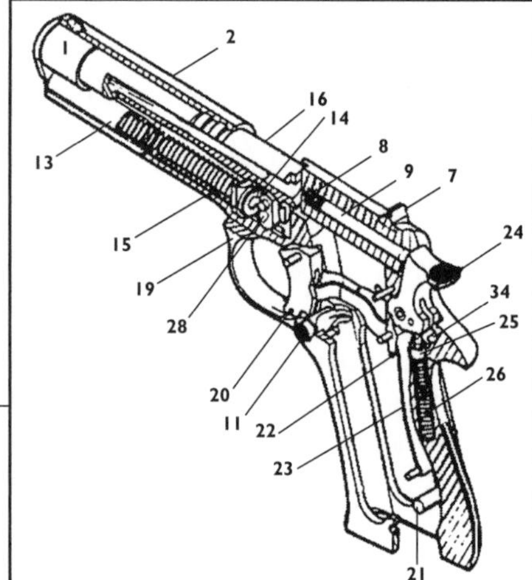

PARTS LEGEND

1. Barrel bushing
2. Slide
3. Extractor pin
4. Firing pin retaining pin
5. Extractor
6. Extractor spring
7. Rear sight
8. Firing pin spring
9. Firing pin
10. Magazine catch lock spring
11. Magazine catch
12. Magazine catch lock
13. Recoil spring plug
14. Recoil spring guide
15. Recoil spring
16. Barrel w/ link and pin
17. Ejector
18. Disconnector
19. Frame
20. Trigger w/ sear bar
21. Magazine safety
22. Sear
23. Sear spring
24. Hammer w/ strut and pin
25. Hammer spring plunger
26. Hammer spring
27. Grip, right
28. Magazine, complete
29. Grip screws (4)
30. Grip, left
31. Slide stop, complete
32. Trigger pin
33. Ejector pin
34. Thumb safety
35. Safety plunger
36. Safety spring
37. Hammer pin
38. Sear pin

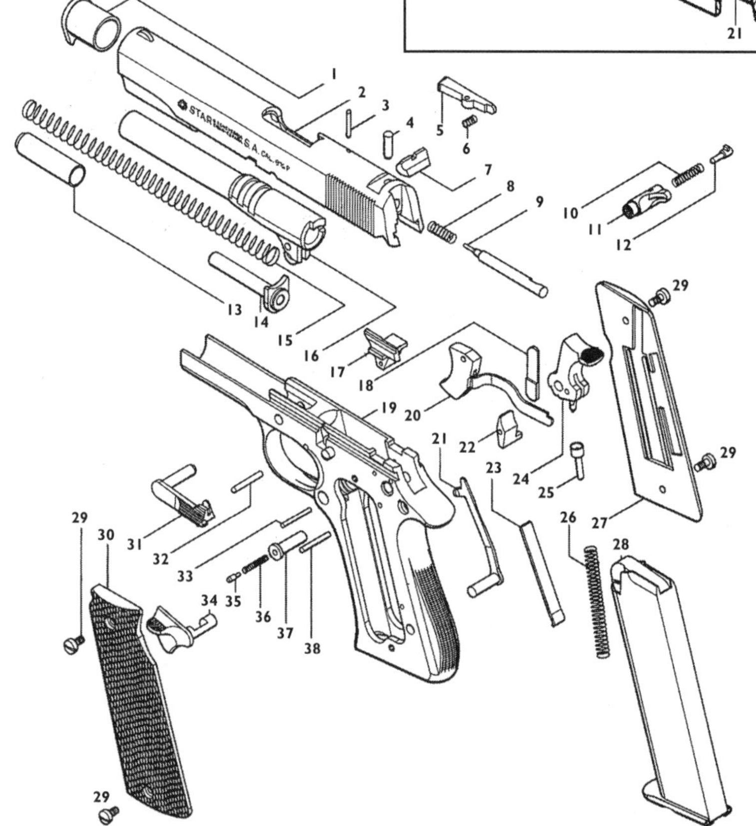

Produced by Star Bonifacio Echeverria of Eibar, Spain, the Star Model Super B pistol is chambered for the 9 mm. Parabellum cartridge and is similar to the earlier Model B manufactured between 1934 and 1975.

The Super B was designed as an autoloader for military, law-enforcement, and personal defense use and is similar to the Colt Model 1911A1 in size and appearance. It encorporates the Colt short-recoil system but the lockwork differs considerably from that of the Colt. An obvious difference between these pistols is that the Star lacks a grip safety and features an exposed extractor (which is actuated by a coil spring) on the right side of the slide. There are internal differences in the firing pin, disconnector, and trigger mechanism. Magazine capacity is 8 rounds.

The thumb safety is on the upper left side of the frame, and locks the hammer and slide when engaged. Other safety devices include a magazine safety and a loaded chamber indicator.

Importation of the Super B by Interarms ended in 1990 and Star Bonifacio Echeverria ceased operation in 1997.

DISASSEMBLY

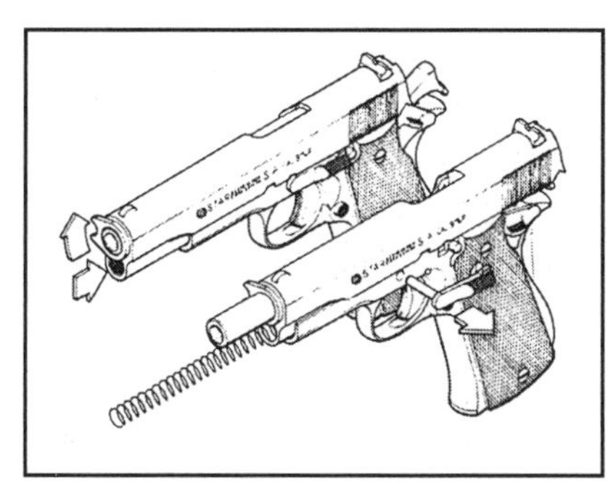

1 Depress magazine catch (11), and remove magazine (28). Draw slide (2) fully rearward to clear chamber and cock hammer (24). Release slide, and engage thumb safety (34). Depress knurled head of recoil spring plug (13), and rotate barrel bushing (1) clockwise (viewed from front) to its stop. Ease plug out of slide and remove. Release safety, and move slide rearward until rounded takedown notch on its left side aligns with lug on slide stop (31). Push inward on slide stop axle protruding from right side of frame (19), and withdraw slide stop to left.

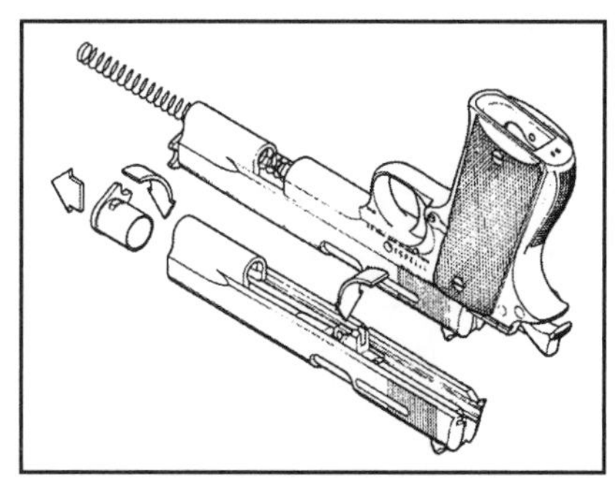

2 Turn pistol upside down, and move slide forward off the frame. Lift recoil spring guide (14), and remove to rear along with the recoil spring (15). Turn barrel bushing counterclockwise to its stop and remove. Lift barrel (16) to unlock from slide, rotate barrel link fully forward, and draw barrel forward out of slide. This completes field stripping for normal cleaning and lubrication.

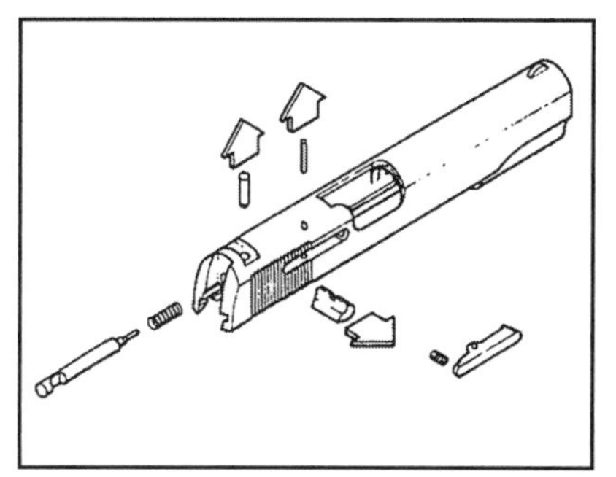

3 For further disassembly, drift extractor pin (3) out through top of slide to release extractor (5) and extractor spring (6). Rear sight (7) must be driven out before firing pin (9) can be removed. Use a brass punch, and remove sight from left to right. Drive firing pin retaining pin (4) upward, and withdraw firing pin and firing pin spring (8).

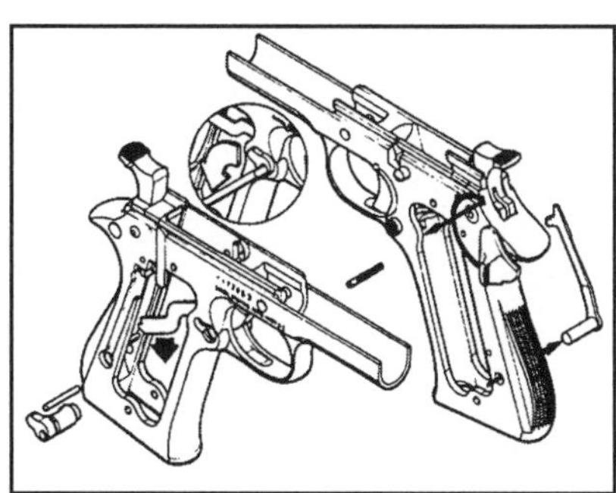

4 Unscrew grip screws (29), and remove grips (27 & 30). Detach magazine safety (21) by drifting out its integral pin. Pull trigger, and lower hammer with thumb. Turn thumb safety downward beyond fire position, and lift out safety plunger (35) and spring (36). Rotate safety upward beyond safe position and withdraw it to the left. Depress magazine catch flush with frame, and turn magazine catch lock (12) fully to left with a small screwdriver (inset). Remove entire magazine catch assembly. Drift out trigger pin (32) from left to right. Pull outward and downward on trigger w/ sear bar (20) until the assembly can be removed through side of magazine well. Slide disconnector (18) downward out of frame.

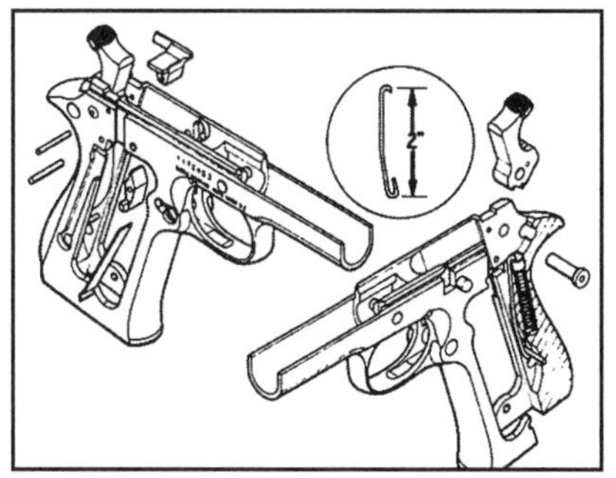

5 Drift out sear pin (38) from right to left, and remove sear (22) and sear spring (23). Drift ejector pin (33) out to the left, and lift off ejector (17). Bend a piece of 1/16 brazing rod as shown (inset). Attach loop of rod to fixed frame pin. Draw back the hammer, and insert hook of rod within cup of hammer spring plunger (25). Adjust hook so that hammer is free of spring tension when fully forward. Push out hammer pin (37) and withdraw hammer. If hammer spring (26) must be removed, depress spring plunger with tapered punch and remove the tool. Then, ease out the plunger and spring cautiously.

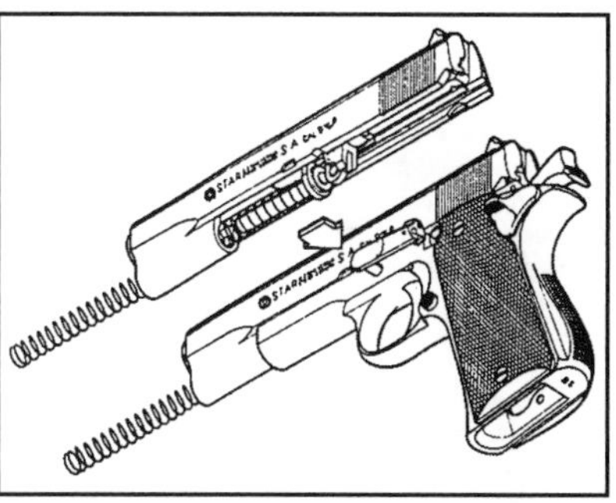

6 Assemble in reverse order. Before replacing the assembled slide, position the barrel link vertically. Start the slide on the inverted frame, align barrel link hole with slide stop hole in frame, and insert the slide stop. Move the slide further rearward to bring takedown notch opposite the slide stop lug, and fully seat the stop.

STEYER MODEL 1912 PISTOL

PARTS LEGEND

1. Front sight
2. Wedge
3. Extractor
4. Slide
5. Firing pin spring
6. Firing pin
7. Trigger bar
8. Hammer
9. Ejector and disconnector
10. Barrel
11. Recoil spring retainer
12. Front recoil spring cap
13. Recoil spring
14. Rear recoil spring cap
15. Trigger
16. Trigger pin
17. Cartridge release
18. Hammer screw
19. Safety
20. Cartridge release spring
21. Left grip
22. Grip and floorplate screw
23. Floorplate
24. Disconnector spring
25. Sear and sear spring
26. Hammer spring
27. Magazine follower
28. Magazine spring
29. Spring retainer pin
30. Receiver
31. Right grip

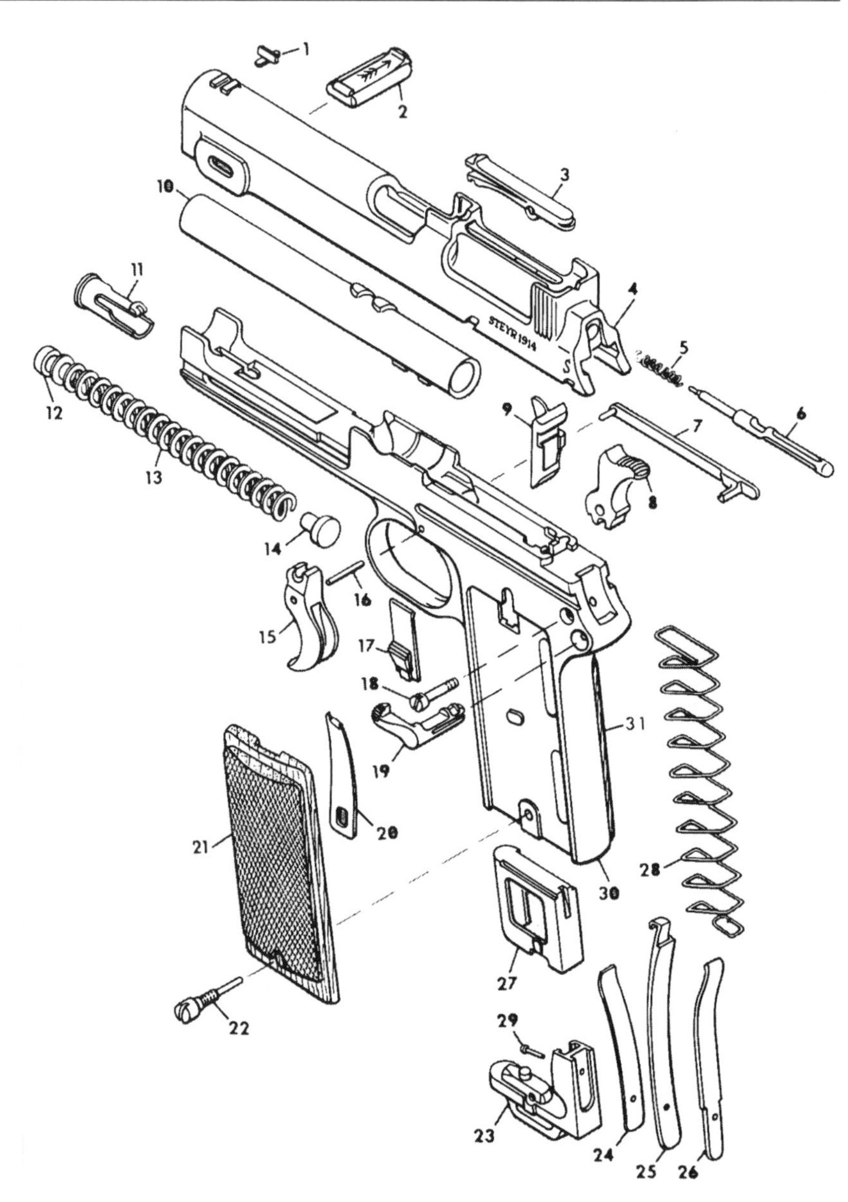

The Steyr Model 1912 9 mm. automatic pistol, designed and produced by the Austrian Arms Co., Steyr, Austria, was the principal Austro-Hungarian handgun during World War I. Introduced by Styer in 1911, it was adopted by the Imperial Austro-Hungarian Army in 1912.

Several references list this exposed-hammer pistol as a Model 1911 (some are marked "M.1911") while other sources call it Model 1912, the designation used by the Austro-Hungarian Army. Another name commonly used is Steyr-Hahn (Steyr-hammer). This unofficial designation distinguishes the pistol from the Austro-Hungarian Roth Steyr Model 1907 hammerless pistol.

One chief characteristic of the Steyr Model 1912 is its short-recoil action with revolving barrel. During the period of high pressure, the barrel is locked to the slide. As the slide and barrel start back, the barrel is revolved about 60 degrees on its axis by a cam, and is unlocked. The barrel length is 5⅛-inch, and over-all length is 8½ inches. Weight empty is 34 ozs.

Another principal feature is the non-detachable magazine in the grip. Accessible only from the top, it is loaded by using an 8-round strip clip, or inserting cartridges singly. After the last round is fired, the slide is locked back by the magazine follower. Cartridges can be released from the magazine by depressing the cartridge release above the left grip.

The 9mm Steyr cartridge is a straight-case rimless design, with a 117-grain full metal-jacketed bullet, with a muzzle velocity of 1,215 feet per second. Muzzle energy is 385 ft-lbs.

In addition to being used by Austria-Hungary, the Steyr Model 1912 was adopted by Rumania and Chile. It was also used by police units in Austria during World War II. Some of these specimens were converted to fire the 9mm Luger (Parabellum) cartridge, and are marked "08," a German military designation for this round.

Sturdy and very well made, this pistol was produced in large quantity, but never achieved widespread popularity. It was discontinued at the end of World War I.

DISASSEMBLY

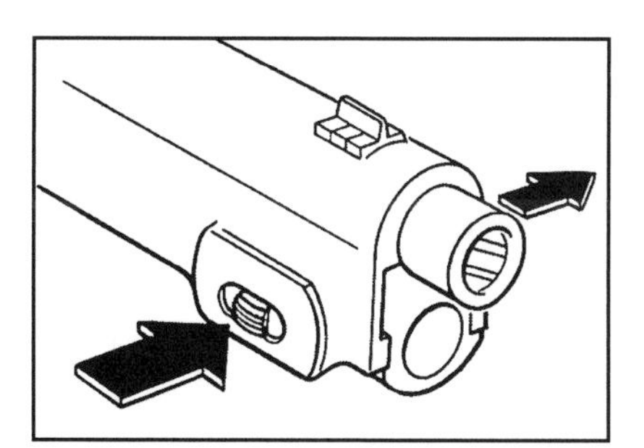

1 To field-strip the pistol, clear the magazine and chamber. Then depress the serrated end of the wedge spring, and push the wedge (2) out of the slide (4) and receiver (30).

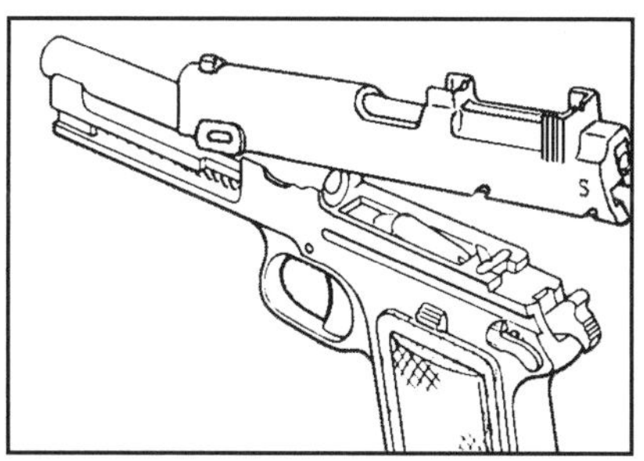

2 Pull the slide all the way back and lift it off the receiver. The barrel (10) can then be removed. In reassembly, the barrel must be positioned so the locking lugs are to the right.

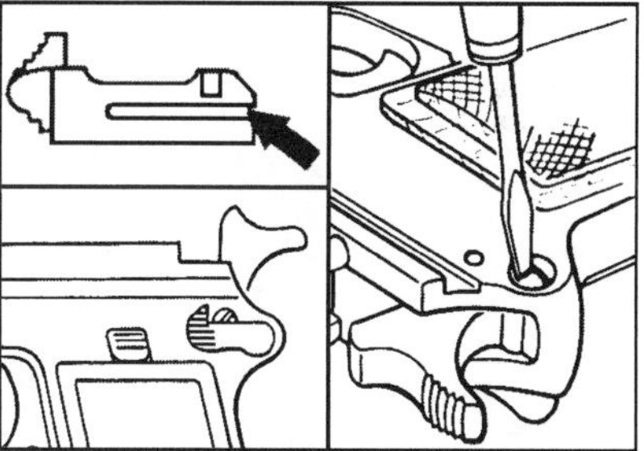

3 For further disassembly, lower the J hammer (8), and remove any dirt from the slotted pin part of the safety (19). Then turn the safety so that it points forward, and use a punch or small screwdriver to push it to the left out of the receiver. Unscrew the hammer screw (18), and remove the hammer. Use a screwdriver to compress the upper rear of the recoil spring retainer (11), and push the retainer out forward. Then remove the recoil spring (13) and recoil spring caps (12 & 14). Slightly depress the ejector and disconnector (9), and use a small screwdriver to gently pry out the trigger bar (7). Then lift out the ejector and disconnector. Turn out the grip and floorplate screw (22), slide the grips (21 & 31) out of the receiver, and remove the floorplate (23) with attached springs, the magazine spring (28), and magazine follower (27). Depress the cartridge release spring (20), turn it forward a quarter turn, and lift from receiver. Also remove the cartridge release (17). Driving out the trigger pin (16) and removing the trigger (15) completes disassembly of the receiver group.

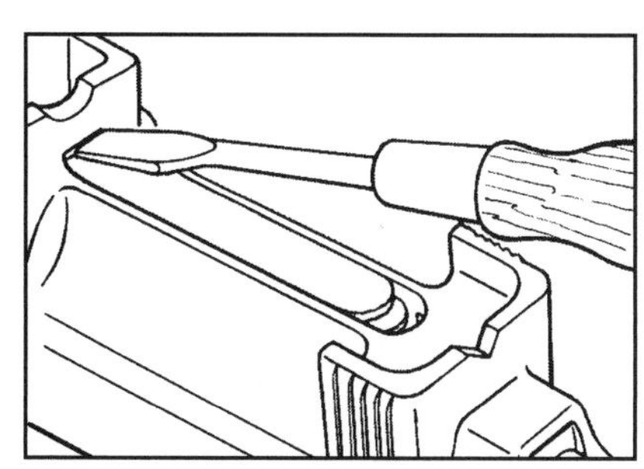

4 Place a screwdriver on the upper front of the extractor (3), and push down and forward. After the extractor is pushed forward, lift it at the rear to free the firing pin (6), and remove the firing pin and firing pin spring (5).

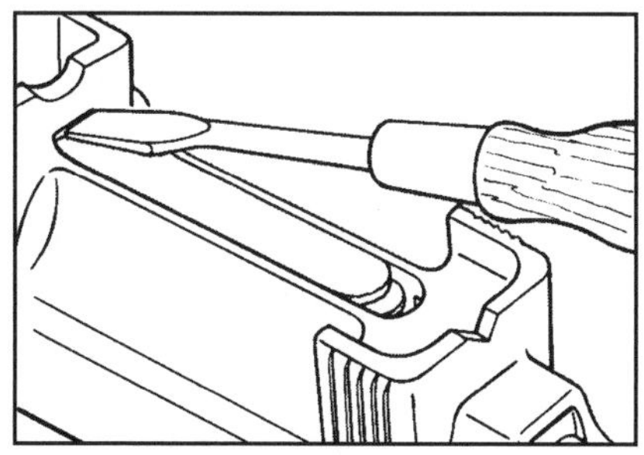

5 Use a needle-nose plier (one with bent jaws is preferable) to compress the extractor limbs at the front. Then push the extractor rearward until the lug on its upper limb is behind the loading port. Push the extractor hook upward with a brass punch or rod, and force the extractor rearward out of the slide. An aid in doing this is to put a pin or nail through the hole in the extractor to provide a finger grip.

STEYER MODEL SP PISTOL

PARTS LEGEND

1. Barrel bushing
2. Slide
3. Rear sight
4. Extractor pin
5. Extractor
6. Extractor spring
7. Firing pin retaining pin
8. Firing pin bushing
9. Firing pin bushing lock screw
10. Firing pin spring
11. Firing pin
12. Recoil spring
13. Trigger pin
14. Sideplate screw
15. Hammer
16. Hammer strut pin
17. Hammer strut
18. Hammer spring
19. Hammer hinge pin
20. Magazine catch
21. Magazine catch pin
22. Right grip
23. Grip screw
24. Frame
25. Magazine
26. Left grip
27. Grip screw
28. Sideplate
29. Trigger spring retaining screw
30. Trigger spring
31. Trigger bar
32. Trigger spring follower
33. Trigger
34. Safety catch
35. Safety catch spring
36. Safety catch detent

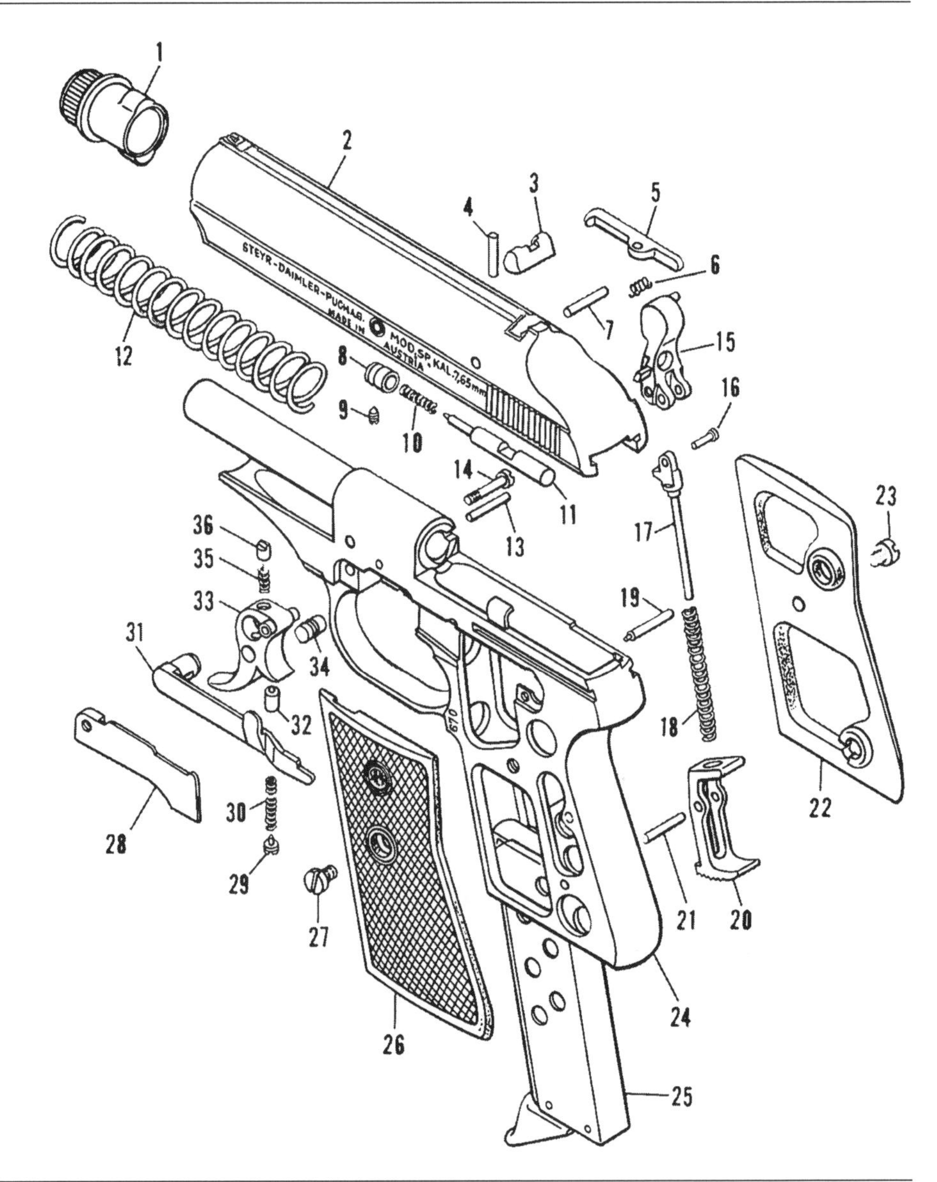

The Steyr Model SP, .32 ACP double- action pistol was introduced in the late 1950s. Manufactured by the Austrian firm of Steyr Daimler-Puch, the Steyr SP is a true double-action design. Since there is no provision in this pistol for single-action operation, the internal hammer does not stay cocked after each shot as in conventional self-loading pistols; the trigger must be pulled through its full cycle to cock and release the hammer for each shot. There is an inertia firing pin within the slide.

A unique feature of the Model SP pistol is the cross-bolt safety catch in the trigger. When pushed to the left with the trigger finger the catch engages the frame to block rearward movement of the trigger. The safety is disengaged by pressing the catch to the right with the thumbnail of the gun hand.

The magazine catch is in the butt of the pistol. Of sheet metal construction,the detachable box magazine holds seven, .32 ACP (7.65 mm) cartridges. When the last shot is fired the slide is held in the open position by the magazine follower. Partially withdrawing the magazine from the grip releases the slide, which is then free to go forward under pressure of the recoil spring. Few Steyr Model SPs were imported into the United States and all importation stopped upon implementation of provisions of the 1968 gun Control Act.

DISASSEMBLY

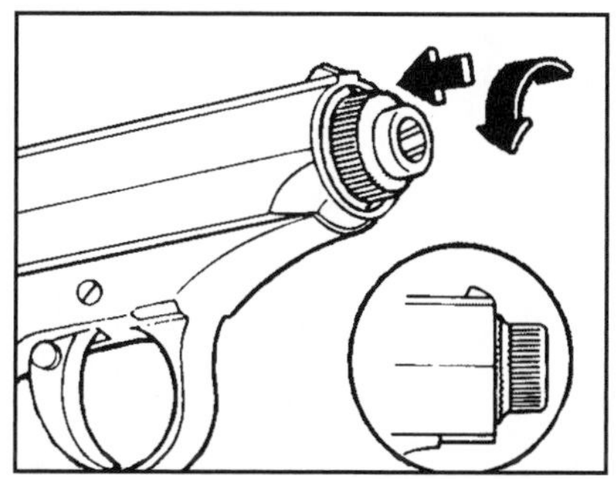

1 To take down the Steyr Model SP pistol, first remove the magazine, and pull back slide and examine chamber to be sure that it is empty. Push in barrel bushing (1) and turn about 15 degrees counterclockwise until it is free to be eased off barrel. Then pull slide (2) to rear and lift it free of frame (24), and slide it off front of barrel.

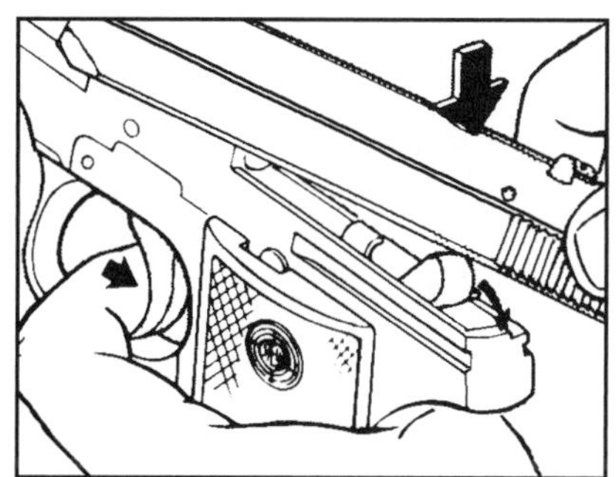

2 When reassembling pistol, put slide back over barrel and pull it back as far as possible. Pull trigger about half way back to partially cock hammer. Then push down on rear of slide until it engages grooves in frame. Install recoil spring (12) and barrel bushing. When barrel bushing is properly seated, it should be flush with end of barrel.

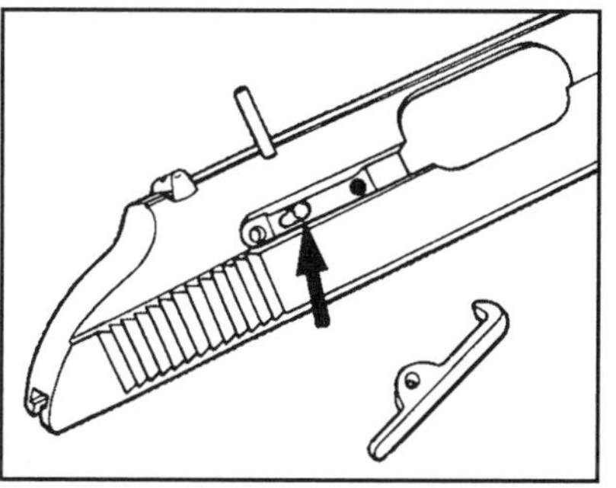

3 To remove firing pin, it is necessary to first remove extractor (5). Drive out extractor pin (4) and remove extractor and extractor spring (6). When extractor is removed, it exposes end of firing pin retaining pin (7) and also exposes a hole that can, if necessary, be of assistance in removing a stuck firing pin bushing (8) or in carrying off gases in event of a punctured primer.

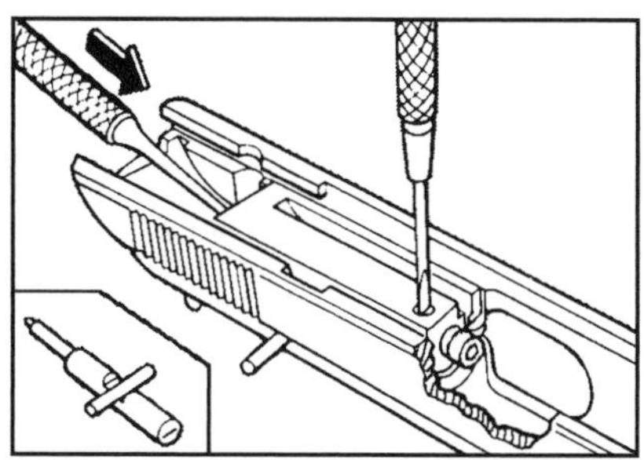

4 To remove firing pin, drive out firing pin retaining pin (7). Then loosen firing pin bushing lock screw (9). Firing pin (11) can now be pushed or tapped out through front of breech. It will in turn push out bushing and firing pin spring (10). Before reassembling firing pin, scribe or pencil a line across large end of pin parallel to flat on pin. Line is an aid in positioning flat to let firing pin retaining pin (7) pass through.

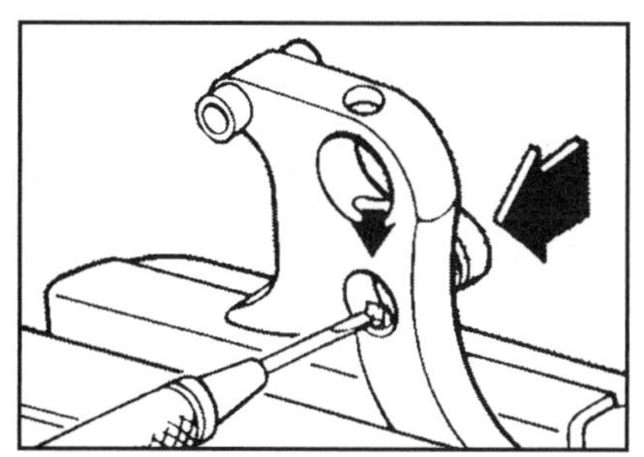

5 Safety catch (34) is a cross-bolt pin that blocks trigger when in "safe" position. To remove it, tap pin out of either side of trigger. Safety is retained by a V-shaped safety catch detent (36) and safety catch spring (35). When replacing safety, install spring and detent in hole in trigger. Hold detent down as shown and tap safety catch into place.

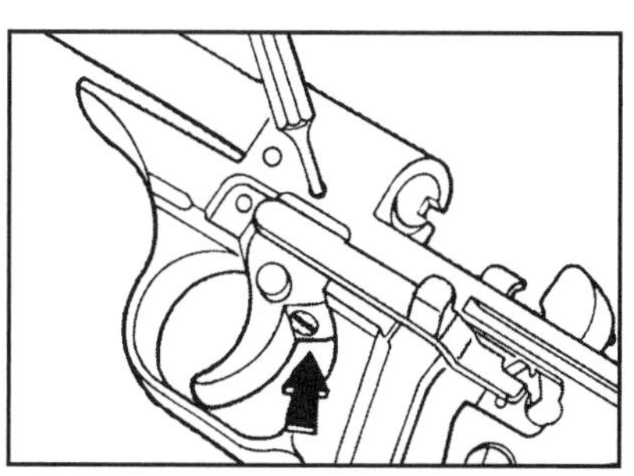

6 After sideplate screw (14) and sideplate (28) and grips have been removed, function of trigger can be studied or disassembled further. First drive out trigger pin (13). Trigger and trigger bar (31) can now be lifted out. To remove trigger bar, remove trigger spring retaining screw (29) on under side of trigger carefully, since it is under spring tension. Remove trigger spring (30) and trigger spring follower (32). Lift out trigger bar.

STOEGER LUGER .22 PISTOL

PARTS LEGEND

1. Bolt stop
2. Bolt stop pin
3. Bolt stop spring
4. Sear
5. Sear spring
6. Safety shoe
7. Hammer
8. Magazine guide pin (2)
9. Sear pin
10. Boltways block pin
11. Hammer spring washer
12. Front sight
13. Barrel
14. Barrel pin
15. Trigger pull pin
16. Trigger
17. Magazine catch anchor plate
18. Magazine catch anchor
19. Trigger pin
20. Trigger pin plunger spring
21. Trigger pin plunger
22. Safety detent plunger
23. Safety spring
24. Safety spring housing
25. Main frame pin
26. Magazine
27. Sear bar
28. Sear bar pin
29. Sear bar guide pin
30. Boltways
31. Magazine guide
32. Hammer strut pin
33. Hammer strut
34. Hammer spring
35. Hammer strut anchor plate
36. Right grip
37. Grip screw (2)
38. Front toggle pin, left hand
39. Front toggle
40. Front toggle pin, right hand
41. Frame
42. Toggle grip pin (2)
43. Toggle grip, left hand
44. Toggle link pin
45. Toggle grip, right hand
46. Rear toggle
47. Rear toggle spring
48. Sear bar retaining screw
49. Extractor
50. Extractor spring
51. Front toggle pin retaining pin (2)
52. Extractor pin
53. Firing pin retaining pin
54. Bolt
55. Magazine catch
56. Magazine catch plunger
57. Magazine catch spring
58. Magazine catch plunger guide
59. Magazine catch pin
60. Rear toggle pivot pin
61. Safety lever
62. Left grip
63. Firing pin spring
64. Drive spring
65. Drive spring guide
66. Firing pin
67. Boltways block
68. Takedown plunger spring
69. Takedown plunger

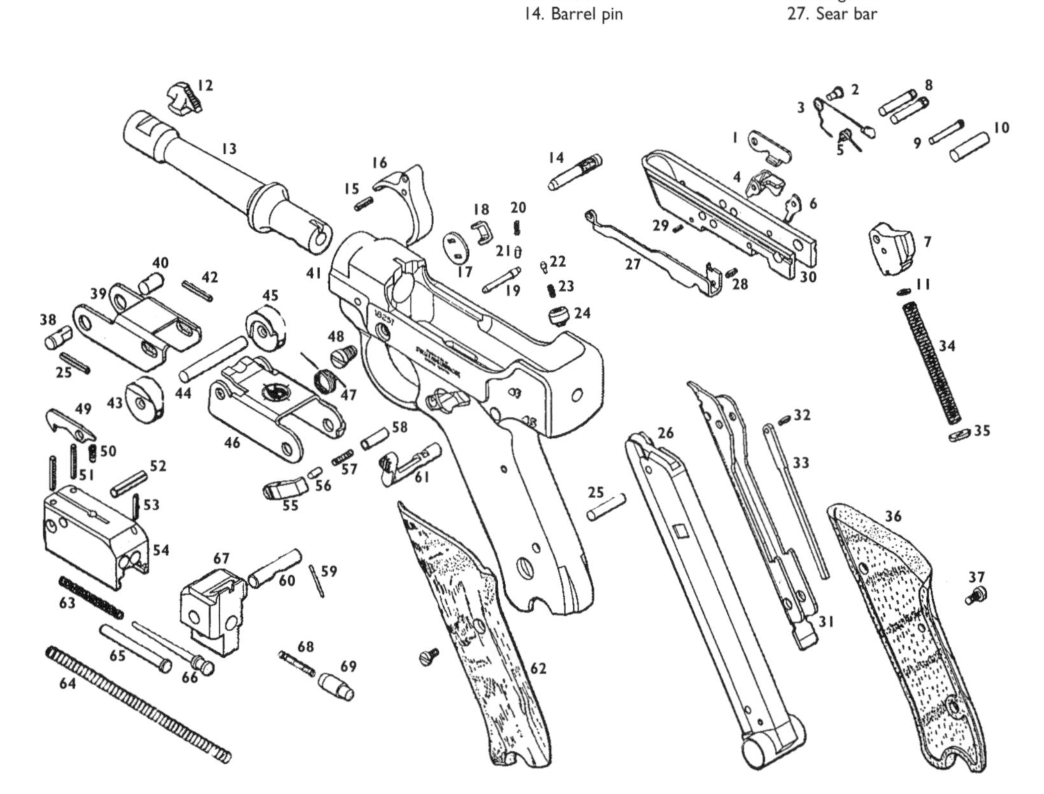

In 1969 Stoeger Arms Corp. introduced a U.S.-made version of the popular Luger pistol. The American Eagle Luger, developed by gun designer Gary Wilhelm, had the same general appearance as the German Model 1908 Luger (P-08) but was chambered for regular or high-velocity .22 Long Rifle ammunition. Barrel lengths were 4½ and 6-inches (Navy Model), with a magazine capacity of 11 rounds. A carbine model was briefly offered in the 1970s.

The mechanical details of the Stoeger Luger differs from the original models. While the Stoeger's toggle-joint breech system resembled that of the center-fire models, the barrel was fixed in the frame and did not recoil. Unlike center-fire Lugers, the lock mechanism had a pivoting hammer powered by a coil spring. A coil-type recoil spring, was contained in the breechbolt. The Stoeger Luger's frame was forged aluminum alloy and the barrel, breechbolt, and other parts subject to wear were steel. The pistol was available in stainless or blued finish. Stoeger discontinued production in 1986.

DISASSEMBLY

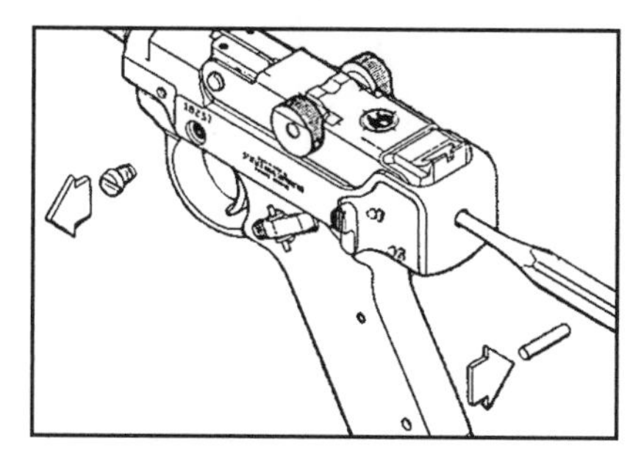

1 Disassemble pistol on a clean, well-lighted bench. Depress magazine catch (55) and remove magazine (26), checking that it is empty. Grasp toggle grips (43, 45) and pull back and up on toggle fully to clear chamber. Release toggle and replace magazine. Move safety lever (61) to fire position, and leave action cocked. Unscrew sear bar retaining screw (48) and grip screws (37). Remove grips (36, 62). Use pin punch to push out main frame pin (25). Then, depress takedown plunger (69). Action will rise slightly as takedown plunger clears frame (41).

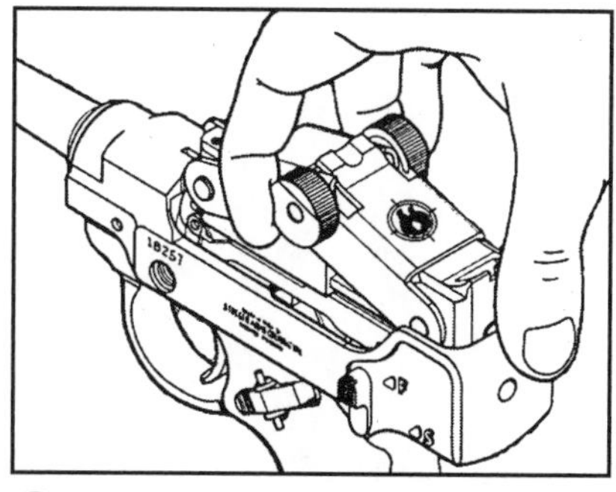

2 Remove magazine and lift out action assembly by pulling straight upward on toggle grips. Rest thumb over rear of frame to catch the spring-loaded take-down plunger as it emerges. Sear bar (27) may not release from trigger pull pin (15). If resistance is felt, move action laterally to free sear bar.

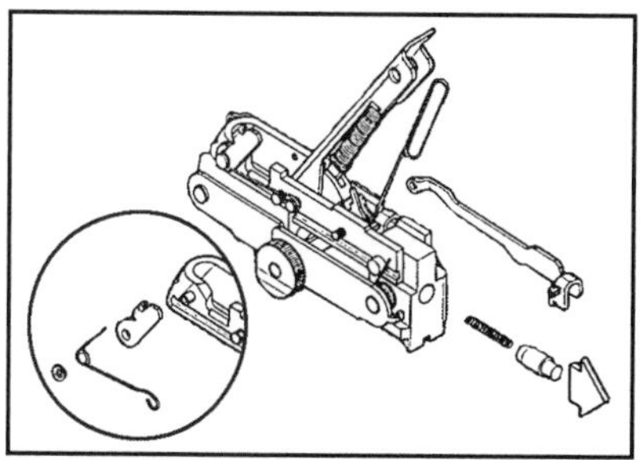

3 Remove takedown plunger and spring (68) so that they are not lost. No further disassembly is required for normal cleaning. If sear bar becomes separated from action assembly, place horseshoe shaped section of the bar in its notch on underside of boltways (30). Bend a small hook in a wire and use to lever the rearward arm of sear spring (5) around and over the sear bar pin (28). On older models, the bolt stop (1) and spring (3) were secured by a separate retainer. Should these parts become displaced, reassemble them over their pin in the order shown (inset).

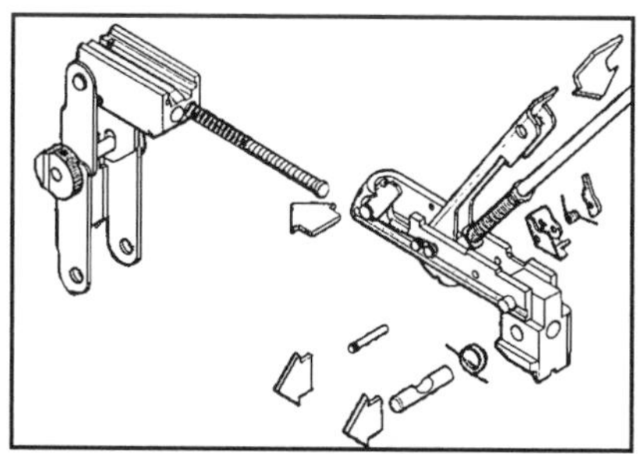

4 To disassemble action, turn assembly upside down and unhook arm of rear toggle spring (47) from boltways block pin (10). Push bolt (54) fully to the rear, in contact with boltways block (67). Push out rear toggle pivot pin (60) with punch. Swing toggle assembly downward and remove rear toggle spring. Ease bolt forward, holding drive spring (64) in alignment so that it is not kinked. Unhook sear spring and remove sear bar. Then, lower hammer (7) cautiously with thumb. Place cleaning rod section or other tube over tip of hammer strut (33), compress hammer spring (34), and pivot assembly clear of magazine guide (31). Drift out swaged pins traversing boltways so that their serrated ends emerge first. Assemble action group in reverse. Longest arms of rear toggle and sear springs bear on boltways block and sear bar pins respectively. Reset both springs with wire hook.

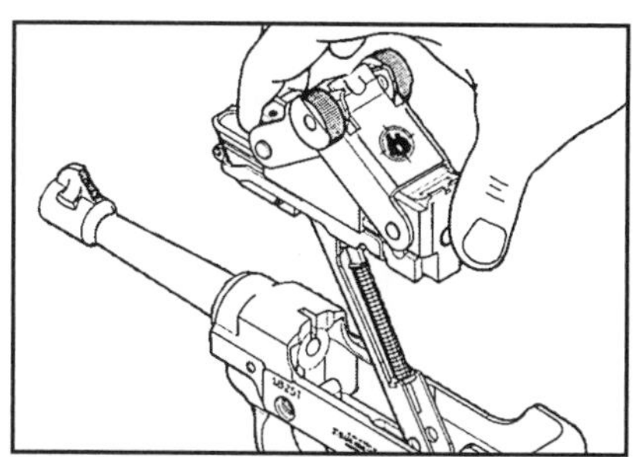

5 To reassemble the field-stripped pistol, first replace takedown plunger and spring. Notch in rear toggle pin must align with takedown plunger. Turn exposed ends of rear toggle pin if necessary. Grasp action between fingers and thumb, compressing drive and takedown plunger springs. Insert tail of magazine guide at rear of magazine well and ease assembly down into place. When fully seated, takedown plunger will snap into its frame recess. Ease toggle closed.

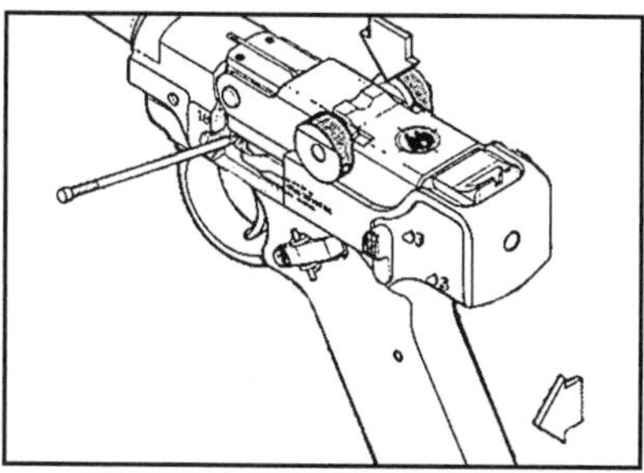

6 Replace magazine and depress rear toggle (46) to align main frame pin holes. Insert frame pin so that it protrudes equally through both sides of frame. Hold trigger (16) fully forward and seat sear bar over trigger pull pin, working through frame hole with the point of a nail. Replace sear bar screw and draw up snugly. Do not use force. Test function of safety and bolt stop. If satisfactory, replace grips and grip screws.

TAURUS PT24/7 PISTOL

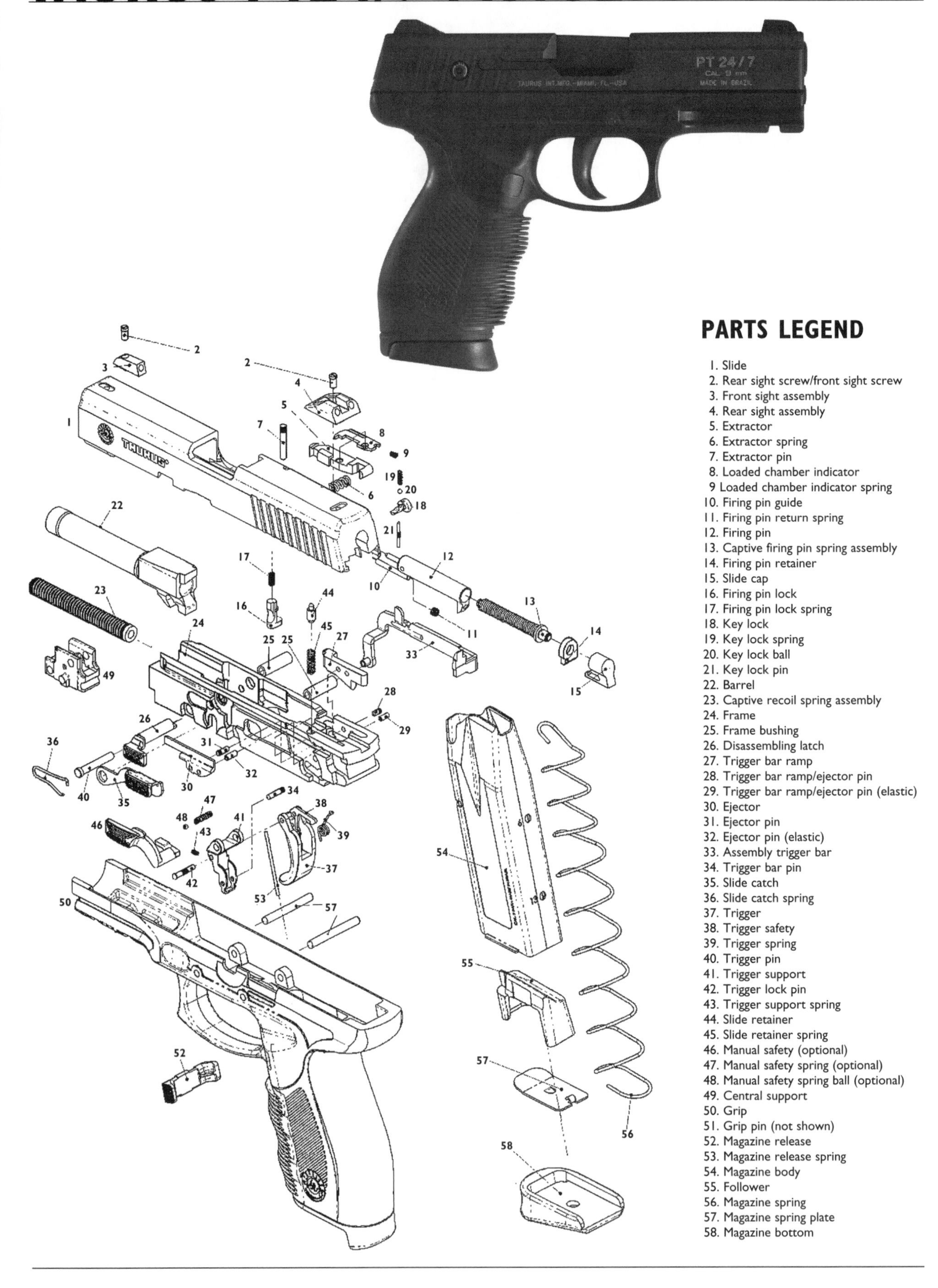

PARTS LEGEND

1. Slide
2. Rear sight screw/front sight screw
3. Front sight assembly
4. Rear sight assembly
5. Extractor
6. Extractor spring
7. Extractor pin
8. Loaded chamber indicator
9. Loaded chamber indicator spring
10. Firing pin guide
11. Firing pin return spring
12. Firing pin
13. Captive firing pin spring assembly
14. Firing pin retainer
15. Slide cap
16. Firing pin lock
17. Firing pin lock spring
18. Key lock
19. Key lock spring
20. Key lock ball
21. Key lock pin
22. Barrel
23. Captive recoil spring assembly
24. Frame
25. Frame bushing
26. Disassembling latch
27. Trigger bar ramp
28. Trigger bar ramp/ejector pin
29. Trigger bar ramp/ejector pin (elastic)
30. Ejector
31. Ejector pin
32. Ejector pin (elastic)
33. Assembly trigger bar
34. Trigger bar pin
35. Slide catch
36. Slide catch spring
37. Trigger
38. Trigger safety
39. Trigger spring
40. Trigger pin
41. Trigger support
42. Trigger lock pin
43. Trigger support spring
44. Slide retainer
45. Slide retainer spring
46. Manual safety (optional)
47. Manual safety spring (optional)
48. Manual safety spring ball (optional)
49. Central support
50. Grip
51. Grip pin (not shown)
52. Magazine release
53. Magazine release spring
54. Magazine body
55. Follower
56. Magazine spring
57. Magazine spring plate
58. Magazine bottom

Taurus began operations as Forjas Taurus (Taurus Forge), a small tool manufacturer in Porto Alegre, Brazil, producing its first revolver, the Model 38101SO, in 1941. In 1968, Taurus began exporting handguns to the United States employing a succession of distributors over the years.

By 1970, the firm of Bangor Punta, owner of Smith & Wesson, purchased 54 percent of Taurus leading to considerable sharing of technology between the two companies. In 1977 Taurus regained ownership and, in 1980, purchased Beretta's Sao Paulo factory that had been built to satisfy a Brazilian military small arms contract. Two years later Taurus opened an affiliated company, Taurus USA, in Miami, Florida.

The Taurus 24/7 was first introduced in 2004. The weapon is a polymer-framed, double-action only, striker-fired pistol with a frame-mounted, 1911-style, manual safety. It features a Single Action/Double Action trigger system that fires normally in single action mode, while providing the ability for a "second try" at firing a faulty cartridge. Taurus also provides a loaded chamber indicator on all PT24/7 Series pistols. The 24/7's grip is designed with an ergonomic profile and fitted with an overmolded/rubberized surface.

All Taurus 24/7s are fitted with the Taurus Security System, which uses a special key to render the pistol inoperable. When the Security System is engaged, the pistol cannot be fired or cocked and the manual safety cannot be disengaged.

Taurus offers 24 different versions of the PT-24, and both long slide and regular models are available in either blue or stainless steel. The 24/7 OSS versions, originally designed as .45 caliber military service sidearms for special forces, are commercially available in .40 S&W and 9mm variants.

DISASSEMBLY

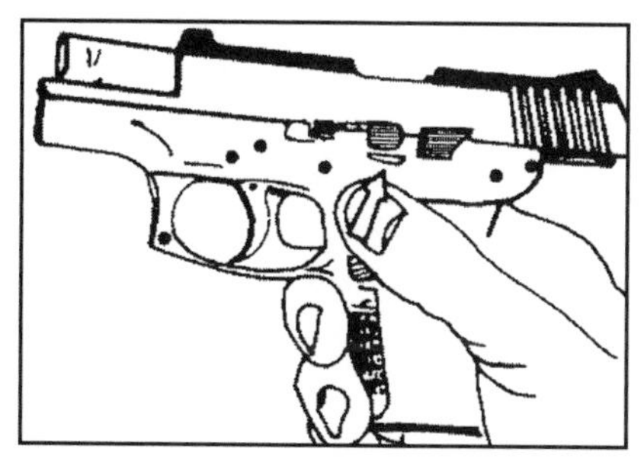

1 Pull slide (1) fully to the rear and push up the slide catch lever (35).

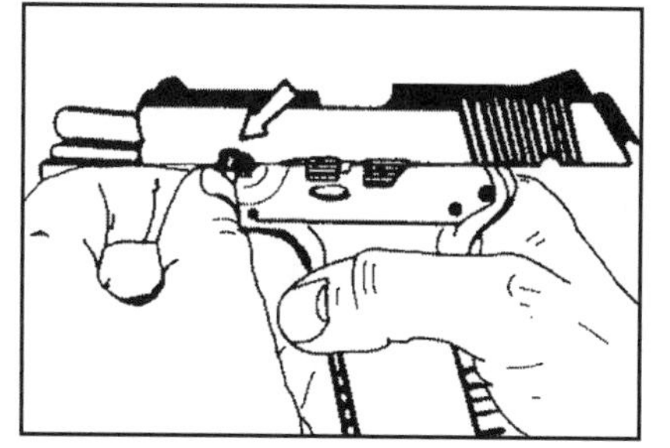

2 With left thumb, rotate slide disassembly latch (26) clockwise until it stops.

Use the key for your Taurus Security System to gently push the slide disassembly latch from the right side of the pistol.

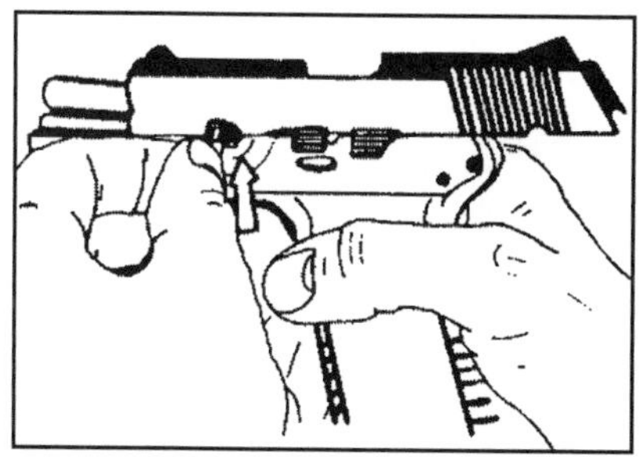

3 With left hand, pull slide disassembly latch or take-down pin out of frame.

4 Carefully release slide catch and with slide under full control, pull slide forward off of frame.

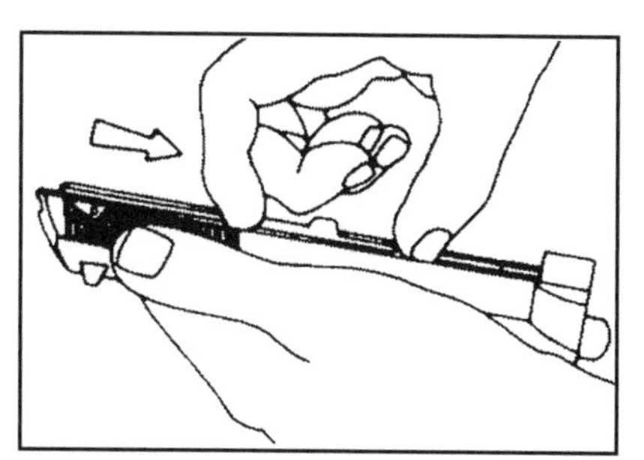

5 Carefully remove slide spring and guide assembly (23) from its position on the bottom of the barrel (22). Spring is under compression so it must be kept under control until removed.

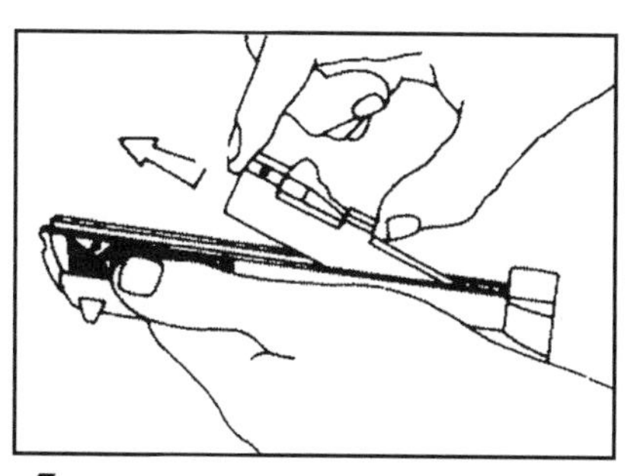

6 Remove barrel (22) from slide by pulling to the rear and up.

NOTE:No further disassembly is recommended unless done by a skilled gunsmith.

TOKAREV MODEL 30 PISTOL

PARTS LEGEND

A. Slide
B. Extractor retaining pin
C. Extractor
D. Extractor spring
E. Rear sight
F. Firing pin spring
G. Firing pin
H. Hammer
I. Hammer spring
J. Hammer mechanism housing
K. Sear spring
L. Sear
M. Disconnector
N. Spring retainer pin
O. Hammer pin
P. Sear pin
Q. Right hand grip
R. Magazine
S. Trigger return spring
T. Spring retainer pin
U. Left hand grip
V. Trigger
W. Magazine catch spring guide
X. Magazine catch spring
Y. Slide stop
Z. Frame (receiver)
AA. Recoil spring guide
BB. Recoil spring retainer
CC. Recoil spring
DD. Slide stop retainer clip
EE. Magazine catch
FF. Barrel link
GG. Barrel link pin
HH. Firing pin retainer pin
II. Barrel
JJ. Barrel bushing

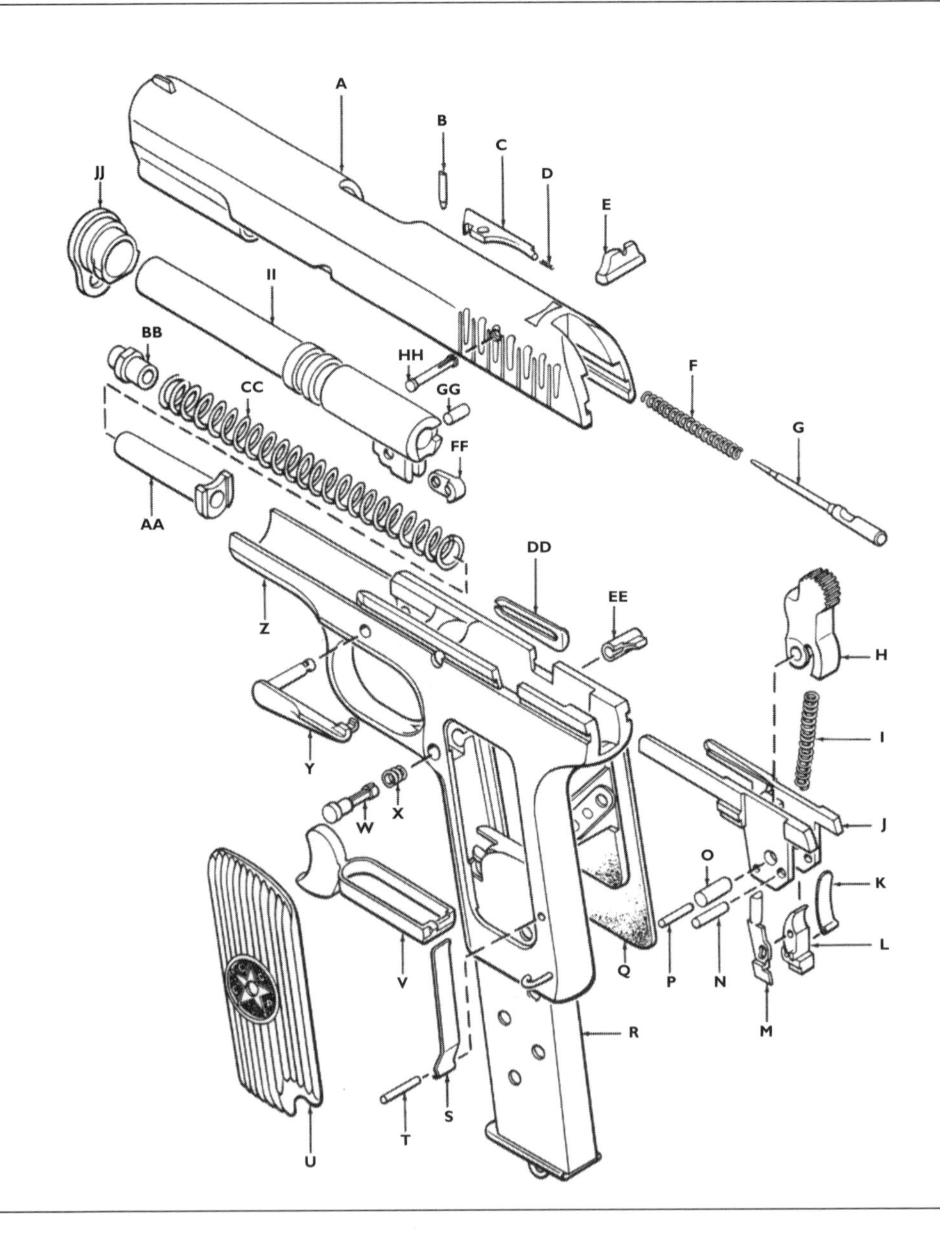

The Tokarev semiautomatic pistol was developed by Fedor V. Tokarev in 1933 and was initially manufactured in a Soviet state factory in Tula, south of Moscow. Designated the TT-33, it was planned to replace the Moisin-Nagant revolver as the standard service handgun of the Red Army.

Chambered for 7.62 Russian or 7.63 Mauser caliber, like other products designed by the Russians during the 1930s, the Tokarev was made with an eye for ease of production. Stalin's Russia, woefully lacking in machine tools, eliminated every unnecessary machining operation. The Tokarev was designed around the time-proven Browning recoil-operated slide lock and stirrup type trigger. The net result was a simple, compact, and dependable automatic pistol, but without manual safety catches or any finely machined parts.

During World War II, Tokarevs were manufactured in the United States for the Soviet Union. The Tokarev remained in service until it was replaced by the Makarov pistol in 1954. The design was widely copied by Soviet bloc nations — China (Type 51), Poland, East Germany, Czechoslovakia, Yugoslavia (M65), North Korea (M68).

Despite manufacturing shortcuts and the lack of a manual safety catch, the Tokarev contains some very interesting points. The most notable is the hammer mechanism which can be lifted out as a unit after the slide has been removed. The unit not only houses the sear, disconnector and hammer, but also acts as feed lips for the 8-round magazine. Since the lips are an integral part of the gun mechanism, they are not subjected to the rough treatment that magazine lips normally get.

There is very little that can wrong with the Tokarev, which weighs one pound fifteen ounces, measures 7 11/16 inches in overall length, and has a barrel 4 9/16 inches long. The weakest parts of the gun are the split pins used to retain the magazine catch and firing pins. These pins have a tendency to break at the bottom of the slot unless they are squeezed together while being removed. All in all, the simplicity of the design and of the parts make this pistol an easy weapon to repair.

DISASSEMBLY

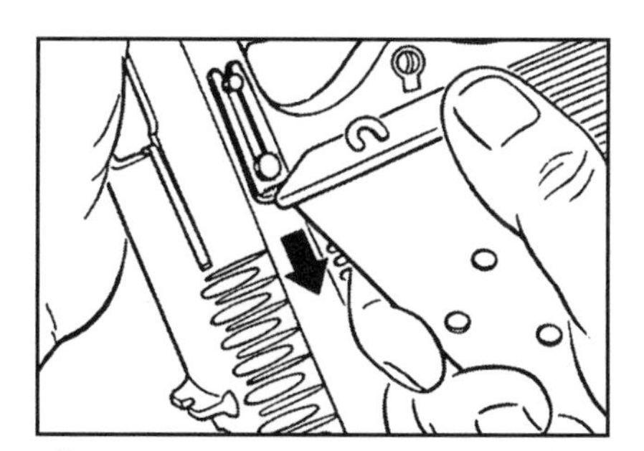

1 Remove the magazine. Draw back the slide to eject any cartridge in the chamber. Using the back edge of the bottom plate of the magazine as a tool, pull back hard on the slide stop retainer clip (DD) until it releases. Then push the slide stop (Y) through from right to left.

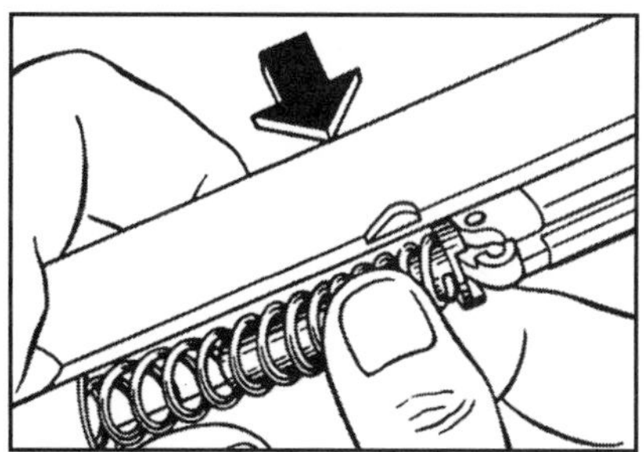

2 Draw the slide off the front of the frame slowly. As soon as the recoil spring is exposed, hold it up against the barrel to prevent it from bending out of the slide. While holding the recoil spring in place, grasp the recoil spring guide (AA) and push it toward the muzzle, while lifting it free of the barrel lug.

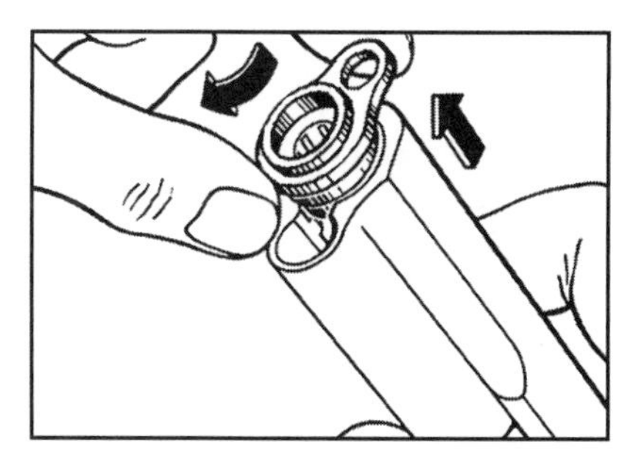

3 The barrel bushing (JJ) can now be turned 180 degrees and then lifted free of the slide. The barrel (II) can now be pulled out the front of the slide. This method of take down will be found much simpler than the one usually recommended for the take down of similar Browning type pistols.

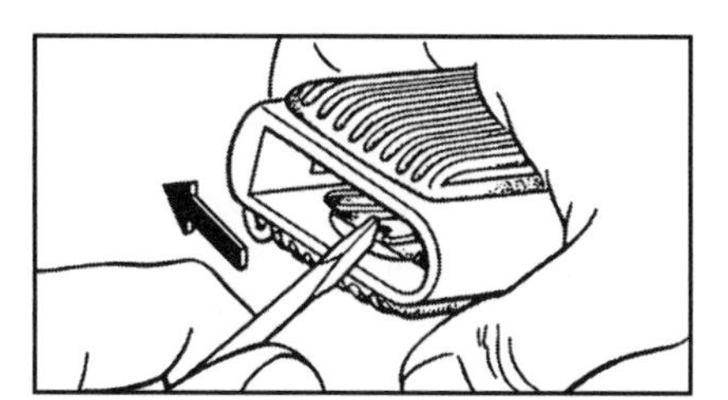

4 The grips on this weapon are held on with a latch arrangement. Holding the gun as shown, a T-shaped piece of steel can be seen. Reach in with a screw driver and push the T-shaped piece toward the rear of the gun grip. The left-hand grip can new be removed by pushing against the inside surface. Do not attempt to pry the grip from the outside—the plastic is a very low grade and will chip along the edges.

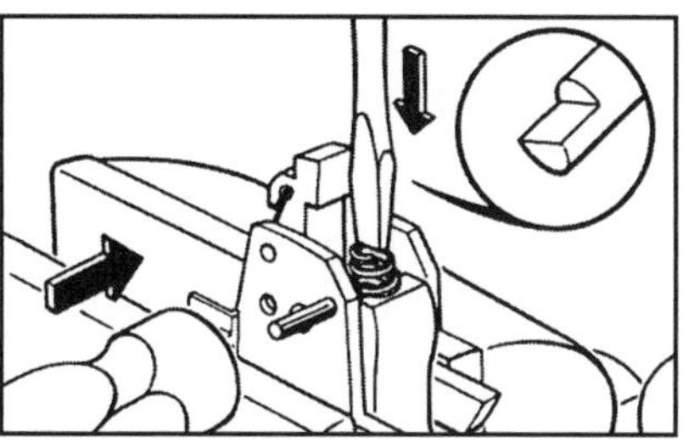

5 The hardest section on this gun to disassemble is the hammer group, but after removing the hammer spring retainer pin (N), the other pins may be removed easily. To reassemble, replace all parts but the hammer spring. Using a screw driver or tool shown in the insert, depress the spring (I) deep enough to allow the pin (N) to hold it. Then tap the pin all the way through.

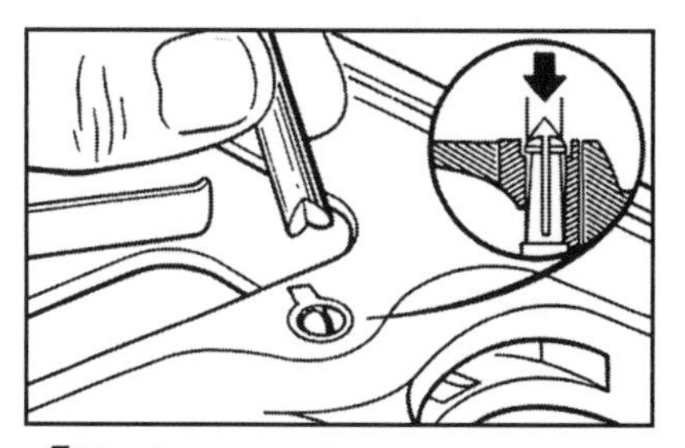

6 The firing pin and the magazine catch are retained by split pins. These split pins (HH & W) can be removed with the aid of the tool shown. This tool forces the pin to close up so that it may be pushed out easily. If an attempt is made to drive the pins out with a flat-end punch, they may be broken or badly deformed.

UNIQUE MILITARY & POLICE PISTOL

PARTS LEGEND

1. Barrel
2. Slide
3. Extractor pin
4. Firing pin retaining pin
5. Extractor
6. Extractor spring
7. Rear sight
8. Firing pin spring
9. Firing pin
10. Hammer with strut & pin
11. Sear
12. Sear spring
13. Grip screws (4)
14. Grip, right
15. Magazine
16. Frame
17. Hammer plunger
18. Hammer spring
19. Hammer catch plunger
20. Magazine catch
21. Magazine catch pin
22. Magazine catch stop pin
23. Hammer pin
24. Sear pin
25. Magazine safety spring
26. Magazine safety
27. Trigger bar
28. Trigger spring
29. Grip, left
30. Trigger bar pin
31. Magazine safety stop pin
32. Trigger pin
33. Trigger
34. Safety
35. Magazine safety stop pin
36. Disconnector
37. Recoil spring assembly

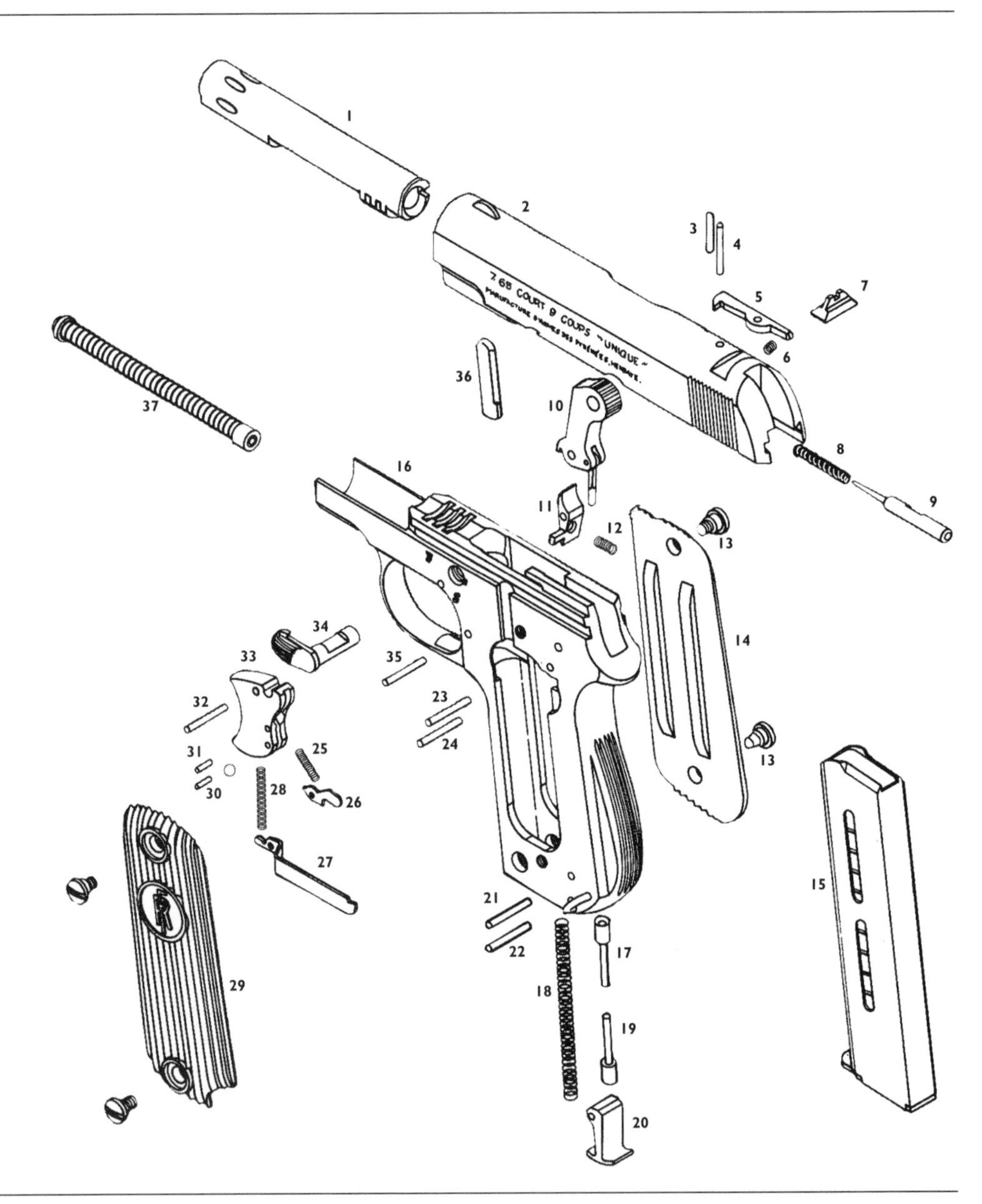

During World War II, the Germans used many substitute-standard small arms, among them the Unique Military & Police Model 7.65 mm, (.32 ACP) automatic pistol. Commonly called the *Kriegsmodell* (War Model), this blowback-operated pistol was produced by Manufacture d'Armes des Pyrénées Françaises in Hendaye, France who designated it the Model "C." It had a 9-round detachable magazine, and weighed 26½ ozs. with a 3¼-inch barrel.

Of simple design, this pistol has an exposed hammer with rounded spur. The safety is on the left of the frame and the hammer has a half-cock notch. When the chamber is loaded, the extractor projects from the slide as a loading indicator. The magazine catch is on the bottom of the handle.

The grips are black plastic with vertical serrations with a circular shield marked with the caliber and magazine capacity. The marking on specimens made for German issue is "7.65 M/M. 9 SCHUSS." On models made for French use, the marking is "7.65 M/M. 9 COUPS." There are also grips with bearing the interlocked letters "RF," for Republique Française.

While wartime pistols were only moderately well made and finished, they were strong, serviceable, and sufficiently accurate for theirr intended purpose.

DISASSEMBLY

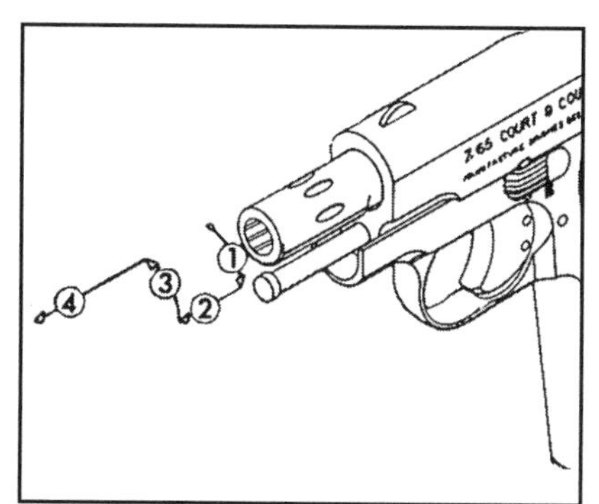

1 Remove the magazine (15) and clear the chamber. Pull the slide (2) to the rear, and engage the safety (34) with the front notch on the slide to lock the slide back. Rotate the barrel clockwise 60 degrees, pull it forward ¾ inch. Rotate it counterclockwise 60 degrees (3), and pull forward (4) out of the slide.

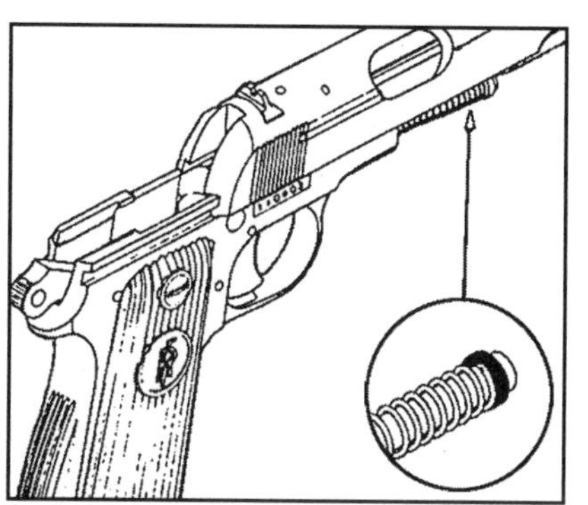

2 While holding the slide firmly, turn the safety downward, and ease the slide forward off the frame (16). Remove the recoil spring assembly (37). This completes field-stripping.

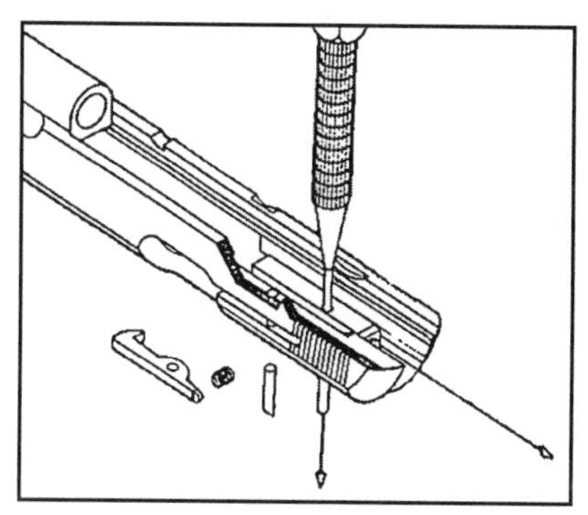

3 For further disassembly, place the slide bottom up in a vise with padded jaws. Drift out the extractor pin (3) and firing retaining pin (4), and remove the extractor (5), extractor spring (6), firing pin (9), and firing pin spring (8). Drift out retaining pins in the slide to the top; those in the frame from right to left.

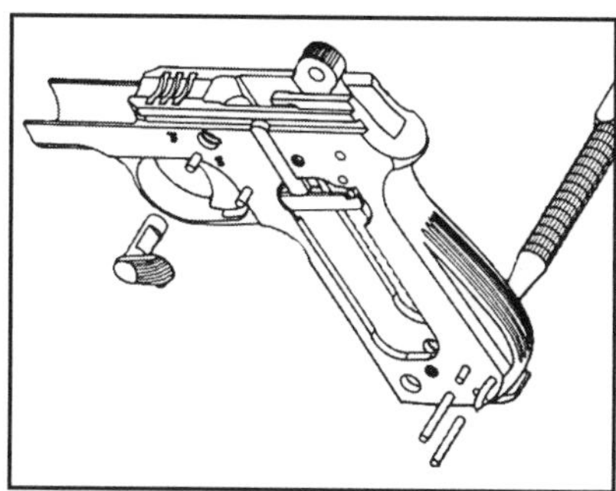

4 Remove grips (14 & 29). Rotate safety a half turn and lift out. Insert magazine, hold hammer (10) and pull trigger (33) to ease hammer down. Place frame in a padded vise and drift out magazine catch stop pin (22). Holding magazine catch (20), drift out magazine catch pin (21), and remove magazine catch, magazine catch plunger (17). Drift out hammer pin (23), and remove hammer.

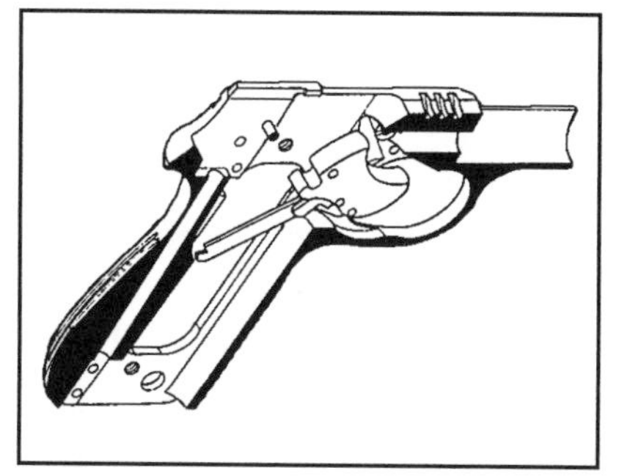

5 Drift out sear pin (24), and remove sear (11) and sear spring (12). Drift out magazine safety stop pin (35) and trigger pin (32). Pull trigger bar (27) inside of frame, and slide disconnector (36) down to remove it. Roll trigger assembly back and down through magazine well. Trigger assembly can be disassembled by drifting out trigger bar pin (30) and magazine safety pin (31) from right to left. Reassemble in reverse. Use a drift punch or slave pin to aid insertion of magazine catch pin. Head of extractor pin is shaped to match rounded top of slide. Drive this pin with a plastic hammer to avoid damaging it. Extractor pin and firing pin retaining pin must not project from bottom of slide.

U.S. MODEL 1842 PISTOL

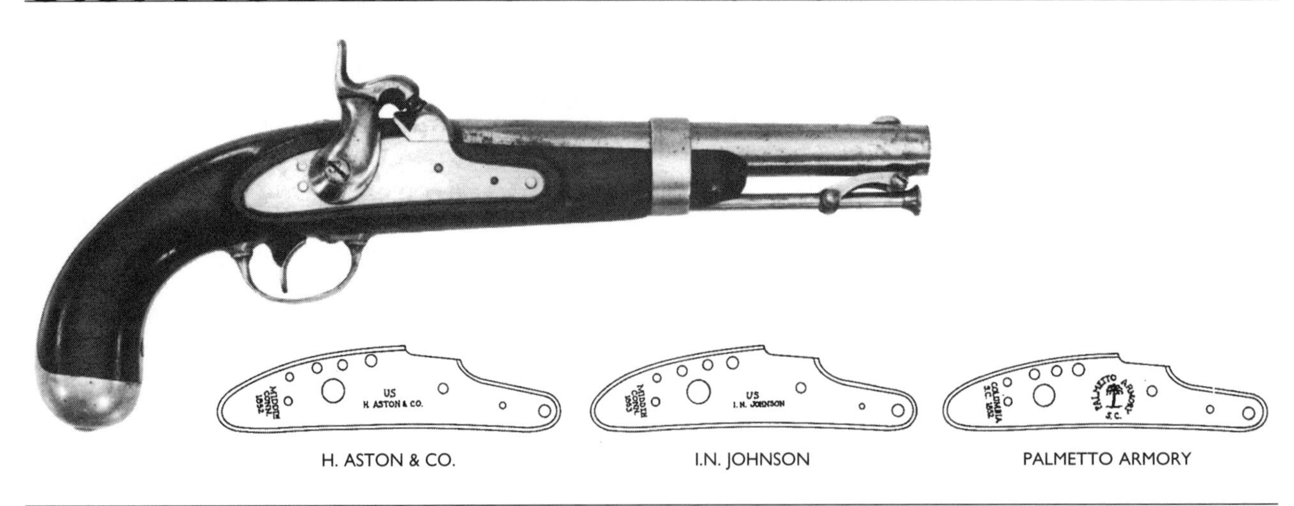

PARTS LEGEND

1. Barrel
2. Front sight
3. Ramrod
4. Anchor stud
5. Link screw
6. Left rammer link
7. Right rammer link
8. Swivel shoulder
9. Swivel
10. Barrel band
11. Front sideplate screw
12. Sideplate
13. Rear sideplate screw
14. Lockplate
15. Mainspring
16. Mainspring screw
17. Bridle screw stop
18. Bridle
19. Bridle screw bottom
20. Sear
21. Sear spring
22. Sear screw
23. Tumbler
24. Hammer screw
25. Hammer
26. Trigger
27. Trigger screw
28. Trigger guard plate
29. Trigger guard bow
30. Rear trigger guard screw
31. Trigger guard nut (2)
32. Buttplate
33. Buttplate screw
34. Stock
35. Tang screw
36. Nipple

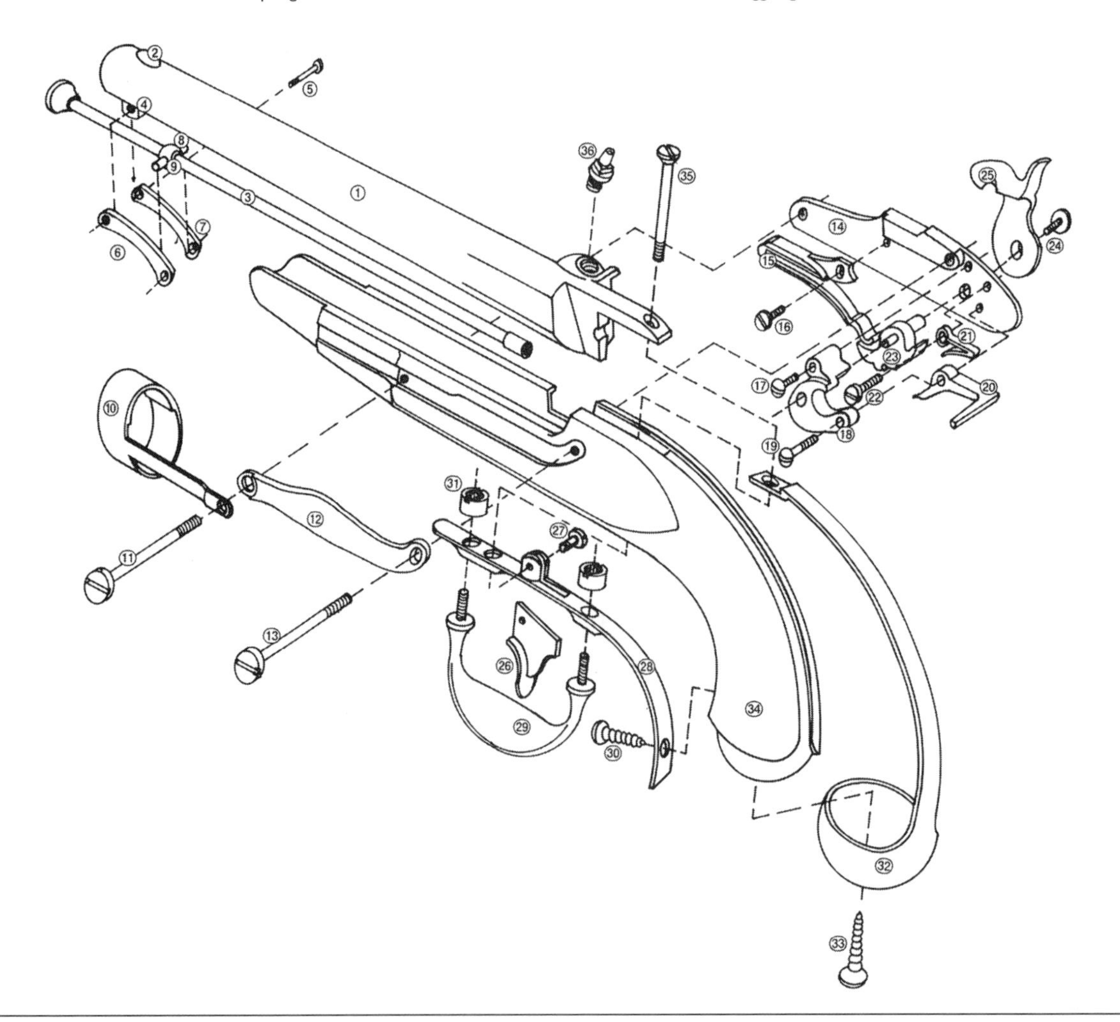

The U.S. Model 1842 .54 caliber percussion pistol with 8-inch barrel was manufactured by Henry Aston and Ira N. Johnson, both operating in Middletown, Connecticut. While the majority of pistols encountered are from either of these two contractors, pattern pistols were produced at Springfield Armory and a variant was made at the Palmetto Armory in South Carolina prior to the Civil War.

The graceful lines of earlier United States martial flintlocks (many of them later converted to percussion) were continued with this percussion smoothbore. Henry Aston, a former employee of Simeon North at Springfield Armory, received a contract for 30,000 pistols at $6.50 each on February 25, 1845. Specifications for the Model 1842 included all brass furniture, even to the blade front sight, and attachment of the trigger guard was by two spanner nuts instead of riveting as in earlier models. After the reorganization of Aston's company in 1850, his former employee, Ira N. Johnson, received an independent contract for 10,000 pistols at $6.75 each.

Date stamping on the barrel tang as well as the lockplate was commonly done by both makers of this 2-lb., 12 oz. pistol. Government inspection stamps are found usually on the barrel tang and on the left side of the stock near the sideplate. Original finishing called for all metal surfaces to be left bright except for the blued trigger.

Firing a half-ounce .54 cal. round ball, the Model 1842 provided a potent single-shot package in the Mexican War period, and the guns saw limited use as late as the Civil War. The rarer Palmetto Armory variation, produced by William Glaze & Co. in Columbia, South Carolina, can be characterized as a Model 1842 pistol with changes in both barrel and lockplate markings and saw service with Southern forces of this period.

Model 1842 pistols were fited with a swiveling mechanism that attached the ramrod to the barrel, a useful component in a pistol primarily intended for issue to mounted troops.

DISASSEMBLY

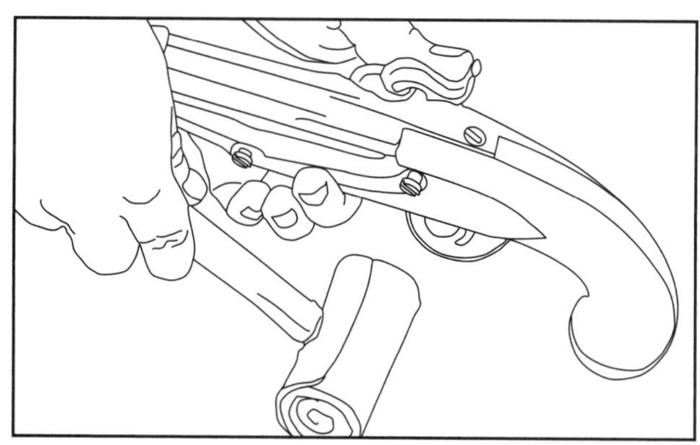

1 After checking the bore for an unfired charge, the hammer (25) should be drawn back to the half-cock position so as to clear the nipple (36). Loosen the front and the rear sideplate screws (11 & 13) slightly. Once the screw heads have risen above the surface of the sideplate (12), a light, non-marring mallet can be used to gently tap them and free the lockplate (14). Prying the lockplate out from the other side may result in scarring of the surrounding wood.

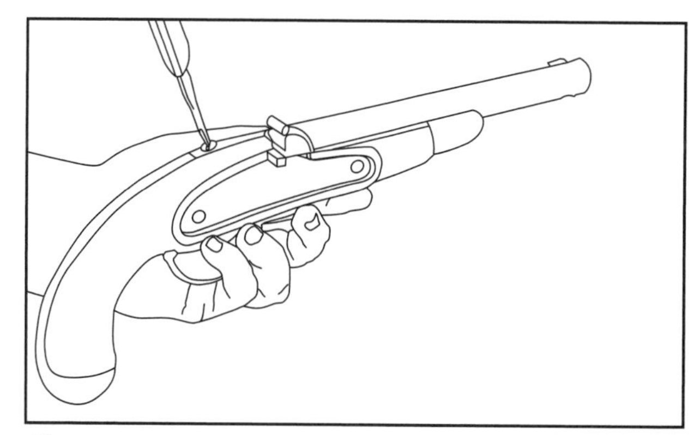

2 After the lockplate mechanism has been removed from the stock (34), pull out the ramrod (3). Unscrewing the link screw (5) will free the ramrod assembly. The barrel band (10) can be tapped off the stock using a wood drift. The barrel (1) is held in place by the tang screw (35) which terminates in the trigger guard plate (28).

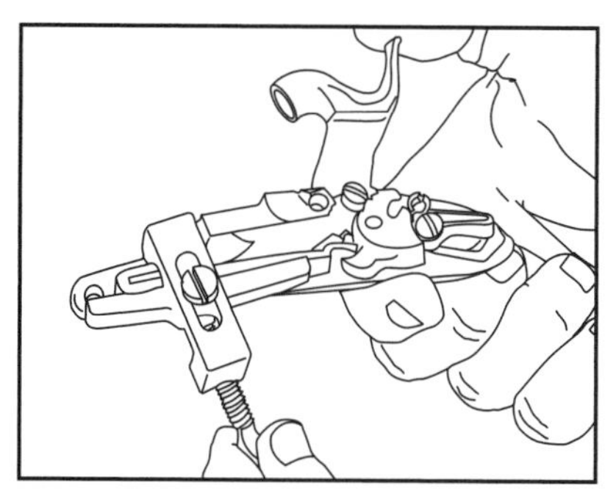

3 To disassemble the lock mechanism, apply pressure to the mainspring (15) with a mainspring vise or a shop vise.

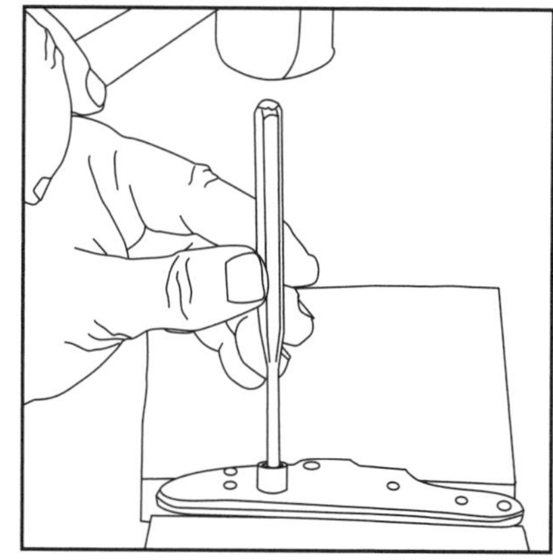

4 After removing the mainspring screw (16) the compressed mainspring can be withdrawn from the lockplate. After removing the bottom bridle screw (19) the sear can be taken out. Remove the top bridle screw (17) and the bridle (18). The hammer (25) is held in place by the hammer screw (24). Remove the sear spring screw (22) and the sear spring (21). Tap the tumbler (23) clear of the lockplate.

U.S. MODEL 1842 NAVY PISTOL

PARTS LEGEND

1. Barrel
2. Cone
3. Barrel screw
4. Swivel screw
5. Left ramrod swivel
6. Ramrod guide
7. Right ramrod swivel
8. Ramrod
9. Ramrod spring
10. Band
11. Band cross pin
12. Stock
13. Lock retaining screw
14. Washer
15. Trigger pin
16. Trigger
17. Trigger guard
18. Trigger guard screw
19. Butt cap
20. Butt cap screw
21. Hammer
22. Lockplate
23. Hammer pin
24. Sear spring
25. Sear
26. Mainspring
27. Bridle
28. Bridle screws (2)

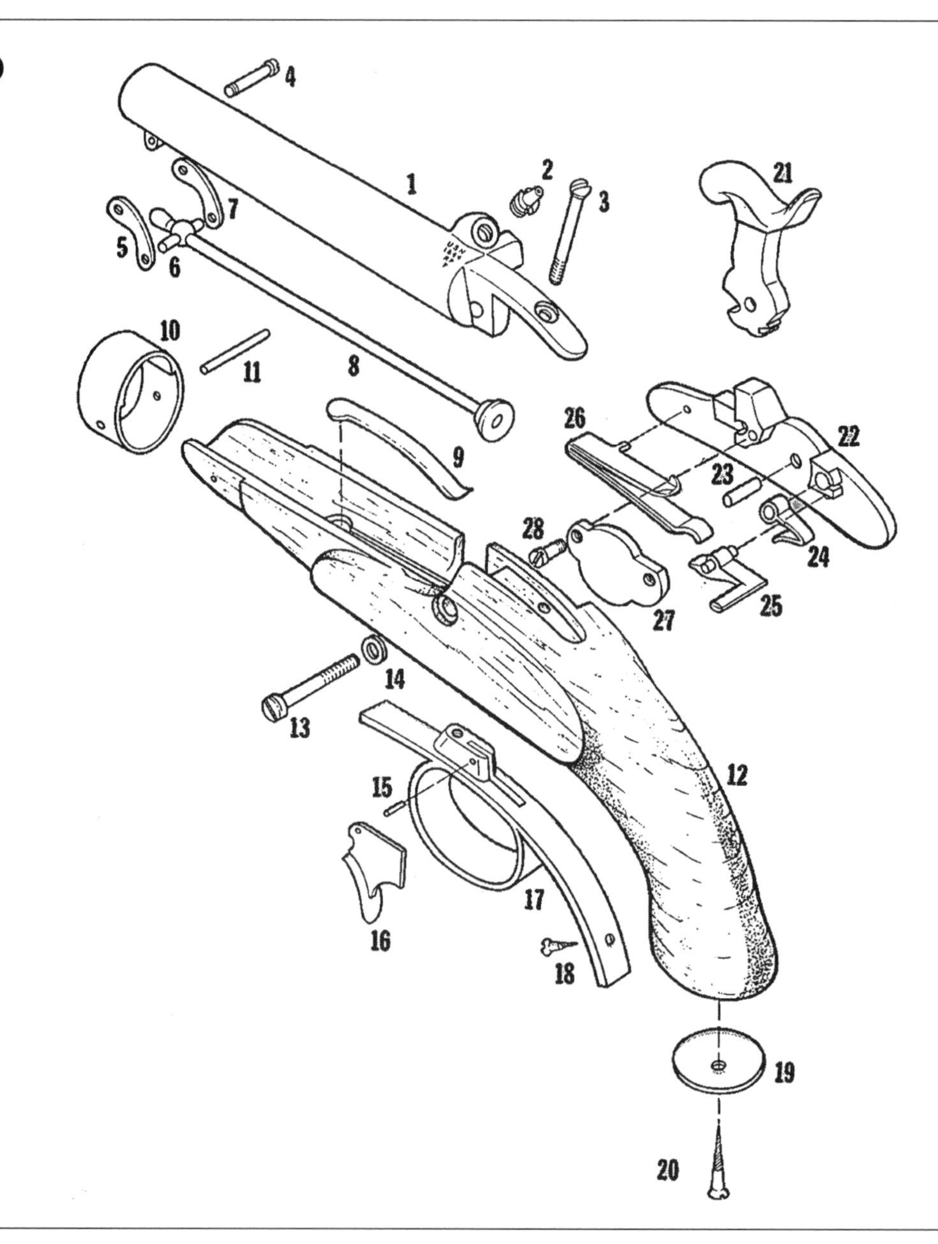

The Navy's Model 1842, .54 caliber percussion pistol, with six-inch round barrel, was made by N.P. Ames of Springfield, Massachusetts and Henry Deringer of Philadelphia.

Those made by Ames are smoothbored and are dated 1842, 1843, 1844 or 1845, according to the year of manufacture. They are found both with and without brass blade front sights. Those made for Navy purchase are marked "U.S.N."

Others, made for the Treasury Department's Revenue Cutter Service, are marked "U.S.R. "

Model 1842 Navy pistols made by Deringer are encountered with both smoothbore and rifled barrels, with the latter having both front and rear sights. Most Deringer guns are unmarked as to the year of production, but a few bear the date 1847.

Box-lock, or inside hammer, mechanisms are uncommon in United States martial arms designs. The idea of the inside hammer was to prevent it from snagging when a sailor thrust a brace of pistols into his belt. This development led to a simplified lock mechanism in which the half- and full-cock notches were cut directly into the hammer and the need for a tumbler and tumbler screw was eliminated — as were the parts.

Another advanced feature of the 1842 Navy pistol was its internal hammer stop. This sturdy projection on the underside of the lockplate prevented the hammer from battering the nipple.

Model 1842 Navy pistols were handsome guns having all brass hardware with case hardened lockplates and hammers. Most barrels were lacquer browned, though some were tinned to prevent salt water corrosion. Relatively few Model 1842 Navy pistols were made. Estimates of the combined production of Ames and Deringer is fewer than 4,000 guns.

DISASSEMBLY

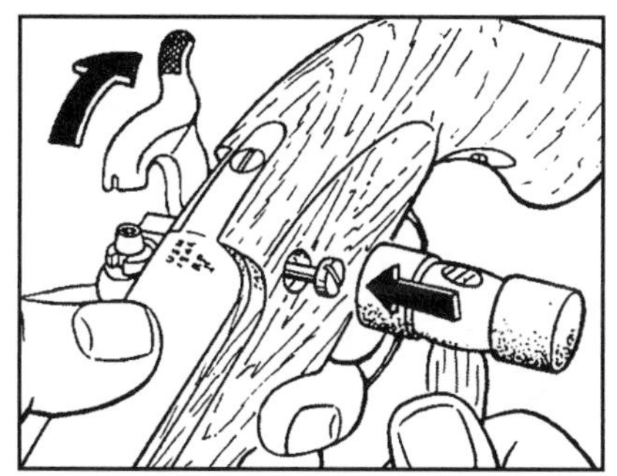

1 To remove the lockplate, first pull the hammer back to half-cock position to clear the cone (2). Loosen the lock retaining screw (13) a few turns and tap it gently with a plastic hammer. If the lock does not come out easily, tap the lock-plate (22) lightly. This will help break the lock loose from rust and grime. Continue to loosen the retaining screw (13) and to tap it until the lock is free of the stock. Never attempt to pry the lock-plate loose, as this may scar the stock.

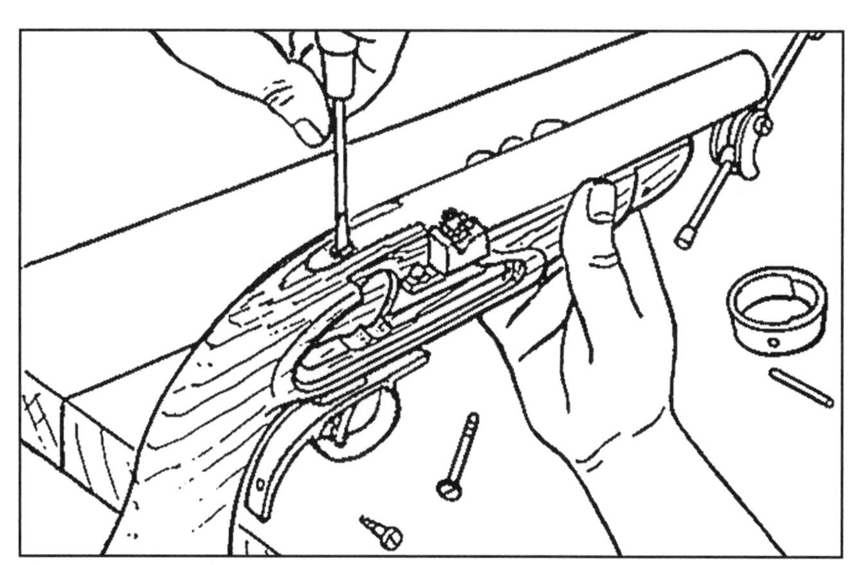

2 After the lock mechanism has been removed, the balance of the gun can be disassembled easily. First pull out the ramrod (8). Drive out the band cross pin (11), and carefully drive off the band (10) with a block of wood or plastic hammer. The barrel screw (3) holds the barrel (1) and the trigger guard (17) together and must be removed completely. Be sure the lock retaining screw is out of the stock, since it, too retains the barrel.

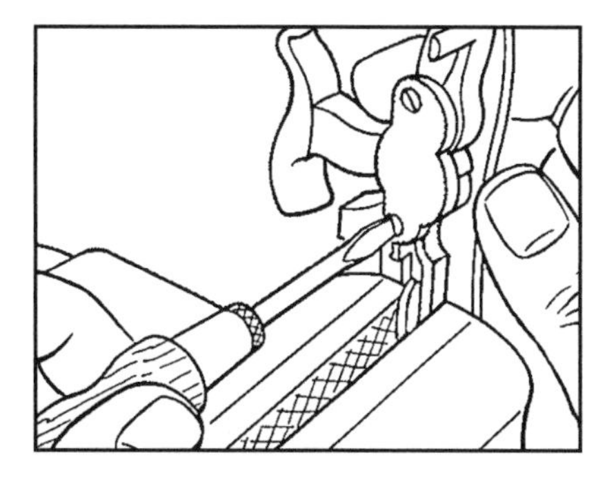

3 Before attempting to disassemble the lock, treat the screws with a good penetrating solvent. Take the tension off the mainspring (26) with an old spring clamp if one is available. If not, clamp the mainspring (26) in a vise as shown. Squeeze the mainspring just enough to relieve the pressure on the hammer. Remove the bridle screws (28) and lift off the bridle (27). Lift out the hammer (21). The mainspring is now free to pivot until the short end is free of its notch in the lockplate. Ease the mainspring out.

WALTHER MODEL 4 PISTOL

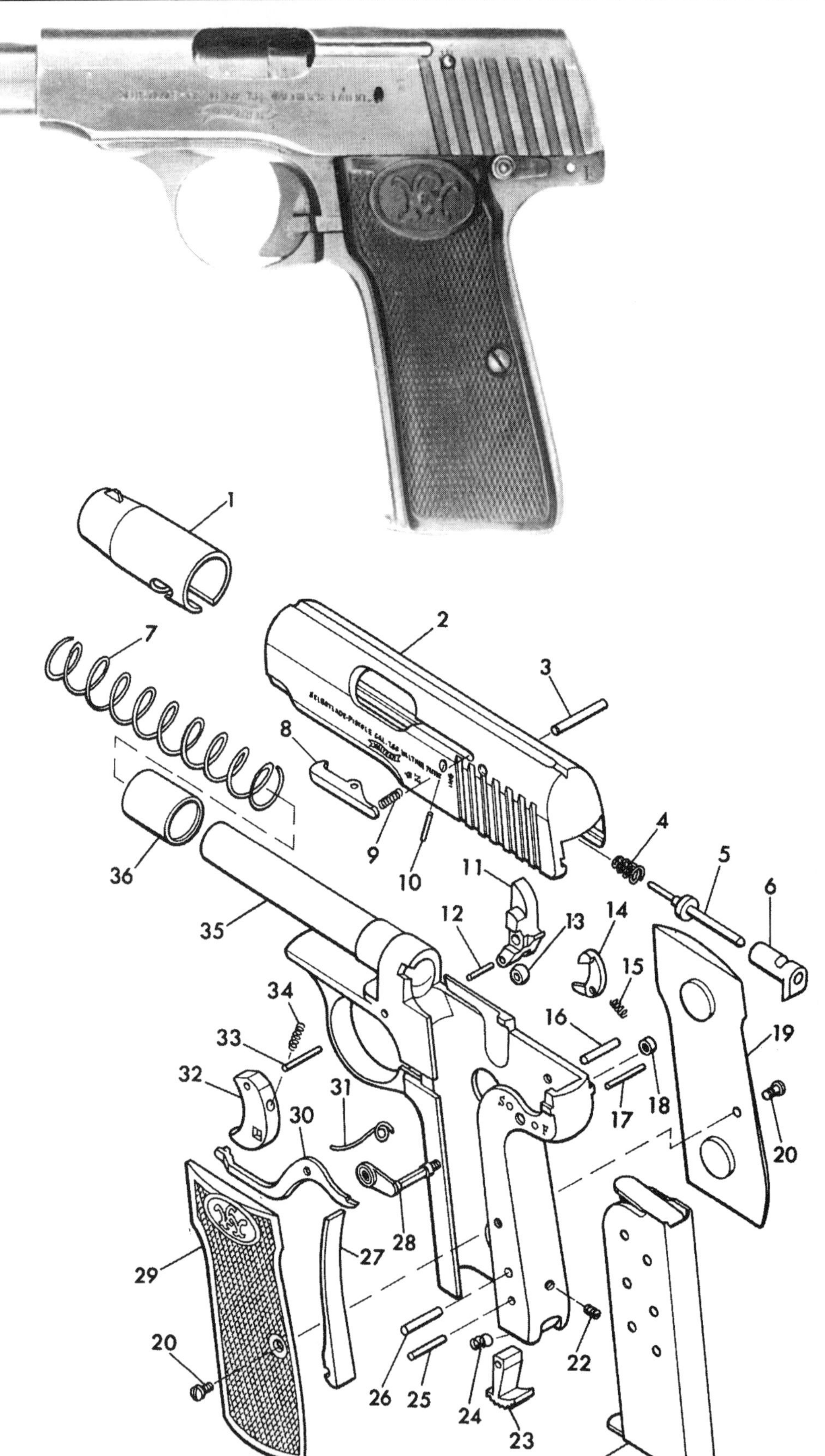

PARTS LEGEND

1. Slide extension
2. Slide
3. Firing pin retainer
4. Firing pin spring
5. Firing pin
6. Firing pin extension
7. Recoil spring
8. Extractor
9. Extractor spring
10. Extractor pin
11. Hammer
12. Hammer roller pin
13. Hammer roller
14. Sear
15. Sear spring
16. Hammer pin
17. Sear pin
18. Safety catch nut
19. Right grip
20. Grip screw (2)
21. Magazine
22. Mainspring retainer screw
23. Magazine catch
24. Magazine catch spring
25. Magazine catch pin
26. Mainspring pin
27. Mainspring
28. Safety catch
29. Left grip
30. Trigger bar
31. Trigger bar spring
32. Trigger
33. Trigger pin
34. Trigger spring
35. Barrel/frame
36. Recoil spring bushing

The Carl Walther firm of Zella St. Basii, Germany, was among the earliest automatic pistol makers. They brought out Germany's first .25 caliber automatic pistol in 1908. In 1910 they introduced the .32 caliber Model 3, then, in the same year, enlarged the Model 3 and called it the Model 4.

In production for only 15 years, the design was revised several times, and over 100,000 were manufactured during World War I. Model 4 pistols were well liked by German officers and large numbers were still in use during World War II.

As stated, the first Model 4 was simply a Model 3 pistol with a longer barrel and grip. The larger size made the pistol much more practical from a military standpoint. Increasing the magazine capacity to eight rounds (plus a round in the chamber) gave the Model 4 a nine-shot capability. Lengthening the barrel resulted in a longer sighting radius.

After the first few hundred guns, the slide was redesigned to simplify the takedown and lighten the pistol. The second version (exploded view) is probably the most common variety of the Model 4. This second variation went through a bewildering number of slide markings and minor changes. The shape of the ejection port was changed and at a later date a rear sight was inserted into a dovetail slot cut into the slide.

Extensive military use in World War I pointed out the need for design changes. On earlier guns the trigger bar, that connects the trigger to the sear, was laid in an open slot milled into the frame. It was exposed to the elements and only retained by the left grip. The last version of the Model 4 moved that trigger bar inside the frame so that it was no longer exposed. Slide serrations were changed from wide flat grooves to a series of 16 sharp "V" serrations.

The Model 4 was eventually replaced in the Walther line by the more modern designs of the late 1920s and '30s.

DISASSEMBLY

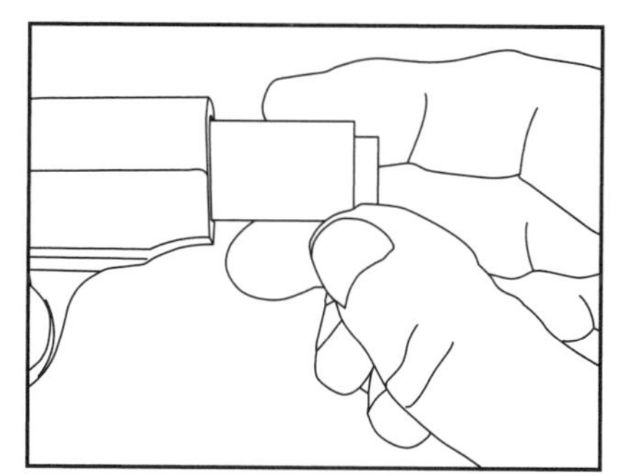

1 Depress the magazine catch (23) and withdraw the magazine (21). Retract the slide (2) and check to be sure that the chamber is empty. Holding the grip in one hand, with the other push in the slide extension (1), turn it counterclockwise to its limit, when viewed from the muzzle end, and allow it to ride forward out of the slide under spring pressure. Remove it, the recoil spring (7) and the recoil spring bushing (36).

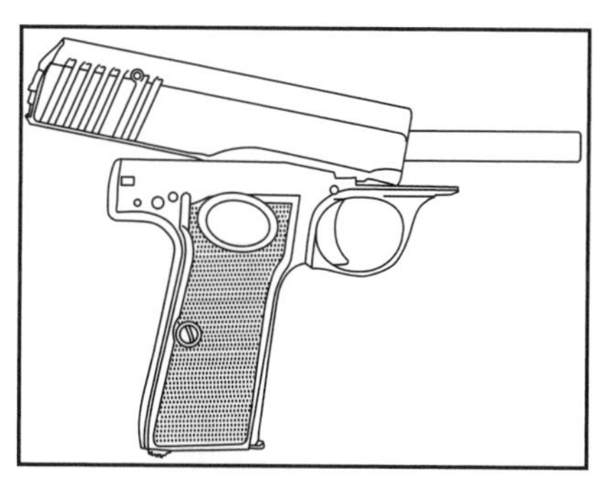

2 The slide (2) can now be drawn fully back, its rear lifted up, and the unit easily pushed forward off the barrel (35).

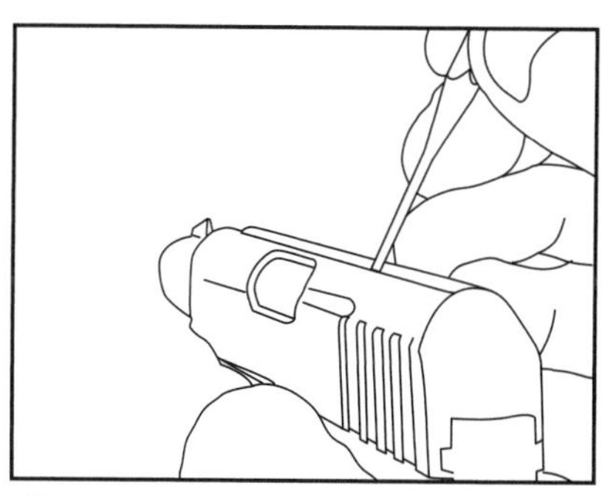

3 With a small drift punch on an angle, drive the extractor pin (10) down from the top of the slide (2) through its oval hole in the left side of the slide. A larger punch can be used to drive out the firing pin retainer (3) from left to right. This frees the firing pin (5), its spring (4), and extension (6).

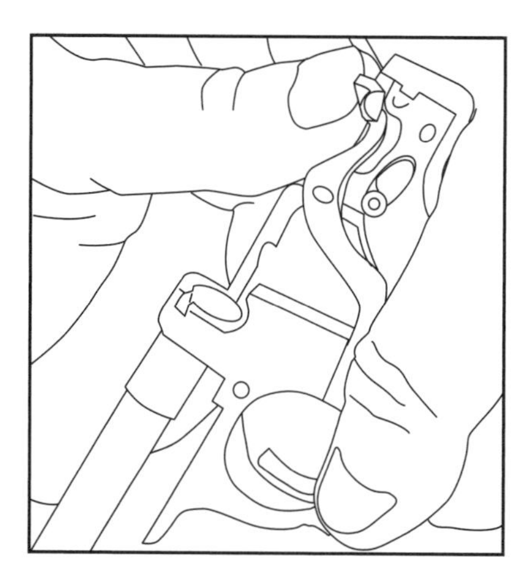

4 Lower the internal hammer (11) by turning the safety (28) to its forward position, placing the thumb on the hammer to cushion its fall, and pulling the trigger (32). Remove the grip screws (20) and grips (19 & 29). This exposes most working parts and allows the manual depression of the trigger bar spring (31), freeing it from its notch in the bottom of the trigger bar (30) which may now be lifted from its recess in the trigger (32).

If further disassembly is required, loosen the mainspring retainer screw (22) and, holding the frame in a padded vise or on a soft wooden block, drive out the magazine catch pin (25) to remove the magazine catch (23) and its spring (24). The mainspring pin (26) and mainspring (27) can be similarly removed and, with a sturdy punch of the correct diameter and the safety (28) in 7 o'clock position, the hammer pin (16) can be drifted out, freeing the hammer (11) with its roller (13) and roller pin (12), the trigger bar spring (31), and safety (28). Drifting out the trigger pin (33) will free the trigger (32) and its spring (34). Removal of the sear pin (17) frees the sear (14) and its spring (15) and completes disassembly.

WALTHER MODEL 6 PISTOL

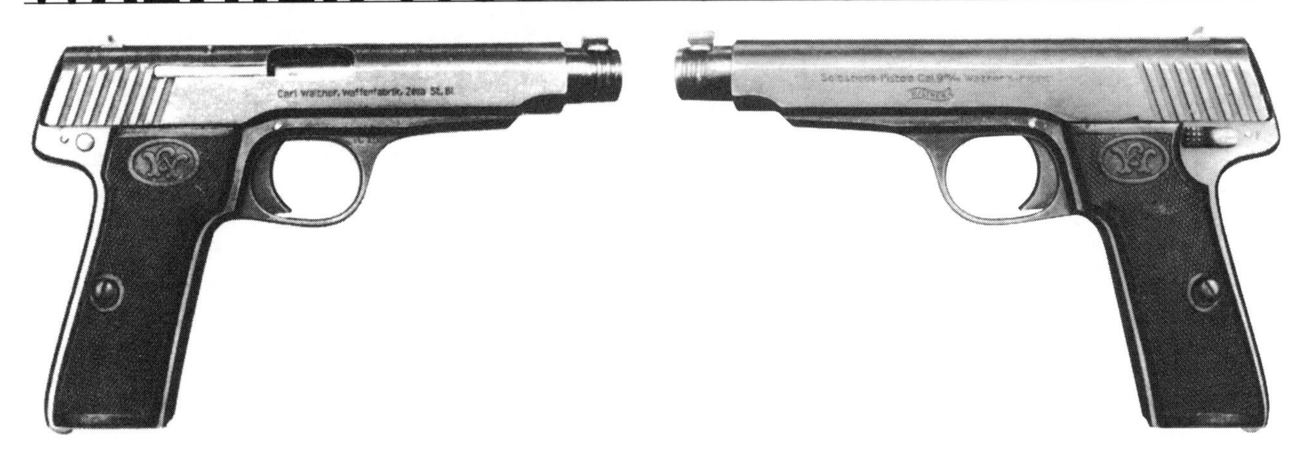

PARTS LEGEND

1. Slide extension
2. Slide
3. Extractor pin
4. Extractor spring
5. Extractor
6. Rear sight
7. Firing pin spring
8. Firing pin
9. Firing pin extension
10. Recoil spring
11. Mainspring tube
12. Hammer
13. Hammer roller pin
14. Hammer roller
15. Sear spring bushing
16. Sear spring
17. Sear
18. Right grip
19. Grip screw (2)
20. Mainspring
21. Mainspring plunger
22. Magazine catch
23. Magazine
24. Magazine catch pin
25. Sear pin
26. Safety catch
27. Hammer pin
28. Left grip
29. Trigger bar
30. Trigger
31. Trigger pin
32. Trigger spring plunger
33. Trigger spring
34. Barrel/frame

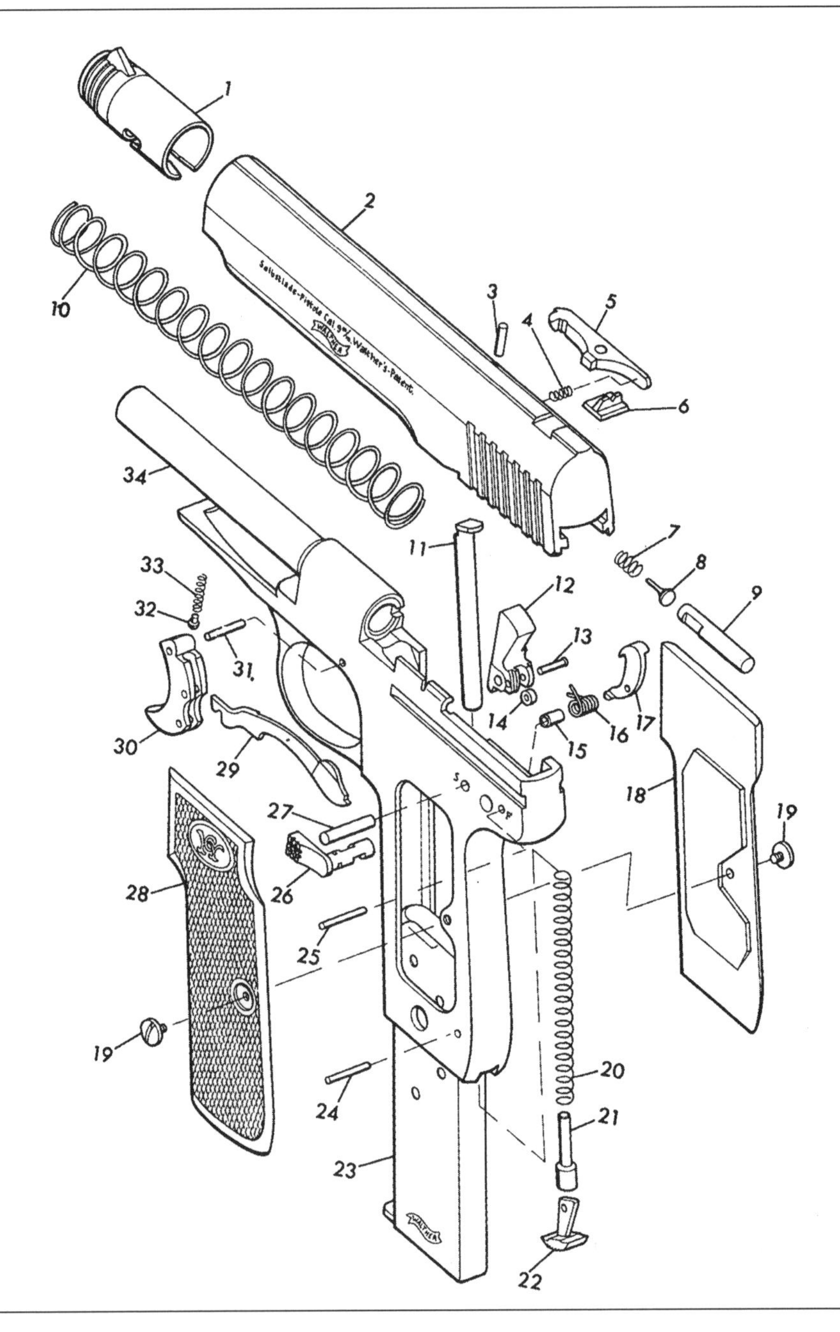

When Germany entered World War I, there was a critical need for military pistols. Walther's Models 1, 2, 3, 4 and 5 were pressed into service, but these pistols were in either .25 or .32 caliber, not the standard 9 mm military caliber.

In an effort to supply a 9 mm Luger caliber pistol that could be produced faster than the Luger P08 or 9 mm Mauser Model 96, Walther developed the Model 6. It was an overgrown Model 4. The barrel was longer, $4\frac{13}{16}$ inches and the grip was longer by about one inch and the slide was lengthened by $2\frac{3}{8}$ inches to add more mass.

The Model 6 is a "blowback" operated pistol or "mass-locked" in German terminology. In this system a heavy slide and a stiff spring compensate for the lack of a breech lock.

The Walther Model 6 was only made from 1915 to the end of the war and less than 2,000 were made. Some pistols were exported after WWI and many of the known specimens have "Germany" stamped on the lower left hand of the slide.

On the left side the slide is marked "Selbstlade-Pistole Cal. 9M/M, Walther's Patent." The right hand side of the slide is marked "Carl Walther, Waffenfabrik, Zella St. BI." Proof marks are found on the right side of the frame, near the end of the barrel support, close to the trigger pin and near the muzzle on the right side of the barrel. The serial number is found at the juncture of the trigger guard and frame.

DISASSEMBLY

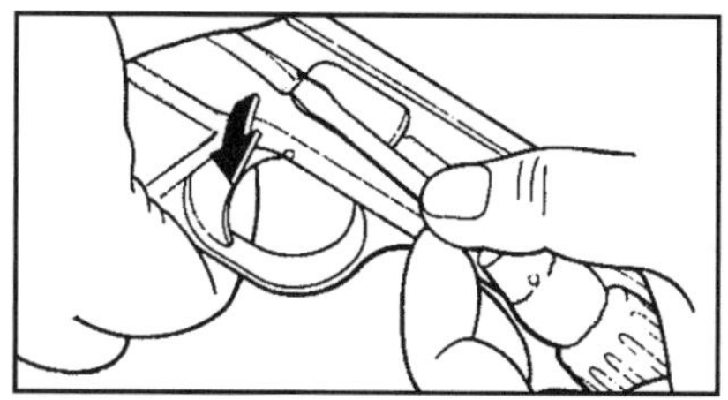

1 CAUTION: Since the Model 6 chambers are very tight, some brands of 9 mm cartridges may stick in the chamber, making it extremely difficult to open the slide. In this case, remove magazine (23), apply safety catch (26), insert a screwdriver tip beneath lip of extractor (5), and pry extractor outward to free it from the chambered round. Then the slide can be retracted and the round removed safely with a cleaning rod.

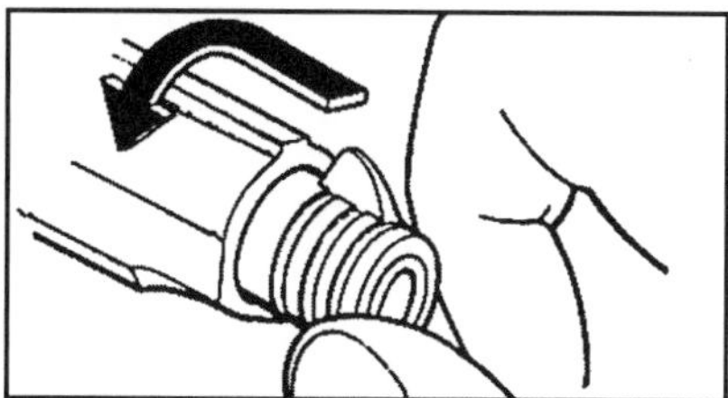

2 To field strip the pistol, depress magazine catch (22) and remove the magazine (23); then clear the chamber, allowing the slide (2) to close. Holding the gun in the left hand, push the slide extension (1) $\frac{1}{8}$ inch into the slide, and turn it 20 degrees counterclockwise. Ease out slide extension and recoil spring (10). (In reassembly, line up the mark on the slide extension with the middle of the slide, push extension in and turn clockwise to lock.)

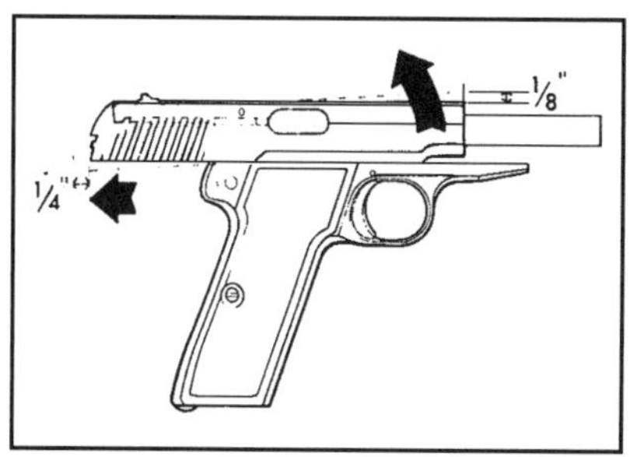

3 Pull the slide rearward until it stops. Lift its forward end $\frac{1}{8}$-inch and move the slide another $\frac{1}{4}$-inch further to the rear, freeing it from its twin grooves in the frame (34). Now lift the rear of the slide and strip it from the frame by drawing it forward, over the barrel.

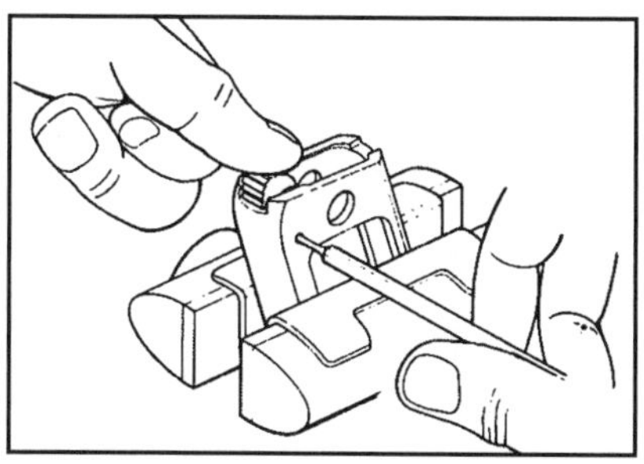

4 Remove the grip screws (19) and grips (18 & 28). Pull the trigger (30) while easing hammer (12) forward with thumb. Hold frame in a soft-jawed vise and drive out the magazine catch pin (24). As the magazine catch is under heavy spring pressure, press it downward, into the frame while removing pin punch, and grasp it firmly as it is eased out of the grip. Drive out sear pin (25) and remove sear (17), sear spring (16), and sear spring bushing (15).

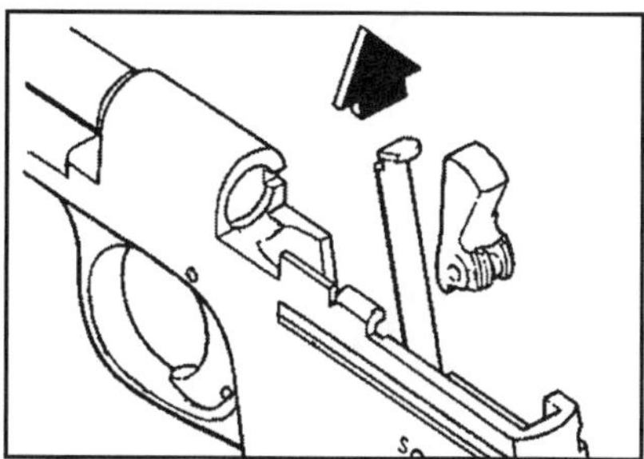

5 The hammer pin (27) is tight, but it can be driven out. If an arbor press is not available, use a punch of almost the same diameter and a few drops of penetrating oil. Remove hammer (12), mainspring (20), and mainspring tube (11). Then the safety catch will come out easily.

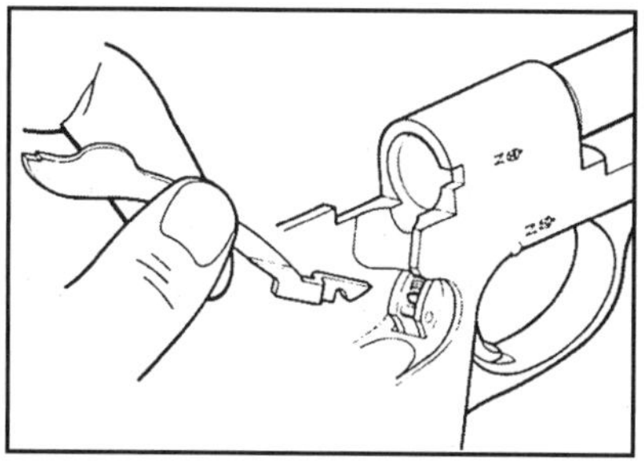

6 Drive out trigger pin (31) and move trigger rearward; then pull trigger bar (29) straight out against pressure of trigger spring (33). Replace by easing the point of the trigger bar into the trigger slot, between the trigger spring plunger (32) and the fixed trigger cross pin. Then push forward until it snaps into place. Reassemble in reverse order.

WALTHER MODEL 8 PISTOL

PARTS LEGEND

A. Slide
B. Extractor
C. Extractor plunger
D. Extractor spring
E. Firing pin spring
F. Firing pin
G. Firing pin housing
H. Retaining plate
I. Retaining plate screw
J. Trigger bar spring
K. Trigger bar
L. Right-hand grip
M. Right-hand grip screw
N. Right-hand grip retainer
O. Sear pin
P. Sear
Q. Sear spring
R. Hammer strut pin
S. Hammer strut
T. Hammer
U. Mainspring plunger
V. Mainspring
W. Magazine latch plunger
X. Magazine latch
Y. Magazine
Z. Left-hand grip
AA. Left-hand grip nut
BB. Left-hand grip retainer
CC. Left-hand grip screw
DD. Safety catch
EE. Trigger
FF. Trigger pin
GG. Trigger guard
HH. Takedown latch pin
II. Takedown latch spring
JJ. Takedown latch
KK. Receiver and barrel assembly
LL. Recoil spring

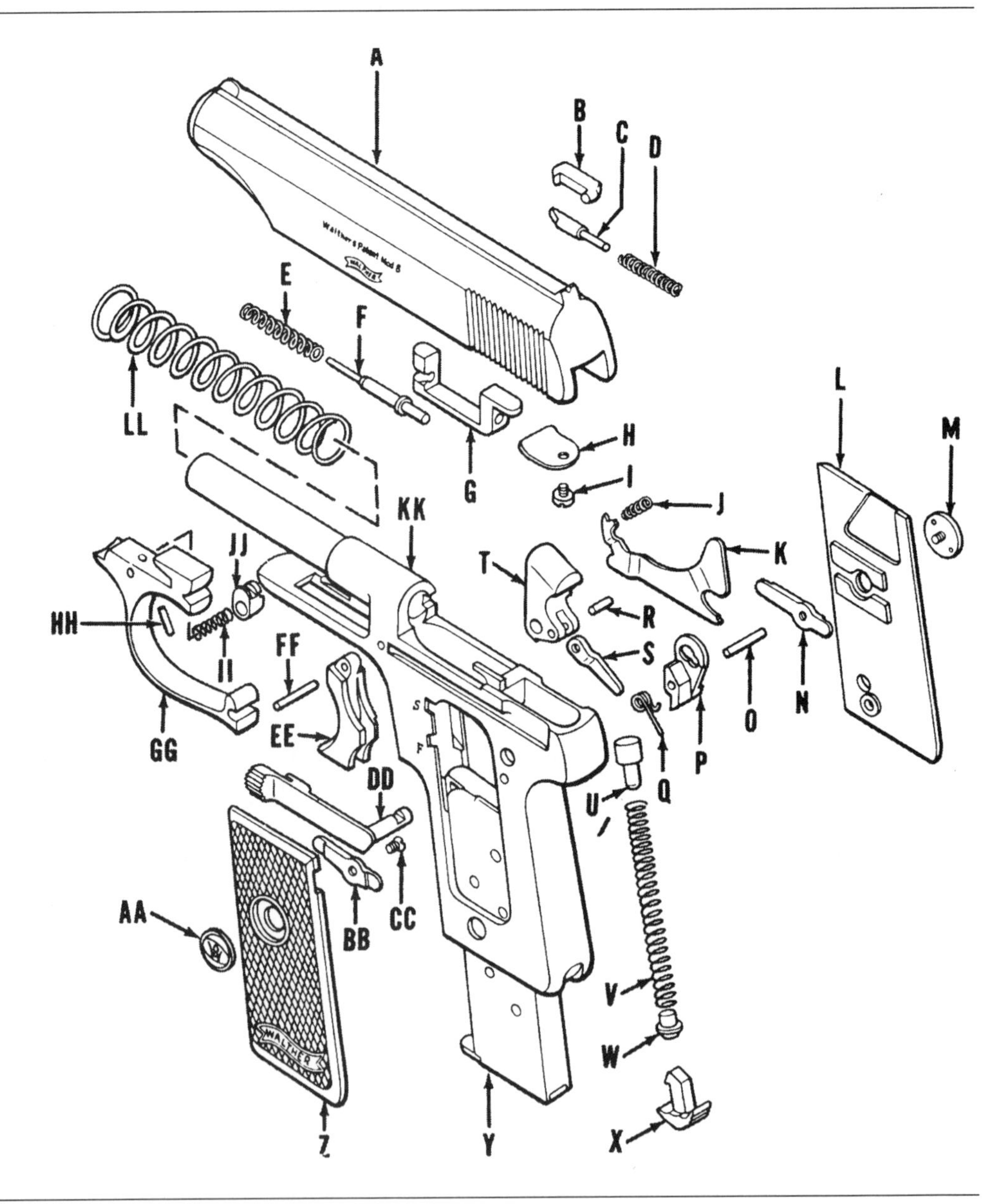

There was a time during the 1920s when many Central European businessmen carried a small-caliber automatic pistol. Europe was in the clutches of the Depression and a compact handgun often came in handy for defense purposes. In order to stay in business, many German firearms manufacturers turned to these popular, inexpensive pocket pistols.

The Walther Model 8 was first marketed in 1920 and caught on almost immediately, and by 1939 more than 200,000 had been sold. Stoeger sold them in America until World War II cut off the supply. The price ranged from $25 for the standard version and up to $92.50 for an engraved, gold-plated model in a presentation case.

When compared with later Walther pistols, such as the PP or PPK, the Model 8 contains nothing very startling in the way of mechanisms. Its popularity was due chiefly to its clean, compact design, to say nothing of the flawless workmanship evident on all pre-war Walther products. The gun is large enough to afford an adequate grip and has a nine-shot capacity, carrying eight in the magazine and one in the chamber. The Model 8 might be called a medium-sized .25 automatic, for while it is smaller than the Mauser Pocket Model .25 caliber, it is larger than the average vest pocket .25 automatic.

As in other Walther pistols, internal design changes were made without much fanfare and at least two variations of the Model 8 are to be found. In the original Model 8, it was possible to pry the entire breech-block assembly out of its seat in the slide. This assembly carried the firing pin, firing pin spring and extractor. The extractor tail acted as a firing pin retainer, and the extractor as a breech-block latch. While this system was simple, it had a tendency to loosen after prolonged use. There is no record of when the gun was revised, but the internal mechanism of the slide was changed. The breech face on later models is an integral part of the slide. A firing pin housing is retained by a screw and plate and the extractor was moved into the slide. The rest of the gun was left unchanged, but the modifications made the new version stronger and easier to clean and repair.

DISASSEMBLY

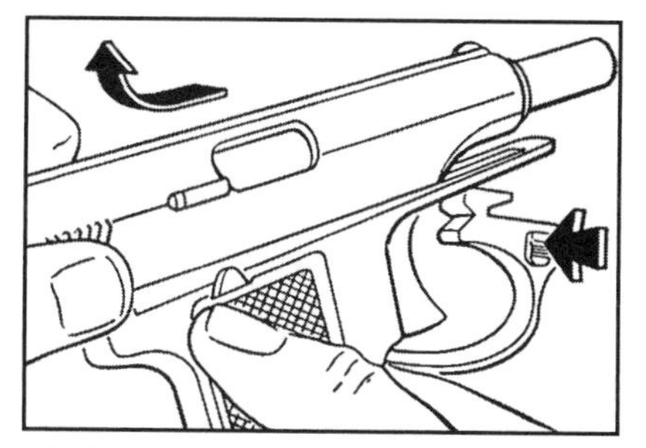

1 Remove the magazine, check the chamber to be sure it is not loaded. Push in the takedown latch (JJ) on the right-hand side of the trigger guard, pulling the guard down as shown. Draw the slide to the rear, lift the end free of the frame, then ease it forward off the barrel.

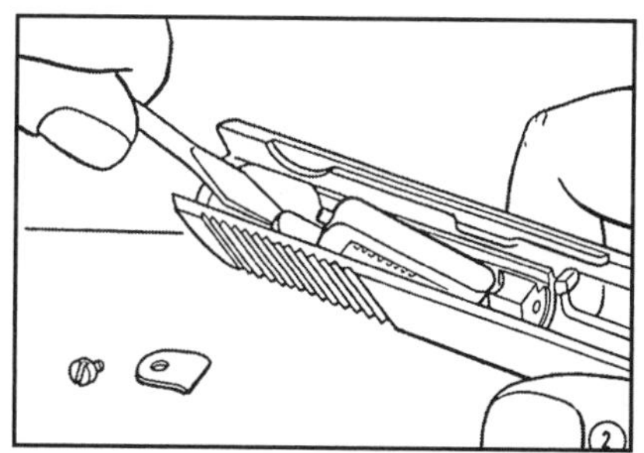

2 To take the firing pin (F) out of the late model, remove the retaining plate screw (I) and the retaining plate (H). The firing pin assembly can then be pried free of the slide. Since the retaining plate screw (I) is usually extremely tight, your screwdriver must fit the screw slot to prevent damage to the head.

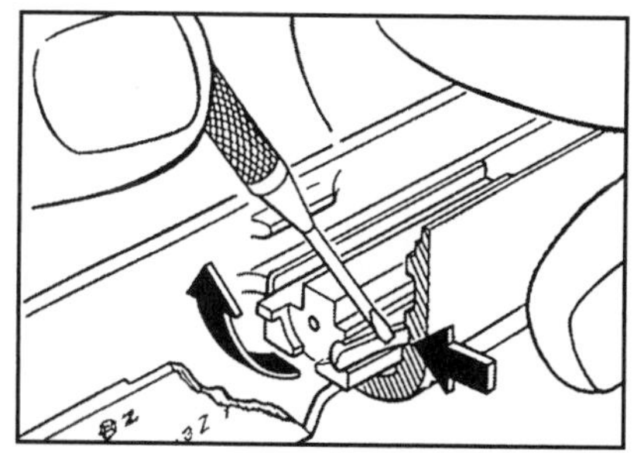

3 Removal of the early model firing pin presents a problem. It is necessary to pry the extractor free of its recess in the slide while prying up the front edge of the breechblock assembly, since the extractor retains the breechblock and a projection on it retains the firing pin.

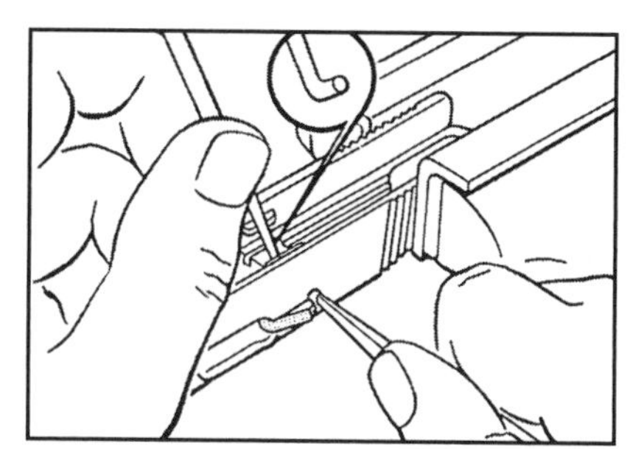

4 The late model extractor (B) is retained by a spring (D) and plunger (C). It may be easily removed by pushing back the spring-loaded plunger with a jeweler's screwdriver. Then, using a tool similar to the one illustrated, push the tail of the extractor out of the slide (A) from the inside.

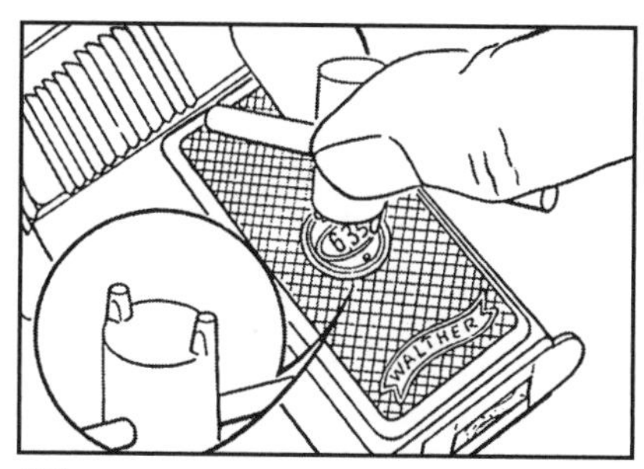

5 Unless a tool similar to the one shown is made, it is difficult to remove the blue medallion (grip screw, M) without damaging it. With this screw out, lift off the right-hand grip (L), remove the magazine (Y), and unscrew the left grip screw from the inside.

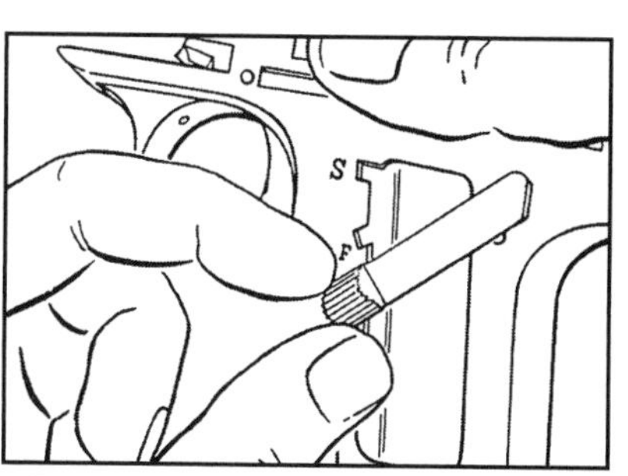

6 In order to remove the safety catch (DD), the grips must be removed. Next, ease the internal hammer (T) to the fired position. Press the safety in toward the receiver out of engagement with the notches, and revolve it to the position shown. Now it can be lifted free of the receiver.

WALTHER MODEL 9 PISTOL

PARTS LEGEND

1. Disconnector bar
2. Ejector
3. Extractor
4. Firing pin
5. Firing pin spring
6. Firing pin spring guide
7. Frame & barrel assembly
8. Grip escutcheon (2)
9. Grip panel, left
10. Grip panel, right
11. Grip screw (2)
12. Grip screw bushing (2)
13. Latch retainer lever
14. Latch retainer pin
15. Magazine base
16. Magazine catch
17. Magazine catch spring
18. Magazine catch spring plunger
19. Magazine follower
20. Magazine housing
21. Magazine spring
22. Recoil spring
23. Recoil spring guide
24. Safety lever
25. Sear
26. Sear lever
27. Sear lever pin
28. Sear pin
29. Slide
30. Takedown latch
31. Takedown latch spring
32. Takedown latch spring plunger
33. Trigger
34. Trigger spring

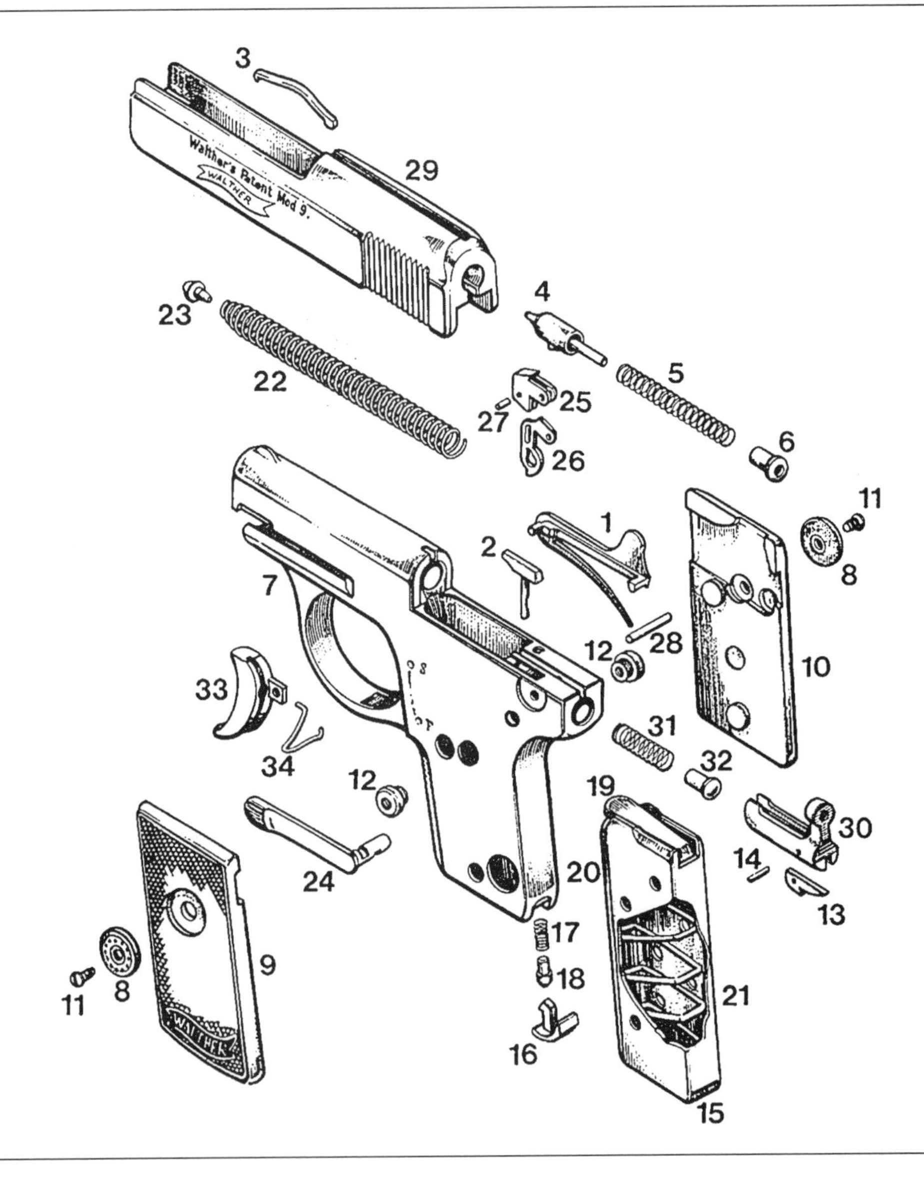

Though best known for double-action police and military pistols (Models PP, PPK and P38 etc.), the Carl Walther firm got its start in 1908 with its Model 1, a single-action .25 caliber pocket pistol.

From 1908 until 1920, eight Walther pistols were introduced, all blowback-operated single-actions, and of these, five were .25s. They were small, with an average weight of 11.3 ozs. and an average barrel and overall length of 2.5 and 4.7 inches, respectively.

In 1920 the Model 9 came on the market and was, by far, the smallest of the lot, weighing less than 9 ozs. with a 2-inch barrel and an overall length of 3.9 inches.

The standard pistol, referred to in Walther's 1936 catalog as the Model 9a, was blued with black composition grip plates and a six-round magazine. The Model 9b was listed as having an etched "engraving" panel on the slide with blue enamel/gold plate grip escutcheons. Full nickel, gold and silver plating were also offered, as was full engraving and mother-of-pearl or ivory grip plates.

The Model 9 was imported into the United States by Stoeger (at $20 for the standard grade in the 1940 *Shooter's Bible* for instance), and many were brought back to the United States by servicemen returning from World War II. The pistol went out of production during the war, but is still valued today as one of the smallest and best made pistols of its type.

DISASSEMBLY

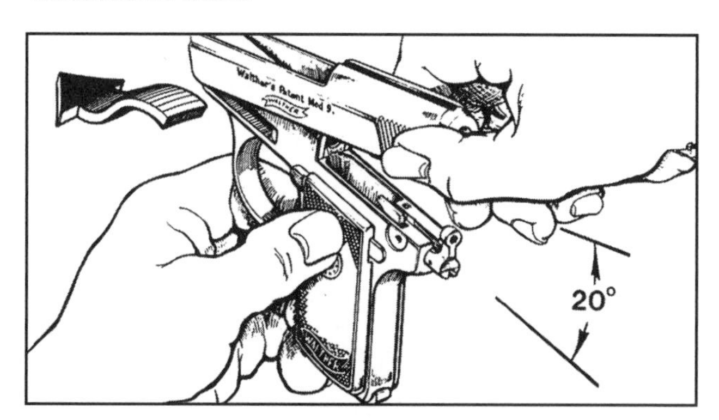

1 Push back the magazine catch (16), remove the magazine (20), retract the slide (29) and check the chamber to insure that the pistol is not loaded. Depress the latch retainer lever (13) to release the takedown latch (30). Raise the rear of the slide about 20 degrees to elevate the breechbolt face above the barrel.

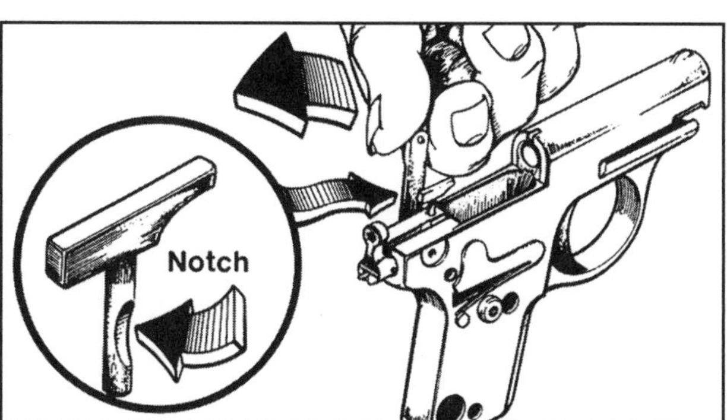

2 Pivot the slide assembly (29) forward and off the frame (7). Remove the firing pin (4) and its spring and guide (5 & 6). The recoil spring (22) and its guide (23) may be removed from the recess in the frame below the barrel. This effectively field strips the pistol for general service and cleaning.

If complete disassembly is required, remove the grip screws (11) and detach both grip panels (9 & 10) to expose the frame and provide access to the components below.

Rotate the safety lever (24) to a vertical position. This cams the ejector post up to clear the safety retaining groove and frees the safety for removal. With the ejector (2) in this elevated position, it may be easily removed, if required.

NOTE: The fitted ejector post is notched with an elliptical cut to provide clearance for the takedown latch. This required cut makes the ejector post susceptible to damage if twisted or levered out. To avoid possible damage, invert the frame and secure the ejector body in a bench vise. To withdraw the ejector, pull straight up on the frame, avoiding all lateral stress.

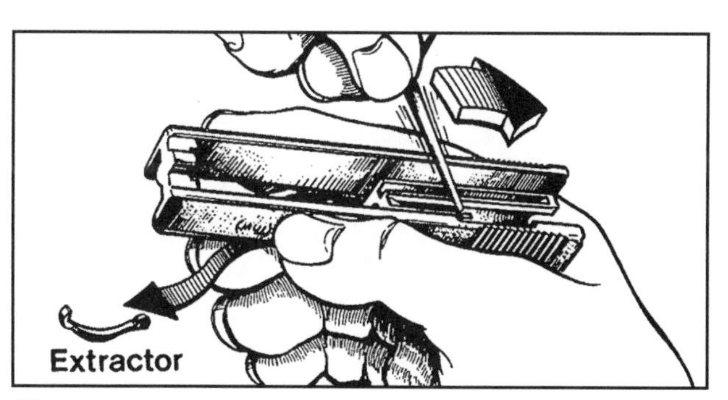

3 Drift out the sear pin (28) to remove the sear group (25, 26 & 27). Note the relationship of these components as they are removed from the frame to facilitate reassembly. Complete disassembly of the sear sub-group is not recommended unless repair or replacement is required.

The takedown latch (30) may now be withdrawn from the rear of the frame. Exercise caution to avoid losing the takedown latch spring and plunger (31 & 32) contained in the latch. The latch retainer pin (14) may be drifted out to free the latch lever (13).

To remove the disconnector (1), lift its lower spring leg to clear the retaining stud in the frame. This allows the disconnector/trigger bar to be removed and frees both the trigger (33) and its spring (34) from the trigger guard.

The extractor (3) may be removed from the breech face by depressing the rear lug of the extractor and levering it forward through the access hole in the underside of the slide.

To remove the magazine catch (16), insert a small screwdriver through the bottom of the magazine well and depress the catch lug located inside the backstrap. This will release the catch its spring and plunger (16, 17&18).

The grip screw bushings (12) are staked in place from inside the magazine well and should be removed only if replacement or repair is required.

WALTHER MODEL P22 PISTOL

PARTS LEGEND

1. Receiver, polymer
2. Sideplate, left
3. Sideplate, right
4. Stove bolt
5. Stove bolt
6. Trigger assembly
7. Straight pin
8. Hammer assembly
9. Sear
10. Sear spring
11. Ejector
12. Magazine catch
13. Straight pin
14. Dowel pin
15. Slide stop lever
16. Slide stop spring
17. Takedown lever
18. Dowel pin
19. Dowel pin
20. Retaining pin
21. Spring guidance rod
22. Recoil spring
23. Magazine safety
24. Magazine safety spring
25. Trigger lock
26. Trigger lock spring
27. Backstrap
28. Backstrap, large
29. Key for trigger lock
30. Slide
31. Breech block
32. Dowel pin
33. Extractor
34. Spring
35. Pin
36. Firing pin
37. Firing pin spring
38. Safety block
39. Safety lever, left
40. Safety lever, right
41. Screw
42. Ball for safety lever
43. Spring for safety lever
44. Firing pin safety
45. Spring
46. Barrel, 3.4 inch
47. Barrel sleeve
48. Barrel nut
49. Spanner
50. Barrel, 5 inch
51. Barrel sleeve, long
52. Stabilizer assembly
53. Allen key
54. Allen key
55. Magazine body
56. Follower
57. Magazine button
58. Magazine buttplate
59. Magazine spring
60. Buttplate retainer
61. Magazine buttplate, large
62. Rear sight
63. Rear sight screw
64. Washer
65. Front sight 3
66. Front sight 2
67. Front sight 4
68. Filler plug
69. Dryfire simulation device
70. Mountain pin
71. Worm screw

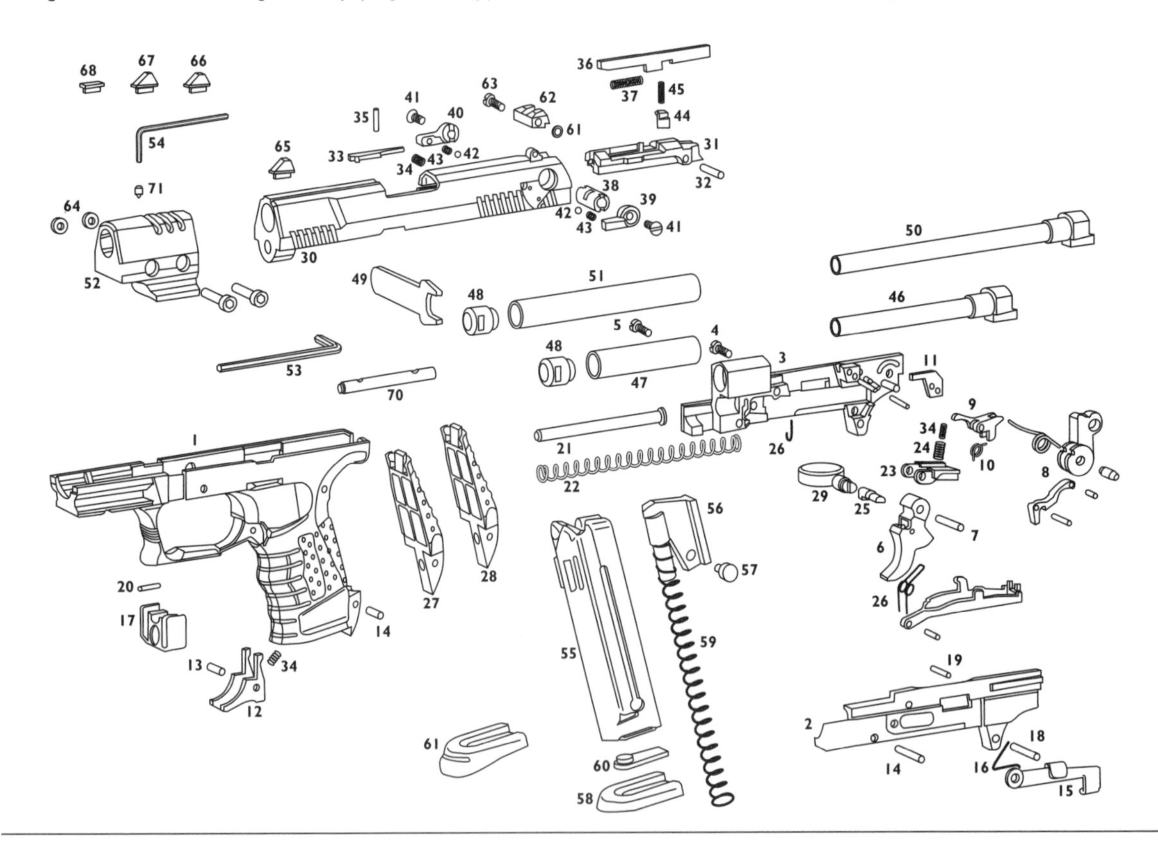

The P-22 is a blowback operated, semi-automatic pistol introduced in 2002 by Walther Sportwaffen. It is similar to the Walther P-99, but is somewhat smaller and is chambered for the .22 Long Rifle cartridge. The P-22 has a slide mounted, ambidextrous safety and external hammer and is manufactured with a polymer frame with slide and frame receiver inserts made from cast zinc alloy.

The barrel is composed of a rifled steel insert in a steel barrel sleeve and is available in 4.4- and 5-inch (target) lengths. The P-22 was designed so that different length barrels could be easily interchanged.

The P-22 is single- and double-action and can be fired double action for the first shot and operates as a single action on successive shots. The hammer can only be de-cocked by pulling the trigger.

A slide mounted safety serves as both hammer block and firing pin lock. The P-22 has a magazine disconnect that prevents the trigger from operating on the sear mechanism unless a magazine is locked into the weapon.

The polymer lower receiver is manufactured in several color variations — black, olive drab, and carbon fiber. The slide assembly is either nickel/stainless or blue-black finish.

DISASSEMBLY

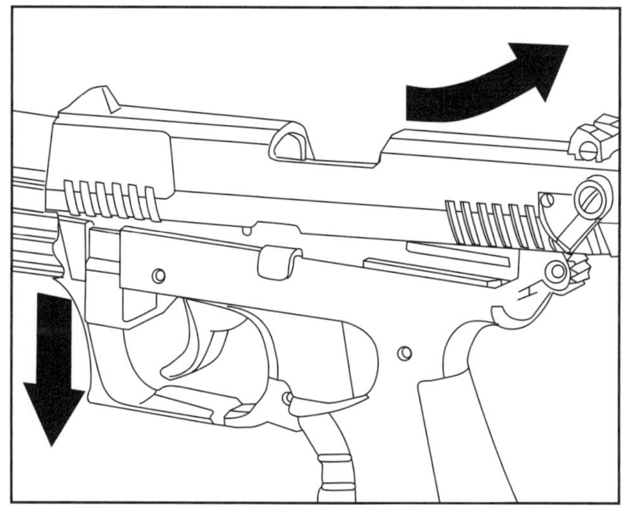

1 With the 5-inch version first remove the stabilizer. Press the takedown lever down and cock the hammer. Fully retract the slide, lift its rear section, and push slide forward off the receiver. Remove guide rod. Assembly is in reverse order.

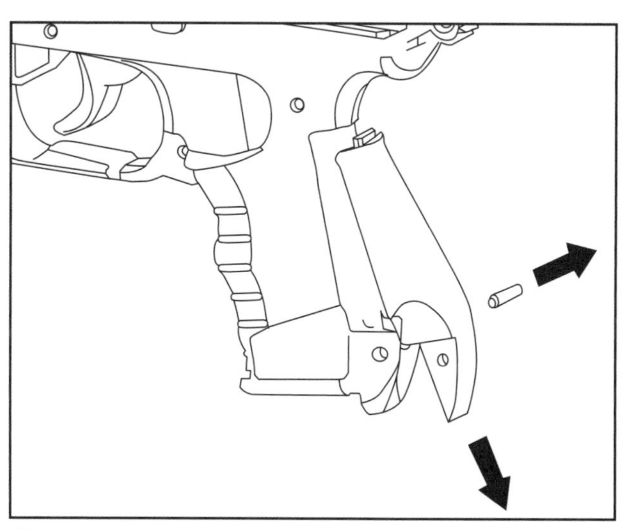

2 In order to adapt the grip of the weapon to your hand, the backstrap of the pistol can be changed. Remove the pin with a punch, change the backstrap and reinsert the pin.

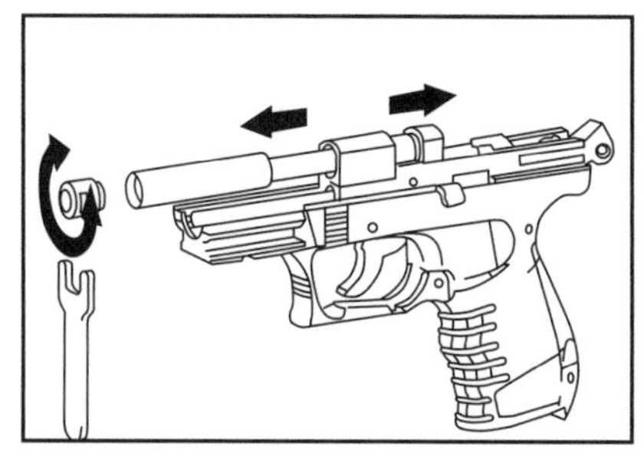

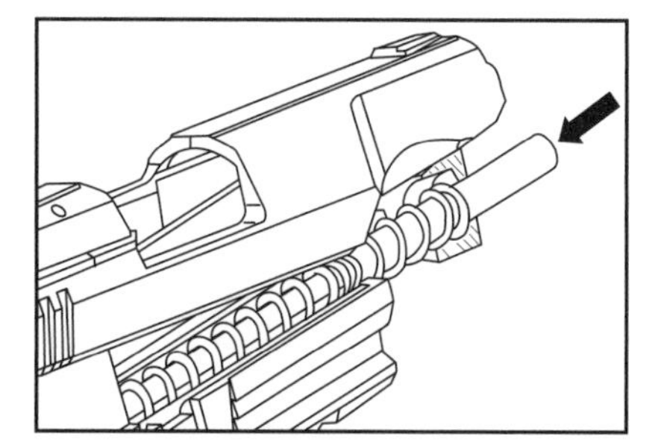

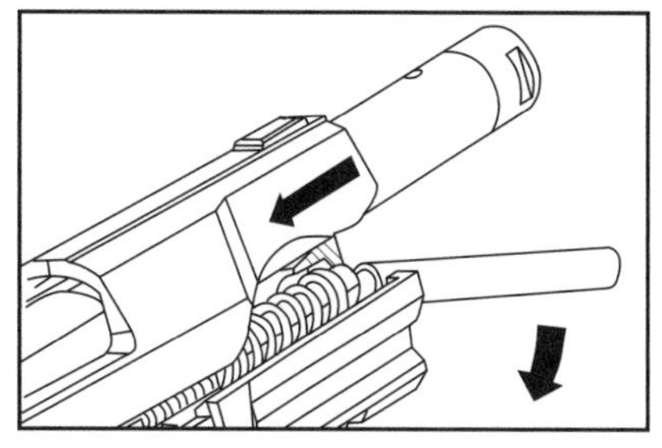

3 A 5 inch or 3.4 inch barrel is available as an accessory. Prior to a barrel change, engage the safety, remove the magazine, and make sure that the weapon is unloaded. Push the takedown lever down, cock the hammer, and remove the slide.

Use the enclosed spanner to release the barrel nut. Remove the barrel sleeve and pull the barrel to the rear out of the receiver.

WALTHER MODEL PP PISTOL

PARTS LEGEND

1. Slide
2. Extractor
3. Extractor plunger
4. Extractor spring
5. Safety catch plunger
6. Rear sight
7. Firing pin spring
8. Firing pin
9. Right-hand grip
10. Grip screw
11. Sear pin
12. Hammer
13. Sear spring
14. Hammer strut pin
15. Sear
16. Hammer strut
17. Hammer spring
18. Hammer spring plug
19. Frame
20. Spring plug pin
21. Trigger guard
22. Trigger guard plunger
23. Trigger guard spring
24. Trigger guard pin
25. Magazine catch spring
26. Magazine catch
27. Trigger pin
28. Trigger
29. Trigger spring
30. Elector
31. Ejector spring
32. Hammer pin
33. Left-hand grip
34. Magazine
35. Recoil spring
36. Safety catch
37. Hammer release
38. Hammer block plunger
39. Trigger bar
40. Cocking piece
41. Hammer block spring
42. Hammer block

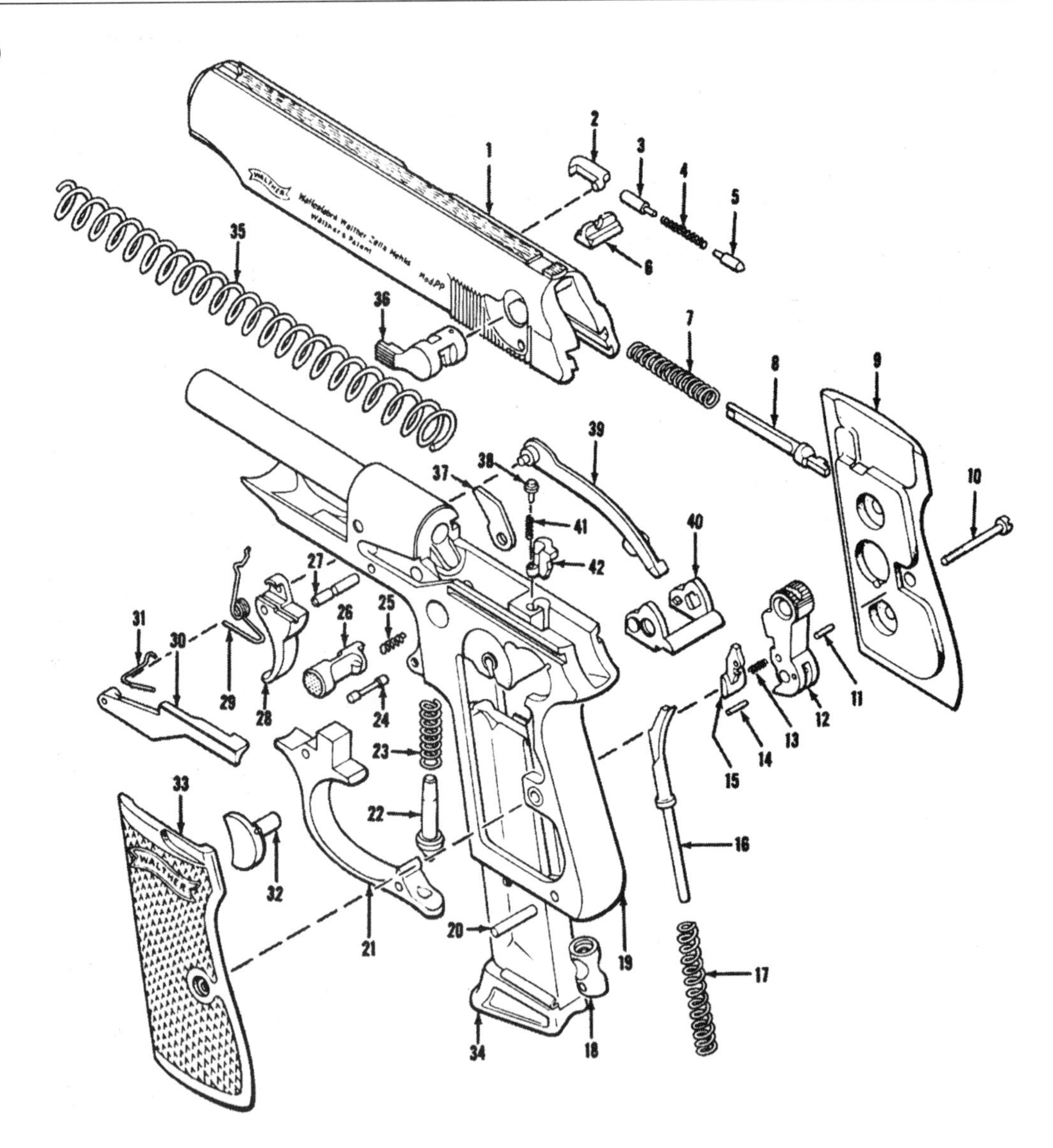

Most GIs who spent time in Europe during and after World War II came home with one or more products of the immense Walther plant at Zella-Mehlis in Thuringia. It might have been a P38 pistol, or a sporting rifle, or it might have been a Model PP or PPK in .32 or .380 ACP, or even a scarce model PP in .22 rimfire. Pre-war Walther guns were made of the finest materials and the finish was the best quality. They could be had in lightweight models with aluminum alloy frames at extra cost.

World War II put Walther out of business and for a time in the late 1950s and early 1960s, Walther pistols were made under license by *Manufacture de Machines du Haut-Rhin* the French firm, better known as *Manurhin,* in Mulhouse, France, and were so marked by United States importers. In 1999, a limited edition Walther Model PP was made by Carl Walther in Germany and imported to the United States by Smith & Wesson. Others in the PP series, the PPK and PPK/S, were also distributed under the agreement. The PP was offered in .22 rimfire and .32 and .380 ACP. The PPK, PPK/S were available in .380 and .32 ACP only. A PPK/E model was offered in .22, .380 ACP and .32 ACP

In addition to its double-action trigger mechanism, the Model PP features a number of safety devices including a chamber loaded indicator (omitted from the .22 caliber and wartime .32 and .380 models) and manual safety catch.

In spite of the intricate shapes of the operating parts, the design of the PP series of pistols is excellent. Any malfunctions on the part of .22 rimfire models can usually be traced to use of standard velocity ammunition instead of the high-speed ammunition for which the pistol was designed.

DISASSEMBLY

1 To strip, remove the magazine and empty the chamber. Pull down the front end of the trigger guard (21) and push it to the right. It will rest against the frame and remain open. Pull the side (1) to the rear as far as it will go. Lift up and ease it forward off the frame.

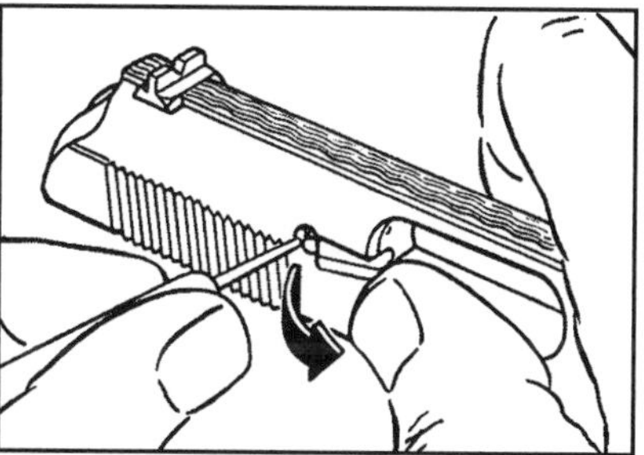

2 To remove the extractor (2) it is necessary to depress the extractor plunger (3) well below the edge of the slide (1). Use a thin awl or a jeweler's screwdriver as shown, and rotate the extractor toward the firing pin.

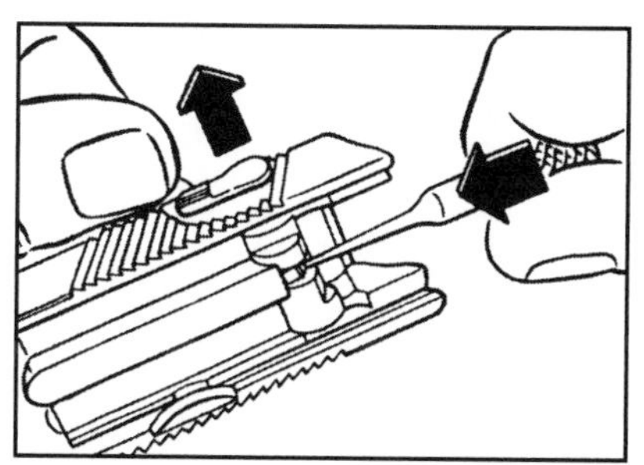

3 After the extractor spring (4) and safety catch plunger (5) have been removed, the safety catch (36) can be easily removed by first rotating it to the off position. Then, while pushing the firing pin deep into the slide, lift out the safety catch as shown.

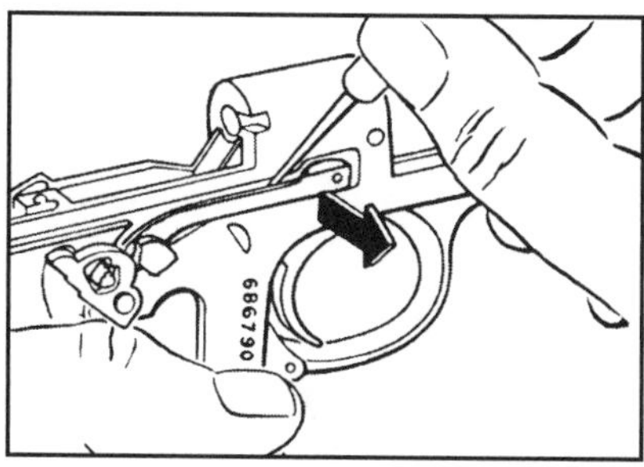

4 The trigger bar (39) should never be pried out. To remove it, first unhook the trigger spring (29) and push it into the frame. Pull the trigger as far as it will go and, using a small screwdriver, lift the trigger bar free of its slot in the frame.

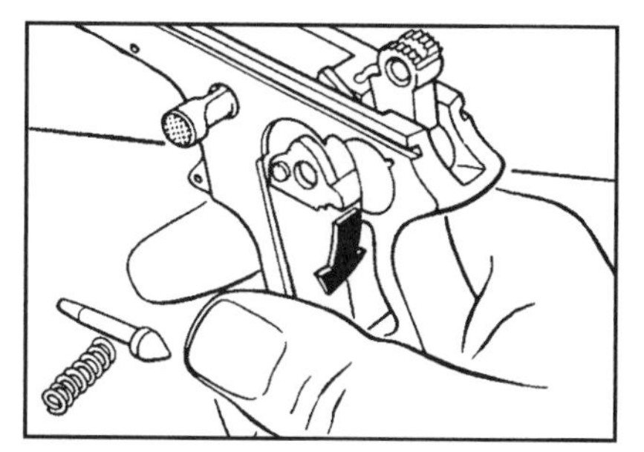

5 The magazine catch (26) is retained by the trigger guard plunger (22). To remove it, first remove the trigger guard pin (24). This will free the trigger guard plunger (22) and spring (23). The cocking piece (40) can be removed by rotating it as shown until it drops free of the frame.

WALTHER P38 PISTOL

PARTS LEGEND

A. Slide
B. Firing Pin Spring
C. Firing Pin and Indicator Cove,
D. Rear Sight
E. Automatic Firing Pin Lock Spring
F. Automatic Firing pin Lock
G. Firing Pin Retainer Pin
H. Cartridge Indicator Pin
I. Cartridge Indicator Spring
J. Firing Pin
K. Extractor
L. Extractor Plunger
M. Extractor Plunger Spring
N. Safety Catch
O. Ejector
P. Firing Pin Lock, Lifter
Q. Safety Hammer Lowering Lever
R. Trigger Bar Spring
S. Trigger Bar
T. Sear
U. Sear Pin
V. Hammer Strut
W. Hammer
X. Hammer Lever Spring
Y. Strut Axle Pin
Z. Hammer Lever Pins
AA. Hammer Lever
BB. Hammer Spring
CC. Magazine Catch
DD. Right Hand Grip
EE. Magazine
FF. Left Hand Grip
GG. Grip Screw
HH. Hammer Pin
II. Slide Stop Return Spring
JJ. Trigger
KK. Slide Stop
LL. Trigger Bushing
MM. Frame (Receiver)
NN. Trigger Spring
OO. Barrel Retaining Latch
PP. Retainer Latch Plunger Spring
QQ. Retainer Latch Plunger
RR. Recoil Spring
SS. Recoil Spring Guide
TT. Locking Block Operating Pin
UU. Locking Block
VV. Locking Block Retainer Spring
WW. Barrel
XX. Front Sight

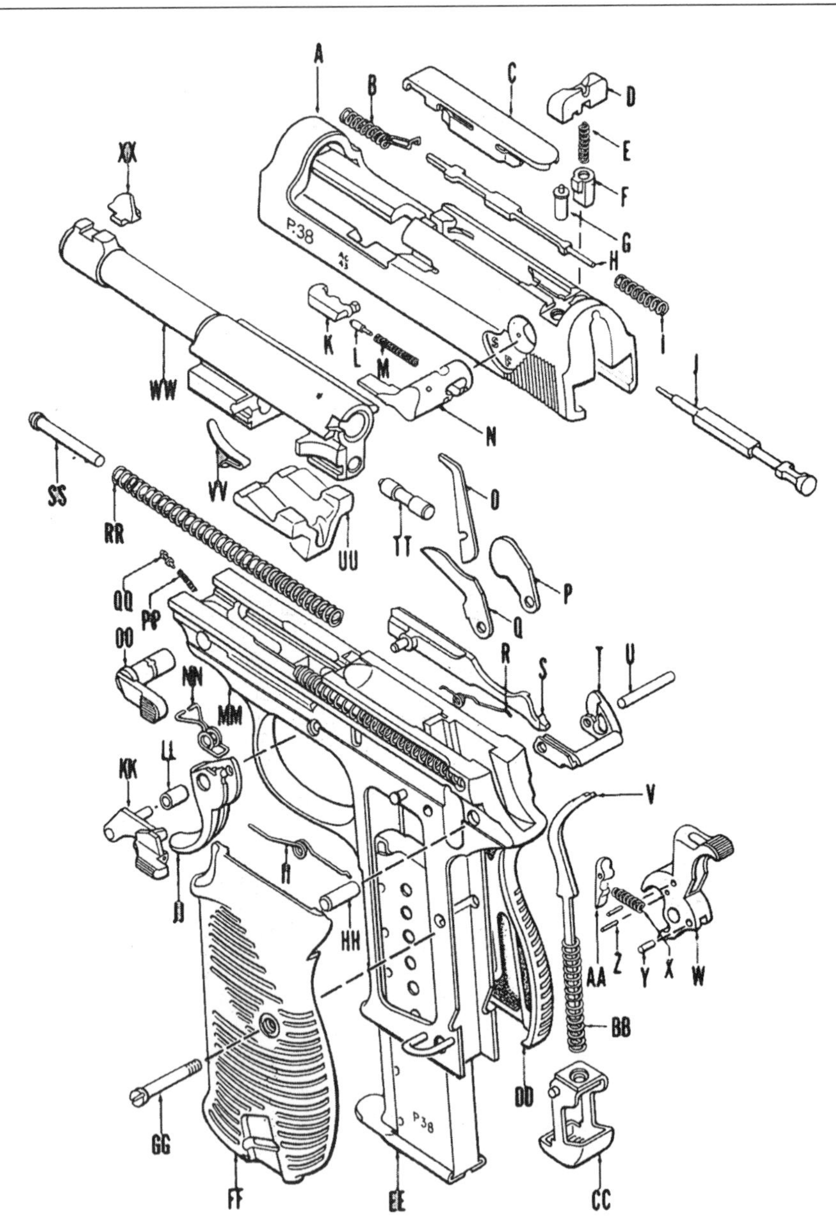

During the 1930s Germany began a modernization program designed to give its armed forces the finest possible tools for war. This extensive program brought forth the famous, dual purpose 8.8 cm gun, the Schmeisser-designed MP38 and MP40 submachine guns, and the MG34 and MG42 light machine guns. Among the best known military arms fielded during this period was the P38 self-loading pistol.

The firm of Karl Walther, in Zella Mehlis, Thuringia was given the task of designing a new self-loading pistol for the German army. Their locked breech, short recoil Model HP (*Heeres Pistole,* or Army Pistol), introduced in 1937, was the result. By 1938 the Model HP had been very slightly modified and accepted by the German army. Its official designation became P38. The new pistol carried eight, 9 mm Parabellum cartridges in the magazine plus one in the chamber and had an overall length of 8½ inches and aweight of 32 ounces.

The P38 was designed from a production point of view. with the use of well-designed but less expensive sheet metal stampings and the use of music wire, coil springs in place of forged flat springs. The coil springs used in the P.38 are quicker to produce, more durable and usually take up less room in a mechanism than do flat springs.

Pre-war Walther HP and P38 pistols were manufactured and finished to the highest shop standards. This is not true of P38s produced later during the war. Inferior materials, shoddy workmanship and outright sabotage by conscripted laborers combine to make some of the pistols produced during 1944 and 1945 dangerous to use.

Manufacture of the Walther P.38 was interrupted at the end of World War II when the Walther plant and the plants of other contract makers fell into Allied hands. In the mid-1950s Walther re-established facilities at Ulm in West Germany and re-instituted manufacture of the P38, but with an aluminum alloy frame instead of steel. In 1957, the West German army, the *Bundeswehr,* adopted the alloy-frame pistol, designating it as the *Pistole 1* or P1. The P1 was issued into the 1980s.

DISASSEMBLY

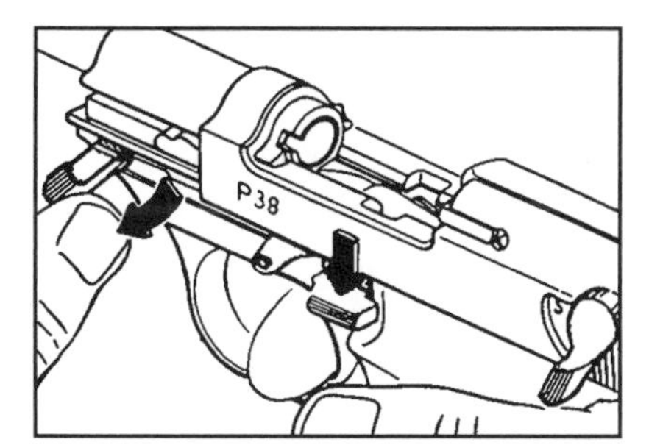

1 Push the safety catch (N) to safe position. Pull back the slide until the slide stop (KK) retains it. Remove the magazine. Revolve the barrel retaining latch (OO) until it stops. Release the slide stop and pull the slide and barrel assembly forward, off the receiver. Push in the exposed end of the locking block pin (TT) to separate the barrel from the slide.

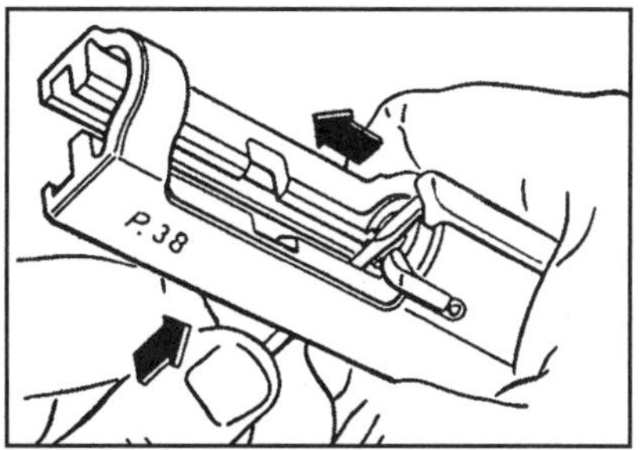

2 To check the firing pin (J) and the indicator pin (H), the cover must be removed. Hold the slide as shown to prevent the rear sight from falling out. Using a small screwdriver, push the indicator pin inside the slide, and insert the blade as shown. A simultaneous push upward and forward will free cover (C) from slide.

3 Remove automatic firing pin lads spring and lock (E & F), firing pin retainer pin (O), and indicator pin and spring (H & I). Safety catch must be in fire position before pushing out firing pin. With safety catch between safe and fire, pry out with screwdriver, as shown.

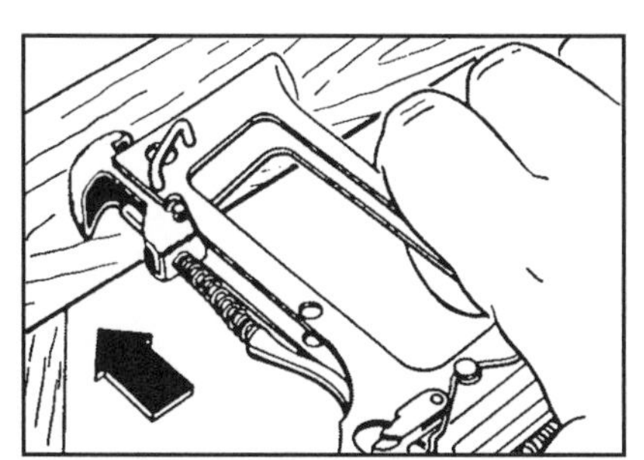

4 To disassemble the trigger mechanism, relieve the tension on the hammer. Remove the grips. Push the magazine catch (CC) firmly against the edge of a bench. When the pivot pin on the magazine catch is free of the frame, ease the pressure and remove the catch and hammer spring.

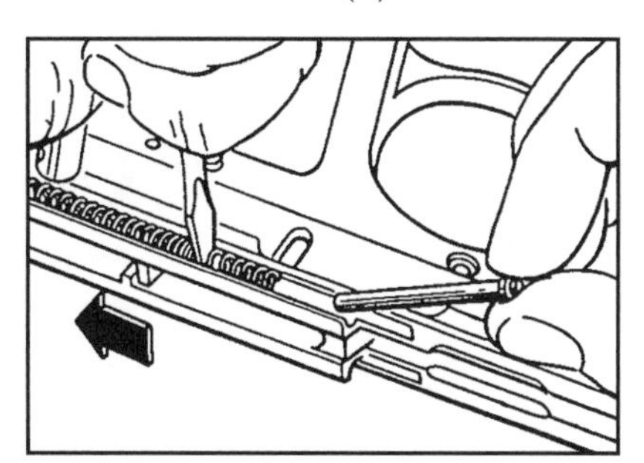

5 Remove the recoil spring (RR) by using a small screwdriver. Insert the screwdriver blade about 6 to 8 coils from the front of the spring guide (SS). Compress the recoil spring as far as possible and remove the guide. Ease up on the spring pressure carefully to avoid losing the spring.

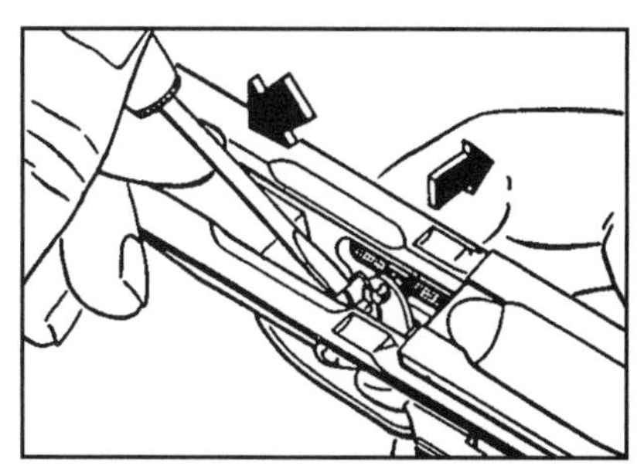

6 The trigger bar (S) is retained by the pressure of the trigger spring (NN) on a small notch in the portion of the bar that engages in the trigger. Use a small screwdriver to hold the trigger spring out of the notch as shown. Pry the trigger bar free with the other hand while the spring is held back.

WALTHER OLYMPIA RAPID-FIRE

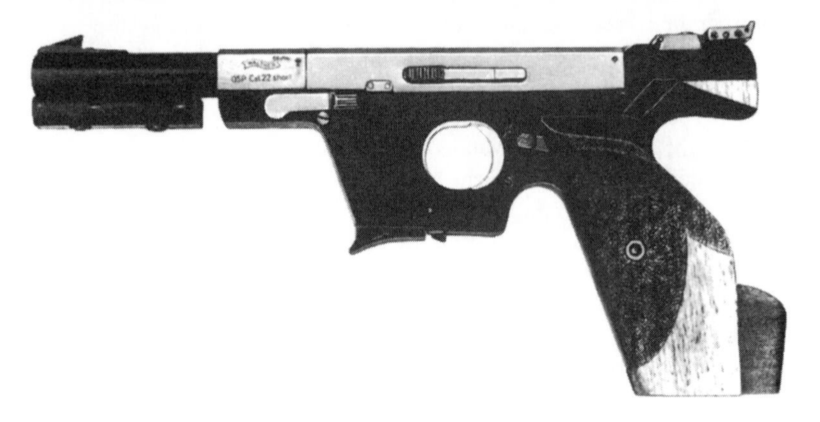

PARTS LEGEND

1. Sight lock screw
2. Front sight
3. Barrel
4. Weight
5. Weight screw (2)
6. Receiver
7. Cocking piece
8. Bolt
9. Extractor pin
10. Extractor
11. Extractor spring
12. Firing pin retainer
13. Firing pin and spring
14. Recoil spring housing
15. Recoil spring
16. Recoil spring guide
17. Bolt stop
18. Plunger spring
19. Stop retaining plunger
20. Trigger assembly
21. Side plate screw
22. Side plate
23. Rear sight leaf assembly
24. Sight leaf pin
25. Click pin
26. Sight elevation screw
27. Rear sight base
28. Rear sight spring
29. Sight retainer screw
30. Washer
31. Sight retainer nuts
32. Safety catch spring
33. Magazine catch spring
34. Magazine catch bushing
35. Magazine catch
36. Safety catch
37. Magazine catch pin
38. Magazine
39. Barrel lock
40. Hold-open latch pin
41. Barrel lock stop screw
42. Barrel lock bushing
43. Lock nut pin
44. Lock nut
45. Spacer
46. Hold-open latch spring
47. Hold-open latch
48. Adjusting screw nut
49. Slide plate
50. Grip
51. Palm rest
52. Adjusting screw
53. Grip screw
54. Frame

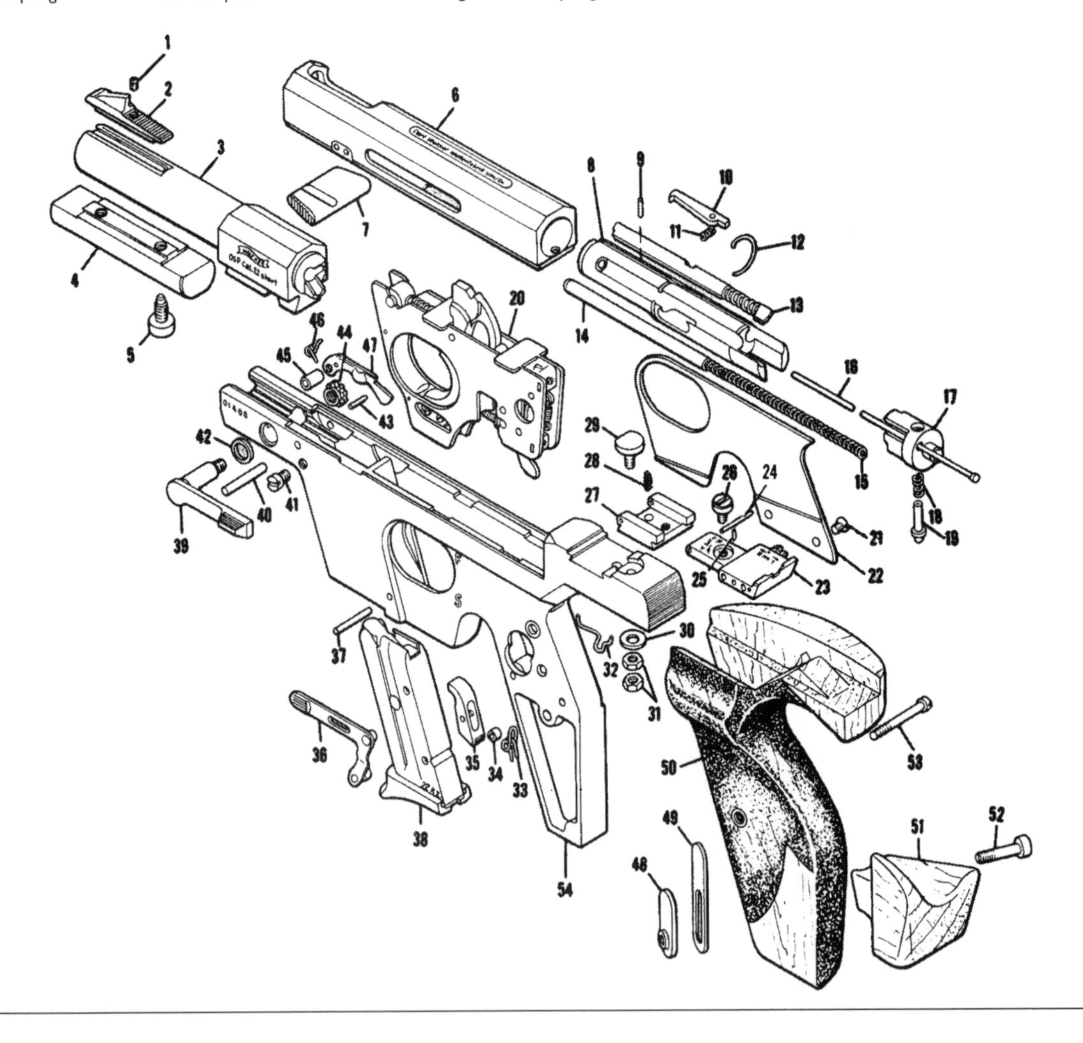

Before World War II, the firm of Carl Walther of Zella-Mehlis, Germany, was foremost in the design and manufacture of Olympic-style rapid-fire pistols. After the war, the factory was taken over by the Russians and Walther then opened a new plant in Ulm/Donau, West Germany. By 1958 a new rapid-fire pistol had been designed for the .22 Short cartridge and a limited number made for test. Production began around 1965 and by 1968 the Model OSP had evolved.

The Model OSP was designed for the Olympic 25-meter rapid fire pistol event. Handling qualities of the Walther rapid-fire pistol are excellent. Its mechanism is similar in some respects to a blowback operated .22 semi-automatic rifle in that the bolt operates inside the receiver to give an unbroken, stationary line of sight. There is no recoiling slide.

The rear sight is fully adjustable. Takedown is simple and the barrel can be quickly detached for cleaning. The fully adjustable trigger mechanism seats down inside the light alloy frame and can be easily removed as a unit.

In 2005, a rule change by the International Shooting Sport Federation ended the use of the .22 Short cartridge and wrap-around grips in the 25 meter rapid fire event and Walther replaced the OSP with the SSP model.

DISASSEMBLY

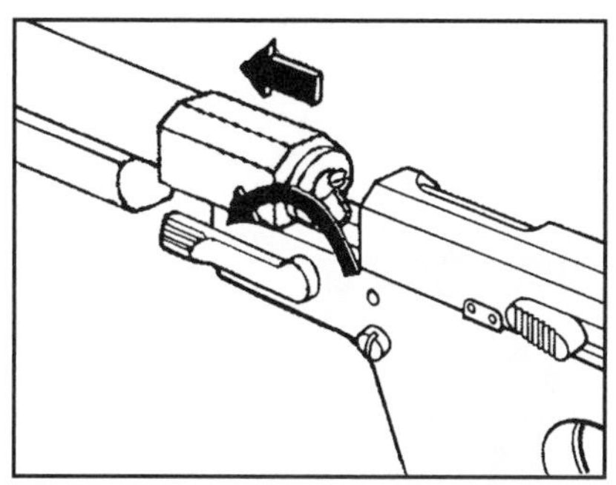

1 To disassemble pistol, first remove magazine (38) and clear chamber. Then pull trigger to drop hammer, since gun must not be cocked when disassembled. Rotate barrel lock (39) forward until it is horizontal as shown. Then pull barrel forward off frame (54). If lock is not horizontal, barrel (3) cannot be removed.

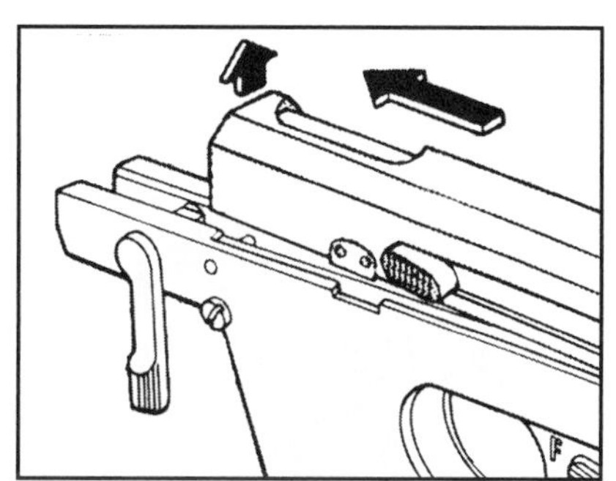

2 After barrel has been removed, receiver (6) and bolt assembly can then be lifted out. Lift end of receiver slightly and pull it forward until it is free of the frame. When reassembling the gun, it may be necessary to push the front of the receiver down tight against the frame to help seat barrel properly.

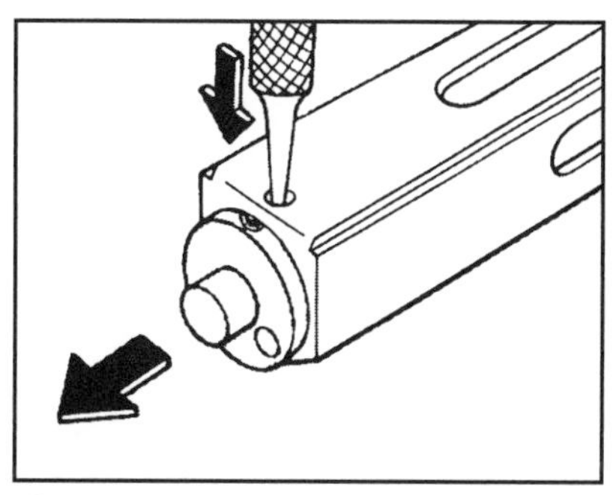

3 Bolt assembly is retained by a spring-loaded plunger (19) in bolt stop (17). To disassemble bolt, push in on plunger as shown and remove bolt stop. When recoil spring (15) and guide (16) are removed, cocking piece (7) can be pulled out through side of bolt and receiver. Balance of bolt assembly can then be removed.

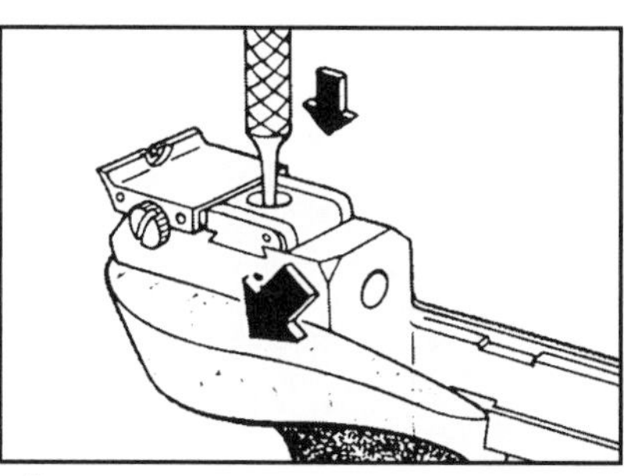

4 Grip (50) is a one-piece wrap-around type made of European walnut. Due to its design, there is a possibility that grip may shrink on the frame. To remove grip, take out grip screw (53). If grip does not slide off easily, strike it gently with heel of hand at point shown. If this does not work, remove rear sight elevation screw (26) and tap grip lightly with a punch small enough to fit through hole in frame.

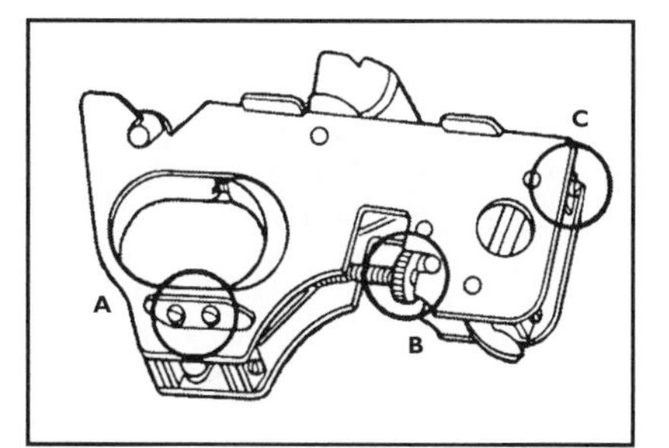

5 When receiver is removed, trigger assembly (20) can be lifted out. To free it, push it up from inside trigger guard and lift it by hammer. Trigger pull can be lightened or increased by turning knurled nut at (8). Screws at (A) are for adjusting position of trigger within trigger guard. Red-colored screw at (C) should not normally be touched. It repositions trigger bar if hammer fails to catch.

WEBLEY MARK IV REVOLVER

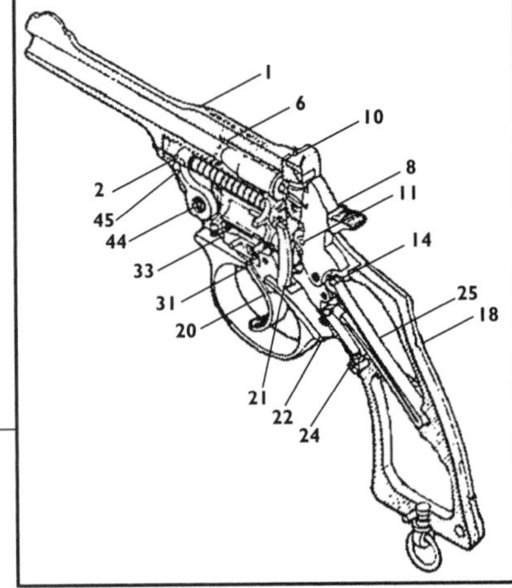

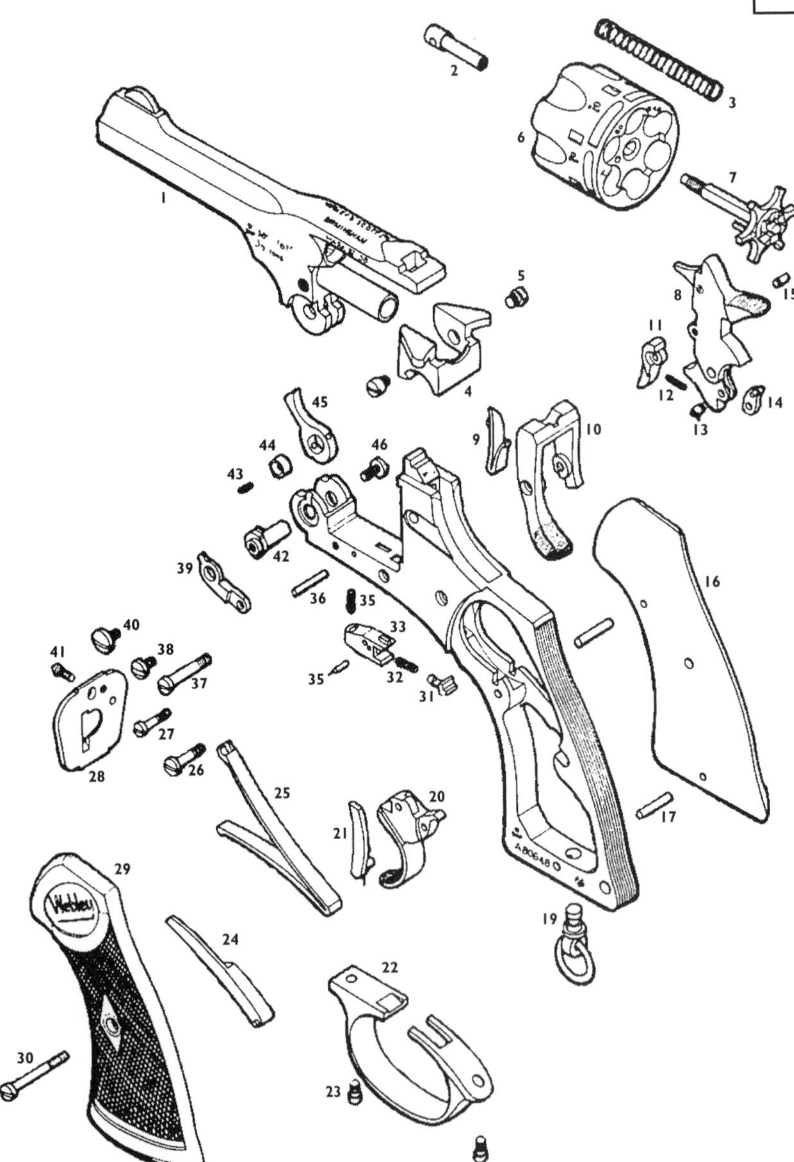

PARTS LEGEND

1. Barrel
2. Extractor nut
3. Extractor spring
4. Cylinder retaining cam
5. Cylinder cam screw (2)
6. Cylinder
7. Extractor
8. Hammer
9. Barrel catch spring
10. Barrel catch
11. Hammer catch
12. Hammer catch spring
13. Hammer swivel screw
14. Hammer swivel
15. Hammer catch screw
16. Right-hand grip
17. Grip pin (2)
18. Frame
19. Lanyard ring
20. Trigger
21. Hand
22. Trigger guard
23. Trigger guard screw (2)
24. Mainspring lever
25. Mainspring
26. Hammer screw
27. Trigger screw
28. Recoil shield
29. Left-hand grip
30. Grip screw
31. Bolt catch
32. Bolt catch spring
33. Bolt
34. Bolt catch pin
35. Bolt spring
36. Bolt pin
37. Barrel catch screw
38. Cam lever lock screw
39. Cam lever
40. Cam lever screw
41. Recoil shield screw
42. Hinge pin
43. Extractor lever spring
44. Extractor lever roller
45. Extractor lever
46. Hinge pin screw

Webley & Scott Ltd., of Birmingham, England were, for neary a century, among the world's leading producers of handguns. They were well known for their excellent top-break, double-action revolvers, offered both commercially and for use by British and Commonwealth military forces.

Webley worked in close cooperation with the British War Office on handgun matters from 1887 until the 1920s. In 1927, the War Office chose its own, Enfield-designed revolver over the Webley entrant in a trial to select a replacement for the .455-caliber Webley revolvers then in use. Despite the army's rejection, Webley introduced its Mark IV revolver, chambered for the .38 S&W cartridge, to the commercial market in 1929.

Like its heavy-caliber predecessors, the Webley Mark IV was a six-shot, double action revolver of top-break design. The revolver weighed 27 ounces and was available with a choice of four- or six-inch barrels.

The Mark IV mechanism was also used for a "Target" version in .22 rimfire or .38 S&W and a "Pocket" model in .32 and .38 S&W. The Target model had a six-inch barrel and adjustable sights. Pocket revolvers had three-inch barrels and came with either small grips, or as the "OP" (Overhand Pocket) variant, with a large grip. Webley Mark IV revolvers gained military acceptance, during World War II when the War Office bought a substantial quantity as supplemental service handguns.

DISASSEMBLY

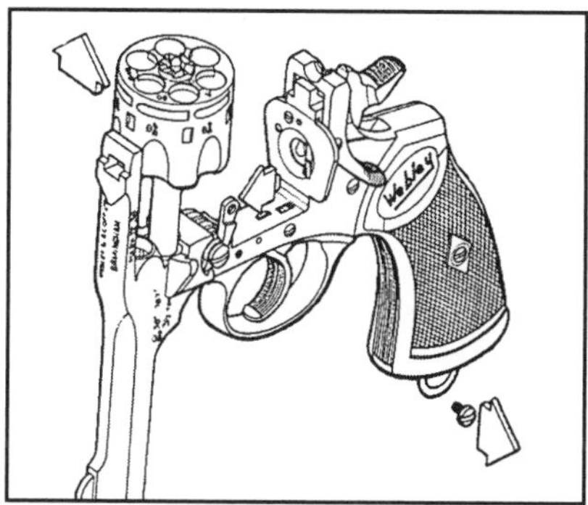

1 To field-strip the Mark IV, depress the thumb lever of barrel catch (10), open revolver, and remove any cartridges. Remove cam lever lock screw (38). Rotate cam lever (39) upward and push it toward barrel (1). Lift cylinder (6) off its axle.

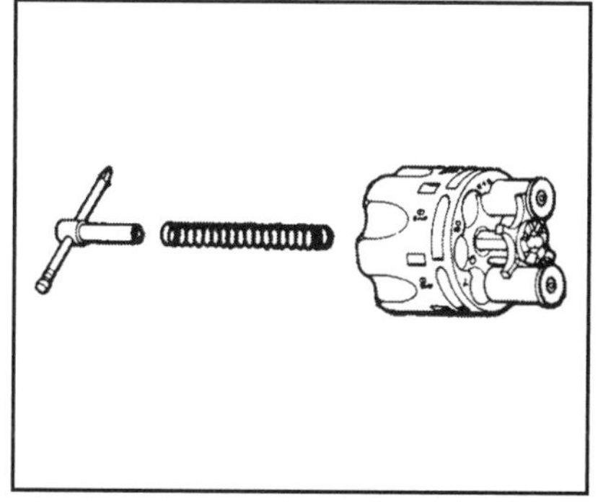

2 Place two empty cartridge cases in opposite chambers of cylinder. Insert a nail through hole in extractor nut (2) and use as a lever to unscrew nut. Remove extractor (7) and extractor spring (3). This is sufficient stripping for normal cleaning.

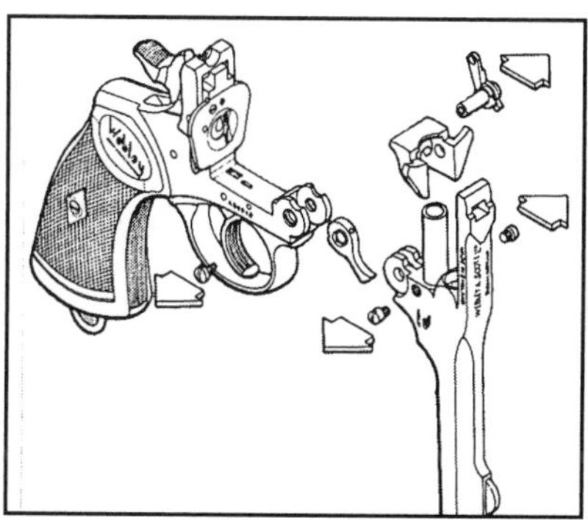

3 For further disassembly, unscrew hinge pin screw (46) and push hinge pin (42) out to left. Barrel and extractor lever (45) can now be removed and separated. Unscrew the two cylinder cam screws (5) and remove cylinder retaining cam (4).

4 Unscrew grip screw (30) and remove grips (16 & 29). Cock the hammer (8). Loop a paper clip around the mainspring (25), securing the wire by twisting with pliers. Pull trigger (20), and lower hammer with thumb. Unhook upper limb of mainspring from hammer swivel (14), and lift out mainspring. Relieve mainspring tension by pinching limb ends together with padded pliers and sliding loop of paper clip toward closed end of spring. Unscrew trigger guard screws (23) and remove trigger guard (22).

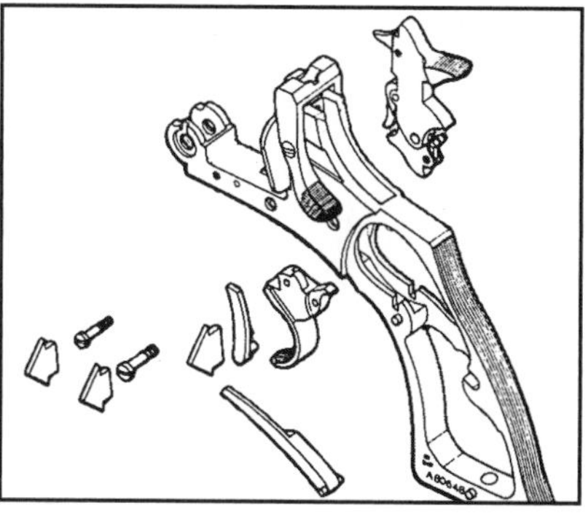

5 Lift mainspring lever (24) from notches in frame (18) and slide out to rear. Unscrew trigger screw (27), and pull trigger and hand (21) downward from the frame and separate. Unscrew hammer screw (26) and lift out hammer.

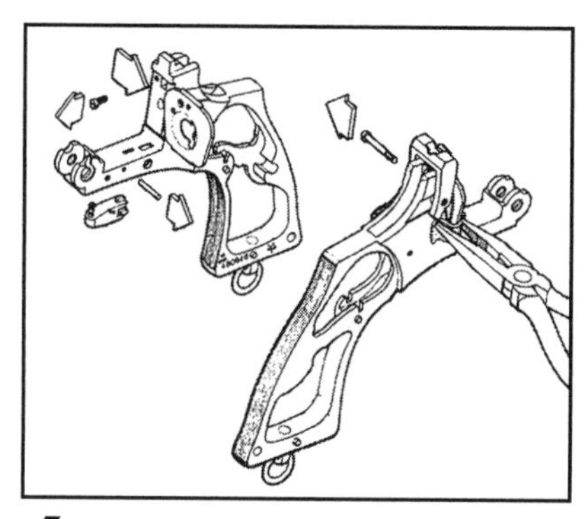

6 Compress barrel catch spring (9) against recoil shield (28) with padded pliers, meanwhile unscrewing barrel catch screw (37). Slide barrel catch and spring off to rear. Unscrew recoil shield screw (41), and drive recoil shield out to left. Use pin punch to drive out bolt pin (36). Bolt (33) and spring (35) fall free as punch is removed, Reassemble in reverse.

WEBLEY MARK VI REVOLVER

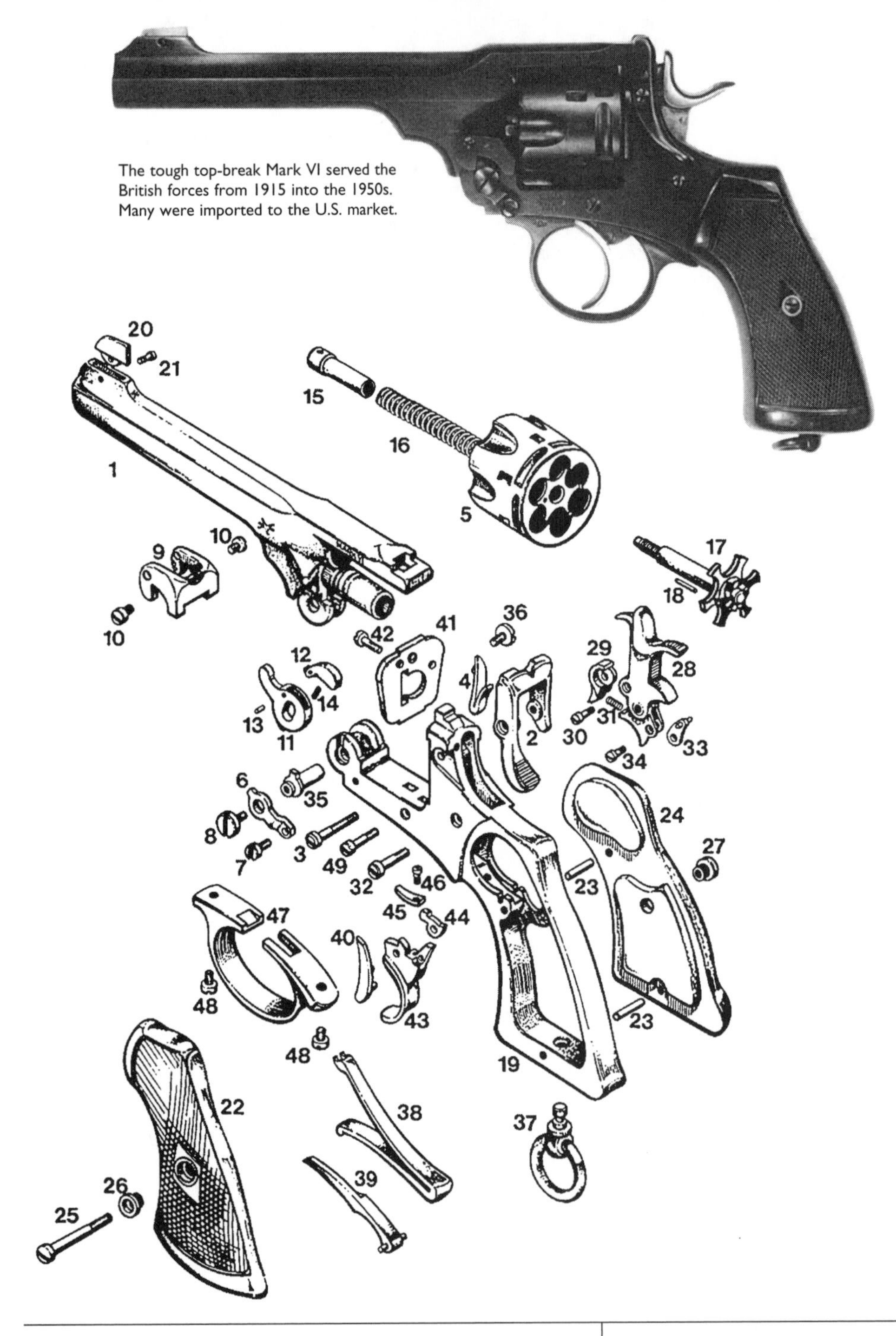

The tough top-break Mark VI served the British forces from 1915 into the 1950s. Many were imported to the U.S. market.

PARTS LEGEND

1. Barrel
2. Barrel latch/rear sight
3. Barrel latch screw
4. Barrel latch spring
5. Cylinder
6. Cylinder cam lever
7. Cylinder cam lever lock screw
8. Cylinder cam lever screw
9. Cylinder cam
10. Cylinder cam screw (2)
11. Extractor lever
12. Extractor lever cam
13. Extractor lever cam pin
14. Extractor lever cam spring
15. Extractor rod retainer
16. Extractor spring
17. Extractor/ratchet
18. Extractor/ratchet index pin
19. Frame
20. Front sight blade
21. Front sight blade screw
22. Grip panel, left
23. Grip panel pin (2)
24. Grip panel, right
25. Grip screw
26. Grip screw escutcheon, left
27. Grip screw escutcheon, right
28. Hammer
29. Hammer catch/sear
30. Hammer catch screw
31. Hammer catch spring
32. Hammer pivot screw
33. Hammer swivel/stirrup
34. Hammer swivel screw
35. Hinge pin
36. Hinge pin screw
37. Lanyard ring
38. Mainspring
39. Mainspring auxiliary lever
40. Pawl/hand
41. Recoil plate
42. Recoil plate screw
43. Trigger
44. Trigger catch/cylinder stop
45. Trigger catch spring
46. Trigger catch spring screw
47. Trigger guard
48. Trigger guard screw (2)
49. Trigger pivot screw

England's most famous handgun, adopted by the British government in 1915, has had several names. As late as 1940 its designer and prime manufacturer, Webley & Scott Ltd. of Birmingham, cataloged the commercial version as the "Mark VI .455 Service Model." It was offered with either a 4- or 6-inch barrel, the latter being the government standard, and a 7½-inch barrelled variation with an adjustable sight in the barrel latch that was listed as the "W.S. Bisley Target."

But the bulk of Webley's sales were to its government that first dubbed the gun "Pistol, Revolver Mark VI." This differentiated it from the similar but bird's head -gripped .455 cal. Webley Marks I through V that had been of British issue beginning in 1887.

In 1926, on the eve of the adoption of a smaller .38 cal. revolver designed by Webley but produced by the Royal Small Arms Factory at Enfield Lock (R.S.A.F.), the .455 was renamed "Pistol, Revolver No. 1 Mark VI" (the "Enfield" became "Pistol, Revolver .38 No. 2 Mark I").

Webley delivered more than 300,000 .455s in the World War I period, where they gained the reputation of being fine military handguns and the strongest break-open revolvers ever made. Following that war, between 1921 and 1926, R.S.A.F.Enfield took up military production of some 25,000 Mark VIs, and Webley continued some commercial assembly so that it was able to refurbish Mark VIs for its government at the outset of World War II.

The Mark VI was standard issue until 1936 and then reclassified as reserve standard until 1948 when it was officially replaced in the army by the .38 Mark I and Mark 1*. and a handful renamed in service through the Korean conflict to 1957, when the adoption of the Browning Hi Power semi-automatic replaced revolvers in British service. Some Marks VIs were permanently converted to .22 Long Rifle cal. for target work while others were fitted with .22 conversion kits.

Surplus .455s of all six Marks were imported into the United States in large quantities and, of these, many had about 1/16" of their cylinders and extractor ratchets lilled off so that they would accept U.S. .45 Auto Rim cartridges or .45 ACP cartridges that could be used with pairs of .45 caliber "half-moon" clips.

DISASSEMBLY

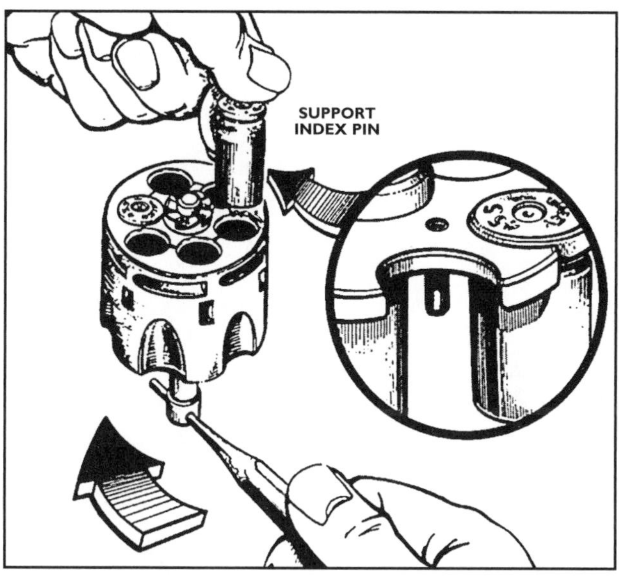

1 Depress the thumb lever of the barrel latch (2) and pivot the barrel assembly down to insure that the revolver is unloaded and safe to service. Remove the cylinder cam lever lock screw (7). Lift the rear of the cam lever (6) to depress the cylinder cam (9) and allow the cylinder (5) to be lifted off the cylinder post. Remove the grip screw (25) and detach both grip panels (22 & 24). This field strips the revolver for general service and cleaning.

If complete takedown is required, support the extactor with wooden dowels or fired cases inserted into opposing chambers of the cylinder (Fig. l) to avoid damage to the extractor pin (18) as you loosen the extractor rod retainer. Insert a drift through the disassembly hole in the extractor rod retainer (15) and rotate counter-clockwise to remove. Lift both the rod and spring (15 & 16) out the face of the cylinder and remove the extractor/ratchet (17) to the rear.

Remove the cylinder cam lever screw (8) and lift off the cylinder cam lever (6) from the left side. Turn out the hinge pin screw (36) from the right side. Push the hinge pin (35) to the left through the frame (19) to free the barrel assembly (1). NOTE: exercise caution not to lose the extractor lever (11) housed in the pivot flange of the barrel assembly. If replacement or repair is required, the extractor lever may be disassembled by drifting out the cam pin (13) to release both the cam and its spring (12 & 14). Remove the right and left cylinder cam screws (10) to separate the cylinder cam (9) from the barrel pivot flange. The front sight blade (20) may be removed by turning out its retaining screw (21) to complete disassembly of the barrel group.

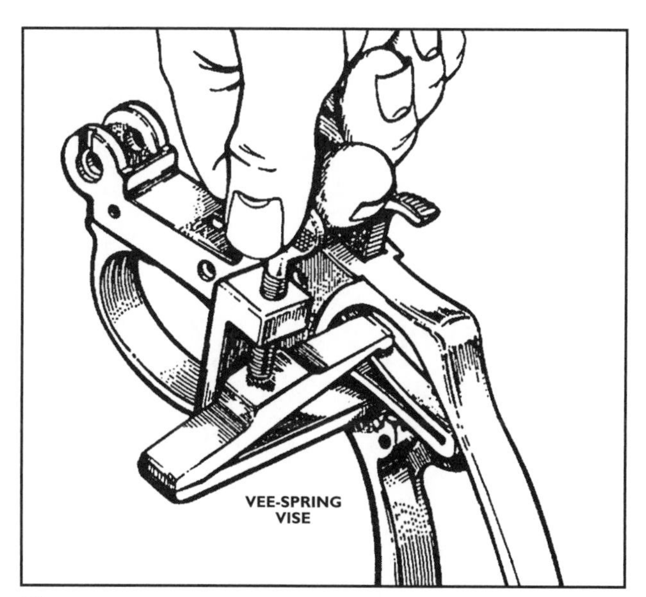

2 To remove the mainspring (38) set the hammer in a full cock position to compress the vee-spring before securing it with a vee-spring vise or locking grip pliers (Fig. 2). Lower the hammer to disengage the spring hooks from the hammer stirrup (33). Lift the secured mainspring to free the spur engaging the frame on the lower side. Raise the mainspring auxiliary lever (39) from its pivot point and remove to the rear. If required, the lanyard ring (37) may be removed by drifting out the lower grip panel pin (23).

Remove the trigger guard and screws (47 & 48). Turn out the hammer pivot screw (32) and with the trigger depressed lift the hammer assembly (28) from its slot. If required, both the hammer catch/sear and the hammer swivel/stirrup (29 & 33) may be detached by removing their respective screws (30 & 34). Remove the trigger pivot screw (49) to free. trigger assembly (43). Lift the pawl/hand (40) from its recess and remove the trigger catch spring screw (46) to detach both the spring and catch (45 & 44).

To remove the barrel latch (2), depress the latch spring (4) to relieve pressure while turning out the latch screw (3). Slide the latch down and back to clear the recesses in the sides of the frame. Lever the latch spring (4) from the retaining hole in the recoil plate. To complete disassembly, turn out the recoil plate screw (42) and drift the recoil plate laterally from its seat.

WEBLEY METROPOLITAN POLICE

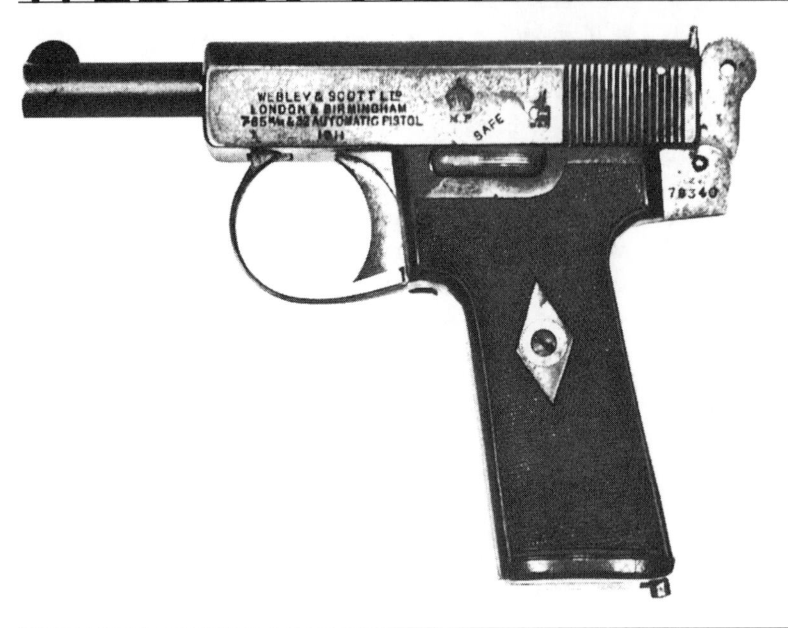

PARTS LEGEND

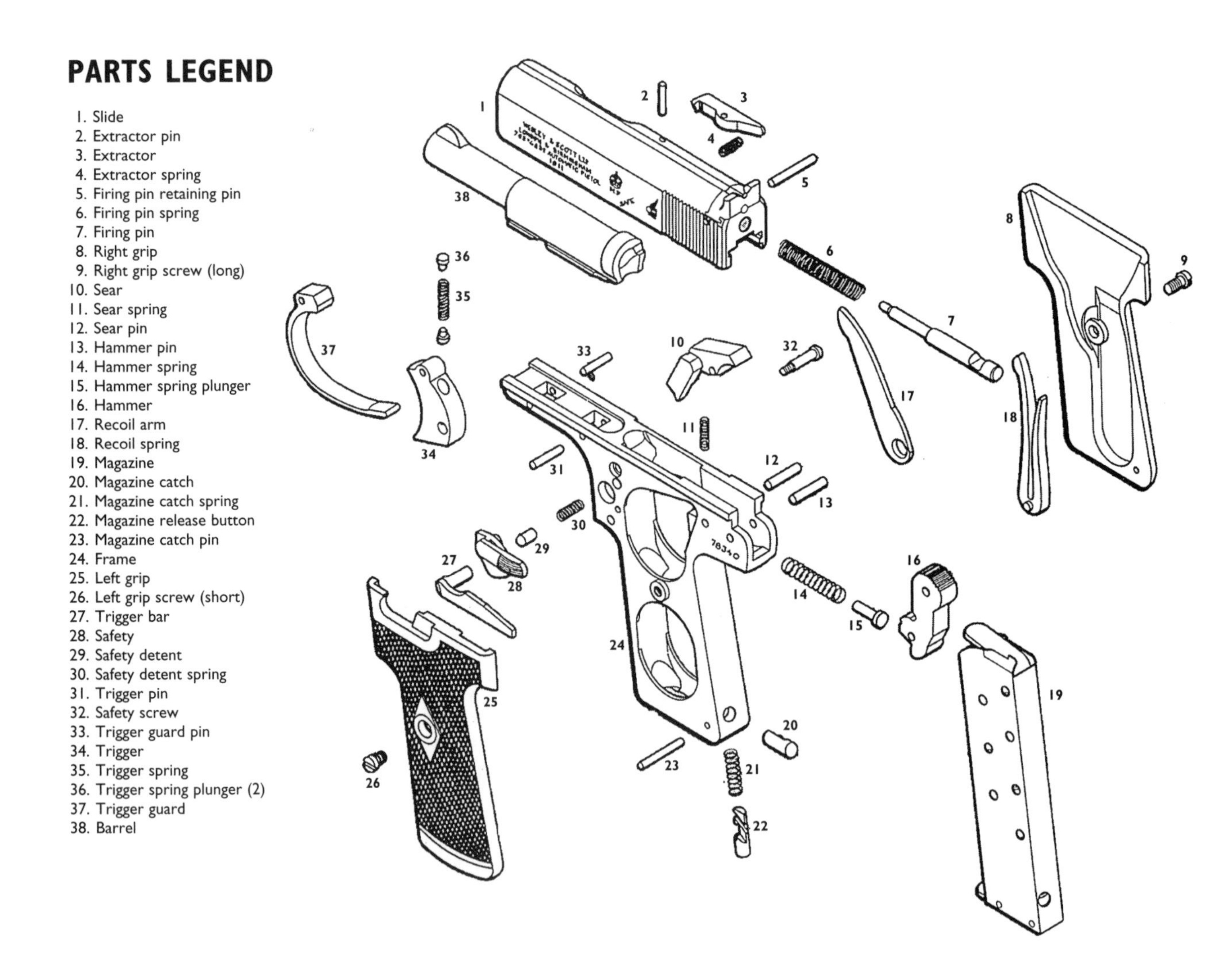

1. Slide
2. Extractor pin
3. Extractor
4. Extractor spring
5. Firing pin retaining pin
6. Firing pin spring
7. Firing pin
8. Right grip
9. Right grip screw (long)
10. Sear
11. Sear spring
12. Sear pin
13. Hammer pin
14. Hammer spring
15. Hammer spring plunger
16. Hammer
17. Recoil arm
18. Recoil spring
19. Magazine
20. Magazine catch
21. Magazine catch spring
22. Magazine release button
23. Magazine catch pin
24. Frame
25. Left grip
26. Left grip screw (short)
27. Trigger bar
28. Safety
29. Safety detent
30. Safety detent spring
31. Trigger pin
32. Safety screw
33. Trigger guard pin
34. Trigger
35. Trigger spring
36. Trigger spring plunger (2)
37. Trigger guard
38. Barrel

Produced by Webley & Scott, Ltd., the Webley Metropolitan Police Model .32 caliber automatic pistol was designed by Webley works manager William Whiting. The first of the Webley automatic pistols, it was manufactured from 1906 to 1940 and was the official handgun of the London Metropolitan Police and many police departments throughout the British Empire.

Typical of automatic pistols chambered for the .32 Automatic cartridge, the Metropolitan Police is blowbackoperated, but the recoil spring is V-shaped and housed under the right grip, an unusual feature. Unlike most center-fire blowback-operated pistols, the barrel extends forward of the slide. In most other respects, this pistol is conventionally designed.

The pistol weighs 20 ozs. and has an eight-round magazine. Well made, it is of simple design, functions reliably, and is very easy to field-strip. Identifying markings are a crown above the letters "M.P." on the left of the slide. There is another .32 caliber Webley automatic pistol similar to the Metropolitan Police Model but without these markings.

DISASSEMBLY

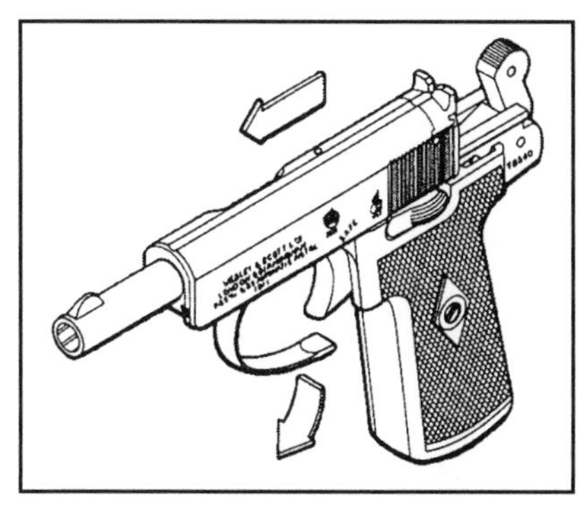

1 To field strip, depress magazine release button (22) and remove magazine (19). Clear the chamber. Lower hammer (16) and move safety (28) to safe position. Snap rear of trigger guard (37) forward and down. Then push slide (1) and barrel (38) forward off frame (24). This is sufficient for cleaning.

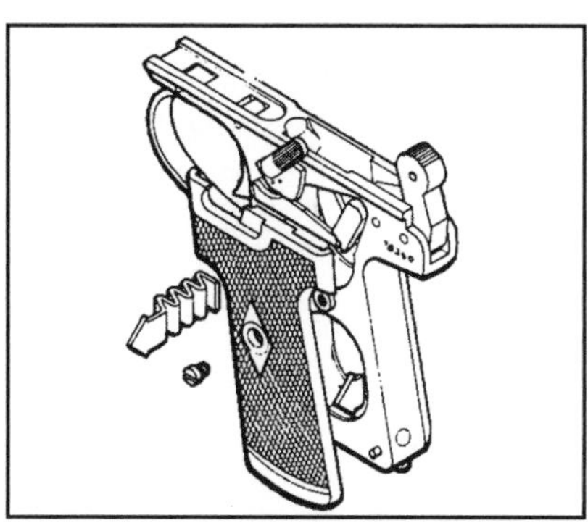

2 To strip slide, use punch to drive out firing pin retaining pin (5), and remove firing pin (7) and firing pin spring (6) to rear. Drive extractor pin (2) downward out of slide, and lift out extractor (3) and extractor spring (4).

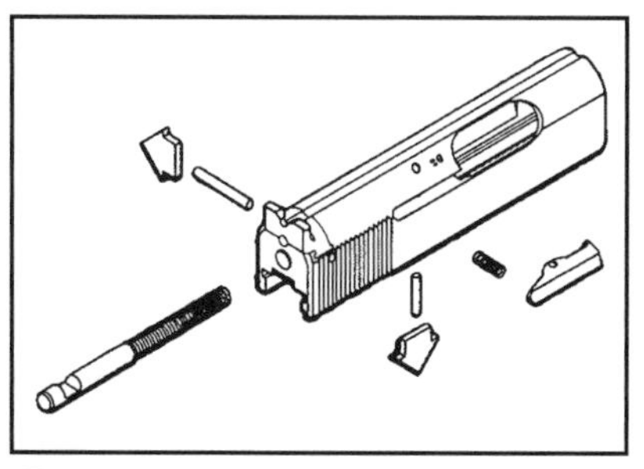

3 The grips are brittle and must be removed with care. Remove left grip screw (26) and rotate safety to its upward position. Magazine catch pin (23) protrudes through both sides of frame and fits grips snugly. Reach upward through bottom of magazine well and apply slight pressure in this area while carefully working left grip (25) off. Use same procedure for right grip (8).

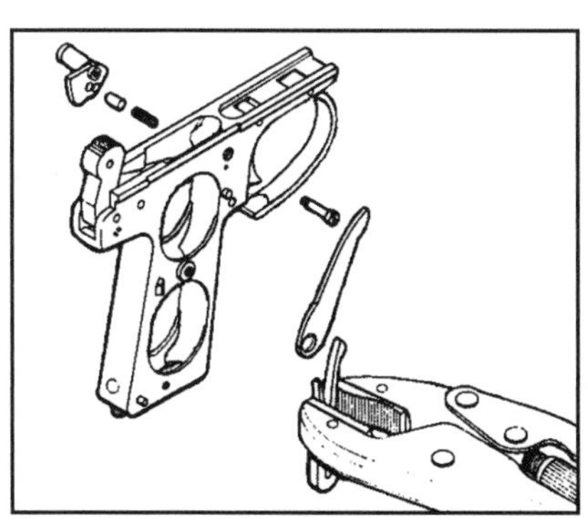

4 Remove recoil spring (18) with locking-jaw pliers or mainspring vise. Grasp spring as high as possible and compress just enough to allow removal. Lift off recoil arm (17) and loosen safety screw (32), releasing safety with its detent (29) and spring (30).

5 Pull trigger bar (27) out through left of frame. Push out trigger guard pin (33) and remove trigger guard. Push out trigger pin (31) to release trigger (34) along with its spring (35) and plungers (36).

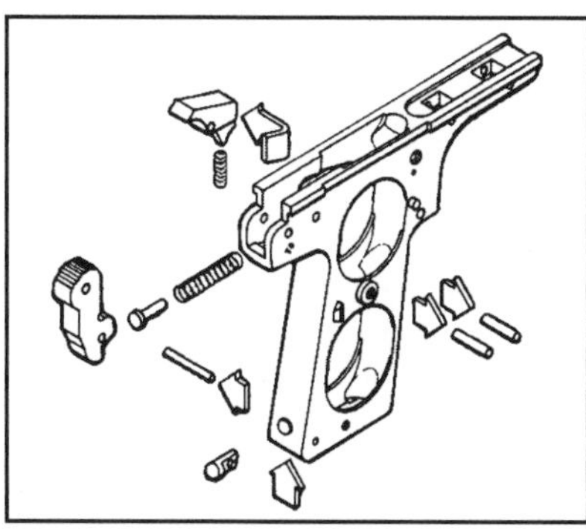

6 Drift out magazine catch pin (23) and depress magazine release button (22). Grasp protruding end of magazine catch (20) and pull it from frame. Ease out magazine release button and magazine catch spring (21). Push out sear pin (12). Pull sear (10) forward and down, and remove to the left. Be careful not to lose sear spring (11). Push out hammer pin (13), and lift out hammer (16), hammer spring (14), and plunger (15). Reassemble in reverse order.

WHITNEY .22 AUTOMATIC PISTOL

PARTS LEGEND

1. Frame
2. Tube
3. Firing pin lock
4. Breech pin
5. Mainspring
6. Barrel
7. Breechblock
8. Firing pin
9. Ejector
10. Extractor
11. Extractor plunger
12. Extractor spring
13. Cocking piece
14. Rear sight
15. Nut
16. Barrel seat washer
17. Barrel key
18. Barrel locking plunger
19. Barrel locking plunger spring
20. Spring seat
21. Trigger
22. Sear bar
23. Trigger connector
24. Trigger pin
25. Trigger spring
26. Trigger spring plunger
27. Side plate
28. Side plate screw
29. Safety
30. Grip screws (2)
31. Magazine catch
32. Magazine catch pin
33. Hammer spring plunger
34. Hammer spring
35. Hammer spring seat
36. Action frame
37. Hammer
38. Strut
39. Strut pin
40. Magazine disconnector safety
41. Hammer pin
42. Sear
43. Sear spring
44. Sear pin
45. Safety lock pin
46. Magazine assembly

Note: Grips are not shown

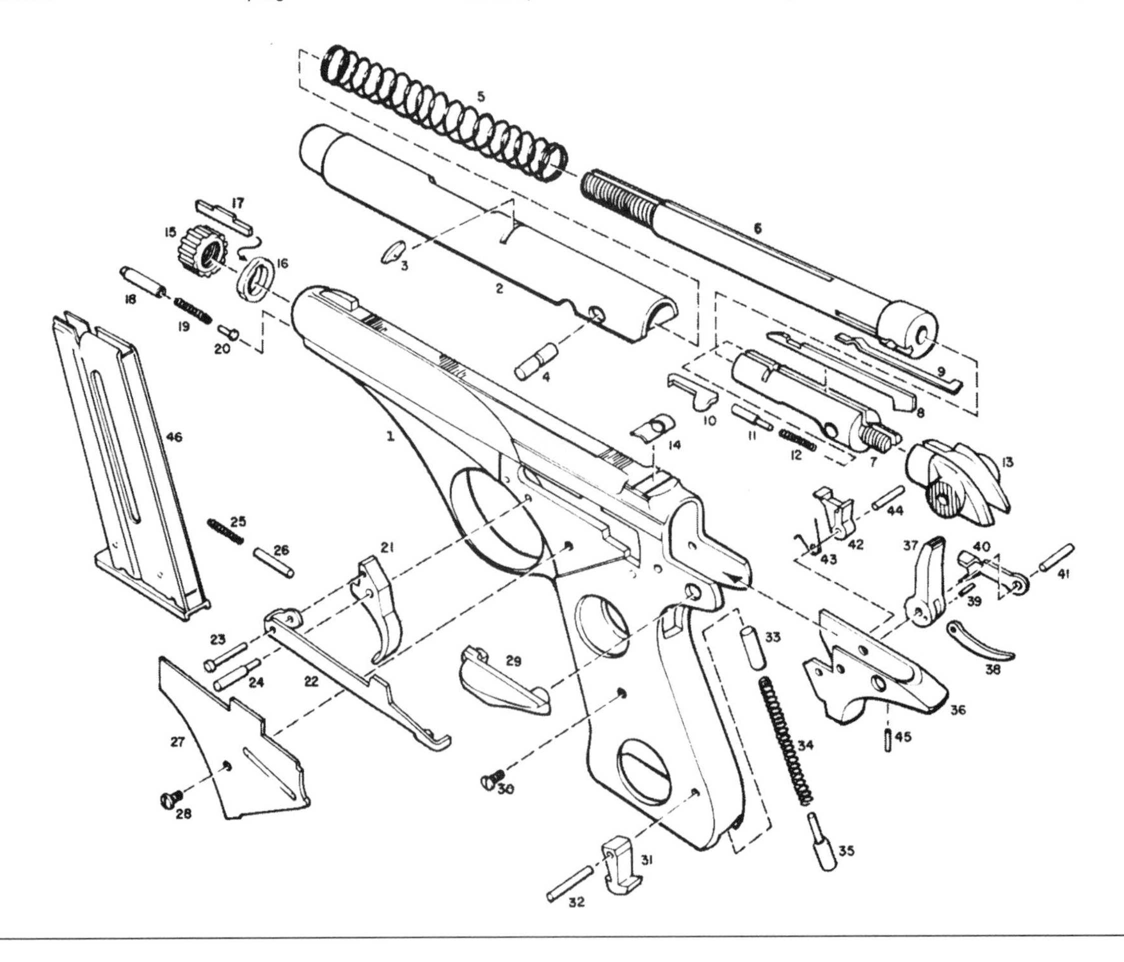

The Whitney .22 long rifle semi-automatic pistol was introduced in 1956. It is blowback operated with detachable 10-round capacity magazine in the grip.

The action mechanism is a self-contained unit retained within the hollow aluminum alloy frame by a serrated nut threaded to the muzzle end of the barrel. By removing this nut the entire action assembly can be slid to the rear and out of the frame. A separate internal washer and key position will align the assembly within the frame.

The mechanical safety on the Whitney is engaged by pushing it down, not up. This is contrary to the usual practice with semi-automatic pistols.

The Whitney pistol was made by Whitney Firearms, Inc., of North Haven, Connecticut, which is no longer in business. There was no connection between this firm and the Whitney Arms Co. which ceased operations in 1888.

DISASSEMBLY

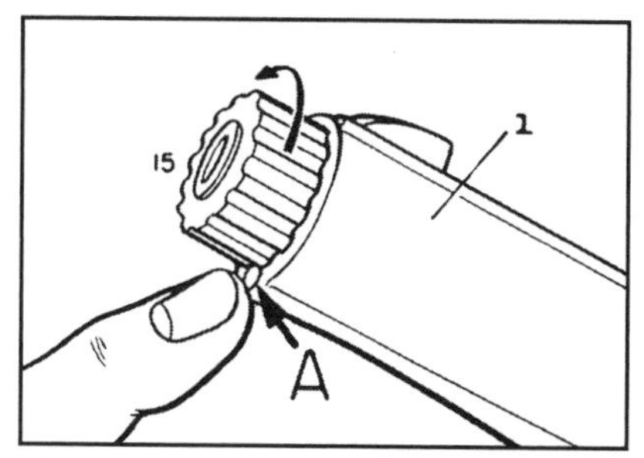

1 While holding barrel locking plunger (18) flush with face of frame as shown at "A", unscrew nut (15) counterclockwise as indicated by arrow.

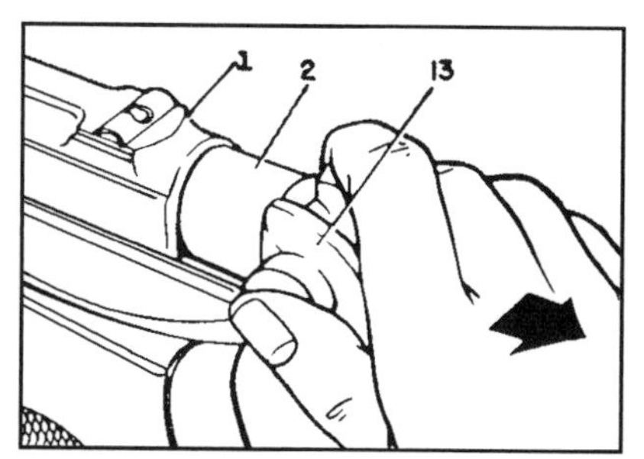

2 With hammer at full cock position, draw tube assembly out of frame (1) to rear by pulling back on cocking piece (13) as shown by arrow.

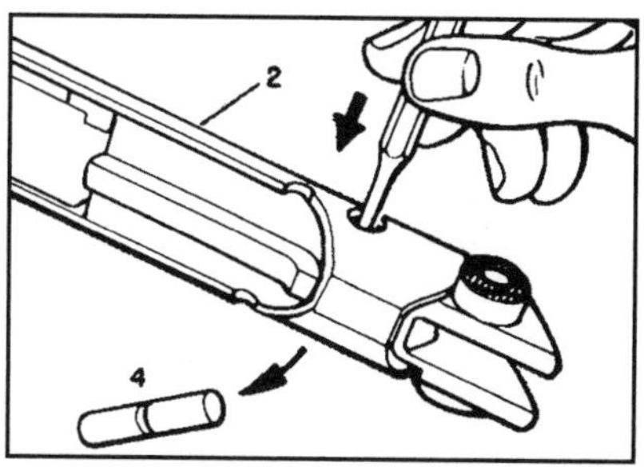

3 While pulling forward on barrel slightly to lessen tension on breech pin (4), push pin out of tube (2) with punch. (Underside of assembly is shown).

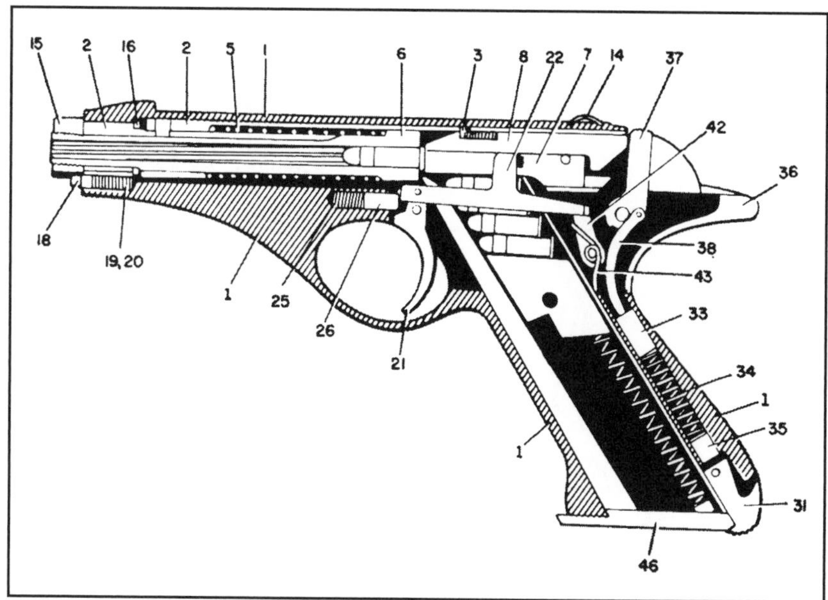

4 The longitudinal section shows the relative position of all parts. Pistol is shown here with a cartridge in the chamber and hammer uncocked.

Remove magazine (46) and check chamber to be sure pistol is unloaded. Replace magazine and pull trigger. Remove magazine once more. Depress barrel locking plunger (18) flush with forward face of frame (1). Unscrew nut (15). Cock hammer (37) and pull tube (2), breechblock (7), and cocking piece (13) assembled out of frame to rear. Remove barrel seat washer (16) and barrel key (17) from front end of frame. Firing pin lock (3) may be removed by rapping inverted tube (2) sharply, causing it to drop out. Pull firing pin (8) out of breech-block (7). Pull barrel (6) forward slightly and push breech pin (4) out of barrel and tube. Remove breechblock (7) and barrel (6) from tube (2). Lift extractor (10) out of breechblock and remove extractor plunger and spring (11 & 12) from breech-block. Disassembly of ejector (9) from barrel is not recommended.

APPENDIX

When setting out to disassemble a firearm, its owner is often challenged to find instructions for the procedure as it applies to the particular gun in question. As a partial solution to this problem, the list that follows contains the brand names and model designations of many pistols and revolvers, represented generally, but not specifically, in this book. These firearms are listed alphabetically with the page number in the book on which a mechanically and operationally similar firearm is described.

Keep in mind, when applying the directions for one firearm to the disassembly of another similar gun, that differences will exist and procedures may need adaptation if disassembly and reassembly are to be done successfully. Discretion, in this instance, may save an embarrassing trip to one's local gunsmith.

INDEX

INDEX

INDEX